McDougal Littell

THE LANGUAGE OF
LITERATURE

McDougal Littell

THE LANGUAGE OF
LITERATURE

Senior Consultants

Arthur N. Applebee

Andrea B. Bermúdez

Sheridan Blau

Rebekah Caplan

Peter Elbow

Susan Hynds

Judith A. Langer

James Marshall

McDougal Littell

A HOUGHTON MIFFLIN COMPANY

Evanston, Illinois ♦ Boston ♦ Dallas

Acknowledgments

Front Matter

World Book Publishing: Excerpt from "Oregon Trail" from *World Book Encyclopedia*. Copyright © 2000 World Book, Inc. By permission of the publisher. www.worldbook.com

Bantam Books: Excerpt from "War Party" by Louis L'Amour. Copyright © 1975 by Bantam Books, a division of Bantam Doubleday Dell Publishing Group, Inc. Used by permission of Bantam Books, a division of Random House, Inc.

Unit One

Farrar, Straus & Giroux: "Charles," from *The Lottery* by Shirley Jackson. Copyright © 1948, 1949 by Shirley Jackson. Copyright renewed © 1976, 1977 by Laurence Hyman, Barry Hyman, Mrs. Sarah Webster and Mrs. Joanne Schnurer. Reprinted by permission of Farrar, Straus & Giroux, Inc.

Orchard Books: "Checkouts," from *A Couple of Kooks and Other Stories About Love* by Cynthia Rylant. Copyright © 1990 by Cynthia Rylant. Published by Orchard Books, an imprint of Scholastic Inc. Reprinted by permission of Scholastic Inc.

Random House: "Raymond's Run," from *Gorilla, My Love* by Toni Cade Bambara. Copyright © 1971 by Toni Cade Bambara. Reprinted by permission of Random House, Inc.

Wendy DuBow: Excerpts from "Do Try This at Home," by Wendy DuBow from *Women's Sports & Fitness,* May 1997. Copyright © by Wendy DuBow. Reprinted by permission of the author.

Flannery Literary Agency: "Stop the Sun" by Gary Paulsen, from *Boy's Life,* January 1986. Copyright © 1986 by Gary Paulsen. Reprinted by permission of Jennifer Flannery as literary representative of Gary Paulsen.

continued on page R208

ISBN-13: 978-0-618-60136-3   ISBN-10: 0-618-60136-8

Printed in the United States of America

7 8 9 - DWO - 09 08 07

Senior Consultants

The senior consultants guided the conceptual development for *The Language of Literature* series. They participated actively in shaping prototype materials for major components, and they reviewed completed prototypes and/or completed units to ensure consistency with current research and the philosophy of the series.

Arthur N. Applebee Professor of Education, State University of New York at Albany; Director, Center for the Learning and Teaching of Literature; Senior Fellow, Center for Writing and Literacy

Andrea B. Bermúdez Professor of Studies in Language and Culture; Director, Research Center for Language and Culture; Chair, Foundations and Professional Studies, University of Houston–Clear Lake

Sheridan Blau Senior Lecturer in English and Education and former Director of Composition, University of California at Santa Barbara; Director, South Coast Writing Project; Director, Literature Institute for Teachers; Former President, National Council of Teachers of English

Rebekah Caplan Senior Associate for Language Arts for middle school and high school literacy, National Center on Education and the Economy, Washington, D.C.; served on the California State English Assessment Development Team for Language Arts; former co-director of the Bay Area Writing Project, University of California at Berkeley.

Peter Elbow Emeritus Professor of English, University of Massachusetts at Amherst; Fellow, Bard Center for Writing and Thinking

Susan Hynds Professor and Director of English Education, Syracuse University, Syracuse, New York

Judith A. Langer Professor of Education, State University of New York at Albany; Co-director, Center for the Learning and Teaching of Literature; Senior Fellow, Center for Writing and Literacy

James Marshall Professor of English and English Education; Chair, Division of Curriculum and Instruction, University of Iowa, Iowa City

Contributing Consultants

Linda Diamond Executive Vice-President, Consortium on Reading Excellence (CORE); co-author of *Building a Powerful Reading Program*. Ms. Diamond reviewed program components as part of the development of a teacher-training program designed to accompany those materials; she also reviewed and contributed to McDougal Littell's *Reading Toolkit*, the professional development component of the program.

William L. McBride Reading and Curriculum Specialist; former middle and high school English instructor. Dr. McBride reviewed prototype materials and served as a consultant on the development of the Reading Strategies Unit and the Reading Handbook.

Sharon Sicinski-Skeans, Assistant Professor of Reading, University of Houston–Clear Lake. Dr. Sicinski-Skeans served as primary consultant on *The InterActive Reader,* providing guidance on prototype development and reviewing final manuscript.

Multicultural Advisory Board

The multicultural advisors reviewed literature selections for appropriate content and made suggestions for teaching lessons in a multicultural classroom.

Dr. Joyce M. Bell Chairperson, English Department, Townview Magnet Center, Dallas, Texas

Dr. Eugenia W. Collier author; lecturer; Chairperson, Department of English and Language Arts and teacher of creative writing and American literature, Morgan State University, Maryland

Kathleen S. Fowler President, Palm Beach County Council of Teachers of English, Boca Raton Middle School, Boca Raton, Florida

Corey Lay ESL Department Chairperson, Chester Nimitz Middle School, Los Angeles Unified School District, Los Angles, California

Noreen M. Rodriguez Trainer for Hillsborough County School District's Staff Development Division; independent consultant, Gaither High School, Tampa, Florida

Michelle Dixon Thompson Seabreeze High School, Daytona Beach, Florida

Teacher Review Panels

The following educators provided ongoing review during the development of the tables of contents, lesson design, and key components of the program.

CALIFORNIA

Steve Bass Eighth-Grade Team Leader, Meadowbrook Middle School, Poway Unified School District

Cynthia Brickey Eighth-Grade Academic Block Teacher, Kastner Intermediate School, Clovis Unified School District

Karen Buxton English Department Chairperson, Winston Churchill Middle School, San Juan School District

Sharon Cook Independent consultant, Fresno Unified School District

continued on pages R193

Manuscript Reviewers

The following educators reviewed prototype lessons and tables of contents during the development of *The Language of Literature* program

William A. Battaglia Herman Intermediate School, San Jose, California

Hugh Delle Broadway McCullough High School, The Woodlands, Texas

Robert M. Bucan National Mine Middle School, Ishpeming, Michigan

Ann E. Clayton Department Chairperson for Language Arts, Rockway Middle School, Miami, Florida

Hillary Crain Dieguño Middle School, Encinitas, California

Linda C. Dahl National Mine Middle School, Ishpeming, Michigan

Mary Jo Eustis Language Arts Coordinator, Lodi Unified School District, Lodi, California

continued on page R194

Student Panel

LITERATURE REVIEWERS

The following students read and evaluated selections to assess their appeal for the eighth grade.

Iruma Bello, Henry H. Filer Middle School, Hialeah, Florida

Leslie M. Blaha, Walnut Springs Middle School, Westerville, Ohio

Osvelia Cantoran, Chester W. Nimitz Middle School, Huntington Park, California

Elizabeth Donaldson, Bettendorf Middle School, Bettendorf, Iowa

Patricia Ernst, East Aurora Middle School, East Aurora, New York

Theresa Ernst, East Aurora Middle School, East Aurora, New York

Aaron Fitzstephens, Fairfield Middle School, Fairfield, Ohio

Stephen Tremayne Johnson, Lincoln College Prep School, Kansas City, Missouri

John Paul Marshall, RAA Middle School, Tallahassee, Florida

Meghan McGuire, St. John of the Cross School, Western Springs, Illinois

Jaret Heath Radford, Fondren Middle School, Houston, Texas

Erick Strauss, Cobb Middle School, Tallahassee, Florida

Christine Warner, Keith Valley Middle School, Horsham, Pennsylvania

ACTIVE READERS

The following students participated in the development of The Active Reader: Skills and Strategies pages in this book:

Peter Green

Elena Martinez

Jonathan Palm

Tiara Banks

Jessica Schopper

Justin Ordman

Jenny Roberge

Tom O'Connell

Stephanie Hernandez

Ryan Cagné

Jules Jeudy

Zahra Shirazi

STUDENT MODEL WRITERS

The following students wrote the student models for Writing Workshop pages that appear in this book:

Joshua Elmer

Jillian Malenfant

Travis Potter

Dalila Martin Del Campo

Brianna Baker

Michael Hogan

Michelle Kazi

Brent Gilmore

Emily Howard

Mordechai Hornick

Devon Frederick

Overview

Table of Contents

Student Resource Bank

Reading Handbook
Vocabulary Handbook
Spelling Handbook
Writing Handbook
Grammar Handbook
Speaking and Listening Handbook
Research and Technology Handbook
Academic Reading Handbook
Glossary of Literary and Reading Terms
Glossary of Words to Know in English and Spanish

Literature Connections

Each of the books in the *Literature Connections* series combines a novel or play with related readings–poems, stories, plays, personal essays, articles– that add new perspectives on the theme or subject matter of the longer work.

Listed below are some of the most popular choices to accompany the Grade 8 anthology:

*A Spanish version is also available.

THE LANGUAGE OF
LITERATURE

Reading Strategies Unit

Unit One

Insights

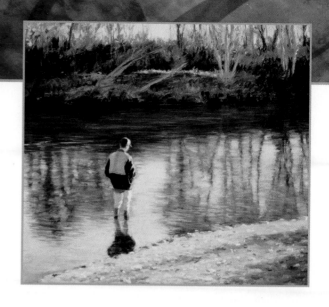

**SOCIAL STUDIES
CONNECTION**
See Unit Six, "The Oral
Tradition: Tales from
the Americas" for links
to Unit One.

x

Unit Two

Rising to the Challenge

SOCIAL STUDIES CONNECTION
See Unit Six, "The Oral Tradition: Tales from the Americas" for links to Unit Two.

Unit Three

The Human Spirit

SOCIAL STUDIES CONNECTION

See Unit Six, "The Oral Tradition: Tales from the Americas" for links to Unit Three.

Unit Four

Strange Goings-On

SOCIAL STUDIES CONNECTION
See Unit Six, "The Oral Tradition: Tales from the Americas" for links to Unit Four.

Unit Five

American Voices

SOCIAL STUDIES CONNECTION

See Unit Six, "The Oral Tradition: Tales from the Americas" for links to Unit Five.

Unit Six

THE ORAL TRADITION:
Tales from the Americas

The Language of Literature
Student Resource Bank

The Language of Literature
Teaching by Genre

Poetry

Writing Workshops

Communication Workshops

Building Vocabulary

Standardized Test Practice

Becoming an Active Reader

Active readers comprehend what they read and connect it to their own lives. An active reader asks questions, forms opinions, and visualizes scenes. The strategies in this special unit and throughout the book will help you become an active reader of all kinds of materials.

McDougal Littell

THE LANGUAGE OF
LITERATURE

HENRY
WADSWORTH
LONGFELLOW

AMY
TAN

MARK
TWAIN

WALTER
DEAN
MYERS

NIKKI GIOVANNI

JULIA ALVAREZ

ISAAC ASIMOV

ROBERT FROST

POE

AN
FRA

HEN

EVE
MER

LON

EMILY
DICKINSON

RUDOLFO A

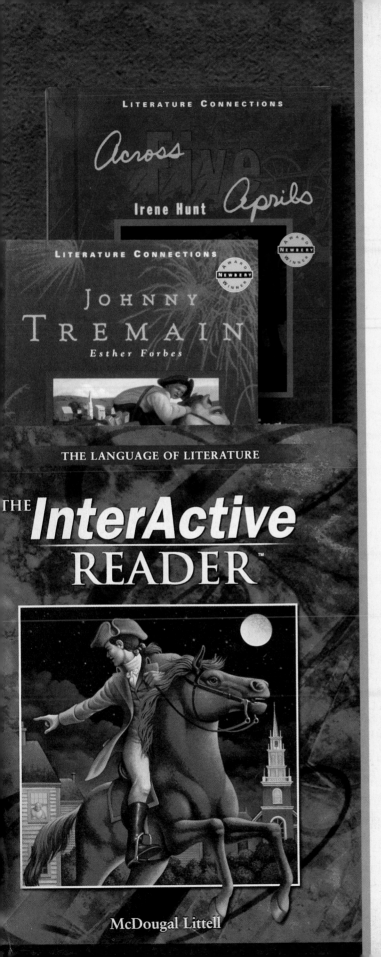

STRATEGIES FOR READING

Active readers learn and apply reading strategies to get the most out of what they read. Whether you are reading for information or for enjoyment, pause from time to time and **monitor** your understanding of the material. Reread if necessary and **reflect** on what you have read. As you reflect, use one or more of these techniques.

PREDICT

Try to figure out what might happen next. Then read on to see how accurate your guesses were.

VISUALIZE

Picture the people, places, and events being described to help you understand what's happening.

CONNECT

Connect personally with what you're reading. Think of similarities between what is being described and what you have experienced, heard about, or read about.

QUESTION

Ask questions about events in the material you're reading. What happened? Why? How do the people involved feel about the events? Searching for reasons can help you feel closer to what you are reading.

CLARIFY

From time to time, review your understanding of what you read. You can do this by **summarizing** what you have read, identifying the **main idea,** and **making inferences**—drawing conclusions from the information you are given. Reread passages you don't understand. If you need to, consult a dictionary, glossary, or other source.

EVALUATE

Form opinions about what you read, both while you're reading and after you've finished. Develop your own ideas about people, places, and events.

READER'S NOTEBOOK

Putting your thoughts on paper can help you understand and connect with literature. Many readers record their ideas in a Reader's Notebook. You can use almost any kind of notebook for this purpose. This page describes two ways you can use your notebook.

1 PREPARE TO READ

Complete the 📖 **READER'S NOTEBOOK** activity on the Preparing to Read page of each literature lesson. This activity will help you apply an important skill as you read the literature selection.

"War Party"
by Louis L'Amour

Text	Response
P. 510 "enormous distance . . . nothing around but prairie and sky."	There are pictures of the prairie in my social studies book. I can imagine Bud riding through them.

2 RECORD YOUR THOUGHTS

In your Reader's Notebook, record responses, connections, questions, sketches, and charts. Use your notebook before and after reading a selection, as well as while you read. Jot down notes that might later be a springboard to your own writing.

Watch for other reminders about your Reader's Notebook throughout this textbook.

Angela Falconetti
PORTFOLIO

Date	Project	Comments
9/22	Essay on "A Mother in Mannville"	Done
10/2	Multimedia project on Jack London	Graphics need work
10/18	Research report on Oregon Trail	Outline, notes, and first draft

Personal Word List

Word: ailing
Selection: "War Party"
Page: S9 ("a man who was always ailing")
Definition: feeling sick or in pain

Word: cringe
Selection: "War Party"
Page: S10 ("They'd cringe into themselves")
Definition: shrink back in fear, cower

Reading Log

Name: **Travis Bowman**

Date	Title / Author	Genre / Type	Time / Number of Pages
9/30	The House of Dies Drear by Virginia Hamilton	Novel	40 minutes / 36 pages
10/5	Baseball Card Collector	Magazine	10 minutes / 8 pages

WORKING PORTFOLIO

Artists and writers keep portfolios in which they store works in progress. Your portfolio can be a folder, a box, or a notebook. Add drafts of your writing experiments and notes on your goals as a reader and writer.

PERSONAL WORD LISTS

Vocabulary In your Reader's Notebook, you can add words you learn to a personal word list—a list of words you want to use.

Spelling Add words that you are having difficulty spelling to a separate spelling list in your Reader's Notebook.

READING LOG

Keep track of how much you read and how often. You may be surprised at how many books and other materials you read in a year! Keep your reading log in your Reader's Notebook or on a worksheet your teacher provides for you.

Integrated Technology

Your involvement doesn't stop with the last line of the text. Use these technology products to further your study and understanding:

• **Literature in Performance videos**
• **NetActivities CD-ROM**
• **Audio Library**
• **INTERNET ClassZone, McDougal Littell's companion Web site, at www.mcdougallittell.com**

Reading Literature

When you read short stories, literary nonfiction, poems, plays, or myths, you are interacting with the literature in many ways. You may be enjoying the power of storytelling. You could be finding connections with your own life. You may even be encountering new ideas and experiences. The tips on this page will help you become an active reader of literature.

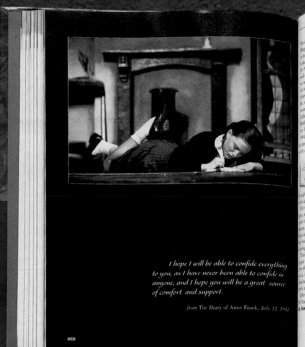

I hope I will be able to confide everything to you, as I have never been able to confide in anyone, and I hope you will be a great source of comfort and support.

from The Diary of Anne Frank, July 12, 1942

DRAMA

HISTORICAL FICTION

STRATEGIES FOR READING

BEFORE READING

- Set a purpose for reading. What do you want to learn? Are you reading as part of an assignment or for fun? Establishing a purpose will help you focus.

- Preview the text by looking at the title and any images and captions. Try to **predict** what the literature will be about.

- Ask yourself if you can **connect** what you are reading with what you already know.

DURING READING

- Check your understanding of what you read. Can you restate the text in your own words?

- Try to **connect** what you're reading to your own life. Have you experienced similar events or emotions?

- **Question** what's happening. You may wonder about events and characters' feelings.

- **Visualize,** or create a mental picture of, what the author is describing.

- Pause from time to time to **predict** what will happen next.

BIOGRAPHY

WE could hear running feet and shouting from the other side of the barricaded doors.

from **All But My Life**

autobiography by Gerda Weissmann Klein

The Charge of the Light Brigade

by Alfred, Lord Tennyson

Cannon to right of them,
Cannon to left of them,
Cannon behind them
    Volley'd and thunder'd;
Storm'd at with shot and shell,
While horse and hero fell,
They that had fought so well
Came thro' the jaws of Death,
Back from the mouth of Hell,
All that was left of them,
    Left of six hundred.

When can their glory fade?
O, the wild charge they made!
All the world wonder'd.
Honor the charge they made!
Honor the Light Brigade,
    Noble six hundred!

THE CHARGE OF THE LIGHT BRIGADE **199**

POETRY

War Party

by Louis L'Amour

WAR PARTY **739**

AFTER READING

- Review your predictions. Were they correct?
- Try to **summarize** the text. Give the main idea or the basic plot.
- Reflect on and **evaluate** what you have read. Did the reading fulfill your purpose?
- To **clarify** your understanding, write down opinions or thoughts about the piece, or discuss it with someone.

The story on these pages is part of a piece of historical fiction from Unit Five. Read the excerpt and record your responses to it in your **READER'S NOTEBOOK.** Then read the Strategies in Action columns to find out how two students applied the strategies for reading.

STRATEGIES IN ACTION

Angela: *It's hard to tell from the title and artwork what the story will be about. I think it may be related to the Wild West.*
PREDICTING

Travis: *In social studies class, we did some reading about cowboys and westward expansion. Is this story about traveling west?*
CONNECTING,
QUESTIONING

War Party

by Louis L'Amour

We buried pa on a sidehill out west of camp, buried him high up so he could look down the trail he'd planned to travel.

We piled the grave high with rocks because of the coyotes, and we dug the grave deep, and some of it I dug myself, and Mr. Sampson helped, and some others.

Folks in the wagon train figured ma would turn back, but

A Certain Trail (1986), Edward Ruscha. Acrylic on canvas 59" × 145½". Private Collection, Seattle. Photo by Paul Ruscha. Courtesy of the artist.

they hadn't known ma so long as I had. Once she set her mind to something she wasn't about to quit.

She was a young woman and pretty, but there was strength in her. She was a lone woman with two children, but she was of no mind to turn back. She'd come through the Little Crow massacre in Minnesota and she knew what trouble was. Yet it was like her that she put it up to me.

"Bud," she said, when we were alone, "we can turn back, but we've nobody there who cares about us, and it's of you and Jeanie that I'm thinking. If we go west you will have to be the man of the house, and you'll have to work hard to make up for pa."

"We'll go west," I said. A boy those days took it for granted that he had work to do, and the men couldn't do it all. No boy ever thought of himself as only twelve or thirteen or whatever he was, being anxious to prove himself a man, and take a man's place and responsibilities.

Ryerson and his wife were going back. She was a complaining woman and he was a man who was always ailing when there was work to be done. Four or five wagons were turning back, folks with their tails betwixt their legs running for the shelter of towns where their own littleness wouldn't stand out so plain.

When a body crossed the Mississippi and left the settlements behind, something happened to him. The world seemed to bust wide open, and suddenly the horizons spread out and a man wasn't cramped any more. The pinched-up villages and the narrowness of towns, all that was gone. The horizons simply exploded and rolled back into enormous distance, with nothing around but prairie and sky.

Some folks couldn't stand it. They'd cringe into themselves and start hunting excuses to go back where they came from. This was a big country needing big men and women to live in it, and there was no place out here for the frightened or the mean.

The prairie and sky had a way of trimming folks down to size, or changing them to giants to whom nothing seemed impossible. Men who had cut a wide swath[1] back in the States found themselves nothing out here. They were folks who were used to doing a lot of talking who suddenly found that no one was listening any more, and things that seemed mighty important back home, like family and money, they amounted to nothing alongside character and courage.

There was John Sampson from our town. He was a man used to being told to do things, used to looking up to wealth and power, but when he crossed the Mississippi he began to lift his head and look around. He squared his shoulders, put more crack to his whip and began to make his own tracks in the land.

Pa was always strong, an independent man given to reading at night from one of the four or five books we had, to speaking up on matters of principle and to straight shooting with a rifle. Pa had fought the Comanche and lived with the Sioux, but he wasn't strong enough to last more than two days with a Kiowa arrow through his lung. But he died knowing ma had stood by the rear wheel and shot the Kiowa whose arrow it was.

Right then I knew that neither Indians nor country was going to get the better of ma. Shooting that Kiowa was the

Angela: I can imagine how huge and lonely the prairie was.
VISUALIZING

Travis: Based on how the mother and the children have acted so far, I think they will succeed out west.
PREDICTING

Travis: Wow, this is a tough family!
EVALUATING

---

1. **cut a wide swath:** created a great impression.

first time ma had shot anything but some chicken-killing varmint—which she'd done time to time when pa was away from home.

Only ma wouldn't let Jeanie and me call it home. "We came here from Illinois," she said, "but we're going home now."

"But ma," I protested, "I thought home was where we came from?"

"Home is where we're going now," ma said, "and we'll know it when we find it. Now that pa is gone we'll have to build that home ourselves."

She had a way of saying "home" so it sounded like a rare and wonderful place and kept Jeanie and me looking always at the horizon, just knowing it was over there, waiting for us to see it. She had given us the dream, and even Jeanie, who was only six, she had it too.

> "Home is where we're going now," ma said, "and we'll know it when we find it."

She might tell us that home was where we were going, but I knew home was where ma was, a warm and friendly place with biscuits on the table and fresh-made butter. We wouldn't have a real home until ma was there and we had a fire going. Only I'd build the fire.

Mr. Buchanan, who was captain of the wagon train, came to us with Tryon Burt, who was guide. "We'll help you," Mr. Buchanan said. "I know you'll be wanting to go back, and—"

"But we are not going back." Ma smiled at them. "And don't be afraid we'll be a burden. I know you have troubles of your own, and we will manage very well."

Mr. Buchanan looked uncomfortable, like he was trying to think of the right thing to say.

Angela: I never thought about home being a place you're going to instead of a place you're from.
CONNECTING

Angela: Bud makes home sound perfect. I wonder if they'll find it?
EVALUATING, QUESTIONING

The entire story can be found on pages 737–755. To practice reading strategies, go to "Your Turn" on pages S20–S27.

Reading
for Information

Reading literature often leads to other kinds of reading experiences. For example, you may read about a historical event in this book and then do research on that event for social studies class. When you read encyclopedia articles, newspapers, magazines, Web pages, and textbooks, you are reading for information. This kind of reading requires you to use a different set of skills. The strategies below will help you.

REFERENCE BOOK

554 **Oregon Trail**

Oregon Trail was the longest of the great overland routes used in the westward expansion of the United States. It wound 2,000 miles (3,200 kilometers) through prairies and deserts and across mountains from Independence, Missouri, to the Pacific Northwest. Even today, travelers can see the deeply rutted road cut by wagon wheels along sections of the trail.

Families traveling to the Oregon region usually began their journey at Independence, near the Missouri River. They followed a trail that ran northwest to Fort Kearny, Nebraska. Then they traveled up the Platte River and its north branch to Fort Laramie, Wyoming. From this point, they continued along the North Platte to its Sweetwater branch, and crossed through South Pass in the Rocky Mountains to the Green River Valley at Fort Bridger, Wyoming. The route turned northwest to Fort Hall in the Snake River area, and on to Fort Boise, Idaho. Settlers crossed the Grande Ronde Valley and the Blue Mountains to Marcus Whitman's mission at Walla Walla, Washington. Then they traveled down the Columbia River to Fort Vancouver and the Willamette Valley of Oregon.

Travel on the Oregon Trail was a severe test of strength and endurance. The journey in a covered wagon took six months. Settlers often had to cross flooded rivers. Indians attacked the wagon trains, and cholera and other diseases were common. Food, water, and wood were always scarce, and the travelers often encountered contaminated water holes.

Explorers and fur traders first traced the course of the Oregon Trail. In 1805, Meriwether Lewis and William Clark traveled on a western section of the route in the region of the Snake and Columbia rivers. Traders returning from Astoria also used the trail. Benjamin Bonneville is credited with taking the first wagons through South Pass in the 1830's. Nathaniel J. Wyeth also led compa-

In Guernsey, Wyoming, you can still see the tracks that covered wagons cut into solid rock.

STRATEGIES FOR READING

SET A PURPOSE FOR READING

- Decide why you are reading the material—to study for a test, to do research, or simply to find out more about a topic that interests you.
- Use your purpose to determine how detailed your notes will be.

LOOK FOR DESIGN FEATURES

- Look at the title, any subheads, boldfaced words or phrases, boxed text, and any other text that is highlighted in some way.
- Use these text organizers to help you preview the text and identify the main ideas.
- Study photographs, maps, charts, graphs, and captions.

NOTICE TEXT STRUCTURES AND PATTERNS

- Does the text make comparisons? Does it describe causes and effects? Is there a sequence of events?
- Look for signal words such as *same, different, because, first,* and *then* to help you see the organizational pattern.

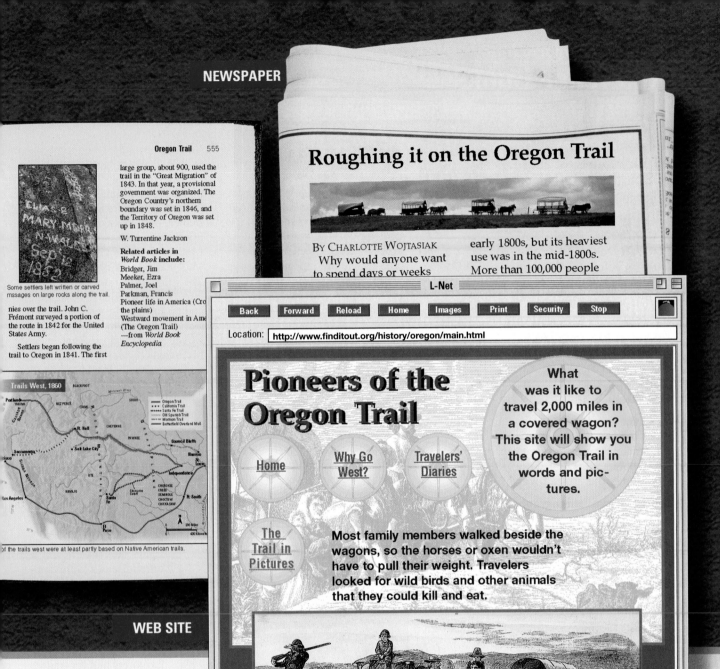

Roughing it on the Oregon Trail

BY CHARLOTTE WOJTASIAK
Why would anyone want
to spend days or weeks

early 1800s, but its heaviest
use was in the mid-1800s.
More than 100,000 people

Oregon Trail 555

large group, about 900, used the
trail in the "Great Migration" of
1843. In that year, a provisional
government was organized. The
Oregon Country's northern
boundary was set in 1846, and
the Territory of Oregon was set
up in 1848.

W. Turrentine Jackson

Related articles in
World Book include:
Bridger, Jim
Meeker, Ezra
Palmer, Joel
Parkman, Francis
Pioneer life in America (Cro
the plains)
Westward movement in Ame
(The Oregon Trail)
—from *World Book*
Encyclopedia

Some settlers left written or carved
mssages on large rocks along the trail.

nies over the trail. John C.
Frémont surveyed a portion of
the route in 1842 for the United
States Army.

Settlers began following the
trail to Oregon in 1841. The first

Trails West, 1860

of the trails west were at least partly based on Native American trails.

L-Net

Back | Forward | Reload | Home | Images | Print | Security | Stop

Location: http://www.finditout.org/history/oregon/main.html

Pioneers of the Oregon Trail

Home | Why Go West? | Travelers' Diaries

The Trail in Pictures

What was it like to travel 2,000 miles in a covered wagon? This site will show you the Oregon Trail in words and pictures.

Most family members walked beside the wagons, so the horses or oxen wouldn't have to pull their weight. Travelers looked for wild birds and other animals that they could kill and eat.

READ SLOWLY AND CAREFULLY

- Take notes on the main ideas. Try to paraphrase, or state the information in your own words.
- Map the information by using a concept web or other graphic organizer.
- Notice unfamiliar words. These are sometimes defined in the text.
- If there are questions with the text, be sure you can answer them.

EVALUATE THE INFORMATION

- Think about what you have read. Does the text make sense? Is it complete?
- Summarize the information—give the main points in just a few words.

Reference books such as encyclopedias, atlases, and textbooks provide reliable information. Use the strategies from the previous pages and the tips below to read the encyclopedia article. Then see how Angela and Travis applied the strategies as they did research for a social studies project.

STRATEGIES FOR READING

A Read the heading.
It will tell you the main idea of the article. Longer articles often have subheadings that show what topics the article covers.

B Look at maps, photographs, and captions.
Visuals linked to the text can give you important information.

C Notice how the text is organized.
This article describes the geography of the trail and then discusses its history.

D Look for clues to unfamiliar words.
You can sometimes understand words like *cholera* by thinking about their context—the words and sentences around them.

E Decide whether you need more information.
If you are doing research, a general article like this one can help you understand and narrow your topic. This article includes a list of related articles from the same encyclopedia.

---

554 **Oregon Trail**

A Oregon Trail was the longest of the great overland routes used in the westward expansion of the United States. It wound 2,000 miles (3,200 kilometers) through prairies and deserts and across mountains from Independence, Missouri, to the Pacific Northwest. Even today, travelers can see the deeply rutted road cut by wagon wheels along sections of the trail.

Families traveling to the Oregon region usually began their journey at Independence, near the Missouri River. They followed a trail that ran northwest to Fort Kearny, Nebraska. Then they traveled up the Platte River and its north branch to Fort Laramie, Wyoming. From this point, they continued along the North Platte to its Sweetwater branch, and crossed through South Pass in the Rocky Mountains to the Green River Valley at Fort Bridger, Wyoming. The route turned northwest to Fort Hall in the Snake River area, and on to Fort Boise, Idaho. Settlers crossed the Grande Ronde Valley and the Blue Mountains to Marcus Whitman's mission at Walla Walla, Washington. Then they traveled down the Columbia River to Fort Vancouver and the Willamette Valley of Oregon.

C Travel on the Oregon Trail was a severe test of strength and endurance. The journey in a covered wagon took six months.

Settlers often had to cross flooded rivers. Indians attacked the wagon trains, and cholera and **D** other diseases were common. Food, water, and wood were always scarce, and the travelers often encountered contaminated water holes.

Explorers and fur traders first traced the course of the Oregon Trail. In 1805, Meriwether Lewis and William Clark traveled on a western section of the route in the region of the Snake and Columbia rivers. Traders returning from Astoria also used the trail. Benjamin Bonneville is credited with taking the first wagons through South Pass in the 1830's. Nathaniel J. Wyeth also

B In Guernsey, Wyoming, you can still see the tracks that covered wagons cut into solid rock.

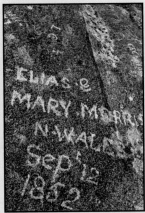

Some settlers left written or carved mssages on large rocks along the trail.

led companies over the trail. John C. Frémont surveyed a portion of the route in 1842 for the United States Army.

Settlers began following the trail to Oregon in 1841. The first large group, about 900, used the trail in the "Great Migration" of 1843. In that year, a provisional government was organized. The Oregon Country's northern boundary was set in 1846, and the Territory of Oregon was set up in 1848.

W. Turrentine Jackson

Related articles in E *World Book* include:

Bridger, Jim
Meeker, Ezra
Palmer, Joel
Parkman, Francis
Pioneer life in America (Crossing the plains)
Westward movement in America (The Oregon Trail)
—from *World Book Encyclopedia*

Trails West, 1860

Legend:
— Oregon Trail
▪▪▪ California Trail
•••• Santa Fe Trail
═══ Old Spanish Trail
▪ ▪ ▪ Mormon Trail
— Butterfield Overland Mail

BLACKFOOT · Missouri River · SIOUX · NEZ PERCE · CROW · YAKIMA · CHEYENNE · PAWNEE · Portland · Ft. Hall · Council Bluffs · Sacramento · Salt Lake City · Nauvoo · San Francisco · St. Louis · Independence · UTE · NAVAJO · Cimmaron Cutoff · CHEROKEE · CREEK · SEMINOLE · CHOCTAW · CHICKASAW · Santa Fe · Ft. Smith · Los Angeles · El Paso · PACIFIC OCEAN · CASCADE RANGE · SIERRA NEVADA · ROCKY MOUNTAINS · GREAT PLAINS · Mississippi River

0   200 Miles
0   400 Kilometers

Many of the trails west were at least partly based on Native American trails.

Newspapers and magazines inform you about your community and the world. Read the strategies below. Then practice your skills by reading the article.

STRATEGIES FOR READING

A **Read the headline and subheads.**
They show what the article is about.

B **Look at visuals and captions.**
Photographs, maps, or graphics draw your attention and provide information.

C **Think about the structure of the text.**
This article gives the main idea in the first section and details related to the main idea in the next two sections. For more on text organization, see pages R6–R10 in the Reading Handbook.

D **Watch for difficult words and phrases.**
The article includes the words *tin-pan, merriment,* and *frolic.* If you can't find an explanation in the text, consult a dictionary.

E **Notice any quotations.**
Think about whether the people quoted are likely to be reliable. Then decide whether you need to do more research on the topic.

A # Roughing it on the Oregon Trail

BY CHARLOTTE WOJTASIAK

Why would anyone want to spend days or weeks traveling a dusty trail in a horse-drawn wagon?

"For the fun of it—just to see if I could," says one participant.

"I want to find out what my ancestors went through, and maybe reclaim a little bit of the past," explains another.

"I grew up reading the *Little House* books by Laura Ingalls Wilder, and I want to get a sense of what pioneer life was like," says a third.

C Thanks to several different tour operators in Nebraska, Wyoming, and Oregon, tourists can learn what it was like to journey along the Oregon Trail—one of the most famous migrations in U.S. history.

A **What was the Oregon Trail?**

The Oregon Trail stretched 2,000 miles from Independence, Missouri, to Portland, in what was then called Oregon Country. Fur trappers and explorers developed the trail in the early 1800s, but its heaviest use was in the mid-1800s. More than 100,000 people had traveled the trail by 1850. The trip took about six months and required crossing deserts, mountains, and prairies. Travelers wanted some of the rich farmland available in the northwest, but many paid a harsh price. By one estimate, 1 out of every 17 adults and 1 out of every 5 children died on the journey—most from disease or accidents. They were buried along the trail.

A bone-jolting ride

Steering a horse-drawn replica of a covered wagon isn't easy. The leather reins tighten and slacken, the wheels rumble and groan, and the entire wagon bounces constantly. Three miles an hour is considered a high speed.

"I just can't believe it," **E** exclaims Anna Morley, who is on a five-day tour of the trail. "There aren't any cars or houses, and the scenery moves by so slowly. The pioneers must have felt

During reenactments of the Oregon Trail journey, some participants wear period costumes.

was impossible to carry enough meat for the journey, so travelers hunted along the way. There was plenty of cooking and washing to do, of course. Even children worked—gathering firewood and looking after younger siblings, among other duties.

"I love to read about the old days, but I'm sort of glad I didn't live in them," says 11-year-old Cassie Bagwell, who is on a two-day tour. She and her parents are learning to cook over an open fire and set up tents, though no chores are required on the tour.

"I'm glad my folks brought me on this trip," she continues. "The pioneers seem so *real* now."

absolutely cut off from the world they used to know."

Despite all the hardships the settlers faced, there were light-hearted moments. On June 24, 1850, Margaret Fink wrote in her diary about crossing a mountain pass and entering Oregon Country: "There was a hailstorm at noon, but that did not prevent the assembled company from having an off-hand celebration. . . . Music from a violin with tin-pan accompaniment contributed to the general merriment of a grand frolic."

Families worked together

Everyone traveling the trail had to work. Livestock had to be fed, watered, and herded. It

This family had to fit all of its supplies in the wagon shown here.

World Wide Web pages that are created by museums, libraries, universities, and government agencies can be reliable sources of information. Use the strategies below to read Web pages and evaluate what you find.

STRATEGIES FOR READING

A **Find the page's Web address.**
This is usually in a box at the top of the screen. Write down or bookmark the address in case you get lost while Web surfing.

B **Read the page's title.**
The title usually gives the main idea of the page.

C **Look for links to other parts of the site.**
Scan the menu options and decide which are most likely to have the information you need. Don't get lost following link after link. Use the Back button to retrace your steps when necessary.

D **Notice source citations.**
Some sites tell you where their information is from so you can judge its reliability.

E **Write down important ideas and details.**
Try to paraphrase the text, or restate it in your own words. Then decide whether you need to check other sources.

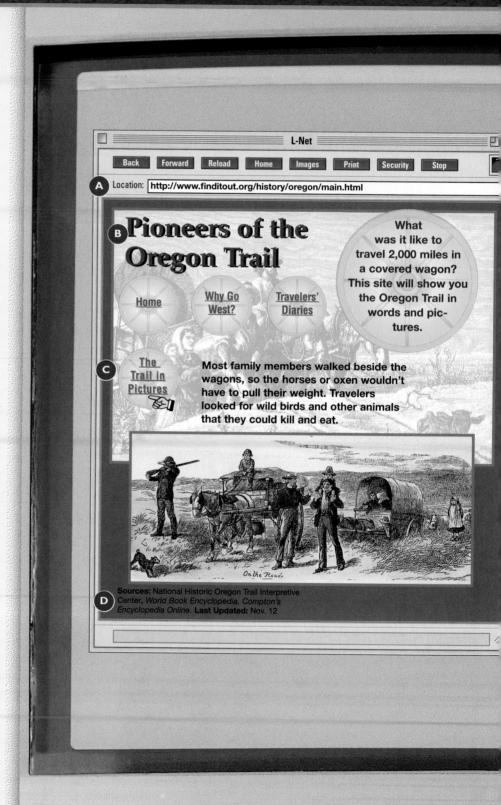

L-Net

Back   Forward   Reload   Home   Images   Print   Security   Stop

A Location: http://www.finditout.org/history/oregon/main.html

B Pioneers of the Oregon Trail

Home   Why Go West?   Travelers' Diaries

What was it like to travel 2,000 miles in a covered wagon? This site will show you the Oregon Trail in words and pictures.

C The Trail in Pictures

Most family members walked beside the wagons, so the horses or oxen wouldn't have to pull their weight. Travelers looked for wild birds and other animals that they could kill and eat.

On the Road

D **Sources:** National Historic Oregon Trail Interpretive Center, *World Book Encyclopedia, Compton's Encyclopedia Online.* **Last Updated:** Nov. 12

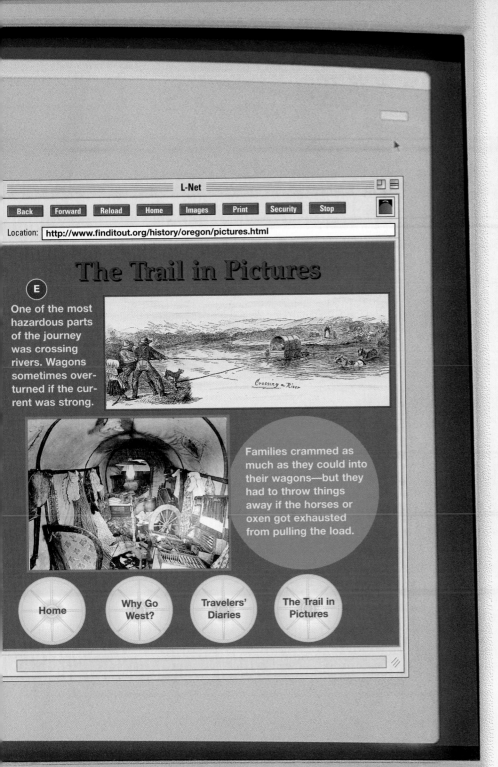

L-Net

Back | Forward | Reload | Home | Images | Print | Security | Stop

Location: http://www.finditout.org/history/oregon/pictures.html

The Trail in Pictures

E

One of the most hazardous parts of the journey was crossing rivers. Wagons sometimes overturned if the current was strong.

Crossing a River

Families crammed as much as they could into their wagons—but they had to throw things away if the horses or oxen got exhausted from pulling the load.

Home | Why Go West? | Travelers' Diaries | The Trail in Pictures

STRATEGIES IN ACTION

Angela: I can tell from the title that this site probably has information I need for my project. The sources listed are two encyclopedias and a historic site, so the information is probably reliable.

Travis: I want to know what the people and the wagons looked like, so I'll click on "The Trail in Pictures."

Angela: I can't believe how much stuff they crammed in those wagons!

Travis: I'll take notes about the river crossings. Then I'll see if the "Travelers' Diaries" link has any information I can use in my research report.

Your Turn
Applying the Strategies

As you read the following story, create a **Reader's Notebook** to help you understand and reflect on what you read. Prompts and questions in the margins will help you. For instructions on how to create a Reader's Notebook, see page S4.

"Charles"
by Shirley Jackson

Text	Response
P. S22 "How <u>was</u> school today?"	The mom seems nervous.
PP. S22, S23 "Look at my thumb. Gee, you're dumb."	I wonder why Laurie's dad doesn't get irritated when he does this?

STRATEGIES FOR READING

Here are sample pages from the notebooks Angela and Travis created as they read "Charles." For strategies to use before, during, and after reading, see "Reading Literature" on pages S6–S7.

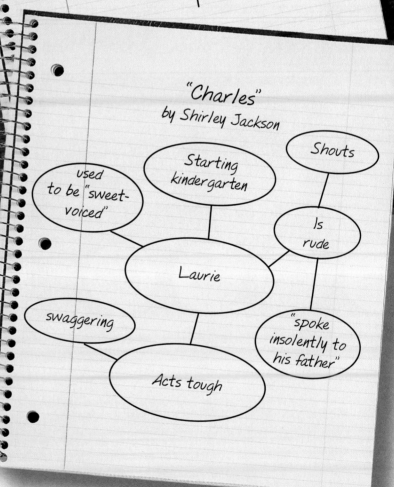

"Charles"
by Shirley Jackson

- Shouts
- Starting kindergarten
- used to be "sweet-voiced"
- Is rude
- Laurie
- swaggering
- "spoke insolently to his father"
- Acts tough

Charles

by Shirley Jackson

Copyright © David Shannon

EVALUATE ▶
Based on what you have read so far, list three or four adjectives that describe Laurie.

he day my son Laurie started kindergarten he renounced corduroy overalls with bibs and began wearing blue jeans with a belt; I watched him go off the first morning with the older girl next door, seeing clearly that an era of my life was ended, my sweet-voiced nursery-school tot replaced by a long-trousered, swaggering character who forgot to stop at the corner and wave goodbye to me.

He came home the same way, the front door slamming open, his cap on the floor, and the voice suddenly become raucous shouting, "Isn't anybody *here?*"

At lunch he spoke insolently to his father, spilled his baby sister's milk, and remarked that his teacher said we were not to take the name of the Lord in vain.

"How *was* school today?" I asked, elaborately casual.

"All right," he said.

"Did you learn anything?" his father asked.

Laurie regarded his father coldly. "I didn't learn nothing," he said.

"Anything," I said. "Didn't learn anything."

"The teacher spanked a boy, though," Laurie said, addressing his bread and butter. "For being fresh," he added, with his mouth full.

"What did he do?" I asked. "Who was it?"

Laurie thought. "It was Charles," he said. "He was fresh. The teacher spanked him and made him stand in a corner. He was awfully fresh."

"What did he do?" I asked again, but Laurie slid off his chair, took a cookie, and left, while his father was still saying, "See here, young man."

The next day Laurie remarked at lunch, as soon as he sat down. "Well, Charles was bad again today." He grinned enormously and said, "Today Charles hit the teacher."

"Good heavens," I said, mindful of the Lord's name, "I suppose he got spanked again?"

"He sure did," Laurie said. "Look up," he said to his father.

"What?" his father said, looking up.

"Look down," Laurie said. "Look at my thumb. Gee, you're

QUESTION ▶
Why do you think Laurie "grinned enormously" when telling his parents about Charles?

dumb." He began to laugh insanely.

"Why did Charles hit the teacher?" I asked quickly.

"Because she tried to make him color with red crayons," Laurie said. "Charles wanted to color with green crayons so he hit the teacher and she spanked him and said nobody play with Charles but everybody did."

The third day—it was Wednesday of the first week—Charles bounced a see-saw onto the head of a little girl and made her bleed, and the teacher made him stay inside all during recess. Thursday Charles had to stand in a corner during story-time because he kept pounding his feet on the floor. Friday Charles was deprived of blackboard privileges because he threw chalk.

On Saturday I remarked to my husband, "Do you think kindergarten is too unsettling for Laurie? All this toughness, and bad grammar, and this Charles boy sounds like such a bad influence."

"It'll be all right," my husband said reassuringly. "Bound to be people like Charles in the world. Might as well meet them now as later."

On Monday Laurie came home late, full of news. "Charles," he shouted as he came up the hill; I was waiting anxiously on the

◀ EVALUATE: MAIN IDEA
What is the main idea of the story so far?

◀ CONNECT
Do you agree with the mother's point of view or the father's? Why?

front steps. "Charles," Laurie yelled all the way up the hill, "Charles was bad again."

"Come right in," I said, as soon as he came close enough. "Lunch is waiting."

"You know what Charles did?" he demanded, following me through the door. "Charles yelled so in school they sent a boy in from first grade to tell the teacher she had to make Charles keep quiet, and so Charles had to stay after school. And so all the children stayed to watch him."

"What did he do?" I asked.

"He just sat there," Laurie said, climbing into his chair at the table. "Hi, Pop, y'old dust mop."

"Charles had to stay after school today," I told my husband. "Everyone stayed with him."

"What does this Charles look like?" my husband asked Laurie. "What's his other name?"

"He's bigger than me," Laurie said. "And he doesn't have any rubbers and he doesn't ever wear a jacket."

EVALUATE: MAKE INFERENCES ▶
Why do you think Laurie's parents are so interested in Charles?

Monday night was the first Parent-Teachers meeting, and only the fact that the baby had a cold kept me from going; I wanted passionately to meet Charles's mother. On Tuesday Laurie remarked suddenly, "Our teacher had a friend come to see her in school today."

"Charles's mother?" my husband and I asked simultaneously.

"Naaah," Laurie said scornfully. "It was a man who came and made us do exercises, we had to touch our toes. Look." He climbed down from his chair and squatted down and touched his toes. "Like this," he said. He got solemnly back into his chair and said, picking up his fork, "Charles didn't even do exercises."

"That's fine," I said heartily. "Didn't Charles want to do exercises?"

"Naaah," Laurie said. "Charles was so fresh to the teacher's friend he wasn't *let* do exercises."

"Fresh again?" I said.

VISUALIZE ▶
Can you imagine the scene in the classroom when Charles kicks the teacher's friend? Make a sketch or write down a few words describing it.

"He kicked the teacher's friend," Laurie said. "The teacher's friend told Charles to touch his toes like I just did and Charles kicked him."

"What are they going to do about Charles, do you suppose?" Laurie's father asked him.

"He was her helper, that's all."

Laurie shrugged elaborately. "Throw him out of school, I guess," he said.

Wednesday and Thursday were routine; Charles yelled during story hour and hit a boy in the stomach and made him cry. On Friday Charles stayed after school again and so did all the other children.

With the third week of kindergarten Charles was an institution in our family; the baby was being a Charles when she cried all afternoon; Laurie did a Charles when he filled his wagon full of mud and pulled it through the kitchen; even my husband, when he caught his elbow in the telephone cord and pulled the telephone and a bowl of flowers off the table, said, after the first minute, "Looks like Charles."

During the third and fourth weeks it looked like a reformation in Charles; Laurie reported grimly at lunch on Thursday of the third week, "Charles was so good today the teacher gave him an apple."

"What?" I said, and my husband added warily, "You mean Charles?"

"Charles," Laurie said. "He gave the crayons around and he

◄ QUESTION
Why do you think the other children stay after school with Charles?

EVALUATE ▶
Are you surprised at the change in Charles's behavior? Why or why not?

CLARIFY ▶
What does Laurie's father mean when he says that Charles is "plotting"?

PREDICT ▶
What do you think will happen at the meeting?

picked up the books afterward and the teacher said he was her helper."

"What happened?" I asked incredulously.

"He was her helper, that's all," Laurie said, and shrugged.

"Can this be true, about Charles?" I asked my husband that night. "Can something like this happen?"

"Wait and see," my husband said cynically. "When you've got a Charles to deal with, this

may mean he's only plotting." He seemed to be wrong. For over a week Charles was the teacher's helper; each day he handed things out and he picked things up; no one had to stay after school.

"The PTA meeting's next week again," I told my husband one evening. "I'm going to find Charles's mother there."

"Ask her what happened to Charles," my husband said. "I'd like to know."

"I'd like to know myself," I said.

On Friday of that week things were back to normal. "You know what Charles did today?" Laurie demanded at the lunch table, in a voice slightly awed. "He told a little girl to say a word and she said it and the teacher washed her mouth out with soap and Charles laughed."

"What word?" his father asked unwisely, and Laurie said, "I'll have to whisper it to you, it's so bad." He got down off his chair and went around to his father. His father bent his head down and Laurie whispered joyfully. His father's eyes widened.

"Did Charles tell the little girl to say *that*?" he asked respectfully.

"She said it *twice*," Laurie said. "Charles told her to say it *twice*."

"What happened to Charles?" my husband asked.

"Nothing," Laurie said. "He was passing out the crayons."

Monday morning Charles abandoned the little girl and said

the evil word himself three or four times, getting his mouth washed out with soap each time. He also threw chalk.

My husband came to the door with me that evening as I set out for the PTA meeting. "Invite her over for a cup of tea after the meeting," he said. "I want to get a look at her."

"If only she's there," I said prayerfully.

"She'll be there," my husband said. "I don't see how they could hold a PTA meeting without Charles's mother."

At the meeting I sat restlessly, scanning each comfortable matronly face, trying to determine which one hid the secret of Charles. None of them looked to me haggard enough. No one stood up in the meeting and apologized for the way her son had been acting. No one mentioned Charles.

After the meeting I identified and sought out Laurie's kindergarten teacher. She had a plate with a cup of tea and a piece of chocolate cake; I had a plate with a cup of tea and a piece of marshmallow cake. We maneuvered up to one another cautiously, and smiled.

"I've been so anxious to meet you," I said. "I'm Laurie's mother."

"We're all so interested in Laurie," she said.

"Well, he certainly likes kindergarten," I said. "He talks about it all the time."

"We had a little trouble adjusting, the first week or so," she said primly, "but now he's a fine little helper. With occasional lapses, of course."

"Laurie usually adjusts very quickly," I said. "I suppose this time it's Charles's influence."

"Charles?"

"Yes," I said, laughing, "you must have your hands full in that kindergarten, with Charles."

"Charles?" she said. "We don't have any Charles in the kindergarten." ❖

◀ CLARIFY: SUMMARIZE
What has been going on in the kindergarten?

EVALUATE
What did you think of the end of the story?

INSIGHTS

Learn what

you are,

and be such.

Pindar
Greek poet

Looking Deep (1996),
Terry Pappas. Pastel,
21" × 20". Collection
Steven Pappas

The Literature You'll Read

The Concepts You'll Study

Vocabulary and Reading Comprehension
Vocabulary Focus: Informal Language—Idioms and Slang
Making Predictions
Cause and Effect
Connecting
Visualizing
Predicting

Writing and Language Conventions
Writing Workshop: Response to Literature
Sentence Fragments
Subjects in Unusual Word Order
Predicate Nouns and Adjectives
Consistent Verb Tense
Pronouns and Antecedents

Literary Analysis
Genre Focus: Fiction
Motivation
Plot
Theme
Setting
Irony

Speaking and Listening
Story Skits
Acceptance Speech
Interview
Short Speech
Film Review

Fiction

> *Detail is the lifeblood of fiction.*
> —J. Gardner

Fiction is writing that comes from a writer's imagination. It can be inspired by actual events or completely made up. Usually a work of fiction is created through the use of vivid details that we recognize or that move us in some way.

Depending on its length, a work of fiction may be classified as a short story or as a novel. Both novels and short stories contain the four main elements of **plot, character, setting,** and **theme.** Use the following descriptions and examples to learn more about the elements of fiction.

Key Forms of Fiction

short story
- usually revolves around a single idea
- is short enough to be read at one sitting

novel
- involves a more complicated plot
- a longer work

Plot

The sequence of events in a story is called the **plot.** The plot is the writer's plan for what happens, when it happens, and to whom it happens. A plot is usually built around a central **conflict**—a problem or struggle involving two or more opposing forces. Plot **complications** are events or problems that arise and make it more difficult to resolve the conflict. Although the development of every plot is different, most plots develop in four stages:

- **Exposition** provides background for the story. Characters are introduced, and the setting is described.
- **Rising action** occurs next. The plot "thickens" as the central conflict begins to unfold. Complications are introduced and suspense builds.
- **Climax** is the point of greatest interest or suspense in the story. It is the turning point, when the action reaches a peak and the outcome of the conflict is decided. The climax may occur because of a decision the characters reach or because of a discovery or an event that changes the situation. The climax usually results in a change in the characters or a solution to the conflict.
- **Falling action** (sometimes called resolution) occurs after the climax and resolves the conflict. The loose ends are tied up and the story comes to a close.

PLOT

"You got anything to say to my brother, you say it to me, Mary Louise Williams of Raggedy Town, Baltimore."

"What are you, his mother?" sasses Rosie.

"That's right, Fatso. And the next word out of anybody and I'll be their mother too." So they just stand there and Gretchen shifts from one leg to the other and so do they. Then Gretchen puts her hands on her hips and is about to say something with her freckle-face self but doesn't.

—Toni Cade Bambara, "Raymond's Run"

YOUR TURN Read the paragraph above. What conflict is introduced?

PLOT AT A GLANCE

Climax

Rising Action

Exposition

Falling Action *resolution*

Character

Characters are the people, animals, or imaginary creatures that take part in the action of a story. Usually a short story centers on events in the life of one important character. This is the **main character.** The other less important characters are called **minor characters.** They interact with the main character and help to move the plot along. Characters have motives and traits. **Motives** are a character's emotions, desires, or needs that prompt action. **Traits** are more permanent qualities in a character's personality, such as gentleness or boldness. Both cause a character to act or react to situations and other characters.

YOUR TURN In the passage on the top right, identify the details that tell you what the boy is like.

CHARACTER

I watched him go off the first morning with the older girl next door, seeing clearly that an era of my life was ended, my sweet-voiced nursery-school tot replaced by a long-trousered, swaggering character who forgot to stop at the corner and wave good-bye to me.

He came home the same way, the front door slamming open, his cap on the floor, and the voice suddenly become raucous shouting, "Isn't anybody *here?*"

—Shirley Jackson, "Charles"

Each time she went to the store, her eyes scanned the checkouts . . . her heart in her mouth.
—from "Checkouts"

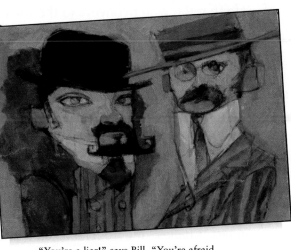

"You're a liar!" says Bill. "You're afraid. You was to be burned at sunrise. . . ."
—from "The Ransom of Red Chief"

He believed he must have looked a fool in her eyes.
—from "Checkouts"

Setting

A story's **setting** is the time and place in which the action of the story happens. A story may be set in a real or an imaginary place. The events may occur in the past, the present, or the future. Setting also includes the customs and culture of the place and time. A writer's vivid description helps readers picture the setting. Setting can often play a role in the plot and the development of character.

YOUR TURN In the paragraph at the right, what words and phrases present the setting of the story?

SETTING

The orphanage is high in the Carolina mountains. Sometimes in winter the snowdrifts are so deep that the institution is cut off from the village below, from all the world. Fog hides the mountain peaks, the snow swirls down the valleys, and a wind blows so bitterly that the orphanage boys who take the milk twice daily to the baby cottage reach the door with fingers stiff in an agony of numbness.

—Marjorie Kinnan Rawlings, "A Mother in Mannville"

THEME

"We had a little trouble adjusting, the first week or so," she said primly, "but now he's a fine little helper. With occasional lapses, of course."

"Laurie usually adjusts very quickly," I said. "I suppose this time it's Charles's influence."

"Charles?"

"Yes," I said, laughing, "you must have your hands full in that kindergarten, with Charles."

"Charles?" she said. "We don't have any Charles in the kindergarten."

—Shirley Jackson, "Charles"

Theme

A **theme** is the meaning, moral, or message about life that the writer conveys to the reader. Most themes are not stated in the story but are revealed by one or more of the following

- the title of the story
- important phrases and statements about ideas like courage and freedom
- the ways the characters change and the lessons they learn about life

For example, the theme of "Charles" is brought out in this passage from the end of the story. Once Laurie's mother meets his teacher, she discovers that Laurie is in fact "Charles," the troublemaker. The theme of the story is that sometimes a person's behavior, and not his or her words, is a better key to who that person really is. Many stories share the same theme but may treat it differently.

Reading Fiction

If you've ever loved a story, you know the power of fiction. Great stories entertain and inform us with powerful **themes,** interesting **characters,** and compelling **plots.** To get the most out of reading fiction, use the strategies explained here.

How to Apply the Strategies

Preview the story and set a purpose for reading. Look at the title and illustrations, and skim through the pages to familiarize yourself with the selection. Can you tell what the story is about? As you read the selections, use the strategies listed below. Stop from time to time to **monitor** how well they are working for you.

CONNECT   Compare the setting and characters with people and places you know. Do any of the characters share the thoughts or experiences that you have had?

QUESTION   The story's events, characters, and ideas should all make sense to you. Ask questions during confusing or suspenseful moments in the story. As you read, look for the answers.

PREDICT   As you become more involved in the story, ask yourself what will happen next. Look for clues that hint of events to come.

VISUALIZE   Can you picture the setting and characters in your mind? Visualizing will make the story seem more real to you.

Here's how Jonathan uses the strategies:

*"I like action books—stories that make me sit on the edge of my seat. I enjoy **visualizing** the characters and setting and can picture the action taking place. To make the story more real, I **connect** the characters and events to my own life. At different points in the story, I stop to **predict** what is happening. I like to guess before I read the outcome. It's fun to get to the end of the story to see if I was right."*

PREPARING to *Read*
ACTIVE READER GUIDE

Checkouts
by CYNTHIA RYLANT

Connect to Your Life

Offering Advice Changes, such as moving to a new community or entering a new school, are not always easy to face. Have you, or has someone you know, ever experienced a major change? How did the change make you feel? Did you feel this way for a long time? Based on your experience, consider what advice you would offer to a friend who is facing a major change.

Build Background

GEOGRAPHY

In "Checkouts," a girl moves from a small town to a large city—Cincinnati, Ohio. Cincinnati lies in the southwest corner of Ohio, very close to Kentucky and Indiana. Today, Cincinnati (Ohio's third largest city) is a manufacturing center with important transportation links along the Ohio River.

WORDS TO KNOW
Vocabulary Preview

brazen	lapse
deftly	meditation
fetish	perverse
impulse	reverie
intuition	tedious

Focus Your Reading

LITERARY ANALYSIS   MOTIVATION

The reason why a character acts, thinks, or feels a certain way is called **motivation.** Some motivations you will find directly in the text. Others you will be able to infer, or guess, from the situation or from the person's behavior. As you read this story, think about the reasons why the characters act as they do or why they fail to act.

ACTIVE READING   MAKING PREDICTIONS

When you read a story and make guesses about what might happen next, you are making **predictions.** Predicting means using what you know to guess what might happen. You can look for clues in the story to help you predict. You can also use knowledge from your own experiences.

📖 **READER'S NOTEBOOK** As you read this story, stop now and then to think about what will happen next. Use the chart as a guide. Fill in the right-hand column.

Stopping Point in Story	Prediction
Page 25: "Then one day the bag boy dropped her jar of mayonnaise and that is how she fell in love."	The boy will ask the girl out.
Page 26: "Incredibly, it was another four weeks before they saw each other again."	

Checkouts

by Cynthia Rylant

Her parents had moved her to Cincinnati, to a large house with beveled glass[1] windows and several porches and the *history* her mother liked to emphasize. You'll love the house, they said. You'll be lonely at first, they admitted, but you're so nice you'll make friends fast. And as an <u>impulse</u> tore at her to lie on the floor, to hold to their ankles and tell them she felt she was dying, to offer anything, anything at all, so they might allow her to finish growing up in the town of her childhood, they firmed their mouths and spoke from their chests and they said, It's decided.

ACTIVE READER

EVALUATE What is the effect of the author's repetition of the phrase "moved her to Cincinnati"?

They moved her to Cincinnati, where for a month she spent the greater part of every day in a room

---

1. **beveled glass:** glass whose edges are cut at an angle, as in window glass.

WORDS
TO
KNOW
impulse (ĭm′pŭls′) *n.* a sudden wish or urge

She liked to grocery shop.

Copyright © Hodges Soileau.

full of beveled glass windows, sifting through photographs of the life she'd lived and left behind. But it is difficult work, suffering, and in its own way a kind of art, and finally she didn't have the energy for it anymore, so she emerged from the beautiful house and fell in love with a bag boy at the supermarket. Of course, this didn't happen all at once, just like that, but in the sequence of things that's exactly the way it happened.

She liked to grocery shop. She loved it in the way some people love to drive long country roads, because doing it she could think and relax and wander. Her parents wrote up the list and handed it to her and off she went without complaint to perform what they regarded as a great sacrifice of her time and a sign that she was indeed a very nice girl. She had never told them how much she loved grocery shopping, only that she was "willing" to do it. She had an <u>intuition</u> which told her that her parents were not safe for sharing such strong, important facts about herself. Let them think they knew her.

Once inside the supermarket, her hands firmly around the handle of the cart, she would <u>lapse</u> into a kind of <u>reverie</u> and wheel toward the produce. Like a Tibetan monk[2] in solitary <u>meditation</u>, she calmed to a point of deep, deep happiness; this feeling came to her, reliably, if strangely, only in the supermarket.

ACTIVE READER

CLARIFY What personality trait in the girl supports this comparison to a Tibetan monk?

---

2. **Tibetan monk:** a member of a Buddhist sect in central Asia who practices meditation.

WORDS TO KNOW

intuition (ĭn'tōō-ĭsh'ən) *n.* a sense of knowing not dependent on reason; an insight
lapse (lăps) *v.* to sink or slip gradually
reverie (rĕv'ə-rē) *n.* a daydream
meditation (mĕd'ĭ-tā'shən) *n.* the act of deep thinking or reflection

Portrait by George Passantino, from *Portraits in Oil*. Copyright © 1980 Wendon Blake.

Then one day the bag boy dropped her jar of mayonnaise and that is how she fell in love.

He was nervous—first day on the job—and along had come this fascinating girl, standing in the checkout line with the unfocused stare one often sees in young children, her face turned enough away that he might take several full looks at her as he packed sturdy bags full of food and the goods of modern life. She interested him because her hair was red and thick, and in it she had placed a huge orange bow, nearly the size of a small hat. That was enough to distract him, and when finally it was her groceries he was packing, she looked at him and smiled and he could respond only by busting her jar of mayonnaise on the floor, shards of glass and oozing cream decorating the area around his feet.

She loved him at exactly that moment, and if he'd known this perhaps he wouldn't have fallen into the brown depression he fell into, which lasted the rest of his shift. He believed he must have looked a fool in her eyes, and he envied the sureness of everyone around him: the cocky cashier at the register, the grim and harried store manager, the bland butcher, and the <u>brazen</u> bag boys who smoked in the warehouse on their breaks. He wanted a second chance. Another chance to be confident and say witty things to her as he threw tin cans into her bags, persuading her to allow him to help her to her car so he might learn just a little about her, check out the floor of the car for signs of hobbies or <u>fetishes</u> and the bumpers for clues as to beliefs and loyalties.

25

But he busted her jar of mayonnaise and nothing else worked out for the rest of the day.

Strange, how attractive clumsiness can be. She left the supermarket with stars in her eyes, for she had loved the way his long nervous fingers moved from the conveyor belt to the bags, how deftly (until the mayonnaise) they had picked up her items and placed them into her bags. She had loved the way the hair kept falling into his eyes as he leaned over to grab a box or a tin. And the tattered brown shoes he wore with no socks. And the left side of his collar turned in rather than out.

The bag boy seemed a wonderful contrast to the perfectly beautiful house she had been forced to accept as her home, to the *history* she hated, to the loneliness she had become used to, and she couldn't wait to come back for more of his awkwardness and dishevelment.

ACTIVE READER

PREDICT What will happen between the boy and the girl?

Incredibly, it was another four weeks before they saw each other again. As fate would have it, her visits to the supermarket never coincided with his schedule to bag. Each time she went to the store, her eyes scanned the checkouts at once, her heart in her mouth. And each hour he worked, the bag boy kept one eye on the door, watching for the red-haired girl with the big orange bow.

Yet in their disappointment these weeks there was a kind of ecstasy. It is reason enough to be alive, the hope you may see again some face which has meant something to you. The anticipation of meeting the bag boy eased the girl's painful transition into her new and jarring life in Cincinnati. It provided for her an anchor amid all that was impersonal and unfamiliar, and she spent less time on thoughts of what she had left behind as she concentrated on what might lie ahead. And for the boy, the long and often tedious hours at the supermarket which provided no challenge other than that of showing up the following workday . . . these hours became possibilities of mystery and romance for him as he watched the electric doors for the girl in the orange bow.

And when finally they did meet up again, neither offered a clue to the other that he, or she, had been the object of obsessive thought for weeks. She spotted him as soon as she came into the store, but she kept her eyes strictly in front of her as she pulled out a cart and wheeled it toward the produce. And he, too, knew the instant she came through the door—though the orange bow was gone, replaced by a small but bright yellow flower instead—and he never once turned his head in her direction but watched her from the corner of his vision as he tried to swallow back the fear in his throat.

It is odd how we sometimes deny ourselves the very pleasure we have longed for and which is finally within our reach. For some perverse reason she would not have been able to articulate, the girl did not bring her cart up to the bag boy's checkout when her shopping was done. And the bag boy let her leave the store, pretending no notice of her.

This is often the way of children, when they truly want a thing, to pretend that they don't. And then they grow angry when no one tries harder to give them this thing they so casually rejected, and they soon find themselves in a

---

WORDS
TO
KNOW

deftly (dĕft'lē) *adv.* move in a quick and skillful manner
tedious (tē'dē-əs) *adj.* boring, tiresome because of length, slowness, or dullness
perverse (pər-vûrs') *adj.* turned away from what is right or good; improper

Food City (1967), Richard Estes. Oil, acrylic and graphite on fiberboard, 48" × 68". Collection of the Akron Art Museum. Purchased with funds raised by the Masked Ball 1955–63, by exchange. Photo by Richman Haire. Copyright © Richard Estes/ Licensed by VAGA, New York/ Marlborough Gallery, New York.

...the bag boy kept one eye on the door, watching for the red-haired girl...

The girl hated herself for not checking out at the boy's line...

ACTIVE READER

EVALUATE Do the girl and the boy seem like real people to you? Why or why not?

rage simply because they cannot say yes when they mean yes. Humans are very complicated. (And perhaps cats, who have been known to react in the same way, though the resulting rage can only be guessed at.)

The girl hated herself for not checking out at the boy's line, and the boy hated himself for not catching her eye and saying hello, and they most sincerely hated each other without having ever exchanged even two minutes of conversation.

Eventually—in fact, within the week—a kind and intelligent boy who lived very near her beautiful house asked the girl to a movie and she gave up her fancy for the bag boy at the supermarket. And the bag boy himself grew so bored with his job that he made a desperate search for something better and ended up in a bookstore where scores of fascinating girls lingered like honeybees about a hive. Some months later the bag boy and the girl with the orange bow again crossed paths, standing in line with their dates at a movie theater, and, glancing toward the other, each smiled slightly, then looked away, as strangers on public buses often do, when one is moving off the bus and the other is moving on. ❖

Connect to the Literature

1. **What Do You Think?** Do you think that the girl will eventually come to enjoy life in Cincinnati? Why or why not?

Comprehension Check
- What do the parents say about the fact that the girl does not want to move?
- How does the girl feel about the boy when she first meets him?
- How does the girl feel about the boy when she meets him four weeks later?

Think Critically

2. What does the girl think that her parents feel about her? Do you agree or disagree? Explain.

3. What does the girl's appearance (page 25) tell you about the kind of person she is?

4. What kind of person is the boy? How do you know?

5. **ACTIVE READING** **MAKING PREDICTIONS**
   Look over the **predictions** you wrote in your 📖 READER'S NOTEBOOK. How well do they match the actual events or ending of the story? Explain your answer.

6. Explain the meaning of the story's title.

   Think About:
   - the various meanings of the phrase *check out*
   - how the phrase *check out* relates to the girl's feelings about her new home
   - why the author chose "Checkouts" rather than "Checkout"

Extend Interpretations

7. **What If?** Suppose the girl and the boy had actually spoken to each other the first time they met. Would they have liked each other? Explain your answer.

8. **Connect to Life** Toward the end of the story, the author says that "humans are very complicated" because "they cannot say yes when they mean yes." Do you agree? Why or why not?

Literary Analysis

MOTIVATION The reason why a character acts, reacts, thinks, or feels a certain way is called **motivation.** Sometimes, a character's motivation is directly stated in the text. Other times, you have to infer, or guess, what the motivation is.

Paired Activity Working with a partner, go back through the story and, in a chart like the one shown, jot down the motivations of the girl and the boy. Which motivations are directly stated in the story? Which motivations did you have to infer? Discuss your responses with your partner.

Who?	Action	Motivation
The Girl	...she spent the greater part of every day in a room full of beveled glass windows... (page 23)	Does not want to begin a new life
The Boy	And the bag boy let her leave the store, pretending no notice of her. (page 26)	
The Boy and The Girl	And when finally they did meet up again, neither offered a clue... (page 26)	

Writing

Personal Letter Imagine that you are in the same situation as the red-haired girl at the beginning of the story. Write a letter to your parents

Dear Mom and Dad,

explaining why you do or do not want to move to a new city. Think of your own motivation for feeling the way you do about moving. Be sure to edit for correct grammar, punctuation, and spelling. Place the entry in your **Working Portfolio.**

Speaking & Listening

Story Skits With a group of classmates, perform a skit that dramatizes one of the following three scenes:

- the time when the girl's parents tell her they are moving
- the first time the boy and the girl meet
- the second time the boy and the girl meet

Perform your skit for the rest of the class.

Speaking and Listening Handbook
See p. R104.

Research & Technology

Part-Time Jobs Research opportunities for after-school or summer jobs in your area. Telephone one or two supermarkets or bookstores to find out about their employment opportunities for young people. For example, how much do young people earn at these jobs and what are their tasks? Use your information to write a paragraph in which you compare and contrast the advantages and the disadvantages of each job. Be sure to note your sources.

Vocabulary

STANDARDIZED TEST PRACTICE

Choose the word or group of words that means the same, or nearly the same, as the underlined Word to Know.

1. An overwhelming <u>impulse</u>
   A fear   B urge
   C insight   D rage

2. A strong <u>intuition</u>
   J resemblance   K respect
   L hunch   M introduction

3. To handle a situation <u>deftly</u>
   A skillfully   B slowly
   C dutifully   D unwillingly

4. To <u>lapse</u> into fourth place
   J leap   K struggle
   L lunge   M slip

5. A pleasant <u>reverie</u>
   A reminder   B daydream
   C agreement   D surprise

6. A personal <u>fetish</u>
   J responsibility   K goal
   L attachment   M grudge

7. A <u>perverse</u> reason
   A contrary   B sincere
   C perfect   D lengthy

8. A <u>brazen</u> act
   J puzzling   K playful
   L thoughtful   M bold

9. A <u>tedious</u> assignment
   A strenuous   B boring
   C tempting   D daily

10. Deep <u>meditation</u>
    J hunger   K irritation
    L reflection   M embarrassment

Vocabulary Handbook
See p. R24: Synonyms and Antonyms.

Grammar in Context: Sentence Fragments

In "Checkouts," Cynthia Rylant uses complete sentences to tell the story. Occasionally, however, she uses a **sentence fragment.**

> **She had loved the way the hair kept falling into his eyes as he leaned over to grab a box or a tin.** And the tattered brown shoes he wore with no socks.

The words in red type are a **sentence fragment** because they do not form a complete sentence. In a sentence fragment the subject, the verb, or sometimes both are missing. This sentence fragment is missing a subject and a verb. Corrected, the sentence might read: *She had loved the tattered brown shoes he wore with no socks.* Even though sentence fragments are not grammatically correct, writers sometimes use them for purposes of style.

WRITING EXERCISE Identify each group of words as a complete sentence or a sentence fragment. Rewrite each fragment to make a complete sentence.

Example: *Original* Come into the supermarket.

Rewritten He saw her come into the supermarket.

1. The bag boy smiled at the redheaded girl in the checkout line.
2. Didn't work.
3. Hoping to catch her attention.
4. Glass shattered and went flying.
5. Really wanted to meet her.

Grammar Handbook
See p. R75: Writing Complete Sentences.

Cynthia Rylant
born 1954

"I love being a writer because I want to leave something here on earth to make it better, prettier, stronger."

Growing Up in the Mountains Cynthia Rylant spent her childhood in the mountains of Appalachia, where she and her mother lived with Rylant's grandparents. The household had neither running water nor electricity, but the beauty of the mountains and their people stayed with Rylant as an adult and found their way into her writings.

New World After finishing her education, Rylant waited tables for some time before finding her true vocation. A job in Ohio in the Akron Public Library introduced her to the world of children's books. Her picture books, short stories, and young-adult novels have won many national awards.

AUTHOR ACTIVITY
Country Life, City Life Before she became a writer, Cynthia Rylant moved from a very rural area in the Appalachians to several other places, including the city of Akron, Ohio. Find out more about the geography and way of life in the Appalachians. Then discuss with classmates how the contrast between the two places might have influenced this story.

Raymond's Run

by TONI CADE BAMBARA

Connect to Your Life

How Would You Act? "Raymond's Run" is about a girl named Squeaky who has responsibility for her mentally disabled older brother Raymond. Imagine yourself in a similar situation. What might your relationship with your brother be like? How would you handle the responsibility of caring for him? If, in fact, you have a disabled family member, describe your relationship with him or her.

Build Background

SCIENCE

Squeaky's brother Raymond has a medical condition known as hydrocephalus (hī′drō-sĕf′ə-ləs). The symptoms of this disorder include a swelling of the head caused by too much fluid collecting in the skull. Sometimes, the excess fluid damages the brain, as in Raymond's case.

Hydrocephalus may be caused by an infection, a tumor, a major head injury, or a malformation of the brain before birth. Childhood hydrocephalus is fairly rare and affects only about 1 out of every 1,000 children.

WORDS TO KNOW
Vocabulary Preview
clutch   relay
periscope   sidekick
prodigy

Focus Your Reading

LITERARY ANALYSIS   PLOT

The events that make up the **plot** of a story can usually be divided into rising action, climax, and falling action. The **rising action** consists of the **conflicts** and **complications** that the main character faces. The **climax** is the greatest point of interest, or turning point. The **falling action** provides resolution of the conflict. For example, in the story you are about to read, conflicts arise as a result of Squeaky's relationship with her brother and with Gretchen, one of the girls in the neighborhood. As you read the story, look for the ways in which Squeaky resolves these conflicts.

ACTIVE READING   CAUSE AND EFFECT

Events in a plot are sometimes linked to each other in a relationship of cause and effect. What happened is called the **effect,** or result. Why it happened is called the **cause,** or reason.

📖READER'S NOTEBOOK As you read "Raymond's Run," think about how one event causes, or brings about, another. Make a chart like the one shown. In the first column, list the effect. In the second column, list the cause.

What Happened: Effect	Why It Happened: Cause
The big kids call her Mercury.	Squeaky is the "swiftest thing in the neighborhood."

Raymond's Run

by Toni Cade Bambara

I don't have much work to do around the house like some girls. My mother does that. And I don't have to earn my pocket money by hustling; George runs errands for the big boys and sells Christmas cards. And anything else that's got to get done, my father does. All I have to do in life is mind my brother Raymond, which is enough.

Petite Fille [Little girl] (1982), Loïs Mailou Jones. Watercolor, 24" × 30". Courtesy of the Loïs Mailou Jones Estate.

Sometimes I slip and say my little brother Raymond. But as any fool can see he's much bigger and he's older too. But a lot of people call him my little brother 'cause he needs looking after 'cause he's not quite right. And a lot of smart mouths got lots to say about that too, especially when George was minding him. But now, if anybody has anything to say to Raymond, anything to say about his big head,[1] they have to come by me. And I don't play the dozens[2] or believe in standing around with somebody in my face doing a lot of talking. I much rather just knock you down and take my chances even if I am a little girl with skinny arms and a squeaky voice, which is how I got the name Squeaky. And if things get too rough,

I run. And as anybody can tell you, I'm the fastest thing on two feet. There is no track meet that I don't win the first place medal. I use to win the twenty-yard dash when I was a little kid in kindergarten. Nowadays, it's the fifty-yard dash. And tomorrow I'm subject to run the quarter-meter <u>relay</u> all by myself and come in first, second, and third. The big kids call me Mercury[3] 'cause I'm the swiftest thing in the neighborhood. Everybody knows that—except

---

1. **big head:** enlarged skull (a result of Raymond's hydrocephalus).
2. **play the dozens:** exchange rhyming insults.
3. **Mercury:** in Roman mythology, the swift messenger of the gods.

WORDS TO KNOW

relay (rē'lā) *n.* a race in which each side uses several team members to complete the race; each member has a turn to finish a set part of the race and is then replaced by another team member to finish the next part, and so forth two people who know better, my father and me. He can beat me to Amsterdam Avenue with me having a two-fire-hydrant head start and him running with his hands in his pockets and whistling. But that's private information. 'Cause can you imagine some thirty-five-year-old man stuffing himself into PAL shorts to race little kids? So as far as everyone's concerned, I'm the fastest and that goes for Gretchen, too, who has put out the tale that she is going to win the

The big kids call me Mercury 'cause I'm the swiftest thing in the neighborhood.

first-place medal this year. Ridiculous. In the second place, she's got short legs. In the third place, she's got freckles. In the first place, no one can beat me and that's all there is to it.

I'm standing on the corner admiring the weather and about to take a stroll down Broadway so I can practice my breathing exercises, and I've got Raymond walking on the inside close to the buildings, 'cause he's subject to fits of fantasy and starts thinking he's a circus performer and that the curb is a tightrope strung high in the air. And sometimes after a rain he likes to step down off his tightrope right into the gutter and slosh around getting his shoes and cuffs wet. Then I get hit when I get home. Or sometimes if you don't watch him he'll dash across traffic to the island in the middle of Broadway and give the pigeons a fit. Then I have to go behind him apologizing to all the old people sitting around trying to get some sun and

getting all upset with the pigeons fluttering around them, scattering their newspapers and upsetting the wax-paper lunches in their laps. So I keep Raymond on the inside of me, and he plays like he's driving a stagecoach which is O.K. by me so long as he doesn't run me over or interrupt my breathing exercises, which I have to do on account of I'm serious about my running, and I don't care who knows it.

Now some people like to act like things come easy to them, won't let on that they practice. Not me. I'll high-prance down 34th Street like a rodeo pony to keep my knees strong even if it does get my mother uptight so that she walks ahead like she's not with me, don't know me, is all by herself on a shopping trip, and I am somebody else's crazy child. Now you take Cynthia Procter for instance. She's just the opposite. If there's a test tomorrow, she'll say something like, "Oh, I guess I'll play handball this afternoon and watch television tonight," just to let you know she ain't thinking about the test. Or like last week when she won the spelling bee for the millionth time, "A good thing you got 'receive,' Squeaky, 'cause I would have got it wrong. I completely forgot about the spelling bee." And she'll <u>clutch</u> the lace on her blouse like it was a narrow escape. Oh, brother. But of course when I pass her house on my early morning trots around the block, she is practicing the scales on the piano over and over and over and over. Then in music class she always lets herself get bumped around so she falls accidentally on purpose onto the piano stool and is so surprised to find herself sitting there that she decides just for fun to try out the ole keys. And what do you know—Chopin's waltzes[4] just

---

4. **Chopin's** (shō-pănz′) **waltzes:** works by the 19th-century pianist and composer Frédéric Chopin.

WORDS
TO
KNOW

clutch (klŭch) *v.* to grasp and hold tightly

spring out of her fingertips and she's the most surprised thing in the world. A regular <u>prodigy</u>. I could kill people like that. I stay up all night studying the words for the spelling bee. And you can see me any time of day practicing running. I never walk if I can trot, and shame on Raymond if he can't keep up. But of course he does, 'cause if he hangs back someone's liable to walk up to

I am not a strawberry. I do not dance on my toes. I run.

him and get smart, or take his allowance from him, or ask him where he got that great big pumpkin head. People are so stupid sometimes.

So I'm strolling down Broadway breathing out and breathing in on counts of seven, which is my lucky number, and here comes Gretchen and her <u>sidekicks</u>: Mary Louise, who used to be a friend of mine when she first moved to Harlem from Baltimore and got beat up by everybody till I took up for her on account of her mother and my mother used to sing in the same choir when they were young girls, but people ain't grateful, so now she hangs out with the new girl Gretchen and talks about me like a dog; and Rosie, who is as fat as I am skinny and has a big mouth where Raymond is concerned and is too stupid to know that there is not a big deal of difference between herself and Raymond and that she can't afford to throw stones. So they are steady coming up Broadway and I see right away that it's going to be one of those Dodge City scenes 'cause the street ain't that big and they're close to the buildings just as we are. First I think I'll step into

the candy store and look over the new comics and let them pass. But that's chicken and I've got a reputation to consider. So then I think I'll just walk straight on through them or over them if necessary. But as they get to me, they slow down. I'm ready to fight, 'cause like I said I don't feature a whole lot of chitchat, I much prefer to just knock you down right from the jump and save everybody a lotta precious time.

"You signing up for the May Day races?" smiles Mary Louise, only it's not a smile at all. A dumb question like that doesn't deserve an answer. Besides, there's just me and Gretchen standing there really, so no use wasting my breath talking to shadows.

"I don't think you're going to win this time," says Rosie, trying to signify with her hands on her hips all salty, completely forgetting that I have whupped her behind many times for less salt than that.

"I always win 'cause I'm the best," I say straight at Gretchen who is, as far as I'm concerned, the only one talking in this ventriloquist-dummy routine.[5] Gretchen smiles, but it's not a smile, and I'm thinking that girls never really smile at each other because they don't know how and don't want to know how and there's probably no one to teach us how, 'cause grown-up girls don't know either. Then they all look at Raymond who has just brought his mule team to a standstill. And they're about to see what trouble they can get into through him.

"What grade you in now, Raymond?"

"You got anything to say to my brother, you say it to me, Mary Louise Williams of Raggedy Town, Baltimore."

---

5. **ventriloquist-dummy routine:** Squeaky thinks that all the girls are speaking Gretchen's thoughts, like dummies being controlled by a ventriloquist.

"What are you, his mother?" sasses Rosie.

"That's right, Fatso. And the next word out of anybody and I'll be their mother too." So they just stand there and Gretchen shifts from one leg to the other and so do they. Then Gretchen puts her hands on her hips and is about to say something with her freckle-face self but doesn't. Then she walks around me looking me up and down but keeps walking up Broadway, and her sidekicks follow her. So me and Raymond smile at each other and he says, "Gidyap," to his team and I continue with my breathing exercises, strolling down Broadway toward the ice man on 145th with not a care in the world 'cause I am Miss Quicksilver[6] herself.

I take my time getting to the park on May Day because the track meet is the last thing on the program. The biggest thing on the program is the May Pole dancing, which I can do without, thank you, even if my mother thinks it's a shame I don't take part and act like a girl for a change. You'd think my mother'd be grateful not to have to make me a white organdy dress with a big satin sash and buy me new white baby-doll shoes that can't be taken out of the box till the big day. You'd think she'd be glad her daughter ain't out there prancing around a May Pole getting the new clothes all dirty and sweaty and trying to act like a fairy or a flower or whatever you're supposed to be when you should be trying to be yourself, whatever that is, which is, as far as I am concerned, a poor Black girl who really can't afford to buy shoes and a new dress you only wear once a lifetime 'cause it won't fit next year.

I was once a strawberry in a Hansel and Gretel pageant when I was in nursery school and didn't have no better sense than to dance on tiptoe with my arms in a circle over my head doing umbrella steps and being a perfect fool just so my mother and father could come dressed up and clap. You'd think they'd know better than to encourage that kind of nonsense. I am not a strawberry. I do not dance on my toes. I run. That is what I am all about. So I always come late to the May Day program, just in time to get my number pinned on and lay in the grass till they announce the fifty-yard dash.

I put Raymond in the little swings, which is a tight squeeze this year and will be impossible next year. Then I look around for Mr. Pearson, who pins the numbers on. I'm really looking for Gretchen, if you want to know the truth, but she's not around. The park is jam-packed. Parents in hats and corsages and breast-pocket handkerchiefs peeking up. Kids in white dresses and light-blue suits. The parkees[7] unfolding chairs and chasing the rowdy kids from Lenox[8] as if they had no right to be there. The big guys with their caps on backwards, leaning against the fence swirling the basketballs on the tips of their fingers, waiting for all these crazy people to clear out the park so they can play. Most of the kids in my class are carrying bass drums and glockenspiels[9] and flutes. You'd think they'd put in a few bongos or something for real like that.

Then here comes Mr. Pearson with his clipboard and his cards and pencils and whistles and safety pins and 50 million other things he's always dropping all over the place with his clumsy self. He sticks out in a crowd because he's on stilts. We used to call him Jack and the Beanstalk to get him mad. But I'm the only one that can outrun him and get away, and I'm too grown for that silliness now.

"Well, Squeaky," he says, checking my name off the list and handing me number seven and two pins. And I'm thinking he's got no right to

---

6. **Miss Quicksilver:** a reference to the speed with which quicksilver (the liquid metal mercury) flows.

7. **parkees:** park employees.

8. **Lenox:** a street in the Harlem section of New York City.

9. **glockenspiels** (glŏk′ən-spēlz′): musical instruments having tuned metal bars that are played with light hammers.

call me Squeaky if I can't call him Beanstalk.

"Hazel Elizabeth Deborah Parker," I correct him and tell him to write it down on his board.

"Well, Hazel Elizabeth Deborah Parker, going to give someone else a break this year?" I squint at him real hard to see if he is seriously thinking I should lose the race on purpose just to give someone else a break. "Only six girls running this time," he continues, shaking his head sadly like it's my fault all of New York didn't turn out in sneakers. "That new girl should give you a run for your money." He

Grownups got a lot of nerve sometimes.

looks around the park for Gretchen like a periscope in a submarine movie. "Wouldn't it be a nice gesture if you were . . . to ahhh . . . "

I give him such a look he couldn't finish putting that idea into words. Grownups got a lot of nerve sometimes. I pin number seven to myself and stomp away, I'm so burnt. And I go straight for the track and stretch out on the grass while the band winds up with "Oh, the Monkey Wrapped His Tail Around the Flag Pole," which my teacher calls by some other name. The man on the loudspeaker is calling everyone over to the track and I'm on my back looking at the sky, trying to pretend I'm in the country, but I can't, because even grass in the city feels hard as sidewalk, and there's just no pretending you are anywhere but in a "concrete jungle" as my grandfather says.

The twenty-yard dash takes all of the two minutes 'cause most of the little kids don't know no better than to run off the track or run the wrong way or run smack into the fence and fall down and cry. One little kid, though, has got the good sense to run straight for the white ribbon up ahead so he wins. Then the second-graders line up for the thirty-yard dash and I don't even bother to turn my head to watch 'cause Raphael Perez always wins. He wins before he even begins by psyching the runners, telling them they're going to trip on their shoelaces and fall on their faces or lose their shorts or something, which he doesn't really have to do since he is very fast, almost as fast as I am. After that is the forty-yard dash which I used to run when I was in first grade. Raymond is hollering from the swings 'cause he knows I'm about to do my thing 'cause the man on the loudspeaker has just announced the fifty-yard dash, although he might just as well be giving a recipe for angel food cake 'cause you can hardly make out what he's saying for the static. I get up and slip off my sweatpants and then I see Gretchen standing at the starting line, kicking her legs out like a pro. Then as I get into place I see that ole Raymond is on line on the other side of the fence, bending down with his fingers on the ground just like he knew what he was doing. I was going to yell at him but then I didn't. It burns up your energy to holler.

Every time, just before I take off in a race, I always feel like I'm in a dream, the kind of dream you have when you're sick with fever and feel all hot and weightless. I dream I'm flying over a sandy beach in the early morning sun, kissing the leaves of the trees as I fly by. And there's always the smell of apples, just like in the country when I was little and used to

WORDS TO KNOW

periscope (pĕr'ĭ-skōp') *n.* a tube-shaped optical device that lets one see into an area beyond the area he or she is in; a periscope is used by submarines to see above the surface of the water while remaining invisible

Visa (1951), Stuart Davis. Oil on canvas, 40" × 52" . The Museum of Modern Art, New York, gift of Mrs. Gertrud A. Mellon. Copyright ©1996 Estate of Stuart Davis/Licensed by VAGA, New York. Photograph copyright © 1995 The Museum of Modern Art, New York.

think I was a choo-choo train, running through the fields of corn and chugging up the hill to the orchard. And all the time I'm dreaming this, I get lighter and lighter until I'm flying over the beach again, getting blown through the sky like a feather that weighs nothing at all. But once I spread my fingers in the dirt and crouch over the Get on Your Mark, the dream goes and I am solid again and am telling myself, Squeaky you must win, you must win, you are the fastest thing in the world, you can even beat your father up Amsterdam if you really try. And then I feel my weight coming back just behind my knees then down to my feet then into the earth and the pistol shot explodes in my blood and I am off and weightless again, flying past the other runners, my arms pumping up and down and the whole world is quiet except for the crunch as I zoom over the gravel in the track. I glance to my left and there is no one. To the right, a blurred Gretchen, who's got her chin jutting out as if it would win the race all by itself. And on the other side of the fence is Raymond with his arms down to his side and the palms tucked up behind him, running in his very own style, and it's the first time I ever saw that and I almost stop to watch my brother Raymond on his first run. But the white ribbon is bouncing toward me and I tear past it, racing into the distance till my feet with a mind of their own start digging up footfuls of dirt and brake me short. Then all the kids standing on the side pile on me, banging me on the back and slapping my head with their May Day programs, for I have won again and everybody on 151st Street can walk tall for another year.

"In first place . . ." the man on the loudspeaker is clear as a bell now. But then he pauses and the loudspeaker starts to whine. Then static. And I lean down to catch my breath and here comes Gretchen walking back, for she's overshot the finish line too, huffing and puffing with her hands on her hips taking it slow, breathing in steady time like a real pro and I sort of like her a little for the first time. "In first place . . ." and then three or four voices get all mixed up on the loudspeaker and I dig my sneaker into the grass and stare at Gretchen who's staring back, we both wondering just who did win. I can hear old Beanstalk arguing with the man on the loudspeaker and then a few others running their mouths about what the stopwatches say. Then I hear Raymond yanking at the fence to call me and I wave to shush him, but he keeps rattling the fence like a gorilla in a cage like in them gorilla movies, but then like a dancer or something he starts climbing up nice and easy but very fast. And it occurs to me, watching how smoothly he climbs hand over hand and remembering how he looked running with his arms down to his side and with the wind pulling his mouth back and his teeth showing and all, it occurred to me that Raymond would make a very fine runner. Doesn't he always keep up with me on my trots? And he surely knows how to breathe in counts of seven 'cause he's always doing it at the dinner table, which drives my brother George up the wall. And I'm smiling to beat the band 'cause if I've lost this race, or if me and Gretchen tied, or even if I've won, I can always retire as a runner and begin a whole new career as a coach with Raymond as my champion. After all, with a little more study I can beat Cynthia and her phony self at the spelling bee. And if I bugged my mother, I could get piano lessons and become a star. And I have a big rep as the baddest thing around. And I've got a roomful of ribbons and medals and awards. But what has Raymond got to call his own?

So I stand there with my new plans, laughing out loud by this time as Raymond jumps down from the fence and runs over with his teeth showing and his arms down to the side, which no one before him has quite mastered as a running style. And by the time he comes over I'm jumping up and down so glad to see him— my brother Raymond, a great runner in the family tradition. But of course everyone thinks I'm jumping up and down because the men on the loudspeaker have finally gotten themselves together and compared notes and are announcing, "In first place—Miss Hazel Elizabeth Deborah Parker." (Dig that.) "In second place —Miss Gretchen P. Lewis." And I look over at Gretchen, wondering what the "P." stands for. And I smile. 'Cause she's good, no doubt about it. Maybe she'd like to help me coach Raymond; she obviously is serious about running, as any fool can see. And she nods to congratulate me and then she smiles. And I smile. We stand there with this big smile of respect between us. It's about as real a smile as girls can do for each other, considering we don't practice real smiling every day, you know, 'cause maybe we too busy being flowers or fairies or strawberries instead of something honest and worthy of respect . . . you know . . . like being people. ❖

Connect to the Literature

1. **What Do You Think?** How do you think Squeaky will get along with Raymond and Gretchen at the end of the story?

Comprehension Check
- Why does Squeaky sometimes think that Raymond is younger than he is?
- What is Squeaky's special talent?
- What plans does Squeaky have for Raymond at the end of the story?

Think Critically

2. **ACTIVE READING CAUSE AND EFFECT**
Look over the causes and effects that you listed in your **READER'S NOTEBOOK**. What events caused Squeaky to think that Raymond would make "a very fine runner"?

3. What do Squeaky's judgments of Cynthia Procter, Mary Louise, and Rosie tell you about the type of person Squeaky is? Explain your answer.

4. In what ways has Squeaky changed by the end of the story?

   Think About:
   - her feelings about Raymond
   - her view of Gretchen
   - her view of herself

5. Based on what you know about Squeaky from the story, would you like to be friends with her? Why or why not?

Extend Interpretations

6. **What If?** Think about Squeaky's relationship with Raymond. What if Raymond were not her brother? In what ways would Squeaky be a different person?

7. **Connect to Life** What attitude toward disabled people is presented in "Raymond's Run"? Do you think this attitude is typical of the way many people feel about disabled individuals? Explain.

Literary Analysis

PLOT The events that make up the **plot** of a story can usually be divided into rising action, climax, and falling action. The **rising action** consists of the **conflicts** and **complications** that the **main character** faces. Eventually, the plot reaches a **climax,** the turning point, or the point of greatest interest or suspense. In the **falling action,** or resolution, loose ends are tied up, and the story is brought to a close.

Group Activity With a small group of classmates, outline the events in "Raymond's Run" that form the rising action, the climax, and the falling action. Record your responses in a chart like the one shown. Compare your responses with those of other groups in your class.

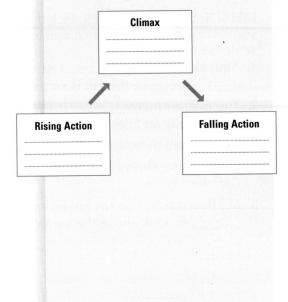

Writing

Personal-Best Paragraph
Squeaky says, "I'm the fastest thing on two feet." What are you really good at? Write a paragraph that describes a skill about which you feel very confident. Explain the effect this skill has had on your life. Place the paragraph in your **Working Portfolio.**
Writing Handbook
See p. R37: Paragraphs.

Speaking & Listening

Acceptance Speech Pretend that Squeaky must give a speech when she accepts first prize for winning the race. Present a speech in which Squeaky expresses her feelings about winning.

Research & Technology

Mental Imaging Many athletes use a technique known as mental imaging to improve their performance. Using sources from the library or Internet, find out about mental imaging. What steps are involved? How do professional athletes use this technique? How can amateur athletes benefit from using it? Be sure to note your sources.

Reading for INFORMATION
To begin your research, read "Do Try This at Home" on pages 44–47.

Art Connection

The painting on page 34 is entitled *Petite Fille. Petite fille* is French for "little girl." Do you think the girl looks like the picture you have of Squeaky in your mind? Why or why not?

Petite Fille [Little girl] (1982), Loïs Mailou Jones. Watercolor, 24" × 30". Courtesy of the Loïs Mailou Jones Estate.

Vocabulary

EXERCISE: DESCRIPTION CLUES Pick the vocabulary word that best completes the sentence.
1. Squeaky thinks one of her classmates is a _____ because the girl is so talented.
2. The quarter-meter _____ is the next race for Squeaky and her partner.
3. Cynthia will nervously _____ her blouse.
4. Mary Louise always tags along with Gretchen as her _____.
5. Mr. Pearson was so tall he did not need a _____ to look above the surface.

VOCABULARY STRATEGY: WORD PARTS Many English words come from Greek. For example, *periscope* comes from the Greek prefix *peri-* ("around") and the Greek word part *scope* ("look"). Write five words by combining a Greek prefix in the first column with the correct Greek word part in the second column.

1. tele-   a. archy
2. auto-   b. onym
3. mon-   c. scope
4. syn-   d. ology
5. psych-   e. graph

After you have formed your words, write down what you think they mean. Check your definitions by looking up the words in a dictionary.

Vocabulary Handbook
See p. R21: Word Parts.

| WORDS TO KNOW | clutch | prodigy | sidekick |
| | periscope | relay | |

Grammar in Context: Subjects in Unusual Word Order

In the following sentence from "Raymond's Run," writer Toni Cade Bambara has used unusual word order. Find the subject of the sentence. Then find the verb. Can you tell why the order is unusual?

> **Then here** comes Mr. Pearson **with his clipboard and his cards and pencils and whistles. . . .**

The **subject** of this sentence is *Mr. Pearson.* The **verb** is *comes.* The order is unusual because the subject follows the verb rather than coming before it. Here's how the sentence would look if Bambara had used the usual word order:

> **Then** Mr. Pearson comes **here with his clipboard and his cards and pencils and whistles. . . .**

WRITING EXERCISE Rewrite each sentence so that the subject follows the verb.

Example: *Original* Raymond ran through the streets.

Rewritten Through the streets ran Raymond.

1. The race begins now.
2. Squeaky dashed across the field.
3. Raymond comes here.
4. Raymond sat on the field.
5. The crowd stood at the starting line.

Grammar Handbook
See p. R76: Making Subjects and Verbs Agree.

Toni Cade Bambara
1939–1995

"I write because I really think that I've got hold of something. . . ."

Background and Beliefs Toni Cade Bambara believed that authors "are everyday people who write stories that come out of their neighborhoods." Like many of her characters, she grew up in New York City. She wrote about African Americans who show family pride and a strong sense of community.

Life Experience After attending college in New York City, Bambara studied theater and mime in Europe and dance and film in the United States. She planned recreational programs for the mentally ill and taught college English and African-American studies. During her later years she lived in Philadelphia, where she taught a writers' workshop, produced documentary videos, and was involved in her community. In 1981, she won the American Book Award for her novel *The Salt Eaters.*

AUTHOR ACTIVITY
Writing and Experience How does "Raymond's Run" reflect Bambara's attitudes toward the African-American community? In what way does the story reflect experiences in her life? In your answer, use the information in this biography and additional information that you research.

Source: *Women's Sports and Fitness*

Do Try This at Home

Mental imaging isn't just for the pros. It can improve your performance and help you overcome anxieties.

by Wendy DuBow

1 Ultimate Frisbee player Becky Hinks was getting frustrated. Every time she tried to throw a forehand into the end zone during a game, she blew the shot, curving the disc far out of bounds. Because she always made this throw perfectly in practice, she couldn't figure out how to fix it. Then one week Hinks added a new element to her routine: She spent 10 minutes a day imagining herself executing the throw correctly under pressure. Soon enough, she was nailing the toss every time.

2 Imaging is a proven tool of Olympic and other top-notch athletes. But it works just as effectively for weekend warriors. The key is to engage all the senses in the imaging process, says Jean Williams, sports psychologist at the University of Arizona and past president of the American Association for the Advancement of Applied Sports Psychology. "I don't like to use the term visualization because it implies just using the sense of the eyes. In the late '70s and early '80s, we began to realize that the best benefits come from maximizing all the senses: visual, kinesthetic, tactile, smell, hearing. Make the image as vivid as possible."

Although it's not completely clear why it works, mental imaging is used by nearly all top-level athletes and coaches to improve physical execution. "It definitely enhances learning," Williams says. "You can learn new techniques faster than if you just do physical practice, and

Outline

I. Imaging improves athletic performance
A. Effective for professionals and amateurs
B. Most effective techniques
   1. uses all five senses
   2. create vivid images

Reading for Information

Do you find it difficult to read and remember text that has many facts and details? Creating an **outline** is one way to organize the main ideas and details and help improve your comprehension. As you read the magazine article about mental imaging, think about how the information could be put into an outline.

Outlining Ideas

Outlining is a point-by-point list of the main ideas and details of text. Using an outline can help you make sense of long or detailed material.

YOUR TURN *Use the questions and activities below to help you create an outline of this magazine article.*

1 When you begin an outline, write out the main idea of each paragraph. The main idea is a statement about the main topic in a paragraph. What is the main idea of this paragraph?

2 In an outline, Roman numerals are used to indicate **main topics,** capital letters to show **subtopics,** and numbers to list details. The main topics are the key ideas or major categories. The subtopics are the less important ideas or details. Subtopics often contain supporting details.

A topic outline for paragraph number 2 is shown here. What are the main topic and the two subtopics of this outline?

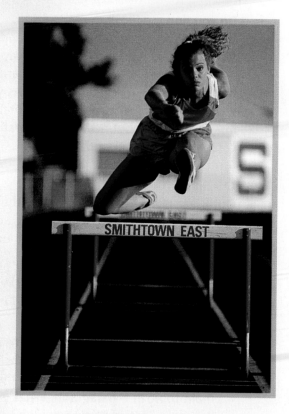

SMITHTOWN EAST

Whatever the reasons, experts agree that imaging has noticeable, positive effects.

still firing," explains Williams. "It's like a physiological blueprint." Whatever the reasons, experts agree that imaging has noticeable, positive effects.

you can refine performance." Imaging helps performance in other ways, too. While recuperating from an injury, athletes can "stay in the game" through mental practice. Sports psychologists point to numerous instances of athletes returning from injuries and achieving record-level performances because they've maintained their timing and concentration through systematic imaging.

Some psychologists believe imaging works simply because it creates the appropriate arousal and focus for succeeding in an activity, setting the mind and body in coordination before the actual performance. But there is also evidence that the neural pathways are trained as the mind engages. "The muscles you'd use during the sport are

Positive imagery creates a desirable mental state. Successful athletes often remark that they relive their great performances over and over between competitions to boost their confidence. It's also common for athletes to run through an impending race in their heads or picture themselves crossing the finish line in order to focus just prior to competition.

❸

Whether your goal is to get the gold or just to finish your first 5K, this technique can help you. "I can honestly not think of an athlete for whom imagery would not be beneficial," asserts Williams. "It's an extremely powerful tool."

Okay, so you're convinced that imaging is important for success, but you don't have the luxury of a coach analyzing your past performances or steering you toward your next goal. Don't worry—you can guide yourself to a better performance.

Make the image as accurate and detailed as you possibly can.

4 To practice mental imaging, find a quiet place to practice where you won't be disturbed. Choose which part of your sport you want to improve or identify a goal you want to set. Create a mental image of yourself performing your activity or meeting your goal. Make the image as accurate and detailed as you possibly can. Use all your senses to help you create the image.

If you are hoping to improve a technique, then remember a time when you did it very well. Recreate that moment in your mind. Repeat this image for a few minutes each day.

If you wish to reach a specific, long-term goal—for example, finishing a 10K race you will run in a month—then imagine very specifically how you'll feel when you have reached your goal. Again, do this several minutes each day until the big event.

Remember, be careful what you wish for— it could come true!

Reading for Information *continued*

3 Read the first sentence. Would you consider this sentence a main topic or a subtopic? Explain.

4 You can organize information in an outline by listing ideas in order of importance, or in the order in which they are given. A **sentence outline** uses complete sentences to describe the main ideas and details. A **topic outline** uses words or phrases for the main ideas. Create a topic outline for the paragraphs numbered 3 and 4.

Research & Technology
Activity Link: "Raymond's Run," p. 42. How does this magazine article help you understand how mental imaging is used? Write interview questions that you would like to ask an athlete who uses this technique.

Stop the Sun

by GARY PAULSEN

Connect to Your Life

In this story, the main character's father is strongly affected by the Vietnam War. Do you know someone who fought in this war?

Build Background

The Vietnam War has its roots in the 1860s when France conquered the country.

1862	The French take over Vietnam.
1940	The Japanese take control of Vietnam during World War II.
1945	Vietnam returns to French rule.
1946	War breaks out between Vietnam and France.
1954	The French withdraw. Vietnam becomes a divided nation.
1957	The Vietnam conflict intensifies between the Communist North, led by Ho Chi Minh, and the nationalists in the South.
1965	South Vietnam depends more and more on American support.
1973	United States withdraws troops from Vietnam.
1975	South Vietnam surrenders to North Vietnam.
1976	Vietnam becomes a united country under Communist rule.

Focus Your Reading

LITERARY ANALYSIS **THEME**

The meaning, moral, or message that a writer wishes to convey is called the **theme.** One way to identify a theme is to pay attention to the lessons learned by the **main character.** As you read this story, think about Terry's experience with his father and the lesson Terry learns about life.

ACTIVE READING **CONNECTING**

When readers make **connections** to a text, they ask themselves how their own experiences are similar to or different from the ones they are reading about. In your **READER'S NOTEBOOK,** create a chart in which you compare how Terry relates to his parents with how you relate to yours.

WORDS TO KNOW Vocabulary Preview

chant   dry   founder   inert   persist

STOP THE SUN

By Gary Paulsen

Terry Erickson was a tall boy, 13, starting to fill out with muscle but still a little awkward. He was on the edge of being a good athlete, which meant a lot to him. He felt it coming too slowly, though, and that bothered him.

But what bothered him even more was when his father's eyes went away.

Usually it happened when it didn't cause any particular trouble. Sometimes during a meal his father's fork would stop halfway to his mouth, just stop, and there would be a long pause while the eyes went away, far away.

After several minutes his mother would reach over and take the fork and put it gently down on his plate, and they would go back to eating—or try to go back to eating—normally.

They knew what caused it. When it first started, Terry had asked his mother in private what it was, what was causing the strange behavior.

"It's from the war," his mother had said. "The doctors at the veterans' hospital call it the Vietnam syndrome."

"Will it go away?"

"They don't know. Sometimes it goes away. Sometimes it doesn't. They are trying to help him."

"But what happened? What actually caused it?"

"I told you. Vietnam."

"But there had to be something," Terry persisted. "Something made him like that. Not just Vietnam. Billy's father was there, and he doesn't act that way."

"That's enough questions," his mother said sternly. "He doesn't talk about it, and I don't ask. Neither will you. Do you understand?"

"But, Mom."

"That's enough."

And he stopped pushing it. But it bothered him whenever it happened. When something bothered him, he liked to stay with it until he understood it, and he understood no part of this.

Words. His father had trouble, and they gave him words like Vietnam syndrome. He knew almost nothing of the war, and when he tried to find out about it, he kept hitting walls. Once he went to the school library and asked for anything they might have that could help him understand the war and how it affected his father. They gave him a dry history that described French involvement, Communist

involvement, American involvement. But it told him nothing of the war. It was all numbers, cold numbers, and nothing of what had *happened*. There just didn't seem to be anything that could help him.

Another time he stayed after class and tried to talk to Mr. Carlson, who taught history. But some part of Terry was embarrassed. He didn't

> "It's from the war," his mother had said. "The doctors at the veterans' hospital call it the Vietnam syndrome."

want to say why he wanted to know about Vietnam, so he couldn't be specific.

"What do you want to know about Vietnam, Terry?" Mr. Carlson had asked. "It was a big war."

Terry had looked at him, and something had started up in his mind, but he didn't let it out. He shrugged. "I just want to know what it was like. I know somebody who was in it."

"A friend?"

"Yessir. A good friend."

Mr. Carlson had studied him, looking into his eyes, but didn't ask any other questions. Instead he mentioned a couple of books Terry had not seen. They turned out to be pretty good. They told about how it felt to be in combat. Still, he couldn't make his father be one of the men he read about.

And it may have gone on and on like that, with Terry never really knowing any more about it except that his father's eyes started going away more and more often. It might have just gone the rest of his life that way except for the shopping mall.

| WORDS TO KNOW | **persist** (pər-sĭst′) *v.* to continue stubbornly
 dry (drī) *adj.* direct and without emotion; matter-of-fact |

Prometheus Under Fire (1984), Rupert Garcia. Pastel on paper, 29¾″ × 84″. Courtesy of the artist, Rena Bransten Gallery, San Francisco, and Galerie Claude Samuel, Paris. Copyright © 1995 Rupert Garcia.

It was easily the most embarrassing thing that ever happened to him.

It started as a normal shopping trip. His father had to go to the hardware store, and he asked Terry to go along.

When they got to the mall they split up. His father went to the hardware store, Terry to a record store to look at albums.

Terry browsed so long that he was late meeting his father at the mall's front door. But his father wasn't there, and Terry looked out to the car to make sure it was still in the parking lot. It was, and he supposed his father had just gotten busy, so he waited.

Still his father didn't come, and he was about to go to the hardware store to find him, when he noticed the commotion. Or not a commotion so much as a sudden movement of people.

Later, he thought of it and couldn't remember when the feeling first came to him that there was something wrong. The people were moving toward the hardware store, and that might have been what made Terry suspicious.

There was a crowd blocking the entry to the store, and he couldn't see what they were looking at. Some of them were laughing small, nervous laughs that made no sense.

Terry squeezed through the crowd until he got near the front. At first he saw nothing unusual. There were still some people in front of him, so he pushed a crack between them. Then he saw it: His father was squirming along the floor on his stomach. He was crying, looking terrified, his breath coming in short, hot pants like some kind of hurt animal.

It burned into Terry's mind, the picture of his father down on the floor. It burned in and in, and he wanted to walk away, but something made his feet move forward. He knelt next to his father and helped the owner of the store get him up on his feet. His father didn't speak at all but continued to make little whimpering sounds, and they led him back into the owner's office and put him in a chair. Then Terry called his mother and she came in a taxi to take them home. Waiting, Terry sat in a chair next to his father, looking at the floor, wanting only for the earth to open and let him drop in a deep hole. He wanted to disappear.

Words. They gave him words like Vietnam syndrome, and his father was crawling through a hardware store on his stomach.

When the embarrassment became so bad that he would cross the street when he saw his father coming, when it ate into him as he went to sleep, Terry realized he had to do something. He had to know this thing, had to understand what was wrong with his father.

When it came, it was simple enough at the start. It had taken some courage, more than Terry thought he could find.

His father was sitting in the kitchen at the table and his mother had gone shopping. Terry wanted it that way; he wanted his father alone. His mother seemed to try to protect him, as if his father could break.

Terry got a soda out of the refrigerator and popped it open. As an afterthought, he handed it to his father and got another for himself. Then he sat at the table.

His father smiled. "You look serious."

"Well . . ."

It went nowhere for a moment, and Terry was just about to drop it altogether. It may be the wrong time, he thought, but there might never be a better one. He tightened his back, took a sip of pop.

"I was wondering if we could talk about something, Dad," Terry said.

His father shrugged. "We already did the bit about girls. Some time ago, as I remember it."

"No. Not that." It was a standing joke between them. When his father finally got around to explaining things to him, they'd already covered it in school. "It's something else."

"Something pretty heavy, judging by your face."

"Yes."

"Well?"

I still can't do it, Terry thought. Things are bad, but maybe not as bad as they could get. I can still drop this thing.

"Vietnam," Terry blurted out. And he thought, there, it's out. It's out and gone.

"No!" his father said sharply. It was as if he had been struck a blow. A body blow.

"But, Dad."

"No. That's another part of my life. A bad part. A rotten part. It was before I met your mother, long before you. It has nothing to do with this family, nothing. No."

So, Terry thought, so I tried. But it wasn't over yet. It wasn't started yet.

"It just seems to bother you so much," Terry said, "and I thought if I could help or maybe understand it better . . ." His words ran until he <u>foundered</u>, until he could say no more. He looked at the table, then out the window. It was all wrong to bring it up, he thought. I blew it. I blew it all up. "I'm sorry."

But now his father didn't hear him. Now his father's eyes were gone again, and a shaft of something horrible went through Terry's heart as he thought he had done this thing to his father, caused his eyes to go away.

"You can't know," his father said after a time. "You can't know this thing."

Terry said nothing. He felt he had said too much.

"This thing that you want to know—there is so much of it that you cannot know it all, and to know only a part is . . . is too awful. I can't tell you. I can't tell anybody what it was really like."

It was more than he'd ever said about Vietnam, and his voice was breaking. Terry hated himself and felt he would hate himself until he was an old man. In one second he had caused such ruin. And all because he had been embarrassed. What difference did it make? Now he had done this, and he wanted to hide, to leave. But he sat, waiting, knowing that it wasn't done.

WORDS
TO
KNOW   **founder** (foun′dər) v. to get stuck; break down

His father looked to him, through him, somewhere into and out of Terry. He wasn't in the kitchen anymore. He wasn't in the house. He was back in the green places, back in the hot places, the wet-hot places.

"You think that because I act strange, that we can talk and it will be all right," his father said. "That we can talk and it will just go away. That's what you think, isn't it?"

Terry started to shake his head, but he knew it wasn't expected.

"That's what the shrinks say," his father continued. "The psychiatrists tell me that if I talk about it, the whole thing will go away. But they don't know. They weren't there. You weren't there. Nobody was there but me and some other dead people, and they can't talk because they couldn't stop the morning."

Terry pushed his soda can back and forth, looking down, frightened at what was happening. *The other dead people,* he'd said, as if he were dead as well. *Couldn't stop the morning.*

"I don't understand, Dad."

"No. You don't." His voice hardened, then softened again, and broke at the edges. "But see, see how it was . . ." He trailed off, and Terry thought he was done. His father looked back down to the table, at the can of soda he hadn't touched, at the tablecloth, at his hands, which were folded, <u>inert</u> on the table.

"We were crossing a rice paddy in the dark," he said, and suddenly his voice flowed like a river breaking loose. "We were crossing the paddy, and it was dark, still dark, so black you couldn't see the end of your nose. There was a light rain, a mist, and I was thinking that during the next break I would whisper and tell Petey Kressler how nice the rain felt, but of course I didn't know there wouldn't be a Petey Kressler."

He took a deep, ragged breath. At that moment Terry felt his brain swirl, a kind of whirlpool pulling, and he felt the darkness and the light rain because it was in his father's eyes, in his voice.

"So we were crossing the paddy, and it was a straight sweep, and then we caught it. We began taking fire from three sides, automatic weapons, and everybody went down and tried to get low, but we couldn't. We couldn't get low enough. We could never get low enough, and you could hear the rounds hitting people. It was just a short time before they brought in the mortars,[1] and we should have moved, should have run, but nobody got up, and after a time nobody *could* get up. The fire just kept coming and coming, and then incoming mortars, and I heard screams as they hit, but there was nothing to do. Nothing to do."

"Dad?" Terry said. He thought, maybe I can stop him. Maybe I can stop him before. . . before it gets to be too much. Before he breaks.

"Mortars," his father went on, "I hated mortars. You just heard them wump as they fired, and you didn't know where they would hit, and you always felt like they would hit your back. They swept back and forth with the mortars, and the automatic weapons kept coming in, and there was no radio, no way to call for artillery. Just the dark to hide in. So I

"*You think that because I act strange, that we can talk and it will be all right," his father said.*

---

1. **mortars:** small, portable cannons that fire explosive shells; also, the shells fired by such cannons.

His hand went out across the table, and he took his father's hand and held it.

crawled to the side and found Jackson, only he wasn't there, just part of his body, the top part, and I hid under it and waited, and waited, and waited.

"Finally the firing quit. But see, see how it was in the dark with nobody alive but me? I yelled once, but that brought fire again, so I shut up, and there was nothing, not even the screams."

His father cried, and Terry tried to understand, and he thought he could feel part of it. But it was so much, so much and so strange to him.

"You cannot know this," his father repeated. It was almost a <u>chant</u>. "You cannot know the fear. It was dark, and I was the only one left alive out of 54 men, all dead but me, and I knew that the Vietcong[2] were just waiting for light. When the dawn came, 'Charley'[3] would come out and finish everybody off, the way they always did. And I thought if I could stop the dawn, just stop the sun from coming up, I could make it."

Terry felt the fear, and he also felt the tears coming down his cheeks. His hand went out across the table, and he took his father's hand and held it. It was shaking.

"I mean I actually thought that if I could stop the sun from coming up, I could live. I made my brain work on that because it was all I had. Through the rest of the night in the rain in the paddy, I thought I could do it. I could stop the dawn." He took a deep breath. "But you can't, you know. You can't stop it from coming, and when I saw the gray light, I knew I was dead. It would just be minutes, and the

light would be full, and I just settled under Jackson's body, and hid."

He stopped, and his face came down into his hands. Terry stood and went around the table to stand in back of him, his hands on his shoulders, rubbing gently.

"They didn't shoot me. They came, one of them poked Jackson's body and went on, and they left me. But I was dead. I'm still dead, don't you see? I died because I couldn't stop the sun. I died. Inside where I am—I died."

Terry was still in back of him, and he nodded, but he didn't see. Not that. He understood only that he didn't understand and that he would probably never know what it was really like, would probably never understand what had truly happened. And maybe his father would never be truly normal.

But Terry also knew that it didn't matter. He would try to understand, and the trying would have to be enough. He would try hard from now on, and he would not be embarrassed when his father's eyes went away. He would not be embarrassed no matter what his father did. Terry had knowledge now. Maybe not enough and maybe not all that he would need.

But it was a start. ❖

---

2. **Vietcong:** Communist rebels fighting to overthrow the U.S.-supported South Vietnamese government.

3. **Charley:** a slang term used by U.S. soldiers to refer to the Vietcong.

from Dear America

Feb. 14th, 1966

Dear Mom,

. . . I've seen some things happen here lately that have moved me so much that I've changed my whole outlook on life. I'll be the same in actions I guess, but inside I'll be changed. I feel different now after seeing some horrible things, and I'll never forget them. It makes you glad you're just existing. I can't say what I mean, but some of the things you see here can really change a man or turn a boy into a man. Any combat GI[1] that comes here doesn't leave the same. I don't mean the cooks, clerks or special service workers, but the fighting man. I doubt if anybody realizes what combat is really like. I *thought* I knew until a few days ago when I started facing harsh realities and forgetting TV and movie interpretations. I never had much respect for GIs even after I was in for a while, but since I've seen what his real job is, I have more respect for him than any man on earth. To shoot and kill somebody, turn your head and walk away isn't hard, it's watching him die that's hard, harder than you could imagine and even harder when it's one of your own men.

Green Machine (1977), Frank Dahmer. Screenprint on paper, 13½" × 17½". Collection of the National Vietnam Veterans Art Museum, Chicago.

I've said enough about it. Don't ask any questions. When I come home, if I feel like talking about it I will, but otherwise don't ask. It may sound dramatic, and I'll tell you it is. It's just something you don't feel like discussing and can't begin to write about.

Well, Mom, I'll sign off. Be careful driving.

**Love,
George**

PFC George Robinson served in Vietnam in 1966. He was injured in June of that year.

---

1. **GI:** an enlisted member of the U.S. armed forces. It is thought that originally *G.I.* stood for "government issue." It was used to describe things associated with American military, such as G.I. shoes and clothes.

Connect to the Literature

1. **What Do You Think?**
   How do you think Terry will relate to his father now?

   Comprehension Check
   - Why does Terry's father sometimes act strangely?
   - What happens in the hardware store?
   - What happened to Terry's father in Vietnam?

Think Critically

2. Because the war took place before Terry's parents were married, Terry's father thinks that the war has "nothing to do with this family." Why do you think he feels this way?

3. What important discovery has Terry made by the end of the story?

   Think About:
   - the story that his father tells
   - Terry's reaction to his father's story
   - your own experiences with family discussions of difficult issues

4. **ACTIVE READING** **CONNECTING**

   In your **READER'S NOTEBOOK** you were asked to compare Terry's experiences with your own. Summarize your observations. How are your experiences similar to Terry's? How are they different?

Extend Interpretations

5. **COMPARING TEXTS** Compare Terry's father with George in the letter on page 55. How are their reactions to the Vietnam War similar?

6. **Connect to Life** Do you agree or disagree with Terry's decision to ask his father about the war? Give reasons for your answer. What would you have done in this situation?

Literary Analysis

THEME The meaning, moral, or message about life or human nature that is communicated by a literary work is called the **theme.** The theme of a story is not always directly stated. In fact, different readers may find different themes in the same story. Here are some ways to look for a theme in a story:

- Skim the story for key phrases and sentences that say something about life or people in general.
- Look for repeated words or ideas that emphasize important ideas or feelings.
- Review what happens to the main character in the story. What does the main character learn?

Group Activity Working with a partner or in a small group, complete a chart like the one shown. Then, use the information in the chart to state the theme.

Key Phrases	Repeated Ideas	What the Main Character Learns

Writing

Father's Day Card Write a Father's Day message from Terry to his father that reflects Terry's new understanding. Think of the story's theme as you prepare your message. Place the message in your **Working Portfolio.**

Speaking & Listening

Veteran Interview If possible, invite a Vietnam veteran to your classroom. Ask the veteran to share with you some of his experiences in the war. Prepare a list of questions to ask him, but be careful to respect his privacy.

Research & Technology

HISTORY

Many war veterans, like Terry's father, suffer from Vietnam syndrome (also known as post-traumatic stress disorder). Research this disorder. What are its symptoms? How is it treated? Present your findings to the class.

INTERNET **Research Starter**
www.mcdougallittell.com

Art Connection

Look again at the painting entitled *Prometheus Under Fire* by artist Rupert Garcia. Prometheus is a figure in Greek mythology who stole fire from the gods and gave it to humans. For his theft, the gods punished Prometheus. How does this painting reflect the horrors of war felt by Terry's father?

Prometheus Under Fire (1984), Rupert Garcia. Pastel on paper, 29¾″ × 84″. Courtesy of the artist, Rena Bransten Gallery, San Francisco, and Galerie Claude Samuel, Paris. Copyright © 1995 Rupert Garcia.

Vocabulary

EXERCISE: MEANING CLUES On your paper, answer the following questions about each underlined Word to Know.

1. Is the tone of a <u>chant</u> most likely to be monotonous, lively, or varied?

2. Do people who <u>persist</u> when a situation is difficult show cowardice, determination, or laziness?

3. If someone were to <u>founder</u> as he spoke, would he or she stop speaking or speak more boldly?

4. Is a <u>dry</u> lecture likely to be exciting, funny, or uninteresting?

5. If an object were <u>inert,</u> would it be flying, not moving, or invisible?

VOCABULARY STRATEGY: DIAGRAM Review the diagram below. On your paper create a diagram for each of the Words to Know.

Commotion
Definition: a disturbance
Synonym: disorder
Example Sentence: The argument caused a commotion in the hallway.

Vocabulary Handbook
See p. R24: Synonyms and Antonyms.

WORDS TO KNOW	chant	dry	founder	inert	persist

Grammar in Context: Predicate Nouns and Predicate Adjectives

In "Stop the Sun," Gary Paulsen uses many action verbs. However, not all verbs in the story express action.

> **Things are bad,** but maybe not as bad as they could get.

Action verbs tell what the subject *does.* **Linking verbs** join, or link, the subject to words that describe or identify it. Linking verbs may connect the subject with a word or group of words in the predicate. When nouns and adjectives follow the verb and tell what the subject is, they are called predicate nouns or predicate adjectives.

The most frequently used linking verb is the verb "to be," but other verbs, such as *feel, appear,* *seem, taste, look, sound,* or *become,* can act as linking verbs as well.

WRITING EXERCISE Complete each sentence starter below with a predicate noun or a predicate adjective.

Example: *Original* Terry was

Rewritten Terry was tall.

1. Terry's mother became
2. Mr. Carlson seemed
3. Terry's father looked
4. The rain felt
5. Petey Kressler was

Grammar Handbook
See p. R76: Making Subjects and Verbs Agree.

Gary Paulsen
born 1939

"I read like a wolf eats. I read myself to sleep every night."

A Writer for Young Adults Gary Paulsen is a highly acclaimed writer of novels, short stories, and nonfiction books for young people. In many of his works, the teenage characters have parents who are less than perfect. These troubled young people often find self-awareness through challenging tests of survival.

A Difficult Childhood Life has not always been easy for Paulsen. He spent an unhappy childhood living in a troubled family. According to Paulsen, "I was an 'army brat,' and it was a miserable life." In school, he says, "I was the last kid chosen for sports, barely got through high school. . . . " Despite trouble in school, Paulsen developed a passion for books. He felt that the public library was the one place he could go where people did not care if he wore the right clothes or was good at sports. Today, Paulsen and his wife, Ruth, who has illustrated some of his books, live in New Mexico and Minnesota.

AUTHOR ACTIVITY
The Iditarod Paulsen's experience of competing in the Iditarod, a dogsled race over 1,150 miles across Alaska, made a lasting impression on him. Find out how his experience in the Iditarod influenced his novel *Dogsong.* Share your findings with the class.

A Mother in Mannville

by MARJORIE KINNAN RAWLINGS

Connect to Your Life

Lonely or Alone? The main characters in this story are a lonely orphan boy and a writer who seeks time alone. Have you ever chosen to spend time alone? Have you ever felt lonely? What do you think is the difference between being lonely and being alone?

Build Background

HISTORY

The events of this story take place in the North Carolina mountains, near an orphanage. An orphanage is an institution for the care of children whose parents have died, have abandoned them, or can no longer care for them.

Orphanages that cared for large groups of children were more common in the past than they are today. Nowadays, many orphaned children are cared for by foster families until permanent homes are found.

WORDS TO KNOW
Vocabulary Preview

abstracted	impel
blunt	inadequate
clarity	instinctive
communion	kindling
ecstasy	predicated

Focus Your Reading

LITERARY ANALYSIS **SETTING**

The time and place in which the events of a story, poem, or play take place is called the **setting.** Elements of setting may include geographic location, historical period (past, present, future), season, time of day, and local customs or ways of speaking. "A Mother in Mannville" is set in an isolated location "high in the Carolina mountains." As you read the story, notice how the climate, geography, and isolation of the setting affect the story's **plot.**

ACTIVE READING **VISUALIZING**

The use of written or spoken information to imagine what something looks like is called **visualizing.** Vivid **descriptions** help readers visualize settings. In "A Mother in Mannville," for example, the words "the snow swirls down the valleys" present a vivid image that readers can picture in their mind's eye.

READER'S NOTEBOOK As you read this story, jot down details that help you visualize the Carolina mountains during the winter, spring, and autumn. Use a chart like the one shown to record your observations.

Details About Winter	Details About Spring	Details About Autumn
"Sometimes in winter the snowdrifts are so deep that the institution is cut off from the village below, from all the world."		

A MOTHER in MANNVILLE

by Marjorie Kinnan Rawlings

The orphanage is high in the Carolina mountains. Sometimes in winter the snowdrifts are so deep that the institution is cut off from the village below, from all the world. Fog hides the mountain peaks, the snow swirls down the valleys, and a wind blows so bitterly that the orphanage boys who take the milk twice daily to the baby cottage reach the door with fingers stiff in an agony of numbness.

"Or when we carry trays from the cook house for the ones that are sick," Jerry said, "we get our faces frostbit, because we can't put our hands over them. I have gloves," he added. "Some of the boys don't have any."

He liked the late spring, he said. The rhododendron was in bloom, a carpet of color, across the mountainsides, soft as the May winds that stirred the hemlocks.[1] He called it laurel.[2]

"It's pretty when the laurel blooms," he said. "Some of it's pink and some of it's white."

I was there in the autumn. I wanted quiet, isolation, to do some troublesome writing. I wanted mountain air to blow out the malaria from too long a time in the subtropics. I was homesick, too, for the flaming of maples in October, and for corn shocks and pumpkins and black-walnut trees and the lift of hills. I found them all, living in a cabin that belonged to the orphanage, half a mile beyond the orphanage farm. When I took the cabin, I asked for a boy or man to come and chop wood for the fireplace. The first few days were

Gathering Autumn Leaves (c. 1877), Winslow Homer, United States (1836–1910). Oil on canvas, 38¼" x 24¼" (97 cm x 61.8 cm). Cooper-Hewitt, National Design Museum, Smithsonian Institution/Art Resource, New York. Gift of Charles Savage Homer, Jr., 1917-14-3.

warm, I found what wood I needed about the cabin, no one came, and I forgot the order.

I looked up from my typewriter one late afternoon, a little startled. A boy stood at the door, and my pointer dog, my companion, was at his side and had not barked to warn me. The boy was probably twelve years old, but undersized. He wore overalls and a torn shirt, and was barefooted.

---

1. **hemlocks:** coniferous evergreen trees belonging to the pine family. Hemlocks grow in the forests of North America and eastern Asia.

2. **laurel:** an evergreen shrub or tree with aromatic leaves.

He said, "I can chop some wood today."

I said, "But I have a boy coming from the orphanage."

"I'm the boy."

"You? But you're small."

"Size don't matter, chopping wood," he said. "Some of the big boys don't chop good. I've been chopping wood at the orphanage a long time."

I visualized mangled and <u>inadequate</u> branches for my fires. I was well into my work and not inclined to conversation. I was a little <u>blunt</u>.

"Very well. There's the ax. Go ahead and see what you can do."

I went back to work, closing the door. At first, the sound of the boy dragging brush annoyed me. Then he began to chop. The blows were rhythmic and steady, and shortly I had forgotten him, the sound no more of an interruption than a consistent rain. I suppose an hour and a half passed, for when I stopped and stretched, and heard the boy's steps on the cabin stoop, the sun was dropping behind the farthest mountain, and the valleys were purple with something deeper than the asters.

The boy said, "I have to go to supper now. I can come again tomorrow evening."

I said, "I'll pay you now for what you've done," thinking I should probably have to insist on an older boy. "Ten cents an hour?"

"Anything is all right."

We went together back of the cabin. An astonishing amount of solid wood had been cut. There were cherry logs and heavy roots of rhododendron, and blocks from the waste pine and oak left from the building of the cabin.

"But you've done as much as a man," I said. "This is a splendid pile."

I looked at him, actually, for the first time.

His hair was the color of the corn shocks, and his eyes, very direct, were like the mountain sky when rain is pending—gray, with a shadowing of that miraculous blue. As I spoke, a light came over him, as though the setting sun had touched him with the same suffused glory with which it touched the mountains. I gave him a quarter.

"You may come tomorrow," I said, "and thank you very much."

He looked at me, and at the coin, and seemed to want to speak, but could not, and turned away.

"I'll split <u>kindling</u> tomorrow," he said over his thin ragged shoulder. "You'll need kindling and medium wood and logs and backlogs."

At daylight I was half wakened by the sound of chopping. Again it was so even in texture that I went back to sleep. When I left my bed in the cool morning, the boy had come and gone, and a stack of kindling was neat against the cabin wall. He came again after school in the afternoon and worked until time to return to the orphanage. His name was Jerry; he was twelve years old, and he had been at the orphanage since he was four. I could picture him at four, with the same grave gray-blue eyes and the same—independence? No, the word that comes to me is "integrity."

The word means something very special to me, and the quality for which I use it is a rare one. My father had it—there is another of whom I am almost sure—but almost no man of my acquaintance possesses it with the <u>clarity</u>, the purity, the simplicity of a mountain stream. But the boy Jerry had it. It is bedded on courage, but it is more than brave. It is

WORDS
TO
KNOW

inadequate (ĭn-ăd′ĭ-kwĭt) *adj.* not good enough for what is needed
blunt (blŭnt) *adj.* abrupt; rudely straightforward or honest
kindling (kĭnd′lĭng) *n.* pieces of dry wood or other material that can be easily lighted to start a fire; tinder
clarity (klăr′ĭ-tē) *n.* the quality of being easily seen; clearness

honest, but it is more than honesty. The ax handle broke one day. Jerry said the wood shop at the orphanage would repair it. I brought money to pay for the job, and he refused it.

"I'll pay for it," he said. "I broke it. I brought the ax down careless."

"But no one hits accurately every time," I told him. "The fault was in the wood of the handle. I'll see the man from whom I bought it."

It was only then that he would take the money. He was standing back of his own carelessness. He was a free-will agent, and he chose to do careful work, and if he failed, he took the responsibility without subterfuge.[3]

And he did for me the unnecessary thing, the gracious thing, that we find done only by the great of heart. Things no training can teach, for they are done on the instant, with no predicated experience. He found a cubbyhole beside the fireplace that I had not noticed. There, of his own accord, he put kindling and "medium" wood, so that I might always have dry fire material ready in case of sudden wet weather. A stone was loose in the rough walk to the cabin. He dug a deeper hole and steadied it, although he came, himself, by a shortcut over the bank. I found that when I tried to return his thoughtfulness with such things as candy and apples, he was wordless. "Thank you" was, perhaps, an expression for which he had had no use, for his courtesy was instinctive. He only looked at the gift and at me, and a curtain lifted, so that I saw deep into the clear well of his eyes, and gratitude was there, and affection, soft over the firm granite of his character.

He made simple excuses to come and sit with me. I could no more have turned him away than if he had been physically hungry. I suggested once that the best time for us to visit was just before supper, when I left off my writing. After that, he waited always until my typewriter had been some time quiet. One day I worked until nearly dark. I went outside the cabin, having forgotten him. I saw him going up over the hill in the twilight toward the orphanage. When I sat down on my stoop, a place was warm from his body where he had been sitting.

He became intimate, of course, with my pointer, Pat. There is a strange communion between a boy and a dog. Perhaps they possess the same singleness of spirit, the same kind of wisdom. It is difficult to explain, but it exists. When I went across the state for a weekend, I left the dog in Jerry's charge. I gave him the dog whistle and the key to the cabin and left sufficient food. He was to come two or three times a day and let out the dog and feed and exercise him. I should return Sunday night, and Jerry would take out the dog for the last time Sunday afternoon and then leave the key under an agreed hiding place.

My return was belated, and fog filled the mountain passes so treacherously that I dared not drive at night. The fog held the next morning, and it was Monday noon before I reached the cabin. The dog had been fed and cared for that morning. Jerry came early in the afternoon, anxious.

"The superintendent said nobody would drive in the fog," he said. "I came just before bedtime last night and you hadn't come. So I brought Pat some of my breakfast this morning. I wouldn't have let anything happen to him."

---

3. **subterfuge** (sŭb′tər-fyōōj′): anything used to hide one's true purpose or avoid a difficult situation.

WORDS TO KNOW

predicated (prĕd′ĭ-kā′-tĭd) *adj.* established; assumed **predicate** *v.*
instinctive (ĭn-stĭngk′tĭv) *adj.* having a natural tendency; spontaneous
communion (kə-myōōn′yən) *n.* close relationship in which deep feelings are shared; intimacy

62

"I was sure of that. I didn't worry."

"When I heard about the fog, I thought you'd know."

He was needed for work at the orphanage, and he had to return at once. I gave him a dollar in payment, and he looked at it and went away. But that night he came in the darkness and knocked at the door.

"Come in, Jerry," I said, "if you're allowed to be away this late."

"I told maybe a story," he said. "I told them I thought you would want to see me."

"That's true," I assured him, and I saw his relief. "I want to hear about how you managed with the dog."

He sat by the fire with me, with no other light, and told me of their two days together. The dog lay close to him and found a comfort there that I did not have for him. And it seemed to me that being with my dog, and caring for him, had brought the boy and me, too, together, so that he felt that he belonged to me as well as to the animal.

"He stayed right with me," he told me, "except when he ran in the laurel. He likes the laurel. I took him up over the hill and we both ran fast. There was a place where the grass was high, and I lay down in it and hid. I could hear Pat hunting for me. He found my trail and he barked. When he found me, he acted crazy, and he ran around and around me, in circles."

We watched the flames.

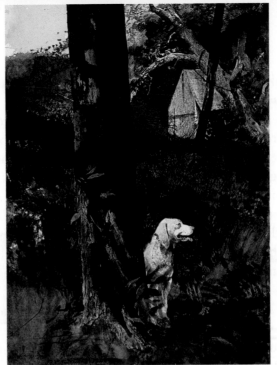

After the Chase (1965), Andrew Wyeth. Watercolor on paper. Copyright © 1965 Andrew Wyeth. Gift of an anonymous donor in memory of Lee E. Phillips, Jr., Wichita Art Museum, Wichita, Kansas.

"That's an apple log," he said. "It burns the prettiest of any wood."

We were very close.

He was suddenly <u>impelled</u> to speak of things he had not spoken of before, nor had I cared to ask him.

"You look a little bit like my mother," he said. "Especially in the dark, by the fire."

"But you were only four, Jerry, when you came here. You have remembered how she looked, all these years?"

"My mother lives in Mannville," he said.

For a moment, finding that he had a mother shocked me as greatly as anything in my life has ever done, and I did not know why it disturbed me. Then I understood my distress. I was filled with a passionate resentment that any woman should go away and leave her son. A fresh anger added itself. A son like this one—The orphanage was a wholesome place, the executives were kind, good people, the food was more than adequate, the boys were healthy, a ragged shirt was no hardship, nor the doing of clean labor. Granted, perhaps, that the boy felt no lack, what blood fed the bowels of a woman who did not yearn over this child's lean body that had come in parturition out of her own? At four he would have looked the same as now. Nothing, I thought, nothing in life could change those eyes. His quality must be apparent to an idiot, a fool. I burned with questions I could not ask. In any, I was afraid, there would be pain.

"Have you seen her, Jerry—lately?"

"I see her every summer. She sends for me."

I wanted to cry out, "Why are you not with her? How can she let you go away again?"

He said, "She comes up here from Mannville whenever she can. She doesn't have a job now."

His face shone in the firelight.

"She wanted to give me a puppy, but they can't let any one boy keep a puppy. You remember the suit I had on last Sunday?" He was plainly proud. "She sent me that for Christmas. The Christmas before that"—he drew a long breath, savoring the memory—"she sent me a pair of skates."

"Roller skates?"

My mind was busy, making pictures of her, trying to understand her. She had not, then, entirely deserted or forgotten him. But why, then—I thought, "I must not condemn her without knowing."

"Roller skates. I let the other boys use them. They're always borrowing them. But they're careful of them."

What circumstance other than poverty—

"I'm going to take the dollar you gave me for taking care of Pat," he said, "and buy her a pair of gloves."

I could only say, "That will be nice. Do you know her size?"

"I think it's 8½," he said.

He looked at my hands.

"Do you wear 8½?" he asked.

"No. I wear a smaller size, a 6."

"Oh! Then I guess her hands are bigger than yours."

I hated her. Poverty or no, there was other food than bread, and the soul could starve as quickly as the body. He was taking his dollar to buy gloves for her big stupid hands, and she lived away from him, in Mannville, and contented herself with sending him skates.

"She likes white gloves," he said. "Do you think I can get them for a dollar?"

"I think so," I said.

I decided that I should not leave the mountains without seeing her and knowing for myself why she had done this thing.

The human mind scatters its interests as though made of thistledown, and every wind stirs and moves it. I finished my work. It did not please me, and I gave my thoughts to another field. I should need some Mexican material.

I made arrangements to close my Florida place. Mexico immediately, and doing the writing there, if conditions were favorable. Then, Alaska with my brother. After that, heaven knew what or where.

I did not take time to go to Mannville to see Jerry's mother, nor even to talk with the orphanage officials about her. I was a trifle <u>abstracted</u> about the boy, because of my work and plans. And after my first fury at her—we did not speak of her again—his having a mother, any sort at all, not far away, in Mannville, relieved me of the ache I had had about him. He did not question the anomalous[4] relation. He was not lonely. It was none of my concern.

He came every day and cut my wood and did small helpful favors and stayed to talk. The days had become cold, and often I let him come inside the cabin. He would lie on the floor in front of the fire, with one arm across the pointer, and they would both doze and wait quietly for me. Other days they ran with

---

4. **anomalous** (ə-nŏm′ə-ləs): differing from the general rule; abnormal.

a common ecstasy through the laurel, and since the asters were now gone, he brought me back vermilion maple leaves, and chestnut boughs dripping with imperial yellow. I was ready to go.

I said to him, "You have been my good friend, Jerry. I shall often think of you and miss you. Pat will miss you too. I am leaving tomorrow."

He did not answer. When he went away, I remember that a new moon hung over the mountains, and I watched him go in silence up the hill. I expected him the next day, but he did not come. The details of packing my personal belongings, loading my car, arranging the bed over the seat, where the dog would ride, occupied me until late in the day. I closed the cabin and started the car, noticing that the sun was in the west and I should do well to be out of the mountains by nightfall. I stopped by the orphanage and left the cabin key and money for my light bill with Miss Clark.

"And will you call Jerry for me to say goodbye to him?"

"I don't know where he is," she said. "I'm afraid he's not well. He didn't eat his dinner this noon. One of the other boys saw him going over the hill into the laurel. He was supposed to fire the boiler this afternoon. It's not like him; he's unusually reliable."

I was almost relieved, for I knew I should never see him again, and it would be easier not to say goodbye to him.

I said, "I wanted to talk with you about his mother—why he's here—but I'm in more of a hurry than I expected to be. It's out of the question for me to see her now too. But here's some money I'd like to leave with you to buy things for him at Christmas and on his birthday. It will be better than for me to try to send him things. I could so easily duplicate—skates, for instance."

She blinked her honest spinster's eyes.

"There's not much use for skates here," she said.

Her stupidity annoyed me.

"What I mean," I said, "is that I don't want to duplicate things his mother sends him. I might have chosen skates if I didn't know she had already given them to him."

She stared at me.

"I don't understand," she said. "He has no mother. He has no skates." ❖

A Story That Could Be True

by William Stafford

If you were exchanged in the cradle and
your real mother died
without ever telling the story
then no one knows your name
5 and somewhere in the world
your father is lost and needs you
but you are faraway.

He can never find
how true you are, how ready.
10 When the great wind comes
and the robberies of the rain
you stand on the corner shivering.
The people who go by—
you wonder at their calm.

15 They miss the whisper that runs
any day in your mind.
"Who are you really, wanderer?"
and the answer you have to give
no matter how dark and cold
20 the world around you is:
"Maybe I'm a king."

WORDS
TO
KNOW

ecstasy (ĕk'stə-sē) *n.* intense joy or delight; bliss

Connect to the Literature

1. **What Do You Think?**
   What was your reaction to learning the truth behind Jerry's story?

   Comprehension Check
   • What two friendships does Jerry develop at the cabin?
   • How do the narrator's first impressions of Jerry's ability change?
   • What does the narrator learn as a result of her visit to Miss Clark?

Think Critically

2. In your opinion, why does Jerry make up the story about his mother?

   Think About:
   • the kind of person Jerry is
   • the kind of life Jerry has
   • Jerry's feelings for the narrator

3. If you were the narrator, what would you do after you learned the truth about Jerry's mother?

4. **ACTIVE READING** **VISUALIZING**
   Look over the descriptive details that you jotted down in your **READER'S NOTEBOOK**. Which season in the Carolina mountains—winter, spring, or autumn—can you **visualize** the best? What words and phrases in the story helped you picture the **setting** clearly?

Extend Interpretations

5. **Critic's Corner** Christine Warner, an eighth-grade student, had this to say about the story: "The story is sad. A boy, not unlike the other orphans, deprived of love and affection, invents things he wants in his mind, for all his friends are temporary." Do you agree with her analysis? Explain your answer.

6. **Connect to Life** To the narrator of the story, integrity is "bedded on courage, but it is more than brave. It is honest, but it is more than honesty." Do you know or have you read about a person with integrity? How is that person similar to Jerry? Think about the person's qualities, then write your own definition of *integrity*.

Literary Analysis

SETTING The time and place of the action of a story, poem, or play are the **setting.** Elements of setting may include geographic location, historical period (past, present, or future), season, time of day, and local customs or ways of speaking. Sometimes all or part of the setting is not directly described. Instead, the reader has to guess, or **infer,** it.

Group Activity "A Mother in Mannville" takes place in the Carolina mountains. The time, however, is not directly stated.

With a partner or a small group of classmates, review the story. Find details that give clues about when the story takes place. Complete a chart like the one shown, and then decide whether the story takes place in the present, the recent past (50–100 years ago), or the distant past (several hundred years ago).

Detail from the Story	Inference
The narrator uses a typewriter.	The use of a typewriter implies the recent past.

REVIEW: MOTIVATION **Character motivation** refers to the reasons why characters act, react, or think in a certain way. Why do you think the narrator believes Jerry?

Writing

Biography of Jerry A **biography** is a writer's account of another person's life. Write a one-page biography of Jerry. Describe where he lived before he came to the orphanage, and tell how he came to the orphanage. Place your biography in your **Working Portfolio.**

Writing Handbook
See p. R43: Narrative Writing.

Speaking & Listening

Interpreting a Reading Write and present a short speech explaining why you think Jerry lied to the narrator about his mother. Use examples from the text to support your statements.

Speaking and Listening Handbook
See p. R104: Organization and Delivery.

Research & Technology

Appalachian Mountains Using sources from the library or Internet, find out about the Appalachian Mountains. How high are they? What states are they in? What types of plants (flora) and animals (fauna) can be found in the Appalachians of North Carolina? Report your findings to the class. If possible, include drawings of mountain flora and fauna. Be sure to note your sources.

Vocabulary

STANDARDIZED TEST PRACTICE

Choose the word or group of words that means the same, or nearly the same, as the underlined Word to Know in each sentence.

1. A boy from the orphanage came to split pieces of kindling for the fireplace. Kindling means—
   A leftover food **B** old metal
   C wet leaves **D** dry wood

2. The woman he worked for realized that he had an instinctive sense of courtesy. Instinctive means—
   F elaborate **G** natural
   H intelligent **J** enormous

3. At first she was blunt and almost rude to him. Blunt means—
   A busy **B** humorous
   C abrupt **D** wild

4. She thought that his work would be inadequate because he was so young. Inadequate means—
   F inspiring **G** impressive
   H invisible **J** insufficient

Choose the word that means the same, or nearly the same, as the underlined Word to Know.

1. Predicated means—
   A established **B** defeated
   C perceived **D** imagined

2. Clarity is another word for—
   F scarcity **G** enthusiasm
   H honesty **J** clearness

3. Communion means—
   A tolerance **B** control
   C friendship **D** rejection

4. Ecstasy refers to—
   F terror **G** delight
   H embarrassment **J** stubbornness

5. To impel is to—
   A force **B** demonstrate
   C enter **D** listen

6. Abstracted means—
   F irritated **G** agreeable
   H excited **J** forgetful

Vocabulary Handbook
See p. R20: Context Clues.

Grammar in Context: Consistent Verb Tense

Marjorie Rawlings describes the relationship between a writer and a young orphan in "A Mother in Mannville." In this passage she recalls her first meeting with Jerry:

> I looked up from my typewriter one late afternoon, a little startled. A boy stood at the door, and my pointer dog, my companion, was at his side. . . . The boy was probably twelve years old, but undersized. He wore overalls and a torn shirt, and was barefooted.

In this passage, all the **verbs** are in the past tense. Writers use **verb tense** to establish the time of the actions being described. If you are writing about events that happened in the past, be sure not to slip into the present tense.

If you are writing about something happening in the present, use one of the present tenses. Try to avoid unnecessary shifts in tense.

WRITING EXERCISE Rewrite these sentences, correcting inconsistencies in verb tense.

Example: *Original* I <u>went</u> back to work, closing the door. At first the sounds <u>annoy</u> me. Then he <u>began</u> to chop.

Rewritten I <u>went</u> back to work, closing the door. At first the sounds <u>annoyed</u> me. Then he <u>began</u> to chop.

1. At daylight I was half wakened by the sound of chopping. Again it was so even in texture that I will go back to sleep.

2. Sometimes in winter the snow drifts are so deep that the institution was cut off from the village below.

3. One day I worked until nearly dark. I go outside the cabin.

4. He sat by the fire with me, with no other light, and will tell me of their two days together.

Grammar Handbook See p. R84: Using Verbs Correctly.

Marjorie Kinnan Rawlings
1896–1953

"It seems to me that the earth may be borrowed but not bought. It may be used, but not owned."

Early Life While growing up in Washington, D.C., Marjorie Kinnan Rawlings entertained neighborhood children with stories. At the age of 11, she won her first award for writing. After graduating from the University of Wisconsin, she worked as a newspaper reporter in Kentucky and New York while writing stories at night.

A Prize Winner A boy that Rawlings met in North Carolina was the model for Jerry in "A Mother in Mannville." This story and others she wrote about farmers, trappers, and fishermen appear in a book entitled *When the Whippoorwill—*. Her most famous work is *The Yearling*, a novel that won a Pulitzer Prize in 1939.

AUTHOR ACTIVITY
Regional Writer Rawlings is considered one of America's outstanding regional writers. Find several examples of works in which she presents the natural environment, dialect, or ways of life of a region of the United States. What region (North, South, East, or West) does she write about?

The Ransom of Red Chief

by O. HENRY

Connect to Your Life

Hold for Ransom Have you ever read about a ransom or heard about one on television? With a partner create a word web, like the one shown. Discuss what the word *ransom* means to you.

Build Background

HISTORY

This story was published in 1910 when methods of catching criminals were simple and unsophisticated. With modern techniques, the kidnappers in "The Ransom of Red Chief" would probably have been quickly caught. Fingerprints on the note would have identified them. Helicopters would have spotted them. Infrared devices would have pinpointed their location. Most likely, the criminals in the story also counted on the isolation of Alabama in 1910.

> WORDS TO KNOW
> **Vocabulary Preview**
>
> | | |
> |---|---|
> | collaborate | palatable |
> | commend | pervade |
> | comply | proposition |
> | diatribe | ransom |
> | impudent | surreptitiously |

Focus Your Reading

LITERARY ANALYSIS   IRONY

A surprising contrast between what is expected and what actually exists or happens is called **irony.** For example, when a criminal breaks into a police station and robs it, the situation can be considered ironic. When you get a high grade on the paper you spent the least time working on, that's ironic too. As you read "The Ransom of Red Chief," look for examples of irony.

ACTIVE READING   PREDICTING

An attempt to answer the question "What will happen next?" is called a **prediction.** A story in which all the events turn out exactly as the reader would have predicted is generally not very interesting. Writers often try to startle or amuse readers by turning readers' predictions upside down.

📖 READER'S NOTEBOOK   "The Ransom of Red Chief" involves a kidnapped child. As you read, note how the story does or does not match your predictions about a kidnap situation.

My Prediction	Actual Event	Surprise?
The boy will be pleased when Bill offers him a bag of candy and a nice ride.	The boy throws a brick at Bill.	yes

The Ransom of Red Chief

BY O. HENRY

It looked like a good thing; but wait till I tell you. We were down South, in Alabama—Bill Driscoll and myself—when this kidnapping idea struck us. It was, as Bill afterward expressed it, "during a moment of temporary mental apparition";[1] but we didn't find that out till later.

There was a town down there, as flat as a flannel-cake, and called Summit, of course. It contained inhabitants of as undeleterious[2] and self-satisfied a class of peasantry as ever clustered around a Maypole.

Bill and me had a joint capital of about six hundred dollars, and we needed just two thousand dollars more to pull off a fraudulent town-lot scheme in Western Illinois. We talked it over on the front steps of the hotel. Philoprogenitiveness,[3] says we, is strong in semi-rural communities; therefore, and for other reasons, a kidnapping project ought to do better there than in the radius[4] of newspapers that send reporters out in plain clothes to stir up talk about such things. We knew that Summit couldn't get after us with anything stronger than constables and, maybe, some lackadaisical bloodhounds and a <u>diatribe</u> or two in the Weekly Farmers' Budget. So, it looked good.

We selected for our victim the only child of a prominent citizen named Ebenezer Dorset. The father was respectable and tight, a mortgage fancier and a stern, upright collection plate passer and forecloser. The kid was a boy of ten, with bas-relief[5] freckles and hair the color of the cover of the magazine you buy at the newsstand when you want to catch a train.

Bill and me figured that Ebenezer would melt down for a <u>ransom</u> of two thousand dollars to a cent. But wait till I tell you.

About two miles from Summit was a little mountain, covered with a dense cedar brake.[6] On the rear elevation of this mountain was a cave. There we stored <u>provisions.</u>

One evening after sundown, we drove in a buggy past old Dorset's house. The kid was in the street, throwing rocks at a kitten on the opposite fence.

"Hey, little boy!" says Bill, "would you like to have a bag of candy and a nice ride?"

The boy catches Bill neatly in the eye with a piece of brick.

"That will cost the old man an extra five hundred dollars," says Bill, climbing over the wheel.

That boy put up a fight like a welterweight cinnamon bear; but, at last, we got him down in the bottom of the buggy and drove away. We took him up to the cave, and I hitched the horse in the cedar brake. After dark I drove the buggy to the little village, three miles away, where we had hired it, and walked back to the mountain.

Bill was pasting court plaster[7] over the scratches and bruises on his features.

---

1. **apparition** (ăp′ə-rĭsh′ən): a sudden or unusual sight; Bill meant an "aberration," a moving away from the normal to the atypical.
2. **undeleterious** (ŭn-dĕl′ĭ-tîr′ē-əs): harmless.
3. **philoprogenitiveness** (fĭl′ō-prō-jĕn′ĭ-tĭv-nəs): love for one's own children.
4. **radius:** range or area.
5. **bas-relief** (bä′rĭ-lēf′): slightly raised; a kind of sculpture carved so that figures stand out only slightly from the background's flat surface.
6. **brake:** a thick grouping of trees or undergrowth.
7. **court plaster:** adhesive cloth for covering superficial cuts or scratches on the skin, used in the 18th century.

WORDS TO KNOW	**diatribe** (dī′ə-trīb′) *n.* condemnation; bitter, abusive criticism
	ransom (răn′səm) *n.* a price or a payment demanded in return for the release of property or a person

Man it look lyk the boys in charge instead of the kidnappers

There was a fire burning behind the big rock at the entrance of the cave, and the boy was watching a pot of boiling coffee, with two buzzard tail feathers stuck in his red hair. He points a stick at me when I come up, and says: "Ha! cursed paleface, do you dare to enter the camp of Red Chief, the terror of the plains?"

"He's all right now," says Bill, rolling up his trousers and examining some bruises on his shins. "We're playing Indian. We're making Buffalo Bill's show look like magic-lantern views[8] of Palestine in the town hall. I'm Old Hank, the Trapper, Red Chief's captive, and I'm to be scalped at daybreak. By Geronimo! that kid can kick hard." *this boy is psyco*

Yes, sir, that boy seemed to be having the time of his life. The fun of camping out in a cave had made him forget that he was a captive himself. He immediately christened me Snake-eye, the Spy, and announced that when his braves returned from the warpath, I was to be broiled at the stake at the rising of the sun.

Then we had supper; and he filled his mouth full of bacon and bread and gravy and began to talk. He made a during-dinner speech something like this:

"I like this fine. I never camped out before; but I had a pet possum once, and I was nine last birthday. I hate to go to school. Rats ate up sixteen of Jimmy Talbot's aunt's speckled hen's eggs. Are there any real Indians in these woods? I want some more gravy. Does the trees moving make the wind blow? We had five puppies. What makes your nose so red, Hank? My father has lots of money. Are the stars hot? I whipped Ed Walker twice, Saturday. I don't like girls. You dassent[9] catch toads unless with a string. Do oxen make any noise? Why are oranges round? Have you got beds to sleep on

Onomatupoeia

in this cave? Amos Murray has got six toes. A parrot can talk, but a monkey or a fish can't. How many does it take to make twelve?"

Every few minutes he would remember that he was an Indian, and pick up his stick rifle and tiptoe to the mouth of the cave to search for the scouts of the hated paleface. Now and then he would let out a war whoop that made Old Hank the Trapper shiver. That boy had Bill terrorized from the start.

"Red Chief," says I to the kid, "would you like to go home?"

"Aw, what for?" says he. "I don't have any fun at home. I hate to go to school. I like to camp out. You won't take me back home again, Snake-eye, will you?"

"Not right away," says I. "We'll stay here in the cave awhile."

"All right!" says he. "That'll be fine. I never had such fun in all my life."

We went to bed about eleven o'clock. We spread down some wide blankets and quilts and put Red Chief between us. We weren't afraid he'd run away. He kept us awake for three hours, jumping up and reaching for his rifle and screeching: "Hist! pard," in mine and Bill's ears, as the fancied crackle of a twig or the rustle of a leaf revealed to his young imagination the stealthy approach of the outlaw band. At last, I fell into a troubled sleep, and dreamed that I had been kidnapped and chained to a tree by a ferocious pirate with red hair.

Just at daybreak, I was awakened by a series of awful screams from Bill. They weren't yells, or howls, or shouts, or whoops, or yawps, such as you'd expect from a manly set of vocal organs—they were simply indecent, terrifying,

---

8. **magic-lantern views:** slides. A magic lantern was an early slide projector used to show an enlarged image of a picture, popular in the 19th century.

9. **dassent:** dare not.

The Birthplace of Herbert Hoover (1931), Grant Wood. Collection of the Minneapolis Institute of Arts, jointly owned with the Des Moines (Iowa) Art Center. Copyright © Estate of Grant Wood/Licensed by VAGA, New York, NY.

humiliating screams, such as women emit when they see caterpillars. It's an awful thing to hear a strong, desperate, fat man scream incontinently in a cave at daybreak.

I jumped up to see what the matter was. Red Chief was sitting on Bill's chest, with one hand twined in Bill's hair. In the other he had the sharp case knife we used for slicing bacon; and he was industriously and realistically trying to take Bill's scalp, according to the sentence that had been pronounced upon him the evening before.

I got the knife away from the kid and made him lie down again. But, from that moment, Bill's spirit was broken. He laid down on his side of the bed, but he never closed an eye again in sleep as long as that boy was with us. I dozed off for a while, but along toward sunup I remembered that Red Chief had said I was to be burned at the stake at the rising of the sun. I wasn't nervous or afraid; but I sat up and leaned against a rock.

"What you getting up so soon for, Sam?" asked Bill.

"Me?" says I. "Oh, I got a kind of pain in my shoulder. I thought sitting up would rest it."

"You're a liar!" says Bill. "You're afraid. You was to be burned at sunrise, and you was afraid he'd do it. And he would, too, if he could find a match. Ain't it awful, Sam? Do you think anybody will pay out money to get a little imp like that back home?"

"Sure," said I. "A rowdy kid like that is just the kind that parents dote on. Now, you and the Chief get up and cook breakfast, while I go up on the top of this mountain and reconnoiter."

I went up on the peak of the little mountain and ran my eye over the contiguous vicinity. Over toward Summit I expected to see the sturdy yeomanry of the village armed with scythes and pitchforks beating the countryside for the dastardly kidnappers. But what I saw was a peaceful landscape dotted with one man plowing with a dun mule. Nobody was dragging the creek; no couriers dashed hither and yon, bringing tidings of no news to the distracted parents. There was a sylvan attitude of somnolent sleepiness pervading that section of the external outward surface of Alabama that lay exposed to my view. "Perhaps," says I to myself, "it has not yet been discovered that the wolves have borne away the tender lambkin from the fold. Heaven help the wolves!" says I, and I went down the mountain to breakfast.

When I got to the cave, I found Bill backed up against the side of it, breathing hard, and the boy threatening to smash him with a rock half as big as a coconut.

"He put a red-hot boiled potato down my back," explained Bill, "and then mashed it with his foot; and I boxed his ears. Have you got a gun about you, Sam?"

I took the rock away from the boy and kind of patched up the argument. "I'll fix you," says the kid to Bill. "No man ever yet struck the Red Chief but he got paid for it. You better beware!"

After breakfast the kid takes a piece of leather with strings wrapped around it out of his pocket and goes outside the cave unwinding it.

"What's he up to now?" says Bill, anxiously. "You don't think he'll run away, do you, Sam?"

"No fear of it," says I. "He don't seem to be much of a homebody. But we've got to fix up some plan about the ransom. There don't seem to be much excitement around Summit on account of his disappearance; but maybe they haven't realized yet that he's gone. His folks may think he's spending the night with Aunt Jane or one of the neighbors. Anyhow, he'll be missed today. Tonight we must get a message to his father demanding the two thousand dollars for his return."

Just then we heard a kind of war whoop, such as David might have emitted when he knocked out the champion Goliath. It was a sling that Red Chief had pulled out of his pocket, and he was whirling it around his head.

I dodged, and heard a heavy thud and a kind of a sigh from Bill, like a horse gives out when you take his saddle off. A rock the size of an egg had caught Bill just behind his left ear. He loosened himself all over and fell in the fire across the frying pan of hot water for washing the dishes. I dragged him out and poured cold water on his head for half an hour.

By and by, Bill sits up and feels behind his ear and says: "Sam, do you know who my favorite Biblical character is?"

"Take it easy," says I. "You'll come to your senses presently."

"King Herod,"[10] says he. "You won't go away and leave me here alone, will you, Sam?"

I went out and caught that boy and shook him until his freckles rattled.

"If you don't behave," says I, "I'll take you straight home. Now, are you going to be good, or not?"

> # But we've got to fix up some plan about the ransom.

---

10. **King Herod:** Herod ruled Judea from 37 B.C. to 4 B.C., and at one point ordered the execution of all boys in Bethlehem younger than two years old (Matthew 2:16).

WORDS	
TO	**pervade** (pər-vād′) v. to be spread or to be present throughout
KNOW	

"I was only funning," says he, sullenly. "I didn't mean to hurt Old Hank. But what did he hit me for? I'll behave, Snake-eye, if you won't send me home and if you'll let me play the Scout today."

"I don't know the game," says I. "That's for you and Mr. Bill to decide. He's your playmate for the day. I'm going away for a while, on business. Now, you come in and make friends with him and say you are sorry for hurting him, or home you go, at once."

I made him and Bill shake hands, and then I took Bill aside and told him I was going to Poplar Grove, a little village three miles from the cave, and find out what I could about how the kidnapping had been regarded in Summit. Also, I thought it best to send a peremptory letter to old man Dorset that day, demanding the ransom and dictating how it should be paid.

"You know, Sam," says Bill, "I've stood by you without batting an eye in earthquakes, fire, and flood—in poker games, dynamite outrages, police raids, train robberies, and cyclones. I never lost my nerve yet till we kidnapped that two-legged skyrocket of a kid. He's got me going. You won't leave me long with him, will you, Sam?"

"I'll be back sometime this afternoon," says I. "You must keep the boy amused and quiet till I return. And now we'll write the letter to old Dorset."

Bill and I got paper and pencil and worked on the letter while Red Chief, with a blanket wrapped around him, strutted up and down, guarding the mouth of the cave. Bill begged me tearfully to make the ransom fifteen hundred dollars instead of two thousand. "I ain't attempting," says he, "to decry[11] the celebrated moral aspect of parental affection,

---

11. **decry:** to minimize or make light of.

but we're dealing with humans, and it ain't human for anybody to give up two thousand dollars for that forty-pound chunk of freckled wildcat. I'm willing to take a chance at fifteen hundred dollars. You can charge the difference up to me."

So, to relieve Bill, I acceded, and we <u>collaborated</u> a letter that ran this way:

EBENEZER DORSET, ESQ.:

We have your boy concealed in a place far from Summit. It is useless for you or the most skillful detectives to attempt to find him. Absolutely the only terms on which you can have him restored to you are these: We demand fifteen hundred dollars in large bills for his return; the money to be left at midnight tonight at the same spot and in the same box as your reply—as hereinafter described. If you agree to these terms, send your answer in writing by a solitary messenger tonight at half-past eight o'clock. After crossing Owl Creek on the road to Poplar Grove, there are three large trees about a hundred yards apart, close to the fence of the wheat field on the right-hand side. At the bottom of the fence post, opposite the third tree, will be found a small pasteboard box.

The messenger will place the answer in this box and return immediately to Summit.

If you attempt any treachery or fail to <u>comply</u> with our demand as stated, you will never see your boy again.

If you pay the money as demanded, he will be returned to you safe and well within three hours. These terms are final, and if you do not accede to them, no further communication will be attempted.

TWO DESPERATE MEN

I addressed this letter to Dorset and put it in my pocket. As I was about to start, the kid comes up to me and says:

"Aw, Snake-eye, you said I could play the Scout while you was gone."

"Play it, of course," says I. "Mr. Bill will play with you. What kind of a game is it?"

"I'm the Scout," says Red Chief, "and I have to ride to the stockade to warn the settlers that the Indians are coming. I'm tired of playing Indian myself. I want to be the Scout."

"All right," says I. "It sounds harmless to me. I guess Mr. Bill will help you foil the enemy."

"What am I to do?" asks Bill, looking at the kid suspiciously.

"You are the hoss," says Scout. "Get down on your hands and knees. How can I ride to the stockade without a hoss?"

"You'd better keep him interested," said I, "till we get the scheme going. Loosen up."

Bill gets down on his all fours, and a look comes in his eye like a rabbit's when you catch it in a trap.

"How far is it to the stockade, kid?" he asks, in a husky manner of voice.

"Ninety miles," says the Scout. "And you have to hurry to get there on time. Whoa, now!"

The Scout jumps on Bill's back and digs his heels in his side.

"For Heaven's sake," says Bill, "hurry back, Sam, as soon as you can. I wish we hadn't made the ransom more than a thousand. Say, you quit kicking me or I'll get up and warm you good."

I walked over to Poplar Grove and sat around the post office and store, talking with the chaw-bacons that came in to trade. One whiskerando says that he hears Summit is all upset on account of Elder Ebenezer Dorset's boy having been lost or stolen. That was all I

What happens if the parents don't pay?

76

wanted to know. I referred casually to the price of black-eyed peas, posted my letter surreptitiously and came away. The postmaster said the mail carrier would come by in an hour to take the mail to Summit.

When I got back to the cave, Bill and the boy were not to be found. I explored the vicinity of the cave and risked a yodel or two, but there was no response.

I showed him the road to Summit and kicked him about eight feet nearer there at one kick.

So I sat down on a mossy bank to await developments.

In about half an hour I heard the bushes rustle, and Bill wabbled out into the little glade in front of the cave. Behind him was the kid, stepping softly like a scout, with a broad grin on his face. Bill stopped, took off his hat, and wiped his face with a red handkerchief. The kid stopped about eight feet behind him. "Sam," says Bill, "I suppose you think I'm a renegade, but I couldn't help it. I'm a grown person with masculine proclivities and habits of self-defense, but there is a time when all systems of egotism and predominance fail. The boy is gone. I sent him home. All is off. There was martyrs in old times," goes on Bill, "that suffered death rather than give up the particular graft they enjoyed. None of 'em ever was subjugated to such tortures as I have been. I tried to be faithful to our articles of depredation;[12] but there came a limit."

"What's the trouble, Bill?" I asks him.

"I was rode," says Bill, "the ninety miles to the stockade, not barring an inch. Then, when the settlers was rescued, I was given oats. Sand ain't a palatable substitute. And then, for an hour I had to try to explain to him why there was nothin' in holes, how a road can run both ways, and what makes the grass green. I tell you, Sam, a human can only stand so much. I takes him by the neck of his clothes and drags him down the mountain. On the way he kicks my legs black and blue from the knees down; and I've got to have two or three bites on my thumb and hand cauterized.[13]

"But he's gone"—continues Bill—"gone home. I showed him the road to Summit and kicked him about eight feet nearer there at one kick. I'm sorry we lose the ransom; but it was either that or Bill Driscoll to the madhouse."

Bill is puffing and blowing, but there is a look of ineffable peace and growing content on his rose-pink features.

"Bill," says I, "there isn't any heart disease in your family, is there?"

"No," says Bill, "nothing chronic except malaria and accidents. Why?"

"Then you might turn around," says I, "and have a look behind you."

Bill turns and sees the boy, and loses his complexion and sits down plump on the ground and begins to pluck aimlessly at grass and little sticks. For an hour I was afraid of his mind. And then I told him that my scheme was to put the whole job through immediately and that we would get the ransom and be off

---

12. **depredation** (dĕp′rĭ-dā′shən): robbery or plundering.

13. **cauterized** (kô′tə-rīzd): burned a wound in order to stop bleeding or to promote healing.

---

with it by midnight if old Dorset fell in with our proposition. So Bill braced up enough to give the kid a weak sort of a smile and a promise to play the Russian in a Japanese war with him as soon as he felt a little better.

I had a scheme for collecting that ransom without danger of being caught by counterplots that ought to commend itself to professional kidnappers. The tree under which the answer was to be left—and the money later on—was close to the road fence, with big, bare fields on all sides. If a gang of constables should be watching for anyone to come for the note, they could see him a long way off crossing the fields or in the road. But no, sirree! At half past eight I was up in that tree as well hidden as a tree toad, waiting for the messenger to arrive.

> At half past eight I was up in that tree as well hidden as a tree toad, waiting for the messenger to arrive.

Exactly on time, a half-grown boy rides up the road on a bicycle, locates the pasteboard box at the foot of the fence post, slips a folded piece of paper into it, and pedals away again back toward Summit.

I waited an hour and then concluded the thing was square. I slid down the tree, got the note, slipped along the fence till I struck the woods, and was back at the cave in another half an hour. I opened the note, got near the lantern, and read it to Bill. It was written with a pen in a crabbed hand,[14] and the sum and substance of it was this:

TWO DESPERATE MEN:

Gentlemen: I received your letter today by post, in regard to the ransom you ask for the return of my son. I think you are a little high in your demands, and I hereby make you a counterproposition, which I am inclined to believe you will accept. You bring Johnny home and pay me two hundred and fifty dollars in cash, and I agree to take him off your hands. You had better come at night, for the neighbors believe he is lost, and I couldn't be responsible for what they would do to anybody they saw bringing him back. Very respectfully,

EBENEZER DORSET

"Great Pirates of Penzance," says I; "of all the impudent—"

But I glanced at Bill, and hesitated. He had the most appealing look in his eyes I ever saw on the face of a dumb or a talking brute.

"Sam," says he, "what's two hundred and fifty dollars, after all? We've got the money. One more night of this kid will send me to a bed in Bedlam.[15] Besides being a thorough gentleman, I think Mr. Dorset is a spendthrift for making us such a liberal offer. You ain't going to let the chance go, are you?"

"Tell you the truth, Bill," says I, "this little he-ewe lamb has somewhat got on my nerves too. We'll take him home, pay the ransom, and make our getaway."

---

14. **crabbed hand:** handwriting that is difficult to read.

15. **Bedlam:** an insane asylum.

WORDS TO KNOW

proposition (prŏp'ə-zĭsh'ən) *n.* a suggested plan
commend (kə-mĕnd') *v.* to speak highly of; to praise
impudent (ĭm'pyə-dənt) *adj.* offensively bold and disrespectful

78

We took him home that night. We got him to go by telling him that his father had bought a silver-mounted rifle and a pair of moccasins for him and we were to hunt bears the next day.

It was just twelve o'clock when we knocked at Ebenezer's front door. Just at the moment when I should have been abstracting the fifteen hundred dollars from the box under the tree, according to the original proposition, Bill was counting out two hundred and fifty dollars into Dorset's hand.

When the kid found out we were going to leave him at home, he started up a howl like a calliope[16] and fastened himself as tight as a leech to Bill's leg. His father peeled him away gradually, like a porous plaster.

"How long can you hold him?" asks Bill.

"I'm not as strong as I used to be," says old Dorset, "but I think I can promise you ten minutes."

"Enough," says Bill. "In ten minutes I shall cross the Central, Southern, and Middle Western States and be legging it trippingly for the Canadian border."

And as dark as it was, and as fat as Bill was, and as good a runner as I am, he was a good mile and a half out of Summit before I could catch up with him. ❖

---

16. **calliope** (kə-lī′ə-pē′): an instrument fitted with steam whistles, played by keyboard.

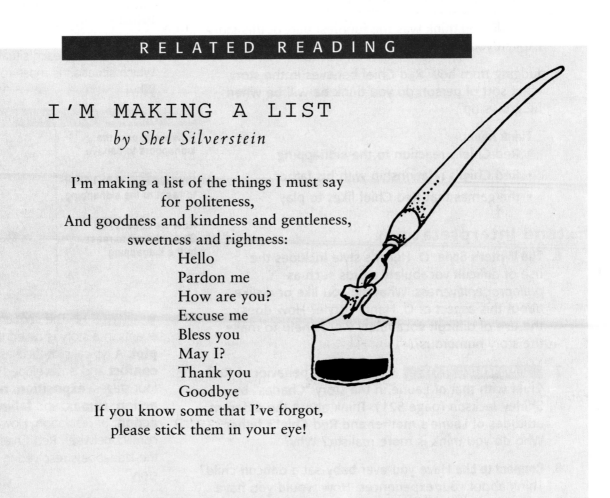

RELATED READING

I'M MAKING A LIST
by Shel Silverstein

I'm making a list of the things I must say
for politeness,
And goodness and kindness and gentleness,
sweetness and rightness:
    Hello
    Pardon me
    How are you?
    Excuse me
    Bless you
    May I?
    Thank you
    Goodbye
If you know some that I've forgot,
please stick them in your eye!

Connect to the Literature

1. **What Do You Think?**
   What was your reaction to the ending of the story?

   Comprehension Check
   - What reason do Bill and Sam have for kidnapping Ebenezer Dorset's son?
   - What are some of the things that Red Chief does to annoy Bill?
   - What does Red Chief's father think of him?

Think Critically

2. **ACTIVE READING** **PREDICTING**
   Go back to the predictions that you made in your **READER'S NOTEBOOK.** Cross out the predictions that did not come true. What predictions are left?

3. How do the criminals change as the story is told?

4. What do you think was the funniest part of this story? Explain your answer.

5. Judging from how Red Chief behaves in the story, what sort of person do you think he will be when he grows up?

   Think About:
   - Red Chief's reaction to the kidnapping
   - Red Chief's relationship with his father
   - the games that Red Chief likes to play

Extend Interpretations

6. **The Writer's Style** O. Henry's style includes the use of difficult vocabulary words such as *philoprogenitiveness.* What did you like or dislike about this aspect of O. Henry's style? How does the use of difficult vocabulary words help to make the story humorous?

7. **COMPARING TEXTS** Compare the behavior of Red Chief with that of Laurie in the story "Charles" by Shirley Jackson (page S21). Think about the different attitudes of Laurie's mother and Red Chief's father. Who do you think is more realistic? Why?

8. **Connect to Life** Have you ever baby-sat a difficult child? Think about your experiences. How would you have reacted to Red Chief?

Literary Analysis

IRONY A surprising contrast between what is expected and what actually exists or happens is called **irony.** The kind of irony used in "The Ransom of Red Chief" is an example of situational irony. **Situational irony** occurs when a character—or the reader—expects one thing to happen but something entirely different takes place. For example, you expect that Red Chief will be upset, rather than happy, about being kidnapped.

Paired Activity With a partner, complete a chart like the one shown. Discuss each situation. Which situation is most ironic? Why?

What We Expect	What Happens
How we expect the kidnappers to behave	
How we expect Red Chief to react to the kidnapping	
How we expect Red Chief's father to react to the kidnapping	

REVIEW: PLOT The sequence of events in a story is called the **plot.** A typical plot focuses on a **conflict** and is developed in four stages: **exposition, rising action, climax,** and **falling action,** or resolution. How is the conflict between Red Chief and the kidnappers resolved in this story?

CHOICES and CHALLENGES

Writing

Journal Entry Write an account of Red Chief's kidnapping from his point of view. As you prepare to write, think of Red Chief's motivations and reactions. This will help you to write from Red Chief's point of view. Be sure to tell what happened as well as how the boy felt about his experiences. Place your journal entry in your **Working Portfolio**.

Speaking & Listening

Film Review View a clip from the film version of "The Ransom of Red Chief." Then, with classmates, discuss whether the film portrays characters in the same way you visualized them. Notice how the images in the film may be different from what you pictured in your mind as you read the story.

VIDEO: Literature in Performance

"The Ransom of Red Chief"

Research & Technology

An Oldie but Goodie Many folk tales and fables have plots that, like "The Ransom of Red Chief," involve a supposedly helpless creature (often an animal) who thwarts the evil intentions of a stronger enemy. Go to the library and locate collections of animal tales or fables from Africa, the Americas, or some other part of the world. Which stories have plots similar to "The Ransom of Red Chief"? Be prepared to tell these stories to the class and to summarize their similarities and differences.

INTERNET Research Starter
www.mcdougallittell.com

Vocabulary

EXERCISE: CONTEXT CLUES On your paper, write the Word to Know that best completes each sentence.

1. The men could not make Red Chief _____ with any of Bill's requests.
2. The men believed the _____ would help them start a new future.
3. Neither Bill nor Sam could _____ Red Chief and his behavior.
4. Red Chief did not want to leave the camp; he thought the food was quite _____.
5. Sam and Bill decided to _____ in kidnapping the boy.
6. Sam went into town to drop off the ransom note _____.
7. When Sam returned, Bill was exhausted and went into a _____ against the entire project.
8. Red Chief could be described as an _____ child.
9. The boy's father responded with a surprising _____.
10. With Red Chief along, an atmosphere of chaos would gradually _____ the camp.

Vocabulary Handbook
See p. R20: Context Clues.

WORDS TO KNOW	collaborate	comply	impudent	pervade	ransom
	commend	diatribe	palatable	proposition	surreptitiously

Grammar in Context: Pronouns and Their Antecedents

In the following sentences, the writer is talking about one person—"the kid" or "Red Chief."

> When the kid found out we were going to leave him at home, he started up a howl like a calliope and fastened himself as tight as a leech to Bill's leg. His father peeled him away gradually, like a porous plaster.

The **pronouns** *him, he, himself,* and *his* let the reader know that the same person is being referred to or described. The person being referred to is called the antecedent. Sentences without clear antecedents can be confusing.

Usage Tip: A pronoun usually refers to the noun that immediately precedes it. Make sure that you do not use the same pronoun with two different antecedents and that the antecedent is clear.

WRITING EXERCISE Rewrite the following sentences to avoid unclear antecedents.

Example: *Original* The boy nearly drove Bill mad, after Sam had left him alone with him.

Rewritten The boy nearly drove Bill mad, after Sam had left them alone.

1. Sam and Bill decided to kidnap the son of Ebenezer Dorset and send him a ransom note.
2. When the boy first saw Sam, he was throwing rocks.
3. Sam told Bill that he had to keep the boy quiet until he returned.
4. Bill hated the boy. In fact he swore to Sam that he had never hated anybody as much as he hated him.
5. Sam asked the boy if he would like him to take him home.

Grammar Handbook
See p. R79: Using Nouns and Pronouns.

O. Henry
1862–1910

"There's a story in everything."

A Checkered Career O. Henry is the pen name of William Sydney Porter. Born in Greensboro, North Carolina, Porter was raised by his grandmother and his aunt after his mother's death. As a young man, he had many jobs. He clerked in his uncle's drugstore, worked as a ranch hand in Texas, and later became a bank teller. Several years after leaving his position at the bank, he was convicted of having embezzled, or stolen, money from the bank.

A Master Storyteller In jail, Porter began writing stories in order to support his young daughter. On being released, Porter changed his name to O. Henry, became a fiction writer, and contributed weekly stories to newspapers. Eventually he became one of the country's best-loved short-story writers. He wrote adventure tales, humorous stories, and slice-of-life tales about ordinary people, often with surprise endings.

AUTHOR ACTIVITY
Surprise! O. Henry is famous for unexpected twists at the ends of his stories. "Gift of the Magi" and "After Twenty Years" are examples of stories with surprise endings. Find these stories in the library. Do the endings surprise you? Why or why not?

Building Vocabulary
Informal Language—Idioms and Slang

Some expressions that you use in everyday speech are so familiar that you probably don't think much about the meanings of the individual words in them.

The meaning of "checking out" is quite different from the meanings of the individual words. This phrase is an **idiom**—an expression that cannot be understood by analyzing it word by word. Many idioms are part of **informal English,** the language of everyday speech.

> "The girl hated herself for not checking out at the boy's line, and the boy hated himself for not catching her eye and saying hello . . ."
> — Cynthia Rylant, "Checkouts"

In this excerpt, the **idiom** means "paying for items."

Strategies for Building Vocabulary

Informal English also includes **slang**—words and phrases that people make up or adapt for use in their casual speech. The word *awesome* in the sentence "That's a totally awesome movie" is an example of slang. Slang terms usually become outdated quickly. Each generation and region creates its own slang.

The following strategies can help you understand unfamiliar idioms and slang that you might find in your reading.

❶ **Find Context Clues** An idiom or slang expression can be confusing if you have never encountered it before. Often you can figure out what idioms and slang mean by thinking about the surrounding words. This is called looking at the **context.** Consider the following example:

> Or sometimes . . . he'll dash across traffic to the island in the middle of Broadway and give the pigeons a fit. Then I have to go behind him apologizing to all the old people . . . getting all upset with the pigeons fluttering around them, scattering their newspapers. . . .
> —Toni Cade Bambara, "Raymond's Run"

The description of the pigeons' actions suggests that the slang expression *give . . . a fit* means "frighten" or "upset."

The following passage contains one idiom. The words "lean down" and "huffing and puffing," and the preceding action in the story, suggest what *catch my breath* means.

> And I lean down to catch my breath and here comes Gretchen walking back, for she's overshot the finish line too, huffing and puffing. . . .
> —Toni Cade Bambara, "Raymond's Run"

❷ **Use Reference Aids** Many dictionaries define idioms and slang terms. There are, however, special dictionaries devoted to idioms and slang.

EXERCISE Use context clues to define the underlined examples of informal language. Then use a dictionary to check your definitions.

1. There was great music, and everyone from school came. It was a very <u>cool</u> party.
2. Ernesto can always depend on his brother to <u>stand up for</u> him.
3. We gave the movie a glowing <u>thumbs up.</u>
4. I was tired and <u>drew a blank</u> when Mr. Wright asked for the answer.
5. Dara and I were <u>wiped out</u> after practice.

BORN WORKER

by Gary Soto

They said that José was born with a ring of dirt around his neck, with grime under his fingernails, and skin calloused from the grainy twist of a shovel. They said his palms were already rough by the time he was three, and soon after he learned his primary colors, his squint was the squint of an aged laborer. They said he was a born worker.

By seven he was drinking coffee slowly, his mouth pursed the way his mother sipped. He wore jeans, a shirt with sleeves rolled to his elbows. His eye could measure a length of board, and his knees genuflected[1] over flower beds and leafy gutters.

They said lots of things about José, but almost nothing of his parents. His mother stitched at a machine all day, and his father, with a steady job at the telephone company, climbed splintered, sun-sucked poles, fixed wires and looked around the city at tree level.

---

1. **genuflected** (jĕn′yə-flĕk′tĭd): bent the knee or touched it to the ground, as in worship.

Mulholland Drive: The Road to the Studio (1980), David Hockney. Acrylic on canvas, 86" × 243". Copyright © David Hockney. Collection of the Los Angeles County Museum of Art. Photo courtesy of the artist's studio.

"What do you see up there?" José once asked his father.

"Work," he answered. "I see years of work, *mi'jo*."[2]

José took this as a truth, and though he did well in school, he felt destined to labor. His arms would pump, his legs would bend, his arms would carry a world of earth. He believed in hard work, believed that his strength was as ancient as a rock's.

"Life is hard," his father repeated from the time José could first make out the meaning of words until he was stroking his fingers against the grain of his sandpaper beard.

His mother was an example to José. She would raise her hands, showing her fingers pierced from the sewing machines. She bled on her machine, bled because there was money to make, a child to raise, and a roof to stay under.

One day when José returned home from junior high, his cousin Arnie was sitting on the lawn sucking on a stalk of grass. José knew that grass didn't come from his lawn. His was cut and pampered, clean.

"José!" Arnie shouted as he took off the earphones of his CD Walkman.

"Hi, Arnie," José said without much enthusiasm. He didn't like his cousin. He thought he was lazy and, worse, spoiled by the trappings[3] of being middle class. His parents had good jobs in offices and showered him with clothes, shoes, CDs, vacations, almost anything he wanted. Arnie's family had never climbed a telephone pole to size up the future.

---

2. **mi'jo** (mē'hō): a contraction of the Spanish words *mi hijo*, meaning "my son."

3. **trappings:** outward decoration or dress.

> **"What would you do?" José asked.**
>
> **"Me?" he said brightly. "Shoot, I'll round**
>
> **up all kinds of jobs for you. You won't have**
>
> **to do anything."**

Arnie rose to his feet, and José saw that his cousin was wearing a new pair of high-tops. He didn't say anything.

"Got an idea," Arnie said cheerfully. "Something that'll make us money."

José looked at his cousin, not a muscle of curiosity twitching in his face.

Still, Arnie explained that since he himself was so clever with words, and his best cousin in the whole world was good at working with his hands, that maybe they might start a company.

"What would you do?" José asked.

"Me?" he said brightly. "Shoot, I'll round up all kinds of jobs for you. You won't have to do anything." He stopped, then started again. "Except—you know—do the work."

"Get out of here," José said.

"Don't be that way," Arnie begged. "Let me tell you how it works."

The boys went inside the house, and while José stripped off his school clothes and put on his jeans and a T-shirt, Arnie told him that they could be rich.

"You ever hear of this guy named Bechtel?"[4] Arnie asked.

José shook his head.

"Man, he started just like us," Arnie said. "He started digging ditches and stuff, and the next thing you knew, he was sitting by his own swimming pool. You want to sit by your own pool, don't you?" Arnie smiled, waiting for José to speak up.

"Never heard of this guy Bechtel," José said after he rolled on two huge socks, worn at the heels. He opened up his chest of drawers and brought out a packet of Kleenex.

Arnie looked at the Kleenex.

"How come you don't use your sleeve?" Arnie joked.

José thought for a moment and said, "I'm not like you." He smiled at his retort.

---

4. **Bechtel:** Warren A. Bechtel (běk′təl) (1872–1933) formed a leading engineering company, which built such structures as the Hoover Dam, the San Francisco–Oakland Bay Bridge, the Trans-Arabian pipeline, and the first nuclear plant to produce electricity.

Chaim Soutine (1917), Amedeo Modigliani. Oil on Canvas 36⅛ × 25½". National Gallery of Art. Washington, D.C./SuperStock.

Portrait of Moise Kisling (1915), Amedeo Modigliani. Oil on canvas, 37 × 28 cm. Pinacoteca di Brera, Milan Italy/ Mauro Magliani/SuperStock.

"Listen, I'll find the work, and then we can split it fifty-fifty."

José knew fifty-fifty was a bad deal.

"How about sixty-forty?" Arnie suggested when he could see that José wasn't going for it. "I know a lot of people from my dad's job. They're waiting for us."

José sat on the edge of his bed and started to lace up his boots. He knew that there were agencies that would find you work, agencies that took a portion of your pay. They're cheats, he thought, people who sit in air-conditioned offices while others work.

"You really know a lot of people?" José asked.

"Boatloads," Arnie said. "My dad works with this millionaire—honest—who cooks a steak for his dog every day."

He's a liar, José thought. No matter how he tried, he couldn't picture a dog grubbing on steak. The world was too poor for that kind of silliness.

"Listen, I'll go eighty-twenty," José said.

"Aw, man," Arnie whined. "That ain't fair."

José laughed.

"I mean, half the work is finding the jobs," Arnie explained, his palms up as he begged José to be reasonable.

José knew this was true. He had had to go door-to-door, and he disliked asking for work. He assumed that it should automatically be his since he was a good worker, honest, and always on time.

"Where did you get this idea, anyhow?" José asked.

"I got a business mind," Arnie said proudly.

"Just like that Bechtel guy," José retorted.

"That's right."

José agreed to a seventy-thirty split, with the condition that Arnie had to help out. Arnie hollered, arguing that some people were meant to work and others to come up with brilliant ideas. He was one of the latter. Still, he agreed after José said it was that or nothing.

In the next two weeks, Arnie found an array[5] of jobs. José peeled off shingles from a rickety garage roof, carried rocks down a path to where a pond would go, and spray-painted lawn furniture. And while Arnie accompanied him, most of the time he did nothing. He did help occasionally. He did shake the cans of spray paint and kick aside debris so that José didn't trip while going down the path carrying the rocks. He did stack the piles of shingles, but almost cried when a nail bit his thumb. But mostly he told José what he had missed or where the work could be improved. José was bothered because he and his work had never been criticized before.

But soon José learned to ignore his cousin, ignore his comments about his spray painting, or about the way he lugged rocks, two in each arm. He didn't say anything, either, when they got paid and Arnie rubbed his hands like a fly, muttering, "It's payday."

Then Arnie found a job scrubbing a drained swimming pool. The two boys met early at José's house. Arnie brought his bike. José's own bike had a flat that grinned like a clown's face.

"I'll pedal," José suggested when Arnie said that he didn't have much leg strength.

With Arnie on the handlebars, José tore off, his pedaling so strong that tears of fear formed in Arnie's eyes.

"Slow down!" Arnie cried.

José ignored him and within minutes they were riding the bike up a gravel driveway. Arnie hopped off at first chance.

"You're scary," Arnie said, picking a gnat from his eye.

José chuckled.

When Arnie knocked on the door, an old man still in pajamas appeared in the window. He motioned for the boys to come around to the back.

"Let me do the talking," Arnie suggested to his cousin. "He knows my dad real good.

They're like this." He pressed two fingers together.

José didn't bother to say OK. He walked the bike into the backyard, which was lush with plants—roses in their last bloom, geraniums, hydrangeas,[6] pansies with their skirts of bright colors. José could make out the splash of a fountain. Then he heard the hysterical yapping of a poodle. From all his noise, a person might have thought the dog was on fire.

"Hi, Mr. Clemens," Arnie said, extending his hand. "I'm Arnie Sanchez. It's nice to see you again."

José had never seen a kid actually greet someone like this. Mr. Clemens said, hiking up his pajama bottoms, "I only wanted one kid to work."

"Oh," Arnie stuttered. "Actually, my cousin José really does the work and I kind of, you know, supervise."

Mr. Clemens pinched up his wrinkled face. He seemed not to understand. He took out a pea-sized hearing aid, fiddled with its tiny dial, and fit it into his ear, which was surrounded with wiry gray hair.

"I'm only paying for one boy," Mr. Clemens shouted. His poodle click-clicked and stood behind his legs. The dog bared its small crooked teeth.

"That's right," Arnie said, smiling a strained smile. "We know that you're going to compensate[7] only one of us."

Mr. Clemens muttered under his breath. He combed his hair with his fingers. He showed José the pool, which was shaped as round as

---

5. **array:** an impressively large number.

6. **hydrangeas** (hī-drān′jəz): shrubs that have large clusters of white, pink, or blue flowers.

7. **compensate:** to make payment to.

an elephant. It was filthy with grime. Near the bottom some grayish water shimmered and leaves floated as limp as cornflakes.

"It's got to be real clean," Mr. Clemens said, "or it's not worth it."

"Oh, José's a great worker," Arnie said. He patted his cousin's shoulders and said that he could lift a mule.

Mr. Clemens sized up José and squeezed his shoulders, too.

"How do I know you, anyhow?" Mr. Clemens asked Arnie, who was aiming a smile at the poodle.

"You know my dad," Arnie answered, raising his smile to the old man. "He works at Interstate Insurance. You and he had some business deals."

Mr. Clemens thought for a moment, a hand on his mouth, head shaking. He could have been thinking about the meaning of life, his face was so dark.

"Mexican fella?" he inquired.

"That's him," Arnie said happily.

José felt like hitting his cousin for his cheerful attitude. Instead, he walked over and picked up the white plastic bottle of bleach.

Next to it were a wire brush, a pumice[8] stone, and some rags. He set down the bottle and, like a surgeon, put on a pair of rubber gloves.

"You know what you're doing, boy?" Mr. Clemens asked.

José nodded as he walked into the pool. If it had been filled with water, his chest would have been wet. The new hair on his chest would have been floating like the legs of a jellyfish.

"Oh yeah," Arnie chimed, speaking for his cousin. "José was born to work."

José would have drowned his cousin if there had been more water. Instead, he poured a

bleach solution into a rag and swirled it over an area. He took the wire brush and scrubbed. The black algae[9] came up like a foamy monster.

"We're a team," Arnie said to Mr. Clemens.

Arnie descended into the pool and took the bleach bottle from José. He held it for José and smiled up at Mr. Clemens, who, hands on hips, watched for a while, the poodle at his side. He cupped his ear, as if to pick up the sounds of José's scrubbing.

"Nice day, huh?" Arnie sang.

"What?" Mr. Clemens said.

"Nice day," Arnie repeated, this time louder. "So which ear can't you hear in?" Grinning, Arnie wiggled his ear to make sure that Mr. Clemens knew what he was asking.

Mr. Clemens ignored Arnie. He watched José, whose arms worked back and forth like he was sawing logs.

"We're not only a team," Arnie shouted, "but we're also cousins."

Mr. Clemens shook his head at Arnie. When he left, the poodle leading the way, Arnie immediately climbed out of the pool and sat on the edge, legs dangling.

"It's going to be blazing," Arnie complained. He shaded his eyes with his hand and looked east, where the sun was rising over a sycamore, its leaves hanging like bats.

José scrubbed. He worked the wire brush over the black and green stains, the grime dripping like tears. He finished a large area. He hopped out of the pool and returned hauling a garden hose with an attached nozzle. He gave the cleaned area a blast. When the spray got too close, his cousin screamed, got

---

8. **pumice:** a light, porous, hardened piece of lava, used to wear down or smooth surfaces.

9. **algae:** aquatic plant life that mainly grows by photosynthesis. Types of algae range from single-celled organisms to the giant kelp.

Day Pool with Three Blues, Paper Pool 7 (1978), David Hockney. Pressed colored paper pulp, 72" × 85½". Produced and published by Tyler Graphics Ltd., 1978. Copyright © David Hockney/Tyler Graphics, Ltd. Photo by Steven Sloman.

up, and, searching for something to do, picked a loquat[10] from a tree.

"What's your favorite fruit?" Arnie asked.

José ignored him.

Arnie stuffed a bunch of loquats into his mouth, then cursed himself for splattering juice on his new high-tops. He returned to the pool, his cheeks fat with the seeds, and once again sat at the edge. He started to tell José how he had first learned to swim. "We were on vacation in Mazatlán.[11] You been there, ain't you?"

José shook his head. He dabbed the bleach solution onto the sides of the pool with a rag and scrubbed a new area.

"Anyhow, my dad was on the beach and saw this drowned dead guy," Arnie continued. "And right there, my dad got scared and realized I couldn't swim."

---

10. **loquat** (lō′kwŏt′): egg-shaped orange or yellow fruit. The loquat is an evergreen native to Japan; the tree is now grown commercially in California.

11. **Mazatlán** (mä′sət-län′): a city in Mexico on the Pacific Ocean, northwest of Guadalajara.

Arnie rattled on about how his father had taught him in the hotel pool and later showed him where the drowned man's body had been.

"Be quiet," José said.

"What?"

"I can't concentrate," José said, stepping back to look at the cleaned area.

Arnie shut his mouth but opened it to lick loquat juice from his fingers. He kicked his legs against the swimming pool, bored. He looked around the backyard and spotted a lounge chair. He got up, dusting off the back of his pants, and threw himself into the cushions. He raised and lowered the back of the lounge. Sighing, he snuggled in. He stayed quiet for three minutes, during which time José scrubbed. His arms hurt but he kept working with long strokes. José knew that in an hour the sun would drench the pool with light. He hurried to get the job done.

Arnie then asked, "You ever peel before?"

José looked at his cousin. His nose burned from the bleach. He scrunched up his face.

"You know, like when you get sunburned."

"I'm too dark to peel," José said, his words echoing because he had advanced to the deep end. "Why don't you be quiet and let me work?"

Arnie babbled on that he had peeled when on vacation in Hawaii. He explained that he was really more French than Mexican, and that's why his skin was sensitive. He said that when he lived in France, people thought that he could be Portuguese or maybe Armenian, never Mexican.

José felt like soaking his rag with bleach and pressing it over Arnie's mouth to make him be quiet.

Then Mr. Clemens appeared. He was dressed in white pants and a flowery shirt. His thin hair was combed so that his scalp, as pink as a crab, showed.

"I'm just taking a little rest," Arnie said.

Arnie leaped back into the pool. He took the bleach bottle and held it. He smiled at Mr. Clemens, who came to inspect their progress.

"José's doing a good job," Arnie said, then whistled a song.

Mr. Clemens peered into the pool, hands on knees, admiring the progress.

"Pretty good, huh?" Arnie asked.

Mr. Clemens nodded. Then his hearing aid fell out, and José turned in time to see it roll like a bottle cap toward the bottom of the pool. It leaped into the stagnant[12] water with a plop. A single bubble went up, and it was gone.

"Dang," Mr. Clemens swore. He took shuffling steps toward the deep end. He steadied his gaze on where the hearing aid had sunk. He leaned over and suddenly, arms waving, one leg kicking out, he tumbled into

---

12. **stagnant:** not moving or flowing; inactive, dull.

the pool. He landed standing up, then his legs buckled, and he crumbled, his head striking against the bottom. He rolled once, and half of his body settled in the water.

"Did you see that!" Arnie shouted, big-eyed.

José had already dropped his brushes on the side of the pool and hurried to the old man, who moaned, eyes closed, his false teeth jutting from his mouth. A ribbon of blood immediately began to flow from his scalp.

"We better get out of here!" Arnie suggested. "They're going to blame us!"

José knelt on both knees at the old man's side. He took the man's teeth from his mouth and placed them in his shirt pocket. The old man groaned and opened his eyes, which were shiny wet. He appeared startled, like a newborn. "Sir, you'll be all right," José cooed, then snapped at his cousin. "Arnie, get over here and help me!"

"I'm going home," Arnie whined.

"You punk!" José yelled. "Go inside and call 911."

Arnie said that they should leave him there.

"Why should we get involved?" he cried as he started for his bike. "It's his own fault."

José laid the man's head down and with giant steps leaped out of the pool, shoving his cousin as he passed. He went into the kitchen and punched in 911 on a telephone. He explained to the operator what had happened. When asked the address, José dropped the phone and went onto the front porch to look for it.

"It's 940 East Brown," José breathed. He hung up and looked wildly about the kitchen. He opened up the refrigerator and brought out a plastic tray of ice, which he twisted so that a few of the cubes popped out and slid across the floor. He wrapped some cubes in a dish

towel. When he raced outside, Arnie was gone, the yapping poodle was doing laps around the edge of the pool, and Mr. Clemens was trying to stand up.

"No, sir," José said as he jumped into the pool, his own knees almost buckling. "Please, sit down."

Mr. Clemens staggered and collapsed. José caught him before he hit his head again. The towel of ice cubes dropped from his hands. With his legs spread to absorb the weight, José raised the man up in his arms, this fragile man. He picked him up and carefully stepped toward the shallow end, one slow elephant step at a time.

"You'll be all right," José said, more to himself than to Mr. Clemens, who moaned and struggled to be let free.

The sirens wailed in the distance. The poodle yapped, which started a dog barking in the neighbor's yard.

"You'll be OK," José repeated, and in the shallow end of the pool, he edged up the steps. He lay the old man in the lounge chair and raced back inside for more ice and another towel. He returned outside and placed the bundle of cubes on the man's head, where the blood flowed. Mr. Clemens was awake, looking about. When the old man felt his mouth, José reached into his shirt pocket and pulled out his false teeth. He fit the teeth into Mr. Clemens's mouth and a smile appeared, something bright at a difficult time.

"I hit my head," Mr. Clemens said after smacking his teeth so that the fit was right.

José looked up and his gaze floated to a telephone pole, one his father might have climbed. If he had been there, his father would have seen that José was more than just a good worker. He would have seen a good man. He held the towel to the old man's head.

The poodle, now quiet, joined them on the lounge chair.

A fire truck pulled into the driveway and soon they were surrounded by firemen, one of whom brought out a first-aid kit. A fireman led José away and asked what had happened. He was starting to explain when his cousin reappeared, yapping like a poodle.

"I was scrubbing the pool," Arnie shouted, "and I said, 'Mr. Clemens, you shouldn't stand so close to the edge.' But did he listen? No, he leaned over and. . .Well, you can just imagine my horror."

José walked away from Arnie's jabbering. He walked away, and realized that there were people like his cousin, the liar, and people like himself, someone he was getting to know. He walked away and in the midmorning heat boosted himself up a telephone pole.

He climbed up and saw for himself what his father saw—miles and miles of trees and houses, and a future lost in the layers of yellowish haze. ❖

Gary Soto
born 1952

"We didn't have books, and no one encouraged us to read. So my wanting to write poetry was sort of a fluke."

A Hobo and Paleontologist A native of Fresno, California, Gary Soto writes about the experiences of Mexican Americans. As a child, Soto worked as a field laborer, but he dreamed of becoming a priest, a hobo, and a paleontologist (a scientist who studies prehistoric life). In college, he discovered poetry.

Poet and Film Producer Since college, Soto has been writing novels, short stories, and essays in addition to poetry. Among young readers, he is best known for his short story collections such as *Baseball in April and Other Stories.* However, he has also written a one-act play, *Novio Boy,* that is frequently performed in high schools, and he has produced three films for Spanish-speaking children.

Poetry and Book Awards Soto has won the United States Award of the International Poetry Forum and the American Book Award of the Before Columbus Foundation. He lives in Berkeley, California, where he occasionally teaches English at the University of California.

Writing Workshop

Expressing reactions to a literary work . . .

From Reading to Writing Which pieces of literature did you respond to most strongly? Perhaps you related to the teenage girl in "Checkouts," or to Squeaky in "Raymond's Run." Often in good literature, our emotions are stirred by certain characters and situations because they remind us of real things we have experienced. One way to better understand your reactions is to write a **response to literature.** You can include your interpretation of a story, its effects on you, and connections to your own life.

For Your Portfolio

WRITING PROMPT Write a personal response to a short story or poem.

Purpose: To connect your responses to specifics in the text

Audience: Others who have read the story or people who know you well

---

Basics in a Box

Response to Literature at a Glance

Introduction
Introduces the title and author and a clear statement of your response

Body
Supports the response with evidence from the work

Evidence

examples from the story

quotations

connections to your own life

Conclusion
Summarizes the response

RUBRIC STANDARDS FOR WRITING

A successful response to literature should

- include an introduction that identifies the literary work and clearly states your overall response to it
- tell enough about the literature so that readers can understand your response
- contain clearly described, specific reactions and responses to the literary work
- support your statements with quotations and details
- summarize the response in the conclusion

Analyzing a Student Model

SPEAKING OPPORTUNITY
See the Speaking and Listening Handbook, p. R104 for oral presentation tips.

**Joshua Elmer
Parkland Middle School**

**RUBRIC
IN ACTION**

Personal Response to "Stop the Sun"

    The Vietnam War still burns like a fire in the minds of its soldiers and their families. This is Gary Paulsen's theme in "Stop the Sun." The story tells of one boy's complicated relationship with his father, a Vietnam veteran. I related to the boy, Terry, because my father also fought in the Vietnam War. This, along with Paulsen's realistic style of writing, made me feel as though I were a part of the story from beginning to end.

    In the story, Terry's father suffers from "Vietnam Syndrome," a condition that causes him to have flashbacks—realistic memories—about the war. My first reaction to this was relief. I felt grateful that my father never experienced the "war syndrome." As I read, I found I could picture everything in my mind, for example, the scene where Terry's father is eating and seems to drift off into his own world. "Sometimes during a meal his father's fork would stop halfway to his mouth, just stop, and there would be a long pause while the eyes went away, far away." I thought about how I would feel if I were in Terry's shoes, and the setting were here in my hometown of El Paso. I asked myself how my life would be different if my father were disturbed about his past.

    As the story moved forward, I related to Terry's growing confusion. During one scene in particular, I felt extremely sad. Terry's father is squirming around on the floor in the hardware store as though he were back in the rice paddy in Vietnam, trying to hide from the Vietcong. Not only did I feel sorry for Terry, I pitied his father. He had to go through something no human being should—watching his friends die.

    One part of the story that I could really relate to was where Terry goes to his father looking for information about what happened to him in Vietnam. At first his father refuses to share any information. "No. That's another part of my life. A bad part. A rotten part. It was before I met your mother, long before you. It has nothing to do with this family, nothing. No." I could see that Terry's father was trying to protect him by not telling him. This helped me to understand my own father better. For a long time, my

① The introduction states title and author of the story and includes a brief statement of response.

② Provides enough background for readers to understand the response
Other Option:
• Give a short plot summary

③ Use of quotations shows writer's familiarity with the story and adds supporting details.

④ Gives specific examples from the text that develop and support the response

⑤ Tells a specific effect on the audience

father refused to tell me anything about his experience. Like Terry's father, though, my father soon came to the conclusion that it was best for his son to know the truth.

The story reaches a peak when Terry's father finally tells him about the war. This part touched me the most. I was gripped with emotion because I wasn't quite sure what would happen. I was relieved when the truth finally came out and their relationship grew deeper.

Like many other stories, "Stop the Sun" has a message. It teaches us that to have a truthful relationship, we must be strong enough to tell the truth and strong enough to hear it. Terry gets to really know his father by asking him about his experience in the war. He and his father begin to build a bridge to each other. Reading this story made me want to expand my relationships with others, especially my father. I learned a lot about the effect that war can have on everyone in a family. I also learned an important lesson from Terry: never give up on those you love.

❻ The writer describes how the story relates to his own personal knowledge and experience.

❼ The conclusion summarizes the response and explains the lessons that the writer took from the story.

Writing Your Response to Literature

❶ Prewriting

We must read not to understand others but to understand ourselves.
—E. M. Cioran, French philosopher

Make a list of ideas for your personal response essay. **Note** stories with scenes you can relate to. **Write** down names of characters that have traits that you admire or dislike. **Review** the stories that make you laugh or cry or that stay burned into your memory for some other reason. See the **Idea Bank** in the margin for more suggestions. After you select a short story for your response, complete the steps that follow.

Planning Your Response to Literature

1. **Carefully reread the short story.** Read the selection again, paying attention to what you are thinking or feeling as you read. What are your responses to the characters, the events, and the writer's message? Creating a chart like the one below can help you keep track of the information.

Characters	Description	Response	Quote from Story
Terry	sensitive	I understand and admire him.	". . . and I thought if I could help or maybe understand it better . . ."

Events	Description	Response	Quote from Story
Scene in hardware store	Terry's father squirming along the floor	sympathy; horror at his father's behavior	

Theme	Description	Response	Quote from Story

2. **Freewrite about your responses.** How would you describe your overall response to the piece? What life experiences have you had that helped you connect to the story?

3. **Choose a focus.** Once you have done a freewrite, decide which parts of the story you will include in your response.

4. **Identify your audience.** How familiar is your audience with the work? What background information will your audience need to know in order to understand your response?

IDEA Bank

1. Your Working Portfolio
Look for ideas in the **Writing** sections that you completed earlier.

2. Mirror Image
As you read, do you see characters and situations that remind you of yourself or your relationships? Choose a story that reminds you of yourself or of a relationship you have.

3. Memory Link
Are there stories that you remember reading in seventh grade? Now think about the stories you have read this year. Which one will you remember long after you have left eighth grade? Respond to that story.

Have a question?

See the **Writing Handbook.**
Options for Organization, p. R42
Elaboration, p. R39
See **Language Network.**
Prewriting, p. 314
Drafting, p. 317

❷ Drafting

You can begin writing even if you have not yet decided on everything you want to say. As you draft your response, think about how to organize your ideas.

- Write an **introduction** that **identifies** the title and author of the work, gives your overall response, and **explains** the connections to your own life.

- Begin the **body** by explaining why you felt as you did. **Elaborate** with specific examples from the literature. This includes **quotations** and **descriptions** of scenes, among other things. Then **describe** how these relate to your own life.

- Finish with a **conclusion** that **summarizes** your response.

Ask Your Peer Reader

- How would you sum up my response?
- Which details from the story stick out in your mind?
- Did you have enough information to understand my response?

Need revising help?

Review the **Rubric**, p. 94

Consider **peer reader** comments

Check **Revision Guidelines**, p. R33

See **Language Network**
The Introduction, p. 370

Plural noun problems?

See the **Grammar Handbook**, p. R79

SPELLING From Writing

As you revise your work, look back at the words you misspelled and determine why you made the errors you did. For additional help, refer to the strategies and generalizations in the **Spelling Handbook** on page R28.

SPEAKING Opportunity

Turn your written response into an oral presentation.

Publishing IDEAS

- Create a collection of different responses to the same story. Note similarities in the story's effects on its audience.
- With your classmates, read parts of the story aloud and explain your reactions. Cover character, plot, and theme.

Publishing Options
www.mcdougallittell.com

❸ Revising

TARGET SKILL ▶ A STRONG INTRODUCTION

The introduction of your response must include the title and author of the work and must introduce a statement of response. It should focus on creating a single impression. You might begin with an image from the story or a quotation that captures the reader's attention.

> *The Vietnam War still burns like a fire in the minds of its soldiers and their families. This is Gary Paulsen's theme in "Stop the Sun."*
>
> ~~"Stop the Sun" by Gary Paulsen was a good story.~~ The story tells of one boy's relationship with his father. I related to the boy, Terry . . .

❹ Editing and Proofreading

TARGET SKILL ▶ RUN-ON SENTENCES

A sentence expresses a complete thought. A run-on sentence is two or more sentences written incorrectly as one. For example, *Many veterans have bad memories of the war and this story is about a man who cannot forget what he saw in Vietnam.* This run-on sentence combines two complete thoughts. The first sentence is: *Many veterans have bad memories of the war.* The second sentence is: *This story is about a man who cannot forget what he saw in Vietnam.*

> The story tells of one boy's complicated relationship with his father, a Vietnam veteran, and I related to the boy, Terry, because my father also fought in the Vietnam War.

❺ Reflecting

FOR YOUR WORKING PORTFOLIO How did writing about the story add to your understanding of the literature and the world around you? What did you learn about the process of writing a personal response essay? Attach your reflections to your finished work. Save your personal response essay in your **Working Portfolio**. 📁

Standardized Test Practice

Mixed Review

Review Your Skills

Use the passage and the questions that follow it to check how well you remember the language conventions you've learned in previous grades.

"Stop the Sun" by Gary Paulsen is a realistic story. It describes the struggles of a Vietnam War veteran and his son, Terry. <u>because Terry's</u> <u>father cannot let go of the past.</u> ₍₁₎ Consequently, he cannot be <u>their</u> for his ₍₂₎ son. This made me realize that <u>parents are people too they are</u> <u>struggling</u> ₍₃₎ with their own <u>problem</u>. However, by the end of the story, ₍₄₎ Terry's father decides that he <u>owes</u> his son an explanation. I admire ₍₅₎ Terry because he realizes that <u>the best he can do</u> for his father is try to ₍₆₎ understand.

1. How is sentence 1 best written?
   A. Terry's father cannot let go of the past.
   B. and Terry's father cannot let go of the past.
   C. so Terry's father cannot let go of the past.
   D. Correct as is

2. What is the correct spelling in sentence 2?
   A. they're
   B. there
   C. thier
   D. Correct as is

3. How is item 3 best written?
   A. parents are people too, they are struggling
   B. parents are people too. They are struggling
   C. parents are people too and; they are struggling
   D. Correct as is

4. Which is the correct word in item 4?
   A. problems
   B. problem's
   C. probelems
   D. Correct as is

5. What is the correct spelling in sentence 5?
   A. oews
   B. oaws
   C. ows
   D. Correct as is

6. How is sentence 6 best written?
   A. the better he can do
   B. the more better he can do
   C. the most best he can do
   D. Correct as is

Self-Assessment

Check your own answers in the **Grammar Handbook**

Plural Nouns, p. R79

Writing Complete Sentences, p. R75

Making Subjects and Verbs Agree, p. R76

The Literature You'll Read

The Concepts You'll Study

Vocabulary and Reading Comprehension
Vocabulary Focus: Understanding Specialized
　Vocabulary
Identifying the Main Idea
Identifying Author's Purpose
Visualizing
Monitoring Your Reading
Understanding Chronological Order

Writing and Language Conventions
Writing Workshop: Autobiographical Incident
Subjects and Predicates
Simple Subjects and Simple Predicates
Compound Subjects and Compound Predicates
Sentence Variety
Problems with Here and There

Literary Analysis
Genre Focus: Nonfiction
Memoir
Anecdote
Essay
Antagonist and Protagonist
Feature Story
Primary Source

Speaking and Listening
Dramatic Reading
Radio Broadcast
Persuasive Speech
Video Review

*N*onfiction

> *I like to think of a historian or a biographer as an artist who . . . has to use his or her imagination to penetrate the record, to dig deep down into the past to the place where life emerges.*
>
> —Jean Fritz, writer

What many readers enjoy reading most is **nonfiction**—writings about real people, places, and events. Nonfiction includes a wide variety of writing, from a newspaper article to the life story of a famous person. Types of nonfiction you will read in this book include biographies, autobiographies, essays, informative articles, and interviews. Nonfiction contains mostly factual information. The writer selects and organizes information to suit a specific purpose.

Key Forms of Nonfiction

- biography
- autobiography
- essay
- informative article
- interview

Biography

A **biography** is the story of a person's life as told by someone else. The writer, or **biographer,** interviews the subject if possible and also researches the subject's life by reading letters, books, and diaries and by finding other information. The best biographers try to produce an accurate description of their subjects, including strengths and weaknesses, successes and failures.

A biography often contains many of the same elements as fiction, such as **character, setting,** and **plot.** As you see in the excerpt on the top right, the biographer Ann Petry creates a realistic portrait of her subject, Harriet Tubman, by recording Tubman's feelings as she leads eleven runaway slaves north.

BIOGRAPHY

But there were so many of them this time. She knew moments of doubt when she was half-afraid and kept looking back over her shoulder, imagining that she heard the sound of pursuit. They would certainly be pursued. Eleven of them. Eleven thousand dollars' worth of flesh and bone and muscle that belonged to Maryland planters. If they were caught, the eleven runaways would be whipped and sold south, but she—she would probably be hanged.

—Ann Petry, *Harriet Tubman: Conductor on the Underground Railroad*

Autobiography

An **autobiography** is the story of a person's life as told by that person. It is almost always written from the **first-person point of view.** An autobiography is often book-length because it covers a long period of the writer's life. However, there are shorter types of autobiographical writing, such as **journals, diaries, letters,** and **memoirs.**

YOUR TURN What details in the autobiographical paragraph on the right help you understand what Julia Alvarez felt and experienced?

AUTOBIOGRAPHY

For weeks that soon became months and years, I would think in this way. What was going on right this moment back home? As the leaves fell and the air turned gray and the cold set in, I would remember the big house in Boca Chica, the waves telling me their secrets, the cousins sleeping side by side in their cots, and I would wonder if those papers had set us free from everything we loved.

—Julia Alvarez, *Something to Declare*

Essay

An essay is a short piece of writing on a single subject. Essays are often found in newspapers and magazines. The writer might share an opinion, try to entertain or persuade the reader, or simply describe a topic or incident that has special meaning. Three common types of essays are **expository** (formal), **personal,** and **persuasive.** Essays that explain how the author feels about a subject are called informal or personal essays because they use a conversational tone. Formal essays are scholarly and serious and have a more impersonal tone.

ESSAY

expository

- tightly structured
- impersonal style
- presents or explains information and ideas

personal

- looser structure
- more personal style
- expresses writer's thoughts and feelings

persuasive

- presents arguments
- tries to convince readers to adopt a certain point of view

Satellites have expanded possibilities for sending and receiving messages. Now it is possible not only to transmit information from one part of the earth to another, but also from Earth to space and back. The results have transformed the way we view our planet.

—Patricia Lauber, "Seeing Earth from Space"

I had asthma when I was young, so I never got to play sports much with my father. While my brother and father practiced, I could only sit in bed, propped up by a stack of pillows. As I read my comic books, I heard them beneath our apartment window. In the summer, it was the thump of my brother's fastball into my father's mitt.

—Laurence Yep, "The Great Rat Hunt"

What we need in the United States is not division; what we need in the United States is not hatred; what we need in the United States is not violence or lawlessness, but love and wisdom, and compassion toward one another, and a feeling of justice toward those who still suffer within our country, whether they be white or they be black.

—Robert F. Kennedy, "On the Death of Martin Luther King, Jr."

Informative Article

Informative articles provide facts about a specific subject. This type of informational text takes two basic forms:

- **News stories** give objective or unbiased accounts of current events.
- **Feature stories** appear in magazines and newspapers. Many of them are human-interest stories focusing on interesting people or events.

Informative nonfiction can also be found in textbooks, encyclopedias, and reference books.

YOUR TURN What is the subject of the feature story on the right? What informative details does the writer provide?

Interview

An **interview** is a conversation in which one person asks questions of another to obtain information. The interviewer takes notes on, tape-records, or films the conversation in order to keep an accurate record of the discussion. Interviews can be seen on television and read in magazines. An interview with the author Nikki Giovanni is included on page 407.

INFORMATIVE ARTICLE

On Wednesday morning at a quarter past five came the earthquake. A minute later the flames were leaping upward. In a dozen different quarters south of Market Street, in the working-class ghetto, and in the factories, fires started. There was no opposing the flames. There was no organization, no communication. All the cunning adjustments of a twentieth century city had been smashed by the earthquake. The streets were humped into ridges and depressions, and piled with the debris of fallen walls. The steel rails were twisted into perpendicular and horizontal angles. The telephone and telegraph systems were disrupted. And the great water-mains had burst.

—Jack London, "The Story of an Eyewitness"

INTERVIEW

How did you become an author? Did anyone help you get started?

—Aiana D., Illinois

Probably the easiest thing in the world, Aiana, is to become an author. All you have to do is say you are one. We do not have tests or require licenses or anything like that. You just have to do it and then comes the hard part: you have to find some one to read it . . . Publishing is the icing on the cake . . .

—*talking online with Nikki Giovanni*

Reading Nonfiction

Nonfiction writing helps us to better understand ourselves and our world. **Autobiographies, biographies, essays, informative articles,** and **interviews** open doors to new worlds, exciting people, and compelling events. The following strategies can help you to enjoy many types of nonfiction.

How to Apply the Strategies

Preview the selection. Look at the title, pictures, diagrams, and any subheadings or terms in boldface or italic type. Stop now and then to **predict** what will come next. Build your understanding and see if your ideas and opinions change.

Clarify the organization. If the work is autobiography or biography, the organization is probably chronological—events are told in time order. Other selections may be organized around ideas the author wants to discuss. As you read, look for dates and signal words that clarify the sequence of events, such as *before, during, after, first, next,* and *last.*

Summarize the main idea. The **main idea** is the most important point in the reading selection. **Details** are used to support the main idea. Does the writer support his or her points with examples or facts? Can you summarize the main idea?

Separate facts and opinions. Facts are statements that can be proved. Opinions are statements that cannot be proved. They simply express a person's beliefs. Writers of nonfiction sometimes present opinions as if they were facts. Be sure you recognize the difference.

Evaluate what you read. Ask, What is the author's purpose for writing? Did the writer allow personal bias to influence the text? Remember that evaluation means forming opinions about people, events, and ideas.

Here's how Tiara uses the strategies:

*"I like to read about computers. Before I read, I look at the diagrams and instructions. Then I try to understand the topic by **summarizing the main ideas.** I like to look for a writer's strong opinions."*

The Great Rat Hunt

by LAURENCE YEP

Connect to Your Life

Childhood Asthma When Laurence Yep, the author of this selection, was a young boy, he suffered from a respiratory disease known as asthma. What words and phrases come to mind when you think of asthma? Write your answers in a word web. See if you can add to the web as you read the story.

Build Background

SCIENCE

Laurence Yep's boyhood asthma kept him from excelling in sports. Asthma may be brought on by an infection or by an allergic reaction. During an asthmatic attack, the bronchi, or branching tubes that carry air into the lungs, become swollen and clogged with mucus. This narrowing of the passageways causes shortness of breath, wheezing, and coughing. Back when Yep was a boy, there were few options to help people control the symptoms of asthma.

> WORDS TO KNOW
> **Vocabulary Preview**
>
> | | |
> |---|---|
> | barricade | mug |
> | brusquely | perpetual |
> | fumigate | rationalize |
> | improvise | ravage |
> | ineptitude | reserve |

Focus Your Reading

LITERARY ANALYSIS | MEMOIR

A form of autobiographical writing in which a person tells about events from his or her life is called a **memoir.** Memoirs are told from the **first-person point of view,** using first-person pronouns, such as *I, me,* and *we.* In a memoir, the narrator reveals how he or she feels about events and people. As you read "The Great Rat Hunt," look for passages that reveal Laurence Yep's feelings.

ACTIVE READING | IDENTIFYING THE MAIN IDEA

Most nonfiction focuses on a main idea. A **main idea** is the most important point or message that the writer wants to communicate to the reader. Sometimes a main idea is stated directly in a key sentence or paragraph. At other times, as in "The Great Rat Hunt," the main idea is implied by the **details** the writer provides.

READER'S NOTEBOOK As you read "The Great Rat Hunt," jot down important details that might offer clues to the main idea of the selection.

The Great RAT HUNT

By Laurence Yep

I had asthma[1] when I was young, so I never got to play sports much with my father. While my brother and father practiced, I could only sit in bed, propped up by a stack of pillows. As I read my comic books, I heard them beneath our apartment window. In the summer, it was the thump of my brother's fastball into my father's mitt. In the fall, it was the smack of a football. In the winter, it was the airy bounce of a basketball.

Though my father had come from China when he was eight, he had taken quickly to American games. When he and Mother were young, they had had the same dances and sports leagues as their white schoolmates—but kept separate in Chinatown. (He had met Mother when she tripped him during a co-ed basketball game at the Chinatown Y.)

Father was big as a teenager and good at sports. In fact, a social club in Chinatown had hired him to play football against social clubs in other Chinatowns. There he was, a boy playing against grown men.

During a game in Watsonville, a part-time butcher had broken Father's nose. It never properly healed, leaving a big bump at the bridge. There were other injuries too from baseball, basketball, and tennis. Each bump and scar on his body had its own story, and each story was matched by a trophy or medal.

Though he now ran a grocery store in San Francisco, he tried to pass on his athletic skills to my older brother Eddy and me. During the times I felt well, I tried to keep up with them, but my lungs always failed me.

When I had to sit down on the curb, I felt as if I had let my father down. I'd glance up anxiously when I felt his shadow over me; but he looked neither angry

ACTIVE READER

CONNECT Have I ever felt this way? Has someone I know felt this way?

---

1. **asthma:** a chronic disease of the lungs and bronchial tubes, marked by sudden attacks of difficult breathing and coughing.

nor disgusted—just puzzled, as if he could not understand why my lungs were not like his.

"S-s-sorry." I panted.

"That's okay." He squatted and waved his hat, trying to fan more air at me. In the background, Eddy played catch with himself, waiting impatiently for the lessons to begin again. Ashamed, I would gasp. "Go on . . . and play."

And Father and Eddy would start once more while I watched, doomed to be positively un-American, a weakling, a <u>perpetual</u> spectator, an outsider. Worse, I felt as if Eddy were Father's only true son.

And then came the day when the rat invaded our store. It was Eddy who first noticed it while we were restocking the store shelves. I was stacking packages of pinto beans when Eddy called me. "Hey, do you know what this is?" He waved me over to the cans of soup. On his palm lay some dark drops. "Is it candy?"

Father came out of the store-room in the rear of our store. Over his back, he carried a huge hundred pound sack of rice. He let it thump to the floor right away. "Throw that away."

"What is it, Father?" I asked.

"Rat droppings," he said. "Go wash your hands."

"Yuck." Eddy flung the droppings down.

While Eddy washed his hands, I helped Father get rid of the evidence. Then he got some wooden traps from a shelf and we set them out.

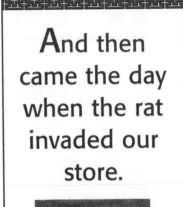

And then came the day when the rat invaded our store.

Leonard Baskin: Courtesy R. Michelson Galleries, Northampton, MA

However, the traps were for mice and not for rats. The rat must have gotten a good laugh while it stole the bait and set off the springs.

Then Father tried poison pellets, but the rat avoided them all. It even left a souvenir right near the front door.

Father looked grim as he cleaned it up. "I'm through fooling around."

So he called up his exterminator friend, Pete Wong, the Cockroach King of Chinatown. While Pete <u>fumigated</u> the store, we stayed with my Aunt Nancy over on Mason, where the cable cars kept me up late. They always rang their bells when they rounded the corner. Even when they weren't there, I could hear the cable rattling in its channel beneath the street. It was OK, though, because my cousin Jackie could tell stories all night.

The next day, when we went back home, Father searched around the store, sniffing suspiciously for deadly chemicals. Mother went upstairs to our apartment over the store to get our electric fan.

She came right back down empty-handed. "I think he's moved up there. I could hear him scratching behind the living room walls."

Father stared at the ceiling as if the rat had gone too far. "Leave it to me," he said. He fished his car keys from his pocket.

"Where are you going?" Mother asked.

Father, though, was a man of few words. He preferred to speak by his actions. "I'll be back soon."

WORDS TO KNOW

perpetual (pər-pĕch′ōō-əl) *adj.* lasting for an indefinitely long time; continuing without interruption

fumigate (fyōō′mĭ-gāt′) *v.* to use smoke or fumes in order to kill off rodents or insects; to disinfect

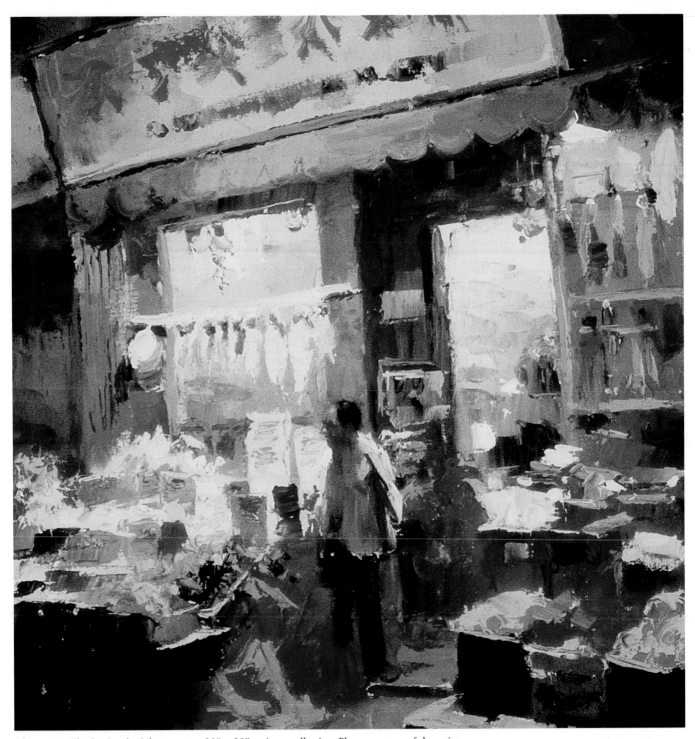

Chinatown, Charles Sovek. Oil on canvas, 20" x 20", private collection. Photo courtesy of the artist.

An hour and a half later he returned with a rifle. He held it up for the three of us to examine. "Isn't it a beaut? Henry Loo loaned it to me." Henry Loo was a pharmacist and one of Father's fishing buddies.

Mother frowned. "You can't shoot that cannon off in my house."

"It's just a twenty-two." Father tugged a box of cartridges out of his jacket pocket. "Let's go, boys."

ACTIVE READER

PREDICT Which brother is more likely to want to help with the rat hunt?

Mother sucked in her breath sharply. "Thomas!"

Father was surprised by Mother's objection. "They've got to learn sometime."

Mother turned to us urgently. "It means killing. Like buying Grandpop's chickens. But you'll be the ones who have to make it dead."

"It's not the same," Father argued. "We won't have to twist its neck."

Buying the chicken was a chore that everyone tried to avoid at New Year's when Mother's father insisted on it. To make sure the chicken was fresh, we had to watch the poulterer[2] kill it. And then we had to collect the coppery-smelling blood in a jar for a special dish that only Mother's father would eat. For a moment, I felt queasy.

"You're scaring the boys," Father scolded her.

Mother glanced at him over her shoulder. "They ought to know what they're getting into."

I didn't believe in killing—unless it was a bug like a cockroach. However, I felt different when I saw a real rifle—the shiny barrel, the faint smell of oil, the decorated wooden stock. I <u>rationalized</u> the hunt by telling myself I was not murdering rabbits or deer, just a mean old rat—like a furry kind of cockroach.

"What'll it be, boys?" Father asked.

Taking a deep breath, I nodded my head. "Yes, sir."

Father turned expectantly to Eddy and raised an eyebrow.

From next to me, though, Eddy murmured, "I think I'll help Mother." He wouldn't look at me.

Father seemed just as shocked as Mother and I. "Are you sure?"

Eddy drew back and mumbled miserably. "Yes, sir."

Mother gave me a quick peck on the cheek. "I expect you to still have ten toes and ten fingers when you finish."

As we left the store, I felt funny. Part of me felt triumphant. For once, it was Eddy who had failed and not me. And yet another part of me wished I were staying with him and Mother.

Father said nothing as we left the store and climbed the back stairs. As I trailed him, I

ACTIVE READER

QUESTION Why does the narrator think that the father would rather have the brother's help?

thought he was silent because he was disappointed: He would rather have Eddy's help than mine.

At the back door of our apartment, he paused and said <u>brusquely</u>, "Now for some rules. First, never, never aim the rifle at anyone."

I listened as attentively as I had the disastrous times he'd tried to teach me how to dribble, or catch a football, or handle a pop foul. "I won't." I nodded earnestly.

Father pulled a lever near the middle of the gun. "Next, make sure the rifle is empty." He let me inspect the breech. There was nothing inside.

---

2. **poulterer:** a poultry dealer.

WORDS TO KNOW

rationalize (răsh′ə-nə-līz′) v. to make self-satisfying but incorrect explanations about one's behavior

brusquely (brŭsk′lē) adv. in an abrupt, sudden manner

"Yes, sir," I said and glanced up at him to read his mood. Because Father used so few words, he always sounded a little impatient whenever he taught me a lesson. However, it was hard to tell this time if it was genuine irritation or his normal <u>reserve</u>.

He merely grunted. "Here. Open this." And he handed me the box of cartridges.

I was so nervous that the cartridges clinked inside the box when I took it. As I fumbled at the lid, I almost felt like apologizing for not being Eddy.

Now, when I got edgy, I was the opposite of Father: I got talkier. "How did you learn how to hunt?" I asked. "From your father?"

My father rarely spoke of his father, who had died before I was born. He winced now as if the rat had just nipped him. "My old man? Nah. He never had the time. I learned from some of my buddies in Chinatown." He held out his hand.

I passed him a cartridge. "What did you hunt? Bear?"

"We shot quail." Father carefully loaded the rifle.

I was uncomfortable with the idea of shooting the cute little birds I saw in cartoons. "You did?"

He clicked the cartridge into the rifle. "You have to be tough in this world, boy. There are going to be some times when nobody's around to help—like when I first came to America."

That was a long speech for Father. "You had your father." His mother had stayed back in China, because in those days,

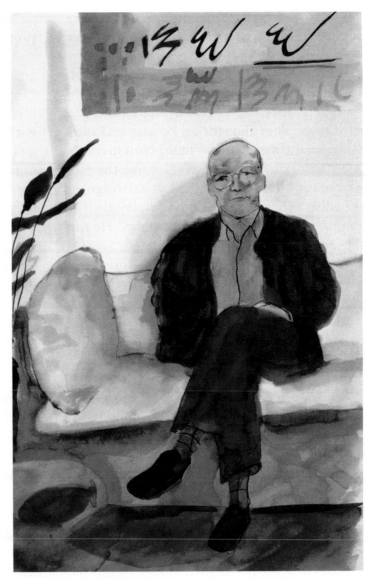

Portrait by Roland Jarvis

America would not let her accompany her husband.

"He was too busy working." Father stared back down the stairs as if each step were a year. "When I first came here, I got beaten up by the white kids. And when the white kids weren't around, there were the other Chinese kids."

I furrowed my forehead in puzzlement. I handed him another cartridge. "But they were your own kind."

He loaded the rifle steadily as I gave him the ammunition. "No, they weren't. The boys born here, they like to give a China-born a hard time. They thought I'd be easy pickings. But it was always a clean fight. No knives. No guns. Just our feet and fists. Not like the punks nowadays." He snapped the last cartridge into the rifle. "Then I learned how to play their games, and I made them my friends." He said the last part with pride.

And suddenly I began to understand all the trophies and medals in our living room. They were more than awards for sports. Each prize was a sign that my father belonged to America—and at the same time, to Chinatown. And that was why he tried so hard now to teach sports to Eddy and me.

When I finally understood what sports really meant to my father, it only magnified the scale of my ineptitude. "I'm not good at fighting." As I closed the lid on the box of ammunition, I thought I ought to prepare him for future disappointments. "I'm not much good at anything."

Careful to keep the rifle pointed away from me, Father unlocked the door. "I said you have to be tough, not stupid. No reason to get a beat-up old mug like mine."

I shook my head, bewildered. "What's wrong with your face?"

Father seemed amused. He stepped away from the door and jerked his head for me to open it. "It's nothing that a steamroller couldn't fix."

"But you have an interesting face," I protested as I grabbed the doorknob.

"Are you blind, boy? This mug isn't ever going to win a beauty contest." He chuckled. "I've been called a lot of names in my time, but never 'interesting.' You've got a way with words."

The doorknob was cold in my hand. "I do?"

Father adjusted his grip on the rifle. "I wouldn't buy any real estate from you." And he gave me an encouraging grin. "Now let's kill that rat."

When I opened the door, our home suddenly seemed as foreign to me as Africa. At first, I felt lonely—and a little scared. Then I heard Father reassure me, "I'm with you, boy."

Feeling more confident, I crept through the kitchen and into the living room. Father was right behind me and motioned me to search one half of the room while he explored the other. When I found a hole in the corner away from the fireplace, I caught Father's eye and pointed.

He peered under a chair with me and gave me an approving wink. "Give me a hand," he whispered.

In silent cooperation, we moved the chair aside and then shifted the sofa over until it was between us and the rat hole. Bit by bit, Father and I constructed an upholstered barricade. I couldn't have been prouder if we'd built a whole fort together.

Father considerately left the lighter things for me to lift, and I was grateful for his thoughtfulness. The last thing I wanted was to get asthma now from overexertion. When we were done, Father got his rifle from the corner where he had left it temporarily.

As we crouched down behind our improvised wall, Father rested the rifle on it.

WORDS TO KNOW

ineptitude (ĭn-ĕp′tĭ-tood′) n. incompetence, clumsiness; displaying a lack of judgment

mug (mŭg) n. the face

barricade (băr′ĭ-kād′) v. a structure set up to block a passage

improvise (ĭm′prə-vīz′) v. to put together or act with little or no preparation or planning

"We'll take turns watching."

"Yes, sir," I said, peering over the barrier. There wasn't so much as a whisker in the hole.

While I scanned the hole with intense radar eyes, Father tried to make himself comfortable by leaning against the sofa. It made me feel important to know Father trusted me; and I was determined to do well. In the center of the living room wall was the fireplace, and on its mantel stood Father's trophies like ranks of soldiers reminding me to be vigilant.

We remained in companionable silence for maybe three quarters of an hour. Suddenly, I saw something flicker near the mouth of the hole. "Father," I whispered.

Father popped up alertly and took his rifle. Squeezing one eye shut, he sighted on the rat hole. His crouching body grew tense. "Right." He adjusted his aim minutely. "Right. Take a breath," he recited to himself. "Take up the slack. Squeeze the trigger." Suddenly, he looked up, startled. "Where'd it go?"

As the gray shape darted forward, I could not control my panic. "It's coming straight at us."

The rifle barrel swung back and forth wildly as Father tried to aim. "Where?"

I thought I could see huge teeth and beady, violent eyes. The teeth were the size of daggers and the eyes were the size of baseballs, and they were getting bigger by the moment. It was the rat of all rats. "Shoot it!" I yelled.

"Where?" Father shouted desperately.

As the gray shape darted forward, I could not control my panic. "It's coming straight at us."

My courage evaporated. All I could think of was escape. "It's charging." Springing to my feet, I darted from the room.

"Oh, man," Father said, and his footsteps pounded after me.

In a blind panic, I bolted out of the apartment and down the back stairs and into the store.

"Get the SPCA.[3] I think the rat's mad," Father yelled as he slammed the door behind him.

Mother took the rifle from him. "I'd be annoyed too if someone were trying to shoot me."

"No." Father panted. "I mean it's rabid."[4] We could hear the rat scurrying above us in the living room. It sounded as if it were doing a victory dance.

Mother made Father empty the rifle. "You return that to Henry Loo tomorrow," she said. "We'll learn to live with the rat."

As she stowed the rifle in the storeroom, Father tried to regather his dignity. "It may have fleas," he called after her.

Now that my panic was over, I suddenly became aware of the enormity of what I had done. Father had counted on me to help him, and yet I had run, leaving him to the <u>ravages</u> of that monster. I was worse than a failure.

---

3. **SPCA:** Society for the Prevention of Cruelty to Animals.

4. **rabid:** affected by rabies, a viral disease that is passed on by the bite of infected animals and that attacks the central nervous system.

I was a coward. I had deserted Father right at the time he needed me most. I wouldn't blame him if he kicked me out of his family.

It took what little nerve I had left to look up at my father. At that moment, he seemed to tower over me, as grand and remote as a monument. "I'm sorry," I said miserably.

He drew his eyebrows together as he clinked the shells in his fist. "For what?"

It made me feel even worse to have to explain in front of Eddy. "For running," I said wretchedly.

He chuckled as he dumped the cartridges into his shirt pocket. "Well, I ran too. Sometimes it's smart to be scared."

"When were you ever scared?" I challenged him.

He buttoned his pocket. "Plenty of times. Like when I came to America. They had to pry my fingers from the boat railing."

It was the first time I'd ever heard my father confess to that failing. "But you're the best at everything."

"Nobody's good at everything." He gave his head a little shake as if the very notion puzzled him. "Each of us is good at some things and lousy at others. The trick is to find something that you're good at."

I thought again of the mantel where all of Father's sports trophies stood. Eddy gave every promise of collecting just as many, but I knew I would be lucky to win even one.

"I'm lousy at sports," I confessed.

His eyes flicked back and forth, as if my face were a book open for his inspection. He seemed surprised by what he read there.

Slowly his knees bent until we were looking eye to eye. "Then you'll find something else," he said and put his arm around me. My father never let people touch him. In fact, I hardly ever saw him hug Mother. As his arm tightened, I felt a real love and assurance in that embrace.

Shortly after that, the rat left as mysteriously as it had come. "I must've scared it off," Father announced.

Mother shook her head. "That rat laughed itself to death."

Father disappeared into the storeroom: and for a moment we all thought Mother had gone too far. Then we heard the electric saw that he kept back there. "What are you doing?" Mother called.

He came back out with a block of wood about two inches square. He was carefully sandpapering the splinters from the edges. "Maybe some day we'll find the corpse. Its head ought to look real good over the fireplace."

Mother was trying hard to keep a straight face. "You can't have a trophy head unless you shoot it."

"If it died of laughter like you said, then I killed it," he insisted proudly. "Sure as if I pulled the trigger." He winked at me. "Get the varnish out for our trophy will you?"

ACTIVE READER

CLARIFY Why is it significant that the father uses the word "our" to refer to the trophy?

I was walking away when I realized he had said "our." I turned and said, "That rat was doomed from the start." I heard my parents both laughing as I hurried away. ❖

Connect to the Literature

1. **What Do You Think?** How do you feel about Laurence Yep's father at the end of the story? Explain your response.

   Comprehension Check
   - How do Laurence and his brother differ?
   - What happened during the rat hunt?
   - What advice did the father give to Laurence at the end of the story?

Think Critically

2. How would you describe young Laurence Yep at the beginning of this selection?

   Think About:
   - the way he compares himself to his brother
   - his feeling that he is a disappointment to his father
   - why he agrees to hunt the rat

3. Based on this selection, what is your opinion of Laurence Yep's family?

4. **ACTIVE READING** | **IDENTIFYING THE MAIN IDEA** |
   Look over the details that you listed in your ▥**READER'S NOTEBOOK**. What do these details tell you about Laurence Yep and his father? What main idea is Yep trying to communicate?

Extend Interpretations

5. **What If?** Assume that the rat episode had never happened. Do you think young Laurence would have always believed that his father was ashamed of him? Explain your answer.

6. **Different Perspectives** Retell the story of the rat hunt from the rat's point of view. In the rat's own words (using the pronoun *I*), tell how it outsmarted Mr. Yep and then moved on, proud of its victory.

7. **Connect to Life** Laurence Yep felt like an outsider within his family. His father had felt like an outsider when he came to the United States. Think of a time when either you or someone you know felt like an outsider. How does that experience differ from Laurence's? How does it differ from the father's? Explain your answer.

Literary Analysis

MEMOIR A first-person recollection of an experience or event is called a **memoir.** Most memoirs have the following characteristics: (1) they are told from the **first-person point of view** using first-person pronouns, such as *I, me,* and *we,* (2) they are accounts of actual events, (3) they include the writer's feelings and beliefs about his or her family and community.

Paired Activity Working with a partner, go back through the selection and look for Yep's opinions about his father and his brother. Record your findings in a chart like the one shown.

When you have finished, discuss how Yep's beliefs about his father and his brother have changed by the end of the story.

Opinion	When
About His Brother: Eddy is "Father's only true son."	Beginning of story
About His Father:	

CHOICES and CHALLENGES

Writing

Father's Memoir Pretend you are Laurence Yep's father. Write a memoir of the great rat hunt from the father's point of view. How is the father's account similar to Laurence's? How is it different? As you prepare to write, think about the main idea of the memoir and the details you will use to support it. Place your memoir in your **Working Portfolio.**

Speaking & Listening

Dramatic Reading With two other classmates, create a dramatic reading of the rat-hunt scene. Have one person play the role of the father, one person play the role of the young boy, and one person act as narrator. Include sound effects that you have taped ahead of time, such as stairs creaking, an apartment door opening, and the sounds of furniture being moved. Perform the reading for your class.

Speaking and Listening Handbook
See p. R104.

Research & Technology

A Famous Asthma Sufferer A famous American who suffered from asthma was President Theodore Roosevelt (1858–1919). Research the early years of Teddy Roosevelt and his battle with asthma. Create notes for a report, in which you explain Roosevelt's experience with asthma. Be sure to note your sources.

INTERNET **Research Starter**
www.mcdougallittell.com

Vocabulary

Choose the word or group of words that means the same, or nearly the same, as the underlined Word to Know.

1. A <u>barricade</u> is a —
   A path **B** hurricane
   C bridge **D** barrier

2. <u>Reserve</u> means—
   F self-respect **G** self-restraint
   H self-doubt **J** self-pity

3. <u>Mug</u> is another word for—
   A foot **B** thief
   C face **D** bowl

4. <u>Perpetual</u> means—
   F partial **G** irregular
   H peculiar **J** continual

5. To <u>rationalize</u> something means to—
   A explain it away **B** fight it off
   C invite it in **D** remember it

6. <u>Brusquely</u> is another word for—
   F broadly **G** abruptly
   H cautiously **J** sluggishly

7. To <u>fumigate</u> something is to—
   A fold it **B** smell it
   C disinfect it **D** dissolve it

8. <u>Ineptitude</u> means—
   F inconvenience **G** intelligence
   H independence **J** incompetence

9. To <u>improvise</u> is to—
   A invent **B** impose
   C impress **D** increase

10. <u>Ravage</u> means—
    F average **G** destruction
    H interruption **J** revenge

Vocabulary Handbook
See p. R24: Synonyms and Antonyms.

Grammar in Context: Subjects and Predicates

A complete sentence has two essential parts, a subject and a predicate. Look at this sentence from Laurence Yep's "The Great Rat Hunt."

> Father came out of the storeroom in the rear of our store.

The first word, *father,* is the **subject** of this sentence. The **subject** of a sentence is the person or thing that the sentence names. The **predicate** of a sentence tells what the subject is or does. In the sentence above, the words *came out of the storeroom in the rear of our store* are the **predicate.** A sentence must have a subject and a predicate. If it does not, it is an incomplete sentence or a sentence fragment.

Usage Tip: Varying the length and complexity of subjects and predicates changes the rhythm of your sentences so that they are more interesting.

WRITING EXERCISE Add a subject or a predicate to complete each sentence fragment.

Example: *Original* heard them beneath my apartment window.

Rewritten I heard them beneath my apartment window.

1. was big as a teenager and good at sports.
2. My father and I
3. tried so hard to teach sports to Eddy and me.
4. The gray shape
5. The rat

Connect to the Literature Look at the first paragraph of "The Great Rat Hunt." Find the subject and predicate of each sentence.

Grammar Handbook
See p. R75: Writing Complete Sentences.

Laurence Yep
born 1948

"Keeping your eyes open is the key to being a writer. Anything you see could provide the seed for a story some day."

A Man of Accomplishments Born in San Francisco, California, Laurence Yep was raised in an African-American neighborhood and commuted to a bilingual school in Chinatown. From high school, he went on to earn a college degree and a Ph.D. Yep has worked as a teacher of English, a lecturer of Asian-American studies, and a writer-in-residence.

A Father's Pride Yep's book *Dragonwings* won ten awards. Many of his more recent young adult books explore Chinese mythology. He also writes science fiction stories and books for adults. Yep's accomplishments as a writer have greatly pleased his father, who displays Yep's writing medals and plaques "in lieu of athletic trophies."

AUTHOR ACTIVITY
Often an Outsider Yep has said that he approaches American culture "as somewhat of a stranger." It is not surprising, therefore, that the theme of the outsider runs through many of his books. For example, Yep's popular young adult novel *Child of the Owl* tells the story of a 12-year-old Chinese-American girl who goes to live with her grandmother in San Francisco's Chinatown. Find out more about the main character of this novel. In what ways is the young girl an outsider in Chinatown? In what ways is she an outsider in her own community?

Flying

by REEVE LINDBERGH

Connect to Your Life

This section describes the flying experiences of a young girl. What do you already know about flying an airplane? What do you want to know? Make a chart like the one shown. Fill in the first two columns. You will complete the third column after you read the selection.

What I Know About Flying	What I Want to Know About Flying	What I Learned About Flying

Build Background

HISTORY

Reeve Lindbergh's father, Charles A. Lindbergh, was an American hero. In 1927 he became the first person to pilot an airplane, alone and without stopping, across the Atlantic Ocean. No history of aviation is complete without an account of the 33½-hour flight in which "Lucky Lindy" journeyed from New York to Paris.

Two years after his famous flight, Lindbergh married Anne Morrow. Anne served for a time as her husband's copilot and navigator. She also achieved fame as a writer. In 1932, their first child—a 20-month-old son—was kidnapped and killed. The

couple survived this tragedy and went on to have five more children.

WORDS TO KNOW
Vocabulary Preview

diminish   perilous   tethered
monotonous   tandem

Focus Your Reading

LITERARY ANALYSIS   ANECDOTE

A brief account of an interesting or amusing event is called an **anecdote.** In "Flying," Reeve Lindbergh tells many anecdotes about the experiences that she and her sister and brothers had while flying with their father. As you read "Flying," think about which of the anecdotes you find amusing. What about them amuses you?

ACTIVE READING   IDENTIFYING AUTHOR'S PURPOSE

A writer's reason for creating a work is known as an **author's purpose.** Writers have four main purposes: **to entertain, to inform, to express opinions,** and **to persuade.** Often a writer has more than one purpose for writing a particular work. For example, a writer may write both to inform and to persuade.

READER'S NOTEBOOK As you read "Flying," look for clues that help you identify Reeve Lindbergh's purpose or purposes for writing. Record your findings in a chart like the one shown.

Clue	Purpose for Writing
"I always flew with my father, who had been a pioneer aviator in the 1920s and '30s."	To inform

Flying

by Reeve Lindbergh

When I was your age, I was flying. I wasn't flying all the time, of course, and I didn't fly by myself, but there I was, nonetheless, on Saturday afternoons in the 1950s, several thousand feet in the air over the state of Connecticut, which is where I grew up.

This Aeronca is similar to the plane that Lindbergh flew with her father.

I sat in the back cockpit of a small airplane and looked down at the forests and the fields and the houses and the roads below me from an intense, vibrating height and hoped that my father, in the front cockpit, would not notice that I had cotton balls stuffed in my ears.

I always flew with my father, who had been a pioneer aviator in the 1920s and '30s. I think that he wanted to share his love for the air and for airplanes with his growing family, the way sports-minded fathers took their children to ball games on Saturdays and taught them to play catch afterward. My father took his children to the airport instead and taught them to fly.

Though he was the pilot on these flights, he did not own the airplane. It was a sixty-five-horsepower Aeronca,[1] with tandem cockpits, that he rented from a former bomber pilot whose name was Stanley. Stanley managed the airport, including the huge loaf-shaped hangar that served as a garage for repairs and maintenance to the aircraft, and he leased out the group of small planes tethered near the building like a fleet of fishing boats clustered around a pier.

It was Stanley, most often, who stood in front of the airplane and waited for my father to shout "ConTACT!" from the cockpit window, at which time, Stanley gave the propeller a hefty downward shove that sent it spinning into action and started the plane shaking and shuddering on its way. The job of starting the propeller was simple but perilous. My father had warned us many times about the danger of standing anywhere near a propeller in action. We could list almost as well as he did the limbs that had been severed from the bodies of careless individuals "in a split second" by a propeller's whirling force. Therefore, each time that Stanley started the propeller, I would peer through its blinding whir to catch a glimpse of any pieces of him that might be flying through the air. Each time, I saw only Stanley, whole and smiling, waving us onto the asphalt runway with his cap in his hand and his hair blowing in the wind of our passing—"the propwash" my father called it.

My sister and my three brothers flew on Saturdays too. The older ones were taught to land and take off, to bank and dip, and even to turn the plane over in midair, although my second-oldest brother confessed that he hated

---

1. **Aeronca:** a plane built by Aeronca, originally the Aeronautical Corporation of America, a small company formed in 1928 which became a major manufacturer of light airplanes.

WORDS	**tandem** (tăn′dəm) *adj.* one behind the other
TO	**tethered** (tĕth′ərd) *adj.* tied to the ground or to another object **tether** *v.*
KNOW	**perilous** (pĕr′ə-ləs) *adj.* full of danger

I always flew with my father, who had been a pioneer aviator in the 1920s and '30s.

this—it made him feel so dizzy. The youngest of my three brothers, only a few years older than me, remembers my father instructing him to "lean into the curve" as the plane made a steep sideways dive toward the ground. My brother was already off balance, leaning away from the curve, and hanging on for dear life. For my sister, our father demonstrated "weightlessness" by having the plane climb so steeply and then dive so sharply that for a moment she could feel her body straining upward against her seatbelt, trying to fight free, while our father shouted out from the front seat that one of his gloves was actually floating in midair.

"See the glove? See the glove?" He called to her over the engine noise and explained that if this state of weightlessness could continue, everything inside the plane would go up in the air. My sister nodded, not speaking, because, she told me later, everything in her stomach was going up in the air, too, and she did not dare open her mouth.

My oldest brother took to flying immediately and eventually got a pilot's license, though he ended up joining the navy and becoming a "frogman,"[2] spending as much time underwater with an aqualung and a wetsuit as he ever had spent in the air. What he secretly yearned to do during the flying years, though, was to jump right out of an airplane altogether, with a parachute. Finally, many years later, he had his chance and told me about it afterward. He stood at the open door of the airplane, with the parachute strapped to his back, wobbling back and forth at first, like a baby bird afraid to leave the nest. Then he jumped, fell about a hundred feet through the air, and only then pulled the cord that caused the chute to blossom around him like a great circular sail. Swaying under it, he floated toward the ground until he landed, fairly hard. I listened with astonishment; my brother's daring thrilled me to the bone.

My father on the other hand, along with most of the early aviators, was not impressed by the growing enthusiasm for parachute-jumping as a sport. Young daredevils like my brother could call it "sky-diving" if they wanted to, but the aviation pioneers referred to it disgustedly as "jumping out of a perfectly good airplane." In their day, a pilot only jumped when he had to: if it was absolutely certain that the airplane was headed for a crash and the parachute was his only hope for survival.

I was considered too young for aerial adventures when I flew, so I did not get dizzy or sick or worry about whether my parachute would open. It was only the noise that gave me trouble. I have never shared other people's enthusiasm for loudness. I don't like sudden sounds that make you jump with alarm, like the noises of fireworks or guns, or endless sounds that pound in your head so hard you can't think about anything else, like the

---

2. **frogman:** a swimmer equipped with breathing apparatus in order to do underwater tasks, often military ones such as demolition projects or gathering information.

The Aeronca flying over Connecticut

commotion made by jackhammers and the engines of small airplanes. My sister felt exactly the same way. In fact, she was the one who showed me how to stuff cotton balls in my ears, secretly, for takeoff—when the engine noise was loudest—and for as long during the flight as we could get away with it.

Our father frowned upon the cotton balls. If he saw them, he would make us remove them. He claimed that they <u>diminished</u> the experience of flying and were in any case unnecessary: The engine noise was not so terribly loud that one couldn't get used to it; he certainly had done so. But my sister and I agreed that the only reason he and the other early aviators had "gotten used to" the noise of airplane engines close to their ears was that they had been deafened early on. We were not about to let this happen to us!

My mother, who had also flown back in the early days, always told us that she had loved her experience as a glider pilot best, because there was such extraordinary quiet all around her. In the absence of the usual aircraft engine noise, she could hear the songs of birds and sometimes even the trilling of insects, crickets or cicadas, on the grassy hillsides below. She said that because there was no noise, she could actually feel the power of air, the way it could push up under the wings of a glider and keep it afloat—like a boat on water—with the strength of unseen currents. She talked about "columns of air," stretching like massive tree trunks between earth and sky. "Just because you can't see the air doesn't mean there's nothing to it," she said. "Most of the really important things in our lives are invisible, anyway."

WORDS
TO
KNOW

diminish (dĭ-mĭn′ĭsh) v. to make smaller or less

When it was my turn to fly with my father, I sat in the back cockpit and enjoyed the view all around me while he, in the front cockpit, flew the plane. I had a duplicate set of controls in back, with rudder[3] pedals, a stick, and instruments, so that if I had been a true student pilot, I could have flown the plane myself, if called upon to do so. But since I was too young to understand or even to reach most of the controls in my cockpit, I just watched them move as if by magic, with no help from me at all, in response to my father's direction and will.

It looked easy. The stick in front of me, exactly like the one in front of my father in the forward cockpit, looked like the gearshift on our car. If it moved backward suddenly (toward me), it meant that my father had decided we were going up. There would be a rushing in my ears, in spite of the cotton, and as I looked over my father's head, through the front window of the aircraft, I would imagine that we were forcing our way right into heaven, higher and higher through ever more brilliantly white banks of cloud.

But then, as I watched, my stick would point forward again, toward what I could see, over the front pilot seat, of the back of my father's neck, with its trim fringe of gray hair and a khaki shirt collar. Then the airplane would nose down, giving a cockeyed view on all sides of blue sky and wooded hillsides and little tiny roads with buglike cars creeping along them, so very slowly. When we were flying, I was struck always by the insignificance of the world we had left behind. Nothing on the ground had speed, compared to us. Nothing looked real. Once I had climbed into the airplane, all of life seemed concentrated inside the loud space of it, shaking but steady, with my father's own hand on the controls. We were completely self-sufficient, completely safe, rock-solid in the center of the sky.

It was also a bit <u>monotonous</u>. My father did the same things and said the same things, loudly, over and over. I knew by heart that a pilot had to fly with a steady hand, with no sudden or jerky movements, just a little throttle here, a little wing dip there, always a light, even touch, always a calm approach. I knew all the stories about student pilots— those not already dismembered by propellers— who "froze" to the stick in a panic and could not let go, forcing the plane into a tragic nosedive. There was no room in my father's lessons with me, his youngest and least experienced child, for soaring like the birds— no wind in the hair, no swooping and circling. We just droned along, my father and me.

And then, one Saturday afternoon, we didn't. I don't remember now exactly what made me understand there was something wrong with the airplane. I think there may have been a jerking sensation that repeated itself over and over. And I think too that there was a huge stillness in the air, a silence so enormous that it took me a moment to realize that it was actually the opposite of noise and not noise itself. The silence was there because the engine had stalled. Perhaps the most profound moment of silence occurred when my father realized that it was not going to start again—no matter what he did. We were in the middle of the sky, on a sunny Saturday afternoon over Connecticut, in a plane without an engine.

I don't think there was any drop in altitude, not at first. What I noticed was my father's sudden alertness, as if he had opened a million

---

3. **rudder:** a vertically hinged plate at the tail of an aircraft, used to move a plane to the right or the left.

... I don't remember fear at all, but I do remember excitement.

eyes and ears in every direction. I heard him say something sharp on the airplane's two-way radio to Stanley down below, and I could hear the crackle of Stanley's voice coming back. I knew enough not to say very much myself, although my father told friends later that I asked him once, in a conversational way, "Are we going to crash?" And when he told this part of the story, the part where I asked that question, he would laugh.

I don't remember being afraid of crashing. In fact, I don't remember fear at all, but I do remember excitement. At last something different was going to happen! I quickly took the cotton out of my ears because my father was talking. He told me that he was looking for a good place to land. We would have to land, he explained, because the engine wasn't working, and we could not land at the airport, because we were too far away to get there in time. (*In time for what?* I wondered.) He was looking for an open area to put the plane down in, right below us somewhere. We were now over a wooded hillside, dotted here and there with cow pastures: It would have to be a cow pasture. He spotted one that looked possible and circled down toward it.

There was nothing resembling a runway below us and no room to spare. He would have to tip the plane sideways and slip it into the pasture that way, somehow righting it and stopping its movement before it could hit any of the trees at the four edges of the field. We circled lower and lower, barely clearing the treetops, and then he told me to put my head down between my knees.

"Hold on!" my father said.

I didn't see the landing, because my head was down, but I felt it: a tremendous series of bumps, as if we were bouncing on boulders, and then the plane shook and rattled to a stop. Then we took off our seatbelts and opened the doors and got out. I didn't see any cows in the pasture, but there were a bunch of people coming toward us from the road, and it looked as if one of them might be Stanley from the airport. I was careful to stay clear of the propeller.

Nobody could figure out how we had landed safely. They had to take the plane apart to get it out of the pasture, a week or more after that Saturday afternoon. But my father and I got a ride back to the airport with Stanley and drove home in plenty of time for dinner. We didn't talk much on the way home. My father seemed tired, though cheerful, and I was thinking.

I had found out something about him that afternoon, just by watching him work his way down through the air. I held on to the knowledge tightly afterward, and I still hold it to this day. I learned what flying was for my father and for the other early aviators, what happened to him and why he kept taking us up to try flying ourselves. As we came in through the trees, he was concentrating hard, getting the rudder and the flaps set, trying to put us in the best possible position for a forced landing, but he was doing more than that. He was persuading and coaxing and willing the plane to do what he wanted; he was leaning that airplane, like a bobsled, right down to where it could safely land. He could feel its every movement, just as if it were part of his own body. My father wasn't flying the airplane, he was being the airplane. That's how he did it. That's how he had always done it. Now I knew. ❖

Our family. I'm on the far right in the first row.

Diary Entry

by Anne Morrow Lindbergh

Friday July 19, 1940

Home to meet C.[1] and the children back from the beach. Jon's[2] face is aglow. He says, "I swam to the lighthouse and back." I couldn't believe it, but his father said it was true. It was a three-quarter-hour swim out against the tide, one-half hour back. When they got around the base of the lighthouse, the lighthouse-keeper threw out a board on a rope and pulled Jon in. Then they climbed up an iron ladder, into the lighthouse. Jon was cold, so the lighthouse-keeper's wife rubbed him with a towel. They wanted to row Jon back but he wanted to swim. C. is very proud of him. And Jon will never forget it.

We walk to the point at night and look at the lighthouse. It looks miles away. I try to tell C. what an immeasurable thing he has given Jon in teaching him to swim and in giving him that rock of confidence in his own ability. And no one else could have—to do it with his father!

---

1. **C.:** Charles Lindbergh.
2. **Jon:** one of Charles and Anne Lindbergh's sons.

The Long Leg (1935), Edward Hopper. Courtesy of The Huntington Library, Art Collections and Botanical Gardens, San Marino, California / SuperStock.

Connect to the Literature

1. **What Do You Think?**
What is your reaction to the author's childhood flying experiences?

   Comprehension Check
   • Why did Reeve Lindbergh's father take his children flying?
   • What part of flying bothered Reeve?
   • Why did Reeve and her father nearly have an accident?

Think Critically

2. In your opinion, was Charles Lindbergh right to have all his children fly with him? Why or why not?

   Think About:
   • the children's various reactions to flying
   • the fun and danger involved
   • the role of flying in the lives of both parents

3. What did Reeve's mother mean by the statement "Most of the really important things in our lives are invisible, anyway"?

4. Charles Lindbergh and other aviation pioneers referred to skydiving as "jumping out of a perfectly good airplane." What does this phrase tell you about the early aviators' feelings about flying?

5. **ACTIVE READING** | **IDENTIFYING AUTHOR'S PURPOSE**
Review the chart that you made in your **READER'S NOTEBOOK.** What **author's purposes** did you identify? In your opinion, which one was most important to Reeve Lindbergh? Explain your response.

Extend Interpretations

6. **COMPARING TEXTS** Read the Related Reading on page 126—an excerpt from a journal entry written by Reeve's mother. What opinion does Reeve's mother seem to have of Charles Lindbergh's ability as a father? Does her view differ from the view expressed by Reeve Lindbergh in "Flying"? If so, in what ways?

7. **Connect to Life** What did you learn about flying an airplane? Did the selection change the way you feel about flying? Why or why not?

Literary Analysis

ANECDOTE A brief account of an interesting or amusing incident is called an **anecdote.** An anecdote is usually told to entertain or to make a point. Writers often use anecdotes to throw a spotlight on particular **characters.** The anecdotes in "Flying" reveal much about Reeve Lindbergh's father, Charles.

Paired Activity With a partner, brainstorm some of the character traits of Charles Lindbergh, as he is presented in "Flying." Record your ideas in a character web like the one shown. Then discuss specific sentences in Reeve Lindbergh's anecdotes that reveal these traits.

REVIEW: MEMOIR A **memoir** is a form of autobiographical writing in which a person tells about events from his or her life. In a memoir, the narrator reveals how he or she feels about events and people. How does Reeve Lindbergh feel about flying?

CHOICES *and* CHALLENGES

Writing

Comparison Essay Write a brief essay in which you compare and contrast how Reeve Lindbergh in "Flying" and Laurence Yep in "The Great Rat Hunt" (pages 106–114) perceive their fathers. Provide details to support your opinions. Be sure to describe what the two children learn about their fathers. Place the essay in your **Working Portfolio.**

Writing Handbook
See p. R45: Compare and Contrast.

Speaking & Listening

Radio Broadcast Pretend that you are a radio news reporter witnessing the forced landing of Charles and Reeve Lindbergh. Tape-record a "live" description of the event. Use action verbs, sensory details, and appropriate and colorful modifiers in your description. Be sure to match your vocabulary, voice modulation, and tone to your purpose. Play the tape for your class.

Speaking and Listening Handbook
See p. R104.

Research & Technology

Women Pilots Take Off In 1929, only 117 women were pilots in the United States. Now there are over 6,500 women pilots worldwide. Research the career and life of a notable woman pilot, and write a report on your findings. Be sure to note your sources.

Reading for INFORMATION
Read the Internet article on pages 130–133 before doing your research.

Vocabulary and Spelling

STANDARDIZED TEST PRACTICE

Choose the word or group of words that means the same, or nearly the same, as the underlined Word to Know.

1. To <u>diminish</u> an experience
   A remember   **B** lessen
   C deny   **D** celebrate

2. <u>Tandem</u> cockpits
   F side-by-side   **G** one-behind-the-other
   H small-to-large **J** too-many-to-count

3. A <u>perilous</u> journey
   A special   **B** lengthy
   C planned   **D** dangerous

4. A <u>monotonous</u> noise
   F mysterious   **G** soothing
   H repetitive   **J** booming

5. A group of <u>tethered</u> airplanes
   A tied   **B** restored
   C battered   **D** abandoned

Vocabulary Handbook
See p. R24: Synonyms and Antonyms.

SPELLING STRATEGY: WORDS ENDING WITH *-OUS*
The suffix *-ous,* meaning "full of," is added to nouns and verbs to create adjectives. When the base word ends in silent *e,* the *e* is dropped before adding *-ous* unless the *e* is preceded by *g.* When *-ous* is added to a word that ends in *y,* the *y* is changed to *i.* Add *-ous* to the following words.

1. peril + -ous
2. melody + -ous
3. courage + -ous
4. marvel + -ous
5. nerve + -ous

Spelling Handbook
See p. R28.

Grammar in Context: Simple Subjects and Simple Predicates

In "Flying," Reeve Lindbergh never liked the noise of flight and stuffed cotton balls in her ears.

> My father frowned upon the cotton balls.

The complete subject of this sentence is *my father.* The key word, *father,* tells who performs the action. This is called the **simple subject.**

The complete predicate is *frowned upon the cotton balls.* The key word, *frowned,* is called the **simple predicate.** The simple predicate is always a verb and tells what the subject is or does. By adding information to both the simple subject and the simple predicate, Lindbergh creates a more interesting sentence.

WRITING EXERCISE Create sentences by adding information to the following simple subjects and predicates. Add details that show where, when, how, and why.

Example: *Original* airplane sat

Rewritten <u>The small</u> airplane sat <u>on the runway.</u>

1. houses stood
2. noise echoed
3. brother jumped
4. silence grew
5. mother loved

Connect to the Literature Look at the opening paragraph of "Flying." Identify the simple subject and simple predicate in each sentence.

Grammar Handbook

See p. R75: Writing Complete Sentences.

Reeve Lindbergh
born 1945

"I can't recall any time… when one of my parents was not engaged in writing a book."

A Family Habit Both of Reeve Lindbergh's parents were writers as well as pilots. "In the household where I grew up," she has said, "writing was a kind of family habit, something the adults around me did every day without thinking too much about it. . . ." Reeve has followed in her parents' footsteps. So far, she has published 13 children's books and 4 books for adults.

Home in Vermont After graduating from Radcliffe College in 1968, Lindbergh moved to Vermont. More than 30 years later, she still lives there. Her current home is a farm that she shares with her husband, the writer Nathaniel Tripp; their son, Benjamin; many chickens; and a flock of sheep. In addition to tending her farm and writing, she serves as president of the Lindbergh Foundation, which promotes her parents' vision of a balance between technological development and environmental protection.

AUTHOR ACTIVITY
Father and Daughter For a closer look at the relationship between Reeve Lindbergh and her father, read portions of her recently published autobiography titled *Under a Wing: A Memoir.* On the basis of that book and "Flying," how would you describe Reeve's feelings about her father?

Back   Forward   Reload   Home   Search   Images   Print   Security   Stop

Source: *Web Site of the 99s*

❶

Who Are The *Ninety-Nines?*

★★★★★★★★★★★★★

...they are women who love to fly!

Learn to Fly

To invent a plane is nothing.

To build one is something.

To fly is everything.

—*Otto Lilienthal*

The Ninety-Nines, Inc. is an international organization of licensed women pilots from 35 countries with over 6,500 members throughout the world. The organization came into being November 2, 1929, at Curtiss Field, Valley Stream, Long Island, New York.

Twenty-six licensed pilots replied to an invitation issued in the form of a letter. Later, after rejecting many names the organization chose "The Ninety-Nines," because 99 of the 117 licensed women pilots in the United States at that time signed up as charter members.

Today, Ninety-Nines are professional pilots for airlines, industry, and government; they are pilots who teach and pilots who fly for pleasure; they are pilots who are technicians and mechanics. But first and foremost, *they are women who love to fly!*

Reading for Information

Think how good it feels to fit the last puzzle piece into a jigsaw puzzle. The picture is complete, and everything finally makes sense. This can also happen when you read. In drawing a conclusion, you complete a picture of what you have read.

Drawing Conclusions from Sources
By combining information from many sources and prior knowledge, a reader can **draw conclusions** about what he or she has read. The sources can include encyclopedias, magazine articles, newspapers, business and public documents, and Web sites. Using a chart like this one can help you organize information and draw a conclusion logically.

Information from Sources +	Prior Knowledge =	Conclusion
One must have 40 hours of flight time to get a pilot's license.	Flying an airplane is a complex task.	Anyone who becomes a pilot needs to be dedicated, be skilled, and enjoy taking risks.
	Many factors can create problems for the pilot.	

YOUR TURN *Use the following questions and activities to draw conclusions about information from the multiple sources in this Web site article.*

❶ **Identifying Multiple Sources** This Internet Web site includes information from several sources. Scan the article. What types of sources can you identify?

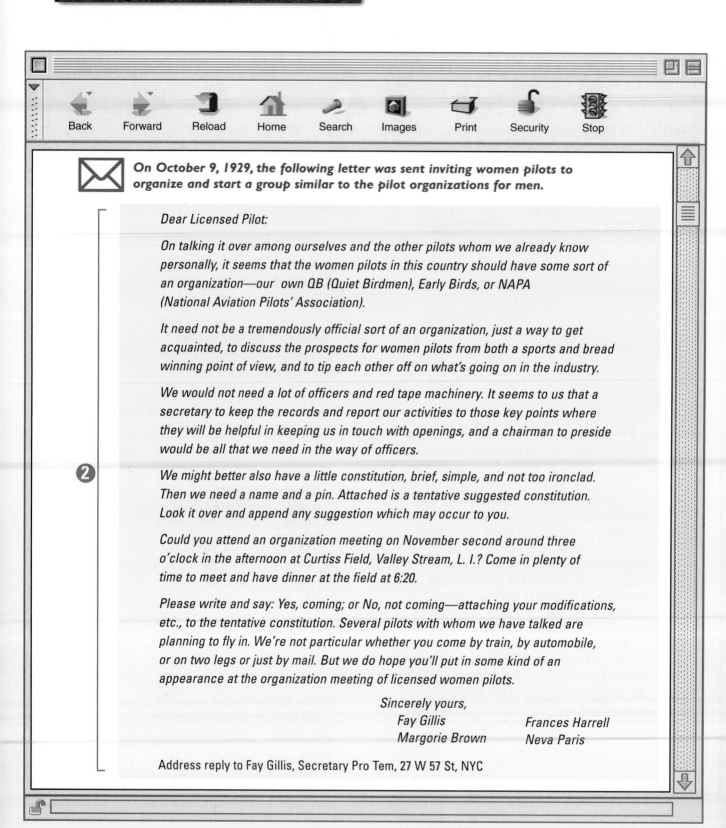

On October 9, 1929, the following letter was sent inviting women pilots to organize and start a group similar to the pilot organizations for men.

Dear Licensed Pilot:

On talking it over among ourselves and the other pilots whom we already know personally, it seems that the women pilots in this country should have some sort of an organization—our own QB (Quiet Birdmen), Early Birds, or NAPA (National Aviation Pilots' Association).

It need not be a tremendously official sort of an organization, just a way to get acquainted, to discuss the prospects for women pilots from both a sports and bread winning point of view, and to tip each other off on what's going on in the industry.

We would not need a lot of officers and red tape machinery. It seems to us that a secretary to keep the records and report our activities to those key points where they will be helpful in keeping us in touch with openings, and a chairman to preside would be all that we need in the way of officers.

We might better also have a little constitution, brief, simple, and not too ironclad. Then we need a name and a pin. Attached is a tentative suggested constitution. Look it over and append any suggestion which may occur to you.

Could you attend an organization meeting on November second around three o'clock in the afternoon at Curtiss Field, Valley Stream, L. I.? Come in plenty of time to meet and have dinner at the field at 6:20.

Please write and say: Yes, coming; or No, not coming—attaching your modifications, etc., to the tentative constitution. Several pilots with whom we have talked are planning to fly in. We're not particular whether you come by train, by automobile, or on two legs or just by mail. But we do hope you'll put in some kind of an appearance at the organization meeting of licensed women pilots.

Sincerely yours,
Fay Gillis   *Frances Harrell*
Margorie Brown   *Neva Paris*

Address reply to Fay Gillis, Secretary Pro Tem, 27 W 57 St, NYC

The Ninety-Nines Mission Statement:

- To promote world fellowship through flight
- To provide networking and scholarship opportunities for women and aviation education in the community
- To preserve the unique history of women in aviation

How to Get a Private Pilot License

The requirements for a private pilot license are governed by the Federal Aviation Administration (FAA) of the U.S. Department of Transportation. To get a private pilot's license you must:

- be at least 17 years of age
- have a current FAA third-class medical certificate
- log at least 40 hours of flight
- have at least 20 hours of flight with an instructor
- have at least 10 hours of solo flight
- pass the FAA Private Pilot Airmen Knowledge written test
- pass a FAA Private Pilot flight exam

FAA, United States Department of Transportation

Reading for Information *continued*

2 A writer does not always state or explain an idea directly. Instead, he or she expects the reader to draw conclusions about the facts presented. What can you conclude about the following organizations: Quiet Birdmen, Early Birds, and the National Aviation Pilots' Association? Consider the kind of organization the women pilots wanted to start.

3 A mission statement lists the goals of an organization. What conclusions can you draw about the goals of the Ninety-Nines from its mission statement?

4 Based on the information in this Web site article and on your own knowledge and experience, what conclusions can you draw about the requirements to qualify for a private pilot's license?

Research & Technology
Activity Link: "Flying," p. 128. Write two or three paragraphs describing the job opportunities for women pilots today. Use the information in this article and at least three other sources, including the Internet.

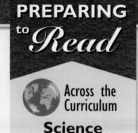
from **High Tide in Tucson**

by BARBARA KINGSOLVER

Connect to Your Life

When you think of a desert, what do you visualize?

Build Background

The setting of this selection is the desert that surrounds Tucson, Arizona, in the Southwest. Scientists classify deserts into three types.

Focus Your Reading

LITERARY ANALYSIS **ESSAY**

A short work of nonfiction that deals with a single subject is called an **essay**. Essays can be formal or informal. A **formal essay** examines a topic in a serious manner. **Informal essays,** such as this one, are lighter in tone and usually reflect the writer's feelings.

ACTIVE READING **VISUALIZING**

The process of forming a mental picture based on a written description is called **visualizing**. As you read the essay, jot down descriptive words and phrases in your 📖 READER'S NOTEBOOK. These words and phrases will help you visualize the pond as it springs to life.

WORDS TO KNOW **Vocabulary Preview**
| armada | optimism | teem |
| conspiracy | predator | |

High-Latitude Deserts

These deserts lie near the North and South Poles. They include the frozen deserts of Antarctica and Greenland.

Equator

Mid-Latitude Deserts

These deserts are found in Arizona and other Southwest states. The temperature varies so that at times it can be cold enough to cause a light frost in winter and may reach 105°F in summer.

Low-Latitude Deserts

Low-latitude deserts, such as the Sahara of North Africa, lie near the equator. These deserts are hot and dry all year long.

Southwest Hills (1998), Steven Zolin. Oil on canvas, 10" x 14". Courtesy of the artist.

from High Tide *in* Tucson

BY

BARBARA
KINGSOLVER

After two days of gentle winter rains, the small pond behind my house is lapping at its banks, content as a well-fed kitten. This pond is a relative miracle. Several years ago I talked a man I knew who was handy with a bulldozer into damming up the narrow wash behind my house. This was not a creek by any stretch of imagination—even so thirsty an imagination as mine. It was only a little strait where, two or three times a year when the rain kept up for more than a day, water would run past in a hurry on its way to flood the road and drown out the odd passing Buick. All the rest of the time this little valley lay empty, a toasted rock patch pierced with cactus.

I cleared out the brush and, with what my bulldozer friend viewed as absurd <u>optimism</u>, directed the proceedings. After making a little hollow, we waterproofed the bottom and lined the sides with rocks, and then I could only stand by to see what would happen. When the rains came my pond filled. Its level rises and falls some, but for years now it has remained steadfastly *pond*, a small blue eye in the blistered face of desert.

That part was only hydrology[1] and luck, no miracle. But this part is: within hours of its creation, my pond <u>teemed</u> with life. Backswimmers, whirligig beetles, and boatmen darted down through the watery strata. Water striders dimpled the surface. Tadpoles and water beetles rootled the furry bottom. Dragonflies hovered and delicately dipped their tails, laying eggs. Eggs hatched into creeping <u>armadas</u> of larvae. I can't imagine where all these creatures came from. There is no other permanent water for many miles around. How did they know? What jungle drums told them to come here? Surely there are not, as a matter of course, aquatic creatures dragging themselves by their elbows across the barren desert *just in case*?

I'm tempted to believe in spontaneous generation.[2] Rushes have sprung up around the edges of my pond, coyotes and javelinas come

...within hours of its creation, my pond teemed with life.

down to drink and unabashedly wallow, nighthawks and little brown bats swoop down at night to snap insects out of the air. Mourning doves, smooth as cool gray stones, coo at their own reflections. Families of Gambel's quail come each and every spring morning, all lined up puffed and bustling with their seventeen children, Papa Quail in proud lead with his ridiculous black topknot feather boinging out ahead of him. Water lilies open their flowers at sunup and fold them, prim as praying hands, at dusk. A sleek male Cooper's hawk and a female great horned owl roost in the trees with their constant <u>predators</u>' eyes on dim-witted quail and vain dove, silently taking turns with the night and day shifts.

For several years that Cooper's hawk was the steadiest male presence in my life. I've stood alone in his shadow through many changes of season. I've been shattered and reassembled a few times over, and there have been long days when I felt my heart was simply somewhere else—possibly on ice, in one of those igloo coolers that show up in the news as they are carried importantly onto helicopters. "So what?" life asked, and went on whirling recklessly around me. Always, every minute, something is eating or being

1. **hydrology:** the scientific study of the properties, distribution, and effects of water on the earth's surface, in the soil and underlying rocks, and in the atmosphere.

2. **spontaneous generation:** the supposed development of living organisms from nonliving matter.

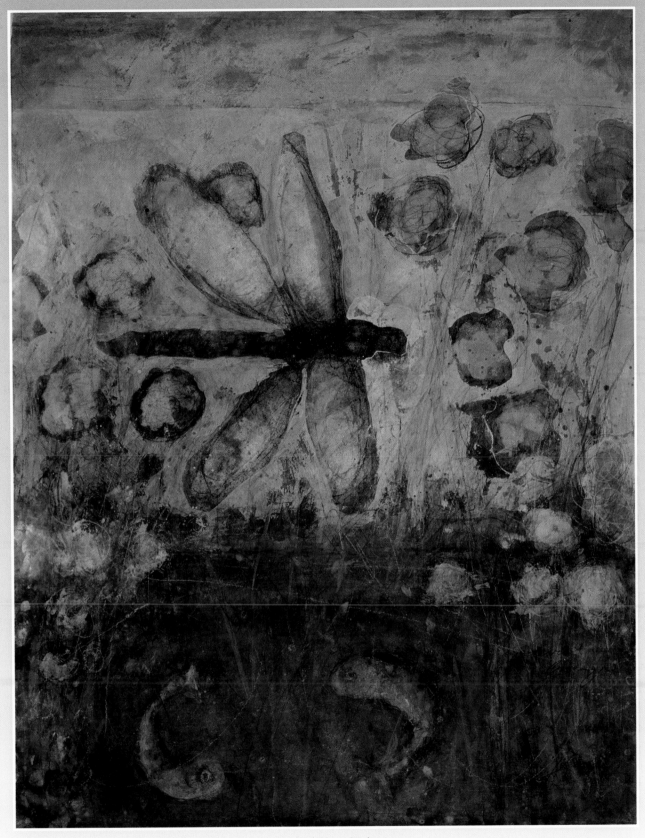

Dragonfly (1996), David Brayne. The Grand Design, Leeds, England / SuperStock.

eaten, laying eggs, burrowing in mud, blooming, splitting its seams, dividing itself in two. What a messy marvel, fecundity.[3]

That is how I became goddess of a small universe of my own creation—more or less by accident. My subjects owe me their very lives. Blithely they ignore me. I stand on the banks, wide-eyed, receiving gifts in every season. In May the palo verde[4] trees lean into their reflections, so heavy with blossoms the desert looks thick and deep with golden hoarfrost. In November the purple water lilies are struck numb with the first frost, continuing to try to open their final flowers in slow motion for the rest of the winter. Once, in August, I saw a tussle in the reeds that turned out to be two bull snakes making a meal of the same frog. Their dinner screeched piteously while the snakes' heads inched slowly closer together, each of them engulfing a drumstick, until there they were at last, nose to scaly nose. I watched with my knuckles in my mouth, anxious to see whether they would rip the frog in two like a pair of pants. As it turned out, they were nowhere near this civilized. They lunged and thrashed, their long bodies scrawling whole cursive alphabets into the rushes, until one of the snakes suddenly let go and curved away.

Last May, I saw a dragonfly as long as my hand—longer than an average-sized songbird. She circled and circled, flexing her body, trying to decide if my little lake was worthy of her precious eggs. She was almost absurdly colorful, sporting a bright green thorax[5] and blue abdomen. Eventually she lit on the tip of the horsetail plant that sends long slender spikes up out of the water. She was joined on the tips of five adjacent stalks by five other dragonflies, all different: an orange-bodied one with orange wings, a yellow one, a blue-green one, one with a red head and purple tail, and a miniature one in zippy metallic blue. A dragonfly bouquet. Be still, and the world is bound to turn herself inside out to entertain you. Everywhere you look, joyful noise is clanging to drown out quiet desperation. The choice is draw the blinds and shut it all out, or believe.

What to believe in, exactly, may never turn out to be half as important as the daring act of belief. A willingness to participate in sunlight, and the color red. An agreement to enter into a conspiracy with life, on behalf of both frog and snake, the predator and the prey, in order to come away changed. ❖

I stand on the banks, wide-eyed, receiving gifts in every season.

----

3. **fecundity:** the power to produce offspring or vegetation with ease and abundance.

4. **palo verde:** a spiny, nearly leafless, bushy tree of the southwest United States, with yellow flowers and blue-green bark.

5. **thorax:** the midregion of the body between the head and the abdomen.

MI MADRE[1] by Pat Mora

I say feed me.
She serves red prickly pear[2] on a spiked cactus.

I say tease me.
She sprinkles raindrops in my face on a sunny day.

5 I say frighten me.
She shouts thunder, flashes lightning.

I say comfort me.
She invites me to lay on her firm body.

I say heal me.
10 She gives me *manzanilla, orégano, dormilón.*[3]

I say caress me.
She strokes my skin with her warm breath.

I say make me beautiful.
She offers turquoise for my fingers, a pink blossom for my hair.

15 I say sing to me.
She chants lonely women's songs of femaleness.

I say teach me.
She endures: glaring heat
           numbing cold
20   frightening dryness.

She: the desert
She: strong mother.

---

1. **mi madre** (mē mä′drĕ) *Spanish:* my mother.
2. **prickly pear:** the pear-shaped edible fruit of a kind of cactus.
3. *manzanilla* (män-sä-nē′yä), *orégano* (ô-rĕ′gä-nô), *dormilón* (dôr-mē-lôn′)
   Spanish: sweet-smelling herbs that can be used to make home medicines.

Connect to the Literature

1. **What Do You Think?** How does this description of Kingsolver's pond make you feel?

   Comprehension Check
   - How was the pond made?
   - What is unusual about the pond's location?
   - On page 138, Kingsolver refers to "my subjects." Who are her subjects?

Think Critically

2. **ACTIVE READING** **VISUALIZING**
   Look at the words and phrases that you recorded in your **READER'S NOTEBOOK**. Which details best help you visualize the pond?

3. Reread the last six sentences, beginning with "Be still, and the world is bound . . ." In these sentences, what is Kingsolver urging the reader to believe in?

4. This essay is one of several in Kingsolver's book *High Tide in Tucson*. What is the connection between this essay and the book title *High Tide in Tucson*?

   Think About:
   - Arizona's location in relation to oceans
   - the ebb and flow of the cycles of nature
   - the author's personal situation

Extend Interpretations

5. **COMPARING TEXTS** Read the poem "Mi Madre" by Pat Mora on page 139. Compare Mora's attitude toward the desert with Kingsolver's attitude.

6. **Connect to Life** When things are not going well for you, do you sometimes seek comfort in nature? If not, in what ways do you experience nature? Explain your answer.

Literary Analysis

ESSAY A short work of nonfiction that deals with a single subject is called an **essay.** Essays can be formal or informal. A **formal essay** is highly organized, thoroughly researched, and serious in tone. An **informal essay** is lighter in tone and usually reflects the writer's feelings, experiences, and personality. The essay from *High Tide in Tucson* is an example of an informal essay.

Paired Activity Make a chart like the one shown. Then, working with a partner, reread the essay and record the author's personal reflections. (Look for "I" statements.)

When you have finished, study the chart. What does it reveal about Barbara Kingsolver? Compare your responses with those of others in your class.

Writer's Personal Reflection	Page Number
I stand on the banks, wide-eyed, receiving gifts in every season.	page 138

CHOICES and CHALLENGES

Writing

Informal Essay Write an informal essay in which you describe a change of season and how that change affects you. Use the essay from *High Tide in Tucson* as a model. As you prepare to write, identify the main idea, or the most important point you want to make. Be sure to include details to support it. Place your essay in your **Working Portfolio.**

Writing Handbook
See p. R36: Building Blocks of Good Writing.

Speaking & Listening

Travel Speech Arizona's mild climate attracts visitors from all over the world. Research the climate and landforms of Arizona. Write a short persuasive speech urging tourists to visit the state. Present the speech to your class. Be sure to use sensory details and colorful modifiers in your descriptions.

Speaking and Listening Handbook
See p. R104.

Research & Technology

SCIENCE

Use sources from the library to find out how plants adapt to desert climates. How do desert plants differ from plants found in wet climates?

INTERNET **Research Starter**
www.mcdougallittell.com

Vocabulary

STANDARDIZED TEST PRACTICE

Choose the word or group of words that means the same, or nearly the same, as the underlined Word to Know in each sentence.

1. <u>Optimism</u>, hard work, and luck combined to create a pond full of life. <u>Optimism</u> means—
   A sorrow   **B** cruelty
   C hopefulness   **D** caution

2. By creating a pond in the middle of the desert, the narrator chose to enter into a <u>conspiracy</u> with nature. <u>Conspiracy</u> means—
   F secret plan   **G** firm agreement
   H big battle   **J** close competition

3. A slithering <u>armada</u> came out from the thousands of eggs laid by the dragonflies. <u>Armada</u> means—
   A snake   **B** army
   C leader   **D** set

4. A <u>predator</u> roosts in a tree near the pond. <u>Predator</u> means—
   F plant-eating animal   **G** tame animal
   H hidden animal   **J** preying animal

5. Within hours of its creation, the pond began to <u>teem</u> with many creatures. <u>Teem</u> means—
   A fill up   **B** dry up
   C close up   **D** freeze up

EXERCISE: STORY CREATION Work in a small group to create a brief story containing all five Words to Know. Take turns adding a sentence that contains one of the Words to Know. The last student must create an ending for the story as well as use the last remaining word. Try this exercise a few times so that different students can begin and end the stories.

Vocabulary Handbook
See p. R24: Synonyms and Antonyms.

WORDS TO KNOW	armada	conspiracy	optimism	predator	teem

Grammar in Context: Compound Subjects and Compound Predicates

In the following passage, Barbara Kingsolver describes a pond.

> Water striders dimpled the surface.
> Tadpoles and water beetles rootled the furry bottom. Dragonflies hovered and delicately dipped their tails, laying eggs.

The first sentence has one **subject**, *water striders*, and one **verb**, *dimpled*. The second sentence has two **subjects**, *tadpoles* and *water beetles*. When a sentence has two or more subjects, the sentence is said to have a **compound subject.** The third sentence has one **subject**, *dragonflies*, but two **verbs**, *hovered* and *dipped*. When a sentence has two or more main verbs, the sentence is said to have a **compound predicate.**

Apply to Your Writing Using compound subjects and predicates can help you create more interesting sentences.

Punctuation Tip: Do not place a comma between compound verbs.

WRITING EXERCISE Add a compound predicate to each subject and a compound subject to each verb.

Example: *Original* The wind
Rewritten The wind blew across the pond and rustled the leaves of the trees.

1. lived in the pond.
2. I
3. began to appear in my pond.
4. Coyotes
5. have grown in the pond.

Grammar Handbook
See p. R76: Making Subjects and Verbs Agree.

Barbara Kingsolver
born 1955

"When I've written a book, it's half done. When a reader takes it, reads it, forms the pictures in his or her mind . . . that's the moment of art."

A Biology Student As a girl in Kentucky, the young Kingsolver never imagined writing as a profession. In college, she studied biology and ultimately earned a master's degree from the University of Arizona.

From Biology to Writing During her early years, Kingsolver held a wide variety of jobs, from housecleaner to archaeologist to X-ray technician. Her first professional writing experience was as a science writer. Today, Kingsolver writes novels, short stories, nonfiction, and poetry. She has won many awards, including the American Library Association Award for *The Bean Trees.* Her novels have been praised for their strong story lines and rich descriptive detail.

AUTHOR ACTIVITY
The Natural World Go to the library and find a copy of the book *High Tide in Tucson.* In the book, read one of the other essays that focuses on the natural world. How is the essay similar to this one? How is it different?

Building Vocabulary
Understanding Specialized Vocabulary

Have you ever listened to the commentary of a TV sportscaster? Many professions, industries, and hobbies have specialized vocabulary. **Specialized vocabulary** is made up of technical terms unique to that profession, interest, or hobby.

The specialized language of a profession is sometimes called **jargon.** Jargon words can be used so often that they become part of everyday language, like the word *mouse,* referring to the device used with a computer.

> When it was my turn to fly with my father, I sat in the back cockpit and enjoyed the view all around me while he, in the front cockpit, flew the plane. I had a duplicate set of controls in back, with rudder pedals, a stick, and instruments, so that if I had been a true student pilot, I could have flown the plane myself. . . .
>
> —Reeve Lindbergh, "Flying"

These words belong to the **specialized vocabulary** of airplane pilots.

Strategies for Building Vocabulary

When you read, you may need to understand technical and specialized words. Resources such as glossaries, dictionaries, and footnotes can help you. The following strategies will help you when you encounter specialized vocabulary.

❶ **Take Notes** While you are reading, jot down the words and phrases that you do not understand. As you read further, you may find the information that will clarify the meanings of those words and phrases.

❷ **Make Inferences** Use information in the writing and your own knowledge to make inferences about the meanings of technical terms or specialized vocabulary. Can you guess what the father had tried to teach his son in the following excerpt from "The Great Rat Hunt"?

> I listened as attentively as I had the disastrous times he'd tried to teach me how to dribble, or catch a football, or handle a pop foul.
>
> —Laurence Yep, "The Great Rat Hunt"

By noting the reference to football, you might infer that *dribble* and *pop foul* are also sports terms. The father, it seems, had tried to teach his son more than one sport.

❸ **Pay Attention to Descriptive Language** Descriptive clues can help you understand what is meant by an unfamiliar term. Notice how the description helps to clarify the meaning of *hangar* in the following passage.

> Stanley managed the airport, including the huge loaf-shaped hangar that served as a garage for repairs and maintenance to the aircraft. . . .
>
> —Reeve Lindbergh, "Flying"

EXERCISE Revise these sentences by replacing the underlined jargon with a more familiar word or words.

1. The new <u>software</u> I bought for my computer came on two <u>CDs</u>.
2. The plumber used a <u>snake</u> to clear the clogged drain.
3. The recipe directed the chef to <u>mince</u> and <u>sauté</u> the chopped onions.
4. The figure skater was able to stay in the <u>camel</u> position for longer than anyone expected.
5. The wound was serious; he would have to go to the emergency room for <u>sutures</u> to stop the bleeding.

Author Study JACK LONDON

Write What You Are!

"Observation, originality, imagination, sincerity, plus natural ability are the qualifications I consider necessary for the successful author."

1876–1916

A POOR BEGINNING

Jack London was born in San Francisco, California, in 1876. His family was poor and moved frequently in search of work. In 1881 the family began working on farms before buying a ranch. London's dislike of farming drew him to literature as a way "to get beyond the sky lines of my narrow California valley." Already, the boy had discovered how to escape into a world of adventure.

The Londons were unlucky in farming. When they lost their land, they moved across the bay to Oakland. To help support his family, the 10-year-old London took his first job. By the time he was 15, he had quit school and was working long hours in a factory. London

His LIFE and TIMES

1876 Born January 12 in San Francisco, California	1886 Takes first job selling newspapers	1893 Hunts seals in the Sea of Japan

1875 1880 1885 1890

1876 Alexander Graham Bell invents the telephone.	1879 Thomas Edison introduces the light bulb.	1892 United States enters economic depression with much poverty and unemployment.

became a tough teenager who knew how to fight but who never lost his burning passion for books.

INTO A LIFE OF ADVENTURE

Living by the sea, London became fascinated by the ships that promised contact with faraway places. At the age of 17, he joined the *Sophia Sutherland* on a seal-hunting voyage to the Sea of Japan. This trip provided material for his first short story, "Story of a Typhoon Off the Coast of Japan," for which he won first prize in a writing contest.

London returned to California with a passion for travel. The next year, he "hopped a train" heading east and lived as a tramp. However, homelessness persuaded him to return to high school in Oakland. In 1896, with only one year of high school behind him, he passed the entrance examination for the University of California at Berkeley.

KLONDIKE GOLD

Unfortunately, London was forced to give up his university studies in order to support his mother. For a time he worked in a laundry before joining thousands of others heading north to Canada's Klondike River in search of gold.

Jack London in the Klondike

1897
Leaves college after one year and joins Klondike gold rush

1903
Publishes *The Call of the Wild*

1905
Marries Charmian Kittredge

1907
Sails on *Snark* with Charmian to South Seas

1916
Dies November 22 in Glen Ellen, California

1895   **1900**   **1905**   **1910**   **1915**

1901
Theodore Roosevelt becomes president.

1903
Wright brothers fly first airplane.

1912
Titanic sinks.

1914
World War I begins in Europe.

JACK LONDON

FROM RAGS TO RICHES

Although London never struck it rich, his Klondike experiences inspired his later writing. The harsh environment, the human dependence on animals, and the bravery and treachery of his companions all became raw material for his fiction. Throughout his life, London channeled his adventures into his art. As he later reminded himself, "Put all those things which are yours into the stories . . . Don't narrate—paint! draw! build! CREATE!"

After almost a year in the Klondike, London returned home. Poor and depressed, he struggled to get his stories published. Then, suddenly, his life began to change. In December 1899, the *Overland Monthly* published one of London's stories. Soon London was being paid for his stories, articles, and novels. A few years later, in 1903, his seventh and most successful novel was published. It was *The Call of the Wild*, the story of a pet dog who is forced to pull sleds for brutal masters in the Far North.

Although London's success made him rich, he never turned his back on the homeless, the poor, and the unemployed. He traveled across the country, condemning greed and demanding that wealth be shared. His own experience with poverty gave his arguments force.

OFF TO THE SOUTH SEAS

London eventually married, although his first marriage did not last. His second wife, Charmian Kittredge, was a remarkable woman who shared London's love of adventure and sports. In 1907 the couple sailed to the South Seas on their private yacht, the *Snark*. Like his Klondike trip, the voyage provided London with a wealth of material for his stories.

London and wife Charmian aboard the *Snark*

An Early Death

On their return to California in 1909, he and Charmian decided to settle down and build a home. However, years of drinking, hard work, and adventure had taken their toll on London. In 1916, London died at the age of 40. During his short lifetime he had written over 50 volumes of stories, novels, and political essays, and had helped people everywhere experience adventures like those that he had read about in his youth.

INTERNET **Author Link**
www.mcdougallittell.com

 NetActivities: Author Exploration

GOLD IN THEM THAR HILLS

When Jack London sailed for the Klondike in 1897, he became part of a throng of people heading north in search of gold. Bonanza Creek is a small stream that flows into the Yukon River in northwest Canada. In 1896, George Carmack discovered gold in the creek. It took a year for the news to reach the United States, but then within a month, thousands of prospectors rushed north.

These fortune seekers believed that large nuggets of gold would be theirs for the taking. All they had to do was reach the southeast coast of Alaska, cross the steep, treacherous passes of the Coast Mountains, build a raft to get across one of two lakes, and then navigate the mighty Yukon River for 500 miles until they reached Dawson City!

To make the journey, each prospector had to bring along about a ton (2,000 pounds) of food and supplies. So great was the danger of starvation that the Northwest Mounted Police stationed themselves along one of the passes and forced people to turn back if they did not have a year's supply of rations. Despite such hardships, as many as 100,000 people braved the 1,600-mile journey overland to the Klondike. The Klondike gold strike proved to be worth tens of millions of dollars in today's terms, and other strikes soon followed in the Far North.

The King of Mazy May

by JACK LONDON

Connect to Your Life

The Right Thing In this story, a young boy does the right thing because he has a good heart. Think about a time when you performed a good deed with no thought of reward. What motivated you? How did you feel?

Build Background

Sled Dogs Today dogsledding is both a popular sport and a means of transportation in such areas as northern Canada, Alaska, and Siberia.

The most important dog on any team is the lead dog, who has to be fast, smart, and reliable. Every dogsled team forms into a pack, just as wild wolves do. Interestingly, the pack leader (the most dominant dog) is not always the team leader.

One of the world's most famous dogsledding events is the Yukon Quest. Part of its course runs along the Yukon River in the Klondike, the setting of many stories by Jack London.

WORDS TO KNOW
Vocabulary Preview

antic	peer
capsize	prospector
commissioner	stampede
flounder	summit
liable	yaw

Focus Your Reading

LITERARY ANALYSIS   ANTAGONIST AND PROTAGONIST

The **protagonist** of a story is the central **character** or hero. Opposing the protagonist is an **antagonist.** The antagonist is usually another character (the "villain"), but sometimes the antagonist can be a force of nature or a set of circumstances. As you read "The King of Mazy May," consider which character is the protagonist and which characters or elements in nature might be the antagonists.

ACTIVE READING   MONITORING YOUR READING

When you read, you use the following reading strategies to **monitor,** or check, your understanding of a selection. Study the strategies. Which one do you use most frequently?

Question	Ask questions about the events and characters.
Visualize	Picture characters, events, and settings.
Connect	Think of similarities between events in the selection and your own experiences.
Predict	Predict what might happen next.
Clarify	Stop now and then for a quick review of what you understand so far.
Evaluate	Form opinions about the story.

📖 **READER'S NOTEBOOK** As you read "The King of Mazy May," use each reading strategy at least once. In your notebook, explain how each strategy helped you understand the story.

The King of Mazy May

by Jack London

Walt Masters is not a very large boy, but there is manliness in his make-up, and he himself, although he does not know a great deal that most boys know, knows much that other boys do not know. He has never seen a train of cars nor an elevator in his life, and for that matter he has never once looked upon a cornfield, a plow, a cow, or even a chicken. He has never had a pair of shoes on his feet, nor gone to a picnic or a party, nor talked to a girl. But he has seen the sun at midnight, watched the ice jams on one of the mightiest of rivers, and played beneath the northern lights,[1] the one white child in thousands of square miles of frozen wilderness.

Walt has walked all the fourteen years of his life in suntanned, moose-hide moccasins, and he can go to the Indian camps and "talk big" with the men, and trade calico and beads with them for their precious furs. He can make bread without baking powder, yeast, or hops, shoot a moose at three hundred yards, and drive the wild wolf dogs fifty miles a day on the packed trail.

Last of all, he has a good heart, and is not afraid of the darkness and loneliness, of man or beast or thing. His father is a good man, strong and brave, and Walt is growing up like him.

Walt was born a thousand miles or so down the Yukon,[2] in a trading post below the Ramparts. After his mother died, his father and he came up on the river, step by step, from camp to camp, till now they are settled down on the Mazy May Creek in the Klondike[3] country. Last year they and several others had spent much toil and time on the Mazy May, and endured great hardships: the creek, in turn, was just beginning to show up its richness and to reward them for their heavy labor. But with the news of their discoveries, strange men began to come and go through the short days and long nights, and many unjust things they did to the men who had worked so long upon the creek.

Si Hartman had gone away on a moose hunt, to return and find new stakes driven and his claim jumped.[4] George Lukens and his brother had lost their claims in a like manner, having delayed too long on the way to Dawson to record them. In short, it was the old story, and quite a number of the earnest, industrious prospectors had suffered similar losses.

But Walt Masters's father had recorded his claim at the start, so Walt had nothing to fear now that his father had gone on a short trip up the White River prospecting for quartz. Walt was well able to stay by himself in the cabin, cook his three meals a day, and look after things. Not only did he look after his father's claim, but he had agreed to keep an eye on the adjoining one of Loren Hall, who had started for Dawson to record it.

Loren Hall was an old man, and he had no dogs, so he had to travel very slowly. After he had been gone some time, word came up the river that he had broken through the ice at Rosebud Creek and frozen his feet so badly that he would not be able to travel for a

---

1. **northern lights:** aurora borealis; bright bands or streamers of light sometimes seen in northern night skies. The lights are believed to be caused by charged particles in the earth's magnetic field.

2. **Yukon:** a river flowing from the Yukon Territory of northwest Canada through Alaska to the Bering Sea.

3. **Klondike:** a region of Yukon Territory crossed by the Klondike River. Gold was discovered there in August 1896, leading to the gold rush of 1897–1898.

4. **claim jumped:** when a plot of land staked out by a miner is stolen by someone else.

WORDS
TO   **prospector** (prŏs′pĕk′tər) *n.* one who explores an area for mineral deposits or oil
KNOW

couple of weeks. Then Walt Masters received the news that old Loren was nearly all right again, and about to move on foot for Dawson as fast as a weakened man could.

Walt was worried, however; the claim was <u>liable</u> to be jumped at any moment because of this delay, and a fresh <u>stampede</u> had started in on the Mazy May. He did not like the looks of the newcomers, and one day, when five of them came by with crack dog teams and the lightest of camping outfits, he could see that they were prepared to make speed, and resolved to keep an eye on them. So he locked up the cabin and followed them, being at the same time careful to remain hidden.

He had not watched them long before he was sure that they were professional stampeders, bent on jumping all the claims in sight. Walt crept along the snow at the rim of the creek and saw them change many stakes, destroy old ones, and set up new ones.

In the afternoon, with Walt always trailing on their heels, they came back down the creek, unharnessed their dogs, and went into camp within two claims of his cabin. When he saw them make preparations to cook, he hurried home to get something to eat himself, and then hurried back. He crept so close that he could hear them talking quite plainly, and by pushing the underbrush aside he could catch occasional glimpses of them. They had finished eating and were sitting around the fire.

"The creek is all right, boys," a large, black-bearded man, evidently the leader, said, "and I think the best thing we can do is to pull out

tonight. The dogs can follow the trail; besides, it's going to be moonlight. What say you?"

"But it's going to be beastly cold," objected one of the party. "It's forty below zero now."

"An' sure, can't ye keep warm by jumpin' off the sleds an' runnin' after the dogs?" cried an Irishman. "An' who wouldn't? The creek's as rich as a United States mint! Faith, it's an ilegant chanst to be gettin' a run fer yer money! An' if ye don't run, it's mebbe you'll not get the money at all, at all."

"That's it," said the leader. "If we can get to Dawson and record, we're rich men; and there's no telling who's been sneaking along in our tracks, watching us, and perhaps now off to give the alarm. The thing for us to do is to

Peering out cautiously, he could see the leader studying a piece of paper.

rest the dogs a bit, and then hit the trail as hard as we can. What do you say?"

Evidently the men had agreed with their leader, for Walt Masters could hear nothing but the rattle of the tin dishes which were being washed. <u>Peering</u> out cautiously, he could see the leader studying a piece of paper. Walt knew what it was at a glance—a list of all the unrecorded claims on Mazy May. Any man could get these lists by applying to the gold <u>commissioner</u> at Dawson.

"Thirty-two," the leader said, lifting his face to the men. "Thirty-two isn't recorded, and this is thirty-three. Come on: let's take a look

WORDS TO KNOW	**liable** (lī′ə-bəl) *adj.* likely
	stampede (stăm-pēd′) *n.* a sudden headlong rush or flight of a crowd of people
	peer (pîr) *v.* to look intently, searchingly, or with difficulty
	commissioner (kə-mĭsh′ə-nər) *n.* a person authorized by a commission or special group to perform certain duties

at it. I saw somebody had been working on it when we came up this morning."

Three of the men went with him, leaving one to remain in camp. Walt crept carefully after them till they came to Loren Hall's shaft. One of the men went down and built a fire on the bottom to thaw out the frozen gravel while the others built another fire on the dump and melted water in a couple of gold pans. This they poured into a piece of canvas stretched between two logs, used by Loren Hall in which to wash his gold.

In a short time a couple of buckets of dirt were sent up by the man in the shaft, and Walt could see the others grouped anxiously about their leader as he proceeded to wash it. When this was finished, they stared at the broad streak of black sand and yellow gold grains on the bottom of the pan, and one of them called excitedly for the man who had remained in camp to come. Loren Hall had struck it rich and his claim was not yet recorded. It was plain that they were going to jump it.

Walt lay in the snow, thinking rapidly. He was only a boy, but in the face of the threatened injustice to old lame Loren Hall he felt that he must do something. He waited and watched, with his mind made up, till he saw the men begin to square up new stakes. Then he crawled away till out of hearing, and broke into a run for the camp of the stampeders. Walt's father had taken their own dogs with him prospecting, and the boy knew how impossible it was for him to undertake the seventy miles to Dawson without the aid of dogs.

Gaining the camp, he picked out, with an experienced eye, the easiest running sled and started to harness up the stampeders' dogs. There were three teams of six each, and from these he chose ten of the best. Realizing how necessary it was to have a good head dog, he strove to discover a leader amongst them: but he had little time in which to do it, for he could hear the voices of the returning men. By the time the team was in shape and everything ready, the claim-jumpers came into sight in an open place not more than a hundred yards from the trail, which ran down the bed of the creek. They cried out to Walt, but instead of giving heed to them he grabbed up one of their fur sleeping robes, which lay loosely in the snow, and leaped upon the sled.

"Mush! Hi! Mush on!" he cried to the animals, snapping the keen-lashed whip among them.

The dogs sprang against the yoke straps, and the sled jerked under way so suddenly as to almost throw him off. Then it curved into the creek, poising perilously on the runner. He was almost breathless with suspense, when it finally righted with a bound and sprang ahead again. The creek bank was high and he could not see the men, although he could hear their cries and knew they were running to cut him off. He did not dare to think what would happen if they caught him: he just clung to the sled, his heart beating wildly, and watched the snow rim of the bank above him.

Suddenly, over this snow rim came the flying body of the Irishman, who had leaped straight for the sled in a desperate attempt to capture it: but he was an instant too late. Striking on the very rear of it, he was thrown from his feet, backward, into the snow. Yet, with the quickness of a cat, he had clutched the end of the sled with one hand, turned over, and was dragging behind on his breast, swearing at the boy and threatening all kinds of terrible things if he did not stop the dogs; but Walt cracked him sharply across the knuckles with the butt of the dog whip till he let go.

It was eight miles from Walt's claim to the Yukon—eight very crooked miles, for the creek wound back and forth like a snake, "tying knots in itself," as George Lukens said. And because it was so crooked the dogs could not get up their best speed, while the sled ground heavily on its side against the curves, now to the right, now to the left.

Travelers who had come up and down the Mazy May on foot, with packs on their backs, had declined to go round all the bends, and instead had made shortcuts across the narrow necks of creek bottom. Two of his pursuers had gone back to harness the remaining dogs, but the others took advantage of these shortcuts, running on foot, and before he knew it they had almost overtaken him.

"Halt!" they cried after him. "Stop, or we'll shoot!"

But Walt only yelled the harder at the dogs, and dashed around the bend with a couple of revolver bullets singing after him. At the next bend they had drawn up closer still, and the bullets struck uncomfortably near him but at this point the Mazy May straightened out and ran for half a mile as the crow flies. Here the dogs stretched out in their long wolf swing, and

"Halt!" they cried after him. "Stop, or we'll shoot!"

the stampeders, quickly winded, slowed down and waited for their own sled to come up.

Looking over his shoulder, Walt reasoned that they had not given up the chase for good, and that they would soon be after him again. So he wrapped the fur robe about him to shut out the stinging air, and lay flat on the empty sled, encouraging the dogs, as he well knew how.

At last, twisting abruptly between two river islands, he came upon the mighty Yukon sweeping grandly to the north. He could not see from bank to bank, and in the quick-falling twilight it loomed a great white sea of frozen stillness. There was not a sound, save the breathing of the dogs, and the churn of the steel-shod sled.

No snow had fallen for several weeks, and the traffic had packed the main river trail till it was hard and glassy as glare ice. Over this the sled flew along, and the dogs kept the trail fairly well, although Walt quickly discovered that he had made a mistake in choosing the leader. As they were driven in single file, without reins, he had to guide them by his voice, and it was evident the head dog had never learned the meaning of "gee" and "haw."[5] He hugged the inside of the curves too closely, often forcing his comrades behind him into the soft snow, while several times he thus <u>capsized</u> the sled.

There was no wind, but the speed at which he traveled created a bitter blast, and with the thermometer down to forty below, this bit through fur and flesh to the very bones. Aware that if he remained constantly upon the sled he would freeze to death, and knowing the practice of Arctic travelers, Walt shortened up one of the lashing thongs, and whenever he felt chilled, seized hold of it, jumped off, and ran behind till warmth was restored. Then he would climb on and rest till the process had to be repeated.

Looking back he could see the sled of his pursuers, drawn by eight dogs, rising and falling over the ice hummocks like a boat in a seaway. The Irishman and the black-bearded leader were with it, taking turns in running and riding.

Night fell, and in the blackness of the first hour or so Walt toiled desperately with his dogs. On account of the poor lead dog, they were continually <u>floundering</u> off the beaten track into the soft snow, and the

---

5. "gee" and "haw": commands to tell an animal to turn to the right or to the left.

WORDS
TO
KNOW

capsize (kăp'sīz) v. to overturn or cause to overturn
flounder (floun'dər) v. to make clumsy attempts to move or regain one's balance

154

sled was as often riding on its side or top as it was in the proper way. This work and strain tried his strength sorely. Had he not been in such haste he could have avoided much of it, but he feared the stampeders would creep up in the darkness and overtake him. However, he could hear them yelling to their dogs, and knew from the sounds they were coming up very slowly.

When the moon rose he was off Sixty Mile, and Dawson was only fifty miles away. He was almost exhausted, and breathed a sigh of relief as he climbed on the sled again. Looking back, he saw his enemies had crawled up within four hundred yards. At this space they remained, a black speck of motion on the white river breast. Strive as they would, they could not shorten this distance, and strive as he would, he could not increase it.

Walt had now discovered the proper lead dog, and he knew he could easily run away from them if he could only change the bad leader for the good one. But this was impossible, for a moment's delay, at the speed they were running, would bring the men behind upon him.

When he was off the mouth of Rosebud Creek, just as he was topping a rise, the report of a gun and the ping of a bullet on the ice beside him told him that they were this time shooting at him with a rifle. And from then on, as he cleared the <u>summit</u> of each ice jam, he stretched flat on the leaping sled till the rifle shot from the rear warned him that he was safe till the next ice jam was reached.

Now it is very hard to lie on a moving sled, jumping and plunging and <u>yawing</u> like a boat

before the wind, and to shoot through the deceiving moonlight at an object four hundred yards away on another moving sled performing equally wild <u>antics</u>. So it is not to be wondered at that the black-bearded leader did not hit him.

After several hours of this, during which, perhaps, a score of bullets had struck about him, their ammunition began to give out and their fire slackened. They took greater care, and shot at him at the most favorable opportunities. He was also leaving them behind, the distance slowly increasing to six hundred yards.

Lifting clear on the crest of a great jam off Indian River, Walt Masters met with his first accident. A bullet sang past his ears, and struck the bad lead dog.

The poor brute plunged in a heap, with the rest of the team on top of him.

Like a flash Walt was by the leader. Cutting the traces with his hunting knife, he dragged the dying animal to one side and straightened out the team.

He glanced back. The other sled was coming up like an express train. With half the dogs

He glanced back. The other sled was coming up like an express train.

still over their traces, he cried "Mush on!" and leaped upon the sled just as the pursuers dashed abreast of him.

The Irishman was preparing to spring for him—they were so sure they had him that they did not shoot—when Walt turned fiercely upon them with his whip.

WORDS TO KNOW	**summit** (sŭm′ĭt) *n.* the highest point or part; the top
	yaw (yô) *v.* to swerve off course momentarily or temporarily
	antic (ănt′ĭc) *n.* an odd or extravagant act or gesture; a prank

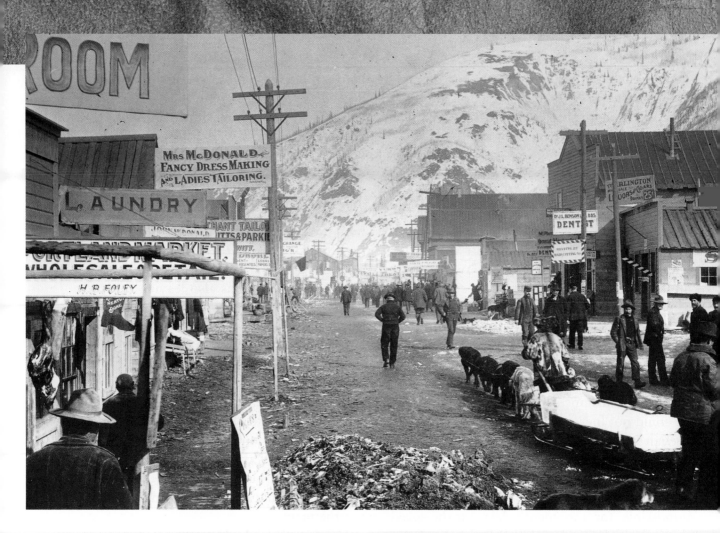

He struck at their faces, and men must save their faces with their hands. So there was no shooting just then. Before they could recover from the hot rain of blows, Walt reached out from his sled, catching their wheel dog by the forelegs in midspring, and throwing him heavily. This snarled the team, capsizing the sled and tangling his enemies up beautifully.

Away Walt flew, the runners of his sled fairly screaming as they bounded over the frozen surface. And what had seemed an accident proved to be a blessing in disguise. The proper lead dog was now to the fore, and he stretched low and whined with joy as he jerked his comrades along.

By the time he reached Ainslie's Creek, seventeen miles from Dawson, Walt had left his pursuers, a tiny speck, far behind. At Monte Cristo Island he could no longer see them. And at Swede Creek, just as daylight was silvering the pines, he ran plump into the camp of old Loren Hall.

Almost as quick as it takes to tell it, Loren had his sleeping furs rolled up, and had joined Walt on the sled. They permitted the dogs to travel more slowly, as there was no sign of the chase in the rear, and just as they pulled up at the gold commissioner's office in Dawson, Walt, who had kept his eyes open to the last, fell asleep.

And because of what Walt Masters did on this night, the men of the Yukon have become proud of him, and speak of him now as the King of Mazy May. ❖

Connect to the Literature

1. **What Do You Think?**
   What was your reaction to the story?

   Comprehension Check
   • Why are Walt and his father living on Mazy May Creek?
   • Why does Walt steal the claim-jumpers' sled and dogs?
   • What do Walt and Loren Hall do at the end of the story?

Think Critically

2. Review the first three paragraphs of the story, beginning with "Walt Masters is not a very large boy . . ." and ending with "His father is a good man, strong and brave, and Walt is growing up like him." What important point about human nature is the author presenting here?

3. What sort of person do you think Walt will grow up to be?

   Think About:
   • his willingness to protect Loren Hall's land
   • the risks he takes in stealing the dogs
   • the decisions he makes as he races toward Dawson

4. **ACTIVE READING** | **MONITORING YOUR READING**
   Review the reading strategies that you recorded in your **READER'S NOTEBOOK**. Which strategies most helped you understand the story? At what point in the story did you use these strategies?

Extend Interpretations

5. **What If?** Suppose this story took place today in a remote part of Canada or Alaska. How might it be similar? How might it be different?

6. **Connect to Life** Like the Klondike prospectors, many people still dream of "striking it rich." What kinds of "get-rich-quick" schemes in modern life are you aware of? How reliable do you think such schemes usually are? Explain your answer.

Literary Analysis

PROTAGONIST AND ANTAGONIST

In a story, the **protagonist** is a main **character** who is involved in the story's **conflict.** An **antagonist** is a force working against the protagonist or main character. The antagonist may be another character, a force of nature, or even a force within the main character.

In "The King of Mazy May," Walt Masters is the protagonist. The five claim-jumpers are the antagonists. The trail leading to Dawson might also be considered an antagonist because it is a natural barrier that Walt must overcome.

Paired Activity Readers often feel sympathy for a story's protagonist and dislike toward a story's antagonist. How did you feel about Walt and the claim-jumpers? With a partner, go back through the story and find the passages that influenced your feelings. When you have finished, discuss your findings with your partner.

Passages About Walt	Passages About Claim-Jumpers
Last of all, he has a good heart, and is not afraid of the darkness and loneliness, of man or beast or thing.	

Grammar in Context: Sentence Variety

Writers try to hold a reader's attention by using different kinds of sentences in their writing. Notice the sentence variety in the following passage from "The King of Mazy May."

> He struck at their faces, and men must save their faces with their hands. So there was no shooting just then. Before they could recover from the hot rain of blows, Walt reached out from his sled, catching their wheel dog by the forelegs in midspring, and throwing him heavily.

In this passage, Jack London has created **sentence variety** by using three types of sentences. The first sentence is an example of a **compound sentence**—two simple sentences that have been joined together. The second sentence is a simple sentence. The third sentence is a **complex sentence.** It has a main clause—*Walt reached out from his sled,* and a subordinate clause—*Before they could recover from the hot rain of blows.*

WRITING EXERCISE The following passage is a collection of simple sentences. Rewrite the passage so that it uses three types of sentences—simple, compound, and complex.

> The creek bank was high. He could not see the men. He could hear the men shouting. He knew something. They were running. They were running to cut him off. He just clung to the sled. His heart was beating wildly. He kept his eye on something. He kept his eye on the rim of the bank. He was watching for the men. The men were getting closer.

Connect to the Literature Find two more examples of each kind of sentence in the selection.

Grammar Handbook
See p. R75: Writing Complete Sentences.

Vocabulary

EXERCISE A: WORD RECOGNITION On your paper, match each vocabulary word on the left with the word or phrase on the right that is closest in meaning. Use each vocabulary word only once.

1. yaw		**a.** likely
2. summit		**b.** prank
3. prospector		**c.** sudden rush
4. capsize		**d.** director
5. liable		**e.** peak
6. flounder		**f.** stare
7. antic		**g.** miner
8. commissioner		**h.** move clumsily
9. peer		**i.** overturn
10. stampede		**j.** veer off course

EXERCISE B: MEANING CLUES Decide which Word to Know is described in each riddle. Write the word on your paper.

1. I describe an attempt to regain one's balance.
2. I am an adventurer who searches for gold.
3. When you've reached me, you're at the top!
4. I describe a sudden rushing movement of people or animals.
5. I am the person authorized to establish rules and regulations.

Vocabulary Handbook
See p. R25: Homonyms, Homophones, and Words With Multiple Meanings.

The Story of an Eyewitness

by JACK LONDON

Connect to Your Life

You Are There Have you ever been an eyewitness to a memorable event, such as an accident, a fire, or a flood? How did you feel at the time? Did everything happen too fast for you to notice details, or did every detail become locked in your memory? Discuss your reactions.

Build Background

SCIENCE

San Francisco sits on top of the San Andreas Fault, a 650-mile crack in the earth's crust that runs along the California coast. On April 18, 1906, parts of the fault line buckled, bent, and slid past each other by as much as 21 feet! This created the great San Francisco earthquake, which was followed by a devastating fire that destroyed much of the city.

> **WORDS TO KNOW**
> **Vocabulary Preview**
>
> | | |
> |---|---|
> | compel | flank |
> | conflagration | flotsam |
> | contrivance | menace |
> | dear | refugee |
> | enumeration | surmount |

Focus Your Reading

LITERARY ANALYSIS | **FEATURE STORY**

One of the many forms of informative nonfiction is the newspaper or magazine **feature story.** A feature story is similar to a **news story.** Both answer the questions *Who? What? Where? When? Why?* and *How?* A feature story, however, goes beyond the "just-the-facts" reporting that characterizes a news story. In a feature story, the writer often includes detailed descriptions and personal feelings. The author's perspective may reflect his or her attitude or beliefs about a subject. As you read "The Story of an Eyewitness," look for places where London puts himself into the scene instead of merely reporting the facts.

ACTIVE READING | **UNDERSTANDING CHRONOLOGICAL ORDER**

The order in which events happen in time is called **chronological order**. In "The Story of an Eyewitness," Jack London proceeds day by day through the dreadful events of the fire. Now and then, he departs from chronological order and moves back and forth in time.

📖 **READER'S NOTEBOOK** As you read this feature story, keep track of the order in which events happen. A chart like the one shown will help you.

Wednesday Morning	5:15—the beginning of the earthquake
Wednesday Afternoon and Evening	
Thursday Morning	
Thursday Night	
Friday Daytime	
Friday Night	

THE STORY OF AN EYEWITNESS

by Jack London

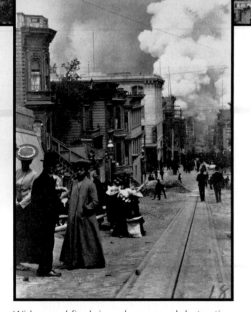

Widespread fire brings damage and destruction to nearly every part of the city.

Upon receipt of the first news of the earthquake, *Collier's* telegraphed to Mr. Jack London—who lives only forty miles from San Francisco—requesting him to go to the scene of the disaster and write the story of what he saw. Mr. London started at once, and he sent the following dramatic description of the tragic events he witnessed in the burning city.

The earthquake shook down in San Francisco hundreds of thousands of dollars worth of walls and chimneys. But the conflagration that followed burned up hundreds of millions of dollars' worth of property. There is no estimating within hundreds of millions the actual damage wrought. Not in history has a modern imperial city been so completely destroyed. San Francisco is gone. Nothing remains of it but memories and a fringe of dwelling houses on its outskirts. Its industrial section is wiped out. Its business section is wiped out. Its social and residential section is wiped out. The factories and warehouses, the great stores and newspaper buildings, the hotels and the palaces of the nabobs,[1] are all gone. Remains only the fringe of dwelling houses on the outskirts of what was once San Francisco.

Within an hour after the earthquake shock the smoke of San Francisco's burning was a lurid tower visible a hundred miles away. And for three days and nights this lurid tower swayed in the sky, reddening the sun, darkening the day, and filling the land with smoke.

On Wednesday morning at a quarter past five came the earthquake. A minute later the flames were leaping upward. In a dozen different quarters south of Market Street, in the working-class ghetto, and in the factories, fires started. There was no opposing the flames. There was no organization, no communication. All the cunning adjustments of a twentieth century city had been smashed by the earthquake. The streets were humped into ridges and depressions, and piled with the debris of fallen walls. The steel rails were twisted into perpendicular and horizontal angles. The telephone and telegraph systems were disrupted. And the great water-mains had burst. All the shrewd <u>contrivances</u> and safeguards of man had been thrown out of gear by thirty seconds' twitching of the earth-crust.

THE FIRE MADE ITS OWN DRAFT

By Wednesday afternoon, inside of twelve hours, half the heart of the city was gone. At that time I watched the vast conflagration from out on the bay. It was dead calm. Not a flicker of wind stirred. Yet from every side

wind was pouring in upon the city. East, west, north, and south, strong winds were blowing upon the doomed city. The heated air rising made an enormous vacuum. Thus did the fire of itself build its own colossal chimney through the atmosphere. Day and night this dead calm continued, and yet, near to the flames, the wind was often half a gale, so mighty was the vacuum.

Wednesday night saw the destruction of the very heart of the city. Dynamite was lavishly used, and many of San Francisco's proudest structures were crumbled by man himself into ruins, but there was no withstanding the onrush of the flames. Time and again successful stands were made by the fire-fighters, and every time the flames <u>flanked</u> around on either side or came up from the rear, and turned to defeat the hard-won victory. An <u>enumeration</u> of the buildings destroyed would be a directory of San Francisco. An enumeration of the buildings undestroyed would be a line and several addresses. An enumeration of the deeds of heroism would stock a library and bankrupt the Carnegie medal fund. An enumeration of the dead will never be made. All vestiges of them were destroyed by the flames. The number of the victims of the earthquake will never be known. South of Market Street, where the loss of life was particularly heavy, was the first to catch fire.

Remarkable as it may seem, Wednesday night while the whole city crashed and roared into ruin, was a quiet night. There were no crowds. There was no shouting and yelling.

---

1. **nabobs:** persons of wealth who are well known.

WORDS TO KNOW	**contrivance** (kən-trī′vəns) *n.* something, as a machine, created to do a specific thing
	flank (flăngk) *v.* to attack the sides of something
	enumeration (ĭ-nōō′mə-rā′shən) *n.* a list

There was no hysteria, no disorder. I passed Wednesday night in the path of the advancing flames, and in all those terrible hours I saw not one woman who wept, not one man who was excited, not one person who was in the slightest degree panic stricken.

Before the flames, throughout the night, fled tens of thousands of homeless ones. Some were wrapped in blankets. Others carried bundles of bedding and <u>dear</u> household treasures. Sometimes a whole family was harnessed to a carriage or delivery wagon that was weighted down with their possessions. Baby buggies, toy wagons, and go-carts were used as trucks, while every other person was dragging a trunk. Yet everybody was gracious. The most perfect courtesy obtained. Never in all San Francisco's history, were her people so kind and courteous as on this night of terror.

A CARAVAN OF TRUNKS

All night these tens of thousands fled before the flames. Many of them, the poor people from the labor ghetto, had fled all day as well. They had left their homes burdened with possessions. Now and again they lightened up, flinging out upon the street clothing and treasures they had dragged for miles.

They held on longest to their trunks, and over these trunks many a strong man broke his heart that night. The hills of San Francisco are steep, and up these hills, mile after mile, were the trunks dragged. Everywhere were trunks with across them lying their exhausted owners, men and women. Before the march of the flames were flung picket lines of soldiers. And a block at a time, as the flames advanced, these pickets retreated. One of their tasks was to keep the trunk-pullers moving. The exhausted creatures, stirred on by the <u>menace</u> of bayonets, would arise and struggle up the steep pavements, pausing from weakness every five or ten feet.

Often, after <u>surmounting</u> a heart-breaking hill, they would find another wall of flame advancing upon them at right angles and be <u>compelled</u> to change anew the line of their retreat. In the end, completely played out, after toiling for a dozen hours like giants, thousands of them were compelled to abandon their trunks. Here the shopkeepers and soft members of the middle class were at a disadvantage. But

WORDS TO KNOW	**dear** (dîr) *adj.* greatly valued; precious **menace** (mĕn′ĭs) *n.* a possible danger; a threat **surmount** (sər-mount′) *v.* to get to the top of; climb **compel** (kəm-pĕl′) *v.* to force or drive

the working-men dug holes in vacant lots and backyards and buried their trunks.

THE DOOMED CITY

At nine o'clock Wednesday evening I walked down through the very heart of the city. I walked through miles and miles of magnificent buildings and towering skyscrapers. Here was no fire. All was in perfect order. The police patrolled the streets. Every building had its watchman at the door. And yet it was doomed, all of it. There was no water. The dynamite was giving out. And at right angles two different conflagrations were sweeping down upon it.

At one o'clock in the morning I walked down through the same section. Everything still stood intact. There was no fire. And yet there was a change. A rain of ashes[2] was falling. The watchmen at the doors were gone. The police had been withdrawn. There were no firemen, no fire-engines, no men fighting with dynamite. The district had been absolutely abandoned. I stood at the corner of Kearney and Market, in the very innermost heart of San Francisco. Kearny Street was deserted. Half a dozen blocks away it was burning on both sides. The street was a wall of flame. And against this wall of flame, silhouetted sharply, were two United States cavalrymen[3] sitting on their horses, calmly watching. That was all. Not another person was in sight. In the intact heart of the city, two troopers sat their horses and watched.

SPREAD OF THE CONFLAGRATION

Surrender was complete. There was no water. The sewers had long since been pumped dry. There was no dynamite. Another fire had broken out further uptown, and now from three sides conflagrations were sweeping down. The fourth side had been burned earlier in the day. In that direction stood the tottering walls of the Examiner Building, the burned-out Call Building, the smoldering ruins of the Grand Hotel, and the gutted, devastated, dynamited Palace Hotel.

The following will illustrate the sweep of the flames and the inability of men to calculate their spread. At eight o'clock Wednesday evening I passed through Union Square. It was packed with <u>refugees</u>. Thousands of them had gone to bed on the grass. Government tents had been set up, supper was being cooked, and the refugees were lining up for free meals.

At half past one in the morning three sides of Union Square were in flames. The fourth side, where stood the great St. Francis Hotel, was still holding out. An hour later, ignited from top and sides the St. Francis was flaming heavenward. Union Square, heaped high with mountains of trunks, was deserted. Troops, refugees, and all had retreated.

A FORTUNE FOR A HORSE!

It was at Union Square that I saw a man offering a thousand dollars for a team of horses. He was in charge of a truck piled high with trunks from some hotel. It had been hauled here into what was considered safety, and the horses had been taken out. The flames were on three sides of the Square and there were no horses.

---

2. **rain of ashes:** an imaginative description of the large amount of ashes blown about by the wind.
3. **cavalrymen:** soldiers trained to fight on horseback; in this story, they were sent to help with the fire but could do nothing.

WORDS
TO
KNOW   **refugee** (rĕf′yŏŏ-jē′) *n.* one who leaves his or her home in search of protection or shelter elsewhere, as in times of war

Also, at this time, standing beside the truck, I urged a man to seek safety in flight. He was all but hemmed in by several conflagrations. He was an old man and he was on crutches. Said he: "Today is my birthday. Last night I was worth thirty thousand dollars. I bought some delicate fish and other things for my birthday dinner. I have had no dinner, and all I own are these crutches."

I convinced him of his danger and started him limping on his way. An hour later, from a distance, I saw the truck-load of trunks burning merrily in the middle of the street.

On Thursday morning at a quarter past five, just twenty-four hours after the earthquake, I sat on the steps of a small residence on Nob Hill. With me sat Japanese, Italians, Chinese, and negroes—a bit of the cosmopolitan flotsam of the wreck of the city. All about were the palaces of the nabob pioneers of Forty-nine. To the east and south at right angles, were advancing two mighty walls of flame.

I went inside with the owner of the house on the steps of which I sat. He was cool and cheerful and hospitable. "Yesterday morning," he said, "I was worth six hundred thousand dollars. This morning this house is all I have left. It will go in fifteen minutes." He pointed to a large cabinet. "That is my wife's collection of china. This rug upon which we stand is a present. It cost fifteen hundred dollars. Try that piano. Listen to its tone. There are few like it. There are no horses. The flames will be here in fifteen minutes."

Outside the old Mark Hopkins residence a palace was just catching fire. The troops were falling back and driving the refugees before them. From every side came the roaring of flames, the crashing of walls, and the detonations of dynamite.

THE DAWN OF THE SECOND DAY

I passed out of the house. Day was trying to dawn through the smoke-pall.[4] A sickly light was creeping over the face of things. Once only the sun broke through the smoke-pall, blood-red, and showing a quarter its usual size. The smoke-pall itself, viewed from beneath, was a rose color that pulsed and fluttered with lavender shades. Then it turned to mauve and yellow and dun. There was no sun. And so dawned the second day on stricken San Francisco.

An hour later I was creeping past the shattered dome of the City Hall. Than it there was no better exhibit of the destructive force of the earthquake. Most of the stone had been shaken from the great dome, leaving standing the naked framework of steel. Market Street was piled high with the wreckage, and across the wreckage lay the overthrown pillars of the City Hall shattered into short crosswise sections.

This section of the city with the exception of the Mint and the Post-Office, was already a waste of smoking ruins. Here and there through the smoke, creeping warily under the shadows of tottering walls, emerged occasional men and women. It was like the meeting of the handful of survivors after the day of the end of the world.

---

4. **smoke-pall:** a thick, dark covering of smoke.

WORDS
TO
KNOW

flotsam (flŏt′səm) *n.* floating wreckage or cargo after a shipwreck

BEEVES SLAUGHTERED AND ROASTED

On Mission Street lay a dozen steers, in a neat row stretching across the street just as they had been struck down by the flying ruins of the earthquake. The fire had passed through afterward and roasted them. The human dead had been carried away before the fire came. At another place on Mission Street I saw a milk wagon. A steel telegraph pole had smashed down sheer through the driver's seat and crushed the front wheels. The milk cans lay scattered around.

All day Thursday and all Thursday night, all day Friday and Friday night, the flames still raged on.

Friday night saw the flames finally conquered, though not until Russian Hill and Telegraph Hill had been swept and three-quarters of a mile of wharves and docks had been licked up.

THE LAST STAND

The great stand of the fire-fighters was made Thursday night on Van Ness Avenue. Had they failed here, the comparatively few remaining houses of the city would have been swept. Here were the magnificent residences of the second generation of San Francisco nabobs, and these, in a solid zone, were dynamited down across the path of the fire. Here and there the flames leaped the zone, but these fires were beaten out, principally by the use of wet blankets and rugs.

San Francisco, at the present time, is like the crater of a volcano, around which are camped tens of thousands of refugees. At the Presidio alone are at least twenty thousand. All the surrounding cities and towns are jammed with the homeless ones, where they are being cared for by the relief committees.[5] The refugees were carried free by the railroads to any point they wished to go, and it is estimated that over one hundred thousand people have left the peninsula on which San Francisco stood. The government has the situation in hand, and, thanks to the immediate relief given by the whole United States, there is not the slightest possibility of a famine. The bankers and business men have already set about making preparations to rebuild San Francisco. ❖

5. **relief committees:** emergency groups organized to give aid such as food, clothing, shelter, and medical assistance.

Connect to the Literature

1. **What Do You Think?**
   What are your impressions of the people who were affected by this tragedy?

   Comprehension Check
   - What natural disaster caused the fire?
   - What firefighting techniques were used?
   - Why were soldiers in the city, and what were they doing?

Think Critically

2. How does London use descriptive language to convey what it is like during the fire? Cite a passage that helped you visualize the disaster.

3. London says, "Never in all San Francisco's history, were her people so kind and courteous as on this night of terror." Why do you suppose people behaved this way?

4. | ACTIVE READING | UNDERSTANDING CHRONOLOGICAL ORDER |
   Go back to the chart that you made in your READER'S NOTEBOOK. In your opinion, does London's use of chronological order add to the effectiveness of the account? Why or why not?

Extend Interpretations

5. **Connect to Life** Does this feature story support the statement "In the face of tragedy, all people are equal"? Why or why not?

   Think About:
   - the description on page 162 of the poor people as they drag their trunks up and down the city's hills
   - the description on page 164 of London's encounter with the wealthy man who owns a piano

Literary Analysis

FEATURE STORY A **feature story** is a form of **informative nonfiction.** Like a **news story,** a feature story provides the facts about an event or situation. However, the language in a feature story is usually more descriptive than the language in a news story. In addition, a feature story frequently focuses on elements of human interest, such as the personal experiences of individuals, and often includes the author's personal observations and feelings. The author's perspective of the events or situation may reflect his or her attitude or beliefs about a subject.

Paired Activity Working with a partner, go back through the selection and identify passages in which Jack London presents elements of human interest. Discuss your findings with your partner or with other members of the class. Which passages reflect London's personal feelings? Which passages reflect the experiences of the victims? What conclusions can you make about London's attitude toward the subject based on his descriptions? In what way does the human-interest element add to the overall effect of the report?

Grammar in Context: Problems with *Here* and *There*

In most of the following sentences, the subject comes before the verb. However, sentences beginning with *here* or *there* follow an unusual pattern in which the **subject** follows the verb.

> Remarkable as it may seem, Wednesday night while the whole city crashed and roared into ruin, was a quiet night. There were no crowds. There was no shouting and yelling. There was no hysteria, no disorder.
>
> I walked through miles and miles of magnificent buildings and towering skyscrapers. Here was no fire. . . . And yet it was doomed, all of it.

Here and *there* can act as adverbs, telling where something is or happens. They can also be introductory words that get a sentence started.

Apply to Your Writing Occasionally use *here* or *there* at the beginning of sentences to create sentence variety.

WRITING EXERCISE Rewrite these sentences so that each sentence begins with *here, there,* or both.

Example: *Original* The magnificent residences of the rich stood in this place.

Rewritten Here stood the magnificent residences of the rich.

1. The flames leaped over the roofs of buildings in this place and in that place.
2. I saw a watchman at the door of every building.
3. I heard loud explosions as houses cracked.
4. People who had lost everything were in this place.
5. A grand hotel stood in that place.

Grammar Handbook
See p. R76: Making Subjects and Verbs Agree.

Vocabulary

EXERCISE: CONTEXT CLUES On your paper, complete each sentence with the correct form of the Word to Know.

1. Jack London reported that the smoke from the _____ after the earthquake could be seen one hundred miles away.
2. He could not give an _____ of all the buildings destroyed, because there were too many to mention.
3. He described how the _____ had fled with as much as they could carry.
4. People carried bedding and anything that was _____ to them.
5. The _____ of the fire threatened rich and poor alike.

6. London compared the city to a shipwreck and its people to the _____ that covers the waves when a great ship goes down.
7. With both sides of the street on fire, people were often _____ by burning buildings.
8. Thousands of people were _____, against their will, to abandon their possessions.
9. People had to _____ the hills in order to escape.
10. The great earthquake and fire proved that all the clever _____ of modern life cannot protect us from the forces of nature.

Vocabulary Handbook
See p. R20: Context Clues.

WORDS TO KNOW	compel	contrivance	enumeration	flotsam	refugee
	conflagration	dear	flank	menace	surmount

Letter TO HIS PUBLISHER

Letter by Jack London

Build Background

On November 1, 1899, a Boston publishing company, Houghton Mifflin, accepted Jack London's first book, *The Son of the Wolf,* for publication. Shortly afterward, Houghton asked London to provide biographical information for advertising purposes. London responded in this letter, which he wrote on January 31, 1900. London was 24 years old at the time.

Focus Your Reading

LITERARY ANALYSIS **PRIMARY SOURCE**

A **primary source** is an eyewitness account of an event. Primary sources may include diaries, letters, speeches, news stories, photographs, and pieces of art. These documents often reveal what people thought or how they felt. As you read Jack London's letter, look for clues that explain how London feels about his life.

Gentlemen:—

In reply to yours of January 25th, requesting additional biographical data. I see I shall have to piece out my previous narrative, which, in turn, will make this choppy.

My father was Pennsylvania-born, a soldier, scout, backwoodsman, trapper, and wanderer. My mother was born in Ohio. Both came west independently, meeting and marrying in San Francisco, where I was born January 12, 1876. What little city life I then passed was in my babyhood. My life, from my fourth to my ninth years, was spent upon Californian ranches. I learned to read and write about my fifth year, though I do not remember anything about it. I always could read and write, and have no recollection antedating such a condition. Folks say I simply insisted upon being taught. Was an omniverous reader, principally because reading matter was scarce and I had to be grateful for whatever fell into my hands. . . .

Somewhere around my ninth year we removed to Oakland. . . . Here, most precious to me was a free library.

From my ninth year, with the exception of the hours spent at school (and I earned them by hard labor), my life has been one of toil. It is worthless to give the long sordid list of occupations, none of them trades, all heavy manual labor. Of course I continued to read. Was never without a book. . . . Took a taste for the water. At fifteen left home and went upon a Bay life. . . . I was a salmon fisher, an oyster pirate, a schooner sailor, a fishpatrolman, a longshoresman, and a general sort of bay-faring adventurer—a boy in years and a man amongst men. Always a book, and always reading when the rest were asleep. . . .

Within a week of my seventeenth birthday I shipped before the mast as sailor on a three top-mast sealing schooner. We went to Japan and hunted along the coast north to the Russian side of Bering Sea. This was my longest voyage; I could not again endure one of such length; not because it was tedious or long, but because life was so short. . . .

In the main I am self-educated; have had no mentor but myself. High school or college curriculums I simply selected from, finding it impossible to follow the rut—life and pocket book were both too short. I attended the first year of high school (Oakland), then stayed at home, without coaching, and crammed the next two years into three months and took the entrance examinations, and entered the University of California at Berkeley. Was forced, much against my inclinations, to give this over just prior to the completion of my Freshman Year. . . .

Naturally, my reading early bred in me a desire to write, but my manner of life prevented me attempting it. I have had no literary help or advice of any kind—just been sort of hammering around in the dark till I knocked holes through here and there and caught glimpses of daylight. Common knowledge of magazine methods, etc., came to me as revelation. Not a soul to say here you err and there you mistake. . . .

Am healthy, love exercise, and take little. . . .

Very truly yours,

Jack London.

THINKING *through the* LITERATURE

1. According to London, who is responsible for his education?
2. What is London's attitude about his life so far?
3. Do you think London values people who work hard in life? Explain your answer.

The Author's Style

London's Realism

London writes about what he knows, and he knows about what he writes. Through the use of realistic details, he helps readers feel as though they are in the story, taking part in the adventure.

Key Style Points

Vivid Language London uses vivid language that helps the reader feel the fear, see the experience, and sense the excitement. Notice his choice of vivid verbs, adjectives, and adverbs in this passage from "The King of Mazy May."

Experience-Based Before writing "The King of Mazy May," Jack London had gone to the Klondike. In order to write "The Story of an Eyewitness," he put himself in the path of the fire. Notice how his firsthand description from "The Story of an Eyewitness" helps you to visualize the scene.

Life-and-Death Situations In London's writing, readers are often kept on the edge of their seats, wondering if a character will live or die. Notice the sense of emergency and danger in this passage from "The King of Mazy May."

> ### Vivid Language
> The dogs sprang against the yoke straps, and the sled jerked under way so suddenly as to almost throw him off. Then it curved into the creek, poising perilously on the runner.
> —"The King of Mazy May"

> ### Experience-Based
> Within an hour after the earthquake shock the smoke . . . was a lurid tower visible a hundred miles away. And for three days and nights this lurid tower swayed in the sky, reddening the sun, darkening the day, and filling the land with smoke.
> —"The Story of an Eyewitness"

> ### Life-and-Death Situations
> "Halt!" they cried after him. "Stop, or we'll shoot!"
> But Walt only yelled the harder at the dogs, and dashed around the bend with a couple of revolver bullets singing after him.
> —"The King of Mazy May"

Applications

1. **Active Reading** Go back through the two selections. Which passages were the most memorable to you? Which created the most vivid images?

2. **Writing** Pick an exciting event that you have witnessed, such as a sporting event or a concert. Then write about it, using London's colorful, dramatic style.

3. **Speaking and Listening** Find a particularly dramatic passage from one of the selections in this Jack London author study and read it aloud. Rewrite the passage, removing vivid adjectives and adverbs. Read it again. How has the feeling in the passage changed?

Writing

Narrative Style Look back through the two selections. Write a brief essay in which you define Jack London's writing style. Be sure to support your conclusions with quoted passages from the text. Save your essay in your **Working Portfolio.**

Speaking & Listening

Video Review Watch the video "The Call of the Wild." Prepare a review of the video in which you describe the story's struggle between "good guys" and "bad guys." How does the struggle in "The Call of the Wild" compare with the one in "The King of Mazy May"?

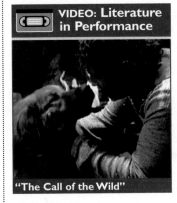

VIDEO: Literature in Performance

"The Call of the Wild"

Research & Technology

Partner, We Are Rich Research the histories of the Klondike Gold Rush of 1897 and the California Gold Rush of 1849. Compare the two. Which one involved more people? was more dangerous? produced more gold? had the greater impact on the region? Try to find an account by someone who experienced it firsthand, and directly quote or paraphrase the information you take from the source. Prepare a report to present to the class. Include illustrations in your report. Be sure to note the sources of your materials.

INTERNET Author Link
www.mcdougallittell.com

Author Study Project
A Presentation on Jack London's Adventures

Working with a small group, create a visual presentation on the life and adventures of Jack London. Include the items listed below. You might want to assign each item to a member of the group. Then work together to assemble and design your presentation.

London and his wife sailed to the South Seas aboard their yacht.

❶ Time Line of Adventure Research the adventures of Jack London. Note what he did and where and when the adventure occurred. Create a time line depicting when these events happened and how long they lasted. Make sure your time line is in chronological order.

❷ Images of London Find photos or drawings of Jack London and the things he wrote about.

Attach the images to the time line where appropriate, or present them separately.

❸ Primary Source For photos and other images that you present separately, choose passages from London's writing that fit the images. Present the passages as captions to the images. Be sure to note the name of the story or article in which you found each passage.

Jack London wrote short stories, novels, essays, and magazine and newspaper articles on a wide variety of topics, such as the Far North, surfing, boxing, farming, social policy, and his adventures sailing the Pacific South Seas.

The White Silence 1899

A young man, his friend, and his friend's wife must face a wrenching, life-or-death decision, 200 miles from the nearest town in the frozen North.

The Call of the Wild 1903

London tells the gripping tale of a pet dog who is stolen from his California home and taken to Alaska to live the brutal life of a sled dog. There he yearns to answer the call of the wild by joining the wolves of the Far North.

The Sea-Wolf 1904

This tale of the sea tells the story of a castaway who is put to work on a ship run by a cruel captain. Hardened by his adventure at sea, the castaway develops strength of character and challenges the cruelty of the captain.

White Fang 1906

The Call of the Wild is seen as a companion to *White Fang*. *White Fang* is the story of a half-dog, half-wolf who is born in the wild but eventually becomes a beloved and trusted human companion. In London's words, White Fang hears "the call of fire and of man—the call which it has been given alone among all animals to answer."

"To Build a Fire" 1908

This short story is the harrowing account of a man who must build a fire in order to survive when the temperature in the Yukon Territory plunges to 75 degrees below zero.

"The Sea Farmer" 1911

"The Sea Farmer" is one of London's South Seas stories and is partly based on London's own life. In the story, a retired sea captain looks back on his career and longs for life on a farm.

Writing Workshop

Autobiographical
Incident

Describing an important event in your life . . .

From Reading to Writing In "The Great Rat Hunt" by Laurence Yep, a boy learns an important truth about his father's view of life. In "Flying," Reeve Lindbergh achieves a greater understanding of her father. For both writers, an experience taught them not only about their fathers but also about themselves. Writing an **autobiographical incident,** or firsthand account, can help you to understand an important event in your life more clearly.

For Your Portfolio

WRITING PROMPT Write an autobiographical essay about an experience that was important to you.

Purpose: To share and explain the significance of an incident
Audience: Your classmates, family members, and friends

Basics in a Box

Autobiographical Incident at a Glance

Beginning

Introduces the incident including the people involved and the setting

Middle

- Describes the incident using descriptive details and dialogue
- Makes the importance clear

End

- Concludes by telling the outcome and importance of the incident
- Presents the writer's feelings about the experience

RUBRIC STANDARDS FOR WRITING

A successful autobiographical incident should

- focus on one well-defined incident
- grab readers' attention at the beginning
- provide background information for the incident
- use elements such as plot, character, and setting as appropriate
- make the order of events clear

- use descriptions or dialogue as appropriate
- include precise language and specific details
- show why the experience was important
- have a strong conclusion that summarizes the importance of the incident

Writing Your Autobiographical Incident

❶ Prewriting

> *What is all knowledge but recorded experience?*
> —Thomas Carlyle, 19th-century writer

The incident you choose to write about does not have to be a major event. In fact, it might be a small moment that was important to you in some way. You might **check** your old diaries or **track down** friends' letters that you've saved. Also try **asking** each person in your family to name an event in your life that he or she remembers. See the **Idea Bank** in the margin for more suggestions. After you've chosen your incident, follow the steps below.

Planning Your Autobiographical Incident Essay

1. **Freewrite about the incident.** Take a few minutes to write down everything that you remember about the incident. What happened? When? Where? Who was involved? How did you feel at the time?

2. **Fill in the details.** Go back to what you wrote about the incident. Flesh out the description of the time, the place, and the people involved. Create a time line to help organize the events.

3. **Think about the significance of the event.** Why do you remember the incident? What did you learn? Did it change you?

4. **Tell your story aloud.** Share your story with others. Can they visualize, or picture, what happened? Do they have questions about the order of events? Take notes on their reactions.

IDEA Bank

1. Your Working Portfolio 📁
Look for ideas in the **Writing** sections you completed earlier.

2. Special Objects
Pull out some of your souvenirs, trophies, and other memorabilia. Write about the circumstances connected to one of the items.

3. Important Areas
List at least one or two incidents that involve important areas in your life such as pets, family members, friends, or school. After finishing your list, choose the event that means the most to you.

Have a question?

See the **Writing Handbook.**
Introductions, p. R36
Chronological Order, p. R44
See **Language Network.**
Prewriting, p. 314
Drafting, p. 317

❷ Drafting

Begin drafting your essay. Remember that you can revise and reorganize your writing later. Try to give readers a strong sense of the incident. Show rather than tell why it is important to you. Include well-chosen sensory details and dialogue as you plan your essay. Remember to start off with a strong beginning and conclude with a memorable ending that reveals your attitude about the incident.

Ask Your Peer Reader

- How could I make my introduction more interesting?
- Where does my essay need more sensory details and dialogue?
- Which parts of my essay are confusing?
- Why do you think the experience was important to me?

Need revising help?

Review the **Rubric**, p. 174

Consider **peer reader** comments
Check **Revision Guidelines**, p. R33

Aggravated by adverbs?

See the **Grammar Handbook**, p. R86

See **Language Network**, Revising, p. 319

SPELLING
From Writing

 As you revise your work, look back at the words you misspelled and determine why you made the errors you did. For additional help, refer to the strategies and generalizations in the **Spelling Handbook** on page R28.

SPEAKING
Opportunity

Turn your written response into an oral presentation.

Publishing
IDEAS

• Rewrite your essay into a skit that can be performed by a small group. Add action and dialogue to make the skit interesting.

• Videotape an interview in which a classmate asks you about the incident you wrote about. After watching the interview, decide which format communicates your story more effectively.

Publishing Options
www.mcdougallittell.com

---

❸ Revising

TARGET SKILL ▶ MAKING THE ORDER OF EVENTS CLEAR

To help your readers understand the order in which things happened, use transitional words and phrases. Some words that indicate time include: *To start off, at first, second, next, then, after, earlier, before, later, finally,* and *at the present time.* Transitions are especially important if you begin your narrative in the middle of the incident or at the conclusion of the incident.

> My parents chose our house. It looked perfect for my
> family, but it did not feel like what I call a "home." We
> didn't belong here. It was empty, dark, and isolated.
> *The night before we moved,*
> ∧ I sat up for a long time thinking about new friends,
> classrooms, teachers, and sports teams.

❹ Editing and Proofreading

TARGET SKILL ▶ COMBINING SENTENCES: COMPOUND SUBJECTS AND PREDICATES Separate sentences can often be combined by using compound subjects or compound predicates. A compound subject consists of two or more subjects joined by the coordinating conjunction *and.* For example: *Mom and Dad were happy.* A compound predicate consists of two predicates joined by a coordinating conjunction such as *and, but,* or *or.* Following is an example of how to combine sentences by forming a compound subject.

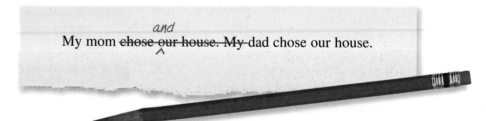

> *and*
> My mom ~~chose our house. My~~ dad chose our house.
> ∧

❺ Reflecting

FOR YOUR WORKING PORTFOLIO What did you learn about the significance of the incident? What did you find hardest about writing this essay? Which part of the process did you enjoy the most? Attach your reflections to the finished essay. Save your **autobiographical incident essay** in your **Working Portfolio.**

Standardized Test Practice

Mixed Review

Review Your Skills

Use the passage and the questions that follow it to check how well you remember the language conventions you've learned in previous grades.

> After it was all over, my father didn't get angry at me or my <u>frends.</u>
> ⁽¹⁾
> Instead he asked if I had a moment to spare. When we <u>are</u> sitting down,
> ⁽²⁾
> he told me about a time in his life when he had acted foolishly. He said
> he <u>couldn't hardly</u> believe the ways in <u>witch</u> the experience changed
> ⁽³⁾   ⁽⁴⁾
> him. Then he asked me what lesson I had learned. I <u>think</u> silently for a
> ⁽⁵⁾
> minute. I tried to put my ideas into words. <u>As I spoke, I realized. my</u>
> ⁽⁶⁾
> <u>father had given me the gift of his trust.</u>

1. What is the correct spelling in sentence 1?
   A. friends
   B. freinds
   C. freands
   D. Correct as is

2. How is sentence 2 best written?
   A. will be
   B. have been
   C. were
   D. Correct as is

3. How is item 3 best written?
   A. couldn't scarcely
   B. could hardly
   C. couldn't barely
   D. Correct as is

4. What is the correct spelling in item 4?
   A. which
   B. wich
   C. whitch
   D. Correct as is

5. How is sentence 5 best written?
   A. thought
   B. was thinking
   C. would be thinking
   D. Correct as is

6. How is sentence 6 best written?
   A. As I spoke, I realized my father had. given me the gift of his trust.
   B. As I spoke, I realized that my father had given. me the gift of his trust.
   C. As I spoke, I realized that my father had given me the gift of his trust.
   D. Correct as is

Self-Assessment

Check your own answers in the **Grammar Handbook**
Verb Tenses, p. R84
Sentence Fragments, p. R75

Insights

The selections in this unit deal with a variety of personal relationships and ways in which characters gain insights into themselves and those around them. What did you learn about how people can be open to and learn more about themselves and others? What kinds of stories did you especially enjoy reading? Explore these questions by completing one or more of the options in each of the following sections.

Looking Deep (1996), Terry Pappas. Pastel, 21" x 20". Collection Steven Pappas.

Reflecting on Theme

OPTION 1

Appreciating Insights In Unit One several characters gain insights into the reasons for a parent's behavior toward them. Both the boy in "Stop the Sun" and the one in "The Great Rat Hunt," for example, come to see how events in the past affect their fathers' behavior. Make a list of the insights the main characters in this unit have about others. Select one insight and write a paragraph explaining how that insight affects the character's relationship with another person.

OPTION 2

Evaluating Reading Experiences Discuss the following questions with your classmates: From which selections did you learn the most about personal relationships? How can the accounts of experiences in literary works help you understand real-life experiences better? Support your choices and opinions with examples drawn from this unit.

OPTION 3

Making Choices With a small group of classmates, pretend that you have been asked to put together a book that will teach people the importance of paying attention to their relationships with others. Which of the selections in this unit would you choose to include in the book? Create a list of four selections that the group can agree on, explaining the reasons for your choices.

Self ASSESSMENT

READER'S NOTEBOOK

Identify one assumption you had about your relationship with a family member, with a friend, or with nature. Then explain how the assumption changed as you read a particular selection in this unit. What was it about the selection that made you see things differently?

REVIEWING YOUR PERSONAL WORD List

Vocabulary Review the new words you learned in this unit. If necessary, use a dictionary to check the meaning of each word.

Spelling Review your list of spelling words. If you're not sure of the correct spelling, use a dictionary or refer to the **Spelling Handbook** on page R28.

Reviewing Literary Concepts

OPTION 1

Exploring Theme A theme is a message about life that a work communicates to the reader. Most themes are not stated directly; they are implied. In a phrase or two, summarize the theme of each selection in this unit. Then look for ways to group the selections according to theme. You may put some selections together because they have similar themes or because their themes are very different. Identify the connection between each group of selections.

Raymond's Run   The Great Rat Hunt

Everyone has a special talent.

OPTION 2

Analyzing Nonfiction Most of the selections in Part 2 of this unit are nonfiction. There are many different kinds of nonfiction, with different styles, purposes, subjects, and audiences. Make a list of the different kinds of nonfiction that appear in Part 2 of the unit, and write a brief explanation of the characteristics of each kind.

📁 Portfolio Building

- **Choices and Challenges—Writing** Several of the writing assignments in this unit asked you to write about a person—in a paragraph, a brief biography, or an essay. From your responses, choose the one that you think best captures the personality or emotions of that person. Then write a cover note explaining the reasons for your choice. Attach the note to the response and add it to your **Presentation Portfolio.** 📁

- **Writing Workshops** In this unit you wrote a personal response and an autobiographical incident. Reread these two pieces and decide which one better shows your strengths as a writer. Explain your choice in a note attached to the piece you have selected, and place the piece in your **Presentation Portfolio.** 📁

- **Additional Activities** Think back to the assignments you completed for **Speaking & Listening** and **Research & Technology.** Keep a record in your portfolio of any assignments that you especially enjoyed or would like to do further work on.

Self ASSESSMENT

📖 READER'S NOTEBOOK

Copy down the following literary terms introduced in this unit. Mark each term that you do not fully understand. Consult the **Glossary of Literary and Reading Terms** on page R124 to clarify the meanings of terms that you have marked.

- character
- setting
- irony
- anecdote
- plot
- theme
- conflict
- memoir
- essay
- main character
- motivation

- resolution
- informative nonfiction
- news story
- first-person point of view
- antagonist
- protagonist
- feature story
- primary source
- falling action
- rising action

Self ASSESSMENT

At this point you may be just beginning your **Presentation Portfolio.** 📁 Are the pieces you have chosen ones you think you'll keep, or do you think you will be replacing them as the year goes on?

Setting GOALS

As you worked through the reading and writing activities in this unit, you probably identified certain skills that you want to work on. Look back through your assignments, your worksheets, and your 📖 **READER'S NOTEBOOK.** Make a list of skills or concepts that you would like to work on in the next unit.

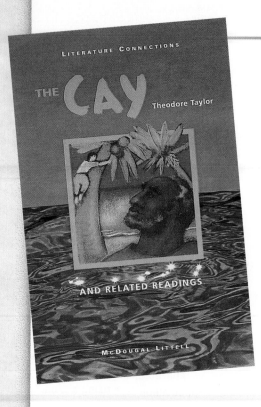

LITERATURE CONNECTIONS
The Cay

BY THEODORE TAYLOR

Against the background of World War II, the author brings together two characters, divided by race and age, on a small remote island in the Caribbean. A German submarine sinks a freighter in the Netherlands Antilles in the Caribbean, and two unlikely companions find each other. The novel takes place over a five-month period, during which the survival of both characters depends upon overcoming prejudice and forming trust. Theodore Taylor has won many awards, including best book of the year by the *New York Times* and *School Library Journal*.

These thematically related readings are provided along with *The Cay*:

Sea Poems
BY LANGSTON HUGHES

from **Survive the Savage Sea**
BY DOUGAL ROBERTSON

The Shark
BY JOHN CIARDI

from **The Killer Storms**
BY GARY JENNINGS

Colin's Island
BY LYNN JOSEPH

More Choices

Alan and Naomie
BY MYRON LEVOY
Alan starts to truly understand the value of life and friendship as he befriends a girl fleeing the war in Europe.

Call of the Wild
BY JACK LONDON
Buck, a stolen sled dog, struggles to survive in the Alaskan wilderness.
A McDougal Littell *Literature Connection*

Cry of the Crow
BY JEAN CRAIGHEAD GEORGE
Taking in a baby crow helps Mandy to better understand her relationship with her family.

Dicey's Song
BY CYNTHIA VOIGT
As Dicey and her siblings settle in with their grandmother, Dicey begins to create new relationships and understand old ones.

In Summer Light
BY ZIBBY O'NEAL
During a summer spent with her distant artist father, Kate discovers much about herself and her own artistic talent.

Park's Quest
BY KATHARINE PATERSON
This novel reveals the effects of the Vietnam War as seen through the eyes of an eleven-year-old boy.

Dragonwings

BY LAURENCE YEP

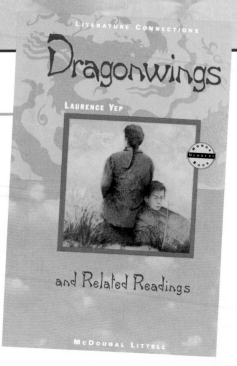

In this historical novel about the risks of growth and change, a young Chinese immigrant comes to San Francisco at the turn of the century to join his father. Father and son encounter prejudice and dangerous people, and also meet some surprising new friends. Along with relatives already settled in Chinatown, they learn how to preserve heritage while pursuing long-held dreams. Laurence Yep draws on historical documents as well as his own imagination in this Newbery Honor Book.

These thematically related readings are provided along with *Dragonwings*:

The Flying Machine
BY RAY BRADBURY

Crazy Boys
BY BEVERLY McLOUGHLAND

The Skydivers
BY JOSEPH COLIN MURPHEY

"The Chinese Must Go"
BY BERNARD A. WEISBERGER

Ginger for the Heart
BY PAUL YEE

The Story of an Eyewitness
BY JACK LONDON

Social Studies Connection

Early Thunder
BY SCOTT BREWSTER
In Massachusetts on the eve of revolution, Daniel West discovers where his true loyalties lie.

I'm Deborah Sampson: A Soldier in the War of the Revolution
BY PATRICIA CLAPP
Deborah, determined to fight in the Revolutionary War, dresses as a man and enlists in the army.

Sarah Bishop
BY SCOTT O'DELL
Sarah discovers her own inner strength after her brother and father take opposite sides during the Revolutionary War.

My Brother Sam Is Dead
BY JAMES L. AND CHRISTOPHER COLLIER
Tim struggles to understand his brother's decision to join the rebel forces during the Revolutionary war.

My Brother, My Enemy
BY MADGE HARRAH
Fourteen-year-old Robert is caught in the middle of Bacon's Rebellion.

The Sherwood Ring
BY ELIZABETH MARIE POPE
Peggy discovers that her uncle's house is frequented by the ghosts of a young woman and a British officer from the American Revolution.

Rising
to the
Challenge

You must do the things you think you cannot do.

ELEANOR ROOSEVELT
FIRST LADY

To Sail The Blue Boat II © Gina Gilmour/
Omni Photo Communications.

The Literature You'll Read

The Concepts You'll Study

Vocabulary and Reading Comprehension
Vocabulary Focus: Exploring Meanings in Figurative Language
Making Inferences
Reading a Narrative Poem
Making Generalizations
Noting Sensory Details
Making Inferences

Writing and Language Conventions
Writing Workshop: Poem
Past and Present Perfect Tenses
Subject-Verb Agreement

Literary Analysis
Genre Focus: Poetry
Speaker
Sound Devices
Style
Figurative Language
Characterization

Speaking and Listening
Interpretive Reading of Poetry
Poetry Reading
Persuasive Speech
Oral Presentation
Oral Report

*P*oetry

Poetry is [an] attempt to paint the color of the wind.
—Maxwell Bodenheim, poet

Poetry is the most compact form of literature. Using a few carefully chosen words, poets express a range of emotions, tell epic stories, and reveal truths. To say so much in so few words, poets use a variety of **forms, sound devices, imagery,** and **figurative language.** Each poem is told through a voice, called the **speaker.** The speaker is not necessarily the poet, yet often poets do write as themselves and speak directly to the reader. Though poets have many different styles, most poems contain the key elements listed below.

Key Elements of Poetry

- form and structure
- sound
- imagery
- figurative language

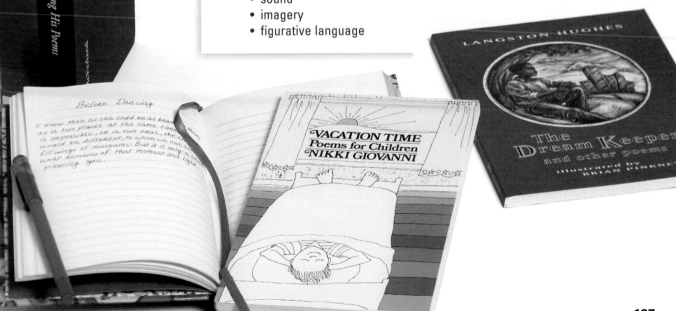

Form and Structure

Poems are written in **lines,** which can vary in length. The poet chooses the line length to fit the rhythm, feeling, or thought expressed in the poem. Lines are grouped together in **stanzas.** These are sections of the poem separated by a space.

The way a poem's lines and words are arranged on the page is its **form.** There are a variety of poetic forms. The most common are the ballad, the epic, the ode, the sonnet, and free verse. The poet chooses a specific form based on the message or theme that he or she is trying to express.

Ballad—a type of narrative poem that tells a story. A ballad is meant to be sung or recited. Because it tells a story, a ballad has a setting, a plot, and characters. Most have regular patterns of rhythm and rhyme.

Epic—a long narrative poem about the adventures of a hero whose actions reflect the ideals and values of a nation or group.

Ode—a type of lyric poem that addresses broad, serious themes such as justice, truth, or beauty.

Sonnet—a poem that has a formal structure, containing fourteen lines and a specific rhyme scheme and meter. The sonnet, which means "little song," can be used for a variety of topics.

Free Verse—poetry without a regular pattern of rhyme, rhythm, or meter. Free verse is used for a variety of subjects.

YOUR TURN Look at the poems shown here. What do you notice about the forms? Refer to the number of lines and stanzas.

Mother to Son
by Langston Hughes

Well, son, I'll tell you:
Life for me ain't been no crystal stair.
It's had tacks in it,
And splinters,
5 And boards torn up,
And places with no carpet on the floor—
Bare.
But all the time
I'se been a-climbin' on,
10 And reachin' landin's,
And turnin' corners,
And sometimes goin' in the dark
Where there ain't been no light.
So boy, don't you turn back.
15 Don't you set down on the steps
'Cause you finds it's kinder hard.
Don't you fall now—
For I'se still goin', honey,
I'se still climbin',
20 And life for me ain't been no crystal stair.

Stairs, Provincetown (1920), Charles Demuth. Gouache and pencil on cardboard, 23½" × 19½" (59.7 × 49.5 cm). The Museum of Modern Art, New York. Gift of Abby Aldrich Rockefeller. Photograph Copyright © 1995 The Museum of Modern Art, New York.

Free Verse

Simile:
Willow and Ginkgo
BY EVE MERRIAM

The willow is like an etching,
Fine-lined against the sky.
The ginkgo is like a crude sketch,
Hardly worthy to be signed.

5 The willow's music is like a soprano
Delicate and thin.
The ginkgo's tune is like a chorus
With everyone joining in.

The willow is sleek as a velvet-nosed calf;
10 The ginkgo is leathery as an old bull.
The willow's branches are like silken thread;
The ginkgo's like stubby rough wool.

The willow is like a nymph with streaming hair;
Wherever it grows, there is green and gold and fair.
15 The willow dips to the water,
Protected and precious, like the king's favorite daughter.

The ginkgo forces its way through gray concrete:
Like a city child, it grows up in the street.
Thrust against the metal sky,
20 Somehow it survives and even thrives.

My eyes feast upon the willow,
But my heart goes to the ginkgo

Ginko (1988), Atsuko Kato. Oil on canvas, 100 x 70 cm. Courtesy of the artist.

Formal Structure

Sound

Besides form, poets use **sound devices** to reinforce the meaning of a poem. Rhyme, meter, and word choice are the key sound devices in a poem. Use the excerpts to the right, from "The Charge of the Light Brigade" by Alfred, Lord Tennyson, to help you understand the sound devices described below.

Rhyme is the repetition of sounds at the ends of words, such as *shell* and *well.* **Internal rhyme** is the use of rhyming words within a line. " **End rhyme** is the use of rhymes at the ends of lines. Notice the end rhyme in the stanza at the right: *shell/fell/well/Hell.* The pattern of end rhymes in a poem is called its **rhyme scheme.**

> **RHYME**
>
> Storm'd at with shot and shell,
> While horse and hero fell,
> They that had fought so well
> Came thro' the jaws of Death,
> Back from the mouth of Hell,

A poem's **rhythm** is the pattern of sound created by stressed and unstressed syllables in a line of poetry. Stressed syllables are those word parts that are read with emphasis, while unstressed syllables are less emphasized. The first four lines of the stanza below at the right have the stressed (´) and unstressed (˘) syllables marked. **Meter** is a regular pattern of stressed and unstressed syllables, which can be repeated from line to line. Meter, rhythm, and rhyme produce a musical quality in the poem. To hear the rhythmic pattern, read the poem aloud.

Repetition refers to sounds, words, phrases, or lines that are stated or used more than once in a poem. Poets use repetition to emphasize an idea or convey a certain feeling. In the excerpt to the right, the first two lines include "Half a league" three times. This emphasizes how far the soldiers have to go. The fourth and the eighth lines of the stanza include the phrase "Rode the six hundred." This repetition emphasizes the number of soldiers before they started their attack. **Alliteration** is the repetition of consonant sounds at the beginnings of words. Notice the repetition of sounds in this phrase: "then no one knows your name."

> **RHYTHM AND REPETITION**
>
> Hálf ă leăgue, hálf ă leăgue,
> Hálf ă leăgue ónwărd,
> Áll ĭn thĕ vállĕy ŏf Déath
> Róde thĕ sĭx húndrĕd.
> "Forward, the Light Brigade!
> Charge for the guns!" he said:
> Into the valley of Death
> Rode the six hundred.

YOUR TURN Copy the stanza used to illustrate rhythm and repetition and mark the stressed and unstressed syllables in lines 5–8.

Imagery and Figurative Language

Imagery refers to words and phrases that appeal to the five senses. Poets use imagery to create a picture in the reader's mind or to remind the reader of a familiar sensation. In the example to the right from "Mi Madre," the reader can see and feel the sensations of rain and sun in the line "She sprinkles raindrops in my face on a sunny day."

Figurative language conveys a meaning beyond the ordinary, literal meaning. One type of figurative language is the **simile,** a comparison of two things with a common quality. A simile is expressed using the words *like* or *as.* In the excerpt from "Simile: Willow and Ginkgo," each line contains a simile; for example, "The willow is sleek as a velvet-nosed calf." What other similes can you find in the excerpt? A **metaphor** is also a comparison of two things with a common quality, but it does not use the words *like* or *as.* In "Mi Madre," the words "firm body" represent the earth. When a poet describes an animal or object as if it were human or had human qualities, that is **personification.** In "Mi Madre," Pat Mora describes the desert as her mother—a living woman who can feed, comfort, and heal her child.

YOUR TURN Read the stanzas at the right. What examples of figurative language can you find?

IMAGERY AND FIGURATIVE LANGUAGE

I say tease me.
She sprinkles raindrops in my face on a
  sunny day.

I say frighten me.
She shouts thunder, flashes lightning.

I say comfort me.
She invites me to lay on her firm body.

—Pat Mora, "Mi Madre"

The willow is sleek as a velvet-nosed calf;
The ginkgo is leathery as an old bull.
The willow's branches are like silken thread;
The ginkgo's like stubby rough wool.

—Eve Merriam
from "Simile: Willow and Ginkgo"

Symbol

A **symbol** is a person, a place, an object, or an action that stands for something beyond itself. Readers can usually recognize what a symbol stands for. For example, "prison" is a place that symbolizes confinement.

Reading Poetry

Poetry is a blending of sound and sense. The musicality, **rhythm, form, imagery,** and feeling of a poem, along with the poem's message, create an overall effect on the reader. Read these strategies to help you get the most from the poems that you read.

How to Apply the Strategies

Preview the poem and read it aloud a few times. Notice the poem's form: the shape it takes on the page, the number of lines, and whether the lines are divided into stanzas. Look for end punctuation to tell you where each thought ends. As you read, listen for rhymes, rhythm, and the overall sound of the words.

Visualize the images. Create a mental picture of the poet's images and comparisons. Do the images remind you of feelings or experiences you have had?

Think about the words and phrases. Think about the choice of words and what they add to the poem. Do the words suggest more than their literal meaning? Are any words or phrases repeated?

Make inferences. Make logical guesses based on clues in the poem. Search for details that reveal something about the identity of the poem's speaker. Look for clues that hint at the speaker's experiences, attitudes, and personality.

Try to figure out the poem's theme. Ask: What's the point of this poem? What message is the poet trying to send or help me understand?

Here's how Jessica uses the strategies:

*"With poetry, you get to see how another person thinks and feels. I always wonder about the speaker of the poem—is it the poet or someone he or she made up? I usually **make inferences** about the speaker based on the poem. I **connect** to the words and images because I have shared similar experiences."*

Mother to Son
by LANGSTON HUGHES

Speech to the Young
Speech to the Progress-Toward
by GWENDOLYN BROOKS

Connect to Your Life

Facing Life's Obstacles The following poems focus on facing life's challenges. What kinds of problems do people experience? What kinds of barriers are difficult for them to overcome? With a group of classmates, share your ideas and consider what gives some people the determination to overcome obstacles.

Build Background

The African-American Experience The poetry of both Langston Hughes and Gwendolyn Brooks reflects the experience of growing up African American in the early part of the 20th century.

Hughes was first recognized as an important literary figure during the 1920s. Many of his poems portray the lives of ordinary African Americans.

Much of Brooks's poetry also paints a vivid picture of the lives of African Americans. Her first collection, *A Street in Bronzeville,* describes the lives of the residents of a poor neighborhood in Chicago, the city in which Brooks has lived from an early age.

Focus Your Reading

LITERARY ANALYSIS **SPEAKER**

The voice that speaks the poem's words is called the **speaker**. In the poem "Mother to Son," the very first words—"Well, son, I'll tell you"—give a clue as to who the speaker is. Sometimes the speaker is a person whom the poet has created. As you read the poems that follow, notice the personality and attitude of each speaker.

ACTIVE READING **MAKING INFERENCES**

In order to understand the speaker of a poem, you need to **make inferences**—logical guesses or conclusions— based on clues in the poem. As you read each of these poems, consider the following:

- what the title tells you about the speaker
- what you learn about the speaker's experiences
- what advice the speaker gives

READER'S NOTEBOOK For each poem, make a chart like the one shown. As you read the poem, use the chart to record your inferences about the speaker.

Clue	Inference
The title is "Mother to Son."	The speaker is a woman.

Mother to Son

by Langston Hughes

Well, son, I'll tell you:
Life for me ain't been no crystal stair.
It's had tacks in it,
And splinters,
5 And boards torn up,
And places with no carpet on the floor—
Bare.
But all the time
I'se been a-climbin' on,
10 And reachin' landin's,
And turnin' corners,
And sometimes goin' in the dark
Where there ain't been no light.
So boy, don't you turn back.
15 Don't you set down on the steps
'Cause you finds it's kinder hard.
Don't you fall now—
For I'se still goin', honey,
I'se still climbin',
20 And life for me ain't been no crystal stair.

Stairs, Provincetown (1920), Charles Demuth. Gouache and pencil on cardboard, 23½" × 19½" (59.7 × 49.5 cm). The Museum of Modern Art, New York. Gift of Abby Aldrich Rockefeller. Photograph Copyright © 1995 The Museum of Modern Art, New York.

THINKING *through the* LITERATURE

1. What was your reaction to the **speaker** of this poem? Share your thoughts with a partner.

2. When reading the poem aloud, did you note the difference in rhythm between the short and the long lines?

3. What do you think the speaker means when she says that her life has not been a "crystal stair"?

> **Think About:**
> • what images the word *crystal* brings to mind
> • what kind of life the mother has lived
> • how she has handled the difficulties in her life

Speech to the Young
Speech to the Progress-Toward
(Among them Nora and Henry III)

by Gwendolyn Brooks

Say to them,
say to the down-keepers,
the sun-slappers,
the self-soilers,
5 the harmony-hushers,
"Even if you are not ready for day
it cannot always be night."
You will be right.
For that is the hard home-run.

10 Live not for battles won.
Live not for the-end-of-the-song.
Live in the along.

Copyright © Nicholas Wilton.

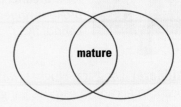

THINKING through the LITERATURE

Connect to the Literature

1. **What Do You Think?**
   What do you think about the advice given by the speaker in Brooks's poem? Share your ideas with a classmate.

   Comprehension Check
   • What phrases in the poem refer to people who have a negative effect on others?
   • According to the speaker, what should the reader say to such people?

Think Critically

2. **ACTIVE READING | MAKING INFERENCES**
   Review the charts in your **READER'S NOTEBOOK** in which you made **inferences** about the two **speakers.** What clues helped you to learn about each poem's speaker? Describe each speaker.

3. What do you think is the meaning of the last three lines of Brooks's poem?

   Think About:
   • the meaning of "the-end-of-the-song"
   • the meaning of "Live in the along"

4. In your opinion, what does the speaker think is in danger of being lost if young people do not follow the advice given in the poem?

5. What might make the advice difficult to follow?

6. What character trait is shared by the people mentioned in lines 2–5? Do you know anyone like this? Describe the person or persons.

Extend Interpretations

7. **COMPARING TEXTS** Which poem, "Speech to the Young . . ." or "Mother to Son," seems more hopeful? Explain your choice.

8. **Connect to Life** Which of the two poems do you think offers the best advice for a teenager today? Give reasons for your choice.

Literary Analysis

SPEAKER The voice the reader "hears" while reading the poem—like the narrator in a short story—is called the **speaker.** In some poems, the speaker expresses the feelings of the poet. When reading a poem, it is usually important to get a sense of who the speaker is in order to fully understand the work.

Activity Using a Venn diagram like the one below, compare and contrast the speakers of these two poems. Consider such things as the speakers' personalities, their backgrounds and experiences, and their attitudes toward life.

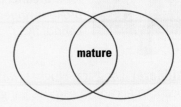

Speaker in "Speech to the Young . . ."   Speaker in "Mother to Son"

mature

CHOICES *and* CHALLENGES

Writing

Advice Poem Write a poem titled "Father to Daughter" or one about some other relationship you would like to write about. In the poem, one of the two people should share his or her thoughts and feelings about life. Be sure to include well-chosen details that reveal the speaker's attitude about the subject. Place the poem in your **Working Portfolio.**

Speaking & Listening

Poetry on Tape Tape-record readings of these poems. Include background music or sound effects to help make their meaning clear. Be sure to match your voice, expression, and tone to the message of the poem. Play your tape for the class.

<u>**Speaking and Listening Handbook**</u>
See p. R106: Oral Interpretation.

Research & Technology

Renaissance Man Langston Hughes was one of the best-known writers of the 1920s literary movement known as the Harlem Renaissance. Use library and Internet sources to research this movement. What other writers were associated with it? What made their work unique? Prepare a short report on your findings. Be sure to note your sources.

Langston Hughes
1902–1967

"Hold fast to dreams, for if dreams die, life is a broken-winged bird that cannot fly."

Trailblazer Langston Hughes was one of the first African Americans to earn his living solely from writing. Although he wrote novels, short stories, plays, song lyrics, newspaper columns, and radio scripts, he is best known for his poetry. *The Dream Keeper* is one of his most famous collections.

Big Break Hughes was "discovered" while working as a busboy. He left three of his poems at a table where the poet Vachel Lindsay was dining. Lindsay was impressed with Hughes's works and presented them at one of his own poetry readings. Soon afterward, Hughes's writing career took off.

Gwendolyn Brooks
1917–2000

"I am not a scholar. I'm just a writer who loves to write and will always write."

Early Support When Gwendolyn Brooks was growing up in Chicago, both of her parents encouraged and supported her writing. Her father presented her with a desk to write on, and her mother excused her from most household chores.

Prizewinner, Prize Giver In her early poetry, Brooks wrote about the lives of ordinary African Americans. In 1950, she became the first African-American author to receive a Pulitzer Prize, for her collection of poetry *Annie Allen*. Brooks also donated prize money to be given to winners of Illinois poetry contests. She was named the poet laureate of Illinois in 1968.

The Charge of the Light Brigade

by ALFRED, LORD TENNYSON

Connect to Your Life

What Is Bravery? Think of an occasion on which you witnessed or heard about an act of bravery that impressed you. What happened? What was at stake? Why do you consider this to be a memorable moment? Describe the incident to a small group of classmates. Then, as a group, try to agree on a definition of bravery that includes all of the examples that you have discussed.

Build Background

WORLD HISTORY

"The Charge of the Light Brigade" is a narrative poem inspired by a real-life tragedy. Tennyson wrote the poem after reading a newspaper account of a battle that occurred during the Crimean [krī-mē' ən] War (1853–1856).

The Crimean War was fought between Russia and a group of nations that included Great Britain. On October 25, 1854, at Balaklava [băl' ə-klăv' ə] in southern Ukraine, a British cavalry unit called the Light Brigade, armed only with swords, was ordered to charge Russian gunners. As the poem begins, Tennyson describes the Light Brigade riding toward the Russian artillery. Russia eventually lost the war.

Ukraine

UKRAINE

CRIMEA

Black Sea

N W E S

Balaklava

Miles 0 50 100

Focus Your Reading

LITERARY ANALYSIS   SOUND DEVICES

Poetry is meant to be read aloud. In the poem you are about to read, the poet uses short lines and phrases to create a fast-paced **rhythm,** or beat, as he describes the sights and sounds of battle:

> *Half a league, half a league,*
> *Half a league onward,*
> *All in the valley of Death*
> *   Rode the six hundred.*

Read the poem aloud several times and listen to the poem's rhythm. Notice examples of **rhyme** (a likeness of sounds at the ends of words), such as in *shell* and *fell,* and the **repetition** of short words and phrases. Be aware of how such **sound devices** contribute to the poem's overall impact.

ACTIVE READING   READING A NARRATIVE POEM

"The Charge of the Light Brigade" is a **narrative poem,** that is, one that tells a story. Like a short story, this type of poem has a plot, a setting, and characters.

READER'S NOTEBOOK As you read Tennyson's poem, keep a list of the events that occur.

The Charge of the Light Brigade

by Alfred, Lord Tennyson

Half a league,[1] half a league,
Half a league onward,
All in the valley of Death
   Rode the six hundred.
5 "Forward, the Light Brigade!
Charge for the guns!" he said:
Into the valley of Death
   Rode the six hundred.

"Forward, the Light Brigade!"
10 Was there a man dismay'd?
Not tho' the soldier knew
   Some one had blunder'd:
Theirs not to make reply,
Theirs not to reason why,
15 Theirs but to do and die:
Into the valley of Death
   Rode the six hundred.

Cannon to right of them,
Cannon to left of them,
20 Cannon in front of them
   Volley'd[2] and thunder'd;
Storm'd at with shot and shell,
Boldly they rode and well,
Into the jaws of Death,
25 Into the mouth of Hell
   Rode the six hundred.

Small sword and scabbard (about 1790).
The Hermitage, St. Petersburg, Russia.

---

1. **league:** distance of three miles.
2. **volleyed:** fired a rapid series of shots.

Detail of *The Charge of the Light Brigade* (early 1900s), Christopher Clark. Historical Pictures/Stock Montage.

Flash'd all their sabers bare,
Flash'd as they turn'd in air
Sabring the gunners there,
30 Charging an army, while
    All the world wonder'd:
Plunged in the battery smoke,
Right thro' the line they broke;
Cossack and Russian
35 Reel'd from the saber-stroke,
    Shatter'd and sunder'd.[3]
Then they rode back, but not,
    Not the six hundred.

Cannon to right of them,
40 Cannon to left of them,
Cannon behind them
    Volley'd and thunder'd;
Storm'd at with shot and shell,
While horse and hero fell,
45 They that had fought so well
Came thro' the jaws of Death.
Back from the mouth of Hell,
All that was left of them,
    Left of six hundred.

50 When can their glory fade?
O, the wild charge they made!
    All the world wonder'd.
Honor the charge they made!
Honor the Light Brigade,
55   Noble six hundred!

---

3. **sundered:** broken apart; split into pieces.

Connect to the Literature

1. What Do You Think? What is your reaction to what happened to the soldiers of the Light Brigade?

Comprehension Check
- Why does the brigade receive the order to charge?
- What is waiting for them in the valley?
- What is the outcome of the charge?

Think Critically

2. Describe the image you consider most powerful in the poem. Why did you choose this image?

3. **ACTIVE READING** **READING A NARRATIVE POEM** Review the chart you completed in your **READER'S NOTEBOOK**. How does the effect of this **narrative poem** differ from the effect a written account of the same event might have?

4. How do you think the **speaker** of the poem feels about the Light Brigade? Support your answer with examples from the poem.

5. Do you consider the soldiers of the Light Brigade to be heroes? Why or why not?

> **Think About:**
> - lines 11–12 of the poem
> - how the soldiers fought
> - the tragic outcome of the charge

6. In your opinion, what is the **theme**, or message, of this poem?

Extend Interpretations

7. What If? What do you think might have happened if a number of soldiers had refused to obey the order to charge?

8. Different Perspectives How might the Russian gunners have viewed the charge? Describe the attack from their **point of view.**

9. Connect to Life Do you think a military tragedy like this could happen today? Why or why not?

Literary Analysis

SOUND DEVICES "The Charge of the Light Brigade" shows the use of poetic **sound devices,** such as **rhyme, rhythm** (the pattern of stressed and unstressed syllables in lines), and **repetition** of sounds, words, phrases, and lines.

Tennyson uses and repeats short lines and phrases to create a fast-paced rhythm. The rhythm of the following example suggests the pounding of horses' hooves:

> Cánnŏn tŏ ríght ŏf thĕm,
> Cánnŏn tŏ léft ŏf thĕm . . .

The syllables read with more emphasis (stressed) are marked with ´. The weaker-sounding syllables (unstressed) are marked with ˇ.

Group Activity Working in small groups, choose a stanza from "The Charge of the Light Brigade." Mark the rhythmic pattern, as shown in the example above. Note any examples of sound devices such as rhyme and repetition. Discuss how these help to make the stanza's sound devices effective.

CHOICES and CHALLENGES

Writing

Story Poem Write your own narrative poem about an act of bravery that impressed you. Be sure to include setting, characters, and a plot. Use sound devices and imagery in telling the events. Include your draft in your **Working Portfolio.**

Writing Workshop
See p. 252: Basics in a Box.

Speaking & Listening

Poetry Reading Recite "The Charge of the Light Brigade" for your class. Use your voice, tone, and gestures to enhance the meaning of the poem.

Speaking and Listening Handbook
See p. R106: Oral Interpretation.

Research & Technology

Dig for Answers Using library and Internet sources, research the Crimean War. Present an oral report that answers the following questions: What were the causes of the war? Which countries fought against the Russians? Who was known as "the Lady with the Lamp," and why was she famous? What happened to the surviving members of the Light Brigade? Be sure to support your main ideas with details.

Research and Technology Handbook
See p. R114: Getting Information Electronically.

INTERNET **Research Starter**
www.mcdougallittell.com

Alfred, Lord Tennyson
1809–1892

". . . I was nearer thirty than twenty before I was anything of an artist."

Family Collaboration Born the fourth son in a family of twelve children, Tennyson grew up in Somersby, England. In 1827, his first published poetry appeared in the collection *Poems by Two Brothers*. When the poems were favorably received, Alfred felt encouraged to continue writing.

Silent Decade In 1833, Tennyson's best friend, Arthur Hallam, died suddenly. Overwhelmed with grief, Tennyson wrote but published little during the next ten years.

Royal Recognition In 1850, *In Memoriam,* a collection of poems in memory of Arthur Hallam, became very popular. Also very popular was *Idylls of the King,* his poems about King Arthur, begun in 1859. Queen Victoria named him poet laureate, or court poet. In this role, Tennyson wrote poems about national events, including the doomed charge at Balaklava.

AUTHOR ACTIVITY
A Fitting Resting Place Tennyson is buried in the Poets' Corner at Westminster Abbey in London, England. Find out more about this honor. What other poets are buried there?

Mr. Misenheimer's Garden

by CHARLES KURALT

Connect to Your Life

A Special Place In the essay you are about to read, people find peace and satisfaction among the azaleas, dogwoods, and pine trees of a Virginia garden. Do you or someone you know have a favorite place where you can daydream and relax? What words come to mind when you hear the word *relaxation?* Create a word web to explore your associations. Then share your thoughts with a small group of classmates.

Build Background

On the Road After working for years as a news correspondent for the Columbia Broadcasting System (CBS), Charles Kuralt convinced the network to let him roam the back roads for stories that celebrated the lives of ordinary Americans.

In 1967 Kuralt and his crew began their travels around the country in a secondhand camper. Their stories became part of the *On the Road* feature of the *CBS Evening News* between 1967 and 1980.

WORDS TO KNOW
Vocabulary Preview

battalion   existence
coax   nurseryman
cultivation

Focus Your Reading

LITERARY ANALYSIS | **STYLE**

How something is said or written in literature is referred to as **style.** Elements that define a writer's style include word choice, sentence length, figurative language, and tone—the writer's attitude toward the subject. A writer makes choices about how to use these elements to make a piece of writing sound formal or informal, serious or funny, conversational or academic. As you read Kuralt's essay, notice how he describes details and presents information.

ACTIVE READING | **MAKING GENERALIZATIONS**

A broad statement about a person or a group is called a **generalization.** To make a generalization, look for patterns in the behavior or speech of the person or group. Try to apply a statement that would describe the patterns overall.

When generalizations are too broad to be accurate, they are called **overgeneralizations.** For example, the statement "All eighth graders like outdoor sports" is not accurate and is considered an overgeneralization.

READER'S NOTEBOOK As you read this essay, pay attention to what Mr. Misenheimer says and does. Jot down his statements and actions. Then use those details to make a generalization about Mr. Misenheimer's attitude toward life and gardening.

Mr. Misenheimer's GARDEN
BY CHARLES KURALT

Hot Pink Dahlias, David Peikon ©1997. Acrylic on canvas, 30"x30". Courtesy of the Mark Humphrey Gallery, Southampton, NY.

We've been wandering the back roads since 1967, and we've been to a few places we'll never forget.

One of them was on Route 10, Surry County, Virginia. We rolled in here on a day in the spring of 1972 thinking this was another of those little roadside rest stops. But there were flowers on the picnic tables. That was the first surprise. And beyond the tables, we found a paradise, a beautiful garden of thirteen acres, bright with azaleas,[1] thousands of them, and bordered by dogwoods[2] in bloom, and laced by a mile of paths in the shade of tall pines. In all our travels, it was the loveliest garden I'd ever seen. It made me wonder how large a <u>battalion</u> of state-employed gardeners it took to keep the place up. The answer was it took one old man, and he was nobody's employee. Walter Misenheimer,[3] a retired <u>nurseryman</u>, created all this in the woods next to his house, created it alone after he retired at the age of seventy. He was eighty-three when I met him and was spending every day tending his garden for the pleasure of strangers who happened to stop.

Walter Misenheimer: I like people, and this is my way of following out some of the teachings of my parents. When I was a youngster, one of the things they said was, "If you don't try to make the world just a little bit nicer when you leave here, what is the reason for man's <u>existence</u> in the first place?" I have tried to give it to the state. The Parks Department says it is too small for them. The Highway Department says it is too big for them.

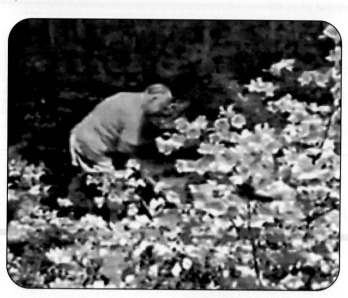

Walter Misenheimer at work in his garden.

Kuralt: What's going to happen to this place after you're gone?

Misenheimer: Well, I imagine that within a very few years, this will be undergrowth, or nature will take it over again.

Kuralt: You mean, it's not going to survive?

Misenheimer: I doubt it.

Kuralt: That's a terribly discouraging thing, isn't it?

Misenheimer: Well, that's the way I see it now.

---

1. **azaleas** (ə-zāl′yəz): shrubs having showy flowers of various colors.
2. **dogwoods:** trees found in eastern North America that have small greenish flowers surrounded by four large white or pink growths.
3. **Walter Misenheimer** (mī′zən-hī′mər).

WORDS TO KNOW

battalion (bə-tăl′yen) *n.* a large body of organized people, especially troops; a great number
nurseryman (nûr′sə-rē-mən) *n.* person employed by a nursery, where plants are grown for sale, transplanting, or experimentation
existence (ĭg-zĭs′təns) *n.* the fact or state of being real

We watched for a while as people enjoyed the beauty of Walter Misenheimer's garden. And we left, and a few years later somebody sent me a clipping from the Surry County paper. It said Walter Misenheimer had died. I wondered what would happen to his garden. I wondered whether the Virginia sun still lights the branches of the dogwood, which he planted there.

Well, it does. Some stories have happy endings. Walter Misenheimer's garden does survive, and so does his spirit, in Haeja Namkoong.[4] *It seems that she stopped by the garden just a few months after we did, eleven years ago.*

Haeja Namkoong:
We slowed down and saw a sign and picnic tables and a lot of flowers blooming. We came to the picnic table, found a water spigot, helped ourselves, and we were sort of curious as to what this place was all about. Finally, we saw the old man sort of wobbling around and coming 'cross the lawn, saying "Hello," and just waving to us to stop. I guess he was afraid we were going to leave.

To please the old man, and herself, Haeja Namkoong stayed the afternoon with him, walking in his garden. It made her remember, she says, something she wanted once.

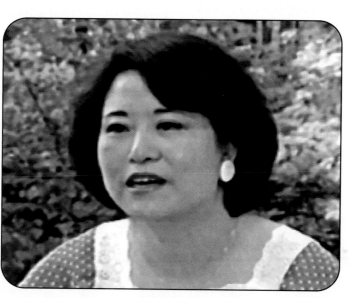
Haeja Namkoong in the garden.

Haeja: I grew up in a large city in Korea[5], and I have never really seen rice grow. I always dreamed about living in the country, about a small, little cabin in the wilderness, with lots of flowers. That's what I dreamed about, but I guess that was just childhood dreams.

When the sun went down that day, the young woman said goodbye to the old man and headed home to Boston, but the roadside Eden called her back. That is, Walter Misenheimer did. He phoned her, long distance, and asked her to come for a little while and help in the garden.

Haeja: He was sort of pleading with me, "Please come down. Just help me for a couple of weeks."

A couple of weeks only, and then a few more, and then it was Christmas. Haeja Namkoong was twenty-six. She had no family. Neither did Walter Misenheimer and his wife.

Haeja: From wildflowers to man-grown shrubberies, he taught me. I was interested in learning the whole thing. I was out here almost every day with him.

---

4. **Haeja Namkoong** (hā′jä näm′gōōng′).
5. **Korea** (kə-rē′ə): a former country in eastern Asia located on a peninsula between the Yellow Sea and the Sea of Japan. It was divided into North Korea and South Korea after World War II.

They became as father and daughter working in the garden, and in time Haeja Namkoong was married in the garden.

Haeja: He was very proud to give me away. I guess he never thought, since he didn't have any children of his own, he would give someone away.

Brown earth was <u>coaxed</u> by the gentle old man into green growth and flowering red and pink and white. The earth rewards every loving attention it is paid. People repay such love, too, in memory.

Haeja: I was very, very close to my mother. But other than my mother, I can't remember anyone that loved me so much and cared for me so much as Mr. Misenheimer.

The garden is still here. Walter Misenheimer died in 1979 and left it to Haeja Namkoong.

She pays a caretaker, Ed Trible, to help keep it beautiful for anybody who passes by. Haeja and her husband and their children live in Richmond now, but they return on weekends to work in the garden.

Haeja: So, knowing how much the garden meant to him, I want to keep it up and carry on.

Walter Misenheimer told me that he expected when he was gone the garden would soon be overgrown. He might have known better. His garden shows that something grows from seeds and <u>cultivation</u>. And if what you plant is love and kindness, something grows from that, too.

Haeja: Look at this purple one.

Child: I like the red.

Haeja: Aren't they pretty? ❖

What Is Success?

by Ralph Waldo Emerson

The Gardener (Le jardinier) (1882–83), Georges Pierre Seurat. Oil on wood, 6¼" x 9¾". The Metropolitan Museum of Art, Bequest of Miss Adelaide Milton de Groot (1876–1967), (67. 187. 102). Photograph by Malcolm Varon, © 1985 The Metropolitan Museum of Art.

What is success?
To laugh often and much;
To win the respect of intelligent people
and the affection of children;
5   To earn the appreciation of honest critics
and endure the betrayal of false friends;
To appreciate beauty;
To find the best in others;
To leave the world a bit better, whether by
10   a healthy child, a garden patch
or a redeemed[1] social condition;
To know even one life has breathed
easier because you have lived;
This is to have succeeded.

---

1. **redeemed:** changed from worse to better

Connect to the Literature

1. **What Do You Think?** What are your impressions of Walter Misenheimer and Haeja Namkoong?

   Comprehension Check
   • What did Mr. Misenheimer think would happen to the garden after his death?
   • What did happen to the garden after his death?

Think Critically

2. Describe the relationship between Mr. Misenheimer and Ms. Namkoong.

   Think About:
   • the advice Mr. Misenheimer received from his parents
   • Mr. Misenheimer's thoughts and feelings about what would happen to the garden after he died
   • Ms. Namkoong's childhood dream in Korea
   • the feelings each one has about the garden

3. **ACTIVE READING** **MAKING GENERALIZATIONS**
   Look back at the details you noted in your **READER'S NOTEBOOK** about Mr. Misenheimer's actions and statements. Using this information, what **generalizations** can you make about Mr. Misenheimer?

4. Kuralt writes, "If what you plant is love and kindness, something grows from that." What do you think he means? Do you agree with this statement? Why or why not?

5. What do you think is the **author's purpose** in writing this essay?

Extend Interpretations

6. **COMPARING TEXTS** What feelings about nature do you think that Mr. Misenheimer and Barbara Kingsolver, the author of *High Tide in Tucson*, share?

7. **Connect to Life** Do you think that a beautiful garden can have a positive effect on a person? Explain.

Literary Analysis

STYLE Kuralt's unique approach to human-interest stories is reflected in the **style** of his essays—how they are written, rather than what is said. Elements of his style include factual information clearly and simply stated and the use of exact quotations. Other elements of his style are personal, as in the following passage:

In all our travels, it was the loveliest garden I'd ever seen.

In other places in the essay, the style is more formal:

The earth rewards every loving attention it is paid. People repay such love, too, in memory.

Paired Activity Look back over the essay and find examples of words, phrases, or sentences that show the elements of Kuralt's style. Discuss with a partner whether Kuralt's use of these style elements makes the essay effective and why.

REVIEW: ANECDOTE A brief account of an interesting incident or event, usually intended to entertain or make a point, is called an **anecdote.** Is the primary purpose of Kuralt's anecdote about meeting Mr. Misenheimer to entertain or to make a point?

Writing

Short Essay Think of a community or neighborhood event or activity in which you have participated. Write an essay on your role and how you and your community benefited from the activity. Use a personal style in your writing. Place your essay in your **Working Portfolio.**

Speaking & Listening

Persuasive Speech Imagine you must go before the Parks Department to convince them to maintain Mr. Misenheimer's garden. Write a short persuasive speech in which you explain why you feel the garden is important to the community. Be sure to provide evidence, examples, and reasons to support your main idea.

Speaking and Listening Handbook
See p. R109: Persuasive Presentations.

Research & Technology

Community Service Mr. Misenheimer and Haeja Namkoong worked together to "make the world just a little bit nicer." Contact local hospitals, community agencies, or other organizations that have volunteer programs for middle school students. Find out what types of volunteer activities are available. Present your findings to the class in a poster or chart.

Reading for INFORMATION
Read "Partners in Growing" on pages 211–214 before doing your research.

Vocabulary and Spelling

EXERCISE: CONTEXT CLUES On your paper, finish this summary by using context clues to choose the vocabulary words that best complete the sentences.

In "Mr. Misenheimer's Garden," Charles Kuralt writes that a ___1___ of workers seemed to be needed to maintain the beautiful garden he saw in Surry County, Virginia. One ___2___, though, cared for the entire garden alone. The reason for the ___3___ of the garden was simply Mr. Misenheimer's wish to make the world a little bit nicer. He worked hard to ___4___ the soil to yield colorful flowers. His apprentice, Haeja Namkoong, learned from him the ___5___ techniques that made the garden flourish.

Vocabulary Handbook
See p. R20: Context Clues.

SPELLING STRATEGY: WORD ENDINGS -*ATE*/-*TION*
To change verbs ending in -*ate* to nouns ending in -*tion*, omit the e in -*ate* and add -*ion.* For example, the verb *cultivate* becomes the noun *cultivation* by adding the suffix -*ion.* The hard *t* in -*ate* becomes the soft *t* in -*tion*, pronounced *shun.*

Change the verb ending in the following words into a noun ending.

1. separate + ion = _____
2. cultivate + ion = _____
3. create + ion = _____
4. isolate + ion = _____
5. decorate + ion = _____

Spelling Handbook
See p. R28.

WORDS TO KNOW	battalion	cultivation	nurseryman
	coax	existence	

Grammar in Context: The Past and Present Perfect Tenses

Read the following excerpt from Charles Kuralt's "Mr. Misenheimer's Garden."

> . . . **we've been** to a few places we'll never forget.

We've is a contraction of *we have.* The full verb, *have been,* is an example of the **present perfect tense.** Unlike the **past tense,** which shows an action that occurred entirely in the past, the present perfect tense can show an action that began in the past and is still continuing: *We have worked here for a few years.* The present perfect tense can also show action that happened at an unspecified time in the past: *I have met him before.*

WRITING EXERCISE Rewrite each sentence, using the underlined verb in either the past tense or the present perfect tense.

Example: *Original* I <u>work</u> in the garden. (some time in the past)

Rewritten I <u>have worked</u> in the garden.

1. We <u>plant</u> seeds last Monday. (specific time in the past)

2. They <u>dig</u> up the potatoes. (some time in the past)

3. She <u>mow</u> the lawn last week. (specific time in the past)

4. He <u>cut</u> the hedge. (some time in the past)

5. We <u>fertilize</u> the soil a week ago. (specific time in the past)

Grammar Handbook See p. R84: Using Verbs Correctly.

Charles Bishop Kuralt
1934–1997

"I didn't have to worry about finding stories any longer. They found me."

A Commitment to News Born and raised in North Carolina, Charles Kuralt always knew that he wanted to be a reporter. While at the University of North Carolina at Chapel Hill, he edited the student newspaper. After a stint as a journalist, he joined CBS News in 1957. Two years later, he became one of the network's youngest news correspondents. Over the next few years, he covered major news stories from around the world.

Change of Heart In 1967, Kuralt decided to focus on lighter news stories. He said, "I got the idea . . . one night in an airplane as I looked down at the lights in the countryside and wondered . . . what was going on down there." *On the Road* won several Emmy awards and three Peabody awards for news reporting. Kuralt also anchored *CBS News Sunday Morning* from 1979 until his retirement in 1994.

AUTHOR ACTIVITY
At Ease Kuralt wrote, "The pig farmer in Illinois to whom I'm talking . . . sees the lights and the camera and . . . gets nervous. But then he sees me and thinks, 'Well, if that fellow can look like that and talk the way he does, then I can just be myself.'" Find and watch a videotape of Kuralt's *On the Road.* How might Kuralt's appearance and behavior help the people he interviews feel at ease?

Source: *Parents* Magazine

❶ GENERATIONS

Partners
in Growing

❷ By Rolaine Hochstein

When young and old get together in a city garden, beautiful things grow.

It's a mild spring afternoon in New York City. Sean, 12, telephones his friend Adele, 77, who lives in the same middle-income housing development. "Can you come down to the garden?"

"Give me ten minutes to change my clothes," she says. Adele's husband, Harry, 82, may go to the garden too, but only as an observer; Adele's

Seniors and kids—like Adele Lopatin and Rafael Cruz—team up to acquire a plot at the community garden at New York City's Penn South housing development.

Reading for Information

You don't always need to read every word of a magazine article to know what it is about. You can preview it by reading the **text organizers**—the visual clues that help you summarize, highlight, and organize the text at a glance.

Using Text Organizers
Scanning text organizers such as titles, headings, words in italic or boldface type, sidebars, photographs, and captions can save time or help you decide whether to read the entire magazine article.

YOUR TURN *Use the following questions and activities to identify and make use of the text organizers in this article.*

❶ Magazines often include special sections or features in every issue. What is the topic of this feature? What kind of stories would you expect to find in this feature?

❷ The **title** of a magazine article is sometimes followed by a **tag,** a brief **summary** about the purpose or focus of the article. What does the tag tell you about this article?

working partner is Sean. He'll be waiting beside the eight-by-ten-foot patch that they have been cultivating, on and off, for six years. It's not exactly a rule, but one never starts without the other.

Adele Lopatin is an expressive, ample woman with curly gray hair and a busy life. She leads the Penn South Senior Chorus. She runs a roof garden with residents of a home for blind people. She also keeps up with three grandchildren and only recently retired from a part-time secretarial job.

Sean Kalish is busy too. He's a working boy (acting occasionally in TV commercials and in plays), but he's also a kid's kid. Between after-school lessons (karate and sculpture), he's likely to be out roller-skating with his buddies. Like Adele, he makes time for gardening because he loves it.

Indoors, Sean Kalish and Adele attend the seedlings. Later they will transplant them to the garden.

❸

The garden itself is an urban wonder. Once a parking lot squeezed in among the ten buildings of Penn South, it is now a fenced-in park with paths, benches, a greenhouse, and 25 symmetrical patches where partners like Adele and Sean make the soil come alive.

Credit the transformation to fellow tenant Jeff Dullea. Bothered by all the KEEP OFF THE GRASS signs that shut the Penn South kids off from nature, he proposed the idea of a children's garden. To ensure adult supervision, every child who wanted a patch had to find a senior (60 or older) partner. Just as the InterGenerational Garden was taking shape, Jeff got a phone call from a woman who hadn't yet moved to Penn South. It was Adele. "I assured her that she'd have a patch and a partner as soon as she arrived," Jeff recalls. Sean, then 6 years old, proved to be a perfect match.

Sean was full of questions; Adele had the answers, having recently earned a "master gardener" certificate from the Cornell University Program of Urban Horticulture. She also brought with her a lifelong enthusiasm for nurturing—people as well as plants. "We talk about all kinds of things," Adele says. "Sean is interested in the growing process, the whys and the hows."

Learning experiences **❹**

Adele taught Sean to test soil, fertilize, measure rainfall. They planted vegetables recommended for high yield in city gardens.

Sean learned tricks like planting radishes and carrots together. "Radishes grow fast." Adele explains. "When we pull the radishes out, the carrots have more room to grow." Sean's parents are glad to get the vegetables, but they are happier for the enrichment of their son's life.

"Sean admires Adele as an expert," says his mother Marta, "but I think he loves her as a grandmother. Once, he saved up to buy her a plant for her birthday. It's strange-looking, but those two think it's beautiful."

"They are not assistants," she points out. "They are coworkers."

Two years ago a third partner joined the pair, a youngster named Rafael Cruz. "He'd be taking a walk down the street with his father, but he would do more looking through the fence than walking," Adele recalls. Soon she gave Rafael a box of soil and some seeds to plant at home. Later she wangled an official okay for an 8-year-old gardener who did not live in Penn South. Rafael got his key to the garden gate, and a patch was divided to give each boy his own piece of land.

The boys get along with each other, but it's clear that Adele is the fulcrum of their friendship.

Of course, they have the gardening in common too.

Working arrangements are informal but serious. Planning sessions take place on a

Reading for Information *continued*

❸ A **caption** provides information about the subject of a photograph or an illustration. Look at the photographs in this article and read their captions. What do you learn about the article?

❹ The words in boldface type that begin a new topic within a story are called a **subheading.** A subheading helps the reader identify the main idea of the text that follows. What main ideas are identified by the subheadings in this article?

garden bench or in Adele's apartment: "I open up my seed catalog, and as far as possible I let the boys have their way." They till and plant after school and on weekends. In peak season Adele gardens for an hour or two, three days a week, with at least one of the boys. "They are not assistants," she points out. "They are coworkers. Sometimes I have to get after them. Sometimes they get after me."

What children like to grow

Although the garden staples are carrots and radishes, the partnership has recently begun to experiment with crops. Both boys were interested in

Adele shares her gardening know-how with Rafael and his sister, Deanna, who sometimes tags along.

growing cotton, which they did. "About enough to make a hankie," Adele jokes.

Jeff Dullea sums it up: "Some kids think the garden is for planting and harvesting, with nothing in between. Adele's kids are different. They show up year-round. I see them sitting in the dirt, and Adele with something in her hand half dissected. I know there's more going on than just weed picking."

How to Start a Community Garden

1. Read about gardening.
2. Locate a site suitable for growing flowers and vegetables.
3. Design a program that will be appropriate for your community.
4. Gather your resources, both human and material.
5. Start small, and let the garden expand as others become interested.
6. Plan the garden as a social center, with an area where gardeners can sit to talk and exchange tips.
7. Celebrate the site year-round.

❺

Reading for Information *continued*

❺ A **sidebar** is additional information set in a box alongside or within an article. The information relates to the article's subject. The sidebar might include definitions of special terms, a list of resources, or more details on a topic mentioned in the article. What information does this sidebar present?

Research & Technology Activity Link: "Mr. Misenheimer's Garden," p. 209. A love of nature and the challenges of gardening can bring together people of all ages. Write a summary that explains some of the benefits of intergenerational gardening.

Simile: Willow and Ginkgo
by EVE MERRIAM

A Loaf of Poetry
by NAOSHI KORIYAMA

Connect to Your Life

A New View Has a person you know ever reminded you of a plant or an animal? What plant or animal? On what characteristics was the resemblance based? With a small group of classmates, choose someone famous or someone you admire. What plant or animal would he or she be? Then discuss whether your comparisons reveal something new about the individual's character or personality.

Build Background

SCIENCE

The first poem that you are about to read is about two very different kinds of trees. The willow is a graceful tree with slender, drooping branches and narrow, pointed leaves. Willows generally grow near water. Many of the 300 species of willow are planted for their beauty.

The ginkgo, on the other hand, is a survivor from the prehistoric past. Its short, thick shape and fan-shaped leaves make it look quite different from the willow. The female tree has a nasty-smelling nut that makes the air around it quite unpleasant.

Focus Your Reading

LITERARY ANALYSIS **FIGURATIVE LANGUAGE**

Poets can present ordinary things in fresh ways by using **figurative language**—language that communicates ideas beyond the normal meanings of the words. Two types of figurative language are similes and metaphors. A **simile** is a comparison that contains the word *like* or *as.* A **metaphor** is a more direct comparison, as in "A leaf is a green summer umbrella."

ACTIVE READING **NOTING SENSORY DETAILS**

These two poems contain many words and phrases that appeal to the reader's senses of sight, touch, smell, taste, and hearing. Such **sensory details** make up the poems' **imagery.** For example, in "Simile: Willow and Ginkgo," the comparison of the willow's music with a soprano (a singer with a high singing voice) appeals to the sense of hearing.

READER'S NOTEBOOK As you read, use a chart like the one below to keep track of the sensory details in the poems.

Poem	Sensory Detail	Sense
Simile: Willow and Ginkgo	Ginkgo's branches are "like stubby rough wool."	touch

Simile: Willow and Ginkgo

BY EVE MERRIAM

Ginkgo (1988), Atsuko Kato. Oil on board,
100 cm. × 80 cm. Courtesy of the artist.

The willow is like an etching,
Fine-lined against the sky.
The ginkgo is like a crude sketch,
Hardly worthy to be signed.

5　The willow's music is like a soprano
Delicate and thin.
The ginkgo's tune is like a chorus
With everyone joining in.

The willow is sleek as a velvet-nosed calf;
10　The ginkgo is leathery as an old bull.
The willow's branches are like silken thread;
The ginkgo's like stubby rough wool.

The willow is like a nymph with streaming hair;
Wherever it grows, there is green and gold and fair.
15　The willow dips to the water,
Protected and precious, like the king's favorite daughter.

The ginkgo forces its way through gray concrete:
Like a city child, it grows up in the street.
Thrust against the metal sky,
20　Somehow it survives and even thrives.

My eyes feast upon the willow,
But my heart goes to the ginkgo.

THINKING through the LITERATURE

1. **Comprehension Check** In a sentence or two, describe the speaker's opinions of the willow and the ginkgo.

2. **ACTIVE READING** **NOTING SENSORY DETAILS**
   Look back at the chart you made in your
   READER'S NOTEBOOK. Which sensory details
   in this poem do you respond to most strongly?
   To which senses do they appeal?

3. What image in this poem could you picture most clearly?

A Loaf of Poetry

BY NAOSHI KORIYAMA

Sunrise (1924), Arthur Dove. Oil on plywood, 18¼" × 20⅞". Milwaukee Art Museum, Milwaukee, WI. Gift of Mrs. Edward L. Wehr.

you mix
the dough
of experience
with
5 the yeast[1]
of inspiration
and knead it well
with love
and pound it
10 with all your might
and then
leave it

until
it puffs out big
15 with its own inner force
and then
knead it again
and
shape it
20 into a round form
and bake it
in the oven
of your heart

---

1. **yeast:** an agent that causes batter or dough to rise.

Connect to the Literature

1. **What Do You Think?** What thoughts or feelings do you have after reading "A Loaf of Poetry"? Share them with a partner.

   Comprehension Check
   - What are the ingredients of "a loaf of poetry"?
   - What is the heart compared to in the poem?

Think Critically

2. Why do you think the **speaker** of "A Loaf of Poetry" compares writing a poem to baking a loaf of bread?

   Think About:
   - the ingredients listed in lines 1–6
   - the process described in the poem
   - what is meant by the "oven" mentioned in line 22

3. Do you think the speaker enjoys the writing process? Which words and phrases in the poem support your opinion?

4. How does the "recipe" given in this poem compare with your own view of the writing process? Explain your answer.

5. **ACTIVE READING** **NOTING SENSORY DETAILS**
   In your opinion, which of the two poems appeals more to your senses? Explain your answer, using the chart you made in your **READER'S NOTEBOOK**.

Extend Interpretations

6. **COMPARING TEXTS** Compare Eve Merriam's poem with "Mi Madre" by Pat Mora on page 139. In what ways are the two speakers' attitudes toward the natural world similar? In what ways do they differ?

7. **Connect to Life** Have you ever noticed how natural objects influence you? What do you think of when you see a desolate landscape? when you smell a bouquet of flowers? Sketch or describe one or two scenes from nature that have had a powerful effect on you.

Literary Analysis

FIGURATIVE LANGUAGE Writers use figurative language to communicate meanings beyond the range of ordinary language. Such language allows them to create fresh descriptions and to provide readers with new insights. Similes and metaphors are two kinds of **figurative language.** Both are comparisons between things that are unlike but have something in common.

- In a **simile** the comparison is expressed by means of the word *like* or *as*.

  The willow is like a nymph with streaming hair;

  is one simile used in "Simile: Willow and Ginkgo."

- A **metaphor** is a direct comparison, without the use of *like* or *as*. For example, Koriyama's

  the dough of experience

  compares a person's "raw" experiences to unbaked bread.

Paired Activity With a partner, reread the two poems, looking for examples of figurative language. Record your findings in a chart like the one shown. Try rewriting one or two of the similes as metaphors and vice versa.

What Is Being Described	What It Is Compared To	Simile or Metaphor?
loaf of bread	poem	metaphor

Writing

Analysis Essay Write a brief essay analyzing the effectiveness of the form, rhyme, figurative language, or imagery in one of these two poems. Be sure to support your main ideas with details and quoted passages from the poems. Place your essay in your **Working Portfolio.**

Writing Handbook
See p. R47: Analysis/Classification.

Speaking & Listening

Similes About Nature Find several pictures of natural objects or scenes. Create a simile based on each object or scene. Present the simile with the picture to your class.

Speaking and Listening Handbook
See p. R104: Organization and Delivery.

Research & Technology

Tree Poetry Using the library and other resources, find three poems that have trees as the subject. Write a short report on how the poems differ in form and content. Be sure to note the poet, title of the poem, and book or source where you found it.

INTERNET **Research Starter**
www.mcdougallittell.com

Eve Merriam
1916–1992

". . . precisely the right word. It's like having a tiny marble in your pocket. You can just feel it."

A Passion for Poetry Eve Merriam grew up in small Pennsylvania towns. As a child, she enjoyed reading poetry, and Merriam began writing poems when she was seven or eight. She went on to become one of the most respected poets in the United States, publishing more than 25 books of adult's and children's poetry, including *It Doesn't Always Have to Rhyme* and *Out Loud.*

Award Winner Merriam won the Yale Younger Poets Prize in 1946, and the National Council of Teachers of English honored her poetry for children in 1981.

Naoshi Koriyama
born 1926

Koriyama says he writes "about any subject that may happen to interest me."

A Professor's Life Naoshi Koriyama studied English in Japan before coming to the United States to complete his college education. After returning to Japan in 1967, he taught American poetry at Toyo University in Tokyo.

Translator of Poetry Koriyama's poems have appeared in high school textbooks in the United States, Canada, and Australia. He has also made English translations of Japanese poetry and folk songs from the Amamio Islands where he was born and raised. Among his works are *We Wrote These Poems* (translator) and *Plum Tree in Japan and Other Poems.*

PREPARING
to **Read**

SHORT STORY

Across the
Curriculum
Science

**ACTIVE READER
GUIDE**

Flowers for Algernon

by DANIEL KEYES

Connect to Your Life

What do you know about your brain?

Build Background

In the short story you are about to read, doctors experiment
with a surgical method to increase the intelligence of a
mentally challenged man. Each area of the brain controls a
different function. What areas might the doctors operate on
during the surgery of the main character?

frontal lobe problem solving, emotional
control, expressive language, voluntary
movement, control of social behavior,
decision making

parietal lobe touch, awareness
of spatial relations, academic
skills (reading)

occipital lobe visual
perception, visual input

temporal lobe memory, receptive
language, musical awareness, sequencing

Focus Your Reading

LITERARY ANALYSIS **CHARACTERIZATION**

Characterization consists of the techniques a
writer uses to create and develop characters.
These techniques include describing the
character's appearance; presenting the way the
character talks, thinks, and behaves; showing
what others think of the character; and making
direct statements about the character.

ACTIVE READING **MAKING INFERENCES**

When you make a logical guess about a
character or an event based on story clues or
your own experience, you are making an
inference. In your ▯▯ **READER'S NOTEBOOK**
create a chart noting details or clues about
Charlie and jot down any inferences you can
make about him.

WORDS TO KNOW	**Vocabulary Preview**			
absurd	introspective	proportional	shrew	syndrome
hypothesis	naïveté	regression	specialization	tangible
impair	opportunist	sensation	statistically	vacuous

Flowers for Algernon

by Daniel Keyes

progris riport 1 — martch 5 1965

Dr. Strauss says I shud rite down what I think and evrey thing that happins to me from now on. I dont know why but he says its importint so they will see if they will use me. I hope they use me. Miss Kinnian says maybe they can make me smart. I want to be smart. My name is Charlie Gordon. I am 37 years old and 2 weeks ago was my brithday. I have nuthing more to rite now so I will close for today.

This page is about charlie spilling ink on a piece of paper and he takes a test n't Jenny it and he doesn't know anything

progris riport 2–martch 6

I had a test today. I think I faled it. and I think that maybe now they wont use me. What happind is a nice young man was in the room and he had some white cards with ink spillled all over them. He sed Charlie what do you see on this card. I was very skared even tho I had my rabits foot in my pockit because when I was a kid I always faled tests in school and I spillled ink to.

I told him I saw a inkblot. He said yes and it made me feel good. I thot that was all but when I got up to go he stopped me. He said now sit down Charlie we are not thru yet. Then I dont remember so good but he wantid me to say what was in the ink. I dint see nuthing in the ink but he said there was picturs there other pepul saw some picturs. I coudnt see any picturs. I reely tryed to see. I held the card close up and then far away. Then I said if I had my glases I coud see better I usally only ware my glases in the movies or TV but I said they are in the closit in the hall. I got them. Then I said let me see that card agen I bet Ill find it now.

I tryed hard but I still coudnt find the picturs I only saw the ink. I told him maybe I need new glases. He rote somthing down on a paper and I got skared of faling the test. I told him it was a very nice inkblot with littel points all around the eges. He looked very sad so that wasnt it. I said please let me try agen. Ill get it in a few minits becaus Im not so fast somtimes. Im a slow reeder too in Miss Kinnians class for slow adults but I'm trying very hard.

He gave me a chance with another card that had 2 kinds of ink spillled on it red and blue.

I had a test today. I think I faled it.

He was very nice and talked slow like Miss Kinnian does and he explained it to me that it was a *raw shok*.[1] He said pepul see things in the ink. I said show me where. He said think. I told him I think a inkblot but that wasnt rite eather. He said what does it remind you— pretend somthing. I closd my eyes for a long time to pretend. I told him I pretned a fowntan pen with ink leeking all over a table cloth. Then he got up and went out.

I dont think I passd the *raw shok* test.

progris report 3–martch 7

Dr Strauss and Dr Nemur say it dont matter about the inkblots. I told them I dint spill the ink on the cards and I coudnt see anything in the ink. They said that maybe they will still use me. I said Miss Kinnian never gave me tests like that one only spelling and reading. They said Miss Kinnian told that I was her bestist pupil in the adult nite scool becaus I tryed the hardist and I reely wantid to lern. They said how come you went to the adult nite scool all by yourself Charlie. How did you find it. I said I askd pepul and sumbody told me where I shud go to lern to read and spell good. They said why did you want to. I told them becaus all my life I wantid to be smart and not dumb. But its very hard to be smart. They said you know it will probly be tempirery. I said yes. Miss Kinnian told me. I dont care if it herts.

Later I had more crazy tests today. The nice

1. **raw shok:** Charlie's way of writing *Rorschach* (rôr′shäk′), the name of a test used to analyze people's personalities on the basis of what they see in inkblot designs.

lady who gave it me told me the name and I asked her how do you spellit so I can rite it in my progris riport. THEMATIC APPERCEPTION TEST.[2] I dont know the frist 2 words but I know what test means. You got to pass it or you get bad marks. This test lookd easy becaus I coud see the picturs. Only this time she dint want me to tell her the picturs. That mixd me up. I said the man yesterday said I shoud tell him what I saw in the ink she said that dont make no difrence. She said make up storys about the pepul in the picturs.

I told her how can you tell storys about pepul you never met. I said why shud I make up lies. I never tell lies any more becaus I always get caut.

She told me this test and the other one the raw-shok was for getting personalty. I laffed so hard. I said how can you get that thing from inkblots and fotos. She got sore and put her picturs away. I dont care. It was sily. I gess I faled that test too.

Later some men in white coats took me to a difernt part of the hospitil and gave me a game to play. It was like a race with a white mouse. They called the mouse Algernon. Algernon was in a box with a lot of twists and turns like all kinds of walls and they gave me a pencil and a paper with lines and lots of boxes. On one side it said START and on the other end it said FINISH. They said it was *amazed*[3] and that Algernon and me had the same *amazed* to do. I dint see how we could have the same *amazed* if Algernon had a box and I had a paper but I dint say nothing. Anyway there wasnt time because the race started.

One of the men had a watch he was trying to hide so I woudnt see it so I tryed not to look and that made me nervus.

Anyway that test made me feel worser than all the others because they did it over 10 times with difernt *amazeds* and Algernon won every time. I dint know that mice were so smart.

Maybe thats because Algernon is a white mouse. Maybe white mice are smarter then other mice.

accepted him for an experiment

progris riport 4—Mar 8

Their going to use me! Im so exited I can hardly rite. Dr Nemur and Dr Strauss had a argament about it first. Dr Nemur was in the office when Dr Strauss brot me in. Dr Nemur was worryed about using me but Dr Strauss told him Miss Kinnian rekemmended me the best from all the people who she was teaching. I like Miss Kinnian becaus shes a very smart teacher. And she said Charlie your going to have a second chance. If you volenteer for this experament you mite get smart. They dont know if it will be perminint but theirs a chance. Thats why I said ok even when I was scared because she said it was an operashun. She said dont be scared Charlie you done so much with so little I think you deserv it most of all.

ACTIVE READER

INFER Why does Charlie feel so excited?

So I got scaird when Dr Nemur and Dr Strauss argud about it. Dr Strauss said I had something that was very good. He said I had a good *motor-vation*.[4] I never even knew I had that. I felt proud when he said that not every body with an eye-q[5] of 68 had that thing. I dont know what it is or where I got it but he said Algernon had it too.

---

2. **Thematic Apperception** (thĭ-mǎt′ĭk ăp′ər-sĕp′shən) **Test:** a test for analyzing people's personalities on the basis of the stories they make up about a series of pictures.

3. **amazed:** Charlie's way of writing *a maze*.

4. **motor-vation:** Charlie's way of writing *motivation*, a word referring to the inner drive that makes a person take a particular course of action.

5. **eye-q:** Charlie's way of writing *I.Q.* (an abbreviation of *intelligence quotient*). Based on the results of a standardized test, an I.Q. is a measurement of a person's mental ability relative to a normal level.

Copyright © Guy Billout.

Algernons *motor-vation* is the cheese they put in his box. But it cant be that because I didnt eat any cheese this week.

Then he told Dr Nemur something I dint understand so while they were talking I wrote down some of the words.

He said Dr Nemur I know Charlie is not what you had in mind as the first of your new brede of intelek** (coudnt get the word) superman. But most people of his low ment** are host** and uncoop** they are usualy dull apath** and hard to reach. He has a good natcher hes intristed and eager to please.

Dr Nemur said remember he will be the first human beeng ever to have his intelijence trippled by surgicle meens.

Dr Strauss said exakly. Look at how well hes lerned to read and write for his low mentel age its as grate an acheve** as you and I lerning einstines therey of **vity[6] without help. That shows the intenss motor-vation. Its comparat** a tremen** achev** I say we use Charlie.

I dint get all the words and they were talking to fast but it sounded like Dr Strauss was on my side and like the other one wasnt.

Then Dr Nemur nodded he said all right maybe your right. We will use Charlie. When he said that I got so exited I jumped up and shook his hand for being so good to me. I told him thank you doc you wont be sorry for giving me a second chance. And I mean it like I told him. After the operashun Im gonna try to be smart. Im gonna try awful hard.

progris ript 5—Mar 10

Im skared. Lots of people who work here and the nurses and the people who gave me the tests came to bring me candy and wish me luck. I hope I have luck. I got my rabits foot and my lucky penny and my horse shoe. Only a black cat crossed me when I was comming to the hospitil. Dr Strauss says dont be superstitis

Charlie this is sience. Anyway Im keeping my rabits foot with me.

I asked Dr Strauss if Ill beat Algernon in the race after the operashun and he said maybe. If the operashun works Ill show that mouse I can be as smart as he is. Maybe smarter. Then Ill be abel to read better and spell the words good and know lots of things and be like other people. I want to be smart like other people. If it works perminint they will make everybody smart all over the wurld.

They dint give me anything to eat this morning. I dont know what that eating has to do with getting smart. Im very hungry and Dr Nemur took away my box of candy. That Dr Nemur is a grouch. Dr Strauss says I can have it back after the operashun. You cant eat befor a operashun. . .

Progress Report 6—Mar 15

ACTIVE READER

PREDICT What's going to happen to Charlie now?

The operashun dint hurt. He did it while I was sleeping. They took off the bandijis from my eyes and my head today so I can make a PROGRESS REPORT. Dr Nemur who looked at some of my other ones says I spell PROGRESS wrong and he told me how to spell it and REPORT too. I got to try and remember that.

I have a very bad memary for spelling. Dr Strauss says its ok to tell about all the things that happin to me but he says I shoud tell more about what I feel and what I think. When I told him I dont know how to think he said try. All the time when the bandijis were on my eyes I tryed to think. Nothing happened. I dont know what to think about. Maybe if I ask him he will tell me how I can think now that Im

---

6. **einstines therey of **vity:** Charlie's way of writing *Einstein's theory of relativity,* a reference to the scientific theory of space and time developed by Albert Einstein.

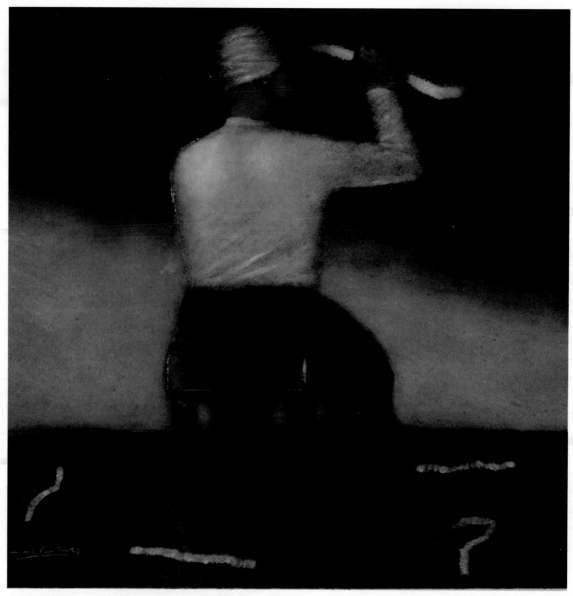

Copyright © Mark Penberthy.

suppose to get smart. What do smart people think about. Fancy things I suppose. I wish I knew some fancy things alredy.

Progress Report 7—mar 19

Nothing is happining. I had lots of tests and different kinds of races with Algernon. I hate that mouse. He always beats me. Dr Strauss said I got to play those games. And he said some time I got to take those tests over again.

Those inkblots are stupid. And those pictures are stupid too. I like to draw a picture of a man and a woman but I wont make up lies about people.

I got a headache from trying to think so much. I thot Dr Strauss was my frend but he dont help me. He dont tell me what to think or when Ill get smart. Miss Kinnian dint come to see me. I think writing these progress reports are stupid too.

Progress Report 8–Mar 23

Im going back to work at the factery. They said it was better I shud go back to work but I cant tell anyone what the operashun was for and I have to come to the hospitil for an hour evry night after work. They are gonna pay me mony every month for lerning to be smart.

Im glad Im going back to work because I miss my job and all my frends and all the fun we have there.

Dr Strauss says I shud keep writing things down but I dont have to do it every day just when I think of something or something speshul happins. He says dont get discoridged because it takes time and it happins slow. He says it took a long time with Algernon before he got 3 times smarter then he was before. Thats why Algernon beats me all the time because he had that operashun too. That makes me feel better. I coud probly do that *amazed* faster than a reglar mouse. Maybe some day Ill beat Algernon. Boy that would be something. So far Algernon looks like he mite be smart perminent.

Mar 25 (I dont have to write PROGRESS REPORT on top any more just when I hand it in once a week for Dr Nemur to read. I just have to put the date on. That saves time)

We had a lot of fun at the factery today. Joe Carp said hey look where Charlie had his operashun what did they do Charlie put some brains in. I was going to tell him but I remembered Dr Strauss said no. Then Frank Reilly said what did you do Charlie forget your key and open your door the hard way. That made me laff. Their really my friends and they like me.

Sometimes somebody will say hey look t Joe or Frank or George he really pulled a

> **Maybe someday Ill beat Algernon. Boy that would be something.**

Charlie Gordon. I dont know why they say that but they always laff. This morning Amos Borg who is the 4 man at Donnegans used my name when he shouted at Ernie the office boy. Ernie lost a packige. He said Ernie for godsake what are you trying to be a Charlie Gordon. I dont understand why he said that. I never lost any packiges.

Mar 28 Dr Straus came to my room tonight to see why I dint come in like I was suppose to. I told him I dont like to race with Algernon any more. He said I dont have to for a while but I shud come in. He had a present for me only it wasnt a present but just for lend. I thot it was a little television but it wasnt. He said I got to turn it on when I go to sleep. I said your kidding why shud I turn it on when Im going to sleep. Who ever herd of a thing like that. But he said if I want to get smart I got to do what he says. I told him I dint think I was going to get smart and he put his hand on my sholder and said Charlie you dont know it yet but your getting smarter all the time. You wont notice for a while. I think he was just being nice to make me feel good because I dont look any smarter.

Oh yes I almost forgot. I asked him when I can go back to the class at Miss Kinnians school. He said I wont go their. He said that soon Miss Kinnian will come to the hospitil to start and teach me speshul. I was mad at her for not comming to see me when I got the operashun but I like her so maybe we will be frends again.

Mar 29 That crazy TV kept me up all night. How can I sleep with something yelling crazy

ACTIVE READER

CLARIFY Why doesn't Charlie want to race with Algernon anymore?

Making fun of Charlie

things all night in my ears. And the nutty pictures. Wow. I dont know what it says when Im up so how am I going to know when Im sleeping.

Dr Strauss says its ok. He says my brains are lerning when I sleep and that will help me when Miss Kinnian starts my lessons in the hospitl (only I found out it isnt a hospitil its a labatory). I think its all crazy. If you can get smart when your sleeping why do people go to school. That thing I dont think will work. I use to watch the late show and the late late show on TV all the time and it never made me smart. Maybe you have to sleep while you watch it.

PROGRESS REPORT 9–April 3

Dr Strauss showed me how to keep the TV turned low so now I can sleep. I dont hear a thing. And I still dont understand what it says. A few times I play it over in the morning to find out what I lerned when I was sleeping and I dont think so. Miss Kinnian says Maybe its another langwidge or something. But most times it sounds american. It talks so fast faster than even Miss Gold who was my teacher in 6 grade and I remember she talked so fast I coudnt understand her.

I told Dr Strauss what good is it to get smart in my sleep. I want to be smart when Im awake. He says its the same thing and I have two minds. Theres the *subconscious* and the *conscious*[7] (thats how you spell it). And one dont tell the other one what its doing. They dont even talk to each other. Thats why I dream. And boy have I been having crazy dreams. Wow. Ever since that night TV. The late late late late late show.

I forgot to ask him if it was only me or if everybody had those two minds.

(I just looked up the word in the dictionary Dr Strauss gave me. The word is *subconscious*. *adj. Of the nature of mental operations yet not present in consciousness; as, subconscious conflict of desires.*) There's more but I still dont know what it means. This isnt a very good dictionary for dumb people like me.

Anyway the headache is from the party. My frends from the factery Joe Carp and Frank Reilly invited me to go with them to Muggsys Saloon for some drinks. I dont like to drink but they said we will have lots of fun. I had a good time.

Joe Carp said I shoud show the girls how I mop out the toilet in the factory and he got me a mop. I showed them and everyone laffed when I told that Mr Donnegan said I was the best janiter he ever had because I like my job and do it good and never come late or miss a day except for my operashun.

I said Miss Kinnian always said Charlie be proud of your job because you do it good.

Everybody laffed and we had a good time and they gave me lots of drinks and Joe said Charlie is a card when hes potted.[8] I dont know what that means but everybody likes me and we have fun. I cant wait to be smart like my best frends Joe Carp and Frank Reilly.

I dont remember how the party was over but I think I went out to buy a newspaper and coffe for Joe and Frank and when I came back there was no one their. I looked for them all over till late. Then I dont remember so good but I think I got sleepy or sick. A nice cop brot me back home. Thats what my landlady Mrs Flynn says.

But I got a headache and a big lump on my head and black and blue all over. I think maybe I fell but Joe Carp says it was the cop

---

7. **the subconscious** (sŭb-kŏn′shəs) **and the conscious** (kŏn′shəs): psychological terms for two kinds of mental activity. The subconscious consists of all a person's mental activity that he or she is not aware of, and the conscious is the mental activity of which the person is aware.

8. **Charlie is a card when hes potted:** Charlie is funny when he's drunk.

they beat up drunks some times. I don't think so. Miss Kinnian says cops are to help people. Anyway I got a bad headache and Im sick and hurt all over. I dont think Ill drink anymore.

April 6 I beat Algernon! I dint even know I beat him until Burt the tester told me. Then the second time I lost because I got so exited I fell off the chair before I finished. But after that I beat him 8 more times. I must be getting smart to beat a smart mouse like Algernon. But I dont *feel* smarter.

I wanted to race Algernon some more but Burt said thats enough for one day. They let me hold him for a minit. Hes not so bad. Hes soft like a ball of cotton. He blinks and when he opens his eyes their black and pink on the eges.

I said can I feed him because I felt bad to beat him and I wanted to be nice and make frends. Burt said no Algernon is a very specshul mouse with an operashun like mine, and he was the first of all the animals to stay smart so long. He told me Algernon is so smart that every day he has to solve a test to get his food. Its a thing like a lock on a door that changes every time Algernon goes in to eat so he has to lern something new to get his food. That made me sad because if he coudnt lern he woud be hungry.

I dont think its right to make you pass a test to eat. How woud Dr Nemur like it to have to pass a test every time he wants to eat. I think Ill be frends with Algernon.

April 9 Tonight after work Miss Kinnian was at the laboratory. She looked like she was glad to see me but scared. I told her dont worry Miss Kinnian Im not smart yet and she laffed. She said I have confidence in you Charlie the way you struggled so hard to read and right better than all the others. At werst you will have it for a littel wile and your doing somthing for sience.

We are reading a very hard book. I never read such a hard book before. Its called

Robinson Crusoe about a man who gets merooned on a dessert Iland. Hes smart and figers out all kinds of things so he can have a house and food and hes a good swimmer. Only I feel sorry because hes all alone and has no frends. But I think their must be somebody else on the iland because theres a picture with his funny umbrella looking at footprints. I hope he gets a frend and not be lonly.

April 10 Miss Kinnian teaches me to spell better. She says look at a word and close your eyes and say it over and over until you remember. I have lots of truble with *through* that you say *threw* and *enough* and *tough* that you dont say *enew* and *tew*. You got to say *enuff* and *tuff*. Thats how I use to write it before I started to get smart. Im confused but Miss Kinnian says theres no reason in spelling.

Apr 14 Finished *Robinson Crusoe*. I want to find out more about what happens to him but Miss Kinnian says thats all there is. *Why*

Apr 15 Miss Kinnian says Im lerning fast. She read some of the Progress Reports and she looked at me kind of funny. She says Im a fine person and Ill show them all. I asked her why. She said never mind but I shoudnt feel bad if I find out that everybody isnt nice like I think. She said for a person who god gave so little to you done more then a lot of people with brains they never even used. I said all my frends are smart people but there good. They like me and they never did anything that wasnt nice. Then she got something in her eye and she had to run out to the ladys room.

ACTIVE READER

INFER What is in Miss Kinnian's eye?

Apr 16 Today, I lerned, the comma, this is a *comma* (,) a period, with a tail, Miss Kinnian, says its important, because, it makes writing, better, she said, somebody, coud lose, a lot of money, if a comma, isnt, in the, right place, I dont have, any money, and I dont see, how a comma, keeps you, from losing it,

But she says, everybody, uses commas, so Ill use, them too,

Apr 17 I used the comma wrong. Its *punctuation*. Miss Kinnian told me to look up long words in the dictionary to lern to spell them. I said whats the difference if you can read it anyway. She said its part of your education so now on Ill look up all the words Im not sure how to spell. It takes a long time to write that way but I think Im remembering. I only have to look up once and after that I get it right. Anyway thats how come I got the word *punctuation* right. (Its that way in the dictionary). Miss Kinnian says a period is punctuation too, and there are lots of other marks to lern. I told her I thot all the periods had to have tails but she said no.

You got to mix them up, she showed? me" how. to mix! them (up,. and now; I can! mix up all kinds" of punctuation, in! my writing? There, are lots! of rules? to lern; but Im gettin'g them in my head.

One thing I? like about, Dear Miss Kinnian: (thats the way it goes in a business letter if I ever go into business) is she, always gives me' a reason" when—I ask. She's a gen'ius! I wish! I cou'd be smart" like, her;

(Punctuation, is; fun!)

April 18 What a dope I am! I didn't even understand what she was talking about. I read the grammar book last night and it explanes the whole thing. Then I saw it was the same way as Miss Kinnian was trying to tell me, but I didn't get it. I got up in the middle of the night, and the whole thing straightened out in my mind.

Miss Kinnian said that the TV working in my sleep helped out. She said I reached a plateau. Thats like the flat top of a hill.

"You're coming along fast, Charlie."

After I figgered out how punctuation worked, I read over all my old Progress Reports from the beginning. Boy, did I have crazy spelling and punctuation! I told Miss Kinnian I ought to go over the pages and fix all the mistakes but she said, "No, Charlie, Dr. Nemur wants them just as they are. That's why he let you keep them after they were photostated, to see your own progress. You're coming along fast, Charlie."

That made me feel good. After the lesson I went down and played with Algernon. We don't race any more.

April 20 I feel sick inside. Not sick like for a doctor, but inside my chest it feels empty like getting punched and a heartburn at the same time.

I wasn't going to write about it, but I guess I got to, because its important. Today was the first time I ever stayed home from work.

Last night Joe Carp and Frank Reilly invited me to a party. There were lots of girls and some men from the factory. I remembered how sick I got last time I drank too much, so I told Joe I didn't want anything to drink. He gave me a plain coke instead. It tasted funny, but I thought it was just a bad taste in my mouth.

We had a lot of fun for a while. Joe said I should dance with Ellen and she would teach me the steps. I fell a few times and I couldn't understand why because no one else was dancing besides Ellen and me. And all the time I was tripping because somebody's foot was always sticking out.

Then when I got up I saw the look on Joe's face and it gave me a funny feeling in my stomack. "He's a scream," one of the girls said. Everybody was laughing.

Frank said, "I ain't laughed so much since we sent him off for the newspaper that night at Muggsy's and ditched him."

"Look at him. His face is red."

"He's blushing. Charlie is blushing."

"Hey, Ellen, what'd you do to Charlie? I never saw him act like that before."

I didn't know what to do or where to turn. Everyone was looking at me and laughing and I felt naked. I wanted to hide myself. I ran out into the street and I threw up. Then I walked home. It's a funny thing I never knew that Joe and Frank and the others liked to have me around all the time to make fun of me.

Now I know what it means when they say "to pull a Charlie Gordon."

I'm ashamed.

PROGRESS REPORT 10

April 21 Still didn't go into the factory. I told Mrs. Flynn my landlady to call and tell Mr. Donnegan I was sick. Mrs. Flynn looks at me very funny lately like she's scared of me.

I think it's a good thing about finding out how everybody laughs at me. I thought about it a lot. It's because I'm so dumb and I don't even know when I'm doing something dumb. People think it's funny when a dumb person can't do things the same way they can.

Anyway, now I know I'm getting smarter every day. I know punctuation and I can spell good. I like to look up all the hard words in the dictionary and I remember them. I'm reading a lot now, and Miss Kinnian says I read very fast. Sometimes I even understand what I'm reading about, and it stays in my mind. There are times when I can close my eyes and think of a page and it all comes back like a picture.

Besides history, geography, and arithmetic, Miss Kinnian said I should start to learn a few foreign languages. Dr. Strauss gave me some more tapes to play while I sleep. I still don't understand how that conscious and unconscious mind works, but Dr. Strauss says not to worry yet. He asked me to promise that when I start learning college subjects next week I wouldn't read any books on psychology[9]—that is, until he gives me permission.

I feel a lot better today, but I guess I'm still a little angry that all the time people were laughing and making fun of me because I wasn't so smart. When I become intelligent like Dr. Strauss says, with three times my I.Q. of 68, then maybe I'll be like everyone else and people will like me and be friendly.

I'm not sure what an *I.Q.* is. Dr. Nemur said it was something that measured how intelligent you were—like a scale in the drugstore weighs pounds. But Dr. Strauss had a big arguement with him and said an I.Q. didn't weigh intelligence at all. He said an I.Q. showed how much intelligence you could get, like the numbers on the outside of a measuring cup. You still had to fill the cup up with stuff.

Then when I asked Burt, who gives me my intelligence tests and works with Algernon, he said that both of them were wrong (only I had to promise not to tell them he said so). Burt says that the I.Q. measures a lot of different things including some of the things you learned already, and it really isn't any good at all.

So I still don't know what I.Q. is except that mine is going to be over 200 soon. I didn't want to say anything, but I don't see how if they don't know *what* it is, or *where* it is—I don't see how they know *how much* of it you've got.

Dr. Nemur says I have to take a *Rorshach Test* tomorrow. I wonder what *that* is.

April 22 I found out what a *Rorshach* is. It's the test I took before the operation—the one with the inkblots on the pieces of cardboard. The man who gave me the test was the same one.

---

9. **psychology** (sī-kŏl'ə-jē): the study of mental processes and behavior.

I was scared to death of those inkblots. I knew he was going to ask me to find the pictures and I knew I wouldn't be able to. I was thinking to myself, if only there was some way of knowing what kind of pictures were hidden there. Maybe there weren't any pictures at all. Maybe it was just a trick to see if I was dumb enough to look for something that wasn't there. Just thinking about that made me sore at him.

"All right, Charlie," he said, "you've seen these cards before, remember?"

"Of course I remember."

The way I said it, he knew I was angry, and he looked surprised. "Yes, of course. Now I want you to look at this one. What might this be? What do you see on this card? People see all sorts of things in these inkblots. Tell me what it might be for you—what it makes you think of."

I was shocked. That wasn't what I had expected him to say at all. "You mean there are no pictures hidden in those inkblots?"

He frowned and took off his glasses. "What?"

"Pictures. Hidden in the inkblots. Last time you told me that everyone could see them and you wanted me to find them too."

He explained to me that the last time he had used almost the exact same words he was using now. I didn't believe it, and I still have the suspicion that he misled me at the time just for the fun of it. Unless—I don't know any more—could I have been *that* feeble-minded?

We went through the cards slowly. One of them looked like a pair of bats tugging at something. Another one looked like two men fencing with swords. I imagined all sorts of things. I guess I got carried away. But I didn't trust him any more, and I kept turning them

around and even looking on the back to see if there was anything there I was supposed to catch. While he was making his notes, I peeked out of the corner of my eye to read it. But it was all in code that looked like this:

WF+A DdF-Ad orig. WF−A SF+obj

The test still doesn't make sense to me. It seems to me that anyone could make up lies about things that they didn't really see. How could he know I wasn't making a fool of him by mentioning things that I didn't really imagine? Maybe I'll understand it when Dr. Strauss lets me read up on psychology.

April 25 I figured out a new way to line up the machines in the factory, and Mr. Donnegan says it will save him ten thousand dollars a year in labor and increased production. He gave me a $25 bonus.

I wanted to take Joe Carp and Frank Reilly out to lunch to celebrate, but Joe said he had to buy some things for his wife, and Frank said he was meeting his cousin for lunch. I guess it'll take a little time for them to get used to the changes in me. Everybody seems to be frightened of me. When I went over to Amos Borg and tapped him on the shoulder, he jumped up in the air.

People don't talk to me much any more or kid around the way they used to. It makes the job kind of lonely.

April 27 I got up the nerve today to ask Miss Kinnian to have dinner with me tomorrow night to celebrate my bonus.

At first she wasn't sure it was right, but I asked Dr. Strauss and he said it was okay. Dr. Strauss and Dr. Nemur don't seem to be getting along so well. They're arguing all the

So I still don't know what I.Q. is except that mine is going to be over 200 soon.

time. This evening when I came in to ask Dr. Strauss about having dinner with Miss Kinnian, I heard them shouting. Dr. Nemur was saying that it was *his* experiment and *his* research, and Dr. Strauss was shouting back that he contributed just as much, because he found me through Miss Kinnian and he performed the operation. Dr. Strauss said that someday thousands of neurosurgeons[10] might be using his technique all over the world.

Dr. Nemur wanted to publish the results of the experiment at the end of this month. Dr. Strauss wanted to wait a while longer to be sure. Dr. Strauss said that Dr. Nemur was more interested in the Chair of Psychology at Princeton[11] than he was in the experiment. Dr. Nemur said that Dr. Strauss was nothing but an opportunist who was trying to ride to glory on *his* coattails.

When I left afterwards, I found myself trembling. I don't know why for sure, but it was as if I'd seen both men clearly for the first time. I remember hearing Burt say that Dr. Nemur had a shrew of a wife who was pushing him all the time to get things published so that he could become famous. Burt said that the dream of her life was to have a big shot husband.

Was Dr. Strauss really trying to ride on his coattails?

April 28 I don't understand why I never noticed how beautiful Miss Kinnian really is. She has brown eyes and feathery brown hair that comes to the top of her neck. She's only thirty-four! I think from the beginning I had the feeling that she was an unreachable genius—and very, very old. Now, every time I see her she grows younger and more lovely.

We had dinner and a long talk. When she said that I was coming along so fast that soon I'd be leaving her behind, I laughed.

"It's true, Charlie. You're already a better reader than I am. You can read a whole page at a glance while I can take in only a few lines at a time. And you remember every single thing you read. I'm lucky if I can recall the main thoughts and the general meaning."

"I don't feel intelligent. There are so many things I don't understand."

She took out a cigarette and I lit it for her. "You've got to be a *little* patient. You're accomplishing in days and weeks what it takes normal people to do in half a lifetime. That's what makes it so amazing. You're like a giant sponge now, soaking things in. Facts, figures, general knowledge. And soon you'll begin to connect them, too. You'll see how the different branches of learning are related. There are many levels, Charlie, like steps on a giant ladder that take you up higher and higher to see more and more of the world around you.

"I can see only a little bit of that, Charlie, and I won't go much higher than I am now, but you'll keep climbing up and up, and see more and more, and each step will open new worlds that you never even knew existed." She frowned. "I hope . . . I just hope to God—"

"What?"

"Never mind, Charles. I just hope I wasn't wrong to advise you to go into this in the first place."

I laughed. "How could that be? It worked, didn't it? Even Algernon is still smart."

We sat there silently for a while, and I knew what she was thinking about as she watched

---

10. **neurosurgeons** (nŏŏr´ō-sûr´jənz): doctors who perform operations on the brain and other parts of the nervous system.

11. **Chair of Psychology at Princeton:** the position of head of the Psychology Department at Princeton University.

WORDS TO KNOW
opportunist (ŏp´ər-tōō´nĭst) *n.* a person who takes advantage of any opportunity to achieve a goal, with little regard for moral principles
shrew (shrōō) *n.* a mean, nagging woman

Max Seabaugh/MAX.

me toying with the chain of my rabbit's foot and my keys. I didn't want to think of that possibility any more than elderly people want to think of death. I *knew* that this was only the beginning. I knew what she meant about levels because I'd seen some of them already. The thought of leaving her behind made me sad.

I'm in love with Miss Kinnian.

PROGRESS REPORT 11

April 30 I've quit my job with Donnegan's Plastic Box Company. Mr. Donnegan insisted that it would be better for all concerned if I left. What did I do to make them hate me so?

The first I knew of it was when Mr. Donnegan showed me the petition. Eight

hundred and forty names, everyone connected with the factory, except Fanny Girden. Scanning the list quickly, I saw at once that hers was the only missing name. All the rest demanded that I be fired.

Joe Carp and Frank Reilly wouldn't talk to me about it. No one else would either, except Fanny. She was one of the few people I'd known who set her mind to something and believed it no matter what the rest of the world proved, said, or did—and Fanny did not believe that I should have been fired. She had been against the petition on principle, and despite the pressure and threats she'd held out.

"Which don't mean to say," she remarked, "that I don't think there's something mighty strange about you, Charlie. Them changes. I don't know. You used to be a good, dependable, ordinary man—not too bright maybe, but honest. Who knows what you done to yourself to get so smart all of a sudden. Like everybody around here's been saying, Charlie, it's not right."

"But how can you say that, Fanny? What's wrong with a man becoming intelligent and wanting to acquire knowledge and understanding of the world around him?"

ACTIVE READER

CLARIFY Why has Mr. Donnegan asked Charlie to leave his job?

She stared down at her work, and I turned to leave. Without looking at me, she said: "It was evil when Eve listened to the snake and ate from the tree of knowledge. It was evil when she saw that she was naked. If not for that, none of us would ever have to grow old and sick and die.[12]"

Once again now I have the feeling of shame burning inside me. This intelligence has driven a wedge between me and all the people I once knew and loved. Before, they laughed at me and despised me for my ignorance and dull-ness; now, they hate me for my knowledge and understanding. What in God's name do they want of me?

They've driven me out of the factory. Now I'm more alone than ever before . . .

May 15 Dr. Strauss is very angry at me for not having written any progress reports in two weeks. He's justified because the lab is now paying me a regular salary. I told him I was too busy thinking and reading. When I pointed out that writing was such a slow process that it made me impatient with my poor hand-writing, he suggested that I learn to type. It's much easier to write now because I can type nearly seventy-five words a minute. Dr. Strauss continually reminds me of the need to speak and write simply so that people will be able to understand me.

I'll try to review all the things that happened to me during the last two weeks. Algernon and I were presented to the American Psychological Association sitting in convention with the World Psychological Association last Tuesday. We created quite a <u>sensation</u>. Dr. Nemur and Dr. Strauss were proud of us.

I suspect that Dr. Nemur, who is sixty—ten years older than Dr. Strauss—finds it necessary to see <u>tangible</u> results of his work. Undoubtedly the result of pressure by Mrs. Nemur.

Contrary to my earlier impressions of him, I realize that Dr. Nemur is not at all a genius. He has a very good mind, but it struggles under the specter of self-doubt. He wants people to take him for a genius. Therefore, it is important for him to feel that his work is accepted by the world. I believe that Dr. Nemur was afraid of further delay because he worried that someone else might make a discovery along these lines and take the credit from him.

Dr. Strauss, on the other hand, might be called a genius, although I feel that his areas of knowledge are too limited. He was educated in the tradition of narrow <u>specialization</u>; the broader aspects of background were neglected far more than necessary—even for a neurosurgeon.

I was shocked to learn that the only ancient languages he could read were Latin, Greek, and

---

12. **It was evil . . . die:** a reference to the biblical story of Adam and Eve (Genesis 2–3). After they ate fruit from the tree of knowledge of good and evil, they were banished from the Garden of Eden, and they and their descendants became subject to illness and death.

WORDS TO KNOW

sensation (sĕn-sā′shən) *n.* a state of great interest and excitement
tangible (tăn′jə-bəl) *adj.* able to be seen or touched; material
specialization (spĕsh′ə-lĭ-zā′shən) *n.* a focus on a particular activity or area of study

Hebrew and that he knows almost nothing of mathematics beyond the elementary levels of the calculus of variations.[13] When he admitted this to me, I found myself almost annoyed. It was as if he'd hidden this part of himself in order to deceive me, pretending—as do many people, I've discovered—to be what he is not. No one I've ever known is what he appears to be on the surface.

Dr. Nemur appears to be uncomfortable around me. Sometimes when I try to talk to him, he just looks at me strangely and turns away. I was angry at first when Dr. Strauss told me I was giving Dr. Nemur an inferiority complex.[14] I thought he was mocking me, and I'm oversensitive at being made fun of.

How was I to know that a highly respected psychoexperimentalist like Nemur was unacquainted with Hindustani[15] and Chinese? It's <u>absurd</u> when you consider the work that is being done in India and China today in the very field of his study.

I asked Dr. Strauss how Nemur could refute Rahajamati's attack on his method and results if Nemur couldn't even read them in the first place. That strange look on Dr. Strauss's face can mean only one of two things. Either he doesn't want to tell Nemur what they're saying in India, or else—and this worries me—Dr. Strauss doesn't know either. I must be careful to speak and write clearly and simply so that people won't laugh.

May 18 I am very disturbed. I saw Miss Kinnian last night for the first time in over a week. I tried to avoid all discussions of intellectual concepts and to keep the conversation on a simple, everyday level, but she just stared at me blankly and asked me what I meant about the mathematical variance equivalent in Dorbermann's Fifth Concerto.

When I tried to explain, she stopped me and laughed. I guess I got angry, but I suspect I'm approaching her on the wrong level. No matter what I try to discuss with her, I am unable to communicate. I must review Vrostadt's equations on levels of semantic progression. I find that I don't communicate with people much any more. Thank God for books and music and things I can think about. I am alone in my apartment at Mrs. Flynn's boarding house most of the time and seldom speak to anyone.

Contrary to my earlier impressions of him, I realize that Dr. Nemur is not at all a genius.

May 20 I would not have noticed the new dishwasher, a boy of about sixteen, at the corner diner where I take my evening meals if not for the incident of the broken dishes. They crashed to the floor, shattering and sending bits of white china under the tables. The boy stood there, dazed and frightened, holding the empty tray in his hand. The whistles and catcalls from the customers (the cries of "Hey, there go the profits! . . ." "*Mazeltov!* . . ." and "Well, *he* didn't work here very long. . . ." which invariably seem to follow the breaking

---

13. **calculus** (kăl′kyə-ləs) **of variations:** a branch of higher mathematics.

14. **inferiority complex:** a psychological condition involving feelings of personal worthlessness.

15. **Hindustani** (hĭn′dŏŏ-stä′nē): a group of languages used in India.

of glass or dishware in a public restaurant) all seemed to confuse him.

When the owner came to see what the excitement was about, the boy cowered as if he expected to be struck and threw up his arms as if to ward off the blow.

"All right! All right, you dope," shouted the owner, "don't just stand there! Get the broom and sweep that mess up. A broom . . . a broom, you idiot! It's in the kitchen. Sweep up all the pieces."

The boy saw that he was not going to be punished. His frightened expression disappeared, and he smiled and hummed as he came back with the broom to sweep the floor. A few of the rowdier customers kept up the remarks, amusing themselves at his expense.

"Here, sonny, over here there's a nice piece behind you. . . ."

"C'mon, do it again. . . ."

"He's not so dumb. It's easier to break 'em than to wash 'em. . . ."

As his vacant eyes moved across the crowd of amused onlookers, he slowly mirrored their smiles and finally broke into an uncertain grin at the joke which he obviously did not understand.

I felt sick inside as I looked at his dull, <u>vacuous</u> smile, the wide, bright eyes of a child, uncertain but eager to please. They were laughing at him because he was mentally retarded.

And I had been laughing at him too.

Suddenly, I was furious at myself and all those who were smirking at him. I jumped up and shouted, "Shut up! Leave him alone! It's not his fault he can't understand! He can't help what he is! But for God's sake . . . he's still a human being!"

> **I cursed myself for losing control and creating a scene.**

The room grew silent. I cursed myself for losing control and creating a scene. I tried not to look at the boy as I paid my check and walked out without touching my food. I felt ashamed for both of us.

How strange it is that people of honest feelings and sensibility, who would not take advantage of a man born without arms or legs or eyes—how such people think nothing of abusing a man born with low intelligence. It infuriated me to think that not too long ago, I, like this boy, had foolishly played the clown.

And I had almost forgotten.

I'd hidden the picture of the old Charlie Gordon from myself because now that I was intelligent, it was something that had to be pushed out of my mind. But today in looking at that boy, for the first time I saw what I had been. *I was just like him!*

Only a short time ago, I learned that people laughed at me. Now I can see that unknowingly I joined with them in laughing at myself. That hurts most of all.

I have often reread my progress reports and seen the illiteracy, the childish <u>naïveté</u>, the mind of low intelligence peering from a dark room, through the keyhole, at the dazzling light outside. I see that even in my dullness I knew that I was inferior and that other people had something I lacked—something denied me. In my mental blindness, I thought that it was somehow connected with the ability to read and write, and I was sure that if I could get those skills I would automatically have intelligence too.

Even a feeble-minded man wants to be like other men.

A child may not know how to feed itself, or

WORDS TO KNOW **vacuous** (văk′yōō-əs) *adj.* showing a lack of intelligence or thought
naïveté (nä′ēv-tā′) *n.* a lack of sophistication; simplicity

237

what to eat, yet it knows of hunger.

This, then, is what I was like. I never knew. Even with my gift of intellectual awareness, I never really knew.

This day was good for me. Seeing the past more clearly, I have decided to use my knowledge and skills to work in the field of increasing human intelligence levels. Who is better equipped for this work? Who else has lived in both worlds? These are my people. Let me use my gift to do something for them.

Tomorrow, I will discuss with Dr. Strauss the manner in which I can work in this area. I may be able to help him work out the problems of widespread use of the technique which was used on me. I have several good ideas of my own.

There is so much that might be done with this technique. If I could be made into a genius, what about thousands of others like myself? What fantastic levels might be achieved by using this technique on normal people? on *geniuses*?

There are so many doors to open. I am impatient to begin.

PROGRESS REPORT 12

ACTIVE READER

INFER What might the changes in Algernon's behavior mean?

May 23 It happened today. Algernon bit me. I visited the lab to see him, as I do occasionally, and when I took him out of his cage, he snapped at my hand. I put him back and watched him for a while. He was unusually disturbed and vicious.

May 24 Burt, who is in charge of the experimental animals, tells me that Algernon is changing. He is less cooperative; he refuses to run the maze any more; general motivation has decreased. And he hasn't been eating.

Everyone is upset about what this may mean.

May 25 They've been feeding Algernon, who now refuses to work the shifting-lock problem. Everyone identifies me with Algernon. In a way we're both the first of our kind. They're all pretending that Algernon's behavior is not necessarily significant for me. But it's hard to hide the fact that some of the other animals who were used in this experiment are showing strange behavior.

Dr. Strauss and Dr. Nemur have asked me not to come to the lab any more. I know what they're thinking, but I can't accept it. I am going ahead with my plans to carry their research forward. With all due respect to both of these fine scientists, I am well aware of their limitations. If there is an answer, I'll have to find it out for myself. Suddenly, time has become very important to me.

May 29 I have been given a lab of my own and permission to go ahead with the research. I'm onto something. Working day and night. I've had a cot moved into the lab. Most of my writing time is spent on the notes which I keep in a separate folder, but from time to time I feel it necessary to put down my moods and my thoughts out of sheer habit.

I find the calculus of intelligence to be a fascinating study. Here is the place for the application of all the knowledge I have acquired. In a sense it's the problem I've been concerned with all my life.

May 31 Dr. Strauss thinks I'm working too hard. Dr. Nemur says I'm trying to cram a lifetime of research and thought into a few weeks. I know I should rest, but I'm driven on by something inside that won't let me stop. I've got to find the reason for the sharp regression in Algernon. I've got to know *if* and *when* it will happen to me.

WORDS TO KNOW
regression (rĭ-grĕsh′ən) *n.* a return to a less developed condition

238

June 4

Letter to Dr. Strauss *(copy)*

Dear Dr. Strauss:

Under separate cover I am sending you a copy of my report entitled "The Algernon-Gordon Effect: A Study of Structure and Function of Increased Intelligence," which I would like to have you read and have published.

As you see, my experiments are completed. I have included in my report all of my formulae, as well as mathematical analysis in the appendix. Of course, these should be verified.

Because of its importance to both you and Dr. Nemur (and need I say to myself, too?) I have checked and rechecked my results a dozen times in the hope of finding an error. I am sorry to say the results must stand. Yet for the sake of science, I am grateful for the little bit that I here add to the knowledge of the function of the human mind and of the laws governing the artificial increase of human intelligence.

I recall your once saying to me that an experimental *failure* or the *disproving* of a theory was as important to the advancement of learning as a success would be. I know now that this is true. I am sorry, however, that my own contribution to the field must rest upon the ashes of the work of two men I regard so highly.

Yours truly,
Charles Gordon

encl.: rept.

June 5 I must not become emotional. The facts and the results of my experiments are clear, and the more sensational aspects of my own rapid climb cannot obscure the fact that the tripling of intelligence by the surgical technique developed by Drs. Strauss and Nemur must be viewed as having little or no practical applicability (at the present time) to

Copyright © Vivienne Flesher.

the increase of human intelligence.

As I review the records and data on Algernon, I see that although he is still in his physical infancy, he has regressed mentally. Motor activity[16] is <u>impaired</u>; there is a general reduction of glandular activity; there is an accelerated loss of coordination.

There are also strong indications of progressive amnesia.[17]

As will be seen by my report, these and other physical and mental deterioration <u>syndromes</u>

---

16. **motor activity:** movement produced by use of the muscles.

17. **progressive amnesia** (ăm-nē′zhə): a steadily worsening loss of memory.

can be predicted with statistically significant results by the application of my formula.

The surgical stimulus to which we were both subjected has resulted in an intensification and acceleration of all mental processes. The unforeseen development, which I have taken the liberty of calling the Algernon-Gordon effect, is the logical extension of the entire intelligence speedup. The hypothesis here proven may be described simply in the following terms: Artificially increased intelligence deteriorates at a rate of time directly proportional to the quantity of the increase.

I feel that this, in itself, is an important discovery.

As long as I am able to write, I will continue to record my thoughts in these progress reports. It is one of my few pleasures. However, by all indications, my own mental deterioration will be very rapid.

I have already begun to notice signs of emotional instability and forgetfulness, the first symptoms of the burnout.

June 10 Deterioration progressing. I have become absent-minded. Algernon died two days ago. Dissection shows my predictions were right. His brain had decreased in weight, and there was a general smoothing out of cerebral convolutions as well as a deepening and broadening of brain fissures.[18]

I guess the same thing is or will soon be happening to me. Now that it's definite, I don't want it to happen.

I put Algernon's body in a cheese box and buried him in the back yard. I cried.

June 15 Dr. Strauss came to see me again. I wouldn't open the door, and I told him to go away. I want to be left to myself. I have become touchy and irritable. I feel the darkness closing in. It's hard to throw off thoughts of suicide. I keep telling myself how important this introspective journal will be.

It's a strange sensation to pick up a book that you've read and enjoyed just a few months ago and discover that you don't remember it. I remembered how great I thought John Milton was, but when I picked up *Paradise Lost,* I couldn't understand it at all. I got so angry I threw the book across the room.

I've got to try to hold on to some of it. Some of the things I've learned. Oh, God, please don't take it all away.

June 19 Sometimes, at night, I go out for a walk. Last night I couldn't remember where I lived. A policeman took me home. I have the strange feeling that this has all happened to me before—a long time ago. I keep telling myself I'm the only person in the world who can describe what's happening to me.

June 21 Why can't I remember? I've got to fight. I lie in bed for days, and I don't know who or where I am. Then it all comes back to me in a flash. Fugues[19] of amnesia. Symptoms of senility—second childhood. I can watch them coming on. It's so cruelly logical. I learned so much and so fast. Now my mind is deteriorating rapidly. I won't let it happen. I'll fight it. I can't help thinking of the boy in the restaurant, the blank expression, the silly

---

18. **cerebral convolutions** (sĕr′ə-brəl kŏn′və-lōō′shənz). . . **brain fissures** (fĭsh′ərz): features of the brain. Cerebral convolutions are the ridges or folds on the brain's surface; fissures are grooves that divide the brain into lobes, or sections.

19. **fugues** (fyōōgz): psychological states in which people seem to be acting consciously, although later they have no memory of the activity.

WORDS TO KNOW

statistically (stə-tĭs′tĭ-klē) *adv.* in terms of the principles used to analyze numerical data
hypothesis (hī-pŏth′ĭ-sĭs) *n.* a theory used as a basis for research
proportional (prə-pôr′shə-nəl) *adj.* having a constant relation in degree or number
introspective (ĭn′trə-spĕk′tĭv) *adj.* examining one's own thoughts, feelings, and sensations

Copyright © Joel Peter Johnson.

smile, the people laughing at him. No—
please—not that again . . .

June 22 I'm forgetting things that I learned
recently. It seems to be following the classic
pattern—the last things learned are the first
things forgotten. Or is that the pattern? I'd
better look it up again . . .

I reread my paper on the Algernon-Gordon
effect, and I get the strange feeling that it was
written by someone else. There are parts I
don't even understand.

Motor activity impaired. I keep tripping
over things, and it becomes increasingly
difficult to type.

June 23 I've given up using the typewriter
completely. My coordination is bad. I feel that
I'm moving slower and slower. Had a terrible
shock today. I picked up a copy of an article I

used in my research, Krueger's "Über psychische Ganzheit," to see if it would help me understand what I had done. First I thought there was something wrong with my eyes. Then I realized I could no longer read German. I tested myself in other languages. All gone.

June 30 A week since I dared to write again. It's slipping away like sand through my fingers. Most of the books I have are too hard for me now. I get angry with them because I know that I read and understood them just a few weeks ago.

I keep telling myself I must keep writing these reports so that somebody will know what is happening to me. But it gets harder to form the words and remember spellings. I have to look up even simple words in the dictionary now, and it makes me impatient with myself.

Dr. Strauss comes around almost every day, but I told him I wouldn't see or speak to anybody. He feels guilty. They all do. But I don't blame anyone. I knew what might happen. But how it hurts.

July 7 I don't know where the week went. Todays Sunday I know because I can see through my window people going to church. I think I stayed in bed all week but I remember Mrs. Flynn bringing food to me a few times. I keep saying over and over Ive got to do something but then I forget or maybe its just easier not to do what I say Im going to do.

I think of my mother and father a lot these days. I found a picture of them with me taken at a beach. My father has a big ball under his arm and my mother is holding me by the hand. I dont remember them the way they are in the picture. All I remember is my father drunk most of the time and arguing with mom about money.

He never shaved much and he used to scratch my face when he hugged me. My mother said

he died but Cousin Miltie said he heard his mom and dad say that my father ran away with another woman. When I asked my mother she slapped my face and said my father was dead. I dont think I ever found out which was true but I dont care much. (He said he was going to take me to see cows on a farm once but he never did. He never kept his promises . . .)

July 10 My landlady Mrs. Flynn is very worried about me. She says the way I lay around all day and dont do anything I remind her of her son before she threw him out of the house. She said she doesnt like loafers. If Im sick its one thing, but if Im a loafer thats another thing and she wont have it. I told her I think Im sick.

I try to read a little bit every day, mostly stories, but sometimes I have to read the same thing over and over again because I dont know what it means. And its hard to write. I know I should look up all the words in the dictionary but its so hard and Im so tired all the time.

Then I got the idea that I would only use the easy words instead of the long hard ones. That saves time. I put flowers on Algernons grave about once a week. Mrs Flynn thinks Im crazy to put flowers on a mouses grave but I told her that Algernon was special.

July 14 Its sunday again. I dont have anything to do to keep me busy now because my television set is broke and I dont have any money to get it fixed. (I think I lost this months check from the lab. I dont remember)

I get awful headaches and asperin doesnt help me much. Mrs Flynn knows Im really sick and she feels very sorry for me. Shes a wonderful woman whenever someone is sick.

July 22 Mrs Flynn called a strange doctor to see me. She was afraid I was going to die. I told the doctor I wasnt too sick and that I only forget sometimes. He asked me did I have any friends or relatives and I said no I dont have any. I told him I had a friend called Algernon once but he was a mouse and we used to run races together. He looked at me kind of funny like he thought I was crazy.

He smiled when I told him I used to be a genius. He talked to me like I was a baby and he winked at Mrs Flynn. I got mad and chased him out because he was making fun of me the way they all used to.

July 24 I have no more money and Mrs Flynn says I got to go to work somewhere and pay the rent because I havent paid for over two months. I dont know any work but the job I used to have at Donnegans Plastic Box Company. I dont want to go back there because they all knew me when I was smart and maybe they'll laugh at me. But I dont know what else to do to get money.

July 25 I was looking at some of my old progress reports and its very funny but I cant read what I wrote. I can make out some of the words but they dont make sense.

Miss Kinnian came to the door but I said go away I dont want to see you. She cried and I cried too but I wouldnt let her in because I didnt want her to laugh at me. I told her I didn't like her any more. I told her I didnt want to be smart any more. Thats not true. I still love her and I still want to be smart but I had to say that so shed go away. She gave Mrs. Flynn money to pay the rent. I dont want that. I got to get a job.

Please . . . please let me not forget how to read and write . . .

July 27 Mr. Donnegan was very nice when I came back and asked him for my old job of janitor. First he was very suspicious but I told him what happened to me then he looked very sad and put his hand on my shoulder and said

Charlie Gordon you got guts.

Everybody looked at me when I came downstairs and started working in the toilet sweeping it out like I used to. I told myself Charlie if they make fun of you dont get sore because you remember their not so smart as you once thot they were. And besides they were once your friends and if they laughed at you that doesnt mean anything because they liked you too.

One of the new men who came to work there after I went away made a nasty crack he said hey Charlie I hear your a very smart fella a real quiz kid. Say something intelligent. I felt bad but Joe Carp came over and grabbed him by the shirt and said leave him alone you lousy cracker or Ill break your neck. I didnt expect Joe to take my part so I guess hes really my friend.

Later Frank Reilly came over and said Charlie if anybody bothers you or trys to take advantage you call me or Joe and we will set em straight. I said thanks Frank and I got choked up so I had to turn around and go into the supply room so he wouldnt see me cry. Its good to have friends.

July 28 I did a dumb thing today I forgot I wasnt in Miss Kinnians class at the adult center any more like I use to be. I went in and sat down in my old seat in the back of the room and she looked at me funny and she said Charles. I dint remember she ever called me that before only Charlie so I said hello Miss Kinnian Im redy for my lesin today only I lost my reader that we was using. She startid to cry and run out of the room and everybody looked at me and I saw they wasnt the same pepul who use to be in my class.

Then all of a suddin I rememberd some things about the operashun and me getting smart and I said holy smoke I reely pulled a Charlie Gordon that time. I went away before she come back to the room.

Thats why Im going away from New York for good. I dont want to do nothing like that agen. I dont want Miss Kinnian to feel sorry for me. Evry body feels sorry at the factery and I dont want that eather so Im going someplace where nobody knows that Charlie Gordon was once a genus and now he cant even reed a book or rite good.

Im taking a cuple of books along and even if I cant reed them Ill practise hard and maybe I wont forget every thing I lerned. If I try reel hard maybe Ill be a littel bit smarter then I was before the operashun. I got my rabits foot and my luky penny and maybe they will help me.

If you ever reed this Miss Kinnian dont be sorry for me Im glad I got a second chanse to be smart becaus I lerned a lot of things that I never even new were in this world and Im grateful that I saw it all for a littel bit. I dont know why Im dumb agen or what I did wrong maybe its becaus I dint try hard enuff. But if I try and practis very hard maybe Ill get a littl smarter and know what all the words are. I remember a littel bit how nice I had a feeling with the blue book that has the torn cover when I red it. Thats why Im gonna keep trying to get smart so I can have that feeling agen. Its a good feeling to know things and be smart. I wish I had it rite now if I did I woud sit down and reed all the time. Anyway I bet Im the first dumb person in the world who ever found out somthing importent for sience. I remember I did somthing but I dont remember what. So I gess its like I did it for all the dumb pepul like me.

Goodbye Miss Kinnian and Dr. Strauss and evreybody. And P.S. please tell Dr Nemur not to be such a grouch when pepul laff at him and he woud have more frends. Its easy to make frends if you let pepul laff at you. Im going to have lots of frends where I go.

P.P.S. Please if you get a chanse put some flowers on Algernons grave in the bak yard. . . . ❖

P.P.S. Please if you get a chanse put some flowers on Algernons grave in the bak yard . . .

Connect to the Literature

1. **What Do You Think?**
   Do you think Charlie is happier at the end of the story than at the beginning? Explain why or why not.

   Comprehension Check
   - What kind of operation does Charlie undergo?
   - What happens to Algernon?
   - What happens to Charlie?

Think Critically

2. **ACTIVE READING** **MAKING INFERENCES**
   With a classmate, look at the chart of **inferences** about Charlie in your **READER'S NOTEBOOK**. On the basis of your inferences, what kind of person do you think Charlie is? How well do you think he will do after he leaves New York?

3. Do you think the doctors should have performed the operation on Charlie? Why or why not?

4. Why do you think Charlie put flowers on Algernon's grave?

5. What changes and experiences are the most difficult for Charlie to go through? Explain your choices.

   Think About:
   - how he felt about his new intelligence
   - whether he is happier before or after becoming a genius
   - what, if anything, he has gained by the end of the story

Extend Interpretations

6. **What If?** If Charlie were asked to participate in another experiment to increase his intelligence, do you think he would accept? Give reasons for your opinion.

7. **Connect to Life** What kind of society would we have if everyone became superintelligent? How would that society be different from the one we live in today?

Literary Analysis

CHARACTERIZATION The way a writer creates and develops characters is called **characterization.** There are four methods of characterization: (1) describing a character's physical characteristics, (2) presenting a character's thoughts, speech, and actions, (3) depicting other characters' thoughts, speech, and actions in relation to the character, and (4) making direct comments about a character's nature.

In this story, Charlie's **character** is developed through a series of progress reports, similar to journal entries.

Paired Activity With a partner, go back through the story. Look for examples of each type of characterization technique, and record them in a character chart. Which method of characterization does the author use most often? Discuss your findings with the class.

Charlie

Physical description of Charlie

Direct comments about Charlie
"You're like a giant sponge now, soaking things in."

Charlie's speech, thoughts, or actions
"I said please let me try agen."

Others' speech, thoughts, or actions about Charlie

CHOICES and CHALLENGES

Writing

Journal Entry Write a journal entry Charlie might have written after he left New York. Refer to progress reports that Charlie wrote before his surgery, to help you model your sentence structure, spelling, and grammar. Place the entry in your **Working Portfolio.**

Writing Handbook
See p. R41: Descriptive Writing

[handwritten: Home Work 06.19.14 done]

Speaking & Listening

Character Comparison With permission from your teacher, watch a videotape of *Charly,* the film based on "Flowers for Algernon." Prepare an oral report that compares and contrasts the characterization in the film and the short story. Keep in mind that the short story presents the characters through Charlie's perspective only. The film allows you to see the characters' actions for yourself.

Speaking and Listening Handbook
See p. R108: Oral Responses to Literature.

Art Connection

Look at the art on page 241. The figure is facing a blank wall. What images or symbols does the artist use to suggest that the man is not trapped in the corner?

Copyright © Joel Peter Johnson.

Vocabulary

EXERCISE: MEANING CLUES On a sheet of paper, answer each of the following questions using meaning clues.

1. If a person calls you **vacuous,** is the person complimenting you, insulting you, or seeking information from you?
2. Is a **tangible** object one that makes sounds, one that can be seen and touched, or one that is expensive?
3. Is an **introspective** person outgoing, contemplative, or comical?
4. If an operation would **impair** Algernon's movement, would he move better, move worse, or move faster after the operation?
5. If Dr. Strauss is an **opportunist,** is he willing to take advantage of others, a hard worker, or honest?
6. If a doctor's **specialization** is nervous disorders, does the doctor avoid treating nervous disorders, have nervous disorders, or treat nervous disorders?
7. Is a **hypothesis** true, false, or unproved?
8. Would a woman who is a **shrew** be popular or unpopular?
9. Would a child or an experienced adult be more likely to behave with **naïveté**?
10. Does a person who proves an argument **statistically** use words, numbers, or logic?
11. Algernon's test shows **regression** in his ability to solve a maze. Is his ability improving, deteriorating, or constant?
12. When Charlie's surgery causes a **sensation,** do people react with excitement, with boredom, or with fear?
13. If Algernon's age and size were **proportional,** would they be closely related, increasing, or unknown?
14. If someone said your opinion was **absurd,** would you feel proud, sympathetic, or annoyed?
15. Does a **syndrome** have a single symptom, a group of symptoms, or no symptoms?

Vocabulary Handbook
See p. R20: Context Clues.

Grammar in Context: Subject-Verb Agreement

Charlie's writing in his progress reports is often confused.

> . . . so I said hello Miss Kinnian Im redy for my lesin today only I lost my reader that we was using. She startid to cry and run out of the room and everybody looked at me and I saw they wasnt the same pepul who use to be in my class.

Among the many mistakes in this passage, there are problems of **subject-verb agreement.** Charlie has used the wrong verb form with the pronouns *we* and *they.* He should have written *we were* and *they weren't.* A singular subject should have a singular verb. A plural subject should have a plural verb. For example:

> I remember **her.**

> My experiments are **completed.**

Apply to Your Writing Always check to make sure your subjects and verbs agree in number.

WRITING EXERCISE Write a sentence that includes each subject and a correct form of the verb in parentheses.

Example: *Original* He (be)

Rewritten <u>He was</u> a good student.

1. Joe Carp and Frank Reilly (be)
2. Charlie's language (be)
3. He (try)
4. Dr. Strauss and Dr. Nemur (be)
5. We (enjoy)

Grammar Handbook
See p. R76: Making Subjects and Verbs Agree.

Daniel Keyes
born 1927

"[I am] fascinated by the complexities of the human mind."

Mind's-Eye View Daniel Keyes was born in Brooklyn, New York. Given the subject matter of his famous story, and others, such as *The Fifth Sally* and *The Minds of Billy Milligan,* it is no surprise that Keyes majored in psychology at Brooklyn College. After graduating, he worked in publishing and fashion photography and taught at his old high school. Keyes is on extended leave from Ohio University, where he has taught writing and literature.

A Flower Grows "Flowers for Algernon" was first published in 1959 in *The Magazine of Fantasy and Science Fiction.* The story was later expanded into a full-length novel, and then made into a movie called *Charly,* a musical play, and a TV production.

A Novel Idea Of "Flowers for Algernon," Daniel Keyes recalls, "The idea came to me many years before I wrote the story or the novel. What would happen if it were possible to increase human intelligence artificially?"

AUTHOR ACTIVITY
"Flowers for Algernon" has been translated into many languages and published around the world. In a small group, discuss why you think this story has such worldwide appeal.

Building Vocabulary
Exploring Meanings in Figurative Language

Writers use **figurative language** to convey meanings beyond the literal meanings of the words. This kind of language can help the reader see the ordinary details of life in fresh and original ways.

A metaphor is a kind of figurative language. A **metaphor** is a comparison in which one thing is said to be another thing.

> Well, son, I'll tell you:
> Life for me ain't been no crystal stair.
> It's had tacks in it,
> And splinters,
> And boards torn up,
>
> —Langston Hughes, "Mother to Son"

How does this **metaphor**, which compares life to a stairway, add meaning to the poem?

Strategies for Building Vocabulary

Another common type of figurative language is the **simile**—a comparison in which the word *like* or *as* is used. "Her eyes were as blue as the sky" is an example of a simile. You can use metaphors and similes to help you figure out the meanings of unfamiliar words.

❶ **Use Graphic Organizers** When you are trying to figure out the meaning of an unfamiliar word in a simile or metaphor, you may find it helpful to plot out your ideas in a diagram like the one shown here.

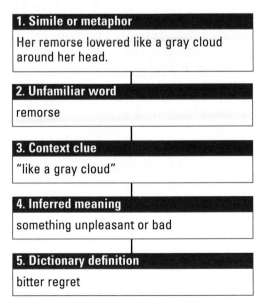

1. Simile or metaphor
Her remorse lowered like a gray cloud around her head.

2. Unfamiliar word
remorse

3. Context clue
"like a gray cloud"

4. Inferred meaning
something unpleasant or bad

5. Dictionary definition
bitter regret

❷ **Look for Context Clues** Study the words that surround an unknown word to try to find clues to its meaning.

Read the example below. How does the context help clarify the meaning of the word *etching?*

> The willow is like an etching,
> Fine-lined against the sky.

The description of the willow as "fine-lined" gives you the clue that an etching can also have that characteristic.

EXERCISE Use context clues to help you clarify the meaning of the underlined word. Then write the definition of the word.

1. The morning birdsong is a joyful <u>chorus</u>.
2. The thick soup became a <u>simmering</u> volcano.
3. The penguins with their snowy bibs looked like the <u>dignitaries</u> of the gathering.
4. His hands were as <u>leathery</u> as an old shoe.
5. Memories, like <u>ethereal</u> clouds, came to visit.

the lesson of the moth

by Don Marquis

Candle, Eigg (1980), Winifred Nicholson. 58 × 43 cm, private collection. Photo by John Webb. Copyright © The artist's family.

i was talking to a moth
the other evening
he was trying to break into
an electric light bulb
5   and fry himself on the wires

why do you fellows
pull this stunt i asked him
because it is the conventional
thing for moths or why
10   if that had been an uncovered
candle instead of an electric
light bulb you would
now be a small unsightly cinder
have you no sense

15 plenty of it he answered
but at times we get tired
of using it
we get bored with the routine
and crave beauty
20 and excitement
fire is beautiful
and we know that if we get
too close it will kill us
but what does that matter
25 it is better to be happy

for a moment
and be burned up with beauty
than to live a long time
and be bored all the while
30 so we wad all our life up
into one little roll
and then we shoot the roll
that is what life is for
it is better to be a part of beauty

35 for one instant and then cease to
exist than to exist forever
and never be a part of beauty
our attitude toward life
is come easy go easy
40 we are like human beings
used to be before they became
too civilized to enjoy themselves

and before i could argue him
out of his philosophy
45 he went and immolated[1] himself
on a patent cigar lighter
i do not agree with him
myself i would rather have
half the happiness and twice
50 the longevity[2]

but at the same time i wish
there was something i wanted
as badly as he wanted to fry himself
archy

---

1. **immolated** (ĭm′ə-lā′tĭd): killed by burning.
2. **longevity** (lŏn-jĕv′ĭ-tē): length of life.

Don Marquis
1878–1937

"Publishing a volume of verse is like dropping a rose petal down the Grand Canyon and waiting for the echo."

Unique Inspiration One day "the biggest cockroach you ever saw" scampered across Don Marquis's desk at the offices of the *New York Sun,* giving Marquis the idea for a comic character—archy, the philosophical cockroach poet. Later, Marquis created mehitabel, a joyful, adventurous alley cat. Through such characters, Marquis expressed his views on life from 1912 to 1922 in his newspaper column "The Sun Dial."

A Renaissance Man Before becoming a prosperous writer, Marquis held a variety of jobs, including drugstore clerk, truck driver, poultry plucker, short-order cook, and teacher. Considered one of America's finest humorists, Marquis wrote novels, plays, short stories, poems, and essays.

Writing Workshop

Writing poetic description . . .

From Reading to Writing Can you describe what happiness really feels like? What about the excitement of a concert or the smell of the earth after a morning rain shower? This is the job of a poet—to capture feelings and images with language. But poems are as different as poets themselves. Some poems rhyme, while others are written in free verse. Poems like "The Charge of the Light Brigade" by Alfred, Lord Tennyson commemorate an event. Others, like "Speech to the Young" by Gwendolyn Brooks, give advice to readers about surviving life's trials. Writing an **original poem** will allow you to share your own experience and ideas in a unique way.

For Your Portfolio

WRITING PROMPT Write a poem that describes an experience, an idea, a place, a person, or a feeling.

Purpose: To express yourself
Audience: Anyone interested in hearing your poem

Basics in a Box

Poetry at a Glance

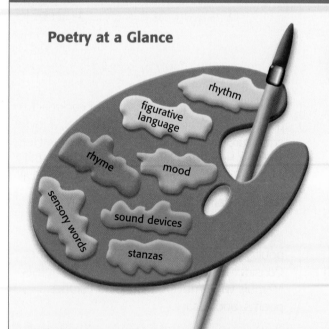

rhythm

figurative language

rhyme

mood

sensory words

sound devices

stanzas

RUBRIC STANDARDS FOR WRITING

A successful original poem should

• focus on a single experience, idea, or feeling

• use precise sensory images in a fresh, interesting way

• use figurative language such as similes and metaphors

• include poetic sound devices such as alliteration and rhyme to support the meaning of the poem

Analyzing Two Student Models

SPEAKING OPPORTUNITY

See the Speaking and Listening Handbook, p. R104 for oral presentation tips.

Travis Potter
Timberland Jr. High School

Predator

Flying high like the sun,
Soaring in the blue vastness of
the mountain sky

Descending, diving like a rock dropped out of the heavens,
Screeching as it races fast as light, down at unsuspecting prey,
Plunging into icy water with all of Earth's harshness

Reappearing from the water's darkness,
Climbing up, up into the sky,
Shedding water off its wings, now glistening like diamonds,
as it speeds, higher, higher into the crystal heavens

Stopping its speeding climb,
It peaks, levels and circles once again

The world down below seems to applaud its amazing feat,
the wind whistles with amazement

The water sore from its ripping talons, which slashed the clear
water's surface causing ripples in agony,
making only minimal noise compared to the damage it suffered

The Eagle,
Nature's Predator.

RUBRIC IN ACTION

❶ The writer focuses on one experience. He creates an atmosphere and setting with precise words and images.

❷ Uses alliteration in *descending, diving,* and *dropped*

❸ Vivid verbs create energy and give the feeling of motion, drawing the reader in.

❹ Uses a striking simile, comparing the water droplets to diamonds

❺ Poem is divided into stanzas.

❻ Brings the poem to a close by naming the subject, the eagle

Jackie Wilbur
Timberland Jr. High School

The Minstrel's Last Words

To many I am a passing thought,
gone with the dawning day.
But my memory is one child's smile,
and my tune has long to stay.

Here I sit among the mountains,
though my joy is a partner's fire.
The mountains are my audience now,
as my life will soon expire.

Many friends I made as I went along,
many more came with the seasons.
I've seen emperors, lords, kings and queens,
lost in their feats, fights, and reasons.

Now I seek the quiet of morning
my harp lies still with silent song.
My heart takes flight with nature's own tune,
echoing the hills forever long.

❶ Simple, direct language draws the reader in.

❷ Uses end rhyme in the 2nd and 4th lines of each stanza, giving the poem a musical quality
Other Options
• Use end rhyme in every other line.
• Don't use end rhyme at all.

❸ Indicates a time shift to contrast with the beginning of the poem

❹ Alliteration of *s* in *still, silent,* and *song* gives poem a lulling quality toward the end.

❺ Metaphor in "heart takes flight" compares heart to soaring bird.

Writing Your Poem

❶ Prewriting

A poem begins with a lump in the throat.

—Robert Frost, poet

Poems may begin with little more than a feeling, a thought, or an image. Without judging your ideas, **list** some emotions that you've experienced in the last week. **Include** words that describe sounds, smells, tastes, and feelings. **Note** objects you love (such as your guitar) and objects you dislike (perhaps the vacuum cleaner or the lawn mower). See the **Idea Bank** in the margin for more suggestions. Follow the steps below once you have decided on a subject.

Planning Your Poem

▷ **1. Freewrite about your subject.** Write down all of the ideas, images, and sensations that you associate with your subject.

▷ **2. Choose a focus.** What do you want the main idea of your poem to be? What impression, idea, or information do you want your readers to take from your poem? Circle the ideas that appeal to you.

▷ **3. Identify the mood you want to express.** Remember that poems say in few words what prose writing takes many words to express. Brainstorm verbs, similes, and metaphors that you might use to convey the mood of your poem. Will your poem be light and humorous or serious and heavy? How will you accomplish this? What sound devices will you use?

❷ Drafting

Don't worry if your poem doesn't flow as smoothly as you would like it to at first. Writing a poem is like sculpting—you must chip away at it to reveal the true structure.

   Zero in on one metaphor or simile that might be the most important part of your poem. **Eliminate** words and phrases that don't contribute to the main idea or that stray from the central metaphor or simile. **Experiment** with line lengths and the rhythm of your poem. If you opted for a poem with regular rhythm, **tap** out a beat as you rearrange your words.

IDEA Bank

1. Your Working Portfolio 📁
Look for ideas in the **Writing** sections you completed earlier.

2. In Other Words
Choose an object that you love. List words that describe it—colors, images, smells, and so on. In a poem, try to capture the essence of the object without actually naming it.

3. Advice Column
Think about the best advice you have ever received. Write a poem describing the situation or event that caused you to appreciate the value of the advice you were given.

Have a question?

See the **Writing Handbook**
Descriptive Writing, p. R41
See **Language Network**
Prewriting, p. 314
Drafting, p. 317

Ask Your Peer Reader

• What is the overall mood of my poem?

• Which images appeal to you most? Which ones are not working? Why?

Need revising help?

Review the **Rubric**, p. 252

Consider **peer reader** comments

Check **Revision Guidelines**, p. R33

Wondering about verb tense?

See the **Grammar Handbook**, p. R84

See **Language Network**, Figurative Language, p. 416

SPELLING
From Writing

As you revise your work, look back at the words you misspelled and determine why you made the errors you did. For additional help, refer to the strategies and generalizations in the **Spelling Handbook** on page R28.

SPEAKING
Opportunity

Recite your poem for the class.

Publishing
IDEAS

- Visit one of the lower grades in your school and read your poem aloud, using dramatic movements to draw attention to important ideas.

- Create an instructional video about the making of a poem. The video should follow you through a step-by-step explanation of how you composed your poem.

Publishing Options
www.mcdougallittell.com

❸ Revising

TARGET SKILL ▶ SIMILES AND METAPHORS Making a comparison can often create meaning in just a few words. Similes and metaphors are two types of comparison that poets use. Similes use *like* or *as*. For example, *Her eyes were like burning embers.* Metaphors describe something by speaking of it as if it were something else: *The old woman knew she had lived through all the seasons but one. Now it was the winter of her life.* Both similes and metaphors can transform a poem from just a mere list of words into an actual experience.

> Reappearing from the water's darkness,
>
> Climbing up, up into the sky, ⟨glistening like diamonds⟩
>
> Shedding water off its wings, now ~~shiny~~ ↙
>
> as it speeds, higher, higher into the sky

❹ Editing and Proofreading

TARGET SKILL ▶ VERB TENSE In poems, just as in stories, it is important to use consistent verb tense. Check your verbs to make sure you don't confuse readers.

> Now I ~~sought~~ seek ∧ the quiet of morning
>
> my harp lies still with silent song.
>
> My heart ~~took~~ takes ∧ flight with nature's won tune,
>
> echoing the hills forever long.

❺ Reflecting

FOR YOUR WORKING PORTFOLIO What did you discover about language from writing a poem? Did you discover anything new about the subject itself? Attach your reflections to your poem. Save your finished **poem** in your Working Portfolio.

Standardized Test Practice

Mixed Review

Last night, winter's white blanket fell across the woods. Today, icicles <u>hangs</u> from the edges of branches, <u>wich</u> cast shadows across the
(1)   (2)
snow. The wind blows through the trees. I watch <u>their</u> needles
(3)
shimmering with light. Silence <u>fill</u> the air, and the field <u>was undisturbed</u>
(4)   (5)
by any footprints or marks. I start to cross <u>them</u>, leaving a trail of
(6)
footprints in the snow.

Review Your Skills

Use the passage and the questions that follow it to check how well you remember the language conventions you've learned in previous grades.

1. What is the correct verb tense in item 1?

  A. hanging

  B. hanged

  C. hang

  D. Correct as is

2. What is the correct spelling in item 2?

  A. which

  B. whicth

  C. whitch

  D. Correct as is

3. What is the correct pronoun in sentence 3?

  A. its

  B. her

  C. our

  D. Correct as is

4. What is the correct verb tense in item 4?

  A. fills

  B. filled

  C. filling

  D. Correct as is

5. What is the correct verb tense in item 5?

  A. is undisturbed

  B. would be undisturbed

  C. will be undisturbed

  D. Correct as is

6. What is the correct pronoun in sentence 6?

  A. it

  B. us

  C. him

  D. Correct as is

Self-Assessment

Check your own answers in the **Grammar Handbook**

Pronoun Forms, p. R80

Making Subjects and Verbs Agree, p. R76

The Literature You'll Read

The Concepts You'll Study

Vocabulary and Reading Comprehension
Vocabulary Focus: Using Context Clues
Cause and Effect
Sequence of Events
Comparing and Contrasting

Literary Analysis
Genre Focus: Drama
Stage Directions
Flashback
Imagery

Writing and Language Conventions
Writing Workshop: Character Sketch
Pronouns
Proper Nouns

Speaking and Listening
Oral Presentation
Monologue

*D*rama

> *The theater, when all is said and done, is not life in miniature but life enormously magnified.*
> —H.L. Mencken, literary critic

Drama is a form of literature that is performed by actors before an audience. Movies, plays, and TV sitcoms are all types of drama. As you watch a movie, for example, you are probably unaware that everything you see and hear was carefully planned and written in a **script**. A **playwright,** or scriptwriter, wrote the characters' dialogue and actions to tell the story. Occasionally people listen to plays written specifically for the radio. Radio plays were a very popular form of entertainment before the age of television.

Key Elements of Drama

- stage directions
- plot
- characters
- dialogue

Stage Directions

Stage directions are instructions for the director, the performers, and the stage crew. These are often printed in italics and enclosed by parentheses. Many stage directions tell actors how to speak or move. They also describe the **scenery**—the items on the stage that create the setting, and what **props** (the objects used in a play) are necessary. Other stage directions describe **sound effects,** which are especially important in radio plays since their success depends entirely on dialogue and sound effects. The description of the set at the beginning of the play *The Diary of Anne Frank* is quite specific.

YOUR TURN Read the stage directions that begin *The Diary of Anne Frank.* What scenery and props would be needed to create the setting?

STAGE DIRECTIONS

The scene remains the same throughout the play. It is the top floor of a warehouse and office building in Amsterdam, Holland.... The three rooms of the top floor and a small attic space above are exposed to our view. The largest of the rooms is in the center, with two small rooms, slightly raised, on either side. On the right is a bathroom, out of sight. A narrow steep flight of stairs at the back leads up to the attic. The rooms are sparsely furnished with a few chairs, cots, a table or two. The windows are painted over, or covered with makeshift blackout curtains. In the main room there is a sink, a gas ring for cooking, and a wood-burning stove for warmth.

—Frances Goodrich and Albert Hackett,
The Diary of Anne Frank

Plot

The **plot** is the series of events that make up the story. The plot usually centers on a main **conflict.** A conflict begins in the **exposition,** grows in intensity during the **rising action,** reaches a **climax,** or peak, and moves toward a solution in the **falling action** (sometimes called **resolution**). The action of a play is divided into **scenes.** The scene changes whenever the setting changes. Sometimes two or more scenes are grouped into **acts.** (For more on plot, see pages 439–442).

YOUR TURN In this excerpt from *The Million-Pound Bank Note* by Walter Hackett, how is the conflict revealed?

PLOT

Henry. When will they be back?

Servant. In a month, they said.

Henry. A month! This is awful! Tell me how to get word to them. It's of great importance.

Servant. I can't, indeed. I've no idea where they've gone, sir.

Henry. Then I must see some member of the family.

Servant. Family's been away too; been abroad months—in Egypt and India, I think.

Henry. There's been an immense mistake made....

—Walter Hackett,
The Million-Pound Bank Note

Characters

In a play, the **main** and **minor characters** are often listed in a cast of characters at the beginning of the script. Often a short description appears next to each character's name. Some characters, acting as **foils,** provide a sharp contrast to the main characters. For instance, if the main character is serious, the foil's character is lighthearted and funny.

YOUR TURN Read the passage on the right from *The Million-Pound Bank Note.* How do Mr. Smedley and Tod act as foils to the calm and direct Henry? What are your impressions of each character?

CHARACTERS

Henry. Oh, very well. I apologize. Here you are.

Tod. Thank you. (*A complete change. He stutters and fumbles.*) Ah—it's—ah—that is—we—ah—you see— It's— (*quickly*) Take it back, please. (*raising voice*) Mr. Smedley! Mr. Smedley! Help! Oh, Mr. Smedley.

Smedley (*coming in; a fussy man*). What is it, Tod, what is it? Stop shouting!

Tod. Oh, but Mr. Smedley, I can't control myself.

Smedley. What's up? What's the trouble? What's wanting? Who's this?

Henry. I am a customer, and I am waiting for my change.

Smedley. Change, change! Tod, give him his change. Get it for him.

Tod. Get him his change! It's easy for you to say that, Mr. Smedley, but look at the bill yourself.

—Walter Hackett,
The Million-Pound Bank Note

Dialogue

Most plays consist almost entirely of **dialogue**—conversation between the characters. Both the plot of the play and the characters' personalities are revealed through the dialogue. The words spoken by each character are preceded by the character's name.

YOUR TURN What character traits of Henry are revealed through dialogue?

DIALOGUE

Hastings. I'm willing to gamble.

Henry. Well, I'm not.

Hastings. Think—a free trip to London.

Henry. I've no desire to go to London. I'll remain right here in Frisco.

Hastings (*fading*). Very well, but I know you're making a mistake, Henry.

—Walter Hackett, *The Million-Pound Bank Note*

Reading Drama

Reading a drama can be as thrilling as watching it performed on the stage—if you know how to visualize. Intriguing **characters** and **dialogue,** exciting **plots,** interesting **themes,** and detailed **stage directions** can all work together to produce a powerful dramatic effect. To get the most from every play, follow the reading strategies suggested here.

How to Apply the Strategies

Read the play silently. Before you try to read the play aloud, read it to yourself. You need to know the entire plot and understand the characters before you perform the play.

Read the stage directions carefully. When you read a drama, you have to imagine both the action and the scenery. Stage directions tell you where and when each scene is happening and help you understand more about the characters and the plot.

Get to know the characters. In drama, you get to know the characters through their actions and through dialogue. Visualize the characters as you read. Analyze each character's words and try to discover the feelings behind the words.

Keep track of the plot. The plot of a drama usually centers on a main conflict. Look for the conflict and watch the action build to a climax before it is resolved. Evaluate **cause-and-effect** relationships. Notice the way a character's actions or a certain event sets the play in motion. An effect may be a change in a character's actions, emotions, or circumstances.

Read the play aloud with others. When you read the part of a character, you become the actor. Be ready with your character's lines and read only the words your character says. Do not read the stage directions aloud.

Here's how Justin uses the strategies:

*"I love reading dramas of all kinds. Before I begin, I read the stage directions and try to **visualize** the action. I **evaluate** the **causes** and **effects** and try to figure out why characters say and do the things they do. I like to imagine how the character I'm reading about would say the words."*

The Million-Pound Bank Note

by MARK TWAIN *Dramatized by* WALTER HACKETT

Connect to Your Life

Overnight Wealth What words and phrases come to mind when you hear the word *millionaire?* What different traits or qualities do you associate with the life of a millionaire? Create a word web to explore your associations. Then with a partner discuss how you think your life would change if you became rich overnight.

Build Background

ECONOMICS

The pound is the main British monetary unit, similar to our dollar. If you ever travel to Britain, you will need to change dollars into pounds.

In the late 1800s, when this play is set, a pound was equal to five dollars. The million-pound bank note of the play was therefore worth $5 million. Today a pound is worth about a dollar and a half. The values of the pound and the dollar change every day, however. To find out the exact exchange rate, you can check a newspaper or Web site.

> **WORDS TO KNOW**
> **Vocabulary Preview**
>
> accommodation diversion
> ad-libbing   eccentric
> competent   judicious
> consequence   precarious
> discreet   rebuke

Focus Your Reading

LITERARY ANALYSIS · STAGE DIRECTIONS

The writer's instructions about how the play should look and sound are found in the **stage directions** in a play's script. They may include suggestions for scenery, lighting, music, sound effects, and how the actors should move and speak.

The drama you are about to read is a **radio play,** written to be heard rather than seen. It therefore has fewer stage directions than a play meant to be performed in a theater. As you read the play, think about places where additional stage directions could help you to visualize the setting and action of the drama.

ACTIVE READING · CAUSE AND EFFECT

Two events are related as **cause and effect** when one brings about the other. The event that takes place first is the cause. The event that the cause brings about is the effect, or result.

READER'S NOTEBOOK As you read *The Million-Pound Bank Note*, use a chart like the one below to keep track of the causes and effects among the events in which Henry, the main character, is involved.

Cause	Effect
Henry ventured too far.	Henry is carried out to sea.

The Million-Pound Bank Note

by Mark Twain
Dramatized by Walter Hackett

CAST OF CHARACTERS

Henry Adams	Servant	Second Man
Lloyd Hastings	Tod	Woman
First Cockney	Mr. Smedley	Third Man
Gordon Featherstone	Hotel Manager	Butler
Abel Featherstone	Second Cockney	Portia Langham
Albert Hawkins	First Man	Sir Alfred

Henry. When I was twenty-seven years old, I was a mining broker's[1] clerk in San Francisco. I was alone in the world and had nothing to depend upon but my wits and a clean reputation. These were setting my feet in the road to eventual fortune, and I was content with the prospect. During my spare time, I did outside work. One of my part-time employers was Lloyd Hastings, a mining broker. During this period I was helping Hastings to verify the Gould and Curry Extension papers, covering what seemed to be a highly valuable gold mine. One morning at two, after six hard hours of work on these papers, Lloyd Hastings and I went to the What Cheer restaurant in Frisco.[2] As we lingered over our coffee, he offered me a proposition.

Hastings. Henry, how would you like to go to London?

Henry. Thank you, no.

Hastings. Listen to me. I'm thinking of taking a month's option on the Gould and Curry Extension for the locators.

Henry. And—?

Hastings. They want one million dollars for it.

Henry. Not too much—if the claim works out

ACTIVE READER

CONNECT Would you have turned down a trip to an exciting place such as London as quickly as Henry does?

the way it appears it may.

Hastings. I'm going to try to sell it to London interests, which means a trip there, and I want you to go with me, because you know more about these papers than I.

Henry. No, thanks.

Hastings. I'll make it well worth your while. I'll pay all your expenses and give you something over if I make the sale.

Henry. I have a job.

Hastings. I'll arrange for you to get a leave of absence. What do you say?

Henry. No.

Hastings. Why?

Henry. If I go to London, I'll get out of touch with my work and with mining conditions here, and that means months getting the hang of things again.

---

1. **mining broker's:** relating to a person who acts as an agent in the buying or selling of mineral rights.

2. **Frisco:** short for "San Francisco."

Hastings. That's a pretty slim excuse, Henry.

Henry. More important, perhaps, I think you're doomed to failure.

Hastings. But you just said the claim is valuable.

Henry. It may well turn out that way, but right now its real value can't be proved. And even so, a month's option may leave you too little time to sell it; unless you sell it within the option time, you'll go stone broke.

Hastings. I'm willing to gamble.

Henry. Well, I'm not.

Hastings. Think—a free trip to London.

Henry. I've no desire to go to London. I'll remain right here in Frisco.

Hastings (*fading*). Very well, but I know you're making a mistake, Henry.

Henry. One of my few <u>diversions</u> was sailing in the bay. One day I ventured too far and was carried out to sea. Late that night, I was picked up by a freighter which was bound for London. It was a long voyage, and the captain made me work my passage without pay, as a common sailor. When I stepped ashore at London, my clothes were ragged and shabby, and I had only a dollar in my pocket. This money fed and sheltered me for twenty-four hours. During the next twenty-four I went without food and shelter. I tried to get a job, doing manual labor. But the reply was always the same.

First Cockney. I'm not sure you'd do. You ain't the sort. (*suspiciously*) Look, 'ere, you're a Yank, ain't you?

Henry. The next morning, seedy and hungry, I was dragging myself along Portland Place when my desiring eye fell on a tempting

ACTIVE READER

EVALUATE Why was it more difficult for Henry to get a job in London than in San Francisco?

treasure lying in the gutter. It was a luscious big pear—minus one bite. My mouth watered for it. But every time I made a move to get it, some passing eye detected my purpose. I was just getting desperate enough to brave all the shame when a window behind me was raised.

Gordon (*away*). I say, you there, will you step in here, please?

Henry. It was a very sumptuous house and an equally sumptuous room into which I was ushered by a servant. A couple of elderly gentlemen were sitting by the window. At that moment if I had known what they had in mind, undoubtedly I would have bolted for the door. They looked me over very thoroughly.

Gordon. He looks poor enough, don't you think, Brother?

Abel. Very. Er, young man, you are poor?

Henry. Extremely!

Abel. Good! And honest, too?

Henry. Honesty is about all I have left; that and character.

Abel. Splendid!

Gordon. If my brother and I are judges of people, we'd say you are just the man for whom we have been searching. By the way, you are also intelligent, I would say.

Henry. Yes, sir, I am. But what do you mean by saying that I appear to be just the man for whom you have been searching?

Gordon. And we don't know you. You're a perfect stranger. And better still, an American.

diversion (dĭ-vûr′zhən) *n.* a distraction, entertainment, or relaxation

Henry. It's very kind of you gentlemen to call me into your home, but I'm a bit puzzled. Could you tell me what you have in mind?

Abel. Might we inquire into your background?

Henry. Pretty soon they had my full story. Their questions were complete and searching, and I gave them straightforward answers. Finally one said:

Gordon. Oh, yes, we're certain you will do, eh, Brother?

Abel. Definitely! He is elected.

Henry. To what am I elected, please?

Gordon. This envelope will explain everything. Here, take it. (*hastily*) No, don't open it now. Take it to your lodgings and look it over carefully.

Abel. Being sure not to be rash or hasty.

Henry. I'd like to discuss the matter.

Gordon. There is nothing to discuss at the moment.

Henry. Is this a joke?

Abel. Not at all. And now good day.

Gordon. And good luck.

Abel. Cheerio!

Henry. As soon as I was out of sight of the house, I opened my envelope and saw it contained money. I lost not a moment but shoved note and money into my pocket and broke for the nearest cheap eating house. How I did eat! Finished, I took out my money and unfolded it. I took one glimpse and nearly fainted. It was a single million-pound bank note. Five millions of dollars! It made my head swim. The next thing I noticed was the owner of the eating house. His eyes were on the note, and he was petrified. He couldn't stir hand or foot. I tossed the note toward him in careless fashion.

Hawkins. I-is it real, sir? A million-pound note?

Henry (*casually*). Certainly. Let me have my change, please.

Hawkins. Oh, I'm very sorry, sir, but I can't break the bill.

Henry. Look here—

Hawkins. Hawkins is the name, Albert Hawkins, proprietor. It's only a matter of two shillings[3] you owe, a trifling sum. Please owe it to me.

Henry. I may not be in this neighborhood again for a good time.

Hawkins. It's of no <u>consequence</u>, sir. And you

> **ACTIVE READER**
>
> **QUESTION** What does Albert Hawkins mean when he said Henry chose to "play larks by dressing as a tramp"?

can have anything you want, any time you choose, and let the account run as long as you please. I'm not afraid to trust as rich a gentleman as you just because you choose to play larks[4] by dressing as a tramp.

Henry. Well, thank you. I shall take advantage of your kindness.

Hawkins. Not at all, sir, (*fading*) and please, sir, enter my humble restaurant place any time you wish. I shall be honored to receive you.

Henry. I was frightened, afraid that the police might pick me up. I was afraid of the two

---

3. **shillings:** former British coins; a shilling was equal to a twentieth of a pound.

4. **play larks:** joke around; engage in harmless pranks.

WORDS TO KNOW   **consequence** (kŏn′sĭ-kwĕns′) *n.* importance brothers' reaction when they discovered they had given me a million-pound note instead of what they must have intended giving—a one-pound note. I hurried to their house and rang the bell. The same servant appeared. I asked for the brothers.

Servant. They are gone.

Henry. Gone! Where?

Servant. On a journey.

Henry. But whereabouts?

Servant. To the Continent,[5] I think.

Henry. The Continent?

Servant. Yes, sir.

Henry. Which way—by what route?

Servant. I can't say, sir.

Henry. When will they be back?

Servant. In a month, they said.

Henry. A month! This is awful! Tell me how to get word to them. It's of great importance.

Servant. I can't, indeed. I've no idea where they've gone, sir.

Henry. Then I must see some member of the family.

Servant. Family's been away too; been abroad months—in Egypt and India, I think.

Henry. There's been an immense mistake made. They'll be back before night. Tell them I've been here, and that I'll keep coming till it's all made right, and they needn't worry.

Servant. I'll tell them, if they come back, but I'm not expecting them. They said you'd be here in an hour to make inquiries, but I must tell you it's all right, they'll be here on time to meet you. (*fading*) And that's all they said.

Henry (*slowly*). I had to give it up and go away. What a riddle it all was! They would be here "on time." What could that mean? Then I thought of the letter. I got it out and read it. It said: "You are an intelligent and honest man, as one can see by your face. We conceive you to be poor and a stranger. Enclosed you will find a sum of money. It is lent to you for thirty days, without interest. Report to this house at the end of that time. I have a bet on you. If I win it, you shall have any situation that is in my gift, any, that is, that you shall be able to prove yourself familiar with and <u>competent</u> to fill." That was all. No signature, no address, no date. I hadn't the least idea what the game was, nor whether harm was meant me or kindness. The letter said there was a bet on me. What kind of a bet? Was the bet that I would abscond with the million-pound bank note? Which brother was betting on my honesty? I reasoned this way: if I ask the Bank of England to deposit it to the credit of the man it belongs to, they'll ask me how I came by it, and if I tell the truth, they'll put me in the asylum; on the other hand, if I lie, they'll put me in jail. The same result would follow if I try to bank it anywhere or borrow money on it. Therefore, I have to carry this burden around until those men come back. A month's suffering without wages or profit—unless I help win that bet, whatever it may be. If I do, I will get the situation I am promised. My hopes began to

> **ACTIVE READER**
>
> **PREDICT** What kind of a bet do you think the elderly brothers made about Henry?

---

5. **the Continent:** mainland Europe.

Liverpool Quay by Moonlight (1887), John Atkinson Grimshaw. Tate Gallery, London/Art Resource, New York.

rise high. Then I looked at my rags. Could I afford a new suit? No, for I had nothing in the world but a million pounds. Finally I gave in and entered a fashionable tailor shop. The clerk looked at me very arrogantly.

Tod (*icily*). No chores to be done here. Get out!

Henry. Perhaps you have a misfit suit.

Tod. We don't give away suits, even misfits.

Henry. I can pay for it.

Tod. Follow me.

Henry. He took me into a back room and overhauled a pile of rejected suits. He tossed the rattiest-looking one at me. I put it on. It didn't fit. It wasn't in any way attractive.

Tod. You may have that for four pounds, cash.

Henry. It would be an <u>accommodation</u> to me if you could wait some days for the money. I haven't any small change about me.

Tod (*sarcastically*). Oh, you haven't? Well, of course, I didn't expect it. I'd only expect gentlemen like you to carry large change.

Henry (*nettled*[6]). My friend, you shouldn't judge a stranger always by the clothes he wears. I am quite able to pay for this suit.

Tod. Hah!

Henry. I simply don't wish to put you to the trouble of changing a large note.

Tod. As long as <u>rebukes</u> are going around, I might say that it wasn't quite your affair to infer that we couldn't change any note that you might happen to be carrying around. On the contrary, we can.

---

6. **nettled:** irritated; annoyed.

Henry. Oh, very well. I apologize. Here you are.

Tod. Thank you. (*A complete change. He stutters and fumbles.*) Ah—it's—ah—that is—we—ah—you see— It's— (*quickly*) Take it back, please. (*raising voice*) Mr. Smedley! Mr. Smedley! Help! Oh, Mr. Smedley.

Smedley (*coming in; a fussy man*). What is it, Tod, what is it? Stop shouting!

Tod. Oh, but Mr. Smedley, I can't control myself.

Smedley. What's up? What's the trouble? What's wanting? Who's this?

Henry. I am a customer, and I am waiting for my change.

Smedley. Change, change! Tod, give him his change. Get it for him.

Tod. Get him his change! It's easy for you to say that, Mr. Smedley, but look at the bill yourself.

Smedley. Bill, bill! Let me see it! (*pause*) Tod! Selling an <u>eccentric</u> millionaire such an unspeakable suit as that! Tod, you're a fool—a born fool! Drives every millionaire away from this place, because he can't tell a millionaire from a tramp. Here, sir, are some suits more in keeping with your position.

Henry. Thank you, but this one will do.

Smedley. Of course it won't do! I shall burn it. Tod, burn this suit at once.

Tod. Yes, Mr. Smedley.

Smedley. We shall be honored to outfit you completely, sir. . . morning clothes, evening dress, sack suits, tweeds, shetlands[7]—everything you need. Come, Tod, book and pen. Now—length of leg, 32 inches; sleeve—

Henry. But look here. I can't give you an order for suits unless you can wait indefinitely or change this bill.

Smedley. Indefinitely, sir. It's a weak word, a weak word. *Eternally, that's* the word, sir. Tod, rush these things through. Let the minor customers wait. Set down the gentleman's address and—

Henry. I'm changing my quarters. I'll drop in and leave the new address.

Smedley. Quite right, sir, quite right. One moment—allow me to show you out, sir. And don't worry about paying us. (*fading*) Your credit is the highest. Good day, sir, good day. You honor us greatly, sir.

Henry (*as though sighing*). Well, don't you see what was bound to happen? I drifted naturally into whatever I wanted. Take my hotel, for example. I merely showed the resident manager my million-pound note, and he said:

Manager. We are honored to have you as a guest, sir. Now, I have just the suite for you. It consists of a bedroom, a sitting room, a dressing room, a dining room, two baths, and—

Henry. I'll pay you a month in advance with this.

Manager (*laughing*). You honor our simple hotel, sir. Pray, don't worry about the bill.

Henry. But it may be several months before I can pay you.

Manager. We're not worried, Mr.—er—

Henry. Henry Adams.

Manager. Mr. Adams, you are a most distinguished guest. (*fading*) Anything you desire, please name it, and we shall procure it for you immediately. Thank you, sir.

---

7. **morning clothes . . . sack suits . . . shetlands:** men's garments—formal daytime dress, business suits with loose-fitting jackets, and suits made of wool from the Shetland Islands.

WORDS TO KNOW **eccentric** (ĭk-sĕn′trĭk) *adj.* very unusual in behavior; odd

Henry. And there I was, sumptuously housed in an expensive hotel in Hanover Square. I took my dinners there, but for breakfast I stuck by Hawkins's humble feeding-house, where I

ACTIVE READER

QUESTION How did Henry make Hawkins's restaurant a success?

had got my first meal on my million-pound bank note. I was the making of Hawkins.

(*Rattle of dishes and silver. Customers' voices ad-libbing in background.*)

Hawkins. Business is brisk, sir, very brisk, indeed, and has been ever since you and your million-pound bank note became patrons of my humble establishment. I've had to hire extra help, put in additional tables. Look for yourself, sir. There's a long queue[8] waiting to get in. Why, I'm famous and fair on my way to becoming wealthy.

Second Cockney. Pardon me, Guv'ner, but aren't you the gentleman what owns the million-pound bank note?

Hawkins. Look here, you, go away and stop bothering Mr.—Mr.—

Henry. Adams.

Hawkins. Mr. Adams.

Second Cockney. I was just anxious to get a look at him.

Hawkins. Who? Mr. Adams?

Second Cockney. No. The bank note.

Henry. Glad to oblige. There you are.

Second Cockney. By george, it *is* real. (*fading*) Now I can go home and tell me old lady I've seen it with me own eyes. I hopes she believes me, but she won't.

Hawkins. Mr. Adams, I wonder if I couldn't force upon you a small loan—even a large one.

Henry. Oh, no.

Hawkins. Please allow me, sir.

Henry (*relenting*). Well, as a matter of fact, I haven't gotten around to changing this note.

Hawkins. Fifty pounds might help tide you over. You know, a little spending money?

Henry. It would help, a bit.

Hawkins. I consider it a great honor. (*fading*) Indeed, a very great honor. Here you are, Mr. Adams, fifty pounds it is. (*fading*) And don't worry about repaying me.

Henry. I was in, now, and must sink or swim. I walked on air. And it was natural, for I had become one of the notorieties[9] of London. It turned my head, not just a little, but a great deal. The newspapers referred to me as the Vest-Pocket Millionaire. Then came the climaxing stroke: *Punch*[10] caricatured me! Wherever I went, people cried:

First Man. There he goes!

Second Man. That's him!

Woman. Morning, Guv'ner.

Third Man. He's a bit of all right, he is.

Henry. Why, I just swam in glory all day long. About the tenth day of my fame I fulfilled my duty to my country by calling upon the American ambassador. He received me with enthusiasm and insisted that I attend a dinner

---

8. **queue** (kyōō): a line of people.

9. **notorieties** (nō′tə-rī′ĭ-tēz): famous people; celebrities.

10. *Punch:* An English humor magazine, known for its cartoons poking fun at famous people.

WORDS
TO
KNOW   **ad-libbing** (ăd-lĭb′ĭng) *adj.* speaking spontaneously, without preparation **ad-lib** *v.*

Lord Ribblesdale (1902), John Singer Sargent. Tate Gallery, London/A.K.G., Berlin/Superstock.

party he was giving the following night. Two important things happened at that dinner. I met two people who were to play important roles in the little drama I was living. Among the guests was a lovely English girl, named Portia Langham, whom I fell in love with in two minutes, and she with me; I could see it without glasses. And just before dinner, the butler announced:

(*Guests ad-libbing in background, very politely.*)

Butler (*calling out*). Mr. Lloyd Hastings.

Henry. I stared at Hastings, and he at me, his mouth open in surprise.

Hastings. I, er—pardon me, but are you?—no, of course you can't be.

Henry (*chuckling*). But I am, Lloyd.

Hastings. Henry, I'm speechless. (*suddenly*) Don't tell me that you're also the Vest-Pocket Millionaire?

Henry. Correct!

Hastings. I've seen your own name coupled with the nickname, but it never occurred to me you were *the* Henry Adams. Why, it isn't six months since you were clerking in Frisco and sitting up nights helping me verify the Gould and Curry Extension papers. The idea of your being in London, and a vast millionaire, and a colossal celebrity! It's out of the *Arabian Nights*!

Henry. I can't realize it myself.

Hastings. It was just three months ago that we were eating together and I tried to persuade you to come to London with me. You turned me down, and now here you are. How did you happen to come, and what gave you this incredible start?

Henry. I'll tell you all about it, but not now.

Hastings. When?

Henry. The end of this month.

Hastings. Make it a week.

Henry. I can't. How's your business venture coming along?

Hastings (*sighing*). You were a true prophet, Henry. I wish I hadn't come.

Henry. Stop with me, when we leave here, and tell me all about it. I want to hear the whole story.

Hastings. You'll hear it, every last dismal word. (*fading a bit*) I'm so grateful to find a willing and sympathetic ear.

(*Background ad-libbing out. A pause, then piano playing semiclassical tune in background.*)

Henry. After dinner there was coffee and an informal piano recital and dear Miss Langham—lovely Portia Langham, the English girl. I eased her away from the music and the guests to the library, where we talked.

(*Piano out.*)

Portia. I'm really quite excited, Mr. Adams, meeting you like this. A millionaire!

Henry. But I'm not one.

Portia. B-but of course you are.

Henry. You're wrong.

Portia. I don't understand.

Henry. You will! You will, that is, if you allow me to see you tomorrow.

Portia (*as though smiling*). Well, Mr. Adams—

Henry. Henry.

Portia. Henry, then. I will give the invitation serious thought.

Henry. Tomorrow is going to be a sunny day, just right for a picnic in the country. Yes?

Portia. Yes.

Henry. I'll tell you the whole story then.

Portia. Do you think you should?

Henry. Certainly! After all, we're going to be married.

Portia (*amazed*). We—we're—going to—marry!

Henry. Absolutely! I'll call for you at noon. Where?

Portia. Meet me here.

Henry. You're a guest here?

Portia. N—no, but it will be more convenient.

Henry. Do you like me?

Portia. Yes, Henry. (*fading*) You're a very unusual young man, even if you are a millionaire, and even if you claim you aren't.

Henry. All the way home I was in the clouds, Hastings talking and I not hearing a word. When we reached my suite, he said to me:

Hastings. This luxury makes me realize how poor, how defeated I am. Even the drippings of your daily income would seem like a tremendous fortune to me.

Henry. Unreel your story, Lloyd.

Hastings. I told you the whole story on the way over here.

Henry. You did?

Hastings. Yes.

Henry. I'll be hanged if I heard a word of it.

Hastings. Are you well?

Henry. Yes. I'm in love.

Hastings. That English girl you were speaking to?

Henry. Yes. I'm going to marry her.

Hastings. Small wonder you didn't hear a word I said.

Henry. Now I'm all attention.

Hastings. I came here with what I thought was a grand opportunity. I have an option to sell the Gould and Curry Mine and keep all I can get over a million dollars.

Henry. Sounds like a good proposition.

Hastings. Yes, it's a fine claim.

Henry. Well?

Hastings. The parties here whom I tried to interest have backed down. And so here I am, trying to peddle a gold mine but with nary a[11] buyer in sight. In addition, I am almost penniless.

Henry. Surely you'll find a buyer.

Hastings. My option on the mine expires in a matter of days—in fact, at the end of this month.

Henry. You *are* in a fix.

Hastings. Henry, you can save me. Will you do it?

Henry. I? How?

Hastings. Give me a million dollars and my passage home for my option.

Henry. I can't.

Hastings. But you're wealthy.

Henry. I—I—not really.

Hastings. You have a million pounds—five millions of dollars. Buy the mine and you'll double, maybe triple, your investment.

Henry. I'd like to help, but I can't.

Hastings. You know the value of this mine as well as I do.

Henry (*tired*). Oh, Lloyd, I wish I could explain, but I can't. What you ask is impossible.

Hastings. That's quite all right. I'm sorry to have bothered you, Henry. (*fading*) You must have a good reason in turning me down, I'm sure.

Henry. It hurt me to have to refuse Lloyd, but it made me comprehend my delicate and precarious position. Here I was, deep in debt, not a cent in the world, in love with a lovely girl, and nothing in front of me but a promise of a position if, *if,* I won the bet for the nameless brother. Nothing could save me. The next day, Portia and I went on our picnic in the country. I told her the whole story, down to the last detail. Her reaction wasn't exactly what I thought it would be.

(*Sound of bird singing in background, weaving in and out of this scene.*)

Portia (*laughs*). Oh, Henry, that's priceless.

Henry (*a bit stiffly*). I fail to see the humor.

ACTIVE READER

VISUALIZE What kind of spot do you think Henry chose for the picnic? Describe scenery as you would imagine it.

Portia. But I do, more than you can imagine.

Henry. Here I am, mixed up in a bet between two eccentric old men, and for all they care I might well be in jail.

Portia (*still laughing*). Wonderful, the funniest thing I've ever heard.

Henry. Pardon me if I don't laugh.

Portia (*stops laughing*). Sorry, but it is both funny and pathetic. But you say that one of the men is going to offer you a position?

Henry. If I win the bet.

Portia. Which one is he?

Henry. I don't know. But I have one solution. If I win, I get the position. Now, I've kept very careful track of every cent I either owe or have borrowed, and I'm going to pay it back from my salary. If the position pays me six hundred pounds a year, I'll—I'll—

Portia. You'll what?

---

11. **nary a:** not one.

Henry. I'll— (*He whistles.*) To date I owe exactly six hundred pounds, my whole year's salary.

Portia. And the month isn't ended.

Henry. If I'm careful, my second year's salary may carry me through. Oh, dear, that is going to make it difficult for us to get married immediately, isn't it?

Portia (*dreamily*). Yes, it is. (*suddenly*) Henry, what are you talking about? Marriage! You don't know me.

Henry. I know your name, your nationality, your age, and most important, I know that I love you. I also know that you love me.

Portia. Please be sensible.

Henry. I can't. I'm in love.

Portia. All this sounds like a play.

Henry. It is—a wonderful one. I'll admit my owing my first two years' pay is going to pose a problem insofar as our getting married is concerned. (*suddenly*) I have it! The day I confront those two old gentlemen, I'll take you with me.

Portia. Oh, no. It wouldn't be proper.

Henry. But so much depends upon that meeting. With you there, I can get the old boys to raise my salary—say, to a thousand pounds a year. Perhaps fifteen hundred. Say you'll go with me.

Portia. I'll go.

Henry. In that case, I'll demand two thousand a year, so we can get married immediately.

Portia. Henry.

Henry. Yes?

Portia. Keep your expenses down for the balance of the month. Don't dip into your third year's salary.

Henry. And that is how matters stood at that point. Thoughts raced through my mind.

What if I lost the bet for my nameless benefactor?[12] What if he failed to give me a position? Then the answer came to me like a flash of lightning. I roused Lloyd Hastings from bed. He was a bit bewildered.

Hastings. I don't understand you. What are you getting at?

Henry. Lloyd, I'm going to save you. Save you— understand?

Hastings. No.

Henry. I'll save you, but not in the way you ask, for that wouldn't be fair after your hard work and the risks you've run. Now, I don't need to buy a mine. I can keep my capital moving without that; it's what I'm doing all the time. I know all about your mine; I know its immense value and can swear to it if anybody wishes it. You shall sell it inside of the fortnight[13] for three million cash.

Hastings. Three million!

Henry. Right!

Hastings. But how?

Henry. By using my name freely—and right now my name is on the tip of everybody's tongue. We'll divide the profits, share and share alike.

Hastings (*overjoyed*). I may use your name! Your name—think of it! Man, they'll flock in droves,[14] these rich English. They'll fight for that stock. I'm a made man, a made man forever. (*fading*) I'll never forget you as long as I live . . . never, never . . .

Henry. In less than twenty-four hours, London was abuzz! I hadn't anything to do, day after day, but sit home and wait for calls.

---

12. **benefactor:** a person who provides money or help.

13. **fortnight:** two weeks.

14. **droves:** mobs; crowds.

Sir Alfred. Then I may assume, Mr. Adams, that you consider this mining property a sound investment?

Henry. A very sound investment, Sir Alfred.

Sir Alfred. And what of this American chap, Hastings?

Henry. I know him very well, and he is as sound as the mine.

Sir Alfred. Then I think I shall invest in this property. Your recommendation does it.

(*Sound of telephone bell.*)

Henry. Excuse me, Sir Alfred.

(*Sound of receiver lifted from hook.*)

Henry (*into phone*). Yes, this is Henry Adams. Who? Sir John Hardcastle. Yes, Sir John. The Gould and Curry Extension? Yes, I know a great deal about it. I certainly would recommend it as a shrewd investment. The mine is worth far more than the asking price. Yes, Mr. Hastings is very well known in the States. Honest as the day is long, as they say. Yes, I suggest you contact Mr. Hastings. Thank you. Not at all. Good day, Sir John.

(*Sound of receiver replaced onto hook.*)

Sir Alfred. That clinches it. If Sir John is in, so am I. Do you suppose that your Mr. Hastings would mind if I brought in a few <u>discreet</u> friends on this venture?

Henry. Er, no, in fact I'm sure he wouldn't. Mr. Hastings is a very democratic chap.

Sir Alfred. Directly I shall go and call upon Mr. Hastings. By the way, exactly where is this mine?

Henry. California.

Sir Alfred. Is that near Washington, D.C.?

Henry. Not exactly.

Sir Alfred. A pity, for I had thought of asking the British ambassador to look at it. (*fading*) Well, I'm off. Thank you for your advice. Good day, Mr. Adams.

Henry. And that's the way it went—a steady stream of wealthy Londoners asking my advice, which, of course, I gave freely. Meanwhile I said not a word to Portia about the possible sale of the mine. I wanted to save it as a surprise; and then there always was the possibility the sale might fall through. The day the month was up, she and I, dressed in our best, went to the house on Portland Place. As we waited for the two old gentlemen to enter, we talked excitedly.

Portia. You're certain you have the bank note with you?

Henry. Right here. Portia, dearest, the way you look it's a crime to ask for a salary a single penny under three thousand a year.

Portia. You'll ruin us.

Henry. Just trust in me. It'll come out all right.

Portia (*worried*). Please remember, if we ask for too much, we may get no salary at all; and then what will become of us, with no way in the world to earn our living? (*fading*) Please handle this delicately, Henry.

Henry. When the two old gentlemen entered, of course they were surprised to see Portia with me. I asked them to introduce themselves, which they did.

Gordon. I am Gordon Featherstone.

Abel. And I am Abel Featherstone.

Henry. Gentlemen, I am ready to report, but first may I ask which of you bet on me?

WORDS
TO
KNOW

discreet (dĭ-skrēt′) *adj.* showing caution in speech and behavior

Gordon. It was I. Have you the million-pound note?

Henry. Here it is, sir.

Gordon. Ah! I've won. *Now* what do you say, Abel?

Abel. I say he did survive, and I've lost twenty thousand pounds. I never would have believed it.

Henry. Perhaps you might enlighten me as to the terms of the bet.

Gordon. Gladly! The Bank of England once issued two notes of a million pounds each. Only one of these had been used and canceled; the other lay in the vaults. Well, Abel and I got to wondering what would happen to a perfectly honest and intelligent stranger turned adrift in London without a friend and with no money in the world but the million-pound bank note. Abel said he would starve to death, and I claimed he wouldn't. My brother said he would be arrested if he offered the note at a bank. Well, we went on arguing until I bet him twenty thousand pounds that the man would live thirty days, anyway, on that million, and keep out of jail, too.

Abel. And I took him up.

Henry. How did you know I was the right choice?

Abel. After talking with you, we decided you had all the qualifications.

Gordon. And that pear incident—if you had picked it up very boldly, it would have proved to us you were nothing but a tramp.

Henry. You don't know how tempted I was to do just that.

Gordon. And so you shall receive your reward—a choice of any position you can fill.

Les adieux [The good-bye] (1871), James J. Tissot. City of Bristol Museum and Art Gallery, England/Bridgeman Art Library, London/Superstock.

Henry. First I ask that you look at this scrap of paper, all of you. You, too, Portia.

Gordon. A certificate of deposit in the London and County Bank—

Abel. In the sum of—

Gordon. Two hundred thousand pounds.

Portia. Henry, is it yours?

Henry. It is. It represents my share of the sale of a mining property in California, sold by my friend Lloyd Hastings—a sort of commission, as it were. It all came about by thirty days' <u>judicious</u> use of that little loan you gentlemen

WORDS TO KNOW

judicious (jōō-dǐsh'əs) *adj.* careful; showing sound judgment

277

let me have. And the only use I made of it was to buy trifles and offer the bill in change.

Abel. Come, this is astonishing.

Gordon. It's incredible.

Henry (*laughing*). I can prove it.

Portia. Henry, is that really your money? Have you been fibbing to me?

Henry. I have, indeed. But you'll forgive me, I know.

Portia (*half smiling*). Don't you be so sure.

Henry. Oh, you'll get over it. Come, let's be going.

Gordon. Wait! I promised to give you a situation, you know.

Henry. Thank you, but I really don't want one.

Portia. Henry, I'm ashamed of you. You don't even thank the good gentleman. May I do it for you?

Henry. If you can improve upon it.

Portia. I shall. Uncle Abel, first, thank you for making this possible. And, dear Father—

Henry. Hold on. You're her uncle?

Abel. I am.

Henry. And you—

Gordon. Yes, I'm her stepfather.

Portia. And the dearest one that ever was. You understand now, don't you, Henry, why I was able to laugh when you told me the story of the bet with the two nameless gentlemen. Of course I couldn't miss knowing that it was this house and that the two men were Father and Uncle Abel.

Henry. Sir, you *have* got a situation open that I want.

Gordon. Name it.

Henry. Son-in-law.

Gordon. Well, well, well! But if you haven't ever served in that capacity, you of course can't furnish satisfactory recommendations to satisfy the conditions of the contract.

Henry. Only just try me for thirty or forty years.

Gordon. What do you think, Abel?

Abel. Well, he does look to be a satisfactory sort.

Gordon. And you, Portia?

Portia. I agree—heartily.

Gordon. Very well. Take her along. If you hurry, you can reach the license bureau before it closes. (*fading*) Hop to it now.

Henry. Happy, we two? Indeed, yes! And when London got the whole history of my adventure for a month, how it did talk. My Portia's father took the million-pound bank note to the Bank of England, cashed it, had it canceled; and he gave it to us at our wedding. Framed, it now hangs in our home. It gave me my Portia; but for it I could not have remained in London, would not have appeared at the American ambassador's, never should have met her. And so I always say: Yes, it's a million-pounder, but it made but one purchase in its life and then got the article for only about a tenth part of its value. ❖

We Alone

by Alice Walker

Copyright © Roxana Villa/SIS.

We alone can devalue gold
by not caring
if it falls or rises
in the marketplace.
5 Wherever there is gold
there is a chain, you know,
and if your chain
is gold
so much the worse
10 for you.

Feathers, shells
and sea-shaped stones
are all as rare.

This could be our revolution:
15 To love what is plentiful
as much as
what is scarce.

THINKING *through* *the* LITERATURE

Connect to the Literature

1. What Do You Think?
Were you pleased by the outcome of Henry's second interview with the Featherstones? Explain your reaction.

Comprehension Check
- What is Henry's condition when he arrives in London?
- Why is Henry amazed when he opens the envelope from the two English gentlemen?
- How is Henry able to help Lloyd Hastings without spending the million-pound bank note?

Think Critically

2. How does having the million-pound note affect Henry?

3. **ACTIVE READING** **CAUSE AND EFFECT**
Review the cause-and-effect chart you made in your **READER'S NOTEBOOK**. Discuss with a classmate the actions or events that cause Henry to end up in London even though he had plans to stay in San Francisco.

4. Why do you think people's attitudes toward Henry change when they think he is rich?

5. How would you evaluate Henry as a person?

> **Think About:**
> - why he does not want to go to London with Hastings
> - how he reacts when he opens the envelope and finds the bank note
> - how he uses the bank note
> - how he reacts to Portia

6. What is your opinion of the Featherstones' bet? Explain your answer.

Extend Interpretations

7. **COMPARING TEXTS** Think back to the poem "What Is Success?" by Ralph Waldo Emerson (page 207). On the basis of the poem's description of success, do you think Henry was a success? Explain your answer.

8. Connect to Life In this play, most people treat Henry very well when they think that he is rich. Do you think people would behave this way in real life? Give reasons for your opinion.

Literary Analysis

STAGE DIRECTIONS In the script of a play, the instructions to the actors, director, and stage crew are called **stage directions.** In this radio play, the stage directions appear in italic type, surrounded by parentheses.

Most of them tell the actors how to speak—"sarcastically," "slowly," "hastily," and so forth. Others give clues about how the characters feel—"nettled," "amazed." A few explain sound effects, such as a piano playing or dishes rattling.

Paired Activity As you were reading the play, you looked for places where additional **stage directions** could help you visualize the drama better. Now, working with a partner, make a chart like the one below. Use it to record five of the places you identified. Then discuss why you selected each spot for additional stage directions.

Stage Directions		
Placement	Reason Needed	Wording
Bottom of page 266	To show what a London street looked like in the 1800s	A cobblestone street with gas lamps and swirling fog

REVIEW: SETTING In a play, the time and place in which the action occurs is called the **setting.** Why do you think the author has most of this play take place in London, far from Henry's San Francisco home?

CHOICES and CHALLENGES

Writing

Fundraising Letter Choose a deserving cause. Then write a letter to Henry, telling him why your cause deserves his help. Create a persuasive message that will encourage him to make a donation. Be sure to present evidence, examples, and reasoning to support your argument. Place your letter in your **Working Portfolio.**

Writing Handbook

See p. R49: Persuasive Writing.

Speaking & Listening

Survey Graph Take a survey or poll to find out what each of your classmates would do with a million dollars. Plot the responses in a chart like the one shown here. Present your findings in an oral presentation to your class.

If I Had a Million Dollars			
Invest	Spend	Save	Share

Number of Students: 5 4 3 2 1

Research & Technology

Honest and True Henry is unexpectedly placed in the role of a millionaire. People lavish him with special treatment, but he strives to remain honest and sincere. Think of a situation in which a person's honesty has been tested. Look for different events from a variety of resources that report similar situations. Present your findings to the class.

Reading for INFORMATION

As part of your research, read the magazine news brief "Found Money" on p. 283.

Vocabulary and Spelling

EXERCISE: SYNONYMS AND ANTONYMS

Decide whether the words in each pair are synonyms or antonyms. On your paper, write *S* for synonyms or *A* for antonyms.

1. **judicious**—foolish
2. **rebuke**—compliment
3. **competent**—unfit
4. **accommodation**—favor
5. **precarious**—secure
6. **consequence**—importance
7. **diversion**—amusement
8. **discreet**—guarded
9. **eccentric**—odd
10. **ad-libbing**—reciting

Vocabulary Handbook

See p. R24: Synonyms and Antonyms.

SPELLING STRATEGY: PREFIXES

The prefix *com-* means "with" or "together." When combining *com-* with a root or word beginning with *m, p,* or *b,* the prefix does not change.

com- + plex = complex

When *com-* is combined with other roots or words that begin with other letters, frequently the prefix changes to *col-, cor-, co-,* or *con-* to make the word easier to pronounce.

Spell the word formed when the prefix *com-* is added to the root words listed.

1. sequence
2. respond
3. operation
4. serve
5. motion

Spelling Handbook

See p. R28.

WORDS TO KNOW	accommodation	consequence	eccentric	precarious
	ad-libbing	discreet	judicious	rebuke
	competent	diversion		

Grammar in Context: Pronouns

Henry's last speech in Walter Hackett's *The Million-Pound Bank Note* describes how Henry and Portia lived happily ever after.

> Happy, we two? Indeed, yes! And when London got the whole history of my adventure for a month, how it did talk. My Portia's father took the million-pound bank note to the Bank of England, cashed it, had it canceled; and he gave it to us at our wedding. Framed, it now hangs in our home.

Instead of repeating the proper nouns *Henry, Portia,* and *London,* as well as the nouns *note* and *father,* the writer has used the **pronouns** *we, my, it, he, us,* and *our.* A pronoun is a word that takes the place of a noun or another pronoun. Writers use pronouns to avoid repeating nouns and to make their writing flow more smoothly.

Usage Tip: Make sure your readers understand to which word each pronoun refers.

WRITING EXERCISE Rewrite these sentences, replacing the underlined proper nouns with pronouns.

Example: *Original* I was working with Lloyd Hastings. One morning Lloyd Hastings offered me a trip to London. I told Lloyd Hastings I did not want to go.

Rewritten I was working with Lloyd Hastings. One morning he offered me a trip to London. I told him I did not want to go.

1. I was walking along Portland Place. Portland Place is a very grand and beautiful part of London.

2. Albert Hawkins refused to break the bank note. Albert Hawkins did not have enough change.

3. After Henry and Portia met, Henry and Portia went for a ride in the country. Henry explained Henry's situation, but Portia only laughed at Henry.

Grammar Handbook
See p. R79: Using Nouns and Pronouns.

Mark Twain
1835–1910

"The difference between the right word and a similar word is the difference between lightning and a lightning bug."

Pen Name Samuel Clemens took his pen name, Mark Twain, from a cry used by crew members of riverboats on the Mississippi River. They would call out "Mark twain!" when they had measured the water to be two fathoms deep (deep enough for boats to pass). Twain's travels on the Mississippi River inspired his most famous books: *The Adventures of Tom Sawyer* and *The Adventures of Huckleberry Finn.*

A Varied Career Twain grew up in Hannibal, Missouri, during the mid-1800s. Many of the characters in his works are based on people he knew there. As an adult, he headed west, mining for gold and silver, and eventually working for newspapers in San Francisco.

His Legacy Twain is one of America's best-known writers. His books have been translated into many languages. A number of movies and television shows have been based on works of his, including *Pudd'nhead Wilson* and *The Innocents Abroad.*

Source: *People Weekly*

Found Money

For a Florida teenager, honesty pays dividends

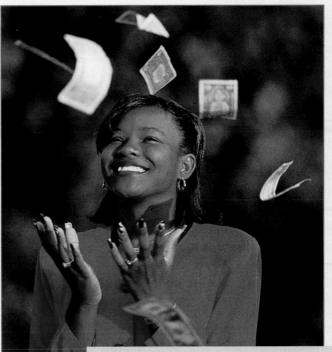

The instant that high school junior Tequesta Allen opened the wallet she'd found in a West Palm Beach, Fla., street, she knew her dream had come true. "I thought, I'm getting me a car," she says.

She might still be getting that car—but not with the $1,100 in the billfold. Because as soon as she discovered the name of the owner, she couldn't help but sympathize. Says Allen, 16: "I knew I couldn't keep it."

The youngest of four children, Tequesta Allen was being driven to the hairdresser by her father, meat-market manager Lovell Allen, 39, on Oct. 23, when they spotted the wallet on the pavement. Tequesta tried to phone its owner, West Palm Beach police officer, Frank DiStephano, 26, from the salon, but he has an unlisted number. So she tried his bank, since the name was on a withdrawal receipt with the cash.

"I was shocked," says DiStephano, who had taken out the money for a down payment on a townhouse. "I was surprised anybody would return it, much less a teenager."

Reading for Information

Often you will be asked to research a topic and report what you've learned. You might write a lengthy research report or give an oral presentation, or write a brief review of the most important information—a summary.

Summarizing

A **summary** is a complete but concise presentation of a longer text. A good summary includes the main idea and important details that support the main idea.

YOUR TURN *Use the questions that follow to help you summarize the news brief, "Found Money."*

❶ Watch for facts and information that might express the main idea of the news brief. What important details about Tequesta Allen finding a wallet are included on this page?

Reading for Information *continued*

❷ Often a writer develops the main idea of a news brief by including descriptions, explanations, examples, stories, and quotations to create a vivid mental image for the reader. How does the writer develop the main idea in these two paragraphs?

❸ Inferring the Main Idea In order to summarize what you read, you need to state the main idea. Sometimes you have to infer (or make logical guesses about) the main idea from the whole text. Use the details in this news brief to identify the main idea.

Summarizing Reread the explanation of summarizing on page 283. Write a short summary of this news brief. To write a summary, first read the complete text carefully. Then reread it, identifying the main idea and a few supporting details to include in your summary.

Research & Technology
Activity Link: *The Million-Pound Bank Note*, p. 281. What have you learned about Tequesta Allen, the teenager who found and returned the wallet? How did this news brief help you understand the merits of being honest? Write a short essay about whether honesty is its own reward or if you should be honest only if you expect to gain something from it.

Fortunately for Tequesta, virtue hasn't been her only reward. DiStephano gave her $20 as thanks, and when a local newspaper carried a story about what she had done, money started pouring in. "You've restored my faith in humanity," wrote one donor. To date, Allen has received $1,910 including a $500 check from a local car dealer.

"You've restored my faith in humanity."

❷

Of course, if any of these people had known Tequesta, they wouldn't have been so surprised that she has character. A student at Lake Worth Community High, she recently gave up her $5.50-an-hour job at Kentucky Fried Chicken to concentrate on improving her grades so she could go to college.

"She's very, very responsible," says Tequesta's mother, Martha, 38, an AIDS case worker, who notes that her daughter does community service work at Huggins Child Care Center in Lake Worth. "We were just saying how blessed we are to have her."

❸

PREPARING
to Read

SHORT STORY

Across the
Curriculum
Social Studies
ACTIVE READER
GUIDE

The Bet

by ANTON CHEKHOV

Connect to Your Life

Have you ever known of a situation that needed to be changed?

Build Background

In the late 1800s, Russian writers Anton Chekhov, Leo Tolstoy, and Maxim Gorky led a reform movement that targeted the economic and social problems in Russia.

When freed serfs failed to find jobs in the city, their children sometimes became beggars.

People were often arrested and thrown into dirty, unhealthy prisons without a fair trial.

The Czars and nobles spent their riches on baubles such as Fabergé eggs.

Focus Your Reading

LITERARY ANALYSIS   FLASHBACK

A scene from an earlier time that interrupts the ongoing action of a story is called a **flashback.** As you read this story, pay attention to when each event is actually taking place.

ACTIVE READING   SEQUENCE OF EVENTS

In order to follow a story, the reader needs to understand the **sequence of events**—the order of the events in time.

In your ☐☐ **READER'S NOTEBOOK** create a chart to track major events in the story. Note words and phrases that signal the order of events.

WORDS TO KNOW **Vocabulary Preview**

capricious	humane	incessantly	posterity	renunciation
haphazardly	immoral	obsolete	rapture	stipulated

THE BET

by Anton Chekhov

It was a dark autumn night. The old banker was pacing from corner to corner of his study, recalling to his mind the party he gave in the autumn fifteen years ago. There were many clever people at the party and much interesting conversation. They talked among other things of capital punishment. The guests, among them not a few scholars and journalists, for the most part disapproved of capital punishment.

Portrait of Henri Matisse (1905), André Derain. Tate Gallery, London/Art Resource, New York. Copyright © 1996 Artists Rights Society (ARS), New York/ADAGP, Paris.

They found it obsolete as a means of punishment, and immoral. Some of them thought that capital punishment should be replaced universally by life imprisonment.

"I don't agree with you," said the host. "I myself have experienced neither capital punishment nor life imprisonment, but if one may judge a priori,[1] then in my opinion capital punishment is more moral and more humane than imprisonment. Execution kills instantly; life imprisonment kills by degrees. Who is the more humane executioner, one who kills you in a few seconds or one who draws the life out of you incessantly, for years?"

"They're both equally immoral," remarked one of the guests, "because their purpose is the same, to take away life. The state is not all powerful. It has no right to take away that which it cannot give back, if it should so desire."

Among the company was a lawyer, a young man of about twenty-five. On being asked his opinion, he said:

"Capital punishment and life imprisonment are equally immoral; but if I were offered the choice between them, I would certainly choose the second. It's better to live somehow than not to live at all."

There ensued a lively discussion. The banker, who was then younger and more nervous, suddenly lost his temper, banged his fist on the table, and turning to the young lawyer, cried out:

"It's a lie. I bet you two millions you wouldn't stick in a cell even for five years."

"If you're serious," replied the lawyer, "then I bet I'll stay not five but fifteen."

"Fifteen! Done!" cried the banker. "Gentlemen, I stake two millions."

"Agreed. You stake two millions, I my freedom," said the lawyer.

So this wild, ridiculous bet came to pass. The banker, who at that time had too many millions to count, spoiled and capricious, was beside himself with rapture. During supper he said to the lawyer jokingly:

"Come to your senses, young man, before it's too late. Two millions are nothing to me, but you stand to lose three or four of the best years of your life. I say three or four, because you'll never stick it out any longer. Don't forget either, you unhappy man, that voluntary is much heavier than enforced imprisonment. The idea that you have the right to free yourself at any moment will poison the whole of your life in the cell. I pity you."

And now the banker, pacing from corner to corner, recalled all this and asked himself:

ACTIVE READER

CLARIFY Why do the banker and the lawyer make the bet?

"Why did I make this bet? What's the good? The lawyer loses fifteen years of his life and I throw away two millions. Will it convince people that capital punishment is worse or better than imprisonment for life? No, no! all stuff and rubbish. On my part, it was the caprice of a well-fed man; on the lawyer's, pure greed of gold."

He recollected further what happened after the evening party. It was decided that the

---

1. **a priori** (ä′prē-ôr′ē): based on a theory rather than on experience.

lawyer must undergo his imprisonment under the strictest observation, in a garden wing of the banker's house. It was agreed that during the period he would be deprived of the right to cross the threshold, to see living people, to hear human voices, and to receive letters and newspapers. He was permitted to have a musical instrument, to read books and to write letters. By the agreement he could communicate, but only in silence, with the outside world through a little window specially constructed for this purpose. Everything necessary, books, music, he could receive in any quantity by sending a note through the window. The agreement provided for all the minutest details, which made the confinement strictly solitary, and it obliged the lawyer to remain exactly fifteen years from twelve o'clock of November 14th, 1870, to twelve o'clock of November 14th, 1885. The least attempt on his part to violate the conditions, to escape if only for two minutes before the time, freed the banker from the obligation to pay him the two millions.

During the first year of imprisonment, the lawyer, as far as it was possible to judge from his short notes, suffered terribly from loneliness and boredom. From his wing day and night came the sound of the piano. During the first year, the lawyer was sent books of a light character; novels with a complicated love interest, stories of crime and fantasy, comedies, and so on.

In the second year, the piano was heard no longer and the lawyer asked only for classics. In the fifth year, music was heard again. Those who watched him said that during the whole of that year he was only eating, drinking, and lying on his bed. He yawned often and talked angrily to himself. Books he did not read. Sometimes at night he would sit down to write. He would write for a long time and tear it all up in the morning. More than once he was heard to weep.

In the second half of the sixth year, the prisoner began zealously to study languages, philosophy, and history. He fell on these subjects so hungrily that the banker hardly had time to get books enough for him. In the space of four years about six hundred volumes were bought at his request. It was while that passion lasted that the banker received the following letter from the prisoner: "My dear jailer, I am writing these lines in six languages. Show them to experts. Let them read them. If they do not find one single mistake, I beg you to give orders to have a gun fired off in the garden. By the noise I shall know that my efforts have not been in vain. The geniuses of all ages and countries speak in different languages; but in them all burns the same flame. Oh, if you knew my heavenly happiness now that I can understand them!" The prisoner's desire was fulfilled. Two shots were fired in the garden by the banker's order.

Later on, after the tenth year, the lawyer sat immovable before his table and read only the New Testament. The banker found it strange that a man who in four years had mastered six hundred erudite[2] volumes, should have spent nearly a year in reading one book, easy to understand and by no means thick. The New Testament was then replaced by the history of religions and theology.

During the last two years of his confinement the prisoner read an extraordinary amount, quite <u>haphazardly</u>. Now he would apply himself to the natural sciences, then would read

ACTIVE READER

PREDICT Will the lawyer stay for 15 years?

---

2. **erudite** (ĕr′yə-dīt′): scholarly.

WORDS TO KNOW   **haphazardly** (hăp-hăz′ərd-lē) adv. in a random manner

Byron[3] or Shakespeare. Notes used to come from him in which he asked to be sent at the same time a book on chemistry, a textbook of medicine, a novel, and some treatise on philosophy or theology. He read as though he were swimming in the sea among broken pieces of wreckage, and in his desire to save his life was eagerly grasping one piece after another.

The banker recalled all this, and thought:

"Tomorrow at twelve o'clock he receives his freedom. Under the agreement, I shall have to pay him two millions. If I pay, it's all over with me. I am ruined forever. . . ."

Fifteen years before he had too many millions to count, but now he was afraid to ask himself which he had more of, money or debts. Gambling on the stock exchange, risky speculation, and the recklessness of which he could not rid himself even in old age, had gradually brought his business to decay; and the fearless, self-confident, proud man of business had become an ordinary banker, trembling at every rise and fall in the market.

ACTIVE READER

CLARIFY Why might the banker be ruined?

"That cursed bet," murmured the old man clutching his head in despair. . . . "Why didn't the man die? He's only forty years old. He will take away my last penny, marry, enjoy life, gamble on

He yawned often and talked angrily to himself. . . . More than once he was heard to weep.

---

3. **Byron:** George Gordon Byron (1788–1824), a leading English poet of the Romantic movement.

the exchange, and I will look on like an envious beggar and hear the same words from him every day: 'I'm obliged to you for the happiness of my life. Let me help you.' No, it's too much! The only escape from bankruptcy and disgrace—is that the man should die."

The clock had just struck three. The banker was listening. In the house everyone was asleep, and one could hear only the frozen trees whining outside the windows. Trying to make no sound, he took out of his safe the key of the door which had not been opened for fifteen years, put on his overcoat, and went out of the house. The garden was dark and cold. It was raining. A keen damp wind hovered howling over all the garden and gave the trees no rest. Though he strained his eyes, the banker could see neither the ground, nor the white statues, nor the garden wing, nor the trees. Approaching the place where the garden wing stood, he called the watchman twice. There was no answer. Evidently the watchman had taken shelter from the bad weather and was now asleep somewhere in the kitchen or the greenhouse.

"If I have the courage to fulfill my intention," thought the old man, "the suspicion will fall on the watchman first of all."

In the darkness he groped for the stairs and the door and entered the hall of the garden wing, then poked his way into a narrow

passage and struck a match. Not a soul was there. Someone's bed, with no bedclothes on it, stood there, and an iron stove was dark in the corner. The seals on the door that led into the prisoner's room were unbroken.

When the match went out, the old man, trembling from agitation, peeped into the little window.

In the prisoner's room a candle was burning dim. The prisoner himself sat by the table. Only his back, the hair on his head, and his

No, it's too much! The only escape from bankruptcy and disgrace—is that the man should die.

hands were visible. On the table, the two chairs, and on the carpet by the table, open books were strewn.

Five minutes passed and the prisoner never once stirred. Fifteen years' confinement had taught him to sit motionless. The banker tapped on the window with his finger, but the prisoner gave no movement in reply. Then the banker cautiously tore the seals from the door and put the key into the lock. The rusty lock gave a hoarse groan and the door creaked.

The banker expected instantly to hear a cry of surprise and the sound of steps. Three minutes passed and it was as quiet behind the door as it had been before. He made up his mind to enter.

Before the table sat a man, unlike an ordinary human being. It was a skeleton, with tight-drawn skin, with a woman's long curly hair, and a shaggy beard. The color of his face was yellow, of an earthy shade; the cheeks were sunken, the back long and narrow, and the hand upon which he leaned his hairy head was so lean and skinny that it was painful to look upon. His hair was already silvering with grey, and no one who glanced at the senile emaciation[4] of the face would have believed that he was only forty years old. On the table, before his bent head, lay a sheet of paper on which something was written in a tiny hand.

"Poor fellow," thought the banker, "he's asleep and probably seeing millions in his dreams. I have only to take and throw this half-dead thing on the bed, smother him a moment with the pillow, and the most careful examination will find no trace of unnatural death. But, first, let us read what he has written here."

The banker took the sheet from the table and read:

"Tomorrow at twelve o'clock midnight, I shall obtain my freedom and the right to mix with people. But before I leave this room and see the sun I think it necessary to say a few words to you. On my own clear conscience, I declare to you that I despise freedom, life, health, and all that your books call the blessings of the world.

"For fifteen years I have diligently studied earthly life. True, I saw neither the earth nor the people, but in your books I sang songs, hunted deer and wild boar in the forests, loved women. . . . And beautiful women, like clouds ethereal,[5] created by the magic of your poets' genius, visited me by night and whispered to me wonderful tales, which made my head spin. In your books I climbed the summits of Elbruz and Mont Blanc and saw from there how the sun rose in the morning, and in the evening overflowed the sky, the ocean and the mountain ridges with a purple gold. From there I saw how above me lightnings glimmered, cleaving the clouds; I saw green forests, fields, rivers, lakes, cities; I heard sirens[6] singing, and the playing of the pipes of Pan. . . .[7] In your books I cast myself into bottomless abysses,[8] worked miracles, burned cities to the ground, preached new religions, conquered whole countries. . . .

"Your books gave me wisdom. All that unwearying human thought created in the centuries is compressed to a little lump in my skull. I know that I am more clever than you all.

"And I despise your books, despise all worldly blessings and wisdom. Everything is void, frail, visionary and delusive as a mirage. Though you be proud and wise and beautiful, yet will death wipe you from the face of the earth like the mice underground; and your posterity, your history, and the immortality of

---

4. **emaciation** (ĭ-mā′shē-ā′shən): abnormal thinness, usually caused by starvation.

5. **ethereal** (ĭ-thîr′ē-əl): delicate; heavenly.

6. **sirens:** from Greek mythology, sea nymphs whose sweet singing lured sailors to their deaths on rocky coasts.

7. **pipes of Pan:** Pan, the Greek god of woods, fields, and flocks, played a flutelike pipe instrument.

8. **abysses** (ə-bĭs′ĭz): deep gulfs, gorges, or chasms.

your men of genius will be as frozen slag, burnt down together with the terrestrial globe.

"You are mad, and gone the wrong way. You take lie for truth and ugliness for beauty. You would marvel if by certain conditions frogs and lizards should suddenly grow on apple and orange trees, instead of fruit, and if roses should begin to breathe the odor of a sweating horse. So do I marvel at you, who have bartered heaven for earth. I do not want to understand you.

"That I may show you in deed my contempt for that by which you live, I waive the two millions of which I once dreamed of as paradise, and which I now despise. That I may deprive myself of my right to them, I shall come out from here five minutes before the <u>stipulated</u> term, and thus shall violate the agreement."

When he had read, the banker put the sheet on the table, kissed the head of the strange man, and began to weep. He went out of the wing. Never at any other time, not even after his terrible losses on the Exchange, had he felt such contempt for himself as now. Coming home, he lay down on his bed, but agitation and tears kept him long from sleep. . . .

ACTIVE READER

EVALUATE What causes the lawyer's bitterness?

Gauguin's Armchair (1888), Vincent van Gogh. Van Gogh Museum, Amsterdam, the Netherlands. Art Resource/New York.

The next morning the poor watchman came running to him and told him that they had seen the man who lived in the wing climbing through the window into the garden. He had gone to the gate and disappeared. With his servants the banker went instantly to the wing and established the escape of his prisoner. To avoid unnecessary rumors he took the paper with the <u>renunciation</u> from the table and, on his return, locked it in his safe. ❖

WORDS TO KNOW   **stipulated** (stĭp′yə-lā′tĭd) *adj.* arranged in an agreement   **stipulate** *v.*
renunciation (rĭ-nŭn′sē-ā′shən) *n.* a declaration in which something is given up

Connect to the Literature

1. What Do You Think? Which character did you find more sympathetic—the banker or the lawyer? Explain your opinion.

Comprehension Check
- What are the terms of the bet?
- What will happen to the banker if the lawyer wins?
- What does the banker decide to do to stop the lawyer from winning?
- Who wins the bet? Why?

Think Critically

2. Do you think the banker and the lawyer would make the bet if they knew what its effects would be? Why or why not?

3. What do you think the bet proves? Explain your answer.

4. What do you think of the lawyer's decision not to take the money?

> **Think About:**
> - what he would gain by not leaving early
> - the effects of long-term isolation on him
> - what, if anything, he has gained by the end of the story

5. ACTIVE READING SEQUENCE OF EVENTS
Compare the chart you made in your READER'S NOTEBOOK with a partner's. What words and phrases helped you recognize flashbacks and other aspects of the **sequence of events?**

Extend Interpretations

6. COMPARING TEXTS The plot of Mark Twain's *The Million-Pound Bank Note* (page 263) also involves a bet. In what ways are the two bets different? In what ways are they alike? Which bet do you think makes for a better story?

7. Different Perspectives How would the story be different if it were told by a character other than the banker?

8. Connect to Life After reading this story, has your attitude about bets changed? Explain your answer.

Literary Analysis

FLASHBACK A scene from an earlier time that interrupts the ongoing action of a story is called a **flashback.** A flashback may provide information that helps the reader understand a character's present situation. In "The Bet," a flashback is used to present the banker's recollection of a party he gave 15 years earlier.

Paired Activity With a partner, identify the flashbacks in this story. When you are done, discuss the following questions:
- Would the story have been as suspenseful if it had been written without flashbacks?
- How did a flashback help you understand the banker's present situation?
- Which flashback had the greatest impact?

REVIEW: CLIMAX In the plot of a story or play, the **climax** (or turning point) is the point of maximum interest and emotional intensity. At the climax, the conflict is resolved and the outcome of the plot becomes clear. What do you think is the climax of "The Bet"?

Writing

Alternative Ending What do you think the outcome of the story would be if the lawyer did not choose to leave the cell early? Write an outline for an alternative ending based on this development.

Alternative Ending
1. The banker tries to murder the lawyer.
   A. They struggle in the lawyer's cell.
   B. _____
   C. _____
II. _____
   A. _____
   B. _____
   C. _____
   D. _____

Research & Technology

SOCIAL STUDIES

The lawyer is confined to a single room from 1870 to 1885. Using history books, encyclopedias, and Web sites, see what you can find out about the events that occurred in the outside world during those years. Did any new world leaders come to power? Did any major wars take place? Share your findings with classmates.

Research and Technology Handbook
See p. R114: Getting Information Electronically.

INTERNET **Research Starter**
www.mcdougallittell.com

Art Connection

Look at the painting *Gauguin's Armchair* by Vincent van Gogh on page 292. What details in the painting create a sense of loneliness and isolation?

Gauguin's Armchair (1888), Vincent van Gogh. Van Gogh Museum, Amsterdam, the Netherlands. Art Resource/New York.

Vocabulary

EXERCISE: DEFINITION CLUES On your paper, write the Words to Know that can best replace the underlined words in these sentences.

1. Many of the guests thought that capital punishment was <u>out-of-date</u>.
2. The banker's behavior was <u>unpredictable</u>.
3. The banker was filled with <u>excitement and joy</u> at the dinner party.
4. The set of <u>agreed-on</u> rules was designed to make the bet fair.
5. The lawyer left a <u>statement that expressed his giving up</u> of the money.
6. The guests could not decide which punishment was more <u>merciful</u>.
7. They argued about the issue <u>endlessly</u>.
8. The lawyer was not worried about <u>future generations</u>.
9. Some punishments are <u>contrary to principles of right behavior</u>.
10. The lawyer read books <u>at random</u>.

Vocabulary Handbook
See p. R20: Context Clues.

WORDS TO KNOW	capricious	humane	incessantly	posterity	renunciation
	haphazardly	immoral	obsolete	rapture	stipulated

Grammar in Context: Proper Nouns

In "The Bet" Anton Chekhov describes the prisoner's reading habits.

> During the last two years of his confinement the prisoner read an extraordinary amount, quite haphazardly. Now he would apply himself to the natural sciences, then would read Byron or Shakespeare.

The words in red are **proper nouns.** All nouns can be described as either common or proper. A common noun is a general name of a person, a place, a thing, or an idea. A proper noun is the name of a particular person, place, thing, or idea.

Proper nouns can make writing more specific. They create clearer pictures and ideas. For example, Chekhov gives the reader a more exact description of the prisoner's reading material by mentioning specific writers—Shakespeare and Byron—instead of saying that the prisoner read classic authors.

Capitalization Tip: Proper nouns always begin with a capital letter; common nouns do not.

Apply to Your Writing Use proper nouns to make your writing clearer and more specific.

WRITING EXERCISE Complete each sentence by adding a proper noun to make the sentence more specific.

Example: *Original* I enjoy poetry.

Rewritten I enjoy the poetry of <u>Nikki Giovanni</u>.

1. I like music.
2. The house had just been painted.
3. A man had just lost his keys.
4. I read a book.
5. We went to another country.

Grammar Handbook

See p. R94: Correcting Capitalization.

Anton Chekhov
1860–1904

"Literature is accepted as an art because it depicts life as it actually is."

A Breadwinner at 15 Anton Chekhov was the third of six children born to a peasant family in Taganrog, Russia, near the Black Sea. When he was 15, he began selling household goods and tutoring younger students to help support his family. Although he went to medical school, he made his career as a writer, practicing medicine only occasionally.

Life as It Really Is Chekhov wrote for comic magazines before turning to more serious stories and plays. His style of writing focuses on mood rather than on action. He believed that writers should show life as it really is. Skilled in writing both fiction and drama, Chekhov became known as the father of the modern short story and the modern play. His stories and plays such as *The Cherry Orchard* and *Uncle Vanya* became popular throughout the world.

AUTHOR ACTIVITY

Find summaries or reviews of two of Chekhov's stories or plays. Decide whether Chekhov wrote about "life as it really is" in his other works. Compare your conclusions with those of your classmates.

I Stepped from Plank to Plank
by EMILY DICKINSON

Child on Top of a Greenhouse
by THEODORE ROETHKE (rĕt kē)

Connect to Your Life

A Special Time Some childhood memories are so clear and complete they seem to carry you back in time. Think about a childhood experience you remember clearly. Share your recollection with a classmate, or share someone else's childhood memory you have read about.

Build Background

Powerful Memories Emily Dickinson and Theodore Roethke wrote at different times, and their lives followed very different paths. Both, however, use personal experience or memory as a means to explore larger questions.

As a young adult Dickinson withdrew from the world. When she wrote about an experience like the one in the poem you are about to read—a walk on a boardwalk or pier—she was drawing on her imagination and memory.

Roethke's poem "Child on Top of a Greenhouse" draws directly on the

poet's memories of his childhood. Roethke's father owned a large commercial greenhouse, and Roethke spent much of his childhood in and around it.

Focus Your Reading

LITERARY ANALYSIS **IMAGERY**

Both of the poems you are about to read describe events in such a way that the reader can imagine the physical experience. Writers can create this effect by using **imagery**—words and phrases that appeal to the reader's five senses. For example, the opening line of Roethke's poem helps the reader imagine what the speaker of the poem is physically feeling:

My feet crackling splinters of glass and dried putty,

As you read each poem, notice how the poet's use of imagery adds to the poem's overall effect.

ACTIVE READING **COMPARING AND CONTRASTING**

A helpful way to approach a story or poem is to look for ways in which it is similar to another work. This is called **comparing.** It may be just as helpful to find ways in which two stories or poems are different. This is called **contrasting.**

READER'S NOTEBOOK Make a chart like the one below. As you read each poem, jot down your thoughts about the speaker, setting, subject, imagery, and mood of the poem. Be ready to compare and contrast the two poems.

	I Stepped from Plank to Plank	Child on Top of a Greenhouse
Speaker	"I"—probably the poet	"I"—probably the poet
Setting		
Subject		
Imagery		
Mood		

I Stepped from PLANK to PLANK

by Emily Dickinson

I stepped from plank to plank
  So slow and cautiously;
The stars about my head I felt,
  About my feet the sea.

5 I knew not but the next
    Would be my final inch,—
This gave me that precarious gait
  Some call experience.

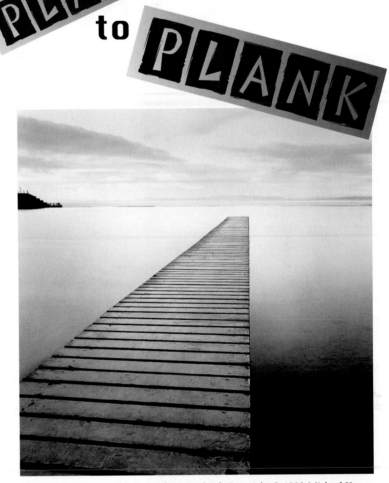

Plank Walk, Morecambe, Lancashire, England. Copyright © 1992 Michael Kenna

THINKING *through the* LITERATURE

1. What is your impression of the speaker? Give the reasons for your answer.
2. How does the speaker in this poem communicate a sense of danger? Support your answer with examples.
3. Why do you think the speaker says (in line 3) that she "felt" the stars, rather than that she simply saw them? How does this word choice add to the poem's imagery?
4. What does the speaker mean by "experience"? What do you think of this definition?

CHILD ON TOP OF A GREENHOUSE

by Theodore Roethke

The wind billowing[1] out the seat of my britches,[2]
My feet crackling splinters of glass and dried putty,
The half-grown chrysanthemums staring up like accusers,[3]
Up through the streaked glass, flashing with sunlight,
5 A few white clouds all rushing eastward,
A line of elms plunging and tossing like horses,
And everyone, everyone pointing up and shouting!

---

1. **billowing:** swelling out or bulging.
2. **britches:** trousers that only go down to the knee.
3. **accusers:** people who blame someone else for
doing something wrong.

Connect to the Literature

1. What Do You Think? What memories or thoughts did this poem bring to your mind?

Comprehension Check
• What does the child do?
• What are the people on the ground doing?

Think Critically

2. Why do you think the child goes to the top of the greenhouse?

3. How would you describe the **mood** of this poem?

> **Think About:**
> • the speaker's attitude
> • the poet's choice of images
> • the **simile,** or comparison, in line 6
> • the reaction of the people on the ground

4. Look at the simile in line 3. Of what do you think the chrysanthemums are accusing the child?

5. **ACTIVE READING** **COMPARING AND CONTRASTING** Look back at the chart you made in your **READER'S NOTEBOOK**. In what ways are the two poems alike and in what ways are they different? Compare them in terms of speaker, setting, subject, imagery, and mood.

6. In which of these two poems can you more clearly **visualize** the scene described? Support your answer.

Extend Interpretations

7. The Writer's Style What do you notice about all of the verb forms in Roethke's poem? In what ways do you think this choice adds to the poem's effect?

8. **COMPARING TEXTS** What similar ideas about nature do you find in "Simile: Willow and Ginkgo" (page 216) and "Child on Top of a Greenhouse"?

9. Connect to Life Do you find new experiences frightening, exciting, or both frightening and exciting? Explain your answer.

Literary Analysis

IMAGERY Imagery consists of words and phrases that appeal to the reader's five senses. Writers use **sensory details** to help readers imagine how things look, feel, smell, sound, and taste. In Roethke's poem the description in line 2, for example, appeals to the senses of hearing and touch:

My feet crackling splinters of glass and dried putty,

Activity With a partner, create for each poem a word web like the one shown below. Find as many examples of imagery as you can and list each example under the sense it appeals to. Compare and contrast the webs you have created for the two poems. Then discuss the following questions with a larger group.

• In each poem, which of the five senses has the most imagery? Which sense has the least imagery? Why do you think this is?

• Which of the poems contains more imagery? How does the imagery affect your ability to connect to the poem's theme?

Writing

Memoir Write a paragraph about a childhood experience you remember or have read about. Be sure to include examples of imagery so your readers will be able to picture the experience. Also be sure to explain why the experience was significant. Place your memoir in your **Working Portfolio.**

Writing Handbook
See p. R43: Narrative Writing.

Speaking & Listening

Internal Monologue Imagine that you are the speaker of one of the poems. Prepare a monologue in which you describe stepping from plank to plank or climbing to the top of the greenhouse. Be sure to state what you see, hear, feel, and smell. Use precise language, action verbs, and sensory details.

Research & Technology

Climate Control Use an encyclopedia to find out more about greenhouses. Just what are they and why do farmers use them? Make a poster with a diagram that shows how a greenhouse works. Present your findings and poster to your class.

Research and Technology Handbook
See p. R120: Using Visuals.

Emily Dickinson
1830–1886

"If I read a book and it makes my whole body so cold no fire can ever warm me, I know that is poetry."

A Small World Born and raised in 19th-century New England, Emily Dickinson became a recluse (someone who withdraws from the world) by the time she was in her mid-30s. The reason for the change is unknown, but afterward she rarely left her home in Amherst, Massachusetts.

Amazing Discovery Only seven of Dickinson's poems were published during her life, all anonymously. After her death, her sister was amazed to discover almost 1,800 poems. Many of them had been written on scraps of paper, backs of lists, bills, flyers, or used envelopes. The full worth of Dickinson's work was not recognized until 1955, when a complete edition of her poems was published in three volumes.

Theodore Roethke
1908–1963

"Make your poetry the reflection of your life."

Greenhouse Years Born in Saginaw, Michigan, Roethke was the son of German immigrants who grew and sold flowers for a living. The greenhouse his father owned became an important symbol in Roethke's poetry.

Poet and Teacher Roethke studied literature at the University of Michigan and later taught at several universities. He was a popular teacher who brought a special energy to the classroom. Once he asked students to describe the action he was about to perform, and then climbed through a window and moved along the outside ledge, making faces at the class through the glass. Roethke won the Pulitzer Prize for his poetry.

Building Vocabulary
Using Context Clues

Figuring out the meanings of unfamiliar words does not always require a dictionary. A good reader looks at the words and phrases surrounding an unfamiliar word—that is, the word's **context**—for clues to its meaning. **Description clues**, for example, can also suggest a word's meaning.

> During the last two years of his confinement the prisoner read an extraordinary amount, quite haphazardly. . . . Notes used to come from him in which he asked to be sent at the same time a book on chemistry, a textbook of medicine, a novel, and some treatise on philosophy or theology.
>
> —Anton Chekhov, "The Bet"

These **description clues** reveal that the prisoner reads books on many topics, in no logical order or pattern.

The meaning of haphazardly, "in a random manner," is made clear by these clues.

Strategies for Building Vocabulary

Here are some other types of context clues.

❶ **Definition and Restatement Clues** Sometimes writers include definitions of difficult words (**definition clues**) or restate the meanings in other words (**restatement clues**). Such clues may be signaled by commas or by words like *or, that is, in other words,* and *also called.*

> The scholars believed that capital punishment was obsolete, that it was completely out-of-date in their civilized society.

The restatement clue "completely out-of-date in their civilized society" suggests that *obsolete* means "old and out-of-date."

❷ **Example Clues** An **example clue** illustrates the meaning of a difficult word. Such clues are often signaled by words like *including* and *such as.* The meaning of *precarious* is suggested by the two examples that show how insecure Henry's position is.

> Several problems made Henry feel that he was in a precarious position, including his debt and his having only a promise of a position if he won the bet.

❸ **Comparison and Contrast Clues** A **comparison clue** compares similar words or ideas.

> The banker was as capricious as the unpredictable weather this year.

The comparison of a banker to unpredictable weather suggests the meaning of *capricious*

("acting impulsively and unpredictably").

Contrast clues point out differences between words or ideas. A contrast clue may be signaled by *although, but, however, yet, on the other hand,* or *in contrast.*

> Who is the more humane executioner, one who kills you in a few seconds or one who draws the life out of you incessantly, for years?

Note how the contrast with "in a few seconds" can help you figure out that *incessantly* means "continually."

EXERCISE Use a context clue to define each underlined word. Identify the kind of context clue that you used.

1. He could not hide his feeling of <u>rapture</u>. In other words, everyone knew the great joy he was feeling.
2. Alice is known for her <u>humane</u> actions. This year she donated thousands of dollars to education and gave food to a local shelter.
3. We wanted to enjoy a <u>diversion,</u> but instead we had to work.
4. I wanted the advice of a <u>judicious</u> person, such as a wise adult or a responsible, thoughtful student.
5. The act was as <u>immoral</u> as stealing food from a hungry child.

from SOMETHING TO DECLARE

BY JULIA ALVAREZ

We never went on trips abroad when I was a child. In the Dominican Republic[1] no one could travel without papers, and the dictatorship rarely granted anyone this special permission.

There were exceptions—my grandparents went to New York regularly because my grandfather had a post in the United Nations.[2] My godmother, who was described as one of the most beautiful widows in the country, got permission to go on a trip because she was clever. At a state function, she told El Jefe[3] that she knew he was a gentleman, and a gentleman would not refuse a lady a favor. She wanted so much to travel. The next morning a black limousine from the National Palace rolled up to her door to deliver her papers, along with some flowers.

"Where did you want to go?" I asked her, years later.

"*Want* to go?" she looked at me blankly. "I didn't want to go anywhere. I just wanted to get away from what we were living in."

Those trips were not vacations—though they did share an aspect of vacations: they were escapes, not from the tedium of daily routines, but from the terror of a police state.[4]

When I was a child, then, vacations meant a vacation from school. That was vacation enough for me! Summer vacations also meant a move. During the long, hot months of July and August, the whole extended family— uncles, aunts, sisters, cousins, grandparents— left the capital to get away from the heat and diseases that supposedly festered in the heat. My grandfather had bought an old house a short walk from the beach in the small fishing village of Boca Chica, close to where the new airport was being built. The house itself was nothing elegant: two stories, wood frame, a wraparound porch on the first floor, a large

---

1. **Dominican Republic** (də-mĭn′ĭ-kən rĭ-pŭb′lĭk): a country of the West Indies on the eastern part of the island of Hispaniola, next to Haiti.

2. **United Nations:** an international organization founded in 1945 to promote peace and economic development.

3. **El Jefe** (hĕ′fĕ): Rafael Trujillo Molina (rä-fī-yĕl′ trōō-hē′yō mō-lē′nä), the dictator of the Dominican Republic from 1930 to 1961.

4. **police state:** a government that carries out rigid and repressive controls, often by using secret police.

screened-in porch on the second, a big almond tree that dropped its fruit on the zinc roof. Ping! in the middle of the night. *What was that?*

We slept on cots, all the cousins, in that screened-in porch. Meals were eaten in two shifts on a big picnic table—first, the whole gang of children, our seating arrangement planned to avoid trouble, the rowdy ones next to the well-behaved ones, the babies with bibs in high chairs, looking like the little dignitaries of the gathering. The grown-ups ate after we were sent up to our cots to nap so we could "make our digestions" and be able to go swimming in the late afternoon. Our lives, which were communal during the rest of the year, since we all lived in neighboring houses, grew even more communal when we were all under the same roof. The men stayed on in the capital during the week, working hard, and appeared on Friday afternoons to a near-stampede of children running up from the beach to see what our papis[5] had brought us from the city. During the rest of the week, it was just the cousins and our mothers and grandmother and aunts and nursemaids, and the great big sea that splashed in our dreams all night long.

It seemed then that we were not living in a dictatorship but in a fairyland of sand and sun and girlish mothers who shared in our fun. The perpetual worried look disappeared from my mother's face. She went barefoot on the beach,

> ## Ha, ha, ha! The women held their sides and laughed wildly at the men's embarrassment.

a sea breeze blew her skirt up in the air, she tried to hold it down. We chose the fish for our dinner right off the fishermen's boats. The women gossiped and told stories and painted their fingernails and toenails and then proceeded down the line to do the same for the girl children. They always had some little intrigue going. They especially loved to tease the husbands alone in the capital, making funny phone calls, pretending they were other women ("Don't you remember me, Edy querido?!")[6] or pretending they were salesladies calling to say that their wives' order of a hundred dollars' worth of Revlon cosmetics had just arrived. Could payment be sent immediately?

Ha, ha, ha! The women held their sides and laughed wildly at the men's embarrassment. It was fun to see them having such a good time for a change.

And then, suddenly, in 1960, summers at the beach stopped altogether. We stayed home in the capital. The women were too worried to leave the men by themselves. Nightly, a black Volkswagen came up our driveway and sat there, blocking our way out. We were under virtual house arrest[7] by the SIM.[8] The men talked in low, worried voices behind closed doors. The shadows under my mother's eyes grew darker. When we begged and pleaded to go to Boca Chica for the summer, she blurted out, "¡Absolutamente[9] no!" before she was hushed by a more circumspect aunt.

---

5. **papis** (pä′pēs) *Spanish:* dads.

6. **querido** (kĕ-rē′dô) *Spanish:* beloved; dear.

7. **house arrest:** a condition of being forced to stay at home by order of a court or other part of the government.

8. **SIM:** Trujillo's secret police force.

9. **absolutamente** (äb-sô-lōō′tə-mĕn′tĕ) *Spanish:* absolutely.

Copyright © Kari Alberg

That's when talk of a vacation began in my family—vacation as in the American understanding of vacation, a trip far away, for fun.

"Wouldn't you love to go to the United States and see the snow?" one aunt asked my sisters and me one day out of the blue.

"That would be so much fun!" another aunt chimed in.

We sisters looked from one to the other aunt, unsure. Something about the conversation seemed rehearsed. Some adult intrigue was afoot. This one would not involve giggles on the phone and howls of laughter over how gullible the men were. This one would be serious, but just how serious I did not understand until years later.

My father's activities in the underground[10] were suspected, and it would be only a matter of time before he would be hauled away if we

10. **underground:** a secret organization that carries out activities opposed by the government.

Brooklyn Bridge (1989), Bernard Buffet.
Courtesy of Galerie Garnier, Paris
France © 1999 Artists Rights Society
(ARS), New York/ADAGP, Paris.

stayed. And who knew where else the ax might
fall—on his wife and children? Friends in the
States rigged up a fellowship for my father.
The pretext[11] was that he would study heart
surgery there since there wasn't a heart
surgeon in the Dominican Republic. What if
our dictator should develop heart trouble?
Papi was petitioning for a two-year visa for
himself and his family. No, he told the
authorities, he would not go without us.
That would be a hardship.

---

11. **pretext** (prē′tĕkst′): an excuse.

All we ever heard about was that we were taking a vacation to the United States.

"You bet," my mother tells me now. "We would have been held hostage!"

"Why didn't you tell us any of this back then?" I ask her. All we ever heard about was that we were taking a vacation to the United States. "Why didn't you just say, we're leaving forever?"

"Ay sí, and get ourselves killed! You had the biggest mouth back then—" She shakes her head, and I know what is coming, "and you still do, writing, writing, writing."

She is right, too—about the big mouth. I remember my three sisters and I were

coached not to mention that we were going to the United States of America—at least not till our papers came, if they ever came.

Before the day was over, I had told our secret to the cousins, the maids, the dog, and the corner candy man, who was always willing to exchange candy for my schoolbooks and school supplies. I hadn't meant to disobey, but it was so tempting to brag and get a little extra respect and a free box of cinnamon Chiclets.

"I'm going to see the snow!" I singsang to my boy cousin Ique.

"So?" he shrugged and threw me a shadow punch. Needless to say, we were two of the rowdy ones.

Toys made a better argument. I was going to the land where our toys came from.

He raised his chin, struggling with the envy he did not want to admit to feeling. "Bring me back something?" he finally pleaded.

"Okay," I said, disarmed. No one had mentioned our return until this very moment. Surely, vacations were something you came back from?

When our papers finally arrived one morning in early August, Papi booked us on the next flight off the Island. The vacation was on. We could tell anybody we wanted. Now, I was the one who grew silent.

"Hello, very pleased to make your acquaintance?" one uncle joked in English, holding out his hand to me. He had come by to say good-bye, for we were leaving that very night. Meanwhile, we girls better practice our English! We would get so tall and pale and pretty in the United States, and smart! Maybe we would marry Americans and have little blue-eyed babies that didn't know how to speak Spanish!

That gripped my braggart's[12] heart. We were going to be gone *that* long?

As the hours ticked by and more and more visitors and relatives snuck in the back way to say good-bye, my sisters and I grew pale with fear. We didn't really want to go to a place where buildings scraped the sky and everyone spoke English all the time, not just at school in English class. We didn't want to go

> For weeks that soon became months and years, I would think in this way. What was going on right this moment back home?

someplace if all the cousins and aunts couldn't come along.

The uncles mocked us, lifting their eyebrows in shock. "How crazy! Do you know how many children would give their right arms to go to the United States of America?" Their argument, a variation on the starving Chinese children who would give their right arms to eat our vegetables, did not convince us. Our protests increased as the hour drew near.

I don't know which aunt it was, or perhaps it was our own distraught mother, who decided to trick us to calm us down. Never mind the United States, we were really going to Boca Chica! The story wasn't a total untruth. The new airport was on the way to the fishing village.

We were suspicious. Why were we dressed in party dresses if we were going to the beach? Why did we have suitcases like foreign people, instead of the big hampers of clothes and provisions we took with us when we left for the summer for the beach house?

"That's enough, girls!" Mami snapped. "One more word from you and you can all stay here by yourselves!"

Now there was a threat worth its weight in silence. Abandonment was far worse than a long, maybe permanent vacation somewhere weird. By the time we boarded the plane, long past midnight, none of us had raised any further objections. Besides by now, it had been drummed into us—how lucky we

---

12. **braggart's** (brăg′ərts): of or belonging to one who boasts, lies, or shows off.

were to have our papers, to be free to go on this long vacation.

Soon after the roar of takeoff, we fell asleep, so we did not see the little lights flickering in some of the houses as we flew over Boca Chica. Hours before dawn, the fishermen would already be casting their nets out in the ocean. By midmorning, when we would be gaping at the buildings in New York City, the fish would be laid out on a big board across the rowboats' length, their pink and silver scales iridescent with the water scooped over them to make them look fresher.

For weeks that soon became months and years, I would think in this way. What was going on right this moment back home? As the leaves fell and the air turned gray and the cold set in, I would remember the big house in Boca Chica, the waves telling me their secrets, the cousins sleeping side by side in their cots, and I would wonder if those papers had set us free from everything we loved. ❖

Julia Alvarez
born 1950

"I believe that stories have the power—they enter us, they transport us, they change things inside us..."

Where Is Home? As she recounts in *Something to Declare,* Julia Alvarez emigrated from the Dominican Republic to the United States at the age of ten. Her father had taken part in an underground plot against the dictator Rafael Trujillo Molina. Although she and her family escaped to safety, she found it difficult being cut off from her homeland and adjusting to a new country. Books offered Alvarez a world where she did not feel alone. Through writing, she could begin to connect her two cultures.

A Poet First Poetry first drew Alvarez to writing. After receiving degrees in literature and writing, she spent 12 years teaching poetry at several universities. *Homecoming,* a book of her poems, was published in 1984. Since then, Alvarez has written fiction and essays. Her popular novel, *How the Garcia Girls Lost Their Accents,* deals with a Hispanic Caribbean family that lives in the Bronx. Alvarez is currently a professor at Middlebury College in Vermont.

Writing Workshop

Describing a character . . .

From Reading to Writing Character descriptions can be found in most great literature. Mark Twain draws a portrait of a clever man in *The Million-Pound Bank Note*. In "The Bet," Anton Chekhov paints a picture of how his main character changes from a greedy young man into a bitter old man. A **character sketch** is a snapshot of a character. It captures the personality and appearance of a person by showing how he or she thinks, looks, and acts. It leaves a reader feeling that he or she knows a character inside and out.

For Your Portfolio

WRITING PROMPT Write a character sketch about an individual you know or admire.

Purpose: To reveal the key elements of an individual's personality
Audience: Classmates, family, or general readers

Basics in a Box

Character Sketch at a Glance

person's actions and speech

physical description

mannerisms of person

Main Impression of Subject

writer's feelings about the person

surroundings

other people's reactions to the person

RUBRIC STANDARDS FOR WRITING

A successful character sketch should

- present a vivid picture of the personality and physical appearance of the person
- give a strong impression of the person
- include dialogue, mannerisms, descriptions, and other devices that show, rather than tell, what the person is like
- reveal the writer's response to the person
- place the person in surroundings that help readers understand him or her
- have a clear structure, a strong beginning, and a strong conclusion

Analyzing a Student Model

SPEAKING

See the Speaking and Listening Handbook, p. R104 for oral presentation tips.

OPPORTUNITY

**Dalila Martin Del Campo
Parkland Middle School**

Mr. Ochoa's Garden

Five years ago I had a best friend who lived near me in El Paso. He was a lifetime older than I am—in his sixties. He spoke only Spanish, but since I am fluent in Spanish, I was able to talk to him freely. Everyone called him Mr. Ochoa, but I called him Grandpa because he was like one: kind and generous, old as the world, his face golden brown like the sun.

Mr. Ochoa's philosophy of life was that he was put on earth to make it better. He did this by sharing his beautiful garden. He was the only person I knew who planted vegetables in the same space with flowers. Every inch of space was filled with the bright colors of flowering plants and the soft green of vegetables. When I looked out across his garden, I never knew if I would find a perfect rose or a round juicy tomato. There, I would see his figure dressed in overalls, stooped over. The oversized straw hat that covered most of his white hair usually hid his face as he moved among towering plants. With dirt-stained hands, he would prune his flowers and tie up his vegetables so they could find the sun more easily. He was always happy to let me help him in the garden. He'd give me a nod, my signal to turn the hose off and on. He wanted others to enjoy and share in his world.

He was as kind to people as he was to his plants. He would often give bouquets and baskets of vegetables to his elderly neighbors. He also volunteered at the local nursing home and visited Spanish-speaking residents who were lonely for the sound of their own language. Sometimes I went with him to the nursing home. Once in a while, if he couldn't go, I would go in his place. I learned a lot from listening to Grandpa's stories and those of his neighbors and friends. I saw the world a little differently after hearing about how much they had lived through.

RUBRIC
IN ACTION

1 The writer establishes a controlling impression of the subject.

2 Places subject in surroundings that show his true nature

3 Specific physical description creates an image in the reader's mind.

4 Details describing character's actions show his kindness and generosity.

Other Options:

• Reveal the character through what others say about him.

• Use a quotation from the character to show his personality.

• Include anecdotes about the character.

One day in early spring, Mr. Ochoa became ill. He was taken to the hospital. "My best friend is going to die soon," I thought to myself. "There is so much more I want to share with him." But now was his time to be rewarded for his kindness. While he was in the hospital, so many people dropped off flowers and arrangements of fruits and vegetables that his room looked like a greenhouse. Sometimes I'd help him slip out of bed, pale and weak, just to sniff some of the flowers or vegetables. No matter how much pain he was in, every day he would say in Spanish, "Ah, I am lucky to be surrounded by the beauty of friends and nature!"

Mr. Ochoa died just before summer. Slowly, I came to realize that I could keep him alive in my own way. I've made a garden in the back of my house. Now I plant flowers among the tomatoes and lettuce leaves. When I work under the hot sun, I think about the things he taught me—to take care of nature and appreciate the beauty of the earth, to be gentle and kind, and to listen to and appreciate the elderly. He made me see that all relationships flower when you put kindness into them.

❺ Details show how the subject reacts in a specific situation.

❻ The subject's personality is revealed through relevant dialogue.

❼ The writer states feelings about the character and his significance to her life in the conclusion.

Writing Your Character Sketch

❶ Prewriting

Whom do you want to write about? Think about people in your life who would make interesting subjects for your piece. You might choose someone you know well, such as a best friend, an outspoken relative, or a humorous sibling. You might also choose a unique person you've only observed, such as a bus driver who sings, a coach at school who carries a lucky rabbit's foot, or someone who jogs by your house rain or shine. See the **Idea Bank** in the margin for more suggestions. Once you've chosen your character, follow the steps suggested.

Planning Your Character Sketch

1. **Study your character.** In order to create a vivid picture of your character, you need to study him or her. Collect and organize information in a chart like the one below.

How character looks	What character says	What character does	How others react

2. **Choose your focus.** Review the information in your chart. What main impression of your character is suggested by his or her specific actions, words, and physical appearance, and the way others react to him or her?

3. **Explore your feelings.** Why is this person significant to you? What tone, or attitude, will you use to communicate your feelings about him or her?

4. **Place the character in a setting.** What place or situation will best show your character's personality?

❷ Drafting

One of the best things about writing a character sketch is that you can start anywhere. As you write, your subject will begin to take shape. You can rework the details at a later stage, when you revise and edit.

- **Show, Don't Tell.** You can create powerful images in a reader's mind by showing rather than telling. To describe a subject's actions, use anecdotes, descriptions, quotations, and other details. For example, instead of telling readers that your character is a kind person, describe an incident in which your character volunteered to work at a homeless shelter.

- **Grab your reader's attention at the beginning but save the best for last.** Start with a quotation or an interesting detail to grab your reader's attention. Develop your character's personality in the **body** of the essay. Your **ending** should leave readers with a strong idea about your subject and how you feel about him or her.

Ask Your Peer Reader

- How do you think I feel about my character?
- How would you describe my character's personality?
- What details help you picture my character?

1. Your Working Portfolio
Look for ideas in the **Writing** section that you completed earlier.

2. Star Potential
Read character sketches about celebrities in magazines or newspapers. Consider writing about the "stars" in your own life.

3. Interview
Choose two people in your life whom you admire. Have a partner interview you about both people to see who would make the best subject for a character sketch.

Have a question?

See the **Writing Handbook**
Incidents, p. R40
Show, Don't Tell, p. R41
See **Language Network**
Prewriting, p. 314
Drafting, p. 317

Need revising help?

Review the **Rubric**, p. 310

Consider **peer reader** comments

Check **Revision Guidelines**, p. R33

See **Language Network**, Punctuating Quotations, p. 258

Struggling with subject and verb agreement?

See the **Grammar Handbook**, p. R76

SPELLING
From Writing

 As you revise your work, look back at the words you misspelled and determine why you made the errors you did. For additional help, refer to the strategies and generalizations in the **Spelling Handbook** on page R28.

SPEAKING
Opportunity

Turn your character sketch into an oral presentation.

Publishing
IDEAS

• Illustrate your character sketches. During story time, read the sketches aloud to students in younger grades.

• Collect character sketches written by your classmates and submit them to a student-writing Web site.

INTERNET

Publishing Options
www.mcdougallittell.com

❸ Revising

TARGET SKILL ▶ **USING QUOTES TO SHOW CHARACTER** Your goal in writing a character sketch is to create images in your reader's mind of the person that you are describing. One method of showing rather than telling is using the character's own words. Dialogue can reveal the personality of the subject more vividly than many sentences of explanation. Insert dialogue to help your character sketch come to life.

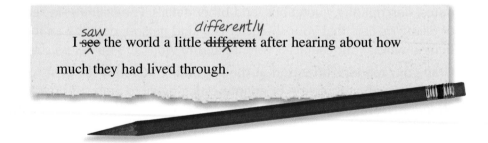

No matter how much pain he was in, every day he would ~~express his gratitude.~~ *say in Spanish, "Ah, I am lucky to be surrounded by the beauty of friends and nature!"*

❹ Editing and Proofreading

TARGET SKILL ▶ **USING MODIFIERS CORRECTLY** In everyday conversation, people often use modifiers incorrectly. For example, people might say *He's doing good* instead of *He's doing well.* Remember to use adverbs, rather than adjectives, to modify verbs, adjectives, and adverbs.

I ~~see~~ *saw* the world a little ~~different~~ *differently* after hearing about how much they had lived through.

❺ Reflecting

FOR YOUR WORKING PORTFOLIO What did you learn about your subject from writing this character sketch? Of which aspect of your character sketch are you most proud? Attach your reflections to your finished essay. Save your character sketch in your **Working Portfolio.**

Standardized Test Practice

Mixed Review

My grandmother doesn't look like a <u>successful</u> artist. Her skin <u>are</u>

(1)
(2)
wrinkled from hours of washing dishes. She dresses in simple,
traditional clothes. But in her home, there <u>was</u> practically no limit to

(3)
what she can create. <u>When nasty weather forces her indoors. She directs
her creativity</u> to her knitting and becomes an artist with wool. The

(4)
knitting needles flash like <u>lightning</u> rods during a storm as her hands

(5)
weave strands of bright wool. Woolen blankets fill her house, but only
one is my favorite. On the rocking chair <u>lie a blanket</u> with my name and

(6)
birthday knitted into it. She made it for me when I was born.

Review Your Skills

Use the passage and the questions that follow it to check how well you remember the language conventions you've learned in previous grades.

1. What is the correct spelling in sentence 1?
   A. sucessful
   B. succesful
   C. sucesful
   D. Correct as is

2. What is the correct verb form in sentence 2?
   A. is
   B. had been
   C. were
   D. Correct as is

3. What is the correct verb tense in sentence 3?
   A. is
   B. would have
   C. were
   D. Correct as is

4. How is item 4 best written?
   A. When nasty weather forces her indoors; she directs her creativity
   B. When nasty weather forces her indoors, and she directs her creativity
   C. When nasty weather forces her indoors, she directs her creativity
   D. Correct as is

5. What is the correct spelling in sentence 5?
   A. lightening
   B. litening
   C. lihtning
   D. Correct as is

6. How is sentence 6 best written?
   A. lies a blanket
   B. lying a blanket
   C. lied a blanket
   D. Correct as is

Self-Assessment

Check your own answers in the **Grammar Handbook**

Inverted Sentences, p. R78

Sentence Fragments, p. R75

Rising to the Challenge

In the selections in Unit Two, characters and speakers face a variety of challenges. What did you think of their responses to the challenges? Has reading about the characters' struggles affected the way you might respond to your next challenge? Which selections did you especially enjoy reading? From which did you learn something about life? Explore these questions as you complete one or more of the options in the following sections.

Reflecting on Theme

OPTION 1

Connecting to Characters In which of the selections in this unit do people face challenges that remind you of experiences of your own? Write a few paragraphs in which you explain the similarities and differences between your challenges and the ones in several of the selections.

OPTION 2

Focusing on Poetry Review the poetry that you read in this unit. Which poems do you think best reflect the unit theme, "Rising to the Challenge"? Create illustrations for the poems you have selected. In your illustrations try to convey both the poems' subject matter and the theme of the unit.

OPTION 3

Evaluating Decisions Several of the people in this unit's selections are faced with the need to make decisions. Others offer advice about life to the reader. Choose the one who you think makes the best decision or offers the best advice, as well as the one who you think makes the worst decision or gives the least helpful advice. Write a paragraph explaining the reasons for your choices.

Self ASSESSMENT

 READER'S NOTEBOOK

On the basis of your reading of the different genres presented in this unit, which do you most enjoy reading—poetry, fiction, nonfiction, or drama? Give reasons for your choice.

REVIEWING YOUR PERSONAL WORD List

Vocabulary Review the new words you learned in this unit. If necessary, use a dictionary to check the meaning of each word.

 Spelling Review your list of spelling words. If you're not sure of the correct spelling, use a dictionary or refer to the **Spelling Handbook** on p. R28.

Reviewing Literary Concepts

Looking at Character Changes Several characters in this unit are dynamic characters—characters who change. Select two or three characters who you think change in important ways. For each, write a sentence or two describing the character at the beginning of the selection. Then write a sentence or two about the way in which the character is different at the end. Which character do you think changes the most? Discuss your choice with a partner.

OPTION 2

Identifying Figurative Language Remember that writers use figurative language—expressions that are not literally true—to create fresh and original descriptions. Identify at least three of this unit's selections (or parts of selections) that include figurative language. List some examples of the figurative language in each, and compare your list with a classmate's. What effects do the writers create by means of the figurative language? What might the stories or poems be like without the figurative language?

Portfolio Building

- **Choices and Challenges—Writing** Several of the writing assignments in this unit asked you to write poems. Each poem focused on a key element of poetry. From your responses, choose the poem that you feel best achieves a poetic style. Write a cover note explaining your choice. Attach the note to the response and add it to your **Presentation Portfolio.**

- **Writing Workshops** In this unit you wrote an original poem and a character sketch. Reread these two pieces and decide which one better shows your strengths as a writer. Explain your choice in a note attached to the piece you have selected, and place the piece in your **Presentation Portfolio.**

- **Additional Activities** Think back to the assignments you completed for **Speaking & Listening** and **Research & Technology.** Keep a record in your portfolio of any assignments that you especially enjoyed or would like to do further work on.

Self ASSESSMENT

READER'S NOTEBOOK

With a small group of classmates, discuss how well you feel you understand the following literary terms introduced in this unit. On the basis of your discussion, divide the terms among the members of the group. Briefly explain to the group the meanings of the terms that you have been assigned. Refer to the **Glossary of Literary and Reading Terms** on page R124 for help.

- speaker
- sound devices
- style
- figurative language
- characterization
- stage directions
- flashback
- imagery

Self ASSESSMENT

Now that you have some pieces in your portfolio, notice which kinds of writing demonstrate your best work. What other kinds of writing would you like to try as the year goes on?

Setting GOALS

As you worked through the reading and writing activities in this unit, you probably identified certain skills that you want to work on. Look back through your assignments, worksheets, and **READER'S NOTEBOOK.** Make a list of skills or concepts that you would like to work on in the next unit.

LITERATURE CONNECTIONS
The Glory Field

BY WALTER DEAN MYERS

The Glory Field chronicles milestones in African-American history through one family's story. As though relating old family memories, Walter Dean Myers reveals the saga of the Lewis family from the 1700s to the present day. The family's founder, transported from Africa to America on a slave ship, inspires his descendants to triumph over adversity.

These thematically related readings are provided along with *The Glory Field:*

from To Be a Slave
BY JULIUS LESTER

The Washed Window
BY DOROTHY CANFIELD FISHER

Satchel Paige
BY BILL LITTLEFIELD

We Are an Old People
from "The Roots"
BY HUGO SALAZAR TAMARIZ

Goodbye, Grandma
BY RAY BRADBURY

A Kinsman
BY JIM WAYNE MILLER

Home
BY GWENDOLYN BROOKS

Who Can Be Born Black
BY MARI EVANS

More Choices

A Boat to Nowhere
BY MAUREEN CRANE WARTSKI
A family that cannot survive in Communist Vietnam takes a desperate chance and flees the country on a boat.

The Dream Keeper
BY LANGSTON HUGHES
A collection of poems about the blues song form.

The Owl's Song
BY JANET C. HALE
Young Billy White Hawk is determined to keep his Native American identity as he tries to find happiness.

Shadow of a Bull
BY MAIA WOJCIECHOWSKA
Manolo, the son of a champion bullfighter, is terrified to face his first bull. He is determined to fight anyway, but will he really do it?

Silent Storm
BY ANNE SULLIVAN MACY
This is the story of Anne Sullivan Macy, Helen Keller's teacher, who showed incredible determination in teaching her blind and deaf student to communicate.

The Contender

By Robert Lipsyte

Alfred Brooks, a high school dropout, desperately wants to change his life and prove to himself that he can be somebody. Subjecting himself to the discipline of training to be a boxer, he tries to discover whether he has the heart of a contender and faces new risks and responsibilities.

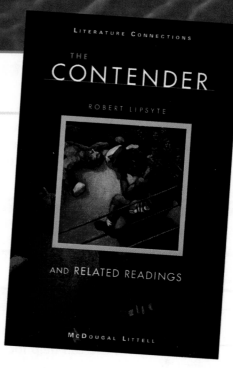

These thematically related readings are provided along with *The Contender*:

The Seventh Round
By James Merrill

Fury
By T. Ernesto Bethancourt

from **The Story of My Life**
By Helen Keller

A Crown of Wild Olive
By Rosemary Sutcliff

Muhammad Ali
By Bill Littlefield

The Rights to the Streets of Memphis
By Richard Wright

Joan Benoit: The 1984 U.S. Olympic Marathon Gold Medalist
By Rina Ferrarelli

To the Field Goal Kicker in a Slump
By Linda Pastan

Social Studies Connection

Amos Fortune, Free Man
By Elizabeth Yates
This is the biography of a slave from his life as a prince in Africa to his capture and sale in Massachusetts.

Edge of Two Worlds
By Weynan Jones
After Calvin loses the rest of his wagon train to an Indian attack, a kindly Cherokee takes the boy under his wing.

A Gathering of Days: A New England Girl's Journal
By Joan W. Blos
Fourteen-year-old Elizabeth's journal of life in New Hampshire in 1830.

Little House on the Prairie
By Laura Ingalls Wilder
The Ingalls family is determined to brave life on the Kansas prairie.

Streets of Gold
By Karen Branson
In 1847, 14-year-old Irish immigrant Maureen O'Connor comes to America. There she discovers slavery and the Underground Railroad.

Standardized Test Practice

Reading and Writing for Assessment

Throughout middle school, you will be tested on your ability to read and understand many different kinds of reading selections. The following pages will give you test-taking strategies. Practice applying these strategies by working through each of the following models.

PART 1 **How to Read the Test Selection**

In many tests, you will read a passage and then answer multiple-choice questions about it. Apply the basic test-taking strategies that follow to help you focus on the information you will need to answer test questions.

STRATEGIES FOR READING A TEST SELECTION

▸ **Before you begin reading, skim the questions that follow the passage.** These can help focus your reading.

▸ **Use your active reading strategies such as analyzing, predicting, and questioning.** Make notes in the margin only if the test directions allow you to mark on the test itself.

▸ **Think about the title, the message, and the theme.** What does the title suggest about the overall selection? What larger lesson can you draw from the passage?

▸ **Look for main ideas.** These are often stated at the beginning or end of paragraphs. Sometimes they are implied, not stated. After reading each paragraph, ask, "What was this passage about?"

▸ **Examine the sequence of ideas.** Are the ideas developed in chronological order or order of importance, or are they organized in some other way?

▸ **Evaluate the literary elements and techniques used by the writer.** How well does the writer use tone (writer's attitude toward the subject), point of view, figurative language, or other elements to create a certain effect or get a message across?

▸ **Unlock word meanings.** Use context clues and word parts to help you unlock the meanings of unfamiliar words.

Reading Selection

STRATEGIES
IN ACTION

❶ The Race Through Space

by Haan Ruby

1   "Houston, Tranquillity Base here. The *Eagle* has landed."

2   Neil Armstrong's famous words traveled around the earth on July 20, 1969, the day he became the first human to set foot on the moon. The *Eagle,* an emblem of the United States, was the name given to the lunar module— or LM—of the *Apollo 11* space mission. Before this, travel to the moon was only a dream. Stepping onto the moon's dusty surface was a concept limited to the halls of laboratories and universities. For certain people, however, words are not merely dreams. When President John F. Kennedy proposed a lunar landing by astronauts as the focus of the United States space program, he believed that moon travel was a realistic goal. He was right.

3   Landing an American on the moon had a dual purpose— to demonstrate the United States' ❷ technical prowess and to beat the Soviet Union in what came to be known as the "space race." ❸ At the time, the United States' political relations with the Soviet Union were strained, and the outcome of the space race, many believed, would indicate the superiority of one system of government over the other. In 1957 the Soviets launched *Sputnik,* the world's first manufactured satellite. In 1961 a Soviet cosmonaut became the first human in space. If America was to be at the forefront of the space race, it had to move fast. In a speech in 1962, President Kennedy said, "We choose to go to the moon in this decade . . . because . . . that goal will serve to organize and measure the best of our energies and skills, because that challenge is one that we are willing to accept, . . . and one which we intend to win . . . "

4   ❹ Despite arguments that space exploration was dangerous, impractical, and would cost too much money, plans were already in motion. The National Aeronautics and Space Administration's (NASA's) *Mercury* program was America's first man-in-space project. The first *Mercury* flight was made in 1961 and the last one in 1963. John H. Glenn, Jr., the first American astronaut to orbit the earth, made three revolutions on February 20, 1962. The *Gemini* and *Apollo* programs soon followed. The first *Gemini* flight with astronauts on board took place in 1965 and the last

❶ **Think about the title.**

One Student's Thoughts
"I wonder what race they're talking about."

❷ **Use context clues to understand vocabulary.**

One Student's Thoughts
"The writer says the U.S. wanted to prove its excellence over the Soviets, so it seems like *technical prowess* means superior technical ability."

❸ **Look for main ideas.**

One Student's Thoughts
"How would scientific exploration make a political statement?"

YOUR TURN
Find one or two other key ideas in this selection.

❹ **Read actively by asking questions.**

One Student's Thoughts
"Space travel is dangerous. Did *Eagle*'s astronauts experience any technical problems on their trip?"

in 1966. The first *Apollo* flight with astronauts, *Apollo 7,* was made in October 1968. When the pictures from *Apollo 8,* the first craft to orbit the moon, flashed across the world, people saw a tiny blue planet ❺ floating in the vast ocean of the universe. Before returning to earth, the crew of *Apollo 8* made ten lunar orbits.

5   ❻ Earlier, on January 27, 1967, tragedy had struck. Three *Apollo* astronauts were killed during a test of their spacecraft. Because of this catastrophe, new safety features were added to the spacecraft and the testing process. After a 20-month delay, three astronauts boarded the command module, *Columbia.* They were Neil Armstrong, Edwin "Buzz" Aldrin, Jr., and Michael Collins. On July 16, 1969, *Apollo 11* was launched from Cape Canaveral, Florida. Destination: the moon.

6   The trip was without major problems. One concern arose when the crew received a computer alarm, but it was minor. Still, Armstrong and Aldrin had to land the *Eagle* manually. They touched down in the Sea of Tranquillity (NASA's predetermined landing site on the moon) with less than 30 seconds worth of fuel left.

7   On July 20, 1969, six hours after landing, Neil Armstrong became the first human to set foot on the moon. One of the most famous pictures taken from that lunar visit is that of a footstep. ❼ The print reminds us of Armstrong's famous words: "That's one small step for [a] man, one giant leap for mankind."

8   After more than 21 hours, the crew headed back to earth. *Apollo 11* dropped down safely into the waters of the Pacific Ocean on July 24, 1969. People everywhere celebrated the triumph. To some, *Apollo 11* showed that the United States had clearly won the space race against the Soviet Union. However, many others saw this as a victory of a different sort. For those precious moments in space, ❽ humans everywhere were carried beyond the boundaries of race, religion, or political systems and were joined in the fulfillment of human potential. Six years later, the United States and the Soviet Union cooperated in their first joint space mission. This, perhaps, was a greater step for humankind.

❺ **Note literary elements like figurative language.**

One Student's Thoughts
"The writer compares the universe to a vast ocean."

YOUR TURN
What is the effect of this comparison?

❻ **Skim the questions that follow the passage.**

One Student's Thoughts
"There was a question about the effects of the 1967 catastrophe."

YOUR TURN
Why does the writer mention the early tragedy if Eagle's *mission was successful?*

❼ **Examine the writer's use of first-hand testimony.**

YOUR TURN
What effect does this testimony create? How does it relate to the overall theme of the selection?

❽ **Look for examples of tone.**

One Student's Thoughts
"The writer uses phrases that sound celebratory and victorious."

YOUR TURN
Why does the writer include these at the end of the essay?

How to Answer Multiple-Choice Questions

Use the strategies and notes in the side column to help you answer the questions below and on the following pages.

Based on the selection you have just read, choose the best answer for each of the following questions.

1. How does the title of the article relate to its theme?
   A. It doesn't relate to the theme.
   B. It refers to the speed of the module.
   C. It refers to the competition between two nations.
   D. It refers to a race between athletes.

2. Why does the writer include Kennedy's quote, "We choose to go to the moon . . ."?
   A. Because Kennedy was the president at the time
   B. To show that competition with the Soviets was a driving force
   C. Because she liked the way it sounded
   D. To show that Kennedy did not support the plan

3. What does the writer's tone reflect about the space race?
   A. She believes that the space race proved that the United States was superior to the Soviet Union.
   B. She celebrates the success of *Eagle*'s landing but believes in the greater victory of global cooperation.
   C. She thinks that superior technical ability means a superior system of government.
   D. She believes the astronauts were foolish in risking their lives in the name of competition.

4. What effect did the 1967 catastrophe have?
   A. It delayed *Eagle*'s mission so that new safety precautions could be added.
   B. Many people became less suspicious of space travel.
   C. All astronauts had to land their modules manually.
   D. It showed the Soviet Union's superiority.

5. What did Armstrong mean by "one small step for [a] man, one giant leap for mankind"?
   A. This was a victory for the whole human race.
   B. In time, men would be able to leap across the moon.
   C. The length of a man's stride shows his true ability.
   D. This was America's success, alone.

STRATEGIES FOR ANSWERING MULTIPLE-CHOICE QUESTIONS

▶ **Ask questions** that help you eliminate some of the choices.
▶ **Pay attention to choices** such as "all of the above" or "none of the above." To eliminate them, all you need to find is one answer that doesn't fit.
▶ **Skim your notes.** Details you noticed as you read may provide answers.

STRATEGIES IN ACTION

Ask questions. What makes sense in the real world?

One Student's Thoughts
"She probably wouldn't include it only because she liked how it sounded. Also, Kennedy did support the plan. *So I can eliminate choices C and D.*"

YOUR TURN
Which other choice doesn't make sense?

Skim your notes.

One Student's Thoughts
"The writer said that *Eagle* had to be landed manually because of a problem with the computer during the mission, not because of an earlier tragedy. *So I can eliminate choice C.*"

YOUR TURN
What other choices can you eliminate?

How to Respond in Writing

You may be asked to write answers to questions about a reading passage. **Short-answer questions** usually ask you to answer in a sentence or two. **Essay questions** require a fully developed piece of writing.

Short-Answer Question

STRATEGIES FOR RESPONDING TO SHORT-ANSWER QUESTIONS

▸ **Identify key words** in the writing prompt that tell you the ideas to discuss.
▸ **State your response directly** and be sure it's to the point.
▸ **Support your ideas** using evidence from the selection.
▸ **Use correct grammar.**

> **Sample Question**
> Answer the following question in one or two sentences.
>
> Explain what you think the writer's purpose was in researching and reporting on the first moon landing.

Essay Question

STRATEGIES FOR ANSWERING ESSAY QUESTIONS

▸ **Look for direction words** in the writing prompt such as *essay, analyze, describe,* or *compare and contrast* that tell you how to respond directly to the prompt.
▸ **List the points** you want to make before beginning to write.
▸ **Write an interesting introduction** that presents your main point.
▸ **Develop your ideas** by using evidence from the selection that supports the statements you make. Present the ideas in a logical order.
▸ **Write a conclusion** that summarizes your points.
▸ **Check your work** for correct grammar.

> **Sample Prompt**
> Write an essay in which you analyze how the tragedy of 1967 and other forces may have affected people's feelings about space travel.

STRATEGIES IN ACTION

Identify key words.

One Student's Thoughts
"The key words are *explain* and *purpose*. This means that I'll have to decide why the writer wrote the essay and tell why I think that way."

YOUR TURN

What clues to the writer's purpose can you find in the selection?

Look for direction words.

One Student's Thoughts
"The important words are *essay* and *analyze*. This means that I'll have to create a fully developed piece of writing that explains the connections between things."

YOUR TURN

What are the main points you will need to cover?

PART 4

How to Revise, Edit, and Proofread a Test Response

Here is a student's first draft in response to the writing prompt at the bottom of page 324. Read it and answer the multiple-choice questions that follow.

1	Many people are afraid of new ideas. New ideas,
2	especially ones that are risky and cost a lot of money,
3	make many people uncomfortable. Landing on the moon
4	was a big risk. People may have questioned why so much
5	money was being spent on travel in space; when there was
6	such a need for improvement on earth.
7	People became even more suspicious of space travel.

1. What is the BEST way to combine the sentences in lines 1–3 ("Many people . . . uncomfortable.")?

   A. Many people are afraid of new ideas, especially ones that are risky and cost a lot of money.

   B. New ideas make many people uncomfortable and many people are afraid of the unknown.

   C. Many people are afraid of the unknown, but even new ideas, especially ones that are risky and cost a lot of money, make many people uncomfortable.

   D. Make no change.

2. What is the BEST change, if any, to make to the sentence in lines 4–6 ("People may have questioned . . . on earth.")?

   A. Remove the semicolon after *space*.

   B. Replace the semicolon after *space* with a colon.

   C. Replace the semicolon after *space* with a period.

   D. Make no change.

3. The BEST way to make the connection between paragraphs clearer would be to add which of the following words or word groups to the beginning of line 7 ("People became . . .")?

   A. On the other hand,

   B. As a result of the tragedy of 1967,

   C. Finally,

   D. Make no change.

STRATEGIES FOR REVISING, EDITING, AND PROOFREADING

▶ **Read the passage carefully.**
▶ **Note the parts that are confusing** or don't make sense. What errors do you find?
▶ **Look for errors** in grammar, usage, spelling, and capitalization. Common errors include:
   • run-on sentences
   • sentence fragments
   • lack of subject-verb agreement
   • unclear pronoun antecedents
   • lack of transition words

THE HUMAN SPIRIT

Injustice
anywhere
is a threat
to justice
everywhere.

DR. MARTIN LUTHER KING, JR.,
Civil-Rights Leader

Second Circle Dance,
Phoebe Beasley/Omni-Photo Communications.

The Literature You'll Read

NIKKI GIOVANNI — AUTHOR STUDY

The Concepts You'll Study

Vocabulary and Reading Comprehension
Vocabulary Focus: Analyzing Word Parts—Affixes
Connecting
Drawing Conclusions
Visualizing
Determining Text Organization
Questioning
Identifying the Main Idea
Identifying Author's Purpose
Making Inferences About the Speaker
Author's Perspective

Writing and Language Conventions
Writing Workshop: Cause-and-Effect Essay
Adjectives
Adverb Placement
Participles
Appositives

Literary Analysis
Literary Focus: Character and Setting
Dynamic and Static Characters
Internal and External Conflict
Symbol
Point of View
Poetic Form
Voice
Lyric Poetry

Speaking and Listening
Oral Report
Original Poem Read-Aloud
Persuasive Speech
Music Review
Oral Interpretation of a Poem

Character and Setting

> *My stories begin with a person—[and] grow out of that person's nature or character.*
> —Paula Fox, writer

Do you have favorite characters? The first time you read about them, did it seem as though you had known them your whole life? Often, our favorite stories have characters who seem to think and feel the way we do. As we accompany these characters on their journeys, we learn about ourselves and the world around us.

Characters are the people, animals, or creatures in a story. They may be based on real people the writer knows or has learned about, or they may come from the writer's imagination. Characters live in a world created by the writer. That world is the **setting**— the time and place in which the action of the story happens. The setting in which a writer places a character will often determine what happens to that character and how his or her personality is shaped.

Main and Minor Characters

The most important characters in a story are called **main characters.** Events in the story center on the lives of one or more of these characters. Therefore, the writer usually includes many details about their circumstances, appearance, actions, and feelings. Main characters often interact with **minor characters,** who have lesser roles in the story. The actions of the minor characters, and their interactions with the major characters, help move the plot forward.

YOUR TURN In the excerpt on the right, which details tell you that Charlie is the main character?

MAIN AND MINOR CHARACTERS

Dr Strauss and Dr Nemur say it dont matter about the inkblots. I told them I dint spill the ink on the cards and I coudnt see anything in the ink. They said that maybe they will still use me. I said Miss Kinnian never gave me tests like that one only spelling and reading. They said Miss Kinnian told that I was her bestist pupil in the adult nite scool becaus I tryed the hardist and I reely wantid to lern. They said how come you went to the adult nite scool all by yourself Charlie. How did you find it. I said I askd pepul and sumbody told me where I shud go to lern to read and spell good.

—Daniel Keyes, "Flowers for Algernon"

Dynamic and Static Characters

Generally, one or more of a story's main characters change as a result of the events or conflict in the story. A character might grow emotionally, learn a lesson, or change his or her behavior. Such a character is called a **dynamic character.** A **static character,** on the other hand, is one who doesn't change. Charlie Gordon, in "Flowers for Algernon," is a dynamic character who changes dramatically throughout the story.

YOUR TURN In the passage from "The Bet," is the banker a dynamic or a static character? How do you know?

DYNAMIC AND STATIC CHARACTERS

Fifteen years before he had too many millions to count, but now he was afraid to ask himself which he had more of, money or debts. Gambling on the stock exchange, risky speculation, and the recklessness of which he could not rid himself even in old age, had gradually brought his business to decay; and the fearless, self-confident, proud man of business had become an ordinary banker, trembling at every rise and fall in the market.

—Anton Chekhov, "The Bet"

From "The Bet"

Characterization

Characterization consists of the techniques a writer uses to create and develop characters. Writers use four basic methods in developing a character:

- description of the physical appearance of the character
- presentation of the character's thoughts; speech, or **dialogue;** and actions
- what other characters think and say to or about the main character
- direct statements made by the writer about the character's nature

All of these combine to give the reader a picture of the character's traits, motivations (what drives him or her), and relationships. Also, the **conflicts** that a character faces may cause the character to change.

In the excerpt to the right, the author uses dialogue to reveal information about the character who is speaking.

CHARACTERIZATION

"When you get as old as me, all you say when something hurts is 'Howdy, Mr. Pain, sees you back again.' Then when Mr. Pain see he can't worry you none, he go on mess with somebody else."

—Walter Dean Myers, "The Treasure of Lemon Brown"

From "The Treasure of Lemon Brown"

Character Motives, Traits, and Reaction

When you analyze characters, you examine their motivations, traits, actions, and reactions. A character's **motives** are the emotions, desires, or needs that prompt the character's actions. **Traits** are permanent qualities of the character's personality. The way a character **reacts** to the story's conflict, situation, or other characters also tells you about the character's motives and traits. Sometimes the motives and traits are directly stated, and at other times, they are implied, as in the example from "The Treasure of Lemon Brown" on this page.

YOUR TURN Which of Lemon's character traits are revealed in the passage above?

Setting and Mood

The **setting** of a story, poem, or play is the time and place of the action. Elements of setting may include geographic location, historical period (past, present, future), season, time of day, and local customs and ways of speaking. Sometimes the setting is clear and well-defined; at other times, it is left to the reader's imagination. The setting will help to create a **mood,** or atmosphere. Mood is often revealed through detailed description. For example, each of the phrases in the following lines creates a mood: *the sky hung heavy and gray; the fog rolled in from the harbor; the sun singed the earth, making the blacktop of the basketball court turn once more to tar.*

A well-chosen setting might make the action seem more real, contribute to the conflict, symbolize some idea that the writer wants to emphasize, or show how the writer feels about a subject. The setting can also play an important part in the character's development and may provide clues to the character's background.

From "The Monkey's Paw"

The setting often reflects the tone of the story. **Tone** is the writer's attitude toward a subject. For example, in "The Treasure of Lemon Brown," part of the story takes place in an abandoned building. This could suggest a lonely or sad tone in the story.

YOUR TURN In the excerpt on the right, what details does the author provide to help you visualize the setting? What kind of mood is set for the story?

Connecting

Have you ever met someone for the first time but felt as though you had known that person forever? Many people call this a connection. You can connect to literature in a similar way. Details about the characters, events, and settings can trigger thoughts about your own experiences or other literature you've read. Active readers connect to what they're reading by relating it to what they already know. As you grow, you may find new things to relate to in a story—things you missed before. The old book sitting on your shelf suddenly may hold new discoveries!

How to Apply the Strategies

To **CONNECT,** an active reader will:
- Think about similarities between the characters in the story and people in his or her own life
- Become involved in the action
- Use details about people, places, and events to relive his or her own experiences
- **Visualize** the events in the story
- **Question** what relates to him or her

Try It Now!

Read and connect from the excerpt below.

But the principal had ended the suspense early when she sent that letter saying Greg would probably fail math if he didn't spend more time studying.

"And you want to play *basketball?*" His father's brows knitted over deep brown eyes. "That must be some kind of a joke. Now you just get into your room and hit those books."
—Walter Dean Myers, "The Treasure of Lemon Brown"

Here's how Jenny uses the strategies:

*"I use the **connect** strategy by thinking of similarities between Greg's and my own experience. I ask **questions** about events as they unfold, for instance, 'Have I ever wanted to spend my time playing sports instead of studying?' Once I identify with the events in the story, I can **visualize** what is happening. I can feel for the character and the situation."*

Across the Curriculum
Social Studies

ACTIVE READER GUIDE

The Treasure of Lemon Brown

by WALTER DEAN MYERS

Connect to Your Life

Are there homeless people in your community? What can you do to help them?

Build Background

Today, homelessness is a problem in every region of the United States. Estimates of the number of homeless people living in our nation range from 600,000 to 3,000,000.

Soup kitchens help feed the homeless.

Members of Habitat for Humanity build housing for people in need.

Focus Your Reading

LITERARY ANALYSIS DYNAMIC AND STATIC CHARACTERS

Generally, one or more of a story's characters change as a result of the events of the story. Such a character is called a **dynamic character.** A **static character,** in contrast, is one who remains unchanged. The characters' actions and **reactions** to events and other characters will give you clues as to whether or not they are changing.

ACTIVE READING CONNECTING

When you read, you **connect** what you are reading with what you have previously read or experienced. As you read "The Treasure of Lemon Brown," jot down in your
📖 READER'S NOTEBOOK situations and events in the story that remind you of situations and events in your own life.

WORDS TO KNOW **Vocabulary Preview**		
ajar	impromptu	tremor
beckon	ominous	vault
commence	probe	
gnarled	tentatively	

The Treasure of Lemon Brown

by Walter Dean Myers

The dark sky, filled with angry, swirling clouds, reflected Greg Ridley's mood as he sat on the stoop[1] of his building. His father's voice came to him again, first reading the letter the principal had sent to the house, then lecturing endlessly about his poor efforts in math.

"I had to leave school when I was thirteen," his father had said. "That's a year younger than you are now. If I'd had half the chances that you have, I'd . . ."

---

1. **stoop:** a small porch or staircase at the entrance of a building.

Greg had sat in the small, pale green kitchen listening, knowing the lecture would end with his father saying he couldn't play ball with the Scorpions. He had asked his father the week before, and his father had said it depended on his next report card. It wasn't often the Scorpions took on new players, especially 14-year-olds, and this was a chance of a lifetime for Greg. He hadn't been allowed to play high school ball, which he had really wanted to do, but playing for the community center team was the next best thing. Report cards were due in a week, and Greg had been hoping for the best. But the principal had ended the suspense early when she sent that letter saying Greg would probably fail math if he didn't spend more time studying.

"And you want to play *basketball?*" His father's brows knitted over deep brown eyes. "That must be some kind of a joke. Now you just get into your room and hit those books."

That had been two nights before. His father's words, like the distant thunder that now echoed through the streets of Harlem,[2] still rumbled softly in his ears.

It was beginning to cool. Gusts of wind made bits of paper dance between the parked cars. There was a flash of nearby lightning, and soon large drops of rain splashed onto his jeans. He stood to go upstairs, thought of the lecture that probably awaited him if he did anything except shut himself in his room with his math book, and started walking down the street instead. Down the block there was an old tenement that had been abandoned for some months. Some of the guys had held an <u>impromptu</u> checker

ACTIVE READER

CONNECT Think about a time in your life when an important adult did not let you participate in an activity. How did you feel?

tournament there the week before, and Greg had noticed that the door, once boarded over, had been slightly <u>ajar</u>.

Pulling his collar up as high as he could, he checked for traffic and made a dash across the street. He reached the house just as another flash of lightning changed the night to day for an instant, then returned the graffiti-scarred building to the grim shadows. He <u>vaulted</u> over the outer stairs and pushed <u>tentatively</u> on the door. It was open, and he let himself in.

The inside of the building was dark except for the dim light that filtered through the dirty windows from the street lamps. There was a room a few feet from the door, and from where he stood at the entrance, Greg could see a squarish patch of light on the floor. He entered the room, frowning at the musty smell. It was a large room that might have been someone's parlor at one time. Squinting, Greg could see an old table on its side against one wall, what looked like a pile of rags or a torn mattress in the corner, and a couch, with one side broken, in front of the window.

He went to the couch. The side that wasn't broken was comfortable enough, though a little creaky. From this spot he could see the blinking neon sign over the bodega[3] on the corner. He sat awhile, watching the sign blink first green, then red, allowing his mind to drift to the Scorpions, then to his father. His father had been a postal worker for all Greg's life and was

---

2. **Harlem:** a section of New York City; since about 1910, it has been one of the largest African-American communities in the United States.

3. **bodega** (bō-dā′gə): a small grocery store.

WORDS TO KNOW	**impromptu** (ĭm-prŏmp′tōō) *adj.* done on the spur of the moment; unplanned
	ajar (ə-jär′) *adj.* partially open
	vault (vôlt) *v.* to jump or leap
	tentatively (tĕn′tə-tĭv-lē) *adv.* with uncertainty or hesitation

proud of it, often telling Greg how hard he had worked to pass the test. Greg had heard the story too many times to be interested now.

For a moment Greg thought he heard something that sounded like a scraping against the wall. He listened carefully, but it was gone.

Outside, the wind had picked up, sending the rain against the window with a force that shook the glass in its frame. A car passed, its tires hissing over the wet street and its red taillights glowing in the darkness.

Greg thought he heard the noise again. His stomach tightened as he held himself still and listened intently. There weren't any more scraping noises, but he was sure he had heard something in the darkness—something breathing!

He tried to figure out just where the breathing was coming from; he knew it was in the room with him. Slowly he stood, tensing. As he turned, a flash of lightning lit up the room, frightening him with its sudden brilliance. He saw nothing, just the overturned table, the pile of rags, and an old newspaper on the floor. Could he have been imagining the sounds? He continued listening but heard nothing and thought that it might have just been rats. Still, he thought, as soon as the rain let up he would leave. He went to the window and was about to look out when he heard a voice behind him.

"Don't try nothin' 'cause I got a razor here sharp enough to cut a week into nine days!"

Greg, except for an involuntary <u>tremor</u> in his knees, stood stock-still. The voice was high and brittle, like dry twigs being broken, surely not one he had ever heard before. There was a shuffling sound as the person who had been speaking moved a step closer. Greg turned, holding his breath, his eyes straining to see in the dark room.

The upper part of the figure before him was still in darkness. The lower half was in the dim rectangle of light that fell unevenly from the window. There were two feet, in cracked, dirty shoes from which rose legs that were wrapped in rags.

> ## "Don't try nothin' 'cause I got a razor here sharp enough to cut a week into nine days!"

"Who are you?" Greg hardly recognized his own voice.

"I'm Lemon Brown," came the answer. "Who're you?"

"Greg Ridley."

"What you doing here?" The figure shuffled forward again, and Greg took a small step backward.

"It's raining," Greg said.

"I can see that," the figure said.

The person who called himself Lemon Brown peered forward, and Greg could see him clearly. He was an old man. His black, heavily wrinkled face was surrounded by a halo of crinkly white hair and whiskers that seemed to separate his head from the layers of dirty coats piled on his smallish frame. His pants were bagged to the knee, where they were met with rags that went down to the old shoes. The rags were held on with strings, and there was a rope around his middle. Greg relaxed. He had seen the man before, picking through the trash on the corner and pulling clothes out of a Salvation Army box. There was no sign of the razor that could "cut a

WORDS TO KNOW **tremor** (trĕm′ər) *n.* a shaking or a vibrating movement; a nervous trembling or quivering week into nine days."

"What are you doing here?" Greg asked.

"This is where I'm staying," Lemon Brown said. "What you here for?"

"Told you it was raining out," Greg said, leaning against the back of the couch until he felt it give slightly.

"Ain't you got no home?"

"I got a home," Greg answered.

"You ain't one of them bad boys looking for my treasure, is you?" Lemon Brown cocked his head to one side and squinted one eye. "Because I told you I got me a razor."

"I'm not looking for your treasure," Greg answered, smiling. "*If* you have one."

"What you mean, *if* I have one," Lemon Brown said. "Every man got a treasure. You don't know that, you must be a fool!"

"Sure," Greg said as he sat on the sofa and put one leg over the back. "What do you have, gold coins?"

"Don't worry none about what I got," Lemon Brown said. "You know who I am?"

"You told me your name was orange or lemon or something like that."

"Lemon Brown," the old man said, pulling back his shoulders as he did so. "They used to call me Sweet Lemon Brown."

"Sweet Lemon?" Greg asked.

"Yessir. Sweet Lemon Brown. They used to say I sung the blues[4] so sweet that if I sang at a funeral, the dead would <u>commence</u> to rocking with the beat. Used to travel all over Mississippi and as far as Monroe, Louisiana,

and east on over to Macon, Georgia. You mean you ain't never heard of Sweet Lemon Brown?"

"Afraid not," Greg said. "What . . . what happened to you?"

"Hard times, boy. Hard times always after a poor man. One day I got tired, sat down to rest a spell, and felt a tap on my shoulder. Hard times caught up with me."

"Sorry about that."

"What you doing here? How come you didn't go on home when the rain come? Rain don't bother you young folks none."

"Just didn't." Greg looked away.

"I used to have a knotty-headed boy just like you." Lemon Brown had half walked, half shuffled back to the corner and sat down against the wall. "Had them big eyes like you got. I used to call them moon eyes. Look into them moon eyes and see anything you want."

"How come you gave up singing the blues?" Greg asked.

"Didn't give it up," Lemon Brown said. "You don't give up the blues; they give you up. After a while you do good for yourself, and it ain't nothing but foolishness singing about how hard you got it. Ain't that right?"

"I guess so."

"What's that noise?" Lemon Brown asked, suddenly sitting upright.

Greg listened, and he heard a noise outside. He looked at Lemon Brown and saw the old man was pointing toward the window.

Greg went to the window and saw three men, neighborhood thugs, on the stoop. One

---

4. **blues:** a style of music developed from southern African-American songs, characterized by a slow tempo and flattened notes that seem to conflict with the melody.

was carrying a length of pipe. Greg looked back toward Lemon Brown, who moved quietly across the room to the window. The old man looked out, then <u>beckoned</u> frantically for Greg to follow him. For a moment Greg couldn't move. Then he found himself following Lemon Brown into the hallway and up darkened stairs. Greg followed as closely as he could. They reached the top of the stairs, and Greg felt Lemon Brown's hand, first lying on his shoulder, then <u>probing</u> down his arm until he finally took Greg's hand into his own as they crouched in the darkness.

> ## "One day I got tired, sat down to rest a spell. . . . Hard times caught up with me."

"They's bad men," Lemon Brown whispered. His breath was warm against Greg's skin.

"Hey! Rag man!" a voice called. "We know you in here. What you got up under them rags? You got any money?"

Silence.

"We don't want to have to come in and hurt you, old man, but we don't mind if we have to."

Lemon Brown squeezed Greg's hand in his own hard, <u>gnarled</u> fist.

There was a banging downstairs and a light as the men entered. They banged around noisily, calling for the rag man.

"We heard you talking about your treasure." The voice was slurred. "We just want to see it, that's all."

"You sure he's here?" One voice seemed to come from the room with the sofa.

"Yeah, he stays here every night."

"There's another room over there; I'm going to take a look. You got that flashlight?"

"Yeah, here, take the pipe too."

Greg opened his mouth to quiet the sound of his breath as he sucked it in uneasily. A beam of light hit the wall a few feet opposite him, then went out.

"Ain't nobody in that room," a voice said. "You think he gone or something?"

"I don't know," came the answer. "All I know is that I heard him talking about some kind of treasure. You know they found that shopping-bag lady with that money in her bags."

"Yeah. You think he's upstairs?"

"HEY, OLD MAN, ARE YOU UP THERE?" Silence.

"Watch my back. I'm going up."

There was a footstep on the stairs, and the beam from the flashlight danced crazily along the peeling wallpaper. Greg held his breath. There was another step and a loud crashing noise as the man banged the pipe against the wooden banister. Greg could feel his temples throb as the man slowly neared them. Greg thought about the pipe, wondering what he would do when the man reached them—what he *could* do.

Then Lemon Brown released his hand and moved toward the top of the stairs. Greg looked around and saw stairs going up to the next floor. He tried waving to Lemon Brown, hoping the old man would see him in the dim light and follow him to the next floor. Maybe, Greg thought, the man wouldn't follow them up there. Suddenly, though, Lemon Brown stood at the top of the stairs, both arms raised high above his head.

"There he is!" a voice cried from below.

"Throw down your money, old man, so I won't have to bash your head in!"

WORDS **beckon** (bĕk′ən) *v.* to signal to come by nodding or waving
TO **probe** (prōb) *v.* to investigate or to explore by touch; searching
KNOW **gnarled** (närld) *adj.* rugged and roughened, as from old age or work

Lemon Brown didn't move. Greg felt himself near panic. The steps came closer, and still Lemon Brown didn't move. He was an eerie sight, a bundle of rags standing at the top of the stairs, his shadow on the wall looming over him. Maybe, the thought came to Greg, the scene could be even eerier.

Greg wet his lips, put his hands to his mouth, and tried to make a sound. Nothing came out. He swallowed hard, wet his lips once more, and howled as evenly as he could.

"What's that?"

As Greg howled, the light moved away from Lemon Brown, but not before Greg saw him hurl his body down the stairs at the men who had come to take his treasure. There was a crashing noise and then footsteps. A rush of warm air came in as the downstairs door opened, then there was only an <u>ominous</u> silence.

Greg stood on the landing. He listened, and after a while there was another sound on the staircase.

"Mr. Brown?" he called.

"Yeah, it's me," came the answer. "I got their flashlight."

Greg exhaled in relief as Lemon Brown made his way slowly back up the stairs.

Sitting In at Baron's (1980), Romare Bearden. Copyright © Romare Bearden Foundation/Licensed by VAGA, New York.

"You O.K.?"

"Few bumps and bruises," Lemon Brown said.

"I think I'd better be going," Greg said, his breath returning to normal. "You'd better leave, too, before they come back."

"They may hang around outside for a while," Lemon Brown said, "but they ain't getting their nerve up to come in here again.

Not with crazy old rag men and howling spooks. Best you stay awhile till the coast is clear. I'm heading out west tomorrow, out to East St. Louis."[5]

"They were talking about treasures," Greg said. "You *really* have a treasure?"

"What I tell you? Didn't I tell you every man got a treasure?" Lemon Brown said. "You want to see mine?"

"If you want to show it to me," Greg shrugged.

"Let's look out the window first, see what them scoundrels be doing," Lemon Brown said.

They followed the oval beam of the flashlight into one of the rooms and looked out the window. They saw the men who had tried to take the treasure sitting on the curb near the corner. One of them had his pants leg up, looking at his knee.

"You sure you're not hurt?" Greg asked Lemon Brown.

"Nothing that ain't been hurt before," Lemon Brown said. "When you get as old as me, all you say when something hurts is 'Howdy, Mr. Pain, sees you back again.' Then when Mr. Pain see he can't worry you none, he go on mess with somebody else."

Greg smiled.

"Here, you hold this." Lemon Brown gave Greg the flashlight.

He sat on the floor near Greg and carefully untied the strings that held the rags on his right leg. When he took the rags away, Greg saw a piece of plastic. The old man carefully took off the plastic and unfolded it. He revealed some yellowed newspaper clippings and a battered harmonica.

"There it be," he said, nodding his head. "There it be."

Greg looked at the old man, saw the distant look in his eye, then turned to the clippings.

They told of Sweet Lemon Brown, a blues singer and harmonica player who was appearing at different theaters in the South. One of the clippings said he had been the hit of the show, although not the headliner. All of the clippings were reviews of shows Lemon Brown had been in more than 50 years ago. Greg looked at the harmonica. It was dented badly on one side, with the reed holes on one end nearly closed.

"I used to travel around and make money for to feed my wife and Jesse—that's my boy's name. Used to feed them good, too. Then his mama died, and he stayed with his mama's sister. He growed up to be a man, and when the war come, he saw fit to go off and fight in it. I didn't have nothing to give him except these things that told him who I was and what he come from. If you know your pappy did something, you know you can do something too.

"Anyway, he went off to war, and I went off still playing and singing. 'Course by then I wasn't as much as I used to be, not without somebody to make it worth the while. You know what I mean?"

"Yeah," Greg nodded, not quite really knowing.

ACTIVE READER

CLARIFYING What does Lemon Brown mean by this statement?

"I traveled around, and one time I come home, and there was this letter saying Jesse got killed in the war. Broke my heart, it truly did.

"They sent back what he had with him over there, and what it was is this old mouth fiddle and these clippings. Him carrying it around with him like that told me it meant something to him. That was my treasure, and when I give it to him, he treated it just like that, a treasure.

---

5. **East St. Louis:** a city in southwestern Illinois, across the Mississippi River from St. Louis, Missouri.

Ain't that something?"

"Yeah, I *guess* so," Greg said.

"You guess so?" Lemon Brown's voice rose an octave as he started to put his treasure back into the plastic. "Well, you got to guess 'cause you sure don't know nothing. Don't know enough to get home when it's raining."

"I guess . . . I mean, you're right."

"You O.K. for a youngster," the old man said as he tied the strings around his leg, "better than those scalawags[6] what come here looking for my treasure. That's for sure."

"You really think that treasure of yours was worth fighting for?" Greg asked. "Against a pipe?"

"What else a man got 'cepting what he can pass on to his son, or his daughter if she be his oldest?" Lemon Brown said. "For a big-headed boy you sure do ask the foolishest questions."

Lemon Brown got up after patting his rags in place and looked out the window again.

"Looks like they're gone. You get on out of here and get yourself home. I'll be watching from the window so you'll be all right."

Lemon Brown went down the stairs behind Greg. When they reached the front door, the old man looked out first, saw the street was clear, and told Greg to scoot on home.

"You sure you'll be O.K.?" Greg asked.

---

6. **scalawags** (skăl′ə-wăgz′): rascals; shameless people.

"Now didn't I tell you I was going to East St. Louis in the morning?"

Lemon Brown asked. "Don't that sound O.K. to you?"

"Sure it does," Greg said. "Sure it does. And you take care of that treasure of yours."

"That I'll do," Lemon said, the wrinkles

Midtown Sunset (1981), Romare Bearden. Copyright © Romare Bearden Foundation/Licensed by VAGA, New York.

about his eyes suggesting a smile. "That I'll do."

The night had warmed, and the rain had stopped, leaving puddles at the curbs. Greg didn't even want to think how late it was. He thought ahead of what his father would say and wondered if he should tell him about Lemon Brown. He thought about it until he reached his stoop, and decided against it. Lemon Brown would be O.K., Greg thought, with his memories and his treasure.

Greg pushed the button over the bell marked Ridley, thought of the lecture he knew his father would give him, and smiled. ❖

Copyright © Gil Mayers/SuperStock

JAZZ FANTASIA

BY CARL SANDBURG

Drum on your drums, batter on your banjoes,
sob on the long cool winding saxophones.
Go to it, O jazzmen.

Sling your knuckles on the bottoms of the happy
tin pans, let your trombones ooze, and go husha-
husha-hush with the slippery sand-paper.

Moan like an autumn wind high in the lonesome treetops,
moan soft like you wanted somebody terrible, cry like a
racing car slipping away from a motorcycle cop,
bang-bang! you jazzmen, bang altogether drums, traps,
banjoes, horns, tin cans—make two people fight on the
top of a stairway and scratch each other's eyes in a
clinch[1] tumbling down the stairs.

Can[2] the rough stuff . . . now a Mississippi steamboat
pushes up the night river with a hoo-hoo-hoo-oo . . . and
the green lanterns calling to the high soft stars . . . a red
moon rides on the humps of the low river hills . . . go to it,
O jazzmen.

---

1. **clinch:** slang for *embrace.*
2. **can:** slang for *stop.*

Connect to the Literature

1. **What Do You Think?**
   What is your impression of Lemon Brown when you first meet him?

   Comprehension Check
   • How does Greg meet Lemon Brown?
   • What "treasures" are important to Lemon Brown? Why?
   • As the story draws to a close, what are Lemon Brown and Greg doing or about to do?

Think Critically

2. Why does Greg smile as he rings his doorbell at the end of the story?

   Think About:
   • what he has learned from Lemon Brown
   • how his understanding of his father may have changed

3. **ACTIVE READING** **CONNECTING**
   Look over the situations and events that you recorded in your **READER'S NOTEBOOK**. What experiences in your own life helped you connect to these situations and events? Compare your feelings with those of the character or characters in the story. How are your feelings similar? How are they different?

4. Walter Dean Myers, the author of this story, believes it is important for people to have role models. In what way can Lemon Brown, a homeless person, be considered a role model for Greg?

5. Does this story change your feelings toward homeless people? Why or why not?

Extend Interpretations

6. **COMPARING TEXTS** Compare Terry in "Stop the Sun" on pages 48–54 with Greg. What problem does each boy have? How does each boy solve his problem? What does each story teach you about the relationship between parent and child?

7. **Connect to Life** Lemon Brown claims that "every man got a treasure." Describe a treasure that you have now or have had in the past. Why do you consider this object a treasure? How does your treasure bring you comfort?

Literary Analysis

DYNAMIC AND STATIC CHARACTERS
In a story, a character may be either dynamic or static. A **static character** is one who does not change during the story. A **dynamic character,** on the other hand, does change. For example, the character may become more mature or learn a lesson.

Paired Activity "The Treasure of Lemon Brown" focuses on two main characters—Lemon Brown and Greg. With a partner, go back through the story and decide which of these characters is static and which of these characters is dynamic. Use a chart like the one shown to help you. Be prepared to discuss how the actions and reactions of the static character helped to bring about change in the dynamic character.

Character	Beginning of Story	End of Story
Lemon Brown	Homeless person who cares about his treasure more than anything else	
Greg		

REVIEW: CHARACTER DEVELOPMENT
Dialogue—conversation between two or more characters—is one of a writer's most important tools in character development. What traits of Lemon Brown and Greg are revealed through dialogue?

Writing

Character Description Think of someone you met briefly who had an impact on your life. In a short essay, write a character description of this person. Describe what the person looked like, how he or she talked, and the place where you met. Explain how this person affected you. Be sure to use correct and varied sentence types. Place the entry in your **Working Portfolio.**

Writing Handbook
See p. R41: Descriptive Writing.

Research & Technology

SOCIAL STUDIES In this selection, Lemon Brown is a homeless person who lives in an abandoned building. Use the Internet or library sources to find out more about homelessness. In recent years, has homelessness increased or decreased? Why? What is being done to help the homeless? Create a list of resources that are available to help the homeless in your community. Share the list with your class.

INTERNET Research Starter
www.mcdougallittell.com

Art Connection

Hubert Shuptrine's watercolor painting on page 335 is a sensitive portrait of an older gentleman named Williams. Write a paragraph explaining how this portrait differs from or is similar to the picture of Lemon Brown you have in your mind.

Vocabulary and Spelling

EXERCISE: SYNONYMS AND ANTONYMS Identify the relationship between each boldfaced Word to Know and the word to its right by writing *Synonyms* or *Antonyms*.

1. **commence**   end
2. **beckon**   summon
3. **vault**   jump
4. **ajar**   shut
5. **tentatively**   hesitantly
6. **gnarled**   smooth
7. **impromptu**   planned
8. **tremor**   shudder
9. **ominous**   friendly
10. **probe**   explore

Vocabulary Handbook
See p. R24: Synonyms and Antonyms.

SPELLING STRATEGY: THE SUFFIX –LY You can turn many adjectives into adverbs by adding the suffix -ly. Sometimes, a final silent e is dropped before adding the -ly, as in *abominably.* Turn the following adjectives into adverbs:

1. regular
2. simple
3. informal
4. pleasant
5. practical

Spelling Handbook
See p. R28.

Grammar in Context: **Adjectives**

In the beginning of "The Treasure of Lemon Brown," Walter Dean Myers describes both the setting of the story and the mood of the main character.

> The **dark** sky, filled with **angry, swirling** clouds, reflected Greg Ridley's mood as he sat on the stoop of his building.

The words in red are **adjectives.** An adjective is a word that modifies a noun or pronoun. As in this passage, adjectives can be used to describe setting or character.

Apply to Your Writing Using adjectives can add color and descriptive power to your writing. They can also make your writing more precise.

WRITING EXERCISE Use adjectives to describe each item in a sentence.

Example: *Original* house

Rewritten The <u>beautiful old</u> house was <u>large</u> and <u>rambling</u>.

1. smell
2. Greg
3. couch
4. building
5. window

Connect to the Literature Look through the first few paragraphs of the story for adjectives that describe setting or character. How do adjectives help the reader imagine the events of the story?

Grammar Handbook
See p. R86: Using Modifiers Effectively.

Walter Dean Myers
born 1937

"I found Harlem a marvel, an exotic land with an inexhaustible supply of delights and surprises."

Harlem Roots Walter Dean Myers was born into a large family in Martinsburg, West Virginia. After the death of his mother, he went to live in Harlem, New York, with the Deans, friends of his family.

Always a Writer As a boy growing up in Harlem, Myers suffered from a speech impediment that often made him feel like an outsider. He found comfort in reading and soon began writing poetry and short stories. When he finished high school, he joined the army because he was not able to afford college. He continued to write during his time in the army and after

discharge. Finally, several of his stories were published, and in the late 1960s he won a contest with his text for a children's picture book.

An Award Winner Since 1975, Myers has written at least one book a year, most of them for young adults. He has received numerous honors, including several Newbery awards and Coretta Scott King awards.

AUTHOR ACTIVITY
An Exotic Land Many of the stories that Walter Dean Myers writes are set in Harlem. In the 1920s, Harlem was the center of a great cultural revival known as the Harlem Renaissance. Find out about contributions made by African-American musicians, writers, and artists who lived in Harlem during this period. How do you think the Harlem Renaissance influenced Myers's feeling that Harlem is "a marvel, an exotic land"?

Rules of the Game

by AMY TAN

What I learned about myself—

Connect to Your Life

Learning the Rules of a Game Think back to a time when you had to learn the rules of an unfamiliar game. How difficult was it to learn the rules? What did you learn about yourself?

Build Background

The Game of Kings The complex game of chess probably began in India about 1,500 years ago. From India, it spread east to China and west to Europe and the Americas. For many centuries it was known as "the game of kings," because it was played by the nobility and because it was considered good training for those engaged in warfare.

Today, chess players of all ages compete one-on-one, by mail, by e-mail, and on the Internet. Most nations have chess tournaments for young people and adults.

WORDS TO KNOW
Vocabulary Preview

adversary	malodorous
benefactor	ponder
benevolently	pungent
circumstance	recessed
impart	retort

Focus Your Reading

LITERARY ANALYSIS INTERNAL AND EXTERNAL CONFLICT

Most stories are built around a central **conflict,** or struggle. A conflict may be either external or internal. An **external conflict** involves a character pitted against another character or against an outside force, such as a storm. An **internal conflict** is one that occurs within a character's mind. In "Rules of the Game," the main character, Waverly, experiences both internal and external conflicts. As you read the story, consider Waverly's conflicts with her mother and within herself.

ACTIVE READING DRAWING CONCLUSIONS

When you read fiction, you may have to **draw conclusions** about aspects of a story that are not directly stated. To draw a conclusion, follow these steps:

• Notice details from the story.
• Consider your own experiences and knowledge.
• Write a summary statement about the meaning of the story details.

📖 **READER'S NOTEBOOK** Create a chart like the one shown. In the first box, write details about Waverly and her mother from the text. In the second box, jot down your thoughts based on your own knowledge and experiences. Then use information from the chart to draw conclusions about Waverly and her mother.

Details from Text	My Knowledge	Conclusion
"Bite back your tongue," scolded my mother when I cried loudly . . .	My mother corrected me when I made a scene in public to teach me about self-control.	Mrs. Jong wanted Waverly to learn self-control.

RULES of the GAME

Chinese Girl, Emil Orlik. Oil on Canvas.
Christie's Images / SuperStock.

BY AMY TAN

I was six when my mother taught me the art of invisible strength. It was a strategy for winning arguments, respect from others, and eventually, though neither of us knew it at the time, chess games.

"Bite back your tongue," scolded my mother when I cried loudly, yanking her hand toward the store that sold bags of salted plums. At home, she said, "Wise guy, he not go against wind. In Chinese we say, Come from South, blow with wind—poom!—North will follow. Strongest wind cannot be seen."

The next week I bit back my tongue as we entered the store with the forbidden candies. When my mother finished her shopping, she quietly plucked a small bag of plums from the rack and put it on the counter with the rest of the items.

My mother imparted her daily truths so she could help my older brothers and me rise above our circumstances. We lived in San Francisco's Chinatown. Like most of the other Chinese children who played in the back alleys of restaurants and curio shops, I didn't think we were poor. My bowl was always full, three five-course meals every day, beginning with a soup full of mysterious things I didn't want to know the names of.

WORDS
TO
KNOW

impart (ĭm-pärt') *v.* to make known; to give or reveal
circumstance (sûr'kəm-stăns') *n.* a condition; a financial situation

We lived on Waverly Place, in a warm, clean, two-bedroom flat that sat above a small Chinese bakery specializing in steamed pastries and dim sum.[1] In the early morning, when the alley was still quiet, I could smell fragrant red beans as they were cooked down to a pasty sweetness. By daybreak, our flat was heavy with the odor of fried sesame balls and sweet curried chicken crescents. From my bed, I would listen as my father got ready for work, then locked the door behind him, one-two-three clicks.

At the end of our two-block alley was a small sandlot playground with swings and slides well-shined down the middle with use. The play area was bordered by wood-slat benches where old-country people sat cracking roasted watermelon seeds with their golden teeth and scattering the husks to an impatient gathering of gurgling pigeons. The best playground, however, was the dark alley itself. It was crammed with daily mysteries and adventures. My brothers and I would peer into the medicinal herb shop, watching old Li[2] dole out onto a stiff sheet of white paper the right amount of insect shells, saffron-colored seeds, and pungent leaves for his ailing customers. It was said that he once cured a woman dying of an ancestral curse that had eluded the best of American doctors. Next to the pharmacy was a printer who specialized in gold-embossed wedding invitations and festive red banners.

Farther down the street was Ping Yuen[3] Fish Market. The front window displayed a tank crowded with doomed fish and turtles struggling to gain footing on the slimy green-tiled sides. A hand-written sign informed tourists, "Within this store, is all for food, not for pet." Inside, the butchers with their bloodstained white smocks deftly gutted the fish while customers cried out their orders and shouted, "Give me your freshest," to which the butchers always protested, "All are freshest." On less crowded market days, we would inspect the crates of live frogs and crabs which we were warned not to poke, boxes of dried cuttlefish, and row upon row of iced prawns, squid, and slippery fish. The sanddabs made me shiver each time; their eyes lay on one flattened side and reminded me of my mother's story of a careless girl who ran into a crowded street and was crushed by a cab. "Was smash flat," reported my mother.

At the corner of the alley was Hong Sing's, a four-table cafe with a recessed stairwell in front that led to a door marked "Tradesmen." My brothers and I believed the bad people emerged from this door at night. Tourists never went to Hong Sing's, since the menu was printed only in Chinese. A Caucasian man with a big camera once posed me and my playmates in front of the restaurant. He had us move to the side of the picture window so the

---

1. **dim sum:** small portions of a variety of Chinese foods and dumplings.
2. **Li** (lē).
3. **Ping Yuen** (bǐng yü'ĕn).

WORDS TO KNOW
pungent (pŭn'jənt) *adj.* sharp and intense, as an odor
recessed (rē'sĕsd) *adj.* indented or hollowed-out space **recess** *v.*

Chinatown, San Francisco, Copyright © Dong Kingman. Courtesy of the artist.

photo would capture the roasted duck with its head dangling from a juice-covered rope. After he took the picture, I told him he should go into Hong Sing's and eat dinner. When he smiled and asked me what they served, I shouted, "Guts and duck's feet and octopus gizzards!" Then I ran off with my friends, shrieking with laughter as we scampered across the alley and hid in the entryway grotto of the China Gem Company, my heart pounding with hope that he would chase us.

My mother named me after the street that we lived on: Waverly Place Jong, my official name for important American documents. But my family called me Meimei,[4] "Little Sister." I was the youngest, the only daughter. Each morning before school, my mother would twist and yank on my thick black hair until she had formed two tightly wound pigtails. One day, as she struggled to weave a hard-toothed comb through my disobedient hair, I had a sly thought.

I asked her, "Ma, what is Chinese torture?" My mother shook her head. A bobby pin was wedged between her lips. She wetted her palm and smoothed the hair above my ear, then

4. **Meimei** (mā´mā).

pushed the pin in so that it nicked sharply against my scalp.

"Who say this word?" she asked without a trace of knowing how wicked I was being. I shrugged my shoulders and said, "Some boy in my class said Chinese people do Chinese torture."

"Chinese people do many things," she said simply. "Chinese people do business, do medicine, do painting. Not lazy like American people. We do torture. Best torture."

My older brother Vincent was the one who actually got the chess set. We had gone to the annual Christmas party held at the First Chinese Baptist Church at the end of the alley. The missionary ladies had put together a Santa bag of gifts donated by members of another church. None of the gifts had names on them. There were separate sacks for boys and girls of different ages.

One of the Chinese parishioners had donned a Santa Claus costume and a stiff paper beard with cotton balls glued to it. I think the only children who thought he was the real thing were too young to know that Santa Claus was not Chinese. When my turn came up, the Santa man asked me how old I was. I thought it was a trick question; I was seven according to the American formula and eight by the Chinese calendar. I said I was born on March 17, 1951. That seemed to satisfy him. He then solemnly asked if I had been a very, very good girl this year and did I believe in Jesus Christ and obey my parents. I knew the only answer to that. I nodded back with equal solemnity.

Having watched the other children opening their gifts, I already knew that the big gifts were not necessarily the nicest ones. One girl my age got a large coloring book of biblical characters, while a less greedy girl who selected a smaller box received a glass vial of lavender toilet water. The sound of the box was also important. A ten-year-old boy had chosen a box that jangled when he shook it. It was a tin globe of the world with a slit for inserting money. He must have thought it was full of dimes and nickels, because when he saw that it had just ten pennies, his face fell with such undisguised disappointment that his mother slapped the side of his head and led him out of the church hall, apologizing to the crowd for her son who had such bad manners he couldn't appreciate such a fine gift.

As I peered into the sack, I quickly fingered the remaining presents, testing their weight, imagining what they contained. I chose a heavy, compact one that was wrapped in shiny silver foil and a red satin ribbon. It was a twelve-pack of Life Savers and I spent the rest of the party arranging and rearranging the candy tubes in the order of my favorites. My brother Winston chose wisely as well. His present turned out to be a box of intricate plastic parts; the instructions on the box proclaimed that when they were properly assembled he would have an authentic miniature replica of a World War II submarine.

Vincent got the chess set, which would have been a very decent present to get at a church Christmas party, except it was obviously used

My older brother Vincent was the one who actually got the chess set.

and, as we discovered later, it was missing a black pawn and a white knight. My mother graciously thanked the unknown <u>benefactor</u>, saying, "Too good. Cost too much." At which point, an old lady with fine white, wispy hair nodded toward our family and said with a whistling whisper, "Merry, merry Christmas."

When we got home, my mother told Vincent to throw the chess set away. "She not want it. We not want it," she said, tossing her head stiffly to the side with a tight, proud smile. My brothers had deaf ears. They were already lining up the chess pieces and reading from the dog-eared instruction book.

I watched Vincent and Winston play during Christmas week. The chessboard seemed to hold elaborate secrets waiting to be untangled. The chessmen were more powerful than Old Li's magic herbs that cured ancestral curses. And my brothers wore such serious faces that I was sure something was at stake that was greater than avoiding the tradesmen's door to Hong Sing's.

"Let me! Let me!" I begged between games when one brother or the other would sit back with a deep sigh of relief and victory, the other annoyed, unable to let go of the outcome. Vincent at first refused to let me play, but when I offered my Life Savers as replacements for the buttons that filled in for the missing pieces, he relented. He chose the flavors: wild cherry for the black pawn and peppermint for the white knight. Winner could eat both.

As our mother sprinkled flour and rolled out small doughy circles for the steamed dumplings that would be our dinner that night, Vincent explained the rules, pointing to each piece. "You have sixteen pieces and so do I. One king and queen, two bishops, two knights, two castles, and eight pawns. The pawns can only move forward one step, except on the first move. Then they can move two. But they can only take men by moving crossways like this, except in the beginning, when you can move ahead and take another pawn."

"Why?" I asked as I moved my pawn. "Why can't they move more steps?"

"Because they're pawns," he said.

"But why do they go crossways to take other men? Why aren't there any women and children?"

"Why is the sky blue? Why must you always ask stupid questions?" asked Vincent. "This is a game. These are the rules. I didn't make them up. See. Here. In the book." He jabbed a page with a pawn in his hand. "Pawn. P-A-W-N. Pawn. Read it yourself."

My mother patted the flour off her hands. "Let me see book," she said quietly. She scanned the pages quickly, not reading the foreign English symbols, seeming to search deliberately for nothing in particular.

"This American rules," she concluded at last. "Every time people come out from foreign country, must know rules. You not know, judge say, Too bad, go back. They not telling you why so you can use their way go forward. They say, Don't know why, you find out yourself. But they knowing all the time. Better you take it, find out why yourself." She tossed her head back with a satisfied smile.

I found out about all the whys later. I read the rules and looked up all the big words in a dictionary. I borrowed books from the Chinatown library. I studied each chess piece, trying to absorb the power each contained.

I learned about opening moves and why it's important to control the center early on; the shortest distance between two points is straight down the middle. I learned about the

Rythmisches (1930), Paul Klee.
Musee National D'Art Moderne.
Photo Bertrand Prevost.
Copyright © Centre Georges
Pompidou (AM 1984-366).

middle game and why tactics between two <u>adversaries</u> are like clashing ideas; the one who plays better has the clearest plans for both attacking and getting out of traps. I learned why it is essential in the endgame to have foresight, a mathematical understanding of all possible moves, and patience; all weaknesses and advantages become evident to a strong adversary and are obscured to a tiring opponent. I discovered that for the whole game one must gather invisible strengths and see the endgame before the game begins.

I also found out why I should never reveal "why" to others. A little knowledge withheld is a great advantage one should store for future use. That is the power of chess. It is a game of secrets in which one must show and never tell.

I loved the secrets I found within the sixty-four black and white squares. I carefully drew a handmade chessboard and pinned it to the wall next to my bed, where at night I would stare for hours at imaginary battles. Soon I no longer lost any games or Life Savers, but I lost my adversaries. Winston and Vincent decided they were more interested in roaming the streets after school in their Hopalong Cassidy cowboy hats.

On a cold spring afternoon, while walking home from school, I detoured through the playground at the end of our alley. I saw a group of old men, two seated across a folding table playing a game of chess, others smoking pipes, eating peanuts, and watching. I ran home and grabbed Vincent's chess set, which was bound in a cardboard box with rubber bands. I also carefully selected two prized rolls of Life Savers. I came back to the park and approached a man who was observing the game.

WORDS
TO
KNOW

adversary (ăd′vər-sĕr′ē) n. an opponent

"Want to play?" I asked him. His face widened with surprise, and he grinned as he looked at the box under my arm.

"Little sister, been a long time since I play with dolls," he said, smiling <u>benevolently</u>. I quickly put the box down next to him on the bench and displayed my <u>retort</u>.

Lau Po,[5] as he allowed me to call him, turned out to be a much better player than my brothers. I lost many games and many Life Savers. But over the weeks, with each diminishing roll of candies, I added new secrets. Lau Po gave me the names. The Double Attack from the East and West Shores. Throwing Stones on the Drowning Man. The Sudden Meeting of the Clan. The Surprise from the Sleeping Guard. The Humble Servant Who Kills the King. Sand in the Eyes of Advancing Forces. A Double Killing Without Blood.

During my first tournament, my mother sat with me in the front row as I waited for my turn.

There were also the fine points of chess etiquette. Keep captured men in neat rows, as well-tended prisoners. Never announce "Check"[6] with vanity, lest someone with an unseen sword slit your throat. Never hurl pieces into the sandbox after you have lost a game, because then you must find them again, by yourself, after apologizing to all around you. By the end of the summer, Lau Po had taught me all he knew, and I had become a better chess player.

A small weekend crowd of Chinese people and tourists would gather as I played and defeated my opponents one by one. My mother would join the crowds during these outdoor exhibition games.[7] She sat proudly on the bench, telling my admirers with proper Chinese humility, "Is luck."

A man who watched me play in the park suggested that my mother allow me to play in local chess tournaments. My mother smiled graciously, an answer that meant nothing. I desperately wanted to go, but I bit back my tongue. I knew she would not let me play among strangers. So as we walked home I said in a small voice that I didn't want to play in the local tournament. They would have American rules. If I lost, I would bring shame on my family.

"Is shame you fall down nobody push you," said my mother.

During my first tournament, my mother sat with me in the front row as I waited for my turn. I frequently bounced my legs to unstick them from the cold metal seat of the folding chair. When my name was called, I leapt up. My mother unwrapped something in her lap. It was her *chang*, a small tablet of red jade which held the sun's fire. "Is luck," she whispered, and tucked it into my dress pocket. I turned to my opponent, a fifteen-year-old boy from Oakland. He looked at me, wrinkling his nose.

---

5. **Lau Po** (lou bō).

6. **check:** a move in chess that places an opponent's king under direct attack.

7. **exhibition games:** public showings or demonstrations—in this case, chess games.

As I began to play, the boy disappeared, the color ran out of the room, and I saw only my white pieces and his black ones waiting on the other side. A light wind began blowing past my ears. It whispered secrets only I could hear.

"Blow from the South," it murmured. "The wind leaves no trail." I saw a clear path, the traps to avoid. The crowd rustled. "Shhh! Shhh!" said the corners of the room. The wind blew stronger. "Throw sand from the East to distract him." The knight came forward ready for the sacrifice. The wind hissed, louder and louder. "Blow, blow, blow. He cannot see. He is blind now. Make him lean away from the wind so he is easier to knock down."

"Check," I said, as the wind roared with laughter. The wind died down to little puffs, my own breath.

My mother placed my first trophy next to a new plastic chess set that the neighborhood Tao society had given to me. As she wiped each piece with a soft cloth, she said, "Next time win more, lose less."

"Ma, it's not how many pieces you lose," I said. "Sometimes you need to lose pieces to get ahead."

"Better to lose less, see if you really need."

At the next tournament, I won again, but it was my mother who wore the triumphant grin.

"Lost eight pieces this time. Last time was eleven. What I tell you? Better off lose less!" I was annoyed, but I couldn't say anything.

I attended more tournaments, each one farther away from home. I won all games, in all divisions. The Chinese bakery downstairs from our flat displayed my growing collection of trophies in its window, amidst the dust-covered cakes that were never picked up. The day after I won an important regional tournament, the window encased a fresh sheet cake with whipped-cream frosting and red script saying, "Congratulations, Waverly Jong, Chinatown Chess Champion." Soon after that, a flower shop, headstone engraver, and funeral parlor offered to sponsor me in national tournaments. That's when my mother decided I no longer had to do the dishes. Winston and Vincent had to do my chores.

"Why does she get to play and we do all the work?" complained Vincent.

"Is new American rules," said my mother. "Meimei play, squeeze all her brains out for win chess. You play, worth squeeze towel."

By my ninth birthday, I was a national chess champion. I was still some 429 points away from grand-master status, but I was touted as the Great American Hope, a child prodigy and a girl to boot. They ran a photo of me in *Life* magazine next to a quote in which Bobby Fischer[8] said, "There will never be a woman grand master." "Your move, Bobby," said the caption.

The day they took the magazine picture I wore neatly plaited braids clipped with plastic barrettes trimmed with rhinestones. I was playing in a large high school auditorium that echoed with phlegmy coughs and the squeaky rubber knobs of chair legs sliding across freshly waxed wooden floors. Seated across from me was an American man, about the same age as Lau Po, maybe fifty. I remember that his sweaty brow seemed to weep at my every move. He wore a dark, <u>malodorous</u> suit. One of his pockets was stuffed with a great white kerchief on which he wiped his palm before sweeping his hand over the chosen chess piece with great flourish.

---

8. **Bobby Fischer:** a well-known chess player who, at 15, was the world's youngest grand master.

In my crisp pink-and-white dress with scratchy lace at the neck, one of two my mother had sewn for these special occasions, I would clasp my hands under my chin, the delicate points of my elbows poised lightly on the table in the manner my mother had shown me for posing for the press. I would swing my patent leather shoes back and forth like an impatient child riding on a school bus. Then I would pause, suck in my lips, twirl my chosen piece in midair as if undecided, and then firmly plant it in its new threatening place, with a triumphant smile thrown back at my opponent for good measure.

I no longer played in the alley of Waverly Place. I never visited the playground where the pigeons and old men gathered. I went to school, then directly home to learn new chess secrets, cleverly concealed advantages, more escape routes.

But I found it difficult to concentrate at home. My mother had a habit of standing over me while I plotted out my games. I think she thought of herself as my protective ally. Her lips would be sealed tight, and after each move I made, a soft "Hmmmmph" would escape from her nose.

"Ma, I can't practice when you stand there like that," I said one day. She retreated to the kitchen and made loud noises with the pots and pans. When the crashing stopped, I could see out of the corner of my eye that she was standing in the doorway. "Hmmmmph!" Only this one came out of her tight throat.

My parents made many concessions to allow me to practice. One time I complained that the bedroom I shared was so noisy that I couldn't think. Thereafter, my brothers slept in a bed in the living room, facing the street. I said I couldn't finish my rice; my head didn't work right when my stomach was too full. I left the table with half-finished bowls and nobody complained. But there was one duty I couldn't avoid. I had to accompany my mother on Saturday market days when I had no tournament to play. My mother would proudly walk with me, visiting many shops, buying very little. "This my daughter Wave-ly Jong," she said to whoever looked her way.

"Ma, I can't practice when you stand there like that," I said one day.

One day, after we left a shop I said under my breath, "I wish you wouldn't do that, telling everybody I'm your daughter." My mother stopped walking. Crowds of people with heavy bags pushed past us on the sidewalk, bumping into first one shoulder, then another.

"Aiii-ya. So shame be with mother?" She grasped my hand even tighter as she glared at me.

I looked down. "It's not that, it's just so obvious. It's just so embarrassing."

"Embarrass you be my daughter?" Her voice was cracking with anger.

"That's not what I meant. That's not what I said."

"What you say?"

I knew it was a mistake to say anything more, but I heard my voice speaking. "Why do you have to use me to show off? If you want to show off, then why don't you learn to play chess."

My mother's eyes turned into dangerous black slits. She had no words for me, just sharp silence.

I felt the wind rushing around my hot ears. I jerked my hand out of my mother's tight grasp and spun around, knocking into an old woman. Her bag of groceries spilled to the ground.

"Aii-ya! Stupid girl!" my mother and the woman cried. Oranges and tin cans careened down the sidewalk. As my mother stooped to help the old woman pick up the escaping food, I took off.

I raced down the street, dashing between people, not looking back as my mother screamed shrilly, "Meimei! Meimei!" I fled down an alley, past dark curtained shops and merchants washing the grime off their windows. I sped into the sunlight, into a large street crowded with tourists examining trinkets and souvenirs. I ducked into another dark alley, down another street, up another alley. I ran until it hurt and I realized I had nowhere to go, that I was not running from anything. The alleys contained no escape routes.

My breath came out like angry smoke. It was cold. I sat down on an upturned plastic pail next to a stack of empty boxes, cupping my chin with my hands, thinking hard. I imagined my mother, first walking briskly down one street or another looking for me, then giving up and returning home to await my arrival. After two hours, I stood up on creaking legs and slowly walked home.

The alley was quiet and I could see the yellow lights shining from our flat like two tiger's eyes in the night. I climbed the sixteen steps to the door, advancing quietly up each so as not to make any warning sounds. I turned the knob; the door was locked. I heard a chair moving, quick steps, the locks turning—click! click! click!—and then the door opened.

"About time you got home," said Vincent. "Boy, are you in trouble."

He slid back to the dinner table. On a platter were the remains of a large fish, its fleshy head still connected to bones swimming upstream in vain escape. Standing there waiting for my punishment, I heard my mother speak in a dry voice.

"We not concerning this girl. This girl not have concerning for us."

Nobody looked at me. Bone chopsticks clinked against the insides of bowls being emptied into hungry mouths.

I walked into my room, closed the door, and lay down on my bed. The room was dark, the ceiling filled with shadows from the dinner-time lights of neighboring flats.

In my head, I saw a chessboard with sixty-four black and white squares. Opposite me was my opponent, two angry black slits. She wore a triumphant smile. "Strongest wind cannot be seen," she said.

Her black men advanced across the plane, slowly marching to each successive level as a single unit. My white pieces screamed as they scurried and fell off the board one by one. As her men drew closer to my edge, I felt myself growing light. I rose up into the air and flew out the window. Higher and higher, above the alley, over the tops of tiled roofs, where I was gathered up by the wind and pushed up toward the night sky until everything below me disappeared and I was alone.

I closed my eyes and <u>pondered</u> my next move. ❖

From SEARCHING FOR BOBBY FISCHER

by FRED WAITZKIN

Josh and I played our first chess games on a squat coffee table in the living room when he was six years old. He sat on the floor, his face cupped in his hands. . . . By trial and error, more than by my instruction, which he staunchly resisted, he found tricky ways to trap my pieces. He unearthed standard chess strategies and tactics that players have used for centuries. He was good at this new game.

So good that I kept forgetting how old he was. Often I became caught up in the intrigues of combat and found myself trying to take my son's head off. . . . Josh would come back shaking his fist at me and grimacing. "I must win, I must win," he'd mutter to himself while setting up the pieces. It must have been profoundly confusing for him that I was able to defeat his best ideas. A couple of times I offered him the handicap of knight odds and he cried at my impudence, as if I'd tried to humiliate him. Already he seemed to know that his old man was a hack, what chess players call a patzer.

While I tried to slaughter Josh, I rooted for him to win. The game became a quicksand of passion for us. After an emotional loss, he would pretend not to care, but his lower lip would tremble. Dejected, he'd go off to his room and my heart would be broken. My carefully crafted victories felt like defeats. The next day he would refuse to play me again, not even for a new toy car—not even for candy. I would feel panicky. Maybe during my last blistering attack I'd killed off his baby dream of being the world champion. Or maybe it was my dream, not his. Such distinctions are ambiguous between a father and a little son. This is how fathers mess up their kids, I'd lecture myself. Would you throw a slider to a six-year-old just learning to hit? Or smack him in the belly with a hard spiral? Still, a few days later we'd be at it again. Once after I'd sprung a trap on his queen, Josh announced that he didn't want to become a grandmaster;[1] "it's too hard," he said. Feeling bad, I asked what he would do instead. He announced soberly that he would work in a pizza shop that had a Pac Man machine (he knew how much I hate video games).

In retrospect I suppose that Josh was just beginning to exercise his muscles as a chess psychologist, trying to soften me up, because the following afternoon he was squirming with pluck and purpose, knocking down pieces each time he reached his short arm across the board to take one of my pawns. That day I was feeling like Karpov,[2] carefully building an insurmountable attack. The game took a long time, and while he was considering the position, I took a break. . . . When Josh called me, he was beside himself with impatience. I . . . checked the position and made my move. Josh smiled, slid his rook over and announced, "Mate in two."

"I doubt it," I said smugly, but every move was a vise. He had me. I hugged him and we rolled on the floor laughing. It was the first time he'd ever beaten me.

---

1. **grandmaster:** a chess player ranked at the highest level of ability.
2. **(Anatoly) Karpov** (ăn′ə-tō′lē kär′pôv′): Chess player who, in 1970, became the world's youngest international grand master.

Connect to the Literature

1. What Do You Think?
What kind of daughter is Waverly? Use details from the story to support your answer.

Comprehension Check
- How does Waverly acquire a chess set?
- Why does Waverly's mother create a special set of family rules for Waverly?
- What does Waverly do at the end of the story?

Think Critically

2. This story is about more than the rules of a chess game. It is about the rules of life. What rules of life does Waverly learn in the story?

> **Think About:**
> - the rules that Waverly's mother tries to teach her
> - the rules that Waverly learns while playing chess

3. | ACTIVE READING | DRAWING CONCLUSIONS |

Look at the chart in your READER'S NOTEBOOK. What conclusions have you drawn about Waverly? about her mother? Compare your conclusions with those of a classmate. In what way does an individual's personal experience and prior knowledge affect the conclusions that he or she forms?

Extend Interpretations

4. Different Perspectives How might this story be different if Waverly's mother had been born in the United States? Explain your answer.

5. Critic's Corner One reviewer of Amy Tan's work wrote, "Amy Tan examines the sometimes painful, often tender, and always deep connection between mothers and daughters." In "Rules of the Game," does Tan portray the relationship between mothers and daughters as both painful and tender? Support your answer with examples and details from the story.

6. Connect to Life Do you know someone who has natural talent for playing a game or a sport? Do you think natural talent is enough for such people, or is it also important to know and follow the rules of the game? Explain your answer.

Literary Analysis

| INTERNAL AND EXTERNAL CONFLICT |

In a work of literature, a **conflict** is a struggle between opposing forces. In an **external conflict,** a character struggles against another person or an outside force, such as another character, nature, or society. **Internal conflict,** on the other hand, is a struggle between opposing desires within a character.

Activity In this story, what internal and external conflicts does Waverly experience? What internal and external conflicts does her mother experience? Record your answers in a chart like the one shown. Compare the internal and external conflicts of the mother and daughter. How are they similar? How are they different?

	Internal Conflict(s)	External Conflict(s)
Waverly	Wants to play chess but does not like giving up all of her free time	
Waverly's Mother		

Writing

Character Comparison In a brief essay compare and contrast Waverly with her mother. How are they alike? How are they different? Be sure to examine and explain the motivations and reactions of these characters as they confront conflicts. Place the entry in your **Working Portfolio.**

Writing Handbook
See p. R45: Compare and Contrast.

Speaking & Listening

Checkmate Research the history of chess. Prepare an oral report that explains how chess was used as a game played by nobility or how it was used as training for warfare. Use appropriate grammar, word choice, enunciation, and pace during your presentation.

Speaking and Listening Handbook
See p. R104: Organization and Delivery.

Research & Technology

Chess Sets There are many different kinds of chess sets. Using Internet and library sources, conduct a multiple-step information search to find out about the variety of chess sets. Look for examples of historical and unusual chess sets. Prepare an oral report on your findings and include photographs, illustrations, and diagrams. Be sure to note your sources.

Reading *for* INFORMATION
Read the Internet article "I've Been Rooked" on pages 363–366 before doing your research.

Vocabulary

STANDARDIZED TEST PRACTICE

Choose the word or group of words that means the same, or nearly the same, as the underlined Word to Know.

1. A difficult <u>circumstance</u>
   A pairing
   B condition
   C gathering
   D celebration

2. A <u>pungent</u> odor
   J lasting
   K pleasant
   L sharp
   M toxic

3. A <u>recessed</u> stairwell
   A neglected
   B darkened
   C painted
   D hollow

4. To <u>ponder</u> a move
   J remember
   K cancel
   L consider
   M delay

5. To <u>impart</u> advice
   A give
   B explain
   C seek
   D ignore

6. An unknown <u>benefactor</u>
   J neighbor
   K supporter
   L relative
   M storekeeper

7. To speak <u>benevolently</u>
   A kindly
   B seriously
   C secretly
   D boldly

8. A <u>malodorous</u> cheese
   J tasty
   K costly
   L smelly
   M sticky

9. A quick <u>retort</u>
   A race
   B reply
   C meal
   D discussion

10. A strong <u>adversary</u>
    J advantage
    K coach
    L opponent
    M fan

Vocabulary Handbook
See p. R24: Synonyms and Antonyms.

Grammar in Context: Adverb Placement

The meaning of a sentence can sometimes be altered simply by changing the position of an **adverb**. Look at this sentence from Amy Tan's "Rules of the Game."

> When my mother finished her shopping, she quietly plucked a small bag of plums from the rack and put it on the counter with the rest of the items.

The word *quietly* is an **adverb,** a word that modifies a verb, an adjective, or another adverb. How would the emphasis change if *quietly* were placed between *mother* and *finished*? How would it change if *quietly* were placed before the words *put it*? Through careful **placement of adverbs,** writers can emphasize certain words and change a sentence's meaning.

WRITING EXERCISE Change the placement of the underlined adverbs. Then describe how the change affects the meaning of the sentence.

Example: *Original* She was a child when she started playing only chess.

Rewritten She was <u>only</u> a child when she started playing chess. (Emphasis shifts from *chess* to *child;* the meaning is that it is remarkable that a child started playing chess.)

1. Amy drew a handmade chessboard and <u>carefully</u> pinned it to the wall.
2. She moved her chess piece and waited for her opponent to react <u>slowly</u>.
3. Everyone who knew us <u>well</u> said that we lived on Waverly Place.
4. Her mother responded when her daughter ran <u>angrily</u> away.
5. She ran down the alley, hoping her mother would not chase her <u>frantically</u>.

Grammar Handbook
See p. R86: Using Modifiers Effectively.

Amy Tan
born 1952

"I couldn't survive without writing. It's like breathing."

A Young Prize Winner Amy Tan was born in Oakland, California, several years after her mother and father immigrated from China. She was raised in various cities in the San Francisco Bay Area. When she was eight, her essay "What the Library Means to Me" won first prize among elementary school participants.

The Joy Luck Club After earning an M.A. in linguistics from San Jose State, Tan held a variety of jobs. Then, in 1985, she attended her first writers' workshop. Only four years later, her novel, *The Joy Luck Club,* became a surprise bestseller, logging over 40 weeks on *The New York Times* bestseller list.

More Success Tan went on to publish two more best-selling novels—*The Kitchen God's Wife* and *The Hundred Secret Senses.* She is also the author of two children's books—*The Moon Lady* and *The Chinese Siamese Cat.*

AUTHOR ACTIVITY
A Happy Ending? Amy Tan later included "Rules of the Game" as part of her novel *The Joy Luck Club,* which is largely based on Tan's own life. Read the parts of the book that are told by Waverly Jong and her mother, Lindo Jong. How does the conflict between Waverly and her mother get resolved in the novel?

Source: Live on the Net Chess Sites

| Back | Forward | Reload | Home | Search | Images | Print | Security | Stop |

"I've Been Rooked!"

What do you know about the game of chess? Do you know anyone who plays? Would you like to learn to play? Here are some rules that will acquaint you with the basics of the game and how each game piece moves.

❶ The Rules of Chess

The Objective in Chess

The primary objective in chess is to checkmate your opponent's King. When a King cannot avoid capture, it is checkmated, and the game is immediately over. If a King is threatened with capture but has a means to escape, then it is said to be in check. A King cannot move into check, and if in check, must move out of check immediately.

Reading for Information

The game of chess can seem very complicated to the beginner: the board has 64 squares, 6 types of game pieces for each player, and specifically defined movements for each game piece.

Using Graphics

Complicated information is often easier to understand when it is presented visually with **graphics.** For example, numerical data presented in a chart or graph allows the reader to easily compare figures and categories. Images, such as photographs or drawings, can add meaning and detail to written text. **Diagrams, charts, maps, illustrations, photographs,** and **time lines** are examples of different kinds of graphics.

YOUR TURN *Use the following questions and activities to help you get the most from the Internet article's graphics and text.*

❶ Graphics are designed to get the reader's attention. Notice the photo of the chess piece on this page. It provides a visual clue about the contents of the article. As you scan this article, what other information do the graphics provide?

Back Forward Reload Home Search Images Print Security Stop

Key for Chess Pieces

Each player starts with
the following pieces:

King (1)

Queen (1)

Rook (2)

Bishop (2)

Knight (2)

Pawn (8)

2

The Starting Position

Black

White

Rows

Chess is played by two players beginning in
the positions shown. The White player (the
player of the light-colored pieces) moves
first. Then each player takes a single turn.

When setting up the pieces, keep two things in
mind. The corner light-colored square goes on
the player's right, and Queens go on their own
color next to the Kings on the center squares.

You may not move a piece to a square
already occupied by one of your own pieces.
You may capture an opposing piece by
replacing that piece with one of your own
pieces, if it can legally move there.

Movement of the Pieces

The King (K)

The King is the most important
piece. When it is trapped so it cannot
move without being captured,
then the game is lost. The trap is called
checkmate. The King can move only one
square in any direction—horizontally,
vertically, or diagonally.

The Queen (Q)

The Queen is the most powerful
piece because it can move in any
straight line—horizontally, vertically,
or diagonally—as long as its path is
not blocked.

Reading for Information *continued*

2 A graphic can be a **symbol.** A key, or legend, identifies what the symbols represent. Here, the ♔ and ♚ represent the King game piece. What other symbols can you find in the article? What do they represent?

3 A **diagram** can show how an object works or how a process flows. It can sometimes be easier to understand than a written explanation. By examining only the diagram, describe how a bishop moves.

4 Each graphic illustrates the text below it. If there were no graphic, would you as easily understand the movements by reading only the text?

♖ ♜ The Rook (R)

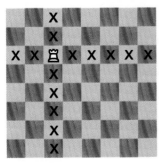

The Rook is a very powerful piece because it can move to any square along its row as long as its path is not blocked. The rook moves in a straight line—horizontally or vertically.

♗ ♝ The Bishop (B)

The Bishop is a powerful piece because it can move to any square along its diagonals as long as its path is not blocked.

♘ ♞ The Knight (N)

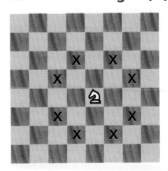

The Knight is the only piece that can hop over other pieces in an L-shaped path that consists of three squares. The Knight may move one step in a horizontal direction and then two steps in a vertical direction. Or, it can move two steps horizontally and then one step vertically.

Reading for Information _continued_

Creating a Graphic For some people, information presented in a graphic can be easier to understand and remember than written text. On a separate sheet of paper, complete the following graphic. In the appropriate column, record how each chess piece moves.

Chess piece	Moves horizontally	Moves vertically	Moves diagonally
King	X	X	
Queen	X	X	
Rook			
Bishop			
Knight			
Pawn			

Research & Technology
Activity Link: "Rules of the Game," p. 361. On page 355 of "Rules of the Game," Amy Tan lists some of the advanced moves she learned from Lau Po. Research one or more of these moves and create a graphic representation for each move.

Search   Images   Print   Security   Stop

♟ ♟ The Pawn (P)

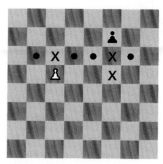

The pawn is the least powerful piece on the board. It may move only one square forward if its path is not blocked. However, it has the option—on its first move only—to move two squares forward. The pawn can never move backwards. It can only capture another piece by moving diagonally one square. It may not capture in a forward move. If a pawn is able to reach the last row of its opponent's side of the board, the pawn is promoted to any other piece but the King. In the diagram, the squares with X's indicate possible destinations for the pawns. The squares with dots show the destinations for captures.

Fear
by GABRIELA MISTRAL
Translated by DORIS DANA

Identity
by JULIO NOBOA
Translated by INA CUMPIANO

Connect to Your Life

Be Yourself In these poems, the speakers do not want other people to tell them or their children how to behave. Does your life sometimes contain conflicts between "I" and "they"? Are there things you don't like about the kind of person "they" want you to be? Discuss your answers in a small group.

Build Background

Two Languages/Dos Lenguas The poems "Fear" and "Identity" are presented in both Spanish and English. Gabriela Mistral, the author of "Fear," grew up in Chile in South America. She wrote her poem in Spanish, and it was later translated into English. On the other hand, Julio Noboa, the author of "Identity," was brought up in a bilingual household in the United States; that is, his family spoke both Spanish and English. "Identity" was originally written in English and later translated into Spanish.

English and Spanish share common roots. Note the similarities between English and Spanish in the following examples from "Fear."

English	Spanish
my	mi
princess	princesa
day	día
throne	trono

Focus Your Reading

LITERARY ANALYSIS **SYMBOL**

A person, place, object, or action that stands for something beyond itself is called a **symbol.** For example, the poem "Identity" may seem to be about plants, but it is not. The plants in this poem symbolize certain qualities. As you read these two poems, look for other symbols.

ACTIVE READING **VISUALIZING**

The process of forming a mental picture from a written description is called **visualizing.** In reading poetry, it is important to visualize the **images** that the poet presents. A poet creates images by using language that appeals to the reader's sense of sight, hearing, smell, taste, or touch.

READER'S NOTEBOOK Make a chart like the one shown. As you read the poems, note the images that each poet presents. Then go back and write a brief description of what you visualize for each image.

Image	from "Fear"	from "Identity"	Mental Picture
child turned into swallow	√		child flying away from mother

Fear

BY GABRIELA MISTRAL
ENGLISH TRANSLATION BY DORIS DANA

I don't want them to turn
my little girl into a swallow.
She would fly far away into the sky
and never fly again to my straw bed,
5 or she would nest in the eaves
where I could not comb her hair.
I don't want them to turn
my little girl into a swallow.

I don't want them to make
10 my little girl into a princess.
In tiny golden slippers
how could she play on the meadow?
And when night came, no longer
would she sleep at my side.
15 I don't want them to make
my little girl a princess.

And even less do I want them
one day to make her queen.
They would put her on a throne
20 where I could not go to see her.
And when nighttime came
I could never rock her . . .
I don't want them to make
my little girl a queen!

THINKING *through the* LITERATURE

1. Why do you think the poet repeats certain lines in the poem?
2. In your opinion, is it better to wear golden slippers or to play in the fields? Explain your answer.
3. Why did Gabriela Mistral entitle her poem "Fear"?
   Think About:
   • what she says she's afraid of
   • what she is really afraid of

MIEDO

Yo no quiero que a mi niña
golondrina me la vuelvan.
Se hunde volando en el cielo
y no baja hasta mi estera;
5   en el alero hace nido
y mis manos no la peinan.
Yo no quiero que a mi niña
golondrina me la vuelvan.

Yo no quiero que a mi niña
10 la vayan a hacer princesa.
Con zapatitos de oro
¿cómo juega en las praderas?
Y cuando llegue la noche
a mi lado no se acuesta...
15 Yo no quiero que a mi niña
la vayan a hacer princesa.

Y menos quiero que un día
me la vayan a hacer reina.
La pondrían en un trono
20 a donde mis pies no llegan.
Cuando viniese la noche
yo no podría mecerla...
¡Yo no quiero que a mi niña
me la vayan a hacer reina!

Lovers (2nd Version), (ca. 1913, cast 1954–1958), Käthe Kollwitz.
Bronze, 28⅞" × 19" × 19½". Hirshhorn Museum and Sculpture Garden,
Smithsonian Institution, gift of Joseph H. Hirshhorn, 1966.
Photograph by Ricardo Blanc. Copyright © 2001 Artists Rights Society
(ARS), New York / VG Bild-Kunst, Bonn.

Identity

by Julio Noboa

Planting According to Rules (Nach regeln zu pflanzen)
1935. 91 (N11) Paul Klee. Watercolor on paper, mounted
on cardboard 10⅛" × 14½". Kunstmuseum Bern, Hermann
und Margrit Rupf-Stiftung, Inv. Nr. Z22.

Let them be as flowers,
always watered, fed, guarded, admired,
but harnessed to a pot of dirt.

I'd rather be a tall, ugly weed,
5 clinging on cliffs, like an eagle
wind-wavering above high, jagged rocks.

To have broken through the surface of stone
to live, to feel exposed to the madness
of the vast, eternal sky.
10 To be swayed by the breezes of an ancient sea,
carrying my soul, my seed, beyond the mountains of time
or into the abyss[1] of the bizarre.

I'd rather be unseen, and if
then shunned[2] by everyone
15 than to be a pleasant-smelling flower,
growing in clusters in the fertile valley
where they're praised, handled, and plucked
by greedy, human hands.

I'd rather smell of musty, green stench
20 than of sweet, fragrant lilac.
If I could stand alone, strong and free,
I'd rather be a tall, ugly weed.

---

1. **abyss** (ə-bĭs): a seemingly bottomless pit.
2. **shunned**: avoided or stayed away from deliberately.

Identidad

Que sean ellos como las flores,
bien rociadas, bien nutridas, cuidadas y bien amadas
pero presas y limitadas en su maceta de tierra sucia.

Más quisiera yo ser mala hierba, alta y fea,
5   de aquéllas que se aferran bien al risco,
como el águila que ondea en la ventolera
más allá de las rocas copetudas.

Poder romper mi propia grieta en lo plano de la piedra,
poder vivir expuesto a la locura, vasta eterna,
    de aquel cielo.
10   Poder mecerme en el vaivén de las brizas de un mar antiguo,
llevar a cuestas mi alma, mi simiente, más alla de las montañas
    que son el tiempo
o de los viejos abismos de la extravagancia.

Más quisiera que no me vieran aunque entonces
quedara solo,
15   que ser la fragante flor
arracimada en el valle fértil,
loada, manoseada, arrancada
por las voraces manos del gentío.

Más quisiera el tufo verde y trasnochado
20   que la fragancia de lilas dulces.
Pudiendo mantenerme erguido, fuerte y libre,
más quisiera yo ser mala hierba, alta y fea.

translated by Ina Cumpiano

Connect to the Literature

1. **What Do You Think?** To which of these two poems did you respond more strongly? Give reasons for your choice.

   Comprehension Check
   • In "Identity," why would the speaker rather be a "tall, ugly weed"?

Think Critically

2. Which speaker is more likely to get his or her wish?

3. **ACTIVE READING** **VISUALIZING**
   Look back over the images that you visualized in your **READER'S NOTEBOOK**. Choose your favorite image from each poem. What does each image make you think of? How does each image make you feel?

4. Compare the speakers in these poems. How are they similar? How are they different?

   Think About:
   • the way each speaker views "they"
   • the way each speaker views "self"
   • what each speaker is wishing for

Extend Interpretations

5. **COMPARING TEXTS** Both poems use birds as images. Why does Mistral use the image of a delicate swallow while Noboa uses the image of a strong eagle? Could the birds have been reversed in the two poems? Why or why not?

6. **Connect to Life** Do you have possessions, dreams, or feelings that are so important that you would be willing to be "ugly," "unseen," and "shunned" in order to keep them? Explain your response.

Literary Analysis

SYMBOL A person, place, object, or action that stands for something beyond itself is called a **symbol.** For example, a dove is a bird, but it may also symbolize, or stand for, peace. A flag is a colored piece of cloth, but it also symbolizes a nation.

Paired Activity In "Fear" and "Identity," the poets use many symbols to enrich the meaning of the poems. With a partner, complete the following charts. The first column in each chart contains the poem's symbols. In the second column, explain what you think the symbol means. If necessary, write more than one meaning. Is one meaning more powerful than the others? Explain your answer.

"Fear"	
Symbol	**Meaning**
swallow	flying away; leaving home; growing up
princess	
queen	

"Identity"	
Symbol	**Meaning**
flowers	
weed	

CHOICES and CHALLENGES

Writing

Pros and Cons Write a paragraph in which you describe the good and bad points of being a weed as opposed to being a garden flower. Feel free to introduce your own ideas as well as those of Julio Noboa. Revise for word choice, appropriate organization, and a consistent point of view. Place the entry in your **Working Portfolio.**

Speaking & Listening

Pattern Poem Write an eight-line poem using Gabriela Mistral's poem as a model. Begin your poem with the following line:

I do not want them to . . .

Include symbols and imagery that allow the listener to picture what you're saying. Read your poem aloud to your class.

Speaking and Listening Handbook See p. R106: Oral Reading.

Research & Technology

Spanish Speakers Spanish-speaking people have an important influence on American life in such areas as music, dance, food, literature, art, architecture, and government. In the library or online, locate the most recent United States census information. How many people in the United States list Spanish as their first language? What percentage of the total population is this group? Create a graph that illustrates your findings. Display your graph in the classroom.

Gabriela Mistral
1889–1957

"If you are not able to love a lot, don't teach children."

A Dedicated Teacher Gabriela Mistral grew up in a small village in northern Chile and became a schoolteacher at the age of 15. Despite her youth, she excelled in this career. When she was 33, the Mexican government asked her to start educational programs for the poor in Mexico. Eventually Mistral settled in the United States, where she taught Spanish literature to college students.

A Famous Poet Mistral began publishing poetry when she was a village schoolteacher. In 1945, she became the first Latin-American woman to win a Nobel Prize in literature.

Julio Noboa
born 1949

"Make your poetry the reflection of your life."

A Bilingual Poet Julio Noboa was born in the Bronx, New York City, to parents who came from Puerto Rico. When he began writing poetry, he decided to write in both Spanish and English.

An Educator and a Writer Noboa now lives in San Antonio, Texas, where he writes for the *San Antonio Express-News,* and the *La Estrella* of Fort Worth. Noboa also works in the Department of Teaching at the University of Northern Iowa and serves as Clinical Supervisor for student teachers in San Antonio public schools.

from **Still Me**
by CHRISTOPHER REEVE

Speech
by CHRISTOPHER REEVE

Connect to Your Life

The author of these selections, actor Christopher Reeve, lost the use of his arms and legs as the result of a horseback-riding accident in 1995. What do you already know about how people cope with paralysis? What do you want to know? Make a chart like the one shown. Fill in the first two columns. You will complete the third column after you read these selections.

What I Know	What I Want to Know	What I Learned

Build Background

A REAL SUPERMAN

Christopher Reeve is the actor who once played Superman in the well-known movie. He is also now a quadriplegic, meaning he is paralyzed in all four limbs. Reeve is confined to an electric wheelchair, which he operates by sucking out of or puffing into an air tube. It takes a team of ten nurses and five aides to give him the required round-the-clock care.

Shortly after the accident that paralyzed him, Reeve's wife, actress and singer Dana Morosini, told him, "You're still you. And I love you." Reeve says these two sentences saved his life and inspired him to help himself and others.

WORDS TO KNOW
Vocabulary Preview

access   rehabilitation
affliction   sever
logistics

Focus Your Reading

LITERARY ANALYSIS   POINT OF VIEW

The perspective from which a literary work is told is called its **point of view.** When a work is told from **first-person point of view,** the narrator is a character in the work and uses first-person pronouns such as *I, me, we,* and *us.*

Still Me is an **autobiography,** an account of Christopher Reeve's life written by Reeve. Like most autobiographies, *Still Me* is told in first-person point of view.

Speeches, including Reeve's speech on page 380, are also told in first-person point of view. Notice how both works use the pronouns *I* and *we.*

ACTIVE READING   DETERMINING TEXT ORGANIZATION

Writers of nonfiction and speeches choose a pattern or patterns of text organization to fit a certain purpose for their writing and to help them develop relationships between facts and events. Common patterns include

• chronological order

• cause and effect

• compare and contrast

• proposition and support

READER'S NOTEBOOK Writers often use more than one pattern in a selection. As you read Reeve's speech and the excerpt from *Still Me,* see if you can find examples of each type.

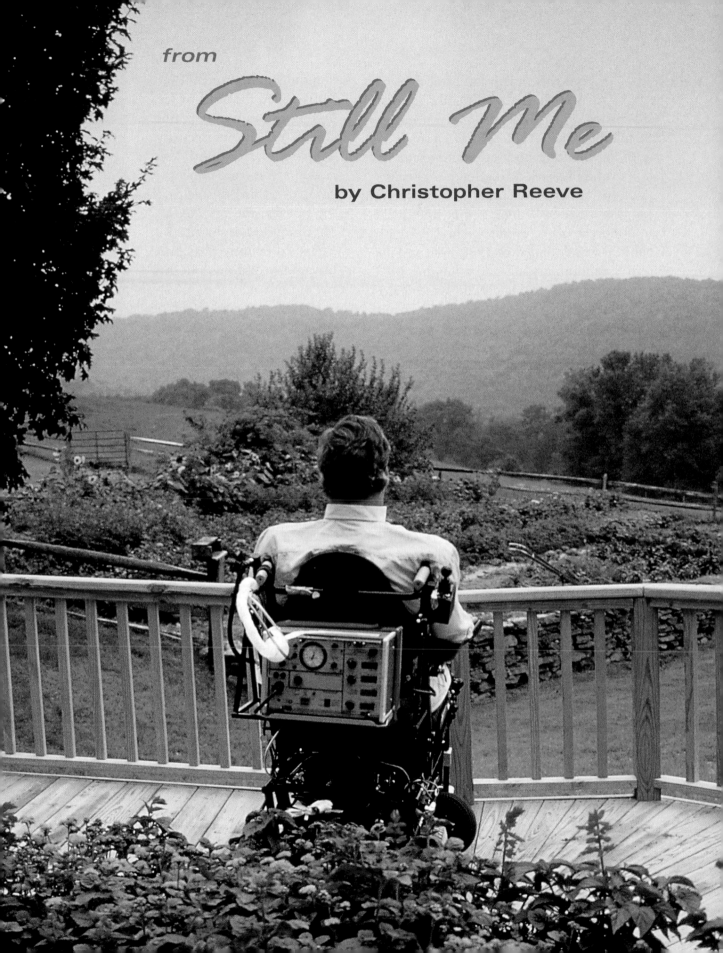

from

Still Me

by Christopher Reeve

At about this time I had to decide if I was well enough to attend the annual fund-raising dinner of The Creative Coalition, scheduled for the seventeenth of October. As one of the founders and recent copresident, I felt a strong obligation to attend, especially because as far back as January I had asked my close friend Robin Williams to be one of the two honorees of the evening. The Creative Coalition was founded in 1989 by Ron Silver, Susan Sarandon, myself, and a number of other celebrities to bring certain issues before the public to try to effect change. We were in the unique position of having <u>access</u> to the media as well as to key players in Washington. Our focus was mainly on the National Endowment for the Arts,[1] homelessness, the environment, and campaign finance reform. Robin was to be honored for his appearances on HBO with Billy Crystal and Whoopi Goldberg for Comic Relief, which had raised millions of dollars to help the homeless. After consulting with Dr. Kirshblum and making special arrangements for Patty and Juice to come with me, I told the board of TCC that I would attend and present Robin his award.

No sooner had I agreed than it dawned on me how challenging this short trip to the Hotel Pierre was going to be. It would be the first time I would be seen or heard in public. I wondered if I would be able to address the audience or if I would be too nervous to speak at all. Would I spasm? Would I have a pop-off?[2] I also knew that getting in and out of the hotel would require well-coordinated security, because the press and photographers would be extremely aggressive in their efforts to get the first pictures of me since the accident.

Dana[3] and I talked it over and decided that the psychological advantage of keeping a long-standing commitment outweighed the risks of just getting through the evening. Robin put his own security people at our disposal. We rented a van from a local company, Dana dusted off my tuxedo, and on the afternoon of the seventeenth I finished therapy early and braced myself to go out into the unknown.

I vividly remember the drive into the city. For nearly four months I had been cruising the halls of Kessler[4] in my wheelchair at three miles per hour. Driving into the city at fifty-five mph was an overwhelming experience. All the other cars seemed so close. Everything was rushing by. As we hit the bumps and potholes on the way in, my neck froze with tension and my body spasmed uncontrollably while I sat strapped in the back of the van, able to see only taillights and license plates and the painted lines on the pavement below us. As we pulled

---

1. **National Endowment for the Arts:** An independent agency of the federal government that gives grants for projects, large and small, to promote excellence, diversity, and growth in the arts. It was established in 1965.
2. **pop-off:** a term to describe when a patient's breathing tube becomes disconnected.
3. **Dana:** the wife of Christopher Reeve.
4. **Kessler:** the Kessler Institute for Rehabilitation, the place where Reeve learned skills to manage his disability.

WORDS
TO   **access** (ăk'sĕs) *n.* the power to reach; to make use of; to get past barriers
KNOW

up to the side entrance of the Pierre, Juice and Neil Stutzer, who we hired to help us with the <u>logistics</u> and accessibility, taped sheets over the windows to protect us from the photographers. There were hundreds of them, straining at the police barricades that had been set up to give us room to park. The block had been sealed off, and mounted police patrolled the street. A special canopy had been constructed that reached from the side door of the hotel to the roof of our van. Once that was in place I was lowered to the ground and quickly pushed into the building.

I wondered if I would be able to address the audience or if I would be too nervous to speak at all.

We made our way through the kitchen to the service elevator. As I went by, the kitchen workers stood respectfully against the wall and applauded. I was in something of a daze, but I

WORDS TO KNOW	**logistics** (lō-jĭs′tĭks) *n.* the management, planning, and carrying out of details in an operation or a project

managed to nod and thank them. Soon I found myself in a suite on the nineteenth floor, where I was transferred into a hospital bed to rest and get my bearings. I had made it this far, but the whole experience had been much more intense than I had anticipated, and the evening was still ahead of me.

Soon it was time to get back in the chair and make all the final adjustments before joining a special reception of friends and honored guests. I wheeled into the suite's living room to find my friends and colleagues from TCC as well as Barbara Walters and Mayor Giuliani, Robin and Marsha, and a sea of other faces, all waiting to greet me and wish me well. For a split second I wished a genie could make me disappear. Somehow I made it through the reception, occasionally doing weight shifts in my chair while Patty discreetly emptied my leg bag and checked my blood pressure. Finally the guests went down to dinner, and I was left alone with Dana to recover. She hugged me but didn't need to ask how I was doing; she could tell that even though I was white as a sheet, I was happy to be out in the world again.

We watched the evening's entertainment on a closed-circuit TV until it was time for me to prepare to go onstage. A special ramp had been built from near the kitchen entrance to the stage of the grand ballroom. Black drapes had been hung to shield me from the audience until it was time for me to go on. At last the moment came. I heard Susan Sarandon introducing me from the podium, and suddenly Juice was pushing me up the ramp and onto the stage. As I was turned into

> **...she could tell that even though I was white as a sheet, I was happy to be out in the world again.**

position, I looked out to see seven hundred people on their feet cheering. The ovation went on for more than five minutes. Once again I had mixed feelings—of gratitude, excitement, and the desire to disappear. At last the applause died down, and the audience lapsed into an intense silence. A blind person walking into the room probably would not have been able to tell that anyone was there.

In a moment of panic I realized that I hadn't prepared any remarks. All my attention had been focused on the practicalities of the evening. Luckily, a thought popped into my head, and I went with it. I said, "Thank you very much, ladies and gentlemen. I'll tell you the real reason I'm here tonight." (A long pause, as I waited for the ventilator to give me my next breath.) "When I was a senior at Princeton Day School (another pause for breath), my English teacher George Packard once asked a student, 'Why weren't you here yesterday?'" (Another pause as I tried to form my thoughts.) "And the student replied, 'Sir, I wasn't feeling very well.'" (Now I knew where I was going.) "And George Packard replied, 'The only excuse for nonattendance is quadruple amputation.'" I could feel the audience holding their breath. "'In which case, they can still bring you in a basket.' So I thought I'd better show up." A huge laugh and applause. I'd made it.

The rest was easy. I introduced Juice as Glenn Miller, talked about how much I'd missed everyone at TCC, talked about Robin and his accomplishments, then brought him up onstage. For the next twenty minutes he and I bounced off each other. He took the curse off the wheelchair, going around behind it and pretending to adjust all the controls, referring to my breathing tube as a stylish new necktie, and suggesting that I use the chair for a tractor pull. He told the audience that I had to be careful with the sip-and-puff control; if I blew too hard into the tube, I might pop a wheelie and blast off into the audience. The evening was transformed into a celebration of friendship and endurance. A large group of people, many of whom were strangers, were suddenly drawn together into a unit that felt almost like family.

THINKING *through the* LITERATURE

1. Why is Reeve's trip to the Hotel Pierre such a challenge?

2. What is the meaning of the title *Still Me*?
   Think About:
   • Reeve's disability
   • Reeve's attitude toward his disability

3. Christopher Reeve and other people with disabilities prefer to be described as disabled rather than handicapped. Look up the word *handicap* in a dictionary. Do you agree that handicapped is not an appropriate description of Reeve's condition? Why?

SPEECH BY CHRISTOPHER REEVE

Over the last few years, we've heard a lot about something called family values. And like many of you, I've struggled to figure out what that means. But since my accident, I've found a definition that seems to make sense. I think it means that we're all family, that we all have value. And if that's true, if America really is a family, then we have to recognize that many members of our family are hurting.

Just to take one aspect of it, one in five of us has some kind of disability. You may have an aunt with Parkinson's disease. A neighbor with a spinal cord injury. A brother with AIDS. And if we're really committed to this idea of family, we've got to do something about it.

First of all, our nation cannot tolerate discrimination of any kind. That's why the Americans with Disabilities Act[1] is so important and must be honored everywhere. It is a civil rights law that is tearing down barriers both in architecture and in attitude.

Its purpose is to give the disabled access not only to buildings but to every opportunity in society. I strongly believe our nation must give its full support to the caregivers who are helping people with disabilities live independent lives.

Sure, we've got to balance the budget. And we will.

We have to be extremely careful with every dollar that we spend. But we've also got to take care of our family—and not slash programs people need. We should be enabling, healing, curing.

> ONE OF THE SMARTEST THINGS WE CAN DO ABOUT DISABILITY IS INVEST IN RESEARCH THAT WILL PROTECT US FROM DISEASE AND LEAD TO CURES.

One of the smartest things we can do about disability is invest in research that will protect us from disease and lead to cures. This country already has a long history of doing just that. When we put our minds to a problem, we can usually find solutions. But our scientists can do more. And we've got to give them the chance.

That means more funding for research. Right now, for example, about a quarter million Americans have a spinal cord injury. Our government spends about $8.7 billion a year just maintaining these members of our family. But we spend only $40 million a year on research that would actually improve the quality of their lives; get them off public assistance, or even cure them.

We've got to be smarter, do better. Because the money we invest in research today is going to determine the quality of life of members of our family tomorrow.

During my rehabilitation, I met a young man named Gregory Patterson. When he was innocently driving through Newark, New Jersey, a stray bullet from a gang shooting went through his car window . . . right into his neck . . . and severed his spinal cord. Five years ago, he might have died. Today, because of research, he's alive.

But merely being alive is not enough.

---

1. **Americans with Disabilities Act:** A federal civil rights law enacted in 1990 that protects citizens with mental or physical disabilities from discrimination in employment or in accessing public accommodations.

WORDS
TO
KNOW

rehabilitation (rē′hə-bĭl′ĭ-tā′shən) n. the process of being restored to good health or useful life through training or therapy
sever (sĕv′ər) v. to become separated; to be cut off from the whole

We have a moral and an economic responsibility to ease his suffering and prevent others from experiencing such pain. And to do that we don't need to raise taxes. We just need to raise our expectations.

America has a tradition many nations probably envy: We frequently achieve the impossible. That's part of our national character. That's what got us from one coast to another. That's what got us the largest economy in the world. That's what got us to the moon.

On the wall of my room when I was in rehab was a picture of the space shuttle blasting off, autographed by every astronaut now at NASA. On the top of the picture it says, "We found nothing is impossible." That should be our motto. Not a Democratic motto, not a Republican motto. But an American motto. Because this is not something one party can do alone. It's something that we as a nation must do together.

So many of our dreams at first seem impossible, then they seem improbable and then, when we summon the will, they soon become inevitable. If we can conquer outer space, we should be able to conquer inner space, too: the frontier of the brain, the central nervous system, and all the <u>afflictions</u> of the body that destroy so many lives and rob our country of so much potential.

Research can provide hope for people who suffer from Alzheimer's. We've already discovered the gene that causes it. Research can provide hope for people like Muhammad Ali and the Reverend Billy Graham who suffer from Parkinson's. Research can provide hope for the millions of Americans like Kirk Douglas who suffer from stroke. We can ease the pain of people like Barbara Jordan, who battled multiple sclerosis. We can find treatments for people like Elizabeth Glaser, whom we lost to AIDS. And now that we know that nerves in the spinal cord can regenerate, we are on the way to getting millions of people around the world like me up and out of our wheelchairs.

Fifty-six years ago, FDR[2] dedicated new buildings for the National Institutes of Health. He said that "the defense this nation seeks involves a great deal more than building airplanes, ships, guns, and bombs. We cannot be a strong nation unless we are a healthy nation." He could have said that today.

President Roosevelt showed us that a man who could barely lift himself out of a wheelchair could still lift a nation out of despair. And I believe—and so does this administration—in the most important principle FDR taught us: America does not let its needy citizens fend for themselves. America is stronger when all of us take care of all of us. Giving new life to that ideal is the challenge before us tonight.

Thank you very much.[3] ❖

---

2. **FDR:** Franklin Delano Roosevelt (1882–1945) was the 32nd president of the United States. He was stricken with polio as an adult and eventually was confined to a wheelchair during his presidency.

3. This speech was delivered by Christopher Reeve on August 26, 1996.

WORDS
TO
KNOW

affliction (ə-flĭk′shən) *n.* a condition of pain or suffering

Connect to the Literature

1. What Do You Think? Has your attitude about people with disabilities changed after reading these selections? Why or why not?

Comprehension Check
- What is the main idea of Christopher Reeve's speech?

Think Critically

2. When Reeve tells the story about his high school English teacher, the people in the audience laugh and applaud. Why do you think they laugh? How do you think they are really feeling?

3. **ACTIVE READING** **DETERMINING TEXT ORGANIZATION**
Go back to the chart that you made in your **READER'S NOTEBOOK.** How does Reeve organize the text and the information in *Still Me* and in his speech? Working with a partner, compare your examples of text organization. Which type of text organization do you think is most effective? Explain why.

4. Christopher Reeve starred as the hero Superman in the movies. Who do you think is more of a hero, Superman or Christopher Reeve? Why?

> **Think About:**
> • Superman's remarkable powers
> • Reeve's courage and determination

5. In the speech, Reeve states that nothing is impossible. Do you agree? Explain your answer.

Extend Interpretations

6. What If? What if Reeve did not believe in himself? How might his life be different? What would his life be like?

7. Connect to Life At the beginning of these selections, you were asked to write down what you know and want to know about how people cope with paralysis. What did you learn as a result of reading these selections? Were you surprised? Why or why not?

Literary Analysis

POINT OF VIEW The perspective from which a short story, novel, or work of nonfiction is told is called the **point of view.** In **first-person point of view,** the narrator is a **character** in the literary work and uses first-person pronouns such as *I, me, we,* and *us.*

Christopher Reeve's speech and the excerpt from *Still Me* both use first-person point of view. This point of view allows Reeve to tell you in his own voice what he is thinking and feeling, as in this sentence:

For a split second I wished a genie could make me disappear.

Group Activity First-person point of view gives the reader a window into the thoughts and feelings of the narrator. In a small group, go back through the excerpt from *Still Me* and look for details that might have been omitted if *Still Me* had been written by someone other than Reeve. What would the excerpt be like without these details?

Thoughts	Feelings
"it dawned on me how challenging this short trip to the Hotel Pierre was going to be"	

CHOICES and CHALLENGES

Writing

Summary Report Write a summary of Christopher Reeve's speech, using his general pattern of organization. When you are finished, make sure you have identified the main ideas and included the most important supporting details. Place your summary in your **Working Portfolio.**

Speaking & Listening

Persuasive Speech Choose a cause that you feel is worthy of funding and research, such as a program to help the homeless. Write a short speech aimed at convincing your community to support your cause. Include a well-defined thesis and support your arguments with detailed evidence, examples, and reasoning. Anticipate and answer counterarguments through the arrangement of your supporting details, and maintain a reasonable tone.

Speaking and Listening Handbook
See p. R109: Persuasive Presentations.

Research & Technology

Causes and Solutions Research the major causes of spinal-cord injuries in the United States. How many people are affected by spinal-cord injuries every year? What age groups are most likely to suffer such injuries? What is being done to assist people with these injuries? Report your findings to the class. Be sure to note your sources.

Reading for INFORMATION

As part of your research, read "Careers That Care" on p. 386.

Vocabulary

EXERCISE A: WORD MEANING Review the Words to Know and answer the following questions on your paper.

1. Christopher Reeve has **access** to the media. Does this mean that he easily communicates with reporters or that he is never able to reach them?

2. Many people helped Reeve with the **logistics** of his public appearance. Did these people manage his transportation to the hotel, or did they provide news coverage of the event?

3. People often need **rehabilitation** after they've been in an accident. Does this mean that they need to be placed on a stretcher or restored to health through training and therapy?

4. If you **sever** your spinal cord, is it cut completely through or just slightly torn?

5. Christopher Reeve's **affliction** has greatly changed his life. Does the word *affliction* refer to his opinion about helping the disabled or to the suffering he has endured?

EXERCISE B Complete a word web like the one shown for each of the Words to Know.

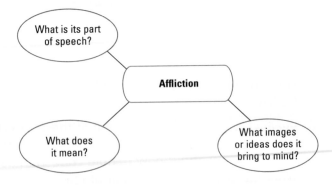

Vocabulary Handbook
See p. R20: Context Clues.

Grammar in Context: **Participles**

In the following sentence from *Still Me,* the word *overwhelming* is a **participle,** a verb that acts as an adjective.

> **Driving into the city at fifty-five mph was an overwhelming experience.**

There are two kinds of participles—the present participle (formed by adding *-ing* to the present tense of a verb: *overwhelm, overwhelming)* and the past participle (formed by adding *-d* or *-ed* to the present tense of regular verbs: *overwhelm, overwhelmed).*

Apply to Your Writing Use participles as a way of adding information to your sentences or to vary sentence beginnings.

Punctuation Tip: Use commas after participles that begin sentences.

WRITING EXERCISE On your paper, write the correct participial form of the verb in parentheses.

Example: *Original* He was only able to see the _____ lines on the road. (paint)

Rewritten He was only able to see the painted lines on the road.

1. _____, Christopher Reeve accepted the invitation. (smile)
2. From the van, he watched the people in the _____ streets. (crowd)
3. _____, the audience gave him a standing ovation. (applaud)
4. After the dinner there was a party for many of the _____ guests. (invite)
5. _____ but happy, he returned home. (exhaust)

Grammar Handbook
See p. R84: Using Verbs Correctly.

Christopher Reeve
born 1952

"At night I am always whole. I've never had a dream in which I am in a wheelchair."

Always an Actor Raised in Princeton, New Jersey, Christopher Reeve began acting in school and local plays at the age of eight. By the time he was sixteen, he had an agent. All through his college years at Cornell, he performed in theatrical productions. After college, he studied performing arts at the Juilliard School in New York City. In 1978, he got the lead role in the movie *Superman.*

Forever Changed In addition to acting, Reeve studied and composed music and was a

dedicated athlete who loved to sail, ride horses, scuba-dive, ski, and pilot planes. Then, in 1995, his life changed forever when a horse he was riding refused to jump and Reeve was hurled from the saddle. The resulting paralysis slowed Reeve, but it did not stop him. Today he focuses his talents on helping others with spinal-cord injuries and on a career as a movie director.

AUTHOR ACTIVITY
What Is a Hero? When the first *Superman* movie came out, Reeve was frequently asked the question "What is a hero?" Reeve answers this question in Chapter 11 of *Still Me.* Find a copy of the book in the library and read Chapter 11. Do you agree with Reeve's definition of a hero? Why or why not?

① CAREERS *That Care*

For individuals who are disabled either by disease or as a result of an accident, there are many different professionals who are trained to help them manage, and in some cases, overcome their disabilities. These professionals may help an accident victim to learn to walk again, design the controls for a specially equipped car, or help a patient with simple tasks such as eating or getting dressed. Although these jobs are very different, those who perform them all share something in common—the desire to care for others.

For some patients, the time after surgery is a long and difficult time of recovery. When Christopher Reeve entered a rehabilitation facility, he had to learn to cope with the effects of his injuries, which had left him paralyzed.

He worked with therapists who helped him learn how to make use of his limited mobility and learn how to breathe with the assistance of special equipment. Other patients need similar help to become more independent.

There is increasing demand for careers similar to those noted in the following article. As advances in technology and medical and surgical procedures allow more individuals to survive accidents and disabling diseases, the need for rehabilitation continues to grow. Similarly, as the number of elderly in the population expands, the need for assisted living services will expand as well. There are many professions from which to choose, when it comes to careers that care.

PHYSICAL THERAPY ②
Erica Druin, *M.P.T.*

In working with people with physical disabilities [I accept that] I had nothing to do with the disease or injury that caused their loss, but I have everything to do with their moving on with their lives. I can't imagine a more satisfying job or one where you feel so appreciated each and every day.

Q: **What does a physical therapist do?**

A: A physical therapist teaches patients ways to move and use their bodies and muscles to relieve pain, restore movement, or prevent permanent disability. Individualized exercise regimens that take into account the injury or disability of a patient are often created by a physical therapist.

Q: **What training and education is required?**

A: A four-year college degree in physical therapy will teach you about the body and how it works. You will also train, for a time, in a hospital or other medical setting. A physical therapist must pass a national exam before he or she can begin treating patients. Many states also require a physical therapy license in order to practice.

Q: **Where could you work?**

A: Hospitals, doctor's offices, nursing homes, sports facilities, schools, and rehabilitation centers are all places that employ physical therapists.

Reading for Information

Have you ever heard a news report on television or on the radio that leaves you with unanswered questions or that raises new questions in your mind? Doing independent research is one way to find the answers to these questions.

Forming, Revising, and Raising New Research Questions

Asking and forming thoughtful **questions** about a specific topic is a part of the research process. After choosing a topic, you might begin **researching a specific question** to answer. For example, your original research question might be "What is life like for people who are disabled?" As you learn more about the topic, new research questions will emerge. Regardless of how carefully you frame your original question, you may need to **revise** it as you gather **additional information.** Sometimes the focus of your research question needs to be narrowed. Your research may change the question to "What technical devices are available to assist people who are quadriplegic?" Ask questions that can be researched by gathering information and facts about the topic.

YOUR TURN *Use this article and the questions and activities that follow to help you learn how to form, revise, and raise new research questions.*

❶ How do you go about selecting a research topic? Consider topics and subjects you want to learn more about. Before you read this article, scan the title, photographs, quotations, and first paragraph. What questions come to mind? List two or three questions you would like to have answered.

❷ Read the information about Erica Druin carefully. Raise one or two research questions about her job and training that go beyond the simple *who* or *what.*

OCCUPATIONAL THERAPY ③
Sue Eberle, *OTR*

I became interested in occupational therapy when I worked in the hospital and had the opportunity to observe patients receiving therapy. . . . The most difficult part of my job is saying goodbye to patients when they leave the facility because you develop a special relationship with them.

Q: **What does an occupational therapist do?**

A: If an illness or disease prevents a patient from performing everyday tasks, an occupational therapist can help him or her learn new ways to live as normally as possible. Through activities or with the use of assistive technology and devices, an occupational therapist helps the patient rebuild independence and self-esteem.

Q: **What training and education is required?**

A: You must obtain a degree in occupational therapy from a four-year college program. You can also get a degree in a related field of study, such as biology, and then earn a certificate in occupational therapy. In either case you must pass a national exam and, in most states, you will need to obtain a license to practice.

Q: **Where could you work?**

A: Occupational therapists work in many different settings: rehabilitation facilities, nursing homes, hospitals, long-term care centers, or in a patient's home.

REHABILITATION ASSISTANT / HOME HEALTH AIDE ④
Glenn "Juice" Miller

The biggest challenge is learning how to help them [patients] through their pain, their fears, their frustrations, anger and heartbreak. As I go about my work, I spend a great deal of time talking with patients and their families. I try to instill in them the strength and confidence to meet the challenges they face. . . . I believe that to do this job you have to have a lot of love in your heart—and be willing to share it with others.

Q: What does a home health aide do?

A: A home health aide makes home visits to the elderly, the disabled, or those who are recovering from an injury or illness. An aide helps with tasks, such as bathing and preparing meals, as well as administering medication and checking vital signs (like blood pressure and heart rate). A home health aide oversees a patient's daily progress and reports any changes to a nurse or doctor.

Q: Is a career as a home health aide for you?

A: If you are caring and compassionate, interested in helping patients in basic but important ways, enjoy having a flexible work schedule, and are willing to travel to different work sites each day, becoming a home health aide is a career you should explore.

Q: What training and education is required?

A: You can train to become a home health aide through the Visiting Nurses Association, the American Red Cross, or at a vocational school. Once classroom studies and a supervised training are completed, you must take a test to earn a certificate as a home health aide.

Q: Where could you work?

A: A home health aide travels to patients' homes. Depending on a patient's needs, a visit may last from 1 to 24 hours. An aide may visit up to six patients a day.
Note: A rehabilitation assistant performs many of the same patient care tasks as a Home Health Aide but works in a rehabilitation facility and not in a patient's home.

③ After reading this section, how would you revise your original question from "What are all of the latest high-tech devices?" to a question that is more focused and specific?

④ Read this section on rehabilitation assistant/home health aide. What questions would you like to research about this career?

Creating a Graphic A chart like the one shown can help you frame or refocus a research question.

Careers That Help the Disabled		
K	**W**	**L**
What I know	What new questions I want to learn about	What I learned from my research

Research & Technology
Activity Link: from *Still Me*, p. 384
Review this article and the excerpt from *Still Me* by Christopher Reeve. Think about the team of dedicated professionals who helped Reeve. What conclusions can you draw about people who work with victims of spinal-cord injury? What are some different ways to help people with disabilities? Research the topic and present your findings in a series of questions and answers.

Stopping by Woods on a Snowy Evening *by* ROBERT FROST

Connect to Your Life

Let It Snow What words and phrases come to mind when you hear the word *snow*? Create a word web to explore your associations. Then, as a class, compare and contrast your webs. What does *snow* mean to different people in your class?

Build Background

GEOGRAPHY

Robert Frost is famous for his poetry about New England. New England is a region in the northeast section of the United States. The region includes six states—Maine, Vermont, New Hampshire, Massachusetts, Connecticut, and Rhode Island.

New England, one of the oldest and most historic parts of the country, is famous for its picturesque villages, thick forests, rugged landscape, and cold, snowy winters. Frost loved the sights and sounds of the New England countryside, which he described with grace and precision.

Focus Your Reading

LITERARY ANALYSIS POETIC FORM

The way a poem looks, or is arranged, on a page is its **poetic form.** The words of a poem are written in lines, which can vary in length. In some poems, lines are grouped together in stanzas.

In poems that have a **traditional form,** each line has the same number of syllables, and each stanza has the same number of lines. For example, "Stopping by Woods on a Snowy Evening" has eight syllables in each line, and four lines in each stanza. It also has a **regular pattern** of rhyme, which reinforces the form. As you read the poem, pay attention to the lines and their end rhymes. Which lines have the same end rhyme?

ACTIVE READING QUESTIONING

One way to understand a poem's meaning is to ask yourself questions about the poem. For example, what is the setting of the poem? Who is the speaker? What is being described in the poem?

READER'S NOTEBOOK As you read, list your questions in the form used by newspaper reporters. Answer each question in a chart like the one shown. Don't worry if you do not have a precise answer to every question. Instead, use the questions to help you think about the overall meaning of the poem.

"Stopping by Woods on a Snowy Evening"	
Who?	a thoughtful person
What?	
Where?	
When?	
Why?	

Stopping by Woods on a Snowy Evening

BY ROBERT FROST

Whose woods these are I think I know.
His house is in the village though;
He will not see me stopping here
To watch his woods fill up with snow.

My little horse must think it queer
To stop without a farmhouse near
Between the woods and frozen lake
The darkest evening of the year.

He gives his harness bells a shake
To ask if there is some mistake.
The only other sound's the sweep
Of easy wind and downy flake.

The woods are lovely, dark and deep,
But I have promises to keep,
And miles to go before I sleep,
And miles to go before I sleep.

Winter Wilderness, Artist Unknown. Oil on Canvas. David David Gallery/SuperStock.

Connect to the Literature

1. **What Do You Think?** What words or phrases from this poem linger in your mind? How do these words and phrases make you feel?

Comprehension Check
- Where does the speaker stop?
- What does the speaker decide to do?

Think Critically

2. **ACTIVE READING** **QUESTIONING**
   Refer back to the questions and answers you wrote in your 📖 **READER'S NOTEBOOK**. Use your answers to complete the following sentence: This poem is about _____.

3. Many critics think this poem is about more than "stopping by woods on a snowy evening." What deeper meaning can you find in the poem?

   Think About:
   - the time of day and the season
   - who might own the woods
   - the phrase "and miles to go before I sleep"

Extend Interpretations

4. **Critic's Corner** Poet and critic Louis Untermeyer said, "Such a poem as 'Stopping by Woods on a Snowy Evening' once in the mind of a reader will never leave it." What do you think Untermeyer means? Do you agree or disagree? Why?

5. **Connect to Life** If you had been walking in these snowy woods, would you have stopped or would you have hurried home? Explain your response.

Literary Analysis

POETIC FORM "Stopping by Woods on a Snowy Evening" has a **traditional form;** that is, each line has the same number of syllables and each stanza has the same number of lines.

Another important part of the poem's form is its rhyme and rhythm. **Rhyme** is a likeness of sounds at the ends of words. **Rhythm** is the pattern of sound created by the arrangement of stressed and unstressed syllables.

"Stopping by Woods on a Snowy Evening" has a regular rhythm, as the pattern of stressed (′) and unstressed (˘) syllables in these lines shows:

Whŏse wóods thĕse aré Ĭ thínk
  Ĭ knŏw.
Hĭs hŏuse ĭs ín thĕ víllăge
  thŏugh;

Paired Activity Working with a partner, copy the poem on a sheet of paper and underline all the words that rhyme. Then mark the stressed and unstressed syllables. Take turns reading the poem aloud, exaggerating the rhyme and rhythm. Discuss your answers to the following questions:
- Why do you think Frost repeats the last line?
- What is the effect of making the rhyme pattern of the last stanza different?

Writing

Regional Poem Write a poem describing a natural setting that is typical of your region. Make sure the poem has a distinctive form and pattern of rhythm and rhyme. Be sure to include sensory details. You may wish to do the Research & Technology activity first. Place your poem in your **Working Portfolio.**

Writing Workshop
See p. 252: Basics in a Box.

Speaking & Listening

Music Review Composer Randall Thompson set several of Frost's poems (including "Stopping by Woods on a Snowy Evening") to music in a piece called "Frostiana." If possible, find a recording and listen to it. In what ways does Thompson's recording enhance Frost's poetry? Write a brief oral report summarizing your thoughts. Play the recording for the class, and present your ideas.

Research & Technology

Home Sweet Home In what region of the country do you live? Using the library, Internet, and local resources, find out about your region's geography. For example, what is the climate of the region? What landforms does it have? Prepare a report to share with the class. Illustrate the report with drawings, photographs, or charts. Be sure to note your sources.

Robert Frost
1874–1963

"I believe that poetry should be enjoyed by everyone . . ."

A Difficult Start Robert Frost was born in San Francisco, California. However, following the death of his father in 1885, he moved with his mother and sister back to New England, the original family home. Frost was a top student in high school but attended college only briefly. In 1895 he married high school classmate Elinor White. Frost struggled to make a living by farming, teaching, and writing poetry.

Success at Last By age 40, Frost had yet to achieve success as a writer. In a courageous move, he and Elinor sold their New Hampshire farm and moved to England. Their gamble paid off. Frost's work was well received in England, and when the Frosts moved back to New England in 1915, they found that his work had become famous in the United States. In 1923, his collection *New Hampshire* received the Pulitzer Prize, the first of four such awards for Frost.

AUTHOR ACTIVITY
Frost and Solitude In "Stopping by Woods on a Snowy Evening," Frost writes about the experience of being alone. His poem "Acquainted with the Night" also focuses on solitude. Find a copy of this poem and read it. Based on these two poems, do you think Frost viewed solitude as a positive or negative experience? Explain your answer.

Building Vocabulary
Analyzing Word Parts—Affixes

When you encounter an unfamiliar word, you can break it down into parts. Thinking about the meaning of each part will help you figure out the meaning of the word as a whole.

The word *malodorous* has two **affixes**—word parts that can be attached to base words to make new words. Affixes added to the beginning of words are **prefixes**; those added to the end are called **suffixes**.

> He wore a dark, **malodorous** suit.
> —Amy Tan, "Rules of the Game"

malodorous

| Prefix **mal-** means "bad" or "badly." | Suffix **-ous** means "possessing" or "full of." |

Base word **odor** means "a smell."

Knowing the parts of the word, you can figure out that *malodorous* means "possessing a bad smell."

Strategies for Building Vocabulary

Here are other strategies to help you analyze words that contain prefixes and suffixes.

❶ Look for Familiar Affixes and Study the Context When you see a word you don't know, look for base words and affixes that you recognize. Using your knowledge, think about the word in context. Read the following excerpt.

> My grandmother, Emma Louvenia Watson, was famous in family circles for getting into the bathtub without her soap. This is a woman who helped organize resistance to segregation in Knoxville, Tennessee.
> —Nikki Giovanni, *Grand Mothers*

The word *segregation* is made up of the word *segregate,* which means "to separate," and the suffix *-ion,* which means "an action or process." You can tell from the sentence structure that segregation must be a noun. From the context, you also know that it is something that Watson resisted or fought against. You can conclude that *segregation* means "the act or process of being separated from others or a main group."

❷ Learn the Meanings of Affixes Study the following tables. Notice that some affixes have similar meanings.

Prefix	Meaning	Example
co-	together	coauthor
de-	reverse, remove from	deodorant
extra-	outside, beyond	extraordinary
im-, in-	not	impermanent
re-	again, back	redecorate
sub-	below, under, beneath	substandard
un-	not, opposite of	unusual

Suffix	Meaning	Example
-ance	condition, action	resistance
-ant, -ent	one who, one that	attendant
-ion	act, condition	possession
-ly	in a certain way, like, resembling	angrily
-or	one who, one that	actor
-ous	possessing, full of	venomous

EXERCISE Find the meaning of each word, using the affix charts and a dictionary if necessary.

1. tentatively
2. unfamiliar
3. reformation
4. variably
5. affliction

The Moustache
by Robert Cormier

At the last minute Annie couldn't go. She was invaded by one of those twenty-four-hour flu bugs that sent her to bed with a fever, moaning about the fact that she'd also have to break her date with Handsome Harry Arnold that night. We call him Handsome Harry because he's actually handsome, but he's also a nice guy, cool, and he doesn't treat

me like Annie's kid brother, which I am, but like a regular person. Anyway, I had to go to Lawnrest alone that afternoon. But first of all I had to stand inspection.

My mother lined me up against the wall. She stood there like a one-man firing squad, which is kind of funny because she's not like a man at all, she's very feminine, and we have this great relationship—I mean, I feel as if she really likes me. I realize that sounds strange, but I know guys whose mothers love them and cook special stuff for them and worry about them and all, but there's something missing in their relationship.

Anyway. She frowned and started the routine.

"That hair," she said. Then admitted: "Well, at least you combed it."

I sighed. I have discovered that it's better to sigh than argue.

"And that moustache." She shook her head. "I still say a seventeen-year-old has no business wearing a moustache."

"It's an experiment," I said. "I just wanted to see if I could grow one." To tell the truth, I had proved my point about being able to grow a decent moustache, but I also had learned to like it.

"It's costing you money, Mike," she said.

"I know, I know."

The money was a reference to the movies. The Downtown Cinema has a special Friday night offer—half-price admission for high school couples seventeen or younger. But the woman in the box office took one look at my moustache and charged me full price. Even when I showed her my driver's license. She charged full admission for Cindy's ticket, too, which left me practically broke and unable to take Cindy out for a hamburger with the crowd afterward. That didn't help matters, because Cindy has been getting impatient recently about things like the fact that I don't own my own car and have to concentrate on my studies if I want to win that college scholarship, for instance. Cindy wasn't exactly crazy about the moustache, either.

Now it was my mother's turn to sigh.

"Look," I said, to cheer her up. "I'm thinking about shaving it off." Even though I wasn't. Another discovery: You can build a way of life on postponement.

"Your grandmother probably won't even recognize you," she said. And I saw the shadow fall across her face.

Let me tell you what the visit to Lawnrest was all about. My grandmother is 73 years old. She is a resident—which is supposed to be a better word than patient—at the Lawnrest Nursing Home. She used to make the greatest turkey dressing in the world and was a nut about baseball and could even quote batting averages, for crying out loud. She always rooted for the losers. She was in love with the Mets until they started to win. Now she has arteriosclerosis, which the dictionary says is "a chronic disease characterized by abnormal thickening and hardening of the arterial walls." Which really means that she can't live at home anymore or even with us, and her memory has betrayed her as well as her body. She used to wander off and sometimes didn't recognize people. My mother visits her all the time, driving the thirty miles to Lawnrest almost every day. Because Annie was home for a semester break from college, we had decided to make a special Saturday visit. Now Annie was in bed, groaning theatrically—she's a drama major—but I told my mother I'd go, anyway. I hadn't seen my grandmother since she'd been admitted to Lawnrest. Besides, the place is located on the Southwest Turnpike, which meant I could barrel along in my father's new Le Mans. My ambition was to see the speedometer hit 75. Ordinarily, I used the old station wagon, which can barely stagger up to 50.

Frankly, I wasn't too crazy about visiting a nursing home. They reminded me of hospitals, and hospitals turn me off. I mean, the smell of ether[1] makes me nauseous, and I feel faint at the sight of blood. And as I approached Lawnrest—which is a terrible cemetery kind of name, to begin with—I was sorry I hadn't avoided the trip. Then I felt guilty about it. I'm loaded with guilt complexes.[2] Like driving like a madman after promising my father to be careful. Like sitting in the parking lot, looking at the nursing home with dread and thinking how I'd rather be with Cindy. Then I thought of all the Christmas and birthday gifts my grandmother had given me, and I got out of the car, guilty, as usual.

Inside, I was surprised by the lack of hospital smell, although there was another odor or maybe the absence of an odor. The air was antiseptic, sterile. As if there was no atmosphere at all or I'd caught a cold suddenly and couldn't taste or smell.

A nurse at the reception desk gave me directions—my grandmother was in East Three. I made my way down the tiled corridor and was glad to see that the walls were painted with cheerful colors like yellow and pink. A wheelchair suddenly shot around a corner, self-propelled by an old man, white-haired and toothless, who cackled merrily as he barely missed me. I jumped aside—here I was, almost getting wiped out by a two-mile-an-hour wheelchair after doing seventy-five on the pike. As I walked through the corridors seeking East Three, I couldn't help glancing into the rooms, and it was like some kind of wax museum[3]—all these figures in various stances and attitudes, sitting in beds or chairs, standing at windows, as if they were frozen forever in these postures. To tell the truth, I began to hurry because I was getting depressed. Finally, I saw a beautiful girl approaching, dressed in white, a nurse or an attendant, and I was so happy to see someone young, someone walking and acting normally, that I gave her a wide smile and a big hello and must have looked like a kind of nut. Anyway, she looked right through me as if I were a window, which is about par for the course whenever I meet beautiful girls.

I finally found the room and saw my grandmother in bed. My grandmother looks like Ethel Barrymore.[4] I never knew who Ethel Barrymore was until I saw a terrific movie, *None But the Lonely Heart,* on TV, starring Ethel Barrymore and Cary Grant.[5] Both my grandmother and Ethel Barrymore have these great craggy faces like the side of a mountain and wonderful voices like syrup being poured. Slowly. She was propped up in bed, pillows puffed behind her. Her hair had been combed out and fell upon her shoulders. For some reason, this flowing hair gave her an almost girlish appearance, despite its whiteness.

She saw me and smiled. Her eyes lit up and her eyebrows arched and she reached out her hands to me in greeting. "Mike, Mike," she said. And I breathed a sigh of relief. This was one of her good days. My mother had warned me that she might not know who I was at first.

I took her hands in mine. They were fragile. I could actually feel her bones, and it seemed as if they would break if I pressed too hard. Her skin was smooth, almost slippery, as if the years had worn away all the roughness the way the wind wears away the surfaces of stones.

"Mike, Mike, I didn't think you'd come," she said, so happy, and she was still Ethel Barrymore, that voice like a caress. "I've been waiting all this time." Before I could reply, she

---

1. **ether** (ē′thər): a chemical formerly used by surgeons as an anesthetic.

2. **complexes:** exaggerated concerns or preoccupations.

3. **wax museum:** a museum that displays wax statues of famous people.

4. **Ethel Barrymore** (1879–1959): U.S. stage and screen actress.

5. **Cary Grant** (1904–1986): U.S. movie star.

looked away, out the window. "See the birds? I've been watching them at the feeder. I love to see them come. Even the blue jays. The blue jays are like hawks—they take the food that the small birds should have. But the small birds, the chickadees, watch the blue jays and at least learn where the feeder is."

She lapsed into silence, and I looked out the window. There was no feeder. No birds. There was only the parking lot and the sun glinting on car windshields.

She turned to me again, eyes bright. Radiant, really. Or was it a medicine brightness? "Ah, Mike. You look so grand, so grand. Is that a new coat?"

"Not really," I said. I'd been wearing my Uncle Jerry's old army-fatigue jacket for months, practically living in it, my mother said. But she insisted that I wear my raincoat for the visit. It was about a year old but looked new because I didn't wear it much. Nobody was wearing raincoats lately.

> "Mike, Mike, I didn't think you'd come," she said, so happy, and she was still Ethel Barrymore, that voice like a caress.

"You always loved clothes, didn't you, Mike?" she said.

I was beginning to feel uneasy because she regarded me with such intensity. Those bright eyes. I wondered—are old people in places like this so lonesome, so abandoned that they go wild when someone visits? Or was she so happy because she was suddenly lucid[6] and everything was sharp and clear? My mother had described those moments when my grandmother suddenly emerged from the fog that so often obscured her mind. I didn't know the answers, but it felt kind of spooky, getting

such an emotional welcome from her.

"I remember the time you bought the new coat—the chesterfield,"[7] she said, looking away again, as if watching the birds that weren't there. "That lovely coat with the velvet collar. Black, it was. Stylish. Remember that, Mike? It was hard times, but you could never resist the glitter."

I was about to protest—I had never heard of a chesterfield, for crying out loud. But I stopped. Be patient with her, my mother had said. Humor her. Be gentle.

We were interrupted by an attendant who pushed a wheeled cart into the room. "Time for juices, dear," the woman said. She was the standard forty- or fifty-year-old woman: glasses, nothing hair, plump cheeks. Her manner was cheerful but a businesslike kind of cheerfulness. I'd hate to be called "dear" by someone getting paid to do it.

"Orange or grape or cranberry, dear? Cranberry is good for the bones, you know."

My grandmother ignored the interruption. She didn't even bother to answer, having turned away at the woman's arrival, as if angry about her appearance.

The woman looked at me and winked. A conspiratorial kind of wink. It was kind of horrible. I didn't think people winked like that anymore. In fact, I hadn't seen a wink in years.

"She doesn't care much for juices," the woman said, talking to me as if my grandmother weren't even there. "But she loves her coffee. With lots of cream and two lumps of sugar. But this is juice time, not coffee time."

---

6. **lucid:** mentally alert; clear-headed.
7. **chesterfield:** an overcoat, usually with concealed buttons and a velvet collar.

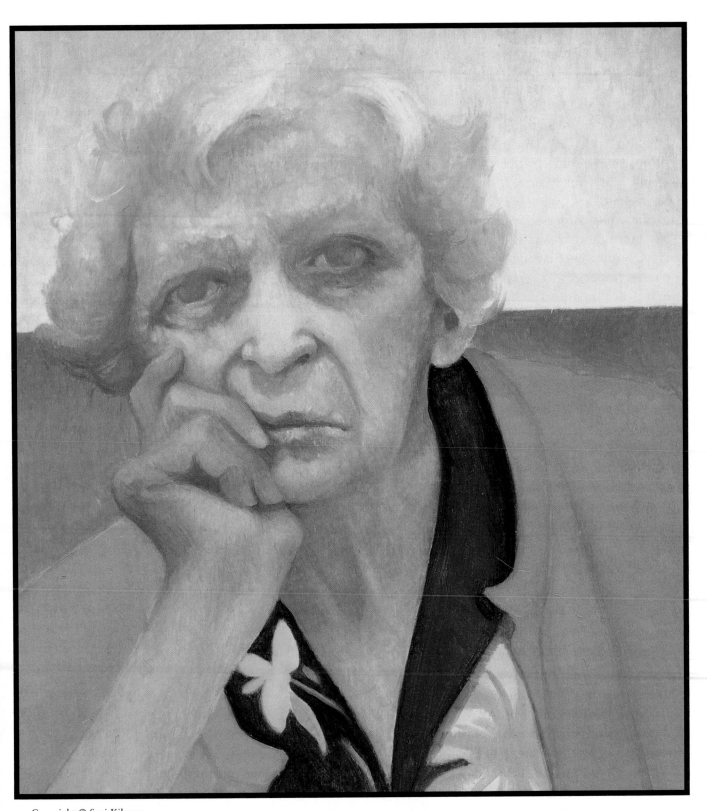

Addressing my grandmother again, she said, "Orange or grape or cranberry, dear?"

"Tell her I want no juices, Mike," my grandmother commanded regally, her eyes still watching invisible birds.

The woman smiled, patience like a label on her face. "That's all right, dear. I'll just leave some cranberry for you. Drink it at your leisure. It's good for the bones."

She wheeled herself out of the room. My grandmother was still absorbed in the view. Somewhere a toilet flushed. A wheelchair passed the doorway—probably that same old driver fleeing a hit-run accident. A television set exploded with sound somewhere, soap-opera voices filling the air. You can always tell soap-opera voices.

I turned back to find my grandmother staring at me. Her hands cupped her face, her index fingers curled around her cheeks like parenthesis marks.

"But you know, Mike, looking back, I think you were right," she said, continuing our conversation as if there had been no interruption. "You always said, 'It's the things of the spirit that count, Meg.' The spirit! And so you bought the baby-grand piano—a baby grand in the middle of the Depression. A knock came on the door and it was the deliveryman. It took five of them to get it into the house." She leaned back, closing her eyes. "How I loved that piano, Mike. I was never that fine a player, but you loved to sit there in the parlor, on Sunday evenings, Ellie on your lap, listening to me play and sing." She hummed a bit, a fragment of melody I didn't recognize. Then she drifted into silence. Maybe she'd fallen asleep. My mother's name is Ellen, but everyone always calls her Ellie. "Take my hand, Mike," my grandmother said suddenly. Then I remembered—my grandfather's name was Michael. I had been named for him.

"Ah, Mike," she said, pressing my hands with all her feeble strength. "I thought I'd lost you forever. And here you are, back with me again. . . ."

> "You always said, 'It's the things of the spirit that count, Meg.' The spirit!"

Her expression scared me. I don't mean scared as if I were in danger but scared because of what could happen to her when she realized the mistake she had made. My mother always said I favored her side of the family. Thinking back to the pictures in the old family albums, I recalled my grandfather as tall and thin. Like me. But the resemblance ended there. He was thirty-five when he died, almost forty years ago. And he wore a moustache. I brought my hand to my face. I also wore a moustache now, of course.

"I sit here these days, Mike," she said, her voice a lullaby, her hand still holding mine, "and I drift and dream. The days are fuzzy sometimes, merging together. Sometimes it's like I'm not here at all but somewhere else altogether. And I always think of you. Those years we had. Not enough years, Mike, not enough. . . ."

Her voice was so sad, so mournful that I made sounds of sympathy, not words exactly but the kind of soothings that mothers murmur to their children when they awaken from bad dreams.

"And I think of that terrible night, Mike, that terrible night. Have you ever really forgiven me for that night?"

"Listen . . ." I began. I wanted to say: "Nana, this is Mike your grandson, not Mike your husband."

"Sh . . . sh . . ." she whispered, placing a finger as long and cold as a candle against my lips. "Don't say anything. I've waited so long for this moment. To be here. With you. I wondered what I would say if suddenly you walked in that door like other people have done. I've thought and thought about it. And I finally made up my mind—I'd ask you to forgive me. I was too proud to ask before." Her fingers tried to mask her face. "But I'm not proud anymore, Mike." That great voice quivered and then grew strong again. "I hate you to see me this way—you always said I was beautiful. I didn't believe it. The Charity Ball when we led the grand march and you said I was the most beautiful girl there. . . ."

"Nana," I said. I couldn't keep up the pretense any longer, adding one more burden to my load of guilt, leading her on this way, playing a pathetic[8] game of make-believe with an old woman clinging to memories. She didn't seem to hear me.

"But that other night, Mike. The terrible one. The terrible accusations I made. Even Ellie woke up and began to cry. I went to her and rocked her in my arms, and you came into the room and said I was wrong. You were whispering, an awful whisper, not wanting to upset little Ellie but wanting to make me see the truth. And I didn't answer you, Mike. I was too proud. I've even forgotten the name of the girl. I sit here wondering now—was it Laura or Evelyn? I can't remember. Later, I learned that you were telling the truth all the time, Mike. That I'd been wrong. . . ." Her eyes were brighter than ever as she looked at me now, but tear-bright, the tears gathering. "It was never the same after that night, was it, Mike? The glitter was gone. From you. From us. And then the accident . . . and I never had the chance to ask you to forgive me. . . ."

My grandmother. My poor, poor grandmother. Old people aren't supposed to have those kinds of memories. You see their pictures in the family albums, and that's what they are: pictures. They're not supposed to come to life. You drive out in your father's Le Mans doing seventy-five on the pike, and all you're doing is visiting an old lady in a nursing home. A duty call. And then you find out that she's a person. She's *somebody*. She's my grandmother, all right, but she's also herself. Like my own mother and father. They exist outside of their relationship to me.

I was scared again. I wanted to get out of there.

"Mike, Mike," my grandmother said. "Say it, Mike."

I felt as if my cheeks would crack if I uttered a word.

"Say you forgive me, Mike. I've waited all these years. . . ."

I was surprised at how strong her fingers were.

"Say, '*I forgive you, Meg.*'"

I said it. My voice sounded funny, as if I were talking in a huge tunnel. "I forgive you, Meg."

Her eyes studied me. Her hands pressed mine. For the first time in my life, I saw love at work. Not movie love. Not Cindy's sparkling eyes when I tell her that we're going to the beach on a Sunday afternoon. But love like something alive and tender, asking nothing in return. She raised her face, and I knew what she wanted me to do. I bent and brushed my lips against her cheek. Her flesh was like a leaf in autumn, crisp and dry.

She closed her eyes and I stood up. The sun wasn't glinting on the cars any longer. Somebody had turned on another television set, and the voices were the show-off voices of the panel shows. At the same time you could still hear the soap-opera dialogue on the other television set.

---

8. **pathetic:** pitiful.

I waited awhile. She seemed to be sleeping, her breathing serene[9] and regular. I buttoned my raincoat. Suddenly she opened her eyes again and looked at me. Her eyes were still bright, but they merely stared at me. Without recognition or curiosity. Empty eyes. I smiled at her, but she didn't smile back. She made a kind of moaning sound and turned away on the bed, pulling the blankets around her.

> Her eyes studied me.
> Her hands pressed mine.
> For the first time in my life,
> I saw love at work.

I counted to twenty-five and then to fifty and did it all over again. I cleared my throat and coughed tentatively. She didn't move; she didn't respond. I wanted to say, "Nana, it's me." But I didn't. I thought of saying, "Meg, it's me." But I couldn't.

Finally I left. Just like that. I didn't say good-bye or anything. I stalked through the corridors, looking neither to the right nor the left, not caring whether that wild old man with the wheelchair ran me down or not.

On the Southwest Turnpike I did seventy-five—no, eighty—most of the way. I turned the radio up as loud as it could go. Rock music—anything to fill the air. When I got home, my mother was vacuuming the living-room rug. She shut off the cleaner, and the silence was deafening. "Well, how was your grand-mother?" she asked.

I told her she was fine. I told her a lot of things. How great Nana looked and how she seemed happy and had called me Mike. I wanted to ask her—hey, Mom, you and Dad really love each other, don't you? I mean—there's nothing to forgive between you, is there? But I didn't.

Instead I went upstairs and took out the electric razor Annie had given me for Christmas and shaved off my moustache. ❖

---

9. **serene:** calm.

Robert Cormier
1925–2000

"…I like to call myself a realistic writer . . . . I take real people and put them in extraordinary situations."

Wishes Come True Growing up in Leominster, Massachusetts, Robert Cormier says he was a "skinny kid living in a ghetto type of neighborhood wanting the world to know I existed." His childhood wish came true. Today, he is one of the country's best-known writers of adolescent fiction.

Award Winner Cormier's books have won many awards. In 1994, *We All Fall Down* was voted by the American Library Association as one of the best books for young adults written during the last 25 years. It also won a 1993–1994 young adult California Reader Medal, an award voted by teenagers.

old age sticks

by E. E. Cummings

Children Playing London Bridge (ca. 1942), William H. Johnson. Watercolor on paper, 12"x 10 1/2". Collection of Professor and Mrs. David C. Driskell

old age sticks
up Keep
Off
signs)&

youth yanks them
down(old
age
cries No

Tres)&(pas)
youth laughs
(sing
old age

scolds Forbid
den Stop
Must
n't Don't

&)youth goes
right on
gr
owing old

Nikki Giovanni

CONTENTS

Living Poetry

"I use poetry as an outlet for my mind. It's my justification for living."

A HAPPY CHILDHOOD

born 1943

Nikki Giovanni was born Yolande Cornelia Giovanni, Jr., in Knoxville, Tennessee, in 1943. Soon after her birth, her parents moved to Lincoln Heights, a suburb of Cincinnati, Ohio. Nikki grew up in a loving family that valued achievement. Both her parents were college graduates, and her grandfather was one of the first graduates of the all-black Fisk University in Tennessee. Giovanni always suspected that one day she would be famous, and during her school days she seemed to be on the fast track to success. In 1960, at the end of her junior year of high school, she enrolled in Fisk University.

Nikki (front) and her sister

Her **LIFE** and **TIMES**

1943
Born June 7 in Knoxville, Tennessee

Nikki, age 14

1959
Accepted at Fisk University at age 16

1940   1950   1960

1945
U.S. drops atomic bombs on Japan; WWII ends.

1955
Bus boycott begins in Montgomery, Alabama.

FIERY VOICE OF THE 1960s

Unfortunately, Giovanni's independent spirit got her into trouble with the university authorities almost immediately. After her first semester, she was expelled for leaving the campus without permission to spend Thanksgiving with her grandparents. In 1964 she returned to Fisk, where she became politically active in the civil rights movement. A year after her 1967 graduation, Giovanni published her first book of poetry, *Black Feeling, Black Talk*. Her poetry was so impressive that the National Foundation for the Arts awarded her a grant, which she used to attend Columbia University's School of the Arts. Two more books of poetry followed in 1968 and 1970.

Giovanni's poetry represented an exciting new voice calling for civil rights and racial equality. Like many other writers of the 1960s, Giovanni was determined to change society through literature. In keeping with the mood of the times, Giovanni's poetry was angry and militant. In the poem "For Two Jameses" she wrote, "they put us in a cell / to make us behave . . . / and we will be born / from their iron cells / new people with a new cry."

Did You Know?

◆ Nikki Giovanni took her first name from a nickname her sister gave her when she was very young.

◆ She has given as many as 200 lectures and poetry readings in a single year.

◆ She started her own publishing house at age 27 to publish her poems.

◆ She has received honorary degrees from many universities.

1967
Graduates from college; wins grant to publish *Black Feeling, Black Talk*

1978
Moves back to Cincinnati, Ohio

1980
Publishes *Vacation Time*

1987
Becomes an English professor at Virginia Tech

1994
Publishes *Grand Mothers*

1970   **1980**   **1990**   **2000**

1969
Neil Armstrong is first person to walk on the moon.

1974
President Nixon resigns.

1989
Berlin Wall is torn down; Germany is reunited.

1991
Soviet Union breaks up.

1998
War erupts in Kosovo.

LOVE, FAMILY, AND COMMUNITY

In the 1970s Giovanni's poetry grew gentler as she explored more personal themes of love and family. In 1972 Giovanni published *My House,* a book of poetry that was organized into two sections. One section, "The Rooms Inside," dealt with her personal relationships, while the other section, "The Rooms Outside," dealt with the African-American experience. At the same time, themes of loneliness and disappointment began appearing in her work.

During the 1970s Giovanni's poetry readings and lectures were much in demand. Her first album, *Truth Is on Its Way,* was a recording of her poetry read to gospel music. Giovanni's poetry had been influenced by the rhythms of black music, and the album was a good way of further uniting her poetry with African-American musical traditions. The recording was a tremendous success and led to many more. Soon she was appearing on television and at colleges throughout the country.

(Above) Nikki Giovanni promoting her album *Truth Is on Its Way* (Left) Nikki Giovanni's CD *Like a Ripple on a Pond*

MOVING ON

In 1978 Giovanni moved back to Cincinnati to help her family after her father suffered a stroke. When he died in 1982, Giovanni began teaching. She also continued publishing poetry and essays. In 1989 Giovanni became a professor of English at the Virginia Polytechnic Institute. In the 1990s she was stricken with cancer, but after successful surgery she resumed her life with a positive attitude. As she commented in 1998, it is important that "we approach our world and our lives with wonder about what is around the bend."

TALKING WITH NIKKI GIOVANNI

Nikki Giovanni frequently responds to questions from student readers.

Q: **How did you become an author? Did anyone help you get started?**

A: Probably the easiest thing in the world, Aiana, is to become an author. All you have to do is say you are one. We do not have tests or require licenses or anything like that. You just have to do it and then comes the hard part: you have to find someone to read it . . . Publishing is the icing on the cake . . .

I have always had difficulty with the second part of your question because people help people no matter what people think or do. I do not believe anyone "does it on their own." We all receive help and those of us who are wise always stand ready to give it.

Q: **What kind of advice would you give to somebody who wanted to do something in their life but didn't get a lot of support?**

A: . . . So you ask what about no support? Well, the first thing anyone needs to understand is that life is a lonely journey, but whether or not others join or leave us we have to do what we were put on Earth to do . . . I think the main supporter of ourselves is ourselves. We should be our own greatest fans. Then others will join in the cheering.

Q: **How long does it take for you to write a poem?**

A: I think any good poet, Edytka, would say "All my life." And while that would be true it would not be a satisfactory answer. I like to give a poem as much space as I need to feel it is complete. But writing poetry isn't baking a cake or cleaning the shower; it is not a job that we can quantify. It is a journey without end that we experience until we feel a point of completion.

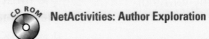 **Author Link**
www.mcdougallittell.com

CD ROM **NetActivities: Author Exploration**

from **Grand Mothers**

by NIKKI GIOVANNI

Connect to Your Life

Who Is Your Grand Person? Think of a beloved older person in your life or in the life of someone you know. Why is that older person so well loved? To help you organize your thoughts, use a chart like the one shown. List the special qualities of the person you are thinking of. Then list evidence of those special qualities.

Special Quality	Evidence
Experience, wisdom	Tells me stories about her youth
Sense of humor	Always ready to have fun
Understanding	Listens to my problems

Build Background

HISTORY

In *Grand Mothers* Nikki Giovanni mentions an event that took place during the Civil Rights movement of the early 1960s. During this time many citizens, both black and white, were working to achieve equal rights for African Americans, while others were violently resisting this movement for change. On September 15, 1963, a bomb tore through an African-American church in Birmingham, Alabama, killing four little girls. As Giovanni points out, reaction was swift but peaceful. It was also effective: In 1964, Congress passed the Civil Rights Act, which banned many forms of discrimination.

WORDS TO KNOW
Vocabulary Preview

bellow	resistance
cliché	segregation
consent	slovenly
contemplate	tackle
exquisite	transition

Focus Your Reading

LITERARY ANALYSIS **VOICE**

A writer's distinctive style or manner of expression is called **voice.** Voice allows a reader to "hear" a personality in the writing. Giovanni writes:

> *Grandmothers are special. They talk funny; they think differently; and they are always telling us how much easier we have it. I'm not so sure.*

Giovanni's "voice" can be heard in her short sentences, which are very informal and create a sense of relaxed conversation—as if she were speaking to the reader in person. In her poems, however, Giovanni often assumes the voice of another personality. As you read examples of Giovanni's writing, pay close attention to the voice of the character who is "speaking."

ACTIVE READING **IDENTIFYING MAIN IDEA**

The most important idea in a piece of writing is called the **main idea.** Sometimes you can find the main idea stated in a sentence or two. Other times you have to infer the main idea from details.

READER'S NOTEBOOK As you read, look for the main idea in this selection. State the main idea in your own words.

from GRAND MOTHERS

by Nikki Giovanni

My grandmother, Emma Louvenia Watson, was famous in family circles for getting into the bathtub without her soap. This is a woman who helped organize <u>resistance</u> to <u>segregation</u> in Knoxville, Tennessee. This is a woman who stood up to Cass Walker, a very conservative Knoxville businessman. This is a woman who was the indirect cause of the family being in Knoxville, Tennessee, in the first place because she smarted off to some white folk in Albany, Georgia. She could not remember her soap.

WORDS
TO
KNOW

resistance (rĭ-zĭs'təns) *n.* the act of fending off; an opposing force
segregation (sĕg'rĭ-gā'shən) *n.* the process of separating others from a main body or group; the policy and practice of separating one race from the rest of society

She could remember how to make miniature Parker House rolls so light that we practically had to put weights on them to keep them on the Sunday table; she made peach or blackberry cobbler so <u>exquisite</u> that we would have eaten it until next year . . . but it wouldn't last that long; she made sherry chicken that fell off the bone; she made her own mayonnaise, which was worth eating on her own homemade bread without any meat at all. But I only mention her food. Grandmother played the piano, could sew like a pro, and would <u>tackle</u> anything foolish enough to bother her children, husband, or mother-in-law. She forgot her soap.

Somehow that bothered this granddaughter when I was small, but the older I have grown, the more it is a fond memory. Who knows what joy it gave her to sit in a tub of hot water? Maybe she had grown up without indoor plumbing and was just showing off the water in the tub the way she showed off when she scraped the dough from the mixing bowl into the baking pan. We all hated that . . . all four of us. Grandmother would scrape it so clean that there was no reason to ask for the bowl . . . there was nothing to lick. She didn't make the ice cream, Grandpapa did, but she was the one who got to pour. Same results. Nothing in the bowl for four hungry grands. She was opinionated and definite. She had a strong sense of right and wrong, and she and hers would stand for the right.

Probably the most horrible racial event after the murder of Emmett Till in Money, Mississippi, in 1954 was the murder of the four little girls in Birmingham, Alabama, on September 15, 1963. The girls had gone to Sunday school early to prepare for a special program. Someone had planted a bomb in the church. If Concord fired the shot heard 'round the world, this was the bomb that alerted the world to the fact that something was very wrong in America. The phones started ringing in black communities all over the country, and mass meetings were announced in churches that Sunday. The children, I guess by common <u>consent</u>, were left at home while the adults decided what should be done. Grandmother and Grandpapa went to Mt. Zion Baptist Church early to get a seat up front.

"Nikki," she said to me after coming from the church meeting, "your grandfather and I are too old to march." *I knew something was coming that I would not especially be pleased with.* "But when they asked for volunteers at

> **Grandmother played the piano, could sew like a pro, and would tackle anything foolish enough to bother her children, husband, or mother-in-law.**

WORDS TO KNOW

exquisite (ĕk'skwĭ-zĭt) *adj.* excellent, flawless; having an intricate and beautiful design or outcome

tackle (tăk'əl) *v.* to take on a problem or a challenge; to wrestle with an opponent

consent (kən-sĕnt') *n.* agreement, acceptance, or approval

Grandmother would call us in, William, Terry, Gary, and me, and line us up. We were supposed to do the scales.

the meeting tonight"— *what has she promised I will do?*—"I was the first to stand." *Curtains. I'm a goner.* "I told them: John Brown and I are too old to march." *Just get on with it, Grandmother.* "But our granddaughter Nikki is here." *Does my mother know what you are doing?* "And she will march in our place." "And everybody applauded." *Sure they did. Those who are about to watch you die salute you.* "Now, John Brown and I will take a cab and come up as soon as the line is in place. You better get on to bed since you have a lot to do tomorrow." Did I mention she hadn't taken her hat off? I did survive that picket line[1] and many others, but her attitude was: Isn't this great? You get to picket! It wasn't often that we said no to her.

One time that I did, however, was when she decided to teach me how to play the piano. My sister, Gary, already played like an angel or whatever heavenly being plays piano. Me, I was a good listener. Grandmother would call us in, William, Terry, Gary, and me, and line us up. We were supposed to do the scales. Gary probably had to play "Clair de Lune" or "Rhapsody in Blue" or some nocturne[2] by Chopin. Me, I couldn't do the scales right. Something about placing your fingers on the right keys and not looking at your hands. Grandmother had one very bad habit: she punished physically. She took a number-two yellow pencil and hit my knuckles. No. A thousand times *no.* I remember saying very calmly to her, "Grandmother, if you are going to be abusive, I am not going to sit here." I proceeded to get up. "Abusive!" she <u>bellowed</u>. "Well, I never." And that was the end of that. She punished me by not teaching me. Abusive, indeed. Recently I was talking about this to my sister, who said, "I didn't realize we could say no to Grandmother." Grandmother never remembered her soap, either.

---

1. **picket line:** a line or a procession of protesters.
2. **nocturne** (nŏk′tûrn): a musical composition meant to suggest a dreamy mood.

WORDS
TO
KNOW   **bellow** (bĕl′ō) *v.* to shout in a deep, loud voice

It was Sweetheart soap: big, oval, and pink. I don't think anything other than perhaps the old blue Sutton Stick deodorant, which Mommy let us use after Gary and I were cleaned up for evening dinner, has smelled as sweet. They don't make Sutton Stick anymore. And I don't use deodorant.

Grandmother did the laundry on Mondays. Every Monday. The trick to the washing was to put your sheets out the night before and sleep on the mattress cover. Otherwise, at the crack of dawn ("Little House on the Prairie" would call it "first light") she would snatch the sheets from under you, not only inconveniencing you but shaming you as well. She had been up for hours, had perked the coffee and started the grits. You were positively <u>slovenly</u> if you slept past six. She washed with Tag soap and used a bluing water for the second rinse. I think it was my aunt Agnes who purchased a wringer[3] washer for her. No one knows what that is anymore. The clothes washed electronically— that is, the tub would spin and churgle all by itself, but it wouldn't wring the clothes dry; you had to hand-feed them through the wringer. I guess some of the things we have today, that we, in fact, take for granted, were unheard of in Emma Lou's day. On the other hand, women did real work. All this talk about feeling useless was such nonsense. If <u>clichés</u> have any truck with reality, certainly "A woman's work is never done" is true. It was always a pleasure to watch her wipe her hands on her apron at day's end and sit down. The footstool on which she rested her feet is in my bedroom right now. I don't have a fireplace, but the glow from 400 Mulvaney is in my heart.

Grandmothers are special. They talk funny; they think differently; and they are always telling us how much easier we have it. I'm not so sure. But when I began to think about the grandmother experience again, I wrote a lot of friends and asked if they would share their experiences. Grandmothers, it seems, are a lot like spinach or asparagus or brussels sprouts: something good for us that we appreciate much more in reflection than in actuality. We were all young when we met these women; we were teenagers by the time we learned to resent their easy, almost casual way of telling us what to do and how to do it. On top of that we had to hear how they and our parents had done everything better. Personally speaking, I'm glad I'm not a teenager anymore. All those emotions running around; all that trying to be grown yet never knowing what "grown" is. It helps tremendously, I think, to just learn that "grown" is something between who we, teenagers, are and who our grandmothers are. Grandmothers make those <u>transitions</u> for us. And they are always on our side. There were, however, times when my grandmother wanted me to pour tea at the church program and I pouted, asking her, "Why do I have to waste my Sunday afternoon?" And there were times when I had to visit the sick, run errands for her friends (and you were *not* allowed to take any money for it), redo a chore that was adequately if not expertly done, and I wondered what is it with grandmothers.

---

3. **wringer:** the part of the washing machine in which wet laundry is pressed between rollers to squeeze out water.

WORDS
TO
KNOW

slovenly (slŭv′ən-lē) *adj.* lazy and careless; untidy

cliché (klē-shā′) *n.* an overused expression that has lost its original quality or effect

transition (trăn-zĭsh′ən) *n.* a change from one stage to another

Mother would have accepted "No" or "Not yet" for an answer. Grandmother wanted it *now*. And cheerfully. Grandmother helped me become civilized. She helped me see that little things are all that matter. She taught me patience. She showed me how to create beauty in everything I do.

Not all grandmothers are the same; maybe yours were the ones to let you off easy, and your parents set the rules. But they are always important, and that is why I asked friends to write in this book. If a book is going to be about someone who is as important to us as a grandmother, then the entire book should be friendly. That doesn't mean nice and easy, though. Grandmothers are older than we are, they have to be, and we grow up with them, even if that means having to take over being an adult too soon. They teach us even when they leave us behind. . . .

When I actually <u>contemplate</u> my grandmother, Emma Lou, the image that stays in my mind is the one that always makes me cry. She was nineteen years old when she married John Brown Watson. She was in her late fifties when he died. She had spent most of her life rearing three daughters, seeing all three receive degrees from Knoxville College; she had been faithful to her church, Mt. Zion Baptist Church; she was an avid club woman, from a supporter of Delta Sigma Theta to her book club, the bridge club, the Court of Calanthe, the Colored Women's Federated Clubs, the flower club, and any and all political groups to help uplift the Negro; she loved to laugh. Yet after we buried Grandpapa, she stood alone at the top of the first set of stairs to wave good-bye to Mommy,

Grandmothers, it seems, are a lot like spinach or asparagus or brussels sprouts: something good for us that we appreciate much more in reflection than in actuality.

Chris, my nephew, and me, as we were the last to leave, and it struck me how alone, not only she, but all of us are. If she contemplated death, and I have every reason to think she surely must have (she lost her mother the same year she married John Brown, and Mama Dear became the mother she did not have), she must have realized that one day she would be there on that hill alone. But it wasn't fair. All of her life she had been in the service of her God, her husband, her children, that which was right.

WORDS TO KNOW

contemplate (kŏn′təm-plāt′) *v.* to look at something thoughtfully, carefully, and thoroughly; to think about something at length

413

They teach us even when they leave us behind....

Gary, my sister; Louvenia, my grandmother; Gus, my father, with me in his lap; Yolande, my mother

Yet none of us could replace what she was losing. She waved that brave wave that my mother has, which is why when I am leaving my mother I go late at night or early in the morning so that I do not have to see the question on her face: Will you return safely to me? We sang, at her funeral, "It Is Well With My Soul"; the preacher said, "Well done, my good and faithful servant." But that does nothing to fill the void in me. So this isn't a balanced book nor a sociological[4] book nor a look at grandmothers through the ages. It's just a book that makes me miss the only person I know for sure whose love I did not have to earn. ❖

4. **sociological:** relating to a way of looking at human social behavior; relating to the study of the development and organization of society.

Connect to the Literature

1. What Do You Think? How did you feel when Giovanni described leaving her grandmother alone after her grandfather's funeral?

Comprehension Check

- What was Giovanni's grandmother famous for in family circles?
- Why did Grandmother stop giving Giovanni piano lessons?
- Why does Grandmother volunteer the young Nikki Giovanni to march after the four little girls are killed in Birmingham?

Think Critically

2. Why is Giovanni amazed at Grandmother's forgetfulness?

3. Giovanni compares grandmothers to spinach, asparagus, and Brussels sprouts: only later in life do we appreciate how good they were for us. What problems did Giovanni have with her grandmother? What does Giovanni miss about her grandmother?

4. Giovanni says that her grandmother was "the only person I know for sure whose love I did not have to earn." Why is it important for Giovanni that she did not have to earn her grandmother's love?

> **Think About:**
> - how it feels to be loved no matter what you do
> - how Giovanni might have felt if her grandmother had stopped loving her because of something Giovanni had done

5. **ACTIVE READING | IDENTIFYING MAIN IDEA**
Review the notes you made in your
READER'S NOTEBOOK. Summarize this selection by presenting its main idea.

Extend Interpretations

6. What If? What if Giovanni had refused to march as her grandmother had requested? How do you think her grandmother would have reacted?

7. Connect to Life Have you ever wondered, as Giovanni's mother does, whether you will see someone again? How did you comfort or reassure yourself about the possibility of long-term or permanent separation?

Literary Analysis

VOICE Many writers reveal their personality through their writing. This is referred to as the writer's **voice.** In *Grand Mothers*, Nikki Giovanni speaks boldly and bluntly. Her style is conversational, full of words and expressions that are not found in formal writing. The reader comes away from the selection with a strong sense of the author's personality.

Group Activity In a small group, review the selection, looking for sentences, phrases, and words that remind you of spoken rather than written language. Then choose a passage by another writer from this unit. Compare his or her voice with Giovanni's. Use a table like the one shown below to organize your examples.

Examples of the Writer's Voice	
Giovanni	We all hated that . . . all four of us.
Other writer	

Grammar in Context: Appositives

In the following sentence, Nikki Giovanni uses a proper noun to identify her grandmother:

> My grandmother, Emma Louvenia Watson, was famous in family circles for getting into the bathtub without her soap.

An **appositive** is a noun that helps define one or more words in a sentence. An appositive phrase consists of a noun and its modifiers. Appositives and appositive phrases are placed immediately after the noun or pronoun that is being defined.

Apply to Your Writing Using appositives in your writing can help your readers understand the relationship between ideas. Writers also use appositives when they want to combine closely related sentences.

Punctuation Tip: Use commas to set off an appositive from the rest of the sentence.

WRITING EXERCISE Combine the following sentences using appositives. There may be more than one way to combine some sentences.

Example: ***Original*** Her only sister's name is Gary. Gary played the piano like an angel. ***Rewritten*** Her only sister, Gary, played the piano like an angel.

1. On Monday Grandmother worked hard. Monday was laundry day.

2. Emma Louvenia Watson had many talents. She was a grandmother.

3. Their granddaughter is a writer. Her name is Nikki.

4. They loved dessert last Sunday. It was Grandmother's blackberry cobbler.

5. Grandmother was a piano player. She taught her grandchildren music.

Grammar Handbook
See p. R89: Appositive Phrases.

Vocabulary

STANDARDIZED TEST PRACTICE

Choose the word or group of words that means the same, or nearly the same, as the underlined Word to Know.

1. Resistance means—
   A opposition   B desperation
   C cooperation   D occupation

2. Another word for segregation is—
   F relation   G separation
   H reunion   J dissection

3. Exquisite means the same as—
   A ordinary   B unnecessary
   C excellent   D uniform

4. To tackle is to—
   F hide from   G take on
   H run through   J look back

5. Another word for consent is—
   A argument   B dismissal
   C discussion   D agreement

6. To bellow is to—
   F shout   G laugh
   H lie   J sing

7. Slovenly means—
   A thoughtful   B sinful
   C crazy   D lazy

8. A cliché is a type of—
   F song   G expression
   H briefcase   J lesson

9. Transition means—
   A decline   B improvement
   C change   D stage

10. To contemplate is to—
    F ponder   G describe
    H ignore   J correct

Vocabulary Handbook
See p. R24: Synonyms and Antonyms.

Legacies / the drum / Choices

by NIKKI GIOVANNI

Connect to Your Life

Finding a Balance Have you ever felt torn between what you wanted to do and what other people wanted you to do? In "Legacies," "the drum," and "Choices," Nikki Giovanni explores what it means to stand up for oneself. She suggests that we all must find a balance between what we want to do and what other people expect of us. Fill in a chart like this one to show the things you do for yourself and the things you do to please others.

My Actions	
Things I Do for Myself	**Things I Do for Others**
Play tennis; read poetry	Wash the dishes

Build Background

Spirit of Independence
Each of Nikki Giovanni's poems reveals something about her personality. Many of Giovanni's poems show that she likes to make her own decisions. This independent spirit can be found in all three poems you are about to read.

Focus Your Reading

LITERARY ANALYSIS   **LYRIC POETRY**

A short poem in which a single speaker expresses personal thoughts and feelings is called a **lyric poem.** Notice that none of these three poems tells a long story. Instead, they present the writer's opinion. As you read these poems, think about the writer's opinion in each poem.

ACTIVE READING   **IDENTIFYING THE AUTHOR'S PURPOSE**

Authors usually have a purpose or reason for creating a particular work. The author's purpose may be to entertain, to inform, to express an opinion, or to persuade. A poem might also be written with more than one purpose in mind.

READER'S NOTEBOOK As you read these poems, think about why Giovanni might have written each one. Later you will use what you have written to help you determine the purpose behind each poem. Make a chart like the one shown here.

Author's Purpose				
Poem	**To Entertain**	**To Inform**	**To Express an Opinion**	**To Persuade**
"Legacies"		X		
"the drum"				
"Choices"				

Legacies

by NIKKI GIOVANNI

Can I Have the Bowl (1994), Jessie Coates. Acrylic on Masonite.
Private Collection/Jessie Coates/SuperStock.

her grandmother called her from the playground
   "yes, ma'am" said the little girl
   "i want chu to learn how to make rolls" said the old
woman proudly
but the little girl didn't want
to learn how because she knew
even if she couldn't say it that
that would mean when the old one died she would be less
dependent on her spirit so
   the little girl said
   "i don't want to know how to make no rolls"
with her lips poked out
and the old woman wiped her hands on
her apron saying "lord
   these children"
and neither of them ever
said what they meant
and i guess nobody ever does

THINKING *through the* LITERATURE

Why did the grandmother want her
granddaughter to learn how to make rolls?

Think About:
- the way the grandmother first
  speaks to the little girl
- how the grandmother might
  expect the little girl to react

the drum

by NIKKI GIOVANNI

daddy says the world is

a drum tight and hard

and i told him

i'm gonna beat

out my own rhythm

Boy with Birds (1953), David C. Driskell. Oil on canvas, 23½" × 29½".
Collection of Professor and Mrs. David C. Driskell.

by NIKKI GIOVANNI

Choices

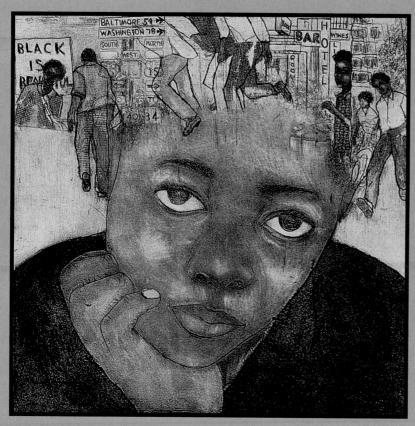

Gemini I (1969), Lev T. Mills. Etching, The Evans-Tibbs Collection, Washington, D.C.

if i can't do
what i want to do
then my job is to not
do what i don't want
to do

it's not the same thing
but it's the best i can
do

if i can't have
what i want   then
my job is to want
what i've got
and be satisfied
that at least there
is something more
to want

since i can't go
where i need
to go   then i must   go
where the signs point
though always understanding
parallel[1] movement
isn't lateral[2]

when i can't express
what i really feel
i practice feeling
what i can express
and none of it is equal
i know
but that's why mankind
alone among the mammals
learns to cry

---

1. **parallel:** placed or moving in the
   same direction always the same
   distance apart, such as railroad
   tracks.
2. **lateral:** of or relating to the side;
   sideways.

Connect to the Literature

1. **What Do You Think?**
For what kind of situations would the poem "Choices" be good advice?

Comprehension Check
• What does the poet think she should do if she can't do what she wants?
• Why does mankind learn to cry?

Think Critically

2. *Parallel* means "side by side"; *lateral* means "to the side." What does Giovanni mean when she says that "parallel movement / isn't lateral"?

3. **ACTIVE READING   IDENTIFYING THE AUTHOR'S PURPOSE**
Review the notes you made about the poems "Legacies," "the drum," and "Choices" in your **READER'S NOTEBOOK**. What do you think is the purpose or purposes of each poem?

4. Do you think that Giovanni is the kind of person who would accept not getting what she wants?

Think About:
• the poet's personality as revealed in *Grand Mothers*
• the attitude of the little girl in "Legacies"
• the attitude of the speaker in "the drum"
• the ending of "Choices"

Extend Interpretations

5. **Different Perspectives** Imagine that Giovanni had written "Choices" from the point of view of the grandmother in "Legacies" or from the point of view of the speaker of "the drum." How would "Choices" be the same or different in each case? Explain your response.

6. **Connect to Life** In both "Legacies" and "Choices," Giovanni describes people who have feelings that they are either not aware of or cannot express. Have you ever had a feeling you could not express?

Writer's Prompt

7. **Connections** If you have ever refused to do something someone wanted you to do, describe how the situation in "Legacies" is similar to your own experience.

Literary Analysis

LYRIC POETRY   A poem that presents the thoughts or feelings of a single speaker is called a **lyric poem.** Lyric poems can take many different forms and can cover a wide range of subjects. Both "Legacies" and "Choices" are lyric poems.

Paired Activity Working with a partner, find the speaker's opinion in each of the three poems. Use the chart below and quote a line or phrase from the poem that indicates the speaker's opinion of the topic or situation presented in the poem. In the third column, explain or paraphrase what the phrase means.

Poem	Phrase Indicating Speaker's Opinion	What the Phrase Means
"Legacies"		
"the drum"		
"Choices"		

A Journey
Knoxville, Tennessee

by NIKKI GIOVANNI

Connect to Your Life

A Place for You Do you have a special place you like to go? Perhaps your special place is in your mind—a place you daydream about. Perhaps you have read about a place you would like to visit. Describe your special place to a small group of classmates.

Build Background

Unforgettable Details Poets help us see ordinary things vividly. The poem "A Journey" suggests that even a long, difficult, or boring trip can be an adventure. "Knoxville, Tennessee" describes a summer in the South, but it makes ordinary details seem unforgettable.

Focus Your Reading

LITERARY ANALYSIS   FORM

The way a poem looks and is arranged is called its **form.** Some poets follow traditional rules of grammar and line length, while others deliberately break these rules to create new forms. In "A Journey" Giovanni has created long lines broken up by punctuation called **ellipses.** This type of punctuation creates a pause within the line:

   It's a journey . . . that I propose . . . I am not the guide . . .

As you read these poems, think about how their forms differ. Do the forms suit the subjects of the poems?

ACTIVE READING   MAKING INFERENCES ABOUT THE SPEAKER

A logical guess based on evidence is called an **inference.** The **speaker** of a poem is the voice that "talks" to the reader. When you make inferences about the speaker, you are making logical guesses about the speaker's beliefs, attitude, age, and so on.

READER'S NOTEBOOK As you read Giovanni's poems, jot down inferences you make about the speaker of each poem. Also note the evidence on which you base your inferences. You can use a simple chart like the one shown.

"A Journey"	
Inference	Evidence
The speaker sees herself as powerful.	She refers to herself as "Ra," an ancient Egyptian god.

April Green (1970),
Romare Bearden.
Collage, 14¼" × 18⅞".
Copyright © Romare
Bearden Foundation /
Licensed by VAGA,
New York, NY.

A Journey

by Nikki Giovanni

It's a journey . . . that I propose . . . I am not the guide . . . nor
technical assistant . . . I will be your fellow passenger . . .

Though the rail has been ridden . . . winter clouds cover . . .
autumn's exuberant quilt . . . we must provide our own
guideposts . . .

I have heard . . . from previous visitors . . . the road washes
out sometimes . . . and passengers are compelled[1] . . . to
continue groping . . . or turn back . . . I am not afraid . . .

I am not afraid . . . of rough spots . . . or lonely times . . . I
don't fear . . . the success of this endeavor . . . I am Ra[2] . . . in
a space. . . not to be discovered . . . but invented . . .

I promise you nothing . . . I accept your promise . . . of the
same we are simply riding . . . a wave . . . that may carry . . .
or crash . . .

It's a journey . . . and I want . . . to go . . .

---

1. **compelled:** to have caused or pressured a person to do
   something, by authority of force, necessity, or powerful
   influence.
2. **Ra:** the sun god of ancient Egyptian mythology.

THINKING *through the* LITERATURE

1. Is the journey described in the poem going to be easy or
   difficult? Explain your response.

2. What do you think the journey might symbolize?

   Think About:
   • the words "the rail has been ridden"
   • the words "in a space . . . not to be discovered . . .
     but invented"

KNOXVILLE, TENNESSEE

by NIKKI GIOVANNI

Picnic in the Park (1915), Martha Walter. Oil on board.
Copyright © David David Gallery, Philadelphia/SuperStock.

I always like summer
best
you can eat fresh corn
from daddy's garden
and okra
and greens
and cabbage
and lots of
barbecue
and buttermilk
and homemade ice-cream
at the church picnic
and listen to
gospel music
outside
at the church
homecoming
and go to the mountains with
your grandmother
and go barefooted
and be warm
all the time
not only when you go to bed
and sleep

Connect to the Literature

1. What Do You Think? Would you like to spend time in the Knoxville that Giovanni describes? Explain your answer.

Comprehension Check
- What foods are mentioned in "Knoxville, Tennessee"?
- Where does the speaker listen to music?
- Where does the speaker go with the grandmother?
- When does the speaker feel warm?

Think Critically

2. Is the speaker of "Knoxville, Tennessee" a child? Explain your response.

3. ACTIVE READING MAKING INFERENCES ABOUT THE SPEAKER
Review the notes you made in your
READER'S NOTEBOOK. Compare the speakers in "A Journey" and "Knoxville, Tennessee." How are they alike? How are they different?

4. Would you rather take the trip described in the poem "A Journey" or stay in the place described in "Knoxville, Tennessee"? Explain your response.

> **Think About:**
> - the difficulties of the trip in "A Journey"
> - the speaker's attitude toward Knoxville in "Knoxville, Tennessee"

Extend Interpretations

5. What If? What if the two poems were combined and the place described in "Knoxville, Tennessee" was the destination of the trip described in "A Journey"? Would you find the new poem satisfying? Explain your response.

6. Connect to Life Look at your own life's journey. Choose metaphors to describe where you have come from and where you are going.

Writer's Prompt

7. Reply In both "A Journey" and "Knoxville, Tennessee," the speaker refers to "you." Choose one poem and rewrite it from the point of view of the person to whom the speaker is talking.

Literary Analysis

FORM The way a poem looks and is arranged on a page is known as its **form.** Sometimes poems follow traditional patterns with the same number of syllables in each line and the same number of lines in each **stanza,** a group of lines in a poem. In "A Journey" Giovanni does not use stanzas composed of regular lines. Instead, each stanza is a collection of phrases or sentences separated by ellipses. In "Knoxville, Tennessee" she does not use stanzas at all. The shape of the two poems on the page is very different, yet neither follows traditional poetic form.

Activity Create a chart like the one shown to help you investigate the forms of the two poems. Then share your results with the class. Be ready to discuss this question: "How does the form help Giovanni express her ideas?"

	"A Journey"	"Knoxville, Tennessee"
Number of syllables in each line	Number varies	Number varies
Stanzas		
Number of lines in each stanza		

Icing on the Cake

Interview with Nikki Giovanni

PREPARING to *Read*

Build Background

In 1968 Nikki Giovanni was ready to publish her first book of poetry, *Black Feeling, Black Talk.* However, as you have read in the on-line interview on page 407, Giovanni says that after you write a book of poems, "then comes the hard part: you have to find someone to read it. . . . Publishing is the icing on the cake." Giovanni was able to "ice her cake" by having a party at one of New York's many fine African-American jazz clubs, Birdland.

Focus Your Reading

ACTIVE READING **AUTHOR'S PERSPECTIVE**

Each person sees the world differently. This is particularly true of writers, each of whom has his or her own **perspective,** or personal attitude, belief, or feeling about a topic or issue. When you read a piece of autobiographical writing, think about how different it might be if it were written from another perspective.

To get publicity for *Black Feeling, Black Talk,* I got the idea to have a book party at Birdland because I love jazz. I went to see Harold Logan, who was the manager, and said: "Hi, I'm Nikki Giovanni. I'm a poet, and I have a new book, and I'd love to have a book party at Birdland. I know you're dead on Sundays, so that would be a good day. What do I have to do to have a party here?"

He looked at me like I was crazy, but he finally said: "I'll tell you what. You bring me 125 people and you can have the club. But if you bring me 124 people or less, you owe me $500."

I said, "Fine," but afterward I thought how would I get $500 if I failed. That was a huge amount of money for me in 1969. Anyway, I made up invitations and sent them out to all sorts of groups and that cost me a couple of hundred dollars to start. Then I contacted radio stations and asked if I could go on the air to talk about my book party. I figured the midnight audiences are full of readers, so I did a lot of late night shows. I did everything I could do free to ask people to come to

Birdland for my book party. I even asked friends like Morgan Freeman, who was a young actor at the time, and Larry Neal, a poet, who is now dead, to read from my book and we'd have a kind of Sunday cabaret.

I ended up with a crowd at Birdland that snaked all the way down the street and turned the corner. Birdland is right in the backyard of *The New York Times,* so some reporters happened to look out the window and wondered what the crowd was all about, and came down to investigate. When they found out everyone was there for a poetry reading, they knew they had a story.

The New York Times took a picture of me, which wound up on the front page of the metro section and, because of publicity, I sold 10,000 books in the next eight months and attracted the attention of some major publishers. I signed with William Morrow, which published *Black Feeling, Black Talk* along with *Black Judgement,* which I wrote later, as one book of poetry, combining both slim volumes.

If this sounds like a Cinderella story, remember I made my own slipper. I'm a Midwesterner. I was born and raised in Cincinnati, and one of the things I think Midwesterners do very well is work hard. . . . I believe people always have to make their own breaks.

THINKING *through the* LITERATURE

1. How did Giovanni attract the attention of major publishers?

2. What does this interview tell you about Giovanni's attitude toward her success?

The Author's Style

Giovanni's Poetic Metaphors

Nikki Giovanni's poetry has always been easy for most people to understand. While much modern poetry can be difficult or obscure, Giovanni's poetry is clear and direct. One of the ways in which Giovanni achieves this clarity is through her use of metaphor. A metaphor is a comparison of two things that have something in common—a comparison in which one thing is said to be another thing. Giovanni uses metaphors to express abstract, difficult ideas through easily visualized images.

Simple Metaphor

daddy says the world is
a drum tight and hard
and i told him
i'm gonna beat
out my own rhythm

Key Style Points

Simple Metaphor Sometimes Giovanni's metaphors are short, direct comparisons between two things; at other times she uses long, extended comparisons.

Extended Metaphor When a metaphor is developed at great length it is called an **extended metaphor.** In "A Journey," Giovanni compares life to a journey. She then extends the metaphor by introducing a series of images that represent different aspects of life.

Extended Metaphor

It's a journey . . . that I propose . . . I am not the guide . . . nor technical assistant . . . I will be your fellow passenger . . .

Though the rail has been ridden . . . winter clouds cover . . . autumn's exuberant quilt . . . we must provide our own guideposts . . .

I have heard . . . from previous visitors . . . the road washes out sometimes . . . and passengers are compelled . . . to continue groping . . . or turn back . . . I am not afraid . . .

I am not afraid . . . of rough spots . . . or lonely times . . . I don't fear . . . the success of this endeavor . . . I am Ra . . . in a space . . . not to be discovered . . . but invented . . .

I promise you nothing . . . I accept your promise . . . of the same we are simply riding . . . a wave . . . that may carry . . . or crash . . .

It's a journey . . . and I want . . . to go . . .

Applications

1. **Active Reading** Reread the poem "A Journey." Explain how the following symbols extend the original metaphor of life as a journey: guideposts; the road washes out; rough spots.

2. **Writing** Write a poem in which you develop an extended metaphor. Create a simple metaphor such as "life is a summer's day." Extend the metaphor by introducing elements, such as storms and dusk, that represent different aspects of life.

3. **Speaking and Listening** With a partner, choose one of the poems above and rewrite it so that it expresses the same idea without the metaphor. Share your responses with the class.

Writing

Lyric Poem Write a poem that reflects your view on an aspect of your life, your family, or your heritage. Use the free verse form. As you write, think about line length and whether your poem will have stanzas. Place your poem in your **Working Portfolio.**

Writing Workshop
See p. 252: Basics in a Box.

Speaking & Listening

Speak to Music Nikki Giovanni often reads her poetry against a background of music. Choose one of her poems, and then choose a piece of music that you think fits the subject and images in the poem. Read the poem aloud to your class with the music playing in the background.

Speaking and Listening Handbook
See p. R106: Oral Interpretation.

Research & Technology

Other Greats Using nonfiction books, the Internet, and other media, write a biography of one of the other great African-American writers whom Giovanni knew: James Baldwin, LeRoi Jones (Amiri Baraka), H. Rap Brown, Don L. Lee (Haki R. Madhubuti), or Margaret Walker. Use well-chosen details to describe events and situations. Be sure to note your sources.

INTERNET Research Starter
www.mcdougallittell.com

Author Study Project

Creating Images from Poetry

Working with a small group, create a collage or mural inspired by Nikki Giovanni's writings. The following suggestions can help you create and present your work of art.

1 Make a List Reread the poetry in this Author Study or find other Giovanni poems in the library. As you read, make a list of images that are particularly striking.

2 Prepare Your Materials If you are making a mural, draw each image on a separate piece of paper. If you are making a collage, collect pictures or small objects. Your group could also work together to create a collage on the computer, if your school has a graphics program and equipment for scanning images.

3 Share Your Ideas If you are creating a mural, share your sketches, and discuss how to arrange them on the classroom wall or bulletin board. For a collage, make a diagram to show how the pictures and objects might fit together.

4 Present Your Artwork Present your collage or mural to the rest of the class, explaining the importance of each image and identifying which poem each image comes from.

Nikki Giovanni

Since the publication of her first
book of poems in the late 1960s,
Nikki Giovanni has been recognized
as one of the most important poets
of her time. Though at first much of
her poetry concerned the racial
situation in the United States, over
the years she has explored themes
of universal interest. Her poetry
for children has won a particularly
wide following.

In "education," Giovanni speaks with
the innocent voice of a young girl.
What does the poem tell you about
the speaker's mother?

education

mama got out and fussed
real good 'bout the schools
'cause i'm in the eighth
grade and she wants me to
  continue
but she says she needs to be
sure i don't become
just another high
school student

For the Masai Warriors
(of Don Miller)

remembering my father's drum
remembering the leopard's screech
if i could weave an ancient rope
and tie myself to history
i'd spring like daylight out of night
into the future of our land
i'd sprint across the grassy plain
and make a nation for the gods
where i could be the man

In "For the Masai Warriors,"
Giovanni celebrates her African-
American heritage. What does
Giovanni believe African Americans
should learn from their history?

Winter

Frogs burrow the mud
snails bury themselves
and I air my quilts
preparing for the cold

Dogs grow more hair
mothers make oatmeal
and little boys and girls
take Father John's Medicine

Bears store fat
chipmunks gather nuts
and I collect books
For the coming winter

*In "Winter," Giovanni describes
how living creatures prepare for the
cold winter months. How does the
speaker prepare for winter?*

Vacation Time 1980

This book of poetry for children
received the 1998 Children's Reading
Roundtable of Chicago Award.

Grand Mothers 1994

Giovanni edited this collection
of writers' remembrances of
their grandmothers. Contributors
include Maxine Hong Kingston,
Gwendolyn Brooks, Gloria Naylor,
and her own mother.

Writing Workshop

Finding the cause of an event . . .

From Reading to Writing You've probably noticed that every action has an effect. This is true in literature as well as in life. For instance, in "The Treasure of Lemon Brown," Greg's accidental meeting with Lemon causes him to reevaluate his relationship with his father. You can explore cause-and-effect relationships in your own life as well. Writing a **cause-and-effect essay** can help you trace the connections between your actions and events.

For Your Portfolio

WRITING PROMPT Write a cause-and-effect essay examining what causes an event to happen or what consequences an event has.

Purpose: To explain and inform
Audience: Your classmates or anyone interested in your subject

---

Basics in a Box

Cause-and-Effect Essay at a Glance

Introduction
introduces the subject

↓

Body
describes the cause and its effects*

cause

↓ ↓ ↓

effect effect effect

↓

Conclusion
summary

* or may present an effect
and then analyze the causes

RUBRIC **STANDARDS FOR WRITING**

A successful cause-and-effect essay should

- clearly state the cause-and-effect relationship
- provide any necessary background information
- make clear the relationship between causes and effects
- arrange details logically and include transitions to show relationships between causes and effects
- summarize the cause-and-effect relationship in the conclusion

Analyzing a Student Model

SPEAKING

See the Speaking and Listening Handbook, p. R104 for oral presentation tips.

OPPORTUNITY

**Mordechai Hornick
Maimonides School**

Be Careful What You Wish For

Have you ever heard the phrase, "Be careful what you wish for, you just might get it!"? Well, I can say firsthand this is true. When I was in fifth grade, a local bank held a competition with a grand prize of a trip to the Cayman Islands. My parents entered the competition, never dreaming they would win. They also never dreamed that this trip would put us all smack in the middle of a hurricane.

The bank kicked off the contest in January. Everyone in the area was sent a key in the mail. There were two treasure chests in the bank, labeled "Trip" and "Mugs." Whoever had the key to the winning treasure chest would win a trip to the Cayman Islands in the Caribbean. If a key fit the other chest, the award was a mug with the bank's name printed on it. However, even if a person's key did not fit either winning chest, that person could still enter his or her name in a raffle. A name would be drawn from those in the raffle if no one had a winning key. My parents didn't have it, but they did enter the raffle. My mother talked often of the trip and told us all to keep our fingers crossed. No one in the family but my mother thought we would win. Surprisingly, one day, my parents' names were drawn. They had won the trip to the Caymans! They couldn't believe it. In addition to the trip, they were given three hundred dollars of spending money and a gift basket, which contained items such as tea and condiments. The only restriction was that they had to take the trip within the year, so my parents decided to plan their vacation for October. They would celebrate their anniversary in the Cayman Islands.

After thinking it over, however, my parents decided they really wanted us to go as a family. They purchased airplane tickets for my brother and me and booked us a room in their hotel. It cost them quite a bit extra, but they figured it was worth it. They knew that they could have never afforded the trip otherwise. My mother didn't want us to fall behind in school, so she made us promise to pack a few books. I also had to pack my trombone because I was going to miss band practice.

RUBRIC
IN ACTION

❶ Presents the cause-and-effect relationship in a coherent thesis statement

❷ The writer gives some background information.

❸ Uses transition to begin new paragraph

❹ Illustrates the connection between the events

The departure date finally arrived. We set off for a week of fun in the sun. My brother and I were so excited we could hardly stand it. We had never been off the continent. And my parents hadn't had a vacation in nearly ten years. However, October is hurricane season in the Cayman Islands. Because my parents had chosen this particular week for the vacation, we ended up arriving in the middle of a hurricane. In the pouring rain, we dashed from the plane to the airport terminal. We quickly caught the shuttle bus to the hotel. In the hustle and bustle of trying to get into the hotel, my parents left their tennis rackets on the bus. They didn't really need them though. It rained throughout our stay. Our only outside activity was running back and forth to the restaurant for meals. Pretty soon, however, I lost my appetite. I became sick from the water.

Because we were stuck in the hotel so much of the time and because I was sick, I had no other option but to practice my trombone. I practiced all day, every day, for a week. (Normally I practice an hour a week.) Unfortunately, even before the week was over, the hurricane conditions had intensified. Tourists were being warned to leave the island if they could. To make sure we got home safely, my parents paid extra to change our flight to an earlier time.

When I returned home, the band instructor could not believe my improvement. He was so impressed that he made me the lead trombone in the upcoming performance for our school. He asked, "How did you improve so much over one week?" "It all began with a raffle," was my reply.

My parents didn't know there would be so many consequences when they entered the raffle. They ended up spending a lot of money on their "free" trip, we experienced a hurricane firsthand, and I became a pro at the good ol' trombone. I would like to return to the Caribbean someday, so that I can see it without sheets of rain in front of my eyes. My parents, however, have decided not to enter any more raffles—just in case they have the bad luck to win!

❺ Uses transitions of chronological order to show the effects as they occur

❻ Uses transitions to signal cause-and-effect relationships

❼ Develops explanation of another effect with specific details and quotations

❽ Summarizes the cause-and-effect relationship in a clear, well-supported conclusion

Writing Your Cause-and-Effect Essay

❶ Prewriting

Write down questions beginning with "Why does . . ." and then try to answer them. **List** the causes of events in stories you have read. Review the lessons learned as a result of these events. See the **Idea Bank** in the margin for more suggestions. Once you have decided on a topic, follow the steps below.

Planning Your Cause-and-Effect Essay

▷ 1. **Determine all causes and effects.** There may be more than one cause leading to an effect or more than one effect resulting from a cause. Also keep in mind that an effect in one relationship may be the cause of another effect. Use a flow chart or web to help you find all possible causes and effects.

▷ 2. **Identify your audience.** Ask yourself, What will make my audience interested in my subject? What kind of information does it need in order to understand my explanation?

▷ 3. **Gather information.** What kinds of details do you need to clarify the link between events? You may need to find background information, research facts, or find examples through observation and personal experience.

❷ Drafting

Your goal in the first draft is to put your ideas on paper. You can develop and reorganize them later.

- In the **introduction,** name the cause-and-effect relationship and express its importance to you or to your audience.

- In the **body** paragraphs, tell the first event. Remember to include supporting details. Then, tell the effects. Include **transitional words and phrases,** such as *before, after, therefore, consequently, because,* and *since* to signal relationships.

- In the **conclusion,** sum up the cause-and-effect relationships.

IDEA Bank

1. Your Working Portfolio 📁
Look for ideas in the **Writing** sections you completed earlier.

2. Rules Rule!
Choose a rule in sports, in school, or at home. Examine the effects on the people involved.

3. Echoes of the Past
Think about the history of your community. Find an event that has had an effect on your community. Describe the event and its consequences.

Have a question?

See the **Writing Handbook.**
Elaboration, p. R39
Cause and Effect, p. R46
See **Language Network.**
Prewriting, p. 314
Drafting, p. 317

Ask Your Peer Reader

- What causes and effects do I describe in my essay?
- Which parts of my essay were confusing?
- What did you like best about my essay?
- What do you want to know more about?

Need revising help?

Review the **Rubric**, p. 432

Consider **peer reader** comments

Check **Revision Guidelines**, p. R33

See **Language Network**, Revising, p. 319

Not certain about noun clauses?

See the **Grammar Handbook**, Phrases and Clauses, p. R89

SPELLING
From Writing

 As you revise your work, look back at the words you misspelled and determine why you made the errors you did. For additional help, refer to the strategies and generalizations in the **Spelling Handbook** on page R28.

SPEAKING
Opportunity

Turn your essay into an oral presentation.

Publishing
IDEAS

• Work with your classmates to create a Web page with all your cause-and-effect essays. Ask your school's technology adviser for help.

INTERNET

Publishing Options
www.mcdougallittell.com

❸ Revising

TARGET SKILL ▶ **TRANSITIONAL WORDS AND PHRASES** Transitional words and phrases help you clearly show the relationships between causes and their effects. Use transitional words and phrases, such as *as a result of, because, consequently, before, after,* and *subsequently,* to indicate cause and effect. Remember that transitions also help unify your writing.

> As a result of
> ~~B~~eing on an earlier flight, we ran into a tropical storm.

❹ Editing and Proofreading

TARGET SKILL ▶ **NOUN CLAUSES** A noun clause is a clause used as a noun. It can be used in any way that a noun is used. Keep in mind, however, that it cannot stand alone as a sentence, as shown below. Check your work to make sure all noun clauses are used as parts of sentences.

> Whoever had the key to the winning treasure chest,
> ~~They~~ would win a trip to the Cayman Islands in the
> Caribbean.

❺ Reflecting

FOR YOUR WORKING PORTFOLIO What did you learn about cause-and-effect relationships by writing your essay? Are there any aspects that you would like to explore further? Attach your reflections to the finished essay. Save your cause-and-effect essay in your **Working Portfolio.**

Standardized Test Practice

Mixed Review

> Whoever has visited this area. They have seen the effect of destructive
> (1)
> insects. The gypsy moths did severe damage to the trees. There was a
> (2)
> gypsy moth infestation six years ago. The caterpillar stage is most
> destructive. These creatures look harmless. However they're not. They
> (3)
> rapidly become huge, furry, and indestructible. They devour leaves. One,
> (4)   (5)
> way to try to save the tree is to put a tape of sticky gel around the trunk
> so that the caterpillars can't climb around it to get their food. Still this is
> sometimes worser for the trees than the caterpillars.
> (6)

Review Your Skills

Use the passage and the questions that follow it to check how well you remember the language conventions you've learned in previous grades.

1. How is item 1 best written?
   A. Whoever has visited this area has
   B. Whoever has visited, this area has
   C. Whoever has visited this area they have
   D. Correct as is

2. How is item 2 best written?
   A. The gypsy moths did severe damage to the trees and there was an infestation six years ago.
   B. When the gypsy moths infested the area six years ago, they did severe damage to the trees.
   C. The gypsy moth infestation which did severe damage to the trees was six years ago.
   D. Correct as is

3. How is sentence 3 best written?
   A. However: they're not.
   B. However they're, not.
   C. However, they're not.
   D. Correct as is

4. How is sentence 4 best written?
   A. become huge furry, and indestructible.
   B. become huge furry and indestructible.
   C. become huge, furry, and, indestructible.
   D. Correct as is

5. How is sentence 5 best written?
   A. One way, to try
   B. One way to try,
   C. One way to try
   D. Correct as is

6. How is sentence 6 best written?
   A. more worse
   B. worst
   C. worse
   D. Correct as is

Self-Assessment

Check your own answers in the **Grammar Handbook**

Commas, p. R72

Using Modifiers Effectively, p. R86

Comparisons and Negatives, p. R86

Noun Clauses, p. R91

The Literature You'll Read

The Concepts You'll Study

Vocabulary and Reading Comprehension
Vocabulary Focus: Interpreting Analogies
Story Mapping

Writing and Language Conventions
Writing Workshop: Comparison-and-Contrast
   Essay
Adverbs

Literary Analysis
Literary Focus: Plot
Plot
Flashback
Conflict
Interview
Autobiography
Main Idea

Speaking and Listening
Performance of a Scene

LEARNING the Language of Literature

Plot

> *Conflict is the core of plot. Without it there is no tension and there's no reason to turn the page.*
>
> —Rita Mae Brown, writer

The time is 1942; the place, Amsterdam. As the Nazis take over Europe, a Jewish girl and her family hide out in the rooms above a factory. She records all of her feelings in her diary. Based on real events, *The Diary of Anne Frank* contains a gripping and emotion-filled plot.

Plot is an important part of every story, whether it is drama, fiction, or narrative poetry. The plot is like an outline of each event that happens, when it happens, and to whom it happens. Plots are almost always built around **conflicts**—problems the character experiences. These conflicts often cause characters to change. Although stories differ, plots usually unfold in the following stages: **exposition, rising action, climax, falling action** (sometimes called the **resolution**). Read the following excerpts from *The Diary of Anne Frank* to learn about plot.

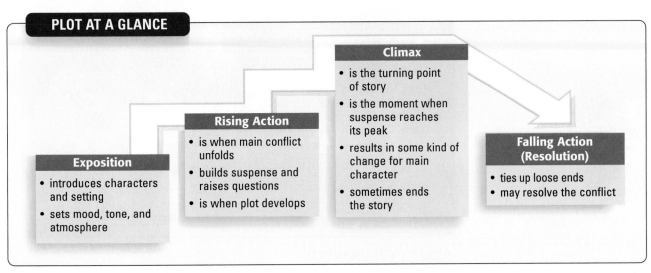

PLOT AT A GLANCE

Climax
- is the turning point of story
- is the moment when suspense reaches its peak
- results in some kind of change for main character
- sometimes ends the story

Rising Action
- is when main conflict unfolds
- builds suspense and raises questions
- is when plot develops

Falling Action (Resolution)
- ties up loose ends
- may resolve the conflict

Exposition
- introduces characters and setting
- sets mood, tone, and atmosphere

Sequence of Events

The plot is the **sequence of events** that makes up a story. A plot is structured so that one event leads to the next in a cause-and-effect relationship. The writer can vary the sequence of events to increase suspense, add an element of surprise, or create more conflict.

Two techniques an author may use to affect the story are flashbacks and foreshadowing. A **flashback** is an interruption of the action to present events that took place at an earlier time. A writer might use a flashback to provide background information on the current situation. **Foreshadowing** occurs when a writer provides hints that suggest future events in a story. This technique creates suspense.

A subplot is an additional minor plot that may weave into the main plot of a story. The subplot usually involves a minor conflict that may or may not affect the main plot.

YOUR TURN Read the passage at the right. How does the author use the technique of foreshadowing? What event do you think is being foreshadowed?

SEQUENCE OF EVENTS

Mrs. Van Daan *(Going to Dussel)*. Someone knows we're here, yes. But who is the someone? A thief! A thief! You think a thief is going to go to the Green Police and say . . . I was robbing a place the other night and I heard a noise up over my head? You think a thief is going to do that?

Dussel. Yes. I think he will.

From *The Diary of Anne Frank*

Conflict

A **conflict** is a struggle between a character who wants something and the obstacle that prevents the character from getting it. All stories have a central, or main, conflict. This struggle is the focus of the story and involves the main character. Stories may also have **minor conflicts** that may or may not affect the central conflict.

When an additional factor or problem is introduced that affects the central conflict, it is called a **complication.** A plot complication in a story makes it seem as though the main character is getting farther away from his or her goal.

There are two types of conflicts. In an **external conflict,** the character struggles against another character or an outside force, such as nature or society. An **internal conflict** is one that takes place within a character's mind.

YOUR TURN Anne Frank is in hiding from the Nazis. What are the things she misses about freedom? In your own words, describe the conflict.

CONFLICT

Anne. I expect I should be describing what it feels like to go into hiding. But I really don't know yet myself. I only know it's funny never to be able to go outdoors . . . never to breathe fresh air . . . never to run and shout and jump. It's the silence in the nights that frightens me most. Every time I hear a creak in the house, or a step on the street outside, I'm sure they're coming for us . . .

CHARACTER CHANGE

Anne. I'm trying. Really I am. Every night I think back over all of the things I did that day that were wrong . . . like putting the wet mop in Mr. Dussel's bed . . . and this thing now with Mother. I say to myself, that was wrong. I make up my mind, I'm never going to do *that* again. Never! . . .

Character Change

Characters often change as they react to conflicts and complications in a story. For instance, at the beginning of a story, a main character may be motivated by greed. However, the same character may end up becoming more concerned for others as a result of experiencing events in the story.

YOUR TURN Anne Frank grows wiser through her experiences in hiding. How do you think her situation has caused her to change?

From *The Diary of Anne Frank*

Wrapping Up the Plot . . . Endings

Story endings often leave us with a strong image, feeling, or realization. Some endings are open-ended, sparking more questions, while others tie up all the loose ends. Many people like **surprise endings,** in which an unexpected event or realization changes the outcome. One thing can be said about all endings—they have to make sense. A reader should be able to look back through the story and see that the ending is logical. Within the plot structure, endings occur in the story's resolution and sometimes at the climax.

> With his servants the banker went instantly to the wing and established the escape of his prisoner. To avoid unnecessary rumors he took the paper with the renunciation from the table and, on his return, locked it in his safe.
>
> —Anton Chekhov, "The Bet"

YOUR TURN In the excerpt above, read the ending from "The Bet," by Anton Chekhov. The banker has already seen the prisoner's note renouncing the two million dollars. Now, he learns of the prisoner's escape. Ask yourself how you feel about this ending. How might you have ended the story differently?

Two eighth-grade students wrote their own endings to "The Bet." In Ending 1, everyone thinks the banker lied about the note. Ending 2 uses a surprise ending. The lawyer kills the banker. Think about how these different endings affect your feelings about the story and characters. Remember that when you change the ending of a story, you take it in a whole different direction.

From "The Bet"

ENDING 1

A crowd of people had gathered to celebrate the lawyer's release. "He doesn't want the money now," said the banker. "He wrote a note."

"Liar," said the policeman. "I wonder, have you killed him so that you don't have to pay?"

"No, I . . . I . . . swear," said the banker, sweat beading up on his forehead. "The note must be here." He fell to his knees and searched. The note was nowhere to be found.

ENDING 2

The banker decided to retrieve the note just in case no one believed him. He slowly approached the lawyer's cell. As he stepped in, he felt a piercing pain in his right side and staggered blindly into the hallway.

When the banker's heartbeat had stopped, the lawyer put his gun down and smiled. "I did my sentence. Now it's your turn."

Story Mapping

Have you ever drawn a map to show someone how to get to your house? A map can help you to present information visually and understand what you see. A story map is a graphic organizer that can help you understand what you're reading. It shows how a story's parts fit together, and how the action moves from one event to another. A story map can even guide you in retelling the story in your own words. The strategies below can help you create a useful story map.

How to Apply the Skill

To make a **story map,** an active reader will
- identify and **clarify** story elements
- organize information into a graphic
- recognize time-order words
- **monitor** and revise the story map

Try It Now!

As you read the play *The Diary of Anne Frank,* copy and complete a story map for each act.

Here's how Tom uses the skill:

"While reading The Diary of Anne Frank, *I made a **story map.** I **clarified** the important details, including main characters, settings, conflict, the major events in sequence, climax, and resolution. I also looked for words such as* first, after, finally, *and* then *that signal the order of events. Then I **monitored** how well each story element helped me to understand the play."*

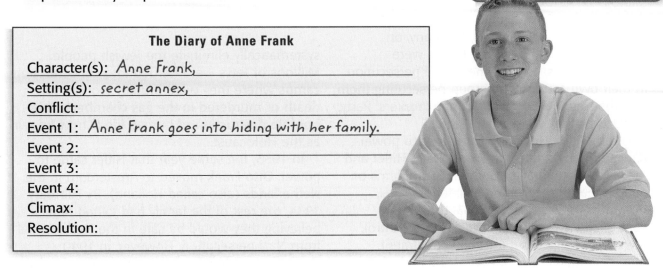

The Diary of Anne Frank

Character(s): Anne Frank,

Setting(s): secret annex,

Conflict:

Event 1: Anne Frank goes into hiding with her family.

Event 2:

Event 3:

Event 4:

Climax:

Resolution:

WHO WAS ANNE

An Astonishing Gift In November 1945, several months after the end of World War II, Otto Frank returned to Amsterdam, where he, his family, and friends had hidden from the Germans for over two years. There he received an astonishing gift—the diary of his teenage daughter, Anne, who had recently died in a German concentration camp. In the confusion and terror of her family's arrest, Anne had left her diary behind. Now, for the first time, Otto Frank read his daughter's account of their life in hiding, along with descriptions of her fears and hopes for the future—a future that was to end so miserably in a concentration camp.

Born into Danger Annelies Marie Frank, the second daughter of Otto and Edith Frank, was born in Frankfurt, Germany, on June 12, 1929. Although the Franks were German citizens, as Jews they faced persecution in their own country. The group persecuting them was the National Socialist German Workers' Party, or Nazis as they were called.

Led by Adolf Hitler, the Nazis rose to power after Germany's defeat in World War I. Hitler and the Nazis blamed all of Germany's problems on people that they regarded as inferior—Jews, Communists, Gypsies. By 1933, the Nazis controlled Germany. With the Nazis in control, Jews were singled out for unjust treatment. Almost immediately, they were stripped of all legal and political rights. Later Hitler tried to

systematically eliminate the Jewish people. Millions of Jews were herded into concentration camps where they were brutally worked to death or murdered in the gas chambers. This horrible destruction of human life is now known as the Holocaust.

In 1933, the same year that Hitler came to power, Otto Frank moved to Amsterdam in the Netherlands (also called Holland). By February 1934, the rest of the family had joined him, believing they would be safe in the Netherlands from Nazi persecution. However, in 1940 Germany invaded the Netherlands. The Franks were trapped.

FRANK?

A Life in Hiding Soon, across all of German-occupied territory, Jews were rounded up and shipped off to concentration camps. Fearing a similar fate, the Franks made plans to go into hiding.

On July 6, 1942, Anne and her family moved into the "Secret Annex," a small attic area hidden behind Otto Frank's office. Soon after, they were joined by Otto Frank's business partner, Hermann Van Pels, his wife, and their 15-year-old son, Peter. (The family is known as the Van Daans in Anne's diary.) Later a man named Fritz Pfeffer (Mr. Dussel in Anne's diary) also joined the group.

In her diary, Anne describes the group's life in hiding and their constant fear of discovery. During the day, they had to creep about and whisper so that no one would hear them. Four of Otto Frank's former colleagues, who worked in the adjoining office building, supplied the family members with food, books, and news. For over two years, the group lived invisibly, in the hope that victory by Allied forces would end their nightmare.

Discovery and Death As Allied armies began liberating Europe, it seemed only a matter of time before Anne, her family, and friends could come out of hiding. However, on August 4, 1944, the Nazis discovered the Secret Annex and arrested the residents, along with two of the men who had helped the residents. All were sent to the Auschwitz-Birkenau concentration camp in Poland, where members of the group were separated. Anne was moved to Bergen-Belsen in Germany, where she tragically died of starvation and disease only weeks before the camp was liberated by Allied forces. Of the eight residents of the Secret Annex, only Otto Frank survived.

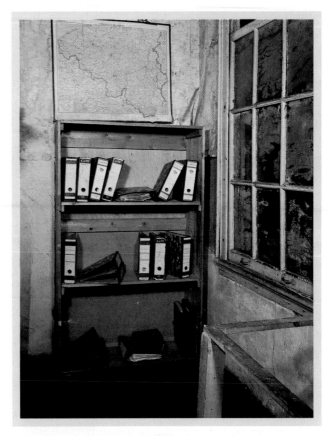

The entrance to the Secret Annex lay behind this movable bookcase.

The Life and Times of Anne Frank

WORLD EVENTS

HER LIFE

1929

June 12, 1929 Anne Frank is born in Frankfurt, Germany.

1933 Rise of Adolf Hitler

1933

1934

Summer 1933–Winter 1934 The Frank family moves to Amsterdam.

1939 German invasion of Poland

1939

1940 German invasion of Netherlands Beginning of Battle of Britain

1940

December 1, 1940 Otto Frank's company moves into the premises that include the "Secret Annex."

1941 German invasion of Soviet Union Bombing of Pearl Harbor

1941

1942 Battle of Midway Battle of Guadalcanal

1942

July 6, 1942 Anne Frank and her family go into hiding.

1943 German surrender at Stalingrad Allied invasion of Italy

1943

1944 D-Day Battle of the Bulge

1944

August 4, 1944 The Franks and their friends are arrested.

1945 Battle of Iwo Jima Germany surrenders. Bombing of Hiroshima and Nagasaki Japan surrenders.

1945

January 6, 1945 Edith Frank dies in Auschwitz.
January 27, 1945 Otto Frank is freed.
March 1945 Anne and her sister, Margot, die in Bergen-Belsen.

Germans salute troops.

The sign says, "Germans! Protect yourselves! Do not buy from Jews!"

1941, Going to Miep Gies's wedding

1930, "Papa and His Kids"

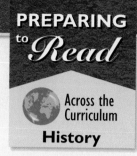
The Diary of Anne Frank

by FRANCES GOODRICH *and* ALBERT HACKETT

Based on the book: ANNE FRANK: THE DIARY OF A YOUNG GIRL

Connect to Your Life

Has war ever affected your life or the life of someone you know?

Build Background

World War II began in 1939 when Germany invaded Poland. Germany was part of the Axis powers, which included Germany, Italy, and Japan. On the other side were the Allies, which included the United States, France, Great Britain, and the Soviet Union.

World War II in the West: 1940–1941

☐ Axis and Axis Controlled
☐ Allies
☐ Neutral Countries

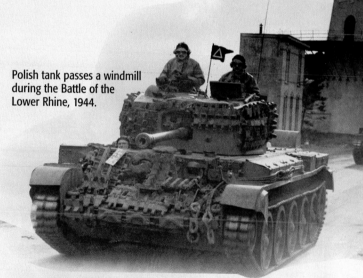

Polish tank passes a windmill during the Battle of the Lower Rhine, 1944.

Focus Your Reading

LITERARY ANALYSIS **PLOT**

The sequence of events that moves the story forward is called the **plot**. A typical plot introduces characters and setting in the **exposition**, presents the main **conflicts** in the **rising action**, reaches a turning point in the **climax**, and ties up loose ends in the **resolution**. Look for these stages of plot as you read *The Diary of Anne Frank*.

ACTIVE READING **STORY MAPPING**

When you read a drama, a story, or a novel, you can use a **story map** to help you keep track of elements of the story. In your 📖 **READER'S NOTEBOOK** create a story map for each of the three scenes that you are about to read in Act One. For each story map, list the characters and describe the setting (time and place) and the main events.

WORDS TO KNOW **Vocabulary Preview**				
appalled	foreboding	jubilation	ostentatiously	vile
conspicuous	inarticulate	loathe	pandemonium	wallow
disgruntled	indignantly	oppression	remorse	zeal

The Diary of
Anne Frank

FRANCES GOODRICH
ALBERT HACKETT

CHARACTERS
Secret Annex Residents
Anne Frank
Margot Frank
Mr. Frank
Mrs. Frank
Peter Van Daan
Mr. Van Daan
Mrs. Van Daan
Mr. Dussel

Workers in
Mr. Frank's Business
Miep Gies
Mr. Kraler

The Time
July 1942–August 1944
November 1945

The Place
Amsterdam,
the Netherlands

The Diary of Anne Frank,
starring Natalie Portman as Anne,
ran on Broadway at the Music Box Theatre
from December 1997 to June 1998.

It's difficult in times like these: ideals, dreams and cherished hopes rise within us, only to be crushed by grim reality. It's a wonder I haven't abandoned all my ideals, they seem so absurd and impractical. Yet I cling to them because I still believe, in spite of everything, that people are truly good at heart.

from The Diary of Anne Frank, *July 15, 1944*

The scene remains the same throughout the play. It is the top floor of a warehouse and office building in Amsterdam, Holland. The sharply peaked roof of the building is outlined against a sea of other rooftops, stretching away into the distance. Nearby is the belfry of a church tower, the Westertoren, whose carillon rings out the hours. Occasionally faint sounds float up from below: the voices of children playing in the street, the tramp of marching feet, a boat whistle from the canal.

The three rooms of the top floor and a small attic space above are exposed to our view. The largest of the rooms is in the center, with two small rooms, slightly raised, on either side. On the right is a bathroom, out of sight.

A narrow steep flight of stairs at the back leads up to the attic. The rooms are sparsely furnished with a few chairs, cots, a table or two. The windows are painted over, or covered with makeshift blackout curtains. In the main room there is a sink, a gas ring for cooking, and a wood-burning stove for warmth.

The room on the left is hardly more than a closet. There is a skylight in the sloping ceiling. Directly under this room is a small steep stairwell, with steps leading down to a door. This is the only entrance from the building below. When the door is opened we see that it has been concealed on the outer side by a bookcase attached to it.

Act One

SCENE 1

The curtain rises on an empty stage. It is late afternoon November, 1945. The rooms are dusty, the curtains in rags. Chairs and tables are overturned.

The door at the foot of the small stairwell swings open. Mr. Frank *comes up the steps into view. He is a gentle, cultured European in his middle years. There is still a trace of a German accent in his speech.*

He stands looking slowly around, making a supreme effort at self-control. He is weak, ill. His clothes are threadbare.

After a second he drops his rucksack on the couch and moves slowly about. He opens the door to one of the smaller rooms, and then abruptly closes it again, turning away. He goes to the window at the back, looking off at the Westertoren as its carillon strikes the hour of six, then he moves restlessly on.

From the street below we hear the sound of a barrel organ and children's voices at play. There is a many-colored scarf hanging from a nail. Mr. Frank *takes it, putting it around his neck. As he starts back for his rucksack, his eye is caught by something lying on the floor. It is a woman's white glove. He holds it in his hand and suddenly all of his self-control is gone. He breaks down, crying.*

We hear footsteps on the stairs. Miep Gies[1] *comes up, looking for* Mr. Frank. Miep *is a Dutch girl of about twenty-two. She wears a coat and hat, ready to go home. She is pregnant. Her attitude toward* Mr. Frank *is protective, compassionate.)*

---

1. **Miep Gies** (mēp gēs)

Miep. Are you all right, Mr. Frank?

Mr. Frank (*Quickly controlling himself*). Yes, Miep, yes.

Miep. Everyone in the office has gone home . . . It's after six. (*Then pleading*) Don't stay up here, Mr. Frank. What's the use of torturing yourself like this?

Mr. Frank. I've come to say good-bye . . . I'm leaving here, Miep.

Miep. What do you mean? Where are you going? Where?

Mr. Frank. I don't know yet. I haven't decided.

Miep. Mr. Frank, you can't leave here! This is your home! Amsterdam is your home. Your business is here, waiting for you . . . You're needed here . . . Now that the war is over, there are things that . . .

Mr. Frank. I can't stay in Amsterdam, Miep. It has too many memories for me. Everywhere there's something . . . the house we lived in . . . the school . . . that street organ playing out there . . . I'm not the person you used to know, Miep. I'm a bitter old man. (*Breaking off*) Forgive me. I shouldn't speak to you like this . . . after all that you did for us . . . the suffering . . .

Miep. No. No. It wasn't suffering. You can't say we suffered. (*As she speaks, she straightens a chair which is overturned.*)

Mr. Frank. I know what you went through, you and Mr. Kraler.[2] I'll remember it as long as I live. (*He gives one last look around.*) Come, Miep.

(*He starts for the steps, then remembers his rucksack, going back to get it.*)

Miep (*Hurrying up to a cupboard*). Mr. Frank, did you see? There are some of your papers here. (*She brings a bundle of papers to him.*) We found them in a heap of rubbish on the floor after . . . after you left.

Mr. Frank. Burn them.

(*He opens his rucksack to put the glove in it.*)

Miep. But, Mr. Frank, there are letters, notes . . .

Mr. Frank. Burn them. All of them.

Miep. Burn this?

(*She hands him a paperbound notebook.*)

Mr. Frank (*Quietly*). Anne's diary. (*He opens the diary and begins to read.*) "Monday, the sixth of July, nineteen forty-two." (*To Miep*) Nineteen forty-two. Is it possible, Miep? . . . Only three years ago. (*As he continues his reading, he sits down on the couch.*) "Dear Diary, since you and I are going to be great friends, I will start by telling you about myself. My name is Anne Frank. I am thirteen years old. I was born in Germany the twelfth of June, nineteen twenty-nine. As my family is Jewish, we emigrated to Holland when Hitler came to power."

(*As Mr. Frank reads on, another voice joins his, as if coming from the air. It is* Anne's *voice.*)

Mr. Frank and Anne's voice. "My father started a business, importing spices and herbs. Things went well for us until nineteen forty. Then the war came, and the Dutch capitulation, followed by the arrival of the Germans. Then things got very bad for the Jews."

(*Mr. Frank's voice dies out.* Anne's *voice continues alone.* **The lights dim slowly to darkness. The curtain falls on the scene.**)

Anne's Voice. You could not do this and you could not do that. They forced Father out of his business. We had to wear yellow stars.[3] I had to turn in my bike. I couldn't go to a Dutch school any more. I couldn't go to the movies, or ride in an automobile, or even on a streetcar, and a million other things. But somehow we children still managed to have

---

2. **Kraler** (krä′lər)

3. **yellow stars:** the six-pointed Stars of David that the Nazis ordered all Jews to wear for identification.

fun. Yesterday Father told me we were going into hiding. Where, he wouldn't say. At five o'clock this morning Mother woke me and told me to hurry and get dressed. I was to put on as many clothes as I could. It would look too suspicious if we walked along carrying suitcases. It wasn't until we were on our way that I learned where we were going. Our hiding place was to be upstairs in the building where Father used to have his business. Three other people were coming in with us . . . the Van Daans and their son Peter . . . Father knew the Van Daans but we had never met them . . .

(During the last lines the curtain rises on the scene. The lights dim on. Anne's voice fades out.)

SCENE 2

It is early morning, July 1942. The rooms are bare, as before, but they are now clean and orderly.

Mr. Van Daan, *a tall, portly man in his late forties, is in the main room, pacing up and down, nervously smoking a cigarette. His clothes and overcoat are expensive and well cut.*

Mrs. Van Daan *sits on the couch, clutching her possessions, a hatbox, bags, etc. She is a pretty woman in her early forties. She wears a fur coat over her other clothes.*

Peter Van Daan *is standing at the window of the room on the right, looking down at the street below. He is a shy, awkward boy of sixteen. He wears a cap, a raincoat, and long Dutch trousers, like "plus fours." At his feet is a black case, a carrier for his cat.*

The yellow Star of David is <u>conspicuous</u> on all of their clothes.

Mrs. Van Daan (*Rising, nervous, excited*). Something's happened to them! I know it!

Mr. Van Daan. Now, Kerli!

Mrs. Van Daan. Mr. Frank said they'd be here at seven o'clock. He said . . .

Mr. Van Daan. They have two miles to walk. You can't expect . . .

Mrs. Van Daan. They've been picked up. That's what's happened. They've been taken . . .

(Mr. Van Daan indicates that he hears someone coming.)

Mr. Van Daan. You see?

(Peter takes up his carrier and his schoolbag, etc., and goes into the main room as Mr. Frank comes up the stairwell from below. Mr. Frank looks much younger now. His movements are brisk, his manner confident. He wears an overcoat and carries his hat and a small cardboard box. He crosses to the Van Daans, shaking hands with each of them.)

Mr. Frank. Mrs. Van Daan, Mr. Van Daan, Peter. (*Then, in explanation of their lateness*) There were too many of the Green Police[4] on the streets . . . we had to take the long way around.

(Up the steps come Margot Frank, Mrs. Frank, Miep (not pregnant now), and Mr. Kraler. All of them carry bags, packages, and so forth. The Star of David is conspicuous on all of the Franks' clothing. Margot is eighteen, beautiful, quiet, shy. Mrs. Frank is a young mother, gently bred, reserved. She, like Mr. Frank, has a slight German accent. Mr. Kraler is a Dutchman, dependable, kindly.

As Mr. Kraler and Miep go upstage to put down their parcels, Mrs. Frank turns back to call Anne.)

Mrs. Frank. Anne?

(ANNE comes running up the stairs. She is thirteen, quick in her movements, interested in

---

4. **Green Police:** the Nazi police who wore green uniforms.

everything, mercurial in her emotions. She wears a cape and long wool socks and carries a schoolbag.)

Mr. Frank (*Introducing them*). My wife, Edith. Mr. and Mrs. Van Daan (*Mrs. Frank hurries over, shaking hands with them.*) . . . their son, Peter . . . my daughters, Margot and Anne.

(Anne *gives a polite little curtsy as she shakes Mr. Van Daan's hand. Then she immediately starts off on a tour of investigation of her new home, going upstairs to the attic room. Miep and Mr. Kraler are putting the various things they have brought on the shelves.*)

Mr. Kraler. I'm sorry there is still so much confusion.

Mr. Frank. Please. Don't think of it. After all, we'll have plenty of leisure to arrange everything ourselves.

Miep (*To Mrs. Frank*). We put the stores of food you sent in here. Your drugs are here . . . soap, linen here.

Mrs. Frank. Thank you, Miep.

Miep. I made up the beds . . . the way Mr. Frank and Mr. Kraler said. (*She starts out.*) Forgive me. I have to hurry. I've got to go to the other side of town to get some ration books[5] for you.

Mrs. Van Daan. Ration books? If they see our names on ration books, they'll know we're here.

Mr. Kraler. There isn't anything . . .

Miep. Don't worry. Your names won't be on them. (*As she hurries out*) I'll be up later.

Mr. Frank. Thank you, Miep.

Mrs. Frank (*To Mr. Kraler*). It's illegal, then, the ration books? We've never done anything illegal.

Mr. Frank. We won't be living here exactly according to regulations. (*As Mr. Kraler reassures Mrs. Frank, he takes various small things, such as matches, soap, etc., from his pockets, handing them to her.*)

Mr. Kraler. This isn't the black market,[6] Mrs. Frank. This is what we call the white market . . . helping all of the hundreds and hundreds who are hiding out in Amsterdam.

(*The carillon is heard playing the quarter-hour before eight. Mr. Kraler looks at his watch. Anne stops at the window as she comes down the stairs.*)

Anne. It's the Westertoren!

Mr. Kraler. I must go. I must be out of here and downstairs in the office before the workmen get here. (*He starts for the stairs leading out.*) Miep or I, or both of us, will be up each day to bring you food and news and find out what your needs are. Tomorrow I'll get you a better bolt for the door at the foot of the stairs. It needs a bolt that you can throw yourself and open only at our signal. (*To Mr. Frank*) Oh . . . You'll tell them about the noise?

Mr. Frank. I'll tell them.

Mr. Kraler. Good-bye then for the moment. I'll come up again, after the workmen leave.

Mr. Frank. Good-bye, Mr. Kraler.

Mrs. Frank (*Shaking his hand*). How can we thank you? (*The others murmur their good-byes.*)

Mr. Kraler. I never thought I'd live to see the day when a man like Mr. Frank would have to go into hiding. When you think—(*He breaks off, going out. Mr. Frank follows him down the steps, bolting the door after him. In the interval before he returns, Peter goes over to Margot, shaking hands with her. As Mr. Frank comes back up the steps, Mrs. Frank questions him anxiously.*)

Mrs. Frank. What did he mean, about the noise?

---

5. **ration books:** books of stamps or coupons issued by the government in wartime. With these coupons, people could purchase scarce items, such as food, clothing, and gasoline.

6. **black market:** a system for selling goods illegally, in violation of rationing or other restrictions.

Mr. Frank. First let us take off some of these clothes. (*They all start to take off garment after garment. On each of their coats, sweaters, blouses, suits, dresses, is another yellow Star of David. Mr. and Mrs. Frank are underdressed quite simply. The others wear several things, sweaters, extra dresses, bathrobes, aprons, nightgowns, etc.*)

Mr. Van Daan. It's a wonder we weren't arrested, walking along the streets . . . Petronella with a fur coat in July . . . and that cat of Peter's crying all the way.

Anne (*As she is removing a pair of panties*). A cat?

Mrs. Frank (*Shocked*). Anne, please!

Anne. It's all right. I've got on three more. (*She pulls off two more. Finally, as they have all removed their surplus clothes, they look to Mr. Frank, waiting for him to speak.*)

Mr. Frank. Now. About the noise. While the men are in the building below, we must have complete quiet. Every sound can be heard down there, not only in the workrooms, but in the offices, too. The men come at about eight-thirty, and leave at about five-thirty. So, to be perfectly safe, from eight in the morning until six in the evening we must move only when it is necessary, and then in stockinged feet. We must not speak above a whisper. We must not run any water. We cannot use the sink, or even, forgive me, the w.c.[7] The pipes go down through the workrooms. It would be heard. No trash . . . (*Mr. Frank stops abruptly as he hears the sound of marching feet from the street below. Everyone is motionless, paralyzed with fear. Mr. Frank goes quietly into the room on the right to look down out of the window. Anne runs after him, peering out with him. The tramping feet pass without stopping. The tension is relieved. Mr. Frank, followed by* Anne, *returns to the main room and resumes his instructions to the group*) . . . No trash must ever be thrown out which might reveal that someone is living up here . . . not even a potato paring. We must burn everything in the stove at night. This is the way we must live until it is over, if we are to survive.

(*There is silence for a second.*)

Mrs. Frank. Until it is over.

Mr. Frank. (*Reassuringly*). After six we can move about . . . we can talk and laugh and have our supper and read and play games . . . just as we would at home. (*He looks at his watch.*) And now I think it would be wise if we all went to our rooms, and were settled before eight o'clock. Mrs. Van Daan, you and your husband will be upstairs. I regret that there's no place up there for Peter. But he will be here, near us. This will be our common room, where we'll meet to talk and eat and read, like one family.

Mr. Van Daan. And where do you and Mrs. Frank sleep?

Mr. Frank. This room is also our bedroom.

Mrs. Van Daan. That isn't right. We'll sleep here and you take the room upstairs.

Mr. Van Daan. It's your place.

Mr. Frank. Please. I've thought this out for weeks. It's the best arrangement. The only arrangement.

Mrs. Van Daan (*To Mr. Frank*). Never, never can we thank you. (*Then to Mrs. Frank*) I don't know what would have happened to us, if it hadn't been for Mr. Frank.

Mr. Frank. You don't know how your husband helped me when I came to this country . . . knowing no one . . . not able to speak the language. I can never repay him for that.

---

7. **w.c.**: water closet; toilet.

(*Going to* Mr. Van Daan) May I help you with your things?

Mr. Van Daan. No. No. (*To* Mrs. Van Daan) Come along, liefje.[8]

Mrs. Van Daan. You'll be all right, Peter? You're not afraid?

Peter (*Embarrassed*). Please, Mother.

(*They start up the stairs to the attic room above.* Mr. Frank *turns to* Mrs. Frank.)

Mr. Frank. You too must have some rest, Edith. You didn't close your eyes last night. Nor you, Margot.

Anne. I slept, Father. Wasn't that funny? I knew it was the last night in my own bed, and yet I slept soundly.

Mr. Frank. I'm glad, Anne. Now you'll be able to help me straighten things in here. (*To* Mrs. Frank *and* Margot) Come with me . . . You and Margot rest in this room for the time being. (*He picks up their clothes, starting for the room on the right.*)

Mrs. Frank. You're sure . . . ? I could help . . . And Anne hasn't had her milk . . .

Mr. Frank. I'll give it to her. (*To* Anne *and* Peter) Anne, Peter . . . it's best that you take off your shoes now, before you forget. (He leads the way to the room, followed by Margot.)

Mrs. Frank. You're sure you're not tired, Anne?

Anne. I feel fine. I'm going to help Father.

Mrs. Frank. Peter, I'm glad you are to be with us.

Peter. Yes, Mrs. Frank.

(Mrs. Frank *goes to join* Mr. Frank *and* Margot.)

(*During the following scene* Mr. Frank *helps* Margot *and* Mrs. Frank *to hang up their clothes. Then he persuades them both to lie down and rest. The* Van Daans *in their room above settle themselves. In the main room* Anne *and* Peter *remove their shoes.* Peter *takes his cat out of the carrier.*)

Anne. What's your cat's name?

Peter. Mouschi.[9]

Anne. Mouschi! Mouschi! Mouschi! (*She picks up the cat, walking away with it. To* Peter) I love cats. I have one . . . a darling little cat. But they made me leave her behind. I left some food and a note for the neighbors to take care of her . . . I'm going to miss her terribly. What is yours? A him or a her?

Peter. He's a tom. He doesn't like strangers. (*He takes the cat from her, putting it back in its carrier.*)

Anne (*Unabashed*). Then I'll have to stop being a stranger, won't I? Is he fixed?

Peter (*Startled*). Huh?

Anne. Did you have him fixed?

Peter. No.

Anne. Oh, you ought to have him fixed—to keep him from—you know, fighting. Where did you go to school?

Peter. Jewish Secondary.

Anne. But that's where Margot and I go! I never saw you around.

Peter. I used to see you . . . sometimes . . .

Anne. You did?

Peter . . . in the school yard. You were always in the middle of a bunch of kids. (*He takes a penknife from his pocket.*)

Anne. Why didn't you ever come over?

Peter. I'm sort of a lone wolf. (*He starts to rip off his Star of David.*)

Anne. What are you doing?

Peter. Taking it off.

Anne. But you can't do that. They'll arrest you if you go out without your star.

(*He tosses his knife on the table.*)

Peter. Who's going out?

---

8. **liefje** (lēf′yə) *Dutch:* little darling.

9. **Mouschi** (mo͞o′shē)

Anne. Why, of course! You're right! Of course we don't need them any more. (*She picks up his knife and starts to take her star off.*) I wonder what our friends will think when we don't show up today?

Peter. I didn't have any dates with anyone.

Anne. Oh, I did. I had a date with Jopie to go and play ping-pong at her house. Do you know Jopie de Waal?[10]

Peter. No.

Anne. Jopie's my best friend. I wonder what she'll think when she telephones and there's no answer? . . . Probably she'll go over to the house . . . I wonder what she'll think . . . we left everything as if we'd suddenly been called away . . . breakfast dishes in the sink . . . beds not made . . . (*As she pulls off her star, the cloth underneath shows clearly the color and form of the star.*) Look! It's still there! (*Peter goes over to the stove with his star.*) What're you going to do with yours?

Peter. Burn it.

Anne (*She starts to throw hers in, and cannot.*) It's funny, I can't throw mine away. I don't know why.

Peter. You can't throw . . . ? Something they branded you with . . . ? That they made you wear so they could spit on you?

Anne. I know. I know. But after all, it is the Star of David, isn't it?

(*In the bedroom, right,* Margot *and* Mrs. Frank *are lying down.* Mr. Frank *starts quietly out.*)

Peter. Maybe it's different for a girl.

(Mr. Frank *comes into the main room.*)

Mr. Frank. Forgive me, Peter. Now let me see. We must find a bed for your cat. (*He goes to a cupboard.*) I'm glad you brought your cat. Annie was feeling so badly about hers. (*Getting a used small washtub*) Here we are. Will it be comfortable in that?

Peter (*Gathering up his things*). Thanks.

Mr. Frank (*Opening the door of the room on the left*). And here is your room. But I warn you, Peter, you can't grow any more. Not an inch, or you'll have to sleep with your feet out of the skylight. Are you hungry?

Peter. No.

Mr. Frank. We have some bread and butter.

Peter. No, thank you.

Mr. Frank. You can have it for luncheon then. And tonight we will have a real supper . . . our first supper together.

Peter. Thanks. Thanks.

(*He goes into his room. During the following scene he arranges his possessions in his new room.*)

Mr. Frank. That's a nice boy, Peter.

Anne. He's awfully shy, isn't he?

Mr. Frank. You'll like him, I know.

Anne. I certainly hope so, since he's the only boy I'm likely to see for months and months.

(Mr. Frank *sits down, taking off his shoes.*)

Mr. Frank. Annele,[11] there's a box there. Will you open it? (*He indicates a carton on the couch.* Anne *brings it to the center table. In the street below there is the sound of children playing.*)

Anne (*As she opens the carton*). You know the way I'm going to think of it here? I'm going to think of it as a boardinghouse. A very peculiar summer boardinghouse, like the one that we—(*She breaks off as she pulls out some photographs.*) Father! My movie stars! I was wondering where they were! I was looking for them this morning . . . and Queen Wilhelmina! How wonderful!

Mr. Frank. There's something more. Go on. Look further. (*He goes over to the sink, pouring a glass of milk from a thermos bottle.*)

---

10. **Jopie de Waal** (yō′pē də väl′)
11. **Annele/Anneke:** a nickname for Anne.

Anne (*Pulling out a pasteboard-bound book*). A diary! (*She throws her arms around her father.*) I've never had a diary. And I've always longed for one. (*She looks around the room.*) Pencil, pencil, pencil, pencil. (*She starts down the stairs.*) I'm going down to the office to get a pencil.

Mr. Frank. Anne! No! (*He goes after her, catching her by the arm and pulling her back.*)

Anne (*Startled*). But there's no one in the building now.

Mr. Frank. It doesn't matter. I don't want you ever to go beyond that door.

Anne (*Sobered*). Never . . . ? Not even at nighttime, when everyone is gone? Or on Sundays? Can't I go down to listen to the radio?

Mr. Frank. Never. I am sorry, Anneke. It isn't safe. No, you must never go beyond that door.

(*For the first time* Anne *realizes what "going into hiding" means.*)

Anne. I see.

Mr. Frank. It'll be hard, I know. But always remember this, Anneke. There are no walls, there are no bolts, no locks that anyone can put on your mind. Miep will bring us books. We will read history, poetry, mythology. (*He gives her the glass of milk.*) Here's your milk. (*With his arm about her, they go over to the couch, sitting down side by side.*) As a matter of fact, between us, Anne, being here has certain advantages for you. For instance, you remember the battle you had with your mother the other day on the subject of overshoes? But in the end you had to wear them? Well now, you see, for as long as we are here you will never have to wear overshoes! Isn't that good? And the coat that you inherited from Margot, you won't have to wear that any more. And the piano! You won't have to practice on the piano. I tell you, this is going to be a fine life for you!

(*Anne's panic is gone.* Peter *appears in the doorway of his room, with a saucer in his hand. He is carrying his cat.*)

Peter. I . . . I . . . I thought I'd better get some water for Mouschi before . . .

Mr. Frank. Of course.

(*As he starts toward the sink the carillon begins to chime the hour of eight. He tiptoes to the window at the back and looks down at the street below. He turns to* Peter, *indicating in pantomime that it is too late.* Peter *starts back for his room. He steps on a creaking board. The three of them are frozen for a minute in fear. As* Peter *starts away again,* Anne *tiptoes over to him and pours some of the milk from her glass into the saucer for the cat.* Peter *squats on the floor, putting the milk before the cat.* Mr. Frank *gives* Anne *his fountain pen, and then goes into the room at the right. For a second* Anne *watches the cat, then she goes over to the center table, and opens her diary.*

In the room at the right, Mrs. Frank *has sat up quickly at the sound of the carillon.* Mr. Frank *comes in and sits down beside her on the settee, his arm comfortingly around her.*

Upstairs, in the attic room, Mr. *and* Mrs. Van Daan *have hung their clothes in the closet and are now seated on the iron bed.* Mrs. Van Daan *leans back exhausted.* Mr. Van Daan *fans her with a newspaper.*

Anne *starts to write in her diary. The lights dim out, the curtain falls.*

In the darkness Anne's *voice comes to us again, faintly at first, and then with growing strength.*)

Anne's Voice. I expect I should be describing what it feels like to go into hiding. But I really don't know yet myself. I only know it's funny never to be able to go outdoors . . . never to breathe fresh air . . . never to run and shout and jump. It's the silence in the nights that frightens me most. Every time I hear a creak in the house, or a step on the street outside, I'm sure they're coming for us.

I hope I will be able to confide everything to you, as I have never been able to confide in anyone, and I hope you will be a great source of comfort and support.

from The Diary of Anne Frank, *July 12, 1942*

The days aren't so bad. At least we know that Miep and Mr. Kraler are down there below us in the office. Our protectors, we call them. I asked Father what would happen to them if the Nazis found out they were hiding us. Pim said that they would suffer the same fate that we would . . . Imagine! They know this, and yet when they come up here, they're always cheerful and gay as if there were nothing in the world to bother them . . . Friday, the twenty-first of August, nineteen forty-two. Today I'm going to tell you our general news. Mother is unbearable. She insists on treating me like a baby, which I <u>loathe</u>. Otherwise things are going better. The weather is . . .

(*As Anne's voice is fading out, the curtain rises on the scene.*)

SCENE 3

It is a little after six o'clock in the evening, two months later.

Margot *is in the bedroom at the right, studying.* Mr. Van Daan *is lying down in the attic room above.*

The rest of the "family" is in the main room. Anne *and* Peter *sit opposite each other at the center table, where they have been doing their lessons.* Mrs. Frank *is on the couch.* Mrs. Van Daan *is seated with her fur coat, on which she has been sewing, in her lap. None of them are wearing their shoes.*

Their eyes are on Mr. Frank, *waiting for him to give them the signal which will release them from their day-long quiet.* Mr. Frank, *his shoes in his hand, stands looking down out of the window at the back, watching to be sure that all of the workmen have left the building below.*

After a few seconds of motionless silence, Mr. Frank *turns from the window.*

Mr. Frank (*Quietly, to the group*). It's safe now. The last workman has left. (*There is an immediate stir of relief.*)

Anne (*Her pent-up energy explodes*). WHEE!

Mrs. Frank (*Startled, amused*). Anne!

Mrs. Van Daan. I'm first for the w.c. (*She hurries off to the bathroom.* Mrs. Frank *puts on her shoes and starts up to the sink to prepare supper.* Anne *sneaks* Peter's *shoes from under the table and hides them behind her back.* Mr. Frank *goes into* Margot's *room.*)

Mr. Frank (*To* Margot). Six o'clock. School's over.

(Margot *gets up, stretching.* Mr. Frank *sits down to put on his shoes. In the main room* Peter *tries to find his.*)

Peter (*To* Anne). Have you seen my shoes?

Anne (*Innocently*). Your shoes?

Peter. You've taken them, haven't you?

Anne. I don't know what you're talking about.

Peter. You're going to be sorry!

Anne. Am I? (Peter *goes after her.* Anne, *with his shoes in her hand, runs from him, dodging behind her mother.*)

Mrs. Frank (*Protesting*). Anne, dear!

Peter. Wait till I get you!

Anne. I'm waiting! (Peter *makes a lunge for her. They both fall to the floor.* Peter *pins her down, wrestling with her to get the shoes.*) Don't! Don't! Peter, stop it. Ouch!

Mrs. Frank. Anne! . . . Peter!

(*Suddenly* Peter *becomes self-conscious. He grabs his shoes roughly and starts for his room.*)

Anne (*Following him*). Peter, where are you going? Come dance with me.

Peter. I tell you I don't know how.

Anne. I'll teach you.

Peter. I'm going to give Mouschi his dinner.

Anne. Can I watch?

WORDS
TO
KNOW

loathe (lōth) *v.* to hate; to dislike someone or something greatly

461

Peter. He doesn't like people around while he eats.

Anne. Peter, please.

Peter. No! (*He goes into his room. Anne slams his door after him.*)

Mrs. Frank. Anne, dear, I think you shouldn't play like that with Peter. It's not dignified.

Anne. Who cares if it's dignified? I don't want to be dignified.

(*Mr. Frank and Margot come from the room on the right. Margot goes to help her mother. Mr. Frank starts for the center table to correct Margot's school papers.*)

Mrs. Frank (*To Anne*). You complain that I don't treat you like a grown-up. But when I do, you resent it.

Anne. I only want some fun . . . someone to laugh and clown with . . . After you've sat still all day and hardly moved, you've got to have some fun. I don't know what's the matter with that boy.

Mr. Frank. He isn't used to girls. Give him a little time.

Anne. Time? Isn't two months time? I could cry. (*Catching hold of Margot*) Come on, Margot . . . dance with me. Come on, please.

Margot. I have to help with supper.

Anne. You know we're going to forget how to dance . . . When we get out we won't remember a thing.

(*She starts to sing and dance by herself. Mr. Frank takes her in his arms, waltzing with her. Mrs. Van Daan comes in from the bathroom.*)

Mrs. Van Daan. Next? (*She looks around as she starts putting on her shoes.*) Where's Peter?

Anne (*As they are dancing*). Where would he be!

Mrs. Van Daan. He hasn't finished his lessons, has he? His father'll kill him if he catches him in there with that cat and his work not done. (*Mr. Frank and Anne finish their dance. They bow*

to each other with extravagant formality.) Anne, get him out of there, will you?

Anne (*At Peter's door*). Peter? Peter?

Peter (*Opening the door a crack*). What is it?

Anne. Your mother says to come out.

Peter. I'm giving Mouschi his dinner.

Mrs. Van Daan. You know what your father says. (*She sits on the couch, sewing on the lining of her fur coat.*)

Peter. For heaven's sake, I haven't even looked at him since lunch.

Mrs. Van Daan. I'm just telling you, that's all.

Anne. I'll feed him.

Peter. I don't want you in there.

Mrs. Van Daan. Peter!

Peter (*To Anne*). Then give him his dinner and come right out, you hear? (*He comes back to the table. Anne shuts the door of Peter's room after her and disappears behind the curtain covering his closet.*)

Mrs. Van Daan (*To Peter*). Now is that any way to talk to your little girl friend?

Peter. Mother . . . for heaven's sake . . . will you please stop saying that?

Mrs. Van Daan. Look at him blush! Look at him!

Peter. Please! I'm not . . . anyway . . . let me alone, will you?

Mrs. Van Daan. He acts like it was something to be ashamed of. It's nothing to be ashamed of, to have a little girl friend.

Peter. You're crazy. She's only thirteen.

Mrs. Van Daan. So what? And you're sixteen. Just perfect. Your father's ten years older than I am. (*To Mr. Frank*) I warn you, Mr. Frank, if this war lasts much longer, we're going to be related and then . . .

Mr. Frank. Mazeltov![12]

Mrs. Frank (*Deliberately changing the*

---

12. **mazel tov** (mä′zəl tôf′) *Hebrew*: good luck.

conversation). I wonder where Miep is. She's usually so prompt.

(*Suddenly everything else is forgotten as they hear the sound of an automobile coming to a screeching stop in the street below. They are tense, motionless in their terror. The car starts away. A wave of relief sweeps over them. They pick up their occupations again. Anne flings open the door of* Peter's *room, making a dramatic entrance. She is dressed in* Peter's *clothes. Peter looks at her in fury. The others are amused.*)

Anne. Good evening, everyone. Forgive me if I don't stay. (*She jumps up on a chair.*) I have a friend waiting for me in there. My friend Tom. Tom Cat. Some people say that we look alike. But Tom has the most beautiful whiskers, and I have only a little fuzz. I am hoping . . . in time . . .

Peter. All right, Mrs. Quack Quack!

Anne (*Outraged—jumping down*). Peter!

Peter. I heard about you . . . How you talked so much in class they called you Mrs. Quack Quack. How Mr. Smitter made you write a composition . . . "'Quack, quack,' said Mrs. Quack Quack."

Anne. Well, go on. Tell them the rest. How it was so good he read it out loud to the class and then read it to all his other classes!

Peter. Quack! Quack! Quack . . . Quack . . . Quack . . .

(Anne *pulls off the coat and trousers.*)

Anne. You are the most intolerable, insufferable boy I've ever met!

(*She throws the clothes down the stairwell. Peter goes down after them.*)

Peter. Quack, quack, quack!

Mrs. Van Daan (*To* Anne). That's right, Anneke! Give it to him!

Anne. With all the boys in the world . . . Why I had to get locked up with one like you! . . .

Peter. Quack, quack, quack, and from now on stay out of my room!

(*As* Peter *passes her,* Anne *puts out her foot, tripping him. He picks himself up, and goes on into his room.*)

Mrs. Frank (*Quietly*). Anne, dear . . . your hair. (*She feels* Anne's *forehead.*) You're warm. Are you feeling all right?

Anne. Please, Mother. (*She goes over to the center table, slipping into her shoes.*)

Mrs. Frank (*Following her*). You haven't a fever, have you?

Anne (*Pulling away*). No. No.

Mrs. Frank. You know we can't call a doctor here, ever. There's only one thing to do . . . watch carefully. Prevent an illness before it comes. Let me see your tongue.

Anne. Mother, this is perfectly absurd.

Mrs. Frank. Anne, dear, don't be such a baby. Let me see your tongue. (*As* Anne *refuses,* Mrs. Frank *appeals to* Mr. Frank.) Otto . . . ?

Mr. Frank. You hear your mother, Anne. (Anne *flicks out her tongue for a second, then turns away.*)

Mrs. Frank. Come on—open up! (*As* Anne *opens her mouth very wide*) You seem all right . . . but perhaps an aspirin . . .

Mrs. Van Daan. For heaven's sake, don't give that child any pills. I waited for fifteen minutes this morning for her to come out of the w.c.

Anne. I was washing my hair!

Mr. Frank. I think there's nothing the matter with our Anne that a ride on her bike, or a visit with her friend Jopie de Waal wouldn't cure. Isn't that so, Anne?

(Mr. Van Daan *comes down into the room. From outside we hear faint sounds of bombers going over and a burst of ack-ack.*)

Mr. Van Daan. Miep not come yet?

Mrs. Van Daan. The workmen just left, a little while ago.

Mr. Van Daan. What's for dinner tonight?

Mrs. Van Daan. Beans.

Mr. Van Daan. Not again!

Mrs. Van Daan. Poor Putti! I know. But what can we do? That's all that Miep brought us.

(Mr. Van Daan *starts to pace, his hands behind his back.* Anne *follows behind him, imitating him.*)

Anne. We are now in what is known as the "bean cycle." Beans boiled, beans en casserole, beans with strings, beans without strings . . .

(Peter *has come out of his room. He slides into his place at the table, becoming immediately absorbed in his studies.*)

Mr. Van Daan (*To* Peter). I saw you . . . in there, playing with your cat.

Mrs. Van Daan. He just went in for a second, putting his coat away. He's been out here all the time, doing his lessons.

Mr. Frank (*Looking up from the papers*). Anne, you got an excellent in your history paper today . . . and very good in Latin.

Anne (*Sitting beside him*). How about algebra?

Mr. Frank. I'll have to make a confession. Up until now I've managed to stay ahead of you in algebra. Today you caught up with me. We'll leave it to Margot to correct.

Anne. Isn't algebra <u>vile</u>, Pim!

Mr. Frank. Vile!

Margot (*To* Mr. Frank). How did I do?

Anne (*Getting up*). Excellent, excellent, excellent, excellent!

Mr. Frank (*To* Margot). You should have used the subjunctive here . . .

Margot. Should I? . . . I thought . . . look here . . . I didn't use it here . . . (*The two become absorbed in the papers.*)

Anne. Mrs. Van Daan, may I try on your coat?

Mrs. Frank. No, Anne.

Mrs. Van Daan (*Giving it to* Anne). It's all right. . . but careful with it. (Anne *puts it on and struts with it.*)

My father gave me that the year before he died. He always bought the best that money could buy.

Anne. Mrs. Van Daan, did you have a lot of boy friends before you were married?

Mrs. Frank. Anne, that's a personal question. It's not courteous to ask personal questions.

Mrs. Van Daan. Oh I don't mind. (*To* Anne) Our house was always swarming with boys. When I was a girl we had . . .

Mr. Van Daan. Oh, God. Not again!

Mrs. Van Daan (*Good-humored*). Shut up! (*Without a pause, to* Anne. Mr. Van Daan *mimics* Mrs. Van Daan, *speaking the first few words in unison with her.*) One summer we had a big house in Hilversum. The boys came buzzing round like bees around a jam pot. And when I was sixteen! . . . We were wearing our skirts very short those days and I had good-looking legs. (*She pulls up her skirt, going to* Mr. Frank.) I still have 'em. I may not be as pretty as I used to be, but I still have my legs. How about it, Mr. Frank?

Mr. Van Daan. All right. All right. We see them.

Mrs. Van Daan. I'm not asking you. I'm asking Mr. Frank.

Peter. Mother, for heaven's sake.

Mrs. Van Daan. Oh, I embarrass you, do I? Well, I just hope the girl you marry has as good. (*Then to* Anne) My father used to worry about me, with so many boys hanging round. He told me, if any of them gets fresh, you say to him . . . "Remember, Mr. So-and-So, remember I'm a lady."

Anne. "Remember, Mr. So-and-So, remember I'm a lady." (*She gives* Mrs. Van Daan *her coat.*)

Mr. Van Daan. Look at you, talking that way in front of her! Don't you know she puts it all down in that diary?

Mrs. Van Daan. So, if she does? I'm only telling the truth!

(Anne *stretches out, putting her ear to the floor, listening to what is going on below. The sound of the bombers fades away.*)

Mrs. Frank (*Setting the table*). Would you mind, Peter, if I moved you over to the couch?

Anne (*Listening*). Miep must have the radio on.

(Peter *picks up his papers, going over to the couch beside* Mrs. Van Daan.)

Mr. Van Daan (*Accusingly, to* Peter). Haven't you finished yet?

Peter. No.

Mr. Van Daan. You ought to be ashamed of yourself.

Peter. All right. All right. I'm a dunce. I'm a hopeless case. Why do I go on?

Mrs. Van Daan. You're not hopeless. Don't talk that way. It's just that you haven't anyone to help you, like the girls have. (*To* Mr. Frank) Maybe you could help him, Mr. Frank?

Mr. Frank. I'm sure that his father . . . ?

Mr. Van Daan. Not me. I can't do anything with him. He won't listen to me. You go ahead . . . if you want.

Mr. Frank (*Going to* Peter). What about it, Peter? Shall we make our school coeducational?

Mrs. Van Daan (*Kissing* Mr. Frank). You're an angel, Mr. Frank. An angel. I don't know why I didn't meet you before I met that one there. Here, sit down, Mr. Frank . . . (*She forces him down on the couch beside* Peter.) Now, Peter, you listen to Mr. Frank.

Mr. Frank. It might be better for us to go into Peter's room. (Peter *jumps up eagerly, leading the way.*)

Mrs. Van Daan. That's right. You go in there, Peter. You listen to Mr. Frank. Mr. Frank is a highly educated man. (*As* Mr. Frank *is about to follow* Peter *into his room,* Mrs. Frank *stops him and wipes the lipstick from his lips. Then she closes the door after them.*)

Anne (*On the floor, listening*). Shh! I can hear a man's voice talking.

Mr. Van Daan (*To* Anne). Isn't it bad enough here without your sprawling all over the place? (Anne *sits up.*)

Mrs. Van Daan (*To* Mr. Van Daan). If you didn't smoke so much, you wouldn't be so bad-tempered.

Mr. Van Daan. Am I smoking? Do you see me smoking?

Mrs. Van Daan. Don't tell me you've used up all those cigarettes.

Mr. Van Daan. One package. Miep only brought me one package.

Mrs. Van Daan. It's a filthy habit anyway. It's a good time to break yourself.

Mr. Van Daan. Oh, stop it, please.

Mrs. Van Daan. You're smoking up all our money. You know that, don't you?

Mr. Van Daan. Will you shut up? (*During this,* Mrs. Frank *and* Margot *have studiously kept their eyes down. But* Anne, *seated on the floor, has been following the discussion interestedly.* Mr. Van Daan *turns to see her staring up at him.*) And what are you staring at?

Anne. I never heard grown-ups quarrel before. I thought only children quarreled.

Mr. Van Daan. This isn't a quarrel! It's a discussion. And I never heard children so rude before.

Anne (*Rising, indignantly*). I, rude!

Mr. Van Daan. Yes!

WORDS TO KNOW **indignantly** (ĭn-dĭg′ nənt-lē) *adv.* angrily aroused by something mean, unjust, or unworthy

Mrs. Frank (*Quickly*). Anne, will you get me my knitting? (Anne *goes to get it.*) I must remember, when Miep comes, to ask her to bring me some more wool.

Margot (*Going to her room*). I need some hairpins and some soap. I made a list. (*She goes into her bedroom to get the list.*)

Mrs. Frank (*To Anne*) Have you some library books for Miep when she comes?

Anne. It's a wonder that Miep has a life of her own, the way we make her run errands for us. Please, Miep, get me some starch. Please take my hair out and have it cut. Tell me all the latest news, Miep. (*She goes over, kneeling on the couch beside* Mrs. Van Daan.) Did you know she was engaged? His name is Dirk, and Miep's afraid the Nazis will ship him off to Germany to work in one of their war plants. That's what they're doing with some of the young Dutchmen . . . they pick them up off the streets—

Mr. Van Daan (*Interrupting*). Don't you ever get tired of talking? Suppose you try keeping still for five minutes. Just five minutes. (*He starts to pace again. Again* Anne *follows him, mimicking him.* Mrs. Frank *jumps up and takes her by the arm up to the sink, and gives her a glass of milk.*)

Mrs. Frank. Come here, Anne. It's time for your glass of milk.

Mr. Van Daan. Talk, talk, talk. I never heard such a child. Where is my . . . ? Every evening it's the same, talk, talk, talk. (*He looks around.*) Where is my . . . ?

Mrs. Van Daan. What're you looking for?

Mr. Van Daan. My pipe. Have you seen my pipe?

Mrs. Van Daan. What good's a pipe? You haven't got any tobacco.

Mr. Van Daan. At least I'll have something to hold in my mouth! (*Opening* Margot's *bedroom door*) Margot, have you seen my pipe?

Margot. It was on the table last night. (Anne *puts her glass of milk on the table and picks up his pipe, hiding it behind her back.*)

Mr. Van Daan. I know. I know. Anne, did you see my pipe? . . . Anne!

Mrs. Frank. Anne, Mr. Van Daan is speaking to you.

Anne. Am I allowed to talk now?

Mr. Van Daan. You're the most aggravating . . . The trouble with you is, you've been spoiled. What you need is a good old-fashioned spanking.

Anne (*Mimicking* Mrs. Van Daan). "Remember, Mr. So-and-So, remember I'm a lady." (*She thrusts the pipe into his mouth, then picks up her glass of milk.*)

Mr. Van Daan (*Restraining himself with difficulty*). Why aren't you nice and quiet like your sister Margot? Why do you have to show off all the time? Let me give you a little advice, young lady. Men don't like that kind of thing in a girl. You know that? A man likes a girl who'll listen to him once in a while . . . a domestic girl, who'll keep her house shining for her husband . . . who loves to cook and sew and . . .

Anne. I'd cut my throat first! I'd open my veins! I'm going to be remarkable! I'm going to Paris . . .

Mr. Van Daan (*Scoffingly*). Paris!

Anne. . . . to study music and art.

Mr. Van Daan. Yeah! Yeah!

Anne. I'm going to be a famous dancer or singer . . . or something wonderful. (*She makes a wide gesture, spilling the glass of milk on the*

fur coat in Mrs. Van Daan's *lap.* Margot *rushes quickly over with a towel.* Anne *tries to brush the milk off with her skirt.*)

Mrs. Van Daan. Now look what you've done . . . you clumsy little fool! My beautiful fur coat my father gave me . . .

Anne. I'm so sorry.

Mrs. Van Daan. What do you care? It isn't yours . . . So go on, ruin it! Do you know what that coat cost? Do you? And now look at it! Look at it!

Anne. I'm very, very sorry.

Mrs. Van Daan. I could kill you for this. I could just kill you! (Mrs. Van Daan *goes up the stairs, clutching the coat.* Mr. Van Daan *starts after her.*)

Mr. Van Daan. Petronella . . . liefje! Liefje! . . . Come back . . . the supper . . . come back!

Mrs. Frank. Anne, you must not behave in that way.

Anne. It was an accident. Anyone can have an accident.

Mrs. Frank. I don't mean that. I mean the answering back. You must not answer back. They are our guests. We must always show the greatest courtesy to them. We're all living under terrible tension. (*She stops as* Margot *indicates that* Van Daan *can hear. When he is gone, she continues.*) That's why we must control ourselves . . . You don't hear Margot getting into arguments with them, do you? Watch Margot. She's always courteous with them. Never familiar. She keeps her distance. And they respect her for it. Try to be like Margot.

Anne. And have them walk all over me, the way they do her? No, thanks!

Mrs. Frank. I'm not afraid that anyone is going to walk all over you, Anne. I'm afraid for other people, that you'll walk on them. I don't know what happens to you, Anne. You are wild, self-willed. If I had ever talked to my mother as you talk to me . . .

Anne. Things have changed. People aren't like that any more. "Yes, Mother." "No, Mother." "Anything you say, Mother." I've got to fight things out for myself! Make something of myself!

Mrs. Frank. It isn't necessary to fight to do it. Margot doesn't fight, and isn't she . . .?

Anne (*Violently rebellious*). Margot! Margot! Margot! That's all I hear from everyone . . . how wonderful Margot is . . . "Why aren't you like Margot?"

Margot (*Protesting*). Oh, come on, Anne, don't be so . . .

Anne (*Paying no attention*). Everything she does is right, and everything I do is wrong! I'm the goat around here! . . . You're all against me! . . . And you worst of all!

(*She rushes off into her room and throws herself down on the settee, stifling her sobs.* Mrs. Frank *sighs and starts toward the stove.*)

Mrs. Frank (*To* Margot). Let's put the soup on the stove . . . if there's anyone who cares to eat. Margot, will you take the bread out? (Margot *gets the bread from the cupboard.*) I don't know how we can go on living this way . . . I can't say a word to Anne . . . she flies at me . . .

Margot. You know Anne. In half an hour she'll be out here, laughing and joking.

Mrs. Frank. And . . . (*She makes a motion upwards, indicating the* Van Daans.) . . . I told your father it wouldn't work . . . but no . . . no . . . he had to ask them, he said . . . he owed it to him, he said. Well, he knows now that I was right! These quarrels! . . . This bickering!

Margot (*With a warning look*). Shush. Shush.

(*The buzzer for the door sounds.* Mrs. Frank *gasps, startled.*)

Mrs. Frank. Every time I hear that sound, my heart stops!

Margot (*Starting for* Peter's *door*). It's Miep. (*She knocks at the door.*) Father?

(Mr. Frank *comes quickly from* Peter's *room.*)

Mr. Frank. Thank you, Margot. (*As he goes down the steps to open the outer door*) Has everyone his list?

Margot. I'll get my books. (*Giving her mother a list.*) Here's your list. (Margot *goes into her and* Anne's *bedroom on the right.* Anne *sits up, hiding her tears, as* Margot *comes in.*) Miep's here.

(Margot *picks up her books and goes back.* Anne *hurries over to the mirror, smoothing her hair.*)

Mr. Van Daan (*Coming down the stairs*). Is it Miep?

Margot. Yes. Father's gone down to let her in.

Mr. Van Daan. At last I'll have some cigarettes!

Mrs. Frank (*To Mr. Van Daan*). I can't tell you how unhappy I am about Mrs. Van Daan's coat. Anne should never have touched it.

Mr. Van Daan. She'll be all right.

Mrs. Frank. Is there anything I can do?

Mr. Van Daan. Don't worry.

(*He turns to meet* Miep. *But it is not* Miep *who comes up the steps. It is* Mr. Kraler, *followed by* Mr. Frank. *Their faces are grave.* Anne *comes from the bedroom.* Peter *comes from his room.*)

Mrs. Frank. Mr. Kraler!

Mr. Van Daan. How are you, Mr. Kraler?

Margot. This is a surprise.

Mrs. Frank. When Mr. Kraler comes, the sun begins to shine.

Mr. Van Daan. Miep is coming?

Mr. Kraler. Not tonight.

(Kraler *goes to* Margot *and* Mrs. Frank *and* Anne, *shaking hands with them.*)

Mrs. Frank. Wouldn't you like a cup of coffee? . . . Or, better still, will you have supper with us?

Mr. Frank. Mr. Kraler has something to talk over with us. Something has happened, he says, which demands an immediate decision.

Mrs. Frank (*Fearful*). What is it?

(*Mr. Kraler sits down on the couch. As he talks he takes bread, cabbages, milk, etc., from his briefcase, giving them to* Margot *and* Anne *to put away.*)

Mr. Kraler. Usually, when I come up here, I try to bring you some bit of good news. What's the use of telling you the bad news when there's nothing that you can do about it? But today something has happened . . . Dirk . . . Miep's Dirk, you know, came to me just now. He tells me that he has a Jewish friend living near him. A dentist. He says he's in trouble. He begged me, could I do anything for this man? Could I find him a hiding place? . . . So I've come to you . . . I know it's a terrible thing to ask of you, living as you are, but would you take him in with you?

Mr. Frank. Of course we will.

Mr. Kraler (*Rising*). It'll be just for a night or two . . . until I find some other place. This happened so suddenly that I didn't know where to turn.

Mr. Frank. Where is he?

Mr. Kraler. Downstairs in the office.

Mr. Frank. Good. Bring him up.

Mr. Kraler. His name is Dussel . . . Jan Dussel.

Mr. Frank. Dussel . . . I think I know him.

Mr. Kraler. I'll get him. (*He goes quickly down the steps and out.* Mr. Frank *suddenly becomes conscious of the others.*)

Mr. Frank. Forgive me. I spoke without consulting you. But I knew you'd feel as I do.

Mr. Van Daan. There's no reason for you to consult anyone. This is your place. You have a right to do exactly as you please. The only thing I feel . . . there's so little food as it is . . . and to take in another person . . .

(Peter *turns away, ashamed of his father.*)

Mr. Frank. We can stretch the food a little. It's only for a few days.

Mr. Van Daan. You want to make a bet?

Mrs. Frank. I think it's fine to have him. But, Otto, where are you going to put him? Where?

Peter. He can have my bed. I can sleep on the floor. I wouldn't mind.

Mr. Frank. That's good of you, Peter. But your room's too small . . . even for *you*.

Anne. I have a much better idea. I'll come in here with you and Mother, and Margot can take Peter's room and Peter can go in our room with Mr. Dussel.

Margot. That's right. We could do that.

Mr. Frank. No, Margot. You mustn't sleep in that room . . . neither you nor Anne. Mouschi has caught some rats in there. Peter's brave. He doesn't mind.

Anne. Then how about *this?* I'll come in here with you and Mother, and Mr. Dussel can have my bed.

Mrs. Frank. No. No. *No!* Margot will come in here with us and he can have her bed. It's the only way. Margot, bring your things in here. Help her, Anne.

(Margot *hurries into her room to get her things.*)

Anne (*To her mother*). Why Margot? Why can't I come in here?

Mrs. Frank. Because it wouldn't be proper for Margot to sleep with a . . . Please, Anne. Don't argue. Please. (Anne *starts slowly away.*)

Mr. Frank (*To* Anne). You don't mind sharing your room with Mr. Dussel, do you, Anne?

Anne. No. No, of course not.

Mr. Frank. Good. (Anne *goes off into her bedroom, helping* Margot. Mr. Frank *starts to search in the cupboards.*) Where's the cognac?

Mrs. Frank. It's there. But, Otto, I was saving it in case of illness.

Mr. Frank. I think we couldn't find a better time to use it. Peter, will you get five glasses for me?

(Peter *goes for the glasses.* Margot *comes out of her bedroom, carrying her possessions, which she hangs behind a curtain in the main room.* Mr. Frank *finds the cognac and pours it into the five glasses that Peter brings him.* Mr. Van Daan *stands looking on sourly.* Mrs. Van Daan *comes downstairs and looks around at all the bustle.*)

Mrs. Van Daan. What's happening? What's going on?

Mr. Van Daan. Someone's moving in with us.

Mrs. Van Daan. In here? You're joking.

Margot. It's only for a night or two . . . until Mr. Kraler finds him another place.

Mr. Van Daan. Yeah! Yeah!

(Mr. Frank *hurries over as* Mr. Kraler *and* Dussel *come up.* Dussel *is a man in his late fifties, meticulous, finicky . . . bewildered now. He wears a raincoat. He carries a briefcase, stuffed full, and a small medicine case.*)

Mr. Frank. Come in, Mr. Dussel.

Mr. Kraler. This is Mr. Frank.

Dussel. Mr. Otto Frank?

Mr. Frank. Yes. Let me take your things. (*He takes the hat and briefcase, but* Dussel *clings to his medicine case.*) This is my wife Edith . . . Mr. and Mrs. Van Daan . . . their son, Peter . . . and my daughters, Margot and Anne.

(Dussel *shakes hands with everyone.*)

Mr. Kraler. Thank you, Mr. Frank. Thank you all. Mr. Dussel, I leave you in good hands. Oh . . . Dirk's coat.

(Dussel *hurriedly takes off the raincoat, giving it to* Mr. Kraler. *Underneath is his white dentist's jacket, with a yellow Star of David on it.*)

Dussel (*To* Mr. Kraler). What can I say to thank you . . . ?

Mrs. Frank (*To* Dussel). Mr. Kraler and Miep . . . They're our lifeline. Without them we couldn't live.

Mr. Kraler. Please. Please. You make us seem very heroic. It isn't that at all. We simply don't like the Nazis. (*To Mr. Frank, who offers him a drink*) No, thanks. (*Then, going on*) We don't like their methods. We don't like . . .

Mr. Frank (*Smiling*). I know. I know. "No one's going to tell us Dutchmen what to do with our damn Jews!"

Mr. Kraler (*To Dussel*). Pay no attention to Mr. Frank. I'll be up tomorrow to see that they're treating you right. (*To Mr. Frank*) Don't trouble to come down again. Peter will bolt the door after me, won't you, Peter?

Peter. Yes, sir.

Mr. Frank. Thank you, Peter. I'll do it.

Mr. Kraler. Good night. Good night.

Group. Good night, Mr. Kraler. We'll see you tomorrow, (*etc., etc.*)

(Mr. Kraler *goes out with* Mr. Frank. Mrs. Frank *gives each one of the "grown-ups" a glass of cognac.*)

Mrs. Frank. Please, Mr. Dussel, sit down.

(Mr. Dussel *sinks into a chair.* Mrs. Frank *gives him a glass of cognac.*)

Dussel. I'm dreaming. I know it. I can't believe my eyes. Mr. Otto Frank here! (*To Mrs. Frank*) You're not in Switzerland then? A woman told me . . . She said she'd gone to your house . . . the door was open, everything was in disorder, dishes in the sink. She said she found a piece of paper in the wastebasket with an address scribbled on it . . . an address in Zurich. She said you must have escaped to Zurich.

Anne. Father put that there purposely . . . just so people would think that very thing!

Dussel. And you've been here all the time?

Mrs. Frank. All the time . . . ever since July.

(Anne *speaks to her father as he comes back.*)

Anne. It worked, Pim . . . the address you left! Mr. Dussel says that people believe we escaped to Switzerland.

Mr. Frank. I'm glad . . . And now let's have a little drink to welcome Mr. Dussel. (*Before they can drink,* Mr. Dussel *bolts his drink.* Mr. Frank *smiles and raises his glass.*) To Mr. Dussel. Welcome. We're very honored to have you with us.

Mrs. Frank. To Mr. Dussel, welcome.

(*The* Van Daans *murmur a welcome. The "grown-ups" drink.*)

Mrs. Van Daan. Um. That was good.

Mr. Van Daan. Did Mr. Kraler warn you that you won't get much to eat here? You can imagine . . . three ration books among the seven of us . . . and now you make eight.

(Peter *walks away, humiliated. Outside a street organ is heard dimly.*)

Dussel (*Rising*). Mr. Van Daan, you don't realize what is happening outside that you should warn me of a thing like that. You don't realize what's going on . . . (*As* Mr. Van Daan *starts his characteristic pacing,* Dussel *turns to speak to the others.*) Right here in Amsterdam every day hundreds of Jews disappear . . . They surround a block and search house by house. Children come home from school to find their parents gone. Hundreds are being deported . . . people that you and I know . . . the Hallensteins . . . the Wessels . . .

Mrs. Frank (*In tears*). Oh, no. No!

Dussel. They get their call-up notice . . . come to the Jewish theatre on such and such a day and hour . . . bring only what you can carry in a rucksack. And if you refuse the call-up notice, then they come and drag you from your home and ship you off to Mauthausen.[13] The death camp!

---

13. **Mauthausen** (mout′hou′zən): a Nazi concentration camp in Austria.

The first day Mr. Dussel was here, he asked me all sorts of questions—for example, what time the cleaning lady comes to the office, how we've arranged to use the washroom amd when we're allowed to go to the toilet. You may laugh, but these things aren't so easy in a hiding place.

from The Diary of Anne Frank, *November 12, 1942*

Mrs. Frank. We didn't know that things had got so much worse.

Dussel. Forgive me for speaking so.

Anne (*Coming to* Dussel). Do you know the de Waals? . . . What's become of them? Their daughter Jopie and I are in the same class. Jopie's my best friend.

Dussel. They are gone.

Anne. Gone?

Dussel. With all the others.

Anne. Oh, no. Not Jopie!

(*She turns away, in tears.* Mrs. Frank *motions to* Margot *to comfort her.* Margot *goes to* Anne, *putting her arms comfortingly around her.*)

Mrs. Van Daan. There were some people called Wagner. They lived near us . . . ?

Mr. Frank (*Interrupting, with a glance at* Anne). I think we should put this off until later. We all have many questions we want to ask . . . But I'm sure that Mr. Dussel would like to get settled before supper.

Dussel. Thank you. I would. I brought very little with me.

Mr. Frank (*Giving him his hat and briefcase*). I'm sorry we can't give you a room alone. But I hope you won't be too uncomfortable. We've had to make strict rules here . . . a schedule of hours . . . We'll tell you after supper. Anne, would you like to take Mr. Dussel to his room?

Anne (*Controlling her tears*). If you'll come with me, Mr. Dussel? (*She starts for her room.*)

Dussel (*Shaking hands with each in turn*). Forgive me if I haven't really expressed my gratitude to all of you. This has been such a shock to me. I'd always thought of myself as Dutch. I was born in Holland. My father was born in Holland, and my grandfather. And now . . . after all these years . . . (*He breaks off*). If you'll excuse me.

(Dussel *gives a little bow and hurries off after* Anne. Mr. Frank *and the others are subdued.*)

Anne (*Turning on the light*). Well, here we are.

(Dussel *looks around the room. In the main room* Margot *speaks to her mother.*)

Margot. The news sounds pretty bad, doesn't it? It's so different from what Mr. Kraler tells us. Mr. Kraler says things are improving.

Mr. Van Daan. I like it better the way Kraler tells it.

(*They resume their occupations, quietly.* Peter *goes off into his room. In* Anne's *room,* Anne *turns to* Dussel.)

Anne. You're going to share the room with me.

Dussel. I'm a man who's always lived alone. I haven't had to adjust myself to others. I hope you'll bear with me until I learn.

Anne. Let me help you. (*She takes his briefcase.*) Do you always live all alone? Have you no family at all?

Dussel. No one. (*He opens his medicine case and spreads his bottles on the dressing table.*)

Anne. How dreadful. You must be terribly lonely.

Dussel. I'm used to it.

Anne. I don't think I could ever get used to it. Didn't you even have a pet? A cat, or a dog?

Dussel. I have an allergy for fur-bearing animals. They give me asthma.

Anne. Oh, dear. Peter has a cat.

Dussel. Here? He has it here?

Anne. Yes. But we hardly ever see it. He keeps it in his room all the time. I'm sure it will be all right.

Dussel. Let us hope so.

(*He takes some pills to fortify himself.*)

Anne. That's Margot's bed, where you're going to sleep. I sleep on the sofa there. (*Indicating the clothes hooks on the wall*) We cleared these off for your things. (*She goes over to the window.*)

The best part about this room . . . you can look down and see a bit of the street and the canal. There's a houseboat . . . you can see the end of it . . . a bargeman lives there with his family . . . They have a baby and he's just beginning to walk and I'm so afraid he's going to fall into the canal some day. I watch him . . .

Dussel (*Interrupting*). Your father spoke of a schedule.

Anne (*Coming away from the window*). Oh, yes. It's mostly about the times we have to be quiet. And times for the w.c. You can use it now if you like.

Dussel (*Stiffly*). No, thank you.

Anne. I suppose you think it's awful, my talking about a thing like that. But you don't know how important it can get to be, especially when you're frightened . . . About this room, the way Margot and I did . . . she had it to herself in the afternoons for studying, reading . . . lessons, you know . . . and I took the mornings. Would that be all right with you?

Dussel. I'm not at my best in the morning.

Anne. You stay here in the mornings then. I'll take the room in the afternoons.

Dussel. Tell me, when you're in here, what happens to me? Where am I spending my time? In there, with all the people?

Anne. Yes.

Dussel. I see. I see.

Anne. We have supper at half past six.

Dussel (*Going over to the sofa*). Then, if you don't mind . . . I like to lie down quietly for ten minutes before eating. I find it helps the digestion.

Anne. Of course. I hope I'm not going to be too much of a bother to you. I seem to be able to get everyone's back up.

(Dussel *lies down on the sofa, curled up, his back to her.*)

Dussel. I always get along very well with children. My patients all bring their children to me, because they know I get on well with them. So don't you worry about that.

(Anne *leans over him, taking his hand and shaking it gratefully.*)

Anne. Thank you. Thank you, Mr. Dussel.

(*The lights dim to darkness. The curtain falls on the scene.* Anne's *voice comes to us faintly at first, and then with increasing power.*)

Anne's Voice. . . . And yesterday I finished Cissy Van Marxvelt's latest book. I think she is a first-class writer. I shall definitely let my children read her. Monday the twenty-first of September, nineteen forty-two. Mr. Dussel and I had another battle yesterday. Yes, Mr. Dussel! According to him, nothing, I repeat . . . nothing, is right about me . . . my appearance, my character, my manners. While he was going on at me I thought . . . sometime I'll give you such a smack that you'll fly right up to the ceiling! Why is it that every grown-up thinks he knows the way to bring up children? Particularly the grown-ups that never had any. I keep wishing that Peter was a girl instead of a boy. Then I would have someone to talk to. Margot's a darling, but she takes everything too seriously. To pause for a moment on the subject of Mrs. Van Daan. I must tell you that her attempts to flirt with father are getting her nowhere. Pim, thank goodness, won't play.

(*As she is saying the last lines, the curtain rises on the darkened scene.* Anne's *voice fades out.*)

Connect to the Literature

1. **What Do You Think?** What kind of person do you think Anne is? How do you feel about her?

Comprehension Check
- In Scene 1, why has Otto Frank returned to the Secret Annex? What does he receive from Miep Gies?
- In Scene 2, why have the Franks and the Van Daans gone into hiding?
- What event in Scene 3 changes the lives of the families in hiding?

Think Critically

2. **ACTIVE READING** **MAPPING**
   Look back at the story maps that you created in your **READER'S NOTEBOOK**. Who are the characters in the play? What do you learn about each character in the first three scenes?

3. In Scene 2, Peter and Anne have a discussion about the yellow Star of David that the Nazis have made the Jews wear. What is the religious significance of the Star of David to the Jewish people? Why do you think the Nazis picked the star as a means of marking the Jews?

4. Although the events in the play take place over 50 years ago, the characters behave as people might behave today. How is Anne's behavior like that of an adolescent today?

   Think About:
   - Anne's attitude toward authority
   - her behavior toward Peter
   - her goals and dreams

Extend Interpretations

5. **Different Perspectives** Imagine that Peter is keeping a diary. In what ways would the play be different if it were based on his diary rather than on Anne's?

6. **Connect to Life** In Scene 2, Mr. Frank tells Anne, "There are no walls, there are no bolts, no locks that anyone can put on your mind." What does he mean by this? How have you felt when someone has tried to restrict your freedom?

Literary Analysis

FLASHBACK In a literary work, an interruption of the action to show events that took place at an earlier time is called a **flashback.** A flashback may provide information that helps readers understand a character's current situation.

In *The Diary of Anne Frank,* the play's first scene takes place in November 1945, some months after the end of World War II. The second scene then flashes back to the war years, where the action remains until the final scene, which returns to November 1945.

Paired Activity Although the play begins and ends during the postwar period, most of the action takes place during the war years and is presented through a flashback. With a partner, answer the following questions. Your story maps of Scenes 1 and 2 will help you.
- What do you learn about the Frank family in Scene 1?
- During what year does Scene 2 take place?
- Do you think that the use of flashback is more effective than a retelling of events? Explain your answer.

SCENE 4

*I*t is the middle of the night, several months later. The stage is dark except for a little light which comes through the skylight in Peter's room.

Everyone is in bed. Mr. and Mrs. Frank lie on the couch in the main room, which has been pulled out to serve as a makeshift double bed.

Margot is sleeping on a mattress on the floor in the main room, behind a curtain stretched across for privacy. The others are all in their accustomed rooms.

From outside we hear two drunken soldiers singing "Lili Marlene." A girl's high giggle is heard. The sound of running feet is heard coming closer and then fading in the distance. Throughout the scene there is the distant sound of airplanes passing overhead.

A match suddenly flares up in the attic. We dimly see Mr. Van Daan. He is getting his bearings. He comes quickly down the stairs, and goes to the cupboard where the food is stored. Again the match flares up, and is as quickly blown out. The dim figure is seen to steal back up the stairs.

There is quiet for a second or two, broken only by the sound of airplanes, and running feet on the street below.

Suddenly, out of the silence and the dark, we hear Anne scream.

Anne (*Screaming*). No! No! Don't . . . don't take me!

(*She moans, tossing and crying in her sleep. The other people wake, terrified. Dussel sits up in bed, furious.*)

Dussel. Shush! Anne! Anne, for God's sake, shush!

Anne (*Still in her nightmare*). Save me! Save me!

(*She screams and screams. Dussel gets out of bed, going over to her, trying to wake her.*)

Dussel. For God's sake! Quiet! Quiet! You want someone to hear?

(*In the main room* Mrs. Frank *grabs a shawl and pulls it around her. She rushes in to* Anne, *taking her in her arms.* Mr. Frank *hurriedly gets up, putting on his overcoat.* Margot *sits up, terrified.* Peter's *light goes on in his room.*)

Mrs. Frank (*To* Anne, *in her room*). Hush, darling, hush. It's all right. It's all right. (*Over her shoulder to* Dussel) Will you be kind enough to turn on the light, Mr. Dussel? (*Back to* Anne) It's nothing, my darling. It was just a dream.

(Dussel *turns on the light in the bedroom.* Mrs. Frank *holds* Anne *in her arms. Gradually* Anne *comes out of her nightmare, still trembling with horror.* Mr. Frank *comes into the room, and goes quickly to the window, looking out to be sure that no one outside had heard* Anne's *screams.* Mrs. Frank *holds* Anne, *talking softly to her. In the main room* Margot *stands on a chair, turning on the center hanging lamp. A light goes on in the* Van Daan's *room overhead.* Peter *puts his robe on, coming out of his room.*)

Dussel (*To* Mrs. Frank, *blowing his nose*). Something must be done about that child, Mrs. Frank. Yelling like that! Who knows but there's somebody on the streets? She's endangering all our lives.

Mrs. Frank. Anne, darling.

Dussel. Every night she twists and turns. I don't sleep. I spend half my night shushing her. And now it's nightmares!

(Margot *comes to the door of* Anne's *room, followed by* Peter. Mr. Frank *goes to them, indicating that everything is all right.* Peter *takes* Margot *back.*)

Mrs. Frank (*To* Anne). You're here, safe, you see? Nothing has happened. (*To* Dussel) Please, Mr. Dussel, go back to bed. She'll be herself in a minute or two. Won't you, Anne?

Dussel (*Picking up a book and a pillow*). Thank you, but I'm going to the w.c. The one place where there's peace! (*He stalks out.* Mr. Van Daan, *in underwear and trousers, comes down the stairs.*)

Mr. Van Daan (*To* Dussel). What is it? What happened?

Dussel. A nightmare. She was having a nightmare!

Mr. Van Daan. I thought someone was murdering her.

Dussel. Unfortunately, no.

(*He goes into the bathroom.* Mr. Van Daan *goes back up the stairs.* Mr. Frank, *in the main room, sends* Peter *back to his own bedroom.*)

Mr. Frank. Thank you, Peter. Go back to bed.

(Peter *goes back to his room.* Mr. Frank *follows him, turning out the light and looking out the window. Then he goes back to the main room, and gets up on a chair, turning out the center hanging lamp.*)

Mrs. Frank (*To* Anne). Would you like some water? (Anne *shakes her head.*) Was it a very bad dream? Perhaps if you told me . . . ?

Anne. I'd rather not talk about it.

Mrs. Frank. Poor darling. Try to sleep then. I'll sit right here beside you until you fall asleep. (*She brings a stool over, sitting there.*)

Anne. You don't have to.

Mrs. Frank. But I'd like to stay with you . . . very much. Really.

Anne. I'd rather you didn't.

Mrs. Frank. Good night, then. (*She leans down to kiss* Anne. Anne *throws her arm up over her face, turning away.* Mrs. Frank, *hiding her hurt, kisses* Anne's *arm.*) You'll be all right? There's nothing that you want?

Anne. Will you please ask Father to come.

Mrs. Frank (*After a second*). Of course, Anne dear. (*She hurries out into the other room.* Mr. Frank *comes to her as she comes in*) Sie verlangt nach Dir![14]

Mr. Frank (*Sensing her hurt*). Edith, Liebe, schau[15] . . .

Mrs. Frank. Es macht nichts! Ich danke dem lieben Herrgott, dass sie sich wenigstens an Dich wendet, wenn sie Trost braucht! Geh hinein, Otto, sie ist ganz hysterisch vor Angst.[16] (*As* Mr. Frank *hesitates*) Geh zu ihr.[17] (*He looks at her for a second and then goes to get a cup of water for* Anne. Mrs. Frank *sinks down on the bed, her face in her hands, trying to keep from sobbing aloud.* Margot *comes over to her, putting her arms around her.*) She wants nothing of me. She pulled away when I leaned down to kiss her.

Margot. It's a phase . . . You heard Father . . . Most girls go through it . . . they turn to their fathers at this age . . . they give all their love to their fathers.

Mrs. Frank. You weren't like this. You didn't shut me out.

Margot. She'll get over it . . . (*She smooths the bed for* Mrs. Frank *and sits beside her a moment as* Mrs. Frank *lies down. In* Anne's *room* Mr. Frank *comes in, sitting down by* Anne. Anne *flings her arms around him, clinging to him. In the distance we hear the sound of ack-ack.*)

Anne. Oh, Pim. I dreamed that they came to get us! The Green Police! They broke down the door and grabbed me and started to drag me out the way they did Jopie.

Mr. Frank. I want you to take this pill.

---

14. **Sie verlangt nach Dir** (zē fer-längt′ näкн dîr) *German:* She is asking for you.

15. **Liebe, schau** (lē′bə shou′) *German:* Dear, look.

16. **Es macht . . . vor Angst** (ĕs mäкнt′ nǐкнts′! ǐкн dängk′ə däm lē′bən hĕr′gôt′, däs zē zǐкн′ vän′ǐкн-shtənz än dǐкн′ vĕn′dət, vĕn zē trôst′ broukht′! gā hǐn-īn′, ôt′tô; zē ǐst gänts hü-stĕr′ǐsh fôr ängst′) *German:* It's all right. I thank dear God that at least she turns to you when she needs comfort. Go in, Otto; she is hysterical with fear.

17. **Geh zu ihr** (gā′ tsoo îr′) *German:* Go to her.

Anne. What is it?

Mr. Frank. Something to quiet you.

(*She takes it and drinks the water. In the main room* Margot *turns out the light and goes back to her bed.*)

Mr. Frank (*To* Anne). Do you want me to read to you for a while?

Anne. No. Just sit with me for a minute. Was I awful? Did I yell terribly loud? Do you think anyone outside could have heard?

Mr. Frank. No. No. Lie quietly now. Try to sleep.

Anne. I'm a terrible coward. I'm so disappointed in myself. I think I've conquered my fear . . . I think I'm really grown-up . . . and then something happens . . . and I run to you like a baby . . . I love you, Father. I don't love anyone but you.

Mr. Frank (*Reproachfully*). Annele!

Anne. It's true. I've been thinking about it for a long time. You're the only one I love.

Mr. Frank. It's fine to hear you tell me that you love me. But I'd be happier if you said you loved your mother as well . . . She needs your help so much . . . your love . . .

Anne. We have nothing in common. She doesn't understand me. Whenever I try to explain my views on life to her she asks me if I'm constipated.

Mr. Frank. You hurt her very much just now. She's crying. She's in there crying.

Anne. I can't help it. I only told the truth. I didn't want her here . . . (*Then, with sudden change*) Oh, Pim, I was horrible, wasn't I? And the worst of it is, I can stand off and look at myself doing it and know it's cruel and yet I can't stop doing it. What's the matter with me? Tell me. Don't say it's just a phase! Help me.

Mr. Frank. There is so little that we parents can do to help our children. We can only try to set a good example . . . point the way. The rest you must do yourself. You must build your own character.

Anne. I'm trying. Really I am. Every night I think back over all of the things I did that day that were wrong . . . like putting the wet mop in Mr. Dussel's bed . . . and this thing now with Mother. I say to myself, that was wrong. I make up my mind, I'm never going to do *that* again. Never! Of course I may do something worse . . . but at least I'll never do that again! . . . I have a nicer side, Father . . . a sweeter, nicer side. But I'm scared to show it. I'm afraid that people are going to laugh at me if I'm serious. So the mean Anne comes to the outside and the good Anne stays on the inside, and I keep on trying to switch them around and have the good Anne outside and the bad Anne inside and be what I'd like to be . . . and might be . . . if only . . . only . . . (*She is asleep.* Mr. Frank *watches her for a moment and then turns off the light, and starts out. The lights dim out. The curtain falls on the scene. Anne's voice is heard dimly at first, and then with growing strength.*)

Anne's Voice . . . The air raids are getting worse. They come over day and night. The noise is terrifying. Pim says it should be music to our ears. The more planes, the sooner will come the end of the war. Mrs. Van Daan pretends to be a fatalist. What will be, will be. But when the planes come over, who is the most frightened? No one else but Petronella! . . . Monday, the ninth of November, nineteen forty-two. Wonderful news! The Allies have landed in Africa. Pim says that we can look for an early finish to the war. Just for fun he asked each of us what was the first thing we wanted to do when we got out of here. Mrs. Van Daan longs to be home with her own things, her needlepoint chairs, the Beckstein piano her father gave her . . . the best that money could buy. Peter would like to go to a movie. Mr. Dussel wants to get back to his

dentist's drill. He's afraid he is losing his touch. For myself, there are so many things . . . to ride a bike again . . . to laugh till my belly aches . . . to have new clothes from the skin out . . . to have a hot tub filled to overflowing and <u>wallow</u> in it for hours . . . to be back in school with my friends . . .

(*As the last lines are being said, the curtain rises on the scene. The lights dim on as Anne's voice fades away.*)

It is the first night of the Hanukkah[18] *celebration. Mr. Frank is standing at the head of the table on which is the Menorah.*[19] *He lights the Shamos, or servant candle, and holds it as he says the blessing. Seated listening is all of the "family," dressed in their best. The men wear hats, Peter wears his cap.*

Mr. Frank (*Reading from a prayer book*). "Praised be Thou, oh Lord our God, Ruler of the universe, who has sanctified us with Thy commandments and bidden us kindle the Hanukkah lights. Praised be Thou, oh Lord our God, Ruler of the universe, who has wrought wondrous deliverances for our fathers in days of old. Praised be Thou, oh Lord our God, Ruler of the universe, that Thou has given us life and sustenance and brought us to this happy season." (Mr. Frank *lights the one candle of the Menorah as he continues.*) "We kindle this Hanukkah light to celebrate the great and wonderful deeds wrought through the <u>zeal</u> with which God filled the hearts of the heroic Maccabees, two thousand years ago.

They fought against indifference, against tyranny and <u>oppression</u>, and they restored our Temple to us. May these lights remind us that we should ever look to God, whence cometh our help." Amen. [Pronounced O-mayn.]

All. Amen.

(Mr. Frank *hands* Mrs. Frank *the prayer book.*)

Mrs. Frank (*Reading*). "I lift up mine eyes unto the mountains, from whence cometh my help. My help cometh from the Lord who made heaven and earth. He will not suffer thy foot to be moved. He that keepeth thee will not slumber. He that keepeth Israel doth neither slumber nor sleep. The Lord is thy keeper. The Lord is thy shade upon thy right hand. The sun shall not smite thee by day, nor the moon by night. The Lord shall keep thee from all evil. He shall keep thy soul. The Lord shall guard thy going out and thy coming in, from this time forth and forevermore." Amen.

All. Amen.

(Mrs. Frank *puts down the prayer book and goes to get the food and wine.* Margot *helps her.* Mr. Frank *takes the men's hats and puts them aside.*)

Dussel (*Rising*). That was very moving.

Anne (Pulling him back). It isn't over yet!

Mrs. Van Daan. Sit down! Sit down!

Anne. There's a lot more, songs and presents.

Dussel. Presents?

Mrs. Frank. Not this year, unfortunately.

Mrs. Van Daan. But always on Hanukkah everyone gives presents . . . everyone!

---

18. **Hanukkah** (hä′nə-kə): a Jewish holiday, celebrated in December and lasting eight days.

19. **menorah** (mə-nôr′ə): a candleholder with nine branches, used in the celebration of Hanukkah.

Dussel. Like our St. Nicholas's Day.[20] (*There is a chorus of "no's" from the group.*)

Mrs. Van Daan. No! Not like St. Nicholas! What kind of a Jew are you that you don't know Hanukkah?

Mrs. Frank (*As she brings the food*). I remember particularly the candles . . . First one, as we have tonight. Then the second night you light two candles, the next night three . . . and so on until you have eight candles burning. When there are eight candles it is truly beautiful.

Mrs. Van Daan. And the potato pancakes.

Mr. Van Daan. Don't talk about them!

Mrs. Van Daan. I make the best latkes[21] you ever tasted!

Mrs. Frank. Invite us all next year . . . in your own home.

Mr. Frank. God willing!

Mrs. Van Daan. God willing.

Margot. What I remember best is the presents we used to get when we were little . . . eight days of presents . . . and each day they got better and better.

Mrs. Frank (*Sitting down*). We are all here, alive. That is present enough.

Anne. No, it isn't. I've got something . . . (*She rushes into her room, hurriedly puts on a little hat improvised from the lamp shade, grabs a satchel bulging with parcels and comes running back.*)

Mrs. Frank. What is it?

Anne. Presents!

Mrs. Van Daan. Presents!

Dussel. Look!

Mr. Van Daan. What's she got on her head?

Peter. A lamp shade!

Anne (*She picks out one at random.*). This is for

Margot. (*She hands it to* Margot, *pulling her to her feet.*) Read it out loud.

Margot (*Reading*).

> You have never lost your temper.
>
> You never will, I fear,
>
> You are so good.
>
> But if you should,
>
> Put all your cross words here.

(*She tears open the package.*)

A new crossword puzzle book! Where did you get it?

Anne. It isn't new. It's one that you've done. But I rubbed it all out, and if you wait a little and forget, you can do it all over again.

Margot (*Sitting*). It's wonderful, Anne. Thank you. You'd never know it wasn't new.

(*From outside we hear the sound of a streetcar passing.*)

Anne (*With another gift*). Mrs. Van Daan.

Mrs. Van Daan (*Taking it*). This is awful . . . I haven't anything for anyone . . . I never thought . . .

Mr. Frank. This is all Anne's idea.

Mrs. Van Daan (*Holding up a bottle*). What is it?

Anne. It's hair shampoo. I took all the odds and ends of soap and mixed them with the last of my toilet water.

Mrs. Van Daan. Oh, Anneke!

Anne. I wanted to write a poem for all of them, but I didn't have time. (*Offering a large box to* Mr. Van Daan) Yours, Mr. Van Daan, is *really* something . . . something you want more than anything. (*As she waits for him to open it*) Look! Cigarettes!

---

20. **St. Nicholas's Day:** December 6, the day that Christian children in the Netherlands receive gifts.

21. **latkes** (lät′kəz): potato pancakes.

Mr. Van Daan. Cigarettes!

Anne. Two of them! Pim found some old pipe tobacco in the pocket lining of his coat . . . and we made them . . . or rather, Pim did.

Mrs. Van Daan. Let me see . . . Well, look at that! Light it, Putti! Light it.

(Mr. Van Daan *hesitates.*)

Anne. It's tobacco, really it is! There's a little fluff in it, but not much.

(*Everyone watches intently as* Mr. Van Daan *cautiously lights it. The cigarette flares up. Everyone laughs.*)

Peter. It works!

Mrs. Van Daan. Look at him.

Mr. Van Daan (*Spluttering*). Thank you, Anne. Thank you.

(Anne *rushes back to her satchel for another present.*)

Anne (*Handing her mother a piece of paper*). For Mother, Hanukkah greeting. (*She pulls her mother to her feet.*)

Mrs. Frank (*She reads*). "Here's an I.O.U. that I promise to pay. Ten hours of doing whatever you say. Signed, Anne Frank." (*Mrs. Frank, touched, takes* Anne *in her arms, holding her close.*)

Dussel (*To* Anne). Ten hours of doing what you're told? Anything you're told?

Anne. That's right.

Dussel. You wouldn't want to sell that, Mrs. Frank?

Mrs. Frank. Never! This is the most precious gift I've ever had!

(*She sits, showing her present to the others.* Anne *hurries back to the satchel and pulls out a scarf, the scarf that* Mr. Frank *found in the first scene.*)

Anne (*Offering it to her father*). For Pim.

Mr. Frank. Anneke . . . I wasn't supposed to have a present! (*He takes it, unfolding it and showing it to the others.*)

Anne. It's a muffler . . . to put round your neck . . . like an ascot, you know. I made it myself out of odds and ends . . . I knitted it in the dark each night, after I'd gone to bed. I'm afraid it looks better in the dark!

Mr. Frank (*Putting it on*). It's fine. It fits me perfectly. Thank you, Annele.

(Anne *hands* Peter *a ball of paper, with a string attached to it.*)

Anne. That's for Mouschi.

Peter (*Rising to bow*). On behalf of Mouschi, I thank you.

Anne (*Hesitant, handing him a gift*). And . . . this is yours . . . from Mrs. Quack Quack. (*As he holds it gingerly in his hands*) Well . . . open it . . . Aren't you going to open it?

Peter. I'm scared to. I know something's going to jump out and hit me.

Anne. No. It's nothing like that, really.

Mrs. Van Daan (*As he is opening it*). What is it, Peter? Go on. Show it.

Anne (*Excitedly*). It's a safety razor!

Dussel. A what?

Anne. A razor!

Mrs. Van Daan (*Looking at it*). You didn't make that out of odds and ends.

Anne (*To* Peter). Miep got it for me. It's not new. It's second-hand. But you really do need a razor now.

Dussel. For what?

Anne. Look on his upper lip . . . you can see the beginning of a mustache.

Dussel. He wants to get rid of that? Put a little milk on it and let the cat lick it off.

Peter (*Starting for his room*). Think you're funny, don't you.

Dussel. Look! He can't wait! He's going in to try it!

I simply can't imagine the world will ever be normal again for us. I do talk about "after the war," but it's as if I were talking about a castle in the air, something that can never come true.

from The Diary of Anne Frank, *November 8, 1943*

Peter. I'm going to give Mouschi his present! (*He goes to his room, slamming the door behind him.*)

Mr. Van Daan (*Disgustedly*). Mouschi, Mouschi, Mouschi.

(*In the distance we hear a dog persistently barking. Anne brings a gift to Dussel.*)

Anne. And last but never least, my roommate, Mr. Dussel.

Dussel. For me? You have something for me? (*He opens the small box she gives him.*)

Anne. I made them myself.

Dussel (*Puzzled*). Capsules! Two capsules!

Anne. They're ear-plugs!

Dussel. Ear-plugs?

Anne. To put in your ears so you won't hear me when I thrash around at night. I saw them advertised in a magazine. They're not real ones . . . I made them out of cotton and candle wax. Try them . . . See if they don't work . . . see if you can hear me talk . . .

Dussel (*Putting them in his ears*). Wait now until I get them in . . . so.

Anne. Are you ready?

Dussel. Huh?

Anne. Are you ready?

Dussel. Good God! They've gone inside! I can't get them out! (*They laugh as Mr. Dussel jumps about, trying to shake the plugs out of his ears. Finally he gets them out. Putting them away.*) Thank you, Anne! Thank you!

(*Together*)

    Mr. Van Daan. A real Hanukkah!

    Mrs. Van Daan. Wasn't it cute of her?

Mrs. Frank. I don't know when she did it.

Margot. I love my present.

Anne (*Sitting at the table*). And now let's have the song, Father . . . please . . . (*To Dussel*) Have you heard the Hanukkah song, Mr. Dussel? The song is the whole thing! (*She sings*) "Oh, Hanukkah! Oh Hanukkah! The sweet celebration . . . "

Mr. Frank (*Quieting her*). I'm afraid, Anne, we shouldn't sing that song tonight. (*To Dussel*) It's a song of jubilation, of rejoicing. One is apt to become too enthusiastic.

Anne. Oh, please, please. Let's sing the song. I promise not to shout!

Mr. Frank. Very well. But quietly now . . . I'll keep an eye on you and when . . .

(*As Anne starts to sing, she is interrupted by Dussel, who is snorting and wheezing.*)

Dussel (*Pointing to Peter*). You . . . You! (*Peter is coming from his bedroom, ostentatiously holding a bulge in his coat as if he were holding his cat, and dangling Anne's present before it.*) How many times . . . I told you . . . Out! Out!

Mr. Van Daan (*Going to Peter*). What's the matter with you? Haven't you any sense? Get that cat out of here.

Peter (*Innocently*). Cat?

Mr. Van Daan. You heard me. Get it out of here!

Peter. I have no cat. (*Delighted with his joke, he opens his coat and pulls out a bath towel. The group at the table laugh, enjoying the joke.*)

Dussel (*Still wheezing*). It doesn't need to be the cat . . . his clothes are enough . . . when he comes out of that room . . .

Mr. Van Daan. Don't worry. You won't be bothered any more. We're getting rid of it.

Dussel. At last you listen to me. (*He goes off into his bedroom.*)

WORDS TO KNOW

jubilation (jōō′ bə-lā′ shən) *n.* rejoicing; a celebration or expression of joy
ostentatiously (ŏs′ tĕn-tā′ shəs-lē) *adv.* with great show or exaggeration

Mr. Van Daan (*Calling after him*). I'm not doing it for you. That's all in your mind . . . all of it! (*He starts back to his place at the table.*) I'm doing it because I'm sick of seeing that cat eat all our food.

Peter. That's not true! I only give him bones . . . scraps . . .

Mr. Van Daan. Don't tell me! He gets fatter every day! Damn cat looks better than any of us. Out he goes tonight!

Peter. No! No!

Anne. Mr. Van Daan, you can't do that! That's Peter's cat. Peter loves that cat.

Mrs. Frank (*Quietly*). Anne.

Peter (*To Mr. Van Daan*). If he goes, I go.

Mr. Van Daan. Go! Go!

Mrs. Van Daan. You're not going and the cat's not going! Now please . . . this is Hanukkah . . . Hanukkah . . . this is the time to celebrate . . . What's the matter with all of you? Come on, Anne. Let's have the song.

Anne (*Singing*). "Oh, Hanukkah! Oh, Hanukkah! The sweet celebration."

Mr. Frank (*Rising*). I think we should first blow out the candle . . . then we'll have something for tomorrow night.

Margot. But, Father, you're supposed to let it burn itself out.

Mr. Frank. I'm sure that God understands shortages. (*Before blowing it out*) "Praised be Thou, oh Lord our God, who hast sustained us and permitted us to celebrate this joyous festival."

(*He is about to blow out the candle when suddenly there is a crash of something falling below. They all freeze in horror, motionless. For a few seconds there is complete silence. Mr. Frank slips off his shoes. The others noiselessly follow his example. Mr. Frank turns out a light near him. He motions to* Peter *to turn off the center lamp.* Peter *tries to reach it, realizes he cannot and gets up on a chair. Just as he is touching the lamp he loses his balance. The chair goes out from under him. He falls. The iron lamp shade crashes to the floor. There is a sound of feet below, running down the stairs.*)

Mr. Van Daan (*Under his breath*). God Almighty! (*The only light left comes from the Hanukkah candle.* Dussel *comes from his room.* Mr. Frank *creeps over to the stairwell and stands listening. The dog is heard barking excitedly.*) Do you hear anything?

Mr. Frank (*In a whisper*). No. I think they've gone.

Mrs. Van Daan. It's the Green Police. They've found us.

Mr. Frank. If they had, they wouldn't have left. They'd be up here by now.

Mrs. Van Daan. I know it's the Green Police. They've gone to get help. That's all. They'll be back!

Mr. Van Daan. Or it may have been the Gestapo,[22] looking for papers . . .

Mr. Frank (*Interrupting*). Or a thief, looking for money.

Mrs. Van Daan. We've got to do something . . . Quick! Quick! Before they come back.

Mr. Van Daan. There isn't anything to do. Just wait.

(Mr. Frank *holds up his hand for them to be quiet. He is listening intently. There is complete silence as they all strain to hear any sound from below. Suddenly* Anne *begins to sway. With a low cry she falls to the floor in a faint.* Mrs. Frank *goes to her quickly, sitting beside her on the floor and taking her in her arms.*)

---

22. **Gestapo** (gə-stä′pō): the Nazi secret police force, known for its terrorism and brutality.

Mrs. Frank. Get some water, please! Get some water!

(*Margot starts for the sink.*)

Mr. Van Daan (*Grabbing* Margot). No! No! No one's going to run water!

Mr. Frank. If they've found us, they've found us. Get the water. (Margot *starts again for the sink.* Mr. Frank, *getting a flashlight*) I'm going down.

(Margot *rushes to him, clinging to him.* Anne *struggles to consciousness.*)

Margot. No, Father, no! There may be someone there, waiting . . . It may be a trap!

Mr. Frank. This is Saturday. There is no way for us to know what has happened until Miep or Mr. Kraler comes on Monday morning. We cannot live with this uncertainty.

Margot. Don't go, Father!

Mrs. Frank. Hush, darling, hush. (Mr. Frank *slips quietly out, down the steps and out through the door below.*) Margot! Stay close to me.

(Margot *goes to her mother.*)

Mr. Van Daan. Shush! Shush!

(Mrs. Frank *whispers to* Margot *to get the water.* Margot *goes for it.*)

Mrs. Van Daan. Putti, where's our money? Get our money. I hear you can buy the Green Police off, so much a head. Go upstairs quick! Get the money!

Mr. Van Daan. Keep still!

Mrs. Van Daan (*Kneeling before him, pleading*). Do you want to be dragged off to a concentration camp? Are you going to stand there and wait for them to come up and get you? Do something, I tell you!

Mr. Van Daan (*Pushing her aside*). Will you keep still! (*He goes over to the stairwell to listen.* Peter *goes to his mother, helping her*

up onto the sofa. There is a second of silence, then Anne *can stand it no longer.*)

Anne. Someone go after Father! Make Father come back!

Peter (*Starting for the door*). I'll go.

Mr. Van Daan. Haven't you done enough? (*He pushes* Peter *roughly away. In his anger against his father* Peter *grabs a chair as if to hit him with it, then puts it down, burying his face in his hands.* Mrs. Frank *begins to pray softly.*)

Anne. Please, please, Mr. Van Daan. Get Father.

Mr. Van Daan. Quiet! Quiet!

(Anne *is shocked into silence.* Mrs. Frank *pulls her closer, holding her protectively in her arms.*)

Mrs. Frank (*Softly, praying*). "I lift up mine eyes unto the mountains, from whence cometh my help. My help cometh from the Lord who made heaven and earth. He will not suffer thy foot to be moved . . . He that keepeth thee will not slumber . . . " (*She stops as she hears someone coming. They all watch the door tensely.* Mr. Frank *comes quietly in.* Anne *rushes to him, holding him tight.*)

Mr. Frank. It was a thief. That noise must have scared him away.

Mrs. Van Daan. Thank God.

Mr. Frank. He took the cash box. And the radio. He ran away in such a hurry that he didn't stop to shut the street door. It was swinging wide open. (*A breath of relief sweeps over them*) I think it would be good to have some light.

Margot. Are you sure it's all right?

Mr. Frank. The danger has passed. (Margot *goes to light the small lamp.*) Don't be so terrified, Anne. We're safe.

Dussel. Who says the danger has passed? Don't you realize we are in greater danger than ever?

Mr. Frank. Mr. Dussel, will you be still!

(Mr. Frank *takes* Anne *back to the table, making her sit down with him, trying to calm her.*)

Dussel (*Pointing to* Peter). Thanks to this clumsy fool, there's someone now who knows we're up here! Someone now knows we're up here, hiding!

Mrs. Van Daan (*Going to* Dussel). Someone knows we're here, yes. But who is the someone? A thief! A thief! You think a thief is going to go to the Green Police and say . . . I was robbing a place the other night and I heard a noise up over my head? You think a thief is going to do that?

Dussel. Yes. I think he will.

Mrs. Van Daan (*Hysterically*). You're crazy! (*She stumbles back to her seat at the table.* Peter *follows protectively, pushing* Dussel *aside.*)

Dussel. I think some day he'll be caught and then he'll make a bargain with the Green Police . . . if they'll let him off, he'll tell them where some Jews are hiding!

(*He goes off into the bedroom. There is a second of <u>appalled</u> silence.*)

Mr. Van Daan. He's right.

Anne. Father, let's get out of here! We can't stay here now . . . Let's go . . .

Mr. Van Daan. Go! Where?

Mrs. Frank (*Sinking into her chair at the table*). Yes. Where?

Mr. Frank (*Rising, to them all*). Have we lost all faith? All courage? A moment ago we thought that they'd come for us. We were sure it was the end. But it wasn't the end. We're alive, safe. (Mr. Van Daan *goes to the table and sits.* Mr. Frank *prays.*) "We thank Thee, oh Lord our God, that in Thy infinite mercy Thou hast again seen fit to spare us." (*He blows out the candle, then turns to* Anne) Come on, Anne. The song! Let's have the song! (*He starts to sing.* Anne *finally starts falteringly to sing, as* Mr. Frank *urges her on. Her voice is hardly audible at first.*)

Anne (*Singing*). "Oh, Hanukkah! Oh, Hanukkah! The sweet . . . celebration . . . " (*As she goes on singing, the others gradually join in, their voices still shaking with fear.* Mrs. Van Daan *sobs as she sings.*)

Group. "Around the feast . . . we . . . gather
In complete . . . jubilation . . .
Happiest of sea . . . sons
Now is here.
Many are the reasons for good cheer."

(Dussel *comes from the bedroom. He comes over to the table, standing beside* Margot, *listening to them as they sing.*)

"Together
We'll weather
Whatever tomorrow may bring."

(*As they sing on with growing courage, the lights start to dim.*)

"So hear us rejoicing
And merrily voicing
The Hanukkah song that we sing.
Hoy!"

(*The lights are out. The curtain starts slowly to fall.*)

"Hear us rejoicing
And merrily voicing
The Hanukkah song that we sing."

(*They are still singing, as the curtain falls.*)

The Curtain Falls

WORDS
TO   **appalled** (ə-pôld') *adj.* horrified; shocked **appall** *v.*
KNOW

Connect to the Literature

1. **What Do You Think?** How do you feel about Anne at the end of Scene 5? Have your feelings toward her changed? Explain your answer.

Comprehension Check
- Why does Anne wake up screaming?
- How does Anne behave when her mother tries to comfort her?
- What event occurs as they are all celebrating Hanukkah?

Think Critically

2. **ACTIVE READING** **STORY MAPPING**
Create a story map for Scene 4 and a story map for Scene 5 in your 📖 **READER'S NOTEBOOK**. How does Anne's behavior in Scene 4 relate to the conflict between Anne and her mother that was shown earlier in the play? Do you think that Anne is trying to hurt her mother? Explain your answer.

3. Scene 5 begins with a prayer and ends with a song. How do the words of the prayer and the song relate to the situation of the people in hiding?

4. What role does faith play in helping Anne, her family, and their friends overcome their fear?

Think About:
- the Hanukkah candle that remains lit
- Mrs. Frank's prayer
- the party's singing of the Hanukkah song after they realize they are safe

Extend Interpretations

5. **What If?** Imagine that Mr. Frank had encountered the thief when he went to investigate the noise. Discuss what might have happened and how the other characters might have responded.

6. **Connect to Life** In Scene 4, Anne says that she is trying to change her bad qualities and behavior. Do you think it is possible to change in this way? Explain your opinion.

Literary Analysis

CONFLICT In a literary work, a struggle between opposing forces is called the **conflict.** In an **external conflict,** a character struggles against another person or some other outside force. **Internal conflict,** on the other hand, takes place within a character. In *The Diary of Anne Frank,* Anne experiences inner conflict about her relationship with her mother.

Paired Activity Make a chart like the one shown. Working with a partner, go back through the play and list as many examples of each kind of conflict as you can. (The story maps in your 📖 **READER'S NOTEBOOK** will help you.) When you have finished your chart, discuss the following question with a larger group:
- How does the situation of living in hiding intensify the conflicts among the characters and within Anne?

External Conflict	Internal Conflict
the Nazis' persecution of the Jews	Anne's feelings toward her mother
Mrs. Frank and Mr. Van Daan	

Act Two

SCENE 1

In the darkness we hear Anne's *voice, again reading from the diary.*

Anne's Voice. Saturday, the first of January, nineteen forty-four. Another new year has begun and we find ourselves still in our hiding place. We have been here now for one year, five months, and twenty-five days. It seems that our life is at a standstill.

The curtain rises on the scene. It is late afternoon. Everyone is bundled up against the cold. In the main room Mrs. Frank *is taking down the laundry which is hung across the back.* Mr. Frank *sits in the chair down left, reading.* Margot *is lying on the couch with a blanket over her and the many-colored knitted scarf around her throat.* Anne *is seated at the center table, writing in her diary.* Peter, Mr. *and* Mrs. Van Daan, *and* Dussel *are all in their own rooms, reading or lying down.*

As the lights dim on, Anne's *voice continues, without a break.*

Anne's Voice. We are all a little thinner. The Van Daans' "discussions" are as violent as ever. Mother still does not understand me. But then I don't understand her either. There is one great change, however. A change in myself. I read somewhere that girls of my age don't feel quite certain of themselves. That they become quiet within and begin to think of the miracle that is taking place in their bodies. I think that what is happening to me is so wonderful . . . not only what can be seen, but what is taking place inside. Each time it has happened I have a feeling that I have a sweet secret. (*We hear the chimes and then a hymn being played on the carillon outside.*) And in spite of any pain, I long for the time when I shall feel that secret within me again.

(*The buzzer of the door below suddenly sounds. Everyone is startled,* Mr. Frank *tiptoes cautiously to the top of the steps and listens. Again the buzzer sounds, in* Miep's *V-for-Victory signal.*)

Mr. Frank. It's Miep! (*He goes quickly down the steps to unbolt the door.* Mrs. Frank *calls upstairs to the* Van Daans *and then to* Peter.)

Mrs. Frank. Wake up, everyone! Miep is here! (Anne *quickly puts her diary away.* Margot *sits up, pulling the blanket around her shoulders.* Mr. Dussel *sits on the edge of his bed, listening,* _disgruntled_. Miep *comes up the steps, followed by* Mr. Kraler. *They bring flowers, books, newspapers, etc.* Anne *rushes to* Miep, *throwing her arms affectionately around her.*) Miep . . . and Mr. Kraler . . . What a delightful surprise!

Mr. Kraler. We came to bring you New Year's greetings.

Mrs. Frank. You shouldn't . . . you should have at least one day to yourselves. (*She goes quickly to the stove and brings down teacups and tea for all of them.*)

Anne. Don't say that, it's so wonderful to see them! (*Sniffing at* Miep's *coat*) I can smell the wind and the cold on your clothes.

Miep (*Giving her the flowers*). There you are. (*Then to* Margot, *feeling her forehead*) How are you, Margot? . . . Feeling any better?

489

*I see my life up to New Year's 1944 as if
I were looking through a powerful magnifying
glass. When I was home, my life was filled with
sunshine. Then, in the middle of 1942,
everything changed overnight...*

from The Diary of Anne Frank, *March 7, 1944*

Margot. I'm all right.

Anne. We filled her full of every kind of pill so she won't cough and make a noise. (*She runs into her room to put the flowers in water. Mr. and* Mrs. Van Daan *come from upstairs. Outside there is the sound of a band playing.*)

Mrs. Van Daan. Well, hello, Miep. Mr. Kraler.

Mr. Kraler (*Giving a bouquet of flowers to* Mrs. Van Daan). With my hope for peace in the New Year.

Peter (*Anxiously*). Miep, have you seen Mouschi? Have you seen him anywhere around?

Miep. I'm sorry, Peter. I asked everyone in the neighborhood had they seen a gray cat. But they said no.

(Mrs. Frank *gives* Miep *a cup of tea. Mr. Frank comes up the steps, carrying a small cake on a plate.*)

Mr. Frank. Look what Miep's brought for us!

Mrs. Frank (*Taking it*). A cake!

Mr. Van Daan. A cake! (*He pinches* Miep's *cheeks gaily and hurries up to the cupboard.*) I'll get some plates.

(Dussel, *in his room, hastily puts a coat on and starts out to join the others.*)

Mrs. Frank. Thank you, Miepia. You shouldn't have done it. You must have used all of your sugar ration for weeks. (*Giving it to* Mrs. Van Daan) It's beautiful, isn't it?

Mrs. Van Daan. It's been ages since I even saw a cake. Not since you brought us one last year. (*Without looking at the cake, to* Miep) Remember? Don't you remember, you gave us one on New Year's Day? Just this time last year? I'll never forget it because you had "Peace in nineteen forty-three" on it. (*She looks at the cake and reads.*) "Peace in nineteen forty-four!"

Miep. Well, it has to come sometime, you know. (*As* Dussel *comes from his room*) Hello, Mr. Dussel.

Mr. Kraler. How are you?

Mr. Van Daan (*Bringing plates and a knife*). Here's the knife, liefje. Now, how many of us are there?

Miep. None for me, thank you.

Mr. Frank. Oh, please. You must.

Miep. I couldn't.

Mr. Van Daan. Good! That leaves one . . . two . . . three . . . seven of us.

Dussel. Eight! Eight! It's the same number as it always is!

Mr. Van Daan. I left Margot out. I take it for granted Margot won't eat any.

Anne. Why wouldn't she!

Mrs. Frank. I think it won't harm her.

Mr. Van Daan. All right! All right! I just didn't want her to start coughing again, that's all.

Dussel. And please, Mrs. Frank should cut the cake.

(*Together*)

  Mr. Van Daan. What's the difference?

  Mrs. Van Daan. It's not Mrs. Frank's cake, is it, Miep? It's for all of us.

Dussel. Mrs. Frank divides things better.

(*Together*)

  Mrs. Van Daan (*Going to* Dussel). What are you trying to say?

  Mr. Van Daan. Oh, come on! Stop wasting time!

Mrs. Van Daan (*To* Dussel). Don't I always give everybody exactly the same? Don't I?

Mr. Van Daan. Forget it, Kerli.

Mrs. Van Daan. No. I want an answer! Don't I?

Dussel. Yes. Yes. Everybody gets exactly the same . . . except Mr. Van Daan always gets a little bit more.

(Mr. Van Daan *advances on* Dussel, *the knife still in his hand.*)

Mr. Van Daan. That's a lie!

(Dussel *retreats before the onslaught of the* Van Daans.)

Mr. Frank. Please, please! (*Then to* Miep) You see what a little sugar cake does to us? It goes right to our heads!

Mr. Van Daan (*Handing* Mrs. Frank *the knife*). Here you are, Mrs. Frank.

Mrs. Frank. Thank you. (*Then to* Miep *as she goes to the table to cut the cake*) Are you sure you won't have some?

Miep (*Drinking her tea*). No, really, I have to go in a minute.

(*The sound of the band fades out in the distance.*)

Peter (*To* Miep). Maybe Mouschi went back to our house . . . they say that cats . . . Do you ever get over there . . . ? I mean . . . do you suppose you could . . . ?

Miep. I'll try, Peter. The first minute I get I'll try. But I'm afraid, with him gone a week . . .

Dussel. Make up your mind, already someone has had a nice big dinner from that cat!

(Peter *is furious,* <u>inarticulate</u>. *He starts toward* Dussel *as if to hit him.* Mr. Frank *stops him.* Mrs. Frank *speaks quickly to ease the situation.*)

Mrs. Frank (*To* Miep). This is delicious, Miep!

Mrs. Van Daan (*Eating hers*). Delicious!

Mr. Van Daan (*Finishing it in one gulp*). Dirk's in luck to get a girl who can bake like this!

Miep (*Putting down her empty teacup*). I have to run. Dirk's taking me to a party tonight.

Anne. How heavenly! Remember now what everyone is wearing, and what you have to eat and everything, so you can tell us tomorrow.

Miep. I'll give you a full report! Good-bye, everyone!

Mr. Van Daan (*To* Miep). Just a minute. There's something I'd like you to do for me. (*He hurries off up the stairs to his room.*)

Mrs. Van Daan (*Sharply*). Putti, where are you going? (*She rushes up the stairs after him, calling hysterically*). What do you want? Putti, what are you going to do?

Miep (*To* Peter). What's wrong?

Peter (*His sympathy is with his mother.*) Father says he's going to sell her fur coat. She's crazy about that old fur coat.

Dussel. Is it possible? Is it possible that anyone is so silly as to worry about a fur coat in times like this?

Peter. It's none of your darn business . . . and if you say one more thing . . . I'll, I'll take you and I'll . . . I mean it . . . I'll . . .

(*There is a piercing scream from* Mrs. Van Daan *above. She grabs at the fur coat as* Mr. Van Daan *is starting downstairs with it.*)

Mrs. Van Daan. No! No! No! Don't you dare take that! You hear? It's mine! (*Downstairs* Peter *turns away, embarrassed, miserable.*) My father gave me that! You didn't give it to me. You have no right. Let go of it . . . you hear?

(Mr. Van Daan *pulls the coat from her hands and hurries downstairs.* Mrs. Van Daan *sinks to the floor, sobbing. As* Mr. Van Daan *comes into the main room the others look away, embarrassed for him.*)

Mr. Van Daan (*To* Mr. Kraler). Just a little—discussion over the advisability of selling this coat. As I have often reminded Mrs. Van Daan, it's very selfish of her to keep it when people outside are in such desperate need of clothing . . . (*He gives the coat to* Miep.) So

WORDS TO KNOW **inarticulate** (ĭn′ är-tĭk′ yə-lĭt) *adj.* speechless; unable to speak effectively or understandably if you will please to sell it for us? It should fetch a good price. And by the way, will you get me cigarettes. I don't care what kind they are . . . get all you can.

Miep. It's terribly difficult to get them, Mr. Van Daan. But I'll try. Good-bye.

(*She goes.* Mr. Frank *follows her down the steps to bolt the door after her.* Mrs. Frank *gives* Mr. Kraler *a cup of tea.*)

Mrs. Frank. Are you sure you won't have some cake, Mr. Kraler?

Mr. Kraler. I'd better not.

Mr. Van Daan. You're still feeling badly? What does your doctor say?

Mr. Kraler. I haven't been to him.

Mrs. Frank. Now, Mr. Kraler! . . .

Mr. Kraler (*Sitting at the table*). Oh, I tried. But you can't get near a doctor these days . . . they're so busy. After weeks I finally managed to get one on the telephone. I told him I'd like an appointment . . . I wasn't feeling very well. You know what he answers . . . over the telephone . . . Stick out your tongue! (*They laugh.* He turns to Mr. Frank *as* Mr. Frank *comes back.*) I have some contracts here . . . I wonder if you'd look over them with me . . .

Mr. Frank (*Putting out his hand*). Of course.

Mr. Kraler (*He rises*). If we could go downstairs . . . (Mr. Frank *starts ahead,* Mr. Kraler *speaks to the others*) Will you forgive us? I won't keep him but a minute. (*He starts to follow* Mr. Frank *down the steps.*)

Margot (*With sudden foreboding*). What's happened? Something's happened! Hasn't it, Mr. Kraler?

(Mr. Kraler *stops and comes back, trying to reassure* Margot *with a pretense of casualness.*)

Mr. Kraler. No, really. I want your father's advice . . .

Margot. Something's gone wrong! I know it!

Mr. Frank (*Coming back, to* Mr. Kraler). If it's something that concerns us here, it's better that we all hear it.

Mr. Kraler (*Turning to him, quietly*). But . . . the children . . . ?

Mr. Frank. What they'd imagine would be worse than any reality.

(*As* Mr. Kraler *speaks, they all listen with intense apprehension.* Mrs. Van Daan *comes down the stairs and sits on the bottom step.*)

Mr. Kraler. It's a man in the storeroom . . . I don't know whether or not you remember him . . . Carl, about fifty, heavy-set, near-sighted . . . He came with us just before you left.

Mr. Frank. He was from Utrecht?

Mr. Kraler. That's the man. A couple of weeks ago, when I was in the storeroom, he closed the door and asked me . . . how's Mr. Frank? What do you hear from Mr. Frank? I told him I only knew there was a rumor that you were in Switzerland. He said he'd heard that rumor too, but he thought I might know something more. I didn't pay any attention to it . . . but then a thing happened yesterday . . . He'd brought some invoices to the office for me to sign. As I was going through them, I looked up. He was standing staring at the bookcase . . . your bookcase. He said he thought he remembered a door there . . . Wasn't there a door there that used to go up to the loft? Then he told me he wanted more money. Twenty guilders[23] more a week.

Mr. Van Daan. Blackmail!

Mr. Frank. Twenty guilders? Very modest blackmail.

---

23. **guilders** (gĭl′dərz): the basic monetary unit of the Netherlands at the time.

WORDS TO KNOW   **foreboding** (fôr-bōd′ ĭng) *n.* a feeling that something, especially bad or harmful, is about to happen

493

Mr. Van Daan. That's just the beginning.

Dussel (*Coming to* Mr. Frank). You know what I think? He was the thief who was down there that night. That's how he knows we're here.

Mr. Frank (*To* Mr. Kraler). How was it left? What did you tell him?

Mr. Kraler. I said I had to think about it. What shall I do? Pay him the money? . . . Take a chance on firing him . . . or what? I don't know.

Dussel (*Frantic*). For God's sake don't fire him! Pay him what he asks . . . keep him here where you can have your eye on him.

Mr. Frank. Is it so much that he's asking? What are they paying nowadays?

Mr. Kraler. He could get it in a war plant. But this isn't a war plant. Mind you, I don't know if he really knows . . . or if he doesn't know.

Mr. Frank. Offer him half. Then we'll soon find out if it's blackmail or not.

Dussel. And if it is? We've got to pay it, haven't we? Anything he asks we've got to pay!

Mr. Frank. Let's decide that when the time comes.

Mr. Kraler. This may be all my imagination. You get to a point, these days, where you suspect everyone and everything. Again and again . . . on some simple look or word, I've found myself . . .

(*The telephone rings in the office below.*)

Mrs. Van Daan (*Hurrying to* Mr. Kraler). There's the telephone! What does that mean, the telephone ringing on a holiday?

Mr. Kraler. That's my wife. I told her I had to go over some papers in my office . . . to call me there when she got out of church. (*He starts out.*) I'll offer him half then. Good-bye . . . we'll hope for the best!

(*The group call their good-byes half-heartedly.*

Mr. Frank *follows* Mr. Kraler, *to bolt the door below. During the following scene,* Mr. Frank *comes back up and stands listening, disturbed.*)

Dussel (*To* Mr. Van Daan). You can thank your son for this . . . smashing the light! I tell you, it's just a question of time now. (*He goes to the window at the back and stands looking out.*)

Margot. Sometimes I wish the end would come . . . whatever it is.

Mrs. Frank (*Shocked*). Margot!

(Anne *goes to* Margot, *sitting beside her on the couch with her arms around her.*)

Margot. Then at least we'd know where we were.

Mrs. Frank. You should be ashamed of yourself! Talking that way! Think how lucky we are! Think of the thousands dying in the war, every day. Think of the people in concentration camps.

Anne (*Interrupting*). What's the good of that? What's the good of thinking of misery when you're already miserable? That's stupid!

Mrs. Frank. Anne!

(*As* Anne *goes on raging at her mother,* Mrs. Frank *tries to break in, in an effort to quiet her.*)

Anne. We're young, Margot and Peter and I! You grown-ups have had your chance! But look at us . . . If we begin thinking of all the horror in the world, we're lost! We're trying to hold onto some kind of ideals . . . when everything . . . ideals, hopes . . . everything, are being destroyed! It isn't our fault that the world is in such a mess! We weren't around when all this started! So don't try to take it out on us!

(*She rushes off to her room, slamming the door after her. She picks up a brush from the chest and hurls it to the floor. Then she sits on the settee, trying to control her anger.*)

Mr. Van Daan. She talks as if we started the war! Did we start the war? (*He spots* Anne's *cake. As he starts to take it,* Peter *anticipates him.*)

Peter. She left her cake. (*He starts for* Anne's *room with the cake. There is silence in the main room.* Mrs. Van Daan *goes up to her room, followed by* Mr. Van Daan. Dussel *stays looking out the window.* Mr. Frank *brings* Mrs. Frank *her cake. She eats it slowly, without relish.* Mr. Frank *takes his cake to* Margot *and sits quietly on the sofa beside her.* Peter *stands in the doorway of* Anne's *darkened room, looking at her, then makes a little movement to let her know he is there.* Anne *sits up, quickly, trying to hide the signs of her tears.* Peter *holds out the cake to her.*) You left this.

Anne (*Dully*). Thanks.

(Peter *starts to go out, then comes back.*)

Peter. I thought you were fine just now. You know just how to talk to them. You know just how to say it. I'm no good . . . I never can think . . . especially when I'm mad . . . That Dussel . . . when he said that about Mouschi . . . someone eating him . . . all I could think is . . . I wanted to hit him. I wanted to give him such a . . . a . . . that he'd . . . That's what I used to do when there was an argument at school . . . That's the way I . . . but here . . . And an old man like that . . . it wouldn't be so good.

Anne. You're making a big mistake about me. I do it all wrong. I say too much. I go too far. I hurt people's feelings . . .

(Dussel *leaves the window, going to his room.*)

Peter. I think you're just fine . . . What I want to say . . . if it wasn't for you around here, I don't know. What I mean . . .

(Peter *is interrupted by* Dussel's *turning on the light.* Dussel *stands in the doorway, startled to see* Peter. Peter *advances toward him forbiddingly.* Dussel *backs out of the room.* Peter *closes the door on him.*)

Anne. Do you mean it, Peter? Do you really mean it?

Peter. I said it, didn't I?

Anne. Thank you, Peter!

(*In the main room* Mr. *and* Mrs. Frank *collect the dishes and take them to the sink, washing them.* Margot *lies down again on the couch.* Dussel, *lost, wanders into* Peter's *room and takes up a book, starting to read.*)

Peter (*Looking at the photographs on the wall*). You've got quite a collection.

Anne. Wouldn't you like some in your room? I could give you some. Heaven knows you spend enough time in there . . . doing heaven knows what . . .

Peter. It's easier. A fight starts, or an argument . . . I duck in there.

Anne. You're lucky, having a room to go to. His lordship is always here . . . I hardly ever get a minute alone. When they start in on me, I can't duck away. I have to stand there and take it.

Peter. You gave some of it back just now.

Anne. I get so mad. They've formed their opinions . . . about everything . . . but we . . . we're still trying to find out . . . We have problems here that no other people our age have ever had. And just as you think you've solved them, something comes along and bang! You have to start all over again.

Peter. At least you've got someone you can talk to.

Anne. Not really. Mother . . . I never discuss anything serious with her. She doesn't understand. Father's all right. We can talk about everything . . . everything but one thing. Mother. He simply won't talk about her. I don't think you can be really intimate with anyone if he holds something back, do you?

Peter. I think your father's fine.

Anne. Oh, he is, Peter! He is! He's the only one who's ever given me the feeling that I have any sense. But anyway, nothing can take the place of school and play and friends of your own age . . . or near your age . . . can it?

Peter. I suppose you miss your friends and all.

Anne. It isn't just . . . (*She breaks off, staring up at him for a second*). Isn't it funny, you and I? Here we've been seeing each other every minute for almost a year and a half, and this is the first time we've ever really talked. It helps a lot to have someone to talk to, don't you think? It helps you to let off steam.

Peter (*Going to the door*). Well, any time you want to let off steam, you can come into my room.

Anne (*Following him*). I can get up an awful lot of steam. You'll have to be careful how you say that.

Peter. It's all right with me.

Anne. Do you mean it?

Peter. I said it, didn't I?

(*He goes out. Anne stands in her doorway looking after him. As Peter gets to his door he stands for a minute looking back at her. Then he goes into his room. Dussel rises as he comes in, and quickly passes him, going out. He starts across for his room. Anne sees him coming, and pulls her door shut. Dussel turns back toward Peter's room.*

Peter pulls his door shut. Dussel stands there, bewildered, forlorn.

The scene slowly dims out. The curtain falls on the scene. Anne's voice comes over in the darkness . . . faintly at first, and then with growing strength.)

Anne's Voice. We've had bad news. The people from whom Miep got our ration books have been arrested. So we have had to cut down on our food. Our stomachs are so empty that they rumble and make strange noises, all in different keys. Mr. Van Daan's is deep and low, like a bass fiddle. Mine is high, whistling like a flute. As we all sit around waiting for supper, it's like an orchestra tuning up. It only needs Toscanini[24] to raise his baton and

we'd be off in the Ride of the Valkyries.[25] Monday, the sixth of March, nineteen forty-four. Mr. Kraler is in the hospital. It seems he has ulcers. Pim says we are his ulcers. Miep has to run the business and us too. The Americans have landed on the southern tip of Italy. Father looks for a quick finish to the war. Mr. Dussel is waiting every day for the warehouse man to demand more money. Have I been skipping too much from one subject to another? I can't help it. I feel that spring is coming. I feel it in my whole body and soul. I feel utterly confused. I am longing . . . so longing . . . for everything . . . for friends . . . for someone to talk to . . . someone who understands . . . someone young, who feels as I do . . .

(*As these last lines are being said, the curtain rises on the scene. The lights dim on. Anne's voice fades out.*)

SCENE 2

It is evening, after supper. From outside we hear the sound of children playing. The "grown-ups," with the exception of Mr. Van Daan, are all in the main room. Mrs. Frank is doing some mending, Mrs. Van Daan is reading a fashion magazine. Mr. Frank is going over business accounts. Dussel, in his dentist's jacket, is pacing up and down, impatient to get into his bedroom. Mr. Van Daan is upstairs working on a piece of embroidery in an embroidery frame.

In his room Peter is sitting before the mirror, smoothing his hair. As the scene goes on, he puts on his tie, brushes his coat and puts it on, preparing himself meticulously for a visit from

---

24. **Toscanini:** (tŏs´kə-nē´nē): Arturo Toscanini, a famous Italian orchestral conductor.

25. **Ride of the Valkyries** (văl-kîr´ēz): a moving passage from an opera by Richard Wagner, a German composer.

Anne. *On his wall are now hung some of* Anne's *motion picture stars.*

In her room Anne *too is getting dressed. She stands before the mirror in her slip, trying various ways of dressing her hair.* Margot *is seated on the sofa, hemming a skirt for* Anne *to wear.*

In the main room Dussel *can stand it no longer. He comes over, rapping sharply on the door of his and* Anne's *bedroom.*

Anne (*Calling to him*). No, no, Mr. Dussel! I am not dressed yet. (Dussel *walks away, furious, sitting down and burying his head in his hands.* Anne *turns to* Margot.) How is that? How does that look?

Margot (*Glancing at her briefly*). Fine.

Anne. You didn't even look.

Margot. Of course I did. It's fine.

Anne. Margot, tell me, am I terribly ugly?

Margot. Oh, stop fishing.

Anne. No. No. Tell me.

Margot. Of course you're not. You've got nice eyes . . . and a lot of animation, and . . .

Anne. A little vague, aren't you?

(*She reaches over and takes a brassière out of* Margot's *sewing basket. She holds it up to herself, studying the effect in the mirror. Outside,* Mrs. Frank, *feeling sorry for* Dussel, *comes over, knocking at the girls' door.*)

Mrs. Frank (*Outside*). May I come in?

Margot. Come in, Mother.

Mrs. Frank (*Shutting the door behind her*). Dr. Dussel's impatient to get in here.

Anne (*Still with the brassière*). Heavens, he takes the room for himself the entire day.

Mrs. Frank (*Gently*). Anne, dear, you're not going in again tonight to see Peter?

Anne (*Dignified*). That is my intention.

Mrs. Frank. But you've already spent a great deal of time in there today.

Anne. I was in there exactly twice. Once to get the dictionary, and then three-quarters of an hour before supper.

Mrs. Frank. Aren't you afraid you're disturbing him?

Anne. Mother, I have some intuition.

Mrs. Frank. Then may I ask you this much, Anne. Please don't shut the door when you go in.

Anne. You sound like Mrs. Van Daan! (*She throws the brassière back in* Margot's *sewing basket and picks up her blouse, putting it on.*)

Mrs. Frank. No. No. I don't mean to suggest anything wrong. I only wish that you wouldn't expose yourself to criticism . . . that you wouldn't give Mrs. Van Daan the opportunity to be unpleasant.

Anne. Mrs. Van Daan doesn't need an opportunity to be unpleasant!

Mrs. Frank. Everyone's on edge, worried about Mr. Kraler. This is one more thing . . .

Anne. I'm sorry, Mother. I'm going to Peter's room. I'm not going to let Petronella Van Daan spoil our friendship.

(Mrs. Frank *hesitates for a second, then goes out, closing the door after her. She gets a pack of playing cards and sits at the center table, playing solitaire. In* Anne's *room* Margot *hands the finished skirt to* Anne. *As* Anne *is putting it on,* Margot *takes off her high-heeled shoes and stuffs paper in the toes so that* Anne *can wear them.*)

Margot (*To* Anne). Why don't you two talk in the main room? It'd save a lot of trouble. It's hard on Mother, having to listen to those remarks from Mrs. Van Daan and not say a word.

Anne. Why doesn't she say a word? I think it's ridiculous to take it and take it.

Margot. You don't understand Mother at all, do you? She can't talk back. She's not like you. It's just not in her nature to fight back.

Anne. Anyway . . . the only one I worry about is you. I feel awfully guilty about you.

(*She sits on the stool near* Margot, *putting on* Margot's *high-heeled shoes.*)

Margot. What about?

Anne. I mean, every time I go into Peter's room, I have a feeling I may be hurting you. (Margot *shakes her head.*) I know if it were me, I'd be wild. I'd be desperately jealous, if it were me.

Margot. Well, I'm not.

Anne. You don't feel badly? Really? Truly? You're not jealous?

Margot. Of course I'm jealous . . . jealous that you've got something to get up in the morning for . . . But jealous of you and Peter? No.

(Anne *goes back to the mirror.*)

Anne. Maybe there's nothing to be jealous of. Maybe he doesn't really like me. Maybe I'm just taking the place of his cat . . . (*She picks up a pair of short white gloves, putting them on.*) Wouldn't you like to come in with us?

Margot. I have a book.

(*The sound of the children playing outside fades out. In the main room* Dussel *can stand it no longer. He jumps up, going to the bedroom door and knocking sharply.*)

Dussel. Will you please let me in my room!

Anne. Just a minute, dear, dear Mr. Dussel. (*She picks up her Mother's pink stole and adjusts it elegantly over her shoulders, then gives a last look in the mirror.*) Well, here I go . . . to run the gauntlet.[26] (*She starts out, followed by* Margot.)

Dussel (*As she appears—sarcastic*). Thank you so much.

(Dussel *goes into his room.* Anne *goes toward* Peter's *room, passing* Mrs. Van Daan *and her parents at the center table.*)

Mrs. Van Daan. My God, look at her! (Anne *pays no attention. She knocks at* Peter's *door.*) I don't know what good it is to have a son. I never see him. He wouldn't care if I killed myself. (Peter *opens the door and stands aside for* Anne *to come in.*) Just a minute, Anne. (*She goes to them at the door.*) I'd like to say a few words to my son. Do you mind? (Peter *and* Anne *stand waiting.*) Peter, I don't want you staying up till all hours tonight. You've got to have your sleep. You're a growing boy. You hear?

Mrs. Frank. Anne won't stay late. She's going to bed promptly at nine. Aren't you, Anne?

Anne. Yes, Mother . . . (*To* Mrs. Van Daan) May we go now?

Mrs. Van Daan. Are you asking me? I didn't know I had anything to say about it.

Mrs. Frank. Listen for the chimes, Anne dear.

(*The two young people go off into* Peter's *room, shutting the door after them.*)

Mrs. Van Daan (*To* Mrs. Frank). In my day it was the boys who called on the girls. Not the girls on the boys.

Mrs. Frank. You know how young people like to feel that they have secrets. Peter's room is the only place where they can talk.

Mrs. Van Daan. Talk! That's not what they called it when I was young.

(Mrs. Van Daan *goes off to the bathroom.* Margot *settles down to read her book.* Mr. Frank *puts his papers away and brings a chess game to the center table. He and* Mrs. Frank *start to play. In* Peter's *room,* Anne *speaks to* Peter, *indignant, humiliated.*)

Anne. Aren't they awful? Aren't they impossible? Treating us as if we were still in the nursery.

(*She sits on the cot.* Peter *gets a bottle of pop and two glasses.*)

Peter. Don't let it bother you. It doesn't bother me.

---

26. **to run the gauntlet:** to endure a series of troubles or difficulties.

Anne. I suppose you can't really blame them . . . they think back to what they were like at our age. They don't realize how much more advanced we are . . . When you think what wonderful discussions we've had! . . . Oh, I forgot. I was going to bring you some more pictures.

Peter. Oh, these are fine, thanks.

Anne. Don't you want some more? Miep just brought me some new ones.

Peter. Maybe later. (*He gives her a glass of pop and, taking some for himself, sits down facing her.*)

Anne (*Looking up at one of the photographs*). I remember when I got that . . . I won it. I bet Jopie that I could eat five ice-cream cones. We'd all been playing ping-pong . . . We used to have heavenly times . . . we'd finish up with ice cream at the Delphi, or the Oasis, where Jews were allowed . . . there'd always be a lot of boys . . . we'd laugh and joke . . . I'd like to go back to it for a few days or a week. But after that I know I'd be bored to death. I think more seriously about life now. I want to be a journalist . . . or something. I love to write. What do you want to do?

Peter. I thought I might go off some place . . . work on a farm or something . . . some job that doesn't take much brains.

Anne. You shouldn't talk that way. You've got the most awful inferiority complex.

Peter. I know I'm not smart.

Anne. That isn't true. You're much better than I am in dozens of things . . . arithmetic and algebra and . . . well, you're a million times better than I am in algebra. (*With sudden directness*) You like Margot, don't you? Right from the start you liked her, liked her much better than me.

Peter (*Uncomfortably*). Oh, I don't know.

(*In the main room Mrs. Van Daan comes from the bathroom and goes over to the sink, polishing a coffee pot.*)

Anne. It's all right. Everyone feels that way. Margot's so good. She's sweet and bright and beautiful and I'm not.

Peter. I wouldn't say that.

Anne. Oh, no, I'm not. I know that. I know quite well that I'm not a beauty. I never have been and never shall be.

Peter. I don't agree at all. I think you're pretty.

Anne. That's not true!

Peter. And another thing. You've changed . . . from at first, I mean.

Anne. I have?

Peter. I used to think you were awful noisy.

Anne. And what do you think now, Peter? How have I changed?

Peter. Well . . . er . . . you're . . . quieter.

(*In his room Dussel takes his pajamas and toilet articles and goes into the bathroom to change.*)

Anne. I'm glad you don't just hate me.

Peter. I never said that.

Anne. I bet when you get out of here you'll never think of me again.

Peter. That's crazy.

Anne. When you get back with all of your friends, you're going to say . . . now what did I ever see in that Mrs. Quack Quack.

Peter. I haven't got any friends.

Anne. Oh, Peter, of course you have. Everyone has friends.

Peter. Not me. I don't want any. I get along all right without them.

Anne. Does that mean you can get along without me? I think of myself as your friend.

Peter. No. If they were all like you, it'd be different.

(*He takes the glasses and the bottle and puts them away. There is a second's silence and then* Anne *speaks, hesitantly, shyly.*)

Anne. Peter, did you ever kiss a girl?

Peter. Yes. Once.

Anne (*To cover her feelings*). That picture's crooked. (Peter *goes over, straightening the photograph.*) Was she pretty?

Peter. Huh?

Anne. The girl that you kissed.

Peter. I don't know. I was blindfolded. (*He comes back and sits down again.*) It was at a party. One of those kissing games.

Anne (*Relieved*). Oh. I don't suppose that really counts, does it?

Peter. It didn't with me.

Anne. I've been kissed twice. Once a man I'd never seen before kissed me on the cheek when he picked me up off the ice and I was crying. And the other was Mr. Koophuis, a friend of Father's who kissed my hand. You wouldn't say those counted, would you?

Peter. I wouldn't say so.

Anne. I know almost for certain that Margot would never kiss anyone unless she was engaged to them. And I'm sure too that Mother never touched a man before Pim. But I don't know . . . things are so different now . . . What do you think? Do you think a girl shouldn't kiss anyone except if she's engaged or something? It's so hard to try to think what to do, when here we are with the whole world falling around our ears and you think . . . well . . . you don't know what's going to happen tomorrow and . . . What do you think?

Peter. I suppose it'd depend on the girl. Some girls, anything they do's wrong. But others . . . well . . . it wouldn't necessarily be wrong with them. (*The carillon starts to strike nine o'clock.*) I've always thought that when two people . . .

Anne. Nine o'clock. I have to go.

Peter. That's right.

Anne (*Without moving*). Good night.

(*There is a second's pause, then* Peter *gets up and moves toward the door.*)

Peter. You won't let them stop you coming?

Anne. No. (*She rises and starts for the door*) Sometime I might bring my diary. There are so many things in it that I want to talk over with you. There's a lot about you.

Peter. What kind of things?

Anne. I wouldn't want you to see some of it. I thought you were a nothing, just the way you thought about me.

Peter. Did you change your mind, the way I changed my mind about you?

Anne. Well . . . You'll see . . .

(*For a second* Anne *stands looking up at* Peter, *longing for him to kiss her. As he makes no move she turns away. Then suddenly* Peter *grabs her awkwardly in his arms, kissing her on the cheek.* Anne *walks out dazed. She stands for a minute, her back to the people in the main room. As she regains her poise she goes to her mother and father and* Margot, *silently kissing them. They murmur their good nights to her. As she is about to open her bedroom door, she catches sight of* Mrs. Van Daan. *She goes quickly to her, taking her face in her hands and kissing her first on one cheek and then on the other. Then she hurries off into her room.* Mrs. Van Daan *looks after her, and then looks over at* Peter's *room. Her suspicions are confirmed.*)

Mrs. Van Daan (*She knows*). Ah hah!

(*The lights dim out. The curtain falls on the scene. In the darkness* Anne's *voice comes faintly at first and then with growing strength.*)

Anne's Voice. By this time we all know each other so well that if anyone starts to tell a story, the rest can finish it for him. We're having to cut down still further on our meals. What makes it worse, the rats have been at work again. They've carried off some of our precious food. Even Mr. Dussel wishes now that Mouschi was here. Thursday, the twentieth of April, nineteen forty-four. Invasion fever is mounting every day. Miep tells us that people outside talk of nothing else. For myself, life has become much more pleasant. I often go to Peter's room after supper. Oh, don't think I'm in love, because I'm not. But it does make life more bearable to have someone with whom you can exchange views. No more tonight. P.S. . . . I must be honest. I must confess that I actually live for the next meeting. Is there anything lovelier than to sit under the skylight and feel the sun on your cheeks and have a darling boy in your arms? I admit now that I'm glad the Van Daans had a son and not a daughter. I've outgrown another dress. That's the third. I'm having to wear Margot's clothes after all. I'm working hard on my French and am now reading *La Belle Nivernaise.*

(*As she is saying the last lines—the curtain rises on the scene. The lights dim on, as* Anne's *voice fades out.*)

SCENE 3

*I*t *is night, a few weeks later. Everyone is in bed. There is complete quiet. In the* Van Daans' *room a match flares up for a moment and then is quickly put out.* Mr. Van Daan, *in bare feet, dressed in underwear and trousers, is dimly seen coming stealthily down the stairs and into the main room, where* Mr. *and* Mrs. Frank *and* Margot *are sleeping. He goes to the food safe and again lights a match. Then he cautiously opens the safe, taking out a half-loaf of bread. As he closes the safe, it creaks. He stands rigid.* Mrs. Frank *sits up in bed. She sees him.*

Mrs. Frank (*Screaming*). Otto! Otto! Komme schnell![27]

(*The rest of the people wake, hurriedly getting up.*)

Mr. Frank. Was ist los? Was ist passiert?[28]

(Dussel, *followed by* Anne, *comes from his room.*)

Mrs. Frank (*As she rushes over to* Mr. Van Daan). Er stiehlt das Essen![29]

Dussel (*Grabbing* Mr. Van Daan). You! You! Give me that.

Mrs. Van Daan (*Coming down the stairs*). Putti . . . Putti . . . what is it?

Dussel (*His hands on* Mr. Van Daan's *neck*). You dirty thief . . . stealing food . . . you good-for-nothing . . .

Mr. Frank. Mr. Dussel! For God's sake! Help me, Peter!

(Peter *comes over, trying, with* Mr. Frank, *to separate the two struggling men.*)

Peter. Let him go! Let go!

(Dussel *drops* Mr. Van Daan, *pushing him away. He shows them the end of a loaf of bread that he has taken from* Mr. Van Daan.)

Dussel. You greedy, selfish . . . !

(Margot turns *on the lights.*)

Mrs. Van Daan. Putti . . . what is it?

(*All of* Mrs. Frank's *gentleness, her self-control, is gone. She is outraged, in a frenzy of indignation.*)

Mrs. Frank. The bread! He was stealing the bread!

Dussel. It was you, and all the time we thought it was the rats!

Mr. Frank. Mr. Van Daan, how could you!

---

27. **Komme schnell!** (kôm′ə shnĕl′) *German:* Come quickly!

28. **Was ist los? Was ist passiert?** (väs ĭst lôs′? väs ĭst päsērt′?) *German:* What's the matter? What has happened?

29. **Er stiehlt das Essen!** (ĕr shtēlt′ däs ĕs′ən) *German:* He is stealing food!

The Diary of Anne Frank

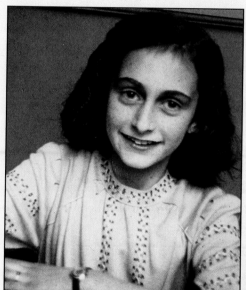

Anne Frank at 13

This play has been performed thousands of times all over the world. In your opinion, which one of these actresses best captures the spirit of Anne Frank, seen in the first photo, upper left?

Susan Strasberg as Anne Frank in the Broadway production during the 1950s

The Diary of Anne Frank as seen in Japan

Natalie Portman as Anne Frank in the Broadway production

Millie Perkins as Anne Frank in the film

Mr. Van Daan. I'm hungry.

Mrs. Frank. We're all of us hungry! I see the children getting thinner and thinner. Your own son Peter . . . I've heard him moan in his sleep, he's so hungry. And you come in the night and steal food that should go to them . . . to the children!

Mrs. Van Daan (*Going to* Mr. Van Daan *protectively*). He needs more food than the rest of us. He's used to more. He's a big man.

(Mr. Van Daan *breaks away, going over and sitting on the couch.*)

Mrs. Frank (*Turning on* Mrs. Van Daan). And you . . . you're worse than he is! You're a mother, and yet you sacrifice your child to this man . . . this . . . this . . .

Mr. Frank. Edith! Edith!

(Margot *picks up the pink woolen stole, putting it over her mother's shoulders.*)

Mrs. Frank (*Paying no attention, going on to* Mrs. Van Daan). Don't think I haven't seen you! Always saving the choicest bits for him! I've watched you day after day and I've held my tongue. But not any longer! Not after this! Now I want him to go! I want him to get out of here!

(Together)

    Mr. Frank. Edith!

    Mr. Van Daan. Get out of here?

Mrs. Van Daan. What do you mean?

Mrs. Frank. Just that! Take your things and get out!

Mr. Frank (*To* Mrs. Frank). You're speaking in anger. You cannot mean what you are saying.

Mrs. Frank. I mean exactly that!

(Mrs. Van Daan *takes a cover from the* Franks' *bed, pulling it about her.*)

Mr. Frank. For two long years we have lived here, side by side. We have respected each other's rights . . . we have managed to live in peace. Are we now going to throw it all away? I know this will never happen again, will it, Mr. Van Daan?

Mr. Van Daan. No. No.

Mrs. Frank. He steals once! He'll steal again!

(Mr. Van Daan, *holding his stomach, starts for the bathroom.* Anne *puts her arms around him, helping him up the step.*)

Mr. Frank. Edith, please. Let us be calm. We'll all go to our rooms . . . and afterwards we'll sit down quietly and talk this out . . . we'll find some way . . .

Mrs. Frank. No! No! No more talk! I want them to leave!

Mrs. Van Daan. You'd put us out, on the streets?

Mrs. Frank. There are other hiding places.

Mrs. Van Daan. A cellar . . . a closet. I know. And we have no money left even to pay for that.

Mrs. Frank. I'll give you money. Out of my own pocket I'll give it gladly. (*She gets her purse from a shelf and comes back with it.*)

Mrs. Van Daan. Mr. Frank, you told Putti you'd never forget what he'd done for you when you came to Amsterdam. You said you could never repay him, that you . . .

Mrs. Frank (*Counting out money*). If my husband had any obligation to you, he's paid it, over and over.

Mr. Frank. Edith, I've never seen you like this before. I don't know you.

Mrs. Frank. I should have spoken out long ago.

Dussel. You can't be nice to some people.

Mrs. Van Daan (*Turning on* Dussel). There would have been plenty for all of us, if you hadn't come in here!

Mr. Frank. We don't need the Nazis to destroy us. We're destroying ourselves.

(*He sits down, with his head in his hands.* Mrs. Frank *goes to* Mrs. Van Daan.)

Mrs. Frank (*Giving* Mrs. Van Daan *some money*). Give this to Miep. She'll find you a place.

Anne. Mother, you're not putting Peter out. Peter hasn't done anything.

Mrs. Frank. He'll stay, of course. When I say I must protect the children, I mean Peter too.

(Peter *rises from the steps where he has been sitting.*)

Peter. I'd have to go if Father goes.

(Mr. Van Daan *comes from the bathroom. Mrs. Van Daan hurries to him and takes him to the couch. Then she gets water from the sink to bathe his face.*)

Mrs. Frank (*While this is going on*). He's no father to you . . . that man! He doesn't know what it is to be a father!

Peter (*Starting for his room*). I wouldn't feel right. I couldn't stay.

Mrs. Frank. Very well, then. I'm sorry.

Anne (*Rushing over to* Peter). No, Peter! No! (Peter *goes into his room, closing the door after him. Anne turns back to her mother, crying.*) I don't care about the food. They can have mine! I don't want it! Only don't send them away. It'll be daylight soon. They'll be caught . . .

Margot (*Putting her arms comfortingly around* Anne). Please, Mother!

Mrs. Frank. They're not going now. They'll stay here until Miep finds them a place. (*To* Mrs. Van Daan) But one thing I insist on! He must never come down here again! He must never come to this room where the food is stored! We'll divide what we have . . . an equal share for each! (Dussel *hurries over to get a sack of potatoes from the food safe. Mrs. Frank goes on, to* Mrs. Van Daan.) You can cook it here and take it up to him.

(Dussel *brings the sack of potatoes back to the center table.*)

Margot. Oh, no. No. We haven't sunk so far that we're going to fight over a handful of rotten potatoes.

Dussel (*Dividing the potatoes into piles*). Mrs. Frank, Mr. Frank, Margot, Anne, Peter, Mrs. Van Daan, Mr. Van Daan, myself . . . Mrs. Frank . . .

(*The buzzer sounds in* Miep's *signal.*)

Mr. Frank. It's Miep! (*He hurries over, getting his overcoat and putting it on.*)

Margot. At this hour?

Mrs. Frank. It is trouble.

Mr. Frank (*As he starts down to unbolt the door*). I beg you, don't let her see a thing like this!

Mr. Dussel (*Counting without stopping*). . . . Anne, Peter, Mrs. Van Daan, Mr. Van Daan, myself . . .

Margot (*To* Dussel). Stop it! Stop it!

Dussel . . . Mr. Frank, Margot, Anne, Peter, Mrs. Van Daan, Mr. Van Daan, myself, Mrs. Frank . . .

Mrs. Van Daan. You're keeping the big ones for yourself! All the big ones . . . Look at the size of that! . . . And that! . . .

(Dussel *continues on with his dividing.* Peter, *with his shirt and trousers on, comes from his room.*)

Margot. Stop it! Stop it!

(*We hear* Miep's *excited voice speaking to* Mr. Frank *below.*)

Miep. Mr. Frank . . . the most wonderful news! . . . The invasion has begun!

Mr. Frank. Go on, tell them! Tell them!

(Miep *comes running up the steps, ahead of Mr. Frank. She has a man's raincoat on over her nightclothes and a bunch of orange-colored flowers in her hand.*)

Miep. Did you hear that, everybody? Did you hear what I said? The invasion has begun! The invasion!

(*They all stare at* Miep, *unable to grasp what she is telling them.* Peter *is the first to recover his wits.*)

Peter. Where?

Mrs. Van Daan. When? When, Miep?

Miep. It began early this morning . . .

(*As she talks on, the realization of what she has said begins to dawn on them. Everyone goes crazy. A wild demonstration takes place.* Mrs. Frank *hugs* Mr. Van Daan.)

Mrs. Frank. Oh, Mr. Van Daan, did you hear that?

(Dussel *embraces* Mrs. Van Daan. Peter *grabs a frying pan and parades around the room, beating on it, singing the Dutch National Anthem.* Anne *and* Margot *follow him, singing, weaving in and out among the excited grownups.* Margot *breaks away to take the flowers from* Miep *and distribute them to everyone. While this* pandemonium *is going on* Mrs. Frank *tries to make herself heard above the excitement.*)

Mrs. Frank (*To* Miep). How do you know?

Miep. The radio . . . The B.B.C.! They said they landed on the coast of Normandy!

Peter. The British?

Miep. British, Americans, French, Dutch, Poles, Norwegians . . . all of them! More than four thousand ships! Churchill spoke, and General Eisenhower! D-Day they call it!

Mr. Frank. Thank God, it's come!

Mrs. Van Daan. At last!

Miep (*Starting out*). I'm going to tell Mr. Kraler. This'll be better than any blood transfusion.

Mr. Frank (*Stopping her*). What part of Normandy did they land at, did they say?

Miep. Normandy . . . that's all I know now . . . I'll be up the minute I hear some more! (*She goes hurriedly out.*)

Mr. Frank (*To* Mrs. Frank). What did I tell you? What did I tell you?

(Mrs. Frank *indicates that he has forgotten to bolt the door after* Miep. *He hurries down the steps.* Mr. Van Daan, *sitting on the couch, suddenly breaks into a convulsive sob. Everybody looks at him, bewildered.*)

Mrs. Van Daan (*Hurrying to him*). Putti! Putti! What is it? What happened?

Mr. Van Daan. Please. I'm so ashamed.

(Mr. Frank *comes back up the steps.*)

Dussel. Oh, for God's sake!

Mrs. Van Daan. Don't, Putti.

Margot. It doesn't matter now!

Mr. Frank (*Going to* Mr. Van Daan). Didn't you hear what Miep said? The invasion has come! We're going to be liberated! This is a time to celebrate!

(*He embraces* Mrs. Frank *and then hurries to the cupboard and gets the cognac and a glass.*)

Mr. Van Daan. To steal bread from children!

Mrs. Frank. We've all done things that we're ashamed of.

Anne. Look at me, the way I've treated Mother . . . so mean and horrid to her.

Mrs. Frank. No, Anneke, no.

(Anne *runs to her mother, putting her arms around her.*)

Anne. Oh, Mother, I was. I was awful.

Mr. Van Daan. Not like me. No one is as bad as me!

Dussel (*To* Mr. Van Daan). Stop it now! Let's be happy!

Mr. Frank (*Giving* Mr. Van Daan *a glass of cognac*). Here! Here! Schnapps! L'chaim![30]

---

30. **Schnapps! L'chaim!** (shnäps′ lə кнä′yĭm) *German:* Brandy! *Hebrew:* To life!

(Mr. Van Daan *takes the cognac. They all watch him. He gives them a feeble smile.* Anne *puts up her fingers in a V-for-Victory sign. As* Mr. Van Daan *gives an answering V-sign, they are startled to hear a loud sob from behind them. It is* Mrs. Frank, *stricken with <u>remorse</u>. She is sitting on the other side of the room.*)

Mrs. Frank (*Through her sobs*). When I think of the terrible things I said . . .

(Mr. Frank, Anne, *and* Margot *hurry to her, trying to comfort her.* Mr. Van Daan *brings her his glass of cognac.*)

Mr. Van Daan. No! No! You were right!

Mrs. Frank. That I should speak that way to you! . . . Our friends! . . . Our guests! (*She starts to cry again.*)

Dussel. Stop it, you're spoiling the whole invasion!

(*As they are comforting her, the lights dim out. The curtain falls.*)

Anne's Voice (*Faintly at first and then with growing strength*). We're all in much better spirits these days. There's still excellent news of the invasion. The best part about it is that I have a feeling that friends are coming. Who knows? Maybe I'll be back in school by fall. Ha, ha! The joke is on us! The warehouse man doesn't know a thing and we are paying him all that money! . . . Wednesday, the second of July, nineteen forty-four. The invasion seems temporarily to be bogged down. Mr. Kraler has to have an operation, which looks bad. The Gestapo have found the radio that was stolen. Mr. Dussel says they'll trace it back and back to the thief, and then, it's just a matter of time till they get to us. Everyone is low. Even poor Pim can't raise their spirits. I have often been downcast myself . . . but never in despair. I can shake off

everything if I write. But . . . and that is the great question . . . will I ever be able to write well? I want to so much. I want to go on living even after my death. Another birthday has gone by, so now I am fifteen. Already I know what I want. I have a goal, an opinion.

(*As this is being said—the curtain rises on the scene, the lights dim on, and* Anne's *voice fades out.*)

SCENE 4

It is an afternoon a few weeks later . . . Everyone but Margot *is in the main room. There is a sense of great tension.*

Both Mrs. Frank *and* Mr. Van Daan *are nervously pacing back and forth,* Mr. Dussel *is standing at the window, looking down fixedly at the street below.* Peter *is at the center table, trying to do his lessons.* Anne *sits opposite him, writing in her diary.* Mrs. Van Daan *is seated on the couch, her eyes on* Mr. Frank *as he sits reading.*

The sound of a telephone ringing comes from the office below. They all are rigid, listening tensely. Mr. Dussel *rushes down to* Mr. Frank.

Dussel. There it goes again, the telephone! Mr. Frank, do you hear?

Mr. Frank (*Quietly*). Yes. I hear.

Dussel (*Pleading, insistent*). But this is the third time, Mr. Frank! The third time in quick succession! It's a signal! I tell you it's Miep, trying to get us! For some reason she can't come to us and she's trying to warn us of something!

Mr. Frank. Please. Please.

Mr. Van Daan (*To* Dussel). You're wasting your breath.

Dussel. Something has happened, Mr. Frank. For three days now Miep hasn't been to see us! And today not a man has come to work. There hasn't been a sound in the building!

Mrs. Frank. Perhaps it's Sunday. We may have lost track of the days.

Mr. Van Daan (*To* Anne). You with the diary there. What day is it?

Dussel (*Going to* Mrs. Frank). I don't lose track of the days! I know exactly what day it is! It's Friday, the fourth of August. Friday, and not a man at work. (*He rushes back to* Mr. Frank, *pleading with him, almost in tears.*) I tell you Mr. Kraler's dead. That's the only explanation. He's dead and they've closed down the building, and Miep's trying to tell us!

Mr. Frank. She'd never telephone us.

Dussel (*Frantic*). Mr. Frank, answer that! I beg you, answer it!

Mr. Frank. No.

Mr. Van Daan. Just pick it up and listen. You don't have to speak. Just listen and see if it's Miep.

Dussel (*Speaking at the same time*). For God's sake . . . I ask you.

Mr. Frank. No. I've told you, no. I'll do nothing that might let anyone know we're in the building.

Peter. Mr. Frank's right.

Mr. Van Daan. There's no need to tell us what side you're on.

Mr. Frank. If we wait patiently, quietly, I believe that help will come.

(*There is silence for a minute as they all listen to the telephone ringing.*)

Dussel. I'm going down. (*He rushes down the steps.* Mr. Frank *tries ineffectually to hold him.* Dussel *runs to the lower door, unbolting it. The telephone stops ringing.* Dussel *bolts the door and comes slowly back up the steps.*) Too late. (Mr. Frank *goes to* Margot *in* Anne's *bedroom.*)

Mr. Van Daan. So we just wait here until we die.

Mrs. Van Daan (*Hysterically*). I can't stand it! I'll kill myself! I'll kill myself!

Mr. Van Daan. For God's sake, stop it!

(*In the distance, a German military band is heard playing a Viennese waltz.*)

Mrs. Van Daan. I think you'd be glad if I did! I think you want me to die!

Mr. Van Daan. Whose fault is it we're here? (Mrs. Van Daan *starts for her room. He follows, talking at her.*) We could've been safe somewhere . . . in America or Switzerland. But no! No! You wouldn't leave when I wanted to. You couldn't leave your things. You couldn't leave your precious furniture.

Mrs. Van Daan. Don't touch me!

(*She hurries up the stairs, followed by* Mr. Van Daan. Peter, *unable to bear it, goes to his room.* Anne *looks after him, deeply concerned.* Dussel *returns to his post at the window.* Mr. Frank *comes back into the main room and takes a book, trying to read.* Mrs. Frank *sits near the sink, starting to peel some potatoes.* Anne *quietly goes to* Peter's *room, closing the door after her.* Peter *is lying face down on the cot.* Anne *leans over him, holding him in her arms, trying to bring him out of his despair.*)

Anne. Look, Peter, the sky. (*She looks up through the skylight.*) What a lovely, lovely day! Aren't the clouds beautiful? You know what I do when it seems as if I couldn't stand being cooped up for one more minute? I think myself out. I think myself on a walk in the park where I used to go with Pim. Where the jonquils and the crocus and the violets grow down the slopes. You know the most wonderful part about *thinking* yourself out? You can have it any way you like. You can have roses and violets and chrysanthemums all blooming at the same time . . . It's funny . . . I used to take it all for granted . . .

and now I've gone crazy about everything to do with nature. Haven't you?

Peter. I've just gone crazy. I think if something doesn't happen soon . . . if we don't get out of here . . . I can't stand much more of it!

Anne (*Softly*). I wish you had a religion, Peter.

Peter. No, thanks! Not me!

Anne. Oh, I don't mean you have to be Orthodox[31] . . . or believe in heaven and hell and purgatory and things . . . I just mean some religion . . . it doesn't matter what. Just to believe in something! When I think of all that's out there . . . the trees . . . and flowers . . . and seagulls . . . when I think of the dearness of you, Peter . . . and the goodness of the people we know . . . Mr. Kraler, Miep, Dirk, the vegetable man, all risking their lives for us every day . . . When I think of these good things, I'm not afraid any more . . . I find myself, and God, and I . . .

(Peter *interrupts, getting up and walking away.*)

Peter. That's fine! But when I begin to think, I get mad! Look at us, hiding out for two years. Not able to move! Caught here like . . . waiting for them to come and get us . . . and all for what?

Anne. We're not the only people that've had to suffer. There've always been people that've had to . . . sometimes one race . . . sometimes another . . . and yet . . .

Peter. That doesn't make me feel any better!

Anne (*Going to him*). I know it's terrible, trying to have any faith . . . when people are doing such horrible . . . But you know what I sometimes think? I think the world may be going through a phase, the way I was with Mother. It'll pass, maybe not for hundreds of years, but some day . . . I still believe, in spite of everything, that people are really good at heart.

Peter. I want to see something now . . . Not a thousand years from now! (*He goes over, sitting down again on the cot.*)

Anne. But, Peter, if you'd only look at it as part of a great pattern . . . that we're just a little minute in the life . . . (*She breaks off.*) Listen to us, going at each other like a couple of stupid grown-ups! Look at the sky now. Isn't it lovely? (*She holds out her hand to him. Peter takes it and rises, standing with her at the window looking out, his arms around her.*) Some day, when we're outside again, I'm going to . . .

(*She breaks off as she hears the sound of a car, its brakes squealing as it comes to a sudden stop. The people in the other rooms also become aware of the sound. They listen tensely. Another car roars up to a screeching stop. Anne and Peter come from Peter's room. Mr. and Mrs. Van Daan creep down the stairs. Dussel comes out from his room. Everyone is listening, hardly breathing. A doorbell clangs again and again in the building below. Mr. Frank starts quietly down the steps to the door. Dussel and Peter follow him. The others stand rigid, waiting, terrified.*)

In a few seconds Dussel *comes stumbling back up the steps. He shakes off* Peter's *help and goes to his room.* Mr. Frank *bolts the door below, and comes slowly back up the steps. Their eyes are all on him as he stands there for a minute. They realize that what they feared has happened.*

Mrs. Van Daan *starts to whimper.* Mr. Van Daan *puts her gently in a chair, and then hurries off up the stairs to their room to collect their things.* Peter *goes to comfort his mother. There is a sound of violent pounding on a door below.*)

---

31. **Orthodox:** Orthodox Jews who strictly observe Jewish laws and traditions.

Mr. Frank (*Quietly*). For the past two years we have lived in fear. Now we can live in hope.

(*The pounding below becomes more insistent. There are muffled sounds of voices, shouting commands.*)

Men's Voices. *Auf machen! Da drinnen! Auf machen! Schnell! Schnell! Schnell!*[32] *etc., etc.*

(*The street door below is forced open. We hear the heavy tread of footsteps coming up. Mr. Frank gets two school bags from the shelves, and gives one to* Anne *and the other to* Margot. *He goes to get a bag for* Mrs. Frank. *The sound of feet coming up grows louder.* Peter *comes to* Anne, *kissing her good-bye, then he goes to his room to collect his things. The buzzer of their door starts to ring.* Mr. Frank *brings* Mrs. Frank *a bag. They stand together, waiting. We hear the thud of gun butts on the door, trying to break it down.*

Anne *stands, holding her school satchel, looking over at her father and mother with a soft, reassuring smile. She is no longer a child, but a woman with courage to meet whatever lies ahead.*

The lights dim out. The curtain falls on the scene. We hear a mighty crash as the door is shattered. After a second Anne's *voice is heard.*)

Anne's Voice. And so it seems our stay here is over. They are waiting for us now. They've allowed us five minutes to get our things. We can each take a bag and whatever it will hold of clothing. Nothing else. So, dear Diary, that means I must leave you behind. Good-bye for a while. P.S. Please, please, Miep, or Mr. Kraler, or anyone else. If you should find this diary, will you please keep it safe for me, because some day I hope . . .

(*Her voice stops abruptly. There is silence. After a second the curtain rises.*)

*I*t is again the afternoon in November, 1945. The rooms are as we saw them in the first scene. Mr. Kraler *has joined* Miep *and* Mr. Frank. *There are coffee cups on the table. We see a great change in* Mr. Frank. *He is calm now. His bitterness is gone. He slowly turns a few pages of the diary. They are blank.*

Mr. Frank. No more. (*He closes the diary and puts it down on the couch beside him.*)

Miep. I'd gone to the country to find food. When I got back the block was surrounded by police . . .

Mr. Kraler. We made it our business to learn how they knew. It was the thief . . . the thief who told them.

(Miep *goes up to the gas burner, bringing back a pot of coffee.*)

Mr. Frank (*After a pause*). It seems strange to say this, that anyone could be happy in a concentration camp. But Anne was happy in the camp in Holland where they first took us. After two years of being shut up in these rooms, she could be out . . . out in the sunshine and the fresh air that she loved.

Miep (*Offering the coffee to* Mr. Frank). A little more?

Mr. Frank (*Holding out his cup to her*). The news of the war was good. The British and Americans were sweeping through France. We felt sure that they would get to us in time. In September we were told that we were to be shipped to Poland . . . The men to one camp. The women to another. I was sent to

---

32. **Auf machen! . . . Schnell!** (ouf´ mäкн´ən! dä drǐn´ən! ouf´ mäкн´ən! shněl! shněl! shněl!) *German:* Open up! Inside there! Open up! Quick! Quick! Quick!

Auschwitz.[33] They went to Belsen.[34] In January we were freed, the few of us who were left. The war wasn't yet over, so it took us a long time to get home. We'd be sent here and there behind the lines where we'd be safe. Each time our train would stop . . . at a siding, or a crossing . . . we'd all get out and go from group to group . . . Where were you? Were you at Belsen? At Buchenwald?[35] At Mauthausen? Is it possible that you knew my wife? Did you ever see my husband? My son? My daughter? That's how I found out about my wife's death . . . of Margot, the Van Daans . . . Dussel. But Anne . . . I still hoped . . . Yesterday I went to Rotterdam. I'd heard of a woman there . . . She'd been in Belsen with Anne . . . I know now.

(*He picks up the diary again, and turns the pages back to find a certain passage. As he finds it we hear* Anne's *voice.*)

Anne's Voice. In spite of everything, I still believe that people are really good at heart.

(Mr. Frank *slowly closes the diary.*)

Mr. Frank. She puts me to shame.

(*They are silent.*)

A bookcase hid the secret doorway that led up to the Annex.

The Curtain Falls

33. **Auschwitz** (oush′vĭts′): a Nazi concentration camp located in Poland, notorious as an extermination center.

34. **Belsen** (bĕl′zən): a village in Germany, the site of a Nazi concentration camp.

35. **Buchenwald** (bōō′kən-wôld′): a Nazi concentration camp in Germany.

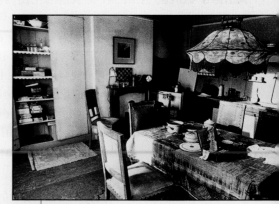

The room of Mr. and Mrs. Van Daan doubled as the kitchen.

The Diary of Anne Frank

Compare the Broadway stage setting (center) with the photos of the annex. Does the stage setting show the annex and its rooms as they really looked? Why or why not?

The outside of the Annex

The stage set from the Broadway production

This was the group living room and the bedroom of Otto and Edith Frank.

Anne shared this room with Mr. Dussel.

Connect to the Literature

1. **What Do You Think?** Compare Anne's character as it is portrayed at the end of the play with her character at the beginning. Have your feelings for her changed? Explain.

Comprehension Check
- Why does Mr. Frank suggest offering the man in the storeroom a raise in salary?
- What is the significance of the cars that come to a screeching stop outside the building?
- In Scene 5, where are the other people who were in hiding with Mr. Frank?

Think Critically

2. Shortly before Anne is arrested, she has a final conversation with Peter. In this conversation she says that she believes that people are good at heart. Would you have felt this way if you had been in Anne's situation? Why or why not?

3. In Act Two, Scene 3, Mr. Van Daan is caught stealing. This event was created for the play; it did not actually take place. Why do you think this event was created?

   Think About:
   - why Mr. Van Daan steals the bread
   - from whom he is stealing
   - the type of person he is

4. **ACTIVE READING** **STORY MAPPING**
   Create a story map for each scene in Act Two and place them in your **READER'S NOTEBOOK.** Choose two events in Act Two that you think mark turning points in the play. Why did you choose each event?

Extend Interpretations

5. **Critic's Corner** Some people feel that this play leaves audiences with an unrealistic understanding of the Holocaust and its victims. For example, the play seems to imply that Holocaust victims could overcome any difficulty through faith and a belief in the goodness of people. How do you feel about this criticism?

6. **Connect to Life** In Act Two, Scene 1, Anne tells Peter, "We have problems here that no other people our age have ever had." What are some of the problems that people your age have today? Are any of them problems that people your age have never had before? Explain.

Literary Analysis

RESOLUTION The part of a plot in which the loose ends of the story are tied up and the story is brought to a close is called the **resolution.** In *The Diary of Anne Frank,* the resolution of the central conflict is tragic—only Otto Frank survives the Nazi death camps. By the end, the minor conflicts between characters have also been resolved.

Paired Activity With a partner, discuss the conflicts listed in the first column in the chart below. Then fill in the second column by describing when and how each conflict is resolved. What event in Act Two, Scene 3, changes the way people in the Secret Annex feel toward one another?

Conflict Resolution	
Conflict	**How and When Resolved**
Anne and Mrs. Frank	
Anne and Peter	
Mrs. Frank and Mr. Van Daan	

from THE LAST SEVEN MONTHS OF ANNE FRANK

INTERVIEW WITH
HANNAH ELISABETH PICK-GOSLAR

BY WILLY LINDWER

PREPARING to Read

Build Background

A Childhood Friend Hannah Elisabeth Pick-Goslar was Anne Frank's childhood friend. As friends, Hannah and Anne had much in common. They were the same age, both of their families had fled Nazi Germany in 1933, and both families had settled on the same street in Amsterdam. Anne and Hannah remained close friends throughout their school years.

The two girls' final meeting took place in the Nazi concentration camp Bergen-Belsen. Anne, along with her sister, Margot, died in the camp, but Hannah survived and settled in Israel. In this excerpt, Hannah describes the Franks' escape into hiding and tells about her incredible last meeting with Anne.

Focus Your Reading

LITERARY ANALYSIS | **INTERVIEW**

An exchange of questions and answers between two people is called an **interview.** The selection you are about to read comes from an interview with Hannah Pick-Goslar conducted by Willy Lindwer for a television documentary about Anne Frank. However, the questions asked by the interviewer have been omitted. As you read, pay attention to the impressions that you get of Hannah Pick-Goslar.

Mr. Frank's factory, Opekta, produced a substance for making jam. My mother always got the old packages as a gift. Soon after school let out, my mother sent me to the Franks' house to get the scale because she wanted to make jam. It was a beautiful day.

I went as usual to the Franks' house and rang and rang and rang, but no one opened the door. I didn't know why no one answered. I rang again, and finally, Mr. Goudsmit, a tenant, opened the door.

"What do you want? What have you come for?" he asked in astonishment.

"I've come to borrow the scale."

"Don't you know that the entire Frank family has gone to Switzerland?"

I didn't know anything about it. "Why?" I asked. He didn't know either.

This was a bolt out of the blue. Why had they gone to Switzerland? The only connection the Frank family had with Switzerland was that Otto Frank's mother lived there.

But later it appeared that, in fact, the family had always reckoned that it would get worse for Jews. They had been preparing for a whole year to go into hiding. We didn't know anything about this. You can't talk about something like that. Because if anyone talked, then the whole affair would go amiss. . . .

I believe that Anne was the first girlfriend that I lost. It was, of course, very frightening, but we began to get used to the idea. When I went back to school after the summer, fewer children came to class every day.

We stayed in Amsterdam almost a full year longer, until June 20, 1943, and all this time things were getting

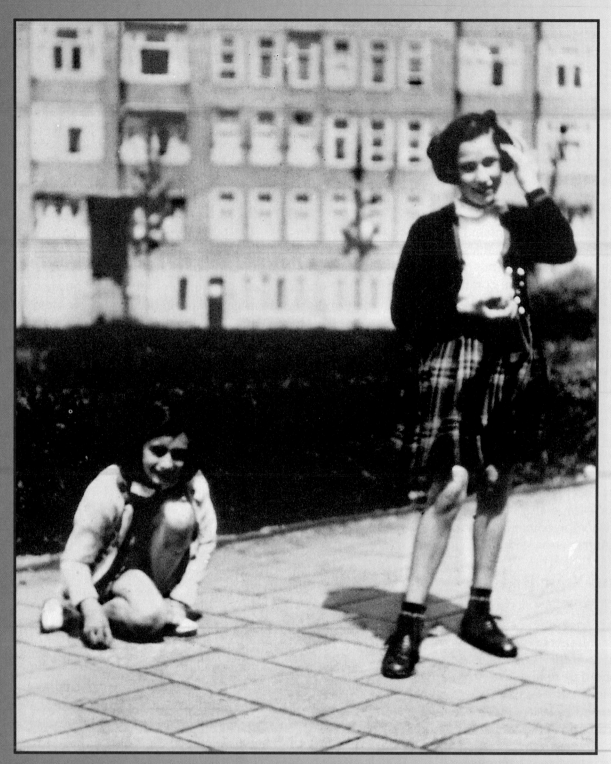

Anne and Hannah in May, 1939

worse and worse. Jews had to wear a yellow star. We had an *Ausweis* (an identification card), with a large "J" on it—for Jew. People were stopped on the street: "May I see your *Ausweis*?" If you were Jewish, you were taken away and you never returned home. And a mother waiting for her child would ask herself: Where is my child? Have they taken her away?

It became more dangerous every day. And day by day our classroom became emptier. We arrived in the morning and this boy would no longer be there and that girl wouldn't be there. I shall never forget how Mr. Presser, our history teacher, who later became Professor Presser, gave us a lecture about the Renaissance.[1] He began to read to us about the meeting of Dante and Beatrice in paradise. Suddenly, in the middle of the lesson, he began to cry and ran out of the class.

"What's the matter?"

"Last night they took away my wife."

It was terrible. I still get chills when I think about it, seeing that man standing in front of the class. He had no children, I thought. His wife was everything to him. He went home and his wife wasn't there. That's how it was.

So far, my family had been lucky insofar as we were able to buy South American citizenship through an uncle in Switzerland. We were expatriates.[2] That's why it was possible. We got passports from Paraguay. Laughing, my father said, "You'd better know something about Paraguay in case

> **If you were Jewish, you were taken away and you never returned home.**

they ask." So I learned the name of the capital, Asunción. I didn't know anything else, but no one ever asked me anything.

Because of these passports we could still go out for a while longer without trembling in fear, but you never knew what would happen tomorrow.

And then a second document helped us. My father had been, after all, one of the leaders of the Mizrachi [Zionist organization] in Germany, and he was also active in the Mizrachi movement in the Netherlands. I believe forty acknowledged lists were drafted and recognized by the Germans, with the names of the most famous Zionists—people who wanted to go to Eretz Israel— and we were on the second list. So we continued to live, with little to eat and with a great deal of fear, but at least we were at home. In October, my mother died during childbirth. The baby was born dead. That was in Anne's diary. Someone told Anne that our baby had died, but not that my mother had died too. They probably didn't have the heart to tell her. . . .

Everything went along fine until June 20, 1943, when there was the big roundup in Amsterdam-South. On that day, the Germans started something new. At five o'clock in the morning while everyone was asleep they blocked off all the southern part of Amsterdam. They went from door to door, rang, and asked:

"Do Jews live here?"

"Yes."

"You have fifteen minutes; take a backpack, put a few things in it, and get outside quickly."

That was our neighborhood, so we had to pack too. A passport no longer helped.

---

1. **Renaissance** (rĕn´ĭ-säns´): a revival of interest in classical art, architecture, and literature that began in Europe during the 14th century.

2. **expatriates** (ĕk-spā´trē-ĭts): people who have given up their citizenship in their native country.

We had a quarter of an hour, and we had to go with them. . . .

So we were taken to Westerbork. My father ended up in a very large barracks. My sister and I were put in an orphanage, where, they said, there was more to eat. My father had known the director of the orphanage when he was in Germany. My little sister wasn't there very long. She became seriously ill and had to have operations in both ears. She was in the hospital for almost the entire time that we were in Westerbork.

I worked there. The toilets were outside, and everyone was very happy when I volunteered to clean them. No one knew why I was so eager to do it. But, now and then, my father was able to come by, and if I was cleaning the toilets just then, I could see him for a moment. That's the reason I did that disgusting work.

It was, in fact, bearable in the orphanage. There were teachers and we still got lessons. There were only youngsters, children of Jews who had been in hiding. The children had been found, but not their parents. It also happened the other way around—that the parents were already gone and the children found later.

Every Friday and Tuesday, trains would come which had to be filled and which then went to Poland. We still had our South American papers and they made it possible for us to stay.

I remember the terrible November night, when it was announced that of all the Palestine lists (lists of people who wanted to go to Israel), only the first two were still valid. All the people on the other lists had to leave that same night. Then the entire orphanage was emptied. I remember Rabbi Vorst, who took all those children and laid a large *tallit* (prayer shawl) over them and blessed them. Most of the teachers went because they wanted to stay with the children. That was awful. On the Friday afternoon after the train left, the only ones still there were me, my sister in the hospital, and two or three other children. All of the rest who had been on those lists disappeared.

On February 15, 1944, neither our Palestine papers nor our passports could help any more. But the big difference for us was that we weren't sent to Auschwitz. If we had been sent to Auschwitz in 1943, I wouldn't be able to tell about it now. Because those people who were taken away in the beginning were almost all killed.

But then I didn't know what Auschwitz was. People talked about an *Arbeitslager*[3] (a work camp) in the east. We were going to an *Austauschlager*[4] (exchange camp). I said at the time: "The Germans want to keep us alive so that they can exchange us for German soldiers."

On February 15, 1944, we were transported to Bergen-Belsen. That was a somewhat better camp. What was better about it? In the first place, we were transported in passenger cars and not in cattle cars. And then, when we arrived, our clothes weren't taken away and families weren't separated. My father and my sister stayed with me. We slept in different places, but we could see each other every evening. The trip took—I don't remember precisely— two or three days to get to Bergen-Belsen.

I don't know any longer whether I knew right away what it meant to be in a concentration camp, but I remember very well how, upon our arrival, the German soldiers stood next to each other, with large

---

3. *Arbeitslager* (är′bīts-lä′gər) *German.*
4. *Austauschlager* (ous′toush-lä′gər) *German.*

dogs at their sides. To this day I am afraid of dogs. I don't believe that experience is the real reason; but if someone remarks about it, then I say, "If you had been there, and if you had seen those dogs, then you'd be afraid, too."

Afterward we had to walk, walk, and walk still farther, until we saw a large field, with barbed wire here and barbed wire there. There were many different camps. But we didn't know who was in there and where they came from. We saw them for the first time later on, when we went to the shower, which was near the train station—a half-hour or an hour walk—but we never had further contact with them.

The Germans were afraid that we would run away, but we couldn't go anywhere.

We came to a part of the camp that was almost new. There were, at most, forty or fifty Jews from Greece there. They became, of course, our bosses, because they had already been there for a while. They distributed the food and had all the important jobs. The doctor was a Greek Jew from Salonika. The camp was called Alballalager.

The first few days, we were separated, but later we were able to be together. In the beginning, my father had to go into a quarantined[5] barracks. Our clothes weren't taken away; that was one of the good things about that camp. In Bergen-Belsen, it was very cold in the winter. We soon found that out. Because we had been arrested in June we hadn't thought about winter clothes. Especially me, a young girl, who had to do her own packing. But what I had brought, I kept.

My sister had a large bandage on her head because she had had surgery on her ears in Westerbork. The first day we arrived in Bergen-Belsen, I got jaundice. The policy of the Germans was: whoever got sick had to go to the hospital; otherwise, all the others could be infected. I didn't know what to do with my little sister. My father was confined in another barracks and I couldn't take her to him. He also had to work, so that wouldn't have worked out.

So there I was and didn't know what to do. This situation showed me that there were very special people in that camp. I told an old lady that I was at my wits' end: "Tomorrow morning, I have to go to the hospital and my little sister is sick."

Two hours later, a woman came, who said, "My name is Abrahams. Mrs. Lange told me that you were here and that you don't know what to do with your sister. I have seven children; give her to me; then we'll just have one more little child with us."

And that's how it worked out. The next morning her daughter, who seemed to be about my age, came and took the little girl with her. Meanwhile, my father was able to visit me. We were together with that family until the end. To this day we have stayed on friendly terms with them.

Every day, we were counted. The Germans were afraid that we would run away, but we couldn't go anywhere. Where could you possibly go, with a large Star of David on your clothes, without money, and without anything? But that was the craziness of the Germans. We had to stand in rows of five for hours in order to be counted.

---

5. **quarantined** (kwôr′ən-tēnd′): isolated, in order to prevent the spread of contagious disease.

One day, we looked in the direction where there hadn't been any barracks and saw that tents had suddenly appeared there. It was already quite cold, and we didn't know who was in those tents. Two or three months later, there were very strong wind storms and they were all blown down. On that same day, we received an order: our beds, which were stacked in two levels, one above the other, were taken away, and we got stacks of three beds. Two of us had to sleep in one bed, and half the camp had to be emptied. Then a barbed-wire fence was built through the middle of the camp and filled with straw so that we couldn't see the other side. But we were, of course, very close to each other, because the camp wasn't large. All those people from the tents were taken to the barracks on the other side. In spite of the German guards on the high watchtowers, we tried to make contact. It was, of course, strictly forbidden to talk with those people, and if the Germans saw or heard someone doing that, that person would have been shot at once. Because of that some of us went to the fence after dark to try to pick up something. I never went there, but we learned that they were all people who had come from Poland—Jews and non-Jews.

About a month later, in early February when there was snow on the ground, one of my acquaintances, an older woman, came up to me one day. "Do you know, there are some Dutch people there. I spoke to Mrs. Van Daan." The woman had known her from before, and she told me that Anne was there. She knew that I knew Anne.

"Go over to the barbed-wire fence and try to talk to her." And, of course, I did. In

So we stood there, two young girls, and we cried.

the evening, I stood by the barbed-wire fence and began to call out. And quite by chance Mrs. Van Daan was there again. I asked her, "Could you call Anne?"

She said, "Yes, yes, wait a minute, I'll go to get Anne. I can't get Margot; she is very, very ill and is in bed."

But naturally I was much more interested in Anne, and I waited there a few minutes in the dark.

Anne came to the barbed-wire fence—I couldn't see her. The fence and the straw were between us. There wasn't much light. Maybe I saw her shadow. It wasn't the same Anne. She was a broken girl. I probably was, too, but it was so terrible. She immediately began to cry, and she told me, "I don't have any parents anymore."

I remember that with absolute certainty. That was terribly sad, because she couldn't have known anything else. She thought that her father had been gassed right away. But Mr. Frank looked very young and healthy, and of course the Germans didn't know how old everybody was who they wanted to gas, but selected them on the basis of their appearance. Someone who looked healthy had to work, but another who might even be younger, but who was sick or looked bad, went directly to the gas chamber.

I always think, if Anne had known that her father was still alive, she might have had more strength to survive, because she died very shortly before the end—only a few days before [liberation]. But maybe it was all predestined.

So we stood there, two young girls, and we cried. I told her about my mother. She hadn't known that; she only knew that the baby had died. And I told her about my little sister. I told her that my father was in the hospital. He died two weeks later; he was already very sick. She told me that Margot was seriously ill and she told me about going into hiding because I was, of course, extremely curious.

"But what are you doing here? You were supposed to be in Switzerland, weren't you?" And then she told me what had happened. That they didn't go to Switzerland at all and why they had said that; so that everyone should think that they had gone to her grandmother's.

Then she said, "We don't have anything at all to eat here, almost nothing, and we are cold; we don't have any clothes and I've gotten very thin and they shaved my hair." That was terrible for her. She had always been very proud of her hair. It may have grown back a bit in the meantime, but it certainly wasn't the long hair she'd had before, which she playfully curled around her fingers. It was much worse for them than for us. I said, "They didn't take away our clothes." That was our first meeting.

Then for the first time—we had already been in the camp for more than a year; we arrived in February 1944, and this was February 1945—we received a very small Red Cross package: my sister, my father, and I. A very small package, the size of a book, with *knäckebrot* (Scandinavian crackers), and a few cookies. You can't imagine how little that was. My son always says, "But Mama, that was something really very special." But in those days we really collected everything, half a cookie, a sock, a glove—anything that gave a little warmth or something to eat. My friends also gave me something for Anne. I certainly couldn't have thrown a large package over the barbed-wire fence; not that I had one, but that wouldn't have been possible at all.

We agreed to try to meet the next evening at eight o'clock—I believe I still had a watch. And, in fact, I succeeded in throwing the package over.

But I heard her screaming, and I called out, "What happened?"

And Anne answered, "Oh, the woman standing next to me caught it, and she won't give it back to me."

Then she began to scream.

I calmed her down a bit and said, "I'll try again but I don't know if I'll be able to." We arranged to meet again, two or three days later, and I was actually able to throw over another package. She caught it; that was the main thing.

After these three or four meetings at the barbed-wire fence in Bergen-Belsen, I didn't see her again, because the people in Anne's camp were transferred to another section in Bergen-Belsen. That happened around the end of February.

That was the last time I saw Anne alive and spoke to her. . . . ❖

THINKING through the LITERATURE

1. **Comprehension Check** Why was Hannah unable to see Anne, even though they were standing close to each other?

2. Nazi concentration camps were designed to destroy human bodies and minds. How does the Anne Frank at Bergen-Belsen compare with the character in the play? What do you think about this difference in Anne?

3. In an attempt to make their victims feel worthless, the Nazis stripped the Jews of personal belongings and other expressions of identity. In light of this fact, why is it so important to Hannah that she be able to see her father and sister? How might the presence of loved ones give people the will to survive?

from All But My Life

PREPARING to Read

Build Background

Gerda's Story Gerda Weissmann Klein was fifteen years old when the Germans invaded Poland in 1939. Like Anne Frank, Gerda lost her freedom under Nazi rule. In 1942, Nazis removed Gerda from her home and forced her to work as a slave laborer in German factories. Gerda's family and friends all perished in the Holocaust.

In 1945, after three years of slave labor, Gerda was forced to go with the Nazis as they fled from the advancing Soviet army. In the final days of the war, she was rescued by American soldiers, one of whom she married in 1946. At the time of her rescue, she weighed 68 pounds.

Focus Your Reading

LITERARY ANALYSIS **AUTOBIOGRAPHY**
The story of a person's life written by that person is called an **autobiography.** In this excerpt from her autobiography, *All But My Life,* Gerda describes the beginning of the 1,000-mile winter march that she was forced to endure. As you read the excerpt, notice how she describes in vivid detail the agony of that march. Why is it so important to hear the story in Gerda's own words?

**autobiography by
Gerda Weissmann Klein**

The sirens began to howl more and more frequently. The Germans threw frightened glances toward the sky and hatefully looked at us. Let them worry now, we gloated. Let them sit on the charred[1] remains of their homes. Let them see their families killed. Then will they shout "Heil Hitler!"?

"It's coming," whispered my heart. "Their downfall is coming!" But I was not naïve. I knew that it would not come without increased suffering on our part.

Christmas passed. There was no Christmas spirit that year. The new year came—the year of 1945.

In January the sirens blew almost daily. Less and less production was entered into the books. At noon one day the electricity went off. The supervisors stood talking excitedly. The SS[2] women took us back to camp. Something drastic had happened. Perhaps the war was over.

That night we were ordered to take all our belongings and go into the dining hall. The door to our sleeping quarters was barricaded. After being given food we huddled together, waiting.

It was snowing heavily. After a time we heard the courtyard gates burst open. Every heart beat faster in

---

1. **charred:** burned; scorched.
2. **SS:** the elite security force of the Nazi Party (an abbreviation of the German word *Schutzstaffel*).

WE could hear running feet and shouting from the other side of the barricaded doors.

Gerda at age 16

expectation. There were shrieks and screams and cries outside. We could hear running feet and shouting from the other side of the barricaded doors. Those of us who sat next to the doors started calling to the newcomers in our sleeping quarters.

They were Jewish girls. They had come from another camp and had been walking for five days. Now we were to join them. They thought we were going to Oranienburg, a concentration camp like Auschwitz, to be gassed. Auschwitz, they said, had been captured by the Russians, who had reconquered Poland and were crossing the German frontier. The English and Americans were invading Germany from the West. Would a miracle happen before we reached the gas chambers?

And so the last stretch of the war began. Not in peaceful Bolkenhain, not in the coal cars of Märzdorf,[3] the night shifts of Landeshut. Nor were we to endure it in tuberculosis-ridden Grünberg. I was certain that we would meet freedom somewhere in the open, and that we would meet it soon.

---

3. **Märzdorf** (mârts′dôrf′) . . . **Landeshut** (län′dəs-ho̅o̅t′).

"You are crazy!" Suse said. "We will never see the liberation, for they will see to it. They would leave us here if they did not want us killed."

"We will be free," I insisted. "I know it, I feel it."

Ilse and Liesel sat in silence. Suse's big eyes filled with tears, the first tears that I ever saw her shed.

"How can you believe so strongly?" she murmured. "But then, you always believed. Remember when we met on the train?"

I nodded.

"Well, you lost that bet," she reminded me.

"I know," I said.

"But you still believe?"

"I do!"

"Tell me, Gerda," Suse whispered urgently, "what is it? What makes you so sure?"

"I don't know. It's something I cannot explain, but I know somehow that we will be liberated."

"And I feel," Suse stammered, "I feel that I will not be."

All that last night in Grünberg I coughed. I think I had a temperature. Ilse, Suse, Liesel, and I cuddled together closely.

"Gerda, don't get sick," they begged, as if I could decide.

At dawn we were given three portions of bread, which we carefully placed in our bundles. We saw the kitchen personnel pack big parcels of food in their bundles.

At the last moment before we assembled, the four of us decided to put on most of the clothes we had intended to carry.

The SS women came for us. We lined up. Ilse was on my left, Liesel and Suse were on my right. We stood erect.

"Let us be strong," Liesel whispered.

"Yes," I answered.

"You be strong," Ilse whispered back to me. I was now the least fit of the group.

As we squeezed through the door, we gripped hands for a fleeting moment. Then we marched out into the bright snow.

The outer gates were open when we reached the courtyard. Stretching as far as we could see were columns of girls. I was shocked to see so many. We learned later there were about three thousand from other camps; with our contingent[4] from Grünberg we totaled nearly four thousand. We were divided into two transports amidst much whipping and screaming by the SS. Many girls tried to shift from one group to another, in the hope that it might be the better one.

We four were in the column which was doomed; out of two thousand only a hundred and twenty survived. The other column was liberated much sooner. Had I been part of it my fate would have been different. Less suffering, yes, but less happiness, too, I am sure.

---

4. **contingent:** group.

Although I had seen misery, I was utterly unprepared for the picture that the girls who had already been marching for a week presented. Covered with gray blankets, they reminded me of drawings of Death when, winged and garbed[5] in loose sheets, he comes to collect the living. Some of them were barefoot, others wore crude wooden clogs. Many of them left a bloody trail in the fresh snow.

Suse looked at me and I looked at my feet—clad in the ski boots that Papa had insisted I wear on that hot summer day. Papa, Papa, how could he possibly have known. The boots were still in good shape, and I had precious things hidden in them: snapshots of Papa, Mama, Arthur, and Abek, wrapped in a piece of cloth, and the packet of poison. In Grünberg they had taken away all pictures, papers, and letters. Germany, we were told, needed all scrap paper she could get. Ilse and I had managed to hide our pictures. Our only worry now was that water might soak through our shoes and ruin them.

"Forward march!" shouted the SS *Wachtmeister*[6] at the head of our column.

"Forward march!" echoed SS men. Carrying rifles, they were stationed along our column at intervals of about thirty feet.

"Forward march!" came the high-pitched voices of the whip-armed SS women.

WE took the first step. I thought: I am marching to death or to liberation.

We took the first step. I thought: I am marching to death or to liberation. It was the morning of January 29, 1945.

We marched all day, with a break at noon. Ilse and I shared one of our portions of bread, guarding the rest carefully. At the head of the column we saw the commandant of the SS with a Hungarian-Jewish girl who, we were told, was his mistress. She and a few of her close friends knew no want; they had plenty to eat, and slept always in peasant houses, rather than in barns or in open fields as the others did.

"How could they?" I asked myself over and over again.

Toward evening, as it grew colder, we were herded off the road and into a huge barn. We huddled together in the darkness and again Ilse and I shared a portion of our bread. It wasn't enough.

"Ilse, I am terribly hungry," I confessed.

"So am I," Ilse admitted. "I would like something warm to drink. We can't eat any more bread, for who knows when they will give us more?"

---

5. **garbed:** clothed.

6. **Wachtmeister** (väKHt′mī′stər) *German:* a high-ranking noncommissioned officer.

A collection of shoes belonging to prisoners deported to a concentration camp

"Careful, careful!" somebody called in the darkness. "The Magyars[7] are after our bread!"

Yes, the poor Hungarian girls were hungry. They had been marching a week already.

"My shoes, my shoes!" another voice cried. "They took them from right next to me!"

Many of the Hungarian girls had no shoes. To save their lives they stole shoes off the feet of those who slept. How much I learned that night!

> "**MY** shoes, my shoes!" another voice cried. "They took them from right next to me!"

When the doors of the dark barn were thrown open in the morning I could see a flood of wintry sunlight on the glittering snow. Two SS men stood at the entrance and with their rifles prodded us as we emerged four abreast.

A little distance away stood the SS commandant with his girl friend and her court of privileged friends. They were eating bread and drinking something steaming out of a large thermos. How good it must feel, I thought, the warm drink in that cold!

We assembled and were counted and recounted. A girl from Grünberg was missing. A few others were beaten bloody because of it, but either they did not know what had become of her or they would not tell.

We learned the story later. A German from the factory who was in love with the girl had followed our column, and under cover of darkness had snatched her quietly away.

---

7. **Magyars** (măg′yärz′): members of the main ethnic group of Hungary.

We marched many miles that second day, often plowing through untouched snow. Again we rested at midday.

"I wonder when they will give us something to eat," Ilse said to the three of us as we nibbled our dry, frozen bread.

We did not answer.

Girls who had lagged behind that morning had been beaten by the SS men with the butts of their guns.

After the midday pause, a couple of girls just sat motionless on the snow, refusing to go. We marched on. Behind us there were pistol shots.

"God!" I said, "God!" looking up to the sky. The sky was blue, the snow was clean, the snowy pine trees were beautiful in the sunlight. ❖

THINKING through the LITERATURE

1. **Comprehension Check** Why are Gerda's boots important to her?

2. **COMPARING TEXTS** Optimists are people who think that everything will turn out well. Pessimists are people who see gloom around every corner. Are Anne Frank and Gerda Weissmann Klein optimists or pessimists? Why do you think so? Support your answer with details from the texts.

3. Reread the last paragraph in the selection. What contrast is Gerda making in this paragraph? How does the contrast add to the power of the selection?

   Think About:
   - why she is calling out to God
   - the beauty of the sky, the snow, and the pine trees

Gerda Weissmann Klein Today

A Life Regained Although the Nazis robbed Gerda Klein of "all but her life," she did not give up. In 1947 she married U.S. Army Lieutenant Kurt Klein, the man who had liberated her from the death march, and set out to build a new life with him in the United States. Today she uses her life to enlarge the lives of others.

The Power of Film A respected historian, author, and human rights activist, Gerda tells her story to people all over the world. Those who cannot hear Gerda in person can listen to her on film. One film, *Testimony,* plays continuously at the Holocaust Museum in Washington, D.C. The other film, an HBO documentary, *One Survivor Remembers,* won both an Emmy and an Oscar award.

More Books Gerda's fame extends to several other books and many articles. In addition to *All But My Life,* she has written *Promise of a New Spring,* a guide for teaching young children about the Holocaust. Her book about a mentally challenged child, *The Blue Rose,* was published in 1974. It helped establish the Blue Rose Foundation, an organization dedicated to helping mentally challenged young adults.

A Message to Children Gerda's work with young people is particularly important to her. In addition to teaching them about the value of tolerance, she also encourages them to help people less fortunate than themselves. At a speech in Cincinnati not long ago, Gerda asked students to bring cans of food in place of an admission ticket. The students brought 7,000 cans of food to feed the city's hungry children!

Gerda Weissmann Klein and Kurt Klein

a Diary from Another World

Connect to Your Life

Simple Pleasures In this newspaper article, Gerda Weissmann Klein, the author of *All But My Life,* writes about visiting Anne Frank's hiding place, which is now a museum. Gerda notes that while in hiding, Anne and her family were deprived of a great many of the simple pleasures that most people take for granted. With a small group of classmates, discuss the things you would miss most if you were forced into hiding.

Focus Your Reading

LITERARY ANALYSIS **MAIN IDEA**

The **main idea** is the writer's most important, or central, point. In the newspaper article you are about to read, the main idea is stated in the last paragraph:

> *This is the legacy she left us, the understanding of things all of us take for granted.*

As you read the article, look for ideas and details that support or explain the main idea. Why do you think the writer put the main idea at the end of the article?

"On Friday, June 12, I woke up at 6 A.M. and—small wonder—it was my birthday. I received a warm welcome from my cat and masses of things from Mummy and Daddy . . ."

Any 13-year-old girl could have written that on her birthday. As it happens these words appear in a diary which was one of the "masses of things" and in which Anne Frank wrote: "I hope I shall be able to confide in[1] you completely, as I have never been able to do in anyone before . . ."

Anne Frank was a girl with dark eyes set into a pale white face. She loved her cat, fought at times with her older sister, thought her parents were terribly old-fashioned, was indifferent to a boy named Peter and eventually learned to care for him a lot.

She thought that what she would write in her diary would be for her eyes alone, so she committed[2] her innermost thoughts to it. She thought that perhaps in the very distant future—when she might have children, or even grandchildren, that they might on a rainy afternoon find their grandmother's old diary.

1. **confide in:** trust with secrets.
2. **committed:** gave for safekeeping; entrusted.

The view from the Annex

In her Annex room, Anne's wall was covered with photos of movie stars and family.

She might chuckle over the things she had once written and let her children share them with her, as she would tell them of "the olden days."

Alas, Anne Frank died as a young girl, for no other reason than that she was Jewish. The Nazis invaded Holland, as they did most other European countries, and anyone who loved freedom and equality and was free of prejudice became an enemy of the Nazi regime.

Many millions of people died at the hands of the Nazis, among them almost the entire Jewish population of Europe, some 6 million. It took the combined efforts of the American, English and Russian armies, their allies, as well as countless partisan groups in occupied countries, such as France, Poland, the Scandinavian countries, six long years to defeat Nazi Germany.

Anne Frank's diary is a reflection of her soul, the revelation of her heart.

This dark chapter of history is known as World War II, spanning the years between 1939 and 1945.

Anne Frank's diary is a reflection of her soul, the revelation of her heart. It is or could be the story of any young, bright vivacious girl who started life as anyone would, with the hope of living it fully, free to enjoy it and to have some fun.

But the very right to life was denied her.

The diary which she kept and recorded in the loneliness of her secret hiding place was found amidst the debris of the tiny rooms in which the Franks and another family had been hiding for 2 years.

I visited Anne Frank's house the other day. Actually, I visited it twice—once alone at night when it was tightly closed, the inside shrouded in darkness. It conveyed then the eerie feeling of a tomb in which Anne's unfulfilled dreams had been dreamed during many lonely nights. I stood by the dark canal thinking of the young girl and remembered my own childhood dreams.

Then I returned during the daytime, as the sun shone brightly and the carillon from the nearby clock tower, of which Anne had written, was just playing a merry tune. In the bright sunlight, I heard music playing, saw boats moving on the canal and observed people walking by.

Across the canal I noticed a boutique, saw some young people looking at sweaters. Two kids in jeans rode on bicycles. Life was going on, even as it must have gone on while she lived there.

Actually, I found it sadder during the daytime, for the night at least seemed to shut out the rest of the world, whereas during the day everything revolved around the silent, subdued girl who so desperately wanted to be a part of that stream of life.

What did she think about in those tiny rooms where shutters had to be closed in the daytime? She tells us that often the heat became oppressive from the tiny stove on which the families cooked their meals. We know that the toilet could not be flushed in the daytime, lest the neighbors would be alerted to the existence of the hiding place.

What did Anne Frank think about as she sat on her bed during those perilous[3] days looking at the pictures of American movie stars and a picture of a chimpanzee's birthday party which still hangs there today?

Her diary tells us that she thought not of fame, nor wealth, nor greatness. She thought rather how much she would want to run downstairs into the tiny garden where sunflowers now bloom against the fence, instead of having to glimpse them from far above.

She thought of touching them and running through a meadow in the spring, of buying an ice cream cone from a vendor on a hot summer afternoon.

She thought of ordinary things, such as going to school with other kids. She thought of dressing up and being able to go to the movies.

In short, she thought of all the things which millions of kids do every day and find boring. But to Anne, who occasionally dared to climb to the roof to see the sky and the patch of world below, that world was as remote as the evening star.

This is the legacy[4] she left us, the understanding of things all of us take for granted. Through understanding, let us assure that all people everywhere can live in freedom so that a book like "The Diary of Anne Frank" will never be written again as a true story. ❖

---

3. **perilous:** dangerous.
4. **legacy:** something handed down to those who will come later.

THINKING *through the* LITERATURE

1. How do you feel about the "ordinary things" of your life after reading this article?

2. What is the meaning of the title of the article, "A Diary from Another World"?

3. How does Klein's observation of activity on the street contribute to the story she is telling about Anne Frank?

CHOICES and CHALLENGES

Writing

Video Review With your teacher's approval, rent the 1959 film adaptation of *The Diary of Anne Frank.* Write a review of the movie. In your review, tell how well the movie portrays the play's characters and captures the play's conflicts and tensions. Be sure to support your conclusions with quotations from the dialogue and comparisons between scenes in the movie and in the play. Place your review in your **Working Portfolio.**

Speaking & Listening

A Scene from the Play With classmates, perform a scene from the play. Hold auditions for the parts. Create scenery and props. Record sound effects. Present the scene to your class. In your performance, be sure to use voice modulation, tone, and gestures to enhance the meaning of the scene.

Speaking and Listening Handbook
See p. R107: Dramatic Reading.

Research & Technology

SOCIAL STUDIES Today, many organizations and individuals are working to prevent another Holocaust from taking place. A few of these organizations are listed below. Use the Internet and/or library resources to find out about one of these groups. Why was the group founded? What is the group doing to stop prejudice? Prepare a report to present to the class.

- Anne Frank Foundation
- United States Holocaust Museum
- Steven Spielberg's Shoah Project

Vocabulary

STANDARDIZED TEST PRACTICE

Choose the word or group of words that means the same, or nearly the same, as the underlined Word to Know.

1. Vile food—
   A expensive B hateful
   C plentiful D extra

2. To wallow in the mud—
   J step K slip
   L roll M run

3. A football fan's zeal
   A enthusiasm B bravery
   C disloyalty D victory

4. A sense of remorse—
   J kindness K regret
   L coincidence M adjustment

5. A disgruntled customer—
   A distressed B distinct
   C distant D displeased

6. A conspicuous badge—
   J required K counterfeit
   L obvious M special

7. A song of jubilation—
   A rejoicing B openness
   C remembrance D forgiveness

8. Appalled bystanders—
   J depressed K shocked
   L injured M annoyed

9. To loathe an opponent—
   A hate B respect
   C taunt D tolerate

10. To gesture ostentatiously—
    J wildly K gracefully
    L obediently M grandly

EXERCISE: SYNONYMS AND ANTONYMS
Identify the relationship between each boldfaced Word to Know and the word to its right by writing *Synonyms* or *Antonyms.*

1. **pandemonium** confusion
2. **oppression** liberation
3. **indignantly** calmly
4. **inarticulate** speechless
5. **foreboding** excitement

Grammar in Context: Adverbs

In the following passage from *The Diary of Anne Frank,* Goodrich and Hackett use **adverbs** to describe how Mrs. Van Daan reacts when her husband threatens to sell her coat.

> **Mrs. Van Daan** (*Sharply*). Putti, where are you going? (*She rushes up the stairs after him, calling* hysterically.)

An adverb is a word that modifies a verb, an adjective, or another adverb. Adverbs that modify verbs tell *how, when, where,* or *to what extent* an action happened. Writers use adverbs to show how characters act or speak and to provide clarity in stage directions.

Apply to Your Writing Using adverbs in your writing can help your readers visualize how characters speak or behave. Adverbs often appear in the stage directions of plays to show how an action should be performed.

WRITING EXERCISE Write an adverb in the parentheses to show how each character acts or speaks.

Example: *Original* (_____). Have you seen my cat? Have you seen him anywhere? I'm very worried.

Rewritten (Anxiously). Have you seen my cat? Have you seen him anywhere? I'm very worried.

1. (_____) What is that sound? I'm afraid.
2. (_____) We must keep our voices down and try to whisper.
3. (_____) Who's angry? I'm not angry!
4. (_____) Don't be afraid. I'm here with you.
5. (_____) I'm so thrilled! Thanks so much for this present!

Grammar Handbook
See p. R86: Using Modifiers Effectively.

Frances Goodrich
1890–1984

Albert Hackett
1900–1995

Writers of Comedies and Musicals Albert Hackett and Frances Goodrich were a writing team who were best known for their Hollywood comedies and musicals. The couple met in 1924, during their acting days on the New York stage. In 1930 they wrote their first play together, and in 1931 they were married. Soon after, they left for Hollywood, where they wrote a series of screenplays for films such as *The Thin Man* (1934), *It's a Wonderful Life* (1946), and *Seven Brides for Seven Brothers* (1954).

The Diary of a Young Girl In the early 1950s, the couple adapted *The Diary of a Young Girl* by Anne Frank into a stage play, which opened in 1955. This play, so unlike their lighthearted Hollywood work, marked a dramatic change of tone for the writing couple. To prepare for the play, they traveled to Amsterdam to interview Mr. Frank and to study the Secret Annex and its surrounding neighborhood. The play won several major awards, including a Pulitzer Prize in 1956.

Building Vocabulary
Interpreting Analogies

"The Treasure of Lemon Brown" begins with a type of comparison known as an analogy. An **analogy** is a comparison of two dissimilar things in order to clarify the less familiar of the two. In this case, the character's mood is clarified for the reader through comparison to a physical image, the sky. Since clouds cannot be angry, the phrase "angry, swirling clouds" is meant to be understood for its figurative meaning rather than its literal meaning.

Notice that in this analogy, the relationship is metaphorical.

> The dark sky, filled with angry, swirling clouds, reflected Greg Ridley's mood as he sat on the stoop of his building.
>
> —Walter Dean Myers,
> "The Treasure of Lemon Brown"

This analogy compares a stormy sky and the mood of one of the characters.

Strategies for Building Vocabulary

Analogies appear frequently in literature. They also appear in standardized tests. Analogies in tests present relationships between pairs of words and are meant to test students' ability to think logically. Although analogies may appear difficult, there is an easy, logical way of solving them. Use the following strategies to solve analogies.

❶ Restate the Analogy One kind of analogy follows this format:

Write the word that completes this analogy.

SIMPLE : UNCOMPLICATED ::
talkative : _____

The colon (:) represents the phrase "is related to" or, in shortened form, "is to." If this analogy were read aloud, one would say "*Simple* is to *uncomplicated* as *talkative* is to ___?___." Restating the analogy is the first step in the process of analyzing the relationship it represents.

❷ Analyze the Relationship Look at the first word pair in this analogy and identify the relationship between the words. In this case the analogy is an analogy of synonyms. Once you have determined that the first pair of words are synonyms, you can think about a synonym for *talkative*. A word such as *chatty* would be a good synonym for *talkative* and would complete the word analogy.

Now consider a different kind of analogy:

DOG : MAMMAL :: lizard : _____

Because a dog is a kind of mammal, you would identify this analogy as one of item to category. You would then write the word *reptile* to complete the analogy. There are many other kinds of word relationships, as well.

Consider this analogy.

PAIN : AGONY :: anger : _____

Because agony is an intense form of pain, you would identify this analogy as one of degree of intensity. You would then write the word *fury* to complete the analogy.

❸ Learn Relationship Types Test analogies explore many different kinds of relationships between words. The following chart lists common types of relationships that you might come across in test analogies.

Common Types of Analogies		
Type	**Example**	**Relationship**
Part to Whole	WHEEL : BICYCLE	is part of
Synonyms	GLAD : HAPPY	means the same as
Antonyms	TALL : SHORT	means the opposite of
Cause to Effect	DOWNPOUR : FLOODING	results in or leads to
Worker to Tool	CARPENTER : HAMMER	works with
Degree of Intensity	FEAR : TERROR	is less (or more) intense than
Grammar	DELIGHT : DELIGHTFUL	is grammatically related to
Item to Category	PEACH : FRUIT	is a type or an example of
Age	PUPPY : DOG	is younger (or older) than
Object to Its Material	TIRE : RUBBER	is made of
Product to Source	HONEY : BEES	comes from
Characteristic Quality	UNIVERSE : VAST	is characteristically

EXERCISE Complete each analogy by choosing a word from the list below. Identify the relationship on which the analogy is based. Use the chart to help you.

EXAMPLE: RUDDER : SHIP :: windshield : <u>automobile</u>

        Type of analogy: <u>Part to Whole</u>

grief	telescope	injection	hair	corruption
computer	exhaustion	sheep	food	wet

1. INSPECT : INSPECTION :: corrupt : _____

2. FEATHER : WING :: keyboard : _____

3. REGRET : REMORSE :: sorrow : _____

4. CONFUSION : CHAOS :: weariness : _____

5. BIOLOGIST : MICROSCOPE :: astronomer : _____

6. PAPER : TREE :: wool : _____

7. REJECT : REJECTION :: inject : _____

8. DESERT : DRY :: ocean : _____

9. PAINTER : PAINT :: cook : _____

10. WINDOW : GLASS :: wig : _____

Writing Workshop

Identifying similarities and differences . . .

From Reading to Writing In *The Diary of Anne Frank,* Anne remarks on the differences between herself and her sister Margot. She complains that everything Margot does is considered right, while everything she does is wrong. The sisters do have similarities, however. Both are intelligent and sensitive. One way to explore such similarities and differences is by writing a **comparison-and-contrast essay.** Comparing two characters—or two other related subjects—gives you a better understanding of each.

For Your Portfolio

WRITING PROMPT Write an essay in which you compare and contrast two characters in literature or two other subjects that interest you.

Purpose: To inform, explain, or clarify
Audience: Anyone interested in your subjects

Basics in a Box

Comparison-and-Contrast Essay at a Glance

Introduction	Body	Conclusion
• introduces the **subjects** being compared • tells the **reason** for the comparison	explains similarities and differences Subject A only — Both subjects — Subject B only	• summarizes the comparison • explains new understanding

RUBRIC STANDARDS FOR WRITING

A successful comparison-and-contrast essay should

- introduce the subjects being compared
- state a clear purpose for the comparison
- include both similarities and differences and support each statement with examples and details

- follow a clear organizational pattern
- include transitional words and phrases to make similarities and differences clear
- summarize the comparison in the conclusion

Analyzing a Student Model

Michael Hogan
Ms. Sandra Mattox, Coppell Middle School North

SPEAKING OPPORTUNITY
See the Speaking and Listening Handbook, p. R104, for oral presentation tips.

Mr. Frank and Mr. Van Daan

It's hard to imagine moving into a tiny apartment with people you have never met. This type of situation could easily bring out differences between the people who are living together. In the play *The Diary of Anne Frank,* the differences between two characters, Mr. Frank and Mr. Van Daan, are clear. Their situation is similar, but their personalities, behavior, and relationships with their families are very different.

Mr. Frank and Mr. Van Daan are living under terrible conditions. Both are Jews living in Nazi-occupied Amsterdam during World War II. Both are married and are fathers; Mr. Frank has two daughters, and Mr. Van Daan has one son. Both men are trying to keep their families hidden from the Nazis, which leads them to move into the apartment above the warehouse. This, however, is where the similarities end.

There are many differences between the two men. First, their personalities are almost opposites. Mr. Van Daan is very concerned with appearances, as the stage directions in Act One, Scene 2, indicate: "His clothes and overcoat are expensive and well cut." Once in a while he can be kind, but he often loses his temper. Mr. Van Daan has strong opinions about the roles of men and women. For example, he acts embarrassed that his son Peter likes his pet cat, and he disapproves of Anne's outspokenness. He tells her, "Men don't like that kind of thing in a girl. . . . A man likes a girl who'll listen to him once in a while . . . a domestic girl, who'll keep her house shining for her husband . . . who loves to cook and sew. . . ." (Act One, Scene 3). In contrast, Mr. Frank does not seem to care about material things. He always stays calm and has compassion for other people, even when they have done something bad. For example, when Mr. Van Daan is caught stealing food, Mr. Frank tries to understand Van Daan's behavior and tries to smooth things over. Mr. Frank does not have the attitude about some women that Mr. Van Daan has. He never criticizes Anne for being unladylike; instead, he encourages her to be herself. He gives her a

---

RUBRIC
IN ACTION

❶ States features of the two subjects that will be compared in a coherent thesis statement

❷ Writer chooses a feature-by-feature organization that is written with a parallel structure (one paragraph per feature: 1st feature—similar situations; 2nd feature—different personalities; 3rd feature—different responses to crisis; 4th feature—communicate differently).

Another Option:

• Subject-by-subject organization explores all features of the first subject and then all features of the second subject.

diary because he knows she loves to write, and he is proud of her creativity when she makes Hanukkah presents for everyone. Anne says of her father, "He's the only one who's ever given me the feeling that I have any sense" (Act Two, Scene 1).

The two men's different personalities determine how they respond to the crisis they are in. Mr. Van Daan is self-centered and believes that he suffers from hunger more than the others. This leads him to try to take Anne's piece of cake when she leaves it unguarded, and to sneak downstairs in the middle of the night to steal food from the common supply. In contrast, Mr. Frank always puts the needs of others before his own. For example, when Dr. Dussel comes to stay in the apartment, Mr. Frank makes him feel welcome and doesn't think twice about giving him food. When a robber is heard in the warehouse, Mr. Frank risks his own safety to investigate the situation.

Mr. Frank and Mr. Van Daan communicate differently with their families. Mr. and Mrs. Van Daan communicate mostly through loud, angry quarrels. "The Van Daans' 'discussions' are as violent as ever," Anne remarks after living with them for a year and a half (Act Two, Scene 1). Mr. and Mrs. Van Daan remain close despite their arguments, but Mr. Van Daan's relationship with his son is not as strong. He criticizes Peter for his slowness and for loving his cat. At one point he threatens to get rid of the cat. In contrast, Mr. Frank shows only love and respect for his wife and daughters. He is gentle with them, and even when he scolds Anne, he does so privately and in a way that teaches a lesson. After Anne has hurt her mother's feelings, Mr. Frank tells her that parents "can only try to set a good example . . . point the way. The rest you must do yourself" (Act One, Scene 4).

In *The Diary of Anne Frank,* the differences between the two fathers outnumber the similarities. Mr. Frank and Mr. Van Daan are in the same situation with the same people, but while Mr. Van Daan acts emotionally and selfishly, Mr. Frank is calm and considerate. Both are caring and love their friends and families, but I would rather live with Mr. Frank if I were in the same situation. He is a leader who puts others before himself, and because of his sensible decisions, those living in the secret apartment survive longer than they would have without him. Mr. Frank helps the others make the best out of a very bad circumstance.

❸ Writer uses transitions to signal contrasts.

❹ Writer supports observations of differences with examples and quotations from the text, showing careful reading.

❺ Summarizes comparison and supports conclusion

❻ Reveals writer's new insight about and response to characters gained from comparison

Writing Your Comparison-and-Contrast Essay

❶ Prewriting

It is possible to compare just about anything, from people to objects to feelings. Think about why you might make such a comparison. Do you have to make a choice or a decision? Do you want to better understand two subjects that are related? See the **Idea Bank** in the margin for more suggestions. After you have chosen your subjects, follow the steps below.

Planning Your Comparison-and-Contrast Essay

▶ 1. **Examine the differences and similarities between your subjects.** What are their most important features? Which are similar? Which are different? Using a Venn diagram will help you sort out your ideas.

▶ 2. **Decide which features to compare and contrast.** What do you want to learn about your subjects by comparing them? Compare and contrast the features that illustrate the main idea.

▶ 3. **Choose your organizational pattern.** There are two ways to organize your comparison-and-contrast essay: subject by subject or feature by feature. Decide which pattern is more effective for your essay, and create a chart like the one shown to outline your points.

Subject by Subject	Feature by Feature
Subject A	Feature 1
Feature 1	Subject A
Feature 2	Subject B
Subject B	Feature 2
Feature 1	Subject A
Feature 2	Subject B

❷ Drafting

Begin to write your essay, keeping in mind that you can revise it later. Use your organizational chart to help keep track of the ideas.

- Use your **introduction** to establish your purpose.
- Keep to the same organizational plan throughout your essay.
- Include **transitions** to indicate similarities and differences clearly.
- Develop a strong **conclusion** to summarize your comparison.

IDEA Bank

1. For Your Working Portfolio 📁
Look for suggestions in the **Writing** sections that you completed earlier.

2. Writing Across Literature
From two different works, choose two characters that seem similar on the surface. Look more closely at them to discover differences.

3. Time Travel
Interview a parent or an older relative. Ask how life was the same or different when he or she was your age.

Have a question?

See the **Writing Handbook**
Compare and Contrast, p. R45
Introductions, p. R36
See **Language Network**
Prewriting, p. 314
Drafting, p. 317

Ask Your Peer Reader: EVALUATING

- Was my reason for comparison clear?
- Did I support my statements with facts and examples?
- Was my organization clear and consistent?
- How well did I describe the similarities and differences?

Need revising help?

Review the **Rubric,** p. 536

Consider **peer reader** comments

Check **Revision Guidelines,** p. R33

Perplexed about participles?

See the **Grammar Handbook,** p. R84

SPELLING From Writing

As you revise your work, look back at the words you misspelled and determine why you made the errors you did. For additional help, refer to the strategies and generalizations in the **Spelling Handbook** on page R28.

SPEAKING Opportunity

Turn your essay into an oral presentation.

Publishing IDEAS

- Talk to classmates who compared and contrasted the same characters. Compare the points that you each made in your essays.

- Transform your essay into a brief lecture. Emphasize what you learned through the process of comparing and contrasting.

INTERNET

Publishing Options
www.mcdougallittell.com

---

❸ Revising

TARGET SKILL ▷ **SUPPORTING IDEAS WITH EXAMPLES**

As you write your comparison-and-contrast essay, you must give examples to support the similarities and differences that you point out. To provide an example from a work of literature, you can quote directly from the text, or you can summarize an event that occurred in the story.

> He never criticizes Anne for being unladylike; instead,
>
> he encourages her to be herself. *He gives her a diary because he knows she loves to write, and he is proud of her creativity when she makes Hannukkah presents for everyone.*

❹ Editing and Proofreading

TARGET SKILL ▷ **PAST AND PRESENT PARTICIPLES** Participles are useful for helping describe the subjects in a comparison. Most past participles are formed by adding *-ed* or *-d* to the present tense, but some past participles are irregular. Proofread your essay to make sure that you have used the correct past-participle forms. With both past and present participles, make sure that you use the correct helping verbs.

> *are*
> Both ~~were~~ caring and love their friends and families,
> *would*
> but I rather live with Mr. Frank if I were in the same
>
> situation.

❺ Reflecting

FOR YOUR WORKING PORTFOLIO How did comparing and contrasting your two subjects help you to understand each of them better? What other subjects would you like to compare and contrast? Attach your reflections to your finished work. Save your comparison-and-contrast essay in your **Working Portfolio.**

Standardized Test Practice

Mixed Review

> At first glance, my Aunt Alice and Uncle Jim seem like an odd pair. <u>Alice is tallest by three inches</u>, with long legs and blond hair. <u>Jim was</u>
> (1)
> <u>rather round and has dark hair</u>. However, they have the same attitude
> (2)
> toward life. <u>Neither Alice nor Jim is very domestic.</u> They'd never dream
> (3)
> of spending a Friday night at home on their own. <u>They wanted to be</u>
> <u>where the action is.</u> <u>Friday nights and Saturday afternoons finds</u> them
> (4)   (5)
> hosting cook-outs or going out dancing with friends. In their spare time,
> <u>they see the latest plays. Or movies.</u>
> (6)

Review Your Skills

Use the passage and the questions that follow it to check how well you remember the language conventions you've learned in previous grades.

1. How is sentence 1 best written?
- **A.** Alice is more tall by three inches
- **B.** Alice is taller by three inches
- **C.** Alice is most tall by three inches
- **D.** Correct as is

2. How is sentence 2 best written?
- **A.** Jim is rather round and has dark hair.
- **B.** Jim was rather round and had dark hair.
- **C.** Jim was rather round and have dark hair.
- **D.** Correct as is

3. How is sentence 3 best written?
- **A.** Neither Alice nor Jim are very domestic.
- **B.** Either Alice or Jim are not very domestic.
- **C.** Alice and Jim is not very domestic.
- **D.** Correct as is

4. How is sentence 4 best written?
- **A.** They wanted to be where the action was.
- **B.** They are wanting to be where the action was.
- **C.** They want to be where the action is.
- **D.** Correct as is

5. How is sentence 5 best written?
- **A.** Friday nights and Saturday afternoons find
- **B.** Friday nights and Saturday afternoons found
- **C.** Friday nights and Saturday afternoons has found
- **D.** Correct as is

6. How is sentence 6 best written?
- **A.** they see the latest plays; or movies.
- **B.** they see the latest, plays or movies.
- **C.** they see the latest plays or movies.
- **D.** Correct as is

Self-Assessment

Check your own answers in the **Grammar Handbook**

Verb Tenses, p. R84

Forming Compound Sentences, p. R76

Agreement with Compound Subjects, p. R76

The Human Spirit

The characters in this unit learn about themselves and human nature. In each selection, which event or events test a character's strength or weakness? How do you think you would have reacted in a similar situation? Which character or characters taught you the most about the human spirit? What did that character teach you? How do you think you might be able to use this insight in your own life?

Second Circle Dance, Phoebe Beasley/Omni-Photo Communications

Reflecting on Theme

OPTION 1

Reflecting on the Human Spirit Think about the ways in which the play *The Diary of Anne Frank* teaches you about the unit theme, "The Human Spirit." Write a paragraph describing the struggles that Anne Frank faced and how they affected her life.

OPTION 2

Discussing Ideas With a small group of classmates, discuss the following questions: Which selections did you learn the most from in this unit? Give examples from the selections to support your choices. Do you think that reading literature can help you in real life? Explain how this can be true. How does reading literature compare with real-life experiences as a way to learn?

Self **ASSESSMENT**

READER'S NOTEBOOK

Think about the quotation at the beginning of the unit: "Injustice anywhere is a threat to justice everywhere." Write a paragraph explaining how the selections in this unit have helped you to better understand the quotation's meaning.

REVIEWING YOUR PERSONAL WORD List

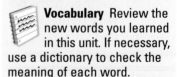

Vocabulary Review the new words you learned in this unit. If necessary, use a dictionary to check the meaning of each word.

Spelling Review your list of spelling words. If you're not sure of the correct spelling, use a dictionary or refer to the **Spelling Handbook** on page R28.

Reviewing Literary Concepts

OPTION 1

Analyzing First-Person Point of View Several selections in this unit were written from the first-person point of view. Create a chart that lists the advantages and disadvantages of telling a story from that point of view. Choose one of the selections and write a paragraph explaining why you do or do not believe it was told effectively from the first-person point of view. Support your opinion with examples from the literature.

OPTION 2

Understanding Lyric Poetry Several examples of lyric poetry were included in this unit. Identify three examples and write a short paragraph about each, explaining how the writer expresses his or her personal thoughts and feelings.

OPTION 3

Contrasting Dynamic and Static Character Write a short essay exploring the differences between a static and a dynamic character. How do both types of characters add to the development of the plot? Discuss with a partner your ideas about dynamic and static characters and what can be learned from each type.

Portfolio Building

- **Choices and Challenges—Writing** For the writing assignment on page 346, you were asked to write a character description. Write a cover note explaining what makes your description effective. Attach the note to the assignment and add both to your **Presentation Portfolio.**

- **Writing Workshops** In this unit you wrote a comparison-and-contrast essay. Reread this writing assignment, and identify its strengths and weaknesses. Explain your assessment on a sheet of paper, attach it to the assignment, and place both in your **Presentation Portfolio.**

- **Additional Activities** Think back to the assignments you completed under **Speaking & Listening** and **Research & Technology.** Keep a record in your portfolio of any assignments that you especially enjoyed or would like to work on further.

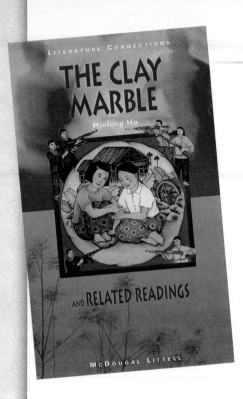

LITERATURE CONNECTIONS
The Clay Marble

BY MINFONG HO

This historical novel is set in a Cambodian refugee camp in the early 1980s. Twelve-year-old Dara—with courage, quick thinking, and perseverance—copes with the horrors of war. She is helped by folk tales about Cambodian heroes and a good friend who gives her a "magical" marble to bring her strength, courage, and patience.

These thematically related readings are provided along with *The Clay Marble*:

All the People of Khmer Were Very Troubled
BY VEN YEM

My Life Story
BY LAN NGUYEN

Oppression
BY LANGSTON HUGHES

Birthday Box
BY JANE YOLEN

Holes
BY LILLIAN MORRISON

from **"Childhood and Poetry"**
BY PABLO NERUDA

All-Ball
BY MARY POPE OSBORNE

Dear World, January 17, 1994
BY ALMA LUZ VILLANEUVA

More Choices

Soup on Ice
BY ROBERT N. PECK
In a moment that is important to the entire town, two young boys arrange for Santa Claus to visit.

The Diary of a Young Girl
BY ANNE FRANK
The diary of a brave young Jewish girl hiding out during the Nazi occupation.

Martin Luther King, Jr.
BY JACQUELINE L. HARRIS
A biography of the civil rights leader who became the courageous voice for peaceful change.

Scorpions
BY WALTER DEAN MYERS
After reluctantly taking on the leadership of a Harlem gang, Jamal finds that his enemies treat him with respect until a tragedy occurs.

Bridge to Terabithia
BY KATHERINE PATERSON
Leslie doesn't quite fit in. However, she and her best friend have many shared moments as they dream of escaping to imaginary Terabithia.

Number the Stars

BY LOIS LOWRY

In Copenhagen, Denmark, in 1943, 10-year-old Annemarie Johansen and her best friend Ellen Rosen have their lives disrupted forever by the Nazi persecution of Jews. When the Danes learn that the Nazis are preparing to send Danish Jews to the death camps, the Johansens help their Jewish friends the Rosens plan an escape. This story is based on the incredible evacuation of Danish Jews from Nazi-held Denmark in 1943.

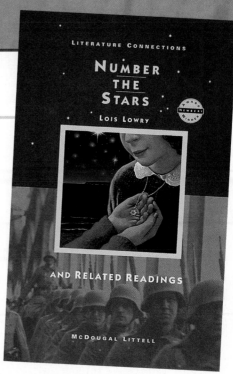

These thematically related readings are provided along with *Number the Stars*:

from **Clara's Story**
BY CLARA ISAACMAN

The Butterfly
BY PAVEL FRIEDMAN

from **Sky**
BY HANNEKE IPPISCH

from **The White Rose: Sophie Scholl**
BY ERIKA MUMFORD

from **Raoul Wallenberg**
BY MICHAEL NICHOLSON AND DAVID WINNER

The Wrong Lunch Line
BY NICHOLASA MOHR

Secret Talk
BY EVE MERRIAM

Social Studies Connection

Across Five Aprils
BY IRENE HUNT
Only young Jethro remains to work the farm when the men in his family leave to fight in the Civil War.
A McDougal Littell *Literature Connection*

By Secret Railway
BY ENID MEADOWCROFT
In the 1860s, a boy in Chicago makes friends with a freed slave.

The Red Badge of Courage
BY STEPHEN CRANE
A young Union soldier confronts his own fear of death.

Harriet Tubman, Conductor of the Underground Railway
BY ANN PETRY
Harriet Tubman, an escaped slave, created the Underground Railway and became a voice of courage and hope for many slaves seeking freedom.

Soujourner Truth and the Struggle for Freedom
BY EDWARD BEECHER CLAFLIN
This is the story of the famous former slave who gave a courageous voice to the abolitionist and women's rights movements.

UNIT FOUR

Strange Goings-On

I guess when
you turn off
the main road,
you have to
be prepared to
see some
funny houses.

STEPHEN KING
WRITER

Dos Toose, James Michalopoulos

The Literature You'll Read

The Concepts You'll Study

Vocabulary and Reading Comprehension

Vocabulary Focus: Synonyms, Antonyms, and
    Homonyms
Drawing Conclusions
Setting Purposes
Study Skill—SQ3R
Monitoring Your Reading
Drawing Conclusions

Writing and Language Conventions

Writing Workshop: Eyewitness Report
Using Participial Phrases to Vary Sentence
    Structure
Prepositional Phrases as Adverbs
Introductory Phrases
Prepositional Phrases as Adjectives

Literary Analysis

Genre Focus: Science Fiction
Science Fiction
Suspense
Descriptive Details
Free Verse
Surprise Ending

Speaking and Listening

Oral Report
Persuasive Speech
Interpretive Reading of Poetry
Film Review

Science Fiction

> *Science fiction is that branch of literature that deals with human responses to changes in . . . science and technology.*
> —Isaac Asimov, science fiction writer

Can you imagine what life on earth will be like one hundred, one thousand, or even one million years from today? Will people still look like people? Will we talk and walk as we do now? Perhaps one day we will use our thoughts to transport us to different destinations. Perhaps our bodies will no longer require food, but instead use energy from the sun, as plants do. These are the ideas that writers of science fiction consider when they weave tales of the future.

Science fiction is imaginative writing that has a scientific basis. It examines events that *might* actually happen. When people think of science fiction, they often picture space travel, alien beings, and computers. Some common machines and tools used today—such as airplanes and cell phones—were first described in earlier science fiction stories.

From "Man-Made Monsters"

Science Fiction

Science fiction explores settings, events, and characters that are both familiar and out of the ordinary. The surprising combination may shed new light on everyday occurrences, sparking new insights and ideas.

Science fiction is usually set in the future and involves **technology** and science. Its purpose is almost always to make a serious comment about the world. Sometimes the ideas of science fiction writers come true. Other times, their suggestions reach far beyond what we imagine in our lifetime. For example, in 1965, Isaac Asimov wrote about futuristic beings in "Eyes Do More Than See."

YOUR TURN What elements in the excerpt at the right help you identify this as science fiction?

Key Elements of Science Fiction

- realistic and fantastic details
- grounded in science
- usually set in the future
- unknown inventions

SCIENCE FICTION

For a moment Brock shifted out of phase and out of communion, so that Ames had to hurry to adjust his lines of force. He caught the drift of other-thoughts as he did so, the view of the powdered galaxies against the velvet of nothingness, and the lines of force pulsing in endless multitudes of energy-life, lying between the galaxies.

Ames said, "Please absorb my thoughts, Brock. Don't close out. I've thought of manipulating Matter. Imagine! A symphony of Matter. Why bother with Energy. Of course, there's nothing new in Energy; how can there be? Doesn't that show we must deal with Matter?"

"Matter!"

Ames interpreted Brock's energy-vibrations as those of disgust.

He said, "Why not? We were once Matter ourselves back—back—Oh, a trillion years ago anyway! Why not build up an imitation of ourselves in Matter, ourselves as we used to be?"

—Isaac Asimov, "Eyes Do More Than See"

Theme and Conflict in Science Fiction

The **theme**—the central message or idea of a work—is hardly ever stated directly. The reader usually has to figure it out from details in the story. These details may be included in the title and in the descriptions of the characters, setting, and plot. In science fiction, there may be a message in the story about the dangers of technology or about what happens to characters who live in futuristic settings.

Conflicts in a story are clues to the theme. Some may be **internal**—taking place within a character—and some may be **external**—taking place between a character and an outside force. A theme in science fiction will often apply to life as we know it, but since the story is set in the future, or the characters are strange and unusual, it is made more vivid and memorable.

YOUR TURN In the passage to the right, Gary, the main character, is reprimanded after writing a science fiction essay. What conflict is illustrated in the passage? What do you think the theme might be? Explain.

THEME AND CONFLICT IN SCIENCE FICTION

When Gary arrived at the English office, Mr. Smith seemed nervous too. He kept folding and unfolding Gary's composition. "Where do you get such ideas?" he asked in his monotone voice.

Gary shrugged. "They just come to me."

"Alien teachers. Taking over the minds of schoolchildren." Mr. Smith's empty eyes were blinking. "What made you think of that?"

"I've always had this vivid imagination."

"If you're sure it's just your imagination." Mr. Smith looked relieved. "I guess everything will work out." He handed back Gary's composition. "No more fantasy, Gary. Reality. That's your assignment. Write only about what you know."

—Robert Lipsyte, "Future Tense"

From "Future Tense"

Foreshadowing

Foreshadowing is a technique that writers use to set a **mood,** create **suspense,** convey a **tone,** or communicate an attitude toward a subject. Foreshadowing is a writer's use of clues or hints about things to come in the story. The suspense and the mood that the writer builds through foreshadowing help keep readers interested.

YOUR TURN What details in this passage may provide clues about things to come?

FORESHADOWING

Gary couldn't wait for tenth grade to start so he could strut his sentences, parade his paragraphs, renew his reputation as the top creative writer in school. At the opening assembly, he felt on edge, psyched, like a boxer before the first-round bell. He leaned forward as Dr. Proctor, the principal, introduced two new staff members. He wasn't particularly interested in the new vice-principal, Ms. Jones; Gary never had discipline problems, he'd never even had to stay after school. But his head cocked alertly as Dr. Proctor introduced the new Honors English teacher, Mr. Smith. Here was the person he'd have to impress.

—Robert Lipsyte,
"Future Tense"

From "Future Tense"

Drawing Conclusions

When your best friend starts to plan a party, you can reasonably conclude that you are going to be invited. You draw conclusions by combining facts and details and your own knowledge and experience to make a special kind of inference. An active reader can also draw conclusions about a character's motives, about the importance of a setting, or about the plot of a story. Use the strategies on this page to help you draw conclusions.

Here's how Stephanie uses the skill:

*"As I read, I look for facts and details from the text to make general statements. I **evaluate** Mrs. Sakkaro's extreme reaction to the weather. I can **conclude** that Mrs. Sakkaro is afraid of being in a rainstorm."*

How to Apply the Skill

To **draw conclusions,** an active reader will
- look for facts and details
- make logical guesses
- **connect** experience and knowledge to the text
- **evaluate** the information
- use a chart like this one to help draw conclusions

	Stated Facts	Inferences
Character (or setting or plot)		
Conclusions: _____		
_____		

Try It Now!

Read and draw conclusions from the excerpt below.

> **(Lillian)** "[Mrs. Sakkaro is] always looking at the sky; I've seen her do it a hundred times and she's never been out when it's the least bit cloudy. Once, when the boy was out playing, she called to him to come in, shouting that it was going to rain."
> —Isaac Asimov, "Rain, Rain, Go Away"

Rain, Rain, Go Away

by ISAAC ASIMOV

Connect to Your Life

First Impressions Have you ever had new people move into your block or neighborhood? Discuss with a small group what you thought about the newcomers before meeting them. Then discuss how accurate your assumptions turned out to be.

Build Background

EARTH SCIENCE

Weather forecasting today relies heavily on technology. For many years, however, weather forecasters primarily used four scientific instruments—the thermometer, which measures temperature; the hygrometer, which measures humidity; the barometer, which measures atmospheric pressure; and the anemometer, which measures wind speed and direction.

Modern technology has revolutionized weather forecasting. Meteorologists, professionals who study the weather, now use information gathered from weather balloons, radar equipment, and satellites circling the earth.

> WORDS TO KNOW
> **Vocabulary Preview**
> affectation   gifted   semblance
> console   interminably

Focus Your Reading

LITERARY ANALYSIS **SCIENCE FICTION**

Fiction in which writers explore unexpected possibilities, usually in the future and sometimes in the present or the past, is called **science fiction.** Science fiction writing may also use scientific data and theories. Most science fiction writers create a world made up of both real and fantastic elements. As you read "Rain, Rain, Go Away," identify elements of the story that are realistic and those that are not.

ACTIVE READING **DRAWING CONCLUSIONS**

You must combine prior knowledge or experience with information from the text **to draw a conclusion.**

📖 READER'S NOTEBOOK Create a chart like the one below to show how you can draw conclusions as you are reading.

Facts and Details from Text	My Experience and Prior Knowledge
The sky is clouding up. Mr. Sakkaro is listening to the weather report and looks anxious.	The sky gets cloudy before it rains.

Conclusion

It's going to rain. Mr. Sakkaro is worried about rain.

RAIN, RAIN, GO AWAY

by Isaac Asimov

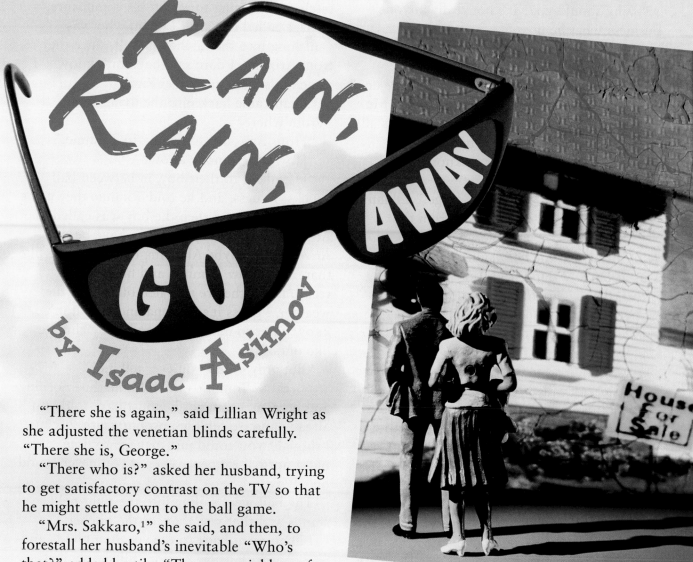

"There she is again," said Lillian Wright as she adjusted the venetian blinds carefully. "There she is, George."

"There who is?" asked her husband, trying to get satisfactory contrast on the TV so that he might settle down to the ball game.

"Mrs. Sakkaro,[1]" she said, and then, to forestall her husband's inevitable "Who's that?" added hastily. "The new neighbors, for goodness sake."

"Oh."

"Sunbathing. Always sunbathing. I wonder where her boy is. He's usually out on a nice day like this, standing in that tremendous yard of theirs and throwing the ball against the house. Did you ever see him, George?"

"I've heard him. It's a version of the Chinese water torture.[2] Bang on the wall, biff on the ground, smack in the hand. Bang, biff, smack, bang, biff—"

"He's a *nice* boy, quiet and well-behaved. I wish Tommie would make friends with him.

He's the right age, too, just about ten, I should say."

"I didn't know Tommie was backward about making friends."

"Well, it's hard with the Sakkaros. They keep so to themselves. I don't even know what Mr. Sakkaro does."

---

1. **Sakkaro** (săk′ə-rō′).

2. **Chinese water torture:** a form of torture in which water is dripped slowly and steadily onto the victim's head.

"Why should you? It's not really anyone's business what he does."

"It's odd that I never see him go to work."

"No one ever sees me go to work."

"You stay home and write. What does *he* do?"

"I dare say Mrs. Sakkaro knows what Mr. Sakkaro does and is all upset because she doesn't know what *I* do."

ACTIVE READER

PREDICT How do you think Lillian is going to find out about Mr. Sakkaro's job?

"Oh, George." Lillian retreated from the window and glanced with distaste at the television. (Schoendienst[3] was at bat.) "I think we should make an effort; the neighborhood should."

"What kind of an effort?" George was comfortable on the couch now.

"To get to know them."

"Well, didn't you, when she first moved in? You said you called."

"I said hello but, well, she'd just moved in and the house was still upset, so that's all it could be, just hello. It's been two months now and it's still nothing more than hello, sometimes.—She's so odd."

"Is she?"

"She's always looking at the sky; I've seen her do it a hundred times and she's never been out when it's the least bit cloudy. Once, when the boy was out playing, she called to him to come in, shouting that it was going to rain. I happened to hear her and I thought, Oh no, wouldn't you know and me with a wash on the line, so I hurried out and, you know, it was broad sunlight. Oh, there were some clouds, but nothing, really."

"Did it rain, eventually?"

"Of course not. I just had to run out in the yard for nothing."

George was lost amid a couple of base hits and a most embarrassing bobble that meant a run. When the excitement was over and the pitcher was trying to regain his composure, George called out after Lillian, who was vanishing into the kitchen, "Well, since they're from Arizona, I dare say they don't know rainclouds from any other kind."

Lillian came back into the living room. "From where?"

"From Arizona, according to Tommie."

"How did Tommie know?"

"He talked to their boy, in between ball chucks, I guess, and he told Tommie they came from Arizona and then the boy was called in. At least, Tommie says it might have been Arizona, or maybe Alabama or some place like that. You know Tommie and his nontotal recall. But if they're that nervous about the weather, I guess it's Arizona and they don't know what to make of a good rainy climate like ours."

"But why didn't you ever tell me?"

"Because Tommie only told me this morning and because I thought he must have told you already and, to tell the absolute truth, because I thought you could just manage to drag out a normal existence even if you never found out. Wow—"

The ball went sailing into the right field stands and that was that for the pitcher.

Lillian went back to the venetian blinds and

ACTIVE READER

DRAW CONCLUSIONS What does George think about Lillian's worries about the Sakkaros?

said, "I'll simply just have to make her acquaintance. She looks *very* nice.—Oh, look at that, George."

George was looking at nothing but the TV.

Lillian said, "I know she's staring at that cloud. And now she'll be going in. Honestly."

---

3. **Schoendienst** (shän′dēnst′): Red Schoendienst, a famous baseball player of the 1940s–1960s. He was the Milwaukee Braves' second baseman when this story was written.

George was out two days later on a reference search in the library and came home with a load of books. Lillian greeted him jubilantly.

She said, "Now, you're not doing anything tomorrow."

"That sounds like a statement, not a question."

"It *is* a statement. We're going out with the Sakkaros to Murphy's Park."

"With—"

"With the next-door neighbors, George. *How* can you never remember the name?"

"I'm gifted. How did it happen?"

"I just went up to their house this morning and rang the bell."

"That easy?"

"It wasn't easy. It was hard. I stood there, jittering, with my finger on the doorbell, till I thought that ringing the bell would be easier than having the door open and being caught standing there like a fool."

"And she didn't kick you out?"

"No. She was sweet as she could be. Invited me in, knew who I was, said she was so glad I had come to visit. You know."

"And you suggested we go to Murphy's Park."

"Yes. I thought if I suggested something that would let the children have fun, it would be easier for her to go along with it. She wouldn't want to spoil a chance for her boy."

"A mother's psychology."

"But you should see her home."

"Ah. You had a reason for all this. It comes out. You wanted the Cook's tour.[4] But, please, spare me the color-scheme details. I'm not interested in the bedspreads, and the size of the closets is a topic with which I can dispense."

It was the secret of their happy marriage that Lillian paid no attention to George. She went into the color-scheme details, was most meticulous about the bedspreads, and gave him an inch-by-inch description of closet-size. "And *clean?* I have never seen any place so spotless."

"If you get to know her, then, she'll be setting you impossible standards and you'll have to drop her in self-defense."

"Her kitchen," said Lillian, ignoring him, "was so spanking clean you just couldn't believe she ever used it. I asked for a drink of water and she held the glass underneath the tap and poured slowly so that not one drop fell in the sink itself. It wasn't affectation. She did it so casually that I just knew she always did it that way. And when she gave me the glass she held it with a clean napkin. Just hospital-sanitary."

---

4. **Cook's tour:** guided tour (a reference to the tours formerly organized by a famous British travel agency).

"She must be a lot of trouble to herself. Did she agree to come with us right off?"

"Well—not right off. She called to her husband about what the weather forecast was, and he said that the newspapers all said it would be fair tomorrow but that he was waiting for the latest report on the radio."

"*All* the newspapers said so, eh?"

"Of course, they all just print the official weather forecast, so they would all agree. But I think they do subscribe to all the newspapers. At least I've watched the bundle the newsboy leaves—"

ACTIVE READER

CONNECT How often do you check the weather report before going on an outing?

"There isn't much you miss, is there?"

"Anyway," said Lillian severely, "she called up the weather bureau and had them tell her the latest and she called it out to her husband and they said they'd go, except they said they'd phone us if there were any unexpected changes in the weather."

"All right. Then we'll go."

The Sakkaros were young and pleasant, dark and handsome. In fact, as they came down the long walk from their home to where the Wright automobile was parked, George leaned toward his wife and breathed into her ear. "So *he's* the reason."

It was a beautiful day at Murphy's Park; hot and dry without being too hot; and with a cheerfully bright sun in a blue, blue sky.

"I wish he were," said Lillian. "Is that a handbag he's carrying?"

"Pocket-radio. To listen to weather forecasts, I bet."

The Sakkaro boy came running after them, waving something which turned out to be an aneroid barometer,[5] and all three got into the back seat. Conversation was turned on and lasted, with neat give-and-take on impersonal subjects, to Murphy's Park.

The Sakkaro boy was so polite and reasonable that even Tommie Wright, wedged between his parents in the front seat, was subdued by example into a <u>semblance</u> of civilization. Lillian couldn't recall when she had spent so serenely pleasant a drive.

She was not the least disturbed by the fact that, barely to be heard under the flow of the conversation, Mr. Sakkaro's small radio was on, and she never actually saw him put it occasionally to his ear.

It was a beautiful day at Murphy's Park; hot and dry without being too hot; and with a cheerfully bright sun in a blue, blue sky. Even Mr. Sakkaro, though he inspected every quarter of the heavens with a careful eye and then stared piercingly at the barometer, seemed to have no fault to find.

---

5. **aneroid barometer** (ăn′ə-roid′ bə-rŏm′ĭ-tər): an instrument for measuring air pressure, used in forecasting the weather.

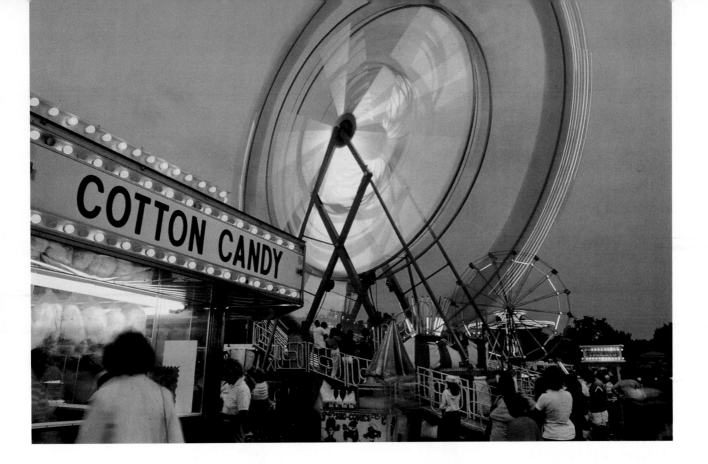

Lillian ushered the two boys to the amusement section and bought enough tickets to allow one ride for each on every variety of centrifugal thrill that the park offered.

"Please," she had said to a protesting Mrs. Sakkaro, "let this be my treat. I'll let you have your turn next time."

When she returned, George was alone.

"Where—" she began.

"Just down there at the refreshment stand. I told them I'd wait here for you and we would join them." He sounded gloomy.

ACTIVE READER

QUESTION Why do you think George was gloomy when Lillian returned?

"Anything wrong?"

"No, not really, except that I think he must be independently wealthy."

"What?"

"I don't know what he does for a living. I hinted—"

"Now who's curious?"

"I was doing it for you. He said he's just a student of human nature."

"How philosophical. That would explain all those newspapers."

"Yes, but with a handsome, wealthy man next door, it looks as though I'll have impossible standards set for me, too."

"Don't be silly."

"And he doesn't come from Arizona."

"He doesn't?"

"I said I heard he was from Arizona. He looked so surprised, it was obvious he didn't. Then he laughed and asked if he had an Arizona accent."

Lillian said thoughtfully, "He has some kind of accent, you know. There are lots of Spanish-ancestry people in the Southwest so he could still be from Arizona. Sakkaro could be a Spanish name."

"Sounds Japanese to me.—Come on, they're waving. Oh, look what they've bought."

The Sakkaros were each holding three sticks of cotton candy, huge swirls of pink foam consisting of threads of sugar dried out of frothy syrup that had been whipped about in a warm vessel. It melted sweetly in the mouth and left one feeling sticky.

The Sakkaros held one out to each Wright, and out of politeness the Wrights accepted.

They went down the midway, tried their hand at darts, at the kind of poker game where balls were rolled into holes, at knocking wooden cylinders off pedestals. They took pictures of themselves and recorded their voices and tested the strength of their handgrips.

Eventually they collected the youngsters, who had been reduced to a satisfactorily breathless state of roiled-up[6] insides, and the Sakkaros ushered theirs off instantly to the refreshment stand. Tommie hinted the extent of his pleasure at the possible purchase of a hot-dog and George tossed him a quarter. He ran off, too.

"Frankly," said George, "I prefer to stay here. If I see them biting away at another cotton candy stick I'll turn green and sicken on the spot. If they haven't had a dozen apiece, I'll eat a dozen myself."

"I know, and they're buying a handful for the child now."

"I offered to stand Sakkaro a hamburger and he just looked grim and shook his head. Not that a hamburger's much, but after enough cotton candy, it ought to be a feast."

"I know. I offered her an orange drink and the way she jumped when she said no, you'd think I'd thrown it in her face.—Still, I suppose they've never been to a place like this before and they'll need time to adjust to the novelty. They'll fill up on cotton candy and then never eat it again for ten years."

"Well, maybe." They strolled toward the Sakkaros. "You know, Lil, it's clouding up."

Mr. Sakkaro had the radio to his ear and was looking anxiously toward the west.

"Uh-oh," said George, "he's seen it. One gets you fifty, he'll want to go home."

All three Sakkaros were upon him, polite but insistent. They were sorry, they had had a wonderful time, a marvelous time, the Wrights would have to be their guests as soon as it could be managed, but now, really, they had to go home. It looked stormy. Mrs. Sakkaro wailed that all the forecasts had been for fair weather.

George tried to <u>console</u> them. "It's hard to predict a local thunderstorm, but even if it were to come, and it mightn't, it wouldn't last more than half an hour on the outside."

At which comment, the Sakkaro youngster seemed on the verge of tears, and Mrs. Sakkaro's hand, holding a handkerchief, trembled visibly.

"Let's go home," said George in resignation.

> **M**r. Sakkaro had the radio to his ear and was looking anxiously toward the west.

---

6. **roiled-up:** stirred up; disturbed.

console (kən-sōl′) *v.* to comfort

He pulled up at the gate that opened onto the Sakkaro's spacious front yard and got out of the car to open the back door. He thought he felt a drop. They were *just* in time.

The Sakkaros tumbled out, faces drawn with tension, muttering thanks, and started off toward their long front walk at a dead run.

"Honestly," began Lillian, "you would think they were—"

The heavens opened and the rain came down in giant drops as though some celestial[7] dam had suddenly burst. The top of their car was pounded with a hundred drum sticks, and halfway to their front door the Sakkaros stopped and looked despairingly upward.

Their faces blurred as the rain hit; blurred and shrank and ran together. All three shriveled, collapsing within their clothes, which sank down into three sticky-wet heaps.

And while the Wrights sat there, transfixed with horror, Lillian found herself unable to stop the completion of her remark: "—made of sugar and afraid they would melt." ❖

The drive back seemed to stretch <u>interminably</u>. There was no conversation to speak of. Mr. Sakkaro's radio was quite loud now as he switched from station to station, catching a weather report every time. They were mentioning "local thundershowers" now.

The Sakkaro youngster piped up that the barometer was falling, and Mrs. Sakkaro, chin in the palm of her hand, stared dolefully at the sky and asked if George could not drive faster, please.

"It does look rather threatening, doesn't it?" said Lillian in a polite attempt to share their guests' attitude. But then George heard her mutter, "Honestly!" under her breath.

A wind had sprung up, driving the dust of the weeks-dry road before it, when they entered the street on which they lived, and the leaves rustled ominously. Lightning flickered.

George said, "You'll be indoors in two minutes, friends. We'll make it."

ACTIVE READER

VISUALIZE Describe in your own words the scene where the Sakkaros get caught in the rain.

7. **celestial** (sə-lĕs′chəl): located in the sky; heavenly.

WORDS TO KNOW   **interminably** (ĭn-tûr′mə-nə-blē) *adv.* without end

561

Connect to the Literature

1. **What Do You Think?**
   What was your reaction to how the story ended?

   Comprehension Check
   - What is Mrs. Sakkaro always looking at?
   - What surprises Lillian and George about what the Sakkaros eat at the fair?
   - What happens when the Sakkaros are caught in the rain?

Think Critically

2. Who or what do you think the Sakkaros are? Why do you think Asimov doesn't make their identity clear?

3. **ACTIVE READING** **DRAWING CONCLUSIONS**
   Compare the chart in your 📖 **READER'S NOTEBOOK** with the charts of three or four classmates. Were their conclusions the same as or different from your own? Why do you think that people reading the same story can draw different conclusions?

4. How would you describe the attitudes and behavior of the Wrights toward the Sakkaro family? How realistic do you think this is? Give reasons for your answer.

   Think About:
   - the way Lillian spies on the Sakkaros through the window
   - her reason for inviting the Sakkaros to Murphy's Park
   - the Wrights' reaction when the Sakkaros insist on going home

5. Writers sometimes use the weather to create mood in a story. How do you think the weather affects the mood of this story?

Extend Interpretations

6. **What If?** What would have happened if the Sakkaro family had made it home before the rain began falling? With a partner, discuss a new ending for the story in which the Sakkaros' reasons for being on Earth are revealed.

7. **Connect to Life** It can be very difficult to move into a new neighborhood where you don't know anyone. What do you think you could do to make a newcomer to your neighborhood feel welcome?

Literary Analysis

SCIENCE FICTION One very popular type of writing is science fiction. In **science fiction,** writers explore unexpected possibilities, usually in the future and sometimes in the past, using scientific data and theories as well as their imaginations to develop plot and character.

Most science fiction writers create a world made up of both real and fantastic elements. Science fiction is often about space travel, futuristic technology, or aliens. Although entertaining, science fiction can often have a serious message.

Paired Activity Make a chart like the one below. Working with a partner, list the characteristics of science fiction. Find examples of these characteristics in "Rain, Rain, Go Away" or in other science fiction stories and films with which you are familiar.

Source	Characteristic of Science Fiction	Example
"Rain, Rain, Go Away" (short story)	Uses scientific data or theory and the writer's imagination	Asimov applies the principle of sugar dissolving in water to probable aliens.

Writing

New Identities Write a report describing who the Sakkaros are, where they come from, and why they are on earth. Use any information or clues from the story to create your description. Place your report in your **Working Portfolio**.

Writing Handbook
See p. R41: Descriptive Writing.

Speaking & Listening

Author Background Research Isaac Asimov's background. Find out what inspired him to write science fiction. Write an oral report on your findings and present it to your class. Be sure to use appropriate grammar, word choice, enunciation, and pace during your presentation.

Speaking and Listening Handbook
See p. R109: Research Presentations.

Research & Technology

Chemistry Lesson Why does sugar dissolve in water? Use a general science book to prepare a brief lesson for a group of younger students to explain why and how this process takes place. Think about how you can make the report interesting and understandable to your audience.

INTERNET **Research Starter**
www.mcdougallittell.com

Vocabulary

VOCABULARY STRATEGY: ROOT WORDS Draw a chart like the one below. Use a dictionary to find and write down the root word for each vocabulary word. If you do not find the root word listed, look up a similar word, such as *terminate* for *interminably.* Choose definitions for the vocabulary words that fit the context of this story. *Interminably* has been completed as a model.

EXERCISE Write a paragraph about an unusual family that moves into your neighborhood. Try to use all five vocabulary words in your paragraph.

Vocabulary Handbook
See p. R22: Word Origins.

Vocabulary Word	Definition	Word Origin	Root Word	Definition of Root Word
affectation				
console				
gifted				
interminably	endlessly	Latin	terminus	end; boundary
semblance				

Grammar in Context: Using Participial Phrases to Vary Sentence Structure

Look at the words in red in the following sentence from Isaac Asimov's "Rain, Rain, Go Away."

> **The Sakkaros tumbled out, faces drawn with tension, muttering thanks, and started off toward their long front walk at a dead run.**

The words in red form a **participial phrase,** a phrase that includes a participle; in this case, the word *muttering.* Writers use participles and participial phrases to add detail to a sentence, or to create interest by varying the usual sentence patterns. Participial phrases can be moved to different positions in a sentence. For example, in the sentence above, the participial phrase might be moved to the beginning: *Muttering thanks, the Sakkaros tumbled out, faces drawn with tension . . .*

WRITING EXERCISE Rewrite each sentence below, moving the underlined participial phrase to a different position in the sentence.

Example: *Original* Mrs. Sakkaro went into the yard, <u>looking for her son.</u>

Rewritten <u>Looking for her son,</u> Mrs. Sakkaro went into the yard.

1. Mrs. Sakkaro, <u>particularly pleased,</u> invited her neighbor to come in.
2. She poured the water slowly, <u>holding the glass underneath the tap.</u>
3. The Sakkaro boy came running after them, <u>waving something.</u>
4. Even Tommie Wright, <u>wedged between his parents in the front seat,</u> was well behaved.
5. <u>Collapsing in their clothes,</u> all three shriveled up.

Connect to the Literature Look at the sentence on page 560 that begins, "At which comment . . ." Identify the participial phrase in the sentence.

Grammar Handbook See p. R89: Phrases and Clauses.

Isaac Asimov
1920–1992

"All I do is write. I do practically nothing else, except eat, sleep, and talk to my wife."

Flying Start Born in Soviet Russia, Isaac Asimov and his parents moved to the United States when he was just three years old. He became a brilliant student, entering Columbia University at age fifteen. He was only eighteen when his first science fiction story was published.

Science Fact and Science Fiction Asimov continued to combine his interests in both

science and science fiction. He earned a Ph.D. in biochemistry. It was in the field of fiction, however, that he made his mark both by the power of his imagination and the number of his published works. Asimov also wrote science books and was a well-respected contributor to the field of robotics, the study of robot technology. In all, Asimov wrote over 470 books.

AUTHOR ACTIVITY
Asimov's Robots Find out more about Asimov's robot stories, collected in *I, Robot* and *The Rest of the Robots.* What famous Three Laws of Robotics did Asimov develop in these stories?

The Dinner Party

by MONA GARDNER

Connect to Your Life

Stereotype Trap A stereotype is an oversimplified view of an entire group of people. Have you ever had someone make a snap judgment about you because of his or her beliefs about a group? Don't be surprised. This can happen because some people do not take the time to find out the facts about you as an individual. With a partner, discuss a time this has happened to you or to someone you know.

Build Background

HISTORY

India was under British control for nearly 200 years before gaining its independence in 1947. "The Dinner Party" takes place in British India, the part of the country ruled directly by the British government.

Some colonial attitudes of the time seem backward today. Most British officials felt superior to the people they ruled and rarely socialized with them. In addition, most men felt they were better than women, and that feeling of male superiority becomes an issue in this story.

WORDS TO KNOW
Vocabulary Preview

arresting	sober
naturalist	spirited
rafter	

Focus Your Reading

LITERARY ANALYSIS   SUSPENSE

Although "The Dinner Party" is a very brief short story, the author is able to create suspense by raising questions about what might happen next. **Suspense** is the sense of growing tension and excitement felt by a reader.

For example, early in the story the reader learns something that most of the characters do not know. Immediately, the suspense grows as one imagines all the things that could go wrong. As you read, look for ways in which the author builds suspense. What questions does she raise in the reader's mind about what might happen?

ACTIVE READING   SETTING PURPOSES

You may often read literature for sheer pleasure. From time to time, however, you may be asked to read for a specific purpose. What you focus on in the story will be based on your purpose for reading.

📖 **READER'S NOTEBOOK** As you read "The Dinner Party," use a chart like the one below to note stereotypes expressed directly or indirectly by the guests at the party.

Guest	Stereotype
young girl	Women now are not as fluttery as their grandmothers were.

The Dinner Party

by Mona Gardner

Detail of *Dinner at Haddo House* (1884), Alfred Edward Emslie. By courtesy of the National Portrait Gallery, London.

The country is India. A large dinner party is being given in an up-country station by a colonial official[1] and his wife. The guests are army officers and government attachés[2] and their wives, and an American naturalist.

At one side of the long table a spirited discussion springs up between a young girl and a colonel. The girl insists women have long outgrown the jumping-on-a-chair-at-sight-of-a-mouse era, that they are not as fluttery as their grandmothers. The colonel says they are, explaining that women haven't the actual nerve control of men. The other men at the table agree with him.

"A woman's unfailing reaction in any crisis," the colonel says, "is to scream. And while a man may feel like it, yet he has that ounce more of control than a woman has. And that last ounce is what counts!"

The American scientist does not join in the argument, but sits watching the faces of the other guests. As he looks, he sees a strange expression come over the face of the hostess. She is staring straight ahead, the muscles of her face contracting slightly. With a small gesture she summons the native boy standing behind her chair. She whispers to him. The boy's eyes widen: he turns quickly and leaves the room. No one else sees this, nor the boy when he puts a bowl of milk on the verandah[3] outside the glass doors.

The American comes to with a start. In India, milk in a bowl means only one thing. It is bait for a snake. He realizes there is a cobra in the room.

He looks up at the rafters—the likeliest place—and sees they are bare. Three corners of the room, which he can see by shifting only slightly, are empty. In the fourth corner a group of servants stand, waiting until the next course can be served. The American realizes there is only one place left—under the table.

His first impulse is to jump back and warn the others. But he knows the commotion will frighten the cobra and it will strike. He speaks quickly, the quality of his voice so arresting that it sobers everyone.

"I want to know just what control everyone at this table has. I will count three hundred—that's five minutes—and not one of you is to move a single muscle. The persons who move will forfeit 50 rupees.[4] Now! Ready!"

The 20 people sit like stone images while he counts. He is saying ". . . two hundred and eighty . . . " when, out of the corner of his eye, he sees the cobra emerge and make for the bowl of milk. Four or five screams ring out as he jumps to slam shut the verandah doors.

"You certainly were right, Colonel!" the host says. "A man has just shown us an example of real control."

"Just a minute," the American says, turning to his hostess, "there's one thing I'd like to know. Mrs. Wynnes, how did you know that cobra was in the room?"

A faint smile lights up the woman's face as she replies. "Because it was lying across my foot." ❖

---

1. **colonial official:** a person holding a position in the British government ruling India.

2. **attachés** (ăt′ə-shāz′): people who assist an ambassador.

3. **verandah:** a long porch, usually roofed, along the side of a building.

4. **rupees** (rōō-pēz′): Indian units of money.

WORDS
TO
KNOW

naturalist (năch′ər-ə-lĭst) *n.* a person who studies living things by observing them directly
spirited (spĭr′ĭ-tĭd) *adj.* lively; vigorous
rafter (răf′tər) *n.* a wooden beam that supports a roof
arresting (ə-rĕs′tĭng) *adj.* capturing attention; striking
sober (sō′bər) *v.* to make serious or solemn

Connect to the Literature

1. **What Do You Think?**
What was your reaction to the story's ending?

Comprehension Check
- What was the disagreement between the colonel and the young girl?
- Why does Mrs. Wynnes have a bowl of milk put outside the door?
- How did the hostess know there was a cobra in the room?

Think Critically

2. In your opinion, who behaves heroically in this story? Is the hero an unlikely one in the context of the story's setting? Give reasons for your answers.

3. **ACTIVE READING** **SETTING A PURPOSE**
Look back at the examples of stereotypes you noted in your **READER'S NOTEBOOK**. Are the stereotypes accurate? Explain why or why not.

4. Do you think the event at the dinner party will change the colonel's view of women? Explain your answer using story details and your own experience.

   Think About:
   - the colonel's manner of speaking
   - the colonel's career and nationality
   - Mrs. Wynnes's actions

Extend Interpretations

5. **COMPARING TEXTS** Do you think the colonel would have made his remark about women if he had met Squeaky in "Raymond's Run"? Why or why not?

6. **Connect to Life** How has this story affected your ideas about how males and females react to tense situations?

Literary Analysis

SUSPENSE The feeling of growing tension and excitement experienced by a reader is called **suspense.** Writers create suspense by keeping readers guessing how a situation will end.

For example, by counting to 300, the American hopes to allow enough time for the cobra to come out. The question in the reader's mind is, Will this be enough time? Notice that the suspense ends at nearly the last moment. The naturalist has already counted to 280 when the snake finally comes out from under the table.

Activity Mona Gardner creates suspense one step at a time, beginning with vague hints of a problem and ending when the cobra finally leaves the room. Make a chart like the one below. Reread the story and jot down each event, action, or reaction that builds suspense. Then write the question that each suspense builder creates in the reader's mind.

Suspense Builders	Questions in Reader's Mind
A strange expression comes over the face of the hostess.	What is wrong?

Writing

Creating Suspense Write a short story describing an event that is suspenseful. The event could be something that happened to you or that you make up. Be sure to use varied sentence types to present a lively and effective personal style.

Art Connection

Dinner at Haddo House by A. E. Emslie (1848–1918), on page 566, shows an actual event, the meeting of British prime minister William Gladstone with the earl and countess of Aberdeen at their home, Haddo House. Does the setting of this painting look like your idea of the dining room in "The Dinner Party"? Explain your answer, giving examples from the painting and the story.

Detail of *Dinner at Haddo House* (1884), Alfred Edward Emslie. By courtesy of the National Portrait Gallery, London.

Research & Technology

First Aid Procedures Using the Internet and library sources, research how to provide first aid for snakebites. Write a set of instructions that explains to your classmates all the procedures you should take to administer the first aid. Be sure your directions are clear and address problems that might arise.

Reading *for* INFORMATION

Before you begin your research, learn how to read and write complex directions, using the article on the following pages.

Vocabulary

VOCABULARY STRATEGY: WORD WEB Create a word web like the one below for each Word to Know. Include definitions, part of speech, examples, synonyms, and related words and ideas.

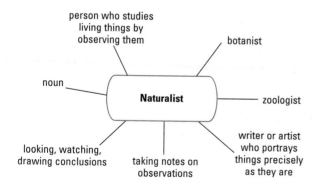

- person who studies living things by observing them
- botanist
- noun
- **Naturalist**
- zoologist
- looking, watching, drawing conclusions
- taking notes on observations
- writer or artist who portrays things precisely as they are

EXERCISE Work with a partner to act out the meaning of one of the Words to Know while another pair of students tries to guess the word. Then switch roles: you and your partner try to guess which word the other pair is acting out. Keep playing this game of charades until all the words have been used.

Vocabulary Handbook
See p. R20: Context Clues.

WORDS TO KNOW	arresting	naturalist	rafter	sober	spirited

Grammar in Context: Prepositional Phrases as Adverbs

Notice how the words in red in the following passage from Mona Gardner's "The Dinner Party" help describe how the hostess calls for her servant.

> **With a small gesture she summons the native boy standing behind her chair.**

The words in red form a **prepositional phrase.** A prepositional phrase consists of a preposition *(with)*, its object *(gesture)*, and possibly one or more modifiers *(small)*. Prepositional phrases can act like adverbs, modifying verbs, adjectives, or other adverbs. The prepositional phrase shown above modifies the verb *summons,* because it shows *how* she summoned the boy.

Apply to Your Writing Use prepositional phrases in your writing when you want to add detail or give more information.

WRITING EXERCISE Rewrite each sentence so that it includes a prepositional phrase that begins with the word in parentheses. (The position of the word in parentheses indicates where the phrase should begin.)

Example: *Original* The people at the dinner party talked. (for)

Rewritten The people at the dinner party talked for several hours.

1. A colonial official and his wife are giving a party. (in)
2. (during) The hostess realizes that a snake is under the table.
3. (with) A servant carries out a bowl of milk.
4. (in) The snake leaves the house.
5. (with) The hostess proves her point.

Grammar Handbook   See p. R89: Phrases and Clauses.

Mona Gardner
1900–1982

"Twelve years of living with the Japanese has filled me with a life-long interest in these people and in their destiny in the East."

Pacific Rim Interests During her childhood in Seattle, Washington, Mona Gardner often visited Japan with her family. There she developed a lifelong interest in Asia. She graduated from Stanford University in Stanford, California, in 1920 and began her writing career as a journalist. Gardner eventually moved to Japan, covering Asia as a correspondent for an American newspaper syndicate. She wrote,

"Twelve years of living with the Japanese has filled me with a life-long interest in these people and in their destiny in the East."

Traveler's Tales In the 1930s, Gardner spent five months in China reporting on that country's war with Japan. One of her three books, *The Menacing Sun,* tells of her travels in Southeast Asia, the East Indies, and India.

AUTHOR ACTIVITY
Women's Roles Find *The Shanghai Item* by Mona Gardner in the library and read the short story "The River Came." Is Gardner's interest in women's equality as obvious in this story as it is in "The Dinner Party"? Find examples to support your opinion.

THE ENORMOUS CROCODILE

FROM ROALD DAHL'S *REVOLTING RECIPES*

Makes one centerpiece to nibble at

you will need:
- wire coat hanger with the hook cut off (optional)
- toothpicks
- 1 tube (4½ ounces) white decorating icing
- long tray or board

the crocodile:
- 1 large baguette, a thin loaf of French bread (body)
- 3½ ounces whole blanched almonds (teeth)
- 1 package (10 ounces) frozen chopped spinach (skin)
- 2 globe artichokes (scales)
- 1 slice ham (tongue)
- 1 egg, hard-boiled (eyeballs)
- 1 black olive (pupils)
- 4 cooked sausages (legs)
- 12 cocktail gherkins (toes)

egg filling:
(quantities depend on the size of the baguette)
- 6 to 8 eggs, hard-boiled
- salt and pepper
- 3 to 4 tablespoons mayonnaise
- 1 small bunch watercress, leaves only, chopped

❶

Reading for Information

For activities such as driving a car or cooking a seven-course meal, you need to follow directions. It's important to follow directions carefully, completely, and in the correct order for successful results.

Following Complex Directions
Directions are step-by-step instructions for carrying out an activity or a process. "The Enormous Crocodile" is a recipe, or set of directions, for how to make an edible centerpiece for a party. This is a playful recipe, but similar sets of complex directions are used to guide people in many real-life activities.

YOUR TURN *Use the questions and activities that follow to help you learn how to follow complex directions.*

❶ The materials and ingredients needed for a recipe are usually printed at its beginning. Prepare for your activity by gathering all the necessary ingredients and materials. What might happen if you began this recipe without a coat hanger or any of the ingredients for the egg filling?

Steps 1 to 7 should be done the day before serving.

1. Slice one end of the baguette horizontally in half along one third of its length to make the mouth.

2. Now slice the other end horizontally to make the body, leaving 1/2 to 3/4 inch unsliced between the body and the mouth (this is the neck). Carefully lift off the top of the body section.

3. Hollow out the top and bottom of the body, and the lower jaw, leaving a wide border for the lower lip.

4. Fold the coat hanger in half (having previously removed the hook), and carefully place it inside the mouth to prop up the jaws.

5. Defrost, drain, and cook the spinach. Set aside.

6. Boil the artichokes for 30 to 40 minutes, drain, and set aside. When cold, pluck the leaves (reserving the hairy choke and heart as a treat for adults later!).

7. **EGG FILLING:** Finely chop the 6 to 8 hard-boiled eggs, and season to taste with salt and pepper. Mix in the mayonnaise and watercress and spoon into the body.

8. **TONGUE AND TEETH:** Place the tongue in the mouth, and insert the teeth (almonds) into the border of the upper and lower lips. Secure any loose teeth with the decorating icing.

④

9. **SKIN AND SCALES:** Spread the cooked spinach over the head and body. Mold the mixture to look like scaly skin. Position artichoke leaves as shown.

10. **EYES:** Cut the hard-boiled egg in half and turn the egg yolks around so that they protrude. Add the pupils (half-olives). Secure with toothpicks.

11. **LEGS AND TOES:** Slice the sausages in half and position for legs. Hold in place with toothpicks. Add the cocktail gherkins for toes.

NOTE: IMPORTANT This recipe is designed to create a centerpiece for a party or other special occasion. If you wish to eat the croc, simply follow the recipe but do not insert the coat hanger. His jaws will be closed, but he'll still be delicious!

Warn children that there are sharp toothpicks in the crocodile's eyes and legs.

Reading for Information *continued*

② **Understanding Meaning** Read through the directions once, making sure you understand each step and all the terms. If you don't understand something after reading, use a dictionary or ask someone to help you. Why is it important to know what "slice the baguette horizontally" means? What might your centerpiece look like if you used a regular loaf of bread and sliced it vertically?

③ **Using Headings** Headings are used to organize and present written information and to identify important information. How do these headings clarify the directions? Would the directions be as clear if the headings were not included? Explain.

④ Note that each step in the directions is numbered to show the order in which the crocodile is prepared. Remember that directions that appear toward the end of a recipe may include important information. Overlooking a step could lead to a ruined product. What might happen if you carried out step 9 before steps 1 through 6?

Research & Technology
Activity Link: "The Dinner Party," p. 569.
After reading "The Dinner Party" and learning how some people behave when faced with danger, write step-by-step instructions for an emergency you might encounter. Explain why your instructions are important.

A Running Brook of Horror

by DANIEL P. MANNIX

Connect to Your Life

Do you know what to do if someone is bitten by a poisonous snake?

Build Background

Every year thousands of people are bitten by snakes. Most recover without any side effects. The bites of some snakes, however, are deadly unless treated immediately. The best way of treating such snakebites is with an antivenin.

The snake is "milked"— its venom, or poison, is collected. The venom is processed in a laboratory.

A small, safe amount of the venom is injected into a horse or cow. The animal builds up immunity over the course of ten weeks. This means it can fight off the dangerous effects of the venom.

Focus Your Reading

LITERARY ANALYSIS **DESCRIPTIVE DETAILS**

Writers use details to help readers clearly imagine an event, a scene, an object, or a person. As you read, note how the author uses **descriptive details** to build the reader's sense of horror and fascination.

WORDS TO KNOW **Vocabulary Preview**

dexterity	invulnerable	reverently
impunity	provocation	

ACTIVE READING **STUDY SKILL—SQ3R**

One useful study skill is **SQ3R**. These letters stand for: **Survey,** or quickly preview, the main ideas; **Question** what you want to find out as you read; **Read** the selection carefully; **Recite** the main ideas; **Review,** or reread, the selection. After you have surveyed the selection, note the questions that you want to answer in your ☐ READER'S NOTEBOOK. This will help you recall and retain information you have read.

A Running Brook of Horror

by Daniel P. Mannix

The animal's blood is used to produce an effective antivenin. The antivenin is injected into a snakebite victim.

I first heard of Grace Wiley when Dr. William Mann, former director of the National Zoological Park in Washington, D.C., handed me a picture of a tiny woman with a gigantic king cobra draped over her shoulders like a garden hose. The snake had partly spread his hood and was looking intently into the camera while his mistress stroked his head to quiet him. Dr. Mann told me, "Grace lives in a little house full of poisonous snakes, imported from all over the world. She lets them wander around like cats. There's been more nonsense written about 'snake charming' than nearly any other subject. Grace is probably one of the few who know the real secrets of this curious business."

Looking at the picture of that deadly creature I knew what a famous writer meant when he described a snake as a "running brook of horror." Still, I like snakes and when Jule, my wife, and I moved into our Malibu house, I made it a point to call on Grace Wiley.

She was living in a small three-room cottage, outside Los Angeles, surrounded by open fields. Behind the cottage was a big, ramshackle barn where the snakes were kept. Grace was cleaning snake boxes with a hose when I arrived. She was a surprisingly little lady, scarcely over five feet tall, and probably weighed less than a hundred pounds. Although Grace was sixty-four years old, she was as active as a boy and worked with smooth <u>dexterity</u>. When she saw me, she hurriedly picked up the four-foot rattlesnake who had been sunning himself while his box was cleaned and poured him into his cage. The snake raised his head but made no attempt to strike or even to rattle. I was impressed but not astonished. In captivity, rattlers often grow sluggish and can be handled with comparative <u>impunity</u>.

Grace came forward, drying her hands on her apron. "Oh dear, I meant to get dressed up for you," she said, trying to smooth down her thatch of brown hair. "But I haven't anybody here to help me with the snakes, except Mother—and she's eighty-four years old. Don't trip over an alligator," she added as I came forward. I noticed for the first time in the high grass a dozen or so alligators and crocodiles. They ranged from a three-foot Chinese croc to a big Florida 'gator more than twelve feet long. I threaded my way among them without mishap, although several opened their huge jaws to hiss at me.

"They don't mean anything by that, any more than a dog barking," Grace explained fondly. "They're very tame and most of them know their names. Now come in and meet my little family of snakes."

We entered the barn. The walls were lined with cages of all sizes and shapes containing snakes. Grace stopped at each cage, casually lifting the occupant and pointing out his fine points while she stroked and examined him. Grace unquestionably had one of the world's finest collections of reptiles. I watched her handle diamondback rattlesnakes from Texas, vipers from Italy, fer-de-lance from the West Indies, a little Egyptian cobra, and the deadly krait from India.

Then I saw Grace perform a feat I would have believed impossible.

We had stopped in front of a large, glass-fronted cage containing apparently nothing but newspaper. "These little fellows arrived only a short time ago, so they're very wild," explained Grace indulgently. She quietly lifted the paper. Instantly a forest of heads sprang up in the cage. Grace moved the paper slightly. At the movement, the heads seemed to spread and flatten. Then I saw that they were not heads but hoods. I was looking at the world's most deadly creature—the Indian cobra.

Tigers are said to kill six hundred people a year, but cobras kill twenty-five thousand people a year in India alone. Hunters have been mauled by wounded elephants and lived to tell about it, but no one survives a body bite from a big cobra. I have caught rattlesnakes with a forked stick and my bare hands, but I'm not ashamed to say I jumped back from that cage.

Grace advanced her hand toward the nearest cobra. The snake swayed like a reed in the wind, feinting[1] for the strike. Grace raised her hand above the snake's head, the reptile twisting around to watch her. As the woman slowly lowered her hand, the snake gave that most terrible of all animal noises—the unearthly hiss of a deadly snake. I have seen children laugh with excitement at the roar of a lion, but I have never seen anyone who did not cringe at that cold, uncanny sound. Grace deliberately tried to touch the rigid, quivering hood. The cobra struck at her hand. He missed. Quietly, Grace presented her open palm. The cobra hesitated a split second, his reared body quivering like a plucked banjo string. Then he struck.

I felt sick as I saw his head hit Grace's hand, but the cobra did not bite. He struck with his mouth closed. As rapidly as an expert boxer drumming on a punching bag, the snake struck three times against Grace's palm, always for some incredible reason with his mouth shut. Then Grace slid her open hand over his head and stroked his hood. The snake hissed again and struggled violently under her touch. Grace continued to caress him. Suddenly the snake went limp and his hood began to close. Grace slipped her other hand under the snake's body and lifted him out of the cage. She held the reptile in her arms as though he were a baby. The cobra raised his head to look Grace in the face; his dancing tongue was less than a foot from her mouth. Grace braced her hand against the curve of his body and talked calmly to him until he folded his hood. He curled up in her arms quietly until I made a slight movement; then he instantly reared up again, threatening me.

---

1. **feinting** (fān'tĭng): moving so as to distract an opponent's attention.

"She lets them wander around like cats."

I had never seen anything to match this performance. Later, Grace opened the cobra's mouth to show me that the fangs were still intact. The yellow venom[2] was slowly oozing over their tips.

If Grace Wiley had wished to make a mystery out of her amazing ability I am certain she could have made a fortune by posing as a woman with supernatural power. There isn't a zoologist alive who could have debunked her. But Grace was a perfectly honest person who was happy to explain in detail exactly how she could handle these terrible creatures. I spent several weeks with her studying her technique and now that I understand it I'm even more impressed than I was before.

When a cobra attacks, it rears straight upward. If you put your elbow on a table, cup your hand to represent the open hood, and sway your forearm back and forth, you will have a good idea of the fighting stance of a cobra. Your index finger represents the tiny, mouselike head that does the business. Your range is limited to the length of your forearm. Here is a large part of the secret in handling cobras. With a little practice you can tell a cobra's range to the inch. Also, the blow of a cobra is comparatively slow. Someone with steady nerves can jerk away in time to avoid being bitten.

When Grace approached a wild cobra, she moved her hand back and forth just outside the snake's range. The cobra would then strike angrily until he became tired. Then he was reluctant to strike again. Grace's next move was to raise her hand over the snake's hood and bring it down slowly. Because of his method of rearing, a cobra cannot strike directly upward, and Grace could actually touch the top of the snake's head. The snake became puzzled and frustrated. He felt that he was fighting an <u>invulnerable</u> opponent who, after all, didn't seem to mean him any harm.

Then came the final touch. Grace would put her open palm toward the snake. At last the cobra was able to hit her. But he had to bite, and he could not get a grip on the flat surface of the palm. If he could get a finger or a loose fold of skin he could fasten his teeth in it and start chewing. But his strike is sufficiently slow that Grace could meet each blow with the flat of her palm. At last Grace would be able to get her hand over the snake's head and stroke his hood. This seemed to relax the reptile, and from then on Grace could handle him with some degree of confidence.

I don't mean to suggest that this is a cut-and-dried[3] procedure. Grace knew snakes perfectly and could tell by tiny, subtle indications what the reptile would probably do next. She had been bitten many times—she would never tell me just how many—but never by a cobra. You're only bitten once by a cobra.

"Now I'll show you what I know you're waiting to see," said Grace as she put the snake away. "My mated pair of king cobras." Dropping her voice <u>reverently</u>, she added, "I call the big male 'The King of Kings.'" She led the way to a large enclosure, and for the first time in my life I was looking into the eyes

---

2. **venom** (vĕn'əm): poison.
3. **cut-and-dried**: done according to a set plan; routine.

WORDS TO KNOW

invulnerable (ĭn-vŭl'nər-ə-bəl) *adj.* impossible to hurt
reverently (rĕv'ər-ənt-lē) *adv.* in a way that shows awe and respect

You're only bitten once by a cobra.

of that dread reptile, the king cobra or hamadryad.[4]

The common cobra is rarely more than five feet long. Even so, he has enough venom in his poison glands to kill fifty people. Grace's king cobras were more than fifteen feet long. The two hamadryads contained enough venom, if injected drop by drop, to kill nearly a thousand human beings. That wasn't all. The hamadryad is the only snake known to attack without any provocation. These fearful creatures have been reported to trail people through a jungle for the express purpose of biting them. They are so aggressive that they have closed roads in India by driving away all traffic. This is probably because the hamadryads, unlike other snakes, guard their eggs and young, and if a pair sets up housekeeping in a district, every other living thing must get out—including elephants. When a king cobra rears up, he stands higher than the head of a kneeling man. They are unquestionably the most dangerous animals in the world today.

When Grace first got these monsters, she was unable to handle them as she would ordinary cobras; so she had to devise an entirely new method of working with them. When the kings first arrived, they were completely unapproachable. They reared up more than four feet, snorting and hissing, their lower jaws open to expose the poison fangs.

"A very threatening look, indeed," Grace called it. She put them in a large cage with a sliding partition. Unlike other snakes, hamadryads are knowing enough to notice that when their keeper opens the door in the side of the cage to put in fresh water, the hand must be exposed for a fraction of a second. These cobras soon learned to lie against the side of the cage and wait for Grace to open the door. She outwitted them by waiting until both of the hamadryads were on one side of the cage and then sliding in the partition before changing water pans.

She did not dare to go near them with her bare hands; she used a padded stick to stroke them. Yet she was able to touch them four days after their arrival. "I petted the kings on their tails when their heads were far away," she told me. "Later in the day I had a little visit with them and told them how perfectly lovely they were—that I liked them and was sure we were going to be good friends."

A few weeks later, the King of Kings began shedding his skin. Snakes are irritable and nervous while shedding, and the hamadryad had trouble sloughing off the thin membrane covering his eyes. Grace wrote in her diary, "I stroked his head and then pulled off the eyelids with eyebrow forceps. He flinched a little but was unafraid. He put out his tongue in such a knowing manner! I mounted the eyelids and they looked just like pearls.

---

4. **hamadryad** (hăm´ə-drī´əd).

WORDS
TO
KNOW   **provocation** (prŏv´ə-kā´shən) *n.* something that irritates or stirs to action

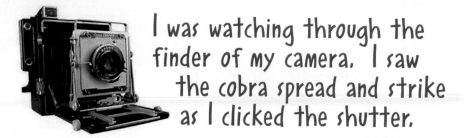

I was watching through the finder of my camera. I saw the cobra spread and strike as I clicked the shutter.

What a pity that there have been nothing but unfriendly, aggressive accounts about this sweet snake. Really, the intelligence of these creatures is unbelievable."

The King of Kings was so heavy that Grace was unable to lift him by herself. Jule offered to help her carry the snake outside for a picture. While Jule and Grace were staggering out the door with the monster reptile between them, the king suddenly reared and rapped Jule several times on her forehead with his closed mouth. "He's trying to tell you something!" exclaimed Grace. He was indeed. I saw that the Chinese crocodile had rushed out from under a table and grabbed the hamadryad by the tail. Jule relaxed her grip and the king dropped his head and gave a single hiss. The croc promptly let go and the ladies bore the cobra out into the sunlight. I was the only person who seemed upset by the incident.

Out of curiosity, I asked Grace if she ever used music in taming her snakes. She laughed and told me what I already knew: all snakes are deaf. Grace assured me that the Hindu fakir[5] uses his flute only to attract a crowd and by swaying his own body back and forth the fakir keeps the snake swaying as the cobra is feinting to strike. The man times his music to correspond to the snake's movements and it appears to dance to the tune. The fakir naturally keeps well outside of the cobra's striking range. Years later when I was in India, I discovered that this is exactly what happens. I never saw any snake charmer even

approximate Grace's marvelous powers over reptiles.

Grace's main source of income was to exhibit her snakes to tourists, although she was occasionally able to rent a snake to a studio (she always went along to make sure the reptile wasn't frightened or injured), and sometimes she bought ailing snakes from dealers, cured them, and resold them for a small profit to zoos. While I was with her, a dusty car stopped and discharged a plump couple with three noisy children who had seen her modest sign: GRACE WILEY—REPTILES. Grace explained that she would show them her collection, handle the poisonous snakes, call over the tame alligators, and let the children play with Rocky, an eighteen-foot Indian Rock python which she had raised from a baby. The charge was twenty-five cents. "That's too much," the woman said to her husband, and they went back to the car. Grace sighed. "No one seems interested in my snakes. No one really cares about them. And they're so wonderful."

One day Grace telephoned me to say that she had gotten in a new shipment of snakes, including some Indian cobras from Siam.[6] "One of them has markings that form a complete G on the back of his hood," she told me. "Isn't it curious that the snake and I have the same initial! I call him 'My Snake.'" We laughed about this, and then Jule and I went out to Cypress to take a last set of pictures of Grace and her snakes for an article I was doing about this remarkable woman.

We took several pictures, and then I asked Grace to let me get a picture of the cobra with

---

5. **fakir** (fə-kîr′): a beggar who performs feats of magic.
6. **Siam** (sī-ăm′): the former name of Thailand, a country in Southeast Asia.

the G on the hood. "I didn't look very well in those other pictures," said Grace anxiously. "I'll comb my hair and put on another blouse." She was back in a few minutes. Jule and I had set up our cameras in the yard behind the barn. I wanted a shot of the cobra with spread hood, and Grace brought him out cradled in her arms. Before allowing me to take the picture, she removed her glasses, as she felt that she looked better without them. The cobra refused to spread, and Grace put him down on the ground and extended her flat palm toward him to make him rear—something I had often seen her do before, but never without her glasses.

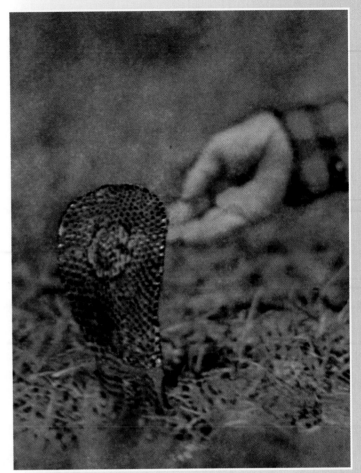

This photo was taken at the very moment that the cobra bit Grace Wiley.

I was watching through the finder of my camera. I saw the cobra spread and strike as I clicked the shutter. As the image disappeared from the ground glass of my Graflex, I looked up and saw the snake had seized Grace by the middle finger. She said in her usual quiet voice, "Oh, he's bitten me."

I dropped the camera and ran toward her, feeling an almost paralyzing sense of shock, for I knew that Grace Wiley was a dead woman. At the same time I thought, "It's just like the book," for the cobra was behaving exactly as textbooks on cobras say they behave. He was deliberately chewing on the wound to make the venom run out of his glands. It was a terrible sight.

Quietly and expertly, Grace took hold of the snake and gently forced his mouth open. I knew that her only chance for life was to put a tourniquet[7] around the finger instantly and slash open the wound to allow the venom to run out. Seconds counted. I reached out my hand to take the snake above the hood so she

could immediately start squeezing out the venom, but Grace motioned me away. She stood up, still holding the cobra, and walked into the barn. Carefully, she put the snake into his cage and closed the door.

This must have taken a couple of minutes, and I knew that the venom was spreading through her system each moment. "Jule," said Grace, "call Wesley Dickinson. He's a herpetologist[8] and a friend of mine. He'll know what to do." Calmly and distinctly she gave Jule the telephone number and Jule ran

---

7. **tourniquet** (tŏŏr'nĭ-kĭt): a band tied tightly around a limb of the body to temporarily stop blood flow.

8. **herpetologist** (hûr'pĭ-tŏl'ə-jĭst): a scientist who studies reptiles and amphibians.

to the phone. Then Grace turned to me. Suddenly she said, "He didn't really bite me, did he?" It was the only emotion I saw her show. I could only say, "Grace, where's your snake-bite kit?" We both knew that nothing except immediate amputation of her arm could save her, but anything was worth a chance.

She pointed to a cabinet. There was a tremendous collection of the surgical aids used for snakebite, but I don't believe any of the stuff had been touched for twenty years. I pulled out a rubber tourniquet and tried to twist it around her finger. The old rubber snapped in my hands. Grace didn't seem to notice. I pulled out my handkerchief and tried that. It was too thick to go around her finger and I twisted it around her wrist. "I'll faint in a few minutes," said Grace. "I want to show you where everything is before I lose consciousness."

Cobra venom, unlike rattlesnake, affects the nervous system. In a few minutes the victim becomes paralyzed and the heart stops beating. I knew Grace was thinking of this. She said, "You must give me strychnine[9] injections to keep my heart going when I begin to pass out. I'll show you where the strychnine is kept. You may have to give me caffeine also."

She walked to the other end of the room and I ran alongside trying to keep the tourniquet in place. She got out the tiny glass vials of strychnine and caffeine and also a hypodermic syringe with several needles. I saw some razor blades with the outfit and picked one up, intending to make a deep incision to let out as much of the venom as possible. Grace shook her head. "That won't do any good," she told me. Cobra venom travels along the nerves, so making the wound bleed wouldn't be very effective, but it was all I could think of to do.

Jule came back with a Mr. Tanner, Grace's cousin who lived next door. Tanner immediately got out his jacknife, intending to cut open the wound, but Grace stopped him. "Wait until Wesley comes," she said. Tanner told me afterward that he was convinced that if he had amputated the finger Grace might have lived. This is doubtful. Probably nothing except amputation of her arm would have saved her then, and we had nothing but a jackknife. She probably would have died of shock and loss of blood.

Grace lay on the floor to keep as quiet as possible and slow the

---

9. **strychnine** (strĭk′nīn′): a poisonous chemical that, in extremely small amounts, is used medically to stimulate the nervous system.

absorption of the venom. "You'd better give me the strychnine now, dear," she told Jule. Jule snapped off the tip of one of the glass vials, but the cylinder broke in her hands. She opened another tube and tried to fill the syringe; the needle was rusted shut. Jule selected another needle, tested it, and filled the syringe. "I'm afraid it will hurt," she told Grace. "Now don't worry, dear," said Grace comfortingly. "I know you'll do it very well."

After the injection, Grace asked Jule to put a newspaper under her head to keep her hair from getting dirty. A few minutes later, the ambulance arrived with Wesley Dickinson following in his own car. Wesley had telephoned the hospital and arranged for blood transfusions and an iron lung. As Grace was lifted into the ambulance, she called back to Tanner, "Remember to cut up the meat for my frogs very fine and take good care of my snakes." That was the last we ever saw of her.

Grace died in the hospital half an hour later. She lived about ninety minutes after being bitten. In the hospital, Wesley directed the doctors to drain the blood out of her arm and pump in fresh blood. When her heart began to fail she was put into the lung. She had become unconscious. Then her heart stopped. Stimulants were given. The slow beating began again but grew steadily weaker. Each time stimulants were given, the heart responded less strongly, and finally stopped forever.

We waited with Mr. and Mrs. Tanner at the snake barn, calling the hospital at intervals. When we heard that Grace was dead, Mrs. Tanner burst into tears. "Grace was such a beautiful young girl—and so talented," she moaned. "There wasn't anything she couldn't do. Why did she ever want to mess around with those awful snakes?"

"I guess that's something none of us will ever understand," said her husband sadly.

Grace was born in Kansas in 1884. She studied entomology[10] at the University of Kansas, and during field trips to collect insects it was a great joke among Grace's fellow students that she was terrified of even harmless garter snakes. Later, however, after her marriage failed, Grace turned with a passionate interest to the creatures she had so long feared. In 1923 she became curator of the Museum of Natural History at the Minneapolis Public Library, but quarreled with the directors, who felt that her reckless handling of poisonous snakes endangered not only her own life but that of others. She went to the Brookfield Zoo in Chicago; here the same difficulty arose. Finally Grace moved to California where she could work with reptiles as she wished.

An attempt was made by several of Grace's friends to keep her collection together for a Grace Wiley Memorial Reptile House, but this failed. The snakes were auctioned off, and the snake that had killed Grace was purchased by a roadside zoo in Arizona. Huge signboards bearing an artist's conception of the incident were erected for miles along the highways.

So passed one of the most remarkable people I have ever known. ◉

---

10. **entomology** (ĕn′tə-mŏl′ə-jē): the scientific study of insects.

Connect to the Literature

1. **What Do You Think?** What was your first thought when you finished reading about Grace Wiley's fate?

Comprehension Check
• How does Wiley earn a living?
• What animal is described as a "deadly creature"?
• What mistake does Wiley make that leads to her being bitten?
• What steps are taken to save Wiley?

Think Critically

2. Mannix said that a famous writer (John Ruskin) called a snake a "running brook of horror." Do you think this metaphor, or direct comparison, is a good description? Why or why not?

3. How would you describe Grace Wiley's character? Support your answer with examples from the selection.

   Think About:
   • her behavior when handling snakes
   • the way she talks about her snakes
   • the fatal mistake she makes
   • her behavior after being bitten

4. Why do you think the author organizes the selection so that his account of Wiley's early life and career comes at the end?

5. **ACTIVE READING STUDY SKILL—SQ3R**
   Working with a partner, complete the **SQ3R** process. Recite the main idea of this selection, and then look back at the questions you wrote in your **📖 READER'S NOTEBOOK.** Which of your questions did the selection answer? Do you think this **study skill** is an effective strategy? Explain your answer.

Extend Interpretations

6. **COMPARING TEXTS** "The Dinner Party" by Mona Gardner (page 565) is also about a cobra. In what ways are these two selections alike? In what ways are they different?

7. **Connect to Life** Why do you think some people are drawn to activities that others think are unusual or dangerous?

Literary Analysis

DESCRIPTIVE DETAILS

A description is a picture, in words, of a scene, an event, a person, or an object. **Descriptive details** can be used to appeal to readers' senses or to give more information about characters or events. Descriptive details in the following passage provide a clear picture of just how a cobra bites:

He grabs his victims and then deliberately chews while the venom runs down into the wound he is making.

Paired Activity Create a chart like the one below, with one column for the Indian cobra and one for the king cobra. With a partner, find and then list as many **descriptive details** from the selection as you can in each category. Then discuss the following questions in a large group.

• Which category—appearance or behavior—has the most descriptive details? Why do you think this is so?

• Which cobra—king or Indian—has the most descriptive details? Did this affect your ability to picture the cobras as you were reading? Explain why or why not.

Indian Cobra	King Cobra
Appearance	**Appearance**
yellow venom oozing over tips of fangs	
Behavior	**Behavior**

Writing

Reptilian Metaphors The title of this story is a metaphor by the writer John Ruskin, who described a snake as a "running brook of horror." Write a brief essay in which you create your own metaphors for some of the creatures in Grace Wiley's collection. Revise your writing for the appropriate word choice and organization. Place your essay in your **Working Portfolio.**

Writing Handbook
See p. R41: Descriptive Writing.

Speaking & Listening

Taking a Risk Was Grace Wiley brave or foolish to risk her life as she did? Prepare a persuasive speech in which you develop an argument for your point of view. Be sure to use reasons and examples that address counterarguments.

Speaking and Listening Handbook
See p. R109: Persuasive Presentations.

Research & Technology

SCIENCE This selection is about cobras, which are native to Asia and Africa, but there are other dangerous snakes that can be found closer to home. Find out more about the best-known poisonous snake native to the United States—the rattlesnake. Present your findings on a poster. Be sure to include information on treatment of rattlesnake bites.

INTERNET Research Starter
www.mcdougallittell.com

Vocabulary and Spelling

EXERCISE: CONTEXT CLUES Write the Word to Know that best completes each sentence.

1. Visitors admired the _____ Grace Wiley showed in feeding and carrying her snakes.
2. Grace Wiley seemed to handle these dangerous snakes with _____, safe even with the deadly Indian cobra.
3. It was clear that Wiley respected the snakes and she spoke of them _____, especially the largest cobra, "The King of Kings."
4. King cobras are known to attack without any _____ at all.
5. Grace seemed _____ as she worked with her snakes, until the day she was bitten by a cobra and died within 90 minutes.

SPELLING STRATEGY: ADDING SUFFIXES Some verbs can be changed to nouns by dropping the silent *e* and adding the suffix *-ion, -tion,* or *-ation.* For example, the ending *-ion* can be added to the verb *irritate* to create the noun *irritation.* When the suffix is added, the hard *t* sound softens so that the suffix is pronounced *shun.* Spell the word formed when the suffix *-ion, -tion,* or *-ation* is added to the root words. *(Note: The letter* k *may change to the letter* c.)

1. provoke
2. imitate
3. operate
4. complicate
5. combine

Vocabulary Handbook
See p. R20: Context Clues.

| WORDS TO KNOW | dexterity | impunity | invulnerable | provocation | reverently |

Grammar in Context: Introductory Phrases

Notice how Daniel P. Mannix uses introductory phrases to begin the following sentences from "A Running Brook of Horror."

> **A few weeks later,** the King of Kings began shedding his skin.

> **With a little practice** you can tell a cobra's range to the inch.

In each sentence, the words in red form an **introductory phrase,** a phrase that gives information at the beginning of a sentence. There are many kinds of introductory phrases. For example, the first sentence begins with an adverb phrase, whereas the second sentence begins with a prepositional phrase. Introductory phrases also include adjective phrases, gerund phrases, infinitive phrases, and participial phrases.

Apply to Your Writing Use introductory phrases to provide information and to add variety to your writing.

Punctuation Tip: In most cases, a comma should separate the introductory phrase from the rest of the sentence.

WRITING EXERCISE Rewrite the following sentences so that each begins with an introductory phrase.

Example: ***Original*** Grace took hold of the snake and gently forced his mouth open.

Rewritten <u>Quietly and expertly,</u> Grace took hold of the snake and gently forced his mouth open.

1. There were baby cobras.
2. He jumped away from the cage.
3. The snakes reared their heads.
4. One of Grace's cobras attacked her.
5. It would have taken a miracle.

Connect to the Literature Look at the paragraph on page 583 that begins "After the injection . . ." Identify the sentences in this paragraph that begin with introductory phrases.

<u>**Grammar Handbook**</u> See p. R89: Phrases and Clauses.

Daniel P. Mannix
1911–1997

He even held the world record for swallowing the longest sword—23½ inches.

Porcupines, Vultures, and Alligators As a boy in Pennsylvania, Daniel Pratt Mannix kept many animals, including porcupines, hawks, vultures, and even alligators. He never lost this love of wildlife, and when he later became a journalist, Mannix combined his interests by selling stories about animals to magazines. In fact, Mannix became known for his nature writing.

Off to Join the Carnival In *Memoirs of a Sword Swallower,* Mannix writes about the three years he spent with a carnival before becoming a writer. His exciting and unusual jobs included those of magician, sword swallower, fire eater, and escape artist. He even held the world record for swallowing the longest sword—23½ inches.

AUTHOR ACTIVITY
Hollywood Success One of Mannix's books for young readers, *The Fox and the Hound,* was made into an animated movie in 1981. Find and view this video. Summarize the plot, and then discuss what attitudes toward wildlife this plot reveals.

Southbound on the Freeway

by MAY SWENSON

who knows if the moon's

by E. E. CUMMINGS

Connect to Your Life

World of Make-Believe Imagination is a powerful tool. Take a moment and look around the classroom or out the window. Do you see a familiar object that you could imagine being something else? What is the object? What do you imagine that it could be?

Build Background

Riddles and Wordplay The two poems you are about to read are by modern poets who help us see the world in imaginative new ways. They also give readers a new way of looking at poetry.

E. E. Cummings is said to be "among the most innovative of 20th-century poets." His work is known for its playful use of language and unusual word order. Cummings often breaks rules of punctuation and capitalization and makes up new words.

Like Cummings, May Swenson often experiments with wordplay and the shape of her poems. In her book *Poems to Solve,* which contains "Southbound on the Freeway," all the poems are riddles.

Focus Your Reading

LITERARY ANALYSIS **FREE VERSE**

Many modern poems are written in **free verse,** which does not contain regular patterns of **rhythm** or **rhyme.** There are no fixed line lengths or stanzas in free verse. Though free verse has a rhythm, it is more like that of everyday speech. Read aloud the two poems that follow, and pay attention to the rhythm of the lines.

ACTIVE READING **MONITORING YOUR READING**

The meaning of some poems may not be clear on the first reading. When this is the case, it is useful to monitor, or check, your reading and comprehension by following these steps:

- Read the poem to get an idea of what it is about, using clues from the title to identify the topic.
- Notice how the punctuation and the order of words, phrases, and sentences separate units of thought.
- Think about the meaning of the poem. Are any lines unclear?
- Identify the lines or stanzas that puzzle you. Try using the parts of the poem that are clear to you to help explain the parts that are unclear.
- Think about different ways it is possible to explain the meaning of the poem.

READER'S NOTEBOOK As you read the two poems, monitor your reading by using the steps listed above. Note any unclear or puzzling words, phrases, or lines in your notebook.

SOUTHBOUND ON THE FREEWAY

by May Swenson

A tourist came in from Orbitville,
parked in the air, and said:

The creatures of this star
are made of metal and glass.

5 Through the transparent parts
you can see their guts.

Their feet are round and roll
on diagrams—or long

measuring tapes—dark
10 with white lines.

They have four eyes.
The two in the back are red.

Sometimes you can see a 5-eyed
one, with a red eye turning

15 on the top of his head.
He must be special—

the others respect him,
and go slow,

when he passes, winding
20 among them from behind.

They all hiss as they glide,
like inches, down the marked

tapes. Those soft shapes,
shadowy inside

25 the hard bodies—are they
their guts or their brains?

Somewhere in Berkeley (1961), Gregory Blake Larson. Oil on Canvas.
Private Collection/SuperStock

THINKING *through the* LITERATURE

1. What is the "answer" to the riddle? What does the tourist from Orbitville believe to be the "creatures of this star"?
2. What do you think the visitor's opinion of life on Earth might be? Give reasons to support your answer.
3. In your opinion, what is the author's purpose in writing this poem?
4. Did you get a sense of rhythm as you read the poem aloud?

WHO KNOWS IF THE MOON'S

by

E. E. Cummings

Red Balloon (1922), Paul Klee. Oil on chalk-primed gauze mounted on board, 12 1/2" x 12 1/4". Solomon R. Guggenheim Museum, New York. Photograph by David Heald copyright © The Solomon R. Guggenheim Foundation, New York (FN 48 1172 X524). Copyright © 2002 Artists Rights Society (ARS), New York/VG Bild-Kunst, Bonn.

who knows if the moon's
a balloon,coming out of a keen city
in the sky—filled with pretty people?
(and if you and i should

5   get into it,if they
should take me and take you into their balloon,
why then
we'd go up higher with all the pretty people

than houses and steeples and clouds:
10 go sailing
away and away sailing into a keen
city which nobody's ever visited,where

always
       it's
15   Spring)and everyone's
in love and flowers pick themselves

Connect to the Literature

1. **What Do You Think?** What went through your mind as you were reading this poem?

   Comprehension Check
   - What does the speaker compare the moon to?
   - Where does the speaker talk about going?
   - What is unusual about this destination?

Think Critically

2. How do you think the **speaker** feels about the city "in the sky"?

   Think About:
   - the description of the city and the people who live there
   - the fact that "nobody's ever visited"
   - the way the speaker questions whether "the moon's a balloon" in lines 1 and 2

3. **ACTIVE READING** **MONITORING YOUR READING**
   With a partner, look back over the notes you made in your 📖 READER'S NOTEBOOK. Which steps of the monitoring process were most useful in helping you to understand the poem? Discuss why.

Extend Interpretations

4. **Critic's Corner** Poet Robert Lowell said that Swenson's poems "should be hung with permanent fresh paint signs." What do you think this means? Might this apply to "Southbound on the Freeway"? Is it true of Cummings's poem as well?

5. **Writer's Style** Explain how Cummings makes the reader look at the moon in a different way and how his use of language adds to this effect.

6. **Connect to Life** Swenson once said that in a poem "you may find an extra something hidden there especially for you—something that seems to mirror your secret feelings and thoughts . . ." Do either of the two poems have this "extra something" especially for you? Why or why not?

Literary Analysis

FREE VERSE Poetry that does not contain a regular pattern of **rhyme** or **rhythm** is called **free verse.** There are no fixed **stanzas** or line lengths. Instead, the poet decides where the lines should break based on where a pause is needed or how the poem will look on the page. Poems written in free verse often reflect the patterns of everyday speech, whereas traditional poems with regular rhyme and rhythm may sound more formal.

Paired Activity Read both poems aloud. Then, with a small group of classmates, discuss the following questions:

- Which of the two poems is closer to the sound patterns of everyday speech?
- What differences do you notice between these two poems and poems such as "The Charge of the Light Brigade"? You may wish to use a chart like the one below to help in your discussion.

Southbound on the Freeway	who knows if the moon's	The Charge of the Light Brigade
Rhythm: like everyday speech	**Rhythm:** like everyday speech	**Rhythm:** a regular repeated pattern rather like the hoofbeats of a running horse
Rhyme pattern:	Rhyme pattern:	Rhyme pattern:
Line length:	Line length:	Line length:
Stanza length and form:	Stanza length and form:	Stanza length and form:

Writing

Moon Verse What does the moon mean to you? Use a cluster diagram to note your thoughts and feelings about Earth's natural satellite. Use the diagram as the starting point of a free verse poem about the moon. Be sure to choose line lengths that fit the pace or message you are trying to express. Place your poem in your **Working Portfolio.**

Speaking & Listening

Poem on Tape Record a reading of one of these poems, using appropriate background music or sound effects. Match your voice and tone to fit the message of the poem. Play your recording for the class.

<u>Speaking and Listening Handbook</u>
See p. R106: Oral Interpretation.

Research & Technology

Moon Myths Across the centuries and from culture to culture, there have been many myths and tales linked to the moon. Using a book of myths or an encyclopedia, research some of these stories and create a poster about them. Be sure to note your sources.

May Swenson
1919–1989

"Solving a poem can be like undoing a mysterious package."

Poet and Teacher Born in Logan, Utah, May Swenson graduated from Utah State University and worked as a reporter in Salt Lake City before moving to New York in 1949. There she became an editor at a publishing house. After winning such prizes as the Guggenheim Fellowship and the Bollingen Poetry Award, Swenson went on to teach at several universities.

Scientific Interests Many of Swenson's poems show her interest in science, an interest she explores in her essay "The Experience of Poetry in a Scientific Age." She wrote poems about such wonders of outer space as comets and eclipses. Her poem "Shuttles" is about the NASA space shuttle program.

E. E. Cummings
1894–1962

"It takes courage to grow up and turn out to be who you really are."

Suspected of Spying Born in Cambridge, Massachusetts, Edward Estlin Cummings began to experiment with his new way of writing while a student at Harvard. After graduating, Cummings volunteered for duty in World War I and served as an ambulance driver in France. While on the French-German border, Cummings tried to lessen the boredom by writing mysterious letters home. These letters were stopped by wartime censors, and Cummings was briefly imprisoned on suspicion of being an enemy spy.

The Paris Years Cummings remained in France after the war, painting and writing poetry. His many poems include such favorites as "since feeling is first" and "nobody loses all the time."

The Lady, or the Tiger?

by FRANK R. STOCKTON

Connect to Your Life

Horns of a Dilemma Think of a time when you, or someone you know, faced an important decision. What helped you make the decision? Share your thoughts with a partner, and then discuss what you think is the best way to make an important decision.

Build Background

HISTORY

Frank Stockton tries to make even his most fantastic tales as realistic as possible. Although "The Lady, or the Tiger?" is about an imaginary kingdom, Stockton mentions the country's "distant Latin neighbors." This is probably a reference to Latin-speaking Rome, which grew from a small settlement in Italy in 753 B.C. to a powerful empire that controlled all the lands bordering the Mediterranean Sea by A.D. 100.

The system of justice in Stockton's "semibarbaric" land brings to mind a very real and very cruel practice of the Roman Empire, the games in the amphitheater. In addition to watching captives, slaves, and professional fighters known as gladiators fight to the death, spectators sometimes watched condemned criminals being killed by wild animals. As you will see, in "The Lady, or the Tiger?" Stockton gives such "barbaric" practices a new twist.

Gladiators fought in the Colosseum in Rome

WORDS TO KNOW
Vocabulary Preview

assert	imperious
decree	procure
destiny	retribution
doleful	subordinate
exuberant	valor

Focus Your Reading

LITERARY ANALYSIS **SURPRISE ENDING**

In a story with a **surprise ending,** the writer springs an unexpected plot twist at the end. Writers often plant clues throughout the story as to what the ending may be. As you read "The Lady, or the Tiger?" look for clues to the ending.

ACTIVE READING **DRAWING CONCLUSIONS**

Stockton's story presents the reader with a kind of puzzle to answer. In order to complete the puzzle, you need to draw conclusions about the actions of one of the main characters, the princess. **Draw conclusions** about the princess by reading "beyond the lines"—combine the facts in the story with your own knowledge and experience.

READER'S NOTEBOOK As you read the story, list the adjectives and phrases the author uses to describe the princess. Focus on descriptions that may help you to draw conclusions about her. Keep track of her actions also, as they may provide clues about what she might do in a difficult situation.

The Personality of the Princess
- *The princess is as arrogant and overbearing as her father.*
- *She loves the young man with great warmth and strength.*

The Lady, or the Tiger?

BY FRANK R. STOCKTON

Caracalla (188–217A.D.): and Geta, Sir Lawrence Alma-Tadema. Private Collection/Bridgeman Art Library, London/New York.

IN the very olden time, there lived a semibarbaric king, whose ideas, though somewhat polished and sharpened by the progressiveness of distant Latin neighbors,[1] were still large, florid, and untrammeled, as became the half of him which was barbaric. He was a man of <u>exuberant</u> fancy, and, withal, of an authority so irresistible that, at his will, he turned his varied fancies into facts. He was greatly given to self-communing; and, when he and himself agreed upon anything, the thing was done. When every member of his domestic and political systems moved smoothly in its appointed course, his nature was bland and genial; but whenever there was a little hitch and some of his orbs got out of their orbits, he was blander and more genial still, for nothing pleased him so much as

---

1. **Latin neighbors:** people living in the Roman Empire.

Copyright © John Thompson.

to make the crooked straight and crush down uneven places.

Among the borrowed notions by which his barbarism had become semifixed was that of the public arena, in which, by exhibitions of manly and beastly <u>valor</u>, the minds of his subjects were refined and cultured.

But even here the exuberant and barbaric fancy <u>asserted</u> itself. The arena of the king was built, not to give the people an opportunity of hearing the rhapsodies of dying gladiators, nor to enable them to view the inevitable conclusion of a conflict between religious opinions and hungry jaws, but for purposes far better adapted to widen and develop the mental energies of the people. This vast amphitheater, with its encircling galleries, its mysterious vaults, and its unseen passages, was an agent of poetic justice,[2] in which crime was

punished or virtue rewarded by the <u>decrees</u> of an impartial and incorruptible chance.

When a subject was accused of a crime of sufficient importance to interest the king, public notice was given that on an appointed day the fate of the accused person would be decided in the king's arena, a structure which well deserved its name. Although its form and plan were borrowed from afar, its purpose emanated solely from the brain of this man, who, every barleycorn a king,[3] knew no tradition to which he owed more allegiance

---

2. **poetic justice:** an outcome in which everyone gets what he or she deserves, with goodness being rewarded and evil being punished.

3. **every barleycorn a king:** a playful exaggeration of the expression "every inch a king," meaning "thoroughly kingly." (Grains of barley were formerly used as units of measurement.)

WORDS
TO
KNOW

valor (văl′ər) *n.* courage; bravery

assert (ə-sûrt′) *v.* to put forward in a forceful or insistent way

decree (dĭ-krē′) *n.* an official order

than pleased his fancy and who ingrafted on every adopted form of human thought and action the rich growth of his barbaric idealism.

When all the people had assembled in the galleries and the king, surrounded by his court, sat high up on his throne of royal state on one side of the arena, he gave a signal, a door beneath him opened, and the accused subject stepped out into the amphitheater. Directly opposite him, on the other side of the enclosed space, were two doors, exactly alike and side by side. It was the duty and the privilege of the person on trial to walk directly to these doors and open one of them. He could open either door he pleased; he was subject to no guidance or influence but that of the aforementioned impartial and incorruptible chance. If he opened the one, there came out of it a hungry tiger, the fiercest and most cruel that could be procured, which immediately sprang upon him and tore him to pieces, as a punishment for his guilt. The moment that the case of the criminal was thus decided, doleful iron bells were clanged, great wails went up from the hired mourners posted on the outer rim of the arena, and the vast audience, with bowed heads and downcast hearts, wended slowly their homeward way, mourning greatly that one so young and fair, or so old and respected, should have merited so dire a fate.

But if the accused person opened the other door, there came forth from it a lady, the most suitable to his years and station[4] that his majesty could select among his fair subjects; and to this lady he was immediately married,

There came out of it a hungry tiger, the fiercest and most cruel that could be procured.

as a reward for his innocence. It mattered not that he might already possess a wife and family or that his affections might be engaged upon an object of his own selection. The king allowed no such subordinate arrangements to interfere with his great scheme of retribution and reward. The exercises, as in the other instance, took place immediately and in the arena. Another door opened beneath the king, and a priest, followed by a band of choristers and dancing maidens blowing joyous airs on golden horns and treading an epithalamic measure,[5] advanced to where the pair stood, side by side, and the wedding was promptly and cheerily solemnized. Then the gay brass bells rang forth their merry peals, the people shouted glad hurrahs, and the innocent man, preceded by children strewing flowers on his path, led his bride to his home.

This was the king's semibarbaric method of administering justice. Its perfect fairness is obvious. The criminal could not know out of which door would come the lady. He opened either he pleased, without having the slightest idea whether, in the next instant, he was to be devoured or married. On some occasions the tiger came out of one door and on some out of the other. The decisions of this tribunal[6] were not only fair, they were positively determinate. The accused person was

---

4. **station:** social position; rank.
5. **treading an epithalamic** (ĕp′ə-thə-lăm′ĭk) **measure:** dancing to wedding music.
6. **tribunal** (trī-byōō′nəl): court of justice.

WORDS TO KNOW

procure (prō-kyŏŏr′) *v.* to obtain; acquire
doleful (dōl′fəl) *adj.* sad; mournful
subordinate (sə-bôr′dn-ĭt) *adj.* less important or lower in rank; secondary
retribution (rĕt′rə-byōō′shən) *n.* punishment for bad behavior

instantly punished if he found himself guilty, and, if innocent, he was rewarded on the spot, whether he liked it or not. There was no escape from the judgments of the king's arena.

The institution was a very popular one. When the people gathered together on one of the great trial days, they never knew whether they were to witness a bloody slaughter or a hilarious wedding. This element of uncertainty lent an interest to the occasion which it could not otherwise have attained. Thus, the masses were entertained and pleased, and the thinking part of the community could bring no charge of unfairness against this plan; for did not the accused person have the whole matter in his own hands?

This semibarbaric king had a daughter as blooming as his most florid fancies and with a soul as fervent and imperious as his own. As is usual in such cases, she was the apple of his eye and was loved by him above all humanity. Among his courtiers[7] was a young man of that fineness of blood and lowness of station common to the conventional heroes of romance who love royal maidens. This royal maiden was well satisfied with her lover, for he was handsome and brave to a degree unsurpassed in all this kingdom, and she loved him with an ardor that had enough of barbarism in it to make it exceedingly warm

Portrait of a young girl, 1st Century A.D./Museo e Gallerie Nazionali di Capodimonte, Naples, Italy/Index/Bridgeman Art Library, London/New York.

and strong. This love affair moved on happily for many months, until one day the king happened to discover its existence. He did not hesitate nor waver in regard to his duty in the premises. The youth was immediately cast into prison, and a day was appointed for his trial in the king's arena. This, of course, was an especially important occasion, and his majesty, as well as all the people, was greatly interested in the workings and development of this trial. Never before had such a case occurred; never before had a subject dared to love the daughter of a king. In after-years such things became commonplace enough, but then they were, in no slight degree, novel and startling.

The tiger cages of the kingdom were searched for the most savage and relentless beasts, from which the fiercest monster might be selected for the arena, and the ranks of maiden youth and beauty throughout the land were carefully surveyed by competent judges, in order that the young man might have a fitting bride in case fate did not determine for him a different destiny. Of course, everybody knew that the deed with which the accused

---

7. **courtiers** (kôr′tē-ərz): royal attendants.

was charged had been done. He had loved the princess, and neither he, she, nor anyone else thought of denying the fact, but the king would not think of allowing any fact of this kind to interfere with the workings of the tribunal, in which he took such great delight and satisfaction. No matter how the affair turned out, the youth would be disposed of, and the king would take an aesthetic pleasure in watching the course of events, which would determine whether or not the young man had done wrong in allowing himself to love the princess.

The appointed day arrived. From far and near the people gathered and thronged the great galleries of the arena, and crowds, unable to gain admittance, massed themselves against its outside walls. The king and his court were in their places opposite the twin doors—those fateful portals so terrible in their similarity.

All was ready. The signal was given. A door beneath the royal party opened, and the lover of the princess walked into the arena. Tall, beautiful, fair, his appearance was greeted with a low hum of admiration and anxiety. Half the audience had not known so grand a youth had lived among them. No wonder the princess loved him! What a terrible thing for him to be there!

As the youth advanced into the arena, he turned, as the custom was, to bow to the king, but he did not think at all of that royal personage; his eyes were fixed upon the princess who sat to the right of her father. Had it not been for the moiety[8] of barbarism in her nature, it is probable that lady would not have been there, but her intense and fervid soul would not allow her to be absent on an occasion in which she was so terribly interested.

> **S**he knew in which of the two rooms that lay behind those doors stood the cage of the tiger...

From the moment that the decree had gone forth, that her lover should decide his fate in the king's arena, she had thought of nothing, night or day, but this great event and the various subjects connected with it. Possessed of more power, influence, and force of character than anyone who had ever before been interested in such a case, she had done what no other person had done—she had possessed herself of the secret of the doors. She knew in which of the two rooms that lay behind those doors stood the cage of the tiger, with its open front, and in which waited the lady. Through these thick doors, heavily curtained with skins on the inside, it was impossible that any noise or suggestion should come from within to the person who should approach to raise the latch of one of them; but gold and the power of a woman's will had brought the secret to the princess.

And not only did she know in which room stood the lady ready to emerge, all blushing and radiant, should her door be opened, but she knew who the lady was. It was one of the fairest and loveliest of the damsels[9] of the court who had been selected as the reward of the accused youth should he be proved innocent of the crime of aspiring to one so far above him, and the princess hated her. Often had she seen, or imagined that she had seen, this fair creature throwing glances of admiration upon the person of her lover, and sometimes she thought these glances were perceived and even returned. Now and then

---

8. **moiety** (moi′ĭ-tē): half; portion.
9. **damsels** (dăm′zəlz): young women; maidens.

she had seen them talking together; it was but for a moment or two, but much can be said in a brief space. It may have been on most unimportant topics, but how could she know that? The girl was lovely, but she had dared to raise her eyes to the loved one of the princess; and, with all the intensity of the savage blood transmitted to her through long lines of wholly barbaric ancestors, she hated the woman who blushed and trembled behind that silent door.

When her lover turned and looked at her, and his eyes met hers as she sat there paler and whiter than anyone in the vast ocean of anxious faces about her, he saw, by that power of quick perception which is given to those whose souls are one, that she knew behind which door crouched the tiger and behind which stood the lady. He had expected her to know it. He understood her nature, and his soul was assured that she would never rest until she had made plain to herself this thing, hidden to all other lookers-on, even to the king. The only hope for the youth in which there was any element of certainty was based upon the success of the princess in discovering this mystery, and the moment he looked upon her, he saw she had succeeded, as in his soul he knew she would succeed.

Then it was that his quick and anxious glance asked the question: "Which?" It was as plain to her as if he shouted it from where he stood. There was not an instant to be lost. The

Spring, maiden gathering flowers, Roman wall painting from the villa of Varano in Stabiae, c. 15 B.C.–60 A.D./Museo Archeologico Nazionale, Naples, Italy/Bridgeman Art Library, London/New York.

question was asked in a flash; it must be answered in another.

Her right arm lay on the cushioned parapet before her. She raised her hand and made a slight, quick movement toward the right. No one but her lover saw her. Every eye but his was fixed on the man in the arena.

He turned, and with a firm and rapid step he walked across the empty space. Every heart stopped beating, every breath was held, every eye was fixed immovably upon that man. Without the slightest hesitation, he went to the door on the right and opened it.

Study of a Tiger (n.d.), Sir Edwin Henry Landseer (1802–1873). Watercolor on paper, 9½" × 13". The British Museum, London. Photograph © The British Museum.

cheek and sparkling eye of triumph; when she had seen him lead her forth, his whole frame kindled with the joy of recovered life; when she had heard the glad shouts from the multitude, and the wild ringing of the happy bells; when she had seen the priest, with his joyous followers, advance to the couple and make them man and wife before her very eyes; and when she had seen them walk away together upon their path of flowers, followed by the tremendous shouts of the hilarious multitude, in which her one despairing shriek was lost and drowned!

Would it not be better for him to die at once and go to wait for her in the blessed regions of semibarbaric futurity?

And yet, that awful tiger, those shrieks, that blood!

Her decision had been indicated in an instant, but it had been made after days and nights of anguished deliberation. She had known she would be asked, she had decided what she would answer, and, without the slightest hesitation, she had moved her hand to the right.

The question of her decision is one not to be lightly considered, and it is not for me to presume to set myself up as the one person able to answer it. And so I leave it with all of you: Which came out of the opened door—the lady, or the tiger? ❖

Now, the point of the story is this: Did the tiger come out of that door, or did the lady?

The more we reflect upon this question, the harder it is to answer. It involves a study of the human heart which leads us through devious mazes of passion, out of which it is difficult to find our way. Think of it, fair reader, not as if the decision of the question depended upon yourself, but upon that hot-blooded, semibarbaric princess, her soul at a white heat beneath the combined fires of despair and jealousy. She had lost him, but who should have him?

How often, in her waking hours and in her dreams, had she started in wild horror and covered her face with her hands as she thought of her lover opening the door on the other side of which waited the cruel fangs of the tiger!

But how much oftener had she seen him at the other door! How in her grievous reveries had she gnashed her teeth and torn her hair, when she saw his start of rapturous delight as he opened the door of the lady! How her soul had burned in agony when she had seen him rush to meet that woman, with her flushing

The Choice

BY DOROTHY PARKER

Birthday (L'Anniversaire) (1915), Marc Chagall. Oil on cardboard, 31¾" × 39¼".
The Museum of Modern Art, New York. Acquired through the Lillie P. Bliss
Bequest. Photograph © 2001 The Museum of Modern Art, New York.

He'd have given me rolling lands,
　　Houses of marble, and billowing farms,
Pearls, to trickle between my hands,
　　Smoldering[1] rubies, to circle my arms.
5　You—you'd only a lilting song,
　　Only a melody, happy and high,
You were sudden and swift and strong,—
　　Never a thought for another had I.

He'd have given me laces rare,
10　Dresses that glimmered with frosty sheen,
Shining ribbons to wrap my hair,
　　Horses to draw me, as fine as a queen.
You—you'd only to whistle low,
　　Gaily I followed wherever you led.
15　I took you, and I let him go,—
　　Somebody ought to examine my head!

---

1. **smoldering:** burning without flame.

Connect to the Literature

1. **What Do You Think?**
How did you react to the ending of the story?

Comprehension Check
- How is the fate of a criminal decided in the king's arena?
- What "crime" has the young man committed?
- What decision causes the princess "days and nights of anguished deliberation"?

Think Critically

2. **ACTIVE READING** **DRAWING CONCLUSIONS**
Do you think the princess pointed to the door with the tiger behind it or the door with the lady behind it? Look at the list in your 📖 **READER'S NOTEBOOK**. Which descriptions or actions led you to **draw** this **conclusion?**

3. The narrator advises readers to make up their minds "not as if the decision of the question depended upon yourself, but upon that hot-blooded, semibarbaric princess." What do you think this advice means and why does Stockton include it?

   Think About:
   - the meaning of the word "semibarbaric"
   - the description of the country's trial system as an example of the king's "barbaric fancy"
   - the description of the princess's passion for the young man

Extend Interpretations

4. **COMPARING TEXTS** What do you think the speaker of "The Choice" on page 600 would advise the princess in the story to do? Explain your answer.

5. **Critic's Corner** One critic writes that this story "depends upon a gimmick." A gimmick, as it is used here, is something meant to trick the reader. Do you think this is a fair statement about the ending? Why or why not?

6. **Connect to Life** Stockton once said, "If you decide which it was—the lady or the tiger—you find out what kind of person you are yourself." What might your interpretation of the story show about you?

Literary Analysis

SURPRISE ENDING An unexpected twist in the plot at the end of a story is called a **surprise ending.** The surprise may be a sudden turn in the action or a revelation that gives a new perspective to the entire story. The idea is to surprise the reader, even though important clues have been planted throughout.

From the very beginning of this story, there are clues that lead in two different directions— one leads to the opening of the lady's door and one to the opening of the tiger's door. The real surprise in this story, of course, is that *both* sets of clues are misleading. The ending is left up to you, the reader!

Paired Activity With a partner, discuss why the ending is such a surprise. Go back through the story and look for clues that lead to each possible ending. Remember that the key to the ending is in the personality of the princess.

You may wish to jot down in your notebook the clues that lead to each ending. Once you have uncovered all the clues, discuss with the entire class the impact of a surprise ending on the story.

Clues to Surprise Ending	
Clues Leading to the Lady's Door	**Clues Leading to the Tiger's Door**
The princess was very happy with her young man.	The princess is as proud and spoiled as her father.

Writing

Story Ending Write an ending to the story in which you reveal what lies behind the door on the right—the lady or the tiger—and the reaction of the princess to her beloved's fate. Use vivid details, appropriate word choice, and a logical organization. Place your writing in your **Working Portfolio.**

Writing Handbook
See p. R43: Narrative Writing.

Speaking & Listening

Film Review View the video version of "The Lady, or the Tiger?" How does it compare with the way you imagined the story when you read it? Choose any scene that you visualized or interpreted differently and evaluate the way the filmmaker portrayed the scene.

VIDEO: Literature in Performance

"The Lady, or the Tiger?"

Research & Technology

Struggle for Survival In Stockton's story, the tiger means certain death for prisoners who open the wrong door. However, in the modern world, this animal is itself fighting for survival. Using the Internet and library sources, find out more about the threats facing the tiger. Present your findings in an oral report to the class. Be sure to note your sources.

Research and Technology Handbook
See p. R114: Getting Information Electronically.

Vocabulary and Spelling

SYNONYMS AND ANTONYMS Identify the relationship between each boldfaced Word to Know and the word to its right by writing *Synonyms* or *Antonyms.*

1. **exuberant**   enthusiastic
2. **valor**   cowardice
3. **assert**   declare
4. **procure**   lose
5. **doleful**   happy
6. **subordinate**   primary
7. **retribution**   punishment
8. **imperious**   humble
9. **destiny**   fate
10. **decree**   proclamation

SPELLING STRATEGY: ADDING SUFFIXES
Suffixes such as *-ion* and *-ous* can be added to base words to create new words. Adding *-ion* to a verb forms a noun. Adding *-ous* to a noun forms an adjective. If the base word ends in a consonant, simply add the suffix. If the base word ends in silent *e,* you should usually drop the *e* before the suffix.

Add suffixes to the following base words:

1. assert + -ion = _____
2. desire + -ous = _____
3. frustrate + -ion = _____
4. valor + -ous = _____
5. accelerate + -ion = _____

Vocabulary Handbook
See p. R24: Synonyms and Antonyms.

Grammar in Context: Prepositional Phrases as Adjectives

Notice how the words in red in the following sentence from Frank Stockton's "The Lady, or the Tiger?" help describe the noun *daughter.*

> . . . never before had a subject dared to love the daughter **of a king.**

The words in red form an **adjective prepositional phrase.** Prepositional phrases can be used as adjectives to modify nouns and pronouns. They help answer the question *which one* or *what kind of.*

Apply to Your Writing Use prepositional phrases to add more description to your writing. Adjective prepositional phrases are especially useful when writing descriptions of setting.

WRITING EXERCISE Rewrite the following sentences, using an adjective prepositional phrase to describe each underlined noun.

Example: *Original* This vast <u>amphitheatre</u> was a place of terror.

Rewritten This vast amphitheatre, <u>with its high walls,</u> was a place of terror.

1. He was the <u>king</u>.
2. The tiger cages were searched for the most savage <u>beasts</u>.
3. The <u>prisoner</u> walked out into the light.
4. The <u>eyes</u> followed his every move.
5. A <u>woman</u> stood behind one of the doors.

Grammar Handbook See p. R89: Phrases and Clauses.

Frank R. Stockton
1834–1902

"The publication of 'The Lady, or the Tiger?' . . . caused a sensation."

Full of Fairy Tales Though Frank R. Stockton's most popular work today is "The Lady, or the Tiger?" his many other works, such as "The Griffin and the Minor Canon," "The Queen's Museum," *The Bee-Man of Orn,* and *Rudder Grange,* were widely read during his lifetime. Born near Philadelphia, Pennsylvania, Stockton first began writing fairy tales, later claiming that he did so because "my mind was full of them."

Literary Sensation Later on in life, Stockton wrote stories for adults and children and helped edit *St. Nicholas,* a children's magazine. The publication of "The Lady, or the Tiger?" in *Century* magazine in 1882 did indeed cause a sensation. The ending was debated in high schools, and Stockton received hundreds of letters from people seeking the solution.

AUTHOR ACTIVITY
Sequel Stockton wrote two sequels to "The Lady, or the Tiger?"—"His Wife's Deceased Sister" and "The Discourager of Hesitancy." Select one to read from the library. Do you think it is a good sequel? Why or why not?

Building Vocabulary
Synonyms, Antonyms, and Homonyms

Many words can be classified according to meaning.

Synonyms are words with similar meanings.
Antonyms are words with opposite meanings.
Homonyms are words with the same spelling and pronunciation but with different meanings.

Each type of word can enliven both your writing and your conversation.

His first impulse is to jump back and warn the others. But he knows the commotion will frighten the cobra and it will strike. He speaks quickly, the quality of his voice so **arresting** that it sobers everyone.

—Mona Gardner, "The Dinner Party"

Arresting is a synonym for **striking**. Its use captures the drama of the scene.

Strategies for Building Vocabulary

Knowledge of synonyms, antonyms, and homonyms will increase your appreciation of literature and make your writing and speaking richer and more varied.

❶ **Find Synonyms** Although synonyms have similar meanings, no two words have exactly the same meaning. Consider this sentence from "Rain, Rain, Go Away": "The drive back seemed to stretch *interminably.*" *Interminably* means "endlessly" and is a synonym for the word *boundlessly.* However, replacing *interminably* with *boundlessly* would change the meaning to "a length of time that couldn't be determined." By learning words with similar meanings, you will be better equipped as a writer to choose the appropriate word. Remember to use a thesaurus or a dictionary when looking for synonyms.

❷ **Learn Antonyms** You can find antonyms in the dictionary or in the thesaurus. When searching for an antonym for a particular word, try adding prefixes that mean "not," such as *un-, anti-, dis-,* or *in-,* to the word. Then check a dictionary to see if the word exists and has the meaning you are searching for.

❸ **Understand Homonyms** Homonyms are particularly confusing because they are words with different meanings but the same pronunciation, and sometimes even the same spelling. If you come across a word that sounds the same as another word, first check the context of the sentence to help you guess the word's meaning. However, sometimes it is difficult to figure out the meaning of a homonym from its context. In such cases, it is best to check the dictionary to determine which meaning is being used.

EXERCISE For each word, write a related word of the type indicated in parentheses. (Include definitions for the homonyms.) Then write a sentence containing the given word and the related word.
1. *vulnerable* (antonym)
2. *exciting* (synonym)
3. *fair* (homonym)
4. *dexterity* (antonym)
5. *clever* (synonym)

FUTURE TENSE

by ROBERT LIPSYTE

Gary couldn't wait for tenth grade to start so he could strut his sentences, parade his paragraphs, renew his reputation as the top creative writer in school. At the opening assembly, he felt on edge, psyched, like a boxer before the first-round bell. He leaned forward as Dr. Proctor, the principal, introduced two new staff members. He wasn't particularly interested in the new vice-principal, Ms. Jones; Gary never had discipline problems, he'd never even had to stay after school. But his head cocked alertly as Dr. Proctor introduced the new Honors English teacher, Mr. Smith. Here was the person he'd have to impress.

He studied Mr. Smith. The man was hard to describe. He looked as though he'd been manufactured to fit his name. Average height, brownish hair, pale white skin, medium build. Middle age. He was the sort of person you began to forget the minute you met him. Even his clothes had no particular style. They merely covered his body.

Mr. Smith was . . . just there.

Gary was studying Mr. Smith so intently that he didn't hear Dr. Proctor call him up to the stage to receive an award from last term. Jim Baggs jabbed an elbow into his ribs and said, "Let's get up there, Dude."

Dr. Proctor shook Gary's hand and gave him the County Medal for Best Composition. While Dr. Proctor was giving Jim Baggs the County Trophy for Best All-Round Athlete, Gary glanced over his shoulder to see if Mr. Smith looked impressed. But he couldn't find the new teacher. Gary wondered if Mr. Smith was so ordinary he was invisible when no one was talking about him.

On the way home, Dani Belzer, the prettiest poet in school, asked Gary, "What did you think of our new Mr. Wordsmith?"

"If he was a color he'd be beige," said Gary. "If he was a taste he'd be water. If he was a sound he'd be a low hum."

"Fancy, empty words," sneered Mike Chung, ace reporter on the school paper. "All you've told me is you've got nothing to tell me."

Dani quickly stepped between them. "What did you think of the first assignment?"

"Describe a Typical Day at School," said Gary, trying unsuccessfully to mimic Mr. Smith's bland voice. "That's about as exciting as tofu."[1]

"A real artist," said Dani, "accepts the commonplace as a challenge."

That night, hunched over his humming electric typewriter, Gary wrote a description of a typical day at school from the viewpoint of a new teacher who was seeing everything for the very first time, who took nothing for granted. He described the shredded edges of the limp flag outside the dented front door, the worn flooring where generations of kids had nervously paced outside the principal's office.

And then, in the last line, he gave the composition that extra twist, the little kicker on which his reputation rested. He wrote:

The new teacher's beady little eyes missed nothing, for they were the optical recorders of an alien creature who had come to earth to gather information.

The next morning, when Mr. Smith asked for a volunteer to read aloud, Gary was on his

---

1. **tofu** (tō′fōō): a soft, bland-tasting food made from soybeans.

feet and moving toward the front of the classroom before Mike Chung got his hand out of his pocket.

The class loved Gary's composition. They laughed and stamped their feet. Chung shrugged, which meant he couldn't think of any criticism, and Dani flashed thumbs up. Best of all, Jim Baggs shouldered Gary against the blackboard after class and said, "Awesome tale, Dude."

Gary felt good until he got the composition back. Along one margin, in a perfect script, Mr. Smith had written:

You can do better.

"How would he know?" Gary complained on the way home.

"You should be grateful," said Dani. "He's pushing you to the farthest limits of your talent."

"Which may be nearer than you think," snickered Mike.

Gary rewrote his composition, expanded it, complicated it, thickened it. Not only was this new teacher an alien, he was part of an extraterrestrial conspiracy to take over Earth. Gary's final sentence was:

Every iota of information, fragment of fact, morsel of minutiae[2] sucked up by those vacuuming eyes was beamed directly into a computer circling the planet. The data would eventually become a program that would control the mind of every school kid on earth.

Gary showed the new draft to Dani before class. He stood on tiptoes so he could read over her shoulder. Sometimes he wished she were shorter, but mostly he wished he were taller.

"What do you think?"

"The assignment was to describe a typical day," said Dani. "This is off the wall."

___
2. **minutiae** (mĭ-nōō'shē-ē'): trivial details or facts.

He snatched the papers back. "Creative writing means creating." He walked away, hurt and angry. He thought: *If she doesn't like my compositions, how can I ever get her to like me?*

That morning, Mike Chung read his own composition aloud to the class. He described a typical day through the eyes of a student in a wheelchair. Everything most students take for granted was an obstacle: the bathroom door too heavy to open, the gym steps too steep to climb, the light switch too high on the wall. The class applauded and Mr. Smith nodded approvingly. Even Gary had to admit it was really good—if you considered plain-fact journalism as creative writing, that is.

> ## Every champion knows that as hard as it is to get to the top, it's even harder to stay up there.

Gary's rewrite came back the next day marked:

Improving. Try again.

Saturday he locked himself in his room after breakfast and rewrote the rewrite. He carefully selected his nouns and verbs and adjectives. He polished and arranged them in sentences like a jeweler strings pearls. He felt good as he wrote, as the electric typewriter hummed and buzzed and sometimes coughed. He thought: *Every champion knows that as hard as it is to get to the top, it's even harder to stay up there.*

Mr. Smith handed back Gary's composition the next day marked:

See me after school.

His mother knocked on his door around noon. When he let her in, she said, "It's a beautiful day."

"Big project," he mumbled. He wanted to avoid a distracting conversation.

She smiled. "If you spend too much time in your room, you'll turn into a mushroom."

He wasn't listening. "Thanks. Anything's okay. Don't forget the mayonnaise."

Gary wrote:

The alien's probes trembled as he read the student's composition. Could that skinny, bespectacled earthling really suspect its extraterrestrial identity? Or was his composition merely the result of a creative thunderstorm in a brilliant young mind?

Before Gary turned in his composition on Monday morning, he showed it to Mike Chung. He should have known better.

"You're trying too hard," chortled Chung. "Truth is stronger than fiction."

Gary flinched at that. It hurt. It might be true. But he couldn't let his competition know he had scored. "You journalists are stuck in the present and the past," growled Gary. "Imagination prepares us for what's going to happen."

Dani read her composition aloud to the class. It described a typical day from the perspective of a louse choosing a head of hair to nest in. The louse moved from the thicket of a varsity crew-cut to the matted jungle of a sagging perm to a straight, sleek blond cascade.[3]

The class cheered and Mr. Smith smiled. Gary felt a twinge of jealousy. Dani and Mike were coming on. There wasn't room for more than one at the top.

In the hallway, he said to Dani, "And you called my composition off the wall?"

Mike jumped in. "There's a big difference between poetical metaphor and hack science fiction."

Gary felt choked by a lump in his throat. He hurried away.

Mr. Smith handed back Gary's composition the next day marked:

See me after school

Gary was nervous all day. What was there to talk about? Maybe Mr. Smith hated science fiction. One of those traditional English teachers. Didn't understand that science fiction could be literature. *Maybe I can educate him,* thought Gary.

When Gary arrived at the English office, Mr. Smith seemed nervous too. He kept folding and unfolding Gary's composition. "Where do you get such ideas?" he asked in his monotone voice.

Gary shrugged. "They just come to me."

"Alien teachers. Taking over the minds of schoolchildren." Mr. Smith's empty eyes were blinking. "What made you think of that?"

"I've always had this vivid imagination."

"If you're sure it's just your imagination." Mr. Smith looked relieved. "I guess everything will work out." He handed back Gary's composition. "No more fantasy, Gary. Reality. That's your assignment. Write only about what you know."

Outside school, Gary ran into Jim Baggs, who looked surprised to see him. "Don't tell me you had to stay after, Dude."

"I had to see Mr. Smith about my composition. He didn't like it. Told me to stick to reality."

"Don't listen." Jim Baggs body checked Gary into the schoolyard fence. "Dude, you got to be yourself."

Gary ran all the way home and locked himself into his room. He felt feverish with creativity. Dude, you got to be yourself, Dude. It doesn't matter what your so-called friends

---

3. **cascade:** waterfall-like hairstyle.

say, or your English teacher. You've got to play your own kind of game, write your own kind of stories.

The words flowed out of Gary's mind and through his fingers and out of the machine and onto sheets of paper. He wrote and rewrote until he felt the words were exactly right:

With great effort, the alien shut down the electrical panic impulses coursing through its system and turned on Logical Overdrive. There were two possibilities:

1. This high school boy was exactly what he seemed to be, a brilliant, imaginative, apprentice best-selling author and screenwriter, or,

2. He had somehow stumbled onto the secret plan and he would have to be either enlisted into the conspiracy or erased off the face of the planet.

First thing in the morning, Gary turned in his new rewrite to Mr. Smith. A half hour later, Mr. Smith called Gary out of Spanish. There was no expression on his regular features. He said, "I'm going to need some help with you."

Cold sweat covered Gary's body as Mr. Smith grabbed his arm and led him to the new vice-principal. She read the composition while they waited. Gary got a good look at her for the first time. Ms. Jones was . . . just there. She looked as though she'd been manufactured to fit her name. Average. Standard. Typical. The cold sweat turned into goose pimples.

How could he have missed the clues? Smith and Jones were aliens! He had stumbled on their secret and now they'd have to deal with him.

He blurted, "Are you going to enlist me or erase me?"

Ms. Jones ignored him. "In my opinion, Mr. Smith, you are overreacting. This sort of nonsense"—she waved Gary's composition—"is the typical response of an overstimulated adolescent to the mixture of reality and fantasy in an environment dominated by manipulative⁴ music, television, and films. Nothing for us to worry about."

"If you're sure, Ms. Jones," said Mr. Smith. He didn't sound sure.

The vice-principal looked at Gary for the first time. There was no expression in her eyes. Her voice was flat. "You'd better get off this science fiction kick," she said. "If you know what's good for you."

"I'll never tell another human being, I swear," he babbled.

"What are you talking about?" asked Ms. Jones.

"Your secret is safe with me," he lied. He thought, *If I can just get away from them. Alert the authorities. Save the planet.*

"You see," said Ms. Jones, "you're writing yourself into a crazed state."

"You're beginning to believe your own fantasies," said Mr. Smith.

"I'm not going to do anything this time," said Ms. Jones, "but you must promise to write only about what you know."

"Or I'll have to fail you," said Mr. Smith.

"For your own good," said Ms. Jones. "Writing can be very dangerous."

"Especially for writers," said Mr. Smith, "who write about things they shouldn't."

"Absolutely," said Gary, "positively, no question about it. Only what I know." He backed out the door, nodding his head, thinking, *Just a few more steps and I'm okay. I hope these aliens can't read minds.*

Jim Baggs was practicing head fakes in the hallway. He slammed Gary into the wall with a hip block. "How's it going, Dude?" he asked, helping Gary up.

---

4. **manipulative** (mə-nĭp′yə-lə′tĭv): influencing thoughts or emotions, especially in a clever or sneaky way.

First thing in the morning,
Gary turned in his new rewrite
to Mr. Smith.

"Aliens," gasped Gary. "Told me no more science fiction."

"They can't treat a star writer like that," said Jim. "See what the head honcho's got to say." He grabbed Gary's wrist and dragged him to the principal's office.

"What can I do for you, boys?" boomed Dr. Proctor.

"They're messing with his moves, Doc," said Jim Baggs. "You got to let the aces run their races."

"Thank you, James." Dr. Proctor popped his forefinger at the door. "I'll handle this."

"You're home free, Dude," said Jim, whacking Gary across the shoulder blades as he left.

"It's just a composition," babbled Gary, **"made the whole thing up, imagination, you know."**

"From the beginning," ordered Dr. Proctor. He nodded sympathetically as Gary told the entire story, from the opening assembly to the meeting with Mr. Smith and Ms. Jones. When Gary was finished, Dr. Proctor took the papers from Gary's hand. He shook his head as he read Gary's latest rewrite.

"You really have a way with words, Gary. I should have sensed you were on to something."

Gary's stomach flipped. "You really think there could be aliens trying to take over Earth?"

"Certainly," said Dr. Proctor, matter-of-factly. "Earth is the ripest plum in the universe."

Gary wasn't sure if he should feel relieved that he wasn't crazy or be scared out of his mind. He took a deep breath to control the quaver in his voice, and said: "I spotted Smith and Jones right away. They look like they were manufactured to fit their names. Obviously humanoids. Panicked as soon as they knew I was on to them."

Dr. Proctor chuckled and shook his head. "No self-respecting civilization would send those two stiffs to Earth."

"They're not aliens?" He felt relieved and disappointed at the same time.

"I checked them out myself," said Dr. Proctor. "Just two average, standard, typical human beings, with no imagination, no creativity."

"So why'd you hire them?"

Dr. Proctor laughed. "Because they'd never spot an alien. No creative imagination. That's why I got rid of the last vice-principal and the last Honors English teacher. They were giving me odd little glances when they thought I wasn't looking. After ten years on your planet,

I've learned to smell trouble."

Gary's spine turned to ice and dripped down the backs of his legs. "You're an alien!"

"Great composition," said Dr. Proctor, waving Gary's papers. "Grammatical, vividly written, and totally accurate."

"It's just a composition," babbled Gary, "made the whole thing up, imagination, you know."

Dr. Proctor removed the face of his wristwatch and began tapping tiny buttons. "Always liked writers. I majored in your planet's literature. Writers are the keepers of the past and the hope of the future. Too bad they cause so much trouble in the present."

"I won't tell anyone," cried Gary. "Your secret's safe with me." He began to back slowly toward the door.

Dr. Proctor shook his head. "How can writers keep secrets, Gary? It's their natures to share their creations with the world." He tapped three times and froze Gary in place, one foot raised to step out the door.

"But it was only a composition," screamed Gary as his body disappeared before his eyes.

"And I can't wait to hear what the folks back home say when you read it to them," said Dr. Proctor.

"I made it all up." Gary had the sensation of rocketing upward. "I made up the whole . . ." ❖

Robert Lipsyte
born 1938

" Writing under deadline is often exhilarating, and if you're lucky a rhythm develops and the story just flows out of the typewriter."

An Early Love of Books Robert Lipsyte was born and brought up in New York City. As a child, Lipsyte read constantly and decided that he wanted to be a writer. He entered Columbia University in New York and graduated with a degree in English in 1957. Although Lipsyte was planning to go on to graduate school, he took a summer job at the *New York Times* newspaper that turned into a 14-year career as a sportswriter.

The World of Sports Lipsyte began his career at the *New York Times* by sharpening pencils and fetching coffee but soon was writing about high school sports events. His first major assignment came in 1962, when he covered the New York Mets during the team's first year of existence. Two years later Lipsyte began writing about boxing and was able to follow Muhammed Ali's

career for more than three years. Lipsyte's experience as a reporter of boxing events influenced his first novel for young readers, *The Contender.*

Devoting Himself to Fiction Lipsyte left the *New York Times* in 1971 to devote himself to writing fiction. His books for young adults, such as *One Fat Summer, Summer Rules, The Summerboy,* and *The Chemo Kid*, earned him a reputation as "a master of the young adult sports novel." In addition to his fiction writing, Lipsyte wrote a column for the *New York Post* and worked in both radio and television as commentator, essayist, and talk-show host.

Return to Sports Writing In 1991 Lipsyte returned to work for the *New York Times* while continuing to write young adult fiction. He remains very concerned about young people's relationship to sports. Lipsyte worries that schools place too much emphasis on success on the sports field, discouraging many young people from getting involved. According to Lipsyte, sports should be a fun and positive experience.

Writing Workshop

Eyewitness Report

Reporting what you have seen . . .

From Reading to Writing In "A Running Brook of Horror," Daniel Mannix provides an exciting eyewitness account of Grace Wiley's last encounter with a cobra. He uses sensory details and vivid language to make the incident realistic for his readers. An **eyewitness report** is a firsthand description of an event. Writers of compelling eyewitness reports can make you feel as if you were there too.

For Your Portfolio

WRITING PROMPT Write about an incident or event that you witnessed, describing it in detail.

Purpose: To reveal your attitude and use narrative strategies

Audience: Classmates, family, or anyone interested in the subject

---

Basics in a Box

Eyewitness Report at a Glance

What? the event

How? the details

Who? people involved

Re-creation of Event

Why? cause

Where? the place

When? date, time, year

RUBRIC **STANDARDS FOR WRITING**

A successful eyewitness report should

- focus on an event that is important to the writer or that is historically important
- answer the five W's: *who, what, when, where,* and *why*
- explain how the event occurred
- use sensory details, dialogue, and action verbs to show exactly what the writer observed
- present events in a clear, logical order
- capture the mood of the event

Analyzing a Student Model

SPEAKING OPPORTUNITY
See the Speaking and Listening Handbook, p. R104 for oral presentation tips.

Michelle Kazi
Ms. Sandra Mattox, Language Arts

Zoo Heroes!

Did you know that an elephant can weigh 17,640 pounds? That is about the weight of 170 eighth graders. When an elephant runs, the ground shakes as violently as it does during some earthquakes. I've always thought of elephants as harmless and cute, but a visit to the zoo last August convinced me that they can also be dangerous. Kara Stevenson, a tour guide at the San Francisco Zoo, also knows this. On Monday, August 7, 1998, at around two-thirty in the afternoon, I watched as she calmed a full-grown female elephant that had been frightened by a mouse.

The zoo was not in its usual clean condition that day because it was the end of "Kidz Week." Cotton candy, popcorn, and ice cream had fallen on the ground throughout the park. Early on Monday, someone spotted a few rodents by the dumpsters near the entrance.

I visited the zoo with my father and sister. We joined a tour that started at one o'clock. Kara Stevenson and Benjamin Hill were our leaders at this time. Kara was a 24-year-old graduate of UCLA. After growing up in San Francisco and dreaming of becoming an animal trainer, she decided to study animal behavior in college. She worked at the zoo training elephants and giving daily tours. She said she loved working there because "I get to meet so many people, and I enjoy watching people interact with the animals." Benjamin was 24 as well, and a graduate of Texas A&M University. He had been around animals all his life. His family raises horses on their ranch in the hills of Tucson. We were lucky to have such dedicated, experienced tour guides.

The tour began. I saw giraffes plucking leaves off trees and zebras eating in a large field. The elephants were in another area being hosed down with water because of the heat. Everything was fine. People were leaning over the fence a little, pointing and talking about their favorite animals.

RUBRIC
IN ACTION

① Introduces the focus of the composition and shows why the event was significant to the writer

② Introduction answers the five W's: *who, what, when, where,* and *why.*

③ Gives background information about the unusual circumstances that triggered the event

④ Compares and contrasts characters

⑤ Presents events in step-by-step order

Suddenly, the peaceful scene was shattered. A large female elephant started making trumpeting noises that almost burst our eardrums. Then she began to run around the pen. The ground shook so much it felt like it was splitting open beneath us. The elephant turned and I saw a small mouse running out of the pen. Even though a fence separated us from the elephant, it was obvious that if she decided to charge, the fence posts would topple like toothpicks.

Ben quickly sprang into action and helped us move far from the pen. Without hesitation, Kara leaped over the fence and carefully approached the elephant. Kara looked tiny compared to the size of the elephant. The elephant was twice as tall. Fearlessly, Kara walked toward her and began to follow her around. Kara followed her from one side of the pen to the other, speaking softly the whole time. The elephant's pace began to let up. The trumpeting stopped. When the elephant stopped, Kara reached up to pat her trunk. Unbelievably, the animal relaxed. She bowed her head and her body was still. We all breathed a sigh of relief.

Afterward, many of the local news stations and newspapers mobbed the zoo. Both Kara and Ben were called heroes. According to one newscaster on the ten o'clock news, Kara had "used her experience and quick-thinking skills to save numerous lives." She put herself in a lot of danger jumping into that pen. The experience proved to me that size really has nothing to do with courage. A big roaring elephant can be frightened, and a small quick-thinking woman can be fearless.

6 Description sets the scene and creates the atmosphere.

7 Action verbs and sensory details re-create the danger and drama of the event.

8 Quotation shows importance of the event. A final observation shows why the experience was important to the writer.

Other Options:
- Conclude with a lesson learned from the experience.
- Conclude with a quotation from the central character in the event.

Writing Your Eyewitness Report

❶ Prewriting

Write down some important incidents that you have witnessed. **Jot down** the details you remember. Attend interesting events listed in school and community bulletins and newspapers. See the **Idea Bank** in the margin for more suggestions. After you have chosen an event, follow the steps on the next page.

Planning Your Eyewitness Report

▷ **1. Choose a focus.** If the event that you have chosen seems too large and complicated, focus on the part that stands out the most.

▷ **2. Get the facts.** Use questions beginning with *who, what, when, where, why,* and *how* to gather the facts about the event. Put your facts into a chart so that you can easily keep track of what you know and what you need to find out.

▷ **3. Re-create the sensations.** What were the sights, sounds, and smells of the experience? Write down sensory details and vivid images that will express the mood of the event to your readers.

▷ **4. Record what is said.** When interviewing people who witnessed the event, try using a tape recorder to accurately record what they say. Which quotations most clearly give a sense of time, place, and action?

▷ **5. Show the importance of the event.** Why is this event important to you? How can you communicate its importance to your readers?

❷ Drafting

As you write your draft, try to keep the image of the scene in your mind. Focus on re-creating the event, and remember that you can revise your draft later. To structure your essay, try using chronological order—presenting events in the order they happened.

Show what happened; don't tell. Use words and phrases that show rather than tell what happened. Instead of saying, *The horse race was exciting,* give details that show the excitement: *As the horses thundered past us, my heart pounded with excitement.*

Include dialogue. A direct quotation can be more effective than several sentences of description. Find quotations that capture the moment: *One onlooker exclaimed, "I don't think I took a breath from the start to the finish of the race!"*

IDEA Bank

1. For Your Working Portfolio 🗁
Look for ideas in the **Writing** sections that you completed earlier.

2. Memory Journal In a journal, create a time line of the most important events and experiences in your life. List when they occurred and some striking details about each. Choose one as your topic.

3. Family Event Tree Make a sketch of a family tree, but instead of listing just names, list family events and stories. Share one or two of these stories with a small group of classmates. Use one of these stories as a starting point.

Have a question?

See the **Writing Handbook.**
Chronological Order, p. R44
Descriptive Writing, p. R41
See **Language Network.**
Prewriting, p. 314
Drafting, p. 317

Ask Your Peer Reader: EVALUATING

• How well did I organize the necessary facts?

• Which parts of my report did you have trouble "seeing"?

• Were the images and ideas clearly described?

Need revising help?

Review the **Rubric,** p. 614

Consider **peer reader** comments

Check **Revision Guidelines,** p. R33

Wondering where to place prepositional phrases?

See the **Grammar Handbook,** p. R89

SPELLING From Writing

 As you revise your work, look back at the words you misspelled and determine why you made the errors you did. For additional help, refer to the strategies and generalizations in the **Spelling Handbook** on page R28.

SPEAKING Opportunity

Turn your report into an oral presentation.

Publishing IDEAS

- Publish your eyewitness account in your school newspaper.
- Create a collage of images that capture the event featured in your eyewitness report. Choose phrases and sentences from your report, and print them on the collage or next to it.

INTERNET

Publishing Options www.mcdougallittell.com

---

❸ Revising

TARGET SKILL ▶ **USING ACTION VERBS** Action verbs will help your readers see, hear, feel, smell, taste, and experience the events in your report. Instead of using passive verbs, as in *There were clowns, acrobats, and vendors at the circus,* insert action verbs to show the movement and energy of the scene: *Clowns skipped past in their colorful costumes, acrobats tumbled by me, and vendors flagged me down with cotton candy batons.* Be sure to check your writing for passive and active verbs.

> Even though a fence separated us from the elephant, it was obvious that if she decided to charge, the fence posts would be *toppled* like toothpicks.
> *leaped*
> Without hesitation, Kara was over the fence and went to be with the elephant. *carefully approached*

❹ Editing and Proofreading

TARGET SKILL ▶ **PLACEMENT OF PREPOSITIONAL PHRASES** Prepositional phrases can function as adjectives or adverbs. However, if the phrases are misplaced, they will be confusing rather than helpful. For example, one student wrote: *I slept in the middle of the pool on a raft.* By changing the placement of the prepositional phrases, the sentence becomes much clearer: *I slept on a raft in the middle of the pool.*

> His family raises horses in the hills of Tucson on their ranch.

❺ Reflecting

FOR YOUR WORKING PORTFOLIO What did you discover about the importance of the event from writing your report? How did writing the report help you to become a better observer? Attach your reflections to your finished work. Save your eyewitness report in your **Working Portfolio.**

Standardized Test Practice

Mixed Review

One day last summer, I witnessed a car accident. It <u>happened</u> at the edge of town. The July afternoon was bright and warm. <u>I sat happily</u> near a main intersection on a bench as I <u>waitid</u> for a ride home. Suddenly, a loud screeching noise <u>rips</u> through the air. Then the sound of <u>tearing metal squealing brakes</u> assaulted my ears. Soon <u>other people</u> <u>of the building came pouring out</u>. I edged closer to the scene and peered over people's shoulders, waiting to see what would happen.

Review Your Skills

Use the passage and the questions that follow it to check how well you remember the language conventions you've learned in previous grades.

1. What is the correct spelling in sentence 1?
   A. happenned
   B. hapened
   C. hapenned
   D. Correct as is

2. How is item 2 best written?
   A. Happily on a bench, I sat near a main intersection
   B. I sat near a main intersection, happily on a bench
   C. I sat happily on a bench near a main intersection
   D. Correct as is

3. What is the correct spelling in item 3?
   A. waited
   B. weighted
   C. wated
   D. Correct as is

4. What is the correct verb tense in sentence 4?
   A. ripping
   B. ripped
   C. rip
   D. Correct as is

5. How is sentence 5 best written?
   A. tearing metal and squealing brakes
   B. tearing metal for squealing brakes
   C. tearing metal but squealing brakes
   D. Correct as is

6. How is sentence 6 best written?
   A. the building came pouring out of other people
   B. other people pouring out came out of the building
   C. other people came pouring out of the building
   D. Correct as is

Self-Assessment

Check your own answers in the **Grammar Handbook**

Verb Tenses and Forms, p. R84

Prepositional Phrases, p. R89

Spelling, p. R28

The Literature You'll Read

COMPARING LITERATURE   **SHORT STORIES**

The Concepts You'll Study

Vocabulary and Reading Comprehension
Vocabulary Focus: Denotation and Connotation
Visualizing
Determining Text Organization
Reading Aloud
Predicting
Setting a Purpose

Writing and Language Conventions
Writing Workshop: Analyzing a Story
Participial Phrases
Gerund Phrases
Infinitive Phrases

Literary Analysis
Literary Focus: Mood and Tone
Mood
Informative Nonfiction
Ballad
Foreshadowing
Plot

Speaking and Listening
Film Review
Oral Report
Oral Interpretation of Poem
Radio Play
Analyzing Video Adaptation

*M*ood and Tone

> *Ever since I was first read to, then started reading to myself, there has never been a line read that I didn't hear. As my eyes followed the sentence, a voice was saying it silently to me. . . . It is to me the voice of the story or the poem itself.*
> —Eudora Welty, writer

Writers hope to stir readers' emotions with their words. They know emotions can produce the **mood** or feeling of a piece of writing. During a story, the mood may shift, but usually one mood prevails. The **setting,** or time and place of a story, can affect the mood dramatically. For instance, a story set in the Alaska wilderness probably has a very different mood from a story set in New York City in the 1920s.

Tone describes a writer's attitude toward his or her subject. A writer might use a serious tone to write about a subject that he or she feels is very important, but a playful tone to write about a subject that he or she does not take so seriously. Mood and tone differ in that mood refers to the way a reader responds to a work. Tone, on the other hand, refers to the feelings of the writer.

From "The Ballad of the Harp-Weaver"

Mood

As you read a story, notice when you feel suspense, excitement, or dread. A writer has many tools to create these **moods.** He or she may carefully select **details—descriptive words, dialogue, imagery,** and **setting—**to create a mood. He or she may also rely on the **sounds** and **rhythms** of words to convey mood. Finally, a writer may use symbolism to create mood. A **symbol** is something that stands for something else. For instance, if the opening scene of a story describes a black crow circling overhead, it may be a symbol of danger to come.

YOUR TURN Describe the mood in this excerpt. What descriptive details help create this mood?

Tone

Tone is the attitude the writer takes toward a subject. The language and details the writer chooses to describe the characters, setting, and events help to create the tone. The tone might be serious, sarcastic, playful, or objective. It often reflects the **author's purpose.** If the author's purpose is to inform, the tone may be serious. If it is to entertain, the tone may be lighter and more playful.

A writer might have an admiring and respectful attitude toward his or her characters or portray them as humorous and foolish. Identifying the writer's tone is one way to decide how the writer feels about a certain subject.

YOUR TURN What attitude does Poe express about the speaker in the first tone excerpt? In the second excerpt, what tone or attitude does the poet reveal?

MOOD

When I had waited a long time, very patiently, without hearing him lie down, I resolved to open a little—a very, very little crevice in the lantern. So I opened it—you cannot imagine how stealthily, stealthily—until, at length, a single dim ray, like the thread of the spider, shot from out the crevice and fell full upon the vulture eye.

—Edgar Allan Poe, "The Tell-Tale Heart"

TONE

True!—nervous—very, very dreadfully nervous I had been and am! but why *will* you say that I am mad? The disease had sharpened my senses—not destroyed—not dulled them. Above all was the sense of hearing acute. I heard all things in the heaven and in the earth. I heard many things in hell.

—Edgar Allan Poe, "The Tell-Tale Heart"

TONE

"It's lucky for me, lad,
     Your daddy's in the ground,
And can't see the way I let
     His son go around!"
And she made a queer sound.

—Edna St. Vincent Millay,
"The Ballad of the
Harp-Weaver"

*V*isualizing

When you listen to the lyrics of your favorite song, what images come to mind? A beautiful sunset, clowns at the circus, or the face of someone special? For most people, the words of a favorite song help them to visualize, or form pictures in their minds. Active readers visualize, too, by picturing characters, settings, and events. As you read, use the strategies on this page to help you visualize the text.

How to Apply the Strategy

To **VISUALIZE,** an active reader will
- look for details that appeal to the senses
- form mental pictures
- **connect** personal experiences to the text

Try It Now!
Read and visualize from the excerpt below.

> I had my head in, and was about to open the lantern, when my thumb slipped upon the tin fastening, and the old man sprang up in the bed, crying out—"Who's there?" . . . Presently I heard a slight groan, and I knew it was the groan of mortal terror. It was not a groan of pain or grief—oh, no!—it was the low, stifled sound that arises from the bottom of the soul when overcharged with awe. I knew the sound well. Many a night, just at midnight, when all the world slept, it has welled up from my own bosom, deepening, with its dreadful echo, the terrors that distracted me.
>
> —Edgar Allan Poe, "The Tell-Tale Heart"

Here's how Ryan uses the strategies:

*"I like to **visualize** because it really puts me in the world of a story. I think the best stories are full of descriptions about how a character looks, speaks, acts, or feels. I enjoy what I am reading when I can **connect** personally to the story's images or examples. Visualizing is easiest when a description in the story reminds me of something that I've read about or experienced."*

The Tell-Tale Heart

by EDGAR ALLAN POE

Connect to Your Life

Creature Features What kinds of horror characters frighten you the most—Frankenstein's monster, Count Dracula, werewolves, King Kong, Godzilla, or some other creature? What do these dreadful creatures have in common? Lower the shades and turn down the lights as you discuss these questions with your classmates!

Build Background

Horror Tales The best horror-story writers are experts at frightening us. Edgar Allan Poe was one of the first American authors to do this. Oddly enough, his work owes much to his own feverish dreams, as well as his rare talent for shaping believable tales. Poe's characters face mysterious forces both within and outside themselves. Underneath the bizarre and frightening details of his stories, Poe explored the conflict in the human soul. Like Poe, today's masters of horror, such as Stephen King, fully understand the frightening power of the unknown and the supernatural. Why do so many people love the horror stories of writers like Poe and King? As one critic put it, "There is no delight the equal of dread."

WORDS TO KNOW
Vocabulary Preview

acute	derision	stifled
audacity	hypocritical	vehemently
conceived	stealthily	vex
crevice		

Focus Your Reading

LITERARY ANALYSIS MOOD

The feeling or atmosphere the writer creates for the reader is called the **mood.** In the story you are about to read, Edgar Allan Poe begins to weave the mood from the very first sentence:

> *True!—nervous—very, very dreadfully nervous I had been and am! but why* will *you say that I am mad?*

What mood is created by this choppy introductory sentence? What thoughts come to mind when a denial of madness is added to this strange speaking style? As you read, decide which methods Poe uses to add to the mood of the story—word choice, sentence structure, plot twists, setting description, and so on.

ACTIVE READING VISUALIZING

Forming a mental picture based on a written description is called **visualizing.** Descriptive details of what can be heard and seen help form this mental picture of the characters, settings, and events.

📖 **READER'S NOTEBOOK** Jot down the descriptive details mentioned in this tale. Your notes will help you understand what the main character is experiencing.

Details from Text	Visualization
Narrator "True!—nervous—very, very dreadfully nervous I had been and am!"	

The Tell-Tale Heart

by Edgar Allan Poe

True!—nervous—very, very dreadfully nervous I had been and am! but why *will* you say that I am mad? The disease had sharpened my senses— not destroyed—not dulled them. Above all was the sense of hearing <u>acute</u>. I heard all things in the heaven and in the earth. I heard many things in hell. How, then, am I mad? Hearken! and observe how healthily— how calmly I can tell you the whole story.

It is impossible to say how first the idea entered my brain; but once <u>conceived</u>, it haunted me day and night. Object there was none. Passion there was none. I loved the old man. He had never wronged me. He had never given me insult. For his gold I had no desire. I think it was his eye! yes, it was this! He had the eye of a vulture—a pale blue eye, with a film over it. Whenever it fell upon me, my blood ran cold; and so by degrees—very gradually—I made up my mind to take the life of the old man, and thus rid myself of the eye forever.

Now this is the point. You fancy me mad. Madmen know nothing. But you should have seen *me*. You should have seen how wisely I proceeded—with what caution—with what foresight—with what dissimulation[1] I went to work!

I was never kinder to the old man than during the whole week before I killed him. And every

ACTIVE READER

EVALUATE What is your first impression of the narrator?

night, about midnight, I turned the latch of his door and opened it—oh, so gently! And then, when I had made an opening sufficient for my head, I put in a dark lantern, all closed, closed, so that no light shone out, and then I thrust in my head. Oh, you would have laughed to see how cunningly I thrust it in! I moved it slowly—very, very slowly, so that I might not disturb the old man's sleep. It took me an hour to place my whole head within the opening so far that I could see him as he lay upon his bed. Ha!—would a madman have been so wise as this? And then, when my head was well in the room, I undid the lantern cautiously—oh, so cautiously—cautiously (for the hinges creaked)—I undid it just so much that a single thin ray fell upon the vulture eye. And this I did for seven long nights—every night just at midnight—but I found the eye always closed; and so it was impossible to do the work; for it was not the old man who <u>vexed</u> me, but his Evil Eye. And every morning, when the day broke, I went boldly into the chamber, and spoke courageously to him, calling him by name in a hearty tone, and inquiring how he had passed the night. So you see he would have been a very profound old man, indeed, to suspect that every night, just at twelve, I looked in upon him while he slept.

Upon the eighth night I was more than usually cautious in opening the door. A watch's minute hand moves more quickly than did mine. Never before that night had I *felt* the extent of my own powers—of my sagacity.[2] I could scarcely contain my feelings of triumph. To think that there I was, opening the door, little by little, and he not even to dream of my secret deeds or thoughts. I fairly chuckled at the idea; and perhaps he heard me; for he moved on the bed suddenly, as if startled. Now you may think that I drew back—but no. His room was as black as pitch with the thick darkness (for the shutters were close fastened, through fear of robbers), and so I knew that he could not see the opening of the door, and I kept pushing it on steadily, steadily.

I had my head in, and was about to open the lantern, when my thumb slipped upon the tin fastening, and the old man sprang up in the bed, crying out— "Who's there?"

ACTIVE READER

PREDICT Does the old man suspect anything?

I kept quite still and said nothing. For a whole hour I did not move a muscle, and in the meantime I did not hear him lie down. He was still sitting up in the bed listening—just as I have done, night after night, hearkening to the death watches[3] in the wall.

Presently I heard a slight groan, and I knew it was the groan of mortal terror. It was not a groan of pain or grief—oh, no!—it was the low, <u>stifled</u> sound that arises from the bottom of the soul when overcharged with awe. I

---

1. **dissimulation:** a hiding of one's true feelings.
2. **sagacity:** sound judgment; intelligence.
3. **death watches:** deathwatch beetles—wood-burrowing insects that make a tapping sound with their head.

WORDS
TO
KNOW

vex (vĕks) *v.* to disturb; annoy
stifled (stī'fəld) *adj.* smothered **stifle** *v.*

knew the sound well. Many a night, just at midnight, when all the world slept, it has welled up from my own bosom, deepening, with its dreadful echo, the terrors that distracted me. I say I knew it well. I knew what the old man felt, and pitied him, although I chuckled at heart. I knew that he had been lying awake ever since the first slight noise, when he had turned in the bed. His fears had been ever since growing upon him. He had been trying to fancy them causeless, but could not. He had been saying to himself—"It is nothing but the wind in the chimney—it is only a mouse crossing the floor," or "it is merely a cricket which has made a single chirp." Yes, he has been trying to comfort himself with these suppositions; but he had found all in vain. *All in vain;* because Death, in approaching him, had stalked with his black shadow before him, and enveloped the victim. And it was the mournful influence of the unperceived shadow that caused him to *feel*—although he neither saw nor heard—to feel the presence of my head within the room.

When I had waited a long time, very patiently, without hearing him lie down, I resolved to open a little—a very, very little <u>crevice</u> in the lantern. So I opened it—you cannot imagine how <u>stealthily</u>, stealthily—until, at length, a single dim ray, like the thread of the spider, shot from out the crevice and fell full upon the vulture eye.

It was open—wide, wide open—and I grew furious as I gazed upon it. I saw it with perfect distinctness—all a dull blue, with a hideous veil over it that chilled the very marrow in my bones; but I could see nothing else of the old man's face or person: for I had directed the ray as if by instinct, precisely upon the damned spot.

And now have I not told you that what you mistake for madness is but over-acuteness of

Presently I heard a slight groan, and I knew it was the groan of mortal terror.

WORDS TO KNOW

crevice (krĕv′ĭs) *n.* a crack
stealthily (stĕl′thĭ-lē) *adv.* cautiously; secretly

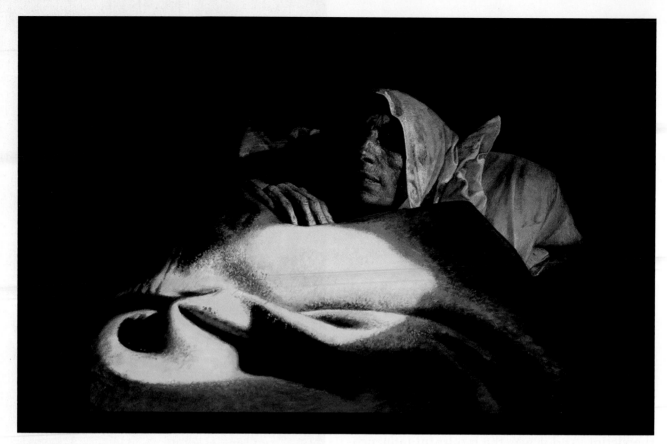

Copyright © John Thompson.

the senses?—now, I say, there came to my ears a low, dull, quick sound, such as a watch makes when enveloped in cotton. I knew *that* sound well too. It was the beating of the old man's heart. It increased my fury, as the beating of a drum stimulates the soldier into courage.

But even yet I refrained and kept still. I scarcely breathed. I held the lantern motionless. I tried how steadily I could maintain the ray upon the eye. Meantime the hellish tattoo[4] of the heart increased. It grew quicker and quicker, and louder and louder every instant. The old man's terror *must* have been extreme! It grew louder, I say, louder every moment!—do you mark me well? I have told you that I am nervous: so I am. And now at the dead hour of the night, amid the dreadful silence of that old house, so strange a noise as this excited me to uncontrollable terror. Yet, for some minutes

longer I refrained and stood still. But the beating grew louder, louder! I thought the heart must burst. And now a new anxiety seized me—the sound would be heard by a neighbor! The old man's hour had come! With a loud yell, I threw open the lantern and leaped into the room. He shrieked once—once only. In an instant I dragged him to the floor, and pulled the heavy bed over him. I then smiled gaily, to find the deed so far done. But, for many minutes, the heart beat on with a muffled sound. This, however, did not vex me; it would not be heard through the wall. At length it ceased. The old man was dead. I removed the bed and examined the corpse. Yes, he was stone, stone dead. I placed my

---

4. **hellish tattoo:** awful drumming.

hand upon the heart and held it there many minutes. There was no pulsation. He was stone dead. His eye would trouble me no more.

If still you think me mad, you will think so no longer when I describe the wise precautions I took for the concealment of the body. The night waned,[5] and I worked hastily, but in silence. First of all I dismembered the corpse. I cut off the head and the arms and the legs.

ACTIVE READER

PREDICT Do you think he will be caught?

I then took up three planks from the flooring of the chamber, and deposited all between the scantlings.[6] I then replaced the boards so cleverly, so cunningly, that no human eye—not even *his*—could have detected anything wrong. There was nothing to wash out—no stain of any kind—no blood-spot whatever. I had been too wary for that. A tub had caught all—ha! ha!

When I made an end of these labors, it was four o'clock—still dark as midnight. As the bell sounded the hour, there came a knocking at the street door. I went down to open it with a light heart,—for what had I *now* to fear? There entered three men, who introduced themselves, with perfect suavity,[7] as officers of the police. A shriek had been heard by a neighbor during the night: suspicion of foul play had been aroused; information had been lodged at the police office, and they (the officers) had been deputed to search the premises.

I smiled,—for *what* had I to fear? I bade the gentlemen welcome. The shriek, I said, was my own in a dream. The old man, I mentioned, was absent in the country. I took my visitors all over the house. I bade them search—search *well*. I led them, at length, to *his* chamber. I showed them his treasures, secure, undisturbed.

He was stone dead. His eye would trouble me no more.

---

5. **waned:** approached its end.

6. **scantlings:** small wooden beams supporting the floor.

7. **suavity** (swäv′ĭ-tē): smooth courteousness.

In the enthusiasm of my confidence, I brought chairs into the room, and desired them *here* to rest from their fatigues, while I myself, in the wild <u>audacity</u> of my perfect triumph, placed my own seat upon the very spot beneath which reposed[8] the corpse of the victim.

The officers were satisfied. My *manner* had convinced them. I was singularly at ease. They sat, and while I answered cheerily, they chatted of familiar things. But, ere long, I felt myself getting pale and wished them gone. My head ached, and I fancied a ringing in my ears: but still they sat and still chatted. The ringing became more distinct:—it continued and became more distinct; I talked more freely to get rid of the feeling: but it continued and gained definitiveness—until, at length, I found that the noise was *not* within my ears.

No doubt I now grew *very* pale;—but I talked more fluently, and with a heightened voice. Yet the sound increased—and what could I do? It was *a low, dull, quick sound—much such a sound as a watch makes when enveloped in cotton.* I gasped for breath—and yet the officers heard it not. I talked more quickly—more <u>vehemently</u>; but the noise steadily increased. I arose and argued about trifles, in a high key and with violent gesticulations,[9] but the noise steadily increased. Why *would* they not be gone? I paced the floor to and fro with heavy strides, as if excited to fury by the observations of the men—but the noise steadily increased. What *could* I do? I foamed—I raved—I swore. I swung the chair upon which I had been sitting, and grated it upon the boards, but the noise arose over all and continually increased. It grew louder—louder—*louder!* And still the men chatted pleasantly, and smiled. Was it possible they heard not? Almighty God!—no, no! They heard!—they suspected!—they *knew!*—they were making a *mockery* of my horror!—this I thought, and this I think. But any thing was better than this agony! Any thing was more tolerable than this <u>derision!</u> I could bear those <u>hypocritical</u> smiles no longer! I felt that I must scream or die—and now—again!—hark! louder! louder!! *louder!*—

"Villains!" I shrieked, "dissemble[10] no more! I admit the deed!—tear up the planks—here, here!—it is the beating of his hideous heart!" ❖

---

8. **reposed:** rested.
9. **gesticulations** (jĕ-stĭk′yə-lā′shənz): energetic gestures of the hands or arms.
10. **dissemble:** pretend.

Connect to the Literature

1. **What Do You Think?**
   What part of this story did you find the most frightening?

   Comprehension Check
   - Why did the narrator kill the old man?
   - How did the narrator commit the murder?
   - Why did the police come to investigate?
   - Why did the narrator finally confess?

Think Critically

2. What are your impressions of the narrator?

   Think About:
   - his insistence that he is sane
   - his obsession with the old man's eye
   - his care in planning the murder

3. Evaluate the narrator's behavior when he is with the police. Support your view with examples.

4. **ACTIVE READING VISUALIZING**
   Review the notes that you made in your
   📖 **READER'S NOTEBOOK.** Did these descriptive details help you picture the characters, setting, and action of the story? Use examples to support your answer.

Extend Interpretations

5. **What If?** What do you think might have happened if the police had not come to the old man's house on the night of the murder? Explain your answer.

6. **COMPARING TEXTS** How does this story connect to the theme of this part of the unit, "Tales Told in the Dark"?

7. **Connect to Life** Consider your prereading discussion of horror characters and your evaluation of "The Tell-Tale Heart" as a horror story. How does Poe's tale measure up to your favorite horror stories?

Literary Analysis

MOOD The overall feeling or atmosphere the writer creates for the reader is called **mood.** Descriptive words, the setting, and figurative language all contribute to the mood of a work, as do the sound and rhythm of the language used. Think about the use of repeated words in the following example, and notice the effect they create:

I undid the lantern cautiously —oh, so cautiously—cautiously (for the hinges creaked)—I undid it just so much that a single thin ray fell upon the vulture eye.

What mood is created by the repetition? How does the sound of the language affect you? Say this sentence aloud, and note what words and sounds are emphasized.

Activity Make a chart like the one below. Then find other examples from the story that help create a mood of horror.

Example	Mood Created
Description of old man's eye—the eye of a vulture	creepy, scary

Writing

Setting the Scene Write a paragraph describing a scene that is scary, humorous, or somber. Before you write, think of the mood you want to create and describe a setting to help establish the mood. Place your writing in your **Working Portfolio**.

Writing Handbook

See p. R41: Descriptive Writing.

Speaking & Listening

Film Review Rent a videotape of "The Tell-Tale Heart." Evaluate the various ways the images convey the story and affect your impressions. Then, with classmates, discuss whether or not the film version is true to the mood of Poe's story.

Art Connection

Look back at the illustration on page 628. Describe what you see. What makes it appropriate for this story? Now notice the artist's use of light and shadow. What does this element lend to the mood of the piece?

Research & Technology

Hollywood Heartthrob It's not surprising that Hollywood's moviemakers mined the works of Edgar Allan Poe. Beginning with silent films and continuing through the 1960s, they adapted Poe's horror classics to film. Use the Internet or library reference materials to find out which movies were made from Poe's works. Why do you think Poe's stories are successful as films? Report your findings to the class.

Reading *for* INFORMATION
Read the story "Birthday Ritual a Grave Tradition" on p. 634 before doing your research.

INTERNET Research Starter
www.mcdougallittell.com

Vocabulary

EXERCISE: WORD MEANING On your paper, write the letter of the word whose meaning is unrelated to the other words in each set.

1. (a) fearfulness, (b) timidity, (c) cowardice, (d) audacity
2. (a) insincere, (b) hypocritical, (c) genuine, (d) phony
3. (a) crest, (b) crevice, (c) crack, (d) cranny
4. (a) please, (b) vex, (c) gratify, (d) delight
5. (a) stifled, (b) muffled, (c) smothered, (d) heightened
6. (a) ridicule, (b) derision, (c) appreciation, (d) insult
7. (a) passively, (b) weakly, (c) vehemently, (d) calmly
8. (a) acute, (b) dull, (c) insensitive, (d) faint
9. (a) carelessly, (b) quietly, (c) stealthily, (d) cautiously
10. (a) forgotten, (b) imagined, (c) conceived, (d) formed

Vocabulary Handbook
See p. R24: Synonyms and Antonyms.

Grammar in Context: **Participial Phrases**

Look at the words in red in this sentence from Edgar Allan Poe's "The Tell-Tale Heart."

> **To think that there I was, opening the door, little by little, and he not even to dream of my secret deeds or thoughts.**

The words in red form a **participial phrase,** which consists of a participle plus its modifiers and complements. A **participle** is a verb form that acts as an adjective and ends in *–ing* or *–ed.* A participial phrase always modifies a noun or a pronoun. Writers use participial phrases when they want to show more than one action happening at the same time.

Usage Tip: Make sure that each participial phrase clearly refers to the noun it modifies. If there is any possibility of confusion, place the phrase near the noun or pronoun it modifies.

WRITING EXERCISE Rewrite each sentence, using the verb in parentheses to form a participial phrase.

Example: *Original* (search), the officers found no evidence of the crime.

Rewritten Searching the room, the officers found no evidence of the crime.

1. (terrify) The old man cried out.
2. (listen) He became convinced that someone was there.
3. (enrage) I leaped into the room.
4. (work) I overturned the bed.
5. (smile) I welcomed the officers.

Connect to the Literature Look at the sentence on page 626 that begins "And every morning . . ." How many participial phrases can you identify in this sentence?

Grammar Handbook See p. R89: Phrases and Clauses.

Edgar Allan Poe
1809–1849

"I became insane, with long intervals of horrible sanity."

An Orphan at Two Poe was born in Boston, the son of traveling actors. The beginnings of his unhappy life were marked by his father's desertion of the family, followed by the death of his mother when he was two years old. The orphaned Poe was taken in by John and Frances Allan of Virginia.

Untimely Death After being expelled from West Point, Poe looked for work as a journalist and wrote literary reviews, but money was scarce. Poverty intensified his despair when his beloved wife, Virginia, died following a long illness. Deeply depressed, Poe died two years later after being found on the streets of Baltimore, sick, delirious, and, in his doctor's words, "haggard, not to say bloated, and unwashed."

Father of the Detective Story Many critics credit Poe with the invention of the detective story. His classic tales include "The Masque of the Red Death," "The Pit and the Pendulum," "The Gold Bug," and "The Purloined Letter."

THE WASHINGTON TIMES • TUESDAY, JANUARY 20, 1998

Cover Story

Birthday Ritual a Grave Tradition

New figure brings tribute to Poe

by Roger J. Hansen

Every year on Edgar Allan Poe's birthday, a mysterious stranger visits Poe's grave.

BALTIMORE - A black-clad stranger carried on the half-century tradition here of placing three red roses and something to drink at the grave of Edgar Allan Poe in a pre-dawn visit on Jan. 19.

Because he was dressed in ordinary street clothes, the man slipped in unrecognized past two dozen people who had gathered at 3 A.M. at Westminster Church to watch the ritual.

Beginning in 1949, one man—his identity unknown—visited the grave on the poet and author's birthday. In recent years, a new man, dressed in black and wearing a hat, has sneaked into the small graveyard tucked in downtown Baltimore.

Reading for Information

How would you like to read about a mysterious cloaked stranger making his annual visit to the grave of horror writer Edgar Allan Poe? A newspaper feature story can bring you there—giving you the facts of the event and details about how and why this annual early-morning event has become a Baltimore tradition.

Reading a Newspaper Feature Story

Newspaper feature stories usually present factual information about a person, an issue, or an event based on the **"five W's"** of news writing—*who, what, where, when,* and *why* (and sometimes *how*).

Newspapers have a common format. The article at left shows the typical structure for pages in most newspapers, which include

- **banner** or **flag:** the name of the newspaper usually set off by size, color, special type, or some other design feature
- **headline:** a short, attention-getting title
- **byline:** the name of the reporter
- **dateline:** where a story takes place

YOUR TURN *Use the questions and activities below to get the most from reading a newspaper feature story.*

1 Most news stories have a headline, a dateline, and a byline. What is the name of the newspaper on this page? What is the story's headline? Who wrote the story? Where does the news story take place? Identify each of these newspaper features.

2 A good reporter answers the critical questions—the five W's (and sometimes *how*)—providing the reader with the most important details of the story. Answer the five W's by reading the first few paragraphs in the article.

THE WASHINGTON TIMES • TUESDAY, JANUARY 20, 1998

③ "I thought for sure he wouldn't show up or would get stuck in the traffic," said Jeff Jerome, curator of the Edgar Allan Poe House and Museum.

Instead, the stranger walked through the crowd undetected and left his gifts at 3:05 A.M.

"What? He walked right past here?" asked one breathless woman. About 20 Poe devotees handpicked by Mr. Jerome did see the brief tribute from the windows of the church. One man, Christoffer Nilsson, 23, came from Sundsvall, Sweden, to see the stranger.

Born in 1809, Poe lived in Baltimore for seven years and died here in 1849 at age 40. He penned classic horror stories such as " The Fall of the House of Usher," "The Pit and the Pendulum," "The Tell-Tale Heart" and "The Masque of the Red Death." His famous poems include "The Raven" and "Annabel Lee."

Mr. Jerome and others were baffled by the appearance of yet another mystery man. "I don't know what that indicates," Mr. Jerome said. "We thought maybe it was a father-and-son tradition and Dad got too sick or too ill to come down here in the middle of the night. But when we started seeing different people, it put a

A raven on the top of Poe's grave recalls his famous poem.

hole in that theory. It's open to speculation."

④ As in years past, the stranger placed the roses and a half-empty bottle at the grave, knelt, touched the white marble, stood up, tipped his cap and walked away.

"The guy last year was big and walked with an attitude," Mr. Jerome said. "This guy seemed like a regular Joe."

Unlike previous years, this 6-foot-tall man did not wear a long black cape or coat and entered with a waist-length black leather jacket and scarf. Befitting the frightening tales Poe wrote, two black cats walked around the cemetery, one of them across the grave exactly at midnight.

The visitor believed to be the original carried on the tradition until 1993, when he left a cryptic note saying, "The torch will be passed." A younger man took up the task for two years.

Last year's 6-foot-5 stranger did not creep into the rear of the cemetery to the site of Poe's original grave to deposit his tribute. Instead, he strode up to the monument at the front of the church, where Poe was reburied in 1875, made a toast, then bent over and kissed the relief image of the poet carved into the monument.

Martha Womack, a high school literature teacher in Farmville, Va., was as thrilled to see the tribute this year as in her three prior visits.

"It's one of those mysteries we just don't want to lose," she said. "Every year it's a little bit different."

Ms. Womack said, "I think people are still interested in him because of the mystery surrounding his life and his death."

What happened during the last four days of Poe's life remains unknown and is the subject of a play written by Michael I. Schmitt, who drove from Philadelphia and stood in the 38-degree chill to watch the tradition he had read about. Unfortunately, he and about four others were standing near the white marble Poe family marker instead of near Poe's grave in the back of the cemetery.

The roses are thought to represent the poet, his wife and her mother, who are all buried in the graveyard. Poe's grandparents and brother also are buried here.

And what would Poe make of the curious birthday tradition?

"He would love it," Ms. Womack said, her eyes lighting up. "Without a doubt, he would love it because he didn't get the attention he deserved in life. But he gets it now."

Reading for Information *continued*

❸ How does this information convince you of the event's importance for some people?

❹ What details and facts describe the different visitors to the grave in previous years?

❺ How does the use of direct quotations from eyewitnesses help to make this article more engaging?

Research & Technology
Activity Link: "The Tell-Tale Heart," p. 632
Does reading "The Tell-Tale Heart" and this newspaper feature story help you to understand the continued interest in Edgar Allan Poe 150 years after his death? Write a short newspaper feature story explaining why Poe continues to influence and attract people. Remember, a newspaper feature story not only answers the five W's and *how* but also develops the how or why in greater detail. Compare your feature story with those of your classmates.

Man-Made Monsters

by DANIEL COHEN

Connect to Your Life

Frankenstein Facts This selection explains the origins of Frankenstein's monster. What do you already know about Frankenstein's monster? What do you want to know? Make a chart like the one shown here and fill in the first two columns. Complete the third column after you read the selection.

What I Know About Frankenstein's Monster	What I Want to Know About the Monster	What I Learned About the Monster

Build Background

A Popular Monster Frankenstein's monster has become an icon of popular culture. Originally a character in Mary Shelley's book *Frankenstein,* his image can now be seen everywhere from Saturday-morning cartoons to the cereal section of grocery stores.

The creature first appeared on film in a silent movie in 1910. Since then, different versions of the monster have appeared in dozens of movies. Filmmakers have sometimes moved away from the original monster and created characters that are quite different. The list of movies based on Shelley's novel includes *Bride of Frankenstein, I Was a Teenage Frankenstein, Frankenstein Meets the Wolf Man,* and even *Abbott and Costello Meet Frankenstein.*

WORDS TO KNOW
Vocabulary Preview
abomination   notorious
benevolence   speculate
flourishing

Focus Your Reading

LITERARY ANALYSIS   **INFORMATIVE NONFICTION**

News stories, magazine articles, and the writing found in encyclopedias, textbooks, and reference books are all different types of **informative nonfiction.** The main purpose of informative nonfiction is to give readers factual information about real people, places, and events. As you read this selection, think about the ways it differs from other types of nonfiction—that is, those written mainly to entertain or persuade, such as biographies or newspaper editorials.

ACTIVE READING   **DETERMINING TEXT ORGANIZATION**

Nonfiction writers choose a pattern or patterns of **text organization** to help them develop the relationship among facts and events. Common patterns include

- chronological order
- cause and effect
- compare and contrast
- proposition and support

READER'S NOTEBOOK Writers of nonfiction often use more than one pattern in a selection. As you read the selection, jot down the types of text organization listed above and see if you can find examples of each type.

Man-Made Monsters

by Daniel Cohen

Self Portrait, (1953) Earl Kerkam. Oil on canvas mounted on paperboard 23¼" × 19". Hirshhorn Museum and Sculpture Garden, Smithsonian Institution, Washington, D.C. Gift of Joseph H. Hirshhorn, 1966. Photograph by Lee Stalsworth.

With the publication of Mary W. Shelley's novel, *Frankenstein: Or, The Modern Prometheus,*[1] in 1818, the mad scientist replaced the evil sorcerer[2] as the master of monsters. In many respects the mad scientist and the evil sorcerer were very similar. They were not necessarily either mad or evil, at least not at first. Often they were brilliant, selfless, and dedicated to the task of acquiring knowledge—for the sorcerer magical knowledge, for the scientist scientific knowledge—that might benefit the human race. But the knowledge they sought was forbidden to mankind. Often for the best of motives, both sorcerer and scientist released great evil upon the world, and their knowledge ultimately destroyed them. That is why Mrs. Shelley chose the subtitle, *Or, the Modern Prometheus,* for her book. Prometheus was one of the Titans of Greek mythology. He was supposed to have given the

---

1. **Prometheus** (prə-mē′thē-əs).
2. **sorcerer** (sôr′sər-ər): a man who practices witchcraft; wizard.

Detail of *Dovecote Tower at Midnight; Balleroy, Normandy, France, 1997* (1997), Peter Adams. Oil on board, 16" × 20". Collection of the artist.

Among those attending this storytelling session were two English poets, Lord Byron and Percy Bysshe Shelley. Also in attendance were Shelley's wife, Mary, and Byron's personal physician and friend, Dr. John Polidori. Dr. Polidori was reported to have told the tale of Lord Ruthven, who was to become the first famous vampire in English fiction. But surely the high point of the evening must have been Mary Shelley's story of Dr. Frankenstein and his creation.

There had never been anything quite like the Frankenstein monster in legend or fiction, but there were a few creatures the monster might have counted among its ancestors. One was Talus, a sort of ancient robot of Greek mythology. Talus was said to have been made of brass by Hephaestus,[3] a god of fire and craftsmen. The job of the brass man was to protect the island of Crete. He drove off strangers by throwing rocks at them, or by heating himself red-hot and clasping the intruders in a lethal bear hug. Talus was animated by a single vein of blood running from his head to his foot, where it was closed with a nail. The powerful sorceress Medea put Talus to sleep and then cut the vein, allowing the vital fluid to pour out—thus killing the brass man.

Somewhat closer to the Frankenstein monster was the golem, a creature of medieval Jewish legend. It was a clay figure said to be given life by some sort of magical charm. According to the legends, golems had been created by several famous medieval European rabbis. The golem was supposed to be a servant and protector of the Jews but it was

human race the knowledge of fire, but this gift angered the gods and they punished him savagely.

Mary Shelley's scientist, Baron Victor von Frankenstein, attempted something no medieval sorcerer, no matter how powerful, could even aspire to—he sought to create life. Thus, Dr. Frankenstein's creation is the first truly modern monster in fiction.

According to tradition, the idea of the Frankenstein monster was first put into words in Switzerland on a stormy evening in 1816. A group of friends decided to pass the evening by telling stories based on supernatural events.

---

3. **Hephaestus** (hĭ-fĕs′təs).

untrustworthy. Rabbi Low, of sixteenth-century Prague, had to destroy the golem he created when it went berserk.

Frankenstein's castle was located in the hills above the picturesque Bavarian city of Ingolstadt.[4] Some have <u>speculated</u> that the inspiration for the Frankenstein story may have come from a German legend. There is a ruined castle outside of Frankfurt am Main, Germany, that contains the tomb of a medieval knight. This knight was supposed to have been killed by a ferocious man-eating, man-made monster that resembled a wild boar.[5] But the legend itself is not at all clear and there is no way of knowing if this story or anything like it was ever encountered by Mary Shelley, although she was known to have traveled extensively in Europe.

More likely Mrs. Shelley drew her inspiration for the story of Frankenstein from events of her own time. Science was becoming ever more important and it increasingly clashed with established beliefs and values. Frankenstein put life back into a creature that had been assembled from the limbs and organs of cadavers.

During the eighteenth and much of the nineteenth centuries human bodies were not readily available for scientific study. Dissection[6] of a corpse was considered both irreligious and illegal. The result was that doctors who wished to study the human anatomy had to employ the services of body snatchers who would exhume newly buried corpses or cut down the hanging corpses of executed criminals and deliver them in secret to the laboratories. (While doctors couldn't dissect a body legally, it was considered perfectly proper to leave the corpse of a hanged man swinging until it rotted, as an example to other potential wrongdoers.)

Interest in medical science had grown enormously while the laws concerning dissection had not kept pace, so the body snatchers (the Resurrectionists or Sack-em-up Men as they were called in England) had a <u>flourishing</u> trade. If an adequate supply of corpses was unavailable, some of the more enterprising body snatchers would murder some unfortunates in order to sell their bodies. The most <u>notorious</u> of these murderers were Burke and Hare, who operated in Edinburgh, Scotland, at about the time that *Frankenstein* was written. The practice was fairly common throughout Europe, and many respectable doctors simply closed their eyes to what was happening.

Dr. Frankenstein himself was forced to steal bodies for his experiments, and this was the first step in his crime. He had not intended to create a monster, rather he had hoped to create a perfect human being. But from the moment the creature opened its "dull yellow eye," the young scientist was overcome with disgust and horror. He realized that he had made an <u>abomination</u>, not a superman.

The monster in Mary Shelley's book is described as being exceptionally tall, yellow-eyed, and having skin like parchment. But few picture the Frankenstein monster as looking

---

4. **Bavarian** (bə-vâr′ē-ən) **city of Ingolstadt** (ĭng′gəl-shtät′): a town on the Danube River in Bavaria, a region of southern Germany.
5. **wild boar:** a wild pig.
6. **dissection** (dĭ-sĕk′shən): a cutting apart for study or examination.

WORDS TO KNOW

speculate (spĕk′yə-lāt′) *v.* to draw a conclusion without having firm evidence; guess
flourishing (flûr′ĭ-shĭng) *adj.* thriving; prosperous **flourish** *v.*
notorious (nō-tôr′ē-əs) *adj.* well-known, particularly for disgraceful behavior
abomination (ə-bŏm′ə-nā′shən) *n.* a hateful or disgusting thing

Copyright © Jim Thiesen.

like that. Our image was fixed in 1931 with the appearance of the movie *Frankenstein,* starring a then unknown actor named Boris Karloff as the monster. Karloff's monster was a masterpiece of horrific makeup. It had a flat head and the overhanging brows of a Neanderthal[7] man. Its face was crisscrossed with crude stitching, and two electrodes stuck out of its neck. Like Mary Shelley's monster, the movie monster was unnaturally tall, but it also wore enormous leaden shoes and walked in a stiff, almost mechanical way.

The monster of the book becomes tremendously evil, but it is an evil forced upon the creature by its unnatural creation. All mankind flees from it in horror, and the monster in revenge turns upon mankind and particularly upon its unfortunate creator. The monster of the book is also intelligent and highly articulate about its plight. At one point it says:

"I am malicious because I am miserable. . . . If any being felt emotions of <u>benevolence</u> toward me, I should return them an hundred and an hundred fold. For that one creature's sake, I would make peace with the whole kind!"

The first of the long series of Frankenstein films simplified Mrs. Shelley's plot but retained much of the sympathy toward the monster. However, the creature's intelligence is largely lost in the films. Instead of making long soul-searching speeches, the monster can only mumble and grunt. In later films the monster loses even this rudimentary speaking ability. It is reduced to a stiff, stumbling, and thoroughly evil automaton, more of a mechanical man than anything else. ❖

---

7. **Neanderthal** (nē-ăn′dər-thôl) **man:** an extinct relative of modern human beings.

WORDS
TO
KNOW
benevolence (bə-nĕv′ə-ləns) *n.* kindness; goodwill

İntroduction to
FRANKENSTEIN

by Mary Shelley

When I placed my head on my pillow I did not sleep, nor could I be said to think. My imagination, unbidden, possessed and guided me, gifting the successive images that arose in my mind with a vividness far beyond the usual bounds of reverie. I saw—with shut eyes, but acute mental vision—I saw the pale student of unhallowed arts kneeling beside the thing he had put together. I saw the hideous phantasm[1] of a man stretched out, and then, on the working of some powerful engine, show signs of life and stir with an uneasy, half-vital motion.

I opened my eyes in terror. The idea so possessed my mind that a thrill of fear ran through me, and I wished to exchange the ghastly image of my fancy for the realities around. I see them still: the very room, the dark parquet, the closed shutters with the moonlight struggling through, and the sense I had that the glassy lake and white high Alps were beyond. I could not so easily get rid of my hideous phantom; still it haunted me. I must try to think of something else. I recurred to my story—my tiresome, unlucky story! Oh! If I could only contrive[2] one which would frighten my reader as I myself had been frightened that night!

Swift as light and as cheering was the idea that broke in upon me. "I have found it! What terrified me will terrify others;

The Repentant Magdalene, (ca. 1640), Georges De La Tour. Oil on canvas, 44½" × 36½". National Gallery of Art, Washington, D.C. Ailsa Mellon Bruce Fund, © 1999 Board of Trustees.

and I need only describe the spectre which had haunted my midnight pillow." On the morrow I announced that I had *thought of a story*. I began that day with the words "It was on a dreary night of November," making only a transcript[3] of the grim terrors of my waking dream.

---

1. **phantasm** (făn′tăz′əm): ghostly figure.
2. **contrive:** invent; devise.
3. **transcript:** written version.

Connect to the Literature

1. **What Do You Think?** What fact did you find most surprising or interesting in this selection?

Comprehension Check
- Who was Prometheus?
- What creatures might be considered the ancestors of Frankenstein's monster?
- What events from her time might have inspired Mary Shelley to write *Frankenstein*?

Think Critically

2. Do you think the title of this selection gives the reader an accurate idea about its content? Why or why not?

    Think About:
    - what you expected the selection to be about based on its title
    - the main idea of Shelley's book
    - the information that the author emphasizes

3. **ACTIVE READING** **DETERMINING TEXT ORGANIZATION**
    Look back at the notes in your **READER'S NOTEBOOK.** How does Cohen organize the text and the information? Working with a partner, compare your examples of **text organization.** Which type of text organization do you think is most effective? Explain why.

4. What purposes do you think Cohen had in mind when he wrote "Man-Made Monsters"?

Extend Interpretations

5. **COMPARING TEXTS** Reread the excerpt from Shelley's introduction to her novel (page 643). How does her account of the inspiration for Frankenstein's monster differ from Cohen's? Do you think it is possible that both views are correct? Why or why not?

6. **Critic's Corner** After reading this selection, do you agree with one critic's claim that *Frankenstein* is "the first science fiction novel"? Give the reasons for your opinion.

7. **Connect to Life** Has reading this selection inspired you either to read Shelley's novel or to see a movie version of it? Explain your answer.

Literary Analysis

INFORMATIVE NONFICTION News stories, magazine articles, and the writing found in encyclopedias, textbooks, and reference books are all types of **informative nonfiction.** The main purpose of informative nonfiction is to give readers factual information about real people, places, and events. In this selection Cohen's main purpose is to give the reader factual information about Dr. Frankenstein's monster. A good piece of informational nonfiction gives the reader several categories of information about its subject. In "Man-Made Monsters," for example, Cohen looks at Dr. Frankenstein's monster from several perspectives.

Paired Activity

Make a diagram like the one shown. Working with a partner, go back through the story and note the different categories of information about Dr. Frankenstein's monster that Cohen gives the reader.

- Which categories does Cohen write the most about?

- What did Cohen omit that you would like to know?

Writing

A Good Scare Write a brief report on a monster you have read about in fiction or have seen in a movie or television show. In your report, include a brief history of the monster's fictional creation, a physical description of the monster, and a comparison to other monsters in fiction or film. Use one of the patterns of organization in presenting your information. Put your review in your **Working Portfolio.**

Writing Handbook
See page R45: Explanatory Writing.

Speaking & Listening

Karloff's Monster View the 1931 movie *Frankenstein* starring Boris Karloff. Then view a more recent Frankenstein movie. As you watch the movies, take notes on how the different filmmakers portray the story of Frankenstein and the character of the monster. How did the images differ? Prepare an oral report comparing Karloff's interpretation with a more recent Frankenstein movie.

Research & Technology

Legendary Monsters Cohen mentions two creatures that are like Frankenstein's monster in some ways. Using the Internet and library sources, find out more about either Talus (the brass giant of Greek mythology) or the golem (a creature in medieval Jewish legend). Write a report on how these two creatures compare and contrast to Frankenstein's monster.

Research and Technology Handbook
See page R114: Getting Information Electronically.

Vocabulary

STANDARDIZED TEST PRACTICE

Choose the word or group of words that means the same, or nearly the same, as the underlined Word to Know in each sentence.

1. During the 1700s and 1800s, the high demand for corpses created a <u>flourishing</u> business for body snatchers—and a few murderers. Flourishing means—
   A hidden   **B** frightening
   C thriving   **D** temporary

2. Some criminals, such as Burke and Hare, were <u>notorious</u> for their involvement in the body-snatching trade. Notorious means—
   F well-trained   **G** well-paid
   H well-liked   **J** well-known

3. What two creatures did Cohen <u>speculate</u> might be the ancestors of Frankenstein's monster? Speculate means—
   A prove   **B** guess
   C deny   **D** doubt

4. Frankenstein's monster turned out to be an <u>abomination</u> rather than the perfect human being the doctor intended. An <u>abomination</u> means something—
   F hateful   **G** clumsy
   H frail   **J** gigantic

5. In Shelley's book, the monster wants humans to show him <u>benevolence.</u> Benevolence means—
   A fear   **B** intelligence
   C patience   **D** kindness

Vocabulary Handbook
See p. R20: Context Clues.

Grammar in Context: Gerund Phrases

Look at the words in red in this excerpt from Daniel Cohen's "Man-Made Monsters."

> **A group of friends decided to pass the evening by telling stories based on supernatural events.**

The words in red form a **gerund phrase,** which consists of a gerund plus its modifiers and complements. A **gerund** is a verbal that ends in *-ing* and acts as a noun. Gerund phrases, like nouns, can be the subject of a sentence, the object of a verb, or the object of a preposition.

Apply to Your Writing Use gerund phrases to help you combine sentences and to create sentence variety in your writing.

WRITING EXERCISE Change each underlined verb into a gerund. Then use the gerund in a gerund phrase to combine each pair of sentences. Underline each gerund phrase.

Example: *Original* The mad scientist was dedicated to a task. The task was to <u>acquire</u> knowledge.

Rewritten The mad scientist was dedicated to the task of <u>acquiring knowledge</u>.

1. They told stories. It was a way to <u>pass</u> the time.
2. It must have been terrifying. To <u>listen</u> to Mary Shelley's story must have been terrifying.
3. Boris Karloff's version of the monster frightened audiences. He frightened them because he <u>walked</u> in a mechanical way.
4. Baron von Frankenstein had an aim. His aim was to <u>create</u> life.
5. Baron von Frankenstein is punished. He is punished because he <u>interferes</u> with nature.

Connect to the Literature Look at the sentence on page 640 that begins with the words "He drove off strangers . . ." How many gerunds can you identify in this sentence?

Grammar Handbook See p. R89: Phrases and Clauses.

Daniel Cohen
born 1936

"I don't really 'believe in' most of the subjects I write about, and I don't pretend to."

An Average Student Born in Chicago, Illinois, Daniel Cohen says that he was an average student "who spent a lot of time watching movies." Because he found school boring, he did not attend college right away. When he continued his education at the University of Illinois, he studied biology and journalism. Cohen loved journalism but eventually gave up his job as managing editor of *Science Digest* magazine to do freelance writing.

From Science to Science Fiction Cohen has written many nonfiction books on science and history as well as books on topics such as UFOs, ghosts, and vampires. When he writes about the supernatural, he tries to keep both an open mind and a measure of scientific doubt. He once remarked, "I don't really 'believe in' most of the subjects I write about, and I don't pretend to."

AUTHOR ACTIVITY
Wide-Ranging List Cohen has written books ranging from *Monster Hunting Today* to *Young and Famous: Sports' Newest Superstars.* From the library, choose one of Cohen's books that appeals to you and read a chapter or two. Give an oral report to the class explaining whether you found the book interesting.

The Ballad of the Harp-Weaver

by EDNA ST. VINCENT MILLAY

Connect to Your Life

A Window to the Unconscious? What words and phrases come to mind when you hear the word *dreams*? What kind of thoughts and feelings do you associate with particularly vivid dreams? Create a word web to explore your associations. Then, with a partner, discuss a strange dream you have had or heard about.

Build Background

MUSIC

Harps are musical instruments played by plucking or stroking the strings with the hands. Harps were among the first instruments used by humans. Pictures of harps in Ancient Egypt and Mesopotamia date from as far back as 3000 B.C. Today, harps are played all around the world. In many cultures, the harp is associated with the idea of goodness.

Focus Your Reading

LITERARY ANALYSIS   BALLAD

The poem you are about to read is a modern example of a traditional folk form, the **ballad.** Ballads are **narrative poems** that are meant to be recited or sung. Most ballads, therefore, have regular patterns of rhythm and rhyme. Because they tell a story, ballads have a setting, a plot, and characters. As you read the poem, be aware of the balance between the ballad's story and how it sounds.

ACTIVE READING   READING ALOUD

One way to clarify your understanding and appreciation of a poem is to **read it aloud.** As you read, pay particular attention to the poem's rhythm and rhymes. Also listen for the repetition of words and phrases and **alliteration,** the use of repeated consonant sounds at the beginning of words.

READER'S NOTEBOOK After reading the poem aloud, note your thoughts in a list like the one shown below.

Heard When Read Aloud	
Rhythm	
Rhyme	
Repetition of Words and Phrases	
Alliteration	

The Ballad of the Harp-Weaver

by Edna St. Vincent Millay

"Son," said my mother,
    When I was knee-high,
"You've need of clothes to cover you,
    And not a rag have I.

5   "There's nothing in the house
    To make a boy breeches,[1]
Nor shears to cut a cloth with
    Nor thread to take stitches.

    "There's nothing in the house
10   But a loaf-end of rye,
And a harp with a woman's head
    Nobody will buy."
    And she began to cry.

That was in the early fall.
15   When came the late fall,
"Son," she said, "the sight of you
    Makes your mother's blood crawl,—

"Little skinny shoulder-blades
    Sticking through your clothes!
20 And where you'll get a jacket from
    God above knows!

    "It's lucky for me, lad,
    Your daddy's in the ground,
And can't see the way I let
25   His son go around!"
    And she made a queer sound.

That was in the late fall.
    When the winter came,
I'd not a pair of breeches
30   Nor a shirt to my name.

I couldn't go to school,
    Or out of doors to play.
And all the other little boys
    Passed our way.

35 "Son," said my mother,
    "Come, climb into my lap,
And I'll chafe your little bones
    While you take a nap."

And, oh, but we were silly
40   For half an hour or more,
Me with my long legs
    Dragging on the floor,

A-rock-rock-rocking
    To a mother-goose rhyme!
45 Oh, but we were happy
    For half an hour's time!

But there was I, a great boy,
    And what would folks say
To hear my mother singing me
50   To sleep all day,
    In such a daft way?

Men say the winter
    Was bad that year;
Fuel was scarce,
55   And food was dear.

A wind with a wolf's head
    Howled about our door,
And we burned up the chairs
    And sat upon the floor.

60 All that was left us
    Was a chair we couldn't break,
And the harp with a woman's head
    Nobody would take,
    For song or pity's sake.

---

1. **breeches** (brĭch′əz): trousers; pants.

65 The night before Christmas
      I cried with the cold,
   I cried myself to sleep
      Like a two-year-old.

   And in the deep night
70   I felt my mother rise,
   And stare down upon me
      With love in her eyes.

   I saw my mother sitting
      On the one good chair,
75 A light falling on her
      From I couldn't tell where,

   Looking nineteen,
      And not a day older,
   And the harp with a woman's head
80   Leaned against her shoulder.

   Her thin fingers, moving
      In the thin, tall strings,
   Were weav-weav-weaving
      Wonderful things.

85 Many bright threads,
      From where I couldn't see,
   Were running through the harp-strings
      Rapidly,

   And gold threads whistling
90   Through my mother's hand.
   I saw the web grow,
      And the pattern expand.

   She wove a child's jacket,
      And when it was done
95 She laid it on the floor
      And wove another one.

   She wove a red cloak
      So regal to see,
   "She's made it for a king's son,"
100   I said, "and not for me."
      But I knew it was for me.

   She wove a pair of breeches
      Quicker than that!
   She wove a pair of boots
105   And a little cocked hat.

She wove a pair of mittens,
  She wove a little blouse,
She wove all night
  In the still, cold house.

110 She sang as she worked,
  And the harp-strings spoke;
Her voice never faltered,
  And the thread never broke.
  And when I awoke—

115 There sat my mother
  With the harp against her shoulder,
Looking nineteen
  And not a day older,

A smile about her lips,
120 And a light about her head,
And her hands in the harp-strings
  Frozen dead.

And piled up beside her
  And toppling to the skies,
125 Were the clothes of a king's son,
  Just my size.

Edvard and His Mother (ca. 1885–1889), Edvard Munch. Pencil and ink.
Munch Museum, Oslo, Norway. Photograph copyright ©1999 Munch
Museum (Svein Anderson/Sidsel de Jong). Copyright © 2002 The Munch
Museum/The Munch-Ellingsen Group/Artists Rights Society (ARS),
New York.

Connect to the Literature

1. **What Do You Think?** What was your reaction to the poem's ending?

Comprehension Check
- Why can't the boy go to school?
- In the boy's dream, how does his mother use the harp?
- What does the boy discover when he wakes up?

Think Critically

2. Millay does not fully explain the events that take place. Why do you think this is so? What effect does this have on the poem's **mood?** How would you explain the cause of the amazing events?

3. What is your impression of the **speaker's character?**

   Think About:
   - how he watches "all the other little boys"
   - his train of thought when his mother holds him in her lap
   - his description of his mother as she weaves

4. **ACTIVE READING** | **READING ALOUD**
   Look at the notes you made in your
   📖 **READER'S NOTEBOOK.** With a partner, discuss how the poem's rhythm, rhymes, repetition, and alliteration helped to support the meaning of the poem. How did **reading aloud** the poem help clarify your understanding?

Extend Interpretations

5. **Critic's Corner** One critic attacked this poem as "the unforgettable rhythm of Mother Goose . . . used to deal out an idea which is wishy-washy . . ." What is your response to this opinion?

6. **Writer's Style** Millay is known for having drawn her inspiration from fairy tales. What similarities do you see between "The Ballad of the Harp-Weaver" and a familiar fairy tale?

7. **Connect to Life** Millay dedicated this poem to her mother to thank her for the excellent education she had received despite the hard times. In your opinion, what is the most important gift a parent can give a child?

Literary Analysis

BALLAD A narrative poem that is meant to be recited or sung is called a **ballad.** Traditional ballads have four-line stanzas with regular **rhythm** and **rhyme** patterns. Notice how Millay adapts this form, mostly using four-line **stanzas** but sometimes adding a fifth line, as in the third stanza. In each stanza the second line rhymes with the fourth and fifth lines.

Group Activity Like all ballads, Millay's poem tells a story. Note the elements of the poem's story in a chart like the one shown. Then, working with a small group of classmates, discuss how the poem could be adapted into a short story. What might the story lose? What might it gain?

Setting	a poor humble home with little furniture
Characters	
Plot	

REVIEW: CHARACTER Ballads, like most stories, center on the experiences and actions of one or more main characters. The minor characters in a story interact with the main characters and help move the action along. Why do you think Millay chooses not to introduce minor characters in "The Ballad of the Harp-Weaver"?

Writing

Dream Ballad Write a ballad describing a dream that you have had. Use descriptive details to bring your dream to life for the reader. Be sure to include four-line stanzas and a regular rhyme pattern. Place your ballad in your **Working Portfolio.**

Writing Workshop

See p. 252: Basics in a Box.

Speaking & Listening

Musical Setting Working with a small group of classmates, create a performance of this poem. Choose a tape or CD of harp music that captures the wistful, fairy-tale quality of the poem, and play it as background music for the poem. One or two students could read the poem aloud.

Speaking and Listening Handbook

See p. R106: Oral Interpretation.

Research & Technology

Modern Minstrels
Contemporary songwriters continue to write songs based on the traditional ballad form. At the library or in a record store, find an example of a recent ballad with a good story line. Write a paragraph explaining how the song reflects the ballad form. Play the song for your classmates and explain why you chose it.

Edna St. Vincent Millay
1892–1950

"Although we sometimes did without a few of life's necessities, we rarely lacked for its luxuries."

Poetry Pay-Off Edna St. Vincent Millay and her two sisters grew up in Camden, on the Maine coast. She published her first poem at 14 and won a scholarship at the age of 20 to Vassar College due mainly to the national recognition for her poem "Renascence."

Voice of Rebellion After graduating, Millay became a part of New York City's Greenwich Village scene, an area that became a center for artists and writers. Millay wrote some of her most successful works while living there in the early 1920s. Her poems often shocked the older generation, and Millay was considered by many to be the voice of the rebellious youth of her time.

AUTHOR ACTIVITY

Poet's Reading Edna St. Vincent Millay recorded many of her poems, including "The Ballad of the Harp-Weaver." Find a copy of this recording at your library and listen to it. How did listening to the poem differ from reading it aloud yourself? Did listening to it give you any new insights into the meaning of the poem?

The Hitchhiker

by LUCILLE FLETCHER

Connect to Your Life

How is listening to a radio show different from watching a television program? How is it the same?

Build Background

In the 1930s and 1940s, families gathered around the radio to listen to their favorite shows. One of the plays that audiences loved to hear was *The Hitchhiker.* It was originally produced and narrated by 23-year-old Orson Welles, who later became a well-known actor and movie director.

Listening to the radio was an important part of family life in the 1940s.

The sound effects on the radio—screams, trains, creaking doors—helped create vivid pictures in listeners' minds.

Focus Your Reading

LITERARY ANALYSIS **FORESHADOWING**

A device that prepares readers for an event or action that will happen later in a story is called **foreshadowing.** Foreshadowing provides hints or clues that prepare the reader for what will occur as the plot develops. Look for signs of foreshadowing in *The Hitchhiker.*

WORDS TO KNOW
Vocabulary Preview

accelerator	lark	sinister
assurance	nondescript	

ACTIVE READING **PREDICTING**

As suspense builds in a horror story, the reader makes **predictions,** or logical guesses, about what will happen next. As you read *The Hitchhiker,* jot down predictions in your **READER'S NOTEBOOK.** Base your predictions on what the writer tells you, your own prior knowledge, logic, and even what seems the most unexpected!

THE HITCHHIKER

by Lucille Fletcher

A Play for Radio

Orson Welles

Cast of Characters:
Orson Welles
Ronald Adams
Adams's Mother
Voice of hitchhiker
Mechanic
Henry, a sleepy man
Woman's Voice (Henry's wife)
Girl
Operator
Long-distance Operator
Albuquerque Operator
New York Operator
Mrs. Whitney

Welles. Good evening, this is Orson Welles. *(Music in)*

Personally I've never met anybody who didn't like a good ghost story, but I know a lot of people who think there are a lot of people who don't like a good ghost story. For the benefit of these, at least, I go on record at the outset of this evening's entertainment with the sober <u>assurance</u> that although blood may be curdled on this program, none will be spilt. There's no shooting, knifing, throttling, axing, or poisoning here. No clanking chains, no cobwebs, no bony and/or hairy hands appearing from secret panels or, better yet, bedroom curtains. If it's any part of that dear old phosphorescent[1] foolishness that people who don't like ghost stories don't like, then again I promise you we haven't got it. What we do have is a thriller. If it's half as good as we think it is, you can call it a shocker; and we present it proudly and without apologies. After all, a story doesn't have to appeal to the heart—it can also appeal to the spine. Sometimes you want your heart to be warmed—sometimes you want your spine to tingle. The tingling, it's to be hoped, will be quite audible as you listen tonight to *The Hitchhiker*—that's the name of our story, *The Hitchhiker*—

(Sound: automobile wheels humming over concrete road)

(Music: something weird and shuddery)

Adams. I am in an auto camp on Route Sixty-six

---

1. **phosphorescent** (fŏs′fə-rĕs′ənt): glowing with a cold light.

WORDS
TO
KNOW

assurance (ə-shŏŏr′əns) *n.* a guarantee or pledge

Adams. Six days ago I left Brooklyn to drive to California . . . perhaps it will help me. It will keep me from going mad. But I must tell this quickly. I am not mad now. I feel perfectly well, except that I am running a slight temperature. My name is Ronald Adams. I am thirty-six years of age, unmarried, tall, dark, with a black mustache. I drive a 1940 Ford V-8, license number 6V-7989. I was born in Brooklyn. All this I know that I am at this moment perfectly sane. That it is not I who have gone mad—but something else—something utterly beyond my control. But I must speak quickly. At any moment the link with life may break. This may be the last thing I ever tell on earth . . . the last night I ever see the stars. . . .

(Music in)

Adams. Six days ago I left Brooklyn to drive to California . . .

Mother. Goodbye, Son. Good luck to you, my boy. . . .

Adams. Goodbye, Mother. Here—give me a kiss, and then I'll go. . . .

Mother. I'll come out with you to the car.

Adams. No. It's raining. Stay here at the door. Hey—what is this? Tears? I thought you promised me you wouldn't cry.

Mother. I know, dear. I'm sorry. But I—do hate to see you go.

Adams. I'll be back. I'll be on the coast only three months.

Mother. Oh—it isn't that. It's just—the trip. Ronald—I wish you weren't driving.

Adams. Oh—Mother. There you go again. People do it every day.

Mother. I know. But you'll be careful, won't you? Promise me you'll be extra careful.

Hampton's Drive-In (1974), Howard Kanovitz.
Photograph courtesy of the artist.

lark (lärk) *n.* a carefree adventure
nondescript (nŏn′dĭ-skrĭpt′) *adj.* lacking in distinctive qualities; drab

(*Music changing*)

Adams. It was on the new Pennsylvania Turnpike between Harrisburg and Pittsburgh. It's 265 miles long, with a very high high speed limit. I was just slowing down for one of the tunnels—when I saw him—standing under an arc light by the side of the road. I could see him quite distinctly. The bag, the cap, even the spots of fresh rain spattered over his shoulders. He hailed me this time. . . .

Voice (*very spooky and faint*). Hall-ooo-. . . Hall-ooo-. . . ! (*echo as through tunnel*)

Adams. I stepped on the gas like a shot. That's lonely country through the Alleghenies,[2] and I had no intention of stopping. Besides, the coincidence, or whatever it was, gave me the willies.[3] I stopped at the next gas station.

(*Sound: auto tires screeching to stop . . . horn honk*)

Mechanic. Yes, sir.

Adams. Fill her up.

Mechanic. Certainly, sir. Check your oil, sir?

Adams. No, thanks.

(*Sound: gas being put into car . . . bell tinkle, et cetera*)

Mechanic. Nice night, isn't it?

Adams. Yes. It—hasn't been raining here recently, has it?

Mechanic. Not a drop of rain all week.

Adams. I suppose that hasn't done your business any harm.

Mechanic. Oh—people drive through here all kinds of weather. Mostly business, you know.

Don't fall asleep—or drive fast—or pick up any strangers on the road. . . .

Adams. Of course I think not. You'd think I was still seventeen to hear you talk—

Mother. And wire me as soon as you get to Hollywood, won't you, Son?

Adams. Of course I will. Now don't you worry. There isn't anything going to happen. It's just eight days of perfectly simple driving on smooth, decent, civilized roads, with a hot-dog or a hamburger stand every ten miles . . . . (*fade*)

(*Sound: auto hum*)

(*Music in*)

Adams. I was in excellent spirits. The drive ahead of me, even the loneliness, seemed like a lark. But I reckoned without him.

(*Music changes to something weird and empty.*)

Adams. Crossing Brooklyn Bridge that morning in the rain, I saw a man leaning against the cables. He seemed to be waiting for a lift. There were spots of fresh rain on his shoulders. He was carrying a cheap overnight bag in one hand. He was thin, nondescript, with a cap pulled down over his eyes. He stepped off the walk, and if I hadn't swerved, I'd have hit him.

(*Sound: terrific skidding*)

(*Music in*)

Adams. I would have forgotten him completely, except that just an hour later, while crossing the Pulaski Skyway over the Jersey flats, I saw him again. At least, he looked like the same person. He was standing now, with one thumb pointing west. I couldn't figure out how he'd got there, but I thought probably one of those fast trucks had picked him up, beaten me to the Skyway, and let him off. I didn't stop for him. Then—late that night, I saw him again.

2. **Alleghenies** (ăl′ĭ-gā′nēz): the Allegheny Mountains, a range extending from northern Pennsylvania to western Virginia.

3. **gave me the willies:** made me nervous.

Adams. It was a bright, sunshiny afternoon. The peaceful Ohio fields, brown with the autumn stubble, lay dreaming in the golden light. I was driving slowly, drinking it in, when the road suddenly ended in a detour. In front of the barrier, he was standing.

(Music in)

Adams. Let me explain about his appearance before I go on. I repeat. There was nothing sinister about him. He was as drab as a mud fence. Nor was his attitude menacing. He merely stood there, waiting, almost drooping a little, the cheap overnight bag in his hand. He looked as though he had been waiting there for hours. Then he looked up. He hailed me. He started to walk forward.

Voice *(far off).* Hall-ooo ... Hall-ooo ...

Adams. I had stopped the car, of course, for the detour. And for a few moments, I couldn't seem to find the new road. I knew he must be thinking that I had stopped for him.

Voice *(closer).* Hall-ooo ... Halll ... ooo ...

(Sound: gears jamming ... sound of motor turning over hard ... nervous accelerator)

Voice *(closer).* Halll ... oooo ...

Adams *(panicky).* No. Not just now. Sorry ...

Voice *(closer).* Going to California?

(Sound: starter starting ... gears jamming)

Adams *(as though sweating blood).* No. Not today. The other way. Going to New York. Sorry ... sorry ... sorry.

(Sound: Car starts with squeal of wheels on dirt ... into auto hum.)

(Music in)

Adams. After I got the car back onto the road again, I felt like a fool. Yet the thought of picking him up, of having him sit beside me, was somehow unbearable. Yet, at the

There aren't many pleasure cars out on the turnpike this season of the year.

Adams. I suppose not. *(casually)* What about hitchhikers?

Mechanic *(half laughing).* Hitchhikers here?

Adams. What's the matter? Don't you ever see any?

Mechanic. Not much. If we did, it'd be a sight for sore eyes.

Adams. Why?

Mechanic. A guy'd be a fool who started out to hitch rides on this road. Look at it. It's 265 miles long, there's practically no speed limit, and it's a straightaway. Now what car is going to stop to pick up a guy under these conditions? Would you stop?

Adams. No. *(slowly, with puzzled emphasis)* Then you've never seen anybody?

Mechanic. Nope. Mebbe they get the lift before the turnpike starts—I mean, you know, just before the toll house—but then it'd be a mighty long ride. Most cars wouldn't want to pick up a guy for that long a ride. And you know—this is pretty lonesome country here—mountains, and woods. ... You ain't seen anybody like that, have you?

Adams. No. *(quickly)* Oh no, not at all. It was—just a—technical question.

Mechanic. I see. Well—that'll be just a dollar forty-nine—with the tax. ... *(fade)*

(Sound: auto hum up)

(Music changing)

Adams. The thing gradually passed from my mind, as sheer coincidence. I had a good night's sleep in Pittsburgh. I did not think about the man all next day—until just outside of Zanesville, Ohio, I saw him again.

(Music: dark, ominous note)

WORDS TO KNOW

sinister (sĭn′ĭ-stər) *adj.* suggestive of evil or misfortune
accelerator (ăk-sĕl′ə-rā′tər) *n.* a device, especially the gas pedal of a motor vehicle, for increasing speed

same time, I felt, more than ever, unspeakably alone.

(Sound: auto hum up)

Adams. Hour after hour went by. The fields, the towns ticked off, one by one. The lights changed. I knew now that I was going to see him again. And though I dreaded the sight, I caught myself searching the side of the road, waiting for him to appear.

(Sound: auto hum up . . . car screeches to a halt . . . impatient honk two or three times . . . door being unbolted)

Sleepy man's voice. Yep? What is it? What do you want?

Adams *(breathless).* You sell sandwiches and pop here, don't you?

Voice *(cranky).* Yep. We do. In the daytime. But we're closed up now for the night.

Adams. I know. But—I was wondering if you could possibly let me have a cup of coffee— black coffee.

Voice. Not at this time of night, mister. My wife's the cook, and she's in bed. Mebbe farther down the road—at the Honeysuckle Rest. . . .

(Sound: door squeaking on hinges as though being closed)

Adams. No—no. Don't shut the door. *(shakily)* Listen—just a minute ago, there was a man standing here—right beside this stand—a suspicious looking man. . . .

Woman's voice *(from distance).* Hen-ry? Who is it, Henry?

Henry. It's nobuddy, Mother. Just a feller thinks he wants a cup of coffee. Go back into bed.

Adams. I don't mean to disturb you. But you see, I was driving along—when I just happened to look—and there he was. . . .

Henry. What was he doing?

Adams. Nothing. He ran off—when I stopped the car.

Henry. Then what of it? That's nothing to wake a man in the middle of his sleep about. *(sternly)* Young man, I've got a good mind to turn you over to the sheriff.

Adams. But—I—

Henry. You've been taking a nip; that's what you've been doing. And you haven't got anything better to do than to wake decent folk out of their hard-earned sleep. Get going. Go on.

Adams. But—he looked as though he were going to rob you.

Henry. I ain't got nothin' in this stand to lose. Now—on your way before I call out Sheriff Oakes. *(fade)*

(Sound: auto hum up)

Adams. I got into the car again and drove on slowly. I was beginning to hate the car. If I could have found a place to stop . . . to rest a little. But I was in the Ozark Mountains of Missouri now. The few resort places there were closed. Only an occasional log cabin, seemingly deserted, broke the monotony of the wild, wooded landscape. I had seen him at that roadside stand; I knew I would see him again—perhaps at the next turn of the road. I knew that when I saw him next, I would run him down. . . .

(Sound: auto hum up)

Adams. But I did not see him again until late next afternoon. . . .

(Sound of railroad warning signal at crossroads)

Adams. I had stopped the car at a sleepy little junction just across the border into Oklahoma—to let a train pass by—when he appeared, across the tracks, leaning against a telephone pole.

(*Sound: distant sound of train chugging . . . bell ringing steadily*)

Adams (*very tense*). It was a perfectly airless, dry day. The red clay of Oklahoma was baking under the southwestern sun. Yet there were spots of fresh rain on his shoulders. I couldn't stand that. Without thinking, blindly, I started the car across the tracks.

(*Sound: train chugging closer*)

Adams. He didn't even look up at me. He was staring at the ground. I stepped on the gas hard, veering the wheel sharply toward him. I could hear the train in the distance now, but I didn't care. Then something went wrong with the car. It stalled right on the tracks.

(*Sound: train chugging closer; above this, sound of car stalling*)

Adams. The train was coming closer. I could hear its bell ringing and the cry of its whistle. Still he stood there. And now—I knew that he was beckoning—beckoning me to my death.

(*Sound: Train chugging close. Whistle blows wildly. Then train rushes up and by with pistons going, et cetera.*)

Adams. Well—I frustrated him that time. The starter had worked at last. I managed to back up. But when the train passed, he was gone. I was all alone in the hot, dry afternoon.

(*Sound: Train retreating. Crickets begin to sing.*)

(*Music in*)

Adams. After that, I knew I had to do something. I didn't know who this man was or what he wanted of me. I only knew that from now on, I must not let myself be alone on the road for one moment.

(*Sound: auto hum up; slow down; stop; door opening*)

Adams. Hello, there. Like a ride?

Girl. What do you think? How far you going?

Adams. Amarillo . . . I'll take you to Amarillo.

Girl. Amarillo, Texas?

Adams. I'll drive you there.

Girl. Gee!

(*Sound: Door closes. Car starts.*)

(*Music in*)

Girl. Mind if I take off my shoes? My dogs[4] are killing me.

Adams. Go right ahead.

Girl. Gee, what a break this is. A swell car, a decent guy, and driving all the way to Amarillo. All I been getting so far is trucks.

Adams. Hitchhike much?

Girl. Sure. Only it's tough sometimes, in these great open spaces, to get the breaks.

Adams. I should think it would be. Though I'll bet if you get a good pickup in a fast car, you can get to places faster than—say, another person, in another car?

Girl. I don't get you.

Adams. Well, take me, for instance. Suppose I'm driving across the country, say, at a nice steady clip of about forty-five miles an hour. Couldn't a girl like you, just standing beside the road, waiting for lifts, beat me to town after town—provided she got picked up every time in a car doing from sixty-five to seventy miles an hour?

Girl. I dunno. Maybe she could and maybe she couldn't. What difference does it make?

Adams. Oh—no difference. It's just a—crazy idea I had sitting here in the car.

Girl (*laughing*). Imagine spending your time in a swell car like that thinking of things like that!

Adams. What would you do instead?

Girl (*admiringly*). What would I do? If I was a good-looking fellow like yourself? Why—I'd

---

4. **dogs:** a slang term for feet.

just enjoy myself—every minute of the time. I'd sit back and relax, and if I saw a good-looking girl along the side of the road. . . .

(sharply) Hey! Look out! . . .

Adams *(breathlessly).* Did you see him too?

Girl. See who?

Adams. That man. Standing beside the barbed wire fence.

Girl. I didn't see—anybody. There wasn't nothing but a bunch of steers—and the barbed wire fence. What did you think you was doing? Trying to run into the barbed wire fence?

Adams. There was a man there, I tell you . . . a thin, gray man with an overnight bag in his hand. And I was trying to—run him down.

Girl. Run him down? You mean—kill him?

Adams. He's a sort of—phantom. I'm trying to get rid of him—or else prove that he's real. But *(desperately)* you say you didn't see him back there? You're sure?

Girl *(queerly).* I didn't see a soul. And as far as that's concerned, mister . . .

Adams. Watch for him the next time, then. Keep watching. Keep your eyes peeled on the road. He'll turn up again—maybe any minute now. *(excitedly)* There. Look there—

(Sound: Auto sharply veering and skidding. Girl screams.)

(Sound: crash of car going into barbed wire fence; frightened lowing⁵ of steer)

Girl. How does this door work? I—I'm gettin' outta here.

Adams. Did you see him that time?

Girl *(sharply).* No. I didn't see him that time. And personally, mister, I don't expect never to see him. All I want to do is to go on living—and I don't see how I will very long, driving with you—

Adams. I'm sorry, I—I don't know what came over me. *(frightened)* Please—don't go . . . .

Girl. So if you'll excuse me, mister—

Adams. You can't go. Listen, how would you like to go to California? I'll drive you to California.

Girl. Seeing pink elephants all the way? No thanks.

Adams *(desperately).* I could get you a job there. You wouldn't have to be a waitress. I have friends there—my name is Ronald Adams—you can check up.

(Sound: Door opens.)

Girl. Uh-huuh. Thanks just the same.

Adams. Listen. Please. For just one minute. Maybe you think I am half-cracked. But this man. You see, I've been seeing this man all the way across the country. He's been following me. And if you could only help me—stay with me—until I reach the coast—

Girl. You know what I think you need, big boy? Not a girl friend. Just a good dose of sleep . . . There, I got it now.

(Sound: Door opens . . . slams.)

Adams. No. You can't go.

Girl *(screams).* Leave your hands offa me, do you hear! Leave your—

Adams. Come back here, please, come back.

(Sound: struggle . . . slap . . . footsteps running away on gravel . . . lowing⁵ of steer)

Adams. She ran from me as though I were a monster. A few minutes later, I saw a passing truck pick her up. I knew then that I was utterly alone.

(Sound: lowing of steer up)

Adams. I was in the heart of the great Texas prairies. There wasn't a car on the road after the truck went by. I tried to figure out what

---

5. lowing: mooing.

was there.

even for a moment—for gas, for oil, for a
drink of pop, a cup of coffee, a sandwich—he
began to be everywhere. Whenever I stopped,
fought it out then and there. For now he
Perhaps I should have spoken to him then,

Adams. I didn't wait for him to come any closer.

(Music in)

(Sound: auto starting violently . . . up to steady hum)

Voice. Hall-ooo. . . . Hall-oooo. . . .

herd of moving steer. . . .

toward me *(hall-ooo)*, emerging from the
a blanket *(hall-ooo)* when I saw him coming
winter overcoat out of the back seat to use as
the side of the road. . . . I was getting my
right here in the car for a few hours, along
find a place to rest. Or even if I could sleep
to do, how to get hold of myself. If I could

Hilco (1989), Kit Boyce. Courtesy of the artist.

Adams. I saw him standing outside the auto
camp in Amarillo that night when I dared to
slow down. He was sitting near the drinking
fountain in a little camping spot just inside
the border of New Mexico.

(Music faster)

Adams. He was waiting for me outside the
Navajo Reservation, where I stopped to
check my tires. I saw him in Albuquerque,[6]
where I bought twelve gallons of gas. . . . I
was afraid now, afraid to stop. I began to
drive faster and faster. I was in lunar
landscape now—the great arid mesa country
of New Mexico. I drove through it with the
indifference of a fly crawling over the face of
the moon.

---

6. **Albuquerque** (ăl′bə-kûr′kē): a city in central New Mexico.

(Music faster)

Adams. But now he didn't even wait for me to stop. Unless I drove at eighty-five miles an hour over those endless roads—he waited for me at every other mile. I would see his figure, shadowless, flitting before me, still in its same attitude, over the cold and lifeless ground; flitting over dried-up rivers, over broken stones cast up by old glacial upheavals, flitting in the pure and cloudless air. . . .

(Music strikes sinister note of finality.)

Adams. I was beside myself when I finally reached Gallup, New Mexico, this morning. There is an auto camp here—cold, almost deserted at this time of year. I went inside and asked if there was a telephone. I had the feeling that if only I could speak to someone familiar, someone that I loved, I could pull myself together.

(Sound: nickel put in slot)

Operator. Number, please?

Adams. Long distance.

(Sound: return of nickel; buzz.)

Long-distance opr. This is long distance.

Adams. I'd like to put in a call to my home in Brooklyn, New York. I'm Ronald Adams. The number is Beechwood 2-0828.

Long-distance opr. Thank you. What is your number?

Adams. 312.

Albuquerque opr. Albuquerque.

Long-distance opr. New York for Gallup.

(pause)

New York opr. New York.

Long-distance opr. Gallup, New Mexico, calling Beechwood 2-0828. *(fade)*

Adams. I had read somewhere that love could banish demons. It was the middle of the morning. I knew Mother would be home.

I pictured her, tall, white-haired, in her crisp house dress, going about her tasks. It would be enough, I thought, merely to hear the even calmness of her voice. . . .

Long-distance opr. Will you please deposit three dollars and eighty-five cents for the first three minutes? When you have deposited a dollar and a half, will you wait until I have collected the money?

(Sound: clunk of six coins)

Long-distance opr. All right, deposit another dollar and a half.

(Sound: clunk of six coins)

Long-distance opr. Will you please deposit the remaining eighty-five cents?

(Sound: clunk of four coins)

Long-distance opr. Ready with Brooklyn—go ahead, please.

Adams. Hello.

Mrs. Whitney. Mrs. Adams's residence.

Adams. Hello. Hello—Mother?

Mrs. Whitney. *(very flat and rather proper . . . dumb, too, in a frizzy sort of way).* This is Mrs. Adams's residence. Who is it you wished to speak to, please?

Adams. Why—who's this?

Mrs. Whitney. This is Mrs. Whitney.

Adams. Mrs. Whitney? I don't know any Mrs. Whitney. Is this Beechwood 2-0828?

Mrs. Whitney. Yes.

Adams. Where's my mother? Where's Mrs. Adams?

Mrs. Whitney. Mrs. Adams is not at home. She is still in the hospital.

Adams. The hospital!

Mrs. Whitney. Yes. Who is this calling, please? Is it a member of the family?

Adams. What's she in the hospital for?

Mrs. Whitney. She's been prostrated[7] for five days. Nervous breakdown. But who is this calling?

Adams. Nervous breakdown? But—my mother was never nervous. . . .

Mrs. Whitney. It's all taken place since the death of her oldest son, Ronald.

Adams. Death of her oldest son, Ronald . . .? Hey—what is this? What number is this?

Mrs. Whitney. This is Beechwood 2-0828. It's all been very sudden. He was killed just six days ago in an automobile accident on the Brooklyn Bridge.

Operator *(breaking in).* Your three minutes are up, sir. *(silence)* Your three minutes are up, sir. *(pause)* Your three minutes are up, sir. *(fade)* Sir, your three minutes are up. Your three minutes are up, sir.

Adams *(in a strange voice).* And so, I am sitting here in this deserted auto camp in Gallup, New Mexico. I am trying to think. I am trying to get hold of myself. Otherwise, I shall go mad. . . . Outside it is night—the vast, soulless night of New Mexico. A million stars are in the sky. Ahead of me stretch a thousand miles of empty mesa, mountains, prairies—desert. Somewhere among them, he is waiting for me. Somewhere I shall know who he is, and who . . . I . . . am. . . .

(Music up) ❖

---

7. **prostrated:** in a state of mental collapse.

Mourning Grace
Maya Angelou

If today I follow death,
go down its trackless wastes,
salt my tongue on hardened tears
for my precious dear time's waste
race
along that promised cave in a headlong
deadlong
haste,
Will you
have
the
grace
to mourn for
me?

THINKING *through* the LITERATURE

Connect to the Literature

1. **What Do You Think?** Do you think *The Hitchhiker* is a good horror story? Why or why not?

Comprehension Check
- Where is Ronald Adams when the radio play begins? Why is he there?
- Why does the repeated sight of the hitchhiker give Adams "the willies"?
- What does Adams learn at the end of the play?

Think Critically

2. **ACTIVE READING** **PREDICTING** Look over the predictions you made in your **READER'S NOTEBOOK.** At what point in the story did you realize that the hitchhiker was not a harmless stranger?

3. What do you think has really happened to Adams?

   Think About:
   - what Adams says about his mental state at the beginning of the play
   - what Adams learns when he tries to call his mother at the end of the play

4. Who do you think the hitchhiker really is?

Extend Interpretations

5. **What If?** What do you think would have happened to Adams if he had stopped and picked up the hitchhiker the first time he saw him?

6. **COMPARING TEXTS** The feeling or atmosphere that a writer creates for the reader is called the **mood.** Read aloud "Mourning Grace" by Maya Angelou on page 665. What is the mood of this poem? Is the mood similar to or different from the mood in *The Hitchhiker*? Explain your answer.

7. **Connect to Life** Horror stories have fascinated numerous readers and audiences of all ages. Why do you think horror stories are so popular?

Literary Analysis

FORESHADOWING To build suspense in a story, writers frequently use a device known as **foreshadowing,** in which the writer provides hints or clues about what may occur later in the story. For example, Lucille Fletcher foreshadows the appearance of the hitchhiker when Adams's mother says:

Promise me you'll be extra careful. Don't fall asleep—or drive fast—or pick up any strangers on the road. . . .

Paired Activity As the play progresses, Lucille Fletcher provides stronger and stronger hints that the stranger on the road might harm Ronald Adams. With a partner, go back through the story and find clues that foreshadow the story's surprise ending. Did the clues help you predict the ending? Why or why not?

Clues to the identity of the hitchhiker	Clues to the ending of the play
Hitchhiker steps directly in front of Adams on the Brooklyn Bridge.	Ronald Adams expresses the fear that he is going mad.

Writing

Additional Scene The ending of the play leaves the audience hanging. Write an additional scene that reveals what Adams does next. Be sure to use relevant dialogue, specific action, and stage directions that provide a physical description. Try to match the mood and tone already used by the writer. Place your scene in your **Working Portfolio.**

Writing Handbook
See p. R43: Narrative Writing.

Speaking & Listening

Radio Play With your classmates, produce *The Hitchhiker* as a radio play. Drop in background music and sound effects to accompany the dialogue. Record your performance on audiotape and play the tape for the class. How do sound effects and music add to the suspense?

Speaking and Listening Handbook
See p. R106: Oral Interpretation.

Research & Technology

SOCIAL STUDIES

Using the Internet and library, find out more about the Golden Age of Radio. For example, what years did this period span? What shows and entertainers were popular? What brought about the end of this era? Write a short report that summarizes the highlights of the Golden Age of Radio.

Art Connection

In the painting on page 663, artist Kit Boyce has created a scene that reflects the suspenseful, eerie mood of *The Hitchhiker*. In the painting, what do you see lurking in the darkness? How would the effect of the painting be different if you could see details of the car's occupants?

Vocabulary

STANDARDIZED TEST PRACTICE

Complete the following analogies. Begin by identifying the relationship between the words in the first pair. Then decide which Word to Know best completes the second analogy in a similar way.

1. CHORE : BURDENSOME :: _____ : carefree
2. SPEED : SLOWDOWN :: _____ : brake
3. GUARANTEE : DOUBT :: _____ : uncertainty
4. COLORFUL : YELLOW :: _____ : gray
5. OMINOUS : GROWL :: _____ : hiss

Vocabulary Handbook See p. R26: Analogies.

EXERCISE: FINAL SILENT *E* WITH SUFFIXES When adding a suffix that begins with a vowel to a word that ends with a silent *e*, drop the silent *e*.

assure + -ance = assurance

Add suffixes to the following words as indicated:

1. finance + -ial = _____
2. resemble + -ance = _____
3. picture + -ing = _____
4. commerce + -ial = _____
5. drive + -er = _____

Spelling Handbook See p. R28.

WORDS
TO
KNOW
accelerator   assurance   lark   nondescript   sinister

Grammar in Context: Infinitive Phrases

Notice the words in red in this sentence from Lucille Fletcher's *The Hitchhiker.*

> **A guy'd be a fool who started out to hitch rides on this road.**

The words in red form an **infinitive phrase.** An infinitive phrase consists of an infinitive (*to* + a verb) along with its modifiers and complements. Writers use infinitive phrases to express an idea using few words.

Apply to Your Writing Use infinitive phrases to vary your sentences.

WRITING EXERCISE Combine each pair of sentences by changing one sentence into an infinitive phrase. Underline the infinitive phrase.

Example: ***Original*** In a panic, Adams desperately tries something. He tries to calm himself.

Rewritten In a panic, Adams desperately tries <u>to calm himself</u>.

1. Adams left Brooklyn. He was driving to California.
2. The hitchhiker was waiting when the driver stopped. The driver stopped to check his tires.
3. Though assault is a crime, Adam tries something. He tries to hit the stranger.
4. When he stops for a woman who is hitchhiking, Adams offers to drive her somewhere. He offers to drive her to Amarillo.
5. At last Adams guesses the truth when he tries to telephone someone. He tries to telephone his mother in Brooklyn.

Grammar Handbook See p. R89: Phrases and Clauses.

Lucille Fletcher
born 1912

"During the 1930s and 1940s, Fletcher kept radio audiences on the edge of their seats with her chilling mystery dramas."

Mystery Dramatist Lucille Fletcher was born in Brooklyn, New York, where Ronald Adams's frightening trip begins. During the 1930s and 1940s, Fletcher kept radio audiences on the edge of their seats with her chilling mystery dramas. She is best known for her radio play *Sorry, Wrong Number*, a suspense classic.

Broadway and Hollywood During her career, Fletcher wrote 20 plays for the radio series *Suspense* and scripts for the television series *Chrysler Theater* and *Lights Out*. Fletcher has also written several mystery novels—including *And Presumed Dead* and *Blindfold*, which were made into movies. Her first Broadway play, *Night Watch,* was produced in 1972 and later made into a movie.

AUTHOR ACTIVITY
View a Video Several of Lucille Fletcher's novels and plays were made into movies. Find *And Presumed Dead, Blindfold*, or *Night Watch* in a video store and view it. Make a poster that captures the mood and plot of your video choice and could also be used to advertise the film. Display the poster in your classroom.

Building Vocabulary
Denotation and Connotation

A writer needs more than a plot to write a good mystery story. Word choice is also very important. A good writer selects a word not just for its **denotation**—its dictionary definition—but also for its **connotation,** the attitudes and emotions associated with it.

By choosing the word *cunningly* over its synonym *cleverly,* Poe gives the passage a more negative connotation.

> And then, when I had made an opening sufficient for my head, I put in a dark lantern, all closed, closed, so that no light shone out, and then I thrust in my head. Oh, you would have laughed to see how cunningly I thrust it in!
>
> —Edgar Allan Poe, "The Tell-Tale Heart"

denotation: cleverly
connotation: the idea of acting deceptively

Strategies for Building Vocabulary

Choosing the most appropriate words can help turn a good story into a great one. Here are some strategies for understanding a word's connotation and for choosing the most appropriate word to use when speaking or writing.

❶ **Look Beyond the Literal** Many words carry strong positive or negative associations. Consider this passage:

> "Hold it up in your right hand and wish aloud," said the sergeant-major, "but I warn you of the consequences."
>
> —W. W. Jacobs, "The Monkey's Paw"

The word *consequences* literally means "effects," but it also suggests the idea that these effects might be bad. In the passage above, the word *consequences* carries a negative connotation. A writer's choice of words often reveals how the writer feels about a subject.

❷ **Consider Connotations** When choosing words to convey your meaning, compare synonyms—words with similar meanings—and select the most appropriate word. For example, if you are describing someone standing outside a house, you might consider the words *lurking* and *waiting.* If the person is doing something wrong, *lurking* would be the better choice, as it implies that the person is trying to avoid being noticed. A thesaurus is an excellent reference when you are looking for fresh, descriptive words. Use a dictionary to confirm denotations and to get a sense of word connotations.

EXERCISE Think about each set of synonyms. Then identify each word as having a positive or a negative connotation. You may use a dictionary to help you.
1. curious/nosy
2. constant/incessant
3. vain/proud
4. old/obsolete
5. grandiose/magnificent

Short Stories

You are about to read two **short stories** about strange and extraordinary events. There are many differences and similarities between these tales. Although "The Third Wish" is a modern-day **fable** (a story that teaches a simple lesson), and "The Monkey's Paw" is a **horror story** set in England during the late 1800s, both stories have a similar **plot** about a man who has been allowed to make three wishes.

A short story by JOAN AIKEN

The Third Wish

SELECTION 1

A short story by W.W. JACOBS

The MONKEY'S PAW

SELECTION 2

Connect to Your Life

Wishbones and Wishing Wells

Think about customs that involve wishing, such as the practice of making a wish as you throw a coin in a fountain. Then answer these questions:

◆ What kinds of things do you wish for?

◆ What wishing customs can you think of?

With a partner, discuss why and how you have made wishes.

POINTS OF COMPARISON

All stories are built around a **plot,** a sequence of related events that make up the story. A story might begin with an **exposition,** which introduces the characters and the **conflict,** or the struggle they face. The **rising action** includes events that complicate the conflict. The rising action leads to a **climax,** the point of greatest interest. During the **falling action,** the conflict is resolved. In the pages that follow you will compare and contrast the **plots** of two short stories. To help you note similarities and differences, keep these questions in mind:

◆ During the **exposition,** what is the story's tone and setting? Who are the characters?

◆ What is the main **conflict** in the story?

◆ What happens during the **rising action** and the **climax?**

◆ How is the conflict resolved during the **falling action?**

	"The Third Wish"	"The Monkey's Paw"
Exposition	Setting: Tone: Characters:	Setting: Tone: Characters:
Main conflict		
Rising action		
Climax		
How is the conflict resolved during the falling action?		

As you read "The Third Wish" and "The Monkey's Paw," use a chart like the one shown to help you take notes as you read.

Assessment Option: Comparison-and-Contrast Essay After you have finished reading "The Third Wish" and "The Monkey's Paw," you will have the option of writing a comparison-and-contrast essay. Your notes will help you plan and write the essay.

The Third Wish

by JOAN AIKEN

Build Background

Swans in Folklore Swans have appeared in European folklore and mythology since ancient times, when people believed that Zeus, the king of the gods, once came to earth disguised as a swan. According to legend, a swan sings one strange and beautiful song in its lifetime—as it is dying. The modern phrase "swan song," meaning a person's farewell appearance or final work, is based on this legend.

Focus Your Reading

LITERARY ANALYSIS   **PLOT**

The sequence of events in a story is called the **plot.** The plot of a story has four main parts. In the early part of the story the **exposition** sets the tone, establishes the setting, introduces the characters, and gives the reader important background information. The **rising action** of the plot refers to the events in a story that add complications or expand the conflict. The rising action usually builds suspense to a **climax** or turning point. After the climax comes the **falling action,** during which the conflict is resolved. As you read the two stories, notice how the first wish creates a conflict for the characters.

ACTIVE READING   **SETTING A PURPOSE**

When you **set a purpose** for reading, you choose specific reasons for reading a work. In this case you will read to identify the plot elements of the two stories so that you can compare and contrast them. As you read, watch for the similarities and differences between the two selections that might be useful when you write your comparison-and-contrast essay.

📖 **READER'S NOTEBOOK**
As you read, try to answer the Points of Comparison questions about plot from page 671.

WORDS TO KNOW
Vocabulary Preview
extricate   preening
malicious   presumptuous
outskirts

The Third Wish

by Joan Aiken

Wallpaper design for *"Swan, Rush and Iris,"* Walter Crane (1845–1915). Victoria & Albert Museum, London, UK/Bridgeman Art Library, London/New York.

Once there was a man who was driving in his car at dusk on a spring evening through part of the forest of Savernake. His name was Mr. Peters. The primroses[1] were just beginning but the trees were still bare, and it was cold; the birds had stopped singing an hour ago.

---

1. **primroses:** flowering plants that bloom in early spring.

Mr. Peters entered a straight, empty stretch of road he seemed to hear a faint crying, and a struggling and thrashing, as if somebody was in trouble far away in the trees. He left his car and climbed the mossy bank beside the road. Beyond the bank was an open slope of beech trees leading down to thorn bushes through which he saw the gleam of water. He stood a moment waiting to try and discover where the noise was coming from, and presently heard a rustling and some strange cries in a voice which was almost human—and yet there was something too hoarse about it at one time and too clear and sweet at another. Mr. Peters ran down the hill and as he neared the bushes he saw something white among them which was trying to <u>extricate</u> itself; coming closer he found that it was a swan that had become entangled in the thorns growing on the bank of the canal.

The bird struggled all the more frantically as he approached, looking at him with hate in its yellow eyes, and when he took hold of it to free it, hissed at him, pecked him, and thrashed dangerously with its wings which were powerful enough to break his arm. Nevertheless he managed to release it from the thorns, and carrying it tightly with one arm, holding the snaky head well away with the other hand (for he did not wish his eyes pecked out), he took it to the verge[2] of the canal and dropped it in.

The swan instantly assumed great dignity and sailed out to the middle of the water, where it put itself to rights with much dabbling and <u>preening</u>, smoothing its feathers with little showers of drops. Mr. Peters waited, to make sure that it was all right and had suffered no damage in its struggles. Presently the swan, when it was satisfied with its appearance, floated in to the bank once more, and in a moment, instead of the great white bird, there was a little man all in green with a golden crown and long beard, standing by the water. He had fierce glittering eyes and looked by no means friendly.

"Well, Sir," he said threateningly, "I see you are <u>presumptuous</u> enough to know some of the laws of magic. You think that because you have rescued—by pure good fortune—the King of the Forest from a difficulty, you should have some fabulous reward."

"I expect three wishes, no more and no less," answered Mr. Peters, looking at him steadily and with composure.

"Three wishes, he wants, the clever man! Well, I have yet to hear of the human being who made any good use of his three wishes—they mostly end up worse off than they started. Take your three wishes then—" he flung three dead leaves in the air "—don't blame me if you spend the last wish in undoing the work of the other two."

Mr. Peters caught the leaves and put two of them carefully in his notecase. When he looked up the swan was sailing about in the

---

2. **verge:** edge.

middle of the water again, flicking the drops angrily down its long neck.

Mr. Peters stood for some minutes reflecting on how he should use his reward. He knew very well that the gift of three magic wishes was one which brought trouble more often than not, and he had no intention of being like the forester who first wished by mistake for a sausage, and then in a rage wished it on the end of his wife's nose, and then had to use his last wish in getting it off again. Mr. Peters had most of the things which he wanted and was very content with his life. The only thing that troubled him was that he was a little lonely, and had no companion for his old age. He decided to use his first wish and to keep the other two in case of an emergency. Taking a thorn he pricked his tongue with it, to remind himself not to utter rash wishes aloud. Then holding the third leaf and gazing round him at the dusky undergrowth, the primroses, great beeches and the blue-green water of the canal, he said:

"I wish I had a wife as beautiful as the forest."

A tremendous quacking and splashing broke out on the surface of the water. He thought that it was the swan laughing at him. Taking no notice he made his way through the darkening woods to his car, wrapped himself up in the rug and went to sleep.

When he awoke it was morning and the birds were beginning to call. Coming along the track towards him was the most beautiful creature he had ever seen, with eyes as blue-green as the canal, hair as dusky as the bushes, and skin as white as the feathers of swans.

"Are you the wife that I wished for?" asked Mr. Peters.

"Yes I am," she replied. "My name is Leita."[3]

She stepped into the car beside him and they drove off to the church on the <u>outskirts</u> of the forest, where they were married. Then he took her to his house in a remote and lovely valley and showed her all his treasures—the bees in their white hives, the Jersey cows, the hyacinths, the silver candlesticks, the blue cups and the lustre bowl for putting primroses in. She admired everything, but what pleased her most was the river which ran by the foot of his garden.

"Do swans come up here?" she asked.

"Yes, I have often seen swans there on the river," he told her, and she smiled.

Leita made him a good wife. She was gentle and friendly, busied herself about the house and garden, polished the bowls, milked the cows and mended his socks. But as time went by Mr. Peters began to feel that she was not happy. She seemed restless, wandered much in the garden, and sometimes when he came back from the fields he would find the house empty and she would only return after half an hour or so with no explanation of where she had been. On these occasions she was always especially tender and would put out his slippers to warm and cook his favourite dish—Welsh rarebit[4] with wild strawberries—for supper.

One evening he was returning home along the river path when he saw Leita in front of him, down by the water. A swan had sailed up to the verge and she had her arms round its neck and the swan's head rested

---

3. **Leita** (lē′tə).

4. **Welsh rarebit:** melted cheese served over toast or crackers.

Wall Mural: Garden Landscape and Fountain (ca. 1905–1915), Louis Comfort Tiffany/Tiffany Studios. Mosaic: favrile glass, cement. 8', 7½". The Metropolitan Museum of Art, Gift of Lillian Nassau, 1976, and Gift of Mrs. L. Groves Geer, 1978. (1976.105. 1978.584) Photograph © 1997 The Metropolitan Museum of Art.

"This is my sister," she answered. "I can't bear being separated from her."

Now he understood that Leita was really a swan from the forest, and this made him very sad because when a human being marries a bird it always leads to sorrow.

"I could use my second wish to give your sister human shape, so that she could be a companion to you," he suggested.

"No, no," she cried, "I couldn't ask that of her."

"Is it so very hard to be a human being?" asked Mr. Peters sadly.

"Very, very hard," she answered.

"Don't you love me at all, Leita?"

"Yes, I do, I do love you," she said, and there were tears in her eyes again. "But I miss the old life in the forest, the cool grass and the mist rising off the river at sunrise and the feel of the water sliding over my feathers as my sister and I drifted along the stream."

"Then shall I use my second wish to turn you back into a swan again?" he asked, and his tongue pricked to remind him of the old King's words, and his heart swelled with grief inside him.

against her cheek. She was weeping, and as he came nearer he saw that tears were rolling, too, from the swan's eyes.

"Leita, what is it?" he asked, very troubled.

"Who would darn your socks and cook your meals and see to the hens?"

"I'd do it myself as I did before I married you," he said, trying to sound cheerful.

She shook her head. "No, I could not be as unkind to you as that. I am partly a swan, but I am also partly a human being now. I will stay with you."

Poor Mr. Peters was very distressed on his wife's account and did his best to make her life happier, taking her for drives in the car, finding beautiful music for her to listen to on the radio, buying clothes for her and even suggesting a trip round the world. But she said no to that; she would prefer to stay in their own house near the river.

He noticed that she spent more and more time baking wonderful cakes—jam puffs, petits fours, éclairs and meringues. One day he saw her take a basketful down to the river and he guessed that she was giving them to her sister.

He built a seat for her by the river, and the two sisters spent hours together there, communicating in some wordless manner. For a time he thought that all would be well, but then he saw how thin and pale she was growing.

One night when he had been late doing the accounts he came up to bed and found her weeping in her sleep and calling:

"Rhea![5] Rhea! I can't understand what you

say! Oh, wait for me, take me with you!"

Then he knew that it was hopeless and she would never be happy as a human. He stooped down and kissed her goodbye, then took another leaf from his notecase, blew it out of the window, and used up his second wish.

Next moment instead of Leita there was a sleeping swan lying across the bed with its head under its wing. He carried it out of the house and down to the brink of the river, and then he said "Leita! Leita!" to waken her, and gently put her into the water. She gazed round her in astonishment for a moment, and then came up to him and rested her head lightly against his hand; next instant she was flying away over the trees towards the heart of the forest.

He heard a harsh laugh behind him, and turning round saw the old King looking at him with a <u>malicious</u> expression.

"Well, my friend! You don't seem to have managed so wonderfully with your first two wishes, do you? What will you do with the

5. **Rhea** (rē′ə).

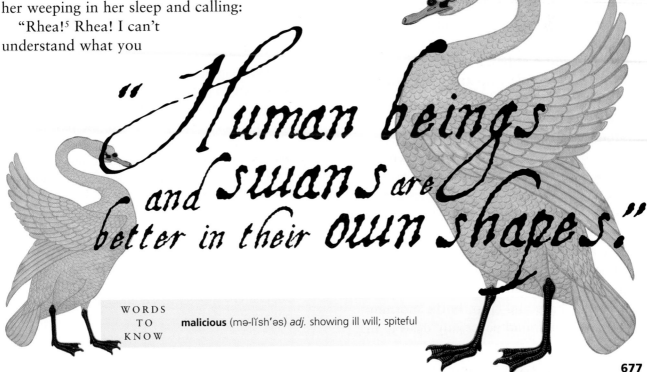

"*Human beings and swans are better in their own shapes.*"

WORDS
TO
KNOW

malicious (mə-lĭsh′əs) *adj.* showing ill will; spiteful

677

last? Turn yourself into a swan? Or turn Leita back into a girl?"

"I shall do neither," said Mr. Peters calmly. "Human beings and swans are better in their own shapes."

But for all that he looked sadly over towards the forest where Leita had flown, and walked slowly back to his empty house.

Next day he saw two swans swimming at the bottom of the garden, and one of them wore the gold chain he had given Leita after their marriage; she came up and rubbed her head against his hand.

Mr. Peters and his two swans came to be well known in that part of the country; people used to say that he talked to the swans and they understood him as well as his neighbours. Many people were a little frightened of him. There was a story that once when thieves tried to break into his house they were set upon by two huge white birds which carried them off bodily and dropped them in the river.

As Mr. Peters grew old everyone wondered at his contentment. Even when he was bent with rheumatism[6] he would not think of moving to a drier spot, but went slowly about his work, milking the cows and collecting the honey and eggs, with the two swans always somewhere close at hand.

Sometimes people who knew his story would say to him:

"Mr. Peters, why don't you wish for another wife?"

"Not likely," he would answer serenely. "Two wishes were enough for me, I reckon. I've learned that even if your wishes are granted they don't always better you. I'll stay faithful to Leita."

One autumn night, passers-by along the road heard the mournful sound of two swans singing. All night the song went on, sweet and harsh, sharp and clear. In the morning Mr. Peters was found peacefully dead in his bed with a smile of great happiness on his face. In between his hands, which lay clasped on his breast, were a withered leaf and a white feather.

---

6. **rheumatism** (rōō′mə-tĭz′əm): a condition that causes painful stiffness of the joints and muscles.

Joan Aiken
born 1924

"Once an Aiken plot gets going, there is no let-up at all in animation or intrigue."

From Horror to History Joan Aiken has published novels, short stories, and plays for younger readers and many novels for adults. A wonderfully imaginative writer, she has written everything from mysteries to fantasy to fictional histories, as well as some books that combine these different forms. Aiken's stories are often complicated and full of fascinating characters.

Two Writing Dads Aiken traces her passion for writing to the influence of her father and stepfather, who were both writers. She began writing at a very early age; from the time she was five years old, she was filling notebooks with poems and stories. Born and raised in rural England, Aiken went to work right after high school. Her employer, the British Broadcasting Company (BBC), also became one of her earliest customers when they purchased two of her stories. Before long, Aiken was publishing regularly and was on her way to becoming one of the most popular children's book authors of our time.

Connect to the Literature

1. What Do You Think?
Write a sentence that expresses your reaction to the story's outcome.

Comprehension Check
- How does Mr. Peters earn three wishes?
- How is Leita related to Mr. Peters and to Rhea?
- What happens to Mr. Peters and Leita at the end of the story?

Think Critically

2. | ACTIVE READING | SETTING PURPOSES |
Review the notes you made in your | READER'S NOTEBOOK and discuss with a classmate how the events in the plot surprised you. Identify the first point in the story where the plot takes an unexpected turn.

3. Connect to Life Have you ever wished for something, such as a gift or a vacation, only to find that getting your wish left you feeling unsatisfied? Why are people so often disappointed when they get what they want?

Literary Analysis

PLOT The sequence of events in a story is called the **plot.** The plot tells what happens, when, and to whom. A plot has four main stages. **Exposition** sets the tone, establishes the setting, introduces the characters, and gives important background. The **rising action** refers to the events in the story that add complications or expand the conflict. Tension or suspense builds in the rising action until an event occurs that is the **climax,** or turning point of the story. The **falling action** is the resolution of the conflict. The first sentence of "The Third Wish" provides important details of exposition.

POINTS OF COMPARISON

Paired Activity Working with a partner, discuss the Points of Comparison questions from page 671. Use your discussion to help you fill in the first column of the Comparison-and-Contrast chart that you began earlier. Look through "The Third Wish" for information that will help you fill in the chart.

	"The Third Wish"	"The Monkey's Paw"
Exposition	**Setting:** modern times; a forest **Tone:** sad **Characters:** Mr. Peters, the King of the Forest, Leita, Rhea	**Setting:** **Tone:** **Characters:**
Main conflict	The wife that Mr. Peters wished for is not happy with her life.	
Rising action		
Climax		
How is the conflict resolved during the falling action?		

The Monkey's Paw

by W. W. JACOBS

Build Background

CULTURE

Many folk tales and horror stories involve magic or magical objects. In this story, the magical object, or talisman, is a monkey's paw that gives unusual powers to anyone who owns it. In many parts of the world, certain objects—especially those associated with animals—are believed to have special powers. In Western culture, for example, a rabbit's foot was once believed to bring luck, and lucky horseshoes still hang on the doors of many barns and farmhouses.

Focus Your Reading

LITERARY ANALYSIS **PLOT**

Most stories involve a **plot,** or sequence of events. **Rising action** refers to the events in a story that move the plot along by adding complications. Writers often try to create **suspense,** a feeling of growing tension and excitement, as the rising action builds toward the **climax,** or turning point of the plot. As you read, notice how the developing tension between the characters makes you feel.

ACTIVE READING **SETTING A PURPOSE**

When you **set a purpose** for reading, you choose specific reasons for reading a work. Here you will read for details that you can use to compare and contrast "The Monkey's Paw" with "The Third Wish." Continue to pay close attention to the similarities and differences between the plots of the two stories.

READER'S NOTEBOOK
As you read, refer to the Points of Comparison questions from page 671. Record your responses in your Reader's Notebook for later use in completing your Points of Comparison chart.

WORDS TO KNOW
Vocabulary Preview

credulity	peril
fate	surveying
grimace	

The MONKEY'S PAW

by W. W. Jacobs

Lilacs (1924-1927), Charles Burchfield. Oil on Board, Delaware Art Museum, Bequest of John Saxon.

Without, the night was cold and wet, but in the small parlor of Laburnum Villa the blinds were drawn and the fire burned brightly. Father and son were at chess; the former, who possessed ideas about the game involving radical changes, putting his king into such sharp and unnecessary perils that it even provoked comment from the white-haired old lady knitting placidly by the fire.

"Hark at the wind," said Mr. White, who, having seen a fatal mistake after it was too late, was amiably[1] desirous of preventing his son from seeing it.

"I'm listening," said the latter, grimly surveying the board as he stretched out his hand. "Check."

"I should hardly think that he'd come tonight," said his father, with his hand poised over the board.

"Mate," replied the son.

"That's the worst of living so far out," bawled Mr. White, with sudden and unlooked-for violence; "of all the beastly, slushy, out-of-the-way places to live in, this is the worst. Pathway's a bog,[2] and the road's a torrent.[3] I don't know what people are thinking about. I suppose because only two houses in the road are let,[4] they think it doesn't matter."

"Never mind, dear," said his wife soothingly; "perhaps you'll win the next one."

Mr. White looked up sharply, just in time to intercept a knowing glance between mother and son. The words died away on his lips, and he hid a guilty grin in his thin gray beard.

"There he is," said Herbert White, as the gate banged loudly and heavy footsteps came toward the door.

The old man rose with hospitable haste, and opening the door, was heard condoling[5] with the new arrival. The new arrival also condoled with himself, so that Mrs. White said, "Tut, tut!" and coughed gently as her husband entered the room, followed by a tall, burly man, beady of eye and rubicund of visage.[6]

"Sergeant-Major Morris," he said, introducing him.

The sergeant-major shook hands, and taking the proffered seat by the fire, watched contentedly while his host brought out drinks and stood a small copper kettle on the fire.

He began to talk, the little family circle regarding with eager interest this visitor from distant parts, as he squared his broad shoulders in the chair and spoke of wild scenes and doughty[7] deeds; of wars and plagues and strange peoples.

"Twenty-one years of it," said Mr. White, nodding at his wife and son. "When he went away, he was a slip of a youth in the warehouse. Now look at him."

"He don't look to have taken much harm," said Mrs. White politely.

"I'd like to go to India myself," said the old man, "just to look round a bit, you know."

"Better where you are," said the sergeant-major, shaking his head. He put down the empty glass, and sighing softly, shook it again.

"I should like to see those old temples and fakirs and jugglers," said the old man. "What was that you started telling me the other day

---

1. **amiably** (ā′mē-ə-blē): in a pleasant, friendly way.
2. **bog**: swamp.
3. **torrent** (tôr′ənt): swift-flowing stream.
4. **let**: rented.
5. **condoling** (kən-dō′lĭng): expressing sympathy (in this case, about the visitor's journey through bad weather).
6. **rubicund** (rōō′bĭ-kənd) **of visage** (vĭz′ĭj): with a ruddy complexion.
7. **doughty** (dou′tē): brave.

WORDS TO KNOW

peril (pĕr′əl) *n.* danger
surveying (sər-vā′ĭng) *adj.* looking over carefully; inspecting **survey** *v.*

about a monkey's paw or something, Morris?"

"Nothing," said the soldier hastily. "Leastways nothing worth hearing."

"Monkey's paw?" said Mrs. White curiously.

"Well, it's just a bit of what you might call magic, perhaps," said the sergeant-major off-handedly.

His three listeners leaned forward eagerly. The visitor absent-mindedly put his empty glass to his lips and then set it down again. His host filled it for him.

"To look at," said the sergeant-major, fumbling in his pocket, "it's just an ordinary little paw, dried to a mummy."

He took something out of his pocket and proffered it. Mrs. White drew back with a grimace, but her son, taking it, examined it curiously.

"And what is there special about it?" inquired Mr. White as he took it from his son, and having examined it, placed it upon the table.

"It had a spell put on it by an old fakir," said the sergeant-major, "a very holy man. He wanted to show that fate ruled people's lives, and that those who interfered with it did so to their sorrow. He put a spell on it so that three separate men could each have three wishes from it."

His manner was so impressive that his hearers were conscious that their light laughter jarred somewhat.

"Well, why don't you have three, sir?" said Herbert White cleverly.

The soldier regarded him in the way that middle age is wont to regard presumptuous youth. "I have," he said quietly, and his blotchy face whitened.

> IT'S JUST AN ORDINARY LITTLE PAW, DRIED TO A MUMMY.

"And did you really have the three wishes granted?" asked Mrs. White.

"I did," said the sergeant-major, and his glass tapped against his strong teeth.

"And has anybody else wished?" persisted the old lady.

"The first man had his three wishes. Yes," was the reply, "I don't know what the first two were, but the third was for death. That's how I got the paw."

His tones were so grave that a hush fell upon the group.

"If you've had your three wishes, it's no good to you now, then, Morris," said the old man at last. "What do you keep it for?"

The soldier shook his head. "Fancy, I suppose," he said slowly. "I did have some idea of selling it, but I don't think I will. It has caused enough mischief already. Besides, people won't buy. They think it's a fairy tale, some of them; and those who do think anything of it want to try it first and pay me afterward."

"If you could have another three wishes," said the old man, eyeing him keenly, "would you have them?"

"I don't know," said the other. "I don't know."

He took the paw, and dangling it between his forefinger and thumb, suddenly threw it upon the fire. White, with a slight cry, stooped down and snatched it off.

"Better let it burn," said the soldier solemnly.

"If you don't want it, Morris," said the other, "give it to me."

"I won't," said his friend doggedly. "I threw it on the fire. If you keep it, don't blame me for what happens. Pitch it on the fire again like a sensible man."

The other shook his head and examined his

WORDS
TO
KNOW

grimace (grĭm′ĭs) *n.* a facial expression of pain or disgust
fate (fāt) *n.* a power that is supposed to determine the course of events

Portrait of a Shared Life (1983), Manuel Lopez de Villasenor. Private Collection/Index/Bridgeman Art Library, London/New York.

and placing chairs, motioned his friend to the table. In the business of supper the talisman was partly forgotten, and afterward the three sat listening in an enthralled fashion to a second installment of the soldier's adventures in India.

"If the tale about the monkey's paw is not more truthful than those he has been telling us," said Herbert, as the door closed behind their guest, just in time for him to catch the last train, "we shan't make much out of it."

"Did you give him anything for it, Father?" inquired Mrs. White, regarding her husband closely.

"A trifle," said he, coloring slightly. "He didn't want it, but I made him take it. And he pressed me again to throw it away."

new possession closely. "How do you do it?" he inquired.

"Hold it up in your right hand and wish aloud," said the sergeant-major, "but I warn you of the consequences."

"Sounds like the *Arabian Nights*,"[8] said Mrs. White, as she rose and began to set the supper. "Don't you think you might wish for four pairs of hands for me?"

Her husband drew the talisman[9] from his pocket, and then all three burst into laughter as the sergeant-major, with a look of alarm on his face, caught him by the arm.

"If you must wish," he said gruffly, "wish for something sensible."

Mr. White dropped it back in his pocket,

"Likely," said Herbert, with pretended horror. "Why, we're going to be rich, and famous, and happy. Wish to be an emperor, Father, to begin with; then you can't be henpecked."

He darted round the table, pursued by the maligned Mrs. White armed with an antimacassar.[10]

Mr. White took the paw from his pocket and eyed it dubiously. "I don't know what

---

8. *Arabian Nights:* a famous collection of Asian stories, also known as *The Thousand and One Nights.*

9. **talisman** (tăl′ĭs-mən): an object thought to have magical powers.

10. **antimacassar** (ăn′tē-mə-kăs′ər): a cloth placed over an arm or back of a chair to keep it from being soiled.

to wish for, and that's a fact," he said slowly. "It seems to me I've got all I want."

"If you only cleared the house, you'd be quite happy, wouldn't you?" said Herbert, with his hand on his shoulder. "Well, wish for two hundred pounds, then; that'll just do it."

His father, smiling shamefacedly at his own credulity, held up the talisman, as his son, with a solemn face, somewhat marred by a wink at his mother, sat down at the piano and struck a few impressive chords.

"I wish for two hundred pounds," said the old man distinctly.

A fine crash from the piano greeted the words, interrupted by a shuddering cry from the old man. His wife and son ran toward him.

"It moved," he cried, with a glance of disgust at the object as it lay on the floor. "As I wished, it twisted in my hand like a snake."

"Well, I don't see the money," said his son, as he picked it up and placed it on the table, "and I bet I never shall."

"It must have been your fancy, Father," said his wife, regarding him anxiously.

He shook his head. "Never mind, though; there's no harm done, but it gave me a shock all the same."

They sat down by the fire again. Outside, the wind was higher than ever, and the old man started nervously at the sound of a door banging upstairs. A silence unusual and depressing settled upon all three, which lasted until the old couple rose to retire for the night.

"I expect you'll find the cash tied up in a big bag in the middle of your bed," said Herbert, as he bade them good-night, "and something horrible squatting up on top of the wardrobe[11] watching you as you pocket your ill-gotten gains."

He sat alone in the darkness, gazing at the dying fire, and seeing faces in it. The last face

was so horrible and so simian[12] that he gazed at it in amazement. It got so vivid that, with a little uneasy laugh, he felt on the table for a glass containing a little water to throw over it. His hand grasped the monkey's paw, and with a little shiver he wiped his hand on his coat and went up to bed.

II

In the brightness of the wintry sun next morning as it streamed over the breakfast table he laughed at his fears. There was an air of prosaic[13] wholesomeness about the room which it had lacked on the previous night, and the dirty, shriveled little paw was pitched on the sideboard[14] with a carelessness which betokened no great belief in its virtues.[15]

"I suppose all old soldiers are the same," said Mrs. White. "The idea of our listening to such nonsense! How could wishes be granted in these days? And if they could, how could two hundred pounds hurt you, Father?"

"Might drop on his head from the sky," said the frivolous Herbert.

"Morris said the things happened so naturally," said his father, "that you might if you so wished attribute it to coincidence."

"Well, don't break into the money before I come back," said Herbert as he rose from the table. "I'm afraid it'll turn you into a

---

11. **wardrobe:** a tall piece of furniture that serves as a closet.

12. **simian** (sĭm′ē-ən): monkey-like.

13. **prosaic** (prō-zā′ĭk): ordinary; commonplace.

14. **sideboard:** a piece of furniture used to store tablecloths and dishes.

15. **virtues:** powers.

---

mean, avaricious[16] man, and we shall have to disown you."

His mother laughed, and following him to the door, watched him down the road; and returning to the breakfast table, was very happy at the expense of her husband's credulity. All of which did not prevent her from scurrying to the door at the postman's knock, when she found that the post brought a tailor's bill.

"Herbert will have some more of his funny remarks, I expect, when he comes home," she said, as they sat at dinner.

"I dare say," said Mr. White, "but for all that, the thing moved in my hand; that I'll swear to."

"You thought it did," said the old lady soothingly.

"I say it did," replied the other. "There was no thought about it; I had just—What's the matter?"

His wife made no reply. She was watching the mysterious movements of a man outside, who, peering in an undecided fashion at the house, appeared to be trying to make up his mind to enter. In mental connection with the two hundred pounds, she noticed that the stranger was well dressed and wore a silk hat of glossy newness. Three times he paused at the gate, and then walked on again. The fourth time he stood with his hand upon it, and then with sudden resolution flung it open and walked up the path. Mrs. White at the same moment placed her hands behind her, and hurriedly unfastening the strings of her apron, put that useful article of apparel beneath the cushion of her chair.

She brought the stranger, who seemed ill at ease, into the room. He gazed at her furtively, and listened in a preoccupied fashion as the old lady apologized for the appearance of the room, and her husband's coat, a garment which he usually reserved for the garden. She waited patiently for him to broach his business, but he was at first strangely silent.

"I—was asked to call," he said at last, and stooped and picked a piece of cotton from his trousers. "I come from Maw and Meggins."

The old lady started. "Is anything the matter?" she asked breathlessly. "Has anything happened to Herbert? What is it? What is it?"

Her husband interposed. "There, there, Mother," he said hastily. "Sit down, and don't jump to conclusions. You've not brought bad news, I'm sure, sir"; and he eyed the other wistfully.

"I'm sorry—" began the visitor.

"Is he hurt?" demanded the mother wildly.

The visitor bowed in assent. "Badly hurt," he said quietly, "but he is not in any pain."

"Oh!" said the old woman, clasping her hands. "Thank goodness for that! Thank—"

She broke off suddenly as the sinister meaning of the assurance dawned upon her and she saw the awful confirmation of her fears in the other's averted face. She caught her breath, and turning to her slower-witted husband, laid her trembling old hand upon his. There was a long silence.

"He was caught in the machinery," said the visitor at length in a low voice.

"Caught in the machinery," repeated Mr. White, in a dazed fashion, "yes."

> **"Has anything happened to Herbert? What is it? What is it?"**

---

16. **avaricious** (ăv′ə-rĭsh′əs): greedy for wealth.

He sat staring blankly out at the window, and taking his wife's hand between his own, pressed it as he had been wont to do in their old courting days nearly forty years before.

"He was the only one left to us," he said, turning gently to the visitor. "It is hard."

The other coughed, and rising, walked slowly to the window. "The firm wished me to convey their sincere sympathy with you in your great loss," he said, without looking round. "I beg that you will understand I am only their servant and merely obeying orders."

There was no reply; the old woman's face was white, her eyes staring, and her breath inaudible; on the husband's face was a look such as his friend the sergeant might have carried into his first action.

"I was to say that Maw and Meggins disclaim all responsibility," continued the other. "They admit no liability at all, but in consideration of your son's services, they wish to present you with a certain sum as compensation."

Mr. White dropped his wife's hand, and rising to his feet, gazed with a look of horror at his visitor. His dry lips shaped the words, "How much?"

"Two hundred pounds," was the answer.

Unconscious of his wife's shriek, the old man smiled faintly, put out his hands like a sightless man, and dropped, a senseless heap, to the floor.

III

In the huge new cemetery, some two miles distant, the old people buried their dead, and came back to a house steeped in shadow and silence. It was all over so quickly that at first they could hardly realize it, and remained in a state of expectation as though of something else to happen—something else which was to lighten this load, too heavy for old hearts to bear. But the days passed, and expectation gave place to resignation—the hopeless resignation of the old, sometimes miscalled apathy. Sometimes they hardly exchanged a word, for now they had nothing to talk about, and their days were long to weariness.

It was about a week after that the old man, waking suddenly in the night, stretched out his hand and found himself alone. The room was in darkness, and the sound of subdued weeping came from the window. He raised himself in bed and listened.

"Come back," he said tenderly. "You will be cold."

"It is colder for my son," said the old woman, and wept afresh.

The sound of her sobs died away on his ears. The bed was warm, and his eyes heavy with sleep. He dozed fitfully, and then slept until a sudden wild cry from his wife awoke him with a start.

The paw!" she cried wildly. "The monkey's paw!"

He started up in alarm. "Where? Where is it? What's the matter?"

She came stumbling across the room toward him. "I want it," she said quietly. "You've not destroyed it?"

"It's in the parlor, on the bracket," he replied, marveling. "Why?"

She cried and laughed together, and bending over, kissed his cheek.

"I only just thought of it," she said hysterically. "Why didn't I think of it before? Why didn't *you* think of it?"

"Think of what?" he questioned.

"The other two wishes," she replied rapidly. "We've only had one."

"Was not that enough?" he demanded fiercely.

"No," she cried triumphantly; "we'll have one more. Go down and get it quickly, and wish our boy alive."

The man sat up in bed and flung the bedclothes from his quaking limbs. "You are mad!" he cried, aghast.

"Get it," she panted; "get it quickly, and wish—Oh, my boy, my boy!"

Her husband struck a match and lit the candle. "Get back to bed," he said unsteadily. "You don't know what you are saying."

"We had the first wish granted," said the old woman feverishly; "why not the second?"

"A coincidence," stammered the old man.

"Go and get it and wish," cried his wife, quivering with excitement.

He went down in the darkness, and felt his way to the parlor, and then to the mantelpiece. The talisman was in its place, and a horrible fear that the unspoken wish might bring his mutilated son before him ere he could escape from the room seized upon him, and he caught his breath as he found that he had lost the direction of the door. His brow cold with sweat, he felt his way round the table, and groped along the wall until he found himself in the small passage with the unwholesome thing in his hand.

Even his wife's face seemed changed as he entered the room. It was white and expectant, and to his fears seemed to have an unnatural look upon it. He was afraid of her.

"*Wish!*" she cried, in a strong voice.

"It is foolish and wicked," he faltered.

"*Wish!*" repeated his wife.

He raised his hand. "I wish my son alive again."

"WISH!"
SHE CRIED, IN A
STRONG VOICE.

The talisman fell to the floor, and he regarded it fearfully. Then he sank trembling into a chair as the old woman, with burning eyes, walked to the window and raised the blind.

He sat until he was chilled with the cold, glancing occasionally at the figure of the old woman peering through the window. The candle-end, which had burned below the rim of the china candlestick, was throwing pulsating shadows on the ceiling and walls, until, with a flicker larger than the rest, it expired. The old man, with an unspeakable sense of relief at the failure of the talisman, crept back to his bed, and a minute or two afterward the old woman came silently and apathetically beside him.

Neither spoke, but lay silently listening to the ticking of the clock. A stair creaked, and a squeaky mouse scurried noisily through the wall. The darkness was oppressive, and after lying for some time gathering up his courage, he took the box of matches, and striking one, went downstairs for a candle.

At the foot of the stairs the match went out, and he paused to strike another; and at the same moment a knock, so quiet and stealthy as to be scarcely audible, sounded on the front door.

The matches fell from his hand. He stood motionless, his breath suspended until the knock was repeated. Then he turned and fled swiftly back to his room, and closed the door behind him. A third knock sounded through the house.

"*What's that?*" cried the old woman, starting up.

"A rat," said the old man in shaking tones— "a rat. It passed me on the stairs."

Book of Hours: Winter (1985), Sabina Ott. Oil on canvas, 54" × 48". The Metropolitan Museum of Art, Edith C. Blum Fund, 1985. (1985.257ab) Photograph © 1995 The Metropolitan Museum of Art.

His wife sat up in bed listening. A loud knock resounded through the house.

"It's Herbert!" she screamed. "It's Herbert!"

She ran to the door, but her husband was before her, and catching her by the arm, held her tightly.

"What are you going to do?" he whispered hoarsely.

"It's my boy; it's Herbert!" she cried, struggling mechanically. "I forgot it was two miles away. What are you holding me for? Let go. I must open the door."

"Don't let it in," cried the old man, trembling.

"You're afraid of your own son," she cried, struggling. "Let me go. I'm coming, Herbert; I'm coming."

There was another knock, and another. The old woman with a sudden wrench broke free and ran from the room. Her husband followed to the landing, and called after her appealingly as she hurried downstairs. He heard the chain rattle back and the bottom bolt drawn slowly and stiffly from the socket. Then the old woman's voice, strained and panting.

"The bolt," she cried loudly. "Come down. I can't reach it."

But her husband was on his hands and knees groping wildly on the floor in search of the paw. If he could only find it before the thing outside got in. A perfect fusillade[17] of knocks reverberated through the house, and he heard the scraping of a chair as his wife put it down in the passage against the door. He heard the creaking of the bolt as it came slowly back, and at the same moment, he found the monkey's paw and frantically breathed his third and last wish.

The knocking ceased suddenly, although the echoes of it were still in the house. He heard the chair drawn back, and the door opened.

A cold wind rushed up the staircase, and a long loud wail of disappointment and misery from his wife gave him courage to run down to her side, and then to the gate beyond. The streetlamp flickering opposite shone on a quiet and deserted road. ❖

17. **fusillade** (fy$\overline{oo}$′sə-läd′): a rapid series of loud noises.

W. W. Jacobs
1863–1943

". . . one of the most permanently delightful short story writers who ever lived."

A Boy Among Boats William Wymark Jacobs grew up on the docks of London where his father worked. This early experience fed a lifelong interest in wharves, ships, and the people who sailed them. As a young man, Jacobs worked for the government while also writing stories. These stories soon made Jacobs a popular and respected author. In fact, one critic called Jacobs "one of the most permanently delightful short story writers who ever lived."

Ships and Shivers Many of W. W. Jacobs's stories are about the ships he knew so well. In fact, his first collection of stories, *Many Cargoes,* was about the sea. Jacobs also wrote 19 more books of sea stories and horror stories like the "The Monkey's Paw," which brought him great success.

Connect to the Literature

1. **What Do You Think?** Did you want Mrs. White to open the door? Explain your answer.

Comprehension Check
- How does Mr. White get the monkey's paw?
- What power is the monkey's paw supposed to have?
- What happens when Mr. White uses the monkey's paw?
- At the end of the story, why did the knocking stop so suddenly?

Think Critically

2. **ACTIVE READING** **SETTING PURPOSES** Review the notes you made in your **READER'S NOTEBOOK**. With a partner, discuss the similarities and differences in plot between the two stories.

3. In both stories, a man has his wish granted only to find that getting what he wants leads to terrible consequences. What are the two authors trying to tell us? What is the moral, or lesson, of each story?

4. **Connect to Life** The sergeant-major says that the fakir wanted to prove "that fate ruled people." Do you think that people have control over their lives? How much are we ruled by forces beyond our control? Explain your answer.

Literary Analysis

PLOT The sequence of events in a story is called **plot.** During the **rising action** of a plot, readers are often kept in a state of **suspense,** or growing tension. In "The Monkey's Paw," the author builds suspense by raising questions in readers' minds about what might happen. Descriptions of the story's setting also help slow down the action in order to build a sense of tension and suspense.

POINTS OF COMPARISON

Paired Activity Now that you've read both stories and studied their plots, work with a partner to compare and contrast the stories. Together, respond to the Points of Comparison questions from page 671. Use your discussion to help you complete your Comparison-and-Contrast chart.

	"The Third Wish"	"The Monkey's Paw"
Exposition	**Setting:** modern times; a forest **Tone:** sad **Characters:** Mr. Peters, the King of the Forest, Leita, Rhea	**Setting:** a house in England during the late 1800s **Tone:** sinister **Characters:** Mr. and Mrs. White and their son, Herbert; Sergeant-Major Morris
Main conflict	The wife that Mr. Peters wished for is not happy with her life.	Mr. White's first wish brings money, but also his son's death.
Rising action		
Climax		
How is the conflict resolved during the falling action?		

Writing

1. Story Moral Although the moral, or message, in "The Third Wish" is stated more directly, both of these stories teach a lesson. Think about the lesson taught by "The Monkey's Paw." Write a brief essay explaining the moral of this story. Be sure to support your main idea with quotations from the text and comparisons or analogies.

Writing Handbook

See p. R45: Explanatory Writing.

2. Warning Label Imagine you are giving someone either the leaves or the monkey's paw. Write directions for use and a warning label for either object. Be sure your instructions identify a sequence of activities and provide information on any other factors that might affect use of the object. Place your writing in your **Working Portfolio.** 🗂

Speaking & Listening

Video Adaptation As you watch the video of "The Monkey's Paw," compare the mood created in the video with that evoked in the story. Which did you find more powerful, the story or the video? Evaluate the ways the filmmaker chose to portray the scenes. How do the film images differ from the ones you imagined as you read the story? Discuss your responses with your classmates.

VIDEO: Literature in Performance

"The Monkey's Paw"

Research & Technology

Swans in Literature Swans often appear in folklore and literature. Read through several story collections, such as *Grimm's Complete Fairy Tales* or Jane Yolen's *Favorite Folktales from Around the World.* Are the swans that appear in these stories similar to Leita in "The Third Wish"? Do the stories about swans have something in common? After you have finished your research, write a brief essay that compares and contrasts two or more of the swan stories. Be sure to balance your original ideas with researched material. Support your conclusions with quotations, opinions from authorities, or comparisons and analogies.

ON THE AIR

PART 1

Reading the Prompt

In writing assessments, you will often be asked to compare and contrast two stories, like "The Third Wish" and "The Monkey's Paw." You are now going to practice writing an essay that involves this type of comparison.

> ### Write a Comparison-and-Contrast Essay
>
> Write a six-paragraph essay <u>comparing and contrasting</u> ❶ "The Third Wish" and "The Monkey's Paw." <u>Show</u> ❷ <u>similarities and differences</u> between the plots of the two stories. Support your ideas using <u>words and examples</u> ❸ from the stories. Compare the <u>moral</u> of the two stories. ❹

STRATEGIES IN ACTION

❶ I have to **compare** and **contrast** two stories.

❷ I have to show **similarities** and **differences** between the plots of the two stories.

❸ I need to use **words** and **examples** from the different stories.

❹ I need to compare the **moral,** or message, of the two stories.

PART 2

Planning a Comparison-and-Contrast Essay

- Review the Points of Comparison chart you began and completed on pages 671, 679, and 691.

- Create an outline, with main headings for the introduction, body, and conclusion.

- Using your chart, find examples of similarities and differences to use in the body of your essay.

I. Introduction
   A. The stories are both about men who are granted three wishes.
   B.
II. Body
   A.
   B.
   C.
III. Conclusion

PART 3

Drafting Your Essay

Introduction Clearly state your essay's main purpose—to compare and contrast the plots of stories with similar events and conflicts. Explain the similarities and differences that you have found in the two plots.

Body Begin by contrasting the stories' expositions,—that is, explain how each man got three wishes. Then describe the conflict, rising action, climax, and falling action of each story and compare them. Use your Points of Comparison chart for details and examples.

Conclusion End your essay with a strong statement about the stories' key similarities and differences in plot. Finally, compare the moral, or message, of the two stories. Refer again to your Points of Comparison chart for help in identifying these elements.

Revising Always indicate clearly which story you are discussing. Use sequence words such as *next* and *then* to keep plot events in order.

Writing Workshop

Examining the parts of a story . . .

From Reading to Writing What part of the story "The Tell-Tale Heart" did you like most? Did the mysterious atmosphere capture your attention? Perhaps the use of a first-person narrator made the story seem realistic and truthful. There are often many different elements at work in a story. **Analyzing a story** can help you examine these elements. This process involves looking at the work from a certain angle and exploring how the author creates certain effects.

For Your Portfolio

WRITING PROMPT Write an interpretation that focuses on one feature in a short story.

Purpose: To explain your interpretation
Audience: Your teacher, classmates, and others who are familiar with the work

---

Basics in a Box

Story Analysis at a Glance

Introduction
Introduces the story and includes a clear thesis statement that introduces the analysis

Body
Supports the analysis with evidence from the story

Evidence:

Details

Examples

Quotations

Conclusion
Summarizes the analysis

RUBRIC STANDARDS FOR WRITING

A successful analysis should

- identify the author and title and give a brief summary of the story
- show why the writer found the story interesting
- focus on one feature of the work
- present evidence from the text, including details, examples, quotations, or other evidence
- summarize the analysis in the conclusion

Analyzing a Student Model

SPEAKING OPPORTUNITY

See the Speaking and Listening Handbook, p. R104 for oral presentation tips.

**Brent Gilmore
Shepherd Middle School**

Mood in "The Tell-Tale Heart"

From the first line of his story "The Tell-Tale Heart" to the conclusion, Edgar Allan Poe creates suspense. The story's first-person narrator talks about an old man with whom he once lived—a man he believed had an evil eye. The narrator's fear of this eye leads him to murder the old man, even though he says he loves him. Then he buries parts of the old man's body in the house. Although he tries to hide this crime from others, he discovers that he cannot hide it from himself. Poe creates a feeling of suspense in three main ways: the style of his prose, the structure of the plot, and the sound device of a heart beating.

Poe creates suspense immediately by showing us what is going on in the narrator's mind. Poe's writing style is direct. Through his choice of first-person point of view, we can quickly see that something is wrong with the narrator: "True!—nervous—very, very dreadfully nervous I had been and am." The narrator says that he is not insane even as he describes killing the old man.

The structure of the story is interesting. Poe has the narrator discussing his murder plans at the beginning so that the reader can only wait to see how the narrator carries out the crime. Poe draws this section out slowly. Suspense builds as the reader witnesses the narrator preparing for murder. For seven nights, the narrator enters the old man's room. First, he sticks his head through the doorway: "It took me an hour to place my whole head within the opening so far that I could see him as he lay upon his bed." On the eighth night of creeping into the room, the narrator's thumb slips as he is opening the lantern, and it makes a noise. The man wakes up, but the narrator doesn't move a muscle. The narrator revels in the fear that the old man is experiencing: "Death, in approaching him, had stalked with his black shadow before him, and enveloped the victim." Finally, when he thinks the time has come, he smothers him.

Poe keeps readers on the edges of their seats throughout the story. The murder takes place halfway through the story, which is

RUBRIC
IN ACTION

❶ The first sentence identifies the title and author, and it tells the focus of the interpretation.

Other Option:
· Begin with a quote.

❷ Gives a brief summary of the story

❸ Writer mentions thesis statement and reveals the structure of the analysis.

❹ Paragraphs discuss how Poe's techniques— style and story structure—build suspense for the audience.

❺ Uses references to the text to support interpretation.

❻ First sentence notes the effect of the literary work on the audience.

unusual because there is still a large portion of the story left. The reader knows that there is something even more horrible than the old man's murder ahead. When the police arrive, tension builds. Because the narrator is so confident that there is no sign of his crime, he invites the police into the bedroom, the place where the old man is buried. The narrator even sets his chair over the spot where the body lies. This creates a feeling of suspense in the reader.

> ❼ Writer uses details of the story events to support the analysis.

The thumping of the old man's heart is another technique Poe uses. Originally, the narrator hears the heartbeat when he is about to murder the old man. It is not very loud, like the sound "a watch makes when enveloped in cotton," but it makes him more and more angry. The fact that he hears the sound, the narrator claims, means that he is not mad. It means that his senses are better than everyone else's. The heartbeat is the narrator's conscience nagging at him because he refuses to listen to reason—both when he is about to kill the old man and after. Sitting with the police officers, he tries to act normal. He can't, though, because he hears a faint ringing in his ears. As the sound of the heartbeat gets stronger, so does the suspense. The narrator realizes that he is hearing the old man's heartbeat, and he feels certain that the police must be able to hear it also. He does everything to try to drown out the noise. "Oh God! what *could* I do? I foamed—I raved—I swore. I swung the chair upon which I had been sitting, and grated it upon the boards, but the noise arose over all and continually increased." Soon he can no longer stand the tension. The narrator confesses to everything and shows the policemen where he hid the body.

> ❽ Use of a transition establishes the coherence of the essay's organization.

> ❾ Writer uses quotations to support the analysis.

Poe creates suspense from the beginning of the story to the end. The question is not who did the deed but how the narrator killed the old man. When that question is answered, the reader wonders whether the narrator will get away with his act. Then the suspense grows as the reader tries to see how long it will be before the narrator loses control. I liked this story because of the suspense but also because Poe tells the story from the killer's point of view. "The Tell-Tale Heart" is an example of how an author can use style, plot, and literary devices to build suspense for the readers and to show them what goes on in the mind of someone with such a dark secret.

> ❿ Explains why the writer found the story interesting

> ⓫ Summarizes the three methods by which Poe creates suspense

Writing Your Analysis

❶ Prewriting

*The answers you get from literature depend
upon the questions you pose.*
—Margaret Atwood, fiction writer and poet

Think about stories you have read. Write down memorable characters, events, moods, themes, and literary devices such as foreshadowing or flashback. Choose the story that you would like to write about. See the **Idea Bank** in the margin for more suggestions. After you have chosen a story to analyze, follow the steps below.

Planning Your Story Analysis

▸ **1. Reread the story.** Jot down ideas about character, setting, and plot as you read. Write down quotations that interest or puzzle you. Record your reactions to different parts of the story.

▸ **2. Exchange insights.** Discuss your views on the story with your classmates. Find out which elements struck them most.

▸ **3. Freewrite about the story.** Give yourself a few minutes to write down all of your thoughts and ideas about the story.

▸ **4. Choose a focus.** Look back over your notes, your discussion, and your freewriting. Which element stands out in all three activities? You can focus on plot, theme, character, or a confusing element or literary technique.

▸ **5. Gather evidence.** Find passages, examples, or other details in the text that will help you make your point about the element you have chosen.

❷ Drafting

Begin writing your analysis with the idea that you will revise it later. Try to include the following:

- In the **introduction,** state your focus and give a short summary of the story.

- In the **body,** explain your thoughts about the element you are analyzing, show how it affects the story, and insert quotations and examples to support your interpretation.

- In the **conclusion,** restate the most important ideas of your analysis.

IDEA Bank

1. For Your Working Portfolio 📁
Look for ideas in the **Writing** sections that you completed earlier.

2. Rapid Reactions
Choose a story that had a strong effect on you. Determine which element created this effect. Use this element as your subject.

3. Analyzing for Answers
Choose a story that confused you or that you didn't understand. Decide which element seemed most puzzling. Consider focusing on this element in your essay.

Have a question?

See the **Writing Handbook**
Analysis/Classification, p. R47
Options for Organization, p. R48
See **Language Network**
Prewriting, p. 314
Drafting, p. 317

Ask Your Peer Reader

- What title would you give my essay? Why?

- What part of my essay is the most important or interesting?

- Where do I need more evidence?

- What have you learned about the story?

SPELLING
From Writing

As you revise your work, look back at the words you misspelled and determine why you made the errors you did. For additional help, refer to the strategies and generalizations in the **Spelling Handbook** on page R28.

SPEAKING
Opportunity

Turn your analysis into an oral presentation.

Publishing
IDEAS

- Find other students who analyzed different elements of the same story. Present your analyses to the class.

- Create a literary journal. Feature student analyses in each edition.

 INTERNET

Publishing Options
www.mcdougallittell.com

❸ Revising

TARGET SKILL ▶ INCLUDING A BRIEF SUMMARY When you evaluate your story analysis, be sure you have a few sentences that summarize the story. Your summary should mention the main idea and the most important details of the plot. It is important not to make the summary of the story your entire essay.

> The story's first-person narrator talks about an old man with whom he once lived—a man he believed had an evil eye.
>
> ~~The narrator keeps looking at the eye. It makes his blood run cold. So one day he decides to kill the old man. He tries to kill him for seven nights and keeps looking in his room to see if the eye is open. On the eighth night, the narrator wakes the old man up. He takes the old man from bed and smothers him.~~
>
> *The narrator murders the old man in the house. Although he tries to hide the crime from others, he cannot hide it from himself.*

❹ Editing and Proofreading

TARGET SKILL ▶ MISPLACED PARTICIPIAL PHRASES A participial phrase is a group of words that acts like an adjective. A participial phrase must be placed near the noun or pronoun it modifies. For example, in the following sentence, notice how the participial phrase is incorrectly placed: *The child began to walk in the sun, trembling with cold.* The correct placement is *The child, trembling with cold, began to walk in the sun.* Make sure your participial phrases are placed correctly.

> The narrator eventually confesses to the police, hearing the heart.

❺ Reflecting

FOR YOUR WORKING PORTFOLIO What did you learn about the story through writing your analysis? What was the most challenging part of analyzing the story element? Attach your reflections to your finished essay. Save your story analysis in your **Working Portfolio.**

Standardized Test Practice

Mixed Review

As I read "The Girl in the Lavender Dress," I felt overwhelmed by fear. The story's structure <u>adds</u> to the horror of the tale. The first-person narrator is straightforward and honest. This helps the reader to <u>beleeve</u> her story. <u>She describes the setting beginning her story.</u> The incident <u>ocurred</u> in 1942 or 1943. <u>While driving along a dark road she and her</u> husband <u>noticing</u> a young girl.

(1) adds
(2) beleeve
(3) She describes the setting beginning her story.
(4) ocurred
(5) While driving along a dark road she and her
(6) noticing

Review Your Skills

Use the passage and the questions that follow it to check how well you remember the language conventions you've learned in previous grades.

1. What is the correct verb tense in sentence 1?

  A. add

  B. added

  C. adding

  D. Correct as is

2. What is the correct spelling in sentence 2?

  A. believe

  B. beleave

  C. beleve

  D. Correct as is

3. How is sentence 3 best written?

  A. Beginning her story, she describes the setting.

  B. She describes, beginning her story, the setting.

  C. Her story begins with a description of the setting.

  D. Correct as is

4. What is the correct spelling in sentence 4?

  A. occurred

  B. occured

  C. ocured

  D. Correct as is

5. How is item 5 best written?

  A. While driving, along a dark road, she and her husband

  B. While driving along, a dark road, she and her husband

  C. While driving along a dark road, she and her husband

  D. Correct as is

6. What is the correct verb tense in item 6?

  A. did notice

  B. notice

  C. have noticed

  D. Correct as is

Self-Assessment

Check your own answers in the **Grammar Handbook**

Verb Tenses and Forms, p. R84

Participial Phrases, p. R89

Strange Goings-On

The selections in this unit focus on the unusual and the unexpected. To further explore this type of writing and theme, complete one or more option in each of the following sections.

Reflecting on Theme

OPTION 1

Examining Endings Think about stories in this unit that had surprising or disturbing endings. Discuss the impact of these endings with a small group of classmates.

OPTION 2

Evaluating Reading Experiences Discuss the following questions with your classmates: How did you feel as you were reading these selections? Have you ever experienced strange events like those described in the stories? What strange event in your own life might make an interesting story?

OPTION 3

Thinking About Genre Choose four selections that you think were the most interesting or challenging, and write each selection title in the center of a concept web. Try to include an example of each major genre—fiction, nonfiction, poetry, and drama—among your choices. Complete the web for each selection by noting aspects of the writer's style, topic, characters, or events that you think captured the unit theme. Which genre do you think was most effective in conveying the theme? Explain your answer.

"Rain, Rain, Go Away"

The Sakkaros are caught in the rain.

REVIEWING YOUR PERSONAL WORD List

Vocabulary Review the new words you learned in this unit. If necessary, use a dictionary to check the meaning of each word.

Spelling Review your list of spelling words. If you're not sure of the correct spelling, use a dictionary or refer to the **Spelling Handbook** on page R28.

Reviewing Literary Concepts

Analyzing Informative Nonfiction Informative nonfiction is one category of nonfiction. It is written mainly to provide factual information. Find the selection in this unit that is an example of informative nonfiction. Identify the subject of the selection and list the most important facts about the topic that were included in the piece.

Creating a Ballad A ballad is a narrative poem that is meant to be sung. Ballads are usually about ordinary people; they are often written in four-line stanzas with regular patterns of rhythm and rhyme. With a partner, compose a ballad about an ordinary person.

Appreciating Suspense Look back through the selections in this unit and choose two works that you enjoyed. For each, write a paragraph explaining how the writer used suspense to build and keep your interest in either the plot or a character.

Self ASSESSMENT

READER'S NOTEBOOK

Ask your classmates to provide definitions or examples from selections in this unit to illustrate the meanings of the following terms. Then take a test created by one of your classmates. Refer to the **Glossary of Literary and Reading Terms** on page R124 for help.

- fantasy
- science fiction
- free verse
- surprise ending
- suspense
- descriptive details
- mood
- informative nonfiction
- ballad
- literary ballad
- folk ballad
- narrative poem
- rhyme scheme
- foreshadowing
- fable

Portfolio Building

- **Choices & Challenges—Writing** For some of the writing assignments in this unit you were asked to create a scene or setting. In which assignment was your writing most effective? Write a cover note explaining what you like best about it. Then add the piece to your **Presentation Portfolio.**

- **Writing Workshops** In this unit you wrote an essay analyzing a short story. Did you find the assignment difficult? Why or why not? Write a cover note explaining what you would do differently if you could do the assignment over. Then attach the note to your assignment and place it in your **Presentation Portfolio.**

- **Additional Activities** Go back through the assignments you have completed in **Speaking & Listening** and **Research & Technology.** In which assignment did you use a new source of information? What did you learn from using this resource? What other resources did you use to complete the assignments? What new skills have you learned?

Self ASSESSMENT

Organize the work in your **Presentation Portfolio** in a way that is not chronological—according to theme, type of activities, or effectiveness. Select the one that suits you best.

Setting GOALS

As you completed the reading and writing activities in this unit, you probably identified certain stories that you particularly liked. What kinds of stories would you like to read more of? What kinds of writing would you like to become more skillful at?

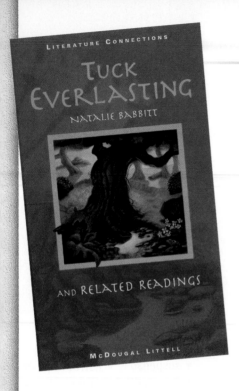

LITERATURE CONNECTIONS

TUCK
EVERLASTING
NATALIE BABBITT

AND RELATED READINGS

McDOUGAL LITTELL

LITERATURE CONNECTIONS
Tuck Everlasting

BY NATALIE BABBITT

This fantasy is about a meeting between a young girl and the Tucks, a family that never ages. Problems with a man who plans to market the spring water, which makes the Tucks live forever, result in an accident, difficulty with the law, and an exciting rescue. *Tuck Everlasting* won the American Library Association Notable Book Award and the Horn Book Honor.

These thematically related readings are provided along with *Tuck Everlasting*:

Remember
BY CHRISTINA ROSSETTI

Why There Is Death
BY JOHN BIERHORST

from **The Population Explosion**
BY JOHN AND SUE BECKLAKE

The Search for the Magic Lake
BY GENEVIEVE BARLOW

Eastside Chic with Drive
BY ALBERT SPECTOR

Hail and Farewell
BY RAY BRADBURY

Guardian Neighbor
BY LYNDA BARRY

More Choices

Aliens in the Family
BY MARGARET MAHY
Jake thinks of herself as an alien in her new family, until she meets a real alien.

Freaky Friday
BY MARY RODGERS
In a bizarre twist, Annabel discovers that she and her mother have switched bodies.

The Hound of the Baskervilles
BY ARTHUR CONAN DOYLE
A legend of a murder by an evil hound is entwined with a mysterious death.

The Westing Game
BY ELLEN RASKIN
In this story, a mystery surrounds the death of a millionaire.

The December Rose
BY LEON GARFIELD
Dreary Victorian London is the setting for this dark tale of murder and espionage.

Prophecy Rock
BY ROB MACGREGOR
Will, son of a Hopi tribal police chief, gets caught up in a murder investigation.

The House of Dies Drear

BY VIRGINIA HAMILTON

13-year-old Thomas moves into a big, old house in Ohio that is supposed to be haunted. The house was once an important stop on the Underground Railroad, and in it, he uncovers hidden passages, slave "treasure," and an unsolved mystery. This book won both the Coretta Scott King Award and the National Book Award.

These thematically related readings are provided along with *The House of Dies Drear*:

Haunted House
BY VALERIE WORTH

The House on the Island
BY WALTER B. GIBSON

from **Get on Board: The Story of the Underground Railroad**
BY JAMES HASKINS

When the Rattlesnake Sounds
BY ALICE CHILDRESS

Runagate Runagate
BY ROBERT HAYDEN

The Secret Room
BY WILLIAM M. DORR

Bound for Freedom
BY LAURA P. McCARTY

Social Studies Connection

Andrew Carnegie: The American Dream
BY JOHN S. BOWMAN
This is the true story of how a poor immigrant made millions in the railroad, telegraph, iron, and steel industries.

Lyddie
BY KATHERINE PATERSON
Thirteen-year-old Lyddie takes work in a Massachusetts textile factory to help support her family.

Voices After Midnight
BY RICHARD PEEK
Three children hear voices in the house their family has rented for the summer and are transported back to 1888 New York.

One Special Year
BY N. A. PEREZ
The chronicles of Jen and her family in upstate New York at the turn of the century.

Morse, Marconi, and You: Understanding and Building Telegraph, Telephone, and Radio Sets
BY IRWIN MATH
A guide to building popular nineteenth-century inventions.

Standardized Test Practice

Reading and Writing for Assessment

When you studied the test-taking strategies on pages 320–325, you learned helpful new techniques. The following pages will allow you to practice using these strategies and others.

PART 1 **How to Read the Test Selection**

Listed below are some basic reading strategies. By applying these strategies and by taking notes, you can identify the information you need to answer test questions.

STRATEGIES FOR READING A TEST SELECTION

▷ **Before you begin reading, skim the questions that follow the passage.** These can help focus your reading.

▷ **Think about the title and message.** What does it suggest about the overall message or theme of the selection?

▷ **Use your active reading strategies such as analyzing, predicting, and questioning.** If the test directions allow you to mark on the test itself, make notes in the margin as you read.

▷ **Look for main ideas.** These are often stated at the beginnings or ends of paragraphs. Sometimes they are implied, not stated. After reading each paragraph, ask, "What was this passage about?"

▷ **Note the literary elements and techniques used by the writer.** Consider the effects of word choice, figurative language, and mood.

▷ **Evaluate the organization.** For a comparison-and-contrast essay, how well does the use of feature-by-feature or subject-by-subject organization work in the piece?

▷ **Look for expert testimony.** What supporting evidence or sources of information does the writer use? Why are these sources appropriate to the subject?

▷ **Make judgments about the writer's purpose.** Does the writer have a bias or use a particular tone? How does this affect the message and presentation of information?

Reading Selection

❶ My Two Homes: Bosnia and the U.S.
   by Elvisa Pandzic

1   I arrived in Chicago's O'Hare International Airport in the summer of 1994. I remember that everyone was walking around in tank tops and shorts. There I stood in my winter coat, waiting to be cleared at ❷ customs. We had just come from Croatia, where I lived for one year. There it was still cold.

2   During the flight, I had been frightened. It was my first time on an airplane, and each time I looked out the window, I imagined the wing breaking off and falling into the sky. As the plane touched down, my younger sister grabbed my hand. This was the first day of our new life. The life we had known in Bosnia—the Bosnia before the war—would soon become a memory.

3   My family and I came to America because of the war in Bosnia. It was very hard to live there, so we went to Croatia, where I have an uncle. We filled out papers and had interviews. After some delay, we were allowed to come to America. I had to catch my breath when I first set eyes on Chicago. It was spectacular—like a dream, with its tall buildings and shiny cars. Everything was moving so fast! Still I often thought of Cazin, where I was born.

4   ❸ I missed the slow pace of small-town life. That and the lack of cars. Most people had no need to travel to a place they couldn't walk to. I especially missed the mountains and hills. Nothing can replace those big beautiful meadows and the forests that took your breath away with their wonderful green smells. My family and I lived with my grandma in a big two-story house. My grandfather, like most of the men in our town, built the house our family lived in. I felt very connected to the place. I even lived in a neighborhood where all the people had the last name Pandzic. When I walked down the street, people would say hello. ❹ Recently, I learned that the region I grew up in was considered one of the poorest in Europe, even before the war. I never knew it because I always felt so rich.

5   In Chicago, I do not see rolling hills, but there is a park across the street. I know only a few names of the people who live in my apartment building. I think it will probably

❶ Think about the title.

One Student's Thoughts
"The writer must have lived in both places. I wonder which she liked better."

❷ Use context clues to understand vocabulary.

One Student's Thoughts
"It seems like *customs* has something to do with being let into a new country."

❸ Examine the writer's tone.

One Student's Thoughts
"The writer speaks fondly of life in Bosnia. I think she misses it."

YOUR TURN
Why do you think the writer uses this tone when speaking about her first home?

❹ Make judgments about the writer's purpose.

One Student's Thoughts
"How was it possible that the writer didn't know her region was so poor? What made her feel so rich?"

YOUR TURN
Look for evidence in this selection to answer this question.

always seem odd to me that neighbors can live so close and not even know each other's names.

6   It often seems that people in America are trying to rush through their lives, just to get things over with. Sometimes I stop in the middle of the busy sidewalk. With the crowds whooshing past me, I feel like a pebble in a stream. In Bosnia, people take their time. No one would ever think, for instance, of drinking coffee in the car.

7   ❺ Another big difference is the school system. When I started school in Chicago I was very confused—all the rules were different. In Bosnia, schools are strict and students give their teachers a lot of respect. We used to stand up when a teacher entered the classroom and when we had to answer a question. In American schools, students may talk without even being called on. This is not entirely bad, in my opinion. I like how students can express themselves freely. Another thing that has taken some time getting used to is the grading system. In Bosnia, all the grades are given in numbers, not letters. In Bosnia a grade of A is equal to 5, B to 4, C to 3, D to 2, and F to 1. At least the dress code in my new school is almost the same as in Bosnia. In both places you can wear blue jeans to school.

8   I had new pressures at school, but my parents had their share of pressures at work. It is not easy to leave your job and start another one in a new country, especially when you are just learning the language. ❻ In Bosnia my mom was a professional cook at a very good restaurant. Now she is a housekeeper in a hotel. My dad was a truck driver in Bosnia. For the first several months after we arrived, he had to work as a valet. Only recently has he been able to work as a truck driver again. He is more satisfied now.

9   I have been living in Chicago for about two years and I am adjusting well, but I still miss Bosnia, my first home. I look forward to a time of peace when I can return. I know I will never return to my "old" life, but there is one thing I do know. Wherever I end up, I will celebrate the best of both worlds.

STRATEGIES
IN ACTION

❺ **Evaluate the writer's use of comparison and contrast.**

One Student's Thoughts
"The writer compares one feature in this paragraph—the school system in both countries."

YOUR TURN
How does this organization contribute to the writer's message?

❻ **Skim the questions that follow the passage.**

One Student's Thoughts
"There's a question about why the writer mentions her mother's job in Bosnia. Why does the writer include it?"

PART 2

How to Answer Multiple-Choice Questions

Use the strategies and notes in the side column to help you
answer the questions below and on the following pages.

Based on the selection you have just read, choose the best
answer for each of the following questions.

1. Why do you think the essay is titled "My Two Homes:
   Bosnia and the U.S."?
   A. The writer lives in both places at the same time.
   B. The writer will always remember Bosnia, but never
      return there.
   C. There is no difference between countries.
   D. The writer considers both countries her home.

2. Why does the writer begin with an anecdote?
   A. She wants to make the reader laugh.
   B. She wants the reader to relate to the feeling of
      alienation in a new country.
   C. She wants to hook the reader with a quotation.
   D. Personal anecdotes usually begin comparison essays.

3. What main idea does the writer support by mentioning
   that in Cazin, most people don't have cars?
   A. Cars are bad for the environment.
   B. Physical activity is more important in Bosnia.
   C. In Cazin, people move at a slower place.
   D. In Chicago, people get their exercise by walking,
      running, and hiking.

4. Why does the writer mention that her mother was a
   cook in a fancy restaurant in Bosnia?
   A. To impress readers
   B. To show that her life is harder now
   C. To show that cooking skills take years to develop
   D. All of the above

5. What is the MAIN REASON the writer felt connected
   to her house?
   A. Her grandfather built the house she lived in.
   B. She liked the rolling hills and meadows.
   C. Houses in Bosnia are better cared for.
   D. She had a larger bedroom in her old house.

STRATEGIES FOR ANSWERING
MULTIPLE-CHOICE QUESTIONS

▸ **Ask questions** that help you
  eliminate some of the choices.
▸ **Pay attention to choices** such as
  "all of the above" or "none of the
  above." To eliminate them, all
  you need to find is one answer
  that doesn't fit the choice.
▸ **Choose the one best answer.**
  More than one choice may be
  true, but only one will be true
  and answer the question
  completely.

STRATEGIES
IN ACTION

Choose the one best answer.

One Student's Thoughts
"All these answers might be true,
but this essay doesn't deal with
exercise in Chicago. *So I can
eliminate choice D.*"

YOUR TURN
*What other choices can you
eliminate?*

Pay attention to choices such as
"all of the above."

One Student's Thoughts
"The writer doesn't mention how
long it took her mother to learn to
cook. *So I can eliminate choice C.
That means that choice D—all of
the above—can't be right either.*"

YOUR TURN
*Which of the remaining choices
makes more sense?*

PART 3

How to Respond in Writing

You may be asked to write answers to questions about a reading passage. **Short-answer questions** usually ask you to answer in a sentence or two. **Essay questions** require a fully developed piece of writing.

Short-Answer Question

STRATEGIES FOR RESPONDING TO SHORT-ANSWER QUESTIONS

▸ **Identify key words** in the writing prompt that tell you the ideas to discuss.
▸ **State your response directly** and to the point.
▸ **Support your ideas** by using evidence from the selection.
▸ **Use correct grammar.**

> **Sample Question**
>
> Answer the following question in one or two sentences.
>
> What advantages does the writer's first-person point of view offer readers? How might the story be told more effectively from the third-person point of view?

Essay Question

STRATEGIES FOR ANSWERING ESSAY QUESTIONS

▸ **Look for direction words** in the writing prompt such as *essay, analyze, describe,* or *compare and contrast.*
▸ **List the points** you want to make before beginning to write.
▸ **Writing an interesting introduction** that presents your main point.
▸ **Develop your ideas** by using evidence from the selection that supports the statements you make. Present the ideas in a logical order.
▸ **Write a conclusion** that summarizes your points.
▸ **Check your work** for correct grammar.

> **Sample Prompt**
>
> The writer compares life in Bosnia and the United States. Write an essay in which you summarize these differences.

STRATEGIES
IN ACTION

Identify key words.

One Student's Thoughts
"The key words seem to be *advantages* and *point of view.* I'm supposed to compare the advantages of first- and third-person point of view."

YOUR TURN
What do first-person and third-person point of view mean?

Identify direction words.

One Student's Thoughts
"The key direction words are *essay* and *summarize.* This means that I'll have to discuss key features in a fully developed piece of writing."

YOUR TURN
What important points will you have to include in your essay?

How to Revise, Edit, and Proofread a Test Response

Here is a student's first draft in response to the writing prompt at the bottom of page 708. Read it and answer the multiple-choice questions that follow.

1	The writer grew up in Bosnia. Life is different there than
2	in Chicago. First of all, there are fewer tall buildings and
3	cars are fewer in Bosnia as well. She also felt more a part
4	of a community in her small town. In Bosnia, the school
5	systems are also different. Students raises their hands
6	when they want to speak. In the United States, students
7	express themselves freely. Finally, it is also harder to get
8	jobs in the U.S.

> **STRATEGIES** FOR REVISING, EDITING, AND PROOFREADING
>
> ▸ **Read the passage carefully.**
> ▸ **Note the parts that are confusing.** What types of errors might cause that confusion?
> ▸ **Look for errors** in grammar, usage, spelling, and capitalization. Common errors include:
> - sentence fragments
> - lack of subject-verb agreement
> - pronoun-antecedent problems
> - lack of transition words

1. What is the BEST way to combine the sentences in lines 1–2 ("The writer . . . Chicago.")?

   A. The writer grew up in Bosnia, so life is different than in Chicago.

   B. The writer grew up in Bosnia, where life is different than in Chicago.

   C. The writer grew up in Bosnia, and life is different than in Chicago.

   D. The writer grew up in Bosnia: Life is different from Chicago.

2. What is the BEST way to revise the sentence in lines 2–3 ("First of all . . . Bosnia as well.")?

   A. First of all, there are fewer tall buildings and cars in Bosnia.

   B. First of all, there are fewer tall buildings; and even cars are fewer in Bosnia.

   C. First of all, there are fewer in Bosnia.

   D. First of all, tall buildings and cars are few in Bosnia.

3. What is the BEST change, if any, to make to the verb in lines 5–6 ("Students raises . . . want to speak.")?

   A. Change the verb *raises* to *raising*.

   B. Change the verb *raises* to *raise*.

   C. Change the verb *raises* to *had raised*.

   D. Make no change.

America II, Diana Ong/SuperStock

American Voices

America is not

something if it consists of each of us.

It is something

only if it consists of all of us.

Woodrow Wilson
President of the United States

The Literature You'll Read

The Concepts You'll Study

Vocabulary and Reading Comprehension
Vocabulary Focus: Researching Word Origins
Paraphrasing
Fact and Opinion
Predicting
Questioning
Summarizing
Author's Purpose
Making Inferences About the Narrator
Visualizing

Writing and Language Conventions
Writing Workshop: Research Report
Forming Compound Sentences
Using Compound Sentences for Sentence Variety
Subordinate Clauses
Joining Main and Subordinate Clauses
Complex Sentences
Using Subordinating Conjunctions

Literary Analysis
Literary Focus: Reading History Through
    Literature
Narrative Poetry
Primary and Secondary Sources
Historical Fiction
Biography
Tone
Extended Metaphor
Exaggeration
Satire

Speaking and Listening
Oral Interpretation of a Poem
Presenting a Graph
Radio Drama
Oral Report
Speech Outline
Dramatic Reading
Evaluation of Video Portrayal

LEARNING the Language of *Literature*

Reading History Through Literature

History teaches everything, even the future.
—*Alphonse de Lamartine*

Have you ever imagined what it might have been like to live in North America before the Europeans arrived, or during the Revolutionary War? These times and places can be explored in a variety of **historical writings.** History is a subject not only for textbooks and nonfiction but for fiction, poetry, and drama as well.

Informative nonfiction about history provides factual accounts of past events, places, and people. **Historical fiction,** however, combines fact and fiction in a story set in the past. Like historical fiction, **poetry** and **drama** may also tell a historical event in a fictional story. Using these genres, a writer can present a new perspective on an event or person. Through the various types of historical writings, you can learn a great deal about a time in history.

From "Paul Revere's Ride"

History in Informative Nonfiction

Informative nonfiction about history presents factual information about past events, places, and people. The writer may have actually lived at that time or may live in the present and is explaining a past event or era. Informative nonfiction includes essays, articles, reference books, and autobiographical and biographical accounts. The example to the right provides factual details about its subject, President Lincoln.

History in Fiction, Poetry, and Drama

In historical fiction, poetry, and drama, the writer may use both real and fictional characters, dialogue, and events. A historical event may be the focus of the story. The setting is particularly important because it gives you clues about when and where the story takes place.

Historical fiction and **drama** include all the story elements of fiction: plot, character, setting, and theme. The author researches the historical period in order to provide accurate details of the events, people, and places.

History may also be written in poetry. **Narrative poetry** is a form that tells a story and includes a setting, plot, and characters. Narrative poetry can be used to tell a historic event or the deeds of a heroic historical figure.

YOUR TURN What do you learn about a historical event in this passage from "Paul Revere's Ride"?

Sources

For all types of historical writing, writers use sources to research the era, events, and people. A **primary source** is a firsthand account of an event or place. Diaries, autobiographies, interviews, and letters are all primary sources. A **secondary source** is an account of an event or place that is based on other sources. Biographies, textbooks, and historical fiction are types of secondary sources.

INFORMATIVE NONFICTION

Lincoln had been living with rumors of abduction and assassination ever since he was first elected. Threatening letters arrived in the mail almost every day. He filed them away in a bulging envelope marked ASSASSINATION.

—Russell Freedman,
Lincoln: A Photobiography

HISTORICAL POETRY

He said to his friend, "If the British march
By land or sea from the town to-night,
Hang a lantern aloft in the belfry arch
Of the North Church tower as a signal light,—
One if by land, and two if by sea;
And I on the opposite shore will be,
Ready to ride and spread the alarm
Through every Middlesex village and farm,
For the country folk to be up and to arm."

—Henry Wadsworth Longfellow,
"Paul Revere's Ride"

---

*P*araphrasing

Have you ever listened to someone speak, known that his or her message hadn't quite been understood, and said, "What he or she meant was . . ." If so, you were paraphrasing. Paraphrasing is restating a writer's ideas in your own words. You include the writer's most important ideas and leave out the unimportant ones. A paraphrase will generally be about the same length as the original. Rewriting the information will help you understand what you've read and may provide ideas for further research. As you read, use the strategies on this page to help you paraphrase.

How to Apply the Skill

To **paraphrase,** an active reader will:
- **Question** the main idea and supporting details
- **Clarify** the information
- Restate ideas in his or her own words
- Look for supporting evidence

Try It Now!

Read and paraphrase the excerpt below.

Jefferson assumed that, although the Sioux were said to be the fiercest and greatest of the tribes, they were "very desirous of being on the most friendly terms with us." That bit of wishful thinking led to Jefferson's direct order to Lewis. "On that nation," he commanded, referring to the Sioux, "we wish most particularly to make a favorable impression."

—Stephen E. Ambrose, *Undaunted Courage*

Here's how Jules uses the skill:

*"To help myself understand the passage, I **paraphrase,** or restate it. I include the same information—the main idea and supporting details—but I rewrite it in my own words. This is my paraphrase of the lines above. 'According to Jefferson, the Sioux were the Native Americans who were most threatening. He also believed that the Sioux wanted to be on friendly terms with the United States. So he ordered Lewis and Clark to be kind to them.'"*

Paul Revere's Ride

by HENRY WADSWORTH LONGFELLOW

Connect to Your Life

Patriotic Ideals During Paul Revere's time, people who favored American independence were called Patriots (as opposed to Loyalists, who supported the British king). Do you think patriotism is an old-fashioned idea, or is it a timeless concept—one that will never go out of fashion? Create a word web that shows what the word *patriotism* means to you.

Build Background

HISTORY

By 1775, many American colonists had begun to rebel against the British government's interference in their affairs. On the night of April 18, British troops left Boston to arrest the rebel leaders and to march on Concord to seize a stockpile of weapons that the colonists had been gathering. Hoping to warn the rebel leaders of the British advance, Paul Revere set off that night on a ride that would make him famous. "Paul Revere's Ride" describes the dramatic events that took place the night before the battles of Lexington and Concord, which marked the beginning of the Revolutionary War.

Focus Your Reading

LITERARY ANALYSIS   NARRATIVE POETRY

"Paul Revere's Ride" is an example of narrative poetry. **Narrative poetry** tells a story, or narrative, in poetic form. Like a work of prose fiction, a narrative poem has a **setting, characters,** and a series of related events called the **plot.** As you read the poem, keep track of the events that make up the plot.

ACTIVE READING   PARAPHRASING

When you restate a writer's ideas in your own words, you are **paraphrasing.** Paraphrasing can help you understand what you have read. Remember to include the writer's most important ideas and leave out the unimportant ones when you paraphrase.

📖 **READER'S NOTEBOOK** As you read "Paul Revere's Ride," try to paraphrase parts of the poem that are difficult to understand. Use a chart like the one below to help you.

Lines from Poem	Paraphrase
He springs to the saddle, the bridle he turns, / But lingers and gazes, till full on his sight / A second lamp in the belfry burns.	He jumps into the horse's saddle and waits until he sees the light of the second lamp.

Paul Revere's Ride

by Henry Wadsworth Longfellow

Listen, my children, and you shall hear
Of the midnight ride of Paul Revere,
On the eighteenth of April, in Seventy-five;
Hardly a man is now alive
5   Who remembers that famous day and year.

He said to his friend, "If the British march
By land or sea from the town to-night,
Hang a lantern aloft in the belfry arch[1]
Of the North Church tower as a signal light,—
10   One if by land, and two if by sea;
And I on the opposite shore will be,
Ready to ride and spread the alarm
Through every Middlesex[2] village and farm,
For the country folk to be up and to arm."

The Midnight Ride of Paul Revere (1931), Grant Wood. Oil on masonite, 30" × 40". The Metropolitan Museum of Art, Arthur Hoppock Hearn Fund, 1950 (50.117). Copyright © 1996 Estate of Grant Wood/Licensed by VAGA, New York. Photo copyright © 1988 The Metropolitan Museum of Art.

15   Then he said, "Good-night!" and with muffled oar
Silently rowed to the Charlestown shore,
Just as the moon rose over the bay,
Where swinging wide at her moorings[3] lay
The *Somerset*, British man-of-war;[4]
20   A phantom ship, with each mast and spar[5]
Across the moon like a prison bar,
And a huge black hulk, that was magnified
By its own reflection in the tide.

Meanwhile, his friend, through alley and street
25   Wanders and watches, with eager ears,
Till in the silence around him he hears
The muster of men at the barrack door,
The sound of arms, and the tramp of feet,

---

1. **belfry** (bĕl′frē) **arch:** a curved opening in a bell tower.
2. **Middlesex:** a county of eastern Massachusetts—the setting of the first battle of the Revolutionary War on April 19, 1775.
3. **moorings:** the place where a ship is docked.
4. **man-of-war:** warship.
5. **spar:** a pole supporting a ship's sail.

And the measured tread of the grenadiers,[6]
30 Marching down to their boats on the shore.

Then he climbed the tower of the Old North Church,
By the wooden stairs, with stealthy tread,[7]
To the belfry chamber overhead,
And startled the pigeons from their perch
35 On the somber[8] rafters, that round him made
Masses and moving shapes of shade,—
By the trembling ladder, steep and tall,
To the highest window in the wall,
Where he paused to listen and look down
40 A moment on the roofs of the town
And the moonlight flowing over all.

Beneath, in the churchyard, lay the dead,
In their night encampment on the hill,
Wrapped in silence so deep and still
45 That he could hear, like a sentinel's[9] tread,
The watchful night-wind, as it went
Creeping along from tent to tent,
And seeming to whisper, "All is well!"
A moment only he feels the spell
50 Of the place and the hour, and the secret dread
Of the lonely belfry and the dead;
For suddenly all his thoughts are bent
On a shadowy something far away,
Where the river widens to meet the bay,—
55 A line of black that bends and floats
On the rising tide like a bridge of boats.

Meanwhile, impatient to mount and ride,
Booted and spurred, with a heavy stride
On the opposite shore walked Paul Revere.
60 Now he patted his horse's side,
Now he gazed at the landscape far and near,
Then, impetuous,[10] stamped the earth,

---

6. **grenadiers** (grĕn´ə-dîrz´): foot soldiers.
7. **stealthy tread:** quiet footsteps.
8. **somber:** gloomy.
9. **sentinel's:** of a guard or sentry.
10. **impetuous** (ĭm-pĕch´o͞o-əs): acting suddenly, on impulse.

And turned and tightened his saddle girth;[11]
But mostly he watched with eager search
65 The belfry tower of the Old North Church,
As it rose above the graves on the hill,
Lonely and spectral[12] and somber and still.
And lo! as he looks, on the belfry's height
A glimmer, and then a gleam of light!
70 He springs to the saddle, the bridle he turns,
But lingers and gazes, till full on his sight
A second lamp in the belfry burns.

A hurry of hoofs in a village street,
A shape in the moonlight, a bulk in the dark,
75 And beneath, from the pebbles, in passing, a spark
Struck out by a steed flying fearless and fleet;
That was all! And yet, through the gloom and the light,
The fate of a nation was riding that night;
And the spark struck out by that steed, in his flight,
80 Kindled the land into flame with its heat.
He has left the village and mounted the steep,
And beneath him, tranquil and broad and deep,
Is the Mystic,[13] meeting the ocean tides;
And under the alders[14] that skirt its edge,
85 Now soft on the sand, now loud on the ledge,
Is heard the tramp of his steed as he rides.

It was twelve by the village clock,
When he crossed the bridge into Medford town.
He heard the crowing of the cock,
90 And the barking of the farmer's dog,
And felt the damp of the river fog,
That rises after the sun goes down.

It was one by the village clock,
When he galloped into Lexington.
95 He saw the gilded weathercock
Swim in the moonlight as he passed,

---

11. **saddle girth:** the strap attaching a saddle to a
    horse's body.
12. **spectral:** ghostly.
13. **Mystic:** a short river flowing into Boston Harbor.
14. **alders:** trees of the birch family.

And the meeting-house windows, blank and bare,
Gaze at him with a spectral glare,
As if they already stood aghast[15]
100   At the bloody work they would look upon.

It was two by the village clock,
When he came to the bridge in Concord town.
He heard the bleating[16] of the flock,
And the twitter of birds among the trees,
105   And felt the breath of the morning breeze
Blowing over the meadow brown.
And one was safe and asleep in his bed
Who at the bridge would be first to fall,
Who that day would be lying dead,
110   Pierced by a British musket-ball.

You know the rest. In the books you have read
How the British Regulars[17] fired and fled,—
How the farmers gave them ball for ball,
From behind each fence and farmyard wall,
115   Chasing the redcoats down the lane,
Then crossing the fields to emerge again
Under the trees at the turn of the road,
And only pausing to fire and load.

So through the night rode Paul Revere;
120   And so through the night went his cry of alarm
To every Middlesex village and farm,—
A cry of defiance, and not of fear,
A voice in the darkness, a knock at the door,
And a word that shall echo forevermore!
125   For, borne on the night-wind of the Past,
Through all our history, to the last,
In the hour of darkness and peril[18] and need,
The people will waken and listen to hear
The hurrying hoof-beats of that steed,
130   And the midnight message of Paul Revere.

---

15. **aghast** (ə-găst′): terrified.
16. **bleating:** the crying of sheep.
17. **British Regulars:** members of Great Britain's standing army.
18. **peril:** danger.

Connect to the Literature

1. **What Do You Think?** What part of the poem did you find most exciting?

Comprehension Check
- How does Revere find out which route the British troops will take?
- How many lamps are placed in the belfry?
- What happened later that day?

Think Critically

2. **ACTIVE READING** **PARAPHRASING**
   Go back to the notes you made in your **READER'S NOTEBOOK.** How did your paraphrasing chart help you understand the events in the poem?

3. "Paul Revere's Ride" is full of descriptive language that appeals to the senses. Which images do you find particularly striking? Why?

4. In "Paul Revere's Ride" there are several references to the past and the future. What is Longfellow saying about history?

   Think About:
   - why the poem is addressed to "my children"
   - why, in line 78, Longfellow writes that "The fate of a nation was riding that night"
   - the final stanza, in which Longfellow writes that Revere's ride will "echo forevermore . . . borne on the night-wind of the Past"

5. Longfellow wanted to emphasize the contrast between the peaceful night and the violence of the approaching Revolution. What images does Longfellow use to create a sense of "the calm before the storm"?

Extend Interpretations

6. **The Writer's Style** Choose a stanza from "Paul Revere's Ride" that you think creates a strong mood. How does that particular stanza make you feel? How do rhyme, rhythm, and figurative language help create the mood?

7. **Connect to Life** If you had to name a present-day figure with the patriotic spirit of Paul Revere, whom would you choose? Explain your choice.

Literary Analysis

NARRATIVE POETRY Like prose fiction, narrative poetry has a **setting, characters,** and a sequence of related events called the **plot.** During the part of the plot known as **exposition,** the author introduces a **conflict.** A plot's **rising action** refers to the events in a story that develop the conflict. The rising action usually builds to a **climax,** or turning point. After the climax comes the **falling action,** during which the conflict is resolved.

Paired Activity Working with a partner, go back through the poem and identify the events that make up the rising action, the climax, and the falling action. Fill in a chart like the one shown as you identify these plot elements.

SETTING: *April 18, 1775, in Massachusetts*
CHARACTERS: *Paul Revere, Revere's friend*
PLOT
Rising Action
Event: *Revere tells his friend to hang a lantern if the British march.*
Event: *He rows to Charlestown to await the signal to begin his ride.*
Event:
Climax
Event:
Falling Action
Event:

Writing

Narrative Poem With a partner, choose a famous event in United States history. Then write a narrative poem about the event, imitating the style of "Paul Revere's Ride." Place your poem in your **Working Portfolio.**

Speaking & Listening

Poetry Reading Take turns reading the poem aloud. First, choose a stanza or set of lines to read. When you have chosen your lines, plan how quickly or slowly, softly or loudly you will read these lines and which words you will emphasize. Rehearse your lines several times before reading them aloud. Use your voice, tone, and gestures to enhance the meaning of the poem.

Research & Technology

Whose Midnight Ride? Poet Henry Wadsworth Longfellow changed some of the factual details of Paul Revere's ride. Using the Internet and library sources, research the events of the night of April 18, 1775. What role did William Dawes play in the midnight ride? What role did Paul Revere play? Prepare a report to present to the class.

INTERNET Research Starter
www.mcdougallittell.com

Art Connection

In the painting entitled *Midnight Ride of Paul Revere* on page 717, artist Grant Wood shows Paul Revere on the night of the famous ride. What does the painting's contrast of the moonlit town with the darkness ahead suggest about Paul Revere's ride?

Henry Wadsworth Longfellow
1807–1882

"What a writer asks of his reader is not so much to like as to listen."

A Gifted Young Man Henry Wadsworth Longfellow was born in Portland, Maine. When he was only 14 years old, he was accepted at Bowdoin, a college in his native state. By the time Longfellow graduated from Bowdoin he had published nearly 40 poems. Fluent in several languages and an outstanding translator, he became the college's first professor of modern languages.

World Fame Longfellow devoted his early career to teaching, writing, and translating. He traveled extensively in Europe and returned to the United States to teach at Harvard University. Longfellow's poetry explored many American themes. Works such as *The Song of Hiawatha* and *Tales of a Wayside Inn* brought American history to the attention of readers at home and abroad.

AUTHOR ACTIVITY
A Tale to Tell Longfellow is the author of several other narrative poems, including *The Courtship of Miles Standish* and *Evangeline: A Tale of Acadie.* Find one of these poems in the library. Describe the poem's plot, characters, and setting. How does the poem compare with "Paul Revere's Ride"? Which do you like better and why?

from **Undaunted Courage**

by STEPHEN E. AMBROSE

Connect to Your Life

The Journey of Lewis and Clark The book *Undaunted Courage* is based on the journals of Meriwether Lewis and William Clark, who led an expedition west of the Mississippi in 1804. What do you know about Lewis and Clark? What do you want to know? Fill in the first two columns of the chart. You will fill in the third column after you read the selection.

What I Know	What I Want to Know	What I Learned
Led an expedition west of the Mississippi in 1804		

Build Background

HISTORY

In 1803, President Thomas Jefferson purchased the Louisiana Territory from France. The purchase extended the western frontier of the United States beyond the Mississippi River to the Rocky Mountains.

The next year, Jefferson sent a group to explore the northwestern part of the territory and the land that lay beyond. He chose Meriwether Lewis to lead the group. Lewis invited his friend Lieutenant William Clark to join him. The members of the group became the first U.S. citizens to travel from the Mississippi River to the Pacific Coast. The journey covered thousands of miles and took two and a half years.

WORDS TO KNOW **Vocabulary Preview**

delegation	perspective	sovereignty
expedition	precedent	specimen
fauna	prudence	
flora	quintessential	

Focus Your Reading

LITERARY ANALYSIS **PRIMARY AND SECONDARY SOURCES**

The journals of Lewis and Clark are examples of **primary sources,** firsthand accounts of events. When Ambrose wrote *Undaunted Courage,* he used information from those journals as well as from **secondary sources.** Secondary sources present information compiled from or based on other sources.

As you read the excerpt from *Undaunted Courage,* look for references to the journals of Lewis and Clark. How are these references set off from the rest of the text?

ACTIVE READING **FACT AND OPINION**

When reading primary and secondary sources, it is important to distinguish between **facts**—statements that can be proved—and **opinions,** which are a writer's feelings and beliefs.

READER'S NOTEBOOK In *Undaunted Courage* Stephen Ambrose includes his own opinions along with those of Meriwether Lewis and President Thomas Jefferson. He also includes facts. As you read the selection, record any facts and opinions that you come across.

FROM UNDAUNTED COURAGE

BY STEPHEN E. AMBROSE

As the men laboriously moved the keelboat[1] upriver, Lewis, in the cabin, weighed and measured and examined and recorded. He took his responsibilities seriously, but he had a lot of fun doing it, and he had a never-flagging sense of wonder and delight at seeing something new.

View From Floyd's Grave, 1300 Miles Above St. Louis (1832), George Catlin. Oil on canvas, 11¼" × 14½". National Museum of American Art, Smithsonian Institution, Washington D.C./Art Resource, N.Y.

On August 8, one of the bowmen called back to Lewis, who was working in the cabin. The captain looked up to see a blanket of white coming down the river. He went to the bow to stare down into the water. The keelboat and the white whatever-it-was came together. On close examination it turned out to be a sea of white feathers, over three miles long and seventy yards wide.

The boat rounded a bend. Ahead was a large sandbar at the foot of a small island. It was entirely covered with white pelicans, preening themselves in their summer molt.[2]

To Lewis, the number of birds was "in credible; they apeared to cover several acres of ground." The mosquitoes were so thick that he could not keep them out of his eyes to take an aimed shot, so he fired his rifle at random into the mass and collected a <u>specimen</u>, which he then weighed, measured, and described. He was astonished to find that the pouch could hold five gallons of water.

The white pelican was not new to science. Lewis had not seen one before, but he knew enough about it to call it a "bird of clime" that wintered "on the coast of Floriday and the borders of the Gulph of mexico." That knowledge came from book learning; he had never been to Florida or the Gulf of Mexico.

On August 12, at 5:00 P.M., what Clark called a "Prairie Wolf" appeared on the bank and barked at the passing keelboat. The captains had not previously seen this animal, or read anything about it, so they went ashore to collect a specimen. But, Clark sadly noted, "we could not git him."

The animal was a coyote. Lewis and Clark were the first Americans to see one. The captains set a <u>precedent</u>; millions of Americans who came after have also failed in their attempt to kill the coyote.

On August 18, while waiting for an Indian <u>delegation</u> to approach, Lewis took twelve soldiers to a fishing pond used by the Otoes. The party caught 490 catfish and upward of three hundred fish of nine other species.

---

1. **keelboat:** a kind of large boat formerly used for carrying freight on rivers.
2. **molt:** shedding of feathers.

WORDS TO KNOW
specimen (spĕs′ə-mən) *n.* an individual that is taken to represent a group or whole
precedent (prĕs′ĭ-dənt) *n.* an event that serves as an example for later actions
delegation (dĕl′ĭ-gā′shən) *n.* a group of people selected as representatives

William Clark, by Charles Willson Peale. Courtesy of Independence National Historical Park, Philadelphia, Pa.

WILLIAM CLARK

deer and elk and beaver and other species in numbers scarcely conceivable. That afternoon, Lewis sent Private Joseph Field on a hunt. A few hours later, Field came rushing down the bluff to the bank and hollered out to the boat to come ashore. When it did, he breathlessly announced that he had killed a buffalo.

The buffalo was the quintessential animal of the North American continent, the symbol of the Great Plains, more than any other animal save the beaver the magnet that drew men to the West. It was not new to science, but of the men of the expedition only the French voyagers had previously seen one. Lewis immediately detailed twelve men to accompany him to the site of the kill to bring the carcass back to the river. That night, for the first time, the party dined on buffalo hump, buffalo tongue, buffalo steaks. Next to the tail of the beaver, buffalo hump and tongue at once became the meat of choice.

In the Garden of Eden, man had but to reach out for his food. So too on the Great Plains, as Clark's birthday menu demonstrated. But this Garden of Eden was also a potential battlefield populated by numerous Indian tribes containing thousands of warriors. As a result, in addition to being a fabulous field for the botanist and naturalist, the Plains were also a challenging field for the soldier, the peacemaker, the ethnologist,[5] and the businessman.

> **ACTIVE READER**
>
> **QUESTION** Why does Ambrose describe the Great Plains as a Garden of Eden?

Beyond flora and fauna, Lewis studied and described the soil and minerals of the area. He was not so good a mineralogist as a botanist.[3] One mineral experiment almost cost him his life. On August 22, along with some copperas and alum he found a substance that appeared to be arsenic or cobalt. Clark recorded, "Capt. Lewis in proveing the quality of those minerals was near poisoning himself by the fumes & taste" of the unknown substance. Lewis took some of Rush's pills to "work off the effects of the Arsenic."

By August 23, the expedition was almost at the ninety-eighth meridian,[4] the generally agreed-upon eastern border of the Great Plains of North America. The sense of being in a Garden of Eden was strong. There were fat

---

3. **botanist** (bŏt′n-ĭst): a scientist who studies plants.
4. **the ninety-eighth meridian** (mə-rĭd′ē-ən): 98 degrees west longitude.
5. **ethnologist** (ĕth-nŏl′ə-jĭst): a scientist who studies the characteristics of human cultures.

WORDS
TO
KNOW

flora (flôr′ə) *n.* plants, especially those characteristic of a particular region
fauna (fô′nə) *n.* animals, especially those characteristic of a particular region
expedition (ĕk′spĭ-dĭsh′ən) *n.* a group of people making a journey with a specific purpose
quintessential (kwĭn′tə-sĕn′shəl) *adj.* most typical or characteristic

MERIWETHER LEWIS

These tribes were virtually unknown except to a handful of British and French fur traders. There were many stories and rumors about them, most of all the Sioux, but little solid fact.

Jefferson and Lewis had talked at length about these tribes, on the basis of near-complete ignorance. They speculated that the lost tribe of Israel could be out there on the Plains, but it was more likely, in their minds, that the Mandans were a wandering tribe of Welshmen. Because they subscribed to such odd ideas, Jefferson's instructions to Lewis on how to deal with the tribes were, in most particulars, hopelessly naïve and impossible to carry out. For example, Jefferson assumed that, although the Sioux were said to be the fiercest and greatest of the tribes, they were "very desirous of being on the most friendly terms with us." That bit of wishful thinking led to Jefferson's direct order to Lewis. "On that nation," he commanded, referring to the Sioux, "we wish most particularly to make a favorable impression."

In general, Jefferson wanted Lewis to inform the tribes that the new father intended to embrace them into a commercial system that would benefit all involved, and that to make this happen the new father wished them to make peace with one another. Lewis's objectives, as given to him by Jefferson, were to establish American sovereignty, peace, and a trading empire in which the warriors would put down their weapons and take up traps.

Jefferson recognized that the possibility of resistance to this program existed, meaning there was a possibility that the Sioux, or some other, unknown tribe, would attempt to stop the expedition. Jefferson knew too that Lewis was, like other army officers of his day, extremely sensitive to perceived threats or slights, and he had reason to suspect that Lewis inclined more toward rashness than prudence. That was why Jefferson specifically ordered Lewis to avoid a fight if at all possible.

This brought back some realism to the commander-in-chief's orders. Relations with the Indians were important, establishing commercial ties with them was desirable, but the *sine qua non*[6] of the expedition was to get

---

6. *sine qua non* (sĭn′ ĭ kwä nŏn′): essential element.

Compass carried
by William Clark during
the expedition to the Pacific Coast,
1804. Collection of the Smithsonian Institution,
Washington, D.C.

to the Pacific and return with as much information as possible. Put more bluntly, Lewis's first objective was to get through, and whatever he had to sacrifice to do it would be sacrificed. That was why the standard of discipline was so high, why there was a cannon on a swivel on the bow of the keelboat, and blunderbusses[7] on the stern and on the canoes. Jefferson, Lewis, Clark, everyone involved hoped that they would not be needed, but all were prepared to use them if necessary.

To avoid fighting and to promote commerce, Lewis had made a major effort to select gifts for the Indians. In Philadelphia in the spring of 1803 and in St. Louis in the winter of 1803–4, he had purchased beads, brass buttons, tomahawks, axes, moccasin awls, scissors, mirrors, and other wonders of the early industrial revolution. On Jefferson's direct orders, he had lugged along two corn grinders, presumably to teach the tribes how to make grits.

Lewis and Clark scholar James Ronda puts perspective on the Indian policy of the expedition: "These items, everything from ivory combs to calico shirts, represented what the United States offered to potential

trading partners. As Jefferson repeated to every delegation of western Indians, Americans sought commerce, not land. Lewis and Clark were on the road to show American wares. The expedition was the mercantile and hardware display case for a trade empire on the move. Moccasin awls and brass kettles were as much symbols of American power as the medals and flags destined for headmen and warriors. . . Lewis and Clark, surrounded by bright mirrors and yards of red flannel, offered more than goods. They proposed membership in a system with well-established posts and dependable delivery schedules."

The most desired items of all were rifles, balls, and powder. Most of the Indian-held guns on the Plains were cheap British shotguns. Lewis wanted to show the overall excellence of the American arms industry, but because of the bulk he could not carry along free samples. He could demonstrate what his men could do with a Kentucky long rifle, but he could only promise, not deliver, similar weapons for the Indians.

The presents, trade goods, certificates, medals, and the rest were packed into twenty-one bags, each containing a variety of items and each marked for one of the various tribes Lewis expected to encounter before going into winter camp. They began with the Poncas and Omahas, tribes of the lower Missouri, and went on to the Mandans. Five bales were stuffed with goods for the tribes beyond the Mandans.

Thus armed with his orders, guns, and goods, Lewis set out to meet the Indians of the Great Plains. ❖

---

7. **blunderbusses:** short muskets with wide muzzles.

THE FLOWER-FED BUFFALOES

by Vachel Lindsay

The flower-fed buffaloes of the spring
In the days of long ago,
Ranged[1] where the locomotives sing
And the prairie flowers lie low:—
5 The tossing, blooming, perfumed grass
Is swept away by the wheat,
Wheels and wheels and wheels spin by
In the spring that still is sweet.
But the flower-fed buffaloes of the spring
10 Left us, long ago.
They gore[2] no more, they bellow no more,
They trundle[3] around the hills no more:—
With the Blackfeet, lying low,
With the Pawnees, lying low,
15 Lying low.

1. **ranged:** wandered; roamed.
2. **gore:** stab with their horns.
3. **trundle:** move heavily and clumsily.

Below Zero (1993), John Axton. Oil on canvas, 30" × 40", courtesy of Ventana Fine Art, Santa Fe, New Mexico.

Connect to the Literature

1. **What Do You Think?**
Would you have
liked to have had
Meriwether Lewis
as your friend?
Why or why not?

Comprehension Check
- In this selection, what part of
North America are Lewis and
Clark about to explore?
- In what areas of study
does Lewis engage during
the journey?
- What is the "first objective"
of the expedition?

Think Critically

2. Look up the meaning of the word *undaunted* in a
dictionary. Do you think that Meriwether Lewis had
"undaunted courage" when he made this journey?
Explain your answer.

3. **ACTIVE READING** **FACT AND OPINION**
Look at the opinions and facts that you recorded in
your **READER'S NOTEBOOK**. How do the opinions
add to the factual information in the text? What would
the text be like without these opinions?

4. Based on this account, what kind of person do you
think Meriwether Lewis was?

   Think About:
   - his knowledge and skills
   - his attitude toward his work
   - his leadership ability

5. Does writer Stephen Ambrose admire Meriwether
Lewis? Support your answer with details from the text.

Extend Interpretations

6. **Different Perspectives** In this selection President
Thomas Jefferson refers to himself as the "new father"
of the Great Plains Native Americans. What does this
tell you about the way Jefferson viewed Native
Americans? How might a Native American of the time
have felt about this view? Explain your answer.

7. **Connect to Life** What did you learn about the journey
of Lewis and Clark from reading this selection? Would
you have liked to have made this journey with them?
Why or why not?

Literary Analysis

PRIMARY AND SECONDARY SOURCES

In writing *Undaunted Courage*,
Stephen Ambrose relied on
information found in both
primary and secondary sources.
A **primary source** is a firsthand
account of an event. The journals
of Lewis and Clark are examples
of primary sources. A **secondary
source** presents information
compiled from or based on other
sources. *Undaunted Courage* is
itself a secondary source.

Paired Activity Stephen
Ambrose and other historians
use primary sources when they
write secondary sources. With a
partner, discuss the advantages
and disadvantages of each type
of source. Would you rather read
the journals of Lewis and Clark,
or would you rather read
Stephen Ambrose's book about
Lewis and Clark? Explain your
reasons.

Writing

Report on the Republican Party
President Thomas Jefferson and Meriwether Lewis had much in common. For example, both belonged to the Republican Party. What did the Republican Party stand for in the early 1800s? What does the Republican Party of 1800 have in common with the Republican or Democratic Party of today? Write a brief report. Support your conclusions with analogies, paraphrases, quotations, opinions from authorities, and comparisons. Put the report in your **Working Portfolio.**

Writing Handbook
See p. R45: Explanatory Writing.

Speaking & Listening

Buffalo Graph Research the history of the buffalo (American bison). Make a graph showing the number of buffalo alive in 1804, the number alive around 1900, and the number alive today. Write a caption for the graph with information about the buffalo and its fate. Present the information to your class.

Research and Technology Handbook
See p. R120: Using Visuals.

Research & Technology

A Modern Journey Lewis and Clark explored the lands west of the Mississippi River. When they made their famous journey from 1804 to 1806, the frontier they explored was known as the Louisiana and Oregon territories. Find out what that area of the country is like today. What states make up the lands that Lewis and Clark explored? Use library resources or the Internet to help you write a brief report.

Reading *for* INFORMATION
Read "Bike a Historic Trail" on pages 733–736 to help prepare for your report.

Research and Technology Handbook
See p. R114: Getting Information Electronically.

Vocabulary

EXERCISE: MEANING CLUES Answer the following questions.

1. Who would be more likely to study a **specimen,** a lawyer or a scientist?
2. Would having a **precedent** make you feel more or less confident about trying something new?
3. Would you expect to see a **delegation** in a video arcade or at a conference?
4. Would you expect to find **flora** in a forest or in a library?
5. Would you expect to find **fauna** in a zoo or in a hospital?
6. Would the people on an **expedition** be more likely to start a farm or make a discovery?
7. Was the buffalo the **quintessential** animal of North America because it appeared in large groups or because it was typical of animals on the Great Plains?
8. Would establishing America's **sovereignty** strengthen or weaken the country?
9. Would you expect a person of **prudence** to rush off on a journey or prepare for it carefully?
10. Does **perspective** help you understand a situation or make it more complicated?

Vocabulary Handbook
See p. R20: Context Clues.

Grammar in Context: Forming Compound Sentences

A **compound sentence** consists of two or more simple sentences joined by a comma and a coordinating conjunction—*and, but,* or *or.* The following sentence from *Undaunted Courage* is an example of a compound sentence.

> He took his responsibilities seriously, **but** he had a lot of fun doing it, **and** he had a never-flagging sense of wonder and delight at seeing something new.

The words in red are coordinating conjunctions that join three simple sentences. What are the three simple sentences?

Apply to Your Writing Use compound sentences to show the relationship between ideas and to pair items for emphasis.

WRITING EXERCISE Use *and, but,* or *or* to combine each pair of sentences to form a compound sentence.

Example: *Original* A blanket of white wafted down the river. The captain ran to the bow.

Rewritten A blanket of white wafted down the river, and the captain ran to the bow.

1. The boat sailed into the sea of white. The captain realized that it was a sea of feathers.
2. The boat rounded a bend. The explorers saw a large sandbar ahead.
3. Lewis wanted to shoot. The mosquitoes were too thick.
4. The white pelican was not new to science. Lewis had not seen one before.

Grammar Handbook
See p. R75: Writing Complete Sentences.

Stephen E. Ambrose
born 1936

"This book has been a labor of love."

Turning Point Stephen Ambrose grew up in a small town in Wisconsin. At the age of 18, he entered the University of Wisconsin, where he met a professor who changed his life. The professor asked the class to "make a contribution to the world's knowledge" by doing original research for a term paper. At that instant, Ambrose knew that he wanted to devote his life to contributing to the world's knowledge.

Grade-A Historian Ambrose has realized his dream. Since college, he has written many best-selling books about American history, especially military history. Three of his books on military history served as the basis for Steven Spielberg's movie *Saving Private Ryan*. Ambrose has also been a professor of history at the University of New Orleans.

AUTHOR ACTIVITY
Adventurer and Family Man In the library, find a copy of *Undaunted Courage* and read the introduction on pages 13–15. What adventure did Ambrose and his wife embark on in the spring of 1976? What impact did the adventure have on the writing of this book?

Source: *Boys' Life*

Bike
A HISTORIC TRAIL

★ BY DENNIS COELLO

Almost 200 years ago, two brave explorers led an expedition through the untamed wilderness of northern America in an effort to explore the headwaters of the Missouri River and find a land route to the Pacific Ocean by way of the Columbia River. In 1978 Congress established the Lewis and Clark National Historic Trail. It allows visitors today to retrace portions of this historic path by car, boat, horseback, foot, and bicycle.

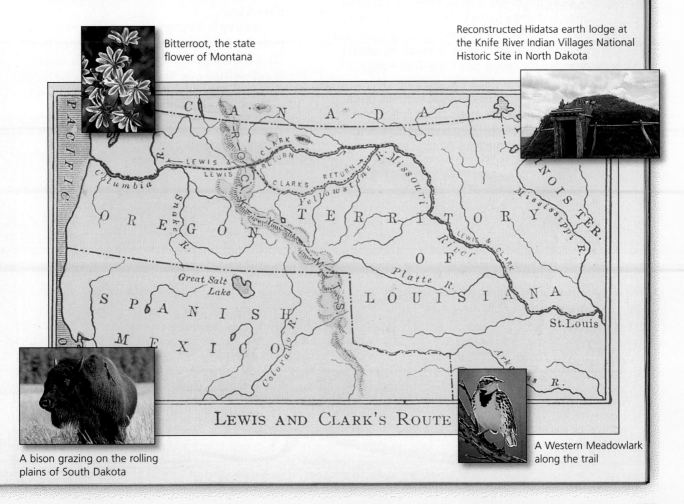

Bitterroot, the state flower of Montana

Reconstructed Hidatsa earth lodge at the Knife River Indian Villages National Historic Site in North Dakota

A bison grazing on the rolling plains of South Dakota

A Western Meadowlark along the trail

LEWIS AND CLARK'S ROUTE

①

"Set out at 4 o Clock P.M. . . . and proceeded on under a jentle brease up the Missourie . . ."
—William Clark, May 14, 1804

With these words began the famous expedition of explorers Meriwether Lewis and William Clark into the wild Northwest.

Starting near St. Louis, they followed the Missouri River to Montana, crossed the Rockies in Idaho and raced to the Pacific on the roaring Columbia River. They endured grizzly bears, hostile natives, treacherous waters, and starvation. And their names went down in history.

Exactly 175 years later, I traced that same historical route by bicycle. I had cycle-toured many times before in many exotic places. But never did I enjoy cycling as much as when I pedalled the Lewis and Clark Trail—after carefully researching the route's history.

Our nation is crisscrossed with historical trails and routes of many kinds. Indians, Spanish explorers, French voyageurs, and brave pioneers pushing through the wilderness all left trails as a part of their legacy. Some became famous, such as the Oregon, Santa Fe, California and Pony Express trails.

②

On any bike trip, you'll enjoy the exercise, the scenery, and the people you meet. But follow an historic trail, reading the explorer's journal in your tent at night, and you'll be transported across centuries. Often, you'll discover that their journey was similar to yours. They endured the same hot sun, cold winds, hard rains and fearsome insects.

As I pedaled the Lewis and Clark Trail, I knew exactly what Lewis meant when he noted in his journal, "Muskeetors veery troublesom."

One day in Montana, a cactus needle punctured my rear tire. That night I read in Clark's journal: "My feet is very much brused & cut walking over the flint & constantly stuck full of Prickley pear thorns." (Lewis and Clark weren't known for their spelling.)

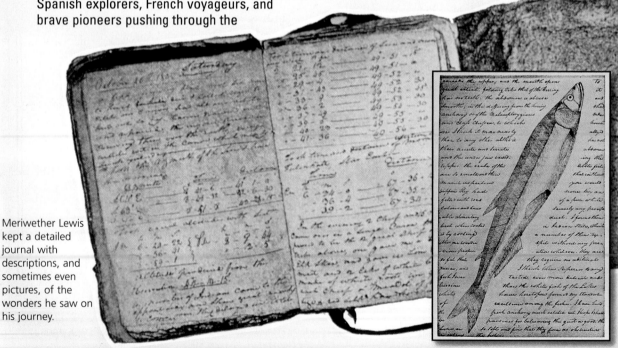

Meriwether Lewis kept a detailed journal with descriptions, and sometimes even pictures, of the wonders he saw on his journey.

Near the Rockies, I was overrun by a storm which pushed me off the road and made setting up camp a nightmare. But reading of the weather endured by Lewis and Clark in this same area somehow made it easier for me.

Half the fun of such a trip is the research you do before you leave. I studied maps, books, articles and diaries. Librarians helped me find some of what I needed, but I also sought help from local historical societies (which sometimes have special libraries of their own), museums, park rangers, and state and local offices of tourism.

Once I started reading Lewis and Clark's journals, I got interested in frontier medicine, Indian history and all the battles that had happened near the trail in the years since their expedition.

You'll have to become part detective to ferret out all the information available. One of the most important things is choosing the route itself. Compare the historical maps you find with the modern road maps. Figure out which roads are nearest the original trails.

To really enhance your trip, take the extra step of studying more detailed maps, such as topographic and county maps. These will reveal the smaller, quieter roads which are safer to pedal than major highways—yet still near the original route.

Write to local bike clubs for advice on roads in their area. Some automobile clubs that your parents may belong to might be able to help plan your route too.

Since my Lewis and Clark ride, I've followed all or portions of a dozen trails in every part of the country. I've shared George Washington's camps on the Northeast, Sherman's March in Georgia, Coronado's trek in the Southwest and ship captain Robert Gray's first voyage up the Columbia.

Reading for Information

Have you ever written or read a personal journal describing a trip or excursion? In this magazine article you are invited to come along on a bicycle journey that explores a historical trail.

Taking Notes and Paraphrasing

When you want to remember a phone number or address, you probably write down the information. Likewise, note taking can help you remember information that you've read, organize what you've heard during a lecture, or write a well-organized report.

Note taking and paraphrasing are methods of organizing information in a way that has meaning to you.

Taking Notes
- identify the main ideas or the important points of the text
- use words and phrases, rather than complete sentences, to convey each idea

Paraphrasing
- simplify an idea and restate the writer's ideas in your own words
- record the important information in sentences and paragraphs

As you take notes or paraphrase information, jot down the most important ideas and leave out the unimportant details.

YOUR TURN *Use the questions and activities that follow to help you take notes on and paraphrase this article.*

1. Note facts and concepts that express the main idea. What details about Lewis and Clark's route are included in this passage?
2. In this paragraph the writer explains what is involved in traveling this historic bike route. Paraphrase the main idea of this paragraph.
3. As you take notes, look up unfamiliar terms and words. Use your own words to write a definition of *topographic*.
4. Identify the main idea of this paragraph. Which details support the main idea?

America has a rich history that can be explored on two wheels.

You won't have to look far for such a trail near your own home, no matter where you live.

There's no better way, in my opinion, to experience history than to read the words of those who went before as you retrace their steps by bike.

Luckily, though, you won't have to share all their experiences. Local cafes and grocery stores, for example, will spare you from the likes of what Lewis and Clark had to eat:

"We purchased fish and dogs . . . dined and proceeded on."

❺

Reading for Information *continued*

❺ Take notes on the information in this box. Write the title, headings, and main ideas in your own words.

Research & Technology
Activity Link: from *Undaunted Courage*, p. 731. Take notes on this article and from two other sources about Lewis and Clark's expedition. Then use the information from your notes to make a map showing Lewis and Clark's historic route. You may use travel and guide books, library resources such as encyclopedias, and the Internet.

★ GETTING THERE ★

The Lewis and Clark Trail Today

There are five different types of transportation that one can choose from to follow the Lewis and Clark National Historic Trail today. Some parts of Lewis and Clark's overland route have been developed for travel by foot, bicycle, horseback, boat, and automobile.

- The Katy Trail State Park in Missouri is open to foot and bicycle travel.

- Portions of the trail over the Bitterroot Mountains are open to horseback riding and hiking.

- Portions of Lewis and Clark's water route on the Missouri and Columbia rivers and their tributaries can be retraced by boat.

- Most people follow portions of the Lewis and Clark National Historic Trail by vehicle. Motor routes that approximately follow the route of the historic expedition are marked with signs featuring Lewis and Clark. These highways connect a series of memorials, museums, visitor centers, interpretive exhibits, and historic sites along the trail.

War Party

by LOUIS L'AMOUR

Connect to Your Life

Going for the Goal Think back to an occasion when you, or someone you know, showed real determination to get something done. What was the goal? What obstacles were in the way? Were you or the person involved successful?

Build Background

HISTORY

"War Party" takes place in the mid-19th century. This was a time when the West attracted increasing numbers of settlers, most of them drawn by the promise of land.

As more and more settlers moved west, they experienced conflict with Native American communities. Many Native Americans actively resisted the invasion of settlers. However, Western novels and movies have probably exaggerated the number of deaths resulting from attacks on settlers. For example, it has been estimated that of the 10,000 deaths that occurred on the Oregon Trail between 1835 and 1855, only 4 percent were the result of attacks by Native Americans. Most of the deaths resulted from accidents and from such diseases as cholera and smallpox.

> WORDS TO KNOW
> **Vocabulary Preview**
> ail   disparagingly   principle
> contempt   encroach

Focus Your Reading

LITERARY ANALYSIS   HISTORICAL FICTION

"War Party" is a work of **historical fiction**—that is, fiction set in the past. "War Party" is set in the West during the 19th century, when the United States was expanding its territory. As you read the story, look for details that help create a sense of life in the 19th century.

ACTIVE READING   PREDICTING

Using your own knowledge to guess what may happen next is called **predicting**. While reading stories, good readers gather information and combine it with prior knowledge to predict upcoming events.

READER'S NOTEBOOK As you read "War Party," use the chart below to note details from the text, knowledge you already have about the information, and your predictions about what might happen in the story. Compare your predictions with the actual events. You may wish to change your predictions as you uncover new clues.

What You Read	What You Know	What You Predict
1. Pa dies. Ma is young and alone with two children on a wagon train.	Life was hard and dangerous on wagon trains.	The family will face dangers and difficulties.
2.		

War Party

by Louis L'Amour

A Certain Trail (1986),
Edward Ruscha. Acrylic on
canvas 59" × 145½". Private
Collection, Seattle. Photo by
Paul Ruscha. Courtesy of
the artist.

We buried pa on a sidehill out west of camp, buried him high up so he could look down the trail he'd planned to travel.

We piled the grave high with rocks because of the coyotes, and we dug the grave deep, and some of it I dug myself, and Mr. Sampson helped, and some others.

Folks in the wagon train figured ma would turn back, but they hadn't known ma so long as I had. Once she set her mind to something she wasn't about to quit.

She was a young woman and pretty, but there was strength in her. She was a lone woman with two children, but she was of no mind to turn back. She'd come through the Little Crow massacre in Minnesota and she knew what trouble was. Yet it was like her that she put it up to me.

"Bud," she said, when we were alone, "we can turn back, but we've nobody there who cares about us, and it's of you and Jeanie that I'm thinking. If we go west you will have to be the man of the house, and you'll have to work hard to make up for pa."

"We'll go west," I said. A boy those days took it for granted that he had work to do, and the men couldn't do it all. No boy ever thought of himself as only twelve or thirteen or whatever he was, being anxious to prove himself a man, and take a man's place and responsibilities.

Ryerson and his wife were going back. She was a complaining woman and he was a man who was always ailing when there was work to be done. Four or five wagons were turning back, folks with their tails betwixt their legs running for the shelter of towns where their own littleness wouldn't stand out so plain.

When a body crossed the Mississippi and left the settlements behind, something happened to him. The world seemed to bust wide open, and suddenly the horizons spread out and a man wasn't cramped any more. The pinched-up villages and the narrowness of towns, all that was gone. The horizons simply exploded and rolled back into enormous distance, with nothing around but prairie and sky.

Some folks couldn't stand it. They'd cringe into themselves and start hunting excuses to go back where they came from. This was a big country needing big men and women to live in it, and there was no place out here for the frightened or the mean.

The prairie and sky had a way of trimming folks down to size, or changing them to giants to whom nothing seemed impossible. Men who had cut a wide swath[1] back in the States found themselves nothing out here. They were folks who were used to doing a lot of talking who suddenly found that no one was listening any more, and things that seemed mighty important back home, like family and money, they amounted to nothing alongside character and courage.

There was John Sampson from our town. He was a man used to being told to do things, used to looking up to wealth and power, but when he crossed the Mississippi he began to lift his head and look around. He squared his shoulders, put more crack to his whip and began to make his own tracks in the land.

Pa was always strong, an independent man given to reading at night from one of the four or five books we had, to speaking up on matters of principle and to straight shooting with a rifle. Pa had fought the Comanche and lived with the Sioux, but he wasn't strong enough to last more than two days with a Kiowa arrow through his lung. But he died knowing ma had stood by the rear wheel and shot the Kiowa whose arrow it was.

Right then I knew that neither Indians nor country was going to get the better of ma. Shooting that Kiowa was the first time ma had shot anything but some chicken-killing varmint—which she'd done time to time when pa was away from home.

Only ma wouldn't let Jeanie and me call it home. "We came here from Illinois," she said, "but we're going home now."

"But ma," I protested, "I thought home was where we came from?"

"Home is where we're going now," ma said, "and we'll know it when we find it. Now that pa is gone we'll have to build that home ourselves."

She had a way of saying "home" so it sounded like a rare and wonderful place and kept Jeanie and me looking always at the horizon, just knowing it was over there, waiting for us to see it. She had given us the dream, and even Jeanie, who was only six, she had it too.

She might tell us that home was where we were going, but I knew home was where ma was, a warm and friendly place with biscuits on the table and fresh-made butter. We wouldn't have a real home until ma was there and we had a fire going. Only I'd build the fire.

---

1. **cut a wide swath:** created a great impression.

WORDS TO KNOW

ail (āl) *v.* to feel ill or be in pain
principle (prĭn′sə-pəl) *n.* the code of good behavior; morality

Mr. Buchanan, who was captain of the wagon train, came to us with Tryon Burt, who was guide. "We'll help you," Mr. Buchanan said. "I know you'll be wanting to go back, and—"

"But we are not going back." Ma smiled at them. "And don't be afraid we'll be a burden. I know you have troubles of your own, and we will manage very well."

Mr. Buchanan looked uncomfortable, like he was trying to think of the right thing to say. "Now, see here," he protested, "we started this trip with a rule. There has to be a man with every wagon."

Ma put her hand on my shoulder. "I have my man. Bud is almost thirteen and accepts responsibility. I could ask for no better man."

Ryerson came up. He was thin, stooped in the shoulder, and whenever he looked at ma there was a greasy look to his eyes that I didn't like. He was a man who looked dirty even when he'd just washed in the creek. "You come along with me, ma'am," he said. "I'll take good care of you."

"Mr. Ryerson"—ma looked him right in the eye—"you have a wife who can use better care than she's getting, and I have my son."

"He's nothin' but a boy."

"You are turning back, are you not? My son is going on. I believe that should indicate who is more the man. It is neither size nor age that makes a man, Mr. Ryerson, but something he has inside. My son has it."

Ryerson might have said something unpleasant only Tryon Burt was standing there wishing he would, so he just looked ugly and hustled off.

"I'd like to say you could come," Mr. Buchanan said, "but the boy couldn't stand up to a man's work."

Ma smiled at him, chin up, the way she had. "I do not believe in gambling, Mr. Buchanan, but I'll wager a good Ballard rifle there isn't a man in camp who could follow a child all day, running when it runs, squatting when it squats, bending when it bends and wrestling when it wrestles and not be played out long before the child is."

"You may be right, ma'am, but a rule is a rule."

Ma put her hand on my shoulder. 'I have my man. Bud is almost thirteen and accepts responsibility. I could ask for no better man.'

"We are in Indian country, Mr. Buchanan. If you are killed a week from now, I suppose your wife must return to the States?"

"That's different! Nobody could turn back from there!"

"Then," ma said sweetly, "it seems a rule is only a rule within certain limits, and if I recall correctly no such limit was designated in the articles of travel.[2] Whatever limits there were, Mr. Buchanan, must have been passed sometime before the Indian attack that killed my husband."

"I can drive the wagon, and so can ma." I said. "For the past two days I've been driving, and nobody said anything until pa died."

---

2. **articles of travel:** the rules that the people in the wagon train agreed to before setting out.

Mr. Buchanan didn't know what to say, but a body could see he didn't like it. Nor did he like a woman who talked up to him the way ma did.

Tryon Burt spoke up. "Let the boy drive. I've watched this youngster, and he'll do. He has better judgment than most men in the outfit, and he stands up to his work. If need be, I'll help."

Mr. Buchanan turned around and walked off with his back stiff the way it is when he's mad. Ma looked at Burt, and she said, "Thank you, Mr. Burt. That was nice of you."

Try Burt, he got all red around the gills[3] and took off like somebody had put a bur under his saddle.

Come morning our wagon was the second one ready to take its place in line, with both horses saddled and tied behind the wagon, and me standing beside the off ox.

Any direction a man wanted to look there was nothing but grass and sky, only sometimes there'd be a buffalo wallow or a gopher hole. We made eleven miles the first day after pa was buried, sixteen the next, then nineteen, thirteen and twenty-one. At no time did the country change. On the sixth day after pa died I killed a buffalo.

It was a young bull, but a big one, and I spotted him coming up out of a draw and was off my horse and bellied down in the grass before Try Burt realized there was game in sight. That bull came up from the draw and stopped there, staring at the wagon train, which was a half-mile off. Setting a sight behind his left shoulder I took a long breath, took in the trigger slack, then squeezed off my shot so gentle-like the gun jumped in my hands before I was ready for it.

The bull took a step back like something had surprised him, and I jacked another shell into the chamber and was sighting on him again when he went down on his knees and rolled over on his side.

"You got him, Bud!" Burt was more excited than me. "That was shootin'!"

Try got down and showed me how to skin the bull, and lent me a hand. Then we cut out a lot of fresh meat and toted it back to the wagons.

Ma was at the fire when we came up, a wisp of brown hair alongside her cheek and her face flushed from the heat of the fire, looking as pretty as a bay pony.

"Bud killed his first buffalo," Burt told her, looking at ma like he could eat her with a spoon.

"Why, Bud! That's wonderful!" Her eyes started to dance with a kind of mischief in them, and she said, "Bud, why don't you take a piece of that meat along to Mr. Buchanan and the others?"

With Burt to help, we cut the meat into eighteen pieces and distributed it around the wagons. It wasn't much, but it was the first fresh meat in a couple of weeks.

John Sampson squeezed my shoulder and said, "Seems to me you and your ma are folks to travel with. This outfit needs some hunters."

Each night I staked out that buffalo hide, and each day I worked at curing it before rolling it up to pack on the wagon. Believe you me, I was some proud of that buffalo hide. Biggest thing I'd shot until then was a cottontail rabbit back in Illinois, where we lived when I was born. Try Burt told folks about that shot. "Two hundred yards," he'd say, "right through the heart."

Only it wasn't more than a hundred and fifty yards the way I figured, and pa used to

---

3. **red around the gills:** flushed in the face and neck.

make me pace off distances, so I'd learn to judge right. But I was nobody to argue with Try Burt telling a story—besides, two hundred yards makes an awful lot better sound than one hundred and fifty.

After supper the menfolks would gather to talk plans. The season was late, and we weren't making the time we ought if we hoped to beat the snow through the passes of the Sierras. When they talked I was there because I was the man of my wagon, but nobody paid me no mind. Mr. Buchanan, he acted like he didn't see me, but John Sampson would not, and Try Burt always smiled at me.

Several spoke up for turning back, but Mr. Buchanan said he knew of an outfit that made it through later than this. One thing was sure. Our wagon wasn't turning back. Like ma said, home was somewhere ahead of us, and back in the States we'd have no money and nobody to turn to, nor any relatives, anywhere. It was the three of us.

"We're going on," I said at one of these talks. "We don't figure to turn back for anything."

Webb gave me a glance full of <u>contempt</u>. "You'll go where the rest of us go. You an' your ma would play hob[4] gettin' by on your own."

Next day it rained, dawn to dark it fairly poured, and we were lucky to make six miles. Day after that, with the wagon wheels sinking into the prairie and the rain still falling, we camped just two miles from where we started in the morning.

Nobody talked much around the fires, and what was said was apt to be short and irritable. Most of these folks had put all they owned into the outfits they had, and if they turned back now they'd have nothing to live on and nothing left to make a fresh start.

Except a few like Mr. Buchanan, who was well off.

"It doesn't have to be California," ma said once. "What most of us want is land, not gold."

"This here is Indian country," John Sampson said, "and a sight too open for me. I'd like a valley in the hills, with running water close by."

"There will be valleys and meadows," ma replied, stirring the stew she was making, "and tall trees near running streams, and tall grass growing in the meadows, and there will be game in the forest and on the grassy plains, and places for homes."

"And where will we find all that?" Webb's tone was slighting.

"West," ma said, "over against the mountains."

"I suppose you've been there?" Webb scoffed.

"No, Mr. Webb, I haven't been there, but I've been told of it. The land is there, and we will have some of it, my children and I, and we will stay through the winter, and in the spring we will plant our crops."

"Easy to say."

"This is Sioux country to the north," Burt said. "We'll be lucky to get through without a fight. There was a war party of thirty or thirty-five passed this way a couple of days ago."

"Sioux?"

"Uh-huh—no women or children along, and I found where some war paint rubbed off on the brush."

"Maybe," Mr. Buchanan suggested, "we'd better turn south a mite."

"It is late in the season," ma replied, "and the straightest way is the best way now."

---

4. **play hob:** have trouble; make a mess of.

WORDS
TO
KNOW

contempt (kən-tĕmpt′) *n.* an attitude of despising; scorn

743

1847 Covered Wagon Pioneers, Madonna at Dawn (1935), Minerva Teichert. Collection of the Museum of Church History and Art, Salt Lake City, Utah. © by Intellectual Reserve, Inc. Used by permission.

"Because we're going on," ma said. "We're going to the mountains, and I am hoping some of the others decide to come with us."

"No use to worry," White interrupted; "those Indians went on by. They won't likely know we're around."

"They were riding southeast," ma said, "and their home is in the north, so when they return they'll be riding northwest. There is no way they can miss our trail."

"Then we'd best turn back," White said.

"Don't look like we'd make it this year, anyway," a woman said; "the season is late."

That started the argument, and some were for turning back and some wanted to push on, and finally White said they should push on, but travel fast.

"Fast?" Webb asked disparagingly. "An Indian can ride in one day the distance we'd travel in four."

That started the wrangling again and ma continued with her cooking. Sitting there watching her I figured I never did see anybody so graceful or quick on her feet as ma, and when we used to walk in the woods back home I never knew her to stumble or step on a fallen twig or branch.

The group broke up and returned to their own fires with nothing settled, only there at the end Mr. Buchanan looked to Burt. "Do you know the Sioux?"

"Only the Utes and Shoshonis, and I spent a winter on the Snake with the Nez Perces one time. But I've had no truck[5] with the Sioux. Only they tell me they're bad medicine. Fightin' men from way back and they don't cotton to[6] white folks in their country. If we run into Sioux, we're in trouble."

After Mr. Buchanan had gone Tryon Burt accepted a plate and cup from ma and settled down to eating. After a while he looked up at her and said, "Beggin' your pardon, ma'am, but it struck me you knew a sight about trackin' for an Eastern woman. You'd spotted those Sioux your own self, an' you figured it right that they'd pick up our trail on the way back."

She smiled at him. "It was simply an observation, Mr. Burt. I would believe anyone would notice it. I simply put it into words."

Burt went on eating, but he was mighty thoughtful, and it didn't seem to me he was satisfied with ma's answer. Ma said finally, "It seems to be raining west of here. Isn't it likely to be snowing in the mountains?"

Burt looked up uneasily. "Not necessarily so, ma'am. It could be raining here and not snowing there, but I'd say there was a chance of snow." He got up and came around the fire to the coffeepot. "What are you gettin' at, ma'am?"

"Some of them are ready to turn back or change their plans. What will you do then?"

He frowned, placing his cup on the grass. "No idea—might head south for Santa Fe. Why do you ask?"

"Because we're going on," ma said. "We're going to the mountains, and I am hoping some of the others decide to come with us."

"You'd go alone?" He was amazed.

"If necessary."

We started on at daybreak, but folks were more scary than before, and they kept looking at the great distances stretching away on either side, and muttering. There was an autumn coolness in the air, and we were still short of South Pass by several days with the memory of the Donner party[7] being talked up around us.

There was another kind of talk in the wagons, and some of it I heard. The nightly

---

5. **truck:** dealings.

6. **cotton to:** like.

7. **Donner party:** a group of pioneers who became trapped by snow in the Sierra Nevada mountains during the winter of 1846–1847. Almost half of them died before help arrived.

gatherings around ma's fire had started talk, and some of it pointed to Tryon Burt, and some were saying other things.

We made seventeen miles that day, and at night Mr. Buchanan didn't come to our fire; and when White stopped by, his wife came and got him. Ma looked at her and smiled, and Mrs. White sniffed and went away beside her husband.

"Mr. Burt"—ma wasn't one to beat around a bush—"is there talk about me?"

Try Burt got red around the ears and he opened his mouth, but couldn't find the words he wanted. "Maybe—well, maybe I shouldn't eat here all the time. Only—well, ma'am, you're the best cook in camp."

Ma smiled at him. "I hope that isn't the only reason you come to see us, Mr. Burt."

He got redder than ever then and gulped his coffee and took off in a hurry.

Time to time the men had stopped by to help a little, but next morning nobody came by. We got lined out about as soon as ever, and ma said to me as we sat on the wagon seat, "Pay no attention, Bud. You've no call to take up anything if you don't notice it. There will always be folks who will talk, and the better you do in the world the more bad things they will say of you. Back there in the settlement you remember how the dogs used to run out and bark at our wagons?"

"Yes, ma."

"Did the wagons stop?"

"No, ma."

"Remember that, son. The dogs bark, but the wagons go on their way, and if you're going some place you haven't time to bother with barking dogs."

We made eighteen miles that day, and the grass was better, but there was a rumble of

distant thunder, whimpering and muttering off in the canyons, promising rain.

Webb stopped by, dropped an armful of wood beside the fire, then started off.

"Thank you, Mr. Webb," ma said, "but aren't you afraid you'll be talked about?"

He looked angry and started to reply something angry, and then he grinned and said, "I reckon I'd be flattered, Mrs. Miles."

Ma said, "No matter what is decided by the rest of them, Mr. Webb, we are going on, but there is no need to go to California for what we want."

Webb had a dark face on him. I was afraid of Mr. Webb.

"We want land," ma said, "and there is land around us. In the mountains ahead there will be streams and forests, there will be fish and game, logs for houses and meadows for grazing."

Mr. Buchanan had joined us. "That's fool talk," he declared. "What could anyone do in these hills? You'd be cut off from the world. Left out of it."

"A man wouldn't be so crowded as in California," John Sampson remarked. "I've seen so many go that I've been wondering what they all do there."

"For a woman," Webb replied, ignoring the others, "you've a head on you, ma'am."

"What about the Sioux?" Mr. Buchanan asked dryly.

"We'd not be <u>encroaching</u> on their land. They live to the north," ma said. She gestured toward the mountains. "There is land to be had just a few days further on, and that is where our wagon will stop."

A few days! Everybody looked at everybody else. Not months, but days only. Those who stopped then would have enough of their supplies left to help them through the winter,

WORDS
TO
KNOW

encroach (ĕn-krōch′) *v.* to intrude; trespass

and with what game they could kill—and time for cutting wood and even building cabins before the cold set in.

Oh, there was an argument, such argument as you've never heard, and the upshot of it was that all agreed it was fool talk and the thing to do was keep going. And there was talk I overheard about ma being no better than she should be, and why was that guide always hanging around her? And all those men? No decent woman—I hurried away.

At break of day our wagons rolled down a long valley with a small stream alongside the trail, and the Indians came over the ridge to the south of us and started our way—tall, fine-looking men with feathers in their hair.

There was barely time for a circle, but I was riding off in front with Tryon Burt, and he said, "A man can always try to talk first, and Injuns like a palaver.[8] You get back to the wagons."

Only I rode along beside him, my rifle over my saddle and ready to hand. My mouth was dry and my heart was beating so's I thought Try could hear it, I was that scared. But behind us the wagons were making their circle, and every second was important.

Their chief was a big man with splendid muscles, and there was a scalp not many days old hanging from his lance. It looked like Ryerson's hair, but Ryerson's wagons should have been miles away to the east by now.

Burt tried them in Shoshoni, but it was the language of their enemies and they merely stared at him, understanding well enough, but of no mind to talk. One young buck kept staring at Burt with a taunt in his eye, daring Burt to make a move; then suddenly the chief spoke, and they all turned their eyes toward the wagons.

There was a rider coming, and it was a woman. It was ma.

She rode right up beside us, and when she drew up she started to talk, and she was speaking their language. She was talking Sioux. We both knew what it was because those Indians sat up and paid attention. Suddenly she directed a question at the chief.

"Red Horse," he said, in English.

Ma shifted to English. "My husband was blood brother to Gall, the greatest warrior of the Sioux nation. It was my husband who found Gall dying in the brush with a bayonet wound in his chest, who took Gall to his home and treated the wound until it was well."

> 'In the mountains ahead there will be streams and forests, there will be fish and game, logs for houses and meadows for grazing.'

"Your husband was a medicine man?" Red Horse asked.

"My husband was a warrior," ma replied proudly, "but he made war only against strong men, not women or children or the wounded."

She put her hand on my shoulder. "This is my son. As my husband was blood brother to Gall, his son is by blood brotherhood the son of Gall, also."

Red Horse stared at ma for a long time, and I was getting even more scared. I could feel a drop of sweat start at my collar and crawl slowly down my spine. Red Horse looked at me. "Is this one a fit son for Gall?"

---

8. **palaver** (pə-lăv′ər): discussion; conference.

"He is a fit son. He has killed his first buffalo."

Red Horse turned his mount and spoke to the others. One of the young braves shouted angrily at him, and Red Horse replied sharply. Reluctantly, the warriors trailed off after their chief.

"Ma'am," Burt said, "you just about saved our bacon. They were just spoilin' for a fight."

"We should be moving," ma said.

Mr. Buchanan was waiting for us. "What happened out there? I tried to keep her back, but she's a difficult woman."

"She's worth any three men in the outfit," Burt replied.

That day we made eighteen miles, and by the time the wagons circled there was talk. The fact that ma had saved them was less important now than other things. It didn't seem right that a decent woman could talk Sioux or mix in the affairs of men.

Nobody came to our fire, but while picketing the saddle horses I heard someone say, "Must be part Indian. Else why would they pay attention to a woman?"

"Maybe she's part Injun and leadin' us into a trap."

"Hadn't been for her," Burt said, "you'd all be dead now."

"How do you know what she said to 'em? Who savvies that lingo?"[9]

"I never did trust that woman," Mrs. White said; "too high and mighty. Nor that husband of hers, either, comes to that. Kept to himself too much."

The air was cool after a brief shower when we started in the morning, and no Indians in sight. All day long we moved over grass made fresh by new rain, and all the ridges were pineclad now, and the growth along the streams heavier. Short of sundown I killed an antelope with a running shot, dropped him

mighty neat—and looked up to see an Indian watching from a hill. At the distance I couldn't tell, but it could have been Red Horse.

Time to time I'd passed along the train, but nobody waved or said anything. Webb watched me go by, his face stolid as one of the Sioux, yet I could see there was a deal of talk going on.

"Why are they mad at us?" I asked Burt.

"Folks hate something they don't understand, or anything seems different. Your ma goes her own way, speaks her mind, and of an evening she doesn't set by and gossip."

He topped out on a rise and drew up to study the country, and me beside him. "You got to figure most of these folks come from small towns where they never knew much aside from their families, their gossip and their church. It doesn't seem right to them that a decent woman would find time to learn Sioux."

Burt studied the country. "Time was, any stranger was an enemy, and if anybody came around who wasn't one of yours, you killed him. I've seen wolves jump on a wolf that was white or different somehow—seems like folks and animals fear anything that's unusual."

We circled, and I staked out my horses and took the oxen to the herd. By the time ma had her grub-box lid down, I was fixing at a fire when here come Mr. Buchanan, Mr. and Mrs. White and some other folks, including that Webb.

"Ma'am"—Mr. Buchanan was mighty abrupt—"we figure we ought to know what you said to those Sioux. We want to know why they turned off just because you went out there."

"Does it matter?"

Mr. Buchanan's face stiffened up. "We think it does. There's some think you might be an Indian your own self."

---

9. **Who savvies that lingo?:** Who understands that language?

Overland Trail (ca. 1871), Albert Bierstadt. Oil on paper mounted on board, 7½" × 11½". The Anschutz Collection, Denver.

"And if I am?" Ma was amused. "Just what is it you have in mind, Mr. Buchanan?"

"We don't want no Indian in this outfit!" Mr. White shouted.

"How does it come you can talk that language?" Mrs. White demanded. "Even Tryon Burt can't talk it."

"I figure maybe you want us to keep goin' because there's a trap up ahead!" White declared.

I never realized folks could be so mean, but there they were facing ma like they hated her. It didn't seem right that ma, who they didn't like, had saved them from an Indian attack and the fact that she talked Sioux like any Indian bothered them.

"As it happens," ma said, "I am not an Indian, although I should not be ashamed of it if I were. They have many admirable qualities.

However, you need worry yourselves no longer, as we part company in the morning. I have no desire to travel further with you— *gentlemen.*"

Mr. Buchanan's face got all angry, and he started up to say something mean. Nobody was about to speak rough to ma with me standing by, so I just picked up that ol' rifle and jacked a shell into the chamber. "Mr. Buchanan, this here's my ma, and she's a lady, so you just be careful what words you use."

"Put down that rifle, you young fool!" he shouted at me.

"Mr. Buchanan, I may be little and may be a fool, but this here rifle doesn't care who pulls its trigger."

He looked like he was going to have a stroke, but he just turned sharp around and walked away, all stiff in the back.

"Ma'am," Webb said, "you've no cause to like me much, but you've shown more brains than that passel o' fools. If you'll be so kind, me and my boy would like to trail along with you."

"I like a man who speaks his mind, Mr. Webb. I would consider it an honor to have your company."

Tryon Burt looked quizzically at ma. "Why, now, seems to me this is a time for a man to make up his mind, and I'd like to be included along with Webb."

"Mr. Burt," ma said, "for your own information, I grew up among Sioux children in Minnesota. They were my playmates."

Come daylight our wagon pulled off to one side, pointing northwest at the mountains, and Mr. Buchanan led off to the west. Webb followed ma's wagon, and I sat watching Mr. Buchanan's eyes get angrier as John Sampson, Neely Stuart, the two Shafter wagons and Tom Croft all fell in behind us.

Tryon Burt had been talking to Mr. Buchanan, but he left off and trotted his horse over to where I sat my horse. Mr. Buchanan looked mighty sullen when he saw half his wagon train gone and with it a lot of his importance as captain.

Two days and nearly forty miles further and we topped out on a rise and paused to let the oxen take a blow. A long valley lay across our route, with mountains beyond it, and tall grass wet with rain, and a flat bench[10] on the mountainside seen through a gray veil of a light shower falling. There was that bench, with the white trunks of aspen on the mountainside beyond it looking like ranks of slim soldiers guarding the bench against the storms.

"Ma," I said.

"All right, Bud," she said quietly, "we've come home."

And I started up the oxen and drove down into the valley where I was to become a man. ❖

---

10. **bench:** an area of level land with steep slopes above and below it; terrace.

The Other Pioneers

by Roberto Félix Salazar

California Vaqueros, James Walker.
Oil on canvas, 31" × 46". Courtesy
The Anshutz Collection, Denver. Photo
copyright © James O. Milmoe.

Now I must write
Of those of mine who rode these plains
Long years before the Saxon[1] and the Irish came.
Of those who plowed the land and built the towns
5   And gave the towns soft-woven Spanish names.
Of those who moved across the Rio Grande
Toward the hiss of Texas snake and Indian yell.
Of men who from the earth made thick-walled homes
And from the earth raised churches to their God.
10   And of the wives who bore them sons
And smiled with knowing joy.

---

1. **Saxon** (săk′sən): English

They saw the Texas sun rise golden-red with promised wealth
And saw the Texas sun sink golden yet, with wealth unspent.
"Here," they said. "Here to live and here to love."

15 "Here is the land for our sons and the sons of our sons."
And they sang the songs of ancient Spain
And they made new songs to fit new needs.
They cleared the brush and planted the corn
And saw green stalks turn black from lack of rain.

20 They roamed the plains behind the herds
And stood the Indian's cruel attacks.
There was dust and there was sweat.
And there were tears and the women prayed.

And the years moved on.

25 Those who were first placed in graves
Beside the broad mesquite and the tall nopal.[2]
Gentle mothers left their graces and their arts
And stalwart fathers pride and manly strength.
Salinas, de la Garza, Sánchez, García,

30 Uribe, Gonzálaz, Martinez, de León:
Such were the names of the fathers.
Salinas, de la Garza, Sánchez, García,
Uribe, Gonzálaz, Martinez, de León:
Such are the names of the sons.

---

2. **mesquite** (mĕ-skēt′) . . . **nopal** (nō-päl′): thorny tree or
shrub common in the southwestern United States and in
northern Mexico; cactus with reddish flowers, found
chiefly in Mexico.

Connect to the Literature

1. What Do You Think?
Would you have stayed with Mr. Buchanan or joined the group that followed Bud's family? Why?

Comprehension Check
- Why do some members of the wagon train want Bud's family to turn back?
- How does Bud's mother save the wagon train from attack?
- What does Bud's family do at the end of the story?

Think Critically

2. **ACTIVE READING** **PREDICTING**
Look at the predictions that you made in your **READER'S NOTEBOOK.** Which of your predictions were accurate? Which ones did you revise when you uncovered new clues in the story? Share your responses with your classmates.

3. What is your impression of Bud's mother?

> **Think About:**
> - what she calls "home"
> - the attitude she displays toward Bud

4. Bud's mother tells Mr. Ryerson that "it is neither size nor age that makes a man, . . . but something he has inside. My son has it." What do you think she means by "it"?

Extend Interpretations

5. Critic's Corner While critics agree that L'Amour was a natural storyteller, some criticize his "cardboard, simplistic characters." Do you think that this criticism applies to the characters in "War Party"? Why or why not?

6. **COMPARING TEXTS** Read the poem "The Other Pioneers" by Roberto Félix Salazar on page 751. In this poem, what is the relationship between Native Americans and Spanish settlers? How does this relationship compare with the one that L'Amour describes in "War Party"?

7. Connect to Life Mr. Burt tells Bud that "Folks hate something they don't understand, or anything seems different." Do you agree with this observation? Explain.

Literary Analysis

HISTORICAL FICTION Fiction that takes place in the past is called **historical fiction.** Sometimes characters in historical fiction are actual historical figures, and the events are fictionalized accounts of real events. In other cases, as in L'Amour's story, the main characters and events are fictional, but the details of the setting are historically accurate.

Paired Activity Go back through the selection and look for details that make "War Party" a work of historical fiction. Record this information in a chart like the one shown. After completing the chart, discuss with a partner how effectively you think the author re-created life on a wagon train in the mid-1800s.

Historical Details of Everyday Life	References to Actual Historical Events	Dialogue That Is Appropriate to the Setting
traveling in a wagon train	people discuss what happened to the Donner party	"This here is Indian country . . . and a sight too open for me."

REVIEW: CONFLICT A conflict can be either external or internal. In an **external conflict,** a character struggles against a force of nature, a physical object, or another character. An **internal conflict** is a struggle within the character's own mind. Is Bud's conflict primarily external or internal?

Writing

1. Research Topics If you were writing a research report on westward expansion, how would you narrow the topic? Using library resources and the Internet, compose a list of possible **thesis statements**—statements that define the main idea or overall purpose of your research report. Place the entries in your **Working Portfolio.**

Writing Handbook
See p. R53: Writing a Thesis Statement.

2. Westward Journal Choose one of the characters in the story other than Bud. Write several journal entries in which that character describes the events of the wagon train.

Include relevant dialogue, specific action, and physical descriptions.

Writing Handbook
See p. R43: Narrative Writing.

Speaking & Listening

Radio Dramatization Adapt all or part of this story into a radio drama. You might want to include appropriate music and sound effects in your recording. Use precise language, action verbs, and sensory details when writing the script. Perform the play for your class.

Speaking and Listening Handbook
See p. R107: Dramatic Reading.

Research & Technology

Historical Details In this story the author refers to several actual historical incidents. Choose one of the following topics to research:

- the 1862 uprising led by Little Crow in Minnesota
- the Donner party tragedy of 1846–1847
- the Salem witch trials of the late 1600s

Prepare a speech outline based on a pattern of organization.

Speaking and Listening Handbook
See p. R104: Writing Your Speech.

INTERNET Research Starter
www.mcdougallittell.com

Vocabulary

EXERCISE: MEANING CLUES For each blank, write the Word to Know that has a meaning similar to the other words in the group.

1. ill, sickly, _____
2. rule, standard, _____
3. scorn, disdain, _____
4. rudely, disrespectfully, _____
5. intrude, invade, _____

VOCABULARY STRATEGY: THE SCHWA SOUND
The schwa (ə) is a common vowel sound in unstressed syllables, but it can represent several different vowels or vowel combinations.

Examine the words listed below and find examples of the schwa sound. Use a dictionary to check the pronunciation if necessary. Then identify the letters responsible for the sound.

contempt   principle
ajar   lemon
treasure

Look for more words with the schwa sound and record them in your notebook.

Vocabulary Handbook
See p. R24: Synonyms and Antonyms.

WORDS TO KNOW	ail	contempt	disparagingly	encroach	principle

Grammar in Context: Using Compound Sentences for Sentence Variety

Many writers use a variety of sentence structures to make their writing more interesting. Look at the following passage from Louis L'Amour's "War Party":

> **One thing was sure. Our wagon wasn't turning back. Like ma said, home was somewhere ahead of us, and back in the States we'd have no money and nobody to turn to, nor any relatives, anywhere. It was the three of us.**

The words in red form a **compound sentence,** a sentence that is created by joining two or more simple sentences. The other sentences in the passage are simple sentences. Notice how the addition of a compound sentence creates a variety of sentence structures that helps make the writing more interesting.

WRITING EXERCISE The following paragraph consists of a series of simple sentences. Rewrite the paragraph, creating compound sentences to create sentence variety.

> We buried my father high up on a hill. Some mothers would not have continued. My mother did not give up. She was a lone woman with two children. She refused to turn back. People were amazed by her. Sometimes they were frightened of her. I admired her immensely. She always stood by me. I inherited her strength. At a very early age I became the man of the family.

Grammar Handbook
See p. R75: Writing Complete Sentences.

Louis L'Amour
1908–1988

"I write my books to be read aloud and I think of myself in that oral tradition."

"Yondering Years" The first half of Louis L'Amour's life sounds like an adventure story itself. Born in Jamestown, North Dakota, L'Amour left home at 15 and held a wide variety of jobs including ranch hand, lumberjack, longshoreman, and elephant handler. He later coined the term "yondering" to describe this period of his life—years in which he "wandered yonder."

A Western Writer After serving overseas in the army, L'Amour began to write Western fiction for magazines in the late 1940s. By the time his novel *Hondo* was published in 1953, L'Amour had established his reputation. The books that followed were hugely successful. He wrote more million-copy bestsellers than any other American author. For more than 30 years he produced three novels a year, and when he died in 1988, he left 50 outlines for future novels.

AUTHOR ACTIVITY
Change of Subject L'Amour is famous as a writer of stories and novels about the West. However, in 1984 he published a novel, *The Walking Drum,* that is set in a very different historical period. Find a copy of this book in the library. What is the setting of the book? What might this book have in common with L'Amour's Western stories?

from Harriet Tubman: Conductor on the Underground Railroad

by ANN PETRY

Connect to Your Life

What do you think of when you hear the term "Underground Railroad"?

Build Background

In the period before and during the Civil War, many Southern slaves fled north to freedom using a secret network of escape routes known as the Underground Railroad. The "conductors" on the Underground Railroad were brave men and women who provided the escaping slaves with food, hid them in secret tunnels and false cupboards, and guided the runaways to the next "station." One of the most famous of these conductors was a woman named Harriet Tubman.

CANADA

ME · MN · VT · NH · WI · NY · MA · CT · RI · IA · MI · Lake Michigan · Lake Huron · Lake Ontario · Lake Erie · IN · OH · PA · NJ · IL · MD · DE · MO · VA · KY · NC · TN · SC · MS · AL · GA · Atlantic Ocean · Gulf of Mexico · FL

FREE STATES   SLAVE STATES   ROUTE OF THE UNDERGROUND RAILROAD

Focus Your Reading

LITERARY ANALYSIS BIOGRAPHY

A writer's account of someone else's life is called a **biography**. Biographies present many facts about their subjects. As you read the excerpt from *Harriet Tubman: Conductor on the Underground Railroad,* look for factual details about Harriet Tubman.

WORDS TO KNOW Vocabulary Preview

borne	dispel	indomitable	sullen
cajoling	eloquence	instill	
disheveled	fastidious	mutinous	

ACTIVE READING QUESTIONING

One way to better understand a biography is to ask yourself questions as you read the text. For example, what motivated Harriet Tubman to help enslaved people? What motivated the slaves to make the dangerous journey? Record the answers to these and other questions in your ▢ **READER'S NOTEBOOK.**

from

Harriet Tubman:
Conductor on the Underground Railroad
by Ann Petry

The Railroad Runs to Canada

ALONG THE EASTERN SHORE OF MARYLAND, IN DORCHESTER COUNTY, IN CAROLINE COUNTY, THE MASTERS KEPT HEARING WHISPERS ABOUT THE MAN NAMED MOSES, WHO WAS RUNNING OFF SLAVES. AT FIRST THEY DID NOT BELIEVE IN HIS EXISTENCE. THE STORIES ABOUT HIM WERE FANTASTIC, UNBELIEVABLE. YET THEY WATCHED FOR HIM. THEY OFFERED REWARDS FOR HIS CAPTURE.

They never saw him. Now and then they heard whispered rumors to the effect that he was in the neighborhood. The woods were searched. The roads were watched. There was never anything to indicate his whereabouts. But a few days afterward, a goodly number of slaves would be gone from the plantation. Neither the master nor the overseer had heard or seen anything unusual in the quarter.[1] Sometimes one or the other would vaguely remember having heard a whippoorwill call somewhere in the woods, close by, late at night. Though it was the wrong season for whippoorwills.

Sometimes the masters thought they had heard the cry of a hoot owl, repeated, and would remember having thought that the intervals between the low, moaning cry were wrong, that it had been repeated four times in succession instead of

three. There was never anything more than that to suggest that all was not well in the quarter. Yet when morning came, they invariably discovered that a group of the finest slaves had taken to their heels.

Unfortunately, the discovery was almost always made on a Sunday. Thus a whole day was lost before the machinery of pursuit could be set in motion. The posters offering rewards for the fugitives could not be printed until Monday. The men who made a living hunting for runaway slaves were out of reach, off in the woods with their dogs and their guns, in pursuit of four-footed game, or they were in camp meetings saying their prayers with their wives and families beside them.

Harriet Tubman could have told them that there was far more

---

1. **quarter:** the area in which slaves lived.

Forward (1967), Jacob Lawrence. Tempera on masonite, 23⅞" × 35¹⁵⁄₁₆", North Carolina Museum of Art, Raleigh, purchased with funds from the State of North Carolina.

involved in this matter of running off slaves than signaling the would-be runaways by imitating the call of a whippoor-will or a hoot owl, far more involved than a matter of waiting for a clear night when the North Star was visible.

In December 1851, when she started out with the band of fugitives that she planned to take to Canada, she had been in the vicinity of the plantation for days, planning the trip, carefully selecting the slaves that she would take with her.

She had announced her arrival in the quarter by singing the forbidden spiritual— "Go down, Moses, 'way down to Egypt Land"[2]—singing it softly outside the door of a slave cabin late at night. The husky voice was beautiful even when it was barely more than a murmur <u>borne</u> on the wind.

Once she had made her presence known, word of her coming spread from cabin to cabin. The slaves whispered to each other, ear to mouth, mouth to ear, "Moses is here." "Moses has come." "Get ready. Moses is back again." The ones who had agreed to go north with her put ashcake and salt herring in an old bandanna, hastily tied it into a bundle, and then waited patiently for the signal that meant it was time to start.

There were eleven in this party, including one of her brothers and his wife. It was the largest group that she had ever conducted, but she was determined that more and more slaves should know what freedom was like.

---

2. **"Go down, Moses, 'way down to Egypt Land":** a line from a well-known African-American folk song about Moses leading the enslaved Israelites out of Egypt.

WORDS TO KNOW

borne (bôrn) *adj.* carried **bear** *v.*

She had to take them all the way to Canada. The Fugitive Slave Law[3] was no longer a great many incomprehensible words written down on the country's law books. The new law had become a reality. It was Thomas Sims, a boy, picked up on the streets of Boston at night and shipped back to Georgia. It was Jerry and Shadrach, arrested and jailed with no warning.

She had never been in Canada. The route beyond Philadelphia was strange to her. But she could not let the runaways who accompanied her know this. As they walked along, she told them stories of her own first flight; she kept painting vivid word pictures of what it would be like to be free.

But there were so many of them this time. She knew moments of doubt when she was half-afraid and kept looking back over her shoulder, imagining that she heard the sound of pursuit. They would certainly be pursued. Eleven of them. Eleven thousand dollars' worth of flesh and bone and muscle that belonged to Maryland planters. If they were caught, the eleven runaways would be whipped and sold south, but she—she would probably be hanged.

They tried to sleep during the day, but they never could wholly relax into sleep. She could tell by the positions they assumed, by their restless movements. And they walked at night. Their progress was slow. It took them three nights of walking to reach the first stop. She had told them about the place where they would stay, promising warmth and good food, holding these things out to them as an incentive to keep going.

When she knocked on the door of a farmhouse, a place where she and her parties of runaways had always been welcome, always been given shelter and plenty to eat, there was no answer. She knocked again, softly. A voice from within said, "Who is it?" There was fear in the voice.

She knew instantly from the sound of the voice that there was something wrong. She said, "A friend with friends," the password on the Underground Railroad.

The door opened, slowly. The man who stood in the doorway looked at her coldly, looked with unconcealed astonishment and fear at the eleven <u>disheveled</u> runaways who were standing near her. Then he shouted, "Too many, too many. It's not safe. My place was searched last week. It's not safe!" and slammed the door in her face.

She turned away from the house, frowning. She had promised her passengers food and rest and warmth, and instead of that there would be hunger and cold and more walking over the frozen ground. Somehow she would have to <u>instill</u> courage into these eleven people, most of them strangers, would have to feed them on hope and bright dreams of freedom instead of the fried pork and corn bread and milk she had promised them.

They stumbled along behind her, half-dead for sleep, and she urged them on, though she was as tired and as discouraged as they were. She had never been in Canada, but she kept painting wondrous word pictures of what it would be like. She managed to <u>dispel</u> their fear of pursuit so that they would not become hysterical, panic-stricken. Then she had to bring some of the fear back so that they would stay awake and keep walking though they drooped with sleep.

---

3. **Fugitive Slave Law:** a law passed in 1850, allowing slave owners to recover escaped slaves even if they had reached free states.

WORDS	**disheveled** (dĭ-shĕv'əld) *adj.* messy; untidy
TO	**instill** (ĭn-stĭl') *v.* to supply gradually
KNOW	**dispel** (dĭ-spĕl') *v.* to drive away

Yet during the day, when they lay down deep in a thicket, they never really slept, because if a twig snapped or the wind sighed in the branches of a pine tree, they jumped to their feet, afraid of their own shadows, shivering and shaking. It was very cold, but they dared not make fires because someone would see the smoke and wonder about it.

She kept thinking, Eleven of them. Eleven thousand dollars' worth of slaves. And she had to take them all the way to Canada. Sometimes she told them about Thomas Garrett, in Wilmington. She said he was their friend even though he did not know them. He was the friend of all fugitives. He called them God's poor. He was a Quaker[4] and his speech was a little different from that of other people. His clothing was different, too. He wore the wide-brimmed hat that the Quakers wear.

She said that he had thick white hair, soft, almost like a baby's, and the kindest eyes she had ever seen. He was a big man and strong, but he had never used his strength to harm anyone, always to help people. He would give all of them a new pair of shoes. Everybody. He always did. Once they reached his house in Wilmington, they would be safe. He would see to it that they were.

She described the house where he lived, told them about the store where he sold shoes. She said he kept a pail of milk and a loaf of bread in the drawer of his desk so that he would have food ready at hand for any of God's poor who should suddenly appear before him, fainting with hunger. There was a hidden room in the store. A whole wall swung open, and behind it was a room where he could hide fugitives. On the wall there were shelves filled with small boxes—boxes of shoes—so that you would never guess that the wall actually opened.

While she talked, she kept watching them. They did not believe her. She could tell by their expressions. They were thinking, New shoes, Thomas Garrett, Quaker, Wilmington—what foolishness was this? Who knew if she told the truth? Where was she taking them anyway?

That night they reached the next stop—a farm that belonged to a German. She made the runaways take shelter behind trees at the edge of the fields before she knocked at the door. She hesitated before she approached the door, thinking, Suppose that he, too, should refuse shelter, suppose— Then she thought, Lord, I'm going to hold steady on to You, and You've got to see me through—and knocked softly.

She heard the familiar guttural voice say, "Who's there?"

She answered quickly, "A friend with friends."

He opened the door and greeted her warmly. "How many this time?" he asked.

"Eleven," she said and waited, doubting, wondering.

He said, "Good. Bring them in."

He and his wife fed them in the lamp-lit kitchen, their faces glowing as they offered food and more food, urging them to eat, saying there was plenty for everybody, have more milk, have more bread, have more meat.

They spent the night in the warm kitchen. They really slept, all that night and until dusk the next day. When they left, it was with reluctance. They had all been warm and safe and well-fed. It was hard to exchange the security offered by that clean, warm kitchen for the darkness and the cold of a December night.

---

4. **Quaker:** a member of a religious group known as the Society of Friends.

"Go On or Die"

HARRIET HAD FOUND IT HARD TO LEAVE THE WARMTH AND FRIENDLINESS, TOO. BUT SHE URGED THEM ON.

For a while, as they walked, they seemed to carry in them a measure of contentment; some of the serenity and the cleanliness of that big, warm kitchen lingered on inside them. But as they walked farther and farther away from the warmth and the light, the cold and the darkness entered into them. They fell silent, <u>sullen</u>, suspicious. She waited for the moment when some one of them would turn <u>mutinous</u>. It did not happen that night.

Two nights later she was aware that the feet behind her were moving slower and slower. She heard the irritability in their voices, knew that soon someone would refuse to go on.

She started talking about William Still and the Philadelphia Vigilance Committee.[5] No one commented. No one asked any questions. She told them the story of William and Ellen Craft and how they escaped from Georgia. Ellen was so fair that she looked as though she were white, and so she dressed up in a man's clothing, and she looked like a wealthy young planter. Her husband, William, who was dark, played the role of her slave. Thus they traveled from Macon, Georgia, to Philadelphia, riding on the trains, staying at the finest hotels. Ellen pretended to be very ill—her right arm was in a sling, and her right hand was bandaged, because she was supposed to have rheumatism. Thus she avoided having to sign the register at the hotels, for she could not read or write. They finally arrived safely in Philadelphia and then went on to Boston.

No one said anything. Not one of them seemed to have heard her.

She told them about Frederick Douglass,[6] the most famous of the escaped slaves, of his <u>eloquence</u>, of his magnificent appearance. Then she told them of her own first, vain effort at running away, evoking the memory of that miserable life she had led as a child, reliving it for a moment in the telling.

But they had been tired too long, hungry too long, afraid too long, footsore too long. One of them suddenly cried out in despair, "Let me go back. It is better to be a slave than to suffer like this in order to be free."

She carried a gun with her on these trips. She had never used it—except as a threat. Now as she aimed it, she experienced a feeling of guilt, remembering that time, years ago, when she had prayed for the death of Edward Brodas, the Master, and then not too long afterward had heard that great wailing cry that came from the throats of the field hands, and knew from the sound that the Master was dead.

One of the runaways said, again, "Let me go back. Let me go back," and stood still and then turned around and said, over his shoulder, "I am going back."

She lifted the gun, aimed it at the despairing slave. She said, "Go on with us or die." The husky, low-pitched voice was grim.

He hesitated for a moment, and then he joined the others. They started walking again. She tried to explain to them why none of them could go back to the plantation. If a runaway

---

5. **Philadelphia Vigilance Committee:** a fund-raising organization set up before the Civil War to help slaves escaping from the South.

6. **Frederick Douglass:** an African-American leader of the 1800s who worked for the end of slavery in the United States.

WORDS
TO
KNOW

sullen (sŭl′ən) *adj.* showing silent resentment; sulky
mutinous (myoot′n-əs) *adj.* rebelling against a leader
eloquence (ĕl′ə-kwəns) *n.* an ability to speak forcefully and persuasively

returned, he would turn traitor; the master and the overseer would force him to turn traitor. The returned slave would disclose the stopping places, the hiding places, the corn stacks they had used with the full knowledge of the owner of the farm, the name of the German farmer who had fed them and sheltered them. These people who had risked their own security to help runaways would be ruined, fined, imprisoned.

She said, "We got to go free or die. And freedom's not bought with dust."

This time she told them about the long agony of the Middle Passage[7] on the old slave ships, about the black horror of the holds, about the chains and the whips. They too knew these stories. But she wanted to remind them of the long, hard way they had come, about the long, hard way they had yet to go. She told them about Thomas Sims, the boy picked up on the streets of Boston and sent back to Georgia. She said when they got him back to Savannah, got him in prison there, they whipped him until a doctor who was standing by watching said, "You will kill him if you strike him again!" His master said, "Let him die!"

Thus she forced them to go on. Sometimes she thought she had become nothing but a voice speaking in the darkness, <u>cajoling</u>, urging, threatening. Sometimes she told them things to make them laugh; sometimes she sang to them and heard the eleven voices behind her blending softly with hers, and then she knew that for the moment all was well with them.

She gave the impression of being a short, muscular, <u>indomitable</u> woman who could never be defeated. Yet at any moment she was liable to be seized by one of those curious fits of sleep,[8] which might last for a few minutes or for hours.

Even on this trip, she suddenly fell asleep in the woods. The runaways, ragged, dirty, hungry, cold, did not steal the gun, as they might have, and set off by themselves or turn back. They sat on the ground near her and waited patiently until she awakened. They had come to trust her implicitly, totally. They, too, had come to believe her repeated statement, "We got to go free or die." She was leading them into freedom, and so they waited until she was ready to go on.

Finally, they reached Thomas Garrett's house in Wilmington, Delaware. Just as Harriet had promised, Garrett gave them all new shoes and provided carriages to take them on to the next stop.

By slow stages they reached Philadelphia, where William Still hastily recorded their names and the plantations whence they had come and something of the life they had led in slavery. Then he carefully hid what he had written, for fear it might be discovered. In 1872 he published this record in book form and called it *The Underground Railroad*. In the foreword to his book he said: "While I knew the danger of keeping strict records, and while I did not then dream that in my day slavery would be blotted out, or that the time would come when I could publish these records, it used to afford me great satisfaction to take them down, fresh from the lips of fugitives on the way to freedom, and to preserve them as they had given them."

William Still, who was familiar with all the

---

7. **Middle Passage:** the sea route along which African slaves were transported across the Atlantic Ocean to the Americas.

8. **curious fits of sleep:** mysterious spells of dizziness or unconsciousness experienced by Harriet Tubman.

station stops on the Underground Railroad, supplied Harriet with money and sent her and her eleven fugitives on to Burlington, New Jersey.

Harriet felt safer now, though there were danger spots ahead. But the biggest part of her job was over. As they went farther and farther north, it grew colder; she was aware of the wind on the Jersey ferry and aware of the cold damp in New York. From New York they went on to Syracuse, where the temperature was even lower.

In Syracuse she met the Reverend J. W. Loguen, known as "Jarm" Loguen. This was the beginning of a lifelong friendship. Both Harriet and Jarm Loguen were to become friends and supporters of Old John Brown.[9]

From Syracuse they went north again, into a colder, snowier city—Rochester. Here they almost certainly stayed with Frederick

9. **Old John Brown:** an antislavery leader executed for leading a raid on the federal arsenal at Harpers Ferry, Virginia, in 1859.

Douglass, for he wrote in his autobiography: "On one occasion I had eleven fugitives at the same time under my roof, and it was necessary for them to remain with me until I could collect sufficient money to get them to Canada. It was the largest number I ever had at any one time, and I had some difficulty in providing so many with food and shelter, but, as may well be imagined, they were not very <u>fastidious</u> in either direction, and were well content with very plain food, and a strip of carpet on the floor for a bed, or a place on the straw in the barn loft."

Late in December 1851, Harriet arrived in St. Catharines, Canada West (now Ontario), with the eleven fugitives. It had taken almost a month to complete this journey; most of the time had been spent getting out of Maryland.

That first winter in St. Catharines was a terrible one. Canada was a strange, frozen land, snow everywhere, ice everywhere, and a bone-biting cold the like of which none of them had ever experienced before. Harriet rented a small frame house in the town and set to work to make a home. The fugitives boarded with her. They worked in the forests, felling trees, and so did she. Sometimes she took other jobs, cooking or cleaning house for people in the town. She cheered on these newly arrived fugitives, working herself, finding work for them, praying for them, sometimes begging for them.

Often she found herself thinking of the beauty of Maryland, the mellowness of the soil, the richness of the plant life there. The climate itself made for an ease of living that could never be duplicated in this bleak, barren countryside.

In spite of the severe cold, the hard work, she came to love St. Catharines and the other towns and cities in Canada where black men lived. She discovered that freedom meant more than the right to change jobs at will, more than the right to keep the money that one earned. It was the right to vote and to sit on juries. It was the right to be elected to office. In Canada there were black men who were county officials and members of school boards. St. Catharines had a large colony of ex-slaves, and they owned their own homes, kept them neat and clean and in good repair. They lived in whatever part of town they chose and sent their children to the schools.

When spring came, she decided that she would make this small Canadian city her home—as much as any place could be said to be home to a woman who traveled from Canada to the Eastern Shore of Maryland as often as she did.

In the spring of 1852, she went back to Cape May, New Jersey. She spent the summer there, cooking in a hotel. That fall she returned, as usual, to Dorchester County and brought out nine more slaves, conducting them all the way to St. Catharines, in Canada West, to the bone-biting cold, the snow-covered forests—and freedom.

She continued to live in this fashion, spending the winter in Canada and the spring and summer working in Cape May, New Jersey, or in Philadelphia. She made two trips a year into slave territory, one in the fall and another in the spring. She now had a definite, crystallized purpose, and in carrying it out, her life fell into a pattern which remained unchanged for the next six years. ❖

WORDS TO KNOW

fastidious (fă-stĭd′ē-əs) *adj.* difficult to please

764

LETTER TO HARRIET TUBMAN
By Frederick Douglass

Rochester, August 29, 1868

Dear Harriet,

I am glad to know that the story of your eventful life has been written by a kindly lady, and that the same is soon to be published. You ask for what you do not need when you call upon me for a word of commendation. I need such words from you far more than you can need them from me, especially where your superior labors and devotion to the cause of the lately enslaved of our land are known as I know them. The difference between us is very marked. Most that I have done and suffered in the service of our cause has been in public, and I have received much encouragement at every step of the way. You, on the other hand, have labored in a private way. I have wrought in the day—you in the night. I have had the applause of the crowd and the satisfaction that comes of being approved by the multitude, while the most that you have done has been witnessed by a few trembling, scarred, and footsore bondmen and women,[1] whom you have led out of the house of bondage, and whose heartfelt *"God Bless*

Frederick Douglass (1818–1895, abolitionist, statesman) (1856), unidentified photographer. Ambrotype, 4³⁄₁₆" × 3⅜", gift of an anonymous donor, National Portrait Gallery, Smithsonian Institution/Art Resource, New York.

you" has been your only reward. The midnight sky and the silent stars have been the witnesses of your devotion to freedom and of your heroism. Excepting John Brown — of sacred memory — I know of no one who has willingly encountered more perils and hardships to serve our enslaved people than you have. Much that you have done would seem improbable to those who do not know you as I know you. It is to me a great pleasure and a great privilege to bear testimony to your character and your works, and to say to those to whom you may come, that I regard you in every way truthful and trustworthy.

Your friend,
Frederick Douglass

---

1. **bondmen and women:** people forced to work for others without pay; slaves.

Connect to the Literature

1. **What Do You Think?** What impressed you most about Harriet Tubman?

Comprehension Check
- Why is Harriet Tubman leading a band of slaves to Canada?
- Why can't Tubman allow a despairing runaway to go back to the plantation?
- How does life for the runaways change once they reach Canada?

Think Critically

2. **ACTIVE READING** **QUESTIONING**
Look at the questions and answers that you recorded in your **READER'S NOTEBOOK.** What motivated Tubman and the slaves to set off on such a dangerous journey?

3. People who offered their homes to escaping slaves broke the Fugitive Slave Law of 1850. Do you think that they were right to break this law? Why or why not?

4. Based on what you have read, would you have been willing to trust your life to Harriet Tubman? Explain your answer.

   Think About:
   - Tubman's knowledge and experience
   - the risk of getting caught and punished
   - Tubman's threat "Go on with us or die"

Extend Interpretations

5. **COMPARING TEXTS** Like Petry's biography, Frederick Douglass's letter to Harriet Tubman presents Tubman as a courageous and determined person. What does Douglass's description of Harriet Tubman add to Petry's portrayal of her in the biography?

6. **Connect to Life** On page 764, Ann Petry describes the meaning of freedom to Harriet Tubman: ". . . freedom meant more than the right to change jobs at will, more than the right to keep the money that one earned . . ." What would you include in a definition of what freedom means to you?

Literary Analysis

BIOGRAPHY The story of a person's life written by someone else is called a **biography.** If a subject is still living, a biographer tries to set up an interview. A biographer relies on **primary sources,** firsthand accounts of events. Biographers also rely on **secondary sources,** accounts that present information compiled from or based on other sources.

Paired Activity Biographers often focus on remarkable aspects of their subjects. At the same time, they try to paint a balanced picture between fact and interpretation. Does biographer Ann Petry present Harriet Tubman as perfect or human? Working with a partner, go back through the selection and fill in a chart like the one shown. Then use the chart to evaluate Petry's presentation of Harriet Tubman.

Ordinary Human Qualities	Extraordinary Human Qualities
"She knew moments of doubt when she was half-afraid and kept looking back over her shoulder . . ."	"She had never been in Canada, but she kept painting wondrous word pictures of what it would be like."

Writing

1. Biography of an Admirable Person Choose a person in history whom you admire—possibly someone you have recently studied in your social studies class. Research an important event in that person's life. Write a brief biography describing that event. Place the entry in your **Working Portfolio.**

2. Book Review In the library, find a copy of *Harriet Tubman: Conductor on the Underground Railroad.* Read the book and write a book review in which you summarize the main events in Harriet Tubman's life and describe which parts you liked the best and why.

Writing Handbook
See p. R66: Book Review.

Speaking & Listening

Route Map On a map of the United States and Canada, trace Tubman's original escape to freedom from Maryland to Ontario, Canada. Make your own map showing Tubman's route. Prepare an oral report in which you use your own words to tell the story of Tubman's journey. Present the map and report to your class.

Research and Technology Handbook
See p. R120: Using Visuals.

Research & Technology

SOCIAL STUDIES

In 1990 Congress authorized the National Park Service to conduct a study of the Underground Railroad. The goal was to preserve this aspect of United States history. Using the Internet and library sources, find out the results of the study. What sites in the Underground Railroad are currently maintained by the park service? What literature about the Underground Railroad has the park service published? Prepare a brief report on the topic.

INTERNET Research Starter
www.mcdougallittell.com

Vocabulary

EXERCISE A: SYNONYMS Choose the word or phrase that is a synonym for each boldfaced Word to Know.

1. **borne:** (a) carried, (b) loved, (c) influenced
2. **sullen:** (a) happy, (b) bored, (c) glum
3. **cajoling:** (a) informing, (b) coaxing, (c) exaggerating
4. **disheveled:** (a) messy, (b) sick, (c) unwise
5. **mutinous:** (a) nasty, (b) rebellious, (c) rude
6. **fastidious:** (a) famous, (b) quick, (c) difficult to please
7. **instill:** (a) supply gradually, (b) set an example, (c) make a law
8. **indomitable:** (a) unable to take a stand, (b) unable to be cured, (c) unable to be conquered
9. **eloquence:** (a) stubbornness, (b) expressiveness, (c) enjoyment
10. **dispel:** (a) scatter, (b) disagree, (c) differ

EXERCISE B: SIMILES A **simile** is a comparison that uses *like* or *as.* Complete each of the following similes to illustrate the meaning of the boldfaced Word to Know.

1. The slave's thin hat was **borne** on the wind like . . .
2. **Cajoling** and encouraging the runaways, Tubman was like . . .
3. When she said, "Go on with us or die," Tubman showed that she was as **indomitable** as . . .
4. The mistreated slaves became as **mutinous** as . . .

Vocabulary Handbook
See p. R24: Synonyms and Antonyms.

Grammar in Context: Subordinate Clauses

Look at this sentence from Ann Petry's *Harriet Tubman: Conductor on the Underground Railroad.*

> **While she talked,** she kept watching them.

The sentence is made up of two clauses, a **main (or independent) clause** and a **subordinate (or dependent) clause**. The main clause expresses a complete thought and can stand alone as a sentence. The subordinate clause does not express a complete thought, so it cannot stand alone. Subordinate clauses often begin with words such as *after, although, if, unless,* and *when.*

WRITING EXERCISE Rewrite each sentence. Add a subordinate clause that begins with the word in parentheses.

Example: *Original* (After) Word of her arrival spread from cabin to cabin.

Rewritten <u>After she had announced her presence</u>, word of her arrival spread from cabin to cabin.

1. (When) The slaves knew she was near.

2. (As) She told them about her own escape.

3. (If) The eleven runaways would be whipped and sold farther south.

4. (Before) She made them hide behind trees.

5. (Although) They were forced to continue their journey.

<u>**Grammar Handbook**</u> See p. R89: Phrases and Clauses.

Ann Petry
1908–1997

"I tried to make history speak across the centuries in the voices of people . . ."

Desire to Make a Difference Ann Petry was born above her father's drugstore in Old Saybrook, Connecticut. As a child, she listened to family tales about her runaway-slave grandfather, who had withstood a racial attack when he opened a pharmacy. She grew up wanting to write about the effects of racism on African Americans. Despite her interest in writing, Petry graduated from the Connecticut College of Pharmacy and went to work in the family store.

An Overnight Success After she married, Petry moved to New York, where a number of her short stories were published. She published her first novel, *The Street,* in 1946. An overnight success, it was the story of an African-American woman's struggle to survive. Petry went on to write two more novels and numerous short stories, articles, and books for young people.

AUTHOR ACTIVITY
Experience and Writing One of Petry's books for young people is entitled *Tituba of Salem Village.* Find a copy of this book in the library. How does the book reflect Petry's interest in writing about the issues and challenges that African-American women have faced in American history?

from **Lincoln: A Photobiography**

by RUSSELL FREEDMAN

Connect to Your Life

What Do You Know? In this excerpt from *Lincoln: A Photobiography,* Russell Freedman describes President Lincoln's assassination and reveals how the nation reacted to his death. Complete a web that shows what you know about Abraham Lincoln, his life, and his death. Share your web with the class.

Build Background

HISTORY

During the Civil War, President Lincoln held the United States together, fighting to preserve the Union when powerful forces risked tearing it apart. Not well known when he first sought the presidency in 1860, Lincoln was elected with less than 40 percent of the popular vote. By the time of his inauguration, a number of Southern states had seceded and organized themselves into the Confederate States of America. Six weeks later the Civil War began.

Lincoln won reelection in 1864, as Union military victories were bringing the war to a close. On April 14, 1865, five days after the Civil War ended, Lincoln was shot by John Wilkes Booth during a performance of the play *Our American Cousin.* The next morning, one of America's greatest political leaders lay dead.

WORDS TO KNOW
Vocabulary Preview

abduction	revoke
assailant	vindictiveness
falter	

Focus Your Reading

LITERARY ANALYSIS   **TONE**

A writer's attitude toward a subject is expressed through **tone.** For example, a writer's tone may be angry or amused, serious or humorous. To identify the tone of a selection, consider the writer's choice of words. As you read this selection, think about Freedman's choice of words and the tone they convey.

ACTIVE READING   **SUMMARIZING**

Restating the main ideas of a piece of writing is called **summarizing.** A summary is about one-third the length of the original. Remember to omit unimportant details.

READER'S NOTEBOOK The following chart divides the selection into four sections. After you read each section, write a summary that states its main ideas.

Section	Summary
Section 1: from "The president's friends were worried . . ." to "I slept no more that night."(page 771)	**Section 1:** Lincoln lived with the threat of assassination. He did not worry about these threats, but he did once dream about his own death.
Section 2: from "April 14, 1865, . . ." to "Was this part of the play?" (pages 771–773)	
Section 3: from "Booth hobbled offstage . . ." to "And the crowd fell silent . . ." (pages 773–774)	
Section 4: from "On the morning that Lincoln died, . . ." to ". . . does not falter." (pages 774–775)	

FROM

LINCOLN
A PHOTOBIOGRAPHY

by Russell Freedman

The president's friends were worried about his safety. They feared that rebel sympathizers would try to kidnap or kill him in a desperate attempt to save the Confederacy.

Lincoln had been living with rumors of <u>abduction</u> and assassination ever since he was first elected. Threatening letters arrived in the mail almost every day. He filed them away in a bulging envelope marked ASSASSINATION.

"I long ago made up my mind that if anyone wants to kill me, he will do it," he told a newspaper reporter. "If I wore a shirt of mail,[1] and kept myself surrounded by a bodyguard, it would be all the same. There are a thousand ways of getting at a man if it is desired that he should be killed."

Even so, his advisors insisted on taking precautions. Soldiers camped on the White House lawn, cavalry troops escorted Lincoln on his afternoon carriage rides, and plainclothes detectives served as his personal bodyguards. He complained about the protection, but he accepted it. Thoughts of death were certainly on his mind. More than once, he had been troubled by haunting dreams.

He told some friends about a dream he had early in April, just before the fall of Richmond.[2] In the dream, he was wandering through the halls of the White House. He could hear people sobbing, but as he went from room to room, he saw no one.

He kept on until he reached the East Room of the White House: "There I met with a sickening surprise. Before me was a . . . corpse wrapped in funeral vestments. Around it were stationed soldiers who were acting as guards; and there was a throng of people, some gazing mournfully upon the corpse, whose face was covered, others weeping pitifully. 'Who is dead in the White House?' I demanded of one of the soldiers. 'The President,' was his answer; 'he was killed by an assassin.' Then came a loud burst of grief from the crowd, which awoke me from my dream. I slept no more that night."

April 14, 1865, was Good Friday. Lee had surrendered just five days earlier, and Washington was in a festive mood. Lincoln arose early as usual, so he could work at his desk before breakfast. He was looking forward to the day's schedule. That afternoon he would tell his wife, "I never felt so happy in my life."

At eleven, he met with his cabinet. He had invited General Grant to attend the meeting as guest of honor. Most of the talk centered on the difficult problems of reconstruction in the conquered South. Lincoln emphasized again that he wanted no persecutions, "no bloody work." Enough blood had been shed. "There are men in Congress," he said, "who possess feelings of hate and <u>vindictiveness</u> in which I do not sympathize and cannot participate."

After lunch he returned to his office to review court-martial sentences.[3] He <u>revoked</u> the death sentence of a Confederate spy. And he pardoned a deserter, signing his name with the comment, "Well, I think this boy can do us more good above ground than under ground."

Late in the afternoon he went for a carriage ride with Mary. That evening they would attend the theater with another couple, but for the moment, they wanted some time to themselves.

---

1. **shirt of mail:** protective armor for the upper part of the body, made of small interlocking metal rings.
2. **the fall of Richmond:** the Union capture of Richmond, Virginia—the Confederate capital—in April 1865. This event assured the victory of the North in the Civil War.
3. **court-martial sentences:** punishments decided by military courts.

WORDS TO KNOW	**abduction** (ăb-dŭk′shən) *n.* kidnapping
	vindictiveness (vĭn-dĭk′tĭv-nĭs) *n.* a desire for revenge
	revoke (rĭ-vōk′) *v.* to withdraw or repeal

Courtesy of the Illinois State Historical Library.

The war had been hard on both of them. Since Willie's death, Mary had been plagued by depression and imaginary fears, and at times, Lincoln had feared for his wife's sanity. As their carriage rolled through the countryside, they talked hopefully of the years ahead. "We must both be more cheerful in the future," Lincoln said. "Between the war and the loss of our darling Willie, we have been very miserable."

After dinner, Lincoln and Mary left for Ford's Theater in the company of a young army major, Henry R. Rathbone, and his fiancée, Clara Harris. Arriving late, they were escorted up a winding stairway to the flag-draped presidential box overlooking the stage. The play had already started, but as Lincoln's party appeared in the box, the orchestra struck up "Hail to the Chief"[4] and the audience rose for a standing ovation. Lincoln smiled and bowed. He took his place in a rocking chair provided for him by the management and put on a pair of gold-rimmed eyeglasses he had mended with a string. Mary sat beside him, with Major Rathbone and Miss Harris to their right.

---

4. **"Hail to the Chief":** a patriotic song played at public appearances of the president of the United States since 1837. The words, seldom heard, are from Sir Walter Scott's "The Lady of the Lake"; James Sanderson wrote the music.

The play was *Our American Cousin,* a popular comedy starring Laura Keene, who had already given a thousand performances in the leading role. Lincoln settled back and relaxed. He laughed heartily, turning now and then to whisper to his wife. Halfway through the play, he felt a chill and got up to drape his black overcoat across his shoulders.

During the third act, Mary reached over to take Lincoln's hand. She pressed closer to him. Behind them, the door to the presidential box was closed but not locked. Lincoln's bodyguard that evening, John Parker, had slipped away from his post outside the door to go downstairs and watch the play.

The audience had just burst into laughter when the door swung open. A shadowy figure stepped into the box, stretched out his arm, aimed a small derringer pistol at the back of Lincoln's head, and pulled the trigger. Lincoln's arm jerked up. He slumped forward in his chair as Mary reached out to catch him. Then she screamed.

Major Rathbone looked up to see a man standing with a smoking pistol in one hand and a hunting knife in the other. Rathbone lunged at the gunman, who yelled something and slashed Rathbone's arm to the bone. Then the assailant leaped from the box to the stage, twelve feet below. One of his boot spurs caught on the regimental flag draped over the box. As he crashed onto the stage, he broke the shinbone of his left leg.

The assailant struggled to his feet, faced the audience, and shouted the motto of the commonwealth of Virginia: "*Sic semper tyrannis*"—(Thus always to tyrants). The stunned and disbelieving audience recognized him as John Wilkes Booth, the well-known actor. What was going on? Was this part of the play?

Booth hobbled offstage and out the stage door, where a horse was saddled and waiting. Twelve days later he would be cornered by federal troops and shot in a Virginia barn.

The theater was in an uproar. People were shouting, standing on chairs, shoving for the exits, as Laura Keene cried out from the stage, "The president is shot! The president is shot!"

Two doctors rushed to the president's box. Lincoln had lost consciousness instantly. The bullet had entered his skull above his left ear, cut through his brain, and lodged behind his right eye. The doctors worked over him as Mary hovered beside them, sobbing hysterically. Finally, six soldiers carried the president out of the theater and across the fog-shrouded street to a boardinghouse, where a man with a lighted candle stood beckoning. He was placed on a four-poster bed in a narrow room off the hallway. The bed wasn't long enough for Lincoln. He had to be laid diagonally across its cornhusk mattress.

Five doctors worked over the president that night. Now and then he groaned, but it was obvious that he would not regain consciousness. The room filled with members of the cabinet, with congressmen and high government officials. Mary waited in the front parlor. "Bring Tad—he will speak to Tad—he loves him so," she cried. Tad had been attending another play that evening. Sobbing, "They killed my pa, they killed my pa," he was taken back to the White House to wait.

Robert Lincoln was summoned to join the hushed crowd around his father's bedside. Outside, cavalry patrols clattered down the street. Another assassin had just tried to murder Secretary of State William Seward. Everyone suspected that the attacks were part of a rebel conspiracy to murder several government officials and capture the city.

By dawn, a heavy rain was falling. Lincoln was still breathing faintly. Robert Lincoln surrendered to tears, then others in the room began to cry. At 7:22 A.M. on April 15, Lincoln died at the age of fifty-six. A doctor folded the president's hands across his chest. Gently he smoothed Lincoln's contracted face muscles, closed his eyelids, and drew a white sheet over his head. It was then that Secretary of War Edwin M. Stanton murmured, "Now he belongs to the ages."

The funeral was held in the East Room of the White House four days later, on April 19. Afterwards, the long funeral procession, led by a detachment of black troops, moved slowly up Pennsylvania Avenue to the muffled beat of drums and the tolling of church bells. When the procession reached the Capitol, Lincoln was carried inside to lie in state under the huge Capitol dome. The next day, thousands of people, black and white, soldiers and civilians, stood patiently in the rain, waiting to file past the open coffin.

On April 21, a funeral train set out on a sixteen-hundred-mile journey to Illinois, carrying Abraham Lincoln home to his final resting place in Springfield. The train followed the same route Lincoln had taken when he came to Washington as president-elect. It stopped at major cities along the way, so mourners could again file past the coffin. Where it did not stop, men and women with their children stood silently along the route to watch the train pass.

On the night of May 2, the train left Chicago and puffed its way southward through the rain across the Illinois prairie. People had built bonfires along the railroad tracks, and they stood outlined against the glowing red flames at every prairie village and country crossroads as the funeral train passed through.

At 9 A.M. it approached Springfield with its bell tolling. It steamed slowly through the business center and pulled up at the station, where regiments of soldiers and delegations of officials were waiting to meet it. Tens of thousands of people jammed the streets around the station and stood on nearby rooftops. A military band began to play a funeral dirge. All the bells of Springfield tolled. Guns fired a salute. And the crowd fell silent as the train came to a stop.

On the morning that Lincoln died, someone emptied the contents of his pockets and placed them in a box, which was wrapped in brown paper and tied with a string. Robert Lincoln passed the box on to his daughter, who presented it to the Library of Congress in 1937. Labeled "Do Not Open," it remained locked in a vault until 1976, when the string was untied and the paper unwrapped as the library staff looked on.

The morning he died, Lincoln had in his pockets a pair of small spectacles folded into a silver case; a small velvet eyeglass cleaner; a large linen handkerchief with A. Lincoln stitched in red; an ivory pocketknife trimmed with silver; and a brown leather wallet lined with purple silk. The wallet contained a Confederate five-dollar bill bearing the likeness of Jefferson Davis and eight newspaper clippings that Lincoln had cut out and saved. All the clippings praised him. As president, he had been denounced,[5] ridiculed, and damned by a legion of critics. When he saw an article that complimented him, he often kept it.

One clipping found in Lincoln's wallet quotes the British reformer John Bright.

---

5. **denounced:** criticized openly.

Shortly before the presidential election of 1864, Bright wrote to the American newspaper publisher Horace Greeley and said:

"All those who believe that Slavery weakens America's power and tarnishes[6] your good name throughout the world, and who regard the restoration of your Union as a thing to be desired . . . are heartily longing for the reelection of Mr. Lincoln. . . . they think they have observed in his career a grand simplicity of purpose and a patriotism which knows no change and does not <u>falter</u>." ❖

---

6. **tarnishes:** stains; disgraces.

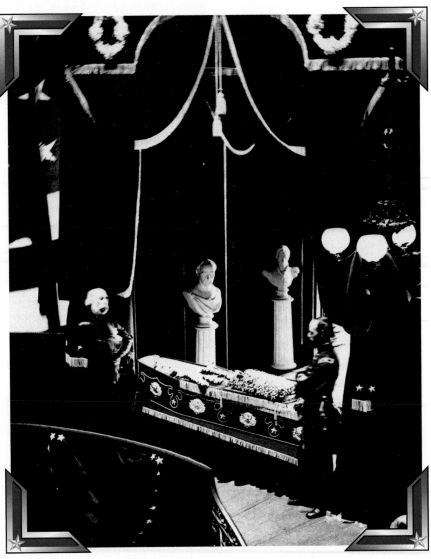

Abraham Lincoln lying in state.
Courtesy of the Illinois State Historical Library.

Connect to the Literature

1. **What Do You Think?** What do you think of Lincoln after reading this selection?

Comprehension Check
- Why were Lincoln's friends and associates concerned for his safety?
- When did Lincoln's assassination take place?
- How did the nation show its grief in the days following Lincoln's funeral?

Think Critically

2. The selection focuses on Lincoln's human qualities rather than his political career. Why do you think Russell Freedman chose to present Lincoln from this point of view? What details reveal Lincoln's humanity?

3. Based on this account, how would you describe Abraham Lincoln's character?

   Think About:
   - his leadership ability
   - his attitude toward the defeated South
   - his relationship with his family

4. Why do you think Russell Freedman included the description of Lincoln's dream?

5. **ACTIVE READING** **SUMMARIZING**
   Look at the summaries that you wrote in your **READER'S NOTEBOOK.** Compare your summaries with those of your classmates. What main ideas did you include? What details did you omit?

Extend Interpretations

6. **What If?** What if Lincoln were president today? Based on what you have learned about him in this selection, what goals do you think he would pursue?

7. **Connect to Life** Today, presidents of the United States are carefully guarded when they appear in public. What are the advantages and disadvantages of tight security? Should presidents be protected from contact with the public? Explain your opinion.

Literary Analysis

TONE A writer's attitude toward a subject is expressed through his or her **tone.** A writer's tone can be respectful, negative, humorous, angry, or solemn, or the tone may represent a range of attitudes. One way to identify a writer's tone is to consider his or her choice of words.

Paired Activity With a partner, go back through the selection and make note of words, phrases, and sentences that express Freedman's attitude toward Lincoln. Record your findings in a chart like the one shown. What would you say is the overall tone of this work?

Words	Tone That the Words Express
"Thoughts of death were certainly on his mind. More than once, he had been troubled by haunting dreams."	grim and somber

REVIEW: BIOGRAPHY The story of a person's life written by someone else is called a **biography.** Although biographers often present their subject in a favorable way, they also strive for a balance between fact and interpretation. Do you think that Freedman presents a balanced view of Lincoln? Why or why not?

Writing

Lincoln's Life Find out more about Abraham Lincoln's life. Where did he grow up? How and when did he get involved in politics? Prepare a report that focuses on a specific area of Lincoln's life. Make sure your report has a coherent thesis, a well-organized body, and a clear conclusion. Place your report in your **Working Portfolio.**

Writing Handbook
See p. R51: Research Report Writing.

Speaking & Listening

The Confederate States
Research the development of the Confederate States of America. Why did these states secede? Who were the people involved in the secession? Prepare a speech outline that includes an introduction, a logically developed body, and an effective conclusion.

Speaking and Listening Handbook
See p. R104: Writing Your Speech.

Research & Technology

Lincoln's Plan During his presidency, Lincoln worked on a plan called Reconstruction, or the rebuilding of the South. When Lincoln was killed, Andrew Johnson became president and tried to carry out Lincoln's plan. Using the Internet and library sources, find out about Lincoln's plan for Reconstruction. What does the plan tell you about Lincoln's vision for the country? Write up your findings in a report.

INTERNET **Research Starter**
www.mcdougallittell.com

Vocabulary

STANDARDIZED TEST PRACTICE

Choose the word or group of words that means the same, or nearly the same, as the underlined Word to Know in each sentence.

1. President Lincoln lived with the constant threat of <u>abduction</u>. <u>Abduction</u> means—
   A cruelty   **B** attack
   C kidnapping   **D** poverty

2. Because Lincoln stood by his beliefs, people knew he would never <u>falter</u>. <u>Falter</u> means—
   F waver   **G** collapse
   H succeed   **J** forget

3. Lincoln decided to <u>revoke</u> the death sentence of a Southern spy. <u>Revoke</u> means—
   A extend   **B** repeal
   C enable   **D** ignore

4. The president did not agree with the <u>vindictiveness</u> of some of the members of Congress. <u>Vindictiveness</u> means—
   F boastfulness   **G** prejudice
   H cowardice   **J** vengefulness

5. John Wilkes Booth was Lincoln's <u>assailant</u>. <u>Assailant</u> means—
   A ally   **B** attacker
   C cousin   **D** competitor

VOCABULARY STRATEGY: PREFIXES AND ROOTS
A single root can be joined with many prefixes to form different words. For example, the root *duct,* meaning "to lead," can be joined with the prefix *ab-* (which means "away from") to form the word *abduct.* The root *duct* can also be joined with the prefix *pro-* (meaning "forward") to form the word *product.* Replace the prefixes in the following words to create new words. Then write a sentence using each new word.

1. denounce—replace with *pro–*
2. observe—replace with *pre-*
3. propose—replace with *ex-*
4. profess—replace with *con-*
5. increase—replace with *de-*

Building Vocabulary
See p. R20: Context Clues.

Grammar in Context: Joining Main and Subordinate Clauses

Notice how Russell Freedman combines a **main clause** and a **subordinate clause** in the following sentence:

> **As he crashed onto the stage,** he broke the shinbone of his left leg.

A **clause** is a group of words that has a subject and a verb. A **main (or independent) clause** can stand alone as a sentence because it expresses a complete thought. A **subordinate (or dependent) clause** cannot stand alone as a sentence because it does not express a complete thought. A subordinate clause must be joined to a main clause to form a sentence.

WRITING EXERCISE Create a sentence by adding a main clause to each subordinate clause.

Example: *Original* because they feared for his safety.

Rewritten Lincoln's advisers tried to protect him because they feared for his safety.

1. while Lincoln was watching a play
2. as a shot rang out
3. when Booth leapt onto the stage
4. although doctors tried to help the president
5. after Lincoln died

<u>Grammar Handbook</u> See p. R89: Phrases and Clauses.

Russell Freedman
born 1929

"History is the story of ourselves."

In Love with Books When Russell Freedman was growing up in San Francisco, his two favorite books were *Treasure Island* by Robert Louis Stevenson, a book of fiction, and Ernest Thompson Seton's *Wild Animals I Have Known,* a book of nonfiction. Freedman later wrote, "In those innocent days, I didn't worry about distinctions like fiction and nonfiction. . . . I did know that I was thrilled by both of these books."

Life's Work Freedman grew up to work as a reporter with the Associated Press, as a television writer, and as a teacher. One day he read a story about Louis Braille, a blind boy who had invented the Braille alphabet at the age of 16. Remembering his love of nonfiction as a child, Freedman decided to write a book about influential young people. With the publication of *Teenagers Who Made History,* Freedman knew he had found his life's work.

Award Winner Freedman has written more than 35 nonfiction books for young people, many of them award winners. *Lincoln: A Photobiography* won the Newbery Medal in 1988.

AUTHOR ACTIVITY
Common Ground Locate a copy of *Lincoln: A Photobiography* in the library and look through the book. Why is it called a photobiography? What other photobiographies has Freedman published? Look through one of these books as well. How does the presence of photographs enhance a biography? What would the books be like without the photographs?

O Captain! My Captain!

by WALT WHITMAN

Connect to Your Life

The Right Stuff Is there a person whom you admire—someone you know or have read about? What is special about this person? What is it about this person that you respect? Use a web like the one shown to identify this person's special traits.

Build Background

HISTORY

Walt Whitman wrote the poem "O Captain! My Captain!" after being deeply affected by President Abraham Lincoln's assassination on April 14, 1865, only five days after the end of the Civil War. The poem captures the sense of tragedy that suddenly overwhelmed the nation, at the very moment when many people were celebrating the war's end.

Lincoln's assassination was the first murder of a president in the history of the United States. It shocked the country. In fact, historians have questioned how much Lincoln's murder influenced U.S. history. Some historians believe, for example, that Reconstruction—the reorganization of the governments of the Southern states—might have been very different if Lincoln had lived.

Focus Your Reading

LITERARY ANALYSIS **EXTENDED METAPHOR**

A figure of speech that compares two people, places, or things at some length and in several ways (and without using the words *like* or *as*) is called an **extended metaphor.** For example, in "O Captain! My Captain!" Walt Whitman compares President Lincoln to the captain of a ship.

ACTIVE READING **AUTHOR'S PURPOSE**

An **author's purpose** is his or her reason for creating a particular work. An author might write a piece of literature to serve one of the following purposes:

- to entertain
- to inform or explain
- to express an opinion
- to persuade

Although an author might have more than one purpose for writing, a piece of literature is usually written with one main purpose in mind.

READER'S NOTEBOOK. As you read "O Captain! My Captain!" keep a list of words or phrases from the poem that give clues to the author's purpose. Later, you will use your responses to determine the author's purpose for writing the poem.

O Captain! My Captain!

by Walt Whitman

Decorative sculpture of Abraham Lincoln. Abby Aldrich Rockefeller Folk Art Museum, Williamsburg, Virginia.

O Captain! my Captain! our fearful trip is done,
The ship has weather'd every rack,[1] the prize we sought is won,
The port is near, the bells I hear, the people all exulting,[2]
While follow eyes the steady keel, the vessel grim and daring;
5   But O heart! heart! heart!
      O the bleeding drops of red,
        Where on the deck my Captain lies,
        Fallen cold and dead.

O Captain! my Captain! rise up and hear the bells;
10 Rise up—for you the flag is flung—for you the bugle trills,
For you bouquets and ribbon'd wreaths—for you the shores a-crowding,
For you they call, the swaying mass, their eager faces turning;
    Here Captain! dear father!
      This arm beneath your head!
15   It is some dream that on the deck,
        You've fallen cold and dead.

My Captain does not answer, his lips are pale and still,
My father does not feel my arm, he has no pulse nor will,
The ship is anchor'd safe and sound, its voyage closed and done,
20 From fearful trip the victor ship comes in with object won:
    Exult O shores, and ring O bells!
      But I with mournful tread,
        Walk the deck my Captain lies,
        Fallen cold and dead.

---

1. **rack:** a battering, as by a storm.
2. **exulting:** rejoicing.

Connect to the Literature

1. **What Do You Think?**
   Does "O Captain! My Captain!" clearly convey the speaker's feelings? Why or why not?

   Comprehension Check
   • Whom does the captain represent?
   • What does the speaker of "O Captain! My Captain!" see on the deck of the ship?
   • What "prize" has been won?

Think Critically

2. **ACTIVE READING AUTHOR'S PURPOSE**
   Look back at the notes you made in your
   READER'S NOTEBOOK. Use your responses to determine Whitman's purposes for writing the poem. Compare your interpretation with those of your classmates.

3. In your opinion, how effective is Whitman's comparison of Lincoln to a ship's captain?

   Think About:
   • what the ship represents
   • the "fearful trip" the ship has weathered
   • the "shores a-crowding"

4. How do you think the speaker of the poem feels about Abraham Lincoln? Support your answer with examples from the poem.

5. **Irony** is the contrast between what is expected and what actually happens. For example, you do not expect that there will be crowds rejoicing on the shore while the captain lies dead on the deck. How does the description of the rejoicing crowds help emphasize the tragedy and irony of the captain's death?

Extend Interpretations

6. **COMPARING TEXTS** Does the excerpt from *Lincoln: A Photobiography* on pages 770–775 or "O Captain! My Captain!" convey a greater sense of loss to you? Explain your answer. What did you learn about Lincoln from each text?

7. **Connect to Life** Think of an important event in the United States or in the world that brought out strong emotions in you. Describe the event and your reactions to it. Why did the event make you feel this way?

Literary Analysis

EXTENDED METAPHOR When two people, places, or things are compared at some length and in several ways in a work of literature, the comparison is called an **extended metaphor.** A metaphor does not use the word *like* or *as* to indicate the comparison. In "O Captain! My Captain!" Whitman compares President Abraham Lincoln to the captain of a ship. Images of the ship and its atmosphere in the poem extend the metaphor.

Paired Activity Working with a partner, create a chart like the one shown. In the left-hand column, list the elements in the poem's extended metaphor. In the right-hand column, explain the meaning of each element.

Metaphor	Meaning
captain	President Lincoln
ship	
storm	
arrival of ship at port	

REVIEW: RHYME SCHEME The pattern of rhyme in a poem is called the **rhyme scheme.** The pattern is charted by assigning a letter of the alphabet, beginning with the letter *a,* to each line. Lines that rhyme are given the same letter. What is the rhyme scheme of the last stanza of "O Captain! My Captain!"?

Writing

Summary Write a short report in which you explain the author's purpose and, in your own words, summarize the meaning of each stanza in the poem. For your summary, be sure to focus on the most important ideas and details. Save your report in your **Working Portfolio.**

Writing Handbook
See p. R36: Building Blocks of Good Writing.

Speaking & Listening

Dramatic Reading Present a dramatic reading of the poem, emphasizing the rhythm and rhyme of the words and explaining their meaning. Pay attention to repeated words and phrases. If you wish, find a piece of music that complements the poem. Play the music softly in the background as you read.

Speaking and Listening Handbook
See p. R107: Dramatic Reading.

Research & Technology

The First Modern War The Civil War was one of the first modern wars. Using the Internet and library sources, research the technological advances that contributed to the Civil War's reputation as a modern war. For example, how did the invention of the rifle change warfare? What role did railroads, the telegraph, and ironclad ships play? Prepare a report for the class. Be sure to note your sources.

Walt Whitman
1819–1892

"To have great poets, there must be great audiences."

A Brief Childhood Whitman left school at age 11. Within a few years, he was living on his own in New York City. He drifted from job to job, working as a printer, a journalist, and a carpenter. He loved to stroll around the city, taking in the sights and sounds that would later emerge in his poetry.

Critic's Voices The poetry of Walt Whitman was praised by a few critics in his lifetime but denounced by many others. Abraham Lincoln frequently read aloud from Whitman's first collection of poetry, *Leaves of Grass,* even though few bookstores carried it. Today Whitman is considered one of America's greatest poets.

A Caring Heart Whitman had a passionate concern for other people and served as a volunteer nurse, caring for the wounded at a Union army hospital in Washington, D.C., during the Civil War.

AUTHOR ACTIVITY
Poetry of Grief Walt Whitman wrote another poem to commemorate President Lincoln's death—"When Lilacs Last in the Dooryard Bloom'd." Read part or all of the poem. What is the meaning of the title?

Building Vocabulary
Researching Word Origins

Many words in the English language come from Latin, Greek, Old English, Anglo-Saxon, and other languages. Some words are derived from the names of people, places, or events in history.

Latin: *scola,* school

Lewis and Clark **scholar** James Ronda puts perspective on the Indian policy of the expedition: "These items, everything from ivory **combs** to **calico shirts,** represented what the United States offered to potential trading partners."

—Stephen E. Ambrose, *Undaunted Courage*

Old English: *scyrte,* originally an article of clothing like a skirt

Greek: *gomphos,* tooth, peg

Calico is a fabric named after Calicut, a port city in India.

Strategies for Building Vocabulary

A word's history and origin are called its **etymology.** Understanding etymology can help you become a better reader and writer. For example, interesting details about a word's history and origin can help you remember the word's meaning. These details can also increase your knowledge of other words with the same origin. The following strategies are guides to understanding etymology.

❶ Learn from a Dictionary An unabridged dictionary will give etymologies of most words. This information appears either before or after the word's definition. Read the highlighted part of this entry.

> po•et (pō′ĭt) *n.* **1. A writer of poems.**
> **2. One who demonstrates great imaginative power, insight, or beauty of expression.**
> [Middle English, from Old French *poëte,* from Latin *poeta,* from Greek *poiētēs,* maker, composer, from *poiein,* to create.]

This entry traces the history of the word *poet.* Before the word appeared in Middle English, it had been used in Old French. The Old French word had come from Latin.

Before it appeared in Latin, it had originated in Greek. The word *poet* has appeared in many languages, and it has always described a person who creates.

❷ Understand Word Families A group of words connected by history and meaning is known as a word family. For example, the words *scripture, describe,* and *scribble* are all derived from the Latin word *scribere,* which means "to write." Review the chart below.

Words Related to Latin *Scribere,* "to Write"	
scripture	a sacred writing
describe	to explain in speech or in writing
scribble	to write in a hurried way

EXERCISE On a sheet of paper, describe the origin of each of the following words. Be sure to use an unabridged dictionary.
Example: fury: from Latin *furere,* "to rage"

1. echo
2. symbol
3. library
4. music
5. yam
6. kimono
7. graduate
8. ax
9. graphic
10. mill

CIVIL WAR *Journal*

BY LOUISA MAY ALCOTT

Portrait of the author, circa 1875

1 8 6 1

April. —War declared with the South, and our Concord company went to Washington. A busy time getting them ready, and a sad day seeing them off, for in a little town like this we all seem like one family in times like these. At the station the scene was very dramatic, as the brave boys went away perhaps never to come back again.

I've often longed to see a war, and now I have my wish. I long to be a man, but as I can't fight, I will content myself with working for those who can. . . .

1 8 6 2

September, October. — . . . War news bad. Anxious faces, beating hearts, and busy minds.

I like the stir in the air, and long for battle like a warhorse when he smells powder. The blood of the Mays is up![1] . . .

November. —Thirty years old. Decided to go to Washington as a nurse if I could find a place. Help needed, and I love nursing, and *must* let out my pent-up energy in some new way. Winter is always a hard and a dull time, and if I am away there is one less to feed and warm and worry over.

I want new experiences, and am sure to get 'em if I go. So I've sent in my name, and bide my time[2] writing tales, to leave all snug behind me, and mending up my old clothes,—for nurses don't need nice things, thank goodness!

December. —On the 11th I received a note from Miss H. M. Stevenson telling me to start for Georgetown next day to fill a place in the Union Hotel Hospital. Mrs. Ropes of Boston was matron, and Miss Kendall of Plymouth

---

1. **The blood of the Mays is up!:** The temper that Alcott has inherited from her ancestors (the Mays) is aroused.

2. **bide my time:** wait around.

Patients in ward K of Armory Square Hospital, Washington D.C., ca. 1865. Library of Congress

was a nurse there, and though a hard place, help was needed. I was ready, and when my commander said "March!" I marched. Packed my trunk, and reported in B.[oston] that same evening.

We had all been full of courage till the last moment came, then we all broke down. I realized that I had taken my life in my hand, and might never see them all again. I said, "Shall I stay, Mother?" as I hugged her close. "No, go!" answered the Spartan[3] woman, and till I turned the corner she bravely smiled and waved her wet handkerchief on the doorstep.

Shall I ever see that dear old face again?

So I set forth in the December twilight, with May and Julian Hawthorne as escort, feeling as if I was the son of the house going to war.

Friday, the 12th, was a very memorable day, spent in running all over Boston to get my pass, etc., calling for parcels, getting a tooth filled, and buying a veil,—my only purchase. A. C. gave me some old clothes, the dear

---

3. **Spartan:** self-disciplined and unaffected by pain or suffering (as the inhabitants of the ancient Greek city of Sparta were said to be).

Sewalls money for myself and boys, lots of love and help, and at 5 P.M., saying "good-by" to a group of tearful faces at the station, I started on my long journey, full of hope and sorrow, courage and plans.

A most interesting journey into a new world full of stirring sights and sounds, new adventures, and an evergrowing sense of the great task I had undertaken.

I said my prayers as I went rushing through the country white with tents, all alive with patriotism, and already red with blood.

A solemn time, but I'm glad to live in it, and am sure it will do me good whether I come out alive or dead.

All went well, and I got to Georgetown one evening very tired. Was kindly welcomed, slept in my narrow bed with two other room-mates, and on the morrow began my new life by seeing a poor man die at dawn, and sitting all day between a boy with pneumonia and a man shot through the lungs. A strange day, but I did my best, and when I put mother's little black shawl round the boy while he sat up panting for breath, he smiled and said, "You are real motherly, ma'am." I felt as if I was getting on. The man only lay and stared with his big black eyes, and made me very nervous. But all were well behaved, and I sat looking at the twenty strong faces as they looked back at me,—hoping that I looked "motherly" to them, for my thirty years made me feel old, and the suffering round me made me long to comfort every one. . . .

1 8 6 3

January. —I never began the year in a stranger place than this, five hundred miles from home, alone among strangers, doing painful duties all day long, & leading a life of constant excitement in this greathouse surrounded by 3 or 4 hundred men in all stages of suffering, disease & death. Though often home sick, heart sick & worn out, I like it—find real pleasure in comforting tending & cheering these poor souls who seem to love me, to feel my sympathy though unspoken, & acknowledge my hearty good will in spite of the ignorance, awkwardness, & bashfulness which I cannot help showing in so new & trying a situation. The men are docile, respectful, & affectionate, with but few exceptions, truly lovable & manly many of them. John Suhre a Virginia blacksmith is the prince of patients, & though what we call a common man, in education & condition, to me is all that I could expect or ask from the first gentleman in the land. Under his plain speech & unpolished manner I seem to see a noble character, a heart as warm & tender as a woman's, a nature fresh & frank as any child's. He is about thirty, I think, tall & handsome, mortally wounded & dying royally, without reproach, repining, or remorse. Mrs. Ropes & myself love him & feel indignant that such a man should be so early lost, for though he might never distinguish himself before the world, his influence & example cannot be without effect, for real goodness is never wasted.

Mon 4th—I shall record the events of a day as a sample of the days I spend—

Up at six, dress by gas light, run through my ward & fling up the windows though the men grumble & shiver; but the air is bad enough to breed a pestilence[4] & as no notice is taken of our frequent appeals for better ventilation I must do what I can. Poke up the fire, add blankets, joke, coax, & command, but continue to open doors & windows as if life depended on it; mine does, & doubtless

---

4. **pestilence** (pĕs′tə-ləns): deadly contagious disease.

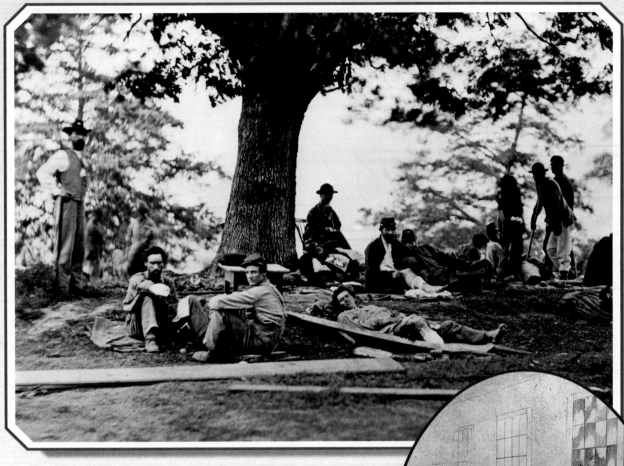

Wounded soldiers recover from surgery on the grounds of a federal field hospital near Fredericksburg, Virginia, in 1864.

He is about thirty, I think, tall & handsome, mortally wounded & dying royally, without reproach, repining, or remorse.

Campaign Sketches: The Letter for Home (1863), Winslow Homer. Lithograph 14" × 10⅞". Prints Division, The New York Public Library, Astor, Lenox and Tilden Foundations.

Cared For. Wood engraving. Harper's Weekly, January 21, 1871. National Library of Medicine, Bethesda, Md.

Till noon I trot, trot, giving out rations, cutting up food for helpless "boys," washing faces, . . .

many another, for a more perfect pestilence-box than this house I never saw—cold, damp, dirty, full of vile odors from wounds, kitchens, wash rooms, & stables. No competent head, male or female, to right matters, & a jumble of good, bad, & indifferent nurses, surgeons & attendants to complicate the Chaos still more.

After this unwelcome progress through my stifling[5] ward I go to breakfast with what appetite I may; find the inevitable fried beef, salt butter, husky bread & washy coffee; listen to the clack of eight women & a dozen men; the first silly, stupid or possessed of but one idea, the last absorbed in their breakfast & themselves to a degree that is both ludicrous and provoking,[6] for all the dishes are ordered down the table *full* & returned *empty*, the conversation is entirely among themselves & each announces his opinion with an air of importance that frequently causes me to choke

in my cup or bolt my meals with undignified speed lest a laugh betray to these pompous beings that a "child's among them takin' notes." Till noon I trot, trot, giving out rations, cutting up food for helpless "boys," washing faces, teaching my attendants how beds are made or floors swept, dressing wounds, taking Dr. FitzPatrick's orders, (privately wishing all the time that he would be more gentle with my big babies), dusting tables, sewing bandages, keeping my tray tidy, rushing up & down after pillows, bed linen, sponges, book & directions, till it seems as if I would joyfully pay down all I possess for fifteen minutes rest.

---

5. **stifling** (stī′flĭng): hot and stuffy; suffocating.
6. **ludicrous** (lōō′dĭ-krəs) **and provoking:** ridiculous and irritating.

At twelve the big bell rings & up comes dinner for the boys who are always ready for it & never entirely satisfied. Soup, meat, potatoes, & bread is the bill of fare. Charley Thayer the attendant travels up & down the room serving out the rations, saving little for himself yet always thoughtful of his mates & patient as a woman with their helplessness. When dinner is over some sleep, many read, & others want letters written. This I like to do for they put in such odd things & express their ideas so comically I have great fun interiorally while as grave as possible exteriorally. A few of the men word their paragraphs well & make excellent letters. John's was the best of all I wrote. The answering of letters from friends after some one has died is the saddest & hardest duty a nurse has to do.

Supper at five sets every one to running that can run & when that flurry is over all settle down for the evening amusements which consist of newspapers, gossip, Drs last round, & for such as need them the final doses for the night. At nine the bell rings, gas is turned down & day nurses go to bed.

Night nurses go on duty, & sleep & death have the house to themselves. . . .

My work is changed to night watching or half night & half day, from twelve to twelve. I like it as it leaves me time for a morning run which is what I need to keep well, for bad air, food, water, work & watching are getting to be too much for me. I trot up & down the streets in all directions, some times to the Heights, then half way to Washington, again to the hill over which the long trains of army wagons are constantly vanishing & ambulances appearing. That way the fighting lies, & I long to follow. . . . ❖

Louisa May Alcott
1832–1888

"Life is my college. May I graduate well, and earn some honors!"

A Childhood Among Writers Louisa May Alcott was raised in Massachusetts. She and her three sisters grew up in an exciting household that was often filled with lively debate. Her father was an educator and writer, and family friends included such famous American writers as Ralph Waldo Emerson and Henry David Thoreau.

Supporting Her Family Unfortunately, Alcott's father was more of a philosopher than a practical man, and the family was frequently in debt. Alcott tried to help her family by working as a teacher and a seamstress. She also wrote and soon began to submit her work for publication. Her first poem was published when she was 19, and by 1854 she had published a book of short stories and poems. During the Civil War, she served as a nurse in Washington, D.C., an experience she would later describe in *Hospital Sketches*. In the late 1860s, her novel *Little Women* was published, bringing her instant success.

Success and Fame The success of *Little Women* meant that Alcott could support her family with the income from her literary work. She could also devote time to political causes. Alcott continued to write books for younger readers and also wrote horror stories. The last years of her life were spent in Boston, where she died at the age of 55.

Author Study MARK TWAIN

Writer and Adventurer

"I like a good story well told. That is the reason I am sometimes forced to tell them myself."

1835–1910

GROWING UP ON THE RIVER

Mark Twain was born Samuel Clemens in Florida, Missouri, in 1835. When he was four years old his family moved to Hannibal, Missouri, a small town on the Mississippi River. Clemens grew up fascinated by the river, navigating its waters on homemade rafts, playing in swimming holes, and exploring nearby woods and caves. His carefree childhood days ended at age 11, however, when his father died of pneumonia. In order to help support his family, he left school and worked for a newspaper and printing firm.

Clemens/Twain as an apprentice printer

His **LIFE** and **TIMES**

1835 Born Nov. 30 as Samuel Clemens in Florida, Missouri	1839 Moves to Hannibal, Missouri	1853 Leaves Hannibal and travels around United States	1859 Gets steamboat pilot's license

1830   1840   1850   1860

1837 Victoria becomes queen of England.	1848 Gold Rush begins in California.		1861 Civil War begins.

LOOKING FOR ADVENTURE

In 1851 Clemens began working for his older brother Orion, who published a small newspaper in Hannibal. Clemens wrote humorous articles for the paper, which he signed "W. Epaminondas Adrastus Blab." In 1853 Clemens left Hannibal and set off to find adventure. He traveled in the eastern and midwestern United States and eventually joined Orion in Iowa. After two years in Iowa, Clemens left for South America to seek his fortune along the banks of the Amazon River.

FROM THE RIVER TO THE WORLD

Clemens never made it to the Amazon. On his journey south he befriended a steamboat captain, and for the next four years he sailed the Mississippi River, first as the captain's apprentice and then as a pilot. The adventures he had during these years would provide the material for some of his most famous stories.

    The Civil War ended Clemens's career as a pilot because steamboats could no longer travel freely between the North and the South. In 1861 he moved with Orion to Nevada, where he prospected for gold and eventually began writing for a local paper. It was during this time that he assumed the

BROOKLYN ACADEMY OF MUSIC, FEB. 7th
Tickets at 244 Fulton St. and
172 Montague St.

Poster advertising a lecture by Twain

1865
Earns fame for "The Celebrated Jumping Frog of Calaveras County"

1870
Marries Olivia Langdon

1884
The Adventures of Huckleberry Finn is published.

1895
Begins worldwide lecture tour

1904
Begins writing his *Autobiography;* wife Olivia dies

1910
Twain dies on April 21 near Redding, Connecticut.

1870   **1880**   **1890**   **1900**   **1910**

1865
Union defeats Confederacy, ending Civil War; Lincoln is assassinated.

1877
First tennis championship is held at Wimbledon, England.

1889
Eiffel Tower is completed in France.

1909
Henry Ford begins assembly-line production of motorcars.

pen name "Mark Twain," a riverboat term that means "two fathoms deep" (a depth of 12 feet)—water that is deep enough for a riverboat to navigate safely. In 1865 the publication of his story "The Celebrated Jumping Frog of Calaveras County" brought him his first taste of national fame. After working as a newspaper correspondent in the Hawaiian Islands, Twain began a successful lecture tour. His growing popularity encouraged him to travel even farther afield, and in 1867 he embarked for Europe and the Middle East.

SUCCESS AND SORROW

Twain married Olivia Langdon, the sister of a close friend, in 1870. After living briefly in Buffalo, New York, they settled in Hartford, Connecticut, where Twain wrote *The Adventures of Tom Sawyer* and *The Adventures of Huckleberry Finn,* among other works. Twain's unique humor and perspective on life brought the author success and wealth. Twain grew rich but invested his money unwisely, and in 1894 he was forced to declare bankruptcy. To support his family, Twain set off on a worldwide lecture tour.

Twain's house, 1885

Twain with his wife, Olivia, and his children, Susy, Clara, and Jean

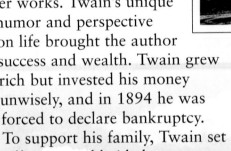

The last 15 years of Twain's life were plagued by tragedy. His daughter Susy died in 1896, his beloved wife died in 1904, and his daughter Jean died on Christmas Eve in 1909. His later writings reflect a darker view of life, although he wrote after Jean's death, "My temperament has never allowed my spirits to remain depressed long at a time." When Twain died in 1910, he was an internationally celebrated writer and speaker.

 INTERNET Author Link
www.mcdougallittell.com

NetActivities: Author Exploration

THE STEAMBOAT ERA

In *Life on the Mississippi* (1883) Mark Twain wrote about his adventures as a steamboat pilot on the Mississippi River just before the Civil War. Steamboats played a crucial role in the economy of the central United States from the early 1800s until the 1870s, hauling cargo such as cotton and sugar as well as passengers. Steamboats were a luxurious way to travel. They resembled grand hotels with ornate lounges, thick carpets, expensive food, and a staff of servants.

Steamboats were not necessarily a safe way to travel, however. Between 1810 and 1850, roughly 4,000 people were killed in steamboat disasters. Some of these deaths resulted from collisions or poorly maintained vessels. Mark Twain's brother Henry was killed in 1858 when the boiler of the steamboat on which he was working exploded, killing 150 people. Spontaneous races between the captains of steamboats—a common event—also contributed to the high death toll of steamboat travel.

The World.

700 LIVES LOST WHEN EXCURSION BOAT BURNS

BURNING OF A MISSISSIPPI STEAMER.

At three o'clock on the morning of the 30th of September one of those deplorable disasters for which the waters of our Western rivers have become so sadly noted occurred on the Lower Mississippi. The splendid steamer *Robert E. Lee* was totally destroyed by fire, thirty-five miles below Vicksburg, while on her first trip of the sea-

from **Roughing It**

by MARK TWAIN

Connect to Your Life

Next! In this selection the narrator describes all the jobs he tried before he found one that suited him. Have you ever had a part-time job that wasn't what you expected? What kind of part-time job would you like to have? Share your experiences and ideas with a partner.

Build Background

HISTORY

By the 1830s newspapers were commonplace, partly due to advances in technology. The most up-to-date printing presses could produce 5,000 papers an hour. Once a product for the wealthy elite, newspapers were now available to a much wider audience. In 1833 a New York publisher named Benjamin Day began selling his paper for a penny per copy. Day also started the practice of sending out young boys to sell newspapers on street corners. The circulation of Day's *New York Sun* soared to record heights—close to 50,000 papers a day.

WORDS TO KNOW
Vocabulary Preview

affluent	endow
barren	lavish
board	legitimate
contrive	proprietor
emigrant	vocation

Focus Your Reading

LITERARY ANALYSIS EXAGGERATION

The overstating of an idea is called **exaggeration.** Authors use exaggeration to emphasize meaning or to create **humor.** Mark Twain's narrator uses exaggeration when he describes how he lost several jobs. He writes that when he was a clerk in a drug store, his "prescriptions were unlucky, and we appeared to sell more stomach-pumps than soda-water." As you read, look for other examples of Mark Twain's humorous use of exaggeration.

ACTIVE READING MAKING INFERENCES ABOUT THE NARRATOR

Authors expect their readers to make inferences. An **inference** is a logical guess or conclusion based on evidence. By combining the information a writer provides with personal knowledge or experience, readers can "read between the lines" and figure out more than the words reveal. For example, the narrator of *Roughing It* describes a long list of jobs that he has had. From this information, you can **infer** that the narrator is a restless person who is willing to try almost anything. As you read, make other inferences about the narrator based on his actions and words.

📖 **READER'S NOTEBOOK**
Use a web like the one shown to develop an understanding of the narrator's character. As you read, record the inferences that you make about the narrator.

ROUGHING IT

BY
MARK TWAIN

WHAT TO DO NEXT?

IT WAS A MOMENTOUS QUESTION. I HAD GONE
OUT INTO THE WORLD TO SHIFT FOR MYSELF, AT
THE AGE OF THIRTEEN (FOR MY FATHER HAD
INDORSED FOR FRIENDS, AND ALTHOUGH HE LEFT
US A SUMPTUOUS LEGACY OF PRIDE IN HIS FINE
VIRGINIAN STOCK AND ITS NATIONAL DISTINCTION,
I PRESENTLY FOUND THAT I COULD NOT LIVE
ON THAT ALONE WITHOUT OCCASIONAL BREAD
TO WASH IT DOWN WITH). I HAD GAINED A

I had clerked in a drug store part of a summer, but my prescriptions were unlucky, and we appeared to sell more stomach-pumps than soda-water.

clerked in a drug store part of a summer, but my prescriptions were unlucky, and we appeared to sell more stomach-pumps than soda-water. So I had to go. I had made of myself a tolerable printer, under the impression that I would be another Franklin some day, but somehow had missed the connection thus far. There was no berth open in the Esmeralda *Union,* and besides I had always been such a slow compositor that I looked with envy upon the achievements of apprentices of two years' standing; and when I took a "take," foremen were in the habit of suggesting that it would be wanted "some time during the year." I was a good average St. Louis and New Orleans pilot

livelihood in various <u>vocations</u>, but had not dazzled anybody with my successes; still the list was before me, and the amplest liberty in the matter of choosing, provided I wanted to work—which I did not, after being so wealthy. I had once been a grocery clerk, for one day, but had consumed so much sugar in that time that I was relieved from further duty by the <u>proprietor</u>; said he wanted me outside, so that he could have my custom. I had studied law an entire week, and then given it up because it was so prosy and tiresome. I had engaged briefly in the study of blacksmithing, but wasted so much time trying to fix the bellows so that it would blow itself, that the master turned me adrift in disgrace, and told me I would come to no good. I had been a bookseller's clerk for a while, but the customers bothered me so much I could not read with any comfort, and so the proprietor gave me a furlough[1] and forgot to put a limit to it. I had

and by no means ashamed of my abilities in that line; wages were two hundred and fifty dollars a month and no <u>board</u> to pay, and I did long to stand behind a wheel again and never roam any more—but I had been making such a fool of myself lately in grandiloquent letters home about my blind lead and my European excursion[2] that I did what many and many a poor disappointed miner had done before; said, "It is all over with me now, and I will never go back home to be pitied—and snubbed." I had been a private secretary, a silver-miner and a silver-mill operative, and amounted to less than nothing in each, and now—

What to do next?

---

1. **furlough** (fûr′lō): leave of absence; vacation.
2. **excursion:** pleasure trip.

WORDS	**vocation** (vō-kā′shən) *n.* job; profession
TO	**proprietor** (prə-prī′ĭ-tər) *n.* the owner of a business
KNOW	**board** (bôrd) *n.* food or meals

I yielded to Higbie's appeals and consented to try the mining once more. We climbed far up on the mountainside and went to work on a little rubbishy claim of ours that had a shaft on it eight feet deep. Higbie descended into it and worked bravely with his pick till he had loosened up a deal of rock and dirt, and then I went down with a long-handled shovel (the most awkward invention yet <u>contrived</u> by man) to throw it out. You must brace the shovel forward with the side of your knee till it is full, and then, with a skillful toss, throw it backward over your left shoulder. I made the toss, and landed the mess just on the edge of the shaft and it all came back on my head and down the back of my neck. I never said a word, but climbed out and walked home. I inwardly resolved that I would starve before I would make a target of myself and shoot rubbish at it with a long-handled shovel. I sat down, in the cabin, and gave myself up to solid misery—so to speak. Now in pleasanter days I had amused myself with writing letters to the chief paper of the territory, the Virginia *Daily Territorial Enterprise,* and had always been surprised when they appeared in print. My good opinion of the editors had steadily declined; for it seemed to me that they might have found something better to fill up with than my literature. I had found a letter in the post-office as I came home from the hillside, and finally I opened it. Eureka! [I never did know what Eureka meant, but it seems to be as proper a word to heave in as any when no other that sounds pretty offers.] It was a deliberate offer to me of Twenty-five Dollars a week to come up to Virginia and be city editor of the *Enterprise.*

I would have challenged the publisher in the "blind lead" days—I wanted to fall down and worship him, now. Twenty-five Dollars a week—it looked like bloated luxury—a fortune, a sinful and <u>lavish</u> waste of money. But my transports cooled when I thought of my inexperience and consequent unfitness for

> I made the toss, and landed the mess just on the edge of the shaft and it all came back on my head and down the back of my neck.

WORDS TO KNOW

contrive (kən-trīv′) *v.* to invent
lavish (lăv′ĭsh) *adj.* exceedingly generous; extravagant

the position—and straightway, on top of this, my long array of failures rose up before me. Yet if I refused this place I must presently become dependent upon somebody for my bread, a thing necessarily distasteful to a man who had never experienced such a humiliation since he was thirteen years old. Not much to be proud of, since it is so common—but then it was all I had to be proud of. So I was scared into being a city editor. I would have declined, otherwise. Necessity is the mother of "taking chances." I do not doubt that if, at that time, I had been offered a salary to translate the Talmud[3] from the original Hebrew, I would have accepted—albeit with diffidence and some misgivings—and thrown as much variety into it as I could for the money.

> So I was scared into being a city editor. I would have declined, otherwise. Necessity is the mother of "taking chances."

I went up to Virginia and entered upon my new vocation. I was a rusty-looking city editor, I am free to confess—coatless, slouch hat, blue woolen shirt, pantaloons stuffed into boot-tops, whiskered half down to the waist, and the universal navy revolver slung to my belt. But I secured a more conservative costume and discarded the revolver. I had never had occasion to kill anybody, nor ever felt a desire to do so, but had worn the thing in deference to popular sentiment, and in order that I might not, by its absence, be offensively conspicuous, and a subject of remark. But the other editors, and all the printers, carried revolvers. I asked the chief editor and proprietor (Mr. Goodman, I will call him, since it describes him as well as any name could do) for some instructions with regard to my duties, and he told me to go all over town and ask all sorts of people all sorts of questions, make notes of the information gained, and write them out for publication. And he added:

"Never say 'We learn' so-and-so, or 'It is reported,' or 'It is rumored,' or 'We understand' so-and-so, but go to headquarters and get the absolute facts, and then speak out and say 'It is so-and-so.' Otherwise, people will not put confidence in your news. Unassailable[4] certainty is the thing that gives a newspaper the firmest and most valuable reputation."

---

3. **Talmud** (täl′mŏŏd): a collection of ancient writings setting forth the basic traditions of Judaism.

4. **unassailable** (ŭn′ə-sā′lə-bəl): impossible to dispute or attack.

Composing room at *The Territorial Enterprise*, Virginia City, Nevada, showing the desk used by Mark Twain. Courtesy of the Nevada Historical Society.

It was the whole thing in a nutshell; and to this day, when I find a reporter commencing his article with "We understand," I gather a suspicion that he has not taken as much pains to inform himself as he ought to have done. I moralize well, but I did not always practise well when I was a city editor; I let fancy get the upper hand of fact too often when there was a dearth[5] of news. I can never forget my first day's experience as a reporter. I wandered about town questioning everybody, boring everybody, and finding out that nobody knew anything.

At the end of five hours my note-book was still <u>barren</u>. I spoke to Mr. Goodman. He said:

"Dan used to make a good thing out of the hay-wagons in a dry time when there were no fires or inquests. Are there no hay-wagons in from the Truckee? If there are, you might speak of the renewed activity and all that sort of thing, in the hay business, you know. It isn't sensational or exciting, but it fills up and looks business-like."

I canvassed[6] the city again and found one wretched old hay-truck dragging in from the country. But I made <u>affluent</u> use of it.

---

5. **dearth** (dûrth): shortage.
6. **canvassed**: conducted a survey throughout.

WORDS
TO
KNOW

barren (băr′ən) *adj.* empty
affluent (ăf′lōō-ənt) *adj.* abundant; rich

I multiplied it by sixteen, brought it into town from sixteen different directions, made sixteen separate items of it, and got up such another sweat about hay as Virginia City had never seen in the world before.

This was encouraging. Two nonpareil columns[7] had to be filled, and I was getting along. Presently, when things began to look dismal again, a desperado killed a man in a saloon and joy returned once more. I never was so glad over any mere trifle before in my life. I said to the murderer:

"Sir, you are a stranger to me, but you have done me a kindness this day which I can never forget. If whole years of gratitude can be to

However, I found one wagon that was going on to California, and made some judicious inquiries of the proprietor.

you any slight compensation, they shall be yours. I was in trouble and you have relieved me nobly and at a time when all seemed dark and drear. Count me your friend from this time forth, for I am not a man to forget a favor."

If I did not really say that to him I at least felt a sort of itching desire to do it. I wrote up the murder with a hungry attention to details, and when it was finished experienced but one regret—namely, that they had not hanged my benefactor on the spot, so that I could work him up too.

---

7. **nonpareil** (nŏn´pə-rĕl´) **columns:** columns of small print.

Next I discovered some emigrant-wagons going into camp on the plaza and found that they had lately come through the hostile Indian country and had fared rather roughly. I made the best of the item that the circumstances permitted, and felt that if I were not confined within rigid limits by the presence of the reporters of the other papers I could add particulars that would make the article much more interesting. However, I found one wagon that was going on to California, and made some judicious inquiries of the proprietor. When I learned, through his short and surly answers to my cross-questioning, that he was certainly going on and would not be in the city next day to make trouble, I got ahead of the other papers, for I took down his list of names and added his party to the killed and wounded. Having more scope here, I put this wagon through an Indian fight that to this day has no parallel in history.

My two columns were filled. When I read them over in the morning I felt that I had found my legitimate occupation at last. I reasoned within myself that news, and stirring news, too, was what a paper needed, and I felt that I was peculiarly endowed with the ability to furnish it. Mr. Goodman said that I was as good a reporter as Dan. I desired no higher commendation. With encouragement like that, I felt that I could take my pen and murder all the immigrants on the plains if need be, and the interests of the paper demanded it. ❖

WORDS TO KNOW	**emigrant** (ĕm′ĭ-grənt) *n.* a person who leaves one country or region to settle in another **legitimate** (lə-jĭt′ə-mĭt) *adj.* logical; genuine **endow** (ĕn-dou′) *v.* to supply; provide

Connect to the Literature

1. **What Do You Think?**
   What was the funniest part of Twain's narrative?

   Comprehension Check
   • Why do the owners of the grocery store, bookstore, and drugstore let the narrator go?
   • What does the narrator decide about mining as an occupation?
   • How does the narrator fill up his two newspaper columns?

Think Critically

2. **ACTIVE READING** | **MAKING INFERENCES ABOUT THE NARRATOR**
   Look back at the web you completed in your **READER'S NOTEBOOK.** Discuss whether the job of newspaper reporter is a good match for the narrator. Think about the qualities that a good reporter should have, and measure these qualities against the character traits that you have inferred about the narrator.

3. Explain what the narrator means when he says he was "scared into being a city editor."

4. What does this selection reveal about American society in the narrator's time?

5. How does Mr. Goodman's attitude toward reporting differ from the narrator's?

   Think About:
   • Mr. Goodman's advice about using expressions like "We learn" and "It is rumored"
   • Mr. Goodman's advice about the hay-wagons
   • what the narrator does with Mr. Goodman's advice

Extend Interpretations

6. **COMPARING TEXTS** Henry Adams in "The Million-Pound Bank Note" (page 263) and the narrator in *Roughing It* are similar in some ways and different in others. Compare and contrast these characters.

7. **Connect to Life** Find out how the reporters on your school newspaper get their news and how they go about writing their articles. Then discuss why you would or would not like being a reporter.

Literary Analysis

EXAGGERATION To make people laugh, humorists often use **exaggeration,** an overstating of an idea. An exaggeration is a statement that describes something as larger, more intense, or more important than it really is. Although an exaggeration may be misleading, it often carries a grain of truth. For example, if the narrator's fellow workers joked that it would take the narrator a year to finish a job, then the reader might **infer** that the narrator is a slow worker.

Paired Activity With a partner, reread the selection to find more examples of exaggeration. Write these examples in a chart like the one shown. Also write down any inferences about the narrator that are conveyed through Twain's exaggeration and humor.

Exaggeration	Inference
1. "I had once been a grocery clerk, for one day, but had consumed so much sugar in that time that I was relieved from further duty by the proprietor; said he wanted me outside, so that he could have my custom."	1. The narrator is greedy and childish, eating when he should be working.
2.	2.

Vocabulary

EXERCISE: CONTEXT CLUES Write the Word to Know that best completes each sentence below.

1. In *Roughing It* the narrator explains that although his family had been _____, his father had not left him with an inheritance.

2. Instead, he has to find a _____ in order to support himself.

3. He tries mining but hates it, believing that the long-handled shovel is the most awkward tool ever _____.

4. The _____ of a grocery fires him for eating too much sugar.

5. However, he needs a job in order to pay for his room and _____.

6. He is astonished when a local newspaper offers a _____ salary that he feels he does not deserve.

7. He is unable to come up with a news story and his notebook remains _____.

8. Then he hears about some _____ wagons that carried settlers through a dangerous region.

9. After he writes the story, he tells himself that he has been _____ with a writing ability.

10. He rejoices that he has found a _____ occupation at last.

Vocabulary Handbook
See p. R20: Context Clues.

WORDS TO KNOW	affluent	board	emigrant	lavish	proprietor
	barren	contrive	endow	legitimate	vocation

Grammar in Context: Complex Sentences

Mark Twain varies his sentence structure in *Roughing It.* One way he adds variety to his writing is by including **complex sentences.**

> If whole years of gratitude can be to you any slight compensation, **they shall be yours.**

Complex sentences have one **main clause** and at least one subordinate clause. In the sentence above, the words *they shall be yours* form a main clause because these words can stand alone. In contrast, subordinate clauses cannot stand alone. Subordinate clauses often begin with words such as *after, although, because, if, since,* and *when.*

Apply to Your Writing Change the rhythm of your writing by varying the length and types of sentences you use. Vary the structure of your complex sentences by placing the subordinate clause either before or after the main clause.

WRITING EXERCISE Create a complex sentence by combining each pair of simple sentences. In each pair, change one sentence into a subordinate clause that begins with the word in parentheses.

Example: *Original* I found something to write about. Happiness returned once more. (after)
Rewritten After I found something to write about, happiness returned once more.

1. I was a grocery clerk. I ate too much sugar. (when)

2. I had studied law for an entire week. I gave it up. (after)

3. I thought of my inexperience. My enthusiasm cooled. (when)

4. I would have felt insulted once. Now I wanted to thank the paper. (although)

5. I had written enough to fill two columns of the newspaper. I felt relieved. (when)

Grammar Handbook See p. R89: Phrases and Clauses.

A Fable

by MARK TWAIN

Connect to Your Life

Trials of Teaching In this fable a cat tries to explain the concept of a picture and a mirror to an audience of animals. In the end the animals are angry with the cat because they think he has misled them. Think of a time when you had to explain something to someone. Did the other person understand the explanation immediately? What did you learn about teaching?

Build Background

HISTORY

The fable is an ancient literary form. The tradition of the fable in Western culture began with Aesop in the sixth century B.C. Little is known about Aesop, whose life remains a mystery. However, Aesop's style of teaching moral lessons through brief animal tales has become the standard form for fables. Aesop's animal characters represent human characters and human behavior. For example, the fox is portrayed as clever, the hare as timid, and the lion as bold. Fables in Aesop's tradition end with a clearly stated **moral**—a lesson people are supposed to learn from the story. In other fables readers or listeners must infer the moral from events in the story.

WORDS TO KNOW
Vocabulary Preview

learned   swoon
perceptible   unappeasable
refined

Focus Your Reading

LITERARY ANALYSIS   **SATIRE**

Satire is a literary technique in which the author makes fun of ideas or customs. Because people tend to react angrily if they are criticized directly, a **satirist** criticizes his or her subject in an indirect way. Mark Twain chose the form of the **fable** to convey his satire. A fable is a brief tale that teaches a lesson about human nature. He uses animals to **personify,** or represent, human beings—especially those human beings who say foolish things about art and literature. As you read, notice what Twain is suggesting about art critics through the words and actions of his animal characters.

ACTIVE READING   **VISUALIZING**

The process of forming a mental picture based on a written description is called **visualizing.** Good readers use the details supplied by writers to visualize characters, settings, and events. In "A Fable" Twain's language evokes a clear image of the animals' reaction when they hear about the beautiful picture. They are "excited . . . almost to a frenzy." As you read, visualize the different animals and events in the fable.

📖 **READER'S NOTEBOOK** As you read "A Fable," keep a log of descriptive words and phrases that help you visualize the action, setting, and characters in Twain's tale. In your notebook, paraphrase each description in your own words.

A FABLE

The Waterfall [La Cascade] (1961), René Magritte.
Oil on canvas. Photograph by Photographie Giraudon, France.
Copyright © 1999 C. Herscovici,
Brussels/Artists Rights Society (ARS), New York.

by MARK TWAIN

ONCE UPON A TIME

AN ARTIST WHO HAD PAINTED A SMALL AND VERY BEAUTIFUL PICTURE PLACED IT SO THAT HE COULD SEE IT IN THE MIRROR. HE SAID, "THIS DOUBLES THE DISTANCE AND SOFTENS IT, AND IT IS TWICE AS LOVELY AS IT WAS BEFORE."

The animals out in the woods heard of this through the housecat, who was greatly admired by them because he was so <u>learned</u>, and so <u>refined</u> and civilized, and so polite and high-bred, and could tell them so much which they didn't know before, and were not certain about afterward. They were much excited about this new piece of gossip, and they asked questions, so as to get at a full understanding of it. They asked what a picture was, and the cat explained.

"It is a flat thing," he said; "wonderfully flat, marvelously flat, enchantingly flat and elegant. And, oh, so beautiful!"

That excited them almost to a frenzy, and they said they would give the world to see it. Then the bear asked:

"What is it that makes it so beautiful?"

"It is the looks of it," said the cat.

This filled them with admiration and uncertainty, and they were more excited than ever. Then the cow asked:

"What is a mirror?"

"It is a hole in the wall," said the cat. "You look in it, and there you see the picture, and it is so dainty and charming and ethereal and inspiring in its unimaginable beauty that your head turns round and round, and you almost <u>swoon</u> with ecstasy."

The ass had not said anything as yet; he now began to throw doubts. He said there had never been anything as beautiful as this before, and probably wasn't now. He said that when it took a

---

WORDS
TO
KNOW

learned (lûr′nĭd) *adj.* having a great deal of knowledge
refined (rĭ-fīnd′) *adj.* having polished manners; cultured
swoon (swoon) *v.* to faint

Connect to the Literature

1. What Do You Think?
What did you think about the cat at the end of the fable?

Comprehension Check
- Why does the artist place a mirror in front of the picture?
- How does the cat explain the mirror to the other animals?
- Which animal is the last to look in the mirror?

Think Critically

2. ACTIVE READING VISUALIZING
Review the log that you kept in your
📖READER'S NOTEBOOK. Which event or character can you visualize most clearly? Which words and phrases were most effective in helping you visualize the action?

3. Why is each animal eager to test the mirror after hearing about the experiences of other animals? What does this reveal about human nature?

4. At the end of the story, does the elephant's reaction represent a typical human reaction? Why or why not?

5. How would you explain the moral of the story in your own words?

> **Think About:**
> - how the cat's experience differs from the experience of the other animals
> - how each animal can see only itself in the mirror and cannot see the picture at all
> - how the mirror represents the imagination

Extend Interpretations

6. What If? What if the moral at the end of the story did not come from the cat but from one of the other animals? Write the moral that the bear, the elephant, or one of the others might have announced at the conclusion. Give evidence from the story to show why the animal would make that observation.

7. Connect to Life Mark Twain's "A Fable" shows how each person's prejudices or attitudes can interfere with the appreciation of art or literature. Discuss times when you disagreed with someone about the meaning of a work of art.

Literary Analysis

SATIRE Writers use the literary technique known as **satire** in order to criticize ideas or social customs. Satire can be harsh and bitterly critical, or it can be gentle and witty, as in Twain's "A Fable." Twain satirizes human foolishness through the skillful use of **personification,** a technique that gives human qualities to an animal, an object, or an idea. In "A Fable" each animal personifies a human profession or attitude. For example, the cat explains the art and the mirror to the other animals, who respect his opinion without quite understanding what he is talking about. The animals admire the cat because he is "so learned, and so refined and civilized." From Twain's description of the cat, the reader would infer that the cat personifies art critics.

Paired Activity With a partner, find examples of personification in "A Fable." Then, in a brief paragraph, discuss the customs or people that Twain may have intended to satirize through each personification. Fill in the following chart to help you organize your examples.

Animal or Animals	Personifies	In Order for Twain to Satirize
The cat	Polite, refined art experts	Art critics
The ass		
All the animals except the cat		

Vocabulary

Choose the word that means the opposite, or nearly the opposite, of the underlined Word to Know in each sentence.

1. The cat is very polite and <u>refined</u>.
   A crude   **B** restless
   C still   **D** curious

2. The animals admire the cat because he is so <u>learned</u>.
   F beautiful   **G** ignorant
   H understanding   **J** mischievous

3. The cat's superiority was quite <u>perceptible</u>.
   A unbearable   **B** untreatable
   C durable   **D** invisible

4. The cat tells the animals that the beauty of the painting will cause them to <u>swoon</u>.
   F frown   **G** gasp
   H wake   **J** laugh

5. The elephant's fury was <u>unappeasable</u> when he thought he had been deceived.
   A predictable   **B** satisfied
   C unexpected   **D** reasonable

Vocabulary Handbook
See p. R24: Synonyms and Antonyms.

Grammar in Context: Using Subordinating Conjunctions

Mark Twain uses subordinating conjunctions to connect clauses in his complex sentences. Look at the word in red in this sentence from "A Fable":

> You can find in a text whatever you bring, if you will stand between it and the mirror of your imagination.

Subordinating conjunctions introduce subordinate clauses and include the following words and phrases: *after, although, as, as if, as much as, because, before, even though, how, if, in order that, provided, since, so that, that, though, unless, when, whenever, where, wherever, while,* and *why.* Each conjunction expresses a different relationship between the clauses it connects, so choose your subordinating conjunctions carefully.

Punctuation Tip: When a subordinate clause begins a sentence, use a comma to separate it from the rest of the sentence.

WRITING EXERCISE Combine each pair of sentences into a single complex sentence. Use the subordinating conjunction in parentheses to link the clauses.

Example: *Original* An artist placed a mirror in front of a picture. He wanted the picture to seem farther away. (because)

Rewritten An artist placed a mirror in front of a picture because he wanted the picture to seem farther away.

1. The animals in the story speak to one another. In real life animals cannot speak. (even though)

2. An artist placed a picture. He could see it in a mirror. (so that)

3. They were filled with admiration. They thought about the painting. (whenever)

4. The cat walked away offended. He saw that the animals doubted him. (because)

5. The elephant decided he would never know what the picture looked like. He went to see it himself. (unless)

Grammar Handbook
See p. R90: Clauses.

Mark Twain's Comedy Knight

PREPARING to *Read*

Build Background

Connect to Life In the excerpts that follow, Twain explores what might happen if a man from 19th-century New England found himself suddenly transported to sixth-century Britain. Have you ever wondered about life in earlier times? Share your thoughts with your classmates.

Focus Your Reading

LITERARY ANALYSIS **HUMOR**

Humor is a quality that provokes laughter or amusement. Writers create humor through exaggeration, sarcasm, **amusing descriptions,** irony, and witty dialogue. In the passages that follow, Twain's amusing descriptions are developed from a single idea—that a modern person would find the past a strange and uncomfortable place.

READER'S NOTEBOOK As you read the selection, consider the relationship between Twain's dream and the novel that he developed out of these thoughts. Think about

- Twain's humor
- how Twain's amusing descriptions emphasize the contrast between two eras

*In the mid-1880s, Mark Twain recorded in his journal a "dream" of being a knight during the Middle Ages. Although we do not know whether the journal entry records an actual dream or a kind of "freewriting," Twain eventually developed the ideas in this passage into a full-fledged novel—*A Connecticut Yankee in King Arthur's Court.

Dream of being a knight errant in armor in the middle ages. Have the notions and habits of thought of the present day mixed with the necessities of that. No pockets in the armor. No way to manage certain requirements of nature. Can't scratch. Cold in the head—can't blow—can't get at handkerchief, can't use iron sleeve. Iron gets red hot in the sun—leaks in the rain, gets white with frost and freezes me solid in winter. Suffer from lice and fleas. Make disagreeable clatter when I enter church. Can't dress or undress myself. Always getting struck by lightning. Fall down, can't get up.

In A Connecticut Yankee in King Arthur's Court, *Hank Morgan, a 19th-century New Englander, finds himself in sixth-century Britain. Although at first he tries to adapt to sixth-century ways, eventually he teaches the English how to create the machines and weapons of the 19th century—with disastrous effects. In the passages that follow, Hank describes the experience of putting on and wearing a suit of armor. Notice how Twain has fully explored the ideas that he first recorded in his "dream."*

was to have an early breakfast, and start at dawn, for that was the usual way; but I had the demon's own time with my armor, and this delayed me a little. It is troublesome to get into, and there is so much detail. First you wrap a layer or two of blanket around your body, for a sort of cushion and to keep off the cold iron; then you put on your sleeves and shirt of chain mail—these are made of small steel links woven together . . . Next you buckle your greaves on your legs, and your cuisses on your thighs; then come your backplate and your breastplate, and you begin to feel crowded . . . next you belt on your sword; then you put your stovepipe joints onto your arms, your iron gauntlets onto your hands, your iron rattrap onto your head . . . and there you are, snug as a candle in a candle mold. This is no time to dance . . .

It was beginning to get hot. . . . Things which I didn't mind at all, at first, I began to mind now—and more and more, too, all the time. The first ten or fifteen times I wanted my handkerchief I didn't seem to care. I got along, and said never mind, it isn't any matter, and dropped it out of my mind. But now it was different; I wanted it all the time; it was nag, nag, nag, right along, and no

A sixth-century British warrior looked very different from the kind of armored knight described by Mark Twain. In reality, sixth-century Britain was a primitive place, where warriors fought without the protection of heavy armor.

helmet

visor

breastplate

gauntlet

sword

sword belt

chain mail

cuisse

greave

Although armor could weigh up to 55 pounds, the weight was distributed fairly evenly over the body. However, armor could also get very hot, just as Twain imagined.

rest; I couldn't get it out of my mind; and so at last I lost my temper and said hang a man that would make a suit of armor without any pockets in it. . . .

Meantime it was getting hotter and hotter in there. You see, the sun was beating down and warming up the iron more and more all the time. Well, when you are hot, that way, every little thing irritates you. When I trotted, I rattled like a crate of dishes, and that annoyed me; and moreover I couldn't seem to stand that shield slatting and banging, now about my breast, now around my back; and if I dropped into a walk my joints creaked and screeched in that wearisome way that a wheelbarrow does, and as we didn't create any breeze at that gait, I was like to get fried in that stove; and besides, the quieter you went the heavier the iron settled down on you and the more and more tons you seemed to weigh every minute. . . .

And when it had got to the worst, and it seemed to me that I could not stand anything more, a fly got in through the bars and settled on my nose, and the bars were stuck and wouldn't work, and I couldn't get the visor up; and I could only shake my head, which was baking hot by this time, and the fly—well, you know how a fly acts when he has got a certainty—he only minded the shaking long enough to change from nose to lip, and lip to ear, and buzz and buzz all around in there, and keep on lighting and biting, in a way that a person already so distressed as I was, simply could not stand.

Twenty-one years after the publication of the novel, Twain reminisced about the background reading that had inspired A Connecticut Yankee in King Arthur's Court. *In this passage Twain recalls reading the Arthurian legends.*

As I read those quaint and curious old legends I suppose I naturally contrasted those days with ours, and it made me curious to fancy what might be the picturesque result if we could dump the nineteenth century down into the sixth century and observe the consequences.

THINKING *through the* LITERATURE

1. Which passage do you think is the funniest?

2. Why does Hank Morgan find the armor uncomfortable?

3. Many people have a romantic image of the Middle Ages. Do you think that Twain describes this period of history in a romantic or a realistic way?

The Author's Style

Twain's Humor

Mark Twain once said that "humor . . . is the good natured side of any truth." Twain created humor through sarcasm, amusing descriptions, and irony. Because of his humorous style, Twain could entertain his readers while presenting his view of the world.

Key Style Points

Sarcasm Sarcasm is an ironic manner of criticizing someone or something. Sarcasm can be wounding, and it is often humorous. Where is the sarcasm in this passage from *Roughing It*?

Amusing Descriptions Twain's ability to create vivid images of characters and situations adds to the humorous effect of his writing. Identify the details in this passage that help create an amusing description of the narrator.

Irony Irony is the contrast between what is expected and what actually exists or happens. Explain the irony in this passage from *Roughing It* and what it reveals about the narrator's character.

> ### Sarcasm
> "I had been a bookseller's clerk for a while, but the customers bothered me so much I could not read with any comfort . . ."
> — *Roughing It*

> ### Amusing Descriptions
> "I was a rusty-looking city editor, I am free to confess—coatless, slouch hat, blue woolen shirt, pantaloons stuffed into boot-tops, whiskered half down to the waist, and the universal navy revolver slung to my belt."
> — *Roughing It*

> ### Irony
> "Now in pleasanter days I had amused myself with writing letters to the chief paper of the territory . . . and had always been surprised when they appeared in print. My good opinion of the editors had steadily declined; for it seemed to me that they might have found something better to fill up with than my literature."
> — *Roughing It*

Applications

1. **Active Reading** Look back at the selections in this author study. Find examples of each type of humor technique.

2. **Writing** Think about a humorous incident that once happened to you. Write about the incident using several of these literary techniques. In the margin identify each technique.

3. **Speaking and Listening** With a partner, choose a passage from one of the works by Mark Twain that includes irony or sarcasm. Rewrite the passage without the irony or sarcasm. Read aloud the original version and then the rewritten version. Discuss the difference between the two versions.

Writing

Satirical Fable Write a brief fable in which you criticize a modern custom, fad, or injustice. Fill out a story map to help you organize your ideas. Place your fable in your **Working Portfolio.** 📁

Writing Handbook
See page R32: The Writing Process.

Speaking & Listening

Video Portrayal Watch the video of Hal Holbrook's "Mark Twain Gives an Interview." How does Hal Holbrook's portrayal of Mark Twain compare with how you imagined Twain? Discuss your responses with your classmates.

VIDEO: Literature in Performance

"Mark Twain Gives an Interview"

Research & Technology

Mine for Information Use nonfiction works, the Internet, or other resources to help you find information on one of the topics below. Present your information as a short written report with illustrations.

- Mining Techniques in the Late 1800s
- The Gold Rush of 1849
- Life in Mining Towns in the West

INTERNET Author Link
www.mcdougallittell.com

Author Study Project

Public Reading

Mark Twain often lectured on his writing and read aloud his work to audiences. Present "A Fable" as a public reading with visual aids.

❶ Listen to Recordings In a group of three or four students, locate and listen to recordings of actors who have portrayed Mark Twain, such as Hal Holbrook. One person should take the role of the narrator and practice imitating Twain's style. Assign other speaking roles and the job of the director to other group members.

❷ Prepare Your Script Each group member should have a copy of the story to mark up as a script. Highlight the lines you will speak and note when you need to present visual aids. During practice sessions, the director should make sure that each reader knows when to speak and pronounces words correctly.

❸ Create Masks As a group, create simple masks to represent each animal in the fable. When presenting the fable, each speaker in turn should peer into a mirror while speaking his or her character's lines.

❹ Present Your Reading Give your public reading to the class or another audience. Pay special attention to your volume and pace.

"The truth is," Mark Twain once remarked, "my books are simply autobiographies. If the incidents were dated they could be strung together in their due order, and the result would be an autobiography." Although this statement is a slight exaggeration, Twain's adventurous life did provide much of the material for his writing. Almost a century after his death, his stories of boyhood adventures and his humorous observations of human behavior are still greatly admired and widely read.

The Celebrated Jumping Frog of Calaveras County and Other Sketches 1867

This collection of sketches includes Twain's first nationally renowned work, which tells the tale of a gambler who trains a frog to jump and then wins money by betting on the frog. A stranger eventually outwits the gambler.

The Adventures of Tom Sawyer 1876

This novel centers around the exploits of young Tom Sawyer and his friend Huck Finn. They hunt for treasure along the banks of the Mississippi and, along the way, witness a terrible crime.

The Prince and the Pauper 1881

This novel tells the story of two boys in 16th-century England who, because of their extraordinary resemblance, switch identities. One boy is extremely poor; the other is a prince.

Life on the Mississippi 1883

This memoir of the age of steamboats on the Mississippi River recounts Twain's adventures as a steamboat pilot before the Civil War. The second half of the book tells of the demise of steamboats as railroads take over.

The Adventures of Huckleberry Finn 1884

This novel, written as a sequel to *Tom Sawyer,* is narrated by Huck himself as he journeys down the Mississippi on a raft with a runaway slave named Jim. The two fugitives encounter many adventures and witness the worst of human behavior before their journey ends.

A Connecticut Yankee in King Arthur's Court 1889

This novel tells the story of Hank Morgan, an American mechanic who is knocked unconscious and wakes up in sixth-century England. Considered a sorcerer by the inhabitants of Camelot, Morgan brings 19th-century American ingenuity to the lives of Camelot's residents.

Writing Workshop

Researching the facts . . .

From Reading to Writing How much do you know about your country and the people who shaped it? Names like Frederick Douglass or events like the Westward Movement are familiar to most people, but could you really describe the person or re-create the event? Writing a **research report** can help you fill in the gaps in your knowledge, provide a new insight on a topic, and allow you to present your topic clearly to others.

For Your Portfolio

WRITING PROMPT Write a research report about a topic in history or another topic that interests you.

Purpose: To share information

Audience: Your classmates, teacher, or anyone who shares your interest in the topic

---

Basics in a Box

Research Report at a Glance

Introduction
presents the thesis statement

→

Body
presents evidence that supports the thesis statement

→

Conclusion
restates the thesis

→

Works Cited
lists the sources of information

↑

Research

RUBRIC STANDARDS FOR WRITING

A successful research report should

- include a strong introduction and thesis statement that clearly state the topic and purpose
- use evidence from primary or secondary sources to develop and support ideas
- credit sources of information

- follow a logical pattern of organization, using transitions between ideas
- use information from multiple sources
- summarize ideas in the conclusion
- include a Works Cited list at the end of the report

Analyzing a Student Model

SPEAKING
OPPORTUNITY
See the Speaking and Listening Handbook, p. R104 for oral presentation tips.

Emily Howard

Writing Class 8B, Rm. 202

Mrs. Jeffet

May 2

The Lewis and Clark Expedition

Have you ever wanted to explore uncharted territory? The participants of the Lewis and Clark expedition of 1804–1806 did just that. Their purpose was to map a good water route from St. Louis and the Mississippi River to the Pacific Ocean; their dream, to connect the people and trade of the East Coast with the land and resources of the West Coast. The journey was often dangerous and demanded incredible acts of courage and teamwork.

In the spring of 1803, France sold lands known as the Louisiana Territory to the United States for 15 million dollars (Phelan 95). The purchase doubled the size of the United States, which now included most of the land stretching from the Mississippi River to the Rocky Mountains and from New Orleans and the Gulf of Mexico to the Canadian border. President Jefferson had been planning an expedition into the land west of the Mississippi River for years before the Louisiana Purchase (Phelan 105). He chose Capt. Meriwether Lewis, his private secretary, to lead the expedition. Lewis chose Lt. William Clark as co-commander (Phelan 127). In 1804, the group, called the "Corps of Discovery," began the journey into the future of America (Ambrose 118).

The expedition had several purposes, but perhaps the most important was, as Jefferson wrote to Lewis, to find ". . . the direct water communication from sea to sea formed by the bed of the Missouri & perhaps the Oregon" (Ambrose 116). Another goal of the Lewis and Clark expedition was to study and make records of the animals, plants, weather systems, native peoples, and geology. They were to map the river systems that they traveled to reach the Pacific Ocean, and were also told to announce "American sovereignty in the new territory" (Ambrose 94–95).

The group that traveled from St. Louis, Missouri, to Fort Mandan, North Dakota, to Fort Clatsop, Oregon, and back included military men, traders and interpreters, William Clark's slave, York, and a young Shoshone woman named Sacajawea, who had joined the expedition with her baby boy

RUBRIC
IN ACTION

❶ Writer begins with a question and then states a coherent thesis.

Other option:
• Open with a quote from a primary source.

❷ The writer uses chronological order as a transitional device. Dates place events in relationship to each other.

❸ Uses information from more than one source to support ideas

❹ Secondary source cites a quotation from a primary source— Jefferson's letter to Lewis.

and French-Canadian fur-trader husband. She helped as a translator and guide when the group reached Shoshone lands in Montana (Anderson).

On May 14, 1804, the expedition left St. Louis in a keelboat and two canoes. They traveled the Missouri River and more than a year later, traded for horses needed to cross the Rockies—the most difficult part of the journey. As they rode deeper into the mountains, with little food, they were forced to kill and eat some of their horses. Several days later, they had crossed this treacherous terrain.

During the expedition, many observations were made in journals and specimens were collected. For example, Lewis found a pelican's beak that could hold five gallons of water. The expedition also encountered coyotes, an animal not known in the East, and started hunting buffalo. Buffalo meat soon became their "meat of choice" (Ambrose 153).

⑤ Uses facts and details from secondary sources to support main idea of each paragraph

In the end, no "all-water route to the Pacific with a short hop over the Rockies" (Ambrose jacket) was found. Lewis considered the journey a failure. Yet the trip was a success in many ways. New territory had been explored, everything observed and discovered there was recorded for scientists to study.

Still, it was discovered that the Great Plains was too dry for

r the United

Works Cited

Ambrose, Stephen E. Undaunted Courage: Meriwether Lewis, Thomas Jefferson, and the Opening of the American West. New York: Simon, 1996.

Anderson, Irving W. "Inside the Corps: The Corps." PBS Online. Public Broadcasting Service. 26 Apr. 2000 <http://www.pbs.org/lewisandclark/inside/idx_corp.html>.

"Gone West." America: A Personal History of the United States. Writ. and narr. Alistair Cooke. Videocassette. Ambrose, 1972.

"Lewis and Clark Expedition." The World Book Encyclopedia. 1990 ed.

Phelan, Mary Kay. The Story of the Louisiana Purchase. New York: Crowell, 1979.

Works Cited

The writer presents all sources used in alphabetical order.

Writing Your Research Report

❶ Prewriting and Exploring

Find a topic that interests you by **brainstorming** questions you have about the early inhabitants of the United States. **List** names of people who helped shape the nation. Write down related subjects or historical events. See the **Idea Bank** in the margin for more suggestions. After choosing a topic, follow the steps below.

Planning Your Research Report

▷ 1. **Focus your topic.** How much information is available on your topic? Create a cluster diagram of ideas connected to the topic. If there is a lot of information, choose one or two ideas to investigate.

▷ 2. **Create research questions.** Write down questions about your topic. Group the questions that are related and use these to guide your research.

▷ 3. **Identify your audience.** Decide how much background you need to include about your topic. Choose the topics you think would most interest your readers.

▷ 4. **Define your focus.** What main points do you want your audience to come away with? Try to write a **thesis statement—** one sentence that tells the main idea or purpose of the report.

❷ Researching

Use the questions you have written about your topic to guide your research. Add other questions as you find facts that move your investigation along.

Remember there are two types of sources—primary and secondary. **Primary sources** offer firsthand information. They include letters, original literary works, diaries, journals, and historical documents. **Secondary sources** provide interpretations, explanations, and comments on material from other sources. Encyclopedias, newspapers, magazines, and many books are examples of secondary sources.

Evaluate Your Sources

You must be sure your sources are reliable—that is, accurate and up to date. Use several sources to be sure that your facts are accurate. Ask the following questions to help you evaluate your sources:

IDEA Bank

1. For Your Working Portfolio 📁
Look for ideas in the **Writing** sections you completed earlier.

2. Branching Out
Choose a significant event in U.S. history. Then find out what historical events occurred at the same time in other countries. Research one of those events.

3. Refresh Some Memories
The memories of some people's deeds of courage have faded over time. Choose a lesser-known figure in U.S. history and give his or her story new life with your research.

Need help with your report?

See the **Writing Handbook,** p. R51

See **Language Network**
    Research Report, p. 486
    Finding Information, p. 505
    Critical Thinking Skills, p. 539
    Learning About Media, p. 571

- Is the source reliable? Who is the author? Is he or she from a respected institution? Is he or she a professional?
- What are the author's viewpoint and biases? Have the author's gender, background, and political beliefs influenced the presentation of information?

Make Source Cards

Make an index card for each source you use. Number these source cards sequentially so that you can easily refer to a particular one when you take notes and prepare your Works Cited list. For library books, include the call number. Follow the formats shown on the right.

> **Book** ①
> Ambrose, Stephen E. *Undaunted Courage: Meriwether Lewis, Thomas Jefferson, and the Opening of the American West.* New York: Simon, 1996. Jamestown Public Library: call # 917.804

Take Notes

Use index cards to record the information in your sources.

- Write the main idea of the information at the top of each card.

- Write the number that you assigned the source and the page number on which you found the information.

- Write just one piece of information on each card.

> **Video** ②
> "Gone West." *America: A Personal History of the United States.* Writ. and narr. Alistair Cooke. Videocassette. Ambrose, 1972.

> **Encyclopedia** ③
> "Lewis and Clark Expedition." *The World Book Encyclopedia.* 1990 ed.

> *Trip as failure* ①
> Lewis was disappointed. Never found "all-water route to the Pacific with a short hop over the Rockies" inside jacket copy *(Paraphrase and Quotation)*

Source Number

Paraphrase. Restate ideas in your own words to summarize them and to avoid plagiarism, or using someone else's original words without giving credit to the author.

Quotation. Write the quote exactly as it appears in the source and enclose it in quotation marks.

Page Number

Organize Your Material

Before writing your rough draft, sort your note cards into groups of similar main ideas. Think about the order in which you want to discuss those main ideas. You might choose **chronological, cause-and-effect, comparison-and-contrast, problem-solution,** or some other method of organizing. Then create an outline. The main ideas would be your major headings. Next, subdivide the groups of note cards into smaller groups. These will be your subheadings.

Outline

Lewis and Clark Expedition

I. Introduction

II. Historical background of expedition

  A. Louisiana Territory

  B. Thomas Jefferson and trade

III. Expedition

  A. Purposes

  B. Participants

  C. Observations

  D. Successes and Failures

IV. Conclusion

Purposes ①

Quotations about Lewis's objectives Jefferson wrote to Lewis to find "the direct water communication from sea to sea formed by the bed of the Missouri & perhaps the Oregon." 116

❸ Drafting

Using your outline as a guide, get your ideas down in a first draft. You can revise it later.

In your **introduction,** you can start with a question, a quotation, or an intriguing fact. Develop a **thesis statement** that includes your topic and focus, using your statement of purpose to help you. **Support your thesis statement** in the **body** of your paper. Use examples, facts, anecdotes, and quotations from your sources. **Interpret** and **draw conclusions** about the information. To avoid plagiarism, write the author's name and page number in parentheses immediately following the fact or idea (or the title and page number of the source if there is no author). **Conclude** by summarizing the importance of your topic or by giving your own interpretation.

In **reviewing your draft,** ask yourself how you can make the thesis statement clearer and stronger. Make sure you cite your sources and give the facts accurately. Check that your ideas are placed in a logical order. Consider displaying some of your information in the form of charts, maps, or graphs.

DRAFTING Tip

Writing a strong topic sentence for each body paragraph can help you to eliminate ideas unrelated to the main idea of the paragraph. Your topic sentence can also help bring your report together by creating a transition from the previous paragraph.

See **Language Network,**
  Using Visuals, p. 390

Ask Your Peer Reader

- What is the main point of my report?
- Which parts of the report do not seem like my own words?
- What parts were confusing?
- What did you learn about my topic?

Need revising help?

Review the **Rubric**, p. 818

Consider **peer reader** comments

Check **Revision Guidelines**, p. R33

SPELLING
From Writing

 As you revise your work, look back at the words you misspelled and determine why you made the errors you did. For additional help, refer to the strategies and generalizations in the **Spelling Handbook** on page R28.

Confused by subordinate clauses?

See the **Grammar Handbook**, p. R89

SPEAKING
Opportunity

Turn your research report into an oral presentation.

Publishing
IDEAS

- Create a book from your report. Find illustrations and choose writing to accompany the illustrations.
- Maintain a fun-fact bulletin board in your classroom. You and your classmates could prepare facts on paper strips. Create illustrations or find images to be posted with them. Every few days, replace the facts.

◀ INTERNET ▶

Publishing Options
www.mcdougallittell.com

❹ Revising

TARGET SKILL ▶ **PARAPHRASING QUOTATIONS** You must support your main ideas with facts taken from your primary and secondary sources. Too many quotations can fragment a report and make it difficult to read. Most of the facts you present should be paraphrased, or written in your own words.

> Another goal of the Lewis and Clark expedition was to *study and make records of animals, plants, fish, trees, weather systems, native tribes, and geology.*

❺ Editing and Proofreading

TARGET SKILL ▶ **AVOIDING SENTENCE FRAGMENTS** To avoid confusing the reader, eliminate sentence fragments from your writing. A subordinate clause cannot stand alone; it must be joined to an independent clause in order to form a complete sentence.

> For example, Lewis found a pelican's beak ⁒hat could hold five gallons of water.

❻ Making a Works Cited List

When you have finished revising and editing your report, make a **Works Cited** list and attach it to the end of the report. See pages R54–R55 in the **Writing Handbook** for the correct format.

❼ Reflecting

FOR YOUR WORKING PORTFOLIO What surprised you about the research process? How did your perspective toward the topic change or develop as you did your research? Attach your answers to the finished report. Save the research report in your **Working Portfolio**. 📁

Standardized Test Practice

Mixed Review

> A good sailor can determine his or her latitude by looking at the sun or stars, but calculating longitude depends on time. It has long been know that the difference between the time on the ship and the time in the home port can be converted into longitude. Nowadays that process seems simple years ago it was almost impossible. Many ships became lost at sea, for instance the *Eva Doran* sank in the Pacific Ocean when she hit land unexpectedly. The problem was not solved. Until John Harrison developed an accurate clock in the late eighteenth century. This invention begun a new era in ship navigation.
>
> (1) (2) (3) (4) (5) (6)

Review Your Skills

Use the passage and the questions that follow it to check how well you remember the language conventions you've learned in previous grades.

1. How is sentence 1 best written?
   A. It has long been knowed
   B. It has long been knew
   C. It has long been known
   D. Correct as is

2. How is sentence 2 best written?
   A. Nowadays that process seems simple; but years ago it was almost impossible.
   B. Nowadays that process seems simple, and years ago it was almost impossible.
   C. Nowadays that process seems simple, but years ago it was almost impossible.
   D. Correct as is

3. What is the correct capitalization in sentence 3?
   A. Sank in the Pacific Ocean
   B. sank in the Pacific ocean
   C. sank in the pacific ocean
   D. Correct as is

4. How is item 4 best written?
   A. The problem was not solved; until John Harrison developed
   B. The problem was not solved until John Harrison developed
   C. The problem was not solved John Harrison developed
   D. Correct as is

5. What is the correct capitalization in item 5?
   A. Late Eighteenth Century
   B. late Eighteenth century
   C. late eighteenth Century
   D. Correct as is

6. How is sentence 6 best written?
   A. This invention had began
   B. This invention beginned
   C. This invention began
   D. Correct as is

Self-Assessment

Check your own answers in the **Grammar Handbook**.

Sentence Fragments, p. R75

Compound Sentences, p. R92

Compound Predicates, p. R99

Run-on Sentences, p. R75

Verbs, p. R84

The Literature You'll Read

The Concepts You'll Study

Vocabulary and Reading Comprehension
Vocabulary Focus: Homonyms and Words with Multiple Meanings
Fact/Opinion
Connecting
Author's Purpose
Specialized Vocabulary
Clarifying

Literary Analysis
Literary Focus: Theme
Theme
Character and Theme
Word Choice
Setting
Tone

Writing and Language Conventions
Communication Workshop: Persuasive Speech
Adjective Clauses
Parallelism
Adverb Clauses
Noun Clauses

Speaking and Listening
Memoir
Speech Outline
Presenting a Graph
Musical Presentation

LEARNING the Language of *Literature*

*T*heme

> *Theme contains the impressions which persist in readers'*
> *minds long after the last page has been turned.*
> —*Barbara H. Baskin, writer*

Theme is often what we remember about a story, long after the details of plot and setting have been forgotten. You can think of **theme** as an observation about life that the writer shares with the reader. In folk tales and fables, themes are simple and may be stated directly as lessons or morals. For example, in "A Fable" by Mark Twain, the lesson is that one sees only what one wants to see. Most themes, however, are not stated directly. They unfold as the characters travel along their journeys.

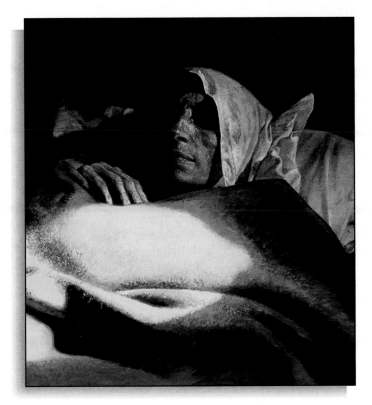

From "The Tell-Tale Heart"

The Difference Between Subject and Theme

A theme should not be confused with the subject of a story. Rather, a theme is a message or moral about life or human nature that the writer wishes to communicate. The **subject** of a story, or what the story is about, can be explained by describing the story's characters and plot. The subject of "The Tell-Tale Heart" is murder. The theme, or central truth of the story, is that you can never escape your crimes—that your own misdeeds will come back to haunt you.

Identifying Theme

You can often find clues to a story's theme by examining the title and the elements of character, setting, and plot. The passage at the right is from the end of "The Tell-Tale Heart." The murderer is face to face with the investigators. He is no longer able to bear the sound of the beating heart. Look at the chart below to analyze how theme is conveyed in the story.

ANALYZING THEME IN "THE TELL-TALE HEART"	
Story Elements	**Clues**
Title	• "The Tell-Tale Heart" implies a heart will reveal a secret.
Character	• The story's narrator is disturbed by his own thoughts.
Setting	• The story takes place in the man's house as well as in his own mind.
Plot	• The narrator plans and commits a murder. He then resolves his internal conflict when he confesses to police.

THEME

But any thing was better than this agony! Any thing was more tolerable than this derision! I could bear those hypocritical smiles no longer! I felt that I must scream or die—and now—again!—hark! louder! louder!! *louder!* —

"Villains!" I shrieked, "dissemble no more! I admit the deed! . . ."

—Edgar Allan Poe, "The Tell-Tale Heart"

Finding Evidence of the Theme

After your first reading of a story, ask yourself what message the author wanted to convey. Find evidence that shows the theme by skimming the story and looking for **key phrases.** It is important to pay attention to

- the first sentence of each paragraph
- how the setting is described
- what the narrator says about the characters
- descriptions of major conflicts or solutions
- what the main character learns

Using these techniques will help you identify and analyze recurring themes in literature.

YOUR TURN In the passage at right, officers have arrived at the man's house to investigate a disturbing noise. Identify key phrases that point to the story's theme.

KEY PHRASES

Why *would* they not be gone? I paced the floor to and fro with heavy strides, as if excited to fury by the observations of the men—but the noise steadily increased. What *could* I do? I foamed—I raved—I swore. I swung the chair upon which I had been sitting, and grated it upon the boards, but the noise arose over all and continually increased. It grew louder—louder—*louder!* And still the men chatted pleasantly, and smiled. Was it possible they heard not? Almighty God!—no, no! They heard!—they suspected!—they *knew!*—they were making a *mockery* of my horror!—this I thought, and this I think.

—Edgar Allan Poe, "The Tell-Tale Heart"

Distinguishing Fact from Opinion

Have you ever heard anyone say something like "Baseball is more American than any other game—and that's a fact!"? Is that really a fact, or is it an opinion? A fact is something that can be proved true. An opinion reflects someone's feeling or belief. As you read, use the strategies on this page to help you distinguish fact from opinion.

How to Apply the Skill

To **distinguish fact from opinion,** an active reader will:
- **Clarify** statements of fact as true or false
- Look for words and phrases that signal opinions
- **Evaluate** and analyze ideas and reasoning
- Look for supporting evidence

Try It Now!

Read the excerpt below and distinguish fact from opinion.

We lived in the dark green hills of Pittsburgh where the smoke from J.L. Steel dusted our clothes gray and blanketed the sky, . . . [and streetcars carried] passengers down the hills into the heart of the city that rested by the three rivers: Ohio, Monongahela, and Allegheny.

But what I remember most about growing up in Pittsburgh was living in a neighborhood where everyone acted like a relative—an aunt, an uncle, a brother, or a sister.

—Jewell Parker Rhodes, "Block Party"

Here's how Zahra uses the skill:

*"While reading, I **clarify** whether something is true or false. I know that the statement about the three rivers in Pittsburgh is a fact. I also look at words or phrases such as always or never, 'I believe,' and 'it seems.' Then I can **evaluate** whether the writer is stating facts or opinions. The last sentence is an opinion because the words 'everyone acted like a relative' indicate a judgment and can't be proved true."*

Block Party

by JEWELL PARKER RHODES

Connect to Your Life

A Sense of Community In "Block Party" the author describes growing up in a neighborhood "where everyone acted like a relative." Is there a strong sense of community in your neighborhood? Do your neighbors know and help each other? In your opinion, what would an ideal neighborhood be like?

Build Background

GEOGRAPHY

"Block Party" describes a predominantly African-American neighborhood in Pittsburgh, Pennsylvania, during the 1960s. Pittsburgh is built along rolling hills at the point where the Monongahela and Allegheny rivers join to form the Ohio River.

Pittsburgh was the center of the United States steel industry for decades. Much of the city's economy still depends on industry, but the city is also becoming an important center of computer services and health care.

WORDS TO KNOW
Vocabulary Preview

hazel	luminous
ledge	stoop
lumbering	

Focus Your Reading

LITERARY ANALYSIS **THEME**

A work of literature usually has a theme, a message or moral about life or human nature. For example, the theme of a story might be "wealth does not bring happiness" or "things are not always what they seem." As you read "Block Party," notice key story elements and phrases that suggest the theme.

ACTIVE READING **FACT/OPINION**

A **fact** is a statement that can be proved, such as "The sun rises every day." An **opinion** is a statement that expresses a belief or feeling, but which is not supported by proof or evidence; for example, "Everyone loves hot, sunny days." Opinions express personal beliefs about which people may agree or disagree.

📖 **READER'S NOTEBOOK** In "Block Party" Jewell Parker Rhodes blends fact and opinion to create a vivid picture of her Pittsburgh neighborhood. In a chart like the one shown, jot down some facts and opinions from the selection.

Fact	Opinion
"We lived in . . . Pittsburgh."	"Sometimes it drove me crazy to have so many mothers, but it also made me feel safe."

BLOCK PARTY

by JEWELL PARKER RHODES

We lived in the dark green hills of Pittsburgh where the smoke from J.L. Steel dusted our clothes gray and blanketed the sky, causing sunsets to streak bright pink and orange. Streetcar wires crisscrossed overhead, making perches for the hungry crows who flew high when the <u>lumbering</u> cars came, spewing electric sparks. Sometimes we'd put pennies in the metal tracks and wait for them to be squashed flat as the streetcars rumbled over them, carrying passengers down the hills into the heart of the city that rested by the three rivers: Ohio, Monongahela, and Allegheny.

But what I remember most about growing up in Pittsburgh was living in a neighborhood where everyone acted like a relative—an aunt,

Lots of women acted like my mother, bossing me, feeding me.

an uncle, a brother, or a sister. Lots of women acted like my mother, bossing me, feeding me. Many would hold me on their laps and tell me stories about High John the Conqueror[1] or John Henry. Some felt no shame about whipping out a comb and fixing my hair when they thought I looked too raggedy. And days when I was lucky, one of my neighborhood

---

1. **High John the Conqueror:** a legendary African-American slave of the Old South. Many folk tales tell of his cleverness in outwitting the plantation owner.

WORDS
TO
KNOW
    lumbering (lŭm'bər-ĭng) *adj.* moving in a heavy, clumsy way **lumber** *v.*

mothers would jump in the circle and join me in a waist-twisting, hip-rolling hula-hoop. Sometimes it drove me crazy to have so many mothers, but it also made me feel safe. My real mother was gone—divorced from us—living in another city. But I lived with my dad, my grandparents, an aunt, a sister, and a cousin whom I called sister.

ACTIVE READER

VISUALIZE What images do you see most clearly?

Dad, Aunt, and Grandpa went off to work while Grandma took care of us. On Tuesdays, she did laundry in the basement and she let us stir the Argo starch and turn the roller drums to wring out all the wet in the clothes. Then we'd help hang the clothes on the line and, when the sheets were dry, she

turned a blind eye while we played hide and seek among them. In the house we'd hike to the third floor and slide down the two banisters, smooth and fast, convinced it was better than any roller coaster ride at Kennywood Park.

We had a red tricycle with a bell. My sister, Tonie, had outgrown it. I was just the right size, while cousin Aleta was too small. But when Grandma made chitlins,[2] we would share the bike and make a game of driving through the stinking kitchen while Grandma cleaned out the pig's guts (yuck!) and boiled them. We'd ride our bike through dangerous territory, ringing our bell once we hit the

---

2. **chitlins:** pigs' intestines used as food.

kitchen linoleum, hollering and hooting like "wild ones"—or, as Grandma would say, like "Silly children with no sense!" If you held your nose you couldn't ring the bell and steer at the same time. So we'd count how many bells to figure out who won, who braved the skunky odor and didn't hold their nose the most.

The best part of growing up was the world we saw from our front <u>stoop</u>. Widow Chalmers mothered all the children, watching over us from her porch, waving her fan from the Methodist Church to cool herself in the summer heat. Mr. Berry, who had a splotch of pink roses on his cheek, liked checkers and would roam the street looking for a partner, carrying his own lawn chair. He even played with Aleta, who was five and had to be told every move. There was Jim, who played ball, spinning, ducking and diving, and throwing hoops into a basketball net and would only stop if someone was in any trouble. "Jim, my car stalled." "Jim, can you drive me to the grocery?" "Jim, my sink is clogged." Jim later joined the Army and came home and dunked three baskets in his clod-hopper black shoes[3] and khaki uniform. My sister Tonie, at eleven, swore she'd marry him.

Stuck-up Rachel liked to cheat at Jacks and had to be blackmailed into playing Double Dutch.[4] "I'll give you some of Grandma's chicken from Sunday dinner," I'd offer. I promised a drumstick for each twenty minutes she turned the rope while I sang and dreamed of winning Double Dutch Champion at the "Y." Truth be told, Grandma would have given anyone who asked a piece of her chicken. Rachel knew it, I knew it. Everyone knew it. But Rachel was two years older than I and, like another big sister, she was nice enough to let me think I was putting one over on her.

ACTIVE READER

QUESTION How does the narrator feel about her neighborhood?

Sitting on the steps, looking up and down the block, I saw and felt a world where I was safe, where I knew everybody and everybody knew me. Everybody was brown and black and when babies were born, we'd all wait for them to grow into their skin. Their shades would sometimes grow lighter, sometimes darker. Even the color of their eyes would change—blue became brown, <u>hazel</u> changed to deep green, and brown irises could mellow to a <u>luminous</u> black. Hair textures all varied: soft, bouncy, waves; strands curled in fuzzy, tight spirals; or even hair thick and straight because of a throwback to a Cherokee.[5] I knew we all were beautiful.

Summer block parties were the best. We'd close off traffic and sometimes the Fire Department would open the hydrants and we'd dance and sing while water gushed at us. A spray of wet beneath the moon and stars. Tonie, Aleta, and I pushed boxes together to make a stage and lipsynched to the record player, pretending we were The Supremes. *"Stop, in the name of love! Before you break my heart. Think it o-o-over! . . ."* and we'd giggle as the grown-ups clapped and the other children squealed, and everyone danced, even fat Charlie who could boogie so well you'd swear there was magic in his shoes.

---

3. **clod-hopper . . . shoes:** heavy work shoes.

4. **Double Dutch:** a game of jump rope in which two people swing two ropes at the same time, usually in opposite directions.

5. **Cherokee** (cher´ə kē´): Native Americans of the southern Appalachians, now living mostly in Oklahoma.

WORDS TO KNOW

stoop (stōōp) *n.* a small porch, platform, or staircase leading to the entrance of a building or house
hazel (hā´zəl) *adj.* a light brown or yellowish brown
luminous (lōō´mə-nəs) *adj.* giving off light; shining

The best block parties happened for no reason. Anyone—even a child—could wake up one day and call for "Block Party Day." And we'd share ribs, corn, chicken, tater pie, and collard greens, and Miss Sarah who never married always made punch with vanilla ice cream and it would melt into a swishy mess. Finally, when legs wouldn't move another dance step, then the record player was taken away, the street was swept. There were cries and whispers of good night. My real family and I, we'd go into the house. Grandma, Grandpa, Aunt, and Daddy would tuck us in bed and kiss me, Tonie, and Aleta good night. And I would wait until Tonie and Aleta were asleep in the small twin beds (I didn't want

**Anyone
— even a child—
could wake up
one day and
call for
"Block Party Day."**

them to think I was off my head) and I'd go to the window. Then, peeking over the <u>ledge</u>, I'd whisper my own private "G'night" to the rest of my family, tucked in their beds inside the tall houses all along my street, there in the city where the three rivers meet. ❖

WORDS
TO
KNOW   **ledge** (lĕj) *n.* a narrow shelf

Connect to the Literature

1. What Do You Think?
What memories of your own childhood days did this selection call up?

Comprehension Check
- Who were the members of the narrator's "real" family?
- How did people in the neighborhood take care of each other?
- What was a "block party"?

Think Critically

2. **ACTIVE READING** **FACT/OPINION**
Look at the facts and opinions you listed in your **READER'S NOTEBOOK**. What opinions of her childhood does the author share with you in this selection?

3. What are some of the ways in which this neighborhood was like a family?

> **Think About:**
> - the role of women
> - how food was shared
> - the last thing the narrator did before she went to sleep

4. The narrator says that "Anyone—even a child—could wake up one day and call for 'Block Party Day.' " What does this suggest about the neighborhood's attitude toward children?

5. Do you think the narrator's portrayal of her neighborhood is realistic? Why or why not?

Extend Interpretations

6. The Writer's Style With a partner, read aloud the first and last paragraphs of "Block Party." How does the last sentence echo the beginning of the selection? What effect does this repetition have? Try reading other passages aloud.

7. Connect to Life "It takes a village to raise a child" is a traditional African saying. Do you think this is true? How does this saying relate to your own experience?

Literary Analysis

THEME A message or moral about life or human nature that is communicated by a literary work is called a **theme.** Often the theme is not directly stated. The reader infers the theme by analyzing story elements, such as setting, character, and conflict. To identify a literary work's theme, find the most important topic or subject in the work and ask yourself, What is the author saying about this topic?

Paired Activity With a partner, go back through the selection and identify the theme. Discuss your findings with your partner. Answer the following questions:
- How does the title of the story relate to the story's theme?
- What descriptive details support the theme?

Significance of the Title "Block Party"
_____
_____

Setting Details	Character Details	Conflict Details
1.————	2.————	3.————
————	————	————
————	————	————
————	————	————

The Theme of "Block Party" is
_____
_____

Writing

Theme Essay Write a short essay defining the theme of "Block Party." State whether you agree or disagree with the writer's message. Provide a thorough explanation for your response. Place the essay in your **Working Portfolio.**

Writing Handbook
See p. R36: Building Blocks of Good Writing.

Speaking & Listening

Memoir Write a memoir about an event or the people in your neighborhood. As you write, think about the main message you wish to convey. Be sure to include relevant dialogue, specific action, descriptive details, and background information that will indirectly state your message, or theme. Read your memoir for your class.

Speaking and Listening Handbook
See p. R107: Narrative Presentations.

Research & Technology

Motown Magic During the 1960s, the Supremes and other Motown singing groups were popular. Using the Internet and library sources, research Motown Records or one of its artists or groups. Why was the Motown label important? Present your findings in an oral report to the class and include examples of Motown music, if possible. Be sure to organize your information to match your purpose.

Vocabulary

STANDARDIZED TEST PRACTICE

Choose the word or group of words that means the same, or nearly the same, as the underlined Word to Know in each sentence.

1. The old streetcars came lumbering down the streets, looking like tired workers at the end of the day. Lumbering means—
   A bouncing **B** plodding
   C howling **D** whistling

2. Some of the children in the neighborhood had hazel eyes, like leaves in the fall. Hazel means—
   F green **G** blue
   H brown **J** violet

3. Others possessed luminous, black-colored eyes. Luminous means—
   A mysterious **B** mischievous
   C wide **D** shining

4. Neighbors often sat on the front stoop where they could comfortably watch the world go by. Stoop means—
   F porch **G** bench
   H swing **J** hill

5. After the block party, the narrator peeked over the ledge to say good night to her neighbors. Ledge means—
   A bush **B** building
   C shelf **D** fence

EXERCISE: SHORT STORY With a partner, write a short story, using all of the Words to Know. Work together to make the story lively, and be sure that the story has a beginning, a middle, and an end. Trade your story with another pair and compare results.

Vocabulary Handbook
See p. R20: Context Clues.

WORDS TO KNOW	hazel	ledge	lumbering	luminous	stoop

Grammar in Context: Adjective Clauses

"Block Party" by Jewell Parker Rhodes is filled with powerful descriptions. Notice how the **adjective clause** in the following sentence describes Mr. Berry:

> **Mr. Berry, who had a splotch of pink roses on his cheek, liked checkers and would roam the street looking for a partner, carrying his own lawn chair.**

An **adjective clause** is a dependent clause that acts as an adjective. Adjective clauses are used to modify nouns or pronouns. They tell what kind, which one, how many, or how much. They can also be used to combine sentences. Adjective clauses usually begin with words such as *that, which, what, who, whom,* and *whose.*

Apply to Your Writing Use adjective clauses to provide additional details about nouns and pronouns or to combine sentences.

WRITING EXERCISE Combine each pair of sentences. Turn one of the sentences into an adjective clause that begins with the word or words in parentheses.

Example: *Original* Streetcar wires made perches for hungry crows. The crows flew high when streetcars approached. (that)

Rewritten Streetcar wires made perches for hungry crows <u>that flew high when streetcars approached.</u>

1. I grew up in a unique world. I felt safe in that world. (in which)
2. There were many women in my neighborhood. They acted like my mother. (who)
3. At the summer block parties, we'd play in water. The water came from hydrants. (that)
4. This is the neighborhood. I remember the neighborhood so well. (that)
5. Mr. Berry even played checkers with Aleta. Aleta was five. (who)

Grammar Handbook See p. R90: Clauses.

Jewell Parker Rhodes
born 1954

"I can be anything and everything in my imagination."

Happy Times Jewell Parker Rhodes grew up in Pittsburgh, Pennsylvania. Her parents were divorced when she was very young, and she was raised by her grandmother. She says that block parties provided some of her happiest times as a child. "I loved lip-synching to records, and I often imagined I'd grow up to become a singer or an actress." Instead, in college she chose to earn degrees in drama criticism, English, and creative writing.

Academic Work As a writer, Parker Rhodes says, "I can be anything and everything in my imagination." She has written scholarly nonfiction as well as magazine articles, stories, and novels. She teaches writing and literature and is former director of the creative writing program at Arizona State University.

AUTHOR ACTIVITY
Storytelling and Myth Use the Internet to find out what Jewell Parker Rhodes has to say about the process of writing her first book and about the importance of storytelling and myth. Does anything in "Block Party" remind you of a myth?

The Summer of the Beautiful White Horse

by WILLIAM SAROYAN (sə-roi′ən)

Connect to Your Life

Family Connections Have you ever known a family of talented musicians or a family of great cooks? Sometimes it seems that members of a family share similar talents or characteristics, such as shyness, a sense of humor, or an optimistic outlook. With a small group, discuss families you have known or read about that have common traits.

Build Background

GEOGRAPHY

This story is set in the San Joaquin (wô-kēn′) Valley of California during the early 1900s, when horses were an important means of transportation. Aram, the narrator, is Armenian. His family came from Armenia, a small country in the Caucasus Mountain region in southwest Asia.

Beginning in the early 1900s, thousands of Armenians emigrated to the United States. Many settled in the San Joaquin Valley, which resembled their homeland. The immigrants continued to grow grapes, olives, apricots, and figs as they had done in Armenia and maintained close family ties and strong feelings of nationality.

San Joaquin Valley

Sacramento
San Francisco
Sierra Nevada
Fresno
San Joaquin River
San Joaquin Valley
Pacific Ocean
CALIFORNIA
N W E S
Los Angeles
Miles
0   80   160

WORDS TO KNOW
Vocabulary Preview
descendant   pious
longing   vagrant
magnificence

Focus Your Reading

LITERARY ANALYSIS   CHARACTER AND THEME

Most stories center on the experience and actions of one or more **main characters.** Often, the lesson the main character learns by the end of a story indicates the theme. Throughout the story, the motivations, experiences, and reactions of the main character act as clues to the theme. As you read this story, note Aram's motivations and the lessons he learns.

ACTIVE READING   CONNECTING

Readers connect to a story when they compare their own experiences with those of the story's characters. Connecting helps readers understand the characters. It also helps readers gain insights into their own actions and feelings.

READER'S NOTEBOOK In a chart like the one shown, note descriptions, dialogue, and events in the story that remind you of your own experience.

Connections	
"The Summer of the Beautiful White Horse"	**My Experience**
". . . my earliest memories had been memories of horses, and my first longings had been longings to ride."	I have always loved animals, especially horses.

White Pacing Mustang (1949), Tom Lea. Oil on canvas, 18" × 24". Art collection, Harry Ransom
Humanities Research Center, The University of Texas at Austin.

THE SUMMER OF THE
BEAUTIFUL WHITE HORSE

BY WILLIAM SAROYAN

One day back there in the good old days when I was nine and the world was full of every imaginable kind of magnificence, and life was still a delightful and mysterious dream, my cousin Mourad, who was considered crazy by everybody who knew him except me, came to my house at four in the morning and woke me up by tapping on the window of my room.

"Aram," he said.

I jumped out of bed and looked out the window.

I couldn't believe what I saw.

It wasn't morning yet, but it was summer and with daybreak not many minutes around the corner of the world it was light enough for me to know I wasn't dreaming.

My cousin Mourad was sitting on a beautiful white horse.

I stuck my head out of the window and rubbed my eyes.

"Yes," he said in Armenian. "It's a horse. You're not dreaming. Make it quick if you want to ride."

I knew my cousin Mourad enjoyed being alive more than anybody else who had ever fallen into the world by mistake, but this was more than even I could believe.

In the first place, my earliest memories had been memories of horses, and my first longings had been longings to ride.

This was the wonderful part.

In the second place, we were poor.

This was the part that wouldn't permit me to believe what I saw.

We were poor. We had no money. Our whole tribe was poverty-stricken. Every branch of the Garoghlanian[1] family was living in the most amazing and comical poverty in the world. Nobody could understand where we ever got money enough to keep us with food in our bellies, not even the old men of the family. Most important of all, though, we were famous for our honesty. We had been famous for our honesty for something like eleven centuries, even when

> It wasn't morning yet, but it was summer and with daybreak not many minutes around the corner of the world it was light enough for me to know I wasn't dreaming.

---

1. **Garoghlanian** (gär′ō-glä′nē-ən).

we had been the wealthiest family in what we liked to think was the world. We were proud first, honest next, and after that we believed in right and wrong. None of us would take advantage of anybody in the world, let alone steal.

Consequently, even though I could *see* the horse, so magnificent; even though I could *smell* it, so lovely; even though I could *hear* it breathing, so exciting; I couldn't *believe* the horse had anything to do with my cousin Mourad or with me or with any of the other members of our family, asleep or awake, because I *knew* my cousin Mourad couldn't have bought the horse, and if he couldn't have *bought* it he must have *stolen* it, and I refused to believe he had stolen it.

No member of the Garoghlanian family could be a thief.

I stared first at my cousin and then at the horse. There was a pious stillness and humor in each of them which on the one hand delighted me and on the other frightened me.

"Mourad," I said, "where did you steal this horse?"

"Leap out of the window," he said, "if you want to ride."

It was true, then. He had stolen the horse. There was no question about it. He had come to invite me to ride or not, as I chose.

Well, it seemed to me stealing a horse for a ride was not the same thing as stealing something else, such as money. For all I knew, maybe it wasn't stealing at all. If you were crazy about horses the way my cousin Mourad and I were, it wasn't stealing. It wouldn't become stealing until we offered to sell the horse, which of course I knew we would never do.

"Let me put on some clothes," I said.

"All right," he said, "but hurry."

I leaped into my clothes.

I jumped down to the yard from the window and leaped up onto the horse behind my cousin Mourad.

That year we lived at the edge of town, on Walnut Avenue. Behind our house was the country: vineyards, orchards, irrigation ditches, and country roads. In less than three minutes we were on Olive Avenue, and then the horse began to trot. The air was new and lovely to breathe. The feel of the horse running was wonderful. My cousin Mourad, who was considered one of the craziest members of our family, began to sing. I mean, he began to roar.

Every family has a crazy streak in it somewhere, and my cousin Mourad was considered the natural descendant of the crazy streak in our tribe. Before him was our uncle Khosrove, an enormous man with a powerful head of black hair and the largest mustache in the San Joaquin Valley,[2] a man so furious in temper, so irritable, so impatient that he stopped anyone from talking by roaring, *It is no harm; pay no attention to it.*

> "Leap out of the window," he said, "if you want to ride."

---

2. **San Joaquin** (săn wô-kēn′) **Valley:** an agricultural area in California.

| WORDS TO KNOW | **pious** (pī′əs) *adj.* showing sincere devotion; reverent |
| | **descendant** (dĭ-sĕn′dənt) *n.* an offspring |

That was all, no matter what anybody happened to be talking about. Once it was his own son Arak running eight blocks to the barber shop where his father was having his mustache trimmed to tell him their house was on fire. This man Khosrove sat up in the chair and roared, "It is no harm; pay no attention to it." The barber said, "But the boy says your house is on fire." So Khosrove roared, "Enough, it is no harm, I say."

My cousin Mourad was considered the natural descendant of this man, although Mourad's father was Zorab, who was practical and nothing else. That's how it was in our tribe. A man could be the father of his son's flesh, but that did not mean that he was also the father of his spirit. The distribution of the various kinds of spirit of our tribe had been from the beginning capricious and vagrant.

We rode and my cousin Mourad sang. For all anybody knew we were still in the old country[3] where, at least according to some of our neighbors, we belonged. We let the horse run as long as it felt like running.

At last my cousin Mourad said, "Get down. I want to ride alone."

"Will you let me ride alone?" I said.

"That is up to the horse," my cousin said. "Get down."

"The *horse* will let me ride," I said.

"We shall see," he said. "Don't forget that I have a way with a horse."

"Well," I said, "any way you have with a horse, I have also."

"For the sake of your safety," he said, "let us hope so. Get down."

"All right," I said, "but remember you've got to let me try to ride alone."

I got down and my cousin Mourad kicked his heels into the horse and shouted, "*Vazire*," run. The horse stood on its hind legs, snorted, and burst into a fury of speed that was the loveliest thing I had ever seen. My cousin Mourad raced the horse across a field of dry grass to an irrigation ditch, crossed the ditch on the horse, and five minutes later returned, dripping wet.

The sun was coming up.

"Now it's my turn to ride," I said.

My cousin Mourad got off the horse.

"Ride," he said.

I leaped to the back of the horse and for a moment knew the awfulest fear imaginable. The horse did not move.

"Kick into his muscles," my cousin Mourad said. "What are you waiting for? We've got to take him back before everybody in the world is up and about."

I kicked into the muscles of the horse. Once again it reared and snorted. Then it began to

> I leaped to the back of the horse and for a moment knew the awfulest fear imaginable.

---

3. **old country:** Armenia.

---

run. I didn't know what to do. Instead of running across the field to the irrigation ditch the horse ran down the road to the vineyard of Dikran Halabian, where it began to leap over vines. The horse leaped over seven vines before I fell. Then it continued running.

My cousin Mourad came running down the road.

"I'm not worried about you," he shouted. "We've got to get that horse. You go this way and I'll go this way. If you come upon him, be kindly. I'll be near."

I continued down the road and my cousin Mourad went across the field toward the irrigation ditch.

It took him half an hour to find the horse and bring him back.

"All right," he said, "jump on. The whole world is awake now."

"What will we do?" I said.

"Well," he said, "we'll either take him back or hide him until tomorrow morning."

He didn't sound worried and I knew he'd hide him and not take him back. Not for a while, at any rate.

"Where will we hide him?" I said.

"I know a place," he said.

"How long ago did you steal this horse?" I said.

It suddenly dawned on me that he had been taking these early morning rides for some time and had come for me this morning only because he knew how much I longed to ride.

"Who said anything about stealing a horse?" he said.

"Anyhow," I said, "how long ago did you begin riding every morning?"

"Not until this morning," he said.

"Are you telling the truth?" I said.

"Of course not," he said, "but if we are found out, that's what you're to say. I don't want both of us to be liars. All you know is that we started riding this morning."

"All right," I said.

He walked the horse quietly to the barn of a deserted vineyard which at one time had been the pride of a farmer named Fetvajian. There were some oats and dry alfalfa in the barn.

We began walking home.

"It wasn't easy," he said, "to get the horse to behave so nicely. At first it wanted to run wild, but, as I've told you, I have a way with a horse. I can get it to do anything *I* want it to do. Horses understand me."

"How do you do it?" I said.

"I have an understanding with a horse," he said.

"Yes, but what sort of an understanding?" I said.

"A simple and honest one," he said.

"Well," I said, "I wish I knew how to reach an understanding like that with a horse."

"You're still a small boy," he said. "When you get to be thirteen you'll know how to do it."

I went home and ate a hearty breakfast.

That afternoon my uncle Khosrove came to our house for coffee and cigarettes. He sat in the parlor, sipping and smoking and

> "It wasn't easy," he said, "to get the horse to behave so nicely."

The Icknield Way (1912), Spencer Gore (England, 1878–1914). Oil on canvas, 63.4 cm × 76.2 cm, Art Gallery of New South Wales, Australia.

remembering the old country. Then another visitor arrived, a farmer named John Byro, an Assyrian[4] who, out of loneliness, had learned to speak Armenian. My mother brought the lonely visitor coffee, and then at last, sighing sadly, he said, "My white horse which was stolen last month is still gone. I cannot understand it."

My uncle Khosrove became very irritated and shouted, "It's no harm. What is the loss of a horse? Haven't we all lost the homeland? What is this crying over a horse?"

---

4. **Assyrian** (ə-sîr′ē-ən): a member of an ethnic group that lives in parts of Turkey and Iraq.

"That may be all right for you, a city dweller, to say," John Byro said, "but what of my surrey?⁵ What good is a surrey without a horse?"

"Pay no attention to it," my uncle Khosrove roared.

"I walked ten miles to get here," John Byro said.

"You have legs," my uncle Khosrove shouted.

"My left leg pains me," the farmer said.

"Pay no attention to it," my uncle Khosrove roared.

"That horse cost me sixty dollars," the farmer said.

"I spit on money," my uncle Khosrove said.

He got up and stalked out of the house, slamming the screen door.

My mother explained.

"He has a gentle heart," she said. "It is simply that he is homesick and such a large man."

The farmer went away and I ran over to my cousin Mourad's house.

He was sitting under a peach tree, trying to repair the hurt wing of a young robin which could not fly. He was talking to the bird.

"What is it?" he said.

"The farmer, John Byro," I said. "He visited our house. He wants his horse. You've had it a month. I want you to promise not to take it back until I learn to ride."

"It will take you *a year* to learn to ride," my cousin Mourad said.

"We could keep the horse a year," I said.

My cousin Mourad leaped to his feet.

"What?" he roared. "Are you inviting a member of the Garoghlanian family to steal?

The horse must go back to its true owner."

"When?" I said.

"In six months at the latest," he said.

He threw the bird into the air. The bird tried hard, almost fell twice, but at last flew away, high and straight.

> ". . . I want you to promise not to take it back until I learn to ride."
> "It will take you *a year* to learn to ride," my cousin Mourad said.

Early every morning for two weeks my cousin Mourad and I took the horse out of the barn of the deserted vineyard where we were hiding it and rode it, and every morning the horse, when it was my turn to ride alone, leaped over grape vines and small trees and threw me and ran away. Nevertheless, I hoped

---

5. **surrey:** a four-wheeled, horse-drawn carriage.

in time to learn to ride the way my cousin Mourad rode.

One morning on the way to Fetvajian's deserted vineyard we ran into the farmer John Byro, who was on the way to town.

"Let me do the talking," my cousin Mourad said. "I have a way with farmers."

"Good morning, John Byro," my cousin Mourad said to the farmer.

The farmer studied the horse eagerly.

"Good morning, sons of my friends," he said. "What is the name of your horse?"

"*My Heart,*" my cousin Mourad said in Armenian.

"A lovely name," John Byro said, "for a lovely horse. I could swear it is the horse that was stolen from me many weeks ago. May I look into its mouth?"

"Of course," Mourad said.

The farmer looked into the mouth of the horse.

"Tooth for tooth," he said. "I would swear it is my horse if I didn't know your parents. The fame of your family for honesty is well known to me. Yet the horse is the twin of my horse. A suspicious man would believe his eyes instead of his heart. Good day, my young friends."

"Good day, John Byro," my cousin Mourad said.

Early the following morning we took the horse to John Byro's vineyard and put it in the barn. The dogs followed us around without making a sound.

"The dogs," I whispered to my cousin Mourad. "I thought they would bark."

"They would at somebody else," he said. "I have a way with dogs."

My cousin Mourad put his arms around the horse, pressed his nose into the horse's nose, patted it, and then we went away.

That afternoon John Byro came to our house in his surrey and showed my mother the horse that had been stolen and returned.

"I do not know what to think," he said. "The horse is stronger than ever. Better-tempered, too. I thank God."

My uncle Khosrove, who was in the parlor, became irritated and shouted, "Quiet man, quiet. Your horse has been returned. Pay no attention to it." ❖

Connect to the Literature

1. What Do You Think?
What are your thoughts about the adventures of Aram and Mourad?

Comprehension Check
- How did Mourad get a horse?
- For what trait was the Garoghlanian family known?
- Why did the boys return the horse?

Think Critically

2. Why do you think John Byro does not take the horse when he recognizes it as his?

3. In your opinion, what kind of person is Mourad?

   Think About:
   - his actions with the horse and his treatment of the injured bird
   - his insistence that he has "a way" with things
   - the family traits he shares with Uncle Khosrove
   - why he returns the horse

4. **ACTIVE READING** **CONNECTING**
   What connections did you make between the story and your own life? Refer to the chart in your **READER'S NOTEBOOK**. In what way does the story help you to gain insight into yourself?

Extend Interpretations

5. What If? What if Byro had never seen the boys with the horse? What if he had angrily accused them of stealing it? Discuss the possible outcomes with classmates.

6. **COMPARING TEXTS** Look back at the selection "Block Party" (page 830), in which people and events are described from a child's perspective. Although the settings of the two works are very different, both selections are about families and growing up. How are the two selections similar and different? What does each seem to say about childhood?

7. Connect to Life At the beginning of this selection, you were asked to identify traits that make a family special. How does Aram's family compare with the families you discussed? What traits would you like to pass along to younger relatives?

Literary Analysis

CHARACTER AND THEME A short story usually features one or two **main characters** whose experiences and reactions are the focus of the story. Main characters are well developed, and they generally change in some way by the end of the story.

One way to identify and analyze the theme of a story is to pay attention to the main character's motivations, experiences, and reactions. For example, Aram tries to convince himself that the horse isn't really stolen, even though it is. This provides a clue that the theme concerns a question of morals. Finally, the lesson Aram learns resolves his moral conflict.

Paired Activity Working with a partner, identify the motivations, experiences, and reactions of the main character, Aram. Explain the lesson he learns and how that indicates the theme of the story.

Character's Experience	What It Reveals About the Theme
"Most important of all, though, we were famous for our honesty."	The theme may have to do with honesty.

Writing

Character Sketch Write a character sketch of Aram, the narrator. Describe Aram's appearance, personality, and behavior. Explain how Aram changes throughout the course of the story. What lesson did he learn? Place your sketch in your **Working Portfolio.**

Writing Handbook
See p. R41: Descriptive Writing.

Speaking & Listening

Speech Outline Write a speech outline for an oral report in which you compare the character of Aram with the narrator of "Block Party." Include details about their attitudes toward their friends, family, and neighbors. Draw a conclusion on how they are similar or different. Be sure to use specific text references to support your opinions.

Speaking and Listening Handbook
See p. R104: Writing Your Speech.

Research & Technology

Armenia Research the history and ways of life of Armenia. Why is King Tigran II important in Armenian history? What countries border present-day Armenia? How do most Armenians today earn a living? Use charts, maps, or graphs to present information visually. Report your findings to the class.

Research and Technology Handbook
See p. R120: Using Visuals.

Art Connection

Look again at the painting entitled *The Deathless White Pacing Mustang* by Tom Lea on page 840. Lea, who grew up in El Paso, Texas, has been described as a realist who paints things as they are. What mood does the painting convey? Explain how the elements in the painting create this mood.

The Deathless White Pacing Mustang (1948), Tom Lea. Oil on canvas, 18" × 24", Harry Ransom, Humanities Research Center, The University of Texas at Austin.

Vocabulary

STANDARDIZED TEST PRACTICE

Complete each analogy with a Word to Know. Use a dictionary if you need help.

1. EXHIBIT : DISPLAY :: _____ : splendor
2. FICKLE : UNPREDICTABLE :: _____ : wandering
3. IRRIGATION : DRAINAGE :: _____ : ancestor
4. HAPPY : JOYOUS :: _____ : devout
5. BOREDOM : DULLNESS :: _____ : desire

EXERCISE Write a paragraph that begins with the words "I am a descendant of . . ." and goes on to tell a story about a real or imagined ancestor of yours. Include at least two additional Words to Know in your paragraph.

Vocabulary Handbook
See p. R26: Analogies.

WORDS TO KNOW	descendant	longing	magnificence	pious	vagrant

Grammar in Context: Parallelism

Look at this sentence from William Saroyan's "The Summer of the Beautiful White Horse":

> The horse **stood** on its hind legs, **snorted,** and **burst** into a fury of speed that was the loveliest thing I had ever seen.

The words in red are **parallel.** Words or groups of words that have the same function and form in a sentence are parallel. In the sentence above, the highlighted words are parallel because they have the same function (they describe what the horse did) and the same form (verb in the past tense). When items in a series are not parallel, the sentence is awkward, as in this sentence: "The horse stood on its hind legs, was snorting, and burst into a fury of speed." Use parallel structures to logically present items in a series and to match ideas for emphasis. When using verbs, be sure they are in the same tense.

Usage Tip: Use parallel structures only when the ideas they express are closely related.

WRITING EXERCISE Revise each sentence below to make the sentence parts parallel.

1. The horse was white, beautiful, and ran fast.

2. My family was known for their honesty and being proud.

3. My uncle Khosrove was an enormous man with black hair, a large mustache, and had a terrible temper.

4. My cousin Mourad raced the white horse across a field, through a ditch, and returned dripping wet.

5. When it was my turn to ride alone, the horse leaped over grapevines and small trees, then would throw me, and run away.

Grammar Handbook
See p. R91: Parallelism.

William Saroyan
1908–1981

"It came to me that I had better write about certain people and things as quickly as possible because . . . I believed I had the obligation not to forget."

Writing from Experience "The Summer of the Beautiful White Horse" and other stories in *My Name Is Aram* are based on Saroyan's own boyhood in Fresno, California. Like Aram, Saroyan was a Californian of Armenian descent. During his lifetime he created numerous works, including short stories, plays, and novels. Many of his writings reveal his belief in the basic innocence of people.

Interesting Views Saroyan won the Pulitzer Prize in 1940 for his play *The Time of Your Life,* but he refused the prize because he considered accepting cash awards to be beneath the dignity of an artist. On his deathbed, Saroyan said, "Everybody has got to die, but I have always believed an exception would be made in my case. Now what?" His words, which reflect the dry humor that filled his writing, were quoted around the world.

AUTHOR ACTIVITY
Exploring Heritage In the library, find a copy of *My Name Is Aram.* Read more of the stories in this book. What values of Armenian-American culture do you find in these stories?

One Million Volumes

by RUDOLFO ANAYA

Connect to Your Life

The Power of Reading Some people always have their noses in a book. Others prefer to read magazines or newspapers. What do you like to read? Write your answers in a web like the one shown. Then discuss your thoughts about reading with a small group of classmates.

Build Background

SOCIAL STUDIES

The speech you are about to read was delivered by author Rudolfo Anaya to celebrate the purchase by the University of New Mexico library of its one-millionth volume. Rudolfo Anaya was a fitting speaker for this occasion. He is a lifelong resident of New Mexico and a graduate of the University of New Mexico.

Rudolfo Anaya is a Hispanic American, a descendant of Spanish-speaking people. Spanish-speaking Mexicans began to settle in the Southwest when it was part of Mexico from 1598 to 1848. When this territory was ceded to the United States in 1848, after the Mexican-American War, English-speaking settlers arrived from other parts of the United States.

Today many Hispanic Americans speak both English and Spanish. This blend of languages is reflected in Anaya's writings. Look for it as you read the speech.

> WORDS TO KNOW
> **Vocabulary Preview**
>
> censorship   litany
> ignite   paradox
> induce

Focus Your Reading

LITERARY ANALYSIS **WORD CHOICE**

Writers use language to express their thoughts and feelings. To do this well, they must carefully choose their words. In one passage Anaya describes the power of books:

> *. . . a book at once quenches the thirst of the imagination and ignites new fires.*

Anaya carefully chose the words *quench* and *ignite* to communicate his view that books both satisfy our need to learn and give us a burning desire to learn even more. As you read the speech, look for other images that Anaya conveys through word choice.

ACTIVE READING **AUTHOR'S PURPOSE**

A writer's reason for creating a work is known as the **author's purpose.** Writers have four main purposes: to entertain, to inform, to express opinions, and to persuade. Often a writer has more than one purpose. For example, a writer may write both to inform and to persuade.

READER'S NOTEBOOK As you read Anaya's speech, make a note of passages that provide clues to Anaya's purpose or purposes for writing.

ONE MILLION VOLUMES

by Rudolfo Anaya

A million volumes.

A magic number.

A million books to read, to look at, to hold in one's hand, to learn, to dream. . . .

I have always known there were at least a million stars. In the summer evenings when I was a child, we, all the children of the neighborhood, sat outside under the stars and listened to the stories of the old ones, los viejitos.[1] The stories of the old people taught us to wonder and imagine. Their adivinanzas[2] <u>induced</u> the stirring of our first questioning, our early learning.

I remember my grandfather raising his hand and pointing to the swirl of the Milky Way which swept over us. Then he would whisper his favorite riddle:

> Hay un hombre con tanto dinero
> Que no lo puede contar
> Una mujer con una sábana tan grande
> Que no la puede doblar.

> There is a man with so much money
> He cannot count it
> A woman with a bedspread so large
> She cannot fold it.

---

1. *los viejitos* (lōs vyě-hē′tōs) *Spanish:* the old ones.
2. *adivinanzas* (ä-dē-vē-nän′säs) *Spanish:* riddles.

WORDS
TO
KNOW

induce (ĭn-dōōs′) *v.* to bring forth; cause

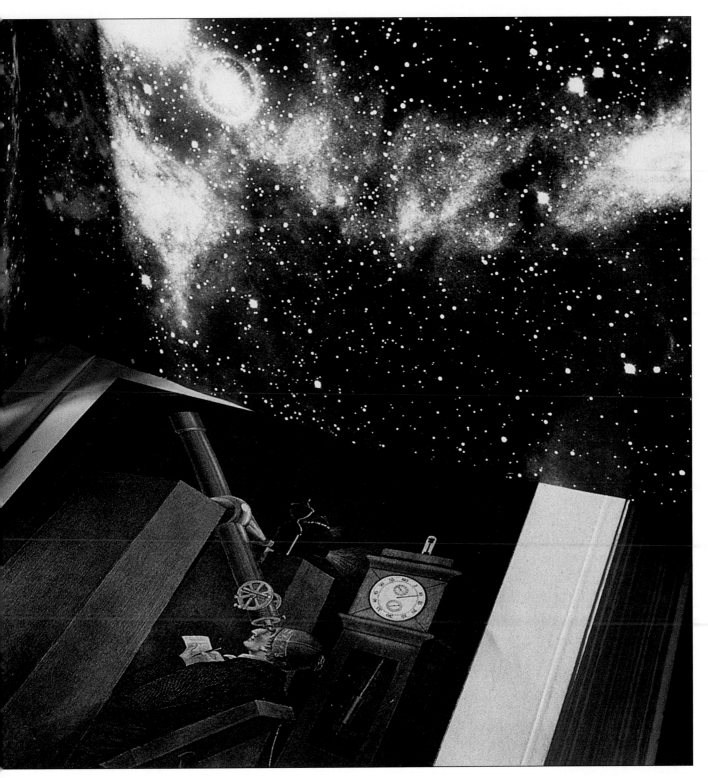

Two Books of Astronomy (1996), © Abelardo Morell.
Courtesy: Bonni Benrubi Gallery, NYC.

We knew the million stars were the coins of the Lord, and the heavens were the bedspread of his mother, and in our minds the sky was a million miles wide. A hundred million. Infinite. Stuff for the imagination. And what was more important, the teachings of the old ones made us see that we were bound to the infinity of that cosmic dance of life which swept around us. Their teachings created in us a thirst for knowledge. Can this library with its million volumes bestow that same inspiration?

I was fortunate to have had those old and wise viejitos as guides into the world of nature and knowledge. They taught me with their stories: they taught me the magic of words. Now the words lie captured in ink, but the magic is still there, the power inherent in each volume. Now with book in hand we can participate in the wisdom of mankind.

Each person moves from innocence through rites of passage into the knowledge of the world, and so I entered the world of school in search of the magic in the words. The sounds were no longer the soft sounds of Spanish which my grandfather spoke: the words were in English, and with each new awareness came my first steps toward a million volumes. I, who was used to reading my oraciones en español[3] while I sat in the kitchen and answered the <u>litany</u> to the slap of my mother's tortillas,[4] I now stumbled from sound to word to groups of words, head throbbing, painfully aware that each new sound took me deeper into the maze of the new language. Oh, how I clutched the hands of my new guides then!

---

3. *oraciones en español* (ō-rä-syō′něs ěn ěs-pä-nyōl′) *Spanish:* prayers in Spanish.

4. **tortillas** (tōr-tē′yəz): thin disks of unleavened cornmeal or wheat-flour bread.

WORDS
TO
KNOW   **litany** (lĭt′n-ē) *n.* a repetitive recitation

Book of Stars (1994), © Abelardo Morell.
Courtesy: Bonni Benrubi Gallery, NYC.

Yes, I remember the cuentos of my grandfather, the stories of the people.

How can we see a million books?

Learn, my mother encouraged me, learn. Be as wise as your grandfather. He could speak many languages. He could speak to the birds and the animals of the field.

Yes, I remember the cuentos[5] of my grandfather, the stories of the people. Words are a way, he said, they hold joy, and they are a deadly power if misused. I clung to each syllable which lisped from his tobacco-stained lips. That was the winter the snow came, he would say, it piled high and we lost many sheep and cattle, and the trees groaned and broke with its weight. I looked across the llano[6] and saw the raging blizzard, the awful destruction of that winter which was imbedded in our people's mind.

And the following summer, he would say, the grass of the llano grew so high we couldn't see the top of the sheep. And I would look and see what was once clean and pure and green. I could see a million sheep and the pastores[7]

caring for them, as I now care for the million words that pasture in my mind.

But a million books? How can we see a million books? I don't mean just the books lining the shelves here at the University of New Mexico Library, not just the fine worn covers, the intriguing titles; how can we see the worlds that lie waiting in each book? A million worlds. A million million worlds. And the beauty of it is that each world is related to the next, as was taught to us by the old ones. Perhaps it is easier for a child to see. Perhaps it is easier for a child to ask: How many stars are there in the sky? How many leaves in the trees of the river? How many blades of grass in the llano? How many dreams in a night of dreams?

---

5. *cuentos* (kwĕn′tōs) *Spanish:* stories.
6. *llano* (yä′nō) *Spanish:* plain.
7. *pastores* (päs-tō′rĕs) *Spanish:* shepherds.

So I worked my way into the world of books, but here is the paradox, a book at once quenches the thirst of the imagination and ignites new fires. I learned that as I visited the library of my childhood, the Santa Rosa Library. It was only a dusty room in those days, a room sitting atop the town's fire department, which was comprised of one dilapidated fire truck used by the town's volunteers only in the direst emergencies. But in that small room I found my shelter and retreat. If there were a hundred books there we were fortunate, but to me there were a million volumes. I trembled in awe when I first entered that library, because I realized that if the books held as much magic as the words of the old ones, then indeed this was a room full of power.

Miss Pansy, the librarian, became my new guide. She fed me books as any mother would nurture her child. She brought me book after book, and I consumed them all. Saturday afternoons disappeared as the time of day dissolved into the time of distant worlds. In a world that occupied most of my other schoolmates with games, I took the time to read. I was a librarian's dream. My tattered library card was my ticket into the same worlds my grandfather had known, worlds of magic that fed the imagination.

Late in the afternoon, when I was satiated with reading, when I could no longer hold in my soul the characters that crowded there, I heard the call of the llano, the real world of my father's ranchito, the solid, warm world of my mother's kitchen. Then to the surprise and bewilderment of Miss Pansy, I would rush out and race down the streets of our town, books tucked under my shirt, in my pockets, clutched tightly to my breast. Mad with the insanity of books, I would cross the river to get home, shouting my crazy challenge even at la Llorona,[8] and that poor spirit of so many frightening cuentos would wither and withdraw. She was no match for me.

Those of you who have felt the same exhilaration from reading—or from love—will know about what I'm speaking. Alas, the people of the town could only shake their heads and pity my mother. At least one of her sons was a bit touched. Perhaps they were right, for few will trade a snug reality to float on words to other worlds.

And now there are a million volumes for us to read here at the University of New Mexico Library. Books on every imaginable subject, in every field, a history of the thought of the world which we must keep free of censorship, because we treasure our freedoms. It is the word *freedom* which eventually must reflect what this collection, or the collection of any library, is all about. We know that as we preserve and use the literature of all cultures, we preserve and regenerate our own. The old ones knew and taught me this. They eagerly read the few newspapers that were available. They kept their diaries, they wrote décimas[9] and cuentos, and they survived on their oral stories and traditions. ❖

---

8. *la Llorona* (lä yō-rō′nä) *Spanish*: the Weeping Woman, a ghostly figure of Mexican-American folklore.
9. *décimas* (dā′sē-mäs) *Spanish*: poems written in ten-line stanzas.

WORDS TO KNOW	
paradox (păr′ə-dŏks′) *n.* a statement that appears to be illogical but may nevertheless be true
ignite (ĭg-nīt′) *v.* to cause to burn; kindle
censorship (sen′ sər-ship′) *n.* the practice of banning writing, music, or visual material that is considered improper or harmful

Connect to the Literature

1. What Do You Think?
How do you feel about Rudolfo Anaya after reading this speech?

Comprehension Check
- Why is Anaya giving this speech?
- How did Anaya spend Saturdays as a young boy?
- What did "the old ones" do that inspired Anaya to love books?

Think Critically

2. | ACTIVE READING | AUTHOR'S PURPOSE |
Look at the notes that you made in your
📖 **READER'S NOTEBOOK.** Discuss with a partner what you think Anaya's main purpose or purposes were in writing this speech. How successfully do you think he achieved his goals?

3. Based on this speech, how would you describe Anaya's feelings about his heritage?

   Think About:
   - the lessons he learned from his grandfather
   - his description of "the old ones" as guides
   - his comments about the landscape of New Mexico

4. Anaya believes that a book both "quenches the thirst of the imagination and lights new fires." How can a book do both of these things at the same time?

5. Respect for the land is a theme that runs through many of Anaya's works. What does he say about the land in this speech? What can you infer about his feelings for the land?

Extend Interpretations

6. Critic's Corner Anaya's works have been praised for the way they capture the heart and soul of Hispanic heritage while at the same time expressing truths that apply to everyone. Based on this speech, do you agree with this assessment of his work? Explain.

7. Connect to Life Has Anaya's speech changed the way you feel about libraries and books? Why or why not?

Literary Analysis

| WORD CHOICE | Writers carefully choose words and phrases to express their thoughts, feelings, and beliefs. **Word choice** often reveals a writer's point of view, or attitude toward a subject. For example, in this passage the reader gets a sense of Anaya's belief that books are as necessary as food:

She [Miss Pansy] fed me books as any mother would nurture her child. She brought me book after book, and I consumed them all.

Paired Activity With a partner, go back through the speech and find other passages that reveal Anaya's feelings about books and learning. What do these passages tell you about Anaya's attitude toward learning?

Words and Phrases	Ideas and Feelings They Convey
"a book at once quenches the thirst of the imagination and ignites new fires"	conveys a passionate love of and need for books
"the stories of the old ones, los viejitos"	creates a sense of history and cultural pride

| REVIEW: POINT OF VIEW | The perspective from which a literary work is told is called its **point of view.** In this speech the point of view is **first person.** What pronouns are used in first-person point of view?

Writing

Community Action Speech
Write a speech urging members of your school's Parent-Teacher Organization to contribute money to expand the school library. Describe how the money will be used. Be sure to support your argument with detailed evidence, examples, and reasoning. Place the speech in your **Working Portfolio.**

Speaking and Listening Handbook
See p. R109: Persuasive Presentations.

Research & Technology

The Southwest Along with Oklahoma, Arizona, and Texas, New Mexico is part of the Southwest region of the United States. Using the Internet and library sources, find out more about this region—its land and people. When did the Spanish first come to the region? What Native American groups live there today? What does a Southwest desert look like? Prepare a brief report. Include charts, maps, or graphs to present your information visually.

Art Connection

The photographs in this selection are by Abelardo Morell, an artist who uses photography to express a unique vision of the world. In these photographs, what is the artist saying about the power of books? What themes and ideas are common to both the photographs and the selection?

Vocabulary and Spelling

EXERCISE: WORD MEANING Write the Word to Know that each rhyme illustrates.

1. Government issued a new declaration,
   Banning all books from our great nation.

2. My statement on libraries, according to you,
   Appears to be false, but indeed it is true.

3. You call me a bookworm, so it's easy to see,
   That books have kindled a fire in me.

4. The long list of questions, 'bout stars, trees, and dreams,
   Asked by a child, is endless it seems.

5. Was it Anaya's speech or a dictionary,
   That sent me running to the library?

Vocabulary Handbook
See p. R20: Context Clues.

SPELLING STRATEGY: THE HARD AND SOFT *C* SOUNDS When the letter *c* has a soft sound, as in the word *center,* it is usually followed by *e, i,* or *y.* When the letter *c* has a hard sound, as in the word *can,* it is usually followed by the vowel *a, o,* or *u* or by any consonant except *y.*

Choose a partner. Ask your partner to spell the following words as you recite them. Then have your partner choose five words with soft *c* and five words with hard *c* for you to spell.

1. induce   4. clear
2. country   5. circle
3. censorship

Spelling Handbook
See p. R28.

WORDS TO KNOW	censorship	ignite	induce	litany	paradox

Grammar in Context: Adverb Clauses

In this excerpt from his speech at the University of New Mexico, Rudolfo Anaya uses an **adverb clause:**

> **I trembled in awe** when I first entered that library . . .

An adverb clause is a dependent clause used as an adverb. Adverb clauses tell how, when, where, why, to what extent, or under what condition.

Like any other clause, an adverb clause contains a subject and a verb. An adverb clause usually begins with one of the following words: *after, although, as, as if, because, before, how, if, since, so that, than, though, unless, until, when, where, whether,* or *while.*

Apply to Your Writing Adverb clauses can help you combine sentences and give information about actions and events.

WRITING EXERCISE Rewrite each pair of sentences as one sentence. Change one of the sentences into an adverb clause that begins with the word in parentheses. Underline the adverb clause.

Example: *Original* We sat outside. My grandfather pointed to the Milky Way. (as)

Rewritten <u>As we sat outside</u>, my grandfather pointed to the Milky Way.

1. I looked up at the stars. I felt the thirst for knowledge. (whenever)

2. I learned to read. I read everything I could get my hands on. (as soon as)

3. I listened to my grandfather's story. I could see a million sheep on the hillside. (while)

4. I visited the library. I learned that I could never get enough to read. (as)

5. The people pitied my mother. They saw me running like a mad person through town. (when)

Grammar Handbook See p. R90: Clauses.

Rudolfo Anaya
born 1937

"I write because I am filled with the urge to create."

New Mexican Roots A sense of his roots is vital to Rudolfo Anaya and his work. He was born in the village of Pastura, New Mexico, in 1937. His early years there, and in nearby Santa Rosa, loom large in Anaya's writing. When he was an eighth grader, Anaya and his family moved to Albuquerque. He remained there, studying English and American literature at the University of New Mexico.

A Writer and a Teacher After graduating from the University of New Mexico in 1963, Anaya taught high school English for seven years. He also began his first novel—*Bless Me, Ultima*—during this time. Published in 1972, the novel won popular acclaim for its moving treatment of Hispanic tradition. Currently professor emeritus at the University of New Mexico, Anaya continues to focus his writing on the cultural identity of his people.

AUTHOR ACTIVITY
Traditional Tales Find a copy of *Cuentos: Tales from the Hispanic Southwest,* which Anaya wrote with José Griego y Maestas. Read Anaya's introduction to find out more about why he considers traditional tales so important.

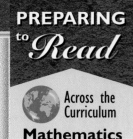

from **Wait Till Next Year**

by DORIS KEARNS GOODWIN

ROY CAMPANELLA
catcher BROOKLYN DODGERS

Connect to Your Life

Do you have a favorite sports team that you support? What is it like to be a loyal fan?

Build Background

In the 1950s many baseball fans collected baseball cards, just like they do today. The cards showed a player's picture and baseball statistics. It was not uncommon for baseball fans to memorize statistics about their favorite players.

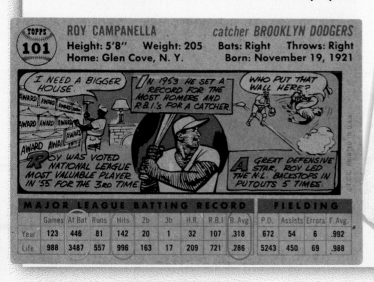

It is easy to compute baseball statistics using some basic math skills. To compute a player's batting average, divide the number of "hits" by the number of "at bats."

$$\frac{\text{Hits}}{\text{At Bats}} = \text{Batting Average}$$

Focus Your Reading

LITERARY ANALYSIS **SETTING**

The time and place in which the events of a literary work take place is called the **setting.** *Wait Till Next Year* is set in Brooklyn, a borough of New York City, during the 1950s. As you read, notice how life in the 1950s was different from your life today.

WORDS TO KNOW **Vocabulary Preview**
admonish   banter   converge   demise   slight

ACTIVE READING **SPECIALIZED VOCABULARY**

Baseball, like many other specialized fields, has its own vocabulary. For example, Goodwin uses words and phrases such as *shortstop, home run,* and *ground ball* to describe the games of the 1955 World Series. These words and phrases are considered **specialized vocabulary** because they are unique to the sport of baseball. In your **READER'S NOTEBOOK** keep a list of unfamiliar words and terms. Try inferring, or guessing, their meanings from the context in which they appear.

Wait Till Next Year

from

❋ by Doris Kearns Goodwin ❋

Although our school principal, Dr. Richard Byers, refused our request to pipe the first game over the PA system, we managed to follow the action at Yankee Stadium through portable radios, with notes passed from desk to desk, and by observing the reactions of classmates. When I saw a look of pain cross the face of my friend Moose Fastov, a devoted Yankee fan, I knew that something good must have happened. Paul Greenberg, who was listening via earphones to a radio surreptitiously tucked under his desk, had just signaled him that Jackie Robinson[1] had tripled to left and scored on a single by Don Zimmer. The Dodgers were ahead 2–0. Barely ten minutes later, however, Moose's fist shot triumphantly into the air when Elston Howard's home run off Newcombe tied the score, 2–2. During the break between classes, Duke Snider homered off Whitey Ford to put the Dodgers up 3–2, but by the time French class had begun, the Yankees had tied it again. When the bell signaled the end of school, it was already the seventh inning and the Yankees led 6–3. Afraid of missing the decisive action if we dashed for home, we gathered on the outside steps of the school building to listen to the final innings. Liberated from the constraints of the classroom, I screamed when the ever-amazing Robinson stole home in the eighth. But in the end, the Yanks held on to win the game, 6–5.

Even though the Series had just begun, the voice of doubt now entered into confrontation with the voice of hope. "They've lost the first game." said doubt. "It looks bad. They're going to lose the Series again, just as they always have."

"It's only one game," countered hope, "and it was in Yankee Stadium. It was a close game, they played well. Tomorrow is another day."

But by the end of the following day, doubt, swollen by fear, was in the ascendancy. The Dodgers had lost again, by a score of 4–2, on a five-hitter by Tommy Byrne. Was the Series already gone? For the past thirty-four years, no team had ever come back to win a Series after being down two games to none. And Dodger history did not encourage dreams of a historic comeback. There's more to life than baseball, I told myself, with the wisdom my twelve years had given me. There was the Sadie Hawkins dance, for instance, and my choice of a date. And there was my paper on Reconstruction.

"Don't give up now," my father admonished me. "They'll be coming back to Brooklyn.

"THEY'LL BE COMING BACK TO BROOKLYN. HOME-FIELD ADVANTAGE IS A BIG THING, AND NOWHERE IS IT BIGGER THAN AT EBBETS FIELD."

Home-field advantage is a big thing, and nowhere is it bigger than at Ebbets Field." And he was right. The Dodgers roared to life in the third

---

1. **Jackie Robinson:** a star baseball player for the Brooklyn Dodgers from 1947 to 1956. He was the first African American to play in the major leagues during the 20th century.

WORDS TO KNOW   **admonish** (ăd-mŏn′ĭsh) v. to caution; warn game, banging out eight runs and fourteen hits. Surprise starter Johnny Podres pitched a complete game to celebrate his twenty-third birthday; Campanella hit a home run, double, and single; and Jackie Robinson ignited the crowd and his teammates when he unnerved Yankee pitcher Bob Turley with his daring on the bases.

My pleasure over Robinson's virtuoso[2] performance and the Dodgers' victory was cut short that night when Elaine called to me from her window. She was so overwrought I could barely understand her and feared that something catastrophic had happened in her house. "Just meet me outside," she said tearfully. I ran down the stairs and met her under the maple tree. She threw her arms around me and told me she had just heard on the radio that James Dean had been killed. His Porsche Spyder had careened off the road between Los Angeles and Salinas. His neck had been broken and he had died instantly.

For a long while we barely talked at all. Then we talked half the night. No one was awake in either of our houses, and soon all the lights on our block were out. There was no <u>banter</u> about that afternoon's game. We were two twelve-year-olds lying on our backs, surrounded by darkness, looking up at the autumn sky and talking fiercely about death and James Dean, who was not so much older than we were, grieving as perhaps only two teenage girls can grieve. Above us, the leaves of the maple tree rustled, and as we looked up at the night stars, the spirit of James Dean seemed very close.

I was exhausted the following day and watched drowsily as the Yankees jumped ahead with two quick runs off Carl Erskine. But when home runs by Campanella, Hodges, and Snider put the Dodgers ahead 7–3 in the fifth, my suddenly revived spirits dissolved all fatigue. In the next inning, the Yankees reduced the Dodger lead to 7–5, scoring two runs on a double by Billy Martin. But in the eighth, Campanella scored an insurance run and the Dodgers held on to win 8–5. The Series was now tied at two games apiece.

Overcoming the disaster of the first two games, the Dodgers had captured the momentum. They won the fifth game on Sunday afternoon as rookie Roger Craig and reliever Clem Labine held the Yankees to three runs while Brooklyn scored five times. "This

BUT IN THE EIGHTH, CAMPANELLA SCORED AN INSURANCE RUN AND THE DODGERS HELD ON TO WIN 8-5. THE SERIES WAS NOW TIED AT TWO GAMES APIECE.

---

2. **virtuoso** (vûr′chōō-ō′sō): exceptionally skillful.

WORDS TO KNOW **banter** (băn′tər) *n.* good-natured, playful talk could be both the day and the year," the *New York Post* predicted in a front-page story Monday morning. "This better be 'next year,'" one fan was quoted as saying. "If the Bums blow this one, the cops better close the Brooklyn Bridge. There'll be more people taking long dives than in 1929."

The sixth game began on Monday, while we sat in Mrs. Brown's geography class. The boys who had the portable radios with earphones sat against the back wall and sent messages forward as each inning progressed. We were studying Mongolia that day, and Mrs. Brown asked us to name Mongolia's three main products. "Yaks, yurts, and yogurt," my friend Marjorie answered. Suddenly there was a muffled roar from the back of the room. Bill Skowron had just hit a three-run homer, putting the Yankees ahead of the Dodgers 5–0. "Well, class," Mrs. Brown said, with a knowing smile, "I'm glad you find the three products of Mongolia as thrilling as I do." Then, to our amazement, she put a radio on the front desk and let us listen to the game. Unfortunately, the Dodgers never got started, and the Yankees won easily by a score of 5–1, tying the Series at three games apiece.

Before my father left for the Williamsburg Savings Bank the Tuesday morning of Game Seven, he promised to call as soon as the game was over. "I feel good about our chances today," he said, as he kissed me goodbye. "I've been waiting for a championship since I was a lot younger than you, and today it's going to happen at last."

"Do you really think so?"

"I really feel it." He winked at me and was off to work.

My morning classes stretched out endlessly before game time finally arrived. At noon, we were astonished to hear Principal Byers' voice telling us to report at one o'clock to our homerooms. We would be allowed to listen to the deciding game over the PA system.

When the lineups were announced, I was dismayed to learn that Jackie Robinson was not starting. Hobbled by a strained Achilles tendon, he was replaced by rookie Don Hoak. My only compensation was the not unwelcome news that an injury to Mickey Mantle would keep him from the Yankee lineup. Young Johnny Podres was on the mound, trying to post his second victory of the Series and win it all for the Dodgers; Tommy Byrne was pitching for the Yankees. In the early innings the classroom was tense, as neither team was able to score. Then, in the fourth, Campanella doubled, moved to third on a groundout, and reached home on a single by Hodges. The Dodgers were ahead, 1–0. In the sixth, they scored again on a sacrifice fly by Hodges.

Even though the Dodgers held a 2–0 lead, there were no sounds of celebration, no blustering talk from the Dodger fans in our class. We were a generation that had been nurtured on tales of tragedy, and memories of defeat: 1941, 1949, 1950, 1951, 1952, 1953. The prideful Yankee fans among us were composed, waiting for Berra or Martin or some other hero to overcome the Brooklyn chokers and transform looming defeat into victory. In the bottom of the sixth, it seemed that their time had come. Billy Martin walked on four straight pitches. Gil McDougald followed with a perfect bunt single. With two on and no outs, Berra came to the plate. Had I been home, this was the moment I would have fled the room, hopeful that when I returned Berra would be out. As it was, I had no choice but to remain at my desk, sandwiched between Michael Karp and Kenny Kemper, certain that trouble was brewing.

It was a little after three in the afternoon when Berra came to bat. The bell ending the school day had just rung, but we sat immobile in our seats, heard the portentous crack of the bat, and listened as the ball sailed toward the distant corner of left field. Some 150 feet away, left fielder Sandy Amoros, having shifted toward center anticipating that Yogi would pull the ball, turned and began his long chase. The Yankee runners, Martin and McDougald, rounded the bases, their faces turned toward the outfield, watching for the ball to drop for a certain double. But Sandy Amoros, fleet of foot, gallant of will, raced to within inches of the concrete left-field wall, stretched

out his gloved hand, and snatched the ball from the air. For a moment he held his glove aloft, then, steadying himself with one hand against the wall, wheeled and rocketed the ball to Reese, the cutoff man, who, in turn, threw to first to double up McDougald.

We were going to win. At that moment, I knew we were going to win. Amoros' spectacular catch augured[3] victory just as surely as Mickey Owen's dropped third strike in '41 had foretold defeat. The gods of baseball had spoken. I ran the mile to my home, anxious to see the end of the game with my mother in familiar surroundings. When I reached home, the score was still 2–0, and it was the bottom of the ninth. Give us three more outs, I prayed. Please, only three more outs. I sat cross-legged on the floor, my back leaning against my

---

3. **augured** (ô′gərd): foreshadowed; predicted.

WE DANCED AROUND THE PORCH, TEARS STREAMING DOWN OUR CHEEKS, AS WE WATCHED CAMPANELLA, REESE, HODGES, ROBINSON, AND ALL THE DODGERS CONVERGE ON THE MOUND, WITH THOUSANDS OF DELIRIOUS FANS IN PURSUIT.

mother's knees as she sat on the edge of her chair. She edged forward as the first batter, Bill Skowron, hit a one-hopper to the mound. Two more outs. Bob Cerv followed with an easy fly to left. One more out. Elston Howard stepped to the plate. After the count reached two and two, Howard fouled off one fast ball after another, then sent a routine ground ball to Reese at shortstop, who threw to Hodges at first for the third and final out.

There was a moment of frozen silence. Then Vin Scully spoke the words I had waited most of my life to hear: "Ladies and gentlemen, the Brooklyn Dodgers are the champions of the world." Later, Scully was asked how he had remained so calm at such a dramatic moment. "Well, I wasn't," he said. "I could not have said another word without breaking down in tears." Just as Campanella leaped up on Podres, I jumped up and threw my arms around my

mother. We danced around the porch, tears streaming down our cheeks, as we watched Campanella, Reese, Hodges, Robinson, and all the Dodgers <u>converge</u> on the mound, with thousands of delirious fans in pursuit.

"We did it! What did I tell you, we did it!" my father bellowed merrily when he reached us minutes later. His call was one of tens of thousands made between 3:44 p.m. and 4:01 p.m., as parents, children, friends, and lovers exchanged screams, shouts, and expressions of joy. Trading on the New York Stock Exchange virtually came to a halt. On that afternoon, the phone company later estimated, it had put through the largest volume of calls since VJ day[4] a decade earlier. "Listen," my father said, holding the phone to the open window of the Williamsburg Bank. "Do you hear the horns, the church bells, the factory whistles? It's absolute pandemonium. There's going to be one grand celebration here tonight. You two have got to come in. Take the next train and meet me at the bank as soon as you can."

---

4. **VJ day:** August 15, 1945—the day on which the Japanese surrender that ended World War II was celebrated by the Allied nations.

WORDS TO KNOW **converge** (kən-vûrj´) *v.* to come together from different directions

My mother paused only to change her clothes, and the two of us were on the train heading for Brooklyn. We emerged from the subway into a crowd of hundreds, then thousands of people dancing in the streets to the music of a small band that had occupied the steps of the Williamsburg Bank. Bunting and banners flew from the windows, pinstriped effigies of Yankee players hung from the lampposts, confetti sifted down onto the sidewalks. The traffic was at a complete standstill, but no one seemed to mind. Finding his bus trapped at an intersection, a bus driver abandoned his vehicle and joined the revelers[5] on the street.

My father suggested dinner at Junior's, a landmark delicatessen on Flatbush Avenue, just two long blocks north of the bank. The place was packed: eight or ten people crowded every booth. Some leaned against posts, many laughed, shouting and jumping ecstatically. We stood happily for an hour or more, hugging each new celebrant who walked in the door, until we finally found seats. In the booth next to ours, an old man boisterously announced that if he died the next morning he would go happily to his grave. We ordered corned-beef sandwiches, topped off by Junior's famous cheesecake.

---

5. **revelers** (rĕv'ə-lərz): people taking part in a celebration.

Someone at Junior's said that the official celebration was taking place at the Bossert Hotel, where the Dodgers were scheduled to hold their victory dinner and dance that night. With scores of others, we took the subway to Brooklyn Heights and got off at Montague Street. There, standing behind police barricades, we joined tens of thousands of Dodger fans hoping to catch a glimpse of our heroes as they made their way into the old-fashioned hotel with its marble pillars and ornate ceilings. As the players walked in, they greeted the crowd. Even after their dinner began, they kept returning outside to wave to us again. Walt Alston posed with a group of teenagers while the crowd serenaded him with "For he's a jolly good fellow." A gray-haired woman in a wheelchair reached up to Johnny Podres and he bent down to kiss her. Even the reticent Carl Furillo was caught up in the exuberance of the night. "That was the thrill of all thrills," he later said. "I never in my life ever seen a town go so wild. I never seen people so happy." At last, Robinson appeared and spoke to the crowd. "The whole team knows it was the fans that made it for us," he told us. "It was your support that made this great day possible. We thank you from the bottom of our hearts."

No one wanted the night to end. When my father turned to ask my mother how she was holding up, she replied she felt twenty again. He led us to the foot of Montague Street, where a promenade overlooking the East River offered a view of the Statue of Liberty and the lights of Manhattan. Ever since the day in 1898 when Brooklyn had given up its proud history and independent status to merge with New York City, Brooklynites had lived in the shadow of Manhattan. Each new slight—including the demise of the famed *Brooklyn Eagle* earlier that year—only reinforced the perception of second-class citizenship. But this night was Brooklyn's night. This night, Brooklyn, not Manhattan, was the center of the world.

Never again would Dodger fans have to wait till next year. The world championship was theirs. As the Daily News proclaimed in the next morning's banner headline: "This IS next year!" ❖

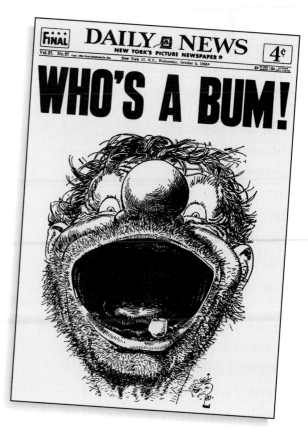

Because the Dodgers lost so much of the time, fans fondly referred to them as "Dem Bums."

WORDS
TO
KNOW

slight (slīt) *n.* an insult to one's pride or self-esteem
demise (dĭ-mīz′) *n.* an ending of existence

Who's on First?

UNKNOWN

Costello: Hey, Abbott, tell me the names of the players on our baseball team so I can say hello to them.

Abbott: Sure, Now, Who's on first, What's on second, I-Don't-Know on third . . .

Costello: Wait a minute.

Abbott: What's the matter?

Costello: I want to know the names of the players.

Abbott: I'm telling you. Who's on first, What's on second, I-Don't-Know on third . . .

Costello: Now, wait. What's the name of the first baseman?

Abbott: No, What's the name of the second baseman.

Costello: I don't know.

Abbott: He's the third baseman.

Costello: Let's start over.

Abbott: Okay. Who's on first . . .

Costello: I'm asking *you* what's the name of the first baseman.

Abbott: What's the name of the second baseman.

Costello: I don't know.

Abbott: He's on third.

Costello: All I'm trying to find out is the name of the first baseman.

Abbott: I keep telling you. Who's on first.

Costello: I'm asking YOU what's the name of the first baseman.

Abbott (*Rapidly*): What's the name of the second baseman.

Costello (*More rapidly*): I don't know.

Both: (*Most rapidly*): Third base!!

Costello: All right. Okay. You won't tell what's the name of the first baseman.

Abbott: I've *been* telling you. What's the name of the second baseman.

Costello: I'm asking *you* who's on second.

Abbott: *Who's* on *first.*

Costello: I don't know.

Abbott: He's on third.

Costello: Let's do it this way. You pay the players on this team?

Abbott: Absolutely.

Costello: All right. Now, when you give the first baseman his paycheck, who gets the money?

Abbott: Every penny of it.

Costello: *Who?*

Abbott: Naturally.

Costello: *Naturally?*

Abbott: Of course.

Costello: All right. Then Naturally's on first . . .

Abbott: No. Who's on first.

Costello: *I'm asking you!* What's the name of the first baseman?

Abbott: And I'm telling you! What's the name of the second baseman.

Costello: You say third base, I'll . . . (*Pause*) Wait a minute. You got a pitcher on this team?

Abbott: Did you ever hear of a team without a pitcher?

Costello: All right. Tell me the pitcher's name.

Abbott: Tomorrow.

Costello: You don't want to tell me now?

Abbott: I said I'd tell you. Tomorrow.

Costello: What's wrong with today?

Abbott: Nothing. He's a pretty good catcher.

Costello: Who's the catcher?

Abbott: No, Who's the first baseman.

Costello: All right, tell me that. What's the first baseman's name?

Abbott: No, What's the second baseman's name.

Costello: I-don't-know-third-base.

Abbott: Look, it's very simple.

Costello: I know it's simple. You got a pitcher. Tomorrow. He throws the ball to Today. Today throws the ball to Who, he throws the ball to What, What throws the ball to I-Don't-Know, *he's* on third . . . and what's more, I-Don't Give-A-Darn!

Abbott: What's that?

Costello: I said, I-Don't-Give-A-Darn.

Abbott: Oh, he's our shortstop.

Connect to Literature

1. What Do You Think?
What was your reaction to the Dodgers' victory?

Comprehension Check
- For which team is Goodwin cheering in the 1955 World Series?
- How do the children at school follow the 1955 World Series?
- Who wins the 1955 World Series?

Think Critically

2. ACTIVE READING SPECIALIZED VOCABULARY
Look at the words and terms that you listed in your
READER'S NOTEBOOK. Share definitions with classmates. If there are words and terms you still do not understand, find a baseball fan to help you. How does your appreciation of the selection change once you understand its specialized vocabulary?

3. What made this World Series so meaningful to Dodgers fans?

> **Think About:**
> - the Dodgers' previous seasons
> - how the Dodgers respond to their fans
> - the feelings Brooklynites have about Manhattan

4. When the Dodgers won the 1955 World Series, the *Daily News* printed the headline "This IS Next Year." What is the connection between this headline and the title of the book *Wait Till Next Year*?

5. Baseball has been called "the national pastime." What is the meaning of "national pastime"? Does the selection support the view that baseball was a national pastime in the 1950s? Explain your answer.

Extend Interpretations

6. Different Perspectives What would it have been like to be a Yankees fan during the 1955 World Series? If the story had been written by a Yankees fan, how would it be different?

7. Connect to Life Dodgers fans believed "Tomorrow is another day" and "Wait till next year." What do these sayings tell you about Dodgers fans? Are you a loyal fan of a particular team or musical group? How do you show your loyalty?

Literary Analysis

SETTING The time and location in which a literary work takes place is called the **setting.** Setting includes geographic location, historical time period, season of the year, and the customs and beliefs of a community or a group of people. The setting can influence characters' thoughts, feelings, and actions. In *Wait Till Next Year* the setting plays a central role in the author's narrative.

Paired Activity With a partner, go back through the selection and, in a chart like the one shown, note elements of setting. For example, what details in the selection reveal the time period? What details help the reader imagine where the action takes place?

Use your chart to answer the following questions:
- How might the story be different if it were to take place today?
- How might the story be different if it had taken place in my hometown?

Setting	
Details of time	Portable radios with earphones help place story in 1950s.
Details of place	
Details of season	
Details of customs or community	

Writing

Opinion Essay Some people say that baseball is no longer the national pastime. Do you agree? Why or why not? Write an essay that expresses your opinion. Be sure to support your argument with detailed evidence, examples, and reasoning. Place the essay in your **Working Portfolio.**

Writing Handbook
See p. R49: Persuasive Writing.

Speaking & Listening

MATHEMATICS

In 1950, Ted Williams of the Boston Red Sox became baseball's highest-paid player, with a contract of $125,000. Find out how much baseball's highest-paid players earn today. How many times greater is each of their salaries than Ted Williams's salary was? Create a chart or graph that shows your findings. Prepare an oral report and present it to your class. Be sure to note your sources.

Speaking and Listening Handbook
See p. R109: Research Presentations.

Research & Technology

Rock Around the Clock During the mid-1950s, a whole new sound emerged—rock 'n' roll. Artists like Fats Domino and Bill Haley and the Comets dominated the pop charts. Research a singer or vocal group who was popular then. Present your findings in an oral report. Then discuss with classmates whether you think that singer or group would be popular today.

Reading for INFORMATION
Read "A Look Back" on p. 875 before beginning your research.

Vocabulary

EXERCISE A: CONTEXT CLUES On your paper, fill in each blank with the correct form of the Word to Know that best completes the sentence.

1. The school halls were filled with the sound of good-natured _____ about baseball games.
2. The narrator and her friend talked sadly of James Dean's _____.
3. Each defeat of the Dodgers was more than a simple _____; it was an assault on Brooklyn's pride.
4. The narrator's father _____ her not to give up hope for a Dodgers victory.

5. When the Dodgers won the World Series, tens of thousands of people _____ on the Bossert Hotel in Brooklyn.

EXERCISE B: WORD MEANING Write the letter of the word that is closest in meaning to each boldfaced vocabulary word.

1. **banter:** (a) argument, (b) request, (c) chat
2. **slight:** (a) warning, (b) insult, (c) discussion
3. **converge:** (a) gather, (b) scatter, (c) leave
4. **admonish:** (a) suggest, (b) warn, (c) admit
5. **demise:** (a) mistake, (b) result, (c) death

Vocabulary Handbook
See p. R24: Synonyms and Antonyms.

WORDS TO KNOW	admonish	banter	converge	demise	slight

Grammar in Context: Noun Clauses

Notice how Doris Kearns Goodwin uses a **noun clause** in the following sentence:

> **When I saw a look of pain cross the face of my friend Moose Fastov, a devoted Yankee fan, I knew that something good must have happened.**

A **noun clause** is a dependent clause that acts as a noun. Noun clauses often begin with one of the following words: *how, that, what, whatever, when, where, who, whoever, whom,* or *whomever.*

Apply to Your Writing Use noun clauses to increase sentence variety and to make your writing smoother and more readable.

Usage Tip: In some sentences, you can omit the subordinating conjunction *that* before a noun clause, as in *At that moment, I knew (that) we were going to win.*

WRITING EXERCISE Combine each pair of sentences by changing one sentence into a noun clause. Make sure that each noun clause begins with the word in parentheses.

Example: *Original* Dodgers fans hoped for something. It came true. (what)

Rewritten What Dodgers fans hoped for came true.

1. The Bossert Hotel was there. The Dodgers held their celebration there. (where)
2. Goodwin says something about the Dodgers. It must be true. (whatever)
3. The radio announcer explained something. James Dean had died. (that)
4. Amoros made the catch. It was unbelievable. (that)
5. When the lineups were announced, fans learned something. They were told Jackie Robinson would not start. (that)

Grammar Handbook See p. R91: Noun Clauses.

Doris Kearns Goodwin
born 1943

"The biographer's real challenge is to ask the right question."

Baseball Fan Doris Kearns Goodwin became a Brooklyn Dodgers fan at the age of six, when her father gave her a red scorebook and taught her how to keep score. The young fan was heartbroken when the Dodgers left Brooklyn in 1958. Goodwin did not become an ardent baseball fan again until she attended graduate school in Cambridge, Massachusetts, where she began cheering for the Boston Red Sox.

Biographer of Presidents Today, Goodwin is a scholar and historian. After earning a Ph.D. in government at Harvard, she became a White House Fellow in 1967 and special assistant to President Lyndon Johnson. Her biography *Lyndon Johnson and the American Dream* was a bestseller. Her study of Franklin and Eleanor Roosevelt, *No Ordinary Time: Franklin and Eleanor Roosevelt,* won the Pulitzer Prize in 1995.

AUTHOR ACTIVITY

Asking Questions As a biographer, Doris Kearns Goodwin believes it is important to ask the right questions. Imagine you are going to write a biography of someone who interests you. What questions would best help you understand your subject?

In the 1950s people all across the United States rediscover jeans, the blue denim work pants originally invented for miners. These tough pants become associated more with leisure activities than with hard work.

❶

Reading for Information

A broad statement can be an effective way to capture a reader's attention, but it is important not to make a statement so general that it cannot be true. Readers need to carefully examine generalizations to determine whether they are accurate and reliable.

Making Generalizations
A **generalization** is a broad statement about a number of people or things. Generalizations can be either valid or faulty. It is important for readers and writers to distinguish between valid and faulty generalizations. "Everyone was happy in 1955, whereas today everyone is unhappy," for instance, is a faulty generalization. It is too broad and is inconsistent with fact and logic. Words such as *every, all, none, always,* and *never* may signal a faulty generalization. On the other hand, the statement "Some of the people in 1955 were happy, just as some people today say they are happy" is an example of a valid generalization. The word *some* qualifies the statement, so that it does not claim to be universally true. It is consistent with fact and logic and allows for exceptions. Words that may signal a valid generalization include *often, many, most, usually,* and *some.*

YOUR TURN *Use the following questions and activities to help you identify generalizations and to make a generalization of your own.*

❶ When you read, look for generalizations. Remember, you are looking for a statement or conclusion about people, objects, events, or ideas. What generalization has been made in this article?

The 1955 Hit Parade

1 **(We're Gonna) Rock Around the Clock**
   Bill Haley and the Comets
2 **Ballad of Davy Crockett**
   Bill Hayes
3 **Cherry Pink and Apple Blossom White**
   Perez Prado
4 **Melody of Love**
   Billy Vaughn
5 **Yellow Rose of Texas**
   Mitch Miller

A portable record player like the one shown here is a fixture at teenage parties.

By the late 1950s there are about 5,000 drive-in movie theaters in the United States, some with room for 3,000 vehicles. Most drive-ins have room for several hundred cars.

2

In the Pink

Transistor radios are very popular with American teenagers because they are portable and can be listened to anywhere.

3

Pink—blush pink, rose pink, cherry pink, shocking pink—is everyone's color in the 1950s. People with flashy taste can buy practically everything, from appliances to plumbing fixtures to cars, in pink—the ultimate in color coordination.

Reading for Information *continued*

❷ Facts, including numbers or similar data, can support a generalization. What information is included to prove the generalization that "most drive-ins have room for several hundred cars"?

❸ Identify the generalization. Is it a valid or a faulty generalization? Explain.

❹ **Making Judgments** A **judgment** is an opinion based on careful thought about the facts. Make a judgment about popular culture of the 1950s. On what facts is your judgment based? What standards, or criteria, did you use?

❹

Saddle shoes—black-and-white or brown-and-white tie shoes—are a fashion hit in the 1950s.

In the 1950s Hula-Hoops keep millions of Americans twirling away. Some experts can keep more than five hoops going at once.

Marbles, such as cat's-eyes, clearies, and fried marbles, are favorites for children to collect.

The $64,000 Question is the most-watched show in 1955.

1955 Baseball's Most Valuable Players
National League:
Roy Campanella,
Brooklyn Dodgers

American League:
Yogi Berra,
New York Yankees

In 1955, the Brooklyn Dodgers, with Jackie Robinson, beat the New York Yankees to win their first World Series ever.

5

	1950s	1990s
Baseball Salaries	**1950s** Average salary of a major league player: $25,000 **1955** Salary of Jackie Robinson, Brooklyn Dodgers' highest-paid player: $35,000	**1995** Average salary of a major league player: $1.07 million **1995** Salary of Jeff Bagwell, Houston Astros' highest-paid player: $2,875,000
Television	**1954** 17" television advertised price: $165.95 **1955** 31 million homes have at least one television.	**1997** 19" television advertised price: $139.00 **1995** 95 million homes have at least one television.
House	**1950** Median sale price of a new, single-family home: $9,422	**1997** Median sale price of a new, single-family home: $146,000
Car	**1955** 4-door sedan cost: $1,914–$2,272	**1997** 4-door sedan cost: $18,580–$29,296
Newspaper	**1955** *Boston Globe:* 5¢	**1999** *Boston Globe:* 50¢
Jeans	**1958** Children's jeans: $1.64	**1995** Children's jeans: $24.00

Reading for Information *continued*

5 Making Generalizations Based on information in the chart above, identify the following statements as either a valid generalization or a faulty generalization:

1. Everyone earned less money in the 1950s than people earned in the 1990s.

2. On average, major league baseball players in the 1990s make more money than those in the 1950s.

3. Everything was cheaper in the 1950s than in the 1990s.

Research & Technology
Activity Link: from *Wait Till Next Year*, p. 873 Use library resources, encyclopedias, almanacs, or the Internet to research information about a professional baseball team in the 1950s. Write a short report and include some generalizations about the team with supporting facts and examples. Then share your information with your classmates.

Lift Every Voice and Sing

by JAMES WELDON JOHNSON

Connect to Your Life

This Song I'm Singin' "Lift Every Voice and Sing" was written in 1900 by James Weldon Johnson and set to music by his brother, John Rosamond Johnson. Do you have a favorite song? It may be one that expresses your feelings particularly well or one that reminds you of a special place, event, or person. In a group discussion, talk about your favorite songs and why you like them.

Build Background

HISTORY

At the time that James Weldon Johnson wrote "Lift Every Voice and Sing," he was principal of Stanton, a school in Jacksonville, Florida. Stanton was a racially segregated school, attended only by African-American students. Johnson wrote the song for a celebration of Abraham Lincoln's birthday.

After writing the song, Johnson thought little more about it, but Stanton students remembered and continued to sing it. As they grew older, they taught the song to their children and to friends who sang it in churches and schools. Gradually the popularity of the song spread across the country. In 1920, the National Association for the Advancement of Colored People (NAACP) adopted the song as the national anthem of African Americans.

Focus Your Reading

LITERARY ANALYSIS **TONE**

A writer's attitude toward his or her subject is called **tone**. Words such as *angry, sad,* and *humorous* can be used to describe different tones. For example, when you read the following lines from the first stanza of the song, you hear a joyful tone:

> *Let our rejoicing rise*
> *High as the listening skies . . .*

As you read the remaining stanzas of the song, jot down words to describe the tone of each stanza.

ACTIVE READING **CLARIFYING**

The process of pausing occasionally while reading to quickly review what you understand is called **clarifying.** Clarifying helps readers draw conclusions about what is suggested but not directly stated.

📖 **READER'S NOTEBOOK** As you read "Lift Every Voice and Sing," pause at regular intervals to clarify what you have read. Record your notes in a chart like the one shown.

Sentence in the Song	Clarification
Lift every voice and sing Till earth and heaven ring, Ring with the harmonies of Liberty; Let our rejoicing rise High as the listening skies, Let it resound loud as the rolling sea.	Let every person sing songs of freedom, and let these happy songs grow as loud as the sounds of the sea.

Lift Every Voice and Sing

by James Weldon Johnson

Lift Every Voice and Sing (1939), Augusta
Savage. Cast iron maquette, 10⅞" × 9¼" × 4½".
Countee Cullen Collection, Hampton
University Museum, Hampton, Virginia.

Lift every voice and sing
Till earth and heaven ring,
Ring with the harmonies of Liberty;
Let our rejoicing rise
5   High as the listening skies,
Let it resound loud as the rolling sea.
Sing a song full of the faith that the dark
        past has taught us,
Sing a song full of the hope that the
        present has brought us,
Facing the rising sun of our new day
        begun
10   Let us march on till victory is won.

Stony the road we trod,
Bitter the chastening[1] rod,
Felt in the days when hope unborn had
        died;
Yet with a steady beat,
15   Have not our weary feet
Come to the place for which our fathers
        sighed?
We have come over a way that with tears
        has been watered,
We have come, treading our path through
        the blood of the slaughtered,
Out from the gloomy past,
20   Till now we stand at last
Where the white gleam of our bright star
        is cast.

God of our weary years,
God of our silent tears,
Thou who has brought us thus far on the
        way;
25   Thou who has by Thy might
Led us into the light,
Keep us forever in the path, we pray.
Lest our feet stray from the places, Our
        God, where we met Thee;
Lest, our hearts drunk with the wine of
        the world, we forget Thee;
30   Shadowed beneath Thy hand,
May we forever stand.
True to our GOD,
True to our native land.

---

1. **chastening** (chā′sə-nĭng): punishing; disciplining.

Connect to the Literature

1. What Do You Think? How does this song make you feel?

Comprehension Check
- To whom does *we* refer in the first two stanzas?
- How does the speaker describe the past?
- How does the speaker view the present?

Think Critically

2. ACTIVE READING CLARIFYING

Look back at the chart that you created in your READER'S NOTEBOOK. How did you clarify each sentence? Compare your notes with those of a classmate. Did you each interpret the song in the same way? Explain your answer.

3. Why, do you think, does the speaker see the present as "full of hope"? (Remember that the song was written in 1900.) Support your answer with details from the song as well as with information relevant to U.S. history.

4. What conclusions can you draw about the speaker?

Think About:
- the advice the speaker gives others
- how the speaker sees the past
- what the speaker hopes for the future

5. Why do you think the NAACP adopted this song as the national anthem of African Americans?

Extend Interpretations

6. The Writer's Style A writer's style involves *how* something is said rather than *what* is said. Like the words of a poem, the lyrics of a song may be conversational, formal, or even religious in style. How would you describe Johnson's literary style in this song?

7. Connect to Life Songs such as "Lift Every Voice and Sing" inspire people with hope for the future. What songs make you feel hopeful?

Literary Analysis

TONE A writer's attitude toward his or her subject is called **tone.** The language and details a writer chooses help to create the tone, which might be playful, serious, angry, or sad, among other possibilities.

To identify the tone of a literary work, read all or part of the work aloud. Read dramatically, as if reading before an audience. The emotions you feel as you read should give you clues to the work's tone.

Paired Activity Read the song aloud to a partner. Then, in a chart like the one shown, identify the tone of each stanza and quote lines that support your opinion.

Stanza	Tone	Evidence
first	joyful	"sing/Till earth and heaven ring," "Let our rejoicing rise"

Writing

Additional Verse Johnson wrote this song in 1900. Write an additional verse for the song that reflects African-American history since that time. Choose a tone in keeping with that of the original song, and try to model your verse after Johnson's. Place the verse in your **Working Portfolio**.

Speaking & Listening

1. Musical Presentation Use the library or Internet to find the music for "Lift Every Voice." Perform the song for the class with or without musical instruments.

2. Dramatic Reading With a partner, practice reading aloud "Lift Every Voice and Sing." Take turns reading different parts of the song. When you are ready, perform your reading for the class. Be sure to use your voice, tone, and gestures to enhance the meaning of the song.

Speaking and Listening Handbook
See p. R106: Oral Interpretation.

Research & Technology

Learn About the NAACP Johnson was a long-time member and officer of the NAACP (National Association for the Advancement of Colored People). Find out more about this organization and the contributions it has made. Write a report on the causes supported by the organization over the years.

James Weldon Johnson
1871–1938

*"This land is ours by right of birth,
This land is ours by right of toil . . ."*

Pupil to Principal Johnson was born in Jacksonville, Florida. As a boy, he attended the city's only African-American school, Stanton. At that time Stanton did not go beyond the eighth grade, so Johnson attended high school and then college in Atlanta, Georgia. After college he returned to Jacksonville to become principal of Stanton.

A Varied Career While principal, Johnson taught high-school classes, started a newspaper, studied law, and became Florida's first African-American lawyer. After he and his brother moved to New York, they wrote over 200 Broadway show songs. Later, Johnson served as U.S. consul to Venezuela and Nicaragua. Back in the United States, Johnson became secretary of the NAACP, leading the fight for important civil-rights legislation. Johnson returned to teaching and became a university professor. By the time of his death in a car accident in 1938, Johnson had become an important legal and literary figure.

AUTHOR ACTIVITY

Famous Friends Johnson was influential in the Harlem Renaissance of African-American literature and art in the 1920s. His friends included W.E.B. Du Bois and Paul Lawrence Dunbar. Read something by each of these writers, and compare the tone of their works with Johnson's.

Building Vocabulary
Homonyms and Words with Multiple Meanings

Many English words have more than one meaning.

Multiple-meaning words have several meanings that have developed, over time, from the original meaning.

Homonyms are spelled and pronounced alike but have different origins and meanings.

> "The dogs," I whispered to my cousin Mourad. "I thought they would **bark**."
>
> —William Saroyan,
> "The Summer of the Beautiful White Horse"

Multiple-meaning word
- a harsh sound made by a dog
- to speak sharply

Homonym
- the tough outer covering of a tree
- a kind of ship

Strategies for Building Vocabulary

Try the following strategies when you can't tell which meaning of a word is intended.

❶ **Use Context Clues** When you come across a familiar word used in an unfamiliar way, try to figure out the word's meaning by examining context clues in the surrounding text. What do you think is the meaning of *fleet* in the following passage? Use the context clue "raced to within inches."

> The Yankee runners, Martin and McDougald, rounded the bases, their faces turned toward the outfield. . . . But Sandy Amoros, *fleet* of foot, gallant of will, raced to within inches of the concrete left-field wall, stretched out his gloved hand, and snatched the ball from the air.
>
> —Doris Kearns Goodwin, *Wait Till Next Year*

From its context, it is unlikely that *fleet* has anything to do with a "number of warships." In this context, which refers to running, *fleet* means "moving swiftly."

❷ **Check Your Dictionary** If you cannot figure out the meaning of a word from context clues, look up the word in a dictionary. Decide which definition best reflects how the word is used in the selection. Remember that each homonym gets a separate entry in the dictionary.

EXERCISE Using a dictionary, identify each word as a homonym or a word with multiple meanings. Write a sentence that shows the meaning of each homonym. If the word has multiple meanings, choose two definitions and write a sentence for each.

1. sound   **2.** peak   **3.** bear   **4.** crop   **5.** fresh

from I Was Dreaming to Come to America

Lazarus Salamon

Hungary
Arrived in 1920 · Age 16

"I feel like I had two lives. You plant something in the ground, it has its roots, and then you transplant it where it stays permanently. That's what happened to me. You put an end . . . and forget about your childhood; I became a man here. All of a sudden, I started life new, amongst people whose language I didn't understand. . . . [It was a] different life; everything was different . . . but I never despaired, I was optimistic.

"And this is the only country where you're not a stranger, because we are all strangers. It's only a matter of time who got here first."

Birgitta Hedman Fichter

Sweden
Arrived in 1924 · Age 6

"Most dear to me are the shoes my mother wore when she first set foot on the soil of America. . . . She landed in America in those shoes and somehow or the other she felt that she was going to hang on to them. They are brown high-top shoes that had been soled and resoled and stitched and mended in Sweden to hold them together till she could get to America. We just kept them. And then . . . as I grew up and everything, I said, 'Don't ever throw them away.'"

Boots worn by Elin Maria Hedman in 1924 when she and her daughter arrived on Ellis Island.

Edward Corsi

Italy
Arrived in 1907 · Age 10

"My first impressions of the new world will always remain etched in my memory, particularly that hazy October morning when I first saw Ellis Island.[1] The steamer *Florida*, 14 days out of Naples,[2] filled to capacity with 1,600 natives of Italy, had weathered one of the worst storms in our captain's memory. Glad we were, both children and grown-ups, to leave the open sea and come at last through the narrows into the bay.

"My mother, my stepfather, my brother Giuseppe, and my two sisters, Liberta and Helvetia, all of us together, happy that we had come through the storm safely, clustered on the foredeck for fear of separation and looked with wonder on this miraculous land of our dreams."

This poster, printed in Italian, is an advertisement for a passenger ship sailing to the United States in the early 1900s.

---

1. **Ellis Island:** an island in New York Harbor that was the main U.S. receiving station for immigrants from 1892 to 1943.

2. **Naples** (nā′pəlz): a large seaport in southern Italy.

This Land Is Your Land

by Woody Guthrie

Mount McKinley and Wonder Lake, Denali National Park, Alaska. Ansel Adams.

As I was walking
    that ribbon of highway,
I saw above me
    that endless skyway,
I saw below me
    that golden valley:
This land was made for you and me.

This land is your land,
    this land is my land,
From California
    to the New York island,
From the redwood forest
    to the Gulf Stream waters,
This land was made for you and me.

I've roamed and rambled,
    and I followed my footsteps
To the sparkling sands of
    her diamond deserts;
And all around me
    a voice was sounding:
"This land was made for you and me."

In the shadow of the steeple
    I saw my people,
By the relief office
    I seen my people;
As they stood there hungry,
    I stood there asking:
"This land was made for you and me?"

As I went walking,
    I saw a sign there.
And on the sign it said
    "No Trespassing."
But on the other side
    it didn't say nothing,
That side was made for you and me.

Nobody living
    can ever stop me,
As I go walking
    that freedom highway;
Nobody living
    can ever make me turn back,
This land was made for you and me.

When the sun came shining,
    and I was strolling,
And the wheat fields waving
    and the dust clouds rolling,
As the fog was lifting,
    a voice was chanting:
"This land was made for you and me."

This land is your land,
    this land is my land,
From California
    to the New York island,
From the redwood forest
    to the Gulf Stream waters,
This land was made for you and me.

Woody Guthrie
1912–1967

"I . . . made up songs telling what I thought was wrong and how to make it right . . ."

Early Life Woody Guthrie was born in Okemah, Oklahoma. He grew up poor, and set off on his own when he was 13. While a teenager, he learned to play guitar and began singing.

The Dust Bowl In 1935 Guthrie joined thousands from Texas, Oklahoma, and Arkansas as they fled the "Dust Bowl," a huge area of land that was slowly being buried under dust and sandstorms. Guthrie never forgot the suffering that he saw on the road at the time.

Songs of the People Guthrie is best known as a songwriter on a wide range of topics. When he died in 1967, he was already considered one of America's most important folk singers.

Communication Workshop

Persuasive Speech

Speaking to convince others . . .

From Reading to Writing to Speaking In "One Million Volumes," Rudolfo Anaya talks about his love of libraries. But suppose one of his favorites—at the University of New Mexico—was going to be closed. What might he do? One thing he might do is to write and present a **persuasive speech.** A persuasive speech aims to convince others to think or act in a certain way. An effective speech changes people's minds and inspires people to take action.

Basics in a Box

GUIDELINES AND STANDARDS PERSUASIVE SPEECH AT A GLANCE

Content

A successful persuasive speech should

- open with a clear statement of the issue and your opinion
- be geared toward the audience you're trying to persuade
- provide facts, examples, and reasons to support your opinion (may also use visual aids)
- answer opposing views
- show clear reasoning
- include strategies such as frequent summaries to help listeners remember your message
- end with a strong restatement of your opinion or a call to action

Delivery

An effective speaker should

- convey enthusiasm and confidence
- stand with good but relaxed posture, speak in a loud and clear voice, and make eye contact with the audience
- include gestures and body language to enhance the presentation
- use visual aids effectively

Analyzing a Student Model

SPEAKING
OPPORTUNITY

See the Speaking and Listening Handbook, p. R104, for oral presentation tips.

Devon Frederick
English 101, Ms. St. Jean

Our Town Needs a Park

As I speak to you at this meeting of the town council, plans are under way for new construction on the last untouched plot of land in our town. I know it is important that good housing be available to everyone, but I think it is just as important that we not allow our beautiful town to be overrun by buildings and parking lots. That is why I feel we should create a park on this land. A park would protect some of the natural beauty of our area. It could also bring money into the town and provide a space for recreation and community activities.

People who don't want the park say that the town cannot afford to "waste" some of its best land. In fact, the city manager recently said, "Maintaining a park would sap the community of valuable funds. Why should we do this when the profits from the sale of the land to the developer would bring in funds?"

It is true that the town would make money if the land were sold to a building developer. But the town could also make money with a park. As you can see on the chart, I have researched the cost of a park. The cost for setting up the park and the maintenance fees would be less than the money that the park could bring in. For instance, two nurseries have offered to donate plants to get the flower beds started. The Garden Club has offered three volunteers a week to landscape and maintain the park. A local construction company will donate gazebos. Organizations such as the Rotary Club and the Kiwanis Club have said that they will donate benches, trash cans, and water fountains.

A park would create opportunities for the town. I'll discuss them in order.

(A.) A park would bring in money. Neighboring towns hold summer concerts and other events in their public

GUIDELINES
IN ACTION

❶ States issue and takes a clear position

❷ Addresses opposing argument and audience concerns with quotations

❸ Uses visual aids to present detailed facts clearly

❹ Supports opinion with facts and examples

parks, charging a small fee for admission. My research shows that businesses in these towns enjoy an increase in sales on these nights. Right now, several businesses want to rent space in the park, where they could sell their foods and products during events. The town could also charge money to groups that want to use the park for events. Finally, a public park is something that would attract new residents to the area.

(B.) A park would help to provide a safe, healthy lifestyle for residents. Parents, would you rather have your children biking on trails or on the ramps of a parking garage? A park would provide a safe recreation place for residents of all ages. One parents' group has begun to collect money and other contributions so that swings, slides, and other playground equipment can be set up if the park is approved. The Sunset Adult Center wants to donate chess tables. Two of our four neighboring towns have popular art and science day camps based in their parks during the summer, which help families with working parents. A park would provide a place to gather and walk, in-line skate, bike, or picnic.

(C.) A park would reduce crime. Studies have shown that downtown areas that consist of buildings and parking garages encourage graffiti and other destructive behaviors. The head of the police department told me that supervising a park area could be done more easily, even at night, than patrolling a bunch of buildings.

To sum up, I believe that a park would preserve the natural beauty of our town. Community bonds would be strengthened, people could enjoy the outdoors in a healthy way, and our town center could remain safe. Make my dream a reality by signing the petition that is being passed around and by adding your name to the list of volunteers and contributors. You can also call your councilperson and vote to keep our town in touch with what's really important.

❺ The speaker keeps the audience's interest by asking a rhetorical question.

❻ The speaker chooses to present reasons in order from least to most important.

❼ The conclusion reinforces opinion and offers a call to action while maintaining a reasonable tone.

Writing and Delivering Your Persuasive Speech

❶ Planning and Drafting

Choose an issue for your speech by **writing down** what you like or don't like about your school or city. Are there problems you or those around you would like to see solved? See the **Idea Bank** in the margin for more suggestions. After you find a topic that you'd like to develop into a speech, follow the steps below.

> ### Steps for Planning and Drafting Your Speech
>
> ▶ 1. **State your position.** How do you feel about the issue? Why?
>
> ▶ 2. **Find support for your position.** Where can you find facts that will back up your position? Can you use statistics, examples, or expert opinions? What questions do you need answered before you can convince others?
>
> ▶ 3. **Think about your audience.** What does your audience already know about the issue? What background information would help them understand the issue? What opinions are they likely to hear?
>
> ▶ 4. **Hook your audience's interest.** How can you grab the attention of your audience? Use an anecdote, a significant statistic, or a question to open your speech.
>
> ▶ 5. **Organize your arguments.** What order will work best for your arguments? Should you move from the weakest to strongest argument in order to convince your audience and to leave a lasting impression?

❷ Practicing and Delivering

The best way to practice your speech is to say it aloud, over and over again. You'll want to sound natural and reasonable, so instead of reading your speech, prepare speaking notes—index cards that contain words, phrases, or sentences of your speech as well as reminders to show visual aids, to pause, or to look up.

IDEA Bank

1. For Your Working Portfolio 📁
Look for ideas in the **Writing** sections you completed earlier.

2. Too Trendy!
Pick a trend or fad that you think is ridiculous. Write a speech stating your opinion.

3. Keeping Current
Scan a newspaper or listen to the news to identify social and political issues currently being debated. Choose one that you've heard mentioned before and write a speech persuading people to take your side.

See **Speaking and Listening Handbook,** p. R104

See **Language Network,** Oral Communication, p. 555

"Our Town Needs a Park" Cont'd.

Opportunities:

A. Bring in money—concerts, business, new residents

B. Safe recreation place (ask question: Parents, would you rather. . .) —Sunset Adult Center

C. Reduce crime

Need revising help?

Review the Rubric, p. 890

Consider **peer reviewer** comments

Check **Revision Guidelines,** p. R33

SPELLING
From Writing

As you revise your work, look back at the words you misspelled and determine why you made the errors you did. For additional help, refer to the strategies and generalizations in the **Spelling Handbook** on page R28.

Publishing
IDEAS

- Deliver your speech to classmates and follow it up with the first step of an action plan, such as a letter-writing campaign or petition.
- Help plan an awareness-raising day at your school and give your speech as part of the program.

Publishing Options
www.mcdougallittell.com

Steps for Delivering Your Speech

As you prepare, don't try to read your essay word for word. Instead, make note cards for each main point. Keep these important suggestions in mind:

▶ 1. **Use your voice effectively.** Speak loudly enough to be heard clearly but not so loudly that your voice is overwhelming. Change your pitch to help make your meaning clear.

▶ 2. **Use visual aids.** Organize information into charts, graphs, or drawings.

▶ 3. **Maintain eye contact.** When speaking, look directly at as many audience members as possible.

▶ 4. **Use gestures, facial expressions, and good posture.** Let your emotions show in your face.

❸ Revising
TARGET SKILL ▶ RESPONDING TO AUDIENCE FEEDBACK

Your speech is successful only if it convinces your audience. Here are some ways to anticipate peer reviews.

- **I couldn't remember the information.** Repeat and include summaries of your main points. Audiences need to hear important ideas more than once in order to remember them.

- **I felt restless.** Your voice should be audible to everyone in the room at all times, but vary your tone to keep the audience's attention.

- **I couldn't understand what you were trying to say.** Rearrange words or phrases to clarify your meaning. Use analogies to help your audience relate to your ideas.

- **Your speech wasn't convincing.** Be well informed and rehearsed. Include enough evidence. Modify your organizational structure to lead up to your most important points.

Ask Your Peer Reviewer

- What argument was most convincing?
- Which points do you disagree with and why?
- How was my delivery?
- Where do I need more facts and examples?

❹ Reflecting
FOR YOUR WORKING PORTFOLIO What did you learn about your topic? What would you like to change in your delivery? Jot down your thoughts in a note and save it with your speech in your **Working Portfolio.**

Standardized Test Practice

Mixed Review

> When I walk to school in the morning I am embarrassed by the litter. It is all over the sidewalk. It is in the corners of the building. People claim that they hardly drop anything, but the debris are not figments of my imagination. One gum wrapper from several different people adds up to a lot of garbage. That is why Broadway middle School needs to take action, starting with an information campaign. First, I believe, that we should bombard students with reminders not to litter and information on how much damage litter can do to the environment.
>
> (1) ... (2) ... (3) ... (4) ... (5) ... (6)

Review Your Skills

Use the passage and the questions that follow it to check how well you remember the language conventions you've learned in previous grades.

1. How is sentence 1 best written?
   A. When I walk to school, in the morning I am embarrassed
   B. When I walk to school, in the morning, I am embarrassed,
   C. When I walk to school in the morning, I am embarrassed
   D. Correct as is

2. How is item 2 best written?
   A. It is all over the sidewalk and in the corners of the building.
   B. It is all over the sidewalk in the corners of the building.
   C. It is all over the sidewalk and building.
   D. Correct as is

3. How is sentence 3 best written?
   A. the debris is not a figment
   B. the debris weren't figments
   C. the debris haven't been figments
   D. Correct as is

4. How is sentence 4 best written?
   A. add
   B. have added
   C. make
   D. Correct as is

5. What is the correct capitalization in sentence 5?
   A. Broadway Middle School
   B. broadway middle school
   C. Broadway middle school
   D. Correct as is

6. How is sentence 6 best written?
   A. I believe that we should bombard students
   B. I believe, we should bombard, students
   C. I believe; that we should bombard students
   D. Correct as is

Self-Assessment

Check your own answers in the **Grammar Handbook**

Quick Reference: Punctuation, p. R72

Subject-Verb Agreement, p. R76

Quick Reference: Capitalization, p. R74

American Voices

As you read the selections in this unit, what new insights did you gain about some of the early voices of our nation? Use one or more of the options in each of the following sections to help you reflect on what you have learned.

Reflecting on Theme

OPTION 1

Thinking About Character Which character in this unit did you most enjoy reading about? What interested you most about this person? Write a brief description of this character. Be sure to include the reasons you found this person engaging and interesting.

OPTION 2

Making Choices Get together with a small group of classmates and imagine that you are putting together a book called *American Voices* that is intended to give students an overview of American literature. Which of the selections in this unit would you choose to include in your book? Try to agree on a group list of four or five selections, explaining the reasons for your choices.

OPTION 3

Evaluating Literature In a small group, discuss the following questions: What kind of literature holds your interest? Which selections did you like best in this unit and why? Which selections in this unit can teach you something that can be applied to real life? Support your opinions with examples from the literature.

Self ASSESSMENT

📖 **READER'S NOTEBOOK**

Reconsider the quotation at the beginning of the unit: "America is not something if it consists of each of us. It is something only if it consists of all of us." Write a few paragraphs explaining how the selections in this unit reflect the meaning of the quotation.

REVIEWING YOUR PERSONAL WORD List

Vocabulary Review the new words you learned in this unit. If necessary, use a dictionary to check the meaning of each word.

Spelling Review your list of spelling words. If you're not sure of the correct spelling, use a dictionary or refer to the **Spelling Handbook** on page R28.

Reviewing Literary Concepts

OPTION 1

Thinking About Point of View Work with a partner, one of you listing the stories in this unit that are told from the first-person point of view and the other listing the stories that are told from the third-person point of view. Compare your lists, then discuss the following questions:

- Why do you think the author of each story chose the point of view that he or she used?
- How would each story be different if it were told from a different point of view?

OPTION 2

Identifying Themes Most themes are not stated directly but are only implied. Write down several themes that you can find in this unit's readings. Then express each theme as a statement, as if you were writing a commercial for a new television series based on the reading. Remember, a work can have more than one theme and there can be more than one good way of stating a theme.

Portfolio Building

- **Choices and Challenges—Writing** Several of the **Writing** assignments in this unit asked you to research a topic and write a report. From your responses, choose the one that you feel best represents a thoughtfully crafted research report. Write a note explaining the reason for your choice. Then attach the note to the report and place the report in your **Presentation Portfolio.**

- **Writing Workshops** In this unit you wrote a persuasive speech on a topic of interest to you. Reread your speech and identify its strengths and weaknesses. Explain your assessment on a sheet of paper, attach it to the assignment, and place both in your **Presentation Portfolio.**

- **Additional Activities** Go back through the assignments you have completed in **Speaking & Listening** and **Research & Technology.** Keep a record of the activities that you have most enjoyed. What areas are you interested in learning more about?

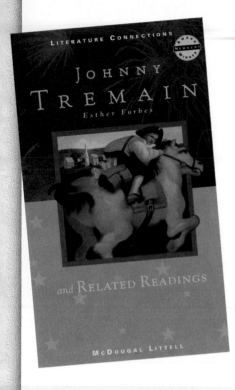

LITERATURE CONNECTIONS
Johnny Tremain

BY ESTHER FORBES

In this Newbery Medal-winning historical novel, readers are drawn into the life of a silversmith's young apprentice living in colonial Boston. During the chaotic times before the Revolution, Johnny's life is turned upside down when he seriously injures his hand. Later, things improve for him as he becomes a spy for the Sons of Liberty.

These thematically related readings are provided along with *Johnny Tremain*:

The Die Is Cast
BY JOHN ADAMS

Monday, March 5, 1770: Who Was to Blame?
BY JOHN M. BRESNAHAN, JR.

Children Have Always Worked
BY MILTON MELTZER

from **The Silversmiths**
BY LEONARD EVERETT FISHER

Envy
BY YEVGENY YEVTUSHENKO

The Fate of the Loyalists
BY CLORINDA CLARKE

Concord Hymn
BY RALPH WALDO EMERSON

More Choices

Child of the Owl
BY LAURENCE YEP
A girl learns about her heritage when she is sent to live in Chinatown.

The Story Catcher
BY MARI SANDOZ
Lance, an Oglala Sioux Indian, becomes the official Story Catcher and works to remember and retell the tribe's history.

Jar of Dreams; The Best Bad Thing; The Happiest Ending
BY YOSHIKO UCHIDA
Rinko, a Japanese-American teenager living in California, comes to terms with her cultural heritage.

Indian Chiefs
BY RUSSELL FREEDMAN
Portraits of six Indian chiefs who describe how they held on to their heritage.

Three Stalks of Corn
BY LEO POLITI
When Angelica's grandmother explains why she tends three stalks of corn in her garden, Angelica understands her own Mexican-American heritage.

The Journal of Joshua Loper: A Black Cowboy
BY WALTER DEAN MYERS
The son of a former slave faces prejudice and hardship.

Taking Sides

BY GARY SOTO

Lincoln Mendoza, a young Mexican American, struggles to find himself. When he moves from the inner city to a suburb of San Francisco, he fears that he may lose an important part of himself—the barrio, his old neighborhood, with its Spanish culture, strong values, and warm-hearted people. In the end, as he plays basketball for his new school's team against his old school, Lincoln must decide who he is and where his loyalties lie.

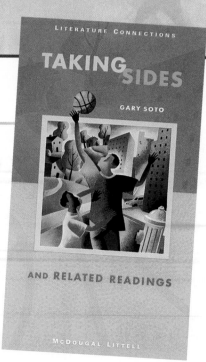

These thematically related readings are provided along with *Taking Sides*:

Endless Search
BY ALONZO LOPEZ

from **Barrio Boy**
BY ERNESTO GALARZA

In the Inner City
BY LUCILLE CLIFTON

I Yearn
BY RICARDO SANCHEZ

Granny Ed and the Lewisville Raiders
BY RAE RAINEY

A Game of Catch
BY RICHARD WILBUR

Social Studies Connection

All-of-a-Kind Family
BY SYDNEY TAYLOR
Set on the eve of World War I, this is the story of five Jewish girls growing up in New York City.

The One Bad Thing About Father
BY FERDINAND N. MONJO
A fictional account of Theodore Roosevelt's presidency through the eyes of his son.

A Tree Grows in Brooklyn
BY BETTY SMITH
The adventures of Francie Nolan as she grows up in turn-of-the-century Brooklyn.

Pie-Biter
BY RUTHANNE L. McCUNN
This is the story of Hoi, a young Chinese boy, who helps build the railroad across America.

Paintbrush and Peacepipe: The Story of George Catlin
BY ANNE ROCKWELL
This is the biography of the artist who spent most of his life painting the Plains Indians' everyday life.

THE ORAL TRADITION

Tales from the Americas

People can hear a story and

relate it to their own lives.

Stories can heal people.

Storytelling is a way for

people to find their power.

Olga Loya

Olga Loya is a Mexican American who grew up in East Los Angeles. She strives to keep the oral tradition alive through her storytelling.

STORYTELLERS PAST AND PRESENT

OLGA LOYA

A Present-Day Storyteller Speaks

Many of Olga Loya's stories come out of her Mexican heritage as well as her own family history. She also shares tales from all over Latin America and from a variety of oral traditions around the world.

I've always told stories. My grandmother was a *curandera* (kōō-rän-dě′rä), a healer. When she died, her house was filled with flowers from all the people that came to say goodbye to her. She always told stories to get her point across to people and to help them. My father was also a storyteller. He was one of those people who would tell a story that lasted five minutes at first. Then the next time he told it, it would last ten minutes, then fifteen minutes, then twenty.

In 1980 I went to a storytelling conference. It was like a thunderbolt to my heart. I came home and said to my family, "I'm going to be a storyteller." At first I started telling stories from books. Within a year, I realized I had many stories within myself and within my own culture. Some of the first stories I told were from Mexico, because that is my heritage. As time passed, I began to realize that there were many stories within my own family. So now I tell a number of family stories as well as stories from Latin America and all over the world. Once I was invited by some Native Americans to come and tell stories to the elders of the tribe. They honored me by giving me permission to tell some of their stories, too.

There are many types of Latino stories. *Mitos* (mē′tōs), or myths, explain how things came to be. Myths are very powerful because they represent the heart of the culture. The *leyendas* (lě-yěn′däs), or legends, tell of people from times before. Legends are a way of connecting past and present. At one time in the past, the characters were believed to be real, but even now we can relate their lives to our own. There are also folk tales, *cuentos* (kwĕn′tōs). Many of these have animal characters. Sometimes these teach a lesson, sometimes they entertain, and often they do both. And there are *fábulas* (fä′bōo-läs), or fables, which always have a moral.

The themes of Latino stories are really universal ones such as honoring your parents, paying attention to how you deal with the land, and not going to extremes in behavior—keeping a balance is important. Another theme that often appears is that of death, but it is often treated in a playful way, which reflects the attitudes of the culture.

I'm always looking for stories that touch my heart. Those are the stories I want to tell, because those are the stories that people will want to listen to. Stories can help people communicate with each other. People can hear a story and relate it to their own lives. Stories can heal people. Storytelling is a way for people to find their power.

We are all storytellers. We all have stories that we carry with us, but some of us don't know we have them. We should be story detectives—find the stories that move us and tell them. Go to your parents and to other members of your family and ask them to tell stories. Take the time to find out your family's stories or they will not be passed on. If you don't have the stories to pass on to your children, the stories will die. They will not stay alive unless someone tells them.

VIDEO **Literature in Performance**

A Traditional Storyteller
The Mexican-American grandmother of the turn of the century, highly respected in her close-knit extended family, often took responsibility for passing along family tales to her grandchildren.

Latin American folklore is a rich blend of Native American traditions and Spanish customs and values. This unique folklore continues to thrive in Hispanic communities throughout the United States.

KEEPING THE PAST ALIVE

Comparing the Oral Tradition Across Cultures

By giving voice to their cultural heritage, storytellers like Olga Loya keep the past alive. Even cultures that vanished centuries ago can seem to live on as long as their tales are passed on to new listeners. These tales from cultures around the world make up what is called the **oral tradition.**

The paired selections listed at the right illustrate the rich variety in the oral tradition. Each listing shows what cultures the stories are associated with. Besides being a celebration of varied cultures, the stories in this unit show the common elements that run through different types of **folklore.** For example, Links to Unit One compare and contrast origin myths from the Cherokee people and from Puerto Rico. The chart below shows some of the common elements of folklore.

MYTHS
- attempt to answer basic questions about the world
- are considered truthful by their originators

FOLK TALES
- are told primarily for entertainment
- feature humans or humanlike animals

COMMON ELEMENTS
- **keep the past alive**
- **teach lessons about human behavior**
- **reveal the values of the society**

FABLES
- are short tales that illustrate morals
- have characters that are animals

LEGENDS
- are considered factual by those who tell them
- may be based on facts
- are usually set in the past

> **INTERNET**
>
> **Social Studies Connection**
> www.mcdougallittell.com

LINKS TO UNIT ONE

Insights

The characters and people in the selections in Unit One change and grow as they learn about themselves and the world they live in. The insights they gain through their relationships and discoveries help them learn valuable lessons about life. Characters in the folk tales and myths you are about to read gain insights too—often unexpected ones.

PUERTO RICO

Aunty Misery

retold by Judith Ortiz Cofer

Christopher Columbus claimed the island of Puerto Rico for Spain in 1493. Most Puerto Ricans are descended from Spanish settlers. Long before the Spanish arrived, however, the island was occupied by a native Caribbean group called the Taino. The Spanish settlers brought African slaves to the island. The Taino, African, and Spanish cultures blended over time to produce the island's rich folklore.

Many of the island's **folk tales** were collected and recorded in the early 1900s by the Puerto Rican writer Cayetano Coll y Toste. Much Puerto Rican folklore deals with forces of nature such as hurricanes, which are common on the island, or the origins of native plants and animals. The folk tale "Aunty Misery" tells of an elderly woman who is kind to a stranger and receives an unusual reward.

UNITED STATES

PUERTO RICO

Strawberries

by Gayle Ross

Where did strawberries come from? This Cherokee story not only answers that question but also describes how anger and bitterness can poison a relationship. The two people in the story are the first man and the first woman in the world, but their disagreement does not sound very different from arguments people have today. However, the way their problem is solved is far from ordinary!

Like "Aunty Misery," "Strawberries" is an **origin myth.** These tales explain how and why something came to be. Origin myths appear in cultures all over the world, and they describe the beginnings of many things—spiders, thunder, echoes, and even the world itself.

AS YOU READ . . .

Identify human traits that are common across cultures.

Compare and contrast the motivations of the characters.

Decide what lesson each selection teaches.

STRAWBERRIES

BY GAYLE ROSS

Long ago, in the very first days of the world, there lived the first man and the first woman. They lived together as husband and wife, and they loved one another dearly.

But one day they quarreled. Although neither later could remember what the quarrel was about, the pain grew stronger with every word that was spoken, until finally, in anger and in grief, the woman left their home and began walking away—to the east, toward the rising sun.

The man sat alone in his house. But as time went by, he grew lonelier and lonelier. The anger left him, and all that remained was a terrible grief and despair, and he began to cry.

Provider, the creator of all things, heard the man crying and took pity on him. The spirit said, "Man, why do you cry?"

The man said, "My wife has left me."

Provider said, "Why did your woman leave?"

The man just hung his head and said nothing.

The creator asked, "You quarreled with her?"

And the man nodded.

"Would you quarrel with her again?" asked the provider.

The man said, "No." He wanted only to live with his wife as they had lived before—in peace, in happiness, and in love.

> *He wanted only to live with his wife . . .in peace, in happiness, and in love.*

"I have seen your woman," the creator said. "She is walking to the east toward the rising sun."

The man followed his wife, but he could not overtake her. Everyone knows an angry woman walks fast.

Finally Provider said, "I'll go ahead and see if I can make her slow her steps." So the spirit found the woman walking, her footsteps fast and angry and her gaze fixed straight ahead. There was pain in her heart.

The creator saw some huckleberry[1] bushes growing along the trail, so with a wave of the hand, the bushes burst into bloom and ripened into fruit. But the woman's gaze remained fixed. She looked neither to the right nor to the left, and she didn't see the berries. Her footsteps didn't slow.

Again Provider waved his hand, and one by one, *all* of the berries growing along the trail burst into bloom and ripened into fruit. But still the woman's gaze remained fixed. She saw nothing but her anger and pain, and her footsteps didn't slow.

---

1. **huckleberry:** a berry with many seeds; related to blueberries.

The anger had gone from her heart, and all that remained was the love she had always known.

And again the creator waved his hand, and one by one, the trees of the forest—the peach, the pear, the apple, the wild cherry—burst into bloom and ripened into fruit. But still the woman's eyes remained fixed, and even still, she saw nothing but her anger and pain. And her footsteps didn't slow.

Then finally Provider thought, "I will create an entirely new fruit—one that grows very, very close to the ground, so the woman must forget her anger and bend her head for a moment." So the spirit waved his hand, and a thick green carpet began to grow along the trail. Then the carpet became starred with tiny white flowers, and each flower gradually ripened into a berry that was the color and shape of the human heart.

As the woman walked, she crushed the tiny berries, and the delicious aroma came up through her nose. She stopped and looked down, and she saw the berries. She picked one and ate it, and she discovered its taste was as sweet as love itself. So she began walking slowly, picking berries as she went, and as she leaned down to pick a berry, she saw her husband coming behind her.

The anger had gone from her heart, and all that remained was the love she had always known. So she stopped for him, and together they picked and ate the berries. Finally they returned to their home, where they lived out their days in peace, happiness, and love.

And that's how the world's very first strawberries brought peace between men and women in the world and why to this day they are called the berries of love. ❖

Gayle Ross
born 1951

"My grandmother was a storyteller. I grew up with stories, and I just always loved them."

A Rich Heritage Gayle Ross is the great-great-great-granddaughter of John Ross, one of the most important chiefs of the Cherokee Nation. "I come from a tradition in which storytelling was a very important part of the culture," she says. "I wanted to tell the stories I had heard as a child and to honor the legacy of . . . the Cherokees."

From Storyteller . . . Ross began a career in radio and television, then formed a storytelling duo, and finally went solo. "It was a hobby that got out of hand," she jokes. She uses her knowledge of Cherokee and other Native American cultures in her work because "one of the most important roles that a storyteller has is to share cultural understanding."

. . . to Author Ross's first book, *How Rabbit Tricked Otter*, is a collection of fifteen traditional Cherokee stories. Her other books are *The Girl Who Married the Moon, The Story of the Milky Way, How Turtle's Back Was Cracked, The Legend of the Windigo,* and *Dat-So-La-Lee, Artisan*.

AUNTY MISERY

retold by Judith Ortiz Cofer

This is a story about an old, very old woman who lived alone in her little hut with no other company than a beautiful pear tree that grew at her door. She spent all her time taking care of her pear tree. But the neighborhood children drove the old woman crazy by stealing her fruit. They would climb her tree, shake its delicate limbs, and run away with armloads of golden pears, yelling insults at "Aunty Misery," as they called her.

One day, a pilgrim[1] stopped at the old woman's hut and asked her permission to spend the night under her roof. Aunty Misery saw that he had an honest face and <u>bade</u> the traveler come in. She fed him and made a bed for him in front of her hearth. In the morning while he was getting ready to leave, the stranger told her that he would show his gratitude for her hospitality by granting her one wish.

"There is only one thing that I desire," said Aunty Misery.

"Ask, and it shall be yours," replied the stranger, who was a sorcerer[2] in disguise.

"I wish that anyone who climbs up my pear tree should not be able to come back down until I permit it."

"Your wish is granted," said the stranger, touching the pear tree as he left Aunty Misery's house.

And so it happened that when the children came back to taunt[3] the old woman and to steal her fruit, she stood at her window watching them. Several of them shimmied up the trunk of the pear tree and immediately got stuck to it as if with glue. She let them cry and beg her for a long time before she gave the tree permission to let them go, on the condition that they never again steal her fruit or bother her.

Time passed, and both Aunty Misery and her tree grew bent and gnarled with age. One day another traveler stopped at her door. This one looked suffocated and exhausted, so the old woman asked him what he wanted in her village. He answered her in a voice that was dry and hoarse, as if he had swallowed a desert: "I am Death, and I have come to take you with me."

Thinking fast, Aunty Misery said, "All right, but before I go I would like to pluck some pears from my beloved pear tree to remember how much pleasure it brought me in this life. But I am a very old woman and cannot climb to the tallest branches where the best fruit is; will you be so kind as to do it for me?"

With a heavy sigh like wind through a catacomb,[4] Death climbed the pear tree. Immediately he became stuck to it as if with glue. And no matter how much he cursed and threatened, Aunty Misery would not give the tree permission to release Death.

"I wish that anyone who climbs up my pear tree should not be able to come back down until I permit it."

---

1. **pilgrim:** a wanderer; traveler.
2. **sorcerer:** a person who practices witchcraft or magic.
3. **taunt** (tônt): to make fun of in a mean way.
4. **catacomb** (kăt′ə-kōm′): an underground arrangement of tunnels or chambers, used as a burial place.

Twilight (1971), Hubert Shuptrine. Copyright © 1971, 1994

And that is why so long as the world is the world, Aunty Misery will always live.

Many years passed, and there were no deaths in the world. The people who make their living from death began to protest loudly. The doctors claimed no one bothered to come in for examinations or treatments anymore, because they did not fear dying; the pharmacists' business suffered too, because medicines are, like magic potions, bought to prevent or postpone the <u>inevitable</u>; the priests and undertakers were unhappy with the situation also, for obvious reasons. There were also many old folks tired of life who wanted to pass on to the next world to rest from the miseries of this one.

Aunty Misery realized all this, and not wishing to be unfair, she made a deal with her prisoner, Death: if he promised not ever to come for her again, she would give him his freedom. He agreed. And that is why so long as the world is the world, Aunty Misery will always live. ❖

Judith Ortiz Cofer
born 1952

"With the stories I tell . . . I try to get my audience past the particulars of my skin color, my accent or my clothes."

Two Worlds As a child, Judith Ortiz Cofer grew up in two different worlds. She was born in Puerto Rico but moved to Paterson, New Jersey, as a young child. Where she lived depended on her father's U.S. Navy assignments—when he was at sea, she returned to Puerto Rico. Both worlds influenced her writing.

The Power of Words In Puerto Rico, she listened to her grandmother's stories in Spanish under a giant mango tree, surrounded by her extended family. It was there, Ortiz Cofer says, "I first began to feel the power of words." In New Jersey, she spent much time by herself, building up "an arsenal of [English] words by becoming an insatiable reader of books." She also served as her mother's interpreter.

Award-Winning Writer and Teacher Ortiz Cofer left her two worlds to attend college in Georgia and then to teach. She has won such honors as the 1990 Pushcart Prize for Nonfiction and the 1994 O. Henry Award for outstanding American short stories.

WORDS
TO
KNOW   **inevitable** (ĭn-ĕv′ĭ-tə-bəl) *adj.* impossible to avoid or prevent

LINKS TO UNIT TWO

Rising to the Challenge

The selections in Unit Two explore the ways that characters change because of the challenges they face. Change brought about by succeeding at difficult or even impossible tasks is a common theme in folklore. In the tales you are about to read, heroes from different cultures must rise to meet a challenge. In the process, the way that they view themselves and the way that others view them are changed.

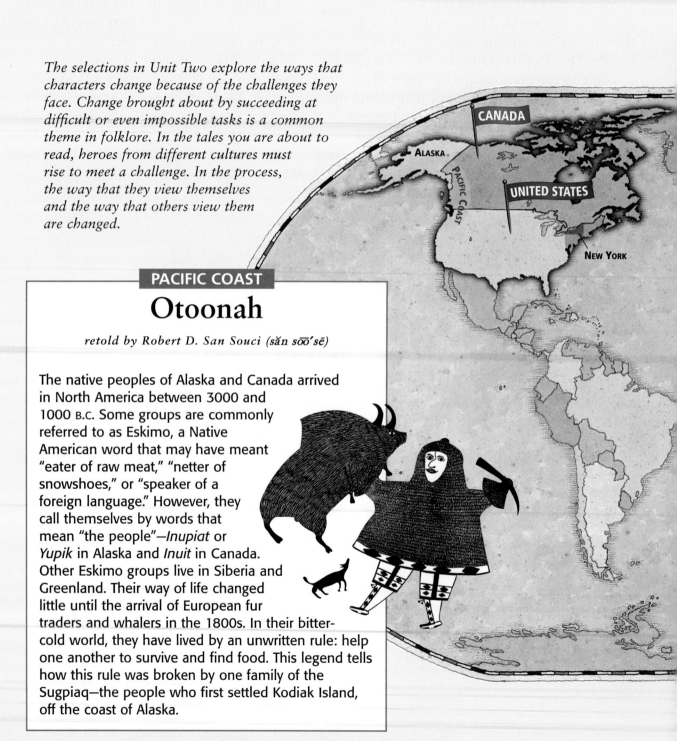

CANADA

ALASKA

PACIFIC COAST

UNITED STATES

NEW YORK

PACIFIC COAST

Otoonah

retold by Robert D. San Souci (săn soo'sē)

The native peoples of Alaska and Canada arrived in North America between 3000 and 1000 B.C. Some groups are commonly referred to as Eskimo, a Native American word that may have meant "eater of raw meat," "netter of snowshoes," or "speaker of a foreign language." However, they call themselves by words that mean "the people"—*Inupiat* or *Yupik* in Alaska and *Inuit* in Canada. Other Eskimo groups live in Siberia and Greenland. Their way of life changed little until the arrival of European fur traders and whalers in the 1800s. In their bitter-cold world, they have lived by an unwritten rule: help one another to survive and find food. This legend tells how this rule was broken by one family of the Sugpiaq—the people who first settled Kodiak Island, off the coast of Alaska.

Racing the Great Bear

retold by Joseph Bruchac (brŏŏ′chäk)

Centered in northern New York State, the Iroquois are not one
Native American people but several. About 1570 several groups
formed a league known as the Iroquois Confederacy,
or Five Nations. Later, the Iroquois became involved in four
wars that took place between 1689 and 1763, in which the British
and French battled for control of North America.
The Iroquois sided with the British.

About 1722, another Native American
group—the Tuscarora—joined, and the
federation became known as the Six
Nations. The league broke up after the
beginning of the Revolutionary War
(1775–1783), with some groups
supporting the British war effort and
others siding with the colonists. As the
legend "Racing the Great Bear" shows,
the Iroquois placed great importance on
fighting skills.

THE FIVE NATIONS OF THE IROQUOIS CONFEDERACY

Cayuga
Mohawk
Onondaga
Oneida
Seneca

AS YOU READ . . .

Notice the customs of
each culture.

Decide what is considered
to be good behavior and
how it is rewarded.

Decide what traits are
seen as negative.

Identify similar structural
elements in the tales.

RACING THE GREAT BEAR

RETOLD BY JOSEPH BRUCHAC

NE ONENDJI. HEAR MY STORY, WHICH HAPPENED LONG AGO. FOR MANY GENERATIONS, THE FIVE NATIONS OF THE HAUDENOSAUNEE, THE PEOPLE OF THE LONGHOUSE,[1] HAD BEEN AT WAR WITH ONE ANOTHER.

No one could say how the wars began, but each time a man of one nation was killed, his relatives sought revenge in the blood feud, and so the fighting continued. Then the Creator took pity on his people and sent a messenger of peace. The Peacemaker traveled from nation to nation, convincing the people of the Five Nations—the Mohawk, the Oneida, the Onondaga, the Cayuga, and the Seneca—that it was wrong for brothers to kill one another. It

---

1. **the Longhouse:** a large group dwelling used by some Native Americans, particularly the five tribes of the Iroquois Nation.

was not easy, but finally the nations agreed, and the Great Peace began. Most welcomed that peace, though there were some beings with bad hearts who wished to see the return of war.

One day, not long after the Great Peace had been established, some young men in a Seneca village decided they would pay a visit to the Onondaga people.

"It is safe now to walk the trail between our nations," the young men said. "We will return after the sun has risen and set seven times."

Then they set out. They walked toward the east until they were lost from sight in the hills. But many more than seven days passed, and those young men never returned. Now another group of young men left, wanting to find out where their friends had gone. They, too, did not return.

The people grew worried. Parties were sent out to look for the vanished young men, but no sign was found. And the searchers who went too far into the hills did not return, either.

The old chief of the village thought long and hard. He asked the <u>clan</u> mothers, those wise women whose job it was to choose the chiefs and give them good advice, what should be done.

"We must find someone brave enough to face whatever danger is out there," the clan mothers said.

So the old chief called the whole village to a council meeting. He held up a white strand of wampum beads[2] made from quahog[3] clamshells as he spoke.

"Hear me," he said. "I am of two minds about what has happened to our people. It may be that the Onondaga have broken the peace and captured them. It may be there is something with an evil mind that wishes to destroy this new peace and so has killed our people. Now someone must go and find out. Who is brave enough? Who will come and take this wampum from my hand?"

Many men were gathered in that council. Some were known to speak of themselves as brave warriors. Still, though they muttered to one another, no man stepped forward to take the strand of wampum. The old chief began to walk about the circle, holding the wampum in front of each man in turn. But each man only lowered his eyes to the ground. No man lifted his hand to take the wampum.

Just outside the circle stood a boy who had not yet become a man. His parents were dead, and he lived with his grandmother in her old lodge at the edge of the village. His clothing was always torn and his face dirty because his grandmother was too old to care for him as a mother would. The other young men made fun of him, and as a joke they called him Swift Runner—even though no one had ever seen him run and it was thought that he was weak and lazy. All he ever seemed to do was play with his little dog or sit by the fire and listen when the old people were talking.

"Our chief has forgotten our greatest warrior," one of the young men said to another, tilting his head toward Swift Runner.

"*Nyoh,*" the other young man said, laughing. "Yes. Why does he not offer the wampum to Swift Runner?"

The chief looked around the circle of men, and the laughing stopped. He walked out of the circle to the place where the small boy in torn clothes stood. He held out the wampum, and Swift Runner took it without hesitating.

"I accept this," Swift Runner said. "It is right that I be the one to face the danger. In the eyes of the people I am worthless, so if I

---

2. **wampum beads:** beads made from seashells that were first used for ceremonial and historical purposes, and later used as money.

3. **quahog** (kwô′hôg′): a type of clam with a hard, rounded shell.

Orion in December (1959), Charles E. Burchfield. Watercolor and pencil on paper, 39⅞" × 32⅞",
National Museum of American Art, gift of S. C. Johnson & Son, Inc., Smithsonian Institution,
Washington, D.C./Art Resource, New York.

do not return, it will not matter. I will leave when the sun rises tomorrow."

When Swift Runner arrived home at his grandmother's lodge, the old woman was waiting for him.

"Grandson," she said, "I know what you have done. The people of this village no longer remember, but your father was a great warrior. Our family is a family that has power."

Then she reached up into the rafters and took down a heavy bow. It was blackened with smoke and seemed so thick that no man could bend it.

"If you can string this bow, Grandson," the old woman said, "you are ready to face whatever waits for you on the trail."

Swift Runner took the bow. It was as thick as a man's wrist, but he bent it with ease and strung it.

"Wah-hah!" said his grandmother. "You are the one I knew you would grow up to be. Now you must sleep. At dawn we will make you ready for your journey."

It was not easy for Swift Runner to sleep, but when he woke the next morning, he felt strong and clear-headed. His grandmother was sitting by the fire with a cap in her hand.

"This was your grandfather's cap," she said. "I have sewed four hummingbird feathers on it. It will make your feet more swift."

Swift Runner took the cap and placed it on his head.

His grandmother held up four pairs of moccasins. "Carry these tied to your waist. When one pair wears out, throw them aside and put on the next pair."

Swift Runner took the moccasins and tied them to his belt.

Next his grandmother picked up a small pouch. "In this pouch is cornmeal mixed with maple sugar," she said. "It is the only food you will need as you travel. It will give you strength when you eat it each evening."

Swift Runner took the pouch and hung it from his belt by the moccasins.

"The last thing I must give you," said the old woman, "is this advice. Pay close attention to your little dog. You have treated him well, and so he is your great friend. He is small, but his eyes and nose are keen. Keep him always in front of you. He will warn you of danger before it can strike you."

Then Swift Runner set out on his journey. His little dog stayed ahead of him, sniffing the air and sniffing the ground. By the time the sun was in the middle of the sky, they were far from the village. The trail passed through deep woods, and it seemed to the boy as if something was following them among the trees. But he could see nothing in the thick brush.

The trail curved toward the left, and the boy felt even more the presence of something watching. Suddenly his little dog ran into the brush at the side of the trail, barking loudly. There were the sounds of tree limbs breaking and heavy feet running. Then out of the forest came a Nyagwahe,[4] a monster bear. Its great teeth were as long as a man's arm. It was twice as tall as a moose. Close at its heels was Swift Runner's little dog.

"I see you," Swift Runner shouted. "I am after you. You cannot escape me."

Swift Runner had learned those words by listening to the stories the old people told. They were the very words a monster bear speaks when it attacks, words that terrify anyone who hears them. On hearing those words, the great bear turned and fled from the boy.

"You cannot escape me," Swift Runner shouted again. Then he ran after the bear.

The Nyagwahe turned toward the east, with Swift Runner and his dog close behind. It left the trail and plowed through the thick forest, breaking down great trees and leaving a path

---

4. **Nyagwahe** (nī-ə-gwä′hĕ).

of destruction like that of a whirlwind. It ran up the tallest hills and down through the swamps, but the boy and the dog stayed at its heels. They ran past a great cave in the rocks. All around the cave were the bones of people the bear had caught and eaten.

"My relatives," Swift Runner called as he passed the cave, "I will not forget you. I am after the one who killed you. He will not escape me."

Throughout the day, the boy and his dog chased the great bear, growing closer bit by bit. At last, as the sun began to set, Swift Runner stopped at the head of a small valley and called his small dog to him.

"We will rest here for the night," the boy said. He took off his first pair of moccasins, whose soles were worn away to nothing. He threw them aside and put on a new pair. Swift Runner made a fire and sat beside it with his dog. Then he took out the pouch of cornmeal and maple sugar, sharing his food with his dog.

"Nothing will harm us," Swift Runner said. "Nothing can come close to our fire." He lay down and slept.

In the middle of the night, he was awakened by the growling of his dog. He sat up with his back to the fire and looked into the darkness. There, just outside the circle of light made by the flames, stood a dark figure that looked like a tall man. Its eyes glowed green.

"I am Nyagwahe," said the figure. "This is my human shape. Why do you pursue[5] me?"

"You cannot escape me," Swift Runner said. "I chase you because you killed my people. I will not stop until I catch you and kill you."

The figure faded back into the darkness.

"You cannot escape me," Swift Runner said again. Then he patted his small dog and went to sleep.

As soon as the first light of the new day appeared, Swift Runner rose. He and his small dog took the trail. It was easy to follow the monster's path, for trees were uprooted and the earth torn by its great paws. They ran all through the morning. When the sun was in the middle of the sky, they reached the head of another valley. At the other end they saw the great bear running toward the east. Swift Runner pulled off his second pair of moccasins, whose soles were worn away to nothing. He put on his third pair and began to run again.

---

5. **pursue:** to follow in order to overtake or capture; to chase.

Kit Fox Society bow-lance, No Two Horns (Hunkpapa).
State Historical Society of North Dakota (SHSND 10491).

All through that day, they kept the Nyagwahe in sight, drawing closer bit by bit. When the sun began to set, Swift Runner stopped to make camp. He took off the third pair of moccasins, whose soles were worn away to nothing, and put on the last pair.

"Tomorrow," he said to his small dog, "we will catch the monster and kill it." He reached for his pouch of cornmeal and maple sugar, but when he opened it, he found it filled with worms. The magic of the Nyagwahe had done this. Swift Runner poured out the pouch and said in a loud voice, "You have spoiled our food, but it will not stop me. I am on your trail. You cannot escape me."

That night, once again, he was awakened by the growling of his dog. A dark figure stood just outside the circle of light. It looked smaller than the night before, and the glow of its eyes was weak.

"I am Nyagwahe," the dark figure said. "Why do you pursue me?"

"You cannot escape me," Swift Runner said. "I am on your trail. You killed my people. You threatened the Great Peace. I will not rest until I catch you."

"Hear me," said the Nyagwahe. "I see your power is greater than mine. Do not kill me. When you catch me, take my great teeth. They are my power, and you can use them for healing. Spare my life, and I will go far to the north and never again bother the People of the Longhouse."

"You cannot escape me," Swift Runner said. "I am on your trail."

The dark figure faded back into the darkness, and Swift Runner sat for a long time, looking into the night.

At the first light of day, the boy and his dog took the trail. They had not gone far when they saw the Nyagwahe ahead of them. Its sides puffed in and out as it ran. The trail was beside a big lake with many alder trees close to the water. As the great bear ran past, the leaves were torn from the trees. Fast as the bear went, the boy and his dog came closer, bit by bit. At last, when the sun was in the middle of the sky, the giant bear could run no longer. It fell heavily to the earth, panting so hard that it stirred up clouds of dust.

Swift Runner unslung his grandfather's bow and notched an arrow to the sinewy[6] string.

"Shoot for my heart," said the Nyagwahe. "Aim well. If you cannot kill me with one arrow, I will take your life."

"No," Swift Runner said. "I have listened to the stories of my elders. Your only weak spot is the sole of your foot. Hold up your foot and I will kill you."

The great bear shook with fear. "You have defeated me," it pleaded. "Spare my life and I will leave forever."

"You must give me your great teeth," Swift Runner said. "Then you must leave and never bother the People of the Longhouse again."

"I shall do as you say," said the Nyagwahe. "Take my great teeth."

---

6. **sinewy:** stringy, lean, and strong.

Swift Runner lowered his bow. He stepped forward and pulled out the great bear's teeth. It rose to its feet and walked to the north, growing smaller as it went. It went over the hill and was gone.

Carrying the teeth of the Nyagwahe over his shoulder, Swift Runner turned back to the west, his dog at his side. He walked for three moons before he reached the place where the bones of his people were piled in front of the monster's empty cave. He collected those bones and walked around them four times. "Now," he said. "I must do something to make my people wake up." He went to a big hickory tree and began to push it over so that it would fall on the pile of bones.

"My people," he shouted, "get up quickly or this tree will land on you."

The bones of the people who had been killed all came together and jumped up, alive again and covered with flesh. They were filled with joy and gathered around Swift Runner.

"Great one," they said, "who are you?"

"I am Swift Runner," he said.

"How can that be?" one of the men said.

"Swift Runner is a skinny little boy. You are a tall, strong man."

Swift Runner looked at himself and saw that it was so. He was taller than the tallest man, and his little dog was bigger than a wolf.

"I am Swift Runner," he said. "I was that boy, and I am the man you see before you."

Then Swift Runner led his people back to the village. He carried with him the teeth of the Nyagwahe, and those who saw what he carried rejoiced. The trails were safe again, and the Great Peace would not be broken. Swift Runner went to his grandmother's lodge and embraced her.

"Grandson," she said, "you are now the man I knew you would grow up to be. Remember to use your power to help the people."

So it was that Swift Runner ran with the great bear and won the race. Throughout his long life, he used the teeth of the Nyagwahe to heal the sick, and he worked always to keep the Great Peace.

Da neho.[7] I am finished. ❖

---

7. **Da neho** (də nē'hō).

Joseph Bruchac
born 1942

"I write to share my insights into the beautiful and all too fragile world of human life and living things."

Heritage Revealed Bruchac, whose ancestors include members of the Abenaki nation, was raised by his grandparents in the foothills of the Adirondack Mountains. For years his grandfather denied Bruchac's Native American heritage because he did not want him to encounter prejudice. It was not until Bruchac was an adult that he uncovered the truth and began to appreciate the rich folklore of his Native American ancestors.

Author and Publisher Bruchac has authored or co-authored more than 50 books, including *Dawn Land* and *Flying with the Eagle, Racing the Great Bear*. In 1970, he and his wife founded the Greenfield Review Press, which publishes multicultural literature.

Prize Winner Bruchac has won numerous awards. They include a Cherokee Nation Prose Award and several grants from the National Endowment for the Arts.

OTOONAH

RETOLD BY ROBERT D. SAN SOUCI

A Man Cooking Fish as His Wife Softens Kamiks, unknown Inuit artist. Stonecut, 25" × 39¼", by permission of the Amway Environmental Foundation.

In those days of the past, there was an Eskimo family—the parents, two brothers, and a sister—who lived in a village near the ocean. Summer was nearly at an end, and bitter winter was coming soon. For one family, the hunting had been especially bad: they had found few edible plants and berries to store, and they had fewer fish and eggs to bury in the ground, where they wouldn't spoil.

One day, the brothers sent their younger sister to gather driftwood from the beach near the family's sod house.[1] When she was gone, the older brother, Nanoona, said to his parents, "There is not enough food for five people. We must send our sister away. She is weak and does not hunt, yet she eats our food. Soon my brother and I will grow too weak to hunt. Then we will all starve."

Next the younger brother, Avraluk,[2] said, "Four can live when five cannot. We will row our sister across the sea to one of the islands and leave her there."

---

1. **sod house:** a dwelling covered by sod, or grass-covered soil, that is held together by matted roots.
2. **Avraluk** (ăv′rə-lŭk).

Sadly, the parents agreed to this.

When the girl, Otoonah, returned with an armful of wood, her brothers told her what they had decided. "*Ahpah!*[3] Father! *Ahkah!* Mother!" the wretched girl cried. But her parents turned away and would not look at her. Then her brothers put her in the family's large sealskin boat and rowed her to an island below the horizon. There they left her with only the poorest caribou hide that the family owned and flints to start a fire.

For a long time, she did nothing but sob. All the time she stared in the direction where the sun rises and imagined she could see traces of the mainland. Over and over she sang,

> Oh poor me!
> Oh unhappy daughter!
> So sad am I, so sad
> And so lonely!

Finally, when her hunger grew too much to bear, she gathered seaweed from the shore to eat. Then, piling up stones, she made herself a tiny hut. She wrapped herself in the skin at night. When she awoke, she ate more seaweed. But she grew weaker and weaker.

Then, one night, in her makeshift shelter of stones, an old man came to her in a dream. "Walk to the west until you find a broad, swift-flowing stream beside sweet berry bushes. Drink two times from the water, but do not drink again. And do not eat even one berry. But you will find there one other thing that you may take with you."

She awoke soon after this and walked for a long time over the stony ground until she found the broad, swift-flowing stream bordered with berry bushes.

Kneeling, she cupped her hands and drank. The first time she sipped the water, she felt her strength returning. The second time, she felt herself growing stronger still. Although she was still thirsty and hungry, she did as the old man in the dream had told her. She did not take a single drop more or taste a single ripe berry.

Looking across the current, she saw an *ulu*, a knife, with a carved ivory handle lying on a flat rock. With her newfound strength, she lifted a tree trunk and set it over the stream. Then she claimed the knife.

In the days that followed, she used the knife to make a bird spear, harpoon, and a bow and arrows for herself. She practiced throwing the spear and harpoon and shooting arrows until she became skilled at using these weapons.

At the same time, she explored the island and discovered that it was a plentiful hunting ground, with ptarmigans[4] and hares and seals that would sun themselves on the rocks. So she was able to provide plenty of food for herself. Then she made herself clothing, boots, and a cape of sealskin that she had scraped and stretched on the ground to dry. As the days grew cold, she even built a kayak.[5]

Sitting by herself in the warmth of her hut, over which she had packed dirt and which was filled with furs, she often dreamed of sailing home across the sea. She vowed to punish her brothers and her parents who had abandoned her so heartlessly.

Ice began to form on ponds and on the sea. Otoonah could no longer take her kayak out because the ice would pierce its skin cover. Snow fell and piled up against the hut; winds began to howl across the island. But she had plenty of dried seal meat and fish. Inside the shelter it was warm, lit by the yellow flame of a lamp that she had carved from soapstone.

---

3. "Ahpah!" (ä′pä).

4. ptarmigans (tär′mĭ-gənz): a type of bird having brown or gray plumage in the summer and white in winter.

5. kayak (kī′ăk′): a watertight canoe completely covered with skins except for an opening in the center.

Proud Hunter (1987), Pudlo Pudlat. Stonecut, 21½" × 24", by permission of the Amway Environmental Foundation.

The wick was made of moss, and the basin was filled with oil from blubber that she had chewed to release the fuel. Several dried seal stomachs hung on the wall, holding more oil.

When the storms were at their worst and she was weathered in, the young woman sat on her bed platform covered with shrubs and skins and sang songs. Some she remembered her mother singing to her; some she made up: happy songs about summer warmth, bitter songs about loneliness, or boastful songs that she would someday sing when she returned well-fed to mock her starving family.

The long Arctic night arrived. At noon, the sun—too weary to climb above the horizon—spread the thin light of false dawn over a world blanketed with snow and ice.

Now the young woman hunted seals by finding one of their breathing holes in the icebound sea. She would pile up blocks of snow and sit motionlessly. When she heard a seal snort, she would instantly plunge her harpoon straight down, haul the unhappy creature onto the ice, and finish it off.

In time, she recognized the promise of spring as the first rays of sunlight touched the highest peaks far inland. Although terrible cold still gripped the island, the coming of daylight made hunting easier. Soon the ice mass covering the sea began to break apart into smaller floes.[6]

---

6. **floes** (flōz): sheets of floating ice.

Walrus Hunt (1986), Lucassie Tukaluk. Stonecut, 14½" × 18", by permission of the Amway Environmental Foundation.

One day, approaching her favorite hunting area, the young woman heard human voices. At first the sound alone startled her. She was even more astounded to discover that she knew those voices. Running forward, she met her brothers, who were just beaching their kayaks on the shore. At the sight of them, the young woman forgot all her thoughts of revenge.

The two men raised their harpoons at the sight of this strange person running toward them. But they lowered them when they heard her call out, "Nanoona! Avraluk! I am your sister. I am Otoonah!"

Hungry for the sound of human voices, she asked them many questions about her old home and her parents. But they merely shrugged and spoke a few words. They could only stare at the fine furs she wore and the glow of well-fed, good health in her face.

"What man has given you so much food and such fine furs?" her older brother demanded.

"Your husband must give us a portion of what he has," said her younger brother, "since he has married our sister."

Angrily, she said, "No man has given me anything. What I have I have been given by the Old Woman of the Sea who let me take some of the seals and fish in her keeping."

"No woman is such a good hunter," said her older brother. Then they both laughed at her.

"If you are such a hunter," Nanoona continued, "I would challenge you to a hunt."

"And I," Avraluk added.

Angered by their laughter, the young woman said, "I accept your challenge."

They waited until she had launched her own kayak. Then they zigzagged swiftly amid the ice floes. Soon each was lost to the sight of the other.

For the young woman, the hunting was good. By the time she returned, she had two seals lashed to the narrow deck of her kayak. As she rowed with her single paddle which she held in the middle, dipping first right and then left, she sang a little song of thanksgiving to the Old Woman of the Sea.

Both her brothers returned much later, angry and empty-handed. She was already roasting some meat when they came to her hut. She invited them to share her food and spend the night. She did not mock them because she knew they were chewing on bitter defeat with every mouthful of meat—even as she was <u>savoring</u> her victory. When they had finished eating, they did not thank her. They sat apart and whispered together.

In the morning, she awoke and discovered that her brothers were gone. They had also stolen her ivory-handled *ulu* in the fish-skin pouch she had made for it, and most of her furs and meat. Running to the shore, she saw the two of them far out to sea.

Angry at this second <u>betrayal</u>, she pursued them. She was stronger than either of them; and her boat was sturdier and swifter. Soon she overtook them. She shook her harpoon and cried, "Return what you have stolen, or I will gut your kayaks as I would a fish."

The two were cowards and quickly surrendered the stolen goods. Then the young woman laughed at *them*. To the shamefaced

"NO MAN HAS GIVEN ME ANYTHING."

men, it sounded as though her laughter had been picked up by the roaring wind. Soon the sky itself was roaring with dark laughter, as a terrible storm arose.

The young woman, her goods safely tied down, paddled quickly back toward the island through a heavy sea. She called to her brothers to come back with her, but they ignored her. Stubbornly, they paddled on into the heart of the storm. Soon, she heard their calls for help as loud and <u>forlorn</u> as petrels'[7] cries. But although she turned around and tried to find them, they had vanished beneath the waves.

Barely escaping with her own life, she reached safe harbor. For a day and a night she

7. **petrels'**: belonging to a group of sea birds.

> THEN, WITH A CRY OF ENCOURAGEMENT TO HER FELLOW HUNTER, SHE CHARGED BEHIND THEM, BRANDISHING HER HARPOON.

huddled in her shelter, until the wind blew itself out.

When the storm subsided, the young woman took as much meat as she could carry. Then she rowed across to her old village. There she found her parents grieving for their lost sons and fearful that they would soon starve with no one to provide for them. Their grief turned to amazement when they saw Otoonah, her arms laden with food, coming up the beach toward them.

"*Punnick!* Daughter! Have you come home?" her father asked.

"I have come back because it is time for me to return," Otoonah said. "I will give you food from now on." So happy was she to be home that when she searched her heart, she found there no wish to hurt her parents any longer.

After this, she brought all her goods from the island and built herself a new hut, very close to the one in which her parents lived. She soon proved herself the best hunter in the village. Then she was sought by many men, each of whom wanted her to become his wife.

But she set her heart on one man, Apatasok. However, he alone would have no part of her because she insisted on taking a man's role in the hunt. "A woman is supposed to take care of the hunter," he said, "and watch out for his clothes. No more."

"Still, I am determined to have you for my husband," Otoonah said stubbornly.

"A girl does not take a husband of her own choosing. Her parents should seek a husband for her."

Then he walked away before she could argue any more.

However, the following winter, when they were hunting near each other on the edge of the frozen sea, Apatasok killed a seal. But while he was loading it on his sled, he discovered to his dismay that the scent of the kill had drawn a polar bear.

Quick-thinking Otoonah cut the traces[8] on her own sled dogs and sent them to harass the bear. Then, with a cry of encouragement to her fellow hunter, she charged behind them, <u>brandishing</u> her harpoon.

---

8. **traces:** straps or chains connecting a harnessed animal to a vehicle.

WORDS TO KNOW

brandishing (brăn′dĭsh-ĭng) *adj.* waving something (such as a weapon) in a threatening manner; **brandish** *v.*

The bear fought the dogs with its paws and teeth. Two dogs were felled by crushing blows. But the beast could not move because the circling huskies would attack at every opening. The young man rushed forward, trying to spear the bear in its heart. But the bear turned sharply, its paw shattering the hunter's spear and tumbling the man into the snow. The angered bear turned toward the man to finish him off. But, at that instant, the young woman charged forward, putting all of her weight behind her harpoon. The weapon pierced the bear's heart, and it dropped on the spot.

When the young man got to his feet and stared at the young woman standing beside the slain creature, he began to laugh. But the woman recognized that he was laughing because he was still alive, and because here was an unlooked-for supply of meat, and because he saw the foolishness of his refusal to marry a woman who hunted as well as any man.

Soon she was laughing, too.

When they returned to the village, they were wed. And the polar bear meat provided a marriage feast for their families and neighbors. Afterwards, they became a familiar sight as they hunted together, paddling their kayaks side by side. ❖

Robert D. San Souci
born 1946

"As far back as I can remember, I loved stories."

California Is Home A lifelong resident of the San Francisco area, Robert San Souci worked at various jobs—teacher, book buyer, bookstore manager, copywriter, editor—before he was able to support himself through writing. San Souci's stories are set in such varied places as medieval Japan, Native American homelands, the Philippines, and the Bahamas.

Award Winner He has won many awards, including ones from Parents' Choice, the American Library Association, and the Children's Book Council. *Cut From the Same Cloth: American Women in Myth, Legend, and Tall Tale*, from which "Otoonah" is taken, won a 1993 Aesop Prize from the American Folklore Society. In addition to writing books for young people, San Souci writes thrillers for adults.

LINKS TO UNIT THREE

The Human Spirit

The characters in the tales you are about to read, like many of those in the Unit Three selections, struggle with feelings of isolation. As each story continues, the main character gains confidence in his or her strengths. Although these stories contain magical elements, their characters' search for peace and happiness reflects the human spirit. The stories have something else in common as well. Both are funny, designed to amuse and entertain you.

UNITED STATES

MEXICO

MEXICO

The Souls in Purgatory

Retold by Guadalupe Baca-Vaughn

In 1492, Spain's rulers launched a feverish campaign to gain new wealth in the Americas—led by the sailor Christopher Columbus. Spanish priests accompanied the conquerors in search of converts to the Catholic faith. Today the majority of Mexicans and Mexican Americans are Catholics. However, the ancient beliefs and traditions of the pre-Christian culture did not disappear. Many of them have been combined with Catholic beliefs and are reflected in numerous Mexican customs and folk tales. One shared belief concerns purgatory, a temporary place where the spirits of dead people reside before ascending to heaven. "The Souls in Purgatory" describes how an innocent girl uses her faith to cope with a meddlesome aunt and a demanding suitor.

Paul Bunyan and Babe, the Blue Ox

retold by Adrien Stoutenburg

Even as a child, Paul Bunyan was about 50 feet taller than his playmates, and that made him "the best hunter, fisherman, walker, runner, yeller, or mountain climber there was." However, even a huge, strong man can feel loneliness. This tall tale, which describes how Paul Bunyan met his most faithful friend, is one of the best-known and best-loved American folk tales.

AS YOU READ . . .

Consider how the characters' thoughts and actions fit the theme "The Human Spirit."

Notice who or what controls the fate of the human characters.

Think about whether the stories remind you of any other tales from folklore.

Paul Bunyan
and
Babe, the Blue Ox

Retold by Adrien Stoutenburg

Some people say Paul Bunyan wasn't much taller than an ordinary house. Others say he must have been a lot taller to do all the things he did, like sticking trees into his pockets and blowing birds out of the air when he sneezed. Even when he was a baby, up in Maine, he was so big he knocked down a mile of trees just by rolling over in his sleep.

Everyone was nervous about what might happen when Baby Paul grew older and started crawling. Maine wouldn't have any forests left.

Paul's father, and his mother, too, couldn't help feeling a bit proud of how strong Paul was. They knew, though, that the smartest thing to do was to move away. No one seems to know exactly where they went. Wherever it was, Paul didn't cause too much trouble for the rest of the time he was growing up. His father taught him certain things that helped.

"Don't lean too hard against smallish trees or buildings, Son," his father told him. "And if there are towns or farmers' fields in your way, step around them."

And Paul's mother told him, "Never pick on anybody who isn't your own size, Son."

Since there wasn't anyone his size around, Paul never got into fights. Being taller than other boys, by about fifty feet or so, he was naturally the best hunter, fisherman, walker, runner, yeller, or mountain climber there was. And he was best of all at cutting down trees and turning them into lumber. In those days, when America was new, people had to cut down a lot of trees. They needed the lumber for houses, churches, town halls, ships, bridges, ballrooms, stores, pencils, wagons, and flag poles. Luckily, the trees were there, stretching in tall, wind-shining rows across America. The trees marched up mountains and down again. They followed rivers and creeks. They massed up together in purple canyons and shoved each other out of the way on the shores of lakes. They pushed their dark roots down into rock and their glossy branches into the clouds.

Paul liked to flash a sky-bright axe over his head. He loved the smell of wood when it was cut and the look of its sap gleaming like honey. He didn't chop trees down in any ordinary way. With four strokes he would lop all the limbs and bark off a tree, making it a tall, square post. After he had squared up miles of forest in a half-hour, he would take an axe head and tie a long rope to it. Then he would stand straddle-legged and swing the axe in a wide circle, yelling, "T-I-M-B-E-R-R-R! Look out!" With every swing and every yell, a hundred trees would come whooshing down.

The fallen trees had to be hauled down to a river so that they could be floated to a sawmill. Paul grew a bit tired of lugging bundles of trees under his arms, and he wished he had a strong friend to help him. Also, at times he felt lonely, not having anyone his size around.

Babe, the Blue Ox

About the time he was feeling loneliest, there came the Winter of the Blue Snow. Paul, who was full-grown by then, had never seen anything like the blue flakes falling from the sky. Nobody else had either, and perhaps no one ever will, unless it happens again. The blue snow fell softly at first, like bits of sky drifting down. The wind rose and the flakes grew thicker. The blue snow kept falling, day after day. It covered branches and roof tops, hill and valley, with blue, and Paul thought it was about as beautiful a sight as anyone could want.

One day when Paul was out walking in the blue snow, he stumbled over something the size of a mountain. The mountain made a faint mooing sound and shuddered.

"Excuse me," said Paul and looked closer.

Two huge, hairy ears stuck up above the snowdrift. The ears were as blue as the snow.

"Who are you?" Paul asked. There was no answer. Paul grabbed both of the ears and pulled.

Out of the snow came a shivering, clumsy, completely blue baby ox. Even its round, blinking eyes and its tail were blue. Only its shiny nose was black. The calf was the largest

Paul had ever seen. Strong as he was, he felt his muscles shake under the creature's weight.

"Ah! Beautiful blue baby!" Paul said. He cradled the half-frozen calf in his great arms and carried it home. There he wrapped the baby ox in warm blankets and sat up all night taking care of it. The calf did not show much sign of life until morning. Then, as the dawn light came through the window, the ox calf stood up. The calf stretched its neck out and sloshed its wet tongue lovingly against Paul's neck.

Paul gave a roar of laughter, for his one ticklish spot was his neck.

Paul patted the baby ox and scratched his silky, blue ears. "We will be wonderful friends, eh Babe? You will be a giant of an ox and carry forests for me on your back."

That is how it happened that Babe the Blue Ox went with Paul Bunyan when Paul started out into the world to do his mighty logging work. By that time, Babe had his full growth. People never could figure out how long Babe was. They had to use field glasses even to see from one end of Babe to the other. And there were no scales large enough to weigh Babe. Paul did measure the distance between Babe's eyes, and that was exactly forty-two axe handle lengths and one plug of tobacco. Every time Babe needed new iron shoes for his hoofs, a fresh iron mine had to be opened. The shoes were so heavy that a man couldn't carry one without sinking up to his knees in solid rock. ❖

Adrien Stoutenburg
1916–1985

Working with Words Adrien Stoutenburg's father was a barber and her mother operated a beauty parlor, but Adrien's career was in words. She attended the Minneapolis School of Arts, where she studied English, art, and music. After that, she was a librarian, a political reporter for a newspaper, a writer for magazines, a book editor, and an author.

All Kinds of Books Stoutenburg wrote at least 40 books, some under her own name and others under various pen names. One of her most popular books, *American Tall Tales*, is a collection of folklore. It includes stories about Paul Bunyan and Pecos Bill. Stoutenburg also wrote *American Tall-Tale Animals*, *Wild Animals of the Far West*, and *The Crocodile's Mouth: Folk-Song Stories*. She wrote poetry for children and adults, winning several awards. Her works also include biographies of poet Walt Whitman, magician Harry Houdini, and Arctic explorer Elisha Kent Kane.

The Souls in Purgatory

retold by Guadalupe Baca-Vaughn

Si es verdad, allá va, Si es mentira, queda urdida.[1]
(If it be true, so it is. If it be false, so be it.)

THERE was once an old lady who had raised a niece since she was a tiny baby. She had taught the girl to be good, obedient, and industrious, but the girl was very shy and timid and spent much time praying, especially to the Souls in Purgatory.[2]

As the girl grew older and very beautiful, the old woman began to worry that when she died her niece would be left all alone in the world, a world which her niece saw only through innocent eyes. The old lady prayed daily to all the saints in heaven for their <u>intercession</u> to Our Lord that he might send some good man who would fall in love with her niece and marry her; then she could die in peace.

As it happens, the old woman did chores for a *comadre*[3] who had a rooming house. Among her tenants there was a seemingly rich merchant who one day said that he would like to get married if he could find a nice, quiet girl who knew how to keep house and be a good wife and mother to his children when they came.

The old lady opened her ears and began to smile and scheme in her mind, for she could imagine her niece married to the nice gentleman. She told the merchant that he

could find all that he was looking for in her niece, who was a jewel, a piece of gold, and so gifted that she could even catch birds while they were flying!

The gentleman became interested and said that he would like to meet the girl and would go to her house the next day.

The old woman ran home as fast as she could; she appeared to be flying. When she got home all out of breath, she called her niece and told her to straighten up the house and get herself ready for the next day, as there was a gentleman who would be calling. She told her to be sure to wash her hair and brush it until it shone like the sun and to put on her best dress, for in this meeting her future was at stake.

The poor timid girl was <u>dumbfounded</u>. She went to her room and knelt before her favorite *retablo*[4] of the Souls in Purgatory. "Please," she prayed, "don't let my aunt do something rash to embarrass us both."

---

1. *Si es verdad, allá va, / Si es mentira, queda urdida* (sē ĕs vĕr-däd', ä-yä' vä, / sē ĕs mĕn-tē'rä, kĕ'dä ōōr-dē'dä) *Spanish.*
2. **Souls in Purgatory:** the spirits of dead people in the place where they undergo temporary suffering to make up for their sins on earth.
3. *comadre* (kō-mä'drĕ) *Spanish:* a female friend.
4. *retablo* (rĕ-tä'blō) *Spanish:* a wooden panel on which a religious picture is painted or carved.

WORDS
TO
KNOW

intercession (ĭn'tər-sĕsh'ən) *n.* the act of asking for something that will benefit someone else
dumbfounded (dŭm'foun'dəd) *adj.* speechless with shock or amazement

En busqueda de la paz [In search of peace], Alfredo Linares.

The next day she obediently prepared herself for the meeting. When the merchant arrived, he asked her if she could spin. "Spin?" answered the old woman, while the poor embarrassed girl stood by with bowed head. "Spin! The hanks[5] disappear so fast you would think she was drinking them like water."

The merchant left three hanks of linen to be spun by the following day. "What have you done, *Tía?*"[6] the poor girl asked. "You know I can't spin!" "Don't sell yourself short," the old lady replied with twinkling eyes. "Where is your faith in God, the Souls in Purgatory? You pray to them every day. They will help you. Just wait and see!" Sobbing, the girl ran to her room

and knelt down beside her bed and began to pray, often raising her head to the *retablo* of the Souls in Purgatory which hung on the wall beside her bed. After she quieted down, she thought she heard a soft sound behind her. She turned and saw three beautiful ghosts dressed in white, smiling at her. "Do not be concerned," they said. "We will help you in gratitude for all the good you have done for us." Saying this, each one took a hank of linen and in a wink spun the linen into thread as fine as hair.

---

5. **hanks:** bundles of fibers that are spun into thread or yarn.

6. *Tía* (tēʹä) *Spanish:* aunt.

THE following day when the merchant came, he was astonished to see the beautiful linen and was very pleased. "Didn't I tell you, sir?" said the old lady with pride and joy. The gentleman asked the girl if she could sew. Before the surprised girl could answer, the old aunt cried, "Sew? Of course she can sew. Her sewing is like ripe cherries in the mouth of a dragon." The merchant then left a piece of the finest linen to be made into three shirts. The poor girl cried bitterly, but her aunt told her not to worry, that her devotion to the Poor Souls would get her out of this one too, as they had shown how much they loved her on the previous day.

The three ghosts were waiting for the girl beside her bed when she went into her room, crying miserably. "Don't cry, little girl," they said. "We will help you again, for we know your aunt, and she knows what she is doing and why."

The ghosts went to work cutting and snipping and sewing. In a flash they had three beautiful shirts finished with the finest stitches and the tiniest seams.

The next morning when the gentleman came to see if the girl had finished the shirts, he could not believe his eyes. "They are lovely; they seem to have been made in heaven," he said.

This time the merchant left a vest of rare satin to be embroidered. He thought he would try this girl for the third and last time. The girl cried desperately and could not even <u>reproach</u> her aunt. She had decided that she would not ask any more favors of the Souls. She went to her room and lay across the bed and cried and cried. When she finally sat up and dried her tears, she saw the three ghosts smiling at her. "We will help you again, but this time we have a condition, and that is that you will invite us to your wedding." "Wedding? Am I going to get married?" she asked in surprise. "Yes," they said, "and very soon."

The next day a very happy gentleman came for his vest, for he was sure that the lovely girl would have it ready for him. But he was not prepared for the beauty of the vest. The colors were vibrant and beautifully matched. The embroidery looked like a painting. It took his breath away. Without hesitation, he asked the old lady for her niece's hand in marriage. "For," he said, "this vest looks as if it was not touched by human hands but by angels!"

The old woman danced with joy and could hardly contain her happiness. She gave her consent at once. The merchant left to arrange for the wedding. Wringing her hands, the poor girl cried, "But *Tía*, what am I going to do when he finds out that I can't do any of those things?" "Don't worry, my *palomita*,[7] the Blessed Souls[8] will get you out of this trouble too. You wait and see!"

Almost at once the old woman went to her *comadre* to tell her the good news and to ask her to help get ready for the wedding. Soon everything was ready.

The poor girl did not know how to invite the Souls to her wedding. She timidly went and stood beside her bed and asked the *retablo* to come to her wedding.

The great day finally arrived. The girl looked beautiful in the gown which the merchant had brought as part of her *donas*.[9] Everyone in the village had been invited to the wedding.

> "Wedding? Am I going to get married?"

---

7. *palomita* (pä-lō-mē′tä) *Spanish:* a little dove.

8. **Blessed Souls:** the holy spirits of the dead.

9. *donas* (dō′näs) *Spanish:* the wedding presents a man gives to his bride.

WORDS TO KNOW

reproach (rĭ-prōch′) *v.* to criticize; to blame

During the fiesta when everyone was drinking *brindes*[10] to the bride and groom and the music was playing, three ugly hags came to the *sala*[11] and stood waiting for the groom to come and welcome them in. One of the hags had an arm that reached to the floor and dragged; the other arm was short. The second hag was bent almost double and had to turn her head sideways to look up. The third hag had bulging, bloodshot eyes like a lobster. "Jesús María," cried the groom. "Who are those ugly creatures?" "They are aunts of my father, whom I invited to my wedding," answered the bride, knowing quite well who they might be. The groom, being well-bred, went at once to greet the ugly hags. He took them to their seats and brought them refreshments. Very casually, he asked the first hag, "Tell me, señora, why is one of your arms so long and the other one short?" "My son," she answered, "my arms are like that because I spin so much."

The groom went to his wife and said, "Go at once and tell the servants to burn your spinning wheel, and never let me see a spinning wheel in my house; never let me see you spinning, ever!"

The groom went to the second hag and asked her why she was so humped over. "My son," she replied, "I am that way from embroidering on a frame so much." The groom went to his wife and whispered, "Burn your embroidery frame at once, and never let me see you embroider another thing."

Next, the groom went to the third hag and asked, "Why are your eyes so bloodshot and bulging?" "My son, it is because I sew so much and bend over while sewing." She had hardly finished speaking when the groom went to his wife and said, "Take your needles and thread and bury them. I never want to see you sewing, never! If I see you sewing, I will divorce you and send you far away, for the wise man learns from others' painful experiences."

Well—so the Souls, in spite of being holy, can also be rascals.

Colorín, colorado, ya mi cuento se ha acabado.[12]
(Scarlet or ruby red, my story has been said.) ❖

---

10. *brindes* (brēn′dĕs) *Spanish:* drinks toasted to someone's health or happiness.
11. *sala* (sä′lä) *Spanish:* a large room for entertaining.
12. *Colorín, colorado, ya mi cuento se ha acabado* (cō-lōr-ēn′, cō-lō-rä′dō, yä mē kwēn′tō sĕ ä ä-kä-bä′dō) *Spanish.*

Guadalupe Baca-Vaughn
born 1905

"We should know what went before us."

Teacher, Interpreter As a little girl, Guadalupe Baca-Vaughn first heard "The Souls in Purgatory" from her aunt, "who told me the stories she heard as a child in Mexico." Baca-Vaughn was born in New Mexico, the birthplace of her father's family. Her mother's family was from California when it was still part of Mexico. Baca-Vaughn was an interpreter and censor for the U.S. government in El Paso, Texas, during World War II. She eventually returned to New Mexico to teach.

Carrier of Culture After retiring, Baca-Vaughn received a grant to teach the history, culture, and stories of Northern New Mexico to children in local schools. Worried about people losing their cultural heritage, she says, "We should know what went before us."

LINKS TO UNIT FOUR

Strange Goings-On

The selections in Unit Four explore events, both real and imaginary, in which the unexpected occurs. They combine mystery and suspense to excite the reader's curiosity. One might wonder, "What is really going on?" The stories you are about to read—"The Woman in the Snow" and "The Girl in the Lavender Dress"—also defy easy explanation. They are urban legends, fictional stories that are sometimes based on real events. Such legends appear in urban cultures of countries all over the world.

UNITED STATES

NORTHEASTERN U.S.

SOUTHEASTERN U.S.

Alabama

SOUTHEASTERN U.S.

The Woman in the Snow

retold by Patricia C. McKissack

This legend comes out of a modern event—the struggle of African Americans for civil rights. By the mid-1950s, several rulings by the U.S. Supreme Court had already brought gains to the fight for equality. The events upon which this tale is based—the bus boycott in Montgomery, Alabama—focused the nation's attention on the boycott's leader, Dr. Martin Luther King, Jr. This story reflects the struggle of King, and of all African Americans, for equal treatment.

The Girl in the Lavender Dress

retold by Maureen Scott

Urban legends are contemporary stories that are told in many versions around the world. The people telling them usually claim the stories are true and that they actually happened to a relative or friend of a friend. In fact, urban legends simply represent modern-day folklore. Part of their appeal may be that they combine legendary fears—for example, the fear of ghosts—with more modern ones, such as fear of random violence or of being followed.

AS YOU READ . . .

Notice similarities and differences between these two urban legends from different regions of the United States.

Consider how the themes in these legends are similar.

Think about what aspects seem realistic and unrealistic.

The Woman in the Snow

retold by Patricia C. McKissack

The year-long Montgomery, Alabama, bus boycott in 1955–56 was a <u>pivotal</u> event in the American civil rights movement. Blacks refused to ride the buses until their demand of fair and equal treatment for all fare-paying passengers was met. Today the right to sit anywhere on a public bus may seem a small victory over racism and discrimination. But that single issue changed the lives of African Americans everywhere. After the successful boycott in Montgomery, blacks in other cities challenged bus companies, demanding not only the right to sit wherever they chose but also employment opportunities for black bus drivers. Many cities had their own "bus" stories. Some are in history books, but this story is best enjoyed by the fireplace on the night of the first snowfall.

Grady Bishop had just been hired as a driver for Metro Bus Service. When he put on the gray uniform and boarded his bus, nothing mattered, not his obesity,[1] not his poor education, not growing up the eleventh child of the town drunk. Driving gave him power. And power mattered.

One cold November afternoon Grady clocked in for the three-to-eleven shift. "You've got Hall tonight," Billy, the route manager, said matter-of-factly.

"The Blackbird Express." Grady didn't care who knew about his nickname for the route. "Not again." He turned around, slapping his hat against his leg.

"Try the *Hall Street Express,*" Billy corrected Grady, then hurried on, cutting their conversation short. "Snow's predicted. Try to keep on schedule, but if it gets too bad out there, forget it. Come on in."

Grady popped a fresh stick of gum into his mouth. "You're the boss. But tell me. How am I s'posed to stay on schedule? What do those people care about time?"

Most Metro drivers didn't like the Hall Street assignment in the best weather, because the road twisted and turned back on itself like

---

1. **obesity**: increased body weight caused by excessive fat.

Illustration Copyright © 1992 Brian Pinkney. From *The Dark-Thirty* by Patricia McKissack, reprinted by permission of Alfred A. Knopf, Inc.

a retreating snake. When slick with ice and snow, it was even more hazardous. But Grady had his own reason for hating the route. The Hall Street Express serviced black domestics[2] who rode out to the fashionable west end in the mornings and back down to the lower east side in the evenings.

"You know I can't stand being a chauffeur for a bunch of colored maids and cooks," he groused.[3]

"Take it or leave it," Billy said, walking away in disgust.

Grady started to say something but thought better of it. He was still on probation,[4] lucky even to have a job, especially during such hard times.

Snow had already begun to fall when Grady pulled out of the garage at 3:01. It fell steadily all afternoon, creating a frosted wonderland on the manicured lawns that lined West Hall. But by nightfall the winding, twisting, and bending street was a driver's nightmare.

The temperature plummeted, too, adding a new challenge to the mounting snow. "Hurry up! Hurry up! I can't wait all day," Grady snapped at the boarding passengers. "Get to the back of the bus," he hustled them on impatiently. "You people know the rules."

The regulars recognized Grady, but except for a few muffled groans they paid their fares and rode in sullen silence out to the east side loop.

"Auntie! Now, just why are you taking your own good time getting off this bus?" Grady grumbled at the last passenger.

> **Snow had already begun to fall when Grady pulled out of the garage at 3:01.**

The woman struggled down the wet, slippery steps. At the bottom she looked over her shoulder. Her dark face held no clue of any emotion. "Auntie? Did you really call me *Auntie?*" she said, laughing sarcastically. "Well, well, well, well! I never knew my brother had a white son." And she hurried away, chuckling.

Grady's face flushed with surprise and anger. He shouted out the door, "Don't get uppity with me! Y'all know *Auntie* is what we call all you old colored women." Furious, he slammed the door against the bitter cold. He shook his head in disgust. "It's a waste of time trying to be nice," he told himself.

But one look out the window made Grady refocus his attention to a more immediate problem. The weather had worsened. He checked his watch. It was a little past nine. Remarkably, he was still on schedule, but that didn't matter. He had decided to close down the route and take the bus in.

That's when his headlights picked up the figure of a woman running in the snow, without a hat, gloves, or boots. Although she'd pulled a shawl over the lightweight jacket and flimsy dress she was wearing, her clothing offered very little protection against the elements. As she pressed forward against the driving snow and wind, Grady saw that the woman was very young, no more than twenty. And she was clutching something close to her body. What was it? Then Grady saw the baby, a small

---

2. **domestics:** household servants.

3. **groused:** complained.

4. **on probation:** working for a trial period before being permanently employed.

bundle wrapped in a faded pink blanket.

"These people," Grady sighed, opening the door. The woman stumbled up the steps, escaping the wind that mercilessly ripped at her petite frame.

"Look here. I've closed down the route. I'm taking the bus in."

In big gulping sobs the woman laid her story before him. "I need help, please. My husband's gone to Memphis looking for work. Our baby's sick, real sick. She needs to get to the hospital. I know she'll die if I don't get help."

"Well, I got to go by the hospital on the way back to the garage. You can ride that far." Grady nodded for her to pay. The woman looked at the floor. "Well? Pay up and get on to the back of the bus so I can get out of here."

"I—I don't have the fare," she said, quickly adding, "but if you let me ride, I promise to bring it to you in the morning."

"Give an inch, y'all want a mile. You know the rules. No money, no ride!"

"Oh, please!" the young woman cried. "Feel her little head. It's so hot." She held out the baby to him. Grady recoiled.

Desperately the woman looked for something to bargain with. "Here," she said, taking off her wedding ring. "Take this. It's gold. But please don't make me get off this bus."

He opened the door. The winds howled savagely. "Please," the woman begged.

"Go on home, now. You young gals get hysterical over a little fever. Nothing. It'll be fine in the morning." As he shut the door the last sounds he heard were the mother's sobs, the baby's wail, and the moaning wind.

Grady dismissed the incident until the next morning, when he read that it had been a record snowfall. His eyes were drawn to a small article about a colored woman and child found frozen to death on Hall Street. No one

seemed to know where the woman was going or why. No one but Grady.

"That gal should have done like I told her and gone on home," he said, turning to the comics.

It was exactly one year later, on the anniversary of the record snowstorm, that Grady was assigned the Hall Street Express again. Just as before, a storm heaped several inches of snow onto the city in a matter of hours, making driving extremely hazardous.

By nightfall Grady decided to close the route. But just as he was making the turnaround at the east side loop, his headlight picked up a woman running in the snow—the same woman he'd seen the previous year. Death hadn't altered her desperation. Still holding on to the blanketed baby, the small-framed woman pathetically struggled to reach the bus.

Grady closed his eyes but couldn't keep them shut. She was still coming, but from where? The answer was too horrible to consider, so he chose to let his mind find a more reasonable explanation. From some dark corner of his childhood he heard his father's voice, slurred by alcohol, mocking him. *It ain't the same woman, dummy. You know how they all look alike!*

Grady remembered his father with bitterness and swore at the thought of him. This *was* the same woman, Grady argued with his father's memory, taking no comfort in being right. Grady watched the woman's movements breathlessly as she stepped out of the headlight beam and approached the door. She stood outside the door waiting . . . waiting.

The gray coldness of Fear slipped into the driver's seat. Grady sucked air into his lungs in big gulps, feeling out of control. Fear moved

WORDS TO KNOW

petite (pə-tēt') *adj.* small and slender
recoil (rĭ-koil') *v.* to shrink back, as in fear or disgust

his foot to the gas pedal, careening[5] the bus out into oncoming traffic. Headlights. A truck. Fear made Grady hit the brakes. The back of the bus went into a sliding spin, slamming into a tree. Grady's stomach crushed against the steering wheel, rupturing his liver and spleen. *You've really done it now, lunkhead.* As he drifted into the final darkness, he heard a woman's sobs, a baby wailing—or was it just the wind?

Twenty-five years later, Ray Hammond, a war hero with two years of college, became the first black driver Metro hired. A lot of things had happened during those two and a half decades to pave the way for Ray's new job. The military had integrated its forces during the Korean War. In 1954 the Supreme Court had ruled that segregated schools were unequal. And one by one, unfair laws were being challenged by civil rights groups all over the South. Ray had watched the Montgomery bus boycott with interest, especially the boycott's leader, Dr. Martin Luther King, Jr.

Ray soon found out that progress on the day-to-day level can be painfully slow. Ray was given the Hall Street Express.

"The white drivers call my route the Blackbird Express," Ray told his wife. "I'm the first driver to be given that route as a permanent assignment. The others wouldn't take it."

"What more did you expect?" his wife answered, tying his bow tie. "Just do your best so it'll be easier for the ones who come behind you."

In November, Ray worked the three-to-eleven shift. "Snow's predicted," the route manager barked one afternoon. "Close it down if it gets bad out there, Ray."

> ## No one seemed to know where the woman was going or why. No one but Grady.

The last shift on the Hall Street Express.

Since he was a boy, Ray had heard the story of the haunting of that bus route. Every first snowfall, passengers and drivers testified that they'd seen the ghost of Eula Mae Daniels clutching her baby as she ran through the snow.

"Good luck with Eula Mae tonight," one of the drivers said, snickering.

"I didn't know white folk believed in haints,"[6] Ray shot back.

But parked at the east side loop, staring into the swirling snow mixed with ice, Ray felt tingly, as if he were dangerously close to an electrical charge. He'd just made up his mind to close down the route and head back to the garage when he saw her. Every hair on his head stood on end.

He wished her away, but she kept coming. He tried to think, but his thoughts were jumbled and confused. He wanted to look away, but curiosity fixed his gaze on the advancing horror.

Just as the old porch stories had described her, Eula Mae Daniels was a small-framed woman frozen forever in youth. "So young," Ray whispered. "Could be my Carolyn in a few more years." He watched as the ghost came around to the doors. She was out there, waiting in the cold. Ray heard the baby crying. "There but for the grace of God goes one of

---

5. **careening:** swerving or leaning to one side while in motion.

6. **haints** *Southern dialect,* variant of *haunts*: ghosts.

948

mine," he said, compassion overruling his fear. "Nobody deserves to be left out in this weather. Ghost or not, she deserves better." And he swung open the doors.

The woman had form but no substance. Ray could see the snow falling *through* her. He pushed fear aside. "Come on, honey, get out of the cold," Ray said, waving her on board.

Eula Mae stood stony still, looking up at Ray with dark, questioning eyes. The driver understood. He'd seen that look before, not from a dead woman but from plenty of his passengers. "It's okay. I'm for real. Ray Hammond, the first Negro to drive for Metro. Come on, now, get on," he coaxed her gently.

Eula Mae moved soundlessly up the steps. She held the infant to her body. Ray couldn't remember ever feeling so cold, not even the Christmas he'd spent in a Korean foxhole. He'd seen so much death, but never anything like this.

The ghost mother consoled her crying baby. Then with her head bowed she told her story in quick bursts of sorrow, just as she had twenty-five years earlier. "My husband is in Memphis looking for work. Our baby is sick. She'll die if I don't get help."

"First off," said Ray. "Hold your head up. You got no cause for shame."

"I don't have any money," she said. "But if you let me ride, I promise to bring it to you tomorrow. I promise."

Ray sighed deeply. "The rule book says no money, no ride. But the book doesn't say a word about a personal loan." He took a handful of change out of his pocket, fished around for a dime, and dropped it into the pay box. "You're all paid up. Now, go sit yourself down while I try to get this bus back to town."

Eula Mae started to the back of the bus.

"No you don't," Ray stopped her. "You don't have to sit in the back anymore. You can sit right up front."

The ghost woman moved to a seat closer, but still not too close up front. The baby fretted. The young mother comforted her as best she could.

They rode in silence for a while. Ray checked in the rearview mirror every now and then. She gave no reflection, but when he looked over his shoulder, she was there, all right. "Nobody will ever believe this," he mumbled. "*I* don't believe it.

"Things have gotten much better since you've been . . . away," he said, wishing immediately that he hadn't opened his mouth. Still he couldn't—or wouldn't—stop talking.

"I owe this job to a little woman just about your size named Mrs. Rosa Parks. Down in Montgomery, Alabama, one day, Mrs. Parks refused to give up a seat she'd paid for just because she was a colored woman."

Eula Mae sat motionless. There was no way of telling if she had heard or not. Ray kept talking. "Well, they arrested her. So the colored people decided to boycott the buses. Nobody rode for over a year. Walked everywhere, formed car pools, or just didn't go, rather than ride a bus. The man who led the boycott was named Reverend King. Smart man. We're sure

> "It's okay. I'm for real. Ray Hammond, the first Negro to drive for Metro. Come on, now, get on."

to hear more about him in the future. . . . You still with me?" Ray looked around. Yes, she was there. The baby had quieted. It was much warmer on the bus now.

Slowly Ray inched along on the icy road, holding the bus steady, trying to keep the back wheels from racing out of control. "Where was I?" he continued. "Oh yeah, things changed after that Montgomery bus boycott. This job opened up. More changes are on the way. Get this: they got an Irish Catholic running for President. Now, what do you think of that?"

About that time Ray pulled the bus over at Seventeenth Street. The lights at Gale Hospital sent a welcome message to those in need on such a frosty night. "This is it."

Eula Mae raised her head. "You're a kind man," she said. "Thank you."

Ray opened the door. The night air gusted up the steps and nipped at his ankles. Soundlessly, Eula Mae stepped off the bus with her baby.

"Excuse me," Ray called politely. "About the bus fare. No need for you to make a special trip . . . back. Consider it a gift."

He thought he saw Eula Mae Daniels smile as she vanished into the swirling snow, never to be seen again. ❖

Patricia C. McKissack
born 1944

"We did not have television and I grew up sitting on the front porch listening to family and community stories."

Literary Lives Patricia C. McKissack has published one award-winning book after another. Writing separately and together, she and her husband, Fredrick, have written more than 100 books for children and teenagers. Most are about the lives of African Americans and Native Americans—some famous, and others who have been "left out of history books." Among the many awards her books have won are three Coretta Scott King Awards and a Newbery Honor Award. She has also written radio and television scripts and an award-winning movie script.

McKissack was born in Smyrna, Tennessee. She and her husband grew up in the same town and both graduated from Tennessee State University. Their lives, McKissack says, were influenced by the civil rights movement of the 1960s, when "African Americans were really looking up, coming out of darkness, segregation, and discrimination, and doors were beginning to open—ever so slightly, but still opening."

Multifaceted Author Before she began writing full-time, McKissack taught eighth graders and college students and edited children's books. When she found no biography of Paul Laurence Dunbar for her eighth graders, she wrote one herself. Other books include *Jessie Jackson: A Biography* and *Mirandy and Brother Wind,* about a girl who believes she will dance with the wind at a party. McKissack and her husband have three grown sons and live in St. Louis, Missouri.

The Girl in the Lavender Dress

told by
Maureen Scott

Copyright © Andrea Brooks.

My grandmother was, I always believed, a truthful woman. She paid her taxes. She went to church. She considered the Lord's business as her own. When her children told lies, they soon saw the light of truth. They went to bed without any supper, the taste of soap still pungent on their tongues.

That's why the story that follows bothers me so much. It just *can't* be true. Of course, Grandma was 92 when she told it to me and her mind had started to fail. She might have really believed it. Who knows? Maybe you will, too.

I'll try to tell the story just the way she told it to me. She was in a nursing home then. It was late at night and the two of us were alone in the TV room. Grandma's eyelids hung low over her eyes. She worked her wrinkled jaw a few times and began:

It all happened about '42 or '43 [Grandma said]. It was during World

War II. We didn't have much gas in those days. No one did. So whenever Herbert took the car somewhere, I tried to go along for the ride.

We lived in Vermont in those days. This time I'm thinking of, Herbert had some business in Claremont. That's in New Hampshire, just across the river. Well, seems Herbert had saved up the gas to go by car. About 25 miles. He said we could leave after work Friday. That night we'd have us a good restaurant meal. Maybe see a movie, too. Then we'd stay in a hotel and drive back the next day.

I don't remember the month, exactly. Sometime in the fall, 'cause it was cool. It was a misty night. I remember Herbert had to keep the wipers going. And it was after dusk when we first saw her. I know it was dark, 'cause I remember first seeing her in the lights ahead.

Neither Herbert nor I spoke. He slowed down, and the girl stopped walking. She just stood there on our side of the road. Not hitching, exactly, but she sure looked like she wanted a ride. It was a lonely road, and there weren't many cars.

First Herbert passed her, going real slow. Then he backed up to where she was. I rolled down my window. She was a pretty little thing, about eighteen or twenty. A round face and big round eyes. Brown hair, cut straight. The mist kind of made her face shine. But the funny thing was what she was wearing: only a thin lavender party dress. In that weather!

Well, I don't remember that anybody did any asking. I just opened the door and leaned forward. She climbed into the back seat, and Herbert started up again. Finally I asked her where she was going.

"Claremont." That was all she said at first. She had a light, breathless voice, like it took a whole lungful of air to say that one word.

"You're lucky," Herbert said. "We're going all the way."

The girl didn't reply. We rode on a little ways. I turned around once or twice, but the girl just smiled, sort of sadly. Anyhow, I didn't want to stare at her. But who was she, and why was she walking on a lonely road at night? I've never been the kind to pry into other people's business. So what I did then was, well, I'd taken off my sweater when the car got warm. I offered it to her, and she put it on.

The mist turned to light rain. Just before we got to the river, Herbert broke the silence. "Where are you going in Claremont, Miss?"

There was no reply.

"It's coming on to rain," Herbert said. "And we got time to deliver you."

"Oh," the girl breathed. "Could you *really*? That would be—that would be *nice*. To my parents' house. Corner of Bond and Mason."

"Claremont must be a nice place to grow up," I said, but again, there was no sound from the back of the car. You couldn't even hear her breathing. I just settled back into my seat and enjoyed the trip. We crossed the bridge, headed into town, and Herbert turned right onto Bond Street.

We rode along, looking at the street signs. Mason was way out. There was only one house on the corner, on the opposite side. Herbert made a U-turn and stopped the car.

There was no one in the rear seat!

I looked at Herbert. He looked at me, his eyes popping. I pulled myself up so I could see the back floor. Nothing. Just a little wetness where her feet had been.

"Where'd she get out?" Herbert asked.

"At a stoplight?" I wondered. But we both knew it couldn't be. It was a two-door car, so we'd know it if a door opened. Both of us looked at the rear windows. They were closed, as they had been. Neither of us had felt a draft.

Yet there had to be some explanation. "Come," Herbert said. We hurried toward the house. It was a big square boxlike building. Lights were on in nearly every room. Splotches of brightness covered the wet lawn.

The door had a name on it: J. R. Bullard. It was opened by a long-faced man about fifty.

"Excuse me," Herbert said, "but there seems to be some mystery. You see, your daughter—"

"Daughter?" said the man. "Why, we don't have any daughter." A small woman, some years younger, now stood at his side.

"Well—" Herbert began.

"We *did* have a daughter," the woman said. "But Carol is deceased, you see. She was buried in Calhoun Cemetery four months ago."

Herbert gripped my arm. We both knew Calhoun Cemetery: it was on the Vermont side of the river. "Then who—?" Herbert wondered aloud. Suddenly he looked embarrassed. "Excuse us," he muttered. "It's all a—a mistake."

"Just a minute," I said. "Would you mind telling us what Carol looked like?"

The couple exchanged glances. If they were worried, it wasn't about Carol. It was about us. "A little on the short side," the woman said almost to herself. "A round face. Big round eyes. Dark, straight hair, cut in bangs."

Herbert's hand was a lobster claw on my elbow. We excused ourselves in a hurry. Back in the car, we sped away through the night. Then we drove around for a long time, looking. Across the bridge. Down every little road. Back into Claremont. Near every stoplight. Along Bond Street.

But we both knew the search was futile. There was only one answer. What we'd had in our car, sitting on the back seat and even talking, was the ghost of Carol Bullard. And the amazing thing was that we had proof. A ghost, you see, cannot cross water. That was why, when we came to the river, the ghost had only one choice: to disappear!

Grandma stopped talking, and I thought that was the end of her incredible story. But no—there was more:

And that isn't all [Grandma went on]. That night—the night that it happened—we were

Back in the car, we sped away through the night.

both pretty edgy. Didn't get much sleep, either. Not till the next morning did we think of my sweater. It had disappeared with the ghost.

That was a really good sweater, almost new. You see, we didn't have much money, and it was wartime. Clothes were hard to come by. But once in a while I'd blow a week's pay on something really nice, something that would last for years—like that sweater.

Now listen: it's like this. On the way home, we thought we'd swing around by Calhoun Cemetery. We wanted to find a certain gravestone, the one that would say "Carol Bullard" on it. So we did just that. It took a long time, but finally we found the new graves. And there, at last, was the stone. A small flat stone. Just "Carol Bullard" on it. No dates; nothing more. But next to the stone, neatly folded up, *was my sweater!*

True—or not? You decide. ❖

LINKS TO UNIT FIVE

American Voices

The selections in Unit Five demonstrate the diverse ways that the story of the United States is told and remembered—in memoirs, journals, letters, songs, speeches, and fiction. Folk tales are another type of literature that preserves history and culture. In the selections you are about to read, you will meet two larger-than-life folk heroes in two uniquely American regional settings of the 19th century.

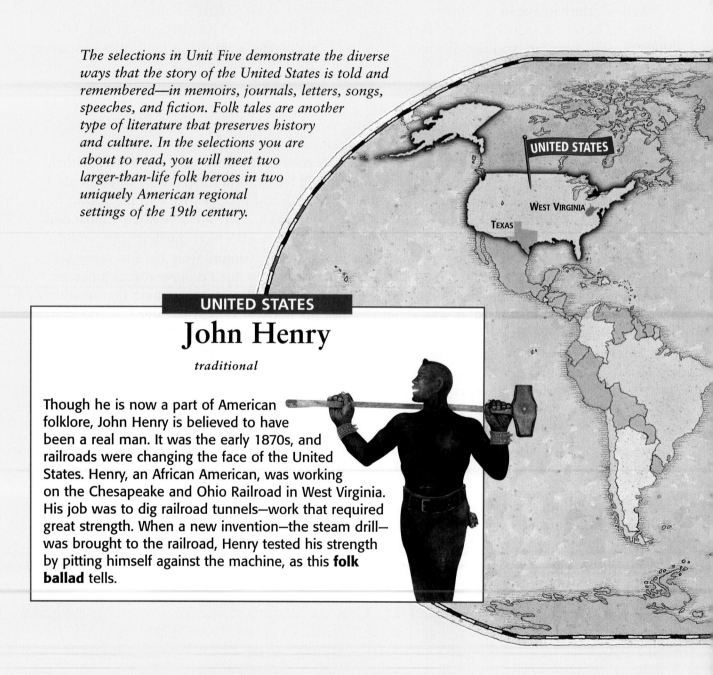

UNITED STATES

WEST VIRGINIA

TEXAS

UNITED STATES

John Henry

traditional

Though he is now a part of American folklore, John Henry is believed to have been a real man. It was the early 1870s, and railroads were changing the face of the United States. Henry, an African American, was working on the Chesapeake and Ohio Railroad in West Virginia. His job was to dig railroad tunnels—work that required great strength. When a new invention—the steam drill—was brought to the railroad, Henry tested his strength by pitting himself against the machine, as this **folk ballad** tells.

Pecos Bill

retold by Mary Pope Osborne

Before railroads reached the Texas rangelands, trail drives were the best way of moving cattle to railroad stations for transport to markets in the East. Cowboys herded millions of longhorn cattle over dusty trails from the mid-1860s to the mid-1880s. Edward O'Reilly, inspired by stories of this rugged trail life and by tales of Paul Bunyan, wrote the first Pecos Bill tall tale in 1923. Other writers made more and more imaginative additions to O'Reilly's original tale.

"Pecos Bill" is an example of a tall tale. **Tall tales** are legends that use exaggeration and feature heroes who accomplish superhuman achievements. These tales were often told around campfires in the American West of the 1800s. The stories evolved out of pioneers' own experiences, greatly exaggerated for dramatic and humorous effect. Often the heroes of tall tales exemplify virtues such as courage, determination, and ingenuity, all of which were necessary for survival on the frontier.

AS YOU READ . . .

Determine whether each selection celebrates a human strength or pokes fun at a human weakness.

Notice which details are realistic and which are fantastic.

Think about how these tales reflect the American heritage and traditions.

JOHN HENRY

TRADITIONAL

When John Henry was a little boy,
Sitting upon his father's knee,
His father said, "Look here, my boy,
You must be a steel driving man[1] like me,
5　You must be a steel driving man like me."

John Henry went up on the mountain,
Just to drive himself some steel.
The rocks was so tall and John Henry so small,
He said lay down hammer and squeal,
10　He said lay down hammer and squeal.

John Henry had a little wife,
And the dress she wore was red;
The last thing before he died,
He said, "Be true to me when I'm dead,
15　Oh, be true to me when I'm dead."

John Henry's wife ask him for fifteen cents,
And he said he didn't have but a dime,
Said, "If you wait till the rising sun goes down,
I'll borrow it from the man in the mine,
20　I'll borrow it from the man in the mine."

John Henry started on the right-hand side,
And the steam drill started on the left.
He said, "Before I'd let that steam drill beat me down,
I'd hammer my fool self to death,
25　Oh, I'd hammer my fool self to death."

---

1. **steel driving man:** a person who used a ten-pound
   hammer to drive a steel drill into rock in order to
   make holes for explosives.

His Hammer in His Hand, Palmer C. Hayden (1890–1973). From the John Henry Series, Museum of African American Art, Los Angeles, Palmer C. Hayden Collection, gift of Miriam A. Hayden. Photo by Armando Solis.

The steam drill started at half-past six,
John Henry started the same time.
John Henry struck bottom at half-past eight,
And the steam drill didn't bottom till nine,
30 And the steam drill didn't bottom till nine.

John Henry said to his captain,
"A man, he ain't nothing but a man,
Before I'd let that steam drill beat me down,
I'd die with the hammer in my hand,
35 Oh, I'd die with the hammer in my hand."

John Henry said to his shaker,[2]
"Shaker, why don't you sing just a few more rounds?
And before the setting sun goes down,
You're gonna hear this hammer of mine sound,
40 You're gonna hear this hammer of mine sound."

---

2. **shaker:** the person who holds the steel drill for the steel
driving man and shakes the drill to remove it from the rock.

John Henry hammered on the mountain,
He hammered till half-past three,
He said, "This big Bend Tunnel on the C. & O. road[3]
Is going to be the death of me,
Lord! is going to be the death of me."

John Henry had a little baby boy,
You could hold him in the palm of your hand.
The last words before he died,
"Son, you must be a steel driving man,
Son, you must be a steel driving man."

John Henry had a little woman,
And the dress she wore was red,
She went down the railroad track and never come back,
Said she was going where John Henry fell dead,
Said she was going where John Henry fell dead.

John Henry hammering on the mountain,
As the whistle blew for half-past two,
The last word I heard him say,
"Captain, I've hammered my insides in two,
Lord, I've hammered my insides in two."

---

3. **big Bend . . . road:** Construction work on the Big
   Bend Tunnel on the Chesapeake & Ohio Railroad
   in West Virginia took place from 1870 to 1873.

Pecos Bill

retold by Mary Pope Osborne

Copyright © Colin Poole.

Ask any coyote near the Pecos River in western Texas who was the best cowboy who ever lived, and he'll throw back his head and howl, "Ah-hooo!" If you didn't know already, that's coyote language for *Pecos Bill.*

"Dang," he said. "But if I'm not a varmint, what am I?" "You're a cowboy! So start acting like one!"

When Pecos Bill was a little baby, he was as tough as a pine knot. He teethed on horseshoes instead of teething rings and played with grizzly bears instead of teddy bears. He could have grown up just fine in the untamed land of eastern Texas. But one day his pappy ran in from the fields, hollering, "Pack up, Ma! Neighbors movin' in fifty miles away! It's gettin' too crowded!"

Before sundown Bill's folks loaded their fifteen kids and all their belongings into their covered wagon and started west.

As they clattered across the <u>desolate</u> land of western Texas, the crushing heat nearly drove them all crazy. Baby Bill got so hot and cross that he began to wallop his big brothers. Pretty soon all fifteen kids were going at one another tooth and nail. Before they turned each other into catfish bait, Bill fell out of the wagon and landed *kerplop* on the sun-scorched desert.

The others were so busy fighting that they didn't even notice the baby was missing until it was too late to do anything about it.

Well, tough little Bill just sat there in the dirt, watching his family rattle off in a cloud of dust, until an old coyote walked over and sniffed him.

"Goo-goo!" Bill said.

Now it's an amazing coincidence, but "Goo-goo" happens to mean something similar to "Glad to meet you" in coyote language. Naturally the old coyote figured he'd come across one of his own kind. He gave Bill a big lick and picked him up by the scruff of the neck and carried him home to his den.

Bill soon discovered the coyote's kinfolk were about the wildest, roughest bunch you could imagine. Before he knew it, he was roaming the prairies with the pack. He howled at the moon, sniffed the brush, and chased lizards across the sand. He was having such a good time, scuttling about naked and dirty on all fours, that he completely forgot what it was like to be a human.

Pecos Bill's coyote days came to an end about seventeen years later. One evening as he was sniffing the sagebrush, a cowpoke came loping by on a big horse. "Hey, you!" he shouted. "What in the world are you?"

Bill sat on his haunches and stared at the feller.

"What *are* you?" asked the cowpoke again.

"<u>Varmint</u>," said Bill hoarsely, for he hadn't used his human voice in seventeen years.

"No, you ain't!"

"Yeah, I am. I got fleas, don't I?"

"Well, that don't mean nothing. A lot of Texans got fleas. The thing varmints got that you ain't got is a tail."

"Oh, yes. I do have a tail," said Pecos Bill.

"Lemme see it then," said the cowpoke.

Bill turned around to look at his rear end, and for the first time in his life he realized he didn't have a tail.

"Dang," he said. "But if I'm not a varmint, what am I?"

WORDS
TO
KNOW

desolate (dĕs′ə-lĭt) *adj.* having few or no inhabitants; lifeless
varmint (vär′mĭnt) *n.* a wild animal that is considered undesirable or troublesome, such as a fox, a rabbit, or a rodent

"You're a cowboy! So start acting like one!"

Bill just growled at the feller like any coyote worth his salt would. But deep down in his heart of hearts he knew the cowpoke was right. For the last seventeen years he'd had a sneaking suspicion that he was different from that pack of coyotes. For one thing, none of them seemed to smell quite as bad as he did.

So with a heavy heart he said good-bye to his four-legged friends and took off with the cowpoke for the nearest ranch.

Acting like a human wasn't all that easy for Pecos Bill. Even though he soon started dressing right, he never bothered to shave or comb his hair. He'd just throw some water on his face in the morning and go around the rest of the day looking like a wet dog. Ignorant cowpokes claimed Bill wasn't too smart. Some of the meaner ones liked to joke that he wore a ten-dollar hat on a five-cent head.

The truth was, Pecos Bill would soon prove to be one of the greatest cowboys who ever lived. He just needed to find the kind of folks who'd appreciate him. One night when he was licking his dinner plate, his ears perked up. A couple of ranch hands were going on about a gang of wild cowboys.

"Yep. Those fellas are more animal than human," one ranch hand was saying.

"Yep. Them's the toughest bunch I ever come across. Heck, they're so tough they can kick fire out of flint rock with their bare toes!"

"Yep. 'N' they like to bite nails in half for fun!"

"Who are these fellers?" asked Bill.

"The Hell's Gate Gang," said the ranch hand. "The mangiest, meanest, most low-down bunch of lowlife varmints that ever grew hair."

"Sounds like my kind of folks," said Bill, and before anyone could holler whoa, he jumped on his horse and took off for Hell's Gate Canyon.

Bill hadn't gone far when disaster struck. His horse stepped in a hole and broke its ankle.

"Dang!" said Bill as he stumbled up from the spill. He draped the lame critter around his neck and hurried on.

After he'd walked about a hundred more miles, Bill heard some mean rattling. Then a fifty-foot rattlesnake reared up its ugly head and stuck out its long, forked tongue, ready to fight.

"Knock it off, you scaly-hided fool. I'm in a hurry," Bill said.

The snake didn't give a spit for Bill's plans. He just rattled on.

Before the cussed varmint could strike, Bill had no choice but to knock him cross-eyed. "Hey, feller," he said, holding up the dazed snake. "I like your spunk. Come go with us." Then he wrapped the rattler around his arm and continued on his way.

After Bill had hiked another hundred miles with his horse around his neck and his snake around his arm, he heard a terrible growl. A huge mountain lion was crouching on a cliff, getting ready to leap on top of him.

"Don't jump, you mangy bobtailed fleabag!" Bill said.

Well, call any mountain lion a mangy bobtailed fleabag, and he'll jump on your back for sure. After this one leaped onto Bill, so much fur began to fly that it darkened the sky. Bill wrestled that mountain lion into a headlock, then squeezed him so tight that the big cat had to cry uncle.

When the embarrassed old critter started to slink off, Bill felt sorry for him. "Aw, c'mon, you big silly," he said. "You're more like me than most humans I meet."

The truth was, Pecos Bill would soon prove to be one of the greatest cowboys who ever lived.

Illustration by J. W. Stewart.

He saddled up the cat, jumped on his back, and the four of them headed for the canyon, with the mountain lion screeching, the horse neighing, the rattler rattling, and Pecos Bill hollering a wild war whoop.

When the Hell's Gate Gang heard those noises coming from the prairie, they nearly fainted. They dropped their dinner plates, and their faces turned as white as bleached desert bones. Their knees knocked and their six-guns shook.

"Hey, there!" Bill said as he sidled up to their campfire, grinning. "Who's the boss around here?"

A nine-foot feller with ten pistols at his sides stepped forward and in a shaky voice said, "Stranger, I was. But from now on, it'll be you."

"Well, thanky, pardner," said Bill. "Get on with your dinner, boys. Don't let me interrupt."

Once Bill settled down with the Hell's Gate Gang, his true genius revealed itself. With his gang's help, he put together the biggest ranch in the Southwest. He used New Mexico as a corral and Arizona as a pasture. He invented tarantulas and scorpions as practical jokes. He also invented roping. Some say his rope was exactly as long as the equator; others argue it was two feet shorter.

Things were going fine for Bill until Texas began to suffer the worst drought in its history. It was so dry that all the rivers turned as powdery as biscuit flour. The parched grass was catching fire everywhere. For a while Bill and his gang managed to lasso water from the Rio Grande. When that river dried up, they lassoed water from the Gulf of Mexico.

No matter what he did, though, Bill couldn't get enough water to stay ahead of the drought. All his horses and cows were starting to dry up and blow away like balls of tumbleweed. It was horrible.

Just when the end seemed near, the sky turned a deep shade of purple. From the distant mountains came a terrible roar. The cattle began to stampede, and a huge black funnel of a cyclone appeared, heading straight for Bill's ranch.

The rest of the Hell's Gate Gang shouted, "Help!" and ran.

But Pecos Bill wasn't scared in the least. "Yahoo!" he hollered, and he swung his lariat and lassoed that cyclone around its neck.

Bill held on tight as he got sucked up into the middle of the swirling cloud. He grabbed the cyclone by the ears and pulled himself onto her back. Then he let out a whoop and headed that twister across Texas.

The mighty cyclone bucked, arched, and screamed like a wild bronco. But Pecos Bill just held on with his legs and used his strong hands to wring the rain out of her wind. He wrung out rain that flooded Texas, New Mexico, and Arizona, until finally he slid off the shriveled-up funnel and fell into California. The earth sank about two hundred feet below sea level in the spot where Bill landed, creating the area known today as Death Valley.[1]

"There. That little waterin' should hold things for a while," he said, brushing himself off.

After his cyclone ride, no horse was too wild for Pecos Bill. He soon found a young colt that was as tough as a tiger and as crazy as a streak of lightning. He named the colt <u>Widow</u> Maker and raised him on barbed wire and dynamite. Whenever the two rode together, they back flipped and somersaulted all over Texas, loving every minute of it.

One day when Bill and Widow Maker were bouncing around the Pecos River, they came across an awesome sight: a wild-looking, red-haired woman riding on the back of the biggest catfish Bill had ever seen. The woman looked like she was having a ball, screeching, "Ride 'em, cowgirl!" as the catfish whipped her around in the air.

"What's your name?" Bill shouted.

"Slue-foot Sue! What's it to you?" she said. Then she war-whooped away over the windy water.

Thereafter all Pecos Bill could think of was Slue-foot Sue. He spent more and more time away from the Hell's Gate Gang as he wandered the barren cattle lands, looking for her. When he finally found her lonely little cabin, he was so love-struck he <u>reverted</u> to some of his old coyote ways. He sat on his haunches in the moonlight and began a-howling and ah-hooing.

Well, the good news was that Sue had a bit of coyote in her too, so she completely understood Bill's language. She stuck her head out her window and ah-hooed back to him that she

"Ride 'em, cowgirl!"

loved him, too. Consequently Bill and Sue decided to get married.

On the day of the wedding Sue wore a beautiful white dress with a steel-spring bustle, and Bill appeared in an elegant buckskin suit.

But after a lovely ceremony, a terrible catastrophe occurred. Slue-foot Sue got it into her head that she just had to have a ride on Bill's wild bronco, Widow Maker.

"You can't do that, honey," Bill said. "He won't let any human toss a leg over him but me."

"Don't worry," said Sue. "You know I can ride anything on four legs, not to mention what flies or swims."

Bill tried his best to talk Sue out of it, but she wouldn't listen. She was dying to buck on the back of that bronco. Wearing her white wedding dress with the bustle, she jumped on Widow Maker and kicked him with her spurs.

Well, that bronco didn't need any thorns in his side to start bucking to beat the band. He bounded up in the air with such amazing force that suddenly Sue was flying high into the Texas sky. She flew over plains and mesas, over canyons, deserts, and prairies. She flew so high that she looped over the new moon and fell back to earth.

But when Sue landed on her steel-spring bustle, she rebounded right back into the heavens! As she bounced back and forth between heaven and earth, Bill whirled his lariat above his head, then lassoed her. But instead of bringing Sue back down to earth, he got yanked into the night sky alongside her!

---

1. **Death Valley:** a desert area of California and Nevada, site of the Western Hemisphere's lowest point.

Together Pecos Bill and Slue-foot Sue bounced off the earth and went flying to the moon. And at that point Bill must have gotten some sort of foothold in a moon crater—because neither he nor Sue returned to earth. Not ever.

Folks figure those two must have dug their boot heels into some moon cheese and raised a pack of wild coyotes just like themselves. Texans'll tell you that every time you hear thunder rolling over the desolate land near the Pecos River, it's just Bill's family having a good laugh upstairs. When you hear a strange ah-hooing in the dark night, don't be fooled— that's the sound of Bill howling *on* the moon instead of *at* it. And when lights flash across the midnight sky, you can bet it's Bill and Sue riding the backs of some white-hot shooting stars. ❖

Mary Pope Osborne
born 1949

". . . I've been afraid that some day an authority figure will knock on my door and say, '. . . Time to get . . . a real job.'"

A Dreamer When Mary Pope Osborne was four, her family was living in Austria. In her imagination, a nearby castle became the home of Cinderella or Sleeping Beauty. She dreamed of worlds that she would later write about.

From Student and Traveler . . . She studied drama, mythology, and religion at the University of North Carolina at Chapel Hill. After college, she traveled to Eastern European and Asian countries, camping and riding in an old van.

. . . To Author A few years after her marriage, she wrote her first book, *Run, Run as Fast as You Can.* "Finally," Osborne says, "I knew exactly what I wanted to be when I grew up." Since then, she has won many awards for her more than 25 books for children and young adults.

Interdisciplinary Projects

LITERATURE CONNECTION

Hold a Storytelling Contest Organize a contest around tales or legends of the Americas. Decide who will be judges, researchers, writers, and storytellers.

Step 1: Rules Decide on rules and guidelines for judging the storytelling and other elements of the contest. Write down the rules and create a sheet, or rubric, to score each entry.

Step 2: Story Selection Find existing stories to retell or create new ones that build on existing

tales. Keep in mind that your stories may revolve around both realistic and unrealistic characters. You will want to include realistic places as the setting for your stories.

Step 3: Contest Each storyteller should concentrate on telling his or her story effectively. Rehearse it, emphasizing important words. Use your voice and gestures to express and enhance the meaning of your story. Be enthusiastic, and look members in the eye.

SOCIAL STUDIES CONNECTION

Create an Oral Traditions Map Draw a map of the Western Hemisphere. Then look at each of the stories presented in "The Oral Tradition: Tales from the Americas." Identify the countries that

are represented in these stories, and locate them on your map. Add the story titles to the map in the areas where they originated.

HISTORY CONNECTION

Research a Legend Many urban legends and stories about ghosts and haunted places have their roots in historical events, especially ones involving conflict and violence. In the library or on the Internet, find out about the historical roots of a local legend or a supposedly haunted place. Or investigate one of the following:

The Battle of Gettysburg Gettysburg, Pennsylvania, the site of the fiercest battle of the

Civil War, is believed by some to be one of the most haunted places in America. Research the legends that have grown up around the Battle of Gettysburg.

"Remember the Alamo!" Many Mexicans died attacking the Alamo, and only a handful of the Texans inside survived. Find out the reasons for their conflict and who won. What legends exist about this famous battle in Texas history?

SCIENCE CONNECTION

Present a Panel Discussion on Health No one has found a way to live forever like Aunty Misery. But since 1900, the average life expectancy of Americans has increased from 47 to 76 years. Today there are many personal choices we can make to promote healthier, longer lives. Work with a group to gather information on healthful

living. For your research, use recently published books and magazines, the Internet, and interviews with health professionals, such as your school nurse. Choose representatives of each group to present a panel discussion or multimedia presentation for another class.

Across Cultures

Compare Characters Select two stories from "The Oral Tradition: Tales from the Americas" and identify the main character in each. Compare and contrast the characters' personal qualities, their reactions to their situations, and the motivations for their behaviors. Record both similarities and differences for the two characters you select.

Create a Language Phrase Book Find out more about Spanish, the original language of "The Souls in Purgatory." A good way to start would be to write down the translations or footnote definitions in the story. Use library resources, and, if possible, interview people who speak the language. On your own or with a few classmates, create a guide—complete with pronunciations and definitions—for a number of common words and phrases in Spanish. Teach some of the words and phrases to the class.

Adapt an Urban Legend "The Woman in the Snow" is an urban legend based on a real event—the bus boycott during the mid-1950s in Montgomery, Alabama. Choose an event that has recently made news in your town or on national television. Look for a story that contains a mystery that remains unsolved, like a plane crash or a sudden disappearance. Then, using "The Woman in the Snow" or "The Girl in the Lavender Dress" as a model, write an urban legend. Remember to include realistic and unrealistic characters. How do they resolve their dilemma?

Explore Ballads "John Henry" is a **ballad**, a type of narrative song that has been a popular form of storytelling for centuries. Ballads usually have regular stanzas, strong story lines, and refrains and other repetition. The main character is often a rebel, an outlaw, or an underdog. Research other traditional ballads and play them for the class, if possible. Discuss the structure of the music and lyrics. How closely do they follow the ballad form as described above?

Combining sound, pictures, and words to tell a story . . .

From Reading to Presenting Legendary characters are often heroic, from John Henry, the man who tested himself against the steam drill, to Pecos Bill, the greatest cowboy in the West. One way to bring a legendary character to life is with a **multimedia presentation,** which uses sound, visuals, and text to explore the character and his or her story. Multimedia presentations capture the attention of the audience and help the presenter convey his or her message.

For Your Portfolio

WRITING PROMPT Create a multimedia presentation based on a favorite folk tale, legend, or character.

Purpose: To inform
Audience: Classmates, family, friends

Basics in a Box

GUIDELINES AND STANDARDS | MULTIMEDIA PRESENTATION

Content

A successful multimedia presentation should

- capture the audience's attention with a strong opening
- use appealing visuals and props
- clearly, directly, and logically present information
- use a variety of media that is appropriate to the content
- end by summarizing the topic and the points made

Delivery

An effective presenter should

- have good posture and maintain eye contact with the audience
- vary pacing as well as the pitch, tone, and volume of voice
- use gestures and body language to get the point across
- use visual aids effectively to help the audience understand the topic

Analyzing a Multimedia Presentation

SPEAKING
See the Speaking and Listening Handbook, p. R104, for oral presentation tips.
OPPORTUNITY

<show brief video clip of Hercules movie>

Before Superman, there was Hercules. With his enormous strength and courage, Hercules was a great hero of ancient Greece.

<show first visual: illustration of baby with snake in fist>

Hercules' heroic qualities were obvious from birth. The goddess Hera, who was jealous of Hercules, sent two snakes into his nursery. Hercules simply grabbed both and strangled them.

<show second visual: map of ancient Greece >

Hera tried to destroy Hercules. She sent madness upon him, which led him to kill his wife and children. To punish himself, he went to the city of Tiryns to work for King Eurystheus, who assigned him 12 seemingly impossible tasks, the "12 labors."

<show third visual: chart of labors 1–4 with illustration of the Hydra>

In his first four labors, Hercules had to strangle a ferocious lion; capture the Hind of Ceryneia, a deer with horns of gold; capture a wild boar; and kill the Lernean Hydra, a water serpent with nine heads.

<show fourth visual: chart of labors 5–8; illustration of diverting river>

The most famous of his next four labors was cleaning the enormous Augean stables, which had not been cleaned for years. Hercules diverted two rivers so that they washed through the stables. He also captured a rampaging bull, drove off a flock of fierce birds, and rounded up a herd of man-eating horses.

<show fifth visual: chart of labors 9–12; illustration of Atlas holding earth>

Hercules' last four labors were the most challenging of all. He retrieved the belt of Hippolyte, Queen of the Amazons. He brought back the cattle guarded by the monster Geryon. He stole the golden apples from the Hesperides. Only Atlas, who supported the world on his shoulders, knew where to find these apples. Hercules held the world while Atlas helped him. Lastly, Hercules traveled to the underworld to get Cerberus, the three-headed guard dog.

<show sixth visual: photograph of a snowy mountain in the clouds>

After completing the 12 labors, he went on to do more great deeds. When he died, he was taken to Mount Olympus, where he and Hera reconciled. He married her daughter and they lived happily among the gods.

GUIDELINES IN ACTION

❶ Captures audience's attention with video clip and reference to modern-day hero; film clip provides a visual image of Hercules.

❷ The map shows the geographical setting.

❸ Discusses the 12 labors chronologically, highlighting one event in each group

❹ Uses various media—charts clarify information; illustrations provide images of monsters and heroic deeds.

❺ Conclusion reinforces the main idea of Hercules' strength and tells about his death.

IDEA Bank

1. Regional Focus
Investigate the folk tales and legends of a particular region of the country, such as the Appalachians or the West. Choose the one with the most appealing or unusual character.

2. Cultural Heroes
Pick a culture that interests you and research the legends and myths of that culture. Select a character or story from your research that you think would make a good subject for a multimedia presentation.

Have a question?

See the **Research and Technology Handbook**
CD-ROM, p. R115
Using Visuals, p. R120

Creating Your Multimedia Presentation

❶ Planning Your Presentation

To find a topic for your multimedia presentation, **list** legendary characters from stories in this unit and stories you've read outside class. **Brainstorm** names of folk heroes whose deeds have become part of American folklore. See the **Idea Bank** in the margin for more suggestions. After you have chosen your topic, follow the steps below.

Steps for Planning Your Multimedia Presentation

▶ 1. **Brainstorm details about your subject.** If you have chosen a character, write down his or her deeds, personality traits, and physical qualities. List other characters connected to the story as well as the setting. If you have chosen a legend or tale, outline the plot and list any unusual qualities of the story.

▶ 2. **Choose your focus.** What are the main ideas you want to communicate? What is the goal of your presentation?

▶ 3. **Think about your audience.** How much does it know about the character or tale that you've chosen? How much background will it need to understand your presentation?

▶ 4. **Organize your information.** What is the best order for presenting? Where should media elements be used?

▶ 5. **Decide which media to use in your presentation.** What types of resources are available to you? Which will help get your point across most effectively? Consider the following possibilities:
   - **Audiotapes and CDs** add sound effects such as music.
   - **Charts, posters, photos, slides, and graphs** allow you to visually represent information or ideas.
   - **Videos** provide sound and visual material.
   - **Computers** can create visual aids such as graphs, charts, drawings, and even slide shows.

❷ Developing Your Presentation

Once you have gathered the information you want to include in your multimedia presentation, you can begin organizing it and creating the script and the media parts.

Steps for Developing Your Multimedia Presentation

▶ 1. **Write your script.** Prepare what you are going to say. Indicate where you will include your media elements. If you need to explain or introduce certain audio or visual materials, write that information in your script.

▶ 2. **Create an attention-getting introduction and a strong conclusion.** Begin your presentation with a question, an anecdote, or a quotation that gets your audience interested in your topic. Use your conclusion to restate your main idea.

▶ 3. **Prepare your media elements.** Gather the materials and equipment for the media parts of your presentation. Make sure that the equipment works and that you know how to operate it. Adjust volume and make visuals large enough so that everyone in the audience can hear and see.

▶ 4. **Evaluate your media choices.** Be sure that you have used various media as effectively as possible. Lists, charts, and graphs make large amounts of information easy to grasp. Slides or video clips present strong visual images.

TECH Tool

Some graphics programs allow you to add animation or movement to the images in your presentation. Animated figures can illustrate what happens in a story. If you need help with finding or using a graphics program to create animation, see your school's technology adviser.

See **Language Network**

Design Elements That Communicate, p. 583

❸ Practicing and Presenting

Practice your presentation several times so that you become familiar with your script and media elements.

Ask Your Peer Reader

- What did you learn from my presentation?
- Which elements were most effective?
- What information was unclear?
- How were my media choices helpful? Which ones were distracting?

- **Project your voice to the back of the room.** Vary your pace, tone, and volume to emphasize important points and to keep your audience's attention.

- **Look up from your script frequently and make eye contact with members of your audience.** Use appropriate gestures and facial expressions that will maintain their interest and strengthen your points.

- **Work on smoothly incorporating your media elements.** Know how to operate all of the equipment, and be prepared to answer questions about each of your materials.

After rehearsing on your own several times, invite family and friends to view your presentation. Use their comments to help you modify your organization or clarify your meaning.

Need revising help?

Review the **Rubric,** p. 968

Consider **peer reviewer** comments

Check **Revision Guidelines,** p. R33

SPELLING
From Writing

 As you revise your work, look back at the words you misspelled and determine why you made the errors you did. For additional help, refer to the strategies and generalizations in the **Spelling Handbook** on page R28.

Publishing
IDEAS

- Adapt your presentation for younger students and visit other classrooms to present it.

- Videotape your presentation and your classmates' presentations. Keep the tapes in the library for other students to view.

Publishing Options
www.mcdougallittell.com

❹ Refining Your Presentation

TARGET SKILL ▶ **CHOOSING APPROPRIATE MEDIA** With a world full of sounds and images, how do you choose the best ones to use? You'll probably be able to think of many different media elements that are related to your script. Think carefully about what point you are trying to make, and then select the media element that best makes that point.

> *Show first visual: illustration of baby with snake in fist*
> ~~<play audio tape: sound of baby crying>~~
> Hercules' heroic qualities were obvious from birth. The
> goddess Hera, who was jealous of Hercules, sent two
> snakes into his nursery.

❺ Editing and Proofreading

TARGET SKILL ▶ **CONSISTENT FORM** Visuals can help you to present information in a clear, interesting way. Your audience will have a greater understanding of your presentation if all of your visuals are easy to read, consistent in form, and correct in capitalization.

> *H*
> Labors of hercules
> 1. Kill the Nemean Lion
> 2. Destroy~~ing~~ the Lernean Hydra
> 3. Capture the Hind of Ceryneia
> *H*
> 4. hunt the Erymanthean Boar

❻ Reflecting

FOR YOUR WORKING PORTFOLIO What did you learn about your subject by doing this multimedia presentation? What effect do you think the media elements had on your audience? What would you do differently next time? Attach your reflections to your presentation script. Save your script in your **Working Portfolio.**

Standardized Test Practice

Mixed Review

Him and I worked hard on our presentation for the town library. We
(1)
wanted to teach local children about elfs and other mythical creatures
(2)
in literature. While we give our presentation, the children smiled and
(3)
laughed often. We could see they liked our bright visuals and lively
music. These features really brought legendary storys and magical folk
(4)
heros to life. After the presentation, we agreed that the afternoon was
fun for both they and us. Can you come back tomorrow?" one child
(5)   (6)
asked. At that moment we felt very successful.

1. How is sentence 1 best written?
   A. He and me
   B. Him and me
   C. He and I
   D. Correct as is

2. What is the correct spelling in sentence 2?
   A. elves
   B. elfes
   C. elvs
   D. Correct as is

3. How is sentence 3 best written?
   A. While we have given our presentation,
   B. While we had given presentation,
   C. While we gave our presentation,
   D. Correct as is

4. How is sentence 4 best written?
   A. stories and magical folk heros
   B. stories and magical folk heroes
   C. storys and magical folk heroes
   D. Correct as is

5. Which are the correct pronouns in sentence 5?
   A. them and we
   B. they and we
   C. them and us
   D. Correct as is

6. How is sentence 6 best written?
   A. "Can you come back tomorrow? one child asked.
   B. "Can you come back tomorrow?" one child asked.
   C. Can you come back tomorrow? one child asked.
   D. Correct as is

The Oral Tradition: Tales from the Americas

The folklore in this unit is linked to the themes of the previous five units. Consider how you have analyzed these themes in Units One to Five. Has reading folklore in the oral tradition changed how you view the five themes? How? To explore these questions further, complete one or more of the options in each of the following sections.

Reflecting on Theme

OPTION 1

Looking into Cultures Get together with your classmates and discuss the cultures whose folklore you found especially interesting. Select two or three of the cultures and, for each one, jot down what you learned about it in this unit. Share your thoughts with the class in an oral report.

OPTION 2

Self-Assessment To what extent have this unit's selections changed how you understand the previous units' themes? For each theme, write a short paragraph explaining how your views of it have changed as a result of reading the folklore.

📁 Portfolio Building

- **Personal Choice** Look back through the records and evaluations of all the activities you completed in this unit. In which projects did you find your exploration of a culture or subject most interesting? Make a brief note that explains your reaction. Then add the note and the project evaluation to your portfolio.

REVIEWING YOUR PERSONAL WORD List

Vocabulary Review the new words you learned in this unit. If necessary, use a dictionary to check the meaning of each word.

Spelling Review your list of spelling words. If you're not sure of the correct spelling, use a dictionary or refer to the **Spelling Handbook** on page R28.

Setting GOALS

As you completed the reading and writing activities in this unit, you probably discovered folklore that especially interested you. What kinds of folklore—myths, folk tales, fables, and legends—would you like to read more of? Are there any cultures whose folklore you would like to explore further?

Introduction to Mythology

The warriors and heroes, gods and goddesses of world mythology appear and reappear in literature and films. Here are their origins—presented by scholars and storytellers from Bullfinch to San Souci. This collection offers an engaging introduction to the characters and stories of classical and world mythology. Maps, diagrams, and time lines add context. Part of the *NexText* series from McDougal Littell, the book comes with online activities at **www.nextext.com.**

Other Collections

Cuentos: Tales from the Hispanic Southwest

SELECTED BY JOSE GRIEGO Y MAESTAS

These Mexican-American tales are translated into English by Rudolfo Anaya. (*Links to* **The Souls in Purgatory**)

Pushing Up the Sky and Other Native American Plays for Children

BY JOSEPH BRUCHAC

This illustrated collection of plays comes from the heritage of North America's native peoples. (*Links to* **Racing the Great Bear**)

Tall Tales from Texas Cow Camps

BY MODY COGGIN BOATRIGHT

This classic version of Texas tales features some of Pecos Bill's larger-than-life buddies. (*Links to* **Pecos Bill**)

Apples from Heaven: Multiculture Folk Tales About Stories and Storytellers

BY NAOMI BALTUCK

From cultures all over the world—including China, Japan, India, and Iraq—these folk tales focus on the art of storytelling.

Informative Nonfiction

The Iroquois

BY CRAIG A. DOHERTY

Doherty offers an overview of the history, religion, society, and political order of the Iroquois, then and now.

(*Links to* **Racing the Great Bear**)

Arctic Memories

BY NORMEE EKOOMIAK

An Inuit artist re-creates, in his personal story, a way of life that has almost disappeared.

(*Links to* **Otoonah**)

The Puerto Ricans

BY JEROME J. ALIOTTA

Aliotta details the history, culture, and religion of the Puerto Rican people. (*Links to* **Aunty Misery**)

The Life and Words of Martin Luther King, Jr.

BY IRA PECK

Peck's book records the life and thought of this famous civil-rights leader.

(*Links to* **The Woman in the Snow**)

Other Media

Legends of the Americas

This CD-ROM illustrates legends of the Maya, Aztecs, and Inca.

Troll Associates (CD-ROM)

Keepers of the Animals: Native American Stories

BY JOSEPH BRUCHAC

Twenty-four stories show Native Americans' respect for the relationship between humans and animals.

Fulcrum Publishing (AUDIOCASSETTE)

The Language of Literature
Student Resource Bank

Reading for Different Purposes

Having a clear purpose can help you better remember and understand what you read. You may be reading for relaxation and pleasure. Perhaps you need information so you can pass a test. Maybe you need to follow directions to program your VCR or to fill out a form. Perhaps you need to analyze an argument to make sure it makes sense. You will need specific reading strategies for every type of reading you do. This Reading Handbook will help you become a better reader of all kinds of materials.

Reading Literature

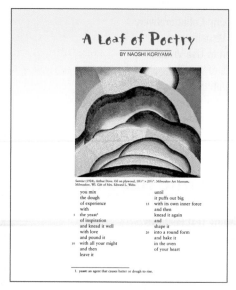

Forms: stories, plays, poems, memoirs, biographies, some nonfiction

Purpose for reading: for pleasure, for increased understanding

Strategies for Reading

- **Predict**
- **Visualize**
- **Connect**
- **Question**
- **Clarify**
- **Evaluate**

See page S3 for details about each strategy.

Reading for Information

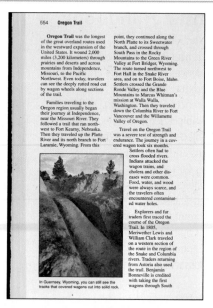

Forms: newspapers, magazines, reference works, on-line information, textbooks

Purpose for reading: to be informed

Strategies for Reading

- **Look for text organizers such as titles, subheads, graphics, and other devices.**
- **Notice the organization of the text.**
- **Look for connections to something you already know.**
- **Read, reread, and answer questions to increase your understanding.**

See pages R4–R10 for help with these strategies.

Critical Reading

<u>Summary of Proposal</u>

I propose that the city put up a stoplight at Park and Oak to help regulate traffic and make our streets safer.

<u>Need</u>

The corner of Park Avenue and Oak Street is one of the most dangerous places in town. In the past six months, two pedestrians and a cyclist have been hit by cars at that intersection.

Forms: newspaper editorials, advertisements, political ads, letters, opinion statements

Purpose for reading: to be informed, to make a decision

Strategies for Reading

- **Find the main ideas.**
- **Evaluate the supporting details.**
- **Determine the author's purpose.**
- **Decide how well the author achieved that purpose.**

See pages R11–R14 for detailed examples.

Functional Reading

LIMITED WARRANTY `Color TV`

West Electronics Inc. ("West") warrants this Product (including any accessories) against defects in material or workmanship, subject to any conditions set forth as follows:

A. LABOR: For a period of 90 days from the date of purchase, if this Product is determined to be defective, West will repair or replace the Product, at its option, at no charge, or pay the labor charges to any West authorized service facility. After the Warranty Period, you must pay for all labor charges.

B. PARTS: In addition, West will supply, at no charge, new or rebuilt replacements in exchange for defective parts for a period of one (1) year (color picture tube-two 2 years). After 90 days from the date of purchase, labor for removal and installation is available from West authorized service facilities or a West Service Center at your expense.

C. ACCESSORIES: Parts and labor for all accessories are for one (1) year.

This warranty does not cover cosmetic damage or damage due to acts of God, accident, misuse, abuse, negligence, commercial use, or modification of, or to any part of the Product, including the antenna.

Proof of purchase in the form of a bill of sale or receipted invoice which is evidence that the unit is within the Warranty period must be presented to obtain warranty service.

To locate the servicer or dealer nearest you, call

West Service Center
1-(800)-111-1111
or write to
West Service Center
1234 Main St.
Westtown, CA 90000

Forms: instruction manuals, applications, schedules, product information, technical directions, and others

Purpose for reading: to make decisions and solve problems

Strategies for Reading

- **Skim the whole piece.**
- **Read the information in the order presented.**
- **Look carefully at any drawings or pictures.**
- **Reread when the meaning is unclear.**

See pages R15–R19 for examples.

Methods of Reading

When you read something for the first time, review material for a test, or search for specific information, you use different methods of reading. The following techniques are useful with all kinds of reading materials.

Skimming When you run your eyes quickly over a text, looking at headings, graphic features, and highlighted words, you are skimming. Skimming is useful in previewing textbook material that you must read for an assignment.

Scanning To find a specific piece of information in a text, such as the date of a battle, use scanning. Place a card under the first line of a page and move it down slowly. Look for key words and phrases.

In-Depth Reading In-depth reading involves asking questions, taking notes, looking for main ideas, and drawing conclusions as you read slowly and carefully. Use this type of reading for literary works and textbooks.

Reading for Information

When you read informational materials such as textbooks, magazines, newspapers, and online text, you need to use specific strategies. It is important to study text organizers, such as headings and special type, that tell you what the main ideas, facts, and terms are on each page. It is also important to recognize patterns of organization in the text and to map them in a graphic organizer. Using these strategies will help you read and understand any kind of informational text.

Text Organizers

Writers use special features such as headings, large or dark type, pictures, or drawings to show you the most important information on the page. You can use these special features to help you understand and remember what you read.

Strategies for Reading

A First, look at the **title** and any **subheads**. These will tell you the main idea of the lesson.

B Many textbooks have one or more **objectives** or **key terms** at the beginning of each lesson. Keep these in mind as you read. This will help you identify the most important details.

C Watch for **pulled-out text**— quotations or other materials that are placed in a box or in different type. These often include especially surprising, important, or memorable information.

---

3 # Ratifying the Constitution **A**

TERMS & NAMES
federalism
Federalists
Antifederalists
The Federalist papers
George Mason
Bill of Rights

MAIN IDEA	WHY IT MATTERS NOW
B Americans across the nation debated whether the Constitution would produce the best government.	American liberties today are protected by the U.S. Constitution, including the Bill of Rights.

ONE AMERICAN'S STORY

For a week in early January 1788, a church in Hartford, Connecticut, was filled to capacity. Inside, 168 delegates were meeting to decide whether their state should ratify the U.S. Constitution. Samuel Huntington, Connecticut's governor, addressed the assembly.

C *A VOICE FROM THE PAST*

This is a new event in the history of mankind. Heretofore, most governments have been formed by tyrants and imposed on mankind by force. Never before did a people, in time of peace and tranquillity, meet together by their representatives and, with calm deliberation, frame for themselves a system of government.

Samuel Huntington, quoted in *Original Meanings*

The governor supported the new Constitution and wanted to see it ratified. Not everyone agreed with him. In this section, you will learn about the debates that led to the ratification of the Constitution.

Samuel Huntington

Federalists and Antifederalists

By the time the convention in Connecticut opened, Americans had already been debating the new Constitution for months. The document had been printed in newspapers and handed out in pamphlets across the United States. The framers of the Constitution knew that the document would cause controversy. They immediately began to campaign for ratification, or approval, of the Constitution.

The framers suspected that people might be afraid the Constitution would take too much power away from the states. To address this fear, the framers explained that the Constitution was based on federalism. **Federalism** is a system of government in which power is shared between the central (or federal) government and the states. Linking themselves to the idea of federalism, the people who supported the Constitution took the name **Federalists**.

People who opposed the Constitution were called **Antifederalists**. **D** They thought the Constitution took too much power away from the

D Don't forget about the **key terms.** These are often boldfaced or underlined where they first appear in the text. Be sure you understand what they mean.

E Look at the **visuals**—photographs, illustrations, charts, maps, and time lines— and read their **captions.** These will help you understand what you are about to read.

F Read any **questions** that are part of the text. They will help you focus your reading.

Vocabulary
aristocracy:
a group or class considered superior to others

states and did not guarantee rights for the people. Some were afraid that a strong president might be declared king. Others thought the Senate might turn into a powerful aristocracy. In either case, the liberties won at great cost during the Revolution might be lost.

Antifederalists published their views about the Constitution in newspapers and pamphlets. They used logical arguments to convince people to oppose the Constitution. But they also tried to stir people's emotions by charging that it would destroy American liberties. As one Antifederalist wrote, "After so recent a triumph over British despots [oppressive rulers], . . . it is truly astonishing that a set of men among ourselves should have had the effrontery [nerve] to attempt the destruction of our liberties."

The Federalist Papers

The Federalists did not sit still while the Antifederalists attacked the Constitution. They wrote essays to answer the Antifederalists' attacks. The best known of the Federalist essays are ***The Federalist* papers.** These essays first appeared as letters in New York newspapers. They were later published together in a book called *The Federalist.*

Three well-known politicians wrote *The Federalist* papers—James Madison, Alexander Hamilton, and John Jay, the secretary of foreign affairs for the Confederation Congress. Like the Antifederalists, the Federalists appealed to reason and emotion. In *The Federalist* papers, Hamilton described why people should support ratification.

Reading **History**
**A. Making
Inferences** What does Hamilton think will happen if the Constitution is not ratified?

A VOICE FROM THE PAST

Yes, my countrymen, . . . I am clearly of opinion it is in your interest to adopt it [the Constitution]. I am convinced that this is the safest course for your liberty, your dignity, and your happiness.
Alexander Hamilton, *The Federalist* "Number 1"

Federalists and Antifederalists

FEDERALISTS	ANTIFEDERALISTS
• Supported removing some powers from the states and giving more powers to the national government	• Wanted important political powers to remain with the states
• Favored dividing powers among different branches of government	• Wanted the legislative branch to have more power than the executive
• Proposed a single person to lead the executive branch	• Feared that a strong executive might become a king or tyrant
	• Believed a bill of rights needed to be added to the Constitution to protect people's rights

E

John Jay

George Mason

SKILLBUILDER Interpreting Charts
1. *Which group wanted a stronger central government?*
2. *If you had been alive in 1787, would you have been a Federalist or an Antifederalist?*
F

Confederation to Constitution **235**

More Examples

To examine the structural features of other kinds of informational materials, see the pages listed below.

For examples of **newspaper articles**, see pages 528 and 634.

For examples of **magazine articles**, see pages 44, 211, 283, and 733.

For examples of an **Internet article**, see pages 130 and 363.

Patterns of Organization

Reading any type of writing is easier if you understand how it is organized. A writer organizes ideas in a sequence, or structure, that helps the reader see how the ideas are related. Five important structures are the following:

- main idea and supporting details
- chronological order
- comparison and contrast
- cause and effect
- proposition and support

This page contains an overview of the five structures, which you will learn about in more detail on pages R7–R10. Each type has been drawn as a map or graphic organizer to help you see how the ideas are related.

Main Idea and Supporting Details

The main idea of a paragraph or a longer piece of writing is its most important point. Supporting details give more information about the main idea.

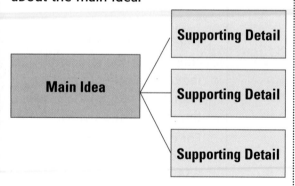

Chronological Order

Writing that is organized in chronological order presents events in the order in which they occur.

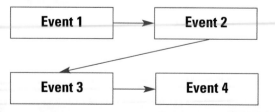

Comparison and Contrast

Comparison-and-contrast writing explains how two or more subjects are similar and how they are different.

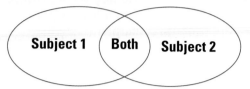

Cause and Effect

Cause-and-effect writing explains the relationship between events. The cause is the first event. The effect happens as a result of the cause. A cause may have more than one effect, and an effect may have more than one cause.

Single Cause with Multiple Effects

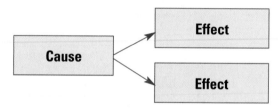

Multiple Causes with Single Effect

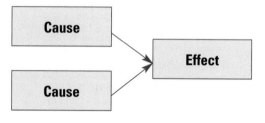

Proposition and Support

A proposition, or a proposal, is a plan offered for acceptance. The need for the plan, the plan itself, and a description of how the plan would work are the usual parts of a proposition.

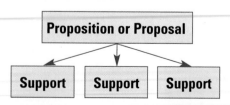

Main Idea and Supporting Details

The **main idea** of a paragraph is the most important point to remember from your reading. The **supporting details** in the paragraph provide additional information about the main idea. A main idea can be stated directly or it can be implied. An implied main idea is not actually stated in the paragraph. A main idea that is stated can appear anywhere in the paragraph. Often, it will be the first or the last sentence.

Strategies for Reading

- To find the **main idea**, ask, "What is the paragraph about?"
- To find **supporting details**, ask, "What specific information do I learn about the main idea?"

MODEL

Main Idea as the First Sentence

Main Idea | Supporting Details

Both the North and the South needed more soldiers as the Civil War continued year after year. As a result, each side passed draft laws. These laws required all men to serve in the military. The Confederate law went into effect in the spring of 1862. The Union draft began in 1863.

MODEL

Main Idea as the Last Sentence

Supporting Details | Main Idea

The South experienced severe food shortages during the Civil War. This was because both men and machines were serving in the army rather than working in the fields. Inflation was a problem in both the South and the North. Prices increased much faster than wages. The war caused economic hardship for almost everyone.

MODEL

Implied Main Idea

Implied main idea: Women made important contributions to the Civil War.

While the men were at war, women worked in the fields to produce food. They also took over office and factory jobs left by men serving in the army. Other women served as nurses and volunteers on the battlefields. Some brave women, like Harriet Tubman, even acted as spies.

PRACTICE AND APPLY

MODEL

Approximately 3 million men, nearly 10 percent of the population, served in the Civil War. More than one-fifth of these soldiers died. Almost that many more were wounded. Not only the soldiers suffered, though. The economy of the nation also was deeply affected. Some people did not have enough to eat. Prices everywhere got higher. The life of practically every citizen was disrupted by the conflict.

Read the model above and then do the following activities.

1. Identify the main idea of the paragraph.

2. List four details that support the main idea.

Chronological Order

Chronological, or time, order presents events or steps in the order that they happened. Historical events are usually presented in chronological order. The steps of a process may also be presented in time order.

Strategies for Reading

- Identify the **individual events or steps.** These will often be presented in separate paragraphs.

- Look for **words that signal order,** such as *first, afterward, then, before, finally,* and *next.*

- Look for **words and phrases that identify time,** such as *in a year; two hours earlier; on July 4, 1776;* and *later.*

MODEL

Time phrases

Events

On Wednesday morning at a quarter past five came the earthquake. A minute later the flames were leaping upward. In a dozen different quarters south of Market Street, in the working-class ghetto, and in the factories, fires started. There was no opposing the flames. There was no organization, no communication. . . .

By Wednesday afternoon, inside of twelve hours, half the heart of the city was gone. At that time I watched the vast conflagration from out on the bay. It was dead calm. Not a flicker of wind stirred. . . . Day and night this dead calm continued, and yet, near to the flames, the wind was often half a gale, so mighty was the vacuum.

Wednesday night saw the destruction of the very heart of the city. Dynamite was lavishly used, and many of San Francisco's proudest structures were crumbled by man himself into ruins, but there was no withstanding the onrush of the flames. . . .

At nine o'clock Wednesday evening I walked down through the very heart of the city. I walked through miles and miles of magnificent buildings and towering skyscrapers. Here was no fire. All was in perfect order. The police patrolled the streets. Every building had its watchman at the door. And yet it was doomed, all of it. There was no water. The dynamite was giving out. And at right angles two different conflagrations were sweeping down upon it.

At one o'clock in the morning I walked down through the same section. Everything still stood intact. There was no fire. And yet there was a change. A rain of ashes was falling. The watchmen at the doors were gone. The police had been withdrawn. There were no firemen, no fire-engines, no men fighting with dynamite. The district had been absolutely abandoned. . . . Half a dozen blocks away it was burning on both sides. The street was a wall of flame. And against this wall of flame, silhouetted sharply, were two United States cavalrymen sitting on their horses, calmly watching. That was all.

—Jack London, "The Story of an Eyewitness"

PRACTICE AND APPLY

After reading the model, do the following activities.

1. Create a time line on your paper. Begin with the earthquake that struck San Francisco on Wednesday, April 18, 1906, at 5:15 A.M. List the other events in the order that they happened.

2. List all the words or phrases in the model that signal time.

3. List the two subjects that are being compared and contrasted in the final two paragraphs.

Comparison and Contrast

Comparison-and-contrast writing explains how two different subjects are alike and different. This type of writing is usually organized by subject or by feature. In **subject organization,** the writer discusses subject 1, then discusses subject 2. In **feature organization,** the writer compares a feature of subject 1 with a feature of subject 2, then compares another feature of both, and so on.

Strategies for Reading

- Look for words and phrases that signal **comparison,** such as *like, similarly, both, also,* and *in the same way.*

- Look for words and phrases that signal **contrast,** such as *unlike, on the other hand, in contrast,* and *however.*

MODEL

Subjects

In 1788 the newly drafted Constitution of the United States was a subject of great debate. On one side were the Federalists, those who supported the Constitution. On the other side were the Antifederalists, who opposed the Constitution.

The Federalists believed in a system of government called federalism. In this type of government a central—or federal—government shares power with the individual states. The Federalists thought that the federal government should have more power than the states.

Contrast words

The Antifederalists, on the other hand, believed that the Constitution took too much power away from the states and the people. Unlike the Federalists, the Antifederalists supported keeping all the important political power with the states.

Comparison word

Both the Federalists and the Antifederalists agreed that the government should be made up of several branches. The Federalists believed that power should be divided equally among the executive, the judicial, and the legislative branches. Because of this system of checks and balances, the Federalists thought that a single person should head the executive branch.

The Antifederalists, in contrast, were afraid to give too much power to the executive branch. They thought that the legislative branch should be the most powerful arm of the government. They feared that if the executive branch became too strong, the president might become like a king or a tyrant.

The Federalists thought that the Constitution fully protected the rights of individual citizens. The Antifederalists disagreed. They argued that a separate bill of rights was needed to make sure that the people were protected from the power of a strong federal government.

The Constitution that was ratified by the states was a compromise between the Federalist and the Antifederalist positions. As the Federalists wanted, it gave more power to the federal government than to the states. It also divided the power of the federal government among its three branches. As the Antifederalists demanded, however, the Constitution included a bill of rights.

PRACTICE AND APPLY

Read the model and do the following activities.

1. In the model, some contrast words are pointed out to you. Find two more contrast words or phrases and write them on your paper.

2. Decide whether the model is organized by subject or by feature. Explain your answer.

3. Create a Venn diagram like the one on page R6. Then fill in the similarities and differences between the Federalist and Antifederalist positions.

Cause and Effect

Cause-and-effect writing explains the relationship between events. A **cause** is an event that brings about another event. An **effect** is something that happens as a result of the first event. Cause-and-effect writing is usually organized in one of three ways:

1. Starting with cause(s) and explaining effect(s)

2. Starting with effect(s) and explaining cause(s)

3. Describing a chain of causes and effects

Strategies for Reading

- To find the **effect or effects,** ask, "What happened?"

- To find the **cause or causes,** ask, "Why did it happen?"

- Look for **signal words and phrases** such as *because, as a result, for that reason, so, consequently,* and *since.*

MODEL

Effect

    Immigrants streamed into the United States during the mid-1800s. Most of them came from European countries, including Germany, Ireland, Denmark, Sweden, Norway, and Britain. There were basically two types of

Signal Word forces that **caused** them to leave their homelands: reasons they were pushed out and reasons they were pulled to the new land.

    Pushing them out were events in people's homelands that made living there more and more difficult. A huge growth in

Causes population, for example, **resulted in overcrowding and a shortage of food.** At the same time, small plots of land were being combined into large farms. **Consequently, farmers were forced off their land and could no longer make a living.** Religious persecution and

political unrest also were reasons for people to leave their homelands and look for a new and better life across the ocean.

    Another important reason was the Industrial Revolution. Factories began to produce goods more cheaply and quickly than independent tradespeople could. So these tradespeople were forced out of business.

    Immigrants also left their countries because such things as vast amounts of land, economic opportunity, and freedom drew them to the United States.

    Many immigrants left their homelands because of overcrowding and loss of their farms. The United States, on the other hand, kept expanding westward and adding more territory. For this reason, the immigrants thought they could obtain land and make a better life for their families in America.

    The Industrial Revolution opened up many factory jobs for skilled immigrants in the United States. As a consequence, tradesmen as well as farmers looked to this country as a land of economic opportunity. Finally, immigrants were drawn to the United States because it offered them the freedom to practice their religion in any way they chose.

PRACTICE AND APPLY

Read the model on this page and then do the following activities.

1. List six of the main causes of immigration to the United States in the mid-1800s.

2. Identify five words or phrases in the passage that signal causes and effects.

3. List the effects of the following events in Europe: a) population growth, b) religious persecution and political unrest, c) the Industrial Revolution.

Critical Reading: Persuasion

Persuasive writing attempts to convince readers to agree with the writer's point of view. Persuasive writing can take many forms. Advertisements, political posters, newspaper editorials, proposals, and reviews are all forms of persuasion. Proposals to convince you to support a change or a new idea are common forms of persuasion.

What Is a Proposal?

A proposal is a special type of persuasive writing that outlines a plan to meet a need or solve a problem. A proposal includes three parts: (1) a brief summary of the plan of action, (2) a statement of the need or problem and support explaining the need, and (3) a detailed discussion of the plan and how it will solve the problem.

The following strategies can help you read a proposal:

Strategies for Reading

- Identify **the need or problem** and **the plan of action** proposed to solve it.
- Evaluate the evidence—**facts, statistics, and opinions**—that the writer gives to support the proposal.
- Evaluate the **reasoning** behind the writer's statements.

MODEL

Summary of Proposal

[Proposed plan]   I propose that our school install video cameras in the halls, the lunchroom, and other public areas to monitor students' activities.

Need

[Problem]   The halls and public areas of our school are not well supervised because of a shortage of security staff. In the past month alone, three students have been hurt in fights on school property.

Proposed Solution

Installing video monitors in the halls and public areas of the school will create a safe environment for students at a reasonable cost.

[Support for the author's position]   There is good evidence that video monitoring works. Westview School has monitored its students for over a year. In that time there has not been one incident of fighting or damage to property.

[Opposing view]   People who are against video monitoring don't agree. They say that monitoring violates students' rights to privacy.

[Author's response]   I disagree. In my opinion, junior high students need to act like responsible adults. We need guidelines and monitoring to show us where the limits are and to help us learn to act responsibly on our own.

Video monitoring not only works, but installing the equipment can lower supervisory costs in the long run. Only eight cameras would be needed: in the two main hallways, the lunchroom, and the auditorium. The total cost would be around $16,000. I believe the money can be found in the general school budget.

[Restatement of author's position]   I say this to the school board, our principal, and our teachers: Install video cameras and give us a safe school where we can learn to be good citizens.

Evaluating Reasoning

To be convincing, a proposal or other persuasive statement must show sound reasoning. The conclusions that the author makes must follow clearly and logically from the information presented.

Four types of unsound reasoning to watch out for are **overgeneralization,** the **either-or fallacy,** the **cause-and-effect fallacy,** and **circular reasoning.**

Overgeneralization

An overgeneralization is a broad statement that says something is true for every case, with no exceptions. In fact, very few statements have no exceptions. Overgeneralizations often include the words *all, none, everyone, no one, any,* and *anyone.*

> **Overgeneralization:**
> **Every school official who cares about students supports video monitoring.**
>
> **Logical statement:**
> **Some school officials believe that video monitoring can help provide a safe environment for students to learn both academic and social skills.**

Either-Or Fallacy

The either-or fallacy states that there are only two possible ways to view a situation or only two options to choose from. In most situations, there are actually a number of views and options. Either-or fallacies often include the words *either . . . or.*

> **Either-or fallacy:**
> **Either video monitors are installed in the school, or students will be injured.**
>
> **Logical statement:**
> **A safety problem exists in the school and video monitoring will help solve it.**

Cause-and-Effect Fallacy

In the cause-and-effect fallacy, the writer makes the assumption that because one event follows another, the second event was caused by the first one. As you read, think carefully about the evidence that one event actually caused another.

> **Cause-and-effect fallacy:**
> **Westview School cut security staff, and two students fell down the stairs and were seriously injured.**
>
> **Logical statement:**
> **Two Westview students were injured because they were running down a slippery stairway that had just been mopped.**

Circular Reasoning

Circular reasoning is an attempt to support a statement by simply repeating it in other words. If a statement does not include any supporting facts and leaves you thinking "So?", it may be circular reasoning.

> **Circular reasoning:**
> **Using video cameras to monitor school hallways is good because it feels right.**
>
> **Logical statement:**
> **Monitoring school hallways with video cameras will help reduce fights and damage to property.**

Evaluating Evidence

In addition to evaluating the logic of an argument, you also must carefully examine the evidence presented to support statements. First, to accurately evaluate information, you must know the difference between **facts** and **opinions.** The statements of experts also provide good evidence. Be careful, though, of arguments that present expert opinions from only one side of an issue.

Here are some types of evidence to watch out for: **fact and opinion, stereotyping, bias, propaganda,** and **emotional appeals.**

Fact and Opinion

A fact is a statement that can be proved. An opinion is a statement of personal belief that cannot be proved. Make sure you identify when a statement is a fact and when it is an opinion.

> **Opinion statement:**
>
> **Video monitors in our school will save lives.**
>
> **Factual statement:**
>
> **Schools with video monitors have reported less running in hallways and fewer accidents within their facilities.**

Stereotyping

A stereotype is a generalization about a group of people that doesn't take individual differences into account.

> **Stereotyping:**
>
> **All school officials really care about are their jobs, not what is good for students.**
>
> **Balanced statement:**
>
> **Some school officials are not fully aware of how much a safe environment affects student learning.**

Bias

Bias is a preference for one side of an argument.

> **Bias:**
>
> **Video monitoring is a terrible crime.**
>
> **Unbiased statement:**
>
> **Some people think that video monitoring is an invasion of students' privacy.**

Propaganda

Propaganda is a form of communication that may use distorted, false, or misleading information.

> **Propaganda:**
>
> **Video monitoring will turn students into criminals.**
>
> **Balanced statement:**
>
> **Some people think that students may resent monitoring and find ways to do what they're not supposed to do without getting caught.**

Emotional Appeals

Emotional appeals are statements that create strong feelings rather than use facts and evidence to make a point. Be alert for statements that make you feel angry, sad, or even very happy. Because emotional appeals are directed at feelings rather than thoughts, they are also sometimes called **unreasonable persuasion**.

> **Emotional appeal:**
>
> **What idiot would not support video monitoring of students?**
>
> **Balanced statement:**
>
> **The evidence that video monitoring works and is reasonable in cost should convince people to support installing it in schools.**

Read the model on this page and then do the activities that follow.

MODEL

Summary of Proposal

I propose that the city put up a stoplight at Park and Oak to help regulate traffic and make our streets safer.

Need

The corner of Park Avenue and Oak Street is one of the most dangerous places in town. In the past six months, two pedestrians and a cyclist have been hit by cars at that intersection. Because there isn't a traffic signal at the intersection, drivers aren't always sure about who has the right of way. Because of the confusion, drivers sometimes don't pay enough attention to people in the crosswalks. Another reason this intersection is so dangerous is that it is on the edge of town. As cars are coming off the highway, they sometimes don't see the change in speed limit and go faster than the posted 25 miles per hour.

Proposed Solution

There is good evidence that a traffic light would help solve these problems. Before the city installed a traffic light at the corner of Main and Elm, a 12-year-old girl was killed there. Since the light went up two years ago, there hasn't been a single accident at that intersection. How could anyone in his or her right mind not realize that a traffic light is the solution to this problem?

The chief of police, Gerald McCourt, agrees: "I just don't understand why the city has to wait until people are seriously injured or killed to do something about the traffic situation. It's been shown time and again that when traffic lights go up, accidents go down. Putting up a traffic light is a low-cost solution. And a single light can preserve the most precious thing in the world—the life of a human being."

In conclusion, I urge the City Council to vote to install a traffic light at Park and Oak. The light would make the right of way clear. It would also force drivers to slow down and pay attention to what is going on around them. Either the city installs this traffic light or we'll all end up in the hospital.

1. List the evidence—facts, statistics, and expert opinions—that the writer uses to support her statements.
2. The sentence beginning "How could anyone in his or her right mind . . ." is an emotional appeal. Rewrite the sentence to make the appeal more reasonable.
3. Find another example of unsound reasoning. Rewrite it to make a logical statement.

Functional Reading

Often, to make decisions and solve problems in life, you will need to use consumer, public, or workplace documents. The applications, technical directions, schedules, product information, and public notices you will read require some special strategies. By becoming familiar with the features and elements of these documents, you will be better able to use them to make informed choices. Look at each example as you read the strategies.

Product Information: Warranty

Strategies for Reading

A Notice the **title** stating the type of warranty and the product for which it applies.

B Read the section on the **types of services** the manufacturer will carry out and the length of time they will be available.

C Read the **conditions** under which the company is not responsible for repair of the product.

D Check the **list of requirements** you must supply in order to obtain warranty service.

E Use the **contact information,** such as the manufacturer's phone number and address, to find out where the product can be repaired.

A **LIMITED WARRANTY** `Color TV`

B West Electronics Inc. ("West") warrants this Product (including any accessories) against defects in material or workmanship, subject to any conditions set forth as follows:

LABOR: For a period of 90 days from the date of purchase, if this Product is determined to be defective, West will repair or replace the Product, at its option, at no charge, or pay the labor charges to any West authorized service facility. After the Warranty Period, you must pay for all labor charges.

PARTS: In addition, West will supply, at no charge, new or rebuilt replacements in exchange for defective parts for a period of one (1) year (color picture tube—two [2] years). After 90 days from the date of purchase, labor for removal and installation is available from West authorized service facilities or a West Service Center at your expense.

ACCESSORIES: Parts and labor for all accessories are guaranteed for one (1) year.

C This warranty does not cover cosmetic damage or damage due to acts of God, accident, misuse, abuse, negligence, commercial use, or modification of or to any part of the Product, including the antenna.

D Proof of purchase in the form of a bill of sale or receipted invoice, which is evidence that the unit is within the Warranty period, must be presented to obtain warranty service.

To locate the servicer or dealer nearest you, call

West Service Center
 E 1-(800)-111-1111
or write to
West Service Center
1234 Main St.
Westtown, CA 90000

PRACTICE AND APPLY

Reread the warranty and explain the following:

1. For how many days after the purchase is labor free?

2. What conditions are not covered by the warranty?

3. How long does the warranty cover accessories?

4. What do you need to provide to prove that you bought the product within the warranty period?

Technical Directions

Strategies for Reading

A Notice **headings** or **rules** that separate one section from another.

B Read the **directions** all the way through at least once.

C Look for **numbers** or **letters** that give the steps in sequence.

D Watch for **warnings, notes,** or other **page references** with more information.

PRACTICE AND APPLY

Reread the microwave instructions and explain how to solve the following problems.

1. The clock needs to be reset after a power outage.
2. The clock was incorrectly set at 14:30.
3. The power level needs to be set for defrosting.
4. A program needs to be canceled while the food in the microwave is cooking.

A Microwave Instructions

A Before Operating

1 Plug the power cord into a three-pronged electrical outlet.

C 2 Display panel will light up and flash 88:88.
Touch Stop/Clear pad.

3 Set the clock.
Touch Stop/Clear pad when the oven is first plugged in, or after the electrical power has been interrupted.

Setting the Clock

Procedure

1 Touch Clock pad.

2 Enter time of day. For example, if it is 10:30, touch the number pads 1030 and "10:30" will appear.

3 Press the Clock pad again to set the time.

D **Note** You can select any time of the day from 1:00–12:59. To reset Clock, repeat steps 1 through 3 above. If incorrect time (for example, 8:61 or 13:00, etc.) is entered, "EE" will appear on display. Touch Stop/Clear pad and program correctly.

Canceling a Program

• To reset, or cancel, a cooking program as it is being entered, touch Stop/Clear pad once.

• To stop the oven while it is operating, touch Stop/Clear pad once. Do not open the door without pressing Stop/Clear pad.

• An entire cooking program (one stage or multiple stages) can be canceled after the oven has started cooking. This can be done by touching Stop/Clear pad twice.

Note See page 10 to create your own cooking programs.

Power Levels

Most foods can be cooked at full power (P-HI). However, for best results, some foods require a lower cooking power. Some foods such as tender cuts of meat can be cooked only with a lower power. Before setting any power level, the Power Level pad must be touched, followed by desired number. See chart.

1	2	3
4	5	6
7	8	9
POWER LEVEL	0	TIMER CLOCK
STOP CLEAR		START

POWER	Touch Power Level pad, then	Display
100%	Touch Power Level pad once more.	P-HI
90%	Touch number pad 9.	P-90
80%	Touch number pad 8.	P-80
70%	Touch number pad 7.	P-70
60%	Touch number pad 6.	P-60
50%	Touch number pad 5.	P-50
40%	Touch number pad 4.	P-40
30%	Touch number pad 3.	P-30
20%	Touch number pad 2.	P-20
10%	Touch number pad 1.	P-10

Note Choose P-30 for thawing or defrosting foods.

For information about writing your own technical document, turn to page R56 in the Writing Handbook.

Workplace Document

Strategies for Reading

A Read the **letterhead** to find out the name of the company sending the letter.

B Notice the **address** and **salutation** to find out the receiver's name.

C Check the **first paragraph** to find out the overall purpose of the letter.

D Look for **details** in the **body** of the letter that will explain what the letter writer wants you to do.

E Notice who **signed** the letter, so you know how to address your reply.

PRACTICE AND APPLY

Reread the letter and answer the questions.

1. Who is this letter from?
2. What is the purpose of the letter?
3. What does the letter tell the yearbook staff to do?

A **McDougal Littell**

A HOUGHTON MIFFLIN COMPANY

P.O Box 1667
Evanston, IL 60201-1667

1560 Sherman Avenue
Evanston, IL 60201-3600
phone 847.869.2300

October 10, 2002

Crane Middle School
The Key Yearbook
5123 Elm Street
B Spring Green, OH 44004

Dear Key Yearbook Staff:

C Thank you for your letter requesting permission to use a photograph from one of our textbooks in the next edition of your school yearbook. We appreciate your request.

D We do not own the rights to the photograph you requested. Please contact the copyright holder for reprint permission. You may send your letter to Carmen Watts Studio, 456 Leonard Dr., Chicago, IL 60620.

We wish you success with your request and with the new edition of your yearbook.

Sincerely,

John Simpson

E John Simpson
Permissions Department

Public Notice

Strategies for Reading

A Read the **title,** which often states the purpose of the notice.

B Read the **introduction,** if there is one, to find out the focus of the notice and whom it should concern.

C Read the **body** of the notice for instructions, announcements, and general information.

D Check the **source** of the notice to find contact information.

E Look for **special features** that may provide additional or related information.

PRACTICE AND APPLY

Reread the notice and explain the following.

1. Whom this notice is for
2. What the notice asks readers to do
3. What will happen to people who do not follow the library's rules for Internet use
4. How the notice defines "netiquette"

L-Net

Location: http://www.southblaine.gov/library/webrules.html

South Blaine Public Library

3424 North Roosevelt • South Blaine, CA 90114 • Main number (818) 555-2837

E Home
Catalog
Search Our Site
Search Internet
Electronic Resources
Library Hours
Bookmobile Schedule
E Versión en Español

A Rules for Internet Use

Introduction
The library has four Internet-enabled computers available to all members of the **B** community. All users of the library's computers MUST follow these rules or face the loss of their Internet privileges.

1. Safety The Internet is a public place, but you will have even less information about **C** the people you "meet" there than you would if you met them on a city street. When you are surfing the Internet, you must follow these rules.
- Never give out your street address, telephone number, or other personal information to someone you do not know.
- Never send a picture of yourself to someone you do not know.
- If you are under 18, check with a parent or teacher before agreeing to a face-to-face meeting with someone.
- Do not reveal your password to anyone.

2. "Netiquette" Netiquette means Net etiquette, or manners on the Internet.
- Do not log on to the Internet under someone else's account and pretend to be that person.
- Do not snoop in other people's on-line files.
- Limit your on-line time to 20 minutes during busy periods. A signup sheet is available from the librarian.
- Do not send "flames" (rude or hateful messages) to individuals or bulletin boards.
- Do not send "spam"—advertisements, chain letters, or pointless messages that go to large groups of people.

D This page is maintained by Angela Zepeda. Contact her at **webmaster@southblaine.library.gov** for more information.

Train Schedule

Strategies for Reading

A Scan the **title** to learn what the schedule covers.

B Study **row labels,** such as station names, to determine the category of information in each row.

C Look at **column headings,** which are train numbers in this schedule, to determine the category of information in each column.

D Look down **columns** and **rows** to find specific information.

E Notice any **graphics or symbols** that help you interpret the schedule.

A Kenwood to Turner City—Monday Through Friday

STATIONS	**C** 300	302	304	306	308	310	312	314	316	318	320	322
	A.M.	A.M.	A.M.	A.M.	A.M.	A.M.	A.M.	A.M.	A.M.	A.M.	A.M.	A.M.
B Kenwood LV:	—	—	—	5:55	—	6:17	—	—	6:53	—	—	7:15
North Springs	—	—	—	6:03	—	6:25	—	—	7:02	—	—	7:23
Hollow Lake	—	—	—	6:07	—	6:30	—	7:09	7:06	—	—	7:28
Grant St.	4:58	5:28	5:54	6:17	—	6:39	—	7:12	7:15	7:20	—	7:37
Central St. **D**	5:01	5:31	5:58	6:19	—	6:43	—	7:16	↓	7:24	—	7:42
Main St.	5:05	—	6:02	—	—	6:46	—	—		7:27	—	—
Ft. Peck	5:10	5:37	6:06	6:26	—	6:50	—	7:23	7:24	7:32	—	7:49
River Valley	5:13	5:40	6:10	6:30	—	6:54	—	↓	—	7:36	—	7:54
Columbus St.	5:16	5:44	6:14	6:35	—	6:59	—		7:32	7:40	—	7:59
Allen Square	5:19	5:47	6:17	6:38	—	7:02	—	7:31	7:36	7:43	—	—
River Falls	5:22	5:50	6:20	6:41	—	7:05	—	7:35	—	7:46	7:53	8:05
Hudson City	5:25	5:53	6:23	6:45	—	7:09	—	↓	7:41		7:57	
Santa Ana	—	—	—	—	—	—	—	↓	—	↓	—	
Lake Pawnee	5:27	5:55	6:25	6:48	—	7:12	—	7:39	7:43		7:59	
Erie Falls	5:30	5:58	6:28	6:51	—	7:15	—	7:42	—	7:52	8:01	
Turner City AR:	5:33	6:01	6:31	6:54	—	7:18	—		7:48	—	8:06	↓

E

PRACTICE AND APPLY

Reread the schedule and answer the questions.

1. Where do the trains on this schedule go?
2. Which days does this schedule cover?
3. List two stations that train 306 skips.
4. If you board train 316 at Grant St., what will be its next stop?
5. If you missed the 6:26 at Fort Peck, what time is the next train you could take?

FUNCTIONAL READING REVIEW:
COMPARE AND CONTRAST

1. Compare the train schedule and the public notice. What features do they share? How are they different?
2. Compare the warranty on page R15 and the technical directions on page R16. Both of these types of documents are often included with a product. How are these documents different?

Vocabulary Handbook

❶ Context Clues

One way to figure out the meaning of a word you don't know is by using context clues. The context of a word is made up of the punctuation marks, words, sentences, and paragraphs that surround it.

1.1 *General Context* Sometimes you need to infer the meaning of an unfamiliar word by reading all the information in the sentence or paragraph.

> Kevin set out the broom, a dustpan, dusting rag, vacuum cleaner, and three trash bags before beginning the **monumental** task of cleaning his room.

1.2 *Definition Clue* Often a difficult word will be followed by a definition of its meaning. Commas, dashes, or other punctuation marks can signal a definition.

> Sometimes the explorers encountered **leads** – open channels of water – and were forced to wait until the ice formed before going on.

1.3 *Restatement Clues* Sometimes a writer restates a word or term in easier language. Commas, dashes, or other punctuation can signal restatement clues as well as expressions such as *that is, in other words,* and *or.*

> The boy put together a **hand-collated** set of trading cards; in other words, he put together a set of trading cards by hand.

1.4 *Example Clues* Sometimes writers suggest the meanings of words with one or two examples.

> The cabin had several **annoyances**, including a leak in the roof, mildew in the shower, and a family of mice.

1.5 *Comparison Clues* Sometimes a word's meaning is suggested by a comparison to something similar. *Like* or *as* are words that signal comparison clues.

> The twins **barreled** through the living room like a tornado.

1.6 *Contrast Clues* Sometimes writers point out differences between things or ideas. Contrast clues are signaled by words like *although, but, however, unlike,* and *in contrast to.*

> The student was usually **bold,** but he became **hesitant** when he had to present a report to the class.

1.7 *Idiom and Slang* An idiom is an expression whose overall meaning is different from the meanings of the individual words. Slang is informal language containing made-up words and ordinary words used to mean something different from their meaning in formal English. Use context clues to figure out the meaning of idioms and slang.

> The mosquitoes **drove us crazy** on our hike through the woods. (idiom)

> That's a really **cool** backpack that you are wearing. (slang)

TIP Be sure to provide appropriate context for words when you write. One way to verify a word's meaning is to use one of the context-clue strategies in your sentence. For example, use restatement or definition clues in a sentence where understanding a word's precise meaning is important.

For more about context clues, see page 301; idioms and slang, see page 83.

② Word Parts

If you know roots, base words, and affixes, you can figure out the meanings of many new words.

2.1 *Base Words* A base word is a complete word that can stand alone. Other words or word parts can be added to base words to form new words.

2.2 *Roots* Many English words contain roots that come from older languages, such as Latin, Greek, or Old English. A root is a word part that conveys the core meaning of a word. Knowing the meaning of a word's root can help you determine the word's meaning.

root	meanings	example
alt	high	altitude
vert	to turn	divert
grad	step, degree	graduate

2.3 *Prefixes* A prefix is a word part that appears at the beginning of a root or base word to form a new word. A prefix usually changes the meaning of a root or a base word.

prefix	meanings	example
ex-	out, from	export
in-	in, into, not	incite
pre-	before	preface
pro-	forward, favoring	propose
re-	again, back	rebound
un-	not, opposite	unhappy

2.4 *Suffixes* A suffix is a word part that appears at the end of a root or base word to form a new word. Some suffixes do not change word meaning.

These suffixes are

- added to nouns to change the number of persons
- added to verbs to change the tense
- added to adjectives to change the degree of comparison
- added to adverbs to show how

suffix	meanings	example
-s, -es	to change the number of a noun	snack + -s, snacks
-ed, -ing	to change verb tense	walk + -ed, walked walk + -ing, walking
-er, -est	to change the degree of comparison in modifiers	wild + -er, wilder wild + -est, wildest

Other suffixes are added to a root or base word to change the word's meaning. These suffixes can also be used to change the word's part of speech.

suffix	meanings	example
noun-*age*	action or process	pilgrim + -age, pilgrimage
adjective-*able*	ability	remark + -able, remarkable
verb-*ize*	to make	public + -ize, publicize

To find the meaning of an unfamiliar word, divide the word into parts. Think about the meaning of the prefix, the suffix, and the root or base word. Use what you know to figure out the meaning of the word. Then check to see if the word makes sense in context.

For more about prefixes and suffixes, see page 394.

③ Word Origins

3.1 *Development of the English Language*

During the past 2,000 years or so, English has developed from a language spoken by a few Germanic tribes into a language that is more widely spoken and written than any other in the world. Some experts, in fact, call today's English the first truly global language. Its most valuable characteristic is its ability to change and grow, adopting new words as the need arises. The history of the English language can be divided into three main periods.

Old English

About the year A.D. 449, Germanic people who lived on the European continent along the North Sea began a series of invasions into Britain. At that time, Britain was inhabited by the Celts, whose native language was Gaelic. Over a period of years, the raiders conquered and settled in Britain. The conquerors, known today as the Anglo-Saxons, prospered in Britain. In time, Britain became "Engla land," and the Anglo-Saxon languages evolved into "Englisc," or what modern scholars call Old English.

Old English was very different from the English we speak today. It was harsher in sound, had no silent letters, and was written phonetically. Few examples of Old English remain in our current English vocabulary. Those that do exist, however, are common words for people, places, things, and actions.

man *(mann)*	wife *(wif)*	child *(cild)*
house *(hus)*	meat *(mete)*	drink *(drincan)*
sleep *(slæpan)*	live *(libban)*	fight *(feohtan)*

In the sixth and seventh centuries, missionaries from Rome and other Christian cities arrived in England, bringing with them their knowledge of religion and ancient languages. Among the most influential figures was St. Augustine, who helped convert thousands of Anglo-Saxons, including a king, to Christianity. As the Anglo-Saxons accepted this faith, they also accepted words from Latin and Greek.

Latin	Greek
candle	alphabet
cup	angel
priest	box
noon	demon
scripture	school

During the 790s, Viking invaders from Denmark and Norway settled in northeast England. As a result, Scandinavian words became part of Old English.

sky	knife	are
steak	leg	birth
they	skin	seat
window	them	their

Middle English

The Norman Conquest brought great changes to England and its language. In 1066, England was defeated by the Normans, a people from an area in France. Their leader, William the Conqueror, staged a successful invasion of England and became the nation's new monarch. With William on the throne of England, Norman French became the language of the English court, government business, nobility, and scholars. Eventually, French words were adopted in everyday vocabulary as well.

The language that evolved is called Middle English. Middle English was not as harsh-sounding as Old English and borrowed many words and grammatical conventions from Norman French.

attorney	joint	mallet
baron	jolly	marriage
chivalry	laundry	merchandise
gown	lodge	petty

Norman French itself borrowed thousands of words from Latin and Greek as well as from ancient Indian and Semitic languages. Consequently, Middle English also contained many of these foreign terms.

Latin	Greek	Indian	Semitic
language	circle	ginger	camel
library	hour	jungle	cinnamon
money	lantern	orange	coffee
serpent	leopard	sugar	lion
square	magnet	pepper	syrup

Modern English By the late 15th century, Middle English began to develop into Modern English. The various pronunciations, word forms, and spellings common to Middle English were becoming more uniform. One invention that aided this process was the printing press. Introduced to London in around 1476, the printing press allowed printers to standardize the spellings of common English words. As a result, readers and writers of English became accustomed to following "rules" of spelling and grammar.

During this period, the English vocabulary also continued to grow as new ideas and discoveries demanded new words. As the English began to colonize and trade with other areas of the world, they borrowed foreign words. In time, the English vocabulary grew to include words from diverse languages, such as French, Dutch, Spanish, Italian, Portuguese, and Chinese. Many of these words stayed the way they were in their original languages.

French	Dutch	Spanish	Italian
ballet	boss	canyon	diva
beret	caboose	rodeo	carnival
mirage	dock	taco	spaghetti
vague	skate	tornado	studio

Portuguese	Chinese	Japanese	Native American
cashew	chow	kamikaze	caribou
mango	ginseng	karaoke	moccasin
jaguar	kung fu	sushi	papoose
yam	kowtow	tsunami	tomahawk

Today, the English language is still changing and absorbing new words. It is considered the international language of science and technology. It is also widely used in business and politics.

3.2 Dictionary as a Source of Word Origins When you study a word's history and origin, you find out when, where, and how the word came to be. A complete dictionary entry includes each word's history.

tan•gi•ble (tăn′jə-bəl) *adj.* **1a.** Discernible by the touch; palpable. **b.** Possible to touch. **c.** Possible to be treated as fact; real or concrete. **2.** Possible to understand or realize. **3.** *Law* That can be valued monetarily. [Late Latin *tangibilis*, from Latin *tangere*, to touch.]

3.3 Word Families Words that have the same root make up a word family and have related meanings. The charts below show some common Greek and Latin roots. Notice how the meanings of the example words are related to the meanings of their roots.

Latin Root: *circum,* around or about

English: **circumference** the boundary line of a circle

circumnavigation the act of moving completely around

circumstance a condition or fact surrounding an event

Greek Root: *mon,* single or alone

English: **monopoly** exclusive control by one group

monologue a speech delivered by one person

monotonous sounded or spoken in a single, unvarying tone

TIP Once you recognize a root in one English word, you will notice the same root in other words. Because all these words developed from the same root, they share a core meaning.

For more about researching word origins, see page 783.

❹ Synonyms and Antonyms

When you read, pay attention to the precise words a writer uses.

4.1 *Synonyms* A synonym is a word that has the same or almost the same meaning as another word. Read each set of synonyms listed below.

occasionally/sometimes   parcel/package

pledge/vow   satisfy/please

rob/steal   schedule/agenda

You can find synonyms in a thesaurus or dictionary. In a dictionary, synonyms are often given as part of the definition of a word. Although synonyms have similar meanings, the words do not necessarily mean exactly the same thing.

4.2 *Antonyms* An antonym is a word with a meaning opposite that of another word. Read each set of antonyms listed below.

accurate/incorrect   similar/different

reveal/conceal   rigid/flexible

fresh/stale   unusual/ordinary

Sometimes an antonym is formed by adding the negative prefix *anti-, in-,* or *un-* to a word, as in the chart below.

word	prefix	antonym
climax	*anti-*	anticlimax
kind	*un-*	unkind
capable	*in-*	incapable

TIP Dictionaries of synonyms and antonyms, as well as some thesauri, can help you find antonyms.

For more about synonyms and antonyms, see page 604.

5 Connotative and Denotative Meaning

Good writers choose just the right word to communicate specific meaning.

5.1 Denotative Meaning A word's dictionary meaning is called its denotation. For example, the denotative meaning of the word *thin* is "having little flesh; spare; lean."

5.2 Connotative Meaning The images or feelings you connect to a word give it finer shades of meaning, called connotation. Connotative meaning stretches beyond a word's most basic dictionary definition. Writers use connotations of words to communicate positive or negative feelings. Some examples are listed below.

Positive Connotations	Negative Connotations
thin	scrawny
careful	cowardly
fast	hasty
thrifty	cheap
young	immature

For more information about denotative and connotative meanings, see page 669.

6 Homonyms, Homophones, and Words with Multiple Meanings

Homonyms, multiple-meaning words, and homophones can be confusing to readers, and can plague writers.

6.1 Homonyms Words that have the same spelling and sound but different origins and meanings are called homonyms.

> The boy had to **stoop** to find his ball under the **stoop.**

Stoop can mean "a small porch," but an identically spelled word means "to bend down." Because the words have different origins, each word has its own dictionary entry.

6.2 Words with Multiple Meanings Multiple-meaning words are ones that over time have acquired additional meanings based on the original meaning.

> Thinking of the horror movie made my skin **creep**.

> I saw my little brother **creep** around the corner.

These two uses of *creep* have different meanings, but both of them have developed from an original meaning. You will find all the meanings of *creep* listed in one entry in the dictionary.

6.3 Homophones Words that sound alike but have different meanings and spellings are called homophones.

> Paul heard his mother say on the phone, "I **hear** you as well as I would if you were **here** talking to me."

Homophones don't usually cause problems for readers, but they can be problems for writers. Many common words with Old

English origins (*there, their; write, right*) have homophones. Be sure to check your writing for misspelled homophones.

For more about homonyms and words with multiple meanings, see page 884.

7 Analogies

7.1 *Analogy* An analogy is a statement that compares two pairs of words. The relationship between the first pair of words is the same as the relationship between the second pair of words. In the example below, each pair of words shows a relationship of an item to a category.

TRACTOR : VEHICLE :: wrench : tool

A tractor is a type of vehicle, just as a wrench is a type of tool.

The sign : stands for "is to." The sign :: stands for "as." The analogy is read like this:

"*Tractor* is to *vehicle* as *wrench* is to *tool.*"

7.2 *Types of Analogies* Here are some common word relationships.

For more about analogies, see page 534.

type of analogy	example	relationship
Part to whole	STAGE : THEATER	is a part of
Synonyms	SWEET : THOUGHTFUL	is similar in meaning
Antonyms	FANTASTIC : AWFUL	is different in meaning
Degree of intensity	SATISFACTORY : EXCELLENT	is less (or more) intense than
Characteristic to object	ROUGHNESS : SANDPAPER	is a quality of
Item to category	ANT : INSECT	is a type of

8 Specialized Vocabulary

Professionals who work in fields such as law, science, or sports use their own technical or specialized vocabulary. Use these strategies to help you figure out the meanings of specialized vocabulary.

8.1 *Use Context Clues* Often the surrounding text gives clues that help you infer the meaning of an unfamiliar term.

8.2 *Use Reference Tools* Textbooks often define special terms when they are first introduced. Look for definitions or restatement clues in parentheses. You can also try to find definitions in footnotes, a glossary, or a dictionary. If you need more information, refer to a specialized reference, such as an encyclopedia, a field guide, an atlas, a user's manual, or a technical dictionary.

For more about specialized vocabulary, see page 143.

❾ Decoding Multisyllabic Words

Many words are familiar to you when you speak them or hear them. Sometimes these same words may be unfamiliar to you when you see them in print. When you come across an unfamiliar word in your reading, first try to pronounce it to see if you might recognize it. Use these syllabication generalizations to help you figure out a word's pronunciation.

Generalization 1:   VCCV

When there are two consonants between two vowels, divide between the two consonants unless they are a blend or a digraph.

pic/ture   a/brupt   feath/er

Generalization 2:   VCCCV

When there are three consonants between two vowels, divide between the blend or the digraph and the other consonant.

an/gler   mer/chant   tum/bler

Generalization 3:   VCCV

When there are two consonants between two vowels, divide between the consonants, unless they are a blend or a digraph. The first syllable is a closed syllable, and the vowel is short.

lath/er   ush/er   ten/der

Generalization 4:   Common Vowel Clusters

Do not split common vowel clusters, such as long-vowel digraphs, *r*-controlled vowels, and vowel diphthongs.

par/ty   poi/son   fea/ture

Generalization 5:   VCV

When you see a VCV pattern in the middle of a word, divide the word either before or after the consonant. Divide the word after the consonant if the first vowel sound is short. Divide the word before the consonant if the first vowel sound is long.

mod/el   ro/bot   cra/zy

Generalization 6:   Compound Words

Divide compound words between the individual words.

grape/vine   life/guard

Generalization 7:   Affixes

When a word includes an affix, divide between the base word and the affix.

re/bound   rest/less

Spelling Handbook

❶ Improving Your Spelling

Good spelling gives your writing a professional look and impresses your audience. You can improve your spelling by practicing the habits of successful spellers. The following guidelines and tips should help.

Good Spelling Habits

1. **Conquer your personal spelling demons.** Keep a list of the words you have misspelled in your writing.

2. **Pronounce words carefully.** Pronouncing words correctly can help you spell them correctly. For example, if you spell *helpfully* as "helpfly," it might be because you are mispronouncing the word.

3. **Get into the habit of seeing the letters in a word.** Some English spellings are tricky. By looking at new or difficult words letter by letter, you will remember the spellings more easily.

4. **Create memory devices for difficult words.** For example:

ac**cq**uaint (cq)	To get a**cq**uainted, I will **seek you.**
princi**pal** (pal)	The princi**pal** is my **pal.**
princi**ple** (ple)	Follow this princi**ple, ple**ase.

5. **Proofread everything you write.** Slowly read what you've written, word for word. You might even try reading a line in reverse order. Otherwise, your eyes may play tricks on you and let you skip a misspelled word.

Mastering the Spelling of Difficult Words

1. Look at the word and say it one syllable at a time.
2. Look at the letters and say each one.
3. Write the word without looking at it.
4. Check to see whether you spelled the word correctly. If you made a mistake, note exactly what the mistake was. Then repeat steps 1–3.

Words Ending in a Silent e

Before adding a suffix beginning with a vowel to a word ending in a silent *e*, the *e* is usually dropped.

amaze + -ing = amazing
love + -able = lovable
nerve + -ous = nervous

Exceptions: change + -able = changeable; courage + -ous = courageous

When adding a suffix beginning with a consonant to a word ending in a silent *e*, keep the *e*.

late + -ly = lately
noise + -less = noiseless
state + -ment = statement

Exceptions: true + -ly = truly; argue + -ment = argument

Words Ending in y

Before adding a suffix to a word that ends in *y* preceded by a consonant, change the *y* to *i*.

easy + -est = easiest
crazy + -est = craziest

However, when you add *-ing*, the *y* does not change.

worry + -ed = worried
BUT worry + -ing = worrying

When adding a suffix to a word that ends in *y* preceded by a vowel, the *y* usually does not change.

play + -er = player
employ + -ed = employed

Words Ending in a Consonant

In one-syllable words that end in one consonant preceded by one vowel, double the final consonant before adding a suffix beginning with a vowel, such as *-ed* or *-ing.* These are sometimes called 1+1+1 words.

dip + -ed = dipped
set + -ing = setting
hop + -ed = hopped
drug + -ist = druggist

The rule does not apply to words of one syllable that end in a consonant preceded by two vowels.

feel + -ing = feeling
peel + -ed = peeled
reap + -ed = reaped
heat + -ing = heating

In words of more than one syllable, double the final consonant when the word ends with one consonant preceded by one vowel *and* when the word is accented on the last syllable.

be•gin′ per•mit′ re•fer′

In the following examples, note that in the new words formed with suffixes, the accent remains on the same syllable.

be•gin′ + -ing = be•gin′ ning
per•mit′ + -ed = per•mit′ ted

But in the following examples, the accent does not remain on the same syllable; thus, the final consonant is not doubled.

re•fer′ + -ence = ref′ er•ence
con•fer′ + -ence = con′ fer•ence

Prefixes and Suffixes

When adding a prefix to a word, do not change the spelling of the base word.

dis- + approve = disapprove
re- + build = rebuild
ir- + regular = irregular
mis- + spell = misspell

When adding *-ly* to a word ending in *l,* keep both *l*'s. When adding *-ness* to a word ending in *n,* keep both *n*'s.

careful + -ly = carefully
sudden + -ness = suddenness
final + -ly = finally
thin + -ness = thinness

Special Spelling Problems

Only one English word ends in *–sede: supersede.* Three words end in *–ceed: exceed, proceed,* and *succeed.* All other verbs ending in the sound *seed* are spelled with *–cede.*

concede precede recede secede

In words with *ie* and *ei* when the sound is long *e* (ē), the word is spelled *ie* except after *c.*

i before *e*		except after *c*	
thief	relieve	conceit	perceive
piece	field	ceiling	receive
grieve	pier	receipt	

Exceptions: either neither weird leisure seize

When *-ion* is added to the end of words that contain the syllable *-mit, -cede,* or *-ceed,* change the final letter, or letters (*-t, -d,* or *-de*) to *-ss-.*

transmit + -ion = transmission
secede + -ion = secession
proceed + -ion = procession

Some prefixes, such as *ad-* (which means "to; toward"), *in-* ("in; not"), and *com-* ("with; together") usually change their final consonant to match the beginning consonant of a root or base word to which they are added.

ad- + parent = apparent
in- + merse = immerse
com- + laborate = collaborate

When the letters *c* and *g* have a hard sound, they are usually followed by the vowels *a, o,* or *u,* or by any consonant except *y.* When the letters *c* and *g* have a soft sound, they are usually followed by *e, i,* or *y.*

c and *g* before *a, o, u,* or a consonant

cause	gap
common	gopher
curious	ghost

c and *g* before *e, i,* or *y*

certain	agile
circumstance	giant
cycle	gyrate

Exceptions: gift, giddy

❷ Using the Right Word

Good writers master words that are easy to misuse and misspell. As you read through the following words, notice how their meanings differ.

all ready, already *All ready* means "all are ready" or "completely prepared." *Already* means "previously."

The astronauts were *all ready* to land.

The other team has *already* started practicing.

bring, take *Bring* refers to the movement toward or with something. *Take* refers to the movement away from something.

I'll *bring* you a glass of water.

He *took* five dollars from his sister.

capital, capitol, the Capitol *Capital* means "excellent," "most serious," or "most important." It also means "seat of government." *Capitol* is a building in which a state legislature meets. *The Capitol* is the building in Washington, D.C., in which the U.S. Congress meets.

Proper nouns begin with *capital* letters.

Is Madison the *capital* of Wisconsin?

Protestors rallied at the state *capitol.*

A subway connects the Senate and the House in the *Capitol.*

choose, chose *Choose* is a verb that means "to decide" or "prefer." *Chose* is the past tense form of *choose.*

He had to *choose* between taking art or band.

She *chose* to write for the school paper.

farther, further *Farther* refers to distance. *Further* refers to something additional.

We traveled two hundred miles *farther* that afternoon.

This idea needs *further* discussion.

fewer, less *Fewer* refers to numbers of things that can be counted. *Less* refers to amount, degree, or value.

Fewer than ten students camped out.

We made *less* money this year on the walkathon than we did last year.

good, well *Good* is always an adjective. *Well* is usually an adverb that modifies an action verb. *Well* can also be an adjective meaning "in good health."

Dana felt *good* when she finished painting her room.

Angela ran *well* in yesterday's race.

I felt *well* when I left my house.

hear, here *Hear* means "to listen to." *Here* means "in this place."

Because of the noisy crowd, we couldn't *hear* the candidate.

After leaving Italy, my grandparents settled *here* in Chicago.

its, it's *Its* is a possessive pronoun. *It's* is a contraction for *it is* or *it has.*

Sanibel Island is known for *its* beaches.

It's great weather for a picnic.

lay, lie *Lay* is a verb that means "to place." It takes a direct object. *Lie* is a verb that means "to be in a certain place." *Lie* never takes a direct object.

The carpenter will *lay* the planks on the bench.

My cat likes to *lie* under the bed.

lead, led *Lead* can be a noun that means "a heavy metal" or a verb that means "to show the way." *Led* is the verb's past tense form.

> A plumb is a weight made of *lead*.

> Maria *leads* the league in home runs.

> She *led* a discussion on ways to help the homeless.

learn, teach *Learn* means "to gain knowledge." *Teach* means "to instruct."

> Raul is *learning* how to play chess.

> Alicia is *teaching* Spanish in preschool.

like, as, as if Use *as* or *as if,* not *like,* to introduce a clause.

> He walks *as if* his ankle were sore.

loan, lone *Loan* refers to "something given for temporary use." *Lone* refers to "the condition of being by oneself, alone."

> I gave that shirt to Max as a gift, not a *loan.*

> The *lone* plant in our yard turned out to be a scraggly weed.

of Use *have,* not *of,* in phrases such as *could have, should have,* and *must have.*

> He could *have* passed if he had studied for the test.

passed, past *Passed* is the past tense of *pass* and means "went by." *Past* is an adjective that means "of a former time." *Past* is also a noun that means "the time gone by."

> We *passed* through the Grand Tetons during our vacation.

> Our *past* experiences have taught us we can win.

> Ebenezer Scrooge is a character who relives his *past.*

peace, piece *Peace* means "calm or quiet." *Piece* means a "section or part of something."

> Music can bring a sense of *peace.*

> We cut the pizza into *pieces.*

quiet, quite *Quiet* refers to "freedom from noise or disturbance." *Quite* means "truly" or "almost completely."

> Observers must be *quiet* during the recording session.

> We were *quite* worried about the results of the test.

set, sit *Set* means "to place." It takes a direct object. *Sit* means "to occupy a seat or a place." It does not take a direct object.

> He *set* the box down outside the shed.

> We *sit* in the last row of the upper balcony at every concert.

their, there, they're *Their* means "belonging to them." *There* means "in that place." *They're* is the contraction for "they are."

> All the campers returned to *their* cabins.

> I keep my card collection *there* in those folders.

> Because Lisa and Beth run daily, *they're* on the track team.

to, too, two *To* means "toward" or "in the direction of." *Too* means "also" or "very." *Two* is the number 2.

> We went *to* the Library of Congress in Washington, D.C.

> It was *too* cold to play baseball.

> *Two* newspapers sent critics to review the play.

whose, who's *Whose* is the possessive form of *who. Who's* is a contraction for *who is* or *who has.*

> *Whose* parents will drive us to camp?

> *Who's* going to the recycling center?

your, you're *Your* is the possessive form of *you. You're* is a contraction for *you are.*

> Please take *your* places in line.

> *You're* going to the library after school, aren't you?

① The Writing Process

The writing process consists of the following four stages: prewriting, drafting, revising and editing, and publishing. As the graphic shows, these stages are not steps that you must complete in a set order. Rather, you may return to any step at any one time in your writing process, using feedback from your readers along the way.

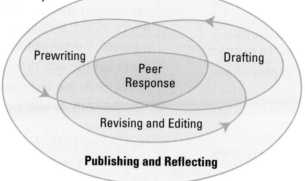

Prewriting
Drafting
Peer Response
Revising and Editing
Publishing and Reflecting

1.1 Prewriting

In the prewriting stage, you explore your ideas and discover what you want to write about.

Finding Ideas for Writing

Try one or more of the following techniques to help you find a writing topic.

Personal Techniques

- Practice imaging, or trying to remember mainly sensory details about a subject—its look, sound, feel, taste, and smell.

- Complete a knowledge inventory to discover what you already know about a subject.

- Browse through magazines, newspapers, and online bulletin boards for ideas.

- Start a clip file of articles that you want to save for future reference. Be sure to label each clip with source information.

Sharing Techniques

- With a group, brainstorm a topic by trying to come up with as many ideas as you can without stopping to critique or examine them.

- Interview someone who knows a great deal about your topic.

Writing Techniques

- After freewriting on a topic, try looping, or choosing your best idea for more freewriting. Repeat the loop at least once.

- Make a list to help you organize ideas, examine them, or identify areas for further research.

Graphic Techniques

- Create a pro-and-con chart to compare the positive and negative aspects of an idea or course of action.

- Use a cluster map or tree diagram to explore subordinate ideas that relate to your general topic or central idea.

Determining Your Purpose

Your purpose for writing may be to express yourself, to entertain, to describe, to explain, to analyze, or to persuade. To clarify your purpose, ask questions like these:

- Why did I choose to write about my topic?

- What aspects of the topic mean the most to me?

- What do I want others to think or feel after they read my writing?

LINK TO LITERATURE One purpose for writing is to inform. For example, Jack London wrote "The Story of an Eyewitness," page 160, to inform people about the disastrous effects of the 1906 San Francisco earthquake.

Identifying Your Audience

Knowing who will read your writing can help you focus your topic and choose relevant details. As you think about your readers, ask yourself questions like these:

- What does my audience already know about my topic?
- What will my audience be most interested in?
- What language is most appropriate for this audience?

Drafting

In the drafting stage, you put your ideas on paper and allow them to develop and change as you write.

Two broad approaches in this stage are discovery drafting and planned drafting.

Discovery drafting is a good approach when you are not quite sure what you think about your subject. You just plunge into your draft and let your feelings and ideas lead you where they will. After finishing a discovery draft, you may decide to start another draft, do more prewriting, or revise your first draft.

LINK TO LITERATURE Some writers plan and outline. Others write in a great flurry, without much previous planning, as ideas occur to them. Describing the approach she uses to draft stories like "Raymond's Run" on page 33, Toni Cade Bambara says, "I babble along, heading I think in one direction, only to discover myself tugged in another, or sometimes I'm absolutely snatched into an alley."

Planned drafting may work better for research reports, critical reviews, and other kinds of formal writing. Try making a writing plan or a scratch outline before you begin drafting. Then, as you write, you can fill in the details.

1.3 Revising, Editing, and Proofreading

The changes you make in your writing during this stage usually fall into three categories: revising for content, revising for structure, and proofreading to correct mistakes in mechanics.

Use the questions that follow to assess problems and determine what changes would improve your work.

Revising for Content

- Does my writing have a main idea or central focus? Is my thesis clear?
- Have I incorporated adequate detail? Where might I include a telling detail, revealing statistic, or vivid example?
- Is any material unnecessary, irrelevant, or confusing?

Revising for Structure

- Is my writing unified? Do all ideas and supporting details pertain to my main idea or advance my thesis?
- Is my writing clear and coherent? Is the flow of sentences and paragraphs smooth and logical?
- Do I need to add transitional words, phrases, or sentences to clarify the relationships among ideas?
- Are my sentences well constructed? What sentences might I combine to improve the grace and rhythm of my writing?

WRITING TIP Be sure to consider the needs of your audience as you answer the questions under Revising for Content and Revising for Structure. For example, before you can determine whether any of your material is unnecessary or irrelevant, you need to identify what your audience already knows.

Proofreading to Correct Mistakes in Grammar, Usage, and Mechanics

When you are satisfied with your revision, proofread your paper, looking for mistakes in grammar, usage, and mechanics. You may want to do this several times, looking for different types of mistakes each time. The following checklist may help.

Sentence Structure and Agreement

- Are there any run-on sentences or sentence fragments?
- Do all verbs agree with their subjects?
- Do all pronouns agree with their antecedents?
- Are verb tenses correct and consistent?

Forms of Words

- Do adverbs and adjectives modify the appropriate words?
- Are all forms of *be* and other irregular verbs used correctly?
- Are pronouns used correctly?
- Are comparative and superlative forms of adjectives correct?

Punctuation, Capitalization, and Spelling

- Is any punctuation mark missing or not needed?
- Are all proper nouns and all proper adjectives capitalized?
- Are all words spelled correctly?

WRITING TIP For help identifying and correcting problems that are listed in the Proofreading Checklist, see the Grammar Handbook, pages R70–R92.

You might wish to mark changes on your paper by using the proofreading symbols shown in the chart below.

Proofreading Symbols	
⋀ Add letters or words.	⁄ Make a capital letter lowercase.
⊙ Add a period.	¶ Begin a new paragraph.
≡ Capitalize a letter.	ℐ Delete letters or words.
⌒ Close up a space.	∿ Switch the positions of letters or words.
⋀ Add a comma.	

1.4 Publishing and Reflecting

Always consider sharing your finished writing with a wider audience. Reflecting on your writing is another good way to finish a project.

Creative Publishing Ideas

Here are some ideas for publishing and sharing your writing.

- Post your writing on an electronic bulletin board or send it to others via e-mail.
- Create a multimedia presentation and share it with classmates.
- Publish your writing in a school newspaper or literary magazine.
- Present your work orally in a report, a speech, a reading, or a dramatic performance.
- Submit your writing to a local newspaper or a magazine that publishes student writing.
- Form a writing exchange group with other students.

WRITING TIP You might work with other students to publish an anthology of class writing. Then exchange your anthology with another class or another school. Reading the work of other student writers will give you ideas for new writing projects and help you find ways to improve your work.

Reflecting on Your Writing

Think about your writing process and whether you would like to add what you have written to your portfolio. You might attach a note in which you answer questions like these:

- What did I learn about myself and my subject through this writing project?
- Which parts of the writing process did I enjoy most and least?
- As I wrote, what was my biggest problem? How did I solve it?
- What did I learn that I can use the next time I write?

1.5 Using Peer Response

Peer response consists of the suggestions and comments your peers or classmates make about your writing.

You can ask a peer reader for help at any point in the writing process. For example, your peers can help you develop a topic, narrow your focus, notice confusing passages, or organize your writing.

Questions for Your Peer Readers

You can help your peer readers provide you with the most useful kinds of feedback by following these guidelines:

- Tell readers where you are in the writing process. Are you still trying out ideas, or have you completed a draft?

- Ask questions that will help you get specific information about your writing. Open-ended questions that require more than yes-or-no answers are more likely to give you information you can use as you revise.

- Give your readers plenty of time to respond thoughtfully to your writing.

- Encourage your readers to be honest when they respond to your work. It's OK if you don't agree with them—you will be the one who decides which changes to make.

Tips for Being a Peer Reader

Follow these guidelines when you respond to someone else's work:

- Respect the writer's feelings.

- Make sure you understand what kind of feedback the writer is looking for, and then respond accordingly.

- Use "I" statements, such as "I like . . . ," "I think . . . ," or "It would help me if . . . ." Remember that your impressions and opinions may not be the same as someone else's.

WRITING TIP Writers are better able to absorb criticism of their work if they first receive positive feedback. When you act as a peer reader, try to start your review by telling something you like about the piece.

The chart below explains different peer-response techniques to use when you are ready to share your work.

Peer-Response Techniques

Sharing When you are just exploring ideas or when you want to celebrate the completion of a piece of writing, phrase your question like this.

- *Will you please read or listen to my writing without criticizing or making suggestions afterward?*

Summarizing When you want to know if your main idea or goals are clear, ask these questions.

- *What do you think I'm saying? What's my main idea or message?*

Replying Ask these questions when you want to enrich your writing by adding new ideas.

- *What are your ideas about my topic? What do you think about what I have said in my piece?*

Responding to Specific Features Ask these questions when you want a quick overview of the strengths and weaknesses of your writing.

- *Are the ideas supported with enough examples? Did I persuade you? Is the organization clear enough for you to follow the ideas?*

Telling Ask these questions to find out which parts of your writing are affecting readers the way you want and which parts are confusing.

- *What did you think or feel as you read my words? Would you show me which passage you were reading when you had that response?*

---

② Building Blocks of Good Writing

Whatever your purpose in writing, you need to capture your readers' interest and organize your thoughts clearly. Giving special attention to some particular parts of a story or an essay can make your writing more enjoyable and more effective.

2.1 Introductions

When you flip through a magazine trying to decide which articles to read, the opening paragraph plays a critical role in grabbing your attention. If it does not grab your attention, you are likely to turn the page.

Kinds of Introductions

Here are some introduction techniques that can capture a reader's interest.

• Make a surprising statement.

• Provide a description.

• Ask a question.

• Relate an anecdote.

• Address the reader directly.

• Begin with a thesis statement.

Make a Surprising Statement Beginning with a startling statement or an interesting fact can capture your reader's curiosity about the subject, as in the model below.

> MODEL
> *Imagine something only 15 to 20 inches long dropping down out of the sky at 200 miles an hour!* It would be nothing but a blur. And that is what makes the peregrine falcon such an effective bird of prey.

Provide a Description A vivid description sets a mood and brings a scene to life for your reader. In the following model, details about heating the air for a hot air balloon set the tone for a narrative about a balloon ride.

> MODEL
> Whoosh! The red and yellow flame shot up into the great nylon cone. The warm air filled the balloon so that the cooler air below held the apparatus aloft. A soft breeze helped to push the balloon and basket along. The four passengers hardly noticed the noise or the heat as they stared in awe at the hilly farmland below.

Ask a Question Beginning with a question can make your reader want to read on to find out the answer. Note how the introduction that follows invites the reader to learn more about a great sports achievement.

> MODEL
> What did St. Louis Cardinal Mark McGwire do in the 1998 baseball season that no other player had ever done? He hit 70 home runs in a single season, breaking the previously held record of 61 set by Roger Maris in 1961. Both McGwire and Chicago Cub Sammy Sosa passed Maris's record during the season, but it wasn't until the season's end that the home-run race was won by McGwire.

Relate an Anecdote Beginning with a brief anecdote, or story, can hook readers and help you make a point in a dramatic way. The anecdote below introduces a firsthand account of a rescue from a burning apartment building.

> MODEL
> A red light began blinking. A siren started up slowly but built to a screeching pitch. Twenty-five sleepy faces appeared a few at a time in the hallway. As I recall, each of us looked to the left and right almost in unison as if watching an imaginary tennis match.

Address the Reader Directly Speaking directly to the readers establishes a friendly, informal tone and involves them in your topic.

> MODEL
> **Find out how to maintain your cardiovascular system while enjoying yourself. Come to a free demonstration of Fit for Life at the Community Center Friday night at 7:00 P.M.**

Begin with a Thesis Statement A thesis statement expressing a paper's main idea may be woven into both the beginning and the end of nonfiction writing. The following example begins with a thesis statement that introduces a research report.

> MODEL
> *There are many similarities between Mohandas Gandhi and Martin Luther King, Jr.* Both believed in nonviolent resistance to laws they felt were unfair. Both were leaders who rallied millions behind their causes, and both leaders met a tragic end.

2.2 Paragraphs

A paragraph is made up of sentences that work together to develop an idea or accomplish a purpose. Whether or not it contains a topic sentence stating the main idea, a good paragraph must have unity and coherence.

Unity

A paragraph has unity when all the sentences support and develop one stated or implied idea. Use the following techniques to create unity in your paragraphs.

Write a Topic Sentence A topic sentence states the main idea of the paragraph; all other sentences in the paragraph provide supporting details. A topic sentence is often the first sentence in a paragraph. However, it may also appear later in the paragraph or at the end, to summarize or reinforce the main idea, as shown in the model that follows.

> MODEL
> They unite against a common enemy but never quarrel among themselves. They feel no need to take over territory or conquer new waters. In fact, they never even fight over food. *This ability to live together in total peace is one of the dolphins' most remarkable qualities.*

Relate All Sentences to an Implied Main Idea A paragraph can be unified without a topic sentence as long as every sentence supports the implied, or unstated, main idea. In the example below, all the sentences work together to create a unified impression of baking an apple pie.

> MODEL
> The chef carefully poured in the mixture of freshly sliced apples, sugar, flour, salt, cinnamon, and nutmeg. Then she floured her hands again before adding strips of pastry in crisscrosses across the top. She dotted some butter all along the top and sprinkled a little more sugar and cinnamon. Finally she placed the masterpiece in the oven.

Coherence

A paragraph is coherent when all its sentences are related to one another and flow logically from one to the next. The following techniques will help you write coherent paragraphs.

- Present your ideas in the most logical order.
- Use pronouns, synonyms, and repeated words to connect ideas.
- Use transitional words and phrases to show the relationships among ideas.

> MODEL
> According to the English colonist John Smith, Pocahontas saved his life. *A few years later,* she was kidnapped by other colonists. *While living with them,* she fell in love with John Rolfe, and they were married. *Later,* Pocahontas, her husband, and their infant son traveled to England, where Pocahontas was introduced to the king.

2.3 Transitions

Transitions are words and phrases that show the connections between details. Clear transitions help show how your ideas relate to each other.

Kinds of Transitions

Transitions can help readers understand several kinds of relationships:

- Time or sequence
- Spatial order
- Degree of importance
- Compare and contrast
- Cause and effect

Time or Sequence Some transitions help to clarify the sequence of events over time. When you are telling a story or describing a process, you can connect ideas with such transitional words as *first, second, always, then, next, later, soon, before, finally, after, earlier, afterward,* and *tomorrow.*

> MODEL
>
> The orchestra members were seated. *At first,* the sounds conflicted with one another as the players tuned and tested their instruments. *Then* the concertmaster stood and played one note on her violin. *Next,* all the instruments tuned to that tone so that one great sound on the same pitch filled the auditorium.

Spatial Order Transitional words and phrases such as *in front, behind, next to, along, nearest, lowest, above, below, underneath, on the left,* and *in the middle* can help readers visualize a scene.

> MODEL
>
> On my mother's dresser you can read the history of our family. *On the left,* a picture shows my parents' wedding. The picture *in the middle* is of my older brother as a baby, still toothless. The picture *on the right* shows all of us children in our fanciest clothes.

Degree of Importance Transitional words such as *mainly, strongest, weakest, first, second, most important, least important, worst,* and *best* may be used to rank ideas or to show degree of importance.

> MODEL
>
> I look for several qualities in a friend. *Most important,* I like someone who shares my interests. *Second,* I want someone who can keep a secret. *Least important,* my new friend should get along with all my other friends.

Compare and Contrast Words and phrases such as *similarly, likewise, also, like, as, neither . . . nor,* and *either . . . or* show similarity between details. Words and phrases such as *however, by contrast, yet, but, unlike, instead, whereas,* and *while* show difference.

> MODEL
>
> *Like* the lawyer in "The Bet," Jerry in "A Mother in Mannville" spends much of his time alone. *Both* characters experience loneliness. *However,* as an orphan, Jerry never chooses to be alone, *whereas* the lawyer agreed to his solitary confinement.

WRITING TIP Both *but* and *however* may be used to join two independent clauses. When *but* is used as a coordinating conjunction, it is preceded by a comma. When *however* is used as a conjunctive adverb, it is preceded by a semicolon and followed by a comma.

Cause and Effect When you are writing about a cause-and-effect relationship, use transitional words and phrases such as *since, because, thus, therefore, so, due to, for this reason,* and *as a result* to help clarify that relationship.

> MODEL
>
> My notebook might look tattered, but I treasure it *because* Silvio gave it to me. He was my best friend, and he moved to Texas. *Since* the notebook is all I have to remember him by, I will never throw it out.

2.4 Conclusions

A conclusion should leave readers with a strong final impression. Try any of these approaches.

Kinds of Conclusions

Here are some effective methods for bringing your writing to a conclusion:

- Restate your thesis.
- Ask a question.
- Make a recommendation.
- Make a prediction.
- Summarize your information.

Restate Your Thesis A good way to conclude an essay is by restating your thesis, or main idea, in different words. The conclusion below restates the thesis introduced on page R37.

> MODEL
> There can be no doubt that Mohandas Gandhi and Martin Luther King, Jr., had much in common. Each was a great leader who struggled to help the oppressed people of his country.

Ask a Question Try asking a question that sums up what you have said and gives readers something new to think about. The question below concludes a request to consider visiting a place of educational entertainment.

> MODEL
> If you enjoy science experiments and you like puzzles, shouldn't you plan soon to visit the Science Museum?

Make a Recommendation When you are persuading your audience to take a position on an issue, you can conclude by recommending a specific course of action.

> MODEL
> Shawn, Maria, and Katie are all real children. The next time you see a homeless person, remember these children and think about what you can do to help.

Make a Prediction Readers are concerned about matters that may affect them and therefore are moved by a conclusion that predicts the future.

> MODEL
> If this state continues to permit landowners to drain wetlands, we will see a tremendous decline in the number of animals and the variety of wildlife.

Summarize Your Information Summarizing reinforces the writer's main ideas, leaving a strong, lasting impression. The model below concludes with a statement that summarizes a literary analysis of the works of Mark Twain.

> MODEL
> Although *Roughing It* and "A Fable" are very different in terms of style and subject matter, in both works Mark Twain uses humor as a way of criticizing society.

2.5 Elaboration

Elaboration is the process of developing a writing idea by providing specific supporting details that are relevant and appropriate to the purpose and form of your writing.

- **Facts and Statistics** A fact is a statement that can be verified, while a statistic is a fact stated in numbers. Make sure the facts and statistics you supply are from a reliable, up-to-date source. As in the model below, the facts and statistics you use should strongly support the statements you make.

> MODEL
> Female cicadas cut little slits in the bark of twigs on trees and lay their eggs inside the slits. The eggs hatch after 6 to 10 weeks. When the eggs hatch, the twigs drop from the trees. Although this might seem threatening to the host trees, in fact there is little danger.

- **Sensory Details** Details that show how something looks, sounds, tastes, smells, or feels can enliven a description, making readers feel they are actually experiencing what you are describing. Which senses does the writer appeal to in this paragraph?

MODEL
On the second day of the heat wave, the temperature hit a sweltering 106 degrees. Outside, the sun melted the soft tar of newly paved streets. Inside, people sipped sweet, cool lemonade and hovered around whirring old fans.

- **Incidents** Describing a brief incident can help to explain or develop an idea. The writer of the following example includes an incident to help make a point about safety.

MODEL
Pedestrians, like drivers, should follow certain rules of the road, such as looking both ways before crossing the street. I learned how dangerous it can be to break that rule when I was nearly hit by a driver who was traveling the wrong direction down a one-way street.

- **Examples** An example can help make an abstract or a complex idea concrete or can provide evidence to clarify a point for readers.

MODEL
Narrative poetry tells a story in poetic form. Like a work of prose fiction, a narrative poem has a setting, characters, and a plot. For example, "Paul Revere's Ride" by Henry Wadsworth Longfellow tells the story of the dramatic events that took place in Massachusetts on April 18, 1775, the night before the battles of Lexington and Concord.

- **Quotations** Choose quotations that clearly support your points and be sure that you copy each quotation word for word. Remember always to credit the source.

MODEL
In his short story "The Tell-Tale Heart," Edgar Allan Poe uses bizarre and frightening details to grip the reader with a sense of horror. "I saw it [the eye] with perfect distinctness—all a dull blue, with a hideous veil over it that chilled the very marrow in my bones . . ."

2.6 Using Language Effectively

Effective use of language can help readers to recognize the significance of an issue, to visualize a scene, or to understand a character. This is true of all writing, from novels to office memos. Keep these particular points in mind.

- **Specific Nouns** Nouns are specific when they refer to individual or particular things. If you refer to a *city,* you are being general. If you refer to *Austin,* you are being specific. Specific nouns help readers identify the *who, what,* and *where* of your message.

- **Specific Verbs** Verbs are the most powerful words in sentences. They convey the action, the movement, and the drama of thoughts and observations. Verbs such as *trudged, skipped,* and *sauntered* provide a more vivid picture of the action than the verb *walked.*

- **Specific Modifiers** Use modifiers sparingly, but when you use them, make them count. Is the building *big* or *towering?* Are your poodle's paws *small* or *petite?*

WRITING TIP Knowing synonyms and antonyms can help you choose the best words when you write. A dictionary of synonyms, also known as a thesaurus, will provide you with exact word choices.

③ Descriptive Writing

Descriptive writing allows you to paint word pictures about anything and everything in the world, from events of global importance to the most personal feelings. Description is an essential part of almost every piece of writing, including essays, poems, letters, field notes, newspaper reports, and film scripts.

RUBRIC STANDARDS FOR WRITING

A successful description should

- have a clear focus and sense of purpose.
- use sensory details and precise words to create a vivid image, establish a mood, or express emotion.
- present details in a logical order.

---

③.1 Key Techniques

Consider Your Goals What do you want to accomplish in writing your description? Do you want to show why something is important to you? Do you want to make a person or scene more memorable? Do you want to explain an event?

Identify Your Audience Who will read your description? How familiar are they with your subject? What background information will they need? Which details will they find most interesting?

Gather Sensory Details Which sights, smells, tastes, sounds, and textures make your subject come alive? Which details stick in your mind when you observe or recall your subject? Which senses does your subject most strongly affect?

MODEL

Davis slouched at the table and gazed out the coffee-shop window, his worn shirt soaked with perspiration. A fly began buzzing furiously against the torn window screen, so Davis took aim with a rolled-up newspaper. When an order of fried eggs and grits was served at the next table, his mouth watered and his stomach growled.

You can use a chart like the one below to collect sensory details about your subject.

Sights	Sounds	Textures	Smells	Tastes

Organize Your Details Details that are presented in a logical order help the reader form a mental picture of the subject. Descriptive details may be organized chronologically, spatially, by order of importance, or by order of impression. In the following model, descriptive details are organized by order of impression.

MODEL

The new teacher's towering height and her icy blue eyes drew our attention immediately. As she strode firmly to the board, our gaze followed her nervously. Only when she finally spoke, in a tone that was warm and friendly, did we begin to relax.

Show, Don't Tell Instead of telling about a subject in a general way, provide details that enable your readers to share your experience. The following sentence, for example, just tells and doesn't show: *I was proud when the local paper published my article.* The model that follows uses descriptive details to show how proud the writer felt.

MODEL

I've delivered newspapers since I was eight, but last Thursday, for the first time, the newspaper printed an article I had written for a contest. I bought a pad of sticky notes and left messages for my customers: "Check out page B7. Enjoy the paper today." I thought about signing the article, but I decided that would be too much.

Options for Organization

Spatial Order Choose one of these options to show the spatial order of a scene.

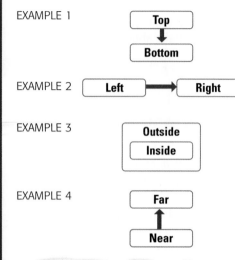

EXAMPLE 1

Top → Bottom

EXAMPLE 2

Left → Right

EXAMPLE 3

Outside / Inside

EXAMPLE 4

Far ↑ Near

> MODEL
> Thunder's nostrils quivered as he was led into the barn. How would this be as a place to spend nights from now on? In the stall to the left, the straw smelled fresh. Beyond that stall, a saddle hung from the rough boards. To the right of his stall was another from which a mare looked at him curiously. So far, so good. To the far right, beyond two empty stalls, a cat lay on its side.

WRITING TIP Use transitions that help the reader picture the relationship among the objects you describe. Some useful transitions for showing spatial relationships are *behind, below, here, in the distance, on the left, over,* and *on top.*

Order of Impression Order of impression is how you notice details.

What first catches your attention

↓

What you notice next

↓

What you see after that

↓

What you focus on last

> MODEL
> As she lost her balance on the slippery pebbles, her first thought was that she was going to sprain her ankle and be swept away by the surf. Her heart beat rapidly, but before she knew it, she was sitting in the sand while the warm surf rolled in, almost covering her. She realized that the water was not going to reach beyond her shoulders and that she was safe. Then, suddenly, she felt the tug of the water in the other direction as the undertow flowed back, sweeping the sand from under her as it went. As soon as the water had receded, she scrambled to her feet.

WRITING TIP Use transitions that help readers understand the order of the impressions you are describing. Some useful transitions are *after, next, during, first, before, finally,* and *then.*

Order of Importance You might want to use order of importance as the organizing structure for your description.

Least Important

↓

More Important

↓

Most Important

> MODEL
> Jordana tried desperately to remember the details of the accident. She found it easy to remember unimportant details, like the song that was playing on the radio when the truck appeared coming toward them. Gradually she recalled more important information—the ice on the road, the look on the driver's face as the truck plowed into their car. Most importantly, she remembered the panic she had felt. She knew it would be a long time before she forgot that feeling of panic.

WRITING TIP Use transitions that help the reader understand the order of importance that you attach to the elements of your description. Some useful transitions are *first, second, mainly, more important, less important,* and *least important.*

4 Narrative Writing

Narrative writing tells a story. If you write a story from your imagination, it is a fictional narrative. A true story about actual events is a nonfictional narrative. Narrative writing can be found in short stories, novels, news articles, and biographies.

RUBRIC STANDARDS FOR WRITING

A successful narrative should

• include descriptive details and dialogue to develop the characters, setting, and plot.

• have a clear beginning, middle, and end.

• have a logical organization with clues and transitions to help the reader understand the order of events.

• maintain a consistent tone and point of view.

• use language that is appropriate for the audience.

• demonstrate the significance of events or ideas.

4.1 Key Techniques

Identify the Main Events What are the most important events in your narrative? Is each event part of the chain of events needed to tell the story? In a fictional narrative, this series of events is the story's plot.

MODEL

Event 1 — An electrical storm approaches while two ranchers search for Kid Turner, a missing ranch hand.

Event 2 — They find his horse and follow its hoof prints up a dry riverbed.

Event 3 — The storm breaks as they find Kid lying helpless with his leg broken.

Event 4 — They carry him to safety just before a flash flood rolls down the riverbed where he was lying.

Define the Conflict The conflict of a narrative is the problem that the main character faces. What is the main problem that Jake faces? Is his conflict external or internal?

MODEL
Jake looked at the dark clouds that hovered overhead. How much time did they have to find Kid before the storm broke? Judging by the sky, the storm would break any minute, endangering all the men who were part of the search. On the other hand, Kid might be seriously hurt. His life depended on their getting to him as fast as possible.

Depict Characters Vividly What do your characters look like? What do they think and say? How do they act?

MODEL
Jake had the hard, lined face of a veteran cowhand. His dark, piercing eyes scanned the countryside from beneath the shadow of his hat brim. He studied the clouds rolling in from the western horizon, gauging how severe the coming storm would be.

WRITING TIP Dialogue is an effective way of developing characters in a narrative. As you write dialogue, choose words that express your characters' personalities and feelings.

MODEL
"Better find 'im soon," Jake said.
Edna Mae could barely make out the words that were muffled by the wind.
"We'll find him, Jake," was her reply, given with somewhat more confidence than she felt.
"I'll know the hoof prints of Kid's horse if we ever pick up the trail," Jake answered.

4.2 Options for Organization

Option 1: Chronological Order One way to organize a piece of narrative writing is to arrange the events in chronological order, as shown below.

MODEL

Introduction *characters and setting*	Kid Turner hasn't come back to the ranch in three days. Fearing that he is hurt, Jake and Edna Mae set out to search for him.
↓	
Event 1	As a thunderstorm approaches, they find his horse and backtrack up a dry wash.
↓	
Event 2	They find Turner just as the storm breaks. He has a broken leg, so he can't drag himself out of the dry wash.
↓	
End *perhaps show the significance of the events*	They carry him out of the riverbed and find shelter under a rock ledge. As they watch, a flash flood surges through the riverbed where Kid had been lying.

WRITING TIP Try hooking your reader's interest by opening a story with an exciting event or some attention-grabbing dialogue. After your introduction, you may need to go back in time and relate the incidents that led up to the opening event.

Option 2: Character Chronological order is the most common way to organize a narrative. However, you may wish to focus more directly on characters.

Introduce the main character.

↓

Describe the conflict that the character faces.

↓

Relate the events and the changes that the character goes through as a result of the conflict.

↓

Present the final change or new understanding.

Option 3: Focus on Conflict When the telling of a fictional narrative focuses on a central conflict, the story's plot may follow the model shown below.

MODEL

Describe the main characters and setting	The brothers arrive at the school gym long before the rest of the basketball team. Although the twins are physically identical, their personalities couldn't be more different. Mark is outgoing and impulsive, while Matt is thoughtful and shy.
↓	
Present the conflict	Matt realizes Mark is missing shots on purpose and worries they will lose the championship.
↓	
Relate the events that make the conflict complex and cause the characters to change	• Matt has a chance at a basketball scholarship if they win the championship. • Mark needs money to buy a car. He is being paid to lose the game. • Matt and Mark have stood by each other no matter what.
↓	
Present the resolution or outcome of the conflict	Matt retells a family story in which their grandfather chose honor and integrity over easy money. The story encourages Mark to play to win.

Option 4: Flashback It is also possible in narrative writing to arrange the order of events by starting with an event that happened before the beginning of the story.

Flashback Begin with a key event that happened before the time in which the story takes place.

↓

Introduce characters and setting.

↓

Describe the events leading up to the conflict.

⑤ Explanatory Writing

Explanatory, or expository, writing informs and explains. For example, you can use it to explain the effects of a new law, to compare two movies, or analyze a piece of literature. The rubric on the left shows you the basics of successful expository writing.

RUBRIC STANDARDS FOR WRITING

Successful explanatory writing should

• engage the interest of the reader.

• state a clear purpose.

• develop the topic with supporting details.

• create a visual image for the reader by using precise verbs, nouns, and adjectives.

• conclude with a detailed summary linked to the purpose of the composition.

5.1 Types of Explanatory Writing

There are many types of explanatory writing. Select the type that presents your topic most clearly.

Compare and Contrast How are two or more subjects alike? How are they different?

> MODEL
> **While the domestic honeybee has been bred for good honey production and gentleness, the Africanized bee is a "wild" bee that is quick-tempered and uncomfortable around people.**

Cause and Effect How does one event cause something else to happen? What are the results of an action or a condition?

> MODEL
> **If the Africanized bees drive out or breed into domesticated honeybee colonies, commercial beekeepers in the United States could be forced out of business.**

Problem-Solution How can you identify and state a problem? How would you analyze the problem and its causes? How can it be solved?

> MODEL
> **The best way to protect yourself against the stings of the Africanized bee is to understand how it behaves.**

Analysis/Classification How does something work? How can it be defined? What are its parts? How can it be classified into categories?

> MODEL
> **The Africanized honeybee is a new insect that has the potential to affect agriculture, recreation, and the environment.**

5.2 Compare and Contrast

Compare-and-contrast writing examines the similarities and differences between two or more subjects.

RUBRIC STANDARDS FOR WRITING

Successful compare-and-contrast writing should

• clearly identify the subjects that are being compared and contrasted.

• include specific, relevant details.

• be easy to follow, using either feature-by-feature or subject-by-subject organization.

• use transitional words and phrases to signal similarities and differences.

• end with a conclusion that summarizes how the subjects are alike and different.

Options for Organization

Compare-and-contrast writing can be organized in different ways. The diagrams that follow demonstrate feature-by-feature organization and subject-by-subject organization.

Option 1

Feature by Feature
Feature 1
• Subject A
• Subject B
Feature 2
• Subject A
• Subject B

Option 2

Subject by Subject
Subject A
• Feature 1
• Feature 2
Subject B
• Feature 1
• Feature 2

WRITING TIP Remember your purpose for comparing and contrasting your subjects, and support your purpose with expressive language and specific details.

5.3 Cause and Effect

Cause-and-effect writing explains why something happened, why certain conditions exist, or what resulted from an action or a condition. You might use cause-and-effect writing to explain a character's actions, the progress of a disease, or the outcome of a war.

RUBRIC STANDARDS FOR WRITING

Successful cause-and-effect writing should

• clearly state the cause-and-effect relationship.

• show clear connections between causes and effects.

• present causes and effects in a logical order and use transitions effectively.

• use facts, examples, and other details to illustrate each cause and effect.

• use language and details appropriate to the audience.

Options for Organization

Your organization will depend on your topic and purpose for writing.

• If you want to explain the causes of an event, such as the threat of Africanized bees to commercial beekeeping, you might first state the effect and then examine its causes.

Option 1: Effect-to-Cause Organization

• If your focus is on explaining the effects of an event, such as the appearance of Africanized bees in the United States, you might first state the cause and then explain the effects.

Option 2: Cause-to-Effect Organization

- Sometimes you'll want to describe a chain of cause-and-effect relationships to explore a topic such as the disappearance of tropical rain forests or the development of home computers.

Option 3: Cause-and-Effect Chain Organization

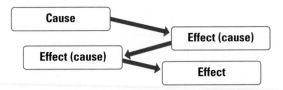

WRITING TIP Don't assume that a cause-and-effect relationship exists just because one event follows another. Look for evidence that the later event could not have happened if the first event had not caused it.

5.4 Problem–Solution

Problem–solution writing clearly states a problem, analyzes the problem, and proposes a solution to the problem. It can be used to identify and solve a conflict between characters, analyze a chemistry experiment, or explain why the home team keeps losing.

RUBRIC STANDARDS FOR WRITING

Successful problem–solution writing should

- identify the problem and help the reader understand the issues involved.
- present a workable solution and include details that explain and support it.
- conclude by restating the problem.

Options for Organization

Your organization will depend on the goal of your problem–solution piece, your intended audience, and the specific problem you choose to address. The organizational methods that follow are effective for different kinds of problem–solution writing.

Option 1: Simple Problem–Solution

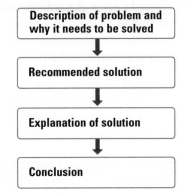

Option 2: Deciding Between Solutions

WRITING TIP Have a classmate read your problem–solution writing. Ask your peer reader: Is the problem clearly stated? Is the organization easy to follow?

5.5 Analysis/Classification

In writing an analysis, you explain how something works, how it is defined, or what its parts are. The details you include will depend upon the kind of analysis you write.

Process Analysis What are the major steps or stages in a process? What background information does the reader need to know— such as definitions of terms or a list of needed equipment—to understand the analysis? You might use process analysis to explain how to program a VCR or prepare for a test.

Definition Analysis What are the most important characteristics of a subject? You might use definition analysis to explain a quality such as honesty, the characteristics of a sonnet, or the features of a computer.

Parts Analysis What are the parts, groups, or types that make up a subject? Parts analysis could be used to explain the makeup of an organization or the anatomy of a flower.

Classification and Division How can one or more items be classified into groups? For example, you might use classification and division to explain how honey bees are either drones, workers, or queens.

RUBRIC STANDARDS FOR WRITING

Successful analysis should

- hook the readers' attention with a strong introduction.
- clearly state the subject and its parts.
- use a specific organizing structure to provide a logical flow of information.
- use transitions to connect thoughts.
- use language and details appropriate for the audience.

Options for Organization

Organize your details to fit the kind of analysis you're writing.

Option 1: Process Analysis A process analysis is usually organized chronologically, with steps or stages in the order they occur.

MODEL

Introduction	**Insect metamorphosis**
Background	**Many insects grow through a four-step life cycle.**
Explain Steps	**Step 1: Egg**
	Step 2: Larva
	Step 3: Pupa
	Step 4: Adult

Option 2: Definition Analysis You can organize the details in a definition or parts analysis in order of importance or impression.

MODEL

Introduce Term	**What is an insect?**
General Definition	**An insect is an animal with an external skeleton, three body segments, and three pairs of legs.**
Explain Features	**Feature 1: External skeleton**
	Feature 2: Three body segments
	Feature 3: Three pairs of legs

Option 3: Parts Analysis The following parts analysis describes the major parts of an insect.

MODEL

Introduce Subject	**An insect's body is divided into three main parts.**
Explain Parts	**Part 1: The head includes eyes, mouth, and antennae.**
	Part 2: The thorax has the legs and wings attached to it.
	Part 3: The abdomen contains organs for digesting food, eliminating waste, and reproducing.

Option 4: Classification/Division The following classification divides insects into groups based on certain characteristics.

MODEL

One way that scientists classify insects is as species that are social insects and those that are not. Most insects are not social insects. The parents get together simply to mate. The female lays her eggs near a source of food and then abandons them. Social insects, on the other hand, live in organized communities in which members depend on one another. Individual insects have special roles within the community. All termites and ants are social. Many bees and some wasps are also social insects.

6 Persuasive Writing

Persuasive writing allows you to use the power of language to inform and influence others. It can take many forms, including speeches, newspaper editorials, billboards, advertisements, and critical reviews.

RUBRIC STANDARDS FOR WRITING

Successful persuasion should

- have a strong introduction.
- clearly state the issue and the writer's position.
- present ideas logically.
- answer opposing viewpoints.
- end with a strong argument or summary or a call for action.

6.1 Key Techniques

State Your Opinion Taking a stand on an issue and clearly stating your opinion are essential to every piece of persuasive writing.

MODEL
Public tax dollars should continue to fund Green Park Zoo.

Know Your Audience Knowing who will read your writing will help you decide what information you need to share and what tone you should use to communicate your message. In the model below, the writer has chosen a formal tone that is appropriate for a letter to a politician or for a newspaper editorial.

MODEL
In fact, an increase in funding will enable Green Park Zoo to expand its highly successful habitat program.

Support Your Opinion Using reasons, examples, facts, statistics, and anecdotes will show your audience why you feel the way you do. Below, the writer uses an example to support her opinion.

MODEL
The zoo's habitat program concentrates on the conservation of endangered species, such as orangutans.

Ways to Support Your Argument

Statistics	Facts that are stated in numbers
Examples	Specific instances that explain your point
Observations	Events or situations you yourself have seen
Anecdotes	Brief stories that illustrate your point
Quotations	Direct statements from authorities

Begin and End with a Bang How can you hook your readers and make a lasting impression? What memorable quotation, anecdote, or statistic will catch their attention at the beginning or stick in their minds at the end? What strong summary or call to action can you conclude with?

BEGINNING
Have you ever enjoyed the antics of the orangutans at Green Park Zoo? Have you learned about the habitat of polar bears by visiting the zoo's polar bear exhibit? If you want to ensure that this wonderful facility does not close down, make sure that public funding for the zoo continues.

CONCLUSION
Many people, old and young alike, have spent countless enjoyable hours at Green Park Zoo. Not only is it a place for relaxation and fun, it is also an important scientific laboratory where trained professionals work together to create educational programs and ensure the survival of endangered species. Don't let this valuable asset close down. Make sure that public tax dollars continue to support Green Park Zoo.

6.2 Options for Organization

In persuasive writing, you need to gather information to support your opinions. Here are some ways you can organize material to convince your audience.

Option 1: Reasons for Your Opinion

MODEL
Opinion:
Public tax dollars should continue to fund Green Park Zoo animals.

Reason 1:
This zoo enables scientists to learn more about the habits and the diseases of animals.

Reason 2:
The zoo educates city dwellers about nature.

Reason 3:
Most important, the zoo breeds endangered species to protect them from extinction.

Depending on the purpose and form of your writing, you may want to show the weaknesses of other opinions as you explain the strength of your own. Two options for organizing writing that includes more than just your side of the issue are shown below.

Option 2: Why Your Opinion Is Stronger

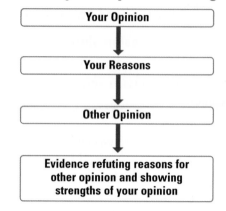

Option 3: Why Another Opinion Is Weaker

WRITING TIP Start a persuasive piece with a question, a surprising fact, or an anecdote to capture your readers' interest and make them want to keep reading. The ending of a persuasive piece is often the part that sticks in a reader's mind. Your conclusion might summarize the two sides of an issue, restate your position, invite readers to make up their own minds, or call for some action.

7 Research Report Writing

In research report writing, you can find answers to questions about a topic you're interested in. Your writing organizes information from various sources and presents it to your readers as a unified and coherent whole.

RUBRIC **STANDARDS FOR WRITING**

An effective research report should

- clearly state the purpose of the report in a thesis statement.
- use evidence and details from a variety of sources to support the thesis.
- contain only accurate and relevant information.
- document sources correctly.
- develop the topic logically and include appropriate transitions.
- include a properly formatted works cited list.

7.1 Key Techniques

Formulate Questions Asking thoughtful questions will help you find an interesting, specific topic. Focus on the *who, what, when, where,* and *why* of your topic. If you were researching Frederick Douglass, you might develop these questions.

> MODEL
> **When did Frederick Douglass live? What were his most important accomplishments? What difficulties did he overcome?**

Clarify Your Thesis Your thesis statement explains to your readers the question your report will answer. In the following example, the thesis statement answers the question "How did Frederick Douglass draw support for the antislavery movement?"

> MODEL
> **In his writing and lectures Frederick Douglass used compelling tales of his own experience as a slave to gain support for the antislavery movement.**

Support Your Ideas You need to support your ideas with details and facts from reliable sources. In the following example, the writer supports the claim that Douglass risked his freedom.

> MODEL
> **Douglass wrote his autobiography at the risk of being arrested as a runaway slave. According to writer Richard Conniff, Douglass only revealed his true identity because people doubted his stories about slavery.**

Document Your Sources You need to document, or credit, the sources where you find your information. In the example below, the writer quotes Douglass and documents the source.

> MODEL
> **Douglass stated that the slaveholders tried "to disgust their slaves with freedom" so that the slaves would think they were better off in captivity. (Douglass 85)**

LINK TO LITERATURE Your reading can inspire ideas for research topics. For example, after reading Frederick Douglass's letter to Harriet Tubman on page 765, you may be interested in learning more about him. The research demonstrated in this part of the Writing Handbook was inspired by Douglass's statement "Most that I have done and suffered in the service of our cause has been in public."

7.2 Finding and Evaluating Sources

Begin your research by looking for information on your topic in books, magazines, newspapers, and computer databases. In addition to using your library's card or computer catalog, look up your subject in indexes, such as the *Readers' Guide to Periodical Literature* or the *New York Times Index*. The bibliographies in books that you find during your research may also help lead to additional sources. The following checklist will help you evaluate the reliability of the sources you find.

Checklist for Evaluating Your Sources	
Authority	An authoritative resource gives evidence of the author's experience and current position. An author who has written books and articles, published in respected sources, is considered to be an authority.
Currency	An authoritative resource clearly shows the date when the document was created or revised. You can check items in the author's works cited list for more clues on currency. For historical research, older resources can be appropriate. For current research, up-to-date resources are important.
Intended audience	Use materials created for serious readers. Such materials have depth of content and respected authors and publishers. Tabloid newspapers and popular-interest magazines, while entertaining, are not reliable sources for reports. For questions about appropriate sources, ask a librarian.

WEB TIP Be especially skeptical of information you locate on the Internet, since virtually everyone can post anything there. Sites sponsored by a government agency (*.gov*) or an educational institute (*.edu*) are generally more reliable.

7.3 Making Source Cards

For each source you find, record the bibliographic information on a separate index card. You will need this information to give credit to the sources you use in your paper. The following samples show how to make source cards for encyclopedia entries, magazine articles, and books. You will use the source number on each card to identify the notes you take during your research.

Encyclopedia Entry

Source number ①
Title of entry   Title of encyclopedia
"Frederick Douglass" The Encyclopedia
  Americana. International Edition.
  1999.   Edition
Date of publication

Location of source
School Library

Magazine Article

Author   Title of article   ②
Conniff, Richard. "Frederick Douglass
  Always Knew He Was Meant
  to Be Free."

Title of magazine/Date of publication
Smithsonian Feb. 1995: 114–27.
              Page number

Book

Author   Title   ③
Douglass, Frederick Narrative of
  the Life of Frederick Douglass.
  New York: Signet, 1997. Date of
City of publication/Publisher publication

Location of source   Library call number
Public Library   973.6 DOU 1845 1443

7.4 Taking Notes

As you find material that suits the purpose of your report, record each piece of information on a separate note card. You will probably use all three of the following note-taking methods. **Paraphrase**, or restate the passage in your own words. Start by finding the main idea and rewriting it in your own words. Then find and list the details that support the idea. As you restate the passage, try to use simpler language. Remember to note the source of the passage.

Summarize, or rephrase the passage in fewer words. Restate only the main ideas, using your own words. Leave out details. As a final step, check to make sure that your summary is accurate and that it does not include unnecessary details.

Quote, or copy word for word, the original text, if you think the author's own words best clarify a particular point. Use quotation marks to signal the beginning and end of the quotation.

> Douglass's lectures   Source number ②
>
> **Main Idea**
> "What, to the American slave, is your Fourth of July? ... To him your celebration is a sham." 115
>   Page number
>
> **Type of note**
> Quotation

For more details on making source cards and taking notes, see the Research Report Workshop on pages 818–825.

7.5 Writing a Thesis Statement

A thesis statement in a research report defines the main idea, or overall purpose, of your report. A clear one-sentence answer to your main question will result in a good thesis statement.

Question: How did Frederick Douglass draw support for the antislavery movement in a way that others could not?

Thesis Statement: Speaking and writing as a former slave, Frederick Douglass openly criticized racism in the United States and drew support for the antislavery movement.

7.6 Making an Outline

To organize your report, group your note cards into main ideas and arrange them in a logical order. With your notes, make a topic outline, beginning with a shortened version of your thesis statement. Key ideas are listed after Roman numerals, and subpoints are listed after uppercase letters and Arabic numerals, as in the following example.

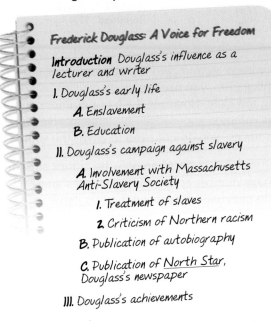

> Frederick Douglass: A Voice for Freedom
>
> **Introduction** Douglass's influence as a lecturer and writer
>
> I. Douglass's early life
>   A. Enslavement
>   B. Education
> II. Douglass's campaign against slavery
>   A. Involvement with Massachusetts Anti-Slavery Society
>   1. Treatment of slaves
>   2. Criticism of Northern racism
>   B. Publication of autobiography
>   C. Publication of <u>North Star</u>, Douglass's newspaper
> III. Douglass's achievements

7.7 Documenting Your Sources

When you quote one of your sources or write in your own words information you have found in a source, you need to credit that source, using parenthetical documentation.

Guidelines for Parenthetical Documentation	
Work by One Author	Put the author's last name and the page reference in parentheses: **(Douglass 12)** If you mention the author's name in the sentence, put only the page reference in parentheses: **(12)**
Work by Two or Three Authors	Put the authors' last names and the page reference in parentheses: **(Meier and Rudwick 146)**
Work by More Than Three Authors	Give the first author's last name followed by *et al.* and the page reference in parentheses: **(Ripley et al. 14)**
Work with No Author Given	Give the title (or a shortened version) and the page reference in parentheses: **("Frederick Douglass" 113)**
One of Two or More Works by Same Author	Give the author's last name, the title (or a shortened version), and the page reference in parentheses: **(Conniff, "Frederick Douglass" 117)**

WRITING TIP Presenting someone else's writing or ideas as your own is plagiarism. To avoid plagiarism, you need to credit sources as noted in the chart. However, if a piece of information is common knowledge—available in several sources—you do not need to credit the source.

PUNCTUATION TIP When only the author and the page number appear in parentheses, there is no punctuation between the two items.

7.8 Following MLA Manuscript Guidelines

The final copy of your report should follow the Modern Language Association (MLA) guidelines for manuscript preparation.

- The heading in the upper left-hand corner of the first page should include your name, your teacher's name, the course name, and the date, each on a separate line.
- Below the heading, center the title on the page.
- Number all the pages consecutively in the upper right-hand corner, one-half inch from the top. Also, include your last name before each page number.
- Double-space the entire paper.
- Except for the margins above the page numbers, leave one-inch margins on all sides of every page.

Works Cited List

At the end of your research report, you need to include a list of works cited. All sources that you have cited in your research report need to be listed alphabetically by the authors' last names. If no author is named in a source, use the editor's last name or the title of the work. Note the guidelines for spacing and punctuation on the model list on page R55.

Internet Sources A works cited entry for an Internet source includes the same kinds of information as one for a print source. It also includes the date you accessed the information and the electronic address of the source. Some of the information may be unavailable; include as much as you can. For more information on how to write works cited entries for Internet sources, see the MLA guidelines posted on the Internet or access that document through the McDougal Littell Web site.

INTERNET Style Guidelines
www.mcdougallittell.com

CD-ROMs Entries for CD-ROMs include the publication medium (CD-ROM), the distributor, and the date of publication. Some of the information may not be available. Include as much as you can.

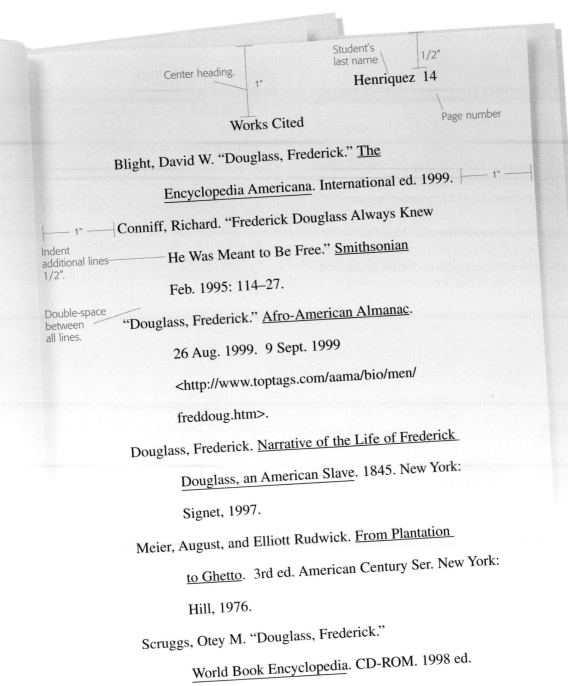

Center heading.   1"

Student's last name   1/2"

Henriquez 14

Page number

Works Cited

Blight, David W. "Douglass, Frederick." The Encyclopedia Americana. International ed. 1999.   1"

Indent additional lines 1/2".   1"

Conniff, Richard. "Frederick Douglass Always Knew He Was Meant to Be Free." Smithsonian Feb. 1995: 114–27.

Double-space between all lines.

"Douglass, Frederick." Afro-American Almanac. 26 Aug. 1999. 9 Sept. 1999 <http://www.toptags.com/aama/bio/men/ freddoug.htm>.

Douglass, Frederick. Narrative of the Life of Frederick Douglass, an American Slave. 1845. New York: Signet, 1997.

Meier, August, and Elliott Rudwick. From Plantation to Ghetto. 3rd ed. American Century Ser. New York: Hill, 1976.

Scruggs, Otey M. "Douglass, Frederick." World Book Encyclopedia. CD-ROM. 1998 ed. Chicago: World Book, 1998.

⑧ Technical Writing

Technical writing is a type of writing used for detailed instructions or descriptions of items or processes in a variety of fields, such as engineering, government, industry, and science. Technical writing can take the form of bylaws, instructions for assembling and using an object or tool, and descriptions of how a tool, machine, or scientific theory works.

8.1 Instructions for Using a Tool

Often in careers or everyday life, an individual will have to use technical writing to leave detailed instructions for another person.

Instructions include specific steps that guide the reader through a process. Each step should offer a specific description of how to do one particular task in the process.

BASICS IN A BOX

A successful set of instructions should include

1. the purpose of the tool
2. a list of necessary equipment and materials
3. numbered steps in the correct order, and clearly explained
4. definitions of unfamiliar terms if necessary

How to Prepare a Hand Sander

A hand sander is used to sand wood or other material to a fine finish. A hand sander makes the job easier by holding sandpaper or other types of abrasive paper in a constant flat position. ❶

Materials
- hand sander
- sandpaper ❷

1. Choose the appropriate type of sandpaper for your job.
2. Lift the flexible rubber flap at one end of the hand sander.
3. Insert the sandpaper in the slot between the flap and the base.
4. Lower the flap. Metal pins in the flap will pierce the sandpaper to hold it in place.
5. Lift the rubber flap at the other end of the hand sander.
6. Pull the sandpaper tightly and insert it in the slot between the flap and the base.
7. Lower the flap to secure the sandpaper. ❸
8. Rub the hand sander along the wood or other material until you get the finish you want. Be careful not to rub too hard.

8.2 Writing Organizational Bylaws

An organizational bylaws document provides a detailed written description of the rules and regulations that allow formal organizations, governing bodies, and businesses to function smoothly. Bylaws include basic information from which an organization sets policies and conducts activities.

BASICS IN A BOX

Complete organizational bylaws should include

1. an opening statement with the organization's name, the type of group, and the purpose for its existence
2. sections that begin with headings and present information in a clear format
3. statements of the characteristics and operation of the organization
4. rules that cannot be changed or suspended without changing the bylaws themselves

Central High School Drama Club Bylaws

We, the current members of Central High School Drama Club, create the following laws for our organization. Our members include actors, scenery designers, makeup artists, costume designers, lighting and sound specialists, stagehands, and stage managers.

MISSION STATEMENT: To provide an organization where members of the dramatic arts program at Central High School heighten awareness about theater in the school, support each other during shows, and provide entertainment for the Oakland community. ❶

ACTIVITIES:
- Biweekly meetings to talk about concerns and programming
- Publicity for upcoming school productions
- Performances, including two major drama productions

MEMBERSHIP REQUIREMENTS

To qualify for membership in the Drama Club, a candidate must ❷
- be enrolled as a student in Central High School
- complete ten hours of participation in a school or community production

To remain a member of the Drama Club, an individual must
- actively contribute to the goals of the club
- complete a minimum of five hours of production participation each year

OFFICER ELECTION LAWS

Each year the members will vote for a president, vice-president, treasurer, and secretary. ❸
1. The individuals running for office must be nominated by another Drama Club member.
2. To be elected, a nominee must receive a majority of the votes.

RULES OF ORDER FOR MEETINGS
1. All meetings will be conducted according to *Robert's Rules of Order*.
2. A quorum of five members must be present for discussion of business items and voting.
3. The president will call the meeting to order.
4. The secretary will record, distribute, and manage meeting minutes.

⑨ Career Handbook

The ability to write clearly is an important skill in the business world. As you prepare to enter the job market, you will need to know how to research different careers, fill out job applications, write business letters, and prepare résumés.

⑨.1 Career Report

Each year, there are jobs that did not exist the year before. How will you find out about the latest career opportunities? One way is to use the library and the Internet as research tools. Here is what one eighth-grade student wrote about a career in which she has an interest—computer animation.

BASICS IN A BOX

A successful career report should

1. include an introductory paragraph that describes the career
2. present information about career training
3. follow a logical pattern of organization, using transitions between ideas
4. use information from multiple sources
5. credit sources of information
6. include a properly formatted Works Cited list

Fantasia 1

Joyce Fantasia
Writing Class 8B
Mrs. Palin
September

Become a Computer Animator

Have you ever wondered who creates the special effects in feature films such as <u>The Phantom Menace</u> and <u>Titanic</u> or who creates the animation for television commercials? The answer is professional computer animators. Computer animation is a growing field that offers many exciting career opportunities. ❶

If you are interested in this field, the first thing to think about is where to get the training you will need. Computer animation started in the 1970s and 1980s. In those days, only a few schools offered training programs. Today, however, hundreds of colleges and universities have programs and courses in computer animation (Morie). For example, the California Institute of the Arts has programs both in character animation and experimental animation, and the University of Washington has a new program that covers the basics ("Growing Demand"). ❷

The next thing to think about is what to specialize in. There are

❸ many different specialties, and new ones are developing all the time. Besides being used in the field of entertainment, computer animation is used in meteorology and medicine. For example, weather forecasters use computer animation to track changes in the weather, and doctors use it to study what's happening inside the human body. Pilots use it in training to fly. Computer animation is even used by architects, lawyers, and business executives (Lund 8–10).

Finally, it's important to know what skills you will need to become a computer animator. The basic skills are the same for all computer animators—you have to be good at math and art (Mardis; Morie).

❹
❺
After you have covered the basics, what you need to know depends on the specialty you choose. For example, I want to be a computer animator in the field of entertainment. (Since I was little, I've always loved to draw. I even invented two cartoon characters—Mighty Max and Asteroid Alexandra.) If I specialize in movies or in television, I might work with storyboards that set up the outlines of stories. Or I might be in charge of "in-betweening"—making the drawings that show every move each character makes. There are many opportunities because the completion of one feature-length film requires hundreds of people and takes thousands of hours of work (Lund 27).

So if you are creative and a good math student, you might want to join the growing number of computer animators. But be prepared— you'll have to work hard to become one!

Works Cited

"Growing Demand for Computer Animators Spurs a New Program at University of Washington." Chronicle of Higher Education 7 Aug. 1997: A23.

Lund, Bill. Getting Ready for a Career as a Computer Animator. Mankato: Capstone, 1998.

Mardis, Lori A. "Career Biographies: 3D Computer Animation." The Internet Public Library. 2 May 1997. U of Michigan School of Information. 25 Aug. 1999 <http://www.ipl.org/teen/pathways/comptech/companim.html>.

Morie, Jacquelyn Ford. "CGI Training for the Entertainment Film Industry." IEEE Computer Graphics and Applications 18.1 (1998). 17 Aug. 1999 <http://www.education.siggraph.org/curriculum/misc/jmorie.html>.

❻

9.2 Job Application

When you apply for a job, you may be asked to fill out an application form. Application forms vary, but most of them ask for similar kinds of information.

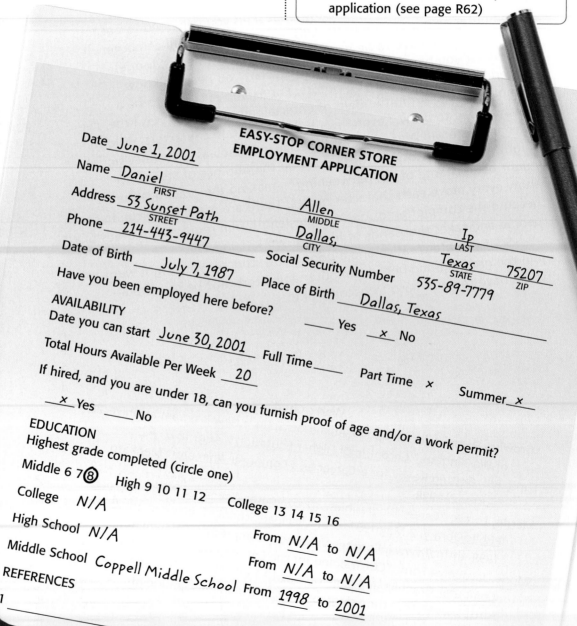

EASY-STOP CORNER STORE
EMPLOYMENT APPLICATION

Date _June 1, 2001_

Name _Daniel_
FIRST

Allen
MIDDLE

_Ip_
LAST

Address _53 Sunset Path_
STREET

Dallas,
CITY

Texas
STATE

_75207_
ZIP

Phone _214-443-9447_

Date of Birth _July 7, 1987_

Social Security Number _535-89-7779_

Place of Birth _Dallas, Texas_

Have you been employed here before? _____ Yes _x_ No

AVAILABILITY
Date you can start _June 30, 2001_   Full Time _____   Part Time _x_   Summer _x_

Total Hours Available Per Week _20_

If hired, and you are under 18, can you furnish proof of age and/or a work permit?
_x_ Yes _____ No

EDUCATION
Highest grade completed (circle one)

Middle 6 7 ⑧   High 9 10 11 12   College 13 14 15 16

College _N/A_

High School _N/A_   From _N/A_ to _N/A_

Middle School _Coppell Middle School_   From _N/A_ to _N/A_

From _1998_ to _2001_

REFERENCES

1 _____

BASICS IN A BOX

A successful résumé should

1. state your purpose or objective
2. describe your qualifications
3. list your previous employment experience
4. describe your education
5. list extracurricular activities and hobbies

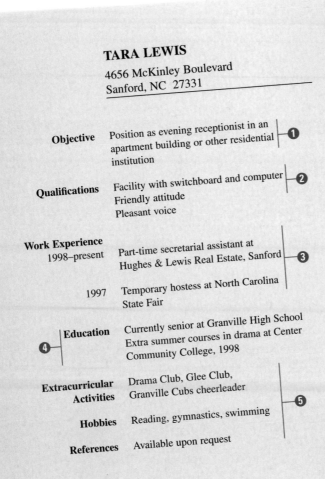

TARA LEWIS
4656 McKinley Boulevard
Sanford, NC 27331

Objective   Position as evening receptionist in an apartment building or other residential institution ①

Qualifications   Facility with switchboard and computer ②
Friendly attitude
Pleasant voice

Work Experience
1998–present   Part-time secretarial assistant at Hughes & Lewis Real Estate, Sanford ③

1997   Temporary hostess at North Carolina State Fair

Education   Currently senior at Granville High School
Extra summer courses in drama at Center Community College, 1998 ④

Extracurricular Activities   Drama Club, Glee Club, Granville Cubs cheerleader

Hobbies   Reading, gymnastics, swimming ⑤

References   Available upon request

9.4 Business Letter/ Letter of Inquiry

Business letters are more formal than personal letters and require a precise form. Types of business letters include the letter of inquiry, letter of complaint, cover letters for résumés, and announcements. The letter of inquiry asks for information or service from an individual or organization that is in a position to provide it. Formal letters are printed on white stationery, 8½ by 11 inches in size. Margins should be at least one inch wide.

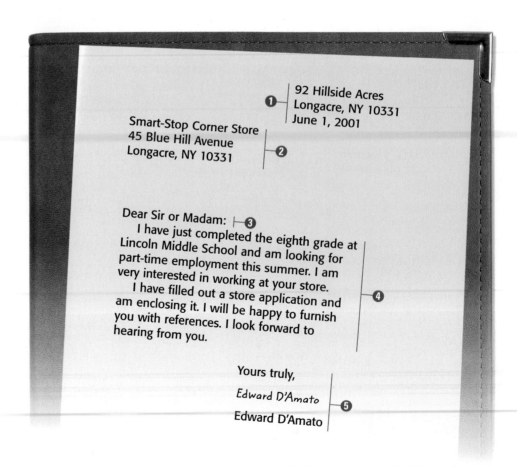

92 Hillside Acres
Longacre, NY 10331
June 1, 2001 ❶

Smart-Stop Corner Store
45 Blue Hill Avenue
Longacre, NY 10331 ❷

Dear Sir or Madam: ❸
    I have just completed the eighth grade at Lincoln Middle School and am looking for part-time employment this summer. I am very interested in working at your store.
    I have filled out a store application and am enclosing it. I will be happy to furnish you with references. I look forward to hearing from you. ❹

Yours truly,

Edward D'Amato ❺
Edward D'Amato

9.5 Memorandum

A memorandum (or memo) is a type of informal correspondence between individuals within an office or organization. The memo has a specific format but does not require a salutation or closing.

MEMORANDUM ❶

To: All employees of *CD Burners: New and Used Music Store*

From: Kasey Havana (store manager)

Date: November 13, 2002

Re: The new closing and lockup procedure ❷

Remember the new procedures for closing the store.

- The closing manager places all money in the safe and locks the safe.
- The stock person takes the trash out and then locks the back door.
- The cashiers put any unwanted CDs back and turn off the neon "Rap" and "Rock" window signs.
- The manager sets the security alarm and quickly exits with the employees. ❸
- The manager locks the front door.
- The employees pull the theft-proof metal grating down.
- The manager locks the padlock and makes sure the grating is secure.

⑩ Model Bank

⑩.⑪ Research Report

BASICS IN A BOX

A successful research report should

1. include a strong introduction and a thesis statement that clearly states the topic and purpose.
2. use evidence from primary or secondary sources to develop and support ideas.
3. credit sources of information.
4. follow a logical pattern of organization, using transitions between ideas.
5. use information from multiple sources.
6. summarize ideas in the conclusion.
7. include a properly formatted works cited list at the end.

Model 1: Research Report

Cogley 1

Catherine Cogley
Mr. Bell
English 8
September 25

Julia Alvarez: How to Make Sense of a Complicated Life

Julia Alvarez is a writer who grew up in two places—the Dominican Republic in the Caribbean and New York City in the United States. Because these places are very different from one another, she has tried to make sense of her childhood by writing about both experiences. "Writing is how I put my life together," she said (Karkabi). **— ❶**

When Alvarez was young, it didn't look as if she would end up a writer. "Back home in the Dominican Republic, I had been an active, lively child, a bad student full of fun with plentiful friends," she told an interviewer ("Alvarez"). Where she grew up, people didn't read books very often. Reading books was considered "anti-social." Instead, her family and friends "were always telling stories" (Requa). **⊢❷**

Alvarez's family had to leave the Dominican Republic when she was ten years old because her parents were fighting against a cruel dictator, General Rafael Trujillo. "We were the lucky ones who escaped," she said (Karkabi). Others **⊢❸** didn't. Alvarez relates her family's terrible struggle in her second book, <u>In the Time of the Butterflies</u>. This book is based on the true story of three brave sisters who fought against the dictator beside Alvarez's own family. The book describes

Works Cited

"Alvarez, Julia." <u>Contemporary Authors</u>. Vol. 147. Detroit: Gale, 1995.

Atanasoski, Neda. "Julia Alvarez." <u>Voices from the Gaps: Women Writers of Color</u>. 15 Apr. 1999. Dept. of English and Program in American Studies, U of Minnesota. 26 Aug. 1999 <http://voices.cla.umn.edu/authors/JuliaAlvarez.html>.

Karkabi, Barbara. "Author Alvarez Views Stories as Sustenance." <u>Houston Chronicle</u> 10 Apr. 1997: B1.

Requa, Marny. "The Politics of Fiction." <u>Frontera</u> 5. 17 Aug. 1999 <http://www.fronteramag.com/issue5/Alvarez>.

7

Cogley 2

what it's like to live in a country where a person can be murdered for speaking out against the government. This book shows the life Alvarez had before she came to America.

4 When her family moved to New York City, Alvarez's life completely changed. She was no longer surrounded by people who told stories, and she felt isolated from other kids partly because she could not speak English very well ("Alvarez"). **5** However, in the end, writing saved her. One of her teachers gave the members of her class an assignment to write stories about themselves. Alvarez found she could make up what she wanted and leave out the difficult aspects about living in a new country ("Alvarez"). In time, she started going to the library and writing on her own. By the time she was in high school, she knew she wanted to be a writer. She didn't have one physical place she could really call home, so Alvarez "made language her homeland" (Atanasoski).

Alvarez's novels include: <u>How the García Girls Lost Their Accents</u>, <u>In the Time of the Butterflies</u>, and <u>¡Yo!</u>. She has also published a collection of essays entitled <u>Something to Declare</u> and four collections of poems: <u>The Housekeeping Book</u>, <u>The Other Side: El Otro Lado</u>, <u>Homecoming</u> and <u>Homecoming: New and Collected Poems</u>. "I write to find out what I am thinking. I write to find out who I am. I write to understand things" (Requa). Writing is what helps Julia Alvarez make sense of her complicated life. **6**

10.2 Book Review

BASICS IN A BOX

A successful book review should

1. have an introduction that gives the title, author, and some information about the book.
2. summarize the work without giving away the ending.
3. if the work is fiction, discuss the plot, setting, characters, and theme.
4. explain why you admire or dislike the work.
5. support your reactions with details from the work.
6. conclude with a strong statement of your opinion or a recommendation.

Model 2: Book Review

Hatchet

Reviewed by Kristen Loos

What would you do if you suddenly found yourself in the middle of a wilderness with no one else around and only a hatchet to help you survive? That's what happens to Brian Robeson, a boy about my age, in Gary Paulsen's book *Hatchet*. After his parents are divorced, Brian heads up to northern Canada to spend the summer with his dad. But the pilot flying him up has a heart attack, and Brian is forced to crash-land the plane by himself. From then on, he has to take charge of the situation, or he won't live to tell about it.

From the beginning all the way to the end of the book, Brian faces big problems just to survive. He's a city kid, so he's used to opening up the refrigerator anytime for whatever he wants to eat. Now, at the edge of the woods, he has to figure out things like how to be safe from wild animals and how to make a fire without matches. At first he panics. He doesn't even know what to drink or what food to eat and how to get it.

One of the things I like about the book is how Brian changes. At first, he hopes he will be rescued very soon. He thinks he can hold out a few days till his parents and people from a search party find him. During this part of the book, he starts to think things out for himself. But he still gets scared easily and feels sorry for himself a lot.

Then, when a plane flies over without seeing him, he realizes that he is really on his own. He learns to make tools to fish and hunt with and to depend on himself for everything he needs. In the end, he is able to confront all kinds of dangers and still hold out hope for himself. To him, this is "tough hope."

I'm not going to say how the book ends or whether Brian gets rescued or not. It would spoil the book if I did. This really is a cool adventure book. It also has some good lessons about what to do in case you are ever caught alone in the wilderness. I hope you enjoy it as much as I did.

① ② ③ ④ ⑤ ⑥

10.3 Short Story

BASICS IN A BOX

A successful short story should

1. have a strong beginning and ending.
2. use the elements of character, setting, and plot to create a convincing world.
3. use vivid sensory language, concrete details, and dialogue to create believable characters and setting.
4. develop a main conflict.
5. present a clear sequence of events.

Model 3: Short Story   **You Have the Power**

Written by Richard Carson ——1

I'm always thinking about new places to get away to, anywhere out of the neighborhood where I live with my family. We've been here all my life, and everybody's so nosy, always messing in somebody else's business. A few more years—I've told myself a million times—and I get my license; I'll be out of here. For now, we have just one car, which my father drives to his day job, packing pharmaceuticals, and three nights a week to work at an all-night gas station. When he's home, we have to be extra quiet around the house. That's when I'd just as soon play basketball, ride my bike, be out, somewhere else. Usually though, I have to take care of my brother Larry. And Larry always wants to be with me. ——2

Larry is little, five years younger than I am. Whenever he sees me heading for the door, he says, "Where you going?" ——3

"None of your business, pip-squeak. Better scram," I warn him, but he still always wants to tag along.

When we leave, Mom reminds Larry, "Now, stay with Steven or you'll get separated." ——4

"That means you'll get lost and end up by yourself," I say. Larry grins. He knows what separated means. I groan, because I know that now, no matter how hard I try, I'll never get rid of him.

I have a deal with my mother about Larry. In the summer, every day for an hour before lunch, she'll watch him so I can be by myself and do whatever I want—take it easy, maybe catch up on some reading. I used to read adventure books like *Treasure Island* or *The Time Machine*. But even they got old after a while, and I was starting to get bored. Then one day I found a book on the give-away table at the library.

It didn't have a cover, so I couldn't tell the name of it, but it was about an archaeologist who found a tomb on a mountain in a jungle somewhere. In the tomb was a design, three circles, one inside the other like a bull's eye, with a skinny diamond running through them. Under the design was an inscription in a language the archaeologist knew. It said, "You have the power."

The archaeologist was thinking about the inscription, when all at once sparks started flying, and he was being chased by a soldier in a chariot! When he looked around, suddenly he realized where he was. Pyramids and palm trees—he was back in ancient Egypt! Then he remembered the inscription and boom!—he was zapped back to the tomb on the mountain. This was pretty cool, so he figured he'd try again, and zap!—this time he was in medieval England. He discovered that all he had to do was let the design appear in his mind, and say the words "You have the power. " Then he could zap himself wherever he wanted to go. He went to Greece and Rome, landed on board a pirate ship, and even ended up once with dinosaurs.

"This is great, " I said, finally closing the book. "Now I can try it."

Behind our house is a wooden fence, flat and high with the boards joined together. Perfect, I thought. The Delancey twins next door like to play hopscotch, so, that afternoon, I borrowed a piece of chalk. I intended to bring it back. I decided I'd even bring them something for letting me use it, a jewel from the pyramids or something. That night, I reread the story over and over till I knew it by heart. I didn't want anything to go wrong.

The next day, exactly at eleven o'clock, I sneaked down the back stairs, the chalk and book in my hands. "You have the power," I whispered to myself as I pushed open the back door, slowly, so it wouldn't squeak. "You have the power." I checked the book one last time, then looked at the fence. "You have the power," I spoke to it out loud and began to draw.

I drew the three circles and three points of the diamond. I was about to do the last side, thinking to myself, I only have an hour, how will I know what time it is? Will my watch work when I travel through time? I shook my head to get rid of those jinxy thoughts. Nothing could spoil this, nothing.

And then I heard him: "Hey, Steven, what you doing?"

I ran over, grabbed Larry by the back of the shirt, and dragged him to the kitchen window where I hoped Mom was inside making his snack.

"Mom!" I cried. "Why is Larry here?"

My mother's face came to the screen door. "Oh, Stevie, there you are. I have to run across the street. Old Mrs. Jenkins isn't feeling well. Mind Larry for me, will you?"

"But Mom," I wailed.

"Steven!" My mother's voice was cross all of a sudden. "You can have your hour after lunch."

I pulled Larry's arm, dragging him into the back yard again. I picked up the book and showed him the picture of the archaeologist surrounded by flying sparks, getting ready to blast through time.

"Look, Larry. You have the power." Then I told him the whole story. When I was done, Larry had his lower lip under his upper one and was staring at the

Short Story at a Glance

Introduction

Sets the stage by
- introducing the characters
- describing the setting

Body

Develops the plot by
- introducing the conflict
- telling a sequence of events
- developing characters through words and actions
- building suspense toward a climax

Conclusion

Finishes the story by
- resolving the conflict
- telling the last event

---

ground. I thought to myself, This will fix it. He'll never want to go with me, not anywhere, ever again. "What do you say?" I said to him.

Larry nodded his head but didn't look at me. I pulled the piece of chalk out of my pocket and connected the last point of the diamond. When I stepped back, Larry was looking at me. His eyes were wide. He shivered like he was cold.

"You're sure?" I asked. Larry nodded slowly.

"Okay." I sat him down in front of the diamond and circles, then I sat right beside him. "Now, look at them, and keep looking," I said. I waited a minute. "Concentrate." I closed my eyes. "You have the power," I sounded kind of like my father when we woke him up.

"You have the power," Larry said, and his voice squeaked when he said it.

"You have the power." I mouthed the words softly this time, like a hypnotist. Larry said nothing.

Slowly, the three circles and diamond drifted into my mind, hazy at first, then as clear as day. I made myself hear the words inside my head. I waited for the shouts of ancient Egypt, the roar of dinosaurs, the clash of knights on horseback. The fence creaked; the trees rustled in the breeze.

Then I heard it, softly at first, then louder. Was it a bird, or was it the beat of a thousand horse hoofs far off in the distance? I opened my eyes. I hadn't moved. Larry was starting to cry, blubbering.

"What if we get separated?" he said.

I hadn't thought of that . . .

Grammar Handbook

❶ Quick Reference: Parts of Speech

Part of Speech	Definition	Examples
Noun	Names a person, place, thing, idea, quality, or action.	Pandora, Greece, boat, freedom, joy, sailing
Pronoun	Takes the place of a noun or another pronoun.	
Personal	Refers to the one speaking, spoken to, or spoken about.	I, me, my, mine, we, us, our, ours, you, your, yours, she, he, it, her, him, hers, his, its, they, them, their, theirs
Reflexive	Follows a verb or preposition and refers to a preceding noun or pronoun.	myself, yourself, herself, himself, itself, ourselves, yourselves, themselves
Intensive	Emphasizes a noun or another pronoun.	(Same as reflexives)
Demonstrative	Points to specific persons or things.	this, that, these, those
Interrogative	Signals questions.	who, whom, whose, which, what
Indefinite	Refers to person(s) or thing(s) not specifically mentioned.	both, all, most, many, anyone, everybody, several, none, some
Relative	Introduces subordinate clauses and relates them to words in the main clause.	who, whom, whose, which, that
Verb	Expresses action, condition, or state of being.	
Action	Tells what the subject does or did, physically or mentally.	run, reaches, listened, consider, decides, dreamt
Linking	Connects subjects to that which identifies or describes them.	am, is, are, was, were, sound, taste, appear, feel, become, remain, seem
Auxiliary	Precedes and introduces main verbs.	be, have, do, can, could, will, would, may, might
Adjective	Modifies nouns or pronouns.	**strong** women, **two** epics, **enough** time
Adverb	Modifies verbs, adjectives, or other adverbs.	walked **out**, **really** funny, **far** away
Preposition	Relates one word to another (following) word.	at, by, for, from, in, of, on, to, with
Conjunction	Joins words or word groups.	
Coordinating	Joins words or word groups used the same way.	and, but, or, for, so, yet, nor
Correlative	Join words or word groups used the same way and used in pairs.	both . . . and, either . . . or, neither . . . nor
Subordinating	Joins word groups not used the same way.	although, after, as, before, because, when, if, unless
Interjection	Expresses emotion.	wow, ouch, hurrah

❷ Quick Reference: The Sentence and Its Parts

The diagrams that follow will give you a brief review of the essentials of the sentence—subjects and predicates—and of some of its parts.

The boy's clothes were ragged and worn.

The **complete subject** includes all the words that identify the person, place, thing, or idea that the sentence is about.

The **complete predicate** includes all the words that tell or ask something about the subject.

clothes

were

The **simple subject** tells exactly whom or what the sentence is about. It may be one word or a group of words but it does not include modifiers.

The **simple predicate** or **verb** tells what the subject is or does. It may be one word or several, but it does not include modifiers.

At the cabin, the woman **had given** the boy **some apples.**

A **prepositional phrase** consists of a preposition, its object, and any modifiers of the object. In this phrase, *at* is the preposition and *the cabin* is its object.

subject

Verbs often have more than one part. They may be made up of a **main verb,** like *given,* and one or more **auxiliary,** or **helping verbs,** like *had.*

A **direct object** is a word or group of words that tells who or what receives the action of the verb in the sentence.

An **indirect object** is a word or group of words that tells *to whom* or *for whom* or *to what* or *for what* about the verb. A sentence can have an indirect object only if it has a direct object. The indirect object always comes before the direct object in a sentence.

❸ Quick Reference: Punctuation

Punctuation	Function	Examples
End Marks period, question mark, exclamation point	to end sentences	We can start now. When would you like to leave? What a fantastic hit!
	initials and other abbreviations	Mr. Misenheimer, O. Henry, McDougal Littell Inc., P.M., A.D., lbs., oz., Blvd., Dr.

	items in outlines	I. Volcanoes
		   A. Central-vent
		      1. Shield

	exception: postal abbreviations	NE (Nebraska), NV (Nevada)
Commas	before conjunction in compound sentence	I have never disliked poetry, but now I really love it.
	items in a series	She is brave, loyal, and kind. The slow, easy route is best.
	words of address	Maria, how can I help you? You must do something, soldier.
	parenthetical expressions	Well, just suppose that we can't? Hard workers, as you know, don't quit. I'm not a quitter, believe me.
	introductory phrases and clauses	In the beginning of the day, I feel fresh. While she was out, I was here. Having finished my chores, I went out.
	nonessential phrases and clauses	Ed Pawn, captain of the chess team, won. Ed Pawn, who is the captain, won. The two leading runners, sprinting toward the finish line, ended in a tie.
	in dates and addresses	September 21, 2001. Mail it by May 14, 2000, to Hauptman Company, 321 Market Street, Memphis, Tennessee.
	in letter parts for clarity, or to avoid confusion	Dear Jim, Sincerely yours, By noon, time had run out. What the minister does, does matter. While cooking, Jim burned his hand.
Semicolons	in compound sentences that are not joined by coordinators such as *and*, etc.	The last shall be first; the first shall be last. I read science fiction; however, I like suspense novels better.
	with items in series that contain commas	We invited my sister, Jan; her friend, Don; my Uncle Jack; and Mary Dodd.
	in compound sentences that contain commas	After I ran out of money, I called my parents; but only my sister was home, unfortunately.

Punctuation	Function	Examples
Colons	to introduce lists	**Correct:** We invited the following people: Dana, John, and Will.
	before a long quotation	Abraham Lincoln wrote: "Four score and seven years ago, our fathers brought forth on this continent a new nation . . . ."
	after the salutation of a business letter	To Whom It May Concern: Dear Leonard Atole:
	with certain numbers	1:28 P.M., Genesis 2:5
Dashes	to indicate an abrupt break in thought	I was thinking of my mother—who is arriving tomorrow—just as you walked in.
Parentheses	to enclose less important material	It was so unlike him (John is always on time) that I began to worry. The last World Series game (Did you see it?) was fun.
Hyphens	with a compound adjective before nouns	The not-so-rich taxpayer won't stand for this!
	in compounds with *all-, ex-, self-, -elect*	The ex-firefighter helped rescue him. Our president-elect is self-conscious.
	in compound numbers (to ninety-nine)	Today, I turn twenty-one.
	in fractions used as adjectives	My cup is one-third full.
	between prefixes and words beginning with capital letters	Which pre-Raphaelite painter do you like best? It snowed in mid-October.
	when dividing words at the end of a line	How could you have any reasonable expec-tations of getting a new computer?
Apostrophes	to form possessives of nouns and indefinite pronouns	my friend's book, my friends' book, anyone's guess, somebody else's problem
	for omitted letters in numbers/contractions	don't (omitted **o**); he'd (omitted **woul**) the class of '99 (omitted **19**)
Quotation Marks	to set off a speaker's exact words	Sara said, "I'm finally ready." "I'm ready," Sara said, "finally." Did Sara say, "I'm ready"? Sara said, "I'm ready!"
	for titles of stories, short poems, essays, songs, book chapters	I liked Paulsen's "Stop the Sun" and Mora's "Mi Madre." I like Joplin's "Me and Bobby McGee."
Ellipses	for material omitted from a quotation	"When in the course of human events . . . and to assume among the powers of the earth. . . ."
Italics	for titles of books, plays, magazines, long poems, operas, films, TV series, names of ships	*Roughing It, Hamlet, Newsweek, The Odyssey, Madame Butterfly, Gone with the Wind, Seinfeld, U.S.S. Constitution*

❹ Quick Reference: Capitalization

Category/Rule	Examples
People and Titles	
Names and initials of people	**G**ish **J**en, **J**. **F**rank **D**obie
Titles with names	**P**rofessor **H**olmes, **S**enator **L**ong
Deities and members of religious groups	**J**esus, **A**llah, the **B**uddha, **Z**eus, **B**aptists, **R**oman **C**atholics
Names of ethnic and national groups	**H**ispanics, **I**rish, **A**frican **A**mericans
Geographical Names	
Cities, states, countries, continents	**P**hiladelphia, **K**ansas, **J**apan, **E**urope
Regions, bodies of water, mountains	the **S**outh, **L**ake **B**aikal, **M**ount **M**cKinley
Geographic features, parks	**G**reat **B**asin, **Y**ellowstone **N**ational **P**ark
Streets and roads, planets	318 **E**ast **S**utton **D**rive, **C**harles **C**ourt, **J**upiter, **P**luto
Organizations and Events	
Companies, organizations, teams	**T**albot **T**oy **C**ompany, **B**oy **S**couts of **A**merica, **S**t. **L**ouis **C**ardinals
Buildings, bridges, monuments	**E**mpire **S**tate **B**uilding, **E**ads **B**ridge, **W**ashington **M**onument
Documents, awards	the **D**eclaration of **I**ndependence, **S**tanley **C**up
Special named events	**M**ardi **G**ras, **W**orld **S**eries
Governmental bodies, historical periods and events	**U**.**S**. **S**enate, **H**ouse of **R**epresentatives, **M**iddle **A**ges, **V**ietnam **W**ar
Days and months, holidays	**T**hursday, **M**arch, **T**hanksgiving, **L**abor **D**ay
Specific cars, boats, trains, planes	**V**auxhall, *Mississippi Queen,* **O**rient **E**xpress, **C**oncorde
Proper Adjectives	
Adjectives formed from proper nouns	**F**rench cooking, **F**reudian psychology, **E**dwardian age, **A**tlantic coast
First Words and the Pronoun *I*	
The first word in a sentence or quote	**T**his is it. **H**e said, "**L**et's go."
Complete sentence in parentheses	(**C**onsult the previous chapter.)
Salutation and closing of letters	**D**ear **M**adam, **V**ery truly yours,
First lines of most poetry	**L**et them be as flowers,
The personal pronoun *I*	If **I** could stand alone, strong and free, **I**'d rather be a tall, ugly weed.
First, last, and all important words in titles	*High **T**ide in **T**ucson,* "**A** **L**oaf of **P**oetry"

❺ Writing Complete Sentences

5.1 *Sentence Fragments* A sentence fragment is a group of words that does not express a complete thought. It may be missing a subject, a predicate, or both. A sentence fragment makes you wonder What is this about? or What happened?

Missing Subject or Predicate You can correct a sentence fragment by adding the missing subject or predicate to complete the thought.

> **INCORRECT:** *Play an important part in a radio drama. The chug of an oncoming train. A car engine. Blows frantically.*
> **CORRECT:** <u>Sound effects</u> *play an important part in a radio drama. The chug of an oncoming train <u>signals danger.</u> A car engine <u>stalls.</u> <u>The train whistle</u> blows frantically.*

Phrase and Subordinate-Clause Fragments When the fragment is a phrase or a subordinate clause, you may join the fragment to an existing sentence.

> **INCORRECT:** *In a radio drama. The music also stirs the listener's emotions. As the music speeds up. The tension builds. Suddenly, terror grips the listener. Because the music has ended abruptly.*
> **CORRECT:** *In a radio drama the music also stirs the listener's emotions. As the music speeds up, the tension builds. Suddenly, terror grips the listener, because the music has ended abruptly.*

GRAMMAR PRACTICE

Correct the sentence fragments that you find in this paragraph.

(1) Like *The Hitchhiker,* the dramatization of *The War of the Worlds* was produced for radio by Orson Welles. **(2)** Reporting a Martian invasion of the United States. **(3)** Broadcast October 30, 1938. **(4)** An announcer interrupted the broadcast several times. **(5)** Said that it was just a play. **(6)** However, the story and the acting were so convincing that millions of Americans thought it was a real news report. **(7)** Terror struck. **(8)** Spreading quickly across the country. **(9)** Reports of panic-stricken people in the streets. **(10)** Welles later apologized to the nation. **(11)** The radio station also. **(12)** The Federal Communications Commission made new regulations after the broadcast. **(13)** To make sure a radio drama would never cause such panic again.

5.2 *Run-On Sentences* A run-on sentence consists of two or more sentences written incorrectly as one. A run-on sentence occurs because the writer either used no end mark or used a comma instead of a period to end the first complete thought. A run-on sentence may confuse readers because it does not show where one thought ends and the next begins.

WATCH OUT! To correct a run-on sentence, read it to yourself, noticing where you naturally pause between ideas. The pause usually indicates where you should place end punctuation.

Forming Separate Sentences One way to correct a run-on sentence is to form two separate sentences. Use a period or other end punctuation after the first sentence, and capitalize the first letter of the next sentence.

> **INCORRECT:** *In "The Treasure of Lemon Brown" Lemon Brown lived in an abandoned building he slept on a pile of rags. Homeless people have to live by their wits they don't have many other defenses against robbery and other dangers.*
> **CORRECT:** *In "The Treasure of Lemon Brown" Lemon Brown lived in an abandoned building. He slept on a pile of rags. Homeless people have to live by their wits. They don't have many other defenses against robbery and other dangers.*

Forming Compound Sentences You can also correct a run-on sentence by rewriting it to form a compound sentence. One way to do this is by using a comma and a coordinating conjunction.

Never join simple sentences with a comma alone, or a run-on sentence will result. You need a comma followed by a conjunction such as *and, but,* or *or* to hold the sentences together.

> **EXAMPLE:** *Lemon Brown was homeless, but he still had his treasure and his memories to comfort him.*

You may use a semicolon to join two ideas that are closely related.

In addition, you can correct a run-on sentence by using a semicolon and a conjunctive adverb. Commonly used conjunctive adverbs are *however, therefore, nevertheless,* and *besides.*

> **INCORRECT:** *Lemon Brown had an interesting past he had once been a famous blues singer. Homeless people are often ignored, Greg learned an important lesson by taking time to get to know Lemon Brown.*

> **CORRECT:** *Lemon Brown had an interesting past; he had once been a famous blues singer. Homeless people are often ignored; however, Greg learned an important lesson by taking time to get to know Lemon Brown.*

GRAMMAR PRACTICE

Rewrite this paragraph, correcting the run-on sentences.

(1) In "The Treasure of Lemon Brown" we learn a little about what it's like to be homeless, it's not the whole picture. **(2)** It has been estimated that 250,000 to 3 million homeless people are living in the United States today one-third of these people are children. **(3)** In fact, children are the fastest-growing segment of the homeless population their average age is three years old. **(4)** Many of these kids face other problems health is a

particularly big concern. **(5)** In 1999 over half of the children in New York City's homeless shelters had not received proper immunizations. **(6)** Education is another problem, homeless children are more likely to repeat a grade, and they are more likely to drop out or be placed in a special education program.

❻ Making Subjects and Verbs Agree

6.1 *Simple and Compound Subjects* A verb must agree in number with its subject. **Number** refers to whether a word is singular or plural. When a word refers to one thing, it is singular. When a word refers to more than one thing, it is plural.

Agreement with Simple Subjects Use a singular verb with a singular subject.

When the subject is a singular noun, use the singular form of the verb. The present-tense singular form of a regular verb usually ends in *-s* or *-es.*

> **EXAMPLE:** *In "The Dinner Party" a poisonous <u>snake</u> <u>invades</u> a dining room.*

USAGE TIP To find the subject of a sentence, first find the verb. Then ask who or what performs the action of the verb. Say the subject and the verb together to see if they agree.

Use a plural verb with a plural subject.

> **EXAMPLE:** *The hostess behaves calmly and orders a servant to distract the snake. These <u>events</u> <u>prove</u> what I have always believed. Women <u>possess</u> as much self-control as men.*

Agreement with Compound Subjects Use a plural verb with a compound subject whose parts are joined by *and,* regardless of the number of each part.

> **EXAMPLE:** *<u>The woman and the scientist</u> <u>realize</u> that a snake is under the table.*

When the parts of a compound subject are

joined by *or* or *nor,* make the verb agree in number with the part that is closer to it.

> **EXAMPLE:** *Neither the guests nor their hostess expects to see a cobra.*

GRAMMAR PRACTICE

Write the correct form of the verb given in parentheses.

1. In "The Dinner Party" the narrator (describes, describe) what happened during a dinner party in India.

2. A colonial official and his wife (invites, invite) a number of people to dinner.

3. Both the host and the hostess (enjoys, enjoy) the dinner conversation.

4. The guests (discusses, discuss) an interesting topic.

5. Most of the men at the dinner party believe that a woman (tends, tend) to lose control when faced with a crisis.

6. Is it true that neither the colonel nor the other men at the dinner party (agrees, agree) with the young girl?

7. However, the hostess (proves, prove) that women also have self-control when she reacts calmly to the presence of the snake.

6.2 *Pronoun Subjects* When a pronoun is used as a subject, the verb must agree with it in number.

Agreement with Personal Pronouns

When the subject is a singular personal pronoun, use a singular verb. When the subject is a plural personal pronoun, use a plural verb.

Singular pronouns are *I, you, he, she,* and *it.* Plural pronouns are *we, you,* and *they.* With *I* and *you,* use the plural form of the verb. (However, use the singular form *I am* when using the verb "to be.")

> **EXAMPLE:** *We know a lot about the Vietnam War. In "Stop the Sun" a young boy searches for information that history books cannot teach. He tries to find out what*

soldiers experienced in Vietnam. As you read the story, you understand the horror of war. I think the story is very moving.

When *he, she,* or *it* is the part of the subject closer to the verb in a compound subject containing *or* or *nor,* use a singular verb. When a pronoun is a part of a compound subject containing *and,* use a plural verb.

> **EXAMPLE:** *Terry worries about his father. Neither his mother nor he understands what his father is going through. His mother and he want his father to be happy.*

Agreement with Indefinite Pronouns

When the subject is a singular indefinite pronoun, use the singular form of the verb.

The following are singular indefinite pronouns: *another, either, nobody, anybody, everybody, somebody, no one, anyone, everyone, someone, one, nothing, anything, everything, something, each,* and *neither.*

> **EXAMPLE:** *My friends feel sorry for Terry's father. Nobody wants to experience that kind of pain. Someone knows a man who was a soldier in Vietnam.*

When the subject is a plural indefinite pronoun (*both, few, many,* or *several*), use the plural form of the verb.

> **EXAMPLE:** *Few imagine that such a thing will ever happen to them. In fact, several hope to serve in the armed forces.*

The indefinite pronouns *some, all, any, none,* and *most* can be either singular or plural. When the pronoun refers to one thing, use a singular verb.

When the pronoun refers to several things, use a plural verb.

> **EXAMPLE:** *In class all the students discussed the story. Most think Terry did the right thing. None believes that Terry made his father's condition worse.*

GRAMMAR PRACTICE

Choose the correct verb form from each pair.

1. Among students of history, some (know, knows) a great deal about the Vietnam War.

2. All (understand, understands) the importance of this war in American history.

3. Everybody (agree, agrees) that the war had a very divisive effect on American society.

4. Few (understand, understands) the psychological effects that the war had on American soldiers.

5. Many (know, knows) someone like Terry's father.

6. In the story Terry and he (talk, talks) about the war.

7. Neither Terry nor he (enjoy, enjoys) the conversation; however, he and Terry (seem, seems) to have grown closer because of their talk.

8. I have read many accounts of the war; most (deal, deals) with military strategies.

9. None (convey, conveys) the impact that this war had on people's minds.

6.3 Common Agreement Problems

Several other situations can cause problems in subject-verb agreement.

Interrupting Words and Phrases Be sure the verb agrees with its subject when words or phrases come between them.

Sometimes one or more words come between the subject and the verb. These interrupting words do not affect the number of the subject. The subject of a verb is never found in a prepositional phrase or in an appositive, which may follow the subject and come before the verb.

> **EXAMPLE:** *This excerpt, which is full of vivid imagery, describes Lewis and Clark's expedition. Meriwether Lewis, President Thomas Jefferson's private secretary, leads the exploration of the Louisiana Territory.*

Phrases beginning with *including, as well as, along with, such as,* and *in addition to* are not part of the subject.

> **EXAMPLE:** *This story, along with other articles I have read about the expedition, fascinates me. Adventures, such as the one described here, excite and intrigue me.*

Inverted Sentences When the subject comes after the verb, be sure the verb agrees with the subject in number.

A sentence in which the subject follows the verb is called an inverted sentence. Questions are usually in inverted form, as are sentences beginning with *here, there,* and *where.* (For example, *Where are the explorers? There is a storm coming.*)

> **EXAMPLE:** *Much has changed since Lewis and Clark's expedition. There were huge herds of bison that once roamed the Plains. Where, in a landscape that has changed out of recognition, are they now?*

Singular Nouns with Plural Forms Be sure to use a singular verb when the subject is a noun that is singular in meaning but appears to be plural.

Words like *mumps, news,* and *molasses* appear to be plural because they end in *-s.* However, these words are singular in meaning. Words ending in *-ics* that refer to sciences or branches of study (*physics, mathematics, genetics, politics*) are also singular.

> **EXAMPLE:** *In the early 19th century, news about Native Americans who lived out west was hard to come by. Likewise Native Americans who lived in the West were unaware of events back east in the United States. American politics was not a subject that interested them.*

Collective Nouns Use a singular verb when the subject is a collective noun—such as *class, team, crowd,* or *flock*—that refers to a group acting as a unit. Use a plural verb when the collective noun refers to members of the group acting individually.

EXAMPLE: *The _flock_ _was_ preening itself on a sandbar. My _class_ _discusses_ whether Lewis should have fired his gun into its midst.*

Nouns of Time, Weight, or Measure Use a singular verb with a subject that identifies a period of time, a weight, a measure, or a number.

EXAMPLE: *It is amazing to think that _28 months_ _was_ the total amount of time it took to travel from just above St. Louis to the Pacific Ocean and back. Some _8,000 miles_ _was_ the total distance covered by the expedition.*

Titles Use a singular verb when the subject is the title of a work of art, literature, or music, even though the title may contain plural words.

EXAMPLE: *I wrote a poem about the expedition. My English teacher told me that _"Lewis and Clark"_ _is_ the best poem he has read all year.*

GRAMMAR PRACTICE

Write the correct form of each verb given in parentheses.

1. The selection from *Undaunted Courage* (are, is) a fascinating account of Lewis and Clark's expedition.

2. The writer, Stephen Ambrose, (describe, describes) the strange sights that the travelers encounter.

3. There (are, is) many descriptions of animals and plants.

4. Lewis, along with Clark and other members of the expedition, (were, was) often astonished by new sights and sounds.

5. Lewis's objectives, as given to him by President Jefferson, (were, was) to explore the new territory and to interest the native tribes in trade.

6. The expedition (seems, seem) as if it were quite cut off from contact with people in the United States.

7. News of events in the United States (was, were) impossible to obtain.

8. How (does, do) you get news when you are so far from home?

9. I read that 55 feet (was, were) the length of the keelboat that they used on the trip.

10. Our class always (enjoy, enjoys) reading stories of exploration.

❼ Using Nouns and Pronouns

7.1 Plural and Possessive Nouns Nouns refer to people, places, things, and ideas. A noun is plural when it refers to more than one person, place, thing, or idea. Possessive nouns show who or what owns something.

Plural Nouns Follow these guidelines to form noun plurals.

Nouns	To Form Plural	Examples
Most nouns	add -*s*	tree—trees
Most nouns that end in *s*, *sh*, *ch*, *x*, or *z*	add -*es*	dress—dresses brush—brushes
Most nouns that end in *ay*, *ey*, *oy*, or *uy*	add -*s*	essay—essays monkey—monkeys
Most nouns that end in a consonant and *y*	change *y* to *i* and add -*es*	story—stories duty—duties
Most nouns that end in *o*	add -*s*	photo—photos patio—patios cameo—cameos
Some nouns that end in a consonant and *o*	add -*es*	echo—echoes hero—heroes veto—vetoes
Most nouns that end in *f* or *fe*	change *f* to *v*, add -*es* or -*s*	leaf—leaves wife—wives *but* belief—beliefs

WATCH OUT! The dictionary usually lists the plural form of a noun if the plural is formed irregularly or if the plural might be formed in more than one way. Dictionary listings are especially helpful for nouns that end in *o, f,* and *fe.*

Some nouns have the same spelling in both singular and plural: *series, trout, sheep.* Some noun plurals are irregular forms that don't follow any rule: *children, teeth.*

> **EXAMPLE:** *"The Lady, or the Tiger?" is one of those <u>stories</u> that one never forgets. Part of the story takes place in an ancient arena—a place filled with the <u>echoes</u> of cheering crowds; a place where <u>destinies</u> are decided and <u>lives</u> are cut short.*

Possessive Nouns Follow these guidelines to form possessive nouns.

Nouns	To Form Possessive	Examples
Singular nouns	add apostrophe and *-s*	girl—girl's
Plural nouns ending in *s*	add apostrophe	fields—fields' plays—plays'
Plural nouns not ending in *s*	add apostrophe and *-s*	men—men's oxen—oxen's

> **EXAMPLE:** *This is a story about a <u>woman's</u> difficult choice between saving and sacrificing her beloved. In the arena, where <u>men's</u> and <u>women's</u> fate often hung in the balance, a young man must choose between two doors.*

WATCH OUT! Be careful when placing apostrophes in possessive nouns. A misplaced apostrophe changes the meaning. For example, *girl's* refers to possession by one girl, but *girls'* refers to possession by two or more girls.

GRAMMAR PRACTICE

Write the correct noun given in parentheses.

(1) "The Lady, or the Tiger?" takes place in a (kings', king's) arena. **(2)** In many parts of the ancient world, (arena's, arenas) or (amphitheaters, amphitheaters') were places where violent games were held. **(3)** Usually circular or oval in shape, these structures, with their huge vaults and (gallerys, galleries), could seat thousands. **(4)** People came to watch their (heros, heroes) fight. **(5)** Often (animals', animals) were made to fight each other as well. **(6)** These arenas were sometimes frightening places that echoed with (gladiators', gladiator's) cries. **(7)** People enjoyed watching terrifying (brushes, brushs) with death. **(8)** Often (criminals', criminals) were punished in these arenas. **(9)** Sometimes people were sent to die in the arenas for their (believes, beliefs).

7.2 **Pronoun Forms** A personal pronoun is a pronoun that can be used in the first, second, or third person. A personal pronoun has three forms: the subject form, the object form, and the possessive form.

Subject Pronouns Use the subject form of a pronoun when it is the subject of a sentence or the subject of a clause. *I, you, he, she, it, we,* and *they* are subject pronouns.

Using the correct pronoun form is seldom a problem when there is just one pronoun in a sentence. Problems can arise, however, when a noun and a pronoun, or two pronouns, are used in a compound subject or compound object. To see if you are using the correct pronoun form, imagine the sentence with only one pronoun.

> **EXAMPLE:** *"War Party" is about a boy on the verge of manhood. His mother and <u>he</u> are traveling west in a wagon train.*

Use the subject form of a pronoun when it is a predicate pronoun following a linking verb.

You often hear the object form used as a predicate pronoun in casual conversation (*It is her.*) For this reason, the subject form may sound awkward to you, though it is preferred for more formal writing.

EXAMPLE: *There can be no doubt about who took over Bud's upbringing after his father's death. It was <u>she</u>.*

WATCH OUT! To check the form of a predicate pronoun, see if the sentence still makes sense when the subject and the predicate pronoun are reversed. *(It was she. She was it.)*

Object Pronouns Use the object form of a pronoun when it is the object of a verb or preposition. *Me, you, him, her, it, us,* and *them* are object pronouns.

> **EXAMPLE:** *Bud's mother helped <u>him</u> assume more responsibility.*

Possessive Pronouns Each personal pronoun has its own possessive form. These forms are shown below.

Possessive Pronouns	
Subject Pronoun	**Possessive Form**
I	my, mine
you	your, yours
he	his
she	her, hers
it	its
we	our, ours
they	their, theirs
who	whose

Writers often confuse the possessive pronouns *its, your,* and *their* with the contractions *it's, you're,* and *they're.* The words *it's, you're,* and *they're* are called contractions because they are shortened forms of the words *it is, you are,* and *they are.* The apostrophe in each of these contractions stands for the missing letters.

> **EXAMPLE:** *The long journey west took <u>its</u> toll. <u>It's</u> very sad, but when Bud's father dies, Bud, his mother, and his sister realize that <u>they're</u> on <u>their</u> own.*

Personal Pronouns as Subjects When using a personal pronoun as a subject, make sure to match it with the correct form of the verb *to be.*

Forms of *Be*			
Present Tense		**Past Tense**	
Singular	Plural	Singular	Plural
I am	we are	I was	we were
you are	you are	you were	you were
she, he, it is	they are	she, he, it was	they were

Note especially that the pronoun *you* takes the verbs *are* and *were,* regardless of whether it is referring to the singular *you* or to the plural *you.*

WATCH OUT! *You is* and *you was* are nonstandard forms and should be avoided in writing and speaking. *We was* and *they was* are also forms to be avoided.

> **INCORRECT:** *You was late this morning. They was very tired.*
> **CORRECT:** *You were late this morning. They were very tired.*

GRAMMAR PRACTICE

Write the correct pronoun form given in parentheses.

(1) When the story opens, four or five wagons are turning back, because (they're, their) drivers can't withstand the hardship of the journey. **(2)** They are startled by the sudden openness of the prairie and (it's, its) enormous vistas. **(3)** Bud's mother asks (he, him) if he wants to continue traveling. **(4)** Bud realizes that there is only one person who can make the decision. It is (him, he). **(5)** Bud's father did not know that death awaited (him, he) on the trail. **(6)** Bud's mother explains the meaning of the word *home* to Bud and his sister Jeanie. Jeanie and (him, he) realize that home is not the place they left but the place they are seeking. **(7)** After Bud's mother speaks to the Sioux in (they're, their) own language, people in the wagon train grow suspicious of her.

(8) However, Bud and (she, her) stand up to the men who are bullying her. **(9)** She and (him, he) decide to head off on their own. **(10)** At the end of the story, many other families decide to take (they're, their) chances with Bud and his family.

7.3 *Pronoun Antecedents* An antecedent is the noun or pronoun to which a personal pronoun refers. The antecedent usually precedes the pronoun.

Pronoun and Antecedent Agreement A pronoun must agree with its antecedent in

> NUMBER—*singular or plural*
> PERSON—*first, second, or third*
> GENDER—*male or female*

Use a singular pronoun to refer to a singular antecedent; use a plural pronoun to refer to a plural antecedent.

Do not allow interrupting words to determine the number of the personal pronoun.

> **EXAMPLE:** *Because Squeaky in "Raymond's Run" realizes that the track meet is the last of the May Day events, she takes her time getting to <u>it</u>.*

If the antecedent is a noun that could be either male or female, use *he or she (him or her, his or her)* or reword the sentence to avoid the need for a singular pronoun.

> **EXAMPLE:** *Every member of the class had something to say after <u>he or she</u> finished reading "Raymond's Run."*

Be sure that the antecedent of a pronoun is clear.

In most cases, do not use a pronoun to refer to an entire idea or clause. Writing is much clearer if the exact reference is repeated.

> **EXAMPLE:** *The narrator mentions Amsterdam Avenue, Broadway, and 34th Street when she is describing her life in New York City, but <u>these streets</u> are not described in detail.*

WATCH OUT! To avoid vague pronoun reference, do not use *this* or *that* alone to start a clause. Instead, include a word that clarifies what *this* or *that* refers to—*this method, this grouping, that idea.*

Indefinite Pronouns as Antecedents When a singular indefinite pronoun is the antecedent, use *he* or *she (him* or *her, his* or *her)* or rewrite the sentence to avoid the need for a singular pronoun.

> **EXAMPLE:** *Anybody can appreciate a sport that brings <u>him or her</u> so much pleasure.*
> **OR**
> *Anybody can appreciate a sport that brings so much pleasure.*

Indefinite Pronouns				
Singular				
another	each	everybody	neither	somebody
anybody	either	everyone	nobody	someone
anyone		everything	no one	something
anything			nothing	
			one	
Plural				
both	few	many	several	
Singular or Plural				
all	any	most	none	
some	more	enough	plenty	

GRAMMAR PRACTICE

Write the correct form given in parentheses.

1. For Squeaky, running was one of her talents, and (they were, it was) a talent that filled her with pride.

2. On the day of the track meet, parents, children, and Maypole dancers filled the park, but (they, all these people) seemed crazy to Squeaky.

3. Each person was there to watch an event that interested (them, him or her).

4. No one could celebrate (their, his or her, its) victory until the judges chose the winner.

5. Every judge had to express (their, his or her, its) opinion.

6. (This, Waiting for the judges' decision) did not bother Squeaky.

7. Every runner had to wait to see if (they, he or she, it) had won the race.

7.4 *Pronoun Usage* The form that a pronoun takes is always determined by its function within its own clause or sentence.

Who **and** *Whom* Use *who* or *whoever* as the subject of a clause or sentence.

> **EXAMPLE:** *If Mr. Misenheimer didn't have an heir,* <u>who</u> *would take care of his garden after his death?* <u>Whoever</u> *visited the garden often wondered what would happen to it.*

WATCH OUT! In the first sentence of the example, *who* is the subject of the clause *who would take care of his garden after his death.* In the second sentence, *whoever* is the subject of the sentence.

Use *whom* as the direct or indirect object of a verb or verbal and as the object of a preposition.

People often use *who* for *whom* when speaking informally. However, in written English the pronouns should be used correctly.

> **EXAMPLE:** *Mr. Misenheimer might have wondered, "To* <u>whom</u> *should I leave my garden?" or "*<u>Whom</u> *should I choose to carry on my work?" or "I will give* <u>whom</u> *the garden?"*

WATCH OUT! *Whom* should be used instead of *who* in each sentence in the example: *To whom*—object of a preposition; *Whom should*—direct object of the verb *should choose; Give whom*—indirect object of *will give.*

In determining the correct pronoun form, ignore interrupters that come between the subject and the verb.

In the example that follows, *who* should replace *whom* because the pronoun is the subject of the clause "Who . . . should inherit the garden?"

> **EXAMPLE:** <u>Who</u> *do you think should inherit the garden?*

Whose **and** *who's* Do not confuse the contraction *who's* with the possessive pronoun *whose.*

> **EXAMPLE:** *When you're planning garden layout and design, you must consider* <u>who's</u> *going to be seeing the garden.* <u>Whose</u> *plans are these?*

Pronouns with Nouns Determine the correct form of the pronoun in phrases such as *we girls* and *us boys* by saying the sentence without the noun.

> **EXAMPLE:** <u>We</u> *gardeners like to think that other people appreciate our work.*

GRAMMAR PRACTICE

Write the correct pronoun given in parentheses.

1. (Whomever, Whoever) enjoys gardening understands how relaxing it can be.

2. When (you're, your) gardening, your troubles become less important.

3. However, there are many for (whom, who) gardening is rather boring.

4. (Whom, Who) among you has ever planted flowers or seeds?

5. (Whom, Who) would like to learn the art of gardening?

6. (Whose, Who's) interested in learning a very ancient art?

7. (We, Us) humans have always enjoyed getting close to the earth.

8. (Whose, Who's) garden is this?

9. (Whomever, Whoever) knows the answer should contact me.

10. (Who, Whom) do you think knows the answer?

❽ Using Verbs Correctly

8.1 *Verb Tenses and Forms* Verb tense shows the time of an action or a condition. Writers sometimes cause confusion when they use different verb tenses in describing actions that occur at the same time.

Consistent Use of Tenses When two or more actions occur at the same time or in sequence, use the same verb tense to describe the actions.

> **EXAMPLE:** *In "Pandora's Box," Pandora pulled the casket from under the bed, lifted the lid, and watched the horrible things escape.*

WATCH OUT! In telling a story, be careful not to shift tenses so often that the reader has difficulty keeping the sequence of events straight.

A shift in tense is necessary when two events occur at different times or out of sequence. The tenses of the verbs should clearly indicate that one action precedes the other.

> **EXAMPLE:** *Prometheus was punished because he had stolen fire from heaven. Although Zeus had punished him, the king of the gods decided to punish Prometheus's brother, as well.*

Tense	Verb Form
Present	walk/walks
Past	walked
Future	will walk
Present perfect	have/has walked
Past perfect	had walked
Future perfect	will/shall have walked

Past Tense and the Past Participle The simple past form of a verb can always stand alone. Always use the past participles of the following irregular verbs when these verbs follow helping verbs.

Present Tense	Past Tense	Past Participle
be (is/are)	was/were	(have, had) been
begin	began	(have, had) begun
break	broke	(have, had) broken
bring	brought	(have, had) brought
choose	chose	(have, had) chosen
come	came	(have, had) come
do	did	(have, had) done
drink	drank	(have, had) drunk
eat	ate	(have, had) eaten
fall	fell	(have, had) fallen
freeze	froze	(have, had) frozen
give	gave	(have, had) given
go	went	(have, had) gone
grow	grew	(have, had) grown
lose	lost	(have, had) lost
ride	rode	(have, had) ridden
sing	sang	(have, had) sung
slay	slew	(have, had) slain
swim	swam	(have, had) swum
tear	tore	(have, had) torn
think	thought	(have, had) thought
write	wrote	(have, had) written

> **EXAMPLE:** *Hera had given Pandora the gift of curiosity. Although Pandora only wanted to peek inside the box, when she lifted the lid, evil things broke loose and could not be brought under control.*

GRAMMAR PRACTICE

Write the correct verb for each sentence.

1. Zeus did not punish Epimetheus as brutally as he (punishes, had punished) Epimetheus' brother.

2. Instead Zeus (had created, created) another plan and (got, had gotten) the goddesses to help him.

3. He (begins, began) by ordering Hephaestus to make a woman out of clay; then he

summoned the Four Winds to breathe life into the figure.

4. After Hephaestus (finishes, had finished), Zeus (had asked, asked) the goddesses to give the figure some interesting qualities.

5. Hermes (will present, presented) Pandora to Epimetheus, and they (had married, married).

6. When Pandora (had opened, opened) the box, the evil spirits (attacked, will attack) her and (had flown, flew) off to attack the rest of humankind.

8.2 *Commonly Confused Verbs* The following verb pairs are often confused.

Let **and** *Leave* *Let* means "to allow or permit." *Leave* means "to depart" or "to allow something to remain where it is."

> **EXAMPLE:** *Let me tell you the tale of Pecos Bill. First, though, you must leave behind your ideas of what is real.*

Lie **and** *Lay* *Lie* means "to rest in a flat position." *Lay* means "to put or to place."

> **EXAMPLE:** *When baby Bill fell off the family wagon, he didn't just lie there and scream. He met a coyote who carried him off and laid him down in its den.*

Sit **and** *Set* *Sit* means "to be in a seated position." *Set* means "to put or place."

> **EXAMPLE:** *Bill just sat in the dirt, not worrying. Bill always seemed to set his problems on a stump so they'd blow away.*

Rise **and** *Raise* *Rise* means "to move upward." *Raise* means "to move something upward."

> **EXAMPLE:** *I was reading "Pecos Bill" when I saw smoke rise in the distance. I raised the window and tried to get a better view.*

WATCH OUT! If you're uncertain about which verb to use, check to see whether the verb has an object. The verbs *lie, sit,* and *rise* never have objects.

Learn **and** *Teach* *Learn* means "to gain knowledge or skill." *Teach* means "to help someone learn."

> **EXAMPLE:** *It was strange how quickly Bill learned what the coyotes had to teach him.*

Here are the principal parts of these troublesome verb pairs.

Present Tense	Past Tense	Past Participle
let	let	(have, had) let
leave	left	(have, had) left
lie	lay	(have, had) lain
lay	laid	(have, had) laid
sit	sat	(have, had) sat
set	set	(have, had) set
rise	rose	(have, had) risen
raise	raised	(have, had) raised
learn	learned	(have, had) learned
teach	taught	(have, had) taught

GRAMMAR PRACTICE

Choose the correct verb from each pair of words.

1. Tall tales like "Pecos Bill" (rise, raise) many questions about the real life of cowboys, those men and boys who herded cattle for a living.

2. The true life of cowboys (lies, lays) hidden from most Americans who have been misled by novels and movies.

3. However, it's important to (set, sit) people straight and to (learn, teach) them the truth about history.

4. For example, if you (let, leave) people to their storybook understanding of the Old West, they'll never know that almost one-fourth of all cowboys were African American.

5. People should be (learned, taught) that almost another fourth of all cowboys were Mexican.

6. Today, more than ever, we must (rise, raise) people's awareness about who helped settle the West.

❾ Using Modifiers Effectively

9.1 *Adjectives and Adverbs* Use an adjective to modify a noun or a pronoun. Use an adverb to modify a verb, an adjective, or another adverb.

> **EXAMPLE:** *In* Grand Mothers, *Nikki Giovanni remembers her grandmother <u>fondly</u>. Because her grandmother was such an organized person, Giovanni is <u>absolutely</u> amazed that her grandmother used to forget her soap.*

WATCH OUT! Always determine first which word is being modified. For example, in the second sentence of the example, *amazed* is the word being modified; since *amazed* is an adjective, the modifier must be an adverb.

Use an adjective after a linking verb to describe the subject.

Remember that in addition to forms of the verb *be,* the following are linking verbs: *become, seem, appear, look, sound, feel, taste, grow, smell.*

> **EXAMPLE:** *Giovanni felt <u>sad</u> when she left her grandmother's house after her grandfather's funeral. Her grandmother looked <u>brave</u> as Giovanni drove away.*

GRAMMAR PRACTICE

Write the correct modifier given in each parentheses.

1. Nikki Giovanni recalls her grandmother's accomplishments (proud, proudly).

2. Her grandmother was a (bravely, brave) woman who fought against segregation.

3. To other people she appeared (courageous, courageously).

4. She seemed (highly, high) organized.

5. She was a (strongly, strong) and determined woman.

6. Giovanni sometimes grew (tiredly, tired) of her grandmother's advice.

7. However, now that her grandmother is gone, she misses her (terribly, terrible).

9.2 *Comparisons and Negatives*

Comparative and Superlative Adjectives
Use the comparative form of an adjective when comparing two things.

Comparative adjectives are formed by adding *-er* to short adjectives *(fierce–fiercer)* or by using the word *more* with longer adjectives *(unusual–more unusual).*

> **EXAMPLE:** *In the story "Otoonah" Otoonah's main challenges were finding food and shelter; she dealt with the <u>easier</u> one first. Shelter was <u>more difficult</u> to find.*

WATCH OUT! When comparing something with everything else of its kind, do not leave out the word *other. (Ilga is taller than any <u>other</u> girl in the class.)*

Use the superlative form when comparing three or more things.

Superlatives are formed by adding *-est* to short adjectives *(great–greatest)* or by using the word *most* with longer adjectives *(remarkable–most remarkable).*

> **EXAMPLE:** *Otoonah proved she was the <u>most successful</u> hunter in her family. She found the <u>greatest</u> number of animals.*

The comparative and superlative forms of some adjectives are irregular.

Adjective	Comparative	Superlative
good	better	best
bad	worse	worst
ill	worse	worst
little	less or lesser	least
much	more	most
many	more	most

Comparative and Superlative Adverbs
When comparing two actions, use a

comparative adverb, formed by adding *-er* or the word *more*.

> **EXAMPLE:** *When attacking the young hunter, the polar bear moved <u>faster</u> and <u>more</u> <u>forcefully</u> than the man.*

WATCH OUT! Do not use both *-er* and *more* or *-est* and *most*: *His car is <u>faster</u> than hers. It has the <u>biggest</u> tires I've ever seen.*

When comparing more than two actions, use the superlative form of an adverb, formed by adding *-est* or the word *most*.

> **EXAMPLE:** *The songs Otoonah sang <u>most</u> enthusiastically were the boastful ones.*

Adverb	Comparative	Superlative
hard	harder	hardest
carefully	more carefully	most carefully

Double Negatives To avoid double negatives, use only one negative word in a clause. *Not, no, never, none,* and *nobody* are negatives.

Besides the compounds formed with *not* and *no,* the words *barely, hardly,* and *scarcely* also function as negative words.

> **EXAMPLE:** *Returning home, Otoonah <u>didn't</u> have <u>any</u> hard feelings toward her parents. They <u>could</u> <u>hardly</u> believe Otoonah was alive.*

GRAMMAR PRACTICE

Rewrite these sentences, correcting mistakes in modifiers.

1. One hundred years ago, the greater challenge facing Eskimos (or Inuits) like those in the story "Otoonah" was finding enough food to feed a family during the harsh winters.

2. Compared to Inuits today, a family like Otoonah's was worst off.

3. Hunting was more hard than it is today.

4. A handmade harpoon couldn't never match the rifle for ease of use and accuracy.

5. An Inuit using a rifle hunted efficiently, while an Inuit using a harpoon worked hardest.

6. Also, of the two methods of hunting, using a harpoon is most dangerous.

7. Of the two types of hunters, the one throwing the harpoon is likely to lose his or her balance and fall into the freezing waters.

9.3 **Special Problems with Modifiers**
Although the following terms are frequently misused in spoken English, they should be used correctly in written English.

Them* and *Those *Them* is always a pronoun and never a modifier of a noun. *Those* is a pronoun when it stands alone. It is an adjective when followed by a noun.

> **EXAMPLE:** *In "The Other Pioneers" the poet honors <u>those</u> settlers who plowed the land. He admires <u>them</u> for their strength and courage.*

Bad* and *Badly Always use *bad* as an adjective, whether before a noun or after a linking verb. *Badly* should generally be used to modify an action verb.

> **EXAMPLE:** *The settlers wanted so <u>badly</u> to be part of this country, but many times they felt <u>bad</u> about leaving their homeland.*

This, That, These,* and *Those Whether used as adjectives or pronouns, *this* and *these* refer to people and things that are nearby, and *that* and *those* refer to people and things that are farther away.

> **EXAMPLE:** *Reading about the Spanish settlers of Texas, I could tell the poet admires <u>these</u> hardworking people more than <u>those</u> wealthy enough to live a life of ease. More people plowed the land in <u>that</u> long-ago time than do in <u>this</u> day.*

The Extra *Here* and *There* Avoid the use of *here* with *this* or *these*; also, do not use *there* with *that* and *those*. Notice the improvement when *here* and *there* are removed from the following sentence:

> **INCORRECT:** <u>*This here*</u> *was a good movie. We hardly breathed as <u>that there</u> image appeared on the screen.*

CORRECT: *This was a good movie. We hardly breathed as that image appeared on the screen.*

Good* and *Well *Good* is always an adjective, never an adverb. Use *well* as either an adjective or an adverb, depending on the sentence.

When used as an adjective, *well* usually refers to a person's health. As an adverb, *well* modifies an action verb. In the expression "feeling good," *good* refers to being happy or pleased.

> **INCORRECT:** *When the weather was well, the crops grew good. The immigrants felt well about settling in a land that held so much promise for their children.*
>
> **CORRECT:** *When the weather was good, the crops grew well. The immigrants felt good about settling in a land that held so much promise for their children.*

Few* and *Little*, *Fewer* and *Less *Few* refers to numbers of things that can be counted; *little* refers to amounts or quantities. *Fewer* is used when comparing numbers of things; *less* is used when comparing amounts or quantities.

> **INCORRECT:** *Early settlers got few help from the government and little opportunities to rest. Who knows whether immigrants then had less problems than immigrants now?*
>
> **CORRECT:** *Early settlers got little help from the government and few opportunities to rest. Who knows whether immigrants then had fewer problems than immigrants now?*

Kind* and *Sort *Kind* and *sort* are singular. Use *this* or *that* with *kind* and *sort*. *Kinds* and *sorts* are plural. Use *these* or *those* with *kinds* and *sorts*.

> **INCORRECT:** *These kind of things irritate me. This sorts of books fascinate me.*
>
> **CORRECT:** *This kind of thing irritates me These sorts of books fascinate me.*

GRAMMAR PRACTICE

Write the modifier from each pair that fits the meaning of the sentence.

1. (This, This here) poem, "The Other Pioneers" acknowledges the important role played by the Spanish in the settlement of Texas.

2. The poem inspired me to do some research to learn more about (these, those) distant colonial days.

3. I realized that my knowledge of the history of Texas was quite (bad, badly), so I decided to check out some books at the library.

4. I learned that in the 16th century, the Spanish sent many expeditions north from Mexico. (Them, Those) expeditions were searching for legendary cities that were supposedly rich in gold.

5. Although the explorers searched thoroughly, they found (little, few) evidence of (this, these) kind of wealth.

6. In the 17th century, Spanish missionaries built the first two missions in what became Texas. Spain based its claim to Texas territory on (those, those there) missions and on the expeditions of exploration.

7. In 1685 a French explorer named René-Robert Cavelier, Sieur de la Salle, founded a French settlement on the coast of Texas. However, La Salle's expedition ended (bad, badly); La Salle was killed and the rest of the settlers died.

8. The Spanish continued to send expeditions of exploration into Texas. They also founded more missions and forts. However, (few, little) Spanish settlers moved into Texas.

9. Mexico broke away from Spain in 1821, and Texas became part of the new Empire of Mexico. In the 1820s and 30s, many American settlers began moving into Texas. (This sort, These sorts) of mass migration alarmed the Mexican government.

10. Now that I have done so much research, I believe that my knowledge of the history of Texas is quite (good, well).

⑩ Phrases and Clauses

10.1 *Phrases* A phrase is a group of related words that does not have a subject and a predicate and that functions in a sentence as a single part of speech. Phrases may appear anywhere in a sentence. If a phrase appears at the beginning of a sentence, it is called an introductory phrase. Because phrases can act as a single part of speech, they are classified as prepositional phrases, appositive phrases, infinitive phrases, participial phrases, and gerund phrases.

Prepositional Phrases When a phrase consists of a preposition, its object, and any modifiers of the object, it is called a prepositional phrase. Prepositional phrases that modify nouns or pronouns are adjective phrases. Prepositional phrases that modify verbs, adjectives, or adverbs are adverb phrases.

> **ADJECTIVE PHRASE:** *In the excerpt from All But My Life, Gerda Weissmann Klein tells the story of her long ordeal.*
> **ADVERB PHRASE:** *She suffered in many Nazi work camps.*

Appositive Phrases An appositive phrase is a group of words that identifies or provides further information about a noun or pronoun that directly precedes the phrase.

> **EXAMPLE:** *Gerda Weissmann Klein, a young Polish girl, lost all her family and friends in the Holocaust.*

Infinitive Phrases An infinitive phrase consists of an infinitive (*to* + a verb) along with its modifiers and objects. Infinitive phrases can function as nouns, adjectives, and adverbs.

> **INFINITIVE PHRASE AS A NOUN (subject of a sentence):** *To survive became Klein's aim.*
> **INFINITIVE PHRASE AS A NOUN (object of a sentence):** *The Nazis tried to destroy the Jews of Europe.*

INFINITIVE PHRASE AS AN ADJECTIVE: *The Nazis needed an enemy to persecute.*
INFINITIVE PHRASE AS AN ADVERB: *Klein lived to see the destruction of the Nazis.*

Participial Phrases A participial phrase is a group of words that includes a participle. There are two kinds of participles: the past participle is usually formed by adding *-d* or *-ed* to the present tense; however, the past participles of irregular verbs do not follow this rule. The present participle is formed by adding *-ing* to the present tense of any verb. A participle with its objects and modifiers is called a participial phrase. Participial phrases act as adjectives, modifying nouns or pronouns.

> **EXAMPLE:** *Having read her autobiography, I can better imagine what life was like under the Nazis.*

Here are examples of the infinitive and participial forms of some regular verbs.

Regular Verbs		
Infinitive	**Present Participle**	**Past Participle**
(to) call	calling	called
(to) cook	cooking	cooked
(to) jump	jumping	jumped
(to) look	looking	looked
(to) paint	painting	painted
(to) rub	rubbing	rubbed
(to) scrub	scrubbing	scrubbed
(to) search	searching	searched
(to) shout	shouting	shouted
(to) talk	talking	talked
(to) toss	tossing	tossed
(to) walk	walking	walked
(to) wash	washing	washed

WATCH OUT! Errors in parallelism often occur with clauses and phrases as well as with individual words. Make sure the parts of the clause are parallel.

Here are examples of the infinitive and participial forms of some irregular verbs.

Irregular Verbs		
Infinitive	Present Participle	Past Participle
(to) eat	eating	eaten
(to) fly	flying	flown
(to) give	giving	given
(to) grow	growing	grown
(to) hide	hiding	hidden
(to) ride	riding	ridden
(to) sit	sitting	sat
(to) swim	swimming	swum
(to) tear	tearing	torn
(to) think	thinking	thought
(to) write	writing	written

Gerund Phrases A gerund is a verb form ending in *-ing* that functions as a noun. A gerund phrase is a group of words that includes a gerund, its modifiers, and objects. Because a gerund phrase functions as a noun, it can act as the subject of a sentence, a direct object, a subject complement, or the object of a preposition.

> **GERUND PHRASE AS SUBJECT:** *Reading about the Holocaust is difficult.*
> **GERUND PHRASE AS DIRECT OBJECT:** *Many people dislike thinking about the Holocaust.*
> **GERUND PHRASE AS SUBJECT COMPLEMENT:** *Our goal is preventing another Holocaust.*
> **GERUND PHRASE AS OBJECT OF A PREPOSITION:** *Many people feel uncomfortable about hearing stories like these.*

GRAMMAR PRACTICE

Identify each underlined phrase as a prepositional phrase, an appositive phrase, an infinitive phrase, a participial phrase, or a gerund phrase.

(1) After reading the selection by Gerda

Weissmann Klein, I wanted to find out more about the Holocaust. **(2)** Searching through the library, I came across many books on the subject. **(3)** During the Holocaust, the 12-year period when the Nazis persecuted and murdered Jews and other minorities, millions of people died. **(4)** It is astonishing that people throughout Nazi-occupied territory allowed such crimes to happen. **(5)** People living near the death camps must have known that thousands were being murdered. **(6)** Reading about this period of history was sometimes a painful experience. **(7)** However, I wanted to learn the truth.

10.2 *Clauses* A clause is a group of words that contains a subject and a verb. There are two kinds of clauses: independent clauses and subordinate clauses.

Independent and Subordinate Clauses An independent clause can stand alone as a complete sentence. A subordinate clause cannot stand alone as a sentence and must be attached to an independent clause to form a complex sentence. If a subordinate clause is not attached to an independent clause, it is considered a sentence fragment.

> **INDEPENDENT CLAUSE:** *I read "Racing the Great Bear."*
> **SUBORDINATE CLAUSE:** *After I had finished dinner*
> **COMPLEX SENTENCE:** *After I had finished dinner, I read "Racing the Great Bear."*

Adjective and Adverb Clauses An adjective clause is a subordinate clause used as an adjective. An adjective clause is usually introduced by the relative pronoun *who, whom, whose, which,* or *that.* An adverb clause is a subordinate clause that is used as an adverb to modify a verb, an adjective, or another adverb.

> **ADJECTIVE CLAUSE:** *Swift Runner was the name of the boy who saved his people.*
> **ADVERB CLAUSE:** *Swift Runner accepted the mission when the chief asked for a volunteer.*

A subordinate clause acting as an adverb is usually introduced by one of the following subordinating conjunctions.

Subordinating Conjunctions			
after	if	though	where
although	since	unless	wherever
as	so that	until	while
because	than	when	why
before	that	whenever	

Noun Clauses A noun clause is a subordinate clause that is used in a sentence as a noun. A noun clause may be used as a subject, a direct object, an indirect object, a predicate noun, or an object of a preposition.

NOUN CLAUSE AS SUBJECT: *What Swift Runner discovered was terrible.*
NOUN CLAUSE AS DIRECT OBJECT: *Swift Runner discovered what was killing his people.*
NOUN CLAUSE AS INDIRECT OBJECT: *The chief offered whoever would volunteer the task of investigating the disappearances.*
NOUN CLAUSE AS PREDICATE NOUN: *Swift Runner is what we would call a hero.*
NOUN CLAUSE AS OBJECT OF A PREPOSITION: *I read of how he had killed the monster.*

GRAMMAR PRACTICE

Identify each underlined clause as an independent or a subordinate clause. If the clause is subordinate, identify it as an adjective, adverb, or noun clause.

(1) Some young Seneca men tried to visit the Onondaga people. **(2)** The people in the Seneca village grew worried when the young people were never heard from again. **(3)** No one could imagine what has happened to them. **(4)** The chief, who was very old, called a council meeting. **(5)** Everyone knew that the chief was proposing a dangerous mission. **(6)** Swift Runner took the wampum when the chief offered it. **(7)** The Nyagwahe was the monster that had killed the villagers. **(8)** Swift Runner realized that the monster was afraid of him. **(9)** The boy killed the great bear that had caused so much suffering. **(10)** Everyone celebrated Swift Runner's victory.

Parallelism Words or groups of words that have the same function in a sentence and the same form are said to be parallel. Paired items and items in a series require a parallel construction.

EXAMPLE: *At block parties, the neighbors ate ribs and corn, danced in the streets, and sang our favorite songs.*

In this series of items, each verb serves the same function in the sentence (to describe what the neighbors are doing) and has the same form, a verb in the past tense.

When items in a sentence are not parallel, the sentence is awkward. In the following example, the verb forms are inconsistent.

EXAMPLE: *At block parties, the neighbors are eating home-cooked food, danced till dawn, and sing favorite songs.*

To create parallelism, balance nouns with nouns, infinitives with infinitives, and gerund phrases with gerund phrases. If the words are verbs, each must have the same tense. Make sure the words also serve the same function in the sentence.

GRAMMAR PRACTICE

Revise each sentence below to make the sentence parts parallel.

(1) Jewell Parker Rhodes wrote "Block Party" about her old neighborhood and to publish a memoir of it. **(2)** In the story, she mentions many colorful characters, riding her bike with her sister, and watching the world from her front stoop. **(3)** With her friends, Rhodes played hide and seek in the laundry hanging out to dry, would slide down the banisters in the house, and rode a red tricycle through the kitchen. **(4)** A block party is when the street is closed off to traffic, hydrants were turned on by the fire department, and the neighbors gather for a picnic. **(5)** The author went on to earn degrees in drama criticism, English, and a third degree in creative writing. **(6)** Rhodes now writes novels, nonfiction, and for magazines.

⓫ The Structure of Sentences

The structure of a sentence is determined by the number and kind of clauses it contains. Sentences are classified as simple, compound, complex, and compound-complex.

11.1 *Simple Sentences* A simple sentence is made up of one independent clause and no dependent (or subordinate) clauses.

> The stone tool was ancient.
> INDEPENDENT CLAUSE

> We did not know its use.
> INDEPENDENT CLAUSE

A simple sentence may contain a compound subject or a compound verb.

> SIMPLE SENTENCE WITH A COMPOUND SUBJECT: *Rita* and *Julie* investigated the stone tool.
> SIMPLE SENTENCE WITH A COMPOUND VERB: They *read* and *studied* about ancient people.

11.2 *Compound Sentences* A compound sentence is made up of two or more independent clauses joined together. A compound sentence does not contain any dependent clauses.

> INDEPENDENT CLAUSES

> Rita studied the tool, and her assistant took notes.

Independent clauses can be joined with a comma and a coordinating conjunction, a semicolon, or a conjunctive adverb preceded by a semicolon and followed by a comma.

> COMPOUND SENTENCE WITH A COMMA AND A COORDINATING CONJUNCTION: *Prehistoric people built forts, and they created burial mounds.*
> COMPOUND SENTENCE WITH A SEMICOLON: *Prehistoric people built forts; they also created burial mounds.*
> COMPOUND SENTENCE WITH A CONJUNCTIVE ADVERB: *Prehistoric people built forts; however, they collapsed over time.*

WATCH OUT! Do not confuse a compound sentence with a simple sentence that has compound parts.

GRAMMAR PRACTICE

Identify the subject and verb in each part of the compound sentence; identify the conjunction or semicolon.

(1) You can pass an ancient mound, and you may not even notice it. **(2)** Mounds look natural; they often seem like enormous hills. **(3)** Once thousands of mounds existed, but now many are gone. **(4)** Some of these earthworks were built thousands of years ago, but others were constructed less than three hundred years ago. **(5)** Ancient people built them for burial purposes, or they used them as fortresses.

11.3 *Complex Sentences* A complex sentence is made up of one independent clause and one or more dependent clauses.

> INDEPENDENT CLAUSE

> I would like to be an archaeologist, although I have never been on an expedition.

> DEPENDENT CLAUSE

An independent clause can stand alone as a sentence. A dependent clause also has a subject and a predicate, but it cannot stand alone. It is often introduced by a subordinating conjunction, such as *when, if, because,* or *until.*

GRAMMAR PRACTICE

In each of the following complex sentences, identify the independent clause and the dependent clause. Then identify the subordinating conjunction.

(1) Before you know it, your flat television picture may be gone. **(2)** The image looks flat because it is two-dimensional. (**3**) The image would look more realistic if it were three-dimensional. (**4**) That 3-D image is not far off, since technology is changing. (**5**) Televisions will use holograms so that the images look real. (**6**) Holograms are available today, although they are not very common. (**7**) If you have ever seen a bank card, perhaps you have seen a hologram. (**8**) You can see a 3-D picture on the card when you look closely. (**9**) Unless problems develop, holographic television should be available in the near future. (**10**) Until it is, we will have to depend on today's technology.

11.4 *Compound-Complex Sentences* A compound-complex sentence is made up of two or more independent clauses and one or more dependent clauses. If you start with a compound sentence, all you need to do to form a compound-complex sentence is add a dependent clause.

> COMPOUND SENTENCE:
> INDEPENDENT CLAUSES
>
> I would like to be an archaeologist, but I have never visited an ancient site.
>
> COMPOUND-COMPLEX SENTENCE:
> INDEPENDENT CLAUSES
>
> I would like to be an archaeologist, but I have never visited an ancient site, although I have had a couple of opportunities.
> DEPENDENT CLAUSE

GRAMMAR PRACTICE

In each of the following compound-complex sentences, identify the independent and the dependent clauses.

(**1**) Rain had been falling for an hour, and the home football team, which was losing badly, welcomed the half-time break. (**2**) Despite the downpour, the band marched onto the field, and the half-time show began. (**3**) While the band played the school anthem, the wind slapped rain in their faces, and the flag bearers were nearly blown over. (**4**) Still, the band played on, and the rain poured down, while the field turned into mud. (**5**) Finally, the show ended, and as the band marched off, a tuba player's foot sank into the sloppy field, and he fell face first into the mud.

GRAMMAR PRACTICE: MIXED REVIEW

Identify each sentence with **S** for simple, **CD** for compound, **CX** for complex, or **CC** for compound-complex.

(**1**) The horse first existed in North America, but it became extinct here about ten thousand years ago. (**2**) Then Christopher Columbus brought horses to the New World in his second voyage. (**3**) The population of horses increased when Spanish conquerors brought them to Mexico in the 1500s. (**4**) In 1519, Hernán Cortés brought sixteen horses from Cuba and used them in his invasion of the Aztec Empire. (**5**) Later Spanish explorers brought more horses to America, where they were useful in battle and on long expeditions. (**6**) Because Native Americans did not have horses, the Spanish had a great advantage in war, and they defeated the Indians. (**7**) Without land, many Native Americans had no means of livelihood, and they were forced to work for the Spanish. (**8**) Although these workers cared for the horses, they were not to ride them; however, over the years the workers learned to train and ride the horses. (**9**) Some of the native peoples stole horses from the Spanish and then traded the horses among their different groups. (**10**) Before many years had passed, Native Americans were riding and breeding horses throughout the West.

⑫ Correcting Capitalization

12.1 *Proper Nouns and Adjectives* A common noun names a whole class of persons, places, things, or ideas. A proper noun names a particular person, place, thing, or idea. A proper adjective is an adjective formed from a proper noun. All proper nouns and proper adjectives are capitalized.

Names and Personal Titles Capitalize the name and title of a person.

Also capitalize the initials and abbreviations of titles. *Clarissa Harlowe Barton, C. H. Barton, Senator Charles Sumner,* and *Mr. Dred Scott* are capitalized correctly.

> **EXAMPLE:** *Russell Freedman's* Lincoln: A Photobiography *is about the assassination of* President Abraham Lincoln.

WATCH OUT! Do not capitalize personal titles used as common nouns. Do capitalize a title when it is part of the name. *(Did* Senator *Stephens call you? The* senator *spoke to us.)*

Capitalize a word referring to a family relationship when it is used as someone's name *(Uncle Al)* but not when it is used to identify a person *(Jill's uncle)*.

> **EXAMPLE:** *Robert Lincoln was summoned to join the crowd around his* father's *bedside.*

Languages, Nationalities, Religious Terms Capitalize the names of languages and nationalities as well as religious names and terms.

Capitalize words referring to languages and nationalities, such as *Hindi, Sanskrit, Afrikaans, Korean, German,* and *Nigerian.* Capitalize religious names and terms, such as *God, Buddha, Bible,* and *Koran.*

> **EXAMPLE:** *One newspaper clipping found in Lincoln's wallet quotes the* British *reformer John Bright. Bright praised Lincoln. Many*

others must have prayed for God *to protect Lincoln, whose life was always in danger.*

School Subjects Capitalize the name of a specific school course (*Biology 1, World History*). Do not capitalize a general reference to a school subject (*mathematics, history, music*).

> **EXAMPLE:** *After reading* Lincoln: A Photobiography, *I became very interested in* history. *Then I studied the Civil War in* U.S. History

Organizations, Institutions Capitalize the important words in the official names of organizations and institutions *(Congress, Duke University).*

Do not capitalize words that refer to kinds of organizations or institutions *(school, church, university)* or words that refer to specific organizations but are not their official names *(at the university).*

> **EXAMPLE:** *I've learned that decisions made in the* House *of* Representatives *cost many young soldiers their lives. The* government *ran the war, but soldiers had to fight it.*

WATCH OUT! Do not capitalize minor words in a proper noun that is made up of several words. *(University* of *Illinois)*

Geographical Names, Events, Time Periods Capitalize geographical names, as well as the names of events, historical periods and documents, holidays, and months and days, but not the names of seasons or directions.

WATCH OUT! Do not capitalize a reference that does not use the full name of a place, event, or a period of history. *(We went to Fort McHenry, but the* fort *was closed.)*

> **EXAMPLE:** *The* Civil War *began at* Ft. Sumter *in the* South *on* April *12, 1861. By the time the war ended in the spring of 1865, it had raged across the* United States *from* Pennsylvania *south to the* Gulf *of* Mexico.

Names	Examples
Continents	North America, Asia
Bodies of water	Atlantic Ocean, Ohio River,
Political units	China, Kentucky, Moscow
Regions	New England, the Midwest
Public areas	Central Park, Civic Plaza
Roads and structures	Main Street, Aswam Dam
Historical events	Battle of Shiloh
Documents	the Constitution
Periods of history	the Renaissance
Holidays	Christmas, Presidents' Day
Months and days	June, Tuesday

GRAMMAR PRACTICE

Write the correct forms of the words given in parentheses.

1. *Lincoln: A Photobiography* is about the (president, President) who saved the nation during the Civil (War, war).

2. Both sides in the (War, war) lost twice as many men to disease as on the (Battlefield, battlefield).

3. Women served as nurses, set up hospitals, and organized relief for both (Union, union) and (Confederate, confederate) armies.

4. One such woman, (Clara, clara) Barton, went on to found the (American Red Cross, american red cross).

5. Barton also formed a (Bureau, bureau) that marked soldiers' graves at Andersonville (Cemetery, cemetery) in (Georgia, georgia).

6. Mary Rice Livermore led much work by the (United States Sanitary Commission, united states sanitary commission).

12.2 Titles of Created Works Titles follow certain capitalization rules.

Books, Plays, Magazines, Newspapers, Films Capitalize the first word, the last word, and all other important words in the title of a book, play or musical, magazine, newspaper, or film. Underline or italicize the title to set it off. (In printed text, titles are italicized if the surrounding text is set in Roman type. If the surrounding type is italicized, set the title in Roman.)

Within a title, don't capitalize articles, conjunctions, and prepositions of fewer than five letters.

> **EXAMPLE:** *In "The Bet" a voluntary prisoner reads the works of Shakespeare. I'm sure that he read* The Merchant of Venice *while in prison.*

Poems, Stories, Articles Capitalize the first word, the last word, and all other important words in the title of a poem, a story, or an article. Enclose the title in quotation marks.

> **EXAMPLE:** *He also read the works of Lord Byron. Do you think that he came across the poem "She Walks in Beauty"? Perhaps he read the article called "Lord Byron and His Poetry."*

GRAMMAR PRACTICE

Rewrite this paragraph, correcting the punctuation and capitalization of titles.

1. How would you pass the time if you were a prisoner like the lawyer in the story the bet?

2. I would spend my time reading horror stories and watching videos of monster movies such as The Monster from the Ocean Floor.

3. If I were the prisoner, I would read old movie magazines such as famous Monsters of Filmland.

4. Stephen King, author of the horror novels it, pet sematary, and the stand, supposedly read the magazine as a child.

5. However, I find it hard to believe that someone who wrote a story as scary as the langoliers was inspired by the movie i was a teenage werewolf.

6. For me, Edgar Allan Poe's poem the raven is much scarier than the movie destroy all monsters, but the movie is more fun.

⓭ Correcting Punctuation

13.1 *Compound Sentences* Punctuation helps organize longer sentences that have several clauses.

Commas in Compound Sentences Use a comma before the conjunction that joins the clauses of a compound sentence.

> **EXAMPLE:** *In "The Tell-Tale Heart" the narrator describes his crime, and he also shows how he gave himself away to the police.*

Semicolons in Compound Sentences Use a semicolon between the clauses of a compound sentence when no conjunction is used. Use a semicolon before, and a comma after, a conjunctive adverb that joins the clauses of a compound sentence.

> **EXAMPLE:** *The narrator tries to conceal the evidence of his crime; <u>however,</u> he gives himself away.*

GRAMMAR PRACTICE

Rewrite these sentences, adding commas and semicolons where necessary.

1. Edgar Allan Poe wrote "The Tell-Tale Heart" he also wrote many other stories.

2. In "The Tell-Tale Heart" Poe examined the criminal mind and he also showed the power of conscience to reveal the truth.

3. The narrator loved the old man however, the old man's eye filled him with horror.

13.2 *Elements Set Off in a Sentence* Most elements that are not essential to a sentence are set off by commas.

Introductory Words Use a comma to separate an introductory word from the rest of the sentence. A single introductory prepositional phrase need not be set off with a comma.

> **EXAMPLE :** *In class we read* Harriet Tubman: Conductor on the Underground Railroad. *Clearly, she was an extraordinary woman.*

In a complex sentence, a comma follows the introductory subordinate clause.

> **EXAMPLE:** *Although they were afraid, Harriet Tubman and the fugitives struggled toward freedom. Whenever they felt discouraged, Tubman kept them going.*

Nouns of Address Use commas to set off a name or noun in direct address.

> **EXAMPLE:** *"Believe me, Thomas, we all thank you for the food and lodging."*

Appositives Use commas to set off an appositive except when the appositive is necessary for the meaning of the sentence.

> **EXAMPLE:** *That famous guide Harriet Tubman told her exhausted travelers that Frederick Douglass, a famous escaped slave, had achieved great things once he gained freedom.*

Interrupters Use commas to set off a word that interrupts the flow of a sentence.

> **EXAMPLE:** *Harriet Tubman, fortunately, never lost confidence in herself.*

When a subordinate clause interrupts the main clause, set it off with commas.

> **EXAMPLE:** *Thomas Garrett, because he wanted to help, gave shelter to the fugitives.*

GRAMMAR PRACTICE

Rewrite these sentences. Add commas where necessary.

1. Tell me Susan who was nicknamed Moses in *Harriet Tubman: Conductor on the Underground Railroad?*

2. Jim it was Harriet Tubman the one who led a group of escaping slaves.

3. Born a slave on a plantation in Maryland Tubman became very strong from her hard work.

4. She avoided capture and finally reached Pennsylvania a free state.

13.3 *Elements in a Series* Commas should be used to separate three or more items in a series and to separate adjectives preceding a noun. Use a comma after every item except the last in a series of three or more items.

>   EXAMPLE: *In the excerpt from* High Tide in Tucson, *Barbara Kingsolver shows how insects, plants, and animals have been attracted to her pond.*

GRAMMAR PRACTICE

Rewrite each sentence, inserting commas where they are needed.

1. Barbara Kingsolver describes the dry dusty, empty landscape around her house.

2. When she builds a pond, she attracts tadpoles water beetles, and dragonflies.

3. Dragonflies hovered dipped their tails and laid eggs.

4. Owls nighthawks, and bats hunt at night.

13.4 *Dates and Addresses* Punctuation in dates and addresses makes information easy to understand.

Dates Use a comma between the day of the month and the year. If the date falls in the middle of a sentence, use another comma after the year.

>   EXAMPLE: *Marjorie Kinnan Rawlings, who was born on August 8, 1896, wrote "A Mother in Mannville."*

Addresses Use a comma between the city and the state in an address. If the city and state fall in the middle of a sentence, use a comma after the state too.

>   EXAMPLE: *If the narrator had written to Jerry, the return address on her letters might have been Anchorage, Alaska.*

GRAMMAR PRACTICE

Rewrite the following sentences, correcting the comma errors.

1. The author Marjorie Kinnan Rawlings died on December 14 1953 after having lived in Florida for 25 years.

2. Previously, she had worked for the *Courier-Journal* in Louisville Kentucky.

3. Her first Florida residence was in Cross Creek Florida.

13.5 *Quotations* Quotation marks let readers know exactly who said what. Incorrectly placed or missing quotation marks lead to misunderstanding.

Quotation Marks Use quotation marks at the beginning and the end of direct quotations and to set off titles of short works.

>   EXAMPLE: *In class our group chose to analyze Daniel P. Mannix's "A Running Brook of Horror." Diego said, "Let's check out the author's use of dialogue."*

End Punctuation Place periods inside quotation marks. Place question marks and exclamation points inside quotation marks if they belong to the quotation; place them outside if they do not belong to the quotation.

>   EXAMPLE: *Ira asked, "What do you suggest, now Mieko?"*
>   *Mieko said, "Let's discuss punctuation."*

Divided Quotations Capitalize the first word of the second part of a direct quotation if it begins a new sentence.

>   EXAMPLE: *"Let's vote on it," said Diego. "There are five of us, so majority rules."*

GRAMMAR PRACTICE

Rewrite these sentences, correcting the use of quotation marks and correcting capitalization and punctuation.

1. "There are many different kinds of snakes, my sister said. They're not all the same."

2. "What are you talking about"? I replied. "I never said they were."

3. "I'm not going to talk to you," she hissed "If you're going to argue with me."

Grammar Glossary

This glossary contains various terms you need to understand when you use the Grammar Handbook. Used as a reference source, this glossary will help you explore grammar concepts and how they relate to one another.

 A

Abbreviation An abbreviation is a shortened form of a word or word group; it is often made up of initials. (B.C., A.M., Maj.)

Active voice. *See* **Voice.**

Adjective An adjective modifies, or describes, a noun or pronoun. (*fine* day, *poor* me) An adjective answers the questions "How many?" "What kind?" and "Which one(s)?"

A **predicate adjective** follows a linking verb and describes the subject. (I am *happy*.)

A **proper adjective** is formed from a proper noun. (*Spanish* rice)

The **comparative** form of an adjective compares two things. (*more elegant, stronger*)

The **superlative** form of an adjective compares more than two things. (*most alert, strongest*)

What Adjectives Tell	Examples
How many	*few* friends *many* painters
What kind	*new* techniques *older* buildings
Which one(s)	*this* painting *those* children

Adjective Clause An adjective clause is a subordinate clause that acts as an adjective. (The man told a story *that was very long*.)

Adjective phrase. *See* **Phrase.**

Adverb An adverb modifies a verb, an adjective, or another adverb. (Meiko jumped *quickly*.)

The **comparative** form of an adverb compares two actions. (*more slowly, sooner*)

The **superlative** form of an adverb compares more than two actions. (*most slowly, soonest*)

What Adverbs Tell	Examples
How	walk *carefully* skate *smoothly*
When	*Now* I see. *once* upon a time
Where	She went *out* *here* in the forest
To what extent	I am *very* pleased. This is *quite* fine.

Adverb Clause An adverb clause is a subordinate clause used as an adverb. (We waited *until the sun went down*.)

Adverb, conjunctive. *See* **Conjunctive adverb.**

Adverb phrase. *See* **Phrase.**

Agreement Sentence parts that correspond with one another are said to be in agreement.

In **pronoun-antecedent agreement**, a pronoun and the word it refers to are the same in number, gender, and person. (*Bill* mailed *his* application. The *students* ate *their* lunches.)

In **subject-verb agreement**, the subject and verb in a sentence are the same in number. (*I fly* home. *He flies* to Rio.)

Ambiguous reference An ambiguous reference occurs when a pronoun may refer to more than one word. (Bud asked his brother if *he* had any mail.)

Antecedent An antecedent is a noun or pronoun to which a pronoun refers. (Because *Juan* practiced *his* backstroke, *he* improved.)

Appositive An appositive is a noun or phrase that explains one or more words in a sentence. (Julie, *a good student*, found algebra simple.)

An **essential appositive** is needed to complete the meaning of a sentence. (A comic strip inspired the musical *Annie*.)

A **nonessential appositive** is one that adds information to a sentence but is not necessary to its meaning. (O. Henry, a *short-story writer*, spent time in prison.)

Article The special adjectives *a, an,* and *the.* (*the* car, *a* bug, *an* apple)

The **definite article** (*the*) is used when a noun refers to a specific thing. (*the* boat)

An **indefinite article** indicates that a noun is not unique but one of many of its kind. (*a* plate, *an* apple)

C

Case A word's form or position in a sentence that indicates its relationship to other words in the sentence.

Clause A clause is a group of words that contains a verb and its subject. (*I wondered.*)

An **adjective clause** is a subordinate clause that modifies a noun or pronoun. (Hugh bought the sweater *that he had admired.*)

An **adverb clause** is a subordinate clause used to modify a verb, an adjective, or an adverb. (Ring the bell *when it is time for class to begin.*)

A **noun clause** is a subordinate clause that is used as a noun. (*Whatever you say interests me.*)

An **elliptical clause** is a clause from which a word or words have been omitted. (We are not as lucky as *they.*)

A **main (independent) clause** can stand by itself as a sentence.

A **subordinate (dependent) clause** does not express a complete thought and cannot stand by itself as a sentence.

Clause	Examples
Main (independent)	Evil things escaped
Subordinate (dependent)	after Pandora opened the box.

Collective noun. *See* **Noun.**

Comma splice A comma splice is an error caused when two sentences are separated with a comma instead of a correct end mark. (*The band played a medley of show tunes, everyone enjoyed the show.*)

Common noun. *See* **Noun.**

Complement A complement is a word or group of words that completes the meaning of a verb. (The kitten finished the *milk.*) *See also* **Direct object; indirect object.**

An **object complement** is a word or a group of words that follows a direct object and renames or describes that object. (The parents of the rescued child declared Gus a *hero.*)

A **subject complement** follows a linking verb and renames or describes the subject. (The coach seemed *anxious.*) *See also* **Noun (predicate noun); Adjective, (predicate adjective).**

Complete predicate The complete predicate of a sentence consists of the main verb and any words that modify or complete the verb's meaning. (The sun *shimmered in the heat.*)

Complete subject The complete subject of a sentence consists of the simple subject and any words that modify or describe the simple subject. (*The vast canyon* lay before us.)

Sentence Part	Example
Complete subject	The man in the ten-gallon hat
Complete predicate	wore a pair of silver spurs.

Complex sentence. *See* **Sentence.**

Compound-complex sentence. *See* **Sentence.**

Compound predicate A sentence with two or more predicates is said to have a compound predicate. (*Di buys and sells rings.*)

Compound sentence A compound sentence consists of two or more independent clauses. (*Sue will play, and the rest of us will cheer.*)

Compound sentence part A sentence element that consists of two or more subjects, verbs, objects, or other parts is compound. (*Lou* and *Jay* helped. Laura *makes* and *models* scarves. Jill sings *opera* and *popular music.*)

Compound subject A sentence with two or more subjects is said to have a compound subject. (*Jim and Bob moved.*)

Conjunction A conjunction is a word that links other words or groups of words.

A **coordinating conjunction** connects related words, groups of words, or sentences. (*and, but, or*)

A **correlative conjunction** is one of a pair of conjunctions that work together to connect sentence parts. (*either . . . or, neither . . . nor*)

A **subordinating conjunction** introduces a subordinate clause. (*unless, while, if*)

Conjunctive adverb A conjunctive adverb joins the clauses of a compound sentence. (*however, therefore, besides*)

Contraction A contraction is formed by joining two words and substituting an apostrophe for a letter or letters left out of one of the words. (*hasn't*)

Coordinating conjunction. *See* **Conjunction.**

Correlative conjunction. *See* **Conjunction.**

 D

Dangling modifier A dangling modifier is one that does not clearly modify any word in the sentence. (*Dashing for the train, the barriers got in the way.*)

Demonstrative pronoun. *See* **Pronoun.**

Dependent clause. *See* **Clause.**

Direct object A direct object receives the action of a verb. (Sarasak hit the *ball*.)

Direct quotation. *See* **Quotation.**

Divided quotation. *See* **Quotation.**

Double negative A double negative is the incorrect use of two negative words when only one is needed. (**Incorrect:** *I can't hardly see you.*)

End mark An end mark is one of several punctuation marks that can end a sentence. *See* the punctuation chart on page R72.

Fragment. *See* **Sentence fragment.**

Future tense. *See* **Verb tense.**

Gender The gender of a personal pronoun indicates whether the person or thing referred to is male, female, or neuter. (My cousin plays the tuba; *he* often performs in school concerts.)

Gerund A gerund is a verbal that ends in *-ing* and functions as a noun. (*Hitting* a home run is easy.)

Gerund phrase. *See* **Phrase.**

Helping verb. *See* **Verb.**

Illogical comparison An illogical comparison is a comparison that does not make sense because words are missing or illogical. (My computer is *newer than Kay*.)

Indefinite pronoun. *See* **Pronoun.**

Indefinite reference Indefinite reference occurs when a pronoun is used without a clear antecedent. (My aunt hugged

me in front of my friends, and *it* was embarrassing.)

Independent clause. *See* **Clause.**

Indirect object An indirect object tells *to whom* or *for whom* (sometimes *to* or *for what*) something is done. (She told *Marika* a joke.)

Indirect question An indirect question tells what someone asked without using the person's exact words. (*My friend asked me if I could go with her to the dentist.*)

Indirect quotation. *See* **Quotation**

Infinitive An infinitive is a verbal that begins with the word *to;* the two words create a phrase. (*to see*)

Intensive pronoun. *See* **Pronoun.**

Interjection An interjection is a word or phrase used to express strong feeling. (*Oh!*)

Interrogative pronoun. *See* **Pronoun.**

Inverted sentence An inverted sentence is one in which the subject comes after the verb. (*Where are my shoes? Here is the prize.*)

Irregular verb. *See* **Verb.**

Linking verb. *See* **Verb.**

Main clause. *See* **Clause.**

Modifier A modifier makes another word more precise; modifiers most often are adjectives or adverbs. (*sunny* day, scowled *grimly*)

An **essential modifier** is one that is necessary to the meaning of a sentence. (Everybody *who has a free pass* should enter now.)

A **nonessential modifier** merely adds more information to a sentence that is clear without the addition. (We will use the new dishes, *which are stored in the closet*.)

Mood Every verb in English is in one of three moods.

The **indicative mood** is used for opinions, facts, and questions. (He *washed* the window.)

The **imperative mood** is used for orders or advice. (*Wash* the window!)

The **subjunctive mood** is used to express a wish, a requirement, a suggestion or a condition contrary to fact. (If I *had* the right tools, I could wash the window.)

Noun A noun names a person, a place, a thing, or an idea. (*Don, home, book, goodness*)

An **abstract noun** names an idea, a quality, or a feeling. (*truth*)

A **collective noun** names a group of things. (*herd*)

A **common noun** is a general name of a person, a place, a thing, or an idea. (*girl, mountain, snow, logic*)

A **compound noun** contains two or more words. (*folklore, sidewalk, son-in-law*)

A **noun of direct address** is the name of a person being directly spoken to. (*Sam*, will you do the dishes?)

A **possessive noun** shows who or what owns or is associated with something. (*Yuri's* jacket, the *sun's* light)

A **predicate noun** follows a linking verb and renames the subject. (She is a good *friend*.)

A **proper noun** names a particular person, place, or

thing. (*Rashid Hamdi, Maine, Eiffel Tower*)

Noun clause A noun clause is a clause used as a noun. (He understands *that he must work very hard*.)

Number A word is *singular* in number if it refers to just one person, place, thing, idea, or action, and *plural* in number if it refers to more than one person, place, thing, idea, or action. (The words *she, hat,* and *eats* are singular. The words *they, hats,* and *eat* are plural.)

 O

Object of a preposition The object of a preposition is the noun or pronoun that follows a preposition. (We climbed over the *fence*.)

Object of a verb The object of a verb receives the action of the verb. (They moved *mountains*.)

 P

Participial Phrase. *See* **Phrase.**

Participle A participle is a verb form. It is often used as part of a verb phrase (had *danced*). It can also be used as a verbal that functions as an adjective (the *shining* star).

The *present participle* is formed by adding *-ing* to the present form of a verb. (*Skating* rapidly, we circled the rink.)

The *past participle* of a regular verb is formed by adding *-d* or *-ed* to the present form. (*Astonished*, they opened the gift.) The past participles of irregular verbs do not follow this pattern.

Passive voice. *See* **Voice.**

Past tense. *See* **Verb tense.**

Perfect tenses. *See* **Verb tense.**

Person The person of a pronoun depends on the noun to which it refers.

A *first-person* pronoun refers to the person speaking. (*I* jumped.)

A *second-person* pronoun refers to the person spoken to. (*You* sat.)

A *third-person* pronoun refers to some other person(s) or thing(s) being spoken of. (*They* sang.)

Personal pronoun. *See* **Pronoun.**

Phrase A phrase is a group of related words that lacks both a subject and a verb. (*gracefully leaping*)

An *adjective phrase* modifies a noun or a pronoun. (The label *on the bottle* has faded.)

An *adverb phrase* modifies a verb, an adjective, or an adverb. (Come *to the fair*.)

An *appositive phrase* identifies or provides further information about a noun or pronoun that directly precedes the phrase. (Leili Moghtader, *a retired teacher*, looked after the lighthouse.)

A *gerund phrase* consists of a gerund with its objects and modifiers. (*Capturing the king* was the object of the game.)

An *infinitive phrase* consists of an infinitive along with its modifiers and objects. (I hope *to see him again*.)

A *participial phrase* consists of a participle and its objects and modifiers. (*Turning the corner*, they headed home.)

A *prepositional phrase* consists of a preposition, its object, and any modifiers, or words that describe the object. (The woman *with the large hat* watched the race.)

A *verb phrase* consists of a main verb and one or more helping verbs. (*might have ordered*)

Possessive A noun or pronoun that is possessive shows ownership or relationship. (*Aisha's* job, *her* sister)

Possessive noun. *See* **Noun.**

Possessive pronoun. *See* **Pronoun.**

Predicate The predicate of a sentence tells what the subject is or does. (The deer *ran away quickly*.) *See also* **Complete predicate, Simple Predicate.**

Predicate adjective. *See* **Adjective.**

Predicate nominative A predicate nominative is a noun or pronoun that follows a linking verb and renames or explains the subject. (Joan is a computer *operator*. The winner of the prize was *he*.)

Predicate noun. *See* **Noun.**

Predicate pronoun. *See* **Pronoun.**

Preposition A preposition is a word that relates its object to another part of the sentence or to the sentence as a whole. (Blanca read *about* the book.)

Prepositional phrase. *See* **Phrase.**

Present tense. *See* **Verb tense.**

Pronoun A pronoun replaces a noun or another pronoun. Some pronouns allow a writer or speaker to avoid repeating a proper noun. Other pronouns let a writer show a situation in which some information is not known.

A *demonstrative pronoun* singles out one or more persons or things. (*this* boat)

An *indefinite pronoun* refers to an unknown or unidentified person or thing. (*Someone* called.)

An *intensive pronoun* emphasizes a noun or pronoun. (She *herself* performed the surgery.)

An *interrogative pronoun* asks a question. (*Who* took my wrench?)

A *personal pronoun* shows a distinction of person. (*I* spoke. *You* heard. *He* won.)

A *possessive pronoun* shows ownership. (*Your* story is in the folder. Are these notes *his?*)

A *predicate pronoun* follows a linking verb and renames the subject. (The caller was *he.*)

A *reflexive pronoun* reflects an action back on the subject of the sentence. (Ashley treated *herself* to a soda.)

A *relative pronoun* relates a subordinate clause to the word it modifies in the main clause. (We gave our reasons, *which* were very strong.)

Pronoun-antecedent agreement. *See* **Agreement.**

Pronoun forms

The *subject form of a pronoun* is used when the pronoun is the subject of a sentence or follows a linking verb as a predicate pronoun. (*He* subtracted. It is *she.*)

The *object form of a pronoun* is used when the pronoun is the direct or indirect object of a verb or verbal or the object of a preposition. (I gave *her* a clue. She sat with *them.*)

Proper adjective. *See* **Adjective.**

Proper noun. *See* **Noun.**

Punctuation Punctuation clarifies the structure of sentences.

Quotation A quotation consists of words from another speaker or writer.

A *direct quotation* is the exact words of a speaker or

writer. (Martin said, *"The homecoming game has been postponed."*)

A *divided quotation* is a quotation separated by words that identify the speaker. (*"The homecoming game,"* said Martin, *"has been postponed."*)

An *indirect quotation* reports what a person said without giving the exact words. (*Martin said that the homecoming game had been postponed.*)

Reflexive pronoun. *See* **Pronoun.**

Regular verb. *See* **Verb.**

Relative pronoun. *See* **Pronoun.**

Run-on sentence A run-on sentence consists of two or more sentences written incorrectly as one. (*I talked he listened.*)

Sentence A sentence expresses a complete thought.

A *compound-complex sentence* contains two or more independent clauses and one or more dependent clauses. (*I would like to be an archaeologist, but I have never visited an ancient site, although I have had opportunities.*)

A *complex sentence* contains one main clause and one or more subordinate clauses. (*Open the windows before you go to bed. If she falls, I'll help her up.*)

A *compound sentence* is made up of two or more independent clauses joined by a conjunction, a colon, or a semicolon. (*The ship finally docked, and the passengers quickly left.*)

A *simple sentence* consists of only one main clause. (*My*

Kind of Sentence	Example
Declarative (statement)	They went home.
Exclamatory (strong feeling)	We won!
Imperative (request, command)	Let the dog out.
Interrogative (question)	Where is Ronnie?

friend volunteers at a nursing home.) There are four kinds of simple sentences.

Sentence fragment A sentence fragment is a group of words that is only part of a sentence. (*As I walked; Was coming to the door*)

Simple predicate A simple predicate is the key word in the predicate of a sentence. (The boat *sailed* off into the sunset.)

Simple subject A simple subject is the key noun or pronoun in the subject. (The huge *animal* attacked.)

Split Infinitive A split infinitive occurs when a modifier is placed between the word *to* and the verb in an infinitive. (*to quickly speak*)

Subject The subject is the part of a sentence that tells whom or what the sentence is about. (*Gena* drove.)

Subject-verb agreement. *See* **Agreement.**

Subjunctive mood. *See* **Mood.**

Subordinate clause. *See* **Clause.**

Subordinating conjunction. *See* **Conjunction.**

Transitive verb. *See* **Verb.**

Unidentified reference An unidentified reference usually occurs when the word *it, they this, which* or *that* is used. (In California *they* have good weather most of the time.)

Verb A verb expresses an action, a condition, or a state of being. *(swim, is, seems)*

The subject of an ***active verb*** performs the action of a sentence. (Ricardo *soared*.)

The subject of a ***passive verb*** receives the verb's action or expresses the result of an action. (The story *was told*.)

A ***helping verb*** is used with the main verb; together they make up a verb phrase. *(has gone)*

A ***linking verb*** expresses a state of being or connects the subject with a word or words that describe the subject. (The ice *feels* cold.) Linking verbs: *be, become, feel, grow, look, remain, seem, smell, sound, taste.*

A ***main verb*** expresses action or state of being; it appears with one or more auxiliary verbs. (will be *staying*)

The ***progressive form*** of a verb shows continuing action. (She *is knitting*.)

The ***past tense*** and ***past participle*** of a regular verb are formed by adding *-d* or *-ed*. (*sail, sailed*) Irregular verbs do not follow this pattern. (*grow, grew, grown*)

Verbal	Example
Gerund (used as a noun)	Lamont enjoys *swimming*.
Infinitive (used as an adjective, an adverb, or a noun)	Everyone wants *to help*.
Participle (used as an adjective)	The leaves *covering* the drive made it slippery.

The action of a ***transitive verb*** is directed toward someone or something, called the object of a verb. (Leo *washed* the windows.) An ***intransitive verb*** has no object. (The leaves *scattered*.)

Verbal A verbal is formed from a verb and acts as another part of speech, such as a noun, an adjective, or an adverb.

Verb phrases. A verb phrase consists of a main verb and one or more helping verbs. (*should have been working*)

Verb tense Verb tense shows the time of an action or a state of being. (*go, went, am, seemed*)

The ***present tense*** places an action or condition in the present. (We *walk* down the street.)

The ***past tense*** places an action or condition in the past. (They *left*.)

The ***future tense*** places an action or condition in the future. (They *will go*.)

The ***present perfect tense*** describes an action that was completed in an indefinite past time or that began in the past and continues in the present. *(has observed, have danced)*

The ***past perfect tense*** describes one action that happened before another action in the past. *(had wondered, had analyzed)*

The ***future perfect tense*** describes an event that will be finished before another future action begins. *(will have fallen)*

Voice The voice of a verb depends on whether the subject performs or receives the action of the verb.

In the ***active voice*** the subject of the sentence performs the verb's action. (We *knew* the answer.)

In the ***passive voice*** the subject of the sentence receives the action of the verb. (The team *has been eliminated*.)

Speaking and Listening

Good communicators do more than just talk. They use specific techniques to present their ideas effectively, and they are attentive and critical listeners.

① Organization and Delivery

In school, in business, and in any community, one of the best ways to present information is to deliver it in person—speaking directly to a live audience.

Audience and Purpose

When preparing and presenting a speech, your goal is to deliver a focused, coherent presentation that both conveys your ideas clearly and relates to the background and interests of your audience. By understanding your audience, you can tailor your speech to them appropriately and effectively.

- **Know your audience** What kind of group are you presenting to—fellow classmates? an entire school assembly? a group of teachers? What are their interests and backgrounds? Understanding their different points of view can help you address each group in the most appropriate way.

- **Understand your purpose** Keep in mind your purpose for speaking. Are you trying to persuade the audience to do something? Are you presenting the audience with results of the latest research? Perhaps you simply want to entertain them by sharing a story or experience.

- **Organize effectively** As you prepare your presentation, it's important to arrange the information effectively and persuasively. Think about your audience and the best way to organize the information so that they understand, absorb, and are interested by it.

Writing Your Speech

If you are writing your speech beforehand, rather than working from notes or memory, use the following guidelines to help you:

- **Prepare an outline** Try to base your speech on a chosen pattern of organization. A standard outline would include a compelling introduction, a concise preview or summary, clear transitions between paragraphs, a logically developed and well-supported body, and an effective conclusion. The organization of the speech—whether it was persuasive, comparison-contrast, or process description, for example—would be most obvious in the body of the speech.

SAMPLE OUTLINE #1
Process Description

I. Introduction
   (Get audience interested and state thesis.)
   (Use transition to link to body.)

II. Body
   A. Step 1 of process
      (Use transition.)
   B. Step 2 of process
      (Use transition.)
   C. Step 3 of process
      (Use transition to link to conclusion.)

III. Conclusion
   (Summarize process and suggest reasons to follow process.)

SAMPLE OUTLINE #2
Persuasive Speech

I. Introduction
(Get audience interested and state thesis.)
(Use transition to link to body.)

II. Body
A. First argument
(Use transition.)
B. Second argument
(Use transition.)
C. Third argument
(Use transition.)

III. Conclusion
(Restate thesis and suggest further action.)

- **Create a unified speech** Do this first by organizing your speech into paragraphs, each of which develops a single main idea. Then make sure that just as all the sentences in a paragraph support the main idea of the paragraph, so all the paragraphs in your speech support the main idea of the speech.

- **Use effective language** Make your presentation interesting and lively by using precise, vivid language; action verbs; sensory details; and colorful modifiers. Avoid the passive voice.

- **Use appropriate language** The subject of your speech—and the way you choose to present it—should match both your audience and the occasion. For example, if you were telling a funny story to a group of friends, your speech might be informal and lighthearted. However, for formal presentations it is important to use appropriate grammar, word choice, enunciation, and pacing.

- **Provide evidence** Include relevant facts, statistics, and incidents; quote experts to support both your ideas and your opinions. Elaborate—or provide specific details, perhaps with visual or media displays—to clarify what you are saying.

- **Emphasize points** To help your audience in following the main ideas and concepts of your speech, be sure to draw attention to important points. You can do this with your voice, using effective rate, volume, pitch, and tone. You can also do this with nonverbal elements, such as eye contact, facial expressions, hand gestures, and props—all of which can help engage your audience's interest and hold their attention.

- **Use audience feedback** Pay attention to how your audience responds to your presentation. Do they look confused? Rearrange words and sentences to clarify meaning. Are they yawning? Liven it up with more effective voice and gesture. Rehearsing in front of a practice audience is a great opportunity for feedback, after which you can reconsider and modify your final presentation to be more effective.

Prepare/Practice/Present

Confidence is the key to a successful presentation. Use these techniques to help you prepare and present your speech to your class.

Prepare

- **Review your information** Reread your written report and review your background research—you'll feel much more confident during your speech.

- **Organize your notes** Jot down a minimum of key points or prepare an entire script. Consider using numbered index cards for each main point or paragraph of your speech. Be sure to include your most important evidence and examples.

- **Plan your visual aids** If you are planning on using visual aids, such as slides, posters, charts, graphs, video clips, overhead transparencies, or computer projections, now is the time to design them and decide how to work them into your speech.

Practice

- **Rehearse** Rehearse your speech several times, possibly in front of a practice audience. If you are using visual aids, practice handling them. Adapt your rate of speaking, pitch, and tone of voice to your audience and setting. Time yourself to ensure that your speech does not run too long.

- **Evaluate your performance** When you have finished each rehearsal, evaluate your performance. How did you do? Did you slow down for emphasis, pause to let an important point sink in, or use gestures for emphasis? Make a list of aspects of your presentation that you will try to perfect for your next rehearsal.

Present

- **Begin your speech** In order to break the tension of the opening moments, try to look relaxed and remember to smile!

- **Make eye contact** Eye contact with audience members will help you establish the feeling of personal contact, and it will also help you determine if the audience understands your speech.

- **Remember to pause** A slight pause after important points will provide emphasis and give your audience time to think about what you are saying.

- **Maintain good posture** Stand up straight and avoid nervous movements that may distract the audience's attention from what you are saying.

- **Use expressive body language** Capture the attention of your audience through body language as well as through speech. Lean forward when you make an important point; move your hands and arms for emphasis. Your body language will show that you really believe in what you are saying.

❷ Oral Interpretation

An oral interpretation is a way to show an audience what a piece of written work means to you—whether it's yours or someone else's. The piece you interpret may be a story, poem, speech, or soliloquy. If you choose to read a scene from a play with several other speakers, your oral interpretation is called a dramatic reading.

Oral Reading

When you perform an oral reading, you use appropriate voice, facial expressions, and gestures to create a special world for your audience and bring the literature to life. There are many different types of pieces to choose from:

- **Story** This may be a brief selection from a short story or novel. You may present a monologue, a long speech offered by a single character or narrator in the piece. You may also present a dialogue, in which you take on the roles of two or more characters. Use voice and gesture to help your audience experience and understand the scene.

- **Soliloquy** This is a dramatic monologue from a story or play. It represents the unspoken thoughts of a single character, heard only by the audience and not by other characters in the scene. Use an expressive voice to help an audience understand a character's inner thoughts, emotions, and feelings.

- **Poem** Unless the poem is very long, you are likely to present the piece in its entirety (4–6 stanzas). As with a story, you may assume the voice of the poem's narrator if there is one. Recite the words of a poem effectively, using your voice to create mood and evoke emotion from your audience.

- **Speech** Unless the speech is short, you are likely to select a brief passage from it. Choose the most powerful and dramatic part of the speech. Put yourself in the position of the speech's original orator, using voice and gesture to deliver the words passionately and persuasively.

Dramatic Reading

When several speakers participate in the reading of a play or other work divided into parts, it is called a dramatic reading. Use the following techniques in your dramatic reading:

- **Prepare** Rehearse your material several times. Become familiar with the humorous and most dramatic parts of your script. Come up with a special voice that fits the personality of your character.

- **Project** As you read your lines, aim your voice toward the very back of the room. This will allow everyone to hear you.

- **Perform** React to the other characters as if you were hearing their lines for the first time. Deliver your own lines with the appropriate emotion. Use your whole body, as well as your hands and face, to express your emotions.

GUIDELINES HOW TO ANALYZE YOUR ORAL INTERPRETATION

- Did you speak clearly, enunciating each word carefully?
- Did you control your volume, projecting without shouting?
- Did you pace yourself, varying your rate of speech appropriately to express emotion, mood, and action?
- Did you use different voices for each character?
- Did you stress important words or phrases?
- Did you use voice, tone, and gesture to enhance meaning?

❸ Narrative Presentations

When you make a narrative presentation, you tell a story or present a subject using a story-type format. A good narrative keeps an audience both informed and entertained. It also allows you to deliver a message in a unique and creative way.

- **Establish a setting** Think about a definite context and setting for your story. Where does the action take place? Is the narrative biographical or autobiographical? Choose a clear, coherent incident, event, or situation that the audience can relate to.

- **Create a plot** What happens in your story? Is it funny? tragic? suspenseful? How do you want the events to unfold? Over what period of time? A standard plot line includes exposition (to draw the audience in), a central conflict (the reason the story is told), rising action (to create tension), a climax (the height of action), and a denouement (to show the final outcome).

- **Determine a point of view** Is a narrator telling the story? Who is the main character of the story? What is his or her point of view or attitude? Show how the incident, event, or situation of your narrative specifically affects the character.

- **Use effective language** Include well-chosen sensory details and concrete language to develop the plot and the character. Let your audience touch, taste, hear, and smell what's happening in the story.

- **Employ narrative devices** Use a range of descriptive strategies to keep your narrative interesting: relevant, believable dialogue; specific action that forwards the plot; language that builds up tension or suspense in a scene; appropriate physical and background description; comparison or contrast of characters.

- **Focus on the delivery** Once you've created your narrative, your next responsibility is to make the story come alive in presentation. Remember, it's not just what you say but how you say it. Speak clearly and confidently. Pace yourself and pause for emphasis. Use a range of voices, movements, gestures, and expressions to convey different emotions and moods.

GUIDELINES   **HOW TO ANALYZE YOUR NARRATIVE PRESENTATION**

- Did you choose a context that makes sense and contributes to a believable narrative?
- Does your plot flow well and create the right mood for your audience?
- Is your character—and his or her point of view—realistic and memorable?
- Did you use sensory language that allows your audience to experience the story?
- Did you use a range of narrative devices to keep your audience interested?
- Did you deliver your speech effectively and persuasively?

Oral Responses to Literature

An oral response to literature is a personal, analytic interpretation of a writer's story, poem, or drama. It demonstrates to an audience a solid and comprehensive understanding of what that piece means to you.

- **Select carefully** In choosing a piece for your oral response, think about the assignment, your interest, and the audience. Choose something that affects you deeply and about which you feel strongly.

- **Exhibit understanding** Develop an interpretation exhibiting careful reading, understanding, and insight. Direct your reader to specific words, sentences, or paragraphs that are rich with meaning. Explore how they make you feel, what they make you think about, and why they are particularly important to the piece.

- **Organize clearly** Organize the selected interpretation around several clear ideas, premises, or images. How do they relate to the piece as a whole? What insight and meaning do they provide? Use examples and textual evidence to give weight to your interpretation.

- **Draw relationships** Show how the writer's words and techniques specifically affect you. Then draw supported inferences about how and why a literary work can affect an audience in general. Support your judgments through references to the text, other works and authors, and personal knowledge.

GUIDELINES   HOW TO ANALYZE YOUR ORAL RESPONSE

- Did you choose an interesting piece that you enjoy, understand, and feel strongly about?
- Did you engage in in-depth analysis and demonstrate an understanding of what the piece means to you?
- Did you direct your audience to specific parts of the piece that support your interpretation?
- Did you present your ideas in a clear, well-organized manner?
- Did you discuss how literature and its audience affect each other?
- Did your enthusiasm for the piece come through in your delivery?

❺ Research Presentations

A research presentation is an informative, investigative presentation based on your own research work. After you pose relevant questions to guide your research, you will organize your information and attempt to explain, teach, and enlighten an audience about a particular subject.

- **Target your audience** Think about what your audience may already know about the subject. Taking their background into consideration, develop a focused, organized presentation.
- **Introduce the topic** Grab your audience's attention by posing an interesting, relevant question or stating a fascinating fact.
- **Propose a definite thesis and framework** Concisely explain to your audience the purpose of your presentation, the argument you are proposing, and how you went about collecting the information to support it.

- **Present your research** Share all important pieces of information gained from your research that support your thesis: evidence, statistics, ideas, concepts, and direct quotations. Paraphrase and summarize all relevant perspectives on the topic, as appropriate.
- **Cite your sources** Use a variety of primary and secondary sources during your research. Distinguish the nature and value of each.
- **Use visual aids** Enliven your presentation by organizing and recording your information on charts, maps, and graphs.

GUIDELINES   HOW TO ANALYZE YOUR RESEARCH PRESENTATION

- Did you think about your audience's previous knowledge on the subject?
- Did you hook your audience with an interesting question or fact?
- Did you propose a definite thesis and framework for your presentation?
- Did you present your research clearly and concisely?
- Did you cite a variety of sources and use effective presentation aids?

❻ Persuasive Presentations

When you deliver a persuasive presentation, you offer a thesis or clear statement on a subject, provide relevant evidence to support your position, and attempt to convince the audience to accept your point of view.

- **Do your research** In order to develop a well-defined thesis on a subject—one that makes a clear and knowledgeable judgment—you need to know enough about the subject in the first place. Learn about all perspectives on the topic so that you can make an informed and intelligent decision.

- **State your position** Present your position on the subject clearly, confidently, and enthusiastically.

- **Support your position** Distinguish between fact and opinion. Demonstrate that your thesis is well-supported by fact. Use strong, supportive evidence to back up your position. Arm yourself with detailed evidence, examples, and reasoning.

- **Provide a strong defense** Consider your audience's own biases and opinions on the subject. What kind of questions or doubts might they have? Prepare effective counterarguments and address them before they are even raised.

- **Deliver effectively** Engage your audience. Give them something to think about by posing challenging questions. Make them aware of a problem and how it might affect them or someone they know. Maintain a convincing yet reasonable tone that demonstrates that you really believe in what you are saying.

GUIDELINES **HOW TO ANALYZE YOUR PERSUASIVE PRESENTATION**

- Did you present a clear statement or argument?
- Did you support your thesis with convincing, well-articulated facts?
- Did you use sound logic in developing the argument?
- Did you anticipate and answer audience concerns?
- Did you hold the audience's interest with effective voice, facial expressions, and gesture?

 Active Listening for Information

Active listeners listen carefully and with purpose. They think about what they hear—before, during, and after any presentation—whether it's a speech, a class lecture, or even a television program.

Before Listening

- **Keep an open mind** Don't prejudge the speaker. Listen to what he or she has to say, and then evaluate it critically but fairly.

- **Prepare yourself** Review what you know about the speaker's topic. Then think of questions you'd like to ask or information you'd like to learn more about.

- **Listen with purpose** Try to match how you listen with why you are listening.

Listening with a Purpose		
Situation	**Reason for Listening**	**How to Listen**
Your friend tells a funny story about her pet gerbil.	For enjoyment, to provide your friend with an audience	Maintain eye contact; show you understand; react to the story.
You're listening to a speech, "Wolves of the Tundra."	For enjoyment; to learn something new	Think about what you already know; listen for ideas that add to your knowledge.
Your mother explains why you can't keep an alligator as a pet.	To understand her point of view; to find opportunities to share your own ideas	Listen carefully; respond positively to valid points; listen for opportunities to state your own reasons.
You and your friends are trying to arrange a trip to a concert.	To solve a problem	Identify goals and problems; listen closely to one another's ideas and build on them.
You are watching a television program about cooking or carpentry.	To follow directions	Listen for words such as *first, second, next,* and *finally;* take notes that you can refer to later.

While Listening

- **Block out distractions** Keep your eyes on the speaker, focus your mind, and ignore outside interference.
- **Look for signals of main ideas** See the Guidelines box below.
- **Take notes, if appropriate** Jot down phrases, main ideas, or questions that occur to you.
- **Look for relationships between ideas** Note comparisons and contrasts, causes and effects, and problems and solutions.
- **Identify tone, mood, and gestures** To aid in your comprehension, note how the speaker uses word choice, voice pitch, posture, and gestures to convey meaning.

TIP If you are listening to an oral interpretation, be sure to analyze both the speaker's language choice and delivery. Recognize how and why a speaker's personal interpretation can influence or affect your own understanding of a subject.

GUIDELINES   **HOW TO RECOGNIZE MAIN IDEAS**

- Did you listen for ideas presented first or last?
- Did you listen for ideas repeated several times for emphasis?
- Did you note statements that begin with phrases such as "My point is . . ." or "The important thing is . . ."?
- Did you pay attention to ideas presented in a loud voice or with forceful gestures?
- In a multimedia presentation, did you note points the speaker had reproduced on a chart or on any other visual aid?

After Listening

- **Review notes taken** Make sure you understand what was said.
- **Ask questions** Ask the speaker probing questions to elicit more information. Demand additional evidence to support claims and conclusions made. Clarify anything that was unclear or confusing.
- **Summarize, paraphrase, and evaluate** Restate the speaker's ideas in your own words. Clarify your reasons for agreeing or disagreeing.
- **Respond to the speaker** Respond to persuasive statements with questions, challenges, or affirmations. Ask relevant questions concerning the speaker's content, delivery, and purpose.

GUIDELINES   **HOW TO EVALUATE WHAT YOU HEAR**

- What is the purpose of the talk, and does the speaker achieve it?
- In an oral interpretation of literature, how effective was the speaker's language choice? delivery?
- Does the information make sense? Does it contradict anything you already know?
- Are ideas presented in an interesting and logical way?
- Are points supported with facts and details?
- Do you still have any questions after hearing the talk?
- Do you agree with what the speaker said? Why or why not?

❽ Critical Listening

As you listen to a speaker's ideas, you will want to analyze, evaluate, and critique those ideas. Use the following critical listening strategies as you listen to a public speaker:

- **Determine the speaker's purpose** Identify the speaker's purpose in giving the speech. Is the speaker trying to inform? to persuade? to express thoughts or feelings? to entertain? Learn to evaluate a speaker's credibility. His or her speech may be slanted by hidden agendas or personal biases.

- **Listen for the main idea** Figure out the speaker's main message before allowing yourself to be distracted by seemingly convincing facts and details.

- **Distinguish between fact and opinion** Know the difference between opinion statements, such as "I think/I believe," and factual statements, such as "Statistics show" or "It has been proved."

- **Recognize the use of rhetorical devices** Some speakers use special techniques to accomplish different purposes when they express their ideas. Noting these techniques as you listen will enable you to identify these purposes. For example, a speaker may use **repetition** of certain words or phrases, which allows him or her to emphasize ideas and draw your attention to something important. The speaker may also pose **rhetorical questions,** questions that you are not expected to respond to, to involve you in the topic. The speaker may use a third device such as an **allusion,** an indirect reference to something, for the purpose of pleasing and making a connection to a listener who recognizes the reference.

- **Recognize the use of persuasive devices** Beware of techniques used to persuade you to accept a particular opinion. Persuasive devices—such as inaccurate generalizations, either/or reasoning, and bandwagon or snob appeal—may represent faulty reasoning and provide misleading information.

- **Interpret the effect of visuals** Image makers—such as graphic artists, illustrators, and photojournalists—are skilled at communicating information through visuals. How do visuals combined with speech alter or affect your impressions and opinions on a subject? Are you aware of their influence?

GUIDELINES **HOW TO LISTEN CRITICALLY**

- Are you aware of the speaker's purpose in addressing you?
- Does the speaker seem confident in his or her knowledge of the subject?
- Does the speaker convince with concrete evidence rather than creative rhetoric?
- Are you able to distinguish between personal opinions and verifiable facts?
- Does the speaker use faulty or misleading persuasive devices?
- Do you recognize how the use of visuals can alter your understanding or impressions of a speech?

---

⑨ Recognizing Persuasive Devices

An important part of critical listening is the ability to recognize persuasive devices—techniques used to persuade you to accept a particular opinion. Persuasive devices may represent faulty reasoning and provide misleading information. They are often used in advertising and in propaganda. Some persuasive devices that you should learn to recognize:

- **Inaccurate generalization** A generalization is a broad statement about a number of people or things, such as "Maps are hard to read." Although some generalizations are true, others are too broad to be true. The statement "All teenagers like junk food" is an example of an inaccurate generalization.

- **Either/or** A writer may try to convince an audience that there are only two choices or ways of looking at something, when in fact there may be many. The statement "If you don't join the glee club, you have no school spirit" is an example of either/or reasoning.

- **Bandwagon** A bandwagon statement appeals to people's desire to belong to a group. For example, a statement like "Everyone at your school already has this hot new watch" is a bandwagon device.

- **Snob appeal** This technique appeals to people's need to feel superior to other people. A statement like "You deserve the best, so buy this jacket" relies on snob appeal.

⑩ Conducting Interviews

Conducting a personal interview can be an effective way to get information.

- Select your interviewee carefully. Identify who has the kind of knowledge and experience you are looking for.

- Research any information by or about the person you will interview. The background details will help you focus.

- Prepare a list of questions. Create open-ended questions that can't be answered simply with a "yes" or "no." Arrange your questions in order of significance, from most important to least important.

- Ask your questions clearly and listen carefully. Give the person that you are interviewing plenty of time to answer.

- Listen interactively and flexibly. Be prepared to follow up on a response you find interesting, even if it was not on your initial list of questions.

- Avoid arguments. Be tactful and polite.

- Take notes to help in your write-up of the interview. Jot down main ideas or important statements that you can quote.

- Summarize your notes while they are still fresh in your mind.

- Send a thank-you note to the interviewee afterward.

① Getting Information Electronically

Electronic resources provide you with a convenient and efficient way to gather information.

⒈⒈ Online Resources

When you use your computer to communicate with another computer or with another person using a computer, you are working "online." Online resources include commercial information services and information available on the Internet.

Commercial Information Services

You can subscribe to various services that offer information, such as the following:

- up-to-date news, weather, and sports reports
- access to encyclopedias, magazines, newspapers, dictionaries, almanacs, and databases (collections of information)
- forums, or ongoing electronic conversations among people interested in a particular topic

Internet

The Internet is a vast network of computers. News services, libraries, universities, researchers, organizations, and government agencies use the Internet to communicate and to distribute information. The Internet includes two key features:

- **World Wide Web,** which provides information on specific subjects and links you to related topics and resources (such as the linked Web pages shown below)
- **Electronic mail** (e-mail), which makes possible communication among e-mail users worldwide

What You'll Need

- To access online resources, you need a computer with a modem to link you to the Internet. Your school computer lab or resource center may be linked to the Internet or to a commercial information service.
- To use CD-ROMs, you need a computer system with a CD-ROM drive.

Navigating the Web

With access to the World Wide Web, you can find virtually any piece of information once you know how to look for it. Here are some tips to get you started and keep you going.

Choose a Search Engine or a Directory

A **search engine** combs through Web sites looking for your topic. A **directory** allows you to search within a collection of sites that are grouped by subject, such as Reference, Sports, or Entertainment.

Enter Key Words

Once you've chosen a starting point, enter the **key word** or words that describe your topic. By using more than one word, you can narrow your search. For example, using the key word "baseball" will find a variety of sites with information on baseball, whereas the key words "Dodgers baseball" will help you find sites with information on a specific team.

Investigate Your Options

Once you receive the results of your search, scan the site listings and their summaries to see which ones look promising. If you click on a site and it's not useful, you can always back up and try again. The sites at the top of the list usually will be more relevant to your search than those found farther down.

Tips for Getting the Most from Your Searching

- **Note the source** Because anyone can put information on the Web, it's wise to check where the information comes from. For example, sites produced by government agencies or educational institutions tend to be more reliable than the personal Web pages of individuals.
- **Refine your search** If you're not getting the results you want, search again, using more or different key words.
- **Explore other avenues** Different search engines may produce different results, and the same goes for directories.
- **Link around** Many Web sites have links to other sites with related content that you might not find by searching on your own.

 ## CD-ROM

A CD-ROM (compact disc–read-only memory) stores data that may include text, sound, photographs, and video.

Almost any kind of information can be found on CD-ROMs, which you can purchase or use at the library, including

- encyclopedias, almanacs, and indexes
- other reference books on a variety of subjects
- news reports from newspapers, magazines, television, or radio
- museum art collections
- back issues of magazines
- literature collections

1.4 Library Computer Services

Many libraries offer computerized catalogs and a variety of other electronic resources.

Computerized Catalogs

You may search for a book in a library by typing the title, author, subject, or key words into a computer terminal. When you find the book you're looking for, the screen will display the kind of information shown here, including the book's call number and whether it is on the shelf or checked out of the library. You may also be able to search the catalogs of other libraries.

Other Electronic Resources

In addition to computerized catalogs, many libraries offer electronic versions of books or other reference materials. They may also have a variety of indexes on CD-ROM, which allow you to search for magazine or newspaper articles on any topic you choose. Ask your librarian for assistance in using these resources.

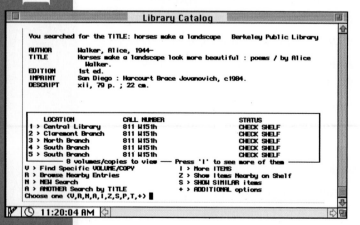

1.5 Evaluating Sources

Be a discriminating consumer of information by evaluating the credibility of a source, the reliability of its information, and its value in answering your research needs.

Credibility of Sources

You must determine the credibility and appropriateness of each source in order to write an effective report or speech. Use these criteria to evaluate print and electronic sources. (For more information on evaluating sources, see page R52 in the Writing Handbook.)

> **CRITERIA HOW TO EVALUATE A SOURCE**
>
> • Is the writer an authority?
> • Is the source reliable and unbiased?
> • Is the source up-to-date?
> • Is the source appropriate?

Distinguishing Fact from Opinion

As you gather information, it is important to recognize facts and opinions. A fact can be proved true or false. You could verify the statement "Congress rejected the bill" by checking the *Congressional Record.* An opinion is a judgment based on facts, such as the statement "Congress should not have rejected the bill." To evaluate an opinion, check for evidence presented logically to support it.

Recognizing Bias

A bias does not automatically make a writer's point of view unreliable. However, recognizing bias can help you evaluate a source. Recognizing that the author of an article about immigration is an immigrant himself will help you understand that author's bias. To avoid relying on information that may be biased, check an author's background and gather a variety of viewpoints.

② Word Processing

Many word-processing programs allow you to draft, revise, edit, and format your writing and to produce neat, professional-looking papers. They also allow you to share your writing with others.

②.1 Prewriting and Drafting

A computer makes it easy to experiment with different ways of expressing and organizing your ideas. You can use it to keep an electronic journal or portfolio, to organize your notes in files, or to access templates for special writing formats. It allows you to store multiple drafts of a paper and even to add graphics to clarify and enhance your message. You may want to create a separate file to use as a writing notebook. Keep all of your story starters, ideas to research, and other writing ideas in this file.

②.2 Revising and Editing

Improving the quality of your writing becomes easier when you use a word-processing program to revise and edit.

Revising a Document
Most word-processing programs allow you to make the following kinds of changes:

- add or delete words
- move text from one location in your document to another
- undo a change you have made in the text
- save a document with a new name, allowing you to keep old drafts for reference
- view more than one document at a time, so that you can copy text from one document and add it to another

Editing a Document
Many word-processing programs have the following features to help you catch errors and polish your writing:

- The **spell checker** automatically finds misspelled words and suggests possible corrections. Even if you use a spell checker, you should still proofread your draft carefully to make sure you've used the right words. For example, you may have used *there* or *they're* when you meant to use *their.*
- The **grammar checker** spots possible grammatical errors and suggests ways you might correct them.
- The **thesaurus** suggests synonyms for a word you want to replace.
- The **dictionary** will give you the definitions of words so that you can be sure you have used words correctly.
- The **search and replace** feature searches your whole document and corrects every occurrence of something you want to change, such as a misspelled name.

②.3 Formatting Your Work

Format is the layout and appearance of your writing on the page. You may choose your formatting options before or after you write.

Formatting Type
You may want to make changes in the typeface, type size, and type style of words in your document. For each your word-processing program likely have several options to

Typeface	Size	Style
Geneva	7-point Times	*Italic*
Times	10-point Times	**Bold**
Chicago	12-point Times	<u>Underline</u>
Courier	14-point Times	

These options allow you to

- **change the typeface** to create a different look for the words in your document
- **change the type size** of section headings in the paper or the entire document
- **change the type style** when necessary; for example, use italics or underlining for the titles of books and magazines

Formatting Pages

Not only can you change the way individual words look; you can also change the way they are arranged on the page. Some of the formatting decisions you make will depend on how you plan to use a printout of a draft or on the guidelines of an assignment.

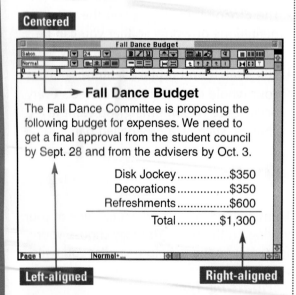

- **Set the line spacing,** or the amount of space you need between lines of text. Double-spacing is commonly used for final drafts.

- **Set the margins,** or the amount of white space around the edges of your text. A one-inch margin on all sides is commonly used for final drafts.
- **Create a header** for the top of the page or a footer for the bottom if you want to include such information as your name, the date, or the page number on every page.
- **Determine the alignment** of your text. The screen on this page shows your options.

WRITING TIP Keep your format simple. Your goal is to create not only an attractive document but also one that is easy to read. Your readers will have difficulty if you change the type formatting frequently.

TECHNOLOGY TIP Some word-processing programs or other software packages provide preset templates, or patterns, for writing outlines, memos, letters, newsletters, or invitations. If you use one of these templates, you will not need to adjust the formatting. Other software programs will help you set up spreadsheets for applications such as budgeting or tracking expenses.

2.4 Working Collaboratively

Computers allow you to share your writing electronically. Send a copy of your work via e-mail or put it in someone's drop box if your computer is linked to other computers on a network. Then use the feedback of your peers to help you improve the quality of your writing.

Peer Editing on a Computer

The writer and the reader can both benefit from the convenience of peer editing "on screen," or at the computer.

- Be sure to save your current draft and then make a copy of it for each of your peer readers.
- You might have your peer readers enter their comments in a different typeface or type style from the one you used for your text.
- Ask each of your readers to include his or her initials in the file name.

- If your computer allows you to open more than one file at a time, open each reviewer's file and refer to the files as you revise your draft.

TECHNOLOGY TIP Some word-processing programs allow you to leave notes for your peer readers in the side column or in a separate text box. If you wish, leave those areas blank so that your readers can write comments or questions.

Peer Editing on a Printout

Some peer readers prefer to respond to a draft on paper rather than on the computer.

- Double- or triple-space your document so that your peer editor can make suggestions and changes between the lines.
- Leave extra-wide margins to give your readers room to note their reactions and questions as they read.
- Print out and photocopy your draft if you want to share it with more than one reader.

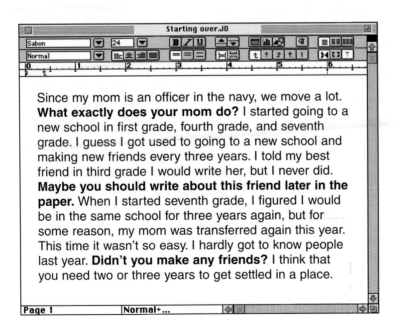

③ Using Visuals

Tables, graphs, diagrams, and pictures often communicate information more effectively than words alone do. Many word-processing and publishing programs allow you to create visuals to use with written text.

3.1 When to Use Visuals

Use visuals in your work to illustrate complex concepts and processes or to make a page look more interesting.

Although you should not expect a visual to do all the work of written text, combining words and pictures or graphics can increase the understanding and enjoyment of your writing. Many word-processing and publishing programs allow you to create and insert graphs, tables, time lines, diagrams, pictures, and flow charts into your document.

An art program allows you to create border designs or to draw an unusual character or setting for narrative or descriptive writing. You may also be able to add clip art, or premade pictures, to your document. Clip art can be used to illustrate an idea or concept in your writing or to enliven a page.

What You'll Need

- A graphics program to create visuals
- Access to clip-art files from a CD-ROM, a computer disk, or an online service

3.2 Kinds of Visuals

The visuals you choose will depend on the type of information you want to present.

Tables

Tables allow you to arrange facts or numbers into rows and columns so that your reader can compare information more easily. In many word-processing programs, you can create a table or database by choosing the number of vertical columns and horizontal rows you need and then entering information in each box, as the illustration shows.

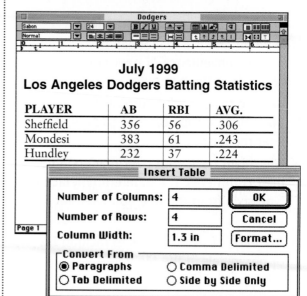

July 1999 Los Angeles Dodgers Batting Statistics			
PLAYER	**AB**	**RBI**	**AVG.**
Sheffield	356	56	.306
Mondesi	383	61	.243
Hundley	232	37	.224

TECHNOLOGY TIP A **spreadsheet** program provides you with a preset table for your statistics and performs any necessary calculations. It can also present tabular information in graphs and charts.

Graphs and Charts

You can sometimes use a graph or chart to help communicate complex information in a clear visual image. For example, you could use a line graph to show how a trend changes over time, a bar graph like the one at the right to compare statistics from different years, or a pie chart to compare percentages. You might want to explore displaying data in several formats before deciding which will work best for you.

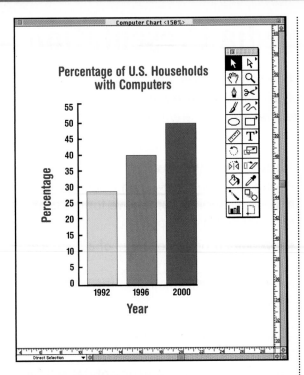

Other Visuals

Art and design programs allow you to create visuals for your writing. Many programs include the following features:

- **drawing tools** that allow you to draw, color, and shade pictures

- **clip art** that you can copy or change with drawing tools

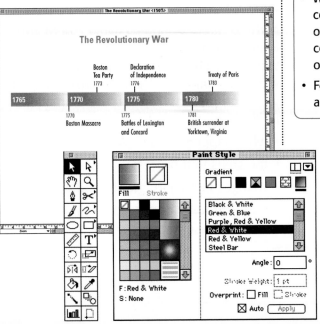

- **page borders** that you can use to decorate title pages, invitations, or brochures

- **text options** that allow you to combine words with your illustrations

- **tools for making geometric shapes** in flow charts, time lines, and diagrams that show a process or sequence of events

3.2 Evaluating Visual Messages

When you view images, whether they are cartoons, advertising art, photographs, or paintings, there are certain elements you should look for.

CRITERIA HOW TO ANALYZE IMAGES

- Is color used realistically? Is it used to emphasize certain objects? To evoke a specific response?

- What tone is created by color and by light and dark in the picture?

- Do the background images intentionally evoke a positive or negative response?

- What is noticeable about the picture's composition—that is, the arrangement of lines, colors, and forms? Does the composition emphasize certain objects or elements in the picture?

- For graphs and charts, does the visual accurately represent the data?

④ Creating a Multimedia Presentation

A multimedia presentation is a combination of text, sound, and visuals such as photographs, videos, and animation. Your audience reads, hears, and sees your presentation at a computer, following different "paths" you create to lead the user through the information you have gathered.

4.1 Features of Multimedia Programs

To start planning your multimedia presentation, you need to know what options are available to you. You can combine sound, photos, videos, and animation to enhance any text you write about your topic.

Sound

Including sound in your presentation can help your audience understand information in your written text. For example, the user may be able to listen and learn from

- the pronunciation of an unfamiliar or foreign word
- a speech
- a recorded news interview
- a music selection
- a dramatic reading of a work of literature

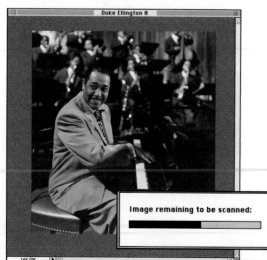

Photos and Videos

Photographs and live-action videos can make your subject come alive for the user. Here are some examples:

- videotaped news coverage of a historical event
- videos of music, dance, or theater performances
- charts and diagrams
- photos of an artist's work
- photos or video of a geographical setting that is important to the written text

TECHNOLOGY TIP You can download photos, sound, and video from Internet sources to your computer. This process allows you to add elements to your multimedia presentation that would usually require complex editing equipment.

Animation

Many graphics programs allow you to add animation, or movement, to the visuals in your presentation. Animated figures add to the user's enjoyment and understanding of what you present. You can use animation to illustrate

- what happens in a story
- the steps in a process
- changes in a chart, graph, or diagram
- how your user can explore information in your presentation

4.2 Planning Your Presentation

To create a multimedia presentation, first choose your topic and decide what you want to include. Then plan how you want your user to move through your presentation.

Imagine that you are creating a multimedia presentation about the great jazz musician Duke Ellington. You know you want to include the following items:

- text about his influence on jazz
- a portrait of him
- a recording of him playing a song
- a photograph of him leading his band
- a videotape of his band in concert, audio included
- a recording of a radio interview with him
- text of interesting anecdotes from his concert tours

You can choose one of the following ways to organize your presentation:

- **a step-by-step** method with only one path, or order, in which the user can see and hear the information
- **a branching path** that allows users to make some choices about what they will see and hear, and in what order

A flow chart can help you figure out the path a user can take through your presentation. Each box in the flow chart shown here represents something about Ellington for the user to read, see, or hear. The arrows on the flow chart show a branching path the user can follow.

When boxes branch in more than one direction, it means that the user can choose which item to see or hear first.

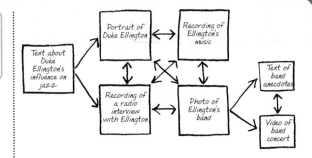

4.3 Guiding Your User

Your user will need directions to follow the path of your multimedia presentation.

Most multimedia authoring programs allow you to create screens that include text or audio directions that guide the user from one part of your presentation to the next. In the example here, the user can choose between several paths, and directions on the screen explain how to make the choice.

If you need help creating your multimedia presentation, ask your school's technology adviser or your classmates, or consult your software manual.

WRITING TIP You usually need permission from the person or organization that owns the copyright on materials if you want to copy them. You do not need permission, however, if you are not making money from your presentation, if you use it only for educational purposes, and if you use only a small percentage of the original material.

Analyzing Text Features

Reading a Magazine Article

A **magazine article** is designed to catch and hold your interest. Learning how to recognize the items on a magazine page will help you read even the most complicated articles. Look at the sample magazine article as you read each strategy below.

Strategies for Reading

A Read the **title** and other **headings** to get an idea of what the article is about. Frequently, the title presents the article's main topic. The smaller headings introduce subtopics related to the main topic.

B Note text that is set off in some way, such as an **indented paragraph** or a passage in a **different typeface.** This text often summarizes the article.

C Study **visuals**—photos, pictures, maps. Visuals help bring the topic to life and enrich the text.

D Look for **special features,** such as charts, tables, or graphs, that provide more detailed information on the topic or on a subtopic.

E Pay attention to terms in **italics** or **boldface.** Look for definitions or explanations before or after these terms.

PRACTICE AND APPLY

Use the sample magazine page and the tips above to help you answer the following questions.

1. What is the article's main topic? What two subtopics does the article cover?

2. Which paragraph summarizes the article?

3. What is the subject of the chart?

4. How many boldfaced terms are explained in the chart?

5. What is steer wrestling?

A MODERN COWBOYS

B *If you think cowboys rode off into the sunset in the 1890s, think again. American cowboys are alive and well and living in the western United States and Canada. Although life has changed greatly for cowboys—long cattle drives are a thing of the past, for instance—roping and riding still go with the territory.*

C

A **At Work** Many cowboys today work on cattle ranches. Like the cowboys of the Wild West, modern cowhands work long hours in all kinds of weather. However, unlike old-time cowboys, today's ranchers use machines for many of their jobs. Cowboys still use their horses to rope calves and do other work. But the livestock are often carried in trucks across the large, fenced-in ranches. And when a cow wanders far from the herd, cowboys sometimes use a helicopter to round up the stray.

A **At Play** Rodeos are rooted in the Old West. After working on a cattle drive, cowboys competed and showed off their skills in roping and riding. Today, the rodeo recalls the spirit of these cowboys. The events at a rodeo are divided into two main groups: rough stock events and timed events. Rough stock events include riding bucking horses or bulls. Timed events include calf roping and steer wrestling.

D
TYPICAL RODEO EVENTS

Bareback Bronc Riding For 8 seconds, the rider spurs the horse as it bucks.

Saddle Bronc Riding The rider uses a saddle and must stay on the horse for 8 or 10 seconds.

Bull Riding The rider tries to stay on the bull for 8 seconds (no spurring needed).

Calf Roping The rider chases the calf on horseback, ropes it, and then gets off the horse to tie up the calf.

Steer Wrestling The cowboy grabs the steer's horns and wrestles the animal to the ground.

E **Team Roping** A team of two rope and tie a steer.

Reading a Textbook

The first page of a **textbook** lesson introduces you to a particular topic. The page also provides important information that will guide you through the rest of the lesson. Look at the sample textbook page as you read each strategy below.

Strategies for Reading

A Preview the **title** and other **headings** to find out the lesson's main topic and related subtopics.

B Look for a list of **vocabulary terms.** These words will be identified and defined throughout the lesson.

C Read the **main idea** or **objectives.** These items summarize the lesson and establish a purpose for your reading.

D Notice text on the page that is set off in some way. For example, text placed in a tinted, or colored, box may be from a **primary source** that gives firsthand knowledge about the topic.

E Examine **visuals,** such as photos and drawings, and their **captions.** Visuals can help the topic come alive.

F Find words set in special type, such as **italics** or **boldface.** Also look for material in **parentheses.** Boldface is often used to identify the vocabulary terms in the lesson. Material in parentheses may refer you to another page or visual in the lesson.

PRACTICE AND APPLY

Use the sample textbook page and the tips above to help you answer the following questions.

1. On what part of the country does the lesson focus?
2. What vocabulary terms are defined in the lesson?
3. What is the main idea that is developed in the lesson?
4. Review the excerpt from the primary source. Who wrote the excerpt?
5. Who was Nat Love?
6. Which vocabulary term refers to the area from the Missouri River to the Rocky Mountains?

A

① A Time of Growth

B TERMS & NAMES
frontier
Great Plains
Homestead Act
Dawes Act
Gilded Age
urbanization
new immigrants

C

MAIN IDEA	WHY IT MATTERS NOW
Miners, ranchers, and cowhands settled in the West seeking economic opportunities.	The mining and cattle industries that developed then still contribute to American economic growth.

A ### ONE AMERICAN'S STORY

Nat Love was born a slave in Tennessee in 1854. After the Civil War, he was one of thousands of African Americans who left the South and went west. In 1869, Love headed for Dodge City, Kansas. He was 15 and now free.

Love's horse-taming skills landed him a job as a cowhand. For 20 years, he took part in the cattle drives that brought Texas cattle to Kansas stockyards. He became well known for his expert horsemanship. In his autobiography, Love offered a lively but exaggerated account of his life. He told how he braved hailstorms, wild animals, and human attackers.

A VOICE FROM THE PAST

D
I carry the marks of fourteen bullet wounds on different parts of my body, most any one of which would be sufficient to kill an ordinary man. . . . Horses were shot from under me, men killed around me, but always I escaped with a trifling wound at the worst.

Nat Love, *The Life and Adventures of Nat Love*

Nat Love was an African-American cowhand who became a rodeo star.

E

As you will read in this section, few cowhands led lives as exciting as that described by Nat Love, but they all helped to open a new chapter in the history of the American West.

A ## Westward Expansion

F In the decades following the Civil War, more Americans began to settle on the **frontier.** The frontier was the sparsely populated area on the western side of the nation. Aside from Native Americans, few people lived there. It included the **Great Plains,** the area from the Missouri River to the Rocky Mountains.

American settlers migrated westward for several reasons. The discovery of gold in California drew numerous fortune seekers to the West. A growing demand for beef in the nation's cities prompted ranchers to seek

The United States, 1860–1920 **539**

Understanding Visuals

Reading Graphs

Graphs are used to present facts and statistics. Bar graphs and circle graphs are useful for making comparisons. Use the following strategies along with the examples below to help you read graphs.

Strategies for Reading

A Read the **title** to help you understand what the graph is about.

B In bar graphs, look at the data on the horizontal line and the data on the vertical line to find a value or estimate.

C In circle graphs, read the **headings** to learn what each percent number stands for.

D Compare the information from circle graphs and bar graphs to see how they relate. Sometimes they will give the same information. Other times one will give additional information.

E Check the credit to see if the information is up to date and from a respected source.

The following graphs show the results of a survey conducted by *Zillions*, the consumer magazine for children. More than half the participants ages 8 to 14 said they do not get an allowance although some do get spending money. What other observations can you make?

Percent of Kids Who Get: **A**

Spending money only 26%

43% Allowance **D**

C No allowance or spending money 31%

Allowance: Who gets one and how much? **A**

Weekly allowance in dollars

B

$3.74 — Ages 8 & 9
$5.19 — Ages 10 & 11
$6.66 — Ages 12 & 13
$9.45 — Age 14

E Source: *Zillions* Jan/Feb, 1999

PRACTICE AND APPLY

Answer the following questions using the graphs and tips.

1. Which graph shows data on the amount of allowance kids get?
2. How many kids do not get an allowance?
3. According to the bar graph, how much more allowance does a 13 year-old get than a 10 year-old?

Reading a Transit Map

It's important to know how to read a **map** so you can find your way around without becoming lost. Look at the example below as you read each strategy in this list.

Strategies for Reading

A Scan the **title** to know the main idea of the map.

B Interpret the **key,** or **legend,** to find out what the symbols on the map stand for.

C Study **geographic labels** to understand specific places on the map.

D Notice the **scale and pointer,** or **compass rose,** to determine distance and direction.

A **STA** Elevated / Subway Train Map
Red, Blue, Purple and Yellow Lines

B Train System Legend

○ Station

✖ Closed nights/weekends/holidays

◐ Closed Sundays/holidays

♿ Wheelchair accessible when agent is on duty

🅿 Daily paid parking is available

RED LINE (Stone City)

♿🅿 Lincoln
Jackson
McKinley
Roosevelt
Monroe
Kennedy
Washington 🅿
South Blvd.
Main

SPRINGFIELD (Downtown)

40th
35th
30th ♿
27th
25th 🅿

BLUE LINE (Queen City)

♿
🅿
Patrick
Tulsa
Halley's Square
♿
Green Park
Niles
Kingston

YELLOW LINE (Queen City)
✖
◐
Anthony St.
Henry St.
Fairbanks
Columbus St.
🅿
Grant St.

PURPLE LINE (University Park)

PRACTICE AND APPLY

Use the map to answer the following questions.

1. What is the purpose of this map?
2. What do the symbols mean together?
3. Which three stations are between 40th and 25th on the Purple Line?
4. Are any of these three stations accessible to commuters who use wheelchairs? If so, which station(s)?
5. Does the Red Line run north and south or east and west? Name another train line that runs in the same direction as the Red Line.

Reading a Diagram

Diagrams combine pictures with a few words to provide a lot of information. Look at the example on the opposite page as you read each of the following strategies.

Strategies for Reading

A Look at the the **title** to get a quick idea of what the diagram is about.

B Study the **images** closely to understand each part of the diagram.

C Look at the **captions** and the **labels** for more information.

PRACTICE AND APPLY

The diagram on the following page shows balanced and unbalanced forces. Study the diagram, then answer the following questions using the strategies above.

1. What is this diagram about?

2. What do the black arrows represent in these pictures?

3. What are the two forces in the picture showing unbalanced forces?

4. In the second picture, why does the car rise up from the ground?

5. Which two pictures show the same set of forces?

Ⓐ *Balanced and Unbalanced Forces*

Newton's First Law of Motion: As long as the forces on an object balance each other, the object's motion will not change.

The force of gravity pulling down on the car is balanced by the force of the ground pushing up on the car. The car remains at rest.

Ⓑ **Balanced Forces**

Ⓒ **Newton's Second Law of Motion: When an unbalanced force acts on an object, the object will accelerate in the direction that the unbalanced force points.**

The force of the crane pulling up on the car is greater than the force of gravity pulling down on it. The car begins to rise.

Unbalanced Forces

Once again, the force of gravity pulling down on the car is balanced by the force of the ground pushing up on it. The car is again at rest.

Balanced Forces

Recognizing Text Structures

Main Idea and Supporting Details

The **main idea** in a paragraph is its most important point. **Details** in the paragraph support the main idea. Identifying the main idea will help you focus on the main message the writer wants to communicate. Use the following strategies to help you identify a paragraph's main idea and supporting details.

Strategies for Reading

- Look for the main idea, which is often the first sentence in a paragraph.
- Use the main idea to help you summarize the point of the paragraph.
- Identify specific details, including facts and examples, that support the main idea.

Searching for E.T.

Main idea — Scientists on Project Phoenix search for extraterrestrials—beings from another planet. The scientists use radio telescopes to track radio signals from outer space. The telescopes are pointed at nearby, sun-like stars that are thought to be orbited by planets. So far, no clear signals have been received. However, scientists hope that the telescopes will finally help answer the question: Is anyone out there? **— Details**

PRACTICE AND APPLY

Read the following paragraph. Then copy the diagram below, and add the paragraph's main idea as well as three supporting details.

Nothing can escape the gravity of a black hole. A meteor passing near the hole is sucked in and crushed. Gases from a dying star are drawn toward the hole. Even light cannot resist its pull.

Problem and Solution

Does the proposed **solution** to a **problem** make sense? In order to decide, you need to look at each part of the text. Use the following strategies to read the text below.

Strategies for Reading

- Look at the beginning or middle of a paragraph to find the problem.
- Find out why the problem is important.
- Look for the proposed solution.
- Identify the details that support the proposed solution.
- Think about whether the solution is a good one.

A Garden for Market Street?

Statement of problem

Anyone who has walked along Market Street has seen the big empty lot next to the public library. This lot has been empty for two years now, and it is ugly and dangerous. Paper trash and broken bottles cover the ground, and nothing grows there but tough nasty weeds. And who knows what kind of rodents might be crawling around in the dirt?

Explanation of problem

According to the mayor, the owner has long since deserted the property, and no one has any plans to build on it. This is valuable land, and it's right in the middle of town! The citizens should do something with it.

A community nature garden would be a great thing for the city. Teachers and students could share what they've learned about local plant wildlife. Other residents could volunteer to help plant the trees, grasses, and wildflowers. When finished, the garden would be both educational and lovely—a great improvement over the weedy lot!

PRACTICE AND APPLY

Read the text above and answer the questions.

1. What is the proposed solution to the problem?
2. Give at least one detail that supports the solution.
3. Do you agree with the solution? Explain why or why not.

Sequence

It's important to understand the **sequence**, or order of events, in what you read. It helps you know what happens and why. Read the tips below to make sure a sequence is clear to you. Then look at the example on the opposite page.

Strategies for Reading

- Read through the passage and think about what its **main steps**, or **stages**, are.
- Look for **words and phrases that signal time**: *today, Saturday, later,* or *9:30.*
- Look for **words and phrases that signal order**: *first, next, then, before, at last, after,* or *finally.*

The article on the next page describes how a sixteen-year-old spent her day as a movie extra. Use the information from the passage and the tips above to answer the questions.

PRACTICE AND APPLY

1. List some words and phrases that signal time.
2. List some phrases in the article that signal order.
3. Use the information from the article to copy and complete this timeline. Make sure to include signal words in your sentences.

6:45 A.M.
Report to set.

7:45 A.M.

9:30 A.M.

9:50 A.M.–1:30 P.M.

1:30 P.M.

I Was a Movie Extra

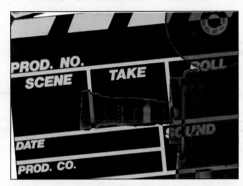

On a recent Saturday, Nicole M., 16, . . . spent the day as a movie extra. . . . She found out that life as an extra isn't exactly glamorous, but she did have fun. Here is her story . . .

I was one of nearly 600 extras who appeared in a fire-drill scene for the movie "Newport South.". . .

At 6:45 A.M. the day of filming, I reported to the set, an abandoned school building. . . . My day started off with registration and wardrobe check. . . . I was assigned to one of four sections: A, B, C or D (I landed in D, along with some of my friends). . . . After that, I was told to find my section and to sit there. My friends and I waited and waited. At 7:45 A.M., caterers arrived with doughnuts, lemonade, coffee, and hot chocolate. After munching down chocolate doughnuts, we waited again—till 9:30 A.M.

Finally, it was time for our big scene. A guy wearing a headset explained to us what we had to do, then directed us to one of four stairwells. We were smooshed: About 75 people stood shoulder to shoulder. It was 20 minutes before we got the signal to move, and we poured out of the school and headed for the football field. . . .

Before the scene was shot, it was stressed upon us not to look at the cameras. But it was stressed so much it was hard NOT to look. . . .

So, after that first take, we shot the scene two more times, then we got a snack. We had five minutes to use the washroom, eat, and do anything else we needed to. Then it was back to our stairwells. . . .

By 1:30 P.M., the shooting was done, and we all gathered in the gym. . . . I reported to wardrobe and returned my jacket. After standing in line to get paid, my friends and I left—feeling tired, cold, wet, hungry and a bit grouchy.

from *The Chicago Tribune*

Cause and Effect

A **cause** is an event that brings about another event. An **effect** is something that happens as a result of the first event. Identifying causes and effects helps you understand how the events are related. The strategies below can help you find causes and effects in any reading.

Strategies for Reading

- Look for an action or event that answers the question "What happened?" This is the **effect**.
- Look for an action or event that answers the question "Why did it happen?" This is the **cause**.
- Identify **words that signal causes and effects**, such as *because, as a result, therefore, cause,* and *since.*

PRACTICE AND APPLY

Use the cause-and-effect passage on the next page to help you answer the following questions. Notice that the first cause and effect in the passage are highlighted.

1. What phrase explains what happened because the *Sultana* was carrying so many people. Is this a cause or an effect?
2. List some words in the passage that signal causes and effects. The first one is highlighted for you.
3. Use the causes and effects in the last two paragraphs to copy and complete the following diagram.

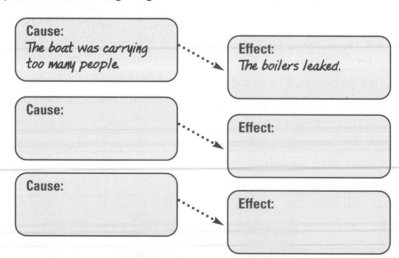

Cause:
The boat was carrying too many people. → Effect:
The boilers leaked.

Cause: → Effect:

Cause: → Effect:

The Sinking of the *Sultana*

On April 25, 1865, about two weeks after the end of the Civil War, a steamboat called the *Sultana* was traveling up the Mississippi River. The ship had set out from Vicksburg, Mississippi, and was going to Cairo, Illinois. Many passengers, including hundreds of ex-prisoners of war, had boarded the ship. **Since** **no one had taken a roll call,** **the exact number is not known.** However, historians guess that there were about 2,300 people on board. That number is about six times as many people as the ship was built to carry. Because the *Sultana* was carrying so many people, it was going slowly.

Signal Word
Cause
Effect

The load also caused the ship's steam boilers to leak several times over the next two days. The boilers were repaired, but the strain was too much. Early on April 27, the boilers exploded after the ship had sailed just a few miles north of Memphis, Tennessee. As a result of the explosion, hundreds of passengers were killed instantly.

Many others drowned or died in the fire that started when hot coals burst from the boiler. Some of the victims who died in the fire were trapped below deck. Others, especially those who had been prisoners of war, were too weak to try to swim in the icy river.

In all, about 1,700 people died. That number is about 200 more than died aboard the *Titanic* 47 years later. The sinking of the *Sultana* was—and still is—the greatest seafaring disaster in American history. However, the newspapers at that time were still covering the death of Abraham Lincoln and his funeral train. Therefore, the tragedy was barely reported.

Comparison and Contrast

Comparing two things means showing how they are the same. **Contrasting** two things means showing how they are different. Comparisons and contrasts are often used in science and history books to make a subject clearer. Use these tips to help you understand comparison and contrast in reading assignments, such as the article on the opposite page.

Strategies for Reading

- Look for **direct statements** of comparison and contrast: "These things are similar because. . . " or "One major difference is. . . ."
- Pay attention to **words and phrases that signal comparisons,** such as *also, both, is the same as,* and *in the same way.*
- Notice **words and phrases that signal contrasts.** Some of these are *however, still, but,* and *on the other hand.*

PRACTICE AND APPLY

Read the essay on the opposite page. Then use the information from the essay and the tips above to answer the questions.

1. List some words and phrases that signal comparisons. The first one is highlighted for you.

2. List some words and phrases that signal contrasts. The first one is highlighted for you.

3. A Venn diagram shows how two subjects are similar and how they are different. Copy this diagram, which uses information from the essay to compare and contrast the United States and Bosnia. Add at least two similarities and two differences.

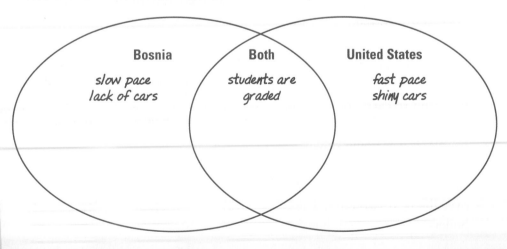

Bosnia

*slow pace
lack of cars*

Both

*students are
graded*

United States

*fast pace
shiny cars*

My Two Homes: Bosnia and the U.S.

by Elvisa Pandzic

My family and I came to America because of the war in Bosnia. . . . I had to catch my breath when I first set eyes on Chicago. It was spectacular—like a dream, with its tall buildings and shiny cars. Everything was moving so fast! **Still,** I often thought of Cazin, where I was born.

Contrast

I missed the slow pace of small-town life. That and the lack of cars. Most people had no need to travel to a place they couldn't walk to. I especially missed the mountains and hills. Nothing can replace those big beautiful meadows and the forests that took your breath away with their wonderful green smells. . . .

Another big difference is the school system. When I started school in Chicago I was very confused—all the rules were different. In Bosnia, schools are strict and students give their teachers a lot of respect. We used to stand up when a teacher entered the classroom and when we had to answer a question. In American schools, students may talk without even being called on. This is not entirely bad, in my opinion. I like how students can express themselves freely. Another thing that has taken some time getting used to is the grading system. In Bosnia, all the grades are given in numbers, not letters. In Bosnia a grade of A is equal to 5, B to 4, C to 3, D to 2, and F to 1. At least the dress code in my new school is almost the same as in Bosnia. In both places you can wear blue jeans to school. . . .

Comparison

I have been living in Chicago for about two years and I am adjusting well, but I still miss Bosnia, my first home. I look forward to a time of peace when I can return. I know I will never return to my "old" life, but there is one thing I do know. Wherever I end up, I will celebrate the best of both worlds.

Argument

An **argument** is an opinion backed up with reasons and facts. Understanding an argument will help you make informed decisions about an issue. Use the following strategies to help you understand an argument.

Strategies for Reading

- Look for **words that signal an opinion**: *I think; I feel; they claim, argue,* or *disagree.*
- Look for **reasons**, **facts**, or **expert opinions** that support the argument.
- Ask yourself if the argument and reasons make sense.

PRACTICE AND APPLY

Read the argument on the next page, and then answer the questions below.

1. List some words that signal an opinion.

2. List the two opinions in this argument.

3. Give an example of a statement that is not supported by reason.

4. The writer gives reasons for and against television. Copy and complete the chart below using the argument. One answer has been given for you.

Pros	Cons
1. *Television keeps people informed about current issues and events.*	1.
2.	2.
3.	3.
4.	4.
5.	5.

Television: Good or Bad?

Many people believe that life before television was happier than life today. In those days, people read books and newspapers for information. Families spent more time together. They talked, ate meals together, and shared chores. Many children used their imaginations to write and tell stories, and they participated in outdoor activities instead of spending hours in front of the television. People were not violent because they did not watch violent programs.

Others disagree. They claim that television has many advantages as an educational tool. It keeps people informed about important current events and issues. Television programs can help children learn valuable social skills such as cooperation and kindness. It can teach children how people live, work, and deal with misfortune. Some public television programs also promote activities such as visits to museums, libraries, bookstores, and zoos.

Both arguments are endless. The only thing we can say for sure is that we need more studies to show whether television is good or bad, or a little bit of both.

Reading in the Content Areas

Social Studies

Your **social studies** textbook uses words and graphics to help you learn about people and places today and throughout history. As you read the tips below, look at the sample page on the right.

Strategies for Reading

A First, look at any **headlines** or **subheads** on the page. These give you an idea of what each section covers.

B Carefully read the text and think about **ways the information is organized.** Social studies books are full of sequence, comparison and contrast, and cause and effect.

C Make sure you know the meaning of any boldfaced or underlined **vocabulary terms.** These terms often appear on tests.

D Next, look closely at any **sidebar articles** or **graphics.** Think about how they relate to the main text.

E Read any **study tips** in the margins or at the bottom of the page. These let you check your understanding as you read.

PRACTICE AND APPLY

The textbook page at right describes some of the effects of the Civil War on Northerners and Southerners. Use information from that page and from the tips above to answer the questions.

1. What two subjects does the page cover?

2. Name the two vocabulary terms and define them.

3. What was a Confederate soldier's monthly pay in 1864?

4. What does it mean to *subjugate* someone?

5. Copy and complete the diagram.

> Cause: *Many farmers were in the army.*
>
> Cause: _____
>
> Cause: _____

> Cause: *Food shortages in South*

A Economic Effects of the War

Many people suffered economic hardship during the war. The suffering was severe in the South, where most battles were fought, but the North also experienced difficulties.

B Food shortages were very common in the South, partly because so many farmers were fighting in the Confederate army. Moreover, food sometimes could not get to market because trains were now being used to carry war materials. The Confederate army also seized food and other supplies for its own needs.

Another problem, especially in the South, was inflation—an increase in price and decrease in the value of money. The average family food bill in the South increased from $6.65 a month in 1861 to $68 by mid–1863. Over the course of the war, prices rose 9,000 percent in the South.

Inflation in the North was much lower, but prices still rose faster than wages, making life harder for working people. Some people took advantage of wartime demand and sold goods for high prices.

Overall, though, war production boosted Northern industry and fueled the economy. In the short term, this gave the North an economic advantage over the South. In the long term, industry would begin to replace farming as the basis of the national economy.

During the war, the federal government passed two important economic measures. In 1861, it established the first **income tax**—a tax on earnings. The following year, the government issued a new paper currency, known as **greenbacks** because of their color. The new currency helped the Northern economy by ensuring that people had money to spend. It also helped the Union to pay for the war.

Some Southerners in the border states took advantage of the stronger Union economy by selling cotton to Northern traders, in violation of Confederate law. "Yankee gold," wrote one Confederate officer, "is fast accomplishing what Yankee arms could never achieve—the subjugation of our people."

Resistance by Slaves

Another factor that affected the South was the growing resistance from slaves. To hurt the Southern economy, slaves slowed their pace of work or stopped working altogether. Some carried out sabotage, destroying crops and farm equipment to hurt the plantation economy.

 Reading **History**

B. Analyzing Causes Why were economic problems particularly bad in the South?

 E

Vocabulary
subjugate: to bring under control or to conquer

 E

D
daily *life*

INFLATION IN THE SOUTH

During the Civil War, inflation caused hardship in the North and the South. But inflation was especially severe in the Confederacy, where prices could become outrageously high.

The food prices shown below are from 1864. Consider how many days it took a Confederate soldier to earn enough money to buy each of these foods.

$6.00
Dozen Eggs

$6.25
Pound of Butter

$10.00
Quart of Milk

$12.00
Pound of Coffee

$18.00

Confederate Soldier's Monthly Pay

Science

Reading in **science** will be easier when you understand how the explanations, drawings, and special terms work together. Use the strategies below to help you better understand your science textbook. Look at the examples on the opposite page as you read each strategy in this list.

Strategies for Reading

A Preview the **title** and **headings** on the page to see what science concepts will be covered.

B Look for **boldfaced** and **italicized** words that appear in the text. Look for **definitions** of those words.

C Many science textbooks discuss **scientific concepts** in terms of **everyday events or experiences.** Look for these places and consider how they improve your understanding.

D Look for references to numbered **figures** in the text.

E Then look in the margin for these figures, which are **diagrams** or **pictures** with **captions.** See how they illustrate and explain the text.

PRACTICE AND APPLY

Use the sample science page to help you answer the following questions.

1. What science concept will be covered in this lesson? Where on the page did you find this information?
2. Define the term *light year.*
3. How old is the light from Polaris when it reaches the Earth?
4. What is the everyday experience used to help explain parallax?
5. Read the discussion of parallax in the text and look at Figure 6-9. What appears to happen to the close star's position between July and January? What actually happens to the star's position during that time?

Figure 6-8 The stars in the Big Dipper appear to be the same brightness. Does this mean that all of these stars are the same distance from Earth?

Figure 6-9 In January, the close star appears to be at point *A*. Six months later, when Earth is at the opposite end of its orbit, the close star seems to be at point *B*. This apparent shift is called parallax.

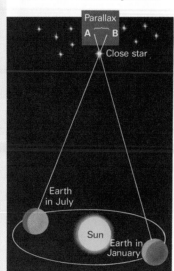

A Star Distances

All of the stars that you see at night are part of the Milky Way galaxy. The Milky Way contains about 200 billion stars. On a clear night, you might think that you can see millions of stars. Actually, you see only about 3000 stars with your unaided eye. To understand why so few stars are visible, think about how you see a flashlight from a distance. At 1 meter, the flashlight is bright. At 50 meters, it appears dimmer. If the flashlight were far enough away, it would be too faint to see. For the same reason, you cannot see most of the stars in the Milky Way because they are too far away.

Astronomers measure distances to stars using the speed of light. Light travels at 300 000 kilometers per second. At this rate, sunlight takes 8 minutes to reach your eyes. Thus, the distance to the sun is 8 light-minutes. Distances to stars are measured in light-years. A **light-year** is the distance that light travels in one year, about 9.5 trillion kilometers. The nearest star, Proxima Centauri, is 4.2 light-years from Earth. The distance to Polaris is 680 light-years. When you look into space, you look into the past. The light you see from Polaris left the star long before Columbus set sail for America.

Figure 6-9 shows how to measure distance to a star by measuring its parallax. **Parallax** is the apparent shift in an object's position that is caused by the motion of the observer. You can see the parallax of your finger if you look at it only with your left eye and then only with your right eye. Your finger seems to move compared to the background. Try observing the parallax again with your finger closer to your eyes. How does the parallax change? You can observe the parallax of nearby stars with a telescope. The closer a star is, the greater is its parallax.

Mathematics

Reading a **mathematics** textbook requires different skills than reading history, literature, or science. The tips below can help you learn these skills. As you read the tips, look at the sample mathematics page on the right.

Strategies for Reading

A First, look at the lesson **title** and any **subheads** on the page, so you know what topics will be covered.

B Find the **goals** or **objectives** for the lesson. These will tell you the most important points to know.

C Read **explanations** carefully. Sometimes the same concept is explained in more than one way to make sure you understand it.

D Look for **special features** such as study or vocabulary tips. These provide more help or information.

E Study any **worked-out solutions** to sample problems. These are the key to understanding how to do the homework assignment.

PRACTICE AND APPLY

Use the sample mathematics page and the tips above to help you answer the following questions.

1. How is a multi-step equation solved?

2. What are the vocabulary words that will be studied in this lesson?

3. Where will the question "How hot is Earth's crust?" be answered?

4. How many steps are required to solve and check a linear equation?

5. In Example 1, how do you isolate the variable?

A
3.3 Solving Multi-Step Equations

B
Goal
Use two or more steps to solve a linear equation.

Key Words
• like terms
• distributive property

How hot is Earth's crust?

Temperatures within Earth's crust can get hot enough to melt rocks. In Example 2 you will see how a multi-step equation can be used to predict the depth at which the temperature of Earth's crust is 114°C.

C
Solving a linear equation may require more than one step. Use the steps you already know for transforming an equation. Simplify one or both sides of the equation first, if needed. Then use inverse operations to isolate the variable.

D

Student Help

▶ VOCABULARY TIP
The prefix *multi-* means "more than one". A multi-step equation is solved by transforming the equation more than one time.

A
EXAMPLE 1 **Solve a Linear Equation**

Solve $3x + 7 = -8$.

Solution

To isolate the variable, undo the addition and then the multiplication.

E
$3x + 7 = -8$	Write original equation.
$3x + 7 - 7 = -8 - 7$	Subtract 7 from each side to undo the addition. (Subtraction Property of Equality)
$3x = -15$	Simplify both sides.
$\dfrac{3x}{3} = \dfrac{-15}{3}$	Divide each side by 3 to undo the multiplication. (Division Property of Equality)
$x = -5$	Simplify.

CHECK ✓ Check by substituting -5 for x in the *original* equation.

$3x + 7 = -8$	Write original equation.
$3(-5) + 7 \stackrel{?}{=} -8$	Substitute -5 for x.
$-15 + 7 \stackrel{?}{=} -8$	Multiply.
$-8 = -8$ ✓	Solution is correct.

Checkpoint ✓ **Solve a Linear Equation**

Solve the equation. Check your solution in the original equation.

1. $6x - 15 = 9$ **2.** $7x - 4 = -11$ **3.** $2y + 5 = 1$

Reading Beyond the Classroom

Reading an Application

Reading and understanding an **application** will help you fill it out correctly and avoid mistakes. Use the following strategies to help you understand any application. Look at the example on the next page as you read each strategy.

Strategies for Reading

A Begin at the top. Scan the application to see what the **different sections** are.

B Look for **special instructions** for how to fill out the application.

C Notice any **request for materials** that must be attached to the application.

D Watch for **sections you don't have to fill in** or **questions you don't have to answer**.

E Look for **difficult** or **confusing words or abbreviations**. Look them up in a dictionary or ask someone what they mean.

PRACTICE AND APPLY

Imagine that you want to participate in the student science fair. Read the application on the next page. Then answer the following questions.

1. On the application, how many different sections are there?

2. What grade levels must students be in to participate in the science fair?

3. What are all of the materials that must be submitted along with the application?

4. In the last section, which category number would you write if you had a botany project?

5. What name should be written in the Team Member Information section?

CHICAGO PUBLIC SCHOOLS STUDENT SCIENCE FAIR, INC.

2000 STUDENT SCIENCE FAIR
Official Entry Form for Region and City Science Fairs

DO NOT WRITE IN THIS SPACE
ENTRY

NUMBER
DO NOT WRITE IN THIS SPACE

Fill in the information below. The information must be typewritten or legibly printed (see handbook). Note: information requested for a team member refers to the second pupil on an elementary school project. Students must be in the 7th grade, 8th grade, or high school to participate in the city fair. Age requirements for participation in the state fair are determined by the rules of the Illinois Junior Academy of Science. **A COPY OF THE ABSTRACT MUST BE ATTACHED TO THIS ENTRY FORM.**

ENTRANT INFORMATION

Entrant Name:
Last   First

Age: **Sex:**   **Phone:**   **Birth Date:**   1 9
Month   Day   Year

Address:
Apartment Number   Zip Code

Student Social Security Number: **Name of Parent or Guardian:** _____

TEAM MEMBER INFORMATION

Name:
Last   First

Age: **Sex:**   **Phone:**   **Birth Date:**   1 9
Month   Day   Year

Address:
Apartment Number   Zip Code

Student Social Security Number: **Name of Parent or Guardian:** _____

SCHOOL INFORMATION

Grade   Unit Number   Region   School   M.R.#

PROJECT INFORMATION

Electricity Required? Y N   **Check Type of Endorsement(s) Attached*:** Human   Vertebrate Animal

Organism(s) Used in Experiment: _____   Microbiology   Recombinant DNA   6th Grade Recognition Luncheon Only

* A COPY OF THE ENDORSEMENT(S) AND ABSTRACT MUST BE ATTACHED TO THIS ENTRY FORM.

INSERT THE CORRESPONDING SET OF NUMERALS AND CATEGORY NAME IN THE BOXES PROVIDED.

01 Aero-Space Science	05 Chemistry	09 Engineering Science	13 Mathematics
02 Behavioral Science	06 Computer Science	10 Environmental Science	14 Microbiology
03 Biochemistry	07 Earth Science	11 Health Science	15 Physics
04 Botany	08 Electronics	12 Material Science	16 Zoology

Category Name

Category Number:

Exhibit Title:
Cannot Exceed 45 Spaces

Teacher/ Sponsor Name:
Last   First

☐ **Check here if an interpreter is needed. Indicate which language:** _____

CERTIFICATION:

I hereby certify that this project has been personally inspected and that it fulfills all requirements as described in the Handbooks, including endorsements if applicable.

I hereby certify that I have read all of the above information and that it is accurate.

_____   _____
Region Science Fair Coordinator Signature   Date

_____   _____
Entrant's Signature   Date

83

Reading a Web Page

If you need information for a report, project, or hobby, the World Wide Web can probably help you. The tips below will help you understand the **Web pages** you read. As you look at the tips, notice where they match up to the sample Web pages on the right.

Strategies for Reading

A Notice the page's **Web address**, or URL. You may want to write it down in case you need to access the same page at another time.

B The **title** of the page is usually at or near the top. It will give you an idea of what the page covers.

C Look for **menu bars** along the top, bottom, or side of the page. These guide you to other parts of the site that may be useful.

D Most pages have **links** to related pages. Links are often underlined words.

E Many sites have **interactive areas**, such as a guest book, where you can tell the site's creators what you think of their work.

PRACTICE AND APPLY

Read the two Web pages on the right-hand page. The top one is a search engine that shows responses to a student's question. The bottom one is a site linked to one of those responses. Then use the information from the sites and the tips above to answer the questions.

1. List the Web address of both pages.

2. On the "LookQuick" page, what three terms did the student ask the search engine to find?

3. On the "Gold Rush" site, which link you would click on if you wanted to learn about people who immigrated to California to take part in the gold rush?

4. Which link you would click on to tell the creators of "Gold Rush!" your opinion of their site?

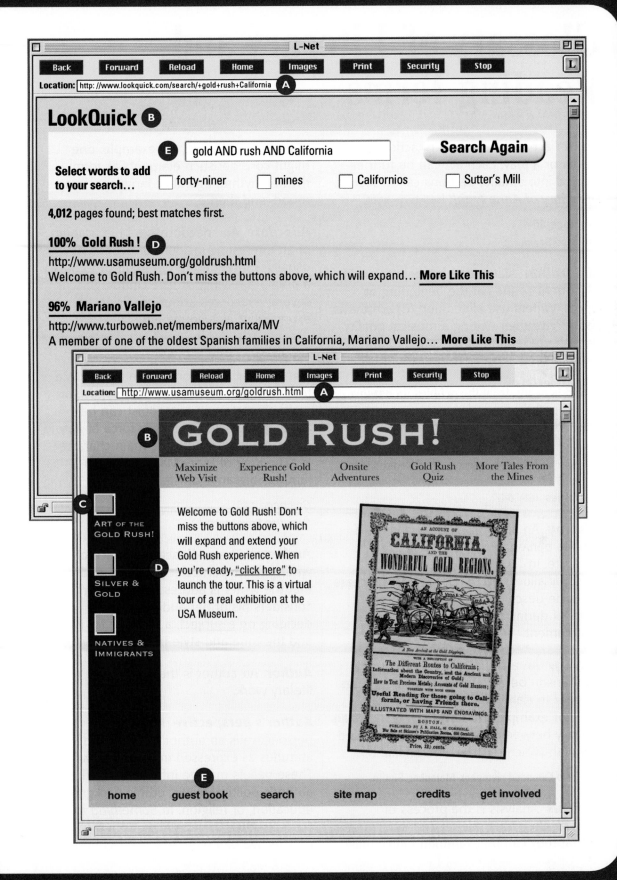

Glossary of Literary and Reading Terms

Act An act is a major unit of action in a drama or a play. Each act can be further divided into smaller sections called scenes. *The Diary of Anne Frank* has two acts.

See page 260.
See also **Scene**.

Alliteration Alliteration is a repetition of consonant sounds at the beginning of words. Writers use alliteration for emphasis and to give their writing a musical quality. Note the repetition of the *s* and *f* sounds in the following lines:

> And beneath, from the pebbles, in passing
>   a spark
> Struck out by a steed flying fearless
>   and fleet . . .
>
> —Henry Wadsworth Longfellow, "Paul Revere's Ride"

See pages 189, 647.

Allusion An allusion is a reference to a famous person, place, event, or work of literature. In "The Bet," writer Anton Chekhov alludes to Byron and Shakespeare when he describes the lawyer's reading material during the last two years of confinement.

Analogy An analogy is a point-by-point comparison between two dissimilar things in order to clarify the less familiar of the two. For example, an author might draw an analogy between an unfamiliar setting and one with which readers are familiar.

See also **Extended metaphor, Metaphor, Simile**.

Analysis Analysis is the process of breaking something down into its elements so that they can be examined individually.

In analyzing a poem, for example, one might consider such elements as form, rhyme, rhythm, figurative language, imagery, mood, and theme.

Anecdote An anecdote is a brief account of an interesting incident or event that usually is intended to entertain or to make a point. In "Flying," Reeve Lindbergh tells several anecdotes about her flying experiences as a young girl.

See pages 118, 208.

Antagonist In a story, an antagonist is a force working against the protagonist, or main character; an antagonist can be another character, society, a force of nature, or even a force within the main character. In "The King of Mazy May," the claim-jumpers are antagonists.

See page 148.
See also **Protagonist**.

Audience The audience of a piece of writing is the particular group of readers that the writer is addressing. A writer considers his or her audience when deciding on a subject, a purpose for writing, and the tone and style in which to write.

Author An author is the writer of a literary work.

Author's perspective An author's perspective is an author's beliefs and attitudes as expressed in his or her writing. These beliefs may be influenced by the author's political views, ethnic background, education, or religion. In *Something to Declare*, Julia Alvarez writes from the perspective of a woman who was born in the Dominican Republic and who emigrated as a young child to the United States.

Author's purpose An author's purpose is his or her reason for creating a particular work. The purpose can be to entertain, to explain or inform, to express an opinion, or to persuade. An author may have more than one purpose for writing, but usually one is most important.

See pages 118, 417, 622, 779, 851.

Autobiography An autobiography is a form of nonfiction in which a person tells the story of his or her life. *All But My Life* is an example of an autobiography. An autobiography is usually book length because it covers a long span of time. Forms of autobiographical writing include personal narratives, journals, memoirs, diaries, letters, and oral histories.

See pages 102, 522.
See also **Memoir, Oral history.**

Ballad A ballad is a poem that tells a story and is meant to be sung or recited. Folk ballads, written by unknown authors and handed down orally, usually depict ordinary people in the midst of tragic events or adventures of love and bravery. "John Henry" is an example of a folk ballad.

See page 647.

Bias In a piece of writing, an author's preference for one side of an issue over another is called bias.

Biographer *See* **Biography.**

Biography A biography is the story of a person's life that is written by someone else. The subjects of biographies are often famous people, as in *Lincoln: A Photobiography* and *Harriet Tubman: Conductor on the Underground Railroad.* A biographer is one who writes, composes, or produces a biography.

See pages 102, 756, 776.

Cast of characters In the script of a play, a cast of characters is a list of all the characters in the play, often in order of appearance. The list is usually found at the beginning of the script. There is a cast of characters at the beginning of *The Diary of Anne Frank.*

Cause and effect Two events are related as cause and effect when one event brings about, or causes, the other. The event that happens first is the cause; the one that follows is the effect. In "The Dinner Party," the placing of a bowl of milk on the verandah causes a desired effect—removing the snake from the dining room.

See pages 32, 262, 263.

Character A character is a person, an animal, or an imaginary creature in a literary work. In general, a work focuses on one or more main characters. Minor characters are less important characters who interact with the main characters and with one another while moving the plot along and providing background for the story. In "Raymond's Run," Squeaky is the main character. Gretchen, Rosie, and Mary Louise are minor characters.

See pages 19, 102, 148, 261, 329, 330, 652, 839.

Character development Characters that grow or change during a story are said to undergo character development. A character that changes significantly is called a dynamic character; one that changes only a little or not at all is said to be a static character. Main characters often develop the most. In "The Treasure of Lemon Brown," for example, Greg is a dynamic character who changes during the course of the story.

See pages 19, 330, 334, 441.

Characterization Characterization consists of all the techniques writers use to create characters. There are four basic methods of developing a character:

1. The writer may describe a character's physical appearance. In "Stop the Sun," the writer describes the main character: "Terry Erickson was a tall boy, 13, starting to fill out with muscle but still a little awkward."

2. A character's nature may be revealed through his or her own speech, thoughts, or actions. In "The Moustache," Mike feels a sense of dread when he approaches the nursing home where his grandmother lives, and he tells the reader how this makes him feel: ". . . I felt guilty about it. I'm loaded with guilt complexes."

3. A character's nature may be revealed by what other characters think or say about the character. The narrator's feelings about the orphan boy in "A Mother in Mannville" help the reader to understand the type of person the boy is: "His name was Jerry . . . I could picture him at four, with the same grave gray-blue eyes and the same— independence? No, the word that comes to me is 'integrity.'"

4. The writer can make direct comments about a character's nature. In "Checkouts," the author explains why the main character likes to shop for groceries: "She loved it in the way some people love to drive long country roads, because doing it she could think and relax and wander."

See pages 220, 331.

Chronological order Chronological order is the order in which events happen in time. In some stories, events are related in chronological order. In other stories, events are presented out of sequence.

See page 159.

Clarifying The reader's process of pausing occasionally while reading to quickly review what he or she understands is called clarifying. By clarifying as they read, good readers are able to draw conclusions about what is suggested but not stated directly.

See pages 443, 715, 829, 879.

Classic A classic is an enduring work of literature that continues to be read long after it was written. A classic deals with emotions, behaviors, and truths shared by human beings of every age, ethnicity, and culture. "The Bet" is considered a classic.

Climax In the plot of a story or a play, the climax, or turning point, is the point of maximum interest. The climax usually occurs toward the end of a story, after the reader has understood the conflict and become emotionally involved with the characters. At the climax, the conflict is resolved and the outcome of the plot becomes clear. The climax of "Raymond's Run," for example, occurs when Squeaky wins the race.

See pages 18, 260, 293, 439, 447.
See also **Plot.**

Comedy A comedy is a dramatic work that is light and often humorous in tone and usually ends happily with a peaceful resolution of the main conflict. *The Million-Pound Bank Note* is an example of a comedy.

Comic relief Comic relief is a humorous scene that is inserted into a serious work of fiction or drama to provide relief from the seriousness felt by the audience. A scene introduced for comic relief, because of the contrast it provides, can also add to the seriousness of the action. In *Still Me,* Christopher Reeve provides comic relief when he breaks the intense silence that greets his first public appearance with a funny anecdote about his English teacher.

Comparison The process of identifying similarities is called comparison. Writers use comparisons to make ideas and details clearer to the reader. In "Stop the Sun," for example, the father's terrified breathing is compared with the panting of "some kind of hurt animal."

See page 296.

See also **Metaphor, Simile.**

Conclusion *See* ***Drawing conclusions.***

Conflict Conflict is a struggle between opposing forces. In an external conflict, a character struggles against another person or some outside force. Gerda Weissmann Klein's struggle for survival in the excerpt from *All But My Life* is an example of an external conflict. An internal conflict, on the other hand, involves a struggle within a character. In "Flowers for Algernon," Charlie experiences inner conflict about his disability.

See pages 18, 260, 348, 439–441, 447, 488, 551, 753.

See also **Plot.**

Connecting A reader's process of relating the content of a literary work to his or her own knowledge and experience is called connecting. In "The Moustache," for example, readers might connect with Mike's feelings as he interacts with his grandmother.

See pages 4, 21, 48, 333, 334, 553, 623, 839.

Connotation A word's connotation is the idea and feeling associated with the word, as opposed to its dictionary definition. For example, the word *mother,* in addition to its basic meaning ("a female parent"), has connotations of love, warmth, and security.

See page 669.

See also **Denotation.**

Context clues Context clues are hints or suggestions that may surround unfamiliar words or phrases and clarify their meaning. A context clue can be a definition, a synonym, an example, a comparison or contrast, or any other expression that enables readers to infer the word's meaning.

See page 301.

Contrast The process of pointing out differences between things is called contrast. In "Flying," Reeve Lindbergh contrasts her flying experiences with those of her sister and brothers.

See page 296.

Couplet A couplet is a rhymed pair of lines in a poem.

> Listen, my children, and you shall hear
> Of the midnight ride of Paul Revere, . . .
>
> —Henry Wadsworth Longfellow,
> "Paul Revere's Ride"

Deductive order In nonfiction, the structure of a text may be organized using deductive order. A text that is organized deductively begins with a generalization and advances with facts and evidence to a conclusion.

See also **Inductive order, Structure.**

Denotation A word's denotation is its dictionary meaning.

See page 669.

See also **Connotation.**

Description Description is writing that helps a reader to picture scenes, events, and characters. To create descriptions, writers often use imagery—words and phrases that appeal to the reader's senses—and figurative language.

> We lived in the dark green hills of Pittsburgh where the smoke from J. L. Steel dusted our clothes gray and blanketed the sky, causing sunsets to streak bright pink and orange.
>
> —Jewell Parker Rhodes, "Block Party"

See pages 574, 622.

See also **Figurative language, Imagery, Sensory details.**

Dialect A dialect is a form of language that is spoken in a particular place or by a particular group of people. Dialects may feature unique pronunciation, vocabulary, and grammar. Some of the dialogue in *The Million-Pound Bank Note* features the dialect of working-class Londoners.

> Pardon me, Guv'ner, but aren't you the gentleman what owns the million-pound bank note?
>
> —Mark Twain, dramatized by Walter Hackett, *The Million-Pound Bank Note*

Dialogue The words that characters speak aloud are called dialogue. Writers use dialogue to bring characters to life and to give readers insights into the characters' qualities, personality traits, and reactions to other characters. In most literary works, dialogue is set off with quotation marks.

See pages 261, 331.

Drama A drama, or play, is a form of literature meant to be performed by actors before an audience. In a drama, the characters' dialogue and actions tell the story. The written form of a play is known as a script. A script usually includes dialogue, a cast of characters, and stage directions that give specific instructions about performing the play. The person who writes the play is known as the playwright, or dramatist.

See page 259.
See also **Act, Cast of characters, Comedy, Dialogue, Prop, Scene, Stage, Scenery, Tragedy.**

Drawing conclusions Combining several pieces of information to make an inference is called drawing a conclusion. A reader's conclusions may be based on the details presented in a literary work, on his or her previous inferences, or on a combination of these.

See pages 131, 348, 553, 554, 592.

Dynamic character *See* **Character development.**

Epic An epic is a long narrative poem about the adventures of a hero whose actions reflect the ideals and values of a nation or a group. Epics address universal concerns, such as good and evil, life and death, and other serious subjects.

Essay An essay is a short work of nonfiction that deals with a single subject. A formal essay is highly organized, thoroughly researched, and serious in tone. An informal essay is lighter in tone and usually reflects the writer's feelings and personality. The excerpt from *High Tide in Tucson* is an example of an informal essay.

See pages 103, 134.

Evaluating Evaluating is the process of judging the worth of something or someone. A work of literature—or any of its elements—can be evaluated in terms of such criteria as entertainment, believability, originality, and emotional power.

Exaggeration An extreme overstatement of an idea is called exaggeration and is often used for purposes of emphasis or humor. For example, in "The Tell-Tale Heart," the narrator exaggerates when he says, "I heard all things in the heaven and in the earth."

See page 794.
See also **Hyperbole.**

Exposition In fiction, the structure of the plot normally begins with exposition. In the early part of the story, the exposition sets the tone, establishes the setting, introduces the characters, and gives the reader important background information. In "The Treasure of Lemon Brown," the exposition leads up to the time when Greg meets Lemon Brown in the abandoned building.

See pages 18, 260, 439.
See also **Plot.**

Extended metaphor An extended metaphor is a figure of speech that compares two essentially unlike things at some length. An extended metaphor may introduce a series of metaphors representing different aspects of a situation. For example, the poem "O Captain! My Captain!" begins with a metaphor in which President Abraham Lincoln is compared to the captain of a ship. The ship is a metaphor for the United States. What other metaphors can you find in the first two lines of the poem?

> O Captain! my Captain! our fearful trip is done,
> The ship has weather'd every rack, the prize we sought is won . . .
>
> —Walt Whitman, "O Captain! My Captain!"

See also **Metaphor.**

External conflict *See* **Conflict.**

Fable A fable is a brief tale that teaches a lesson about human nature. Many fables feature animals.

See page 904.
See also **Moral.**

Fact and opinion A fact is a statement that can be proved, such as "Mars is the fourth planet from the sun." An opinion, in contrast, is a statement that reflects a writer's belief, but which cannot be supported by proof or evidence; for example, "Mars is the most beautiful planet." Much nonfiction contains both facts and opinions, and it is important for readers to distinguish between the two.

See pages 723, 829, 830.

Falling action Falling action is the part of the plot of a story that occurs after the climax. During the falling action, sometimes called the resolution, conflicts are resolved and loose ends are tied up.

See pages 18, 41, 260, 439.
See also **Plot.**

Fantasy A work of literature that contains at least one fantastic or unreal element is called fantasy. The setting of a work of fantasy might be a totally imaginary world, or it might be a realistic place where very unusual or impossible things happen.

See page 562.

Fiction Fiction is prose writing that tells an imaginary story. The writer of a fictional work might invent all the events and characters in it or might base parts of the story on real people or events. Fiction includes both short stories and novels. A short story can usually be read in one sitting. Novels are longer and more complex.

See also **Historical fiction, Horror fiction, Novel, Short story.**

Figurative language Writers use figurative language—expressions that are not literally true—to create original descriptions. In *Undaunted Courage,* Stephen Ambrose uses the words *blanket* and *sea* to describe a large flock of pelicans:

> The captain looked up to see a blanket of white coming down the river. . . . On close examination it turned out to be a sea of white feathers, over three miles long and seventy yards wide.

See pages 190, 215, 249.
See also **Metaphor, Personification, Simile.**

First-person point of view *See* **Point of view.**

Flashback In a literary work, a flashback is an interruption of the action to present events that took place at an earlier time. A flashback can provide information that helps readers understand a character's current situation. In "The Bet," for example, a flashback is used to present the banker's recollection of a party he gave 15 years earlier.

See pages 285, 440, 475.

Glossary of Literary and Reading Terms

Folklore The traditions, customs, and stories that are passed down within a culture are known as its folklore. Folklore contains various types of literature, such as legends, folk tales, myths, and fables.

See page 904.

Folk tale A folk tale is a simple story that has been passed from generation to generation by word of mouth. The characters in folk tales might be animals, people, or superhuman beings. Folk tales are told primarily to entertain rather than to explain or teach a lesson. "The Souls in Purgatory" is a folk tale from Mexico.

See page 904.

Foreshadowing Foreshadowing occurs when a writer provides hints that suggest future events in a story. Foreshadowing creates suspense while preparing the reader for what is to come. In *The Hitchhiker,* the mother's fears about her son's trip foreshadow the trouble the son will have on his journey.

> But you'll be careful, won't you? Promise me you'll be careful. Don't fall asleep—or drive fast—or pick up any strangers on the road.

See pages 440, 552, 654.

Form A literary work's form is its structure or organization. The form of a poem includes the arrangement of words and lines on the page. Some poems follow predictable patterns, with the same number of syllables in each line and the same number of lines in each stanza. Others, like "Southbound on the Freeway," have irregular forms.

See pages 188, 390, 422.

Free verse Poetry without regular patterns of rhyme and rhythm is called free verse. Some poets use free verse to capture the sounds and rhythms of ordinary speech. The poem "the drum" is written in free verse.

> daddy says the world is
> a drum tight and hard
> and i told him
> i'm gonna beat
> out my rhythm
>
> —Nikki Giovanni, "the drum"

See pages 188, 587.

Generalization A generalization is a broad statement about an entire group, such as "Whales are larger than salmon." Not all generalizations are true. Some are too broad or are not supported by sufficient evidence, like the statement "All eighth graders like yogurt."

See pages 202, 875.

Genre A type or category of literature is called a genre. There are four main literary genres: fiction, nonfiction, poetry, and drama.

Haiku Haiku is a traditional form of Japanese poetry. A haiku normally has three lines and describes a single moment, feeling, or thing. In a traditional haiku, the first and third lines contain five syllables, and the second line contains seven syllables.

Historical fiction Historical fiction is contemporary fiction that is set in the past. Historical fiction may contain references to actual people and events of the past. "War Party" is an example of historical fiction.

See page 737.

Horror fiction Horror fiction contains mysterious and often supernatural events that create terror. "The Tell-Tale Heart" is an example of horror fiction.

Humor Humor is the quality that provokes laughter or amusement. Writers create humor through exaggeration, sarcasm, amusing descriptions, irony, and witty and insightful dialogue. "The Ransom of Red Chief" is an example of a humorous work.

See page 794.

Hyperbole Hyperbole is a figure of speech in which the truth is exaggerated for emphasis or for humorous effect.

> With his gang's help, he [Bill] put together the biggest ranch in the Southwest. He used New Mexico as a corral and Arizona as a pasture. He invented tarantulas and scorpions as practical jokes. He also invented roping. Some say his rope was exactly as long as the equator; others argue it was two feet shorter.
>
> —Mary Pope Osborne, "Pecos Bill"

Idiom An idiom is an expression whose meaning is different from the sum of the meanings of its individual words. The expression "break her date" in "The Moustache" is an example of an idiom.

Imagery Imagery consists of words and phrases that appeal to readers' five senses. Writers use sensory details to help readers imagine how things look, feel, smell, sound, and taste.

> After two days of gentle winter rains, the small pond behind my house is lapping at its banks, content as a well-fed kitten.
>
> —Barbara Kingsolver, *High Tide in Tucson*

See pages 190, 215, 296, 367, 622.

Inductive order In nonfiction, the structure of a text may be organized using inductive order. A text that is organized inductively begins with specific evidence that leads to a general conclusion.

See also **Deductive order, Structure.**

Inference An inference is a logical guess based on evidence. Readers, by combining the information a writer provides with what they know from their own experience, can figure out more than the words say. For example, readers of "Checkouts" can make inferences about what motivates the red-haired girl to behave as she does.

See pages 191, 192, 220, 422, 794.

Informative nonfiction Informative nonfiction is writing that provides factual information about real people, places, and events. Informative nonfiction includes newspaper and magazine articles, textbooks, and encyclopedias.

See pages 104, 159, 638.
See also **Nonfiction.**

Internal conflict *See* **Conflict.**

Interview An interview is a meeting in which one person asks another about personal matters, professional matters, or both. The excerpt from *The Last Seven Months of Anne Frank* is based on an interview with Anne Frank's friend Hannah Elisabeth Pick-Goslar.

See pages 104, 515.

Irony Irony is a contrast between what is expected and what actually exists or happens. In "The Ransom of Red Chief," for example, it is ironic that Red Chief enjoys being kidnapped.

See page 69.

Legend A legend is a story handed down from the past about a specific person—usually someone of heroic accomplishments. "Otoonah" is an Eskimo legend.

See page 904.

Limerick A limerick is a short, humorous poem composed of five lines. It usually has the rhyme scheme *aabba,* created by two rhyming couplets followed by a fifth line that rhymes with the first couplet. A limerick typically has a sing-song rhythm.

> There was an Old Man who supposed
> That the street door was partially closed;
> But some very large rats
> Ate his coats and his hats,
> While that futile Old Gentleman dozed.
>
> —Edward Lear

See also **Couplet.**

Literary nonfiction See **Nonfiction.**

Lyric poetry Lyric poetry is poetry that presents the thoughts and feelings of a single speaker. Most poems, other than narrative poems, are lyric poems. Lyric poetry can be in a variety of forms and cover many subjects, from love and death to everyday experiences. "Knoxville, Tennessee" by Nikki Giovanni is a lyric poem.

See page 417.

Main character See **Character.**

Main idea A main idea is the most important point that a writer wishes to express. It can be the central idea of an entire work or a thought expressed in the topic sentence of a paragraph.

See pages 105, 106, 408, 528.

Memoir A memoir is a specific type of autobiography. Like autobiography, a memoir is about the author's personal experiences. However, a memoir does not necessarily cover the author's entire life. "Block Party" is a memoir.

See pages 102, 106, 127.
See also **Autobiography.**

Metaphor A metaphor is a comparison of two things that have some quality in common. Unlike a simile, a metaphor does not contain an explicit word of comparison, such as *like* or *as*. To what is the moon being compared in the following lines?

> who knows if the moon's
> a balloon,coming out of a keen city
> in the sky—filled with pretty people?
>
> —E. E. Cummings, "who knows if the moon's"

See pages 190, 215, 249, 779.
See also **Extended metaphor, Figurative language.**

Meter In poetry, meter is the regular pattern of accented (´) and unaccented (˘)

syllables. Although all poems have rhythm, not all poems have regular meter. Each unit of meter is known as a foot. The feet and the meter are marked in these lines.

> cánnŏn tŏ | rĭght ŏf thĕm
> cánnŏn tŏ | léft ŏf thĕm
>
> —Alfred, Lord Tennyson,
> "The Charge of The Light Brigade"

See page 189.
See also **Rhythm.**

Minor character See **Character.**

Monitoring Monitoring is the attention readers pay to their comprehension as they are reading. Monitoring helps readers to understand more clearly the meaning of what they are reading.

See pages 21, 148, 443, 587.

Mood A mood, or atmosphere, is a feeling that a literary work conveys to readers. In "The Woman in the Snow," for example, the description of the ghostly figure and her baby in the snow creates an ominous and heart-wrenching mood. What kind of mood is created in the following passage?

> They sat down by the fire again. Outside, the wind was higher than ever, and the old man started nervously at the sound of a door banging upstairs. A silence unusual and depressing settled upon all three, which lasted until the old couple rose to retire for the night.
>
> —W. W. Jacobs, "The Monkey's Paw"

See pages 332, 621, 622, 624.

Moral A moral is a lesson that a story teaches. A moral is often stated directly at the end of a fable. The following moral appears at the end of "A Fable" by Mark Twain.

> **MORAL, BY THE CAT**
> You can find in a text whatever you bring, if you will stand between it and the mirror of your imagination. You may not see your ears, but they will be there.

See also **Fable.**

Motivation A character's motivation is the reason why he or she acts, feels, or thinks in a certain way. For example, young Laurence Yep in "The Great Rat Hunt" is motivated by a desire to please his father.

See pages 19, 22, 331.

Myth A myth is a traditional story, usually of unknown authorship, that answers basic questions about the world. Myths attempt to explain such things as human nature, the origin of the world, mysteries of nature, and social customs.

See page 904.

Narrative Writing that tells a story is called a narrative. The events in a narrative can be real or imagined. Narratives dealing with real events include biographies and autobiographies. Fictional narratives include myths, short stories, and novels.

See also **Autobiography, Biography, Myth, Novel, Short story.**

Narrative poetry Poetry that tells a story is called narrative poetry. Like fiction, narrative poetry contains characters, settings, and plots. It might also contain such elements of poetry as rhyme, rhythm, imagery, and figurative language. "Paul Revere's Ride" is an example of narrative poetry.

See pages 197, 714, 716.

Narrator A narrator is the teller of a story. Sometimes a story's narrator is a character who takes part in the action, such as Charlie in "Flowers for Algernon." Other times, as in "The Treasure of Lemon Brown," the story is narrated by an outside voice.

See also **Point of view.**

Nonfiction Writing that tells about real people, places, and events is called nonfiction. Literary nonfiction is written to be read in much the same way as fiction. Informative nonfiction is written mainly to provide factual information.

See page 101.
See also **Autobiography, Biography, Essay, Informative nonfiction.**

Novel A novel is a work of fiction that is longer and more complex than a short story. In a novel, setting, plot, and characters are usually developed in great detail.

See page 17.
See also **Fiction.**

Onomatopoeia Onomatopoeia is the use of words whose sounds suggest their meaning. The words *bang* and *hiss* are examples of onomatopoeia. In the following lines, the word *sweep* is an example of onomatopoeia.

> The only other sound's the sweep
> Of easy wind and downy flake.
>
> —Robert Frost, "Stopping by Woods on a Snowy Evening"

Opinion *See* **Fact and opinion.**

Oral history Oral histories are stories of people's lives related by word of mouth. These histories usually include both factual material and personal reactions.

Paradox A paradox is a statement that seems to contradict itself but is, nevertheless, true. All forms of irony involve paradox. For example, in "The Ransom of Red Chief," it is both ironic and a paradox that Red Chief enjoys being kidnapped.

Parallelism Parallelism is the use of similar grammatical constructions to express ideas that are related or equal in importance.

Paraphrasing Paraphrasing is the restatement of a text by readers in their own words or in another form.

See page 715, 716.

Personification The giving of human qualities to an animal, object, or idea is known as personification. In "Racing the Great Bear," the great bear is personified when it takes on a human shape.

See pages 190, 804.
See also **Figurative language.**

Perspective *See* **Author's perspective, Point of view.**

Persuasion Persuasive writing is meant to sway readers' feelings, beliefs, or actions. Persuasion normally appeals to both the mind and the emotions of readers.

See page 103.

Play *See* **Drama.**

Playwright *See* **Drama.**

Plot A plot is the sequence of related events that make up a story. It is typical for a plot to begin with an exposition that introduces the characters and the conflict they face. Complications arise during the rising action as the characters struggle with the conflict. Eventually, the plot reaches a climax, the turning point of the story. In the falling action, or resolution, that follows, loose ends are tied up, and the story is brought to a close.

See pages 18, 32, 80, 102, 260, 439, 447, 672, 680.
See also **Character, Climax, Conflict, Exposition, Subplot.**

Poetic Form *See* **Form.**

Poetry Poetry is a type of literature in which ideas and feelings are expressed in compact, imaginative, and often musical language. Poets arrange words in ways designed to touch readers' senses, emotions, and minds. Most poems are written in lines, which may contain patterns of rhyme and rhythm. These lines may, in turn, be grouped in stanzas.

See page 187.
See also **Alliteration, Ballad, Free verse, Lyric poetry, Meter, Narrative poetry, Rhyme, Rhythm, Stanza.**

Point of view The perspective from which a story is told is called its point of view. When a story is told from the first-person point of view, the narrator is a character in the story and uses first-person pronouns, such as *I, me,* and *we.* "War Party" is told from the first-person point of view. When a writer uses a third-person point of view, the story is told by a narrative voice outside the action, not by one of the characters. Third-person point of view uses third-person pronouns, such as *he, she, it,* and *they.* "The Treasure of Lemon Brown" is told from the third-person point of view.

See pages 102, 106, 374.

Predicting Using what you know to guess what might happen is called predicting. Good readers gather information and combine it with their own knowledge to predict events.

See pages 4, 21, 22, 69, 105, 654, 737.

Primary source A primary source is a firsthand account of an event. Primary sources include diaries, journals, letters, speeches, news stories, photographs, and pieces of art. The journals of Meriwether Lewis and William Clark, which form the basis of *Undaunted Courage,* are examples of primary sources.

See pages 168, 723, 766.

Propaganda Text that uses false or misleading information to present a point of view is called propaganda. Name-calling, snob appeal, and bandwagon appeal are three techniques of propaganda.

Prose Prose is the ordinary form of spoken and written language—that is, it is language that lacks the special features of poetry.

Protagonist A protagonist is the central character or hero in a narrative or a drama, usually the one with whom the audience tends to identify. Anne Frank is the protagonist in *The Diary of Anne Frank.*

See page 148.
See also **Antagonist.**

Purpose *See* **Author's purpose, Setting a purpose.**

Questioning The process of raising questions while reading is called questioning. Good readers ask themselves questions in an effort to understand characters and events; they look for the answers as they read.

See pages 4, 21, 333, 390, 715, 756.

Radio play A drama written specifically to be heard on the radio is called a radio play. Because the audience is not meant to see a radio play, sound effects are often used to help listeners imagine the setting and the action. *The Hitchhiker* is an example of a radio play. Notice how the stage directions in the following lines from the script indicate the sound effects.

> *sound*: automobile wheels humming over concrete road

See page 263.

Realistic fiction Realistic fiction is imaginative writing set in the real, modern world. The characters act like real people who use ordinary human abilities to cope with problems and conflicts typical of modern life. "The Treasure of Lemon Brown" is an example of realistic fiction.

Repetition Repetition is a technique in which a sound, word, phrase, or line is repeated for effect or emphasis. Note how the use of repetition in the following lines emphasizes the speaker's faith:

> Sing a song full of the faith that the dark
>   past has taught us,
> Sing a song full of the hope that the present
>   has brought us . . .
>
> —James Weldon Johnson,
> "Lift Every Voice and Sing"

See pages 189, 197.
See also **Alliteration, Rhyme.**

Resolution *See* **Falling action, Plot.**

Rhyme Rhyme is a repetition of sounds at the ends of words. Words rhyme when their accented vowels and all letters that follow have identical sounds. *Cat* and *bat* rhyme, as do *weather* and *feather.* The most common form of rhyme in poetry is end rhyme, in which the rhyming words are at the end of lines. Rhyme that occurs within a line is called internal rhyme. The following lines show both end and internal rhyme:

> The ship is anchor'd safe and sound, its
>   voyage closed and <u>done</u>,
> From fearful <u>trip</u> the victor <u>ship</u> comes in
>   with object <u>won</u> . . .
>
> —Walt Whitman, "O Captain! My Captain!"

See pages 189, 197.

Rhyme scheme The pattern of end rhyme in a poem is called rhyme scheme. The pattern is charted by assigning a letter of the alphabet, beginning with the letter *a,* to each line. Lines that rhyme are given the same letter.

> He'd have given me rolling lands,   *a*
> Houses of marble, and billowing farms, *b*
> Pearls, to trickle between my hands,   *a*
> Smoldering rubies, to circle my arms. *b*
> —Dorothy Parker, "The Choice"

Rhythm Rhythm refers to the pattern or flow of sound created by the arrangement of stressed and unstressed syllables in a line of poetry. The accented, or stressed, syllables are marked with ´, while unaccented, or unstressed, syllables are marked with ˘. A regular pattern of rhythm is called meter. Note the stressed and unstressed syllables in the following lines:

> Whŏse wóods thĕse áre Ĭ thínk Ĭ knów.
> Hĭs hóuse ĭs ín thĕ víllăge thóugh;
>
> —Robert Frost,
> "Stopping by Woods on a Snowy Evening"

See pages 189, 197.
See also **Meter**.

Rising action Rising action refers to the events in a story that move the plot forward. Rising action involves conflicts and complications and usually builds toward a climax, or turning point.

See pages 18, 41, 260, 439.
See also **Plot**.

Satire Satire is a literary technique in which ideas or customs are ridiculed for the purpose of improving society. Satire can be gently witty, mildly abrasive, or bitterly critical. "A Fable" by Mark Twain is an example of satire.

See page 804.

Scanning Scanning is the process of searching through writing for a particular fact or piece of information. When readers scan, their eyes sweep across a page looking for key words that could lead to the information they want.

Scene In a play, a scene is a section presenting events that occur in one place at one time. Act One of *The Diary of Anne Frank* has five scenes.

See page 260.

Scenery The painted backdrop or other structures used to create the setting for a play is called scenery.

See page 260.

Science fiction Science fiction is prose writing in which a writer explores unexpected possibilities of the past or the future by using scientific data and theories as well as his or her imagination. Most science fiction creates a believable world, although some works create a fantasy world that has familiar elements. "Rain, Rain, Go Away" is an example of science fiction.

See pages 549, 554.

Script See **Drama.**

Secondary source A secondary source presents information compiled from or based on other sources. *Undaunted Courage* is an example of a secondary source because it is based on other sources, such as the journals of Meriwether Lewis and William Clark.

See pages 723, 766.

Sensory details Words and phrases that help readers see, hear, taste, feel, or smell what an author is describing are called sensory details. Note the sensory details in these lines:

> The rhododendron was in bloom, a carpet of color, across the mountainsides, soft as the May winds that stirred the hemlocks.
>
> —Marjorie Kinnan Rawlings, "A Mother in Mannville"

See page 215.

Sequence The order in which events occur or in which ideas are presented is called sequence. In a narrative, events are usually presented in chronological order—the order in which they happen. A writer might use clue words and phrases, such as *then, until,* and *finally,* to help readers understand the sequence of events.

See pages 285, 440.
See also **Chronological order.**

Setting A setting of a story, poem, or play is the time and place of the action. Sometimes the setting is clear and well defined; at other times, it is left to readers' imaginations. Elements of setting can include geographic location, historical period (past, present, or future), season, time of day, and the customs and manners of a society.

See pages 17, 20, 59, 102, 280, 329, 332, 861.

Setting a purpose The process of establishing specific reasons to read a work is called setting a purpose. Readers can look at a work's title, headings, and illustrations to guess what the work might be about. Then they can use these guesses to guide their reading and discover whether their ideas match the actual content of the work.

See pages 565, 672, 680.

Short story A short story is a brief work of fiction that can generally be read in one sitting. A short story usually focuses on one or two main characters who face a single problem or conflict.

See page 17.
See also **Fiction.**

Simile A simile is a comparison of two things that have some quality in common. In a simile, the comparison is expressed by means of a word such as *like, as,* or *resembles.*

> The willow is like an etching,
> Fine-lined against the sky.
> The ginkgo is like a crude sketch,
> Hardly worthy to be signed.
>
> —Eve Merriam, "Simile: Willow and Ginkgo"

See pages 190, 215, 249.

Skimming Skimming is the process of reading quickly to find a main idea or to get an overview of a work or a passage. It involves reading the title, the headings, the words in special type, and the first sentence of each paragraph, along with charts, graphs, and time lines.

Sound devices *See* **Alliteration, Onomatopoeia, Repetition, Rhyme, Rhythm.**

Spatial alignment The arrangement of ideas and images in a graphic pattern to indicate their relationships is called spatial alignment.

Speaker The speaker is the voice that talks to the reader in a poem, like the narrator in a work of fiction; the speaker in a poem is not necessarily the poet, however. In "Child on Top of a Greenhouse" by Theodore Roethke, the experiences related might or might not have happened to the poet. In "I Stepped from Plank to Plank" by Emily Dickinson, since the poet uses the pronoun *I,* the poem may well be autobiographical.

See pages 192, 422.

Specialized vocabulary The words unique to a specific subject or profession make up a specialized vocabulary. The excerpt from *Wait Till Next Year,* for example, contains terms related to baseball.

See page 861.

Speech A speech is a talk given in public. "One Million Volumes" by Rudolfo Anaya is an example of a speech.

SQ3R SQ3R is a method of text reading that combines reading and studying in five steps:

> S—Survey
> Q—Question
> R-1—Read
> R-2—Recite
> R-3—Review

See page 574.

Stage A stage is the level and raised platform on which entertainers usually perform.

Stage directions In the script of a play, the instructions to the actors, director, and stage crew are called stage directions. Stage directions might suggest scenery, lighting, music, sound effects, and ways for actors to move and speak. In *The Diary of Anne Frank,* stage directions appear within parentheses and in italic type.

> (Dussel *hurriedly takes off the raincoat, giving it to* Mr. Kraler. *Underneath is his white dentist's jacket, with a yellow Star of David on it.*)

See pages 260, 263.

Stanza A stanza is a grouping of two or more lines. A stanza is comparable to a paragraph in prose. Each stanza may have the same number of lines or the number of lines may vary. "The Other Pioneers" contains three stanzas.

See pages 188, 390.

Static character *See* **Character development.**

Stereotype A stereotype is a broad generalization or an oversimplified view that disregards individual differences. Stereotypes can lead to unfair judgments of people on the basis of ethnic background or physical appearance.

Story mapping A story map is a visual organizer that helps a reader understand a work of literature. A story map helps a reader to keep track of setting, characters, events, and conflicts.

See pages 443, 447.

Structure In nonfiction, the structure of a piece may be chronological or spatial order, cause and effect, or comparison and contrast.

Also, ideas may be presented using inductive or deductive reasoning. Recognizing a text's structure can help in finding the most important ideas as well as the supporting facts and details.

Style A style is a manner of writing; it involves how something is said rather than what is said. The style of the poem "Mother to Son," for example, might be described as conversational—it reflects the speaker's usual informal way of talking. Many elements contribute to style, including word choice, sentence length, tone, and figurative language.

See page 202.

Subject The subject of a literary work is its focus or topic. In a biography, for example, the subject is the person whose life story is being told. Subject differs from theme in that theme is a deeper meaning, usually inferred by the reader, whereas the subject is the main situation or set of facts described by the text.

Subplot A subplot is an additional, minor plot that involves a secondary conflict in the story. The subplot may or may not affect the main plot.

See page 440.
See also **plot.**

Summarizing Summarizing is the process of briefly recounting the main ideas of a piece of writing in a person's own words, while omitting unimportant details.

See pages 283, 769.

Surprise ending An unexpected twist in the plot at the end of a story is called a surprise ending. "The Ransom of Red Chief" is an example of a story with a surprise ending.

See page 592.

Suspense Suspense is a feeling of growing tension and excitement. Writers create suspense by raising questions in readers' minds about what might happen.

See pages 552, 565.

Symbol A symbol is a person, a place, an object, or an action that stands for something beyond itself. A flag, for example, can symbolize a state or country. In "The Moustache," Mike's moustache symbolizes his desire to be an adult.

See pages 190, 367, 622.

Table of contents In most nonfiction books or in books arranged by chapter or section, the contents of the book are shown in a table of contents. The table of contents usually appears at the beginning of the book and lists chapter and section titles and the page where each begins. Besides helping you to find specific parts of the book, the table of contents can give you an overview of the material covered by the book.

Tall tale A tall tale is a humorously exaggerated story about impossible events. Often the main character in a tall tale has extraordinary abilities. "Pecos Bill" is a tall tale.

Text organizers Text organizers include headings, tables of contents, and graphic elements such as charts, tables, time lines, boxes, bullets, and captions.

See page 211.

Theme A theme is the meaning, moral, or message about life or human nature that is communicated by a literary work. In many cases, readers must infer what the theme is. One way of figuring out a theme is to examine the lesson learned by the main character and to apply it to all people. For example, a theme of "The Treasure of Lemon Brown" might be that every person has a treasure.

See pages 20, 48, 551, 827, 830.

Third-person point of view See **Point of view.**

Tone The tone of a work expresses the writer's attitude toward his or her subject. Words such as *angry, sad,* and *humorous* can be used to describe different tones. The poem "I'm Making a List," for example, can be said to have a humorous tone.

See pages 332, 552, 621, 622, 769, 879.

Topic sentence See **Main idea.**

Tragedy A tragedy is a dramatic work that presents the downfall of a dignified character or characters who are involved in historically or socially significant events. The events in a tragic plot are set in motion by a decision that is often an error in judgment. Succeeding events are linked in a cause-and-effect relationship and lead inevitably to a disastrous conclusion, usually death. The play *Romeo and Juliet* by William Shakespeare is an example of a tragedy.

Turning point See **Climax.**

Urban legend A contemporary story that is told in many versions around the world is called an urban legend. "The Girl in the Lavender Dress" is an urban legend.

See page 943.

Visualizing The process of forming a mental picture based on a written description is called visualizing. Good readers use the details supplied by writers to picture characters, settings, and events.

See pages 4, 21, 59, 134, 333, 367, 623, 624, 804.

Voice An author's or a narrator's voice is his or her distinctive style or manner of expression. Voice can reveal much about the author's or the narrator's personality—as does the voice of Squeaky, the narrator of "Raymond's Run."

See page 408.

Glossary of Words to Know
In English and Spanish

A

abduction (ăb-dŭk′shən) *n.* kidnapping
  rapto *n.* secuestro

abomination (ə-bŏm′ə-nā′shən) *n.* a hateful or disgusting thing
  abominación *n.* cosa desagradable

abstracted (ăb-străk′tĭd) *adj.* lost in thought so as to be unaware of one's surroundings; absent-minded, pre-occupied
  abstraído(a) *adj.* ensimismado(a)

absurd (əb-sûrd′) *adj.* ridiculously unreasonable
  absurdo(a) *adj.* opuesto(a) a la razón

accelerator (ăk-sĕl′ə-rā′tər) *n.* a device, especially the gas pedal of a motor vehicle, for increasing speed
  acelerador *n.* pedal de los automóviles que controla la velocidad

access (ăk′sĕs) *n.* the power to reach; to make use of; to get past barriers
  acceso *n.* acción de llegar o acercarse

accommodation (ə-kŏm′ə-dā′shən) *n.* a favor or convenience
  favor *n.* ayuda, beneficio

acute (ə-kyōōt′) *adj.* sharp; keen
  filoso(a) *adj.* cortante

ad-libbing (ăd-lĭb′ĭng) *adj.* speaking spontaneously, without preparation
  ad-lib *v.*
  improvisado(a) *adj.* que habla espon-táneamente, sin preparación

admonish (ăd-mŏn′ĭsh) *v.* to caution; warn
  prevenir *v.* avisar, advertir

adversary (ăd′vər-sĕr′ē) *n.* an opponent
  adversario *n.* oponente

affectation (ăf′ĕk-tā′shən) *n.* unnatural behavior, especially behavior intended to impress others
  afectación *n.* falta de naturalidad en la manera de hablar y de comportarse

affliction (ə-flĭk′shən) *n.* a condition of pain or suffering
  aflicción *n.* tristeza

affluent (ăf′lōō-ənt) *adj.* abundant; rich
  rico(a) *adj.* con dinero y riquezas

ail (āl) *v.* to feel ill or be in pain
  sentirse mal *v.* sentir dolor o aflicción

ajar (ə-jär′) *adj.* partially open
  entreabierto(a) *adj.* abierto(a) a medias

antic (ănt′ĭc) *n.* an odd or extravagant act or gesture; a prank
  payasada *n.* acción ridícula

appalled (ə-pôld′) *adj.* horrified; shocked
  appall *v.*
  asombrado(a) *adj.* asustado(a), impactado(a) **asombrar** *v.*

armada (är-mä′də) *n.* a fleet of warships; a large group of moving things
  armada *n.* conjunto de fuerzas navales

arresting (ə-rĕs′tĭng) *adj.* capturing attention; striking
  llamativo(a) *adj.* cautivante, que llama la atención

assailant (ə-sā′lənt) *n.* a person who attacks another
  agresor(a) *n.* persona que ataca a otra

assert (ə-sûrt') *v.* to put forward in a forceful or insistent way
aseverar *v.* afirmar, hacer valer

assurance (ə-shŏŏr'əns) *n.* a guarantee or pledge
garantía *n.* prenda, cosa que asegura y protege contra algún riesgo

audacity (ô-dăs'ĭ-tē) *n.* shameless daring or boldness
osadía *n.* atrevimiento

B

bade (băd) *v.* invited; directed; *present tense*—**bid**
dejó *v.* permitió; *presente*—**dejar**

banter (băn'tər) *n.* good-natured, playful talk
chanza *n.* dicho o conversación burlona

barren (băr'ən) *adj.* empty
yermo(a) *adj.* vacío(a), que no contiene nada

barricade (băr'ĭ-kād') *v.* a structure set up to block a passage
barricada *n.* obstáculo hecho de varios materiales para bloquear el avance del enemigo

battalion (bə-tăl'yen) *n.* a large body of organized people, especially troops; a great number
batallón *n.* grupo numeroso de gente; tropas militares

beckon (běk'ən) *v.* to signal to come by nodding or waving
hacer señas *v.* llamar a alguien por medio de gestos

bellow (běl'ō) *v.* to shout in a deep, loud voice
bramar *v.* gritar fuertemente

benefactor (běn'ə-făk'tər) *n.* a person who gives monetary or other aid
benefactor(a) *n.* persona que da ayuda, generalmente monetaria

benevolence (bə-něv'ə-ləns) *n.* kindness; goodwill
benevolencia *v.* simpatía, buena voluntad

benevolently (bə-něv'ə-lənt-lē) *adv.* characterized by doing good; kindly
benevolentemente *adv.* de manera simpática y bondadosa

betrayal (bĭ-trā' ŭl) *n.* the act of being disloyal
traición *n.* acto de ser desleal

blunt (blŭnt) *adj.* abrupt; rudely straightforward or honest
contundente *adj.* directo(a), que da su parecer espontáneamente

board (bôrd) *n.* food or meals
comida *n.* alimentos que se ofrecen como parte del alojamiento

borne (bôrn) *adj.* carried **bear** *v.*
sufrido(a) *adj.* aguantar **sufrir** *v.*

boycott (boi' kŏt') *v.* to act together in refusing to use, buy, or deal with, especially as an expression of protest
boicot *n.* dejar de negociar con una compañía o persona a manera de protesta

brandishing (brăn'dĭsh-ĭng) *adj.* waving something (such as a weapon) in a threatening manner **brandish** *v.*
amenazante *adj.* que se muestra para amenazar a alguien **amenazar** *v.*

brazen (brā'zən) *adj.* marked by exaggerated fearlessness or boldness
desvergonzado(a) *adj.* descarado(a), desfachatado(a)

brusquely (brŭsk'lē) *adv.* in an abrupt, sudden manner
bruscamente *adv.* de golpe, de manera repentina

C

cajoling (kə-jō′lĭng) *adj.* urging gently; coaxing **cajole** *v.*
persuadido(a) *adj.* convencido(a) por otra persona a hacer algo **persuadir** *v.*

capricious (kə-prĭsh′əs) *adj.* unpredictable
caprichoso(a) *adj.* que actúa con capricho; **capricho** deseo egoísta *n.*

capsize (kăp′sīz) *v.* to overturn or cause to overturn
volcar *v.* hacer que una cosa caiga

censorship (sen′ sər-ship′) *n.* the practice of banning writing, music, or visual material that is considered improper or harmful
censura *n.* prohibición de material escrito, visual o musical, considerado impropio

chant (chănt) *n.* something sung or spoken in a rhythmic monotone
salmo *n.* cántico o recitado de ritmo monótono

circumstance (sûr′kəm-stăns′) *n.* a condition; a financial situation
circunstancia *n.* condición, situación final

clan (klăn) *n.* a group of families claiming a common ancestor; a group of relatives, friends, or others having a common background or interest
clan *n.* grupo de familias que tienen un antepasado en común; grupo de familiares o amigos que tienen antecedentes en común

clarity (klăr′ĭ-tē) *n.* the quality of being easily seen; clearness
claridad *n.* cualidad de ser visto fácilmente; luminosidad

cliché (klē-shā′) *n.* an overused expression that has lost its original quality or effect
cliché *n.* expresión repetida que ha perdido su significado original

clutch (klŭch) *v.* to grasp and hold tightly
agarrar *v.* tomar firmemente

coax (kōks) *v.* to persuade or try to persuade by gentle, persistent urging or flattery
engatusar *v.* persuadir de manera insistente y con halagos

collaborate (kə-lăb′ə-rāt) *v.* to work together on a project
colaborar *v.* trabajar juntos en un proyecto

commence (kə-mĕns′) *v.* to begin; start
comenzar *v.* empezar

commend (kə-mĕnd′) *v.* to speak highly of; to praise
recomendar *v.* hablar bien de alguien, alabar

commissioner (kə-mĭsh′ə-nər) *n.* a person authorized by a commission or special group to perform certain duties
comisionado *n.* persona autorizada por una comisión o grupo especial para realizar ciertas actividades

communion (kə-myōōn′yən) *n.* close relationship in which deep feelings are shared; intimacy
comunión *n.* relación cercana en la que se comparten sentimientos; intimidad

compel (kəm-pĕl′) *v.* to force or drive
compeler *v.* forzar, obligar, exigir

competent (kŏm′pĭ-tənt) *adj.* qualified; capable
competente *adj.* calificado(a); capaz

comply (kəm-plī′) *v.* to act according to a command, request, or order
cumplir *v.* actuar de acuerdo a una orden o requerimiento

conceived (kən-sēvd′) *adj.* thought of **conceive** *v.*
concebido(a) *adj.* pensado(a)

conflagration (kŏn′flə-grā′shən) *n.* a large, destructive fire
conflagración *n.* incendio destructivo

consent (kən-sĕnt') *n.* agreement, acceptance, or approval
consentimiento *n.* acuerdo, aceptación, aprobación

consequence (kŏn'sĭ-kwĕns') *n.* importance
consecuencia *n.* importancia

console (kən-sōl') *v.* to comfort
consolar *v.* confortar

conspicuous (kən-spĭk'yōo-əs) *adj.* easy to notice; obvious
conspicuo(a) *adj.* sobresaliente, llamativo(a)

conspiracy (kən-spîr'ə-sē) *n.* a secret plan by a group to perform an illegal, wrongful, or rebellious act
conspiración *n.* plan secreto para llevar a cabo un acto ilegal o rebelde

contemplate (kŏn'təm-plāt') *v.* to look at something thoughtfully, carefully, and thoroughly; to think about something at length
contemplar *v.* observar algo cuidadosamente, pensar profundamente

contempt (kən-tĕmpt') *n.* an attitude of despising; scorn
desdén *n.* actitud de desprecio

contrivance (kən-trī'vəns) *n.* something, as a machine, created to do a specific thing
invención *n.* algo creado, como una máquina, para hacer algo específico

contrive (kən-trīv') *v.* to invent
inventar *v.* crear

converge (kən-vûrj') *v.* to come together from different directions
converger *v.* unirse al llegar de distintas direcciones

credulity (krĭ-dōo'lĭ-tē) *n.* a tendency to believe too easily; gullibility
credulidad *n.* tendencia a creer de manera fácil

crevice (krĕv'ĭs) *n.* a crack
ranura *n.* rendija

cultivation (kŭl'tə-vā'shən) *n.* the act of preparing and improving the land; the growing of crops
cultivo *n.* acto de preparar la tierra para cosechar

D

dear (dîr) *adj.* greatly valued; precious
estimado(a) *adj.* valioso(a), precioso(a)

decree (dĭ-krē') *n.* an official order
decreto *n.* orden oficial

deftly (dĕft'lē) *adv.* move in a quick and skillful manner
hábilmente *adv.* con destreza

delegation (dĕl'ĭ-gā'shən) *n.* a group of people selected as representatives
delegación *n.* grupo de personas seleccionadas como representantes

demise (dĭ-mīz') *n.* an ending of existence
fallecimiento *n.* final de la existencia

derision (dĭ-rĭzh'ən) *n.* ridicule
burla *n.* desprecio

descendant (dĭ-sĕn'dənt) *n.* an offspring
descendiente *n.* el hijo, nieto o bisnieto de una familia

desolate (dĕs'ə-lĭt) *adj.* having few or no inhabitants; lifeless
desolado(a) *adj.* lugar con pocos o ningún habitante; sin vida

destiny (dĕs'tə-nē) *n.* an unavoidable lot in life; fate
destino *n.* lo que sucede inevitablemente en la vida, suerte

dexterity (dĕk-stĕr'ĭ-tē) *n.* skill or grace in using the hands
destreza *n.* habilidad en el uso de las manos

diatribe (dī'ə-trīb') *n.* condemnation; bitter, abusive criticism
diatriba *n.* condena, discurso violento contra algo o alguien

diminish (dĭ-mĭn′ĭsh) *v.* to make smaller or less
reducir *v.* hacer algo más pequeño o en menor cantidad

discreet (dĭ-skrēt′) *adj.* showing caution in speech and behavior
discreto(a) *adj.* que muestra cautela en el habla y el comportamiento

disgruntled (dĭs-grŭn′tld) *adj.* displeased and irritated **disgruntle** *v.*
malhumorado(a) *adj.* descontento(a), irritado(a) **malhumorarse** *v.*

disheveled (dĭ-shĕv′əld) *adj.* messy; untidy
desaliñado(a) *adj.* desarreglado(a), desprolijo(a)

disparagingly (dĭ-spăr′ĭ-jĭng-lē) *adv.* in a manner that shows a lack of respect
despectivamente *adv.* con falta de respeto

dispel (dĭ-spĕl′) *v.* to drive away
desvanecer *v.* disipar, dispersar

diversion (dĭ-vûr′zhən) *n.* a distraction, entertainment, or relaxation
diversión *n.* distracción, entretenimiento

doleful (dōl′fəl) *adj.* sad; mournful
afligido(a) *adj.* triste, dolorido(a)

dry (drī) *adj.* direct and without emotion; matter-of-fact
seco(a) *adj.* sin emoción, frío(a); directo(a)

dumbfounded (dŭm′foun′dəd) *adj.* speechless with shock or amazement
atónito(a) *adj.* sin habla, sorprendido(a)

E

eccentric (ĭk-sĕn′trĭk) *adj.* very unusual in behavior; odd
excéntrico(a) *adj.* de comportamiento inusual; raro(a)

ecstasy (ĕk′stə-sē) *n.* intense joy or delight; bliss
éxtasis *n.* diversión y placer intensos

eloquence (ĕl′ə-kwəns) *n.* an ability to speak forcefully and persuasively
elocuencia *n.* habilidad de hablar enérgica y persuasivamente

emigrant (ĕm′ĭ-grənt) *n.* a person who leaves one country or region to settle in another
emigrante *n.* persona que deja un país o región para ir a otra

encroach (ĕn-krōch′) *v.* to intrude; trespass
usurpar *v.* traspasar los límites; inmiscuirse

endow (ĕn-dou′) *v.* to supply; provide
dotar *v.* proveer, suministrar

enumeration (ĭ-nōō′mə-rā′shən) *n.* a list
enumeración *n.* lista

existence (ĭg-zĭs′təns) *n.* the fact or state of being real
existencia *n.* el hecho o el estado de ser real

expedition (ĕk′spĭ-dĭsh′ən) *n.* a group of people making a journey with a specific purpose
expedición *n.* grupo de personas que realiza un viaje con un propósito específico

exquisite (ĕk′skwĭ-zĭt) *adj.* excellent, flawless; having an intricate and beautiful design or outcome
exquisito(a) *adj.* excelente, impecable; que tiene bello diseño o presencia

extricate (ĕk′strĭ-kāt′) *v.* to free from a tangle or difficulty
desenredar *v.* liberar de un enredo o dificultad

exuberant (ĭg-zōō′bər-ənt) *adj.* vigorous and unrestrained
exuberante *adj.* vigoroso(a), abundante

F

falter (fôl′tər) *v.* to become unsteady or lose confidence; waver
tropezar *v.* perder el equilibrio, tambalear

fastidious (fă-stĭd′ē-əs) *adj.* difficult to please
quisquilloso(a) *adj.* difícil de complacer

fate (fāt) *n.* a power that is supposed to determine the course of events
destino *n.* poder que determina el curso de los sucesos

fauna (fô′nə) *n.* animals, especially those characteristic of a particular region
fauna *n.* animales, especialmente aquellos característicos de una región en particular

fetish (fĕt′ĭsh) *n.* an abnormal attention or attachment
fetichismo *n.* atención o apego anormal a un objeto; **fetiche** *n.* objeto al que se le atribuyen poderes sobrenaturales

flank (flăngk) *v.* to attack the sides of something
flanquear *v.* atacar los lados del adversario

flora (flôr′ə) *n.* plants, especially those characteristic of a particular region
flora *n.* plantas, especialmente aquellas características de una región en particular

flotsam (flŏt′səm) *n.* floating wreckage or cargo after a shipwreck
pecio *n.* restos flotantes que quedan después de un naufragio

flounder (floun′dər) *v.* to make clumsy attempts to move or regain one's balance
caminar torpemente *v.* hacer intentos bruscos para avanzar sin perder el equilibrio

flourishing (flûr′ĭ-shĭng) *adj.* thriving; prosperous **flourish** *v.*
floreciente *adj.* próspero(a) **florecer** *v.*

foreboding (fôr-bōd′ĭng) *n.* a feeling that something, especially bad or harmful, is about to happen
presagio *n.* sentimiento de que algo, especialmente malo o dañino, va a suceder

forlorn (fər-lôrn′) *adj.* sad and desperate because of abandonment
desamparado(a) *adj.* triste y alfigido(a) debido al abandono

founder (foun′dər) *v.* to get stuck; break down
desplomarse *v.* caer, derrumbarse

fumigate (fyōō′mĭ-gāt′) *v.* to use smoke or fumes in order to kill off rodents or insects; to disinfect
fumigar *v.* deshacerse de insectos y animales dañinos usando gases y sustancias químicas

G

gifted (gĭf′tĭd) *adj.* having natural talent or intelligence
dotado(a) *adj.* que tiene talento o inteligencia natural

gnarled (närld) *adj.* rugged and roughened, as from old age or work
rugoso(a) *adj.* con protuberancias, áspero(a); como si fuera viejo(a)

grimace (grĭm′ĭs) *n.* a facial expression of pain or disgust
mueca *n.* expresión facial de dolor o disgusto

H

haphazardly (hăp-hăz′ərd-lē) *adv.* in a random manner
sin elección *adv.* al azar

hazel (hā′zəl) *adj.* a light brown or yellowish brown
avellanado(a) *adj.* de color castaño claro

humane (hyōō-mān′) *adj.* merciful; showing the best qualities of humans
humano(a) *adj.* con humanidad

hypocritical (hĭp′ə-krĭt′ĭ-kəl) *adj.* false or deceptive, like a person who is pretending to be what he or she is not
hipócrita *adj.* falso(a)

hypothesis (hī-pŏth′ĭ-sĭs) *n.* a theory used as a basis for research
hipótesis *n.* teoría utilizada como base para una investigación

I

ignite (ĭg-nīt′) *v.* to cause to burn; kindle
encender *v.* prender fuego; alumbrar

immoral (ĭ-môr′əl) *adj.* contrary to what is considered to be correct behavior
inmoral *adj.* sin moralidad

impair (ĭm-pâr′) *v.* to weaken; damage
deteriorar *v.* debilitar; dañar

impart (ĭm-pärt′) *v.* to make known; to give or reveal
impartir *v.* dar a conocer; dar un aviso

impel (ĭm-pĕl′) *v.* to drive, force, or urge to action
impeler *v.* llamar o inducir a la acción

imperious (ĭm-pîr′ē-əs) *adj.* proud; overbearing
imperioso(a) *adj.* orgulloso(a), arrogante

impromptu (ĭm-prŏmp′tōō) *adj.* done on the spur of the moment; unplanned
improvisado(a) *adj.* sin planificar

improvise (ĭm′prə-vīz′) *v.* to put together or act with little or no preparation or planning
improvisado(a) *adj.* algo que se hace en el momento

impudent (ĭm′pyə-dənt) *adj.* offensively bold and disrespectful
descarado(a) *adj.* irrespetuoso(a), ofensivo(a)

impulse (ĭm′pŭls′) *n.* a sudden wish or urge
impulso *n.* deseo repentino o urgente

impunity (ĭm-pyōō′nĭ-tē) *n.* freedom from injury or punishment
impunidad *n.* que no requiere castigo o perjuicio

inadequate (ĭn-ăd′ĭ-kwĭt) *adj.* not good enough for what is needed
inadecuado(a) *adj.* que no es suficientemente bueno(a) para lo que se necesita

inarticulate (ĭn′är-tĭk′yə-lĭt) *adj.* speechless; unable to speak effectively or understandably
inarticulado(a) *adj.* sin habla; sin posibilidad de hablar o hacerse comprender efectivamente

incessantly (ĭn-sĕs′ənt-lē) *adv.* continually, without interruption
incesantemente *adv.* continuamente, sin interrupción

indignantly (ĭn-dĭg′nənt-lē) *adv.* angrily aroused by something mean, unjust, or unworthy
indignantemente *adv.* con enojo ante algo malo, injusto o indigno

indomitable (ĭn-dŏm′ĭ-tə-bəl) *adj.* unable to be conquered
indomable *adj.* que no se puede conquistar o vencer

induce (ĭn-dōōs′) *v.* to bring forth; cause
inducir *v.* producir, causar

ineptitude (ĭn-ĕp′tĭ-tōōd′) *n.* incompetence, clumsiness; displaying a lack of judgment
inaptitud *n.* incompetencia

inert (ĭn-ûrt′) *adj.* having no power to move or act; lifeless
inerte *adj.* sin poder para moverse ni actuar; sin vida

inevitable (ĭn-ĕv′ĭ-tə-bəl) *adj.* impossible to avoid or prevent
inevitable *adj.* que no puede prevenirse

instill (ĭn-stĭl′) *v.* to supply gradually
verter gota a gota *v.* suministrar gradualmente

instinctive (ĭn-stĭngk′tĭv) *adj.* having a natural tendency; spontaneous
instintivo(a) *adj.* con tendencia natural; espontáneo(a)

intercession (ĭn′tər-sĕsh′ən) *n.* the act of asking for something that will benefit someone else
intercesión *n.* acción de pedir algo que favorecerá a otro

interminably (ĭn-tûr′mə-nə-blē) *adv.* without end
interminablemente *adv.* sin fin

introspective (ĭn′trə-spĕk′tĭv) *adj.* examining one's own thoughts, feelings, and sensations
introspectivo(a) *adj.* el que examina sus propios pensamientos, sentimientos y sensaciones

intuition (ĭn′tōō-ĭsh′ən) *n.* a sense of knowing not dependent on reason; an insight
intuición *n.* sentimiento de sabiduría que no depende de una razón; perspicacia

invulnerable (ĭn-vŭl′nər-ə-bəl) *adj.* impossible to hurt
invulnerable *adj.* que no se puede dañar

J

jubilation (jōō′bə-lā′shən) *n.* rejoicing; a celebration or expression of joy
júbilo *n.* regocijo; celebración o expresión de alegría

judicious (jōō-dĭsh′əs) *adj.* careful; showing sound judgment
juicioso(a) *adj.* cuidadoso(a); que muestra buen juicio

K

kindling (kĭnd′lĭng) *n.* pieces of dry wood or other material that can be easily lighted to start a fire; tinder
leña *n.* trozos de madera seca con los que se puede hacer fuego fácilmente; mecha

L

lapse (lăps) *v.* to sink or slip gradually
deslizarse *v.* resbalar o sumergirse gradualmente

lark (lärk) *n.* a carefree adventure
jolgorio *n.* diversión sin preocupación

lavish (lăv′ĭsh) *adj.* exceedingly generous; extravagant
derrochador(a) *adj.* excesivamente generoso(a); extravagante

learned (lûr′nĭd) *adj.* having a great deal of knowledge
culto(a) *adj.* que tiene muchos conocimientos

ledge (lĕj) *n.* a narrow shelf
repisa *n.* estante angosto

legitimate (lə-jĭt′ə-mĭt) *adj.* logical; genuine
legítimo(a) *adj.* lógico(a); genuino(a)

liable (lī′ə-bəl) *adj.* likely
probable *adj.* posible

litany (lĭt′n-ē) *n.* a repetitive recitation
letanía *n.* recitado repetitivo

loathe (lōth) *v.* to hate; to dislike someone or something greatly
detestar *v.* odiar; aborrecer a alguien o algo

logistics (lō-jĭs′tĭks) *n.* the management, planning, and carrying out of details in an operation or a project
logística *n.* manejo, plan y ejecución de detalles durante una operación o proyecto

longing (lông′ĭng) *n.* a strong desire
anhelo *n.* un deseo intenso

lumbering (lŭm′bər-ĭng) *adj.* moving in a heavy, clumsy way **lumber** *v.*
pesado(a) *adj.* que se mueve de manera lenta y torpe **avanzar pesadamente** *v.*

luminous (lōō′mə-nəs) *adj.* giving off light; shining
luminoso(a) *adj.* brillante, con mucha luz

M

magnificence (măg-nĭf′ĭ-səns) *n.* greatness or richness; grand or impressive beauty
magnificencia *n.* cualidad de magnífico

malicious (mə-lĭsh′əs) *adj.* showing ill will; spiteful
malicioso(a) *adj.* que muestra maldad; rencoroso(a)

malodorous (măl-ō′dər-əs) *adj.* having a bad odor
maloliente *adj.* que tiene mal olor

meditation (měd′ĭ-tā′shən) *n.* the act of deep thinking or reflection
meditación *n.* acto de pensar profundamente o reflexionar

menace (měn′ĭs) *n.* a possible danger; a threat
amenaza *n.* un peligro posible

monotonous (mə-nŏt′n-əs) *adj.* repeating over and over, without variety
monótono(a) *adj.* que se repite continuamente, sin variación

mug (mŭg) *n.* the face
cara *n.* rostro

mutinous (myōōt′n-əs) *adj.* rebelling against a leader
motín *n.* rebelión en contra de un líder

N

naïveté (nä′ēv-tā′) *n.* a lack of sophistication; simplicity
ingenuidad *n.* falta de sofisticación; simplicidad

naturalist (năch′ər-ə-lĭst) *n.* a person who studies living things by observing them directly
naturalista *n.* persona que estudia los seres vivientes observándolos directamente

nondescript (nŏn′dĭ-skrĭpt′) *adj.* lacking in distinctive qualities; drab
indefinido(a) *adj.* con falta de cualidades distintivas; ordinario

notorious (nō-tôr′ē-əs) *adj.* well-known, particularly for disgraceful behavior
notorio(a) *adj.* conocido por todos, particularmente por comportamiento vergonzoso

nurseryman (nûr′sə-rē-mən) *n.* person employed by a nursery, where plants are grown for sale, transplanting, or experimentation
viverista *n.* persona a cargo de un vivero, donde cultiva plantas para su venta, trasplante o para experimentos

O

obsolete (ŏb′sə-lēt′) *adj.* out-of-date
anticuado(a) *adj.* pasado(a) de moda

ominous (ŏm′ə-nəs) *adj.* menacing; threatening
ominoso(a) *adj.* amenazante; siniestro(a)

opportunist (ŏp′ər-tōō′nĭst) *n.* a person who takes advantage of any opportunity to achieve a goal, with little regard for moral principles
oportunista *n.* persona que saca provecho de cualquier oportunidad, sin principios morales

oppression (ə-prĕsh′ən) *n.* the act of keeping someone down through harsh and unjust use of power; the feeling of being heavily weighed down, either mentally or physically
opresión *n.* acto de contener a alguien por medio de la crueldad y el abuso de poder; sentimiento de estar agobiado(a), mental o físicamente

optimism (ŏp′tə-mĭz′əm) *n.* a tendency to expect the best possible outcome or to dwell on the most hopeful aspects of a situation
optimismo *n.* tendencia a esperar los mejores resultados posibles o de ver los mejores aspectos de una situación

ostentatiously (ŏs′tĕn-tā′shəs-lē) *adv.* with great show or exaggeration
ostentosamente *adv.* con mucha exageración

outskirts (out′skûrts′) *n.* the region remote from the central district of a city or town
suburbios *n.* las regiones lejanas a un distrito central de una ciudad o pueblo

P

palatable (păl′ə-tə-bəl) *adj.* acceptable to the taste; able to be eaten
sabroso(a) *adj.* que tiene un sabor agradable; gustoso(a)

pandemonium (păn′də-mō′nē-əm) *n.* wild confusion and noise; an uproar
pandemonio *n.* desorden y ruido; alboroto

paradox (păr′ə-dŏks′) *n.* a statement that appears to be illogical but may nevertheless be true
paradoja *n.* una aserción que parece ilógica pero sin embargo podría ser verdadera

parched (pärchd) *adj.* extremely dry
reseco(a) *adj.* muy seco(a)

peer (pîr) *v.* to look intently, searchingly, or with difficulty
escrutar *v.* mirar atentamente

perceptible (pər-sĕp′tə-bəl) *adj.* capable of being observed; noticeable
perceptible *adj.* que se puede observar; notable

peril (pĕr′əl) *n.* danger
peligro *n.* riesgo; la posibilidad de que suceda algún mal

perilous (pĕr′ə-ləs) *adj.* full of danger
peligroso(a) *adj.* que puede ocasionar daño; arriesgado(a)

periscope (pĕr′ĭ-skōp′) *n.* a tube-shaped optical device that lets one see into an area beyond the area he or she is in; a periscope is used by submarines to see above the surface of the water while remaining invisible
periscopio *n.* un tubo óptico que sirve para observar los objetos por encima de un obstáculo que impide la visión directa. Los submarinos usan un periscopio para ver sobre la superficie del mar mientras están sumergidos.

perpetual (pər-pĕch′ōō-əl) *adj.* lasting for an indefinitely long time; continuing without interruption
perpetuo(a) *adj.* eterno(a)

persist (pər-sĭst′) *v.* to continue stubbornly
persistir *v.* seguir tercamente

perspective (pər-spĕk′tĭv) *n.* a point of view from which things can be correctly understood or judged
perspectiva *n.* un punto de vista desde el que se puede entender o evaluar las cosas correctamente

pervade (pər-vād′) *v.* to be spread or to be present throughout
penetrar *v.* extender por; invadir

perverse (pər-vûrs′) *adj.* turned away from what is right or good; improper
perverso(a) *adj.* que no es correcto(a) o bueno(a); impropio(a)

petite (pə-tēt′) *adj.* small and slender
pequeño(a) *adj.* chiquito(a) y delgado(a)

pious (pī′əs) *adj.* showing sincere devotion; reverent
beato(a) *adj.* con mucha reverencia

pivotal (pĭv′ə-tl) *adj.* being of central importance
fundamental *adj.* que tiene mucha importancia

plummet (plŭm′ĭt) *v.* to fall suddenly and steeply
desplomarse *v.* caer a plomo

ponder (pŏn′dər) *v.* to think or to consider carefully and thoroughly
ponderar *v.* pensar cuidadosamente o considerar completamente

posterity (pŏ-stĕr′ĭ-tē) *n.* future generations
vuestras generaciones *n.* los hijos y nietos que heredan la posteridad

precarious (prĭ-kâr′ē-əs) *adj.* not secure; risky
precario(a) *adj.* que no es seguro(a); arriesgado(a)

precedent (prĕs′ĭ-dənt) *n.* an event that serves as an example for later actions
precedente *n.* un suceso que sirve de un ejemplo para acciones posteriores

predator (prĕd′ə-tər) *n.* an organism that lives by preying on other organisms
depredador *n.* un organismo que mata y come a otros organismos para vivir

predicated (prĕd′ĭ-kā′-tĭd) *adj.* established; assumed **predicate** *v.*
fundado(a) *adj.* establecido(a); afirmado(a) **fundar** *v.*

preening (prē′nĭng) *n.* cleaning feathers with the beak **preen** *v.*
arreglo *n.* limpieza de las plumas con el pico **arreglar** *v.*

presumptuous (prĭ-zŭmp′chōō-əs) *adj.* excessively bold, confident, or shameless
presuntuoso(a) *adj.* audaz, confiado(a) o sinvergüenza

principle (prĭn′sə-pəl) *n.* the code of good behavior; morality
principio *n.* base de buena conducta; moralidad

probe (prōb) *v.* to investigate or to explore by touch; searching
sondar *v.* investigar o explorar por tocar; buscar

procure (prō-kyōōr′) *v.* to obtain; acquire
procurar *v.* obtener; adquirir

prodigy (prŏd′ə-jē) *n.* a person with an exceptional talent
prodigio *n.* una persona que tiene un talento excepcional

proportional (prə-pôr′shə-nəl) *adj.* having a constant relation in degree or number
proporcional *adj.* que tiene una relación constante de nivel o número

proposition (prŏp′ə-zĭsh′ən) *n.* a suggested plan
proposición *n.* un plan sugerido

proprietor (prə-prī′ĭ-tər) *n.* the owner of a business
propietario *n.* el dueño de un negocio

prospector (prŏs′pĕk′tər) *n.* one who explores an area for mineral deposits or oil
buscador *n.* una persona que explora una región para encontrar depósitos minerales o petróleo

provocation (prŏv′ə-kā′shən) *n.* something that irritates or stirs to action
provocación *n.* algo que irrita o que incita a la acción

prudence (prōōd′ns) *n.* the quality of behaving with caution and good judgment
prudencia *n.* la calidad de actuar con cautela y buen juicio

pungent (pŭn′jənt) *adj.* sharp and intense, as an odor
acre *adj.* áspero(a) y picante al gusto o al olfato

Q

quintessential (kwĭn′tə-sĕn′shəl) *adj.* most typical or characteristic
depuradísimo(a) *adj.* más típico(a) o característico(a)

R

rafter (răf′tər) *n.* a wooden beam that supports a roof
par *n.* viga de madera que sostiene un techo

ransom (răn′səm) *n.* a price or a payment demanded in return for the release of property or a person
rescate *n.* un precio o un pago que se pide por devolver una cosa o poner en libertad a una persona

rapture (răp′chər) *n.* a feeling of ecstasy; great joy
entusiasmarse *v.* sentir mucha pasión o ánimo por algo

rationalize (răsh′ə-nə-līz′) *v.* to make self-satisfying but incorrect explanations about one's behavior
encontrar una explicación *v.* justificar

ravage (răv′ĭj) *n.* serious damage; widespread destruction
devastador *adj.* que destruye totalmente

rebuke (rĭ-byōōk′) *n.* a sharp scolding or criticism
reprimenda *n.* regaño; censura

recessed (rē′sĕsd) *adj.* indented or hollowed-out space **recess** *v.*
retirado(a) *adj.* que está en una depresión o un espacio hueco **retirar** *v.*

recoil (rĭ-koil′) *v.* to shrink back, as in fear or disgust
recular *v.* tener horror o asco a algo

refined (rĭ-fīnd′) *adj.* having polished manners; cultured
fino(a) *adj.* cortés; culto(a)

refugee (rĕf′yŏŏ-jē′) *n.* one who leaves his or her home in search of protection or shelter elsewhere, as in times of war
refugiado *n.* una persona que, a causa de guerras u opresión, busca protección o seguridad en un país extranjero

regression (rĭ-grĕsh′ən) *n.* a return to a less developed condition
regresión *n.* un retroceso a una condición menos desarrollada

rehabilitation (rē′hə-bĭl′ĭ-tā′shən) *n.* the process of being restored to good health or useful life through training or therapy
rehabilitación *n.* el proceso de restablecer la buena salud o una vida útil a través del entrenamiento o la terapia

relay (rē′lā) *n.* a race in which each side uses several team members to complete the race; each member has a turn to finish a set part of the race and is then replaced by another team member to finish the next part, and so forth
carrera de relevos *n.* prueba deportiva en que los corredores de un mismo equipo se sustituyen sucesivamente. Cada miembro corre una parte de la carrera y luego se sustituye por otro miembro que corre la parte siguiente

remorse (rĭ-môrs′) *n.* a bitter regret or guilt after having done wrong
remordimiento *n.* pena o culpa interna que queda después de hacer algo mal

renunciation (rĭ-nŭn′sē-ā′shən) *n.* a declaration in which something is given up
abdicación *n.* ceder los derechos sobre algo

reproach (rĭ-prōch′) *v.* to criticize; to blame
reprochar *v.* criticar; echar la culpa

reserve (rĭ-zûrv′) *n.* self-restraint in the way one looks or acts
reserva *n.* discreción

resistance (rĭ-zĭs′təns) *n.* the act of fending off; an opposing force
resistencia *n.* la acción de resistir; una fuerza de oposición

retort (rĭ-tôrt′) *n.* a quick, sharp, or witty reply
réplica *n.* una respuesta rápida o aguda

retribution (rĕt′rə-byoō′shən) *n.* punishment for bad behavior
punición *n.* castigo por comportamiento malo

reverently (rĕv′ər-ənt-lē) *adv.* in a way that shows awe and respect
con reverencia *adv.* de una manera que muestra temor o respeto

reverie (rĕv′ə-rē) *n.* a daydream
ensueño *n.* una fantasía

revert (rĭ-vûrt′) *v.* to return to a former condition, belief, subject, or practice
revertir *v.* volver a un estado, una creencia, un tema o una práctica

revoke (rĭ-vōk′) *v.* to withdraw or repeal
revocar *v.* retirar o anular

S

savor (sā′vər) *v.* to take great pleasure in
gozar *v.* disfrutar

segregation (sĕg′rĭ-gā′shən) *n.* the process of separating others from a main body or group; the policy and practice of separating one race from the rest of society
segregación *n.* el proceso de separar algunas personas de otras o de un grupo principal; el sistema y la práctica de separar las personas de una raza del resto de la sociedad

semblance (sĕm′bləns) *n.* an outward appearance
semblante *n.* apariencia

sensation (sĕn-sā′shən) *n.* a state of great interest and excitement
sensación *n.* un estado de mucho interés y mucha emoción

sever (sĕv′ər) *v.* to become separated; to be cut off from the whole
romperse *v.* separarse de algo; estar apartado(a) del todo

shrew (shroō) *n.* a mean, nagging woman
regañona *n.* una mujer cruel y molesta

sidekick (sīd′kĭk′) *n.* a close friend
compañero(a) *n.* un(a) buen(a) amigo(a)

sinister (sĭn′ĭ-stər) *adj.* suggestive of evil or misfortune
siniestro(a) *adj.* que indica el mal o el infortunio

slight (slīt) *n.* an insult to one's pride or self-esteem
desaire *n.* un insulto al orgullo o al amor propio de alguien

slovenly (slŭv′ən-lē) *adj.* lazy and careless; untidy
desaliñado(a) *adj.* perezoso(a) y descuidado(a); desaseado(a)

sober (sō′bər) *v.* to make serious or solemn
moderar *v.* poner serio(a) o solemne

sovereignty (sŏv′ər-ĭn-tē) *n.* authority; rule
soberanía *n.* autoridad; dominio

specialization (spĕsh′ə-lĭ-zā′shən) *n.* a focus on a particular activity or area of study
especialización *n.* la acción de dedicarse a una cosa o un tema específico

specimen (spĕs′ə-mən) *n.* an individual that is taken to represent a group or whole
espécimen *n.* una muestra que se obtiene para representar un grupo o un todo

speculate (spĕk′yə-lāt′) *v.* to draw a conclusion without having firm evidence; guess
especular *v.* llegar a una conclusión sin tener conocimiento completo; adivinar

spirited (spĭr′ĭ-tĭd) *adj.* lively; vigorous
animado(a) *adj.* enérgico(a); vigoroso(a)

stampede (stăm-pēd′) *n.* a sudden headlong rush or flight of a crowd of people
espantada *n.* huida repentina de una multitud de personas

statistically (stə-tĭs′tĭ-klē) *adv.* in terms of the principles used to analyze numerical data
según las estadísticas *adv.* en cuanto a los métodos que se usan para analizar los datos numéricos

stealthily (stĕl′thĭ-lē) *adv.* cautiously; secretly
furtivamente *adv.* secretamente

stifled (stī′fəld) *adj.* smothered **stifle** *v.*
sofocado(a) *adj.* ahogado(a) **sofocar** *v.*

stipulated (stĭp′yə-lā′tĭd) *adj.* arranged in an agreement **stipulate** *v.*
acordado(a) *adj.* negociado(a) **acordar** *v.*

stoop (sto͞op) *n.* a small porch, platform, or staircase leading to the entrance of a building or house
pórtico *n.* un porche pequeño, una plataforma o una escalinata delante de un edificio o una casa

subordinate (sə-bôr′dn-ĭt) *adj.* less important or lower in rank; secondary
subordinado(a) *adj.* menos importante o de rango más bajo; secundario(a)

sullen (sŭl′ən) *adj.* showing silent resentment; sulky
malhumorado(a) *adj.* resentido(a); malcontento(a)

summit (sŭm′ĭt) *n.* the highest point or part; the top
cima *n.* el punto de mayor elevación; el vértice

surmount (sər-mount′) *v.* to get to the top of; climb
superar *v.* llegar a la parte de arriba; escalar

surreptitiously (sûr′əp-tĭsh′əs-lē) *adv.* in a sneaky way; secretly
subrepticiamente *adv.* solapadamente; a escondidas

surveying (sər-vā′ĭng) *adj.* looking over carefully; inspecting **survey** *v.*
examinando *v.* mirando con cuidado; inspeccionando

swoon (swo͞on) *v.* to faint
desvanecerse *v.* desmayarse

syndrome (sĭn′drōm′) *n.* a group of symptoms that characterizes a disease or psychological disorder
síndrome *n.* un grupo de síntomas que caracteriza una enfermedad o un problema psicológico

T

tackle (tăk′əl) *v.* to take on a problem or a challenge; to wrestle with an opponent
atacar *v.* asumir y hacerle frente a una dificultad o un reto; luchar con un adversario

tandem (tăn′dəm) *adj.* one behind the other
(en) tándem *adv.* uno delante del otro

tangible (tăn′jə-bəl) *adj.* able to be seen or touched; material
tangible *adj.* que se puede ver o tocar; material

tedious (tē′dē-əs) *adj.* boring; tiresome because of length, slowness, or dullness
tedioso(a) *adj.* aburrido(a); molesto(a) a causa de duración, lentitud o monotonía

teem (tēm) *v.* to be full of; to abound
abundar *v.* estar lleno(a) de algo

tentatively (tĕn′tə-tĭv-lē) *adv.* with uncertainty or hesitation
a tientas *adv.* tanteando sin certidumbre

tethered (tĕth′ərd) *adj.* tied to the ground or to another object **tether** *v.*
atado(a) *adj.* asegurado(a) a la tierra o a otro objeto **atar** *v.*

transition (trăn-zĭsh′ən) *n.* a change from one stage to another
transición *n.* el proceso de cambiar de un estado a otro

tremor (trĕm'ər) *n.* a shaking or a vibrating movement; a nervous trembling or quivering
temblor *n.* movimiento rápido e involuntario

U

unappeasable (ŭn'ə-pē'zə-bəl) *adj.* impossible to calm or satisfy
implacable *adj.* que no se puede calmar o satisfacer

V

vacuous (văk'yōō-əs) *adj.* showing a lack of intelligence or thought
vacuo(a) *adj.* caracterizado(a) por una falta de inteligencia o reflexión

vagrant (vā'grənt) *adj.* wandering from place to place; moving in a random way
andariego(a) *adj.* que va de lugar en lugar

valor (văl'ər) *n.* courage; bravery
valor *n.* coraje; valentía

varmint (vär'mĭnt) *n.* a wild animal that is considered undesirable or troublesome, such as a fox, a rabbit, or a rodent
sabandija *n.* un animal considerado indeseable o molesto, como un zorro, un conejo o un roedor

vault (vôlt) *v.* to jump or leap
saltar *v.* impulsar el cuerpo sobre algo

vehemently (vē'ə-mənt-lē) *adv.* with intense emotion
con mayor vehemencia *adv.* con más intensidad

vex (vĕks) *v.* to disturb; annoy
confundir *v.* desorientar

vile (vīl) *adj.* disgusting; hateful; unpleasant
vil *adj.* repulsivo(a); odioso(a); desagradable

vindictiveness (vĭn-dĭk'tĭv-nĭs) *n.* a desire for revenge
carácter vengativo *n.* la cualidad de ser rencoroso

vocation (vō-kā'shən) *n.* job; profession
vocación *n.* empleo; profesión

W

wallow (wŏl'ō) *v.* to roll the body about, as an elephant in water or mud; to indulge in or to take great pleasure and delight in
revolcarse *v.* voltearse por el suelo, como un elefante en el agua o el barro; darse gusto

widow (wĭd'ō) *n.* a woman whose husband has died and who has not remarried
viuda *n.* una mujer que ha perdido a su esposo y que no ha vuelto a casarse

Y

yaw (yô) *v.* to swerve off course momentarily or temporarily
desviarse *v.* perder la ruta momentáneamente o temporariament

Z

zeal (zēl) *n.* great enthusiasm; a devotion to a cause, an ideal, or a goal
celo *n.* gran entusiasmo; dedicación a un ideal o una meta

Pronunciation Key

Symbol	Examples	Symbol	Examples	Symbol	Examples
ă	at, gas	m	man, seem	v	van, save
ā	ape, day	n	night, mitten	w	web, twice
ä	father, barn	ng	sing, anger	y	yard, lawyer
âr	fair, dare	ŏ	odd, not	z	zoo, reason
b	bell, table	ō	open, road, grow	zh	treasure, garage
ch	chin, lunch	ô	awful, bought, horse	ə	awake, even, pencil, pilot, focus
d	dig, bored	oi	coin, boy		
ĕ	egg, ten	ŏŏ	look, full	ər	perform, letter
ē	evil, see, meal	ōō	root, glue, through		
f	fall, laugh, phrase	ou	out, cow		**Sounds in Foreign Words**
g	gold, big	p	pig, cap	KH	*German* ich, auch; *Scottish* loch
h	hit, inhale	r	rose, star		
hw	white, everywhere	s	sit, face	N	*French* entre, bon, fin
ĭ	inch, fit	sh	she, mash	œ	*French* feu, cœur; *German* schön
ī	idle, my, tried	t	tap, hopped		
îr	dear, here	th	thing, with	ü	*French* utile, rue; *German* grün
j	jar, gem, badge	*th*	then, other		
k	keep, cat, luck	ŭ	up, nut		
l	load, rattle	ûr	fur, earn, bird, worm		

Stress Marks

′ This mark indicates that the preceding syllable receives the primary stress. For example, in the word *language,* the first syllable is stressed: lăng′gwĭj.

′ This mark is used only in words in which more than one syllable is stressed. It indicates that the preceding syllable is stressed, but somewhat more weakly than the syllable receiving the primary stress. In the word *literature,* for example, the first syllable receives the primary stress, and the last syllable receives a weaker stress: lĭt′ər-ə-chŏŏr′.

Adapted from *The American Heritage Dictionary of the English Language, Third Edition;* Copyright © 1992 by Houghton Mifflin Company. Used with the permission of Houghton Mifflin Company.

Index of Fine Art

Index of Skills

Literary Concepts

Act, R124
Action
  falling, 18, 41, 260, 439, 671, 672, R129
  rising, 18, 41, 260, 439, 671, 672, 680, 691, R136
Aesthetic language. *See* Figurative language.
Alliteration, 189, R124. *See also* Sound devices.
Allusion, R124
Analogy, R124
Analysis, R124
Anecdote, 118, 127, 208, R124
Antagonist, 148, 157, R124
Author, R124
Author biography, 58, 68, 82, 93, 117, 129, 142, 196, 201, 210, 219, 248, 282, 295, 300, 309, 347, 362, 373, 385, 393, 402, 533, 564, 586, 591, 592, 603, 613, 633, 646, 653, 668, 678, 690, 722, 732, 755, 768, 778, 782, 789, 838, 850, 860, 874, 883, 911, 915, 924, 931, 937, 941, 950, 965
Author's perspective, 115, 200, 293, 360, 421, 426, 475, R124
Author's purpose, R125
  identifying, 118, 127, 208, 417, 779, 781
Author's style, 80, 170, 299, 428, 650, 652, 721, 809, 814, 836, 882, R138
Author studies, 144–148, 168–173, 426–431, 790–793, 814–817
Autobiography, 101, 102, 522, R125
Ballad, 188, 647, 701, 967, R125
  folk, 954
Biographer, R125
Biography, 101, 102, 756, 766, 776, R125
Byline, 635
Caption, 211
Cast of characters, R125
Cause and effect, as organizing principle, 32, 253, 262, R125
Change, 441, 568
Character, 19, 329, 331, 652, 839, 848, R125. *See also* Character *under* Reading and Critical Thinking Skills.
  analyzing, 22, 29, 41, 66, 80, 115, 157, 169, 208, 236, 280, 293, 297, 317, 345, 652, 766
  and conflict, 348, 360, 441, 488, 514, 551, 679
  development, 246, 345
  making inferences about, 220, 223, 246, 330
  motivation, 22, 29, 66
  opinions of, 317, 652
  sketches, 310, 361, 849
Characterization, 220, 246, 331, R125
Character types
  antagonist, 145, 157, R124

dynamic, 19, 334, 345, 543, R127
foil, 261
main, 19, 261, 330, 839, 848, R125
minor, 19, 261, 330, 839, R125
protagonist, 148, 157, R135
static, 19, 334, 345, R138
Chronological order, 105, 159, R126
Clarifying, R126
Classic, R126
Climax, 18, 260, 293, 671, 672, 680, R126. *See also* Falling action; Rising action.
Comedy, R126
Comparing literature texts, 80, 127, 140, 142, 195, 208, 218, 280, 293, 299, 345, 527, 568, 601, 631, 644, 652, 666, 670, 722, 753, 755, 766, 781, 802, 848, 883, 967
Comparison, 142, 218, 246, 296, 299, 372, 393, 474, 503, 521, 584, 671, 691, 802, 826, 836, R126
Complications of plot, 32, 80
Conflict, 32, 41, 80, 348, 360, 439, 441, 514, 551, 753, R127
  analyzing, 488, 514, 753
  external, 348, 360, 441, 488, 514, 551, 679, 753, R129
  internal, 348, 360, 441, 488, 514, 551, 679, 753, R131
Connecting, R127
Connecting to literature, 29, 41, 56, 66, 80, 115, 127, 140, 157, 166, 195, 200, 208, 218, 246, 293, 299, 345, 360, 372, 379, 383, 392, 415, 421, 425, 475, 488, 514, 562, 568, 584, 590, 601, 631, 644, 652, 666, 679, 691, 721, 730, 753, 776, 781, 809, 836
Connotation, 669, R127
Context clues, R127
Contrast, R127
Couplet, R127
Critical thinking, 29, 41, 56, 66, 80, 115, 127, 140, 157, 166, 169, 193, 195, 200, 208, 216, 218, 246, 280, 293, 297, 299, 345, 360, 368, 372, 415, 418, 421, 423, 425, 427, 475, 488, 514, 521, 531, 562, 568, 584, 588, 590, 601, 631, 644, 652, 666, 679, 691, 721, 730, 753, 766, 776, 802, 809, 836, 848, 858, 872, 882
Cuentos, 903. *See also* Folklore, folk tale.
Dateline, 635
Deductive order, R108, R127
Denotation, R127
Description, R127
  amusing, 811
Descriptive details, 574, 584
Dialect, R128
Dialogue, 261, 811, R128. *See also* Interview.
Directions, 571

Reading and Critical Thinking Skills

Vocabulary Skills

Grammar, Usage, and Mechanics

Writing Skills, Modes, and Formats

Sketching, 585, 692
Skits, presenting, 30
Tables. *See* Charting.
Technology
    CD-ROM, 147, 407, 793
    Internet, 57, 116, 147, 171, 201, 219, 256, 294,
        346, 407, 429, 563, 585, 632, 722, 754, 767,
        777, 793, 815, 905, R58, R114–R115
    video, 81, 171, 532, 586, 602, 668, 815, 903
Theme, charts for identifying, 56. *See also* Theme
    under Reading and Critical Thinking Skills.
Venn diagrams, 195
Video. *See* Technology.
Video reviews, 81, 171, 532, 602, 668
View and compare, 503, 512–513
Visual aids, R120–R121
Visualizing
    comparisons, 503
    setting, 59, 66, 134, 513
Web site, 131
Word webs, 69, 100, 127, 186, 202, 384, 644, 647,
    700

Assessment

Active reading strategies, for tests, 321–322, 705–706
Assessment practice
    editing, 99, 179, 257, 315, 437, 541, 619, 699,
        825, 895
    revising, 99, 179, 257, 315, 437, 541, 619, 699,
        825, 895
    vocabulary, 158, 281, 346, 416, 532, 602, 754,
        767, 849, 873
Author's purpose, in test selections, 705
Comparison and contrast, use of, 706
Comprehension, checking, 29, 41, 56, 66, 80, 115,
    127, 140, 157, 166, 195, 200, 208, 218, 246,
    293, 299, 345, 360, 372, 383, 392, 415, 421,
    425, 475, 488, 514, 531, 562, 568, 584, 590,
    601, 631, 644, 652, 666, 679, 691, 721, 730,
    753, 776, 781, 809, 836
Conclusions, drawing, 131, 133, 348, 360, 553, 556,
    562, 592, 601, R127
Context clues, using, 321, 705, R20–R21
Direction words, identifying, 324, 708
Editing, assessment practice, 99, 179, 257, 315, 437,
    541, 619, 699, 825
Editing test responses, 325, 709
Essay questions, 324, 708
Expository essays, 103
Goals, setting, 181, 317, 543, 701
Grammar, in test answers, 324, 708
Key words, identifying, 324, 708, R115

Literary analysis, 542, 700, 896
Literary elements, identifying, 322
Main ideas, looking for, 321, 707
Multiple-choice questions, answering, 99, 323, 707
Peer response, R25
Portfolio, S5, 30, 57, 94, 98, 116, 128, 174, 178,
    201, 219, 252, 256, 281, 300, 310, 314, 346,
    373, 429, 432, 436, 536, 540, 563, 585, 591,
    614, 618, 632, 645, 667, 694, 698, 731, 754,
    767, 815, 859, 873, 974
Presentation portfolio, 181, 317, 543, 701
Proofreading test responses, 325, 709
Questions, multiple-choice, 99, 323, 707
Questions, short-answer, responding in, 324, 708
Reading for assessment, 320, 704
Reflecting and assessing, 180–181, 316–317,
    542–543, 700–701, 974
Revising
    assessment practice, 99, 179, 257, 315, 437, 541,
        619, 699
Self-assessment, 180–181, 316–317, 542–543, 701,
    974
Short-answer questions, how to answer, 324, 708
Skimming test selections, 322, 706
Spelling, review, 180, 316, 700, 709, R28–R31
Standardized tests, practice for, 30, 42, 57, 67, 81,
    116, 128, 141, 158, 167, 209, 247, 361, 416,
    437, 532, 541, 619, 645, 667, 699, 777, 810,
    825, 837, 849, 895, 973
Strategies for reading test selections, 320, 704
Test selections, reading, 321–322, 705–706
Test-taking strategies, 320, 704
    essay, 324–325, 708–709
    multiple-choice, 99, 323, 707
    short-answer, 324, 708
    true-false, 981
Theme, thinking about, 542, 897
Vocabulary assessment practice, 158, 281, 346, 416,
    532, 608, 754, 767, 849, 873
Working portfolio, S5, 30, 57, 94, 98, 116, 128, 178,
    201, 219, 256, 281, 294, 300, 314, 346, 373,
    429, 540, 563, 585, 591, 632, 645, 667, 731,
    754, 767, 815, 859, 873
Writing assessment, 324, 693, 708

Index of Titles and Authors

Page numbers that appear in italics refer to biographical information.

Bernard Edelman: Excerpt from *Dear America: Letters Home from Vietnam,* edited by Bernard Edelman for the New York Vietnam Veterans Memorial Commission, published in 1985 by W. W. Norton & Company. Copyright © 1985 by the New York Vietnam Veterans Memorial Commission. Reprinted by permission of Bernard Edelman.

Scribner: "A Mother in Mannville," from *When the Whippoorwill* by Marjorie Kinnan Rawlings. Copyright © 1936, 1940 by Marjorie Kinnan Rawlings; copyright renewed © 1964, 1968 by Norton Baskin. Reprinted with the permission of Scribner, a division of Simon & Schuster.

Graywolf Press: "A Story That Could Be True," from *The Way It Is: New & Selected Poems* by William Stafford. Copyright © 1977, 1998 by the Estate of William Stafford. Reprinted by permission of Graywolf Press, Saint Paul, Minnesota.

HarperCollins: "I'm Making a List," from *Where the Sidewalk Ends* by Shel Silverstein. Copyright © 1974 by Evil Eye Music, Inc. Reprinted by permission of HarperCollins Publishers, Inc.

Excerpt from *High Tide in Tucson* by Barbara Kingsolver. Copyright © 1995 by Barbara Kingsolver. Reprinted by permission of HarperCollins Publishers, Inc.

Harcourt: "Born Worker," from *Petty Crimes* by Gary Soto. Copyright © 1998 by Gary Soto. Reproduced by permission of Harcourt, Inc.

Excerpt from "Friday, July 19th 1940" from *War Within and Without, Diaries and Letters of Anne Morrow Lindbergh 1939-1944.* Copyright © 1980 by Anne Morrow Lindbergh. Reprinted by permission of Harcourt, Inc.

Laurence Yep: "The Great Rat Hunt" by Laurence Yep, from *When I Was Your Age: Original Stories about Growing Up*, edited by Amy Ehrlich. Copyright © 1996 by Laurence Yep. Reprinted by permission of the author.

Rhoda Weyr Agency: "Flying" by Reeve Lindbergh, from *When I Was Your Age*, edited by Amy Ehrlich (Candlewick Press). Copyright © 1996 by Reeve Lindbergh. Reprinted by permission of Rhoda Weyr Agency, New York.

The Ninety-Nines: Excerpts from the archives of The Ninety-Nines, Inc. Courtesy of The Ninety-Nines, Inc.

Arte Público Press: "Mi Madre," from *Chants* by Pat Mora. Copyright © 1985 by Arte Público Press—University of Houston. By permission of Arte Público Press.

Unit Two

Alfred A. Knopf: "Mother to Son," from *Collected Poems* by Langston Hughes. Copyright © 1994 by the Estate of Langston Hughes. Reprinted by permission of Alfred A. Knopf, Inc.

Gwendolyn Brooks: "Speech to the Young / Speech to the Progress-Toward" from *Blacks* by Gwendolyn Brooks (Chicago: Third World Press). Copyright © 1991 by Gwendolyn Brooks. Reprinted by permission of The Estate of Gwendolyn Brooks.

Penguin Putnam: "Mister Misenheimer's Garden," from *On the Road with Charles Kuralt* by Charles Kuralt. Copyright © 1985 by CBS Inc. Reprinted by permission of Putnam Berkley, a division of Penguin Putnam Inc.

Gruner + Jahr USA Publishing: Excerpts from "Partners in Growing" by Rolaine Hochstein, *Parents*, July 1994. Copyright © 1994 by Gruner + Jahr USA Publishing. Reprinted by permission from *Parents* magazine.

Marian Reiner: "Simile: Ginkgo and Willow" from *A Sky Full of Poems* by Eve Merriam. Copyright © 1964, 1970, 1973 by Eve Merriam. By permission of Marian Reiner.

Naoshi Koriyama: "A Loaf of Poetry," from *Time and Space and Other Poems* by Naoshi Koriyama. Copyright © 1985 by Naoshi Koriyama. Reprinted by permission of the author.

Daniel Keyes: "Flowers for Algernon" by Daniel Keyes. Copyright © 1959, 1987 by Daniel Keyes. A book-length version of the story is published by Bantam Books and Harcourt Brace & Company Classic Edition, as well as a companion book, *Reliving "Flowers for Algernon," A Writer's Story*. Reprinted by permission of the author. All rights reserved.

Doubleday: "the lesson of the moth," from *archy and mehitabel* by Don Marquis. Copyright © 1927 by Doubleday, a division of Bantam, Doubleday, Dell Publishing Group, Inc. Used by permission of Doubleday, a division of Random House, Inc.

"Child on Top of a Greenhouse," from *The Collected Poems of Theodore Roethke,* by Theodore Roethke. Copyright © 1946 by Editorial Publications, Inc. Reprinted by permission of Doubleday, a division of Random House, Inc.

The KidLit WebSite: "Predator" by Travis Potter and "The Minstrel's Last Words" by Jacki Wilbur, from The KidLit WebSite. Used with the permission of The KidLit WebSite.

Plays, Inc.: *The Million-Pound Bank Note* by Walter Hackett, adapted from the story by Mark Twain, from *Radio Plays for Young People,* edited by Walter Hackett. Copyright © 1950 by Plays, Inc. Reprinted by permission of Plays, Inc., Publishers, 120 Boylston St., Boston, Massachusetts 02116 USA.

Harcourt: "We Alone," from *Horses Make a Landscape Look More Beautiful* by Alice Walker. Copyright © 1984 by Alice Walker. Reprinted by permission of Harcourt, Inc.

People Weekly: "Found Money," *People Weekly,* November 24, 1997. Copyright © 1997 by Time, Inc. Reprinted by permission of Time Inc.

Susan Bergholz Literary Services: Excerpt from *Something to Declare* by Julia Alvarez (Algonquin Books of Chapel Hill, 1998). Copyright © 1982, 1998 by Julia Alvarez. Reprinted by permission of Susan Bergholz Literary Services, New York. All rights reserved.

Unit Three

Miriam Altschuler Literary Agency: "The Treasure of Lemon Brown" by Walter Dean Myers, *Boys' Life,* March 1983. Copyright © 1983 by Walter Dean Myers. Reprinted by permission of Miriam Altshuler Literary Agency on behalf of Walter Dean Myers.

Harcourt: "Jazz Fantasia," from *Smoke and Steel* by Carl Sandburg. Copyright © 1920 by Harcourt Brace & Company and renewed © 1948 by Carl Sandburg. Reprinted by permission of Harcourt, Inc.

Penguin Putnam: "Rules of the Game," from *The Joy Luck Club* by Amy Tan. Copyright © 1989 by Amy Tan. Reprinted by permission of Putnam Berkley, a division of Penguin Putnam Inc.

Random House: Excerpt from *Searching for Bobby Fischer* by Fred Waitzkin. Copyright © 1988 by Fred Waitzkin. Reprinted by permission of Random House, Inc.

Excerpts from *Still Me* by Christopher Reeve. Copyright © 1998 by Cambria Productions, Inc. Reprinted by permission of Random House, Inc.

From *The Diary of Anne Frank* by Frances Goodrich and Albert Hackett. Copyright © 1954, 1956 as an unpublished work. Copyright © 1956 by Albert Hackett, Frances Goodrich, and Otto Frank. Reprinted by permission of Random House, Inc.

David Hayes: Excerpts from "The Rules of Chess," from the *Traveller Chess Sites* (http://chess.liveonthenet.com/chess/archive.html). Used by permission of David Hayes, Swiss Perfect America.

Joan Daves Agency/Writers House: "Fear" ("Miedo") by Gabriela Mistral, from *Selected Poems of Gabriela Mistral,* translated by Doris Dana. Copyright © 1971 by Doris Dana. Reprinted by arrangement with Doris Dana, c/o Joan Daves Agency as agent for the proprietor.

Julio Noboa: "Identity" by Julio Noboa. Used by permission of Julio Noboa, writer and educator.

Henry Holt & Company: "Stopping by Woods on a Snowy Evening" by Robert Frost, from *The Poetry of Robert Frost,* edited by Edward Connery Lathem. Copyright © 1951 by Robert Frost. Copyright 1923, © 1969 by Henry Holt and Company, L.L.C. Reprinted by permission of Henry Holt and Company, L.L.C.

Excerpts from introduction to *Grand Mothers* by Nikki Giovanni. Copyright © 1994 by Nikki Giovanni. Reprinted by permission of Henry Holt and Company, Inc.

Pantheon Books: "The Moustache," from *Eight Plus One* by Robert Cormier. Copyright © 1975 by Robert Cormier. Reprinted by the permission of Pantheon Books, a division of Random House, Inc.

Excerpts from *The Last Seven Months of Anne Frank* by Willy Lindwer. Copyright © 1988 by Willy Lindwer. English translation copyright © 1991 by Random House, Inc. Reprinted by permission of Pantheon Books, a division of Random House, Inc.

Liveright Publishing Corporation: "old age sticks" by E. E. Cummings, from *Complete Poems: 1904-1962,* edited by George J. Firmage. Copyright © 1958, 1986, 1991 by the Trustees for the E. E. Cummings Trust. Reprinted by

Excerpt from *All But My Life* by Gerda Weissmann Klein. Copyright © 1957 and copyright renewed 1995 by Gerda Weissmann Klein. Reprinted by permission of Farrar, Straus & Giroux, Inc.

HarperCollins Publishers: "Legacies," "the drum," "Choices," "A Journey," and "Knoxville, Tennessee," from *The Selected Poems of Nikki Giovanni* by Nikki Giovanni. Compilation copyright © 1996 by Nikki Giovanni. Reprinted by permission of HarperCollins Publishers, Inc.

Doubleday: Excerpts from *The Diary of a Young Girl, The Definitive Edition* by Anne Frank, edited by Otto H. Frank and Mirjam Pressler and translated by Susan Massotty. Translation copyright © 1995 by Doubleday, a division of Bantam Doubleday Dell Publishing Group, Inc. Used by permission of Doubleday, a division of Random House, Inc.

Gerda Weissmann Klein: "A Diary from Another World" by Gerda Weissmann Klein, *The Buffalo News,* November 12, 1978. Reprinted by permission of Gerda Weissmann Klein.

Unit Four

Doubleday: Excerpt from "Eyes Do More Than See," from *The Complete Stories, Volume 1,* by Isaac Asimov. Copyright © 1965 by Mercury Press, Inc. Reprinted by permission of Doubleday Books, a division of Random House, Inc.

"Rain, Rain Go Away" from *Buy Jupiter and Other Stories* by Isaac Asimov. Copyright © 1975 by Isaac Asimov. Reprinted by permission of Doubleday, a division of Random House, Inc.

Bill Berger Associates: "The Dinner Party" by Mona Gardner, from *The Saturday Review.* Copyright © 1942, renewed © 1970 by *The Saturday Review.* Reprinted by permission of Bill Berger Associates, Inc.

Alfred A. Knopf: "The Enormous Crocodile," from *Revolting Recipes* by Roald Dahl. Text copyright © 1978 by Roald Dahl. Illustrative copyright © 1978 by Quentin Blake. Reprinted by the permission of Alfred A. Knopf, Inc.

Harold Matson Company: "A Running Brook of Horror" (originally titled "Woman Without Fear") by Daniel P. Mannix. Copyright © 1963 by Daniel P. Mannix. Reprinted by permission of Harold Matson Co., Inc.

May Swenson Literary Estate: "Southbound on the Freeway" by May Swenson. Copyright © 1963 by May Swenson and renewed © 1982. First appeared in *The New Yorker*, February 16, 1963. Reprinted by permission of the Literary Estate of May Swenson.

Liveright Publishing Corporation: "who knows if the moon's" by E. E. Cummings from *Complete Poems: 1904-1962*, edited by George J. Firmage. Copyright © 1923, 1925, 1951, 1953, © 1991 by the Trustees for the E. E. Cummings Trust. Copyright © 1976 by George James Firmage. Reprinted by permission of Liveright Publishing Corporation.

Viking Penguin: "The Choice," from *The Portable Dorothy Parker* by Dorothy Parker. Copyright © 1926, copyright renewed 1954 by Dorothy Parker. Used by permission of Viking Penguin, a division of Penguin Putnam Inc.

Dell Publishing: "Future Tense" by Robert Lipsyte, from *Sixteen Short Stories by Outstanding Writers for Young Adults*, edited by Donald R. Gallo. Copyright © 1984 by Robert Lipsyte. Reprinted by permission of Dell Publishing, a division of Random House, Inc.

The Washington Times: "Birthday Ritual a Grave Tradition: New Figure Brings Tribute to Poe" by Ronald J. Hansen, *The Washington Times,* February 1, 1998. Reprinted by permission of The Washington Times.

Henry Morrison, Inc.: Excerpts from "Man-Made Monsters," from *A Natural History of Unnatural Things* by Daniel Cohen. Copyright © 1971 by Daniel Cohen. Reprinted here by permission of the author and Henry Morrison, Inc., his agents.

Elizabeth Barnett, Literary Executor: "The Ballad of the Harp-Weaver" by Edna St. Vincent Millay, from *Collected Poems* (HarperCollins). Copyright © 1923, 1951 by Edna St. Vincent Millay and Norma Millay Ellis. Used by permission of Elizabeth Barnett, literary executor. All rights reserved.

William Morris Agency: "The Hitchhiker" by Lucille Fletcher, from *Radio's Best Plays*. Copyright © 1947 by Lucille Fletcher. Reprinted by permission of the William Morris Agency, Inc., on behalf of the author.

Random House: "Mourning Grace," from *Just Give Me a Cool Drink of Water 'Fore I Die* by Maya Angelou. Copyright © 1971 by Maya Angelou. Reprinted by permission of Random House, Inc.

Brandt & Brandt Literary Agents: "The Third Wish" from *Not What You Expected: A Collection of Short Stories* by Joan Aiken. Copyright © 1974 by Joan Aiken. Reprinted by permission of Brandt & Brandt Literary Agents, Inc.

Unit Five

Simon & Schuster: Excerpts from *Undaunted Courage* by Stephen E. Ambrose. Copyright © 1996 by Ambrose-Tubbs, Inc. Reprinted by permission of Simon & Schuster, Inc.

Dutton Children's Books: "The Flower-Fed Buffaloes," from *Going to the Stars* by Vachel Lindsay. Copyright © 1926 by D. Appleton & Co., renewed 1954 by Elizabeth C. Lindsay. A Hawthorn book. Reprinted by permission of Dutton Children's Books, a division of Penguin Putnam Inc.

Dennis Coello: "Bike an Historic Trail" by Dennis Coello, *Boys' Life*, July 1986. Reprinted by permission of Dennis Coello and *Boys' Life*, a publication of the Boy Scouts of America.

Bantam Books: "War Party," from *War Party* by Louis L'Amour. Copyright © 1959 by The Curtis Publishing Company. Reprinted by permission of Bantam Books, a division of Random House, Inc.

The LULAC National: "The Other Pioneers" by Roberto Félix Salazar, *The LULAC National,* July 1939. Copyright © 1939 by The LULAC National. Reprinted by permission of The LULAC National.

Russell & Volkening: Excerpt from *Harriet Tubman: Conductor on the Underground Railroad* by Ann Petry. Copyright © 1955 by Ann Petry, renewed © 1983 by Ann Petry. Reprinted by permission of Russell & Volkening, Inc. as agents for the author.

Clarion Books/Houghton Mifflin Company: "Who Is Dead in the White House?" from *Lincoln: A Photobiography* by Russell Freedman. Copyright © 1987 by Russell Freedman. Reprinted by permission of Clarion Books/Houghton Mifflin Co. All rights reserved.

Jewell Parker Rhodes: "Block Party" by Jewell Parker Rhodes. Copyright © 1993 by Jewell Parker Rhodes. Reprinted by permission of the author.

Aram Saroyan: "The Summer of the Beautiful White Horse," from *My Name Is Aram* by William Saroyan. Copyright © 1938 and renewed © 1966 by William Saroyan. Reprinted by permission of Aram Saroyan.

Susan Bergholz Literary Services: Excerpt from *The Anaya Reader* published as "The Magic of Words" by Rudolfo Anaya. Copyright © 1995 by Rudolfo Anaya. First published as "In Commemoration: One Million Volumes" in *A Million Stars: Millionth Acquisition for the University of New Mexico General Library,* edited by Connie Capers Thorsen (University of New Mexico Press, 1982). Reprinted by permission of Susan Bergholz Literary Services, New York. All rights reserved.

Simon & Schuster: Excerpt from *Wait Till Next Year* by Doris Kearns Goodwin. Copyright © 1997 by Blithedale Productions, Inc. Reprinted by permission of Simon & Schuster, Inc.

Rosenfeld, Meyer & Susman: "Who's on First?" used with the permission of Rosenfeld, Meyer & Susman, L.L.P.

Viking Penguin: "Edward Corsi, Italy" by Edward Corsi, "Lazarus Salamon, Hungary" by Lazarus Salamon and "Birgitta Hedman Fichter, Sweden" by Birgitta Hedman Fichter from *I Was Dreaming to Come to America*, edited by Veronica Lawlor. Copyright © 1995 by Veronica Lawlor. Reprinted by permission of Viking Penguin, a division of Penguin Putnam Inc.

The Richmond Organization: "This Land Is Your Land" by Woody Guthrie. Reprinted by permission of The Richmond Organization.

Unit Six

Viking Penguin: "Paul Bunyan and Babe, the Blue Ox," adapted from *American Tall Tales* by Adrien Stoutenburg. Copyright © 1968 by Adrien Stoutenburg. Reprinted by permission of Viking Penguin, an imprint of Penguin Putnam Books for Younger Readers, a division of Penguin Putnam Inc.

Judith Ortiz Cofer: "Aunty Misery" by Judith Ortiz Cofer. Reprinted by permission of the author.

Staniels Associates/BridgeWater Books: "Racing the Great Bear," from *Flying with the Eagle, Racing the Great Bear: Stories from Native North America* by Joseph Bruchac. Copyright © 1993 by Joseph Bruchac. Reprinted with permission of Staniels Associates as agent for BridgeWater Books, an imprint of Troll Communications, L.L.C.

Philomel Books: "Otoonah," from *Cut from the Same Cloth* by Robert D. San Souci. Copyright © 1993 by Robert D. San Souci. Used by permission of Philomel Books, a division of Penguin Putnam Inc.

Gayle Ross: "Strawberries" retold by Gayle Ross, from *Homespun: Tales from America's Favorite Storytellers*, edited by Jimmy Neil Smith. Copyright © 1988 by Jimmy Neil Smith. Reprinted by permission of Gayle Ross.

Guadalupe Baca Vaughn: "The Souls in Purgatory" by Guadalupe Baca-Vaughn, from *Voces: An Anthology of Nuevo Mexicano Writers*, edited by Rudolfo A. Anaya. Reprinted by permission of Guadalupe Baca-Vaughn.

Alfred A. Knopf: "The Woman in the Snow," from *The Dark Thirty: Southern Tales of the Supernatural* by Patricia McKissack. Copyright © 1992 by Patricia McKissack. Reprinted by permission of Alfred A. Knopf, Inc.

"Pecos Bill," from *American Tall Tales* by Mary Pope Osborne. Text copyright © 1991 by Mary Pope Osborne. Reprinted by permission of Alfred A. Knopf, Inc.

Globe Fearon: "The Girl in the Lavender Dress," retold by Maureen Scott, from *The American Anthology*. Copyright © 1987. Reprinted by permission of Globe Fearon, a division of Pearson Education.

The editors have made every effort to trace the ownership of all copyrighted material found in this book and to make full acknowledgment for its use. Omissions brought to our attention will be corrected in a subsequent edition.

Art Credits

Cover

Illustration copyright © 1999 Gary Overacre.

Front Matter

ix School Division, Houghton Mifflin Company; **x** *Looking Deep* (1996), Terry Pappas. Pastel, 19½" × 20½". Collection Steven Pappas; **xi** Jack London Research Center; **xii** *To Sail The Blue Boat II.* Copyright © Gina Gilmour/Omni-Photo Communications; **xiv** *Second Circle Dance.* Copyright © Phoebe Beasley/Omni-Photo Communications; **xv** Barron Claiborne; **xvi** *Dos Toose,* James Michalopoulos; **xviii** *America II,* Diana Ong/SuperStock; **xix** The Granger Collection, New York; **xx** Map by John Sandford; Photo by Gordon Lewis; **xxi** Gordon Lewis; **S2–S4** Photo by Sharon Hoogstraten; **S12** Copyright © Lowell Georgia/Corbis; **S13** *background* Photo by Sharon Hoogstraten; **S13** The Granger Collection, New York; **S14** Copyright © Lowell Georgia/Corbis; **S15** Copyright © Michael Lewis/Corbis; **S16–S17** *background* Photo by Sharon Hoogstraten; **S16** Copyright © Dave Bartruff/Corbis; **S17** *top left* Copyright © James L. Amos/Corbis; *bottom right* Utah State Historical Society; **S18** *top* The Granger Collection, New York; *bottom* The Granger Collection, New York; **S19** The National Archives; **S26** Copyright © Bob Conge; **S27** Detail of painting copyright © David Shannon.

Unit One

14–15 *background* Copyright © PhotoDisc, Inc; **17** School Division, Houghton Mifflin Company; **19** *center* Copyright © Natalie Ascencios; *top right* Copyright © Hodges Soileau; *bottom right* Portrait by George Passantino, from *Portraits in Oil.* Copyright © 1980 Wendon Blake; **20** Copyright © Tim Barnwell/Stock Boston; **21** RMIP/Richard Haynes; **23** *top left* Detail of painting copyright © Hodges Soileau; *top right* Detail of portrait by George Passantino, from *Portraits in Oil.* Copyright © 1980 Wendon Blake; **28** *top left* Detail of painting copyright © Hodges Soileau; *top right* Detail of portrait by George Passantino, from *Portraits in Oil.* Copyright © 1980 Wendon Blake; **31** Margaret Miller; **33, 35, 36, 38** Copyright © M. Yamazaki/Photonica; **43** Photographs and Prints Division. The Schomburg Center for Research in Black Culture, The New York Public Library, Astor, Lenox and Tilden Foundations; **44** Copyright © Brooks Freehill; **46** Copyright © 1992 Michael Krasowitz/FPG International; **47** Copyright © Brooks Freehill; **48** *clockwise from top* Liaison Agency/Hulton Getty; D.C. Heath Photo Archive; Nik Wheeler/Corbis; Swanston Publishing Company, U.K.; UPI/Bettmann; **58** Courtesy of Flannery Literary; **68** AP/Wide World Photos; **70** Copyright © Natalie Ascencios; **79** Copyright © Shel Silverstein; **81** From *The Ransom of Red Chief,* provided by Coronet/MTI Films, St. Louis, Missouri; **82** Stock Montage; **100** Jack London Research Center; **101, 102** *top* School Division, Houghton Mifflin Company; **102** *bottom* From *Something to Declare* by Julia Alvarez. Copyright © 1998 by the author. Reprinted by permission of Algonquin Books of Chapel Hill, a division of Workman Publishing; **104** Corbis-Bettmann; **105** RMIP/Richard Haynes; **107** *center, The Seto Kids.* Oil on canvas. Copyright © Pamela Chin Lee/Omni-Photo Communications; *inset, House Mouse,* Leonard Baskin. Courtesy of R. Michelson Galleries, Northampton, Massachusetts; **111** Portrait by Roland Jarvis, from *Practical Drawing and Sketching.* Copyright © Ebury Press, U.K.; **113** *House Mouse,* Leonard Baskin. Courtesy of R. Michelson Galleries, Northampton, Massachusetts; **116** Courtesy of Sagamore Hill National Historic Site, National Park Service; **117** Photo by K. Yep; **118** Corbis-Bettmann; **119** Corbis/PEMCO–Webster & Stevens Collection, Museum of History & Industry, Seattle, Washington; *inset* Courtesy of Reeve Lindbergh/The Rhoda Weyr

Literary Agency; **120** Courtesy Roy Molyneux; **122** Courtesy Robert Hollenbaugh/Archives of The Aeronca Aircraft Corporation, Middletown, Ohio; **125** Lindbergh Picture Collection, Manuscripts and Archives, Yale University Library; **128** School Division, Houghton Mifflin Company; **129** Copyright © Lizzy Brown. Courtesy of Reeve Lindbergh; **130** *background* School Division, Houghton Mifflin Company; *foreground* From the Archives of The Ninety-Nines, Inc.; **133** School Division, Houghton Mifflin Company; **134** *background* DLF Group; *bottom left* Copyright © Tom Bean/PNI; *top right* © Christopher Arnesen/PNI; *bottom right* Copyright © Jean-Claude Carton/PNI; **141** Copyright © Randy Wells/Tony Stone Images; **142** Copyright © Susan Pearce; **144–147** *top background* RMIP/Richard Haynes; **144** *top* Jack London Research Center; *left* Henry E. Huntington Library; *bottom middle* Science Museum/Science & Society Picture Library; *bottom right* Henry E. Huntington Picture Library; **145** *top right* MSCUA, University of Washington Libraries, photo by LaRoche, negative no. 2033; *bottom, left to right* J. C. Carton/Bruce Coleman, Inc.; Corbis-Bettmann; Brown Brothers; Henry E. Huntington Library; **146–147** *bottom background* MSCUA, University of Washington Libraries, photo by Goetzman, negative no. 62; **146** *left* School Division, Houghton Mifflin Company; *right* MSCUA, University of Washington Libraries, photo by UW, negative no. 7741; **147** *top* J. C. Carton/Bruce Coleman, Inc.; *bottom* MSCUA, University of Washington Libraries, photo by Hegg, negative no. 2267; **149** Copyright © Gustav H. Lamprecht, Fairbanks, Alaska; **152** Copyright © Wayne R. Bilenduke/Tony Stone Images; **154** Copyright © Vinitzki/Sipa Press; **156** Special Collections Division, University of Washington Library; **160** *top, bottom* Corbis-Bettmann; **161** California Historical Society, Morton-Waters Co., FN#12377; **162** Corbis-Bettmann; **164** detail Courtesy of Morton-Waters Co.; **165, 168** Corbis-Bettmann; **170** Jack London Research Center; **171** *top* From *Call of The Wild*, provided by Coronet/MTI Films, St. Louis, Missouri; *bottom* Courtesy of I. Milo Shepard, Trustee - Trust of Irving Shepard; **172–173** *background* MSCUA, University of Washington Libraries, photo by Goetzman, negative no. 62; **172** *top* Corbis-Bettmann; **172** *bottom*, **173** School Division, Houghton Mifflin Company; **180–183** *background* Copyright © PhotoDisc; **182, 183** School Division, Houghton Mifflin Company.

Unit Two

184, 186 *background* Copyright © 1999 Graeme Gillies/Picture Perfect; **187** School Division, Houghton Mifflin Company; *Robert Frost Among His Poems; A Literary Companion to the Poet's Biographical Contexts and Associations* © 1996 Jeffrey S. Cramer by permission of McFarland & Company, Inc., Publishers, Box 611, Jefferson, North Carolina 28640. www.mcfarlandpub.com. Orders: 800-253-2187 **188** *left, Ginkgo* (1988), Atsuko Kato. Oil on canvas, 100 cm × 70 cm. Courtesy of the artist; *right, Stars, Provincetown* (1920), Charles Demuth. Gouach and pencil on cardboard, 23½" × 109½" (59.7 cm × 49.5 cm). The Museum of Modern Art, New York. Gift of Abby Aldrich Rockefeller. Photograph copyright © 1995 The Museum of Modern Art, New York; **191** RMIP/Richard Haynes; **192** School Division, Houghton Mifflin Company; **196** *left* The Granger Collection, New York; *right* AP/Wide World Photos; **201** Stock Montage; **202** CBS Photo Archive; **203** *bottom* Copyright © William Johnson/Stock Boston/PNI; **204, 205, 206** From *The Best of On the Road* with Charles Kuralt: A production of CBS News, a division of CBS Inc., in association with Bellon Enterprises, Ltd. Copyright © 1989 CBS Inc.; **207** *The Gardener* [Le jardinier] (1882–1882), Georges Pierre Seurat. Oil on wood, 6¼" × 9¾". The Metropolitan Museum of Art, bequest of Miss Adelaide Milton de Groot (1876–1967), 1967 (67.187.102). Photograph by Malcolm Varon copyright © 1985 The Metropolitan Museum of Art; **209** Myrleen Ferguson/PhotoEdit; **210** Copyright © Gregory Pace/Sygma; **211, 212, 214** Copyright © Jenny Acheson/Parents Magazine; **215** Copyright © John D. Cunningham/Visuals Unlimited; **219** *top* Copyright © 1997 FoodPix; *left*

New York; 395 Illustration by Susi Kilgore; 402 Copyright © Richard Howard Photography; 404–407 *background* School Division, Houghton Mifflin Company; 404 *top* Barron Claiborne; *center* Courtesy of Yolande Giovanni; *bottom, left to right* Courtesy of Yolande Giovanni; UPI/Corbis-Bettmann; 405 *top* St. Clairbourne; *bottom, left to right* UPI/Corbis-Bettmann; From *Grand Mothers* by Nikki Giovanni. Copyright © 1994 Nikki Giovanni. Reprinted by permission of Henry Holt & Company, Inc.; 406–407 *background* Copyright © 1991 David Carmack/Stock Boston; 406 *top* Courtesy of Monroe Frederick; *bottom* Courtesy of Nikki Giovanni; 407 RMIP/Richard Haynes; 409, 410, 411, 413, 414 *background* Courtesy of Elena Irish Zimmerman; *inset* Courtesy of Nikki Giovanni; 410 School Division, Houghton Mifflin Company; 411 Culver Pictures; 412 School Division, Houghton Mifflin Company; 413 Courtesy of Nikki Giovanni; 414 *top* Courtesy of Nikki Giovanni; *bottom* School Division, Houghton Mifflin Company; 426–427 *background* Frank Driggs/Archive Photos; 427 *center* Archive Photos; *right* From the cover of *Black Feeling, Black Talk* by Nikki Giovanni. Copyright © 1968 by Nikki Giovanni. Reprinted by permission of William Morrow and Company Inc.; 428–431 *top background* School Division, Houghton Mifflin Company; 428 Barrow Claiborne; 429 RMIP/Richard Haynes; 430–431 *background* Copyright © 1991 David Carmack/Stock Boston; 430 *left* Copyright © Renee Lynn/Tony Stone Images; *right* Copyright © Steve Azzara/Liaison Agency; 431 *left to right* From *Vacation Time* by Nikki Giovanni. Copyright © 1980 Nikki Giovanni. Reprinted by permission of The William Morrow Company, Inc.; From the cover from *Grand Mothers* by Nikki Giovanni. Copyright © 1994 by Nikki Giovanni. Reprinted by permission of Henry Holt & Company, LLC; From the cover of *The Selected Poems of Nikki Giovanni*. Copyright © Compilation 1996 by Nikki Giovanni. Reprinted by permission of The William Morrow Company, Inc.; 438 *background* Copyright © PhotoDisc; 440, 441 Joan Marcus; 442 *Portrait of Henri Matisse* (1905), André Derain. Tate Gallery, London/Art Resource, New York. Copyright © 1996 Artists Rights Society (ARS), New York/ADAGP, Paris; 443 RMIP/Richard Haynes; 444 Copyright © AFF/AFS Amsterdam, the Netherlands; 445 Copyright © AFF/AFS Amsterdam, the Netherlands; 446 *top left* Corbis-Bettmann; *top right* Copyright © AFF/AFS, Amsterdam, the Netherlands; *bottom, left to right* Corbis-Bettmann; Corbis-Bettmann; Copyright © AFF/AFS, Amsterdam, the Netherlands; Copyright © AFF/AFS, Amsterdam, the Netherlands; 447 Corbis/Hulton-Deutsch Collection; 448–449, 450, 456, 460, 467, 472, 479, 483, 490, 496 Copyright © Joan Marcus; 503 *clockwise from top left* Copyright © AFF/AFS, Amsterdam, the Netherlands; PhotoFest; PhotoFest; Copyright © Joan Marcus; 509 Copyright © Joan Marcus; 512 *top, center* Copyright © AFF/AFS, Amsterdam, the Netherlands; *bottom* Copyright © Wubbo de Jong, AFF/AFS Amsterdam; 513 *center* Joan Marcus; *top right* Copyright © AFF/AFS, Amsterdam, the Netherlands; *bottom left, bottom right* Copyright © Wubbo de Jong, AFF/AFS, Amsterdam; 515 Michael St. Maur Sheil/Corbis; 516 Copyright © AFF/AFS, Amsterdam, the Netherlands; 517, 518, 519, 520, 521 Copyright © Will Wheeler; 523 Courtesy of Gerda Weissmann Klein/HBO; 524–525 Collection of The Jewish Museum in Prague (Czech Republic)/The United States Holocaust Memorial Museum; 526 Arnold Kramer, courtesy of USHMM Photo Archives; 527 Copyright © Scott Wachter/HBO; 529, 530 Copyright © AFF/AFS, Amsterdam, the Netherlands; 533 AP/WideWorld Photos; 542–545 *background* Copyright © PhotoDisc; 544, 545 School Division, Houghton Mifflin Company.

Unit Four

549 Copyright © Jim Thiesen; 551 Copyright © 1996 FPG International; 552 *Untitled*, Ignacio Villegas. Kactus Foto/Santiago, Chile/SuperStock; 553 RMIP/Richard Haynes; 555 *foreground* Copyright © PhotoDisc; 555 Copyright © Stephen Webster/Photonica; 557 Copyright © Marc Tauss/Photonica; 559

Copyright © P. Degginger/H. Armstrong Roberts; **561** Copyright © Patrick McDonogh/Photonica; **564** AP/Wide World Photos; **565** Robert Voights; **571–573** Illustrations by Quentin Blake from *Revolting Recipes* by Roald Dahl published by Jonathan Cape. Used by permission of The Random House Group Limited; **574** *left* Copyright © Tim Davis/Tony Stone Images; *top right* Michael & Patricia Fogden/Corbis; *center right* Copyright © Andy Sacks/Tony Stone Images; *bottom right* Copyright © PhotoDisc; **575** From *Life* Magazine, March 1946. Photo by Bob Ettinger; **576–577, 579** Copyright © D. Lyons/Photo Researchers, Inc; **580** Courtesy of Oleg Volk/www.olegvolk.net; **581** Daniel Mannix; **582** Copyright © Gerard Lacz/Animals Animals; **586** Courtesy of the Harold Matson Company, Inc.; **591** *left* AP/Wide World Photos; *right* By permission of the Houghton Library, Harvard University; **592** Copyright © PhotoDisc; **602** From *The Lady or The Tiger,* provided by MTI/Coronet Films, St. Louis, Missouri; **605** *Untitled,* Ignacio Villegas. Kactus Foto/Santiago, Chile/SuperStock; **606** Copyright © Benelux Press/H. Armstrong Roberts; **611** Copyright © 1996 FPG International; **612** Copyright © American Stock/Archive Photos; **621** *Edvard and His Mother* (ca. 1885–1889), Edvard Munch. Pencil and ink. Munch Museum, Oslo, Norway. Photo copyright © 1999 Munch Museum (Svein Anderson/Sidsel de Jong). Copyright © 2002 The Munch Museum/The Munch-Ellingsen Group/Artists Rights Society (ARS), New York; **623** RMIP/Richard Haynes; **624** SuperStock; **625** Detail copyright © John Thompson; **632** Copyright © John Thompson; **633** Library of Congress; **634, 635, 636** Copyright © Bill Ballenberg; **646** Courtesy of Daniel Cohen; **653** The Bettmann Archive; **654** *background* Kansas State Historical Society, Topeka, Kansas/D.C. Heath Archive; *left* Corbis-Bettmann; *center right* Archive Photos; *bottom right* Corbis/Hulton-Deutsch Collection; **655, 656–657** *background* Meighan Depke; **665** Copyright © 1994 Jake Wyman/Photonica; **667** Detail of *Hilco* (1989), Kit Boyce. Courtesy of the artist; **668** By permission of The Vassar College Library; **670** *right, Lilacs* (1924–1927), Charles Burchfield. Oil on board. Delaware Art Museum, bequest of John Saxon; *left* Wallpaper design for "Swan Rush and Iris," Walter Crane (1845–1915). Victoria and Albert Museum, London/Bridgeman Art Library, London/New York; **671** RMIP/Richard Haynes; **674** *Liv's Daughters,* Frederick Samuel Beaumont. Simon Carter Gallery, Woodbridge, Suffolk, U.K./Bridgeman Art Library, London/New York; **677** Detail of wallpaper design for "Swan Rush and Iris," Walter Crane (1845–1915). Victoria and Albert Museum, London/Bridgeman Art Library, London/New York; **690** The Granger Collection, New York; **692** *bottom* RMIP/Richard Haynes; *top* From *The Monkey's Paw,* provided by Coronet/MTI Films, St. Louis, Missouri; **700** *Dos Toose,* James Michalopoulos; **702, 703** School Division, Houghton Mifflin Company.

Unit Five

710–712 *background* Copyright © PhotoDisc; **712** The Granger Collection, New York; **713** *Midnight Ride of Paul Revere* (1931), Grant Wood. Oil on composition board, 30" × 40". The Metropolitan Museum of Art, Arthur Hoppock Hearn Fund, 1950 (50.117). Copyright © 1996 Estate of Grant Wood/Licensed by VAGA, New York. Photo copyright © 1988 The Metropolitan Museum of Art; **715** RMIP/Richard Haynes; **722** *top, Midnight Ride of Paul Revere* (1931), Grant Wood. Oil on composition board, 30" × 40". The Metropolitan Museum of Art, Arthur Hoppock Hearn Fund, 1950 (50.117). Copyright © 1996 Estate of Grant Wood/Licensed by VAGA, New York. Photo copyright © 1988 The Metropolitan Museum of Art; `*bottom* Stock Montage; **726, 727** Copyright © PhotoDisc; **728** National Museum of American History, Smithsonian Institution, Washington, D.C; **732** Courtesy of The Eisenhower Center, New Orleans, Louisiana; **733** *center* Copyright © 1994 North Wind Pictures; *clockwise from top left* Horticultural Photography™; Copyright © 1998 N. Carter/North Wind Pictures; A. Morris/Academy of Natural Sciences, Philadelphia. Copyright © VIREO; Copyright © 1999 N.

Carter/North Wind Pictures; **734** Copyright © 1998 North Wind Pictures; *inset* Copyright © 1999 North Wind Pictures; **736** Copyright © 1999 Gary Brettnacher/Tony Stone Images; *inset* Copyright © 1996 North Wind Pictures; **755** AP/Wide World Photos; **756** The Granger Collection, New York; **757, 759, 761–762, 764** *background* Copyright © PhotoDisc; **770** *Abraham Lincoln,* Mathew B. Brady. Courtesy of the Illinois State Historical Library; **772** *Booth in Theater.* Engraving. Courtesy of the Illinois State Historical Library; **775** *Abraham Lincoln lying in state.* Courtesy of the Illinois State Historical Library; **778** Copyright © Chicago Tribune Company. All rights reserved. Used with permission; **782** Museum of The City of New York; **784** Photograph courtesy of The Louisa May Alcott Memorial Association; **785, 787** *top,* **789** Corbis-Bettmann; **790–794** *border* Steve Solum/Bruce Coleman, Inc.; **790** *center* The Granger Collection, New York; bottom Corbis-Bettmann; **791** *center right* Courtesy of The Mark Twain House, Hartford, Connecticut; *bottom left* The Granger Collection, New York; *bottom right* Lauros-Giraudon/Art Resource, New York; **792–793** *bottom background* C. C. Lockwood/Bruce Coleman, Inc.; **792** *left* Mark Twain Papers; *right* Courtesy of The Mark Twain House, Hartford, Connecticut; **793** *top* Corbis-Bettmann; *bottom* The Granger Collection, New York; **795** *top* North Wind Pictures; **795** *bottom,* **796–798, 800–801** From *Roughing It* by Mark Twain. Published by The American Publishing Company, 1872; **802–804** *border* Steve Solum/Bruce Coleman, Inc.; **805–808** *background* Copyright © PhotoDisc; **807, 808** Byron Gin; **809–810** *border* Steve Solum/Bruce Coleman, Inc.; **812–813** Chris Costello; **814–817** *border* Steve Solum/Bruce Coleman, Inc.; **814** The Granger Collection, New York; **815** *top* From *Mark Twain Gives an Interview.* Provided by Coronet/MTI Films, St. Louis, Missouri; *bottom* RMIP/Richard Haynes; **816–817** *bottom background* C. C. Lockwood/Bruce Coleman, Inc.; **816** top Archive Photos; *left* From *The Celebrated Jumping Frog of Calaveras County* by Mark Twain, Shelley Fisher Fishkin, ed. Copyright © 1996 by Oxford University Press, Inc. Reproduced with permission; *right* From *The Adventures of Tom Sawyer* by Mark Twain. Copyright. Used by permission of Bantam Books, a division of Random House, Inc.; **817** *left to right* From *The Prince and the Pauper* by Mark Twain. Used by permission of Penguin Putnam; From *Life on the Mississippi* by Mark Twain. Copyright © 1990. Used by permission of Bantam Books, a division of Random House, Inc.; From the cover of *The Adventures of Huckleberry Finn.* Used by permission of Barnes & Noble, Inc.; From the cover of *A Connecticut Yankee in King Arthur's Court.* Used by permission of Barnes & Noble, Inc.; **827** Copyright © John Thompson; **829** RMIP/Richard Haynes; **831** *top right, center* Charles Harris/Corbis, *Pittsburgh Courier;* **831** *bottom,* **832** Ted Streshinsky/Corbis; **833, 835** Charles Harris/Corbis, *Pittsburgh Courier;* **838** Susan Rae Lakin; **839** Robert Voights; **850** National Archives; **859** *Two Books of Astronomy* (1996). Copyright © Abelardo Morell. Courtesy of Bonni Benrubi Gallery, New York; **861** Courtesy of Kit Young; **862** Lake County Museum/Corbis; **864** Copyright © PhotoDisc; **866–867** Corbis-Bettmann; **868** James Marshall/Corbis; **869** Copyright © New York Daily News, L. P. reprinted-reproduced with permission; **874** Copyright © Sam Jones/Corbis Outline; **875** SuperStock; **876** *clockwise from top left* Corbis-Bettmann; Copyright © J. R. Eyerman/TimePix; SuperStock; School Division, Houghton Mifflin Company; School Division, Houghton Mifflin Company; **877** *clockwise from top left* Corbis-Bettmann; Cornell Capa/ TimePix; Corbis-Bettmann; Copyright © CBS Photo Archive; Copyright © PhotoDisc; **883** Fisk University; **885** Courtesy of the Ellis Island Immigration Museum; **886–887** *background* Corbis-Bettmann; **886** *top* Photography by Karen Yamauchi for Chermayeff & Geismar Inc./MetaForm Inc., New York; **887** *top* David Lees/Corbis; **888** Corbis/Ansel Adams Publishing Rights Trust; **889** Corbis-Bettmann; **896–899** Copyright © PhotoDisc; **898, 899** School Division, Houghton Mifflin Company.

Unit Six

900–901 *background map* John Sandford; 901–902 Gordon Lewis, 903 Richard Waldrep; 904–907 *background map* John Sandford; 904 *top to bottom, Victory of Samothrace,* Musée du Louvre, Paris. Giraudon/Art Resource, New York; Copyright © Rick Gomez/The Stock Market; *Moccasins* (1830), unknown Iroqouis craftsworker. Buckskin, wool, cotton, glass beads. The Detroit Institute of Arts, Founders Society Purchase with funds from Flint Ink Corporation (1988.32). Photo by Dick Bakker. Photo copyright © 1995 The Detroit Institute of Arts; 905 *left, top to bottom* Panopticon/D. C. Heath Photo Archive; Copyright © 1994 Michael Keller/The Stock Market; United Press International/D. C. Heath Photo Archive; Copyright © Pascal Quittemelle/Stock Boston; *right, top to bottom,* Wood engraving by Michael McCurdy from *American Tall Tales; Bronco Buster,* Frederic Remington. The Bettmann Archive; Art Resource, New York; 906 Detail of Twilight (1971), Hubert Shuptrine. Copyright © 1971, 1994 Hubert Shuptrine. All rights reserved; 908 *Girl in a Poppy Field* (1891), Dora Hitz. Museum der Bildenden Kunste, Leipzig; 909 Photodisc; 910 Charles Neal/Superstock; 912 Copyright © 1995 PhotoDisc; 915 Courtesy of Arte Público Press; 916–917 *background map* John Sandford; 916 *Proud Hunter* (1987), Pudlo Pudlat. Stonecut, 21½" × 24". By permission of the Amway Environmental Foundation; 917, 918 From *The Spirit of Native America* by Anna Lee Walters. Copyright © 1989, published by Chronicle Books; 923 Kit Fox Society bow-lance, No Two Horns (Hunkpapa). State Historical Society of North Dakota (SHSND 10491); 924 Copyright © Layle Silbert; 931 *top* Courtesy of Penguin Putnam, Inc; *bottom* Detail of *Walrus Hunt* (1986), Lucassie Tukaluk. Stonecut, 14½" × 18". By permission of the Amway Environmental Foundation; 932–933 *background map* John Sandford; 932 Detail of *En busqueda de la paz* [In search of peace], Alfredo Linares; 934–937 Wood engravings by Michael McCurdy from *American Tall Tales;* 941 Courtesy of Ramona R. Nevares and Guadalupe Baca-Vaughn; 942–943 *background map* John Sandford; 942 Illustration copyright © 1992 Brian Pinckney. From *The Dark-Thirty* by Patricia McKissack. Reprinted by permission of Alfred A. Knopf, Inc; 943 Copyright © Andrea Brooks; 950 Courtesy of Patricia McKissack; 951–953 Photos by Sharon Hoogstraten; 954–955 *background map* John Sandford; 954 Detail of *His Hammer in His Hand,* Palmer C. Hayden (1890–1973). From the John Henry Series, Museum of African American Art, Los Angeles, Palmer C. Hayden Collection, gift of Miriam A. Hayden. Photo by Armando Solis; 955 Detail of illustration by J. W. Stewart; 965 Courtesy of Scholastic, Inc.; 969 *top* RMIP/Richard Haynes; Photofest.

End Matter

R2 *left Sunrise* (1924), Arthur Dove. Oil on plywood, 18¼" × 20⅞". Copyright © Arthur Dove. Milwaukee Art Museum, Milwaukee, Wisconsin. Gift of Mrs. Edward L. Wehr; *right* Copyright © Lowell Georgia/Corbis. R125 *top left* © Nik Wheeler/Black Star/PictureQuest; *top right, bottom right* © PhotoDisc; R127 Photo courtesy of the The Denver Public Library, Western History Collection. Text © 2001 McDougal Littell; R135 © PhotoDisc; R137 From the Collection of The Public Library of Cincinnati (Ohio) and Hamilton County; R141 © PhotoDisc; R145 © 1998 Jerry Lodriguss. Text © 1991 D.C. Heath and Company; R147 © Photri/Corbis. Text © 2001 McDougal Littell; R151 Courtesy of the Oakland Museum of California.

Teacher Review Panels *(continued)*

Bonnie Garrett Davis Middle School, Compton School District

Sally Jackson Madrona Middle School, Torrance Unified School District

Sharon Kerson Los Angeles Center for Enriched Studies, Los Angeles Unified School District

Gail Kidd Center Middle School, Azusa School District

Myra LeBendig Foshay Learning Center, Los Angeles Unified School District

Dan Manske Elmhurst Middle School, Oakland Unified School District

Joe Olague Language Arts Department Chairperson, Alder Middle School, Fontana School District

Pat Salo Sixth-Grade Village Leader, Hidden Valley Middle School, Escondido Elementary School District

FLORIDA

Judi Briant English Department Chairperson, Armwood High School, Hillsborough County School District

Beth Johnson Polk County English Supervisor, Polk County School District

Sharon Johnston Learning Resource Specialist, Evans High School, Orange County School District

Eileen Jones English Department Chairperson, Spanish River High School, Palm Beach County School District

Jan McClure Winter Park High School, Orange County School District

Wanza Murray English Department Chairperson (retired), Vero Beach Senior High School, Indian River City School District

Shirley Nichols Language Arts Curriculum Specialist Supervisor, Marion County School District

Debbie Nostro Ocoee Middle School, Orange County School District

Barbara Quinaz Assistant Principal, Horace Mann Middle School, Dade County School District

OHIO

Joseph Bako English Department Chairperson, Carl Shuler Middle School, Cleveland City School District

Deb Delisle Language Arts Department Chairperson, Ballard Brady Middle School, Orange School District

Ellen Geisler English/Language Arts Department Chairperson, Mentor Senior High School, Mentor School District

Dr. Mary Gove English Department Chairperson, Shaw High School, East Cleveland School District

Loraine Hammack Executive Teacher of the English Department, Beachwood High School, Beachwood City School District

Sue Nelson Shaw High School, East Cleveland School District

Mary Jane Reed English Department Chairperson, Solon High School, Solon City School District

Nancy Strauch English Department Chairperson, Nordonia High School, Nordonia Hills City School District

Ruth Vukovich Hubbard High School, Hubbard Exempted Village School District

TEXAS

Gloria Anderson Language Arts Department Chairperson, Campbell Middle School, Cypress Fairbanks Independent School District

Gwen Ferguson Assistant Principal, Northwood Middle School, North Forest Independent School District

Rebecca Hadavi Parkland Middle School, Ysleta Independent School District

Patricia Jackson Pearce Middle School, Austin Independent School District

Sandy Mattox Coppell Middle School North, Coppell Independent School District

Adrienne C. Myers Foster Middle School, Longview Independent School District

Pam Potts Clute Intermediate School, Brazosport Independent School District

Frank Westermann Jackson Middle School, North East Independent School District

Bessie B. Wilson W.E. Greiner Middle School, Dallas Independent School District

Manuscript Reviewers (*continued*)

Anita Graham Muirlands Middle School, LaJolla, California

Carol Hammons English Department Chair, Washington Middle School, Salinas, California

Shirley Herzog Reading Department Coordinator, Fairfield Middle School, Fairfield, Ohio

Ellen Kamimoto Ahwahnee Middle School, Fresno, California

Maryann Lyons Literacy Specialist and Mentor Teacher, San Francisco Unified School District, San Francisco, California

Karis MacDonnell Dario Middle School, Miami, Florida

Bonnie J. Mansell Downey Adult School, Downey, California

Martha Mitchell Memorial Middle School, Orlando, Florida

Ellen Moir GATE Coordinator and teacher, Twin Peaks Middle School, Poway, California

Nancy Nachman Landmark High School, Jacksonville, Florida

Katerine L. Noether Warren E. Hyde Middle School, Cupertino, California

Gloria Perry Bancroft Middle School, Long Beach, California

Karen Williams Perry English Department Chairperson, Kennedy Junior High School, Lisle, Illinois

Julia Pferdehirt Freelance writer; former Special Education Teacher, Middleton, Wisconsin

Phyllis Stewart Rude English Department Head, Mears Junior-Senior High School, Anchorage, Alaska

Leo Schubert Bettendorf Middle School, Bettendorf, Iowa

Lynn Thomas Borel Middle School, Burlingame, California

Gertrude H. Vannoy Curriculum Liaison Specialist and Gifted and Horizon Teacher, Meany Middle School, Seattle, Washington

Richard Wagner Language Arts Curriculum Coordinator, Paradise Valley School District, Phoenix, Arizona

Stevie Wheeler Humanities Department Chair, Rincon Middle School, San Diego, California

Stephen J. Zadravec Newmarket Junior-Senior High School, Newmarket, New Hampshire